WHO'S WHO
OF BRITISH
MEMBERS OF PARLIAMENT

Volume
II
1886–1918

Who's Who of British Members of Parliament

VOLUME
II
1886–1918

A Biographical Dictionary of the House of Commons

Based on annual volumes of
'Dod's Parliamentary Companion' and other sources

MICHAEL STENTON
Department of History, University of Bristol

and

STEPHEN LEES
University of Cambridge Library

THE HARVESTER PRESS, SUSSEX

HUMANITIES PRESS, NEW JERSEY

First published in England in 1978 by
THE HARVESTER PRESS LIMITED
Publisher: John Spiers
2 Stanford Terrace,
Hassocks, Sussex, England
and in the USA by
Humanities Press Inc.,
Atlantic Highlands, NJ 07716

Who's Who of British Members of Parliament Volume 2
© 1978 The Harvester Press Limited

Harvester Press
British Library Cataloguing in Publication Data
Who's who of British Members of Parliament.
   Vol. 2: 1886–1918.
   1. Great Britain. Parliament. House of
Commons – Biography
   I. Stenton, Michael II. Lees, Stephen
   328.41'07'30922   JN672

   ISBN 0-85527-315-1

Humanities Press
Library of Congress Cataloging in Publication Data
(Revised)

Stenton, Michael.
   Who's who of British members of Parliament.

   Vol. 2 – by M. Stenton and S. Lees.
   Includes index.
   CONTENTS: v. 1. 1832–1885—v. 2. 1886–1918.
   1. Great Britain Parliament. House of Commons—
Biography.   I. Lees, Stephen.   II. Dod's Parliamentary
companion.   III. Title.
JN672. S73   1976   328.41'092'2 [B]   76-12565

ISBN 0-391-00613-4 (v. 1)

Typeset by Computacomp (UK) Ltd., Fort William
Printed in Great Britain by
Redwood Burn Limited
Trowbridge and Esher

Contents

Preface by Michael Stenton   vii

Acknowledgements   xi

Advice to Readers   xiii

WHO'S WHO OF BRITISH MEMBERS OF PARLIAMENT, 1886–1918   1

Index   387

Preface by Michael Stenton

The principle of this book is to transform what is in fact a contemporary document – the annual editions of *Dod's Parliamentary Companion* – into a compilation of the fullest and most useful entries that Dod provides on each MP's parliamentary career. These little political 'biographies' have been rounded off with material that was no part of Dod's concern: the ostensible cause of a man's departure from the House of Commons, the leading features of his subsequent career, if any, and the date of his death. This book flaunts the vices of hindsight. Anyone seeking to trace a young Member of Parliament making some slight contribution to an unimportant debate will find here the *curriculum vitae* of the fully fledged politician, perhaps swathed in offices and titles, with attention drawn solely to his major attainments and characteristics.

An approach to history and the potentialities of men and periods which depends upon preserving a degree of constructive ignorance about what happens next might be somewhat hampered by this book. Every entry points inflexibly towards success or failure; high office or defeat at the polls. The advantages are as plain as the distortion.

Although the politics of one particular debate may be blurred by a hasty and unconsidered use of a historical work whose Whiggish inclination is always towards the successful aspects of completed careers, the pattern of advancement of two generations of MPs stands out more sharply in this light. Precisely because the book is a collection of the most substantial summaries of parliamentary 'lives', it becomes almost a survey of one generation of Parliamentary history, and in doing so acts as a corrective, in the hands of those reading *Hansard* or manuscript collections, to a tendency of the study of politics towards the merely incidental or even the merely biographical, as well as helping one to grasp these notorious nettles.

The editors have not checked and revised the details of the Dod entries. They start with the assumption that Dod provides first-class material otherwise unavailable in any one place. However when errors were noticed the entry was corrected without giving any note of the change. For example the original Dod entry said that the Rt. Hon. John Atkinson was born at Drogheda in 1842. Both the *DNB* and *Who Was Who* give the date as being 1844. The entry has been corrected to read 1844 but no footnote reference has been given to document the change. There are many minor corrections of this nature which have been incorporated into the original Dod entries and it would be beyond the aim of this book – and the patience of the reader – to document these. A further difficulty arises because *DNB*, *Who Was Who*, and other reference works are not correct in every point of detail. For example *DNB* says of Love Parry Jones Parry from Volume I that he sat for Carmarthen from 1835 to 1840 whereas in fact he sat for Caernarvon district from 1835 to 1837. And in this volume, *Who Was Who* gives the date of death of James Henry Alexander Majendie as 21 July 1932, whereas the Winchester College register gives it as 11 January 1939 and this is confirmed by *The Times* obituary notice of 13 January 1939.

The hazards are many and the editors have needed to make provisional choices between conflicting versions when discrepancies came to their attention while preparing the biographies in Volume I and the biographies in this volume. The editors, on the basis of a great deal of examination, but without attempting the exhaustive task of checking, are convinced that the margin of inaccuracy in *Dod's Parliamentary Companion* is not so great as to provide any cautious scholar with many problems.

Apart from the corrections a not inconsiderable amount of additional information has been given, and a note on this supplementary data is given in 'Advice to Readers' which follows this Preface. As far as death-dates are concerned it was difficult to trace all of these but in Volume I 85 per cent were traced, and in the present volume more than 95 per cent have been traced.

*   *   *

Charles Roger Phipps Dod (1793–1855) was the son of a county Leitrim vicar whose family were of Shropshire origin. He entered the King's Inns, Dublin, in 1816, but soon abandoned his legal studies, became a journalist and gravitated to London. Like several others, he saw in the Great Reform Act a peg on which to hang a new political handbook and launched the *Parliamentary Pocket Companion* in 1833. He was in a strong position in doing this, for Dod was one of the small group of men who lifted *The Times* to its unique position in the history of journalism. During the editorial reigns, first of Thomas Barnes and then, after 1841, of the legendary Delane, Charles Dod served and then succeeded John Tyas as head of the Press Gallery staff at the time when *The Times* was establishing its tradition of comprehensive and reliable Parliamentary reporting. Such a tradition was long thwarted by over-crowding and poor acoustics in the Gallery: problems which Fleet Street overcame only when the place was burnt down in 1834; but the new Gallery contained nineteen press boxes

(*The Times* was allotted three of the best, while *Hansard* made do with one) providing facilities for Dod to organise his team of scribes systematically. With his own pen, Dod produced the daily summaries which readers were reasonably expected to prefer to the prestigious and exhaustive but practically unreadable full reports. Charles Dod (or 'Dodd' before 1847) was also an obituary writer whose use of the columns of *The Times* was considered rather too free and pointed by his superiors.[1]

Dod also produced a *Peerage, Baronetage and Knightage* annually from 1841 and a volume of *Electoral Facts* in 1853. His son, Roger Phipps Dod, later a captain in the Shropshire yeomanry, took over most of the work of producing both the *Peerage* and the retitled *Parliamentary Companion* in 1843. This task he continued after his father's death in 1855 until his own, as a result of a shooting accident, ten years later. *Dod's Parliamentary Companion* then assumed the name under which it has flourished ever since.

There are other nineteenth century annual publications which supplement without supplanting *Dod* as a guide to Parliament. *Vacher's Parliamentary Companion* runs, like *Dod*, from 1833 to the present and provides lists of Members, constituencies, election results and office holders, but it lacks the element of political description. Debrett's *Illustrated House of Commons*, begun in 1867, offers a paragraph on each MP and every member of the judicial bench, but sadly its claim to distinction rests upon the heraldic shields it bestows wherever possible: there are no portraits. One of Charles Dod's most distinguished successors as head of *The Times's* parliamentary staff was Charles Ross, who edited *Ross's Parliamentary Record* from 1875: a periodical cast in the form of a dictionary of Parliamentary business – bills, summaries of debates, major division lists, dates and names of resolutions – which reverted to its original name of the *Parliamentary Record* in 1880. Other relevant publications of this type are listed extensively in H.J. Hanham *Bibliography of British History 1851–1914* (1976) in section II under 'Parliament' and 'The Electoral System'.

Numbers of *Dod's Parliamentary Companion* after 1885 are not as difficult to obtain as the earlier ones. Nevertheless, even major libraries often failed to collect the full sequence from 1885–1918. It is hoped that readers will find this one volume somewhat handier than thirty-three fragile 'pocket' books.

M.S.

1. Mowbray Morris to John Walter 1856, Vol. ii, *History of The Times* (1935–52), pp. 593–4.

Acknowledgements

The Editors must once again express their gratitude to Mavis Thomas for her remarkable performance at the typewriter, and to Tony Stenton for his diligence in preparing the original series of index cards. William Pidduck helped greatly as our assistant at Hassocks, and Ruth Wheatman gave us her usual co-operation from the Palace of Westminster. We are grateful to Dr. D. Menhennet, Librarian of the House of Commons, for his permission to loan copies of *Dod's Parliamentary Companion*, and to the staff of Bristol University Library for their helpful attention. Mr. Alastair Everitt of The Harvester Press was, of course, as patient and as helpful as ever.

Advice to Readers

This is the second volume of four, which taken together will supply biographies of every Member of Parliament to have sat in the House of Commons between 1832–1975. Volume I comprises more than 3050 lives for the years 1832–1885 inclusive. Volume II covers the years 1886–1918. Volumes III and IV will cover the period from 1919–1975.

The foundation of the whole set of reference works is the long run of *Dod's Parliamentary Companion*, published annually (sometimes twice a year) since 1832 and still continuing. The fullest and best entry for each MP has been taken from this source, and supplemented where possible with important additional information. Yet the personal and idiosyncratic style of Charles Dod's original entries has been maintained, with minor adjustment where events he mentions in the present tense have been rendered into the past. The biographies have then been organised into these new volumes, for ease of reference.

The following notes on the location of each biography in particular volumes, party labels, supplementary data which has been specially researched, changes of names and further guidance on supplementary sources will assist the user:

WHICH VOLUME IS AN MP IN?
The biography of an MP is printed in the volume whose dates cover the *end of his career in Parliament*, rather than his year of initial entry. The great majority of those who sat both before and after 1886 have been included in Volume II, and left out of Volume I. Exceptions are some members who sat for most of their parliamentary career prior to 1886. There are also a handful of entries which appear in both Volumes I and II as an extra help to the reader. In Volume II the same ruling applies and

usually the great majority of those who sat both before and after 1918 have been included in Volume III, and left out of Volume II.

The index of names clearly indicates with a dagger those members whose full entries appear in Volume I, and with an asterisk those members who continued to sit after 1918 and whose entries appear in Volume III.

WHICH VOLUME OF 'DOD' IS THE PRINCIPAL SOURCE FOR EACH LIFE?

In the majority of cases the very last entry has been used. After certain general elections Dod ran a second edition. Unless otherwise specified the first edition of Dod is the one which has been used. The year of Dod which has been used as the source has been clearly indicated in square brackets at the end of each entry.

PARTY LABELS

Those given by Charles Dod are used.

SUPPLEMENTARY DATA ADDED

Each entry essentially follows that of Dod but a number of consistent changes have been made to ensure that all the information appears in the same order. Some variations used by Dod have been retained; Brecknockshire and Breconshire are used interchangeably, as also are Salop and Shropshire.

The consistent order that we have followed is: name, address, clubs, birth, details of parentage, marriage, education, career prior to entering Parliament, political principles or affiliations, views on controversial or important questions, full Parliamentary career including every occasion when a person unsuccessfully contested a seat, reason for finally leaving Parliament, subsequent career when known, and the date of death when this can be traced. It was found that Dod was less concerned in giving full information about the occasions when MPs were unsuccessful candidates and a considerable amount of checking and adding of details has been necessary. Neither could Dod include any information about contested seats after an MP had finally left Parliament. This information has been researched and added to the relevant entries.

There were a number of successful candidates who entered and left Parliament between editions and no entries are to be found in Dod. In those cases we have provided all the information about the Parliamentary career, together with full details about any other seats contested either before or after they sat. We have added further information when this has been available. There are also a few entries of people who, while having been elected to Parliament, may not have actually sat in the house as they were unseated shortly after the election. As these are listed in such standard works as McCalmont's *Parliamentary Poll Book* entries for these have been composed from all available material and inserted.

CHANGES OF NAMES

Many individuals changed their family names during this period and there are sometimes discrepancies between the names recorded in standard reference books and those which appeared in *Dod's Parliamentary Companion*. As a general rule we have followed the *Parliamentary Companion* and where necessary cross references are given in the text and in the name index.

In a few cases further information about entries in Volume I has been discovered. This covers points such as incorrect birth-dates given by Dod, death-dates which we were unable to locate previously, additional information about a post-parliamentary career etc. In these few cases we have included a further short entry in Volume II pointing out the error or adding the further information.

OTHER CONVENTIONS FOLLOWED

'Returned in 1852' etc., means elected at the general election in that year. 'Retired in 1859' etc., means that the sitting MP failed to contest his seat. There is no implication that the man took a sober decision to end his political career. Where the word is not used it is because there is something standing in the text constituting the formal cause of the MPs departure from the House of Commons: electoral defeat, a peerage, a government appointment, etc. To 'contest' a seat, or to be 'a candidate', is, by gentlemanly omission, not to be elected.

SUPPLEMENTARY SOURCES

After the convenience of *Dod*, the way is hard. In this book attempts have been made, usually with success, to trace those MPs who left the House of Commons, inherited a title from some distant relative and died in obscurity, or emigrated and changed their names. Peerages and Baronetages are very useful in tracing such people, and some even thornier problems have been solved in using L.G. Pine's *New Extinct Peerage, 1884–1971* (London, 1972).

Other general sources used include *Who's Who*, published annually since 1849, *Who was Who*, which since 1897 has cumulated the entries and usually provided a date of death, F. Boase *Modern English Biography* (Truro, 1892–1921), *Kelly's Handbook ...*, published annually from 1878, *Debrett's Illustrated House of Commons and the Judicial Bench*, an annual publication from 1867 to 1931, *The Constitutional Yearbook*, published between 1885 and 1939 and reprinted by The Harvester Press 1970–1974, and *The Times Guide to the House of Commons*, published after most general elections this century.

Official material of relevance includes the official return of election expenses, published as a Parliamentary Paper after each general election, *The Journal of the House of Commons* (which is useful for checking new writs and the expulsion of members), *London Gazette* (e.g. for the dates of appointments to offices of profit under the Crown), and the lists of members contained in *Hansard*.

Other works have been valuable in confirming or contradicting dubious statements in *Dod*, notably F.W.S. Craig, *British Parliamentary*

Election Results, Vacher's Parliamentary Companion (published at frequent intervals usually monthly or quarterly since 1832), *Whitaker's Almanack* (annually since 1869), D. Butler and A. Sloman, *British Political Facts 1900–1975* (4th edition London, 1975), C. Cook and B. Keith, *British Historical Facts 1830–1900* (London, 1975), and W.P.W. Phillimore, *An Index to Changes of Name ... 1760–1901* (London, 1905). *The Times Index* has often proved invaluable but the lack of an index to other newspapers has limited their usefulness to the checking of information retrieved from other sources. J.A. Venn, *Alumni Cantabrigienses 1752–1900* (Cambridge, 1940–54) and J. Foster, *Alumni Oxonienses 1715–1886* (Oxford, 1888) have been useful for graduates of the older universities and recourse has been made to the registers of other universities, colleges and schools. Membership lists of learned societies and professional bodies have occasionally been helpful but the profession with the most valuable documentation is undoubtedly the law. *The Law List*, the registers of each of the Inns of Court, *Debrett's Illustrated House of Commons and the Judicial Bench* and J. Foster, *Men at the Bar* (London, 1885) have been especially useful.

The Irish members present problems all their own since they appear only haphazardly in the usual biographical sources and there is often conflicting information about those who do appear. Many of the pre-1916 Nationalists passed from public life (and from the pages of *Who's Who*) and died in obscurity whilst the Sinn Feiners fought amongst themselves for the body and soul of the Irish Free State, the successful ones reappearing as members of the Dáil or the Seanad. Further problems are caused by men with similar names. John Daly must not be confused with James Daly nor John Joseph Clancy (Co. Dublin North 1885–1918) with John Joseph Clancy (Sligo North 1918–22). Conversely J.J. Shee and J.J. O'Shee turn out to be the same man. Useful information has been gleaned from *Burke's Irish Family Records* (London, 1976), A. Webb, *Compendium of Irish Biography* (Dublin, 1878), J.S. Crone, *A Concise Dictionary of Irish Biography* (Dublin, 1937), and, for those members who later sat in the Irish Parliament, *Oireachtas Companion* for 1928 and 1930 and *The Free State Parliamentary Companion* for 1932.

Working-class members were not as numerous as the Irish in this period. At first they usually appeared as Liberals but by 1918 there existed a Labour Party which proved almost as capable as Sinn Fein of exploiting the post-war confusions of the great parties. These MPs will eventually all be included in J.M. Bellamy and J. Saville (eds.), *Dictionary of Labour Biography* (London, 1972—) and in the forthcoming Harvester Press publication J.O. Baylen and N.J. Gossman *The Biographical Dictionary of Modern British Radicals since 1770*.

Volumes 3 & 4 of Chris Cook, *Sources of British Political History 1900–51* (London, 1977) list the papers of members who sat between those dates and C. Hazlehurst and C. Woodland, *A Guide to the Papers of British Cabinet Ministers 1900–51* (London, 1974) is also extremely useful. For other members it is necessary to have recourse to the National Register of Archives.

The period 1885–1918 is bounded by two reform acts: from 1885 each constituency had a 'mass' electorate, and the unqualified men who survived the Great War were enfranchised in 1918. The study of elections must begin with H.M. Pelling, *The Social Geography of British Elections 1885–1910* (London, 1967) and M. Kinnear, *The British Voter* (London, 1968).

ABBREVIATIONS
The following abbreviations are used in this book:
B. means born; *Bart.* Baronet; *bro.* brother; *Capt.* Captain; *Co.* county; *Col.* Colonel; *Coll.* College; *d.* daughter; *Dept.* Deputy; *educ.* educated; *E.I.C.* East India Company; *eld.* eldest; *Gen.* General; *Gov.* Governor; *Hon.* Honourable; *jun.* junior; *Lieut.* Lieutenant; *Maj.* Major; *m.* married; *Nr.* near; *PC.* Privy Councillor; *Pres.* President; *Rt.* Right; *Sec.* Secretary; *sen.* senior; *s.* son; *Visct.* Viscount.

Who's Who of British
Members of Parliament, 1886–1918

ABERCROMBY, Robert William. See DUFF, Robert William.

ABRAHAM, William. 26 Ashmount Road, Hornsey Lane, London. B. 1840 at Limerick. Was one of the Treasurers of the Irish Nationalist Party. Took an active part in the Land League agitation 1881. Was Chairman of Limerick Board of Guardians 1882–83 and 1885–86. A Protestant Nationalist. Sat for W. Limerick from 1885 to 1892, when he retired; sat for N.E. Cork from 1893 to Jan. 1910, when he was defeated. First elected for the Harbour division of Dublin in June 1910 and sat until his death 2 Aug. 1915. [1915]

ABRAHAM, Rt. Hon. William ('Mabon'). Bryn-y-Bedw, Pentre, South Wales. Westminster Palace Hotel, Victoria Street, London. S. of a Working Collier and Copper-Smelter. B. 1842. He worked in the mines at ten years of age. From 1873 was a Miners' Agent, and was for many years Vice-President of the Monmouthshire and S. Wales Conciliation Board. At one time President of the S. Wales Miners' Federation; Treasurer of the Miners' Federation of Great Britain 1907. PC. 1911. A Labour Member, in favour of Home Rule for Ireland. Sat for the Rhondda division of Glamorganshire from 1885–1918, elected for the W. Rhondda division of Glamorganshire in Dec. 1918 and sat until he accepted Chiltern Hundreds in 1920. Died 14 May 1922. [1919]

ACLAND, Rt. Hon. Arthur Herbert Dyke. 28 Cheyne Walk, London. Westholme, Scarborough. Reform, Athenaeum, and Cobden. 2nd s. of the Rt. Hon. Sir Thomas Dyke Acland, Bart., at one time MP for the Wellington division of Somerset, by Mary, d. of Sir Charles Mordaunt. B. 1847; m. 1873, Alice Sophia, d. of the Rev. F.H. Cunningham. Educ. at Rugby, and Christ Church, Oxford. Was student of Christ Church and senior bursar at Balliol Coll., Oxford, of which Coll. he was an Honorary Fellow. Lecturer of Keble Coll., Oxford 1871–72 and Tutor 1872–75. Principal of Oxford Military School, Cowley 1875–77. Ordained Deacon in Church of England 1872 but resigned Holy Orders in 1879. Author of a Handbook of English Political History, and of *Working Men Co-operators*. Was Vice-President of the Committee of the Council on Education

with a seat in the Cabinet 1892–95; became a PC. 1892. A Liberal, in favour of Irish Home Rule. Sat for the Rotherham division of the W. Riding of Yorkshire from 1885 until he accepted Chiltern Hundreds in 1899. Succeeded as 13th Bart. in 1919. Died 9 Oct. 1926. [1898]

ACLAND, Sir Charles Thomas Dyke. See ACLAND, Charles Thomas Dyke.

ACLAND, Charles Thomas Dyke. Sprydoncote, Exeter. Athenaeum, Travellers', and Brooks's. Eld. s. of the Rt. Hon. Sir Thomas Dyke Acland, Bart., at one time MP for N. Devon, by his 1st wife, Mary, eld. d. of Sir Charles Mordaunt, Bart. B. in Queen Street, London 1842; m. 1879, Gertrude, 3rd d. of Sir John and the Hon. Lady Walrond. Educ. at St. Andrew's Coll., Bradfield, also at Eton; then at Christ Church, Oxford, and graduated M.A. Was called to the bar at the Inner Temple 1869, and for a short time joined the Western Circuit. A Magistrate for Devon, Cornwall, and Somerset, and Dept.-Lieut. for Somerset. A Dept.-Warden of the Stannaries from 1882. Appointed Lieut.-Col. Royal 1st Devon Yeomanry Cavalry 1885, and commanded the 1st Devon Mounted Rifle Volunteers from 1862 to 1877. Appointed Parliamentary Secretary to the Board of Trade and 2nd Church Estates Commissioner Feb. 1886. Author of an essay on *County Boards*. A Liberal, and supporter of Mr. Gladstone's Home Rule Scheme; in favour of reform in county government, in local taxation, and in the land laws, etc. Unsuccessfully contested W. Somerset in Apr. 1880. Sat for E. Cornwall from Mar. 1882–85, and for the Launceston division of Cornwall from 1885 until he retired in 1892. Succeeded as 12th Bart. in 1898. Alderman of Devon County Council. Died 18 Feb. 1919. [1892]

ACLAND, Rt. Hon. Francis Dyke. Continued in House after 1918: full entry in Volume III.

ACLAND, Rt. Hon. Sir Thomas Dyke, Bart. Retired in 1886: full entry in Volume I, under ACLAND, Sir Thomas Dyke, Bart., jun.

ACLAND-HOOD, Rt. Hon. Sir Alexander Fuller, Bart. St. Audries, Bridgwater. Carlton, Constitutional, and

Guards'. S. of Sir Alexander Acland-Hood, 3rd Bart., MP for W. Somerset, and Isabel, d. of Sir P. Palmer Fuller-Palmer-Acland. B. 1853 at St. Audries; m. 1888, Mildred, d. of Lord Ventry. Educ. at Eton, and Balliol Coll., Oxford; B.A. Capt. Grenadier Guards 1875–1892; served in Egyptian Campaign 1882; Aide-de-Camp to Gov. of Victoria 1889–91. Succeeded father as 4th Bart. 1892 and succeeded kinsman in the Bateman Baronetcy 1905. Member of Somerset County Council. A Dept.-Lieut. for Somerset. Vice-Chamberlain of H.M. Household 1900–02, Patronage Secretary to the Treasury 1902–05, and was chief Conservative Whip 1902–11. PC. 1904. A Unionist. First elected for W. Somerset in 1892 and sat until created Baron St. Audries 1911. Died 4 June 1917.   [1911]

ADAM, Maj. William Augustus. Carlton, and Junior United Service. S. of the Rev. B.W. Adam, D.D., Rector of Bantry, Ireland. B. 27 May 1865 at Dublin. Educ. at Harrow, Dublin University and Royal Military Coll., Sandhurst; 1st honours in Classics and Modern History, M.A. Joined the 5th (Royal Irish) Lancers 1887; Lieut. 1889; Capt. 1893; Maj. 1905. Gen. Staff Officer, Army Headquarters 1909–10; an Interpreter in Russian, French, Hindustani, etc. Served in South African Campaign 1899–1902, and took part in the defence of Ladysmith. Was on special service in Japan, 1903–05. Wrote *Rus Divinum, Horae Fugaces, The Lonely Way, Japanese Conversation,* and other works. Changed his name from Adams to Adam in 1907. A Unionist. Unsuccessfully contested Woolwich in 1906; elected there in Jan. 1910 and sat until defeated in Dec. 1910. Unsuccessfully contested Woolwich W. as Independent Conservative against the official candidate in 1918. Active service 1914–17. Died 18 Oct. 1940.   [1910]

ADAMS, Maj. William Augustus. See ADAM, Maj. William Augustus.

ADAMSON, William. Continued in House after 1918: full entry in Volume III.

ADDISON, Rt. Hon. Christopher. Continued in House after 1918: full entry in Volume III.

ADDISON, John Edmund Wentworth. 32 Norfolk Square, Hyde Park, London.

Carlton. S. of Henry Addison, Esq., of Preston, by Grace, d. of Gen. Sir Robert Barton. B. 1838; m. 1873, Alice, d. of Joseph M'Keand, Esq., of Manchester (she died 1894). Educ. at Preston Grammar School, and Trinity Coll., Dublin, where he became a scholar and moderator. Was called to the bar 1862; Q.C. 1880. Chairman Salford Quarter Session, and Recorder of Preston from 1874 to 1890. A Conservative. Sat for Ashton-under-Lyne from Nov. 1885 (being elected by the Returning Officers' casting vote in the general election of 1886), until he retired in 1895. Appointed County Court Judge same year. Died 22 Apr. 1907.   [1895]

ADKINS, Sir William Ryland Dent. Continued in House after 1918: full entry in Volume III.

AGAR-ROBARTES, Hon. Thomas Charles Reginald. 1 Great Stanhope Street, London. Landydrock, Bodmin. Brooks's, and Bachelors'. Eld. s. of Visct. Clifden. B. 1880. Educ. at Eton, and Christ Church, Oxford. A Lieut. Royal Devonshire Yeomanry. A Liberal. Elected for the Bodmin division of Cornwall in 1906, but was unseated on petition in June 1906. Elected for the St. Austell division of Cornwall in Feb. 1908 and sat until he died of wounds received in action on 28 Sept. 1915.   [1915]

AGG-GARDNER, Sir James Tynte. Continued in House after 1918: full entry in Volume III.

AGNEW, Sir Andrew Noel, Bart. 21 Abingdon Street, London. Lochnaw Castle, Wigtownshire. Brooks's, and United Universities'. S. of Sir Andrew Agnew, 8th Bart., and Lady Louisa Noel, d. of 1st Earl of Gainsborough. B. at Exton Park, Oakham 1850; m. 1889, Gertrude, d. of the Hon. Gowran C. Vernon. Educ. at Harrow, and Trinity Coll., Cambridge; graduated 1871, LL.B. 1872. Called to the bar 1874. A Dept.-Lieut. and J.P. for Wigtownshire and Vice-Lieut. of the Co. Succeeded as 9th Bart. in 1892. A Liberal Unionist, in favour of army reform, old age pensions, temperance reform on the lines of the "Majority" Report, taxation of land values, etc. Unsuccessfully contested Dumfries district July 1892. First elected for Edinburgh S. 1900 and sat until he retired in 1906. President, Royal Scottish

Arboricultural Society. Died 14 July 1928.
[1905]

AGNEW, Sir George William, Bart.
Rougham Hall, Bury St. Edmunds. 269 St.
James's Court, Buckingham Gate, London. Reform, and Devonshire. Eld. s. of Sir
William Agnew, 1st Bart., and Mary, d. of
G.P. Kenworthy, Esq., of Manchester. B.
19 Jan. 1852 at Salford; m. 1878, Fanny, d.
of John Stuart Bolton, Esq., of Oulton
Hall, Aylsham, Norfolk. Educ. at Rugby,
and St. John's Coll., Cambridge. A Partner
in Thomas Agnew and Sons, Fine Art
Dealers, of London, Manchester and
Liverpool. President of the Printsellers'
Association. Gov. of Manchester University and President of Manchester
Children's Hospital. A J.P. for Lancashire
and Suffolk. A Liberal. Elected for W.
Salford in 1906 and sat until he retired in
1918. Succeeded as 2nd Bart. in 1910. High
Sheriff of Suffolk 1922. Died 19 Dec. 1941.
[1918]

AGNEW, William. 11 Great Stanhope
Street, Mayfair. Summer Hill, Pendleton,
Manchester. Reform, and Devonshire. Eld.
s. of Thomas Agnew, Esq., of Manchester,
who was Mayor of Salford in 1851, by Jane,
2nd d. of William Lockett, Esq., of Salford
and of Lytham. B. at Manchester 1825; m.
Mary, eld. d. of George Pixton Kenworthy,
Esq., of Manchester and of Peel Hall,
Astley, Manchester. A well-known
Publisher, head of the firm of Messrs.
Thomas Agnew and Sons, London, Liverpool and Manchester, also Partner of the
firm of Messrs. Bradbury, Agnew and
Company, Whitefriars, London. A Magistrate for Lancashire, also for Manchester
and for Salford. A Liberal, in favour of the
equalisation of the whole franchise of the
country, the reform of the Land Laws, the
abolition of the system of primogeniture,
reform of the licensing system, etc. Sat for
S.E. Lancashire from Apr. 1880 to 1885
and for the Stretford division of Lancashire from 1885 to 1886, when he was
defeated. Unsuccessfully contested Prestwich in 1892. Created Bart. in 1895. Died
31 Oct. 1910. [1886]

AINSLIE, William George. 23 Abingdon
Street, London. 5 Cornwall Gardens, London. Grizedale Hall, Hawkeshead, Nr.
Ulverston. Carlton, and St. Stephen's. 3rd
s. of Montague Ainslie, Esq., J.P. and
Dept.-Lieut. of the Hon. East India Company's Service, and Sophia Mary, d. of
George Poyntz Ricketts, Esq. B. in India
1832. Educ. at Sedbergh School, Yorkshire.
He was in the Iron and Steel trade, being a
Partner of the firm of Harrison, Ainslie
and Company of Ulverston, and Chairman of the North Lonsdale Iron and Steel
Company Limited. A Magistrate for Lancashire, and formerly Capt. in the 37th
Lancashire Volunteers. A Conservative.
Sat for the N. Lonsdale division of Lancashire from 1885 until he retired in 1892.
Died 10 Feb. 1893. [1892]

AINSWORTH, David. 29 Pont Street,
London. The Flosh, Cleator, Cumberland.
National Liberal, Devonshire, and
Reform. Eld. s. of Thomas Ainsworth,
Esq., of the Flosh, Cleator, Cumberland,
by Mary, eld. d. of J. Stirling, Esq., D.D., of
Craigie, Ayrshire. B. at Cleator 1842; m.
1874, Margaret, d. of Henry McConnell,
Esq., of Cressbrook, Derbyshire. Was
educ. at University Coll. School, London,
at Manchester New Coll., and at the London University. Was called to the bar at
Lincoln's Inn June 1870. A Flax Manufacturer and Ironmaster. A J.P. for Lancashire and Cumberland, and a Dept.-
Lieut. for Cumberland. A Director of the
Economic Fire Office, and of the Maryport
and Carlisle Railway. A Liberal, in favour
of Home Rule for Ireland and the Gladstonian programme generally. Unsuccessfully contested Cumberland W. Feb.
1874; sat for Cumberland W. from Apr.
1880 until defeated Nov. 1885; became a
Gladstonian Liberal; unsuccessfully contested Cumberland W. July 1886; returned
for Cumberland W. July 1892 and sat until
defeated July 1895; failed to win back the
seat as a Liberal Oct. 1900. Died 21 Mar.
1906. [1895]

AINSWORTH, Sir John Stirling, Bart.
Ardanaiseig, Kilchrenan, Argyll, N.B.
Harecroft, Gosforth, and The Flosh, Cleator, Cumberland. 55 Eaton Place, London.
Reform. 2nd s. of Thomas Ainsworth,
Esq., of The Flosh, Cleator, Cumberland,
and Mary, d. of the Rev. J. Stirling, D.D., of
Craigie, Ayrshire. B. 1844; m. 1879,
Margaret, d. of R.R. Macredie, Esq. Educ.
at University Coll. School, and University
Coll., London; M.A., LL.B. Was interested
in Iron-Mining in Cumberland. Chairman
of the Cleator and Workington Junction
Railway; member of Royal Commission
on Metalliferous Mines and Quarries; J.P.

3

and Dept.-Lieut. for Argyll, and Cumberland (High Sheriff for Cumberland 1891); created Bart. 1916. Col. (retired) of 8th Battalion Border Regiment. A Liberal, in favour of Free Trade. Unsuccessfully contested Barrow-in-Furness in 1886 and Argyllshire in 1900. Elected for Argyllshire in Aug. 1903 and sat until he retired in 1918. Died 24 May 1923.   [1918]

AIRD, Sir John, Bart. 14 Hyde Park Terrace, London. Junior Carlton, Carlton, Constitutional, Conservative, and St. Stephen's. S. of John Aird, Esq., of Rossshire, Scotland, and Agnes Bennett, his wife. B. in London 3 Dec. 1833; m.; 1854, Sarah, d. of Benjamin Smith, Esq., of Lewisham. Educ. at private schools. A Contractor for Public Works from 1850, and a Partner in the firms of John Aird and Company, and John Aird and Sons, of Great George Street, Westminster. Was on the Court of Lieutenancy of the City of London, and a Col. in the Engineers and Railway Volunteer Staff Corps; Mayor of Paddington 1900-02; he served on the Royal Commission upon Trade. Created Bart. 1901. A Conservative, and a strong upholder of the Union. Sat for Paddington N. from 8 July 1887 until he retired in 1906. Died 6 Jan. 1911.   [1905]

AITKEN, Sir William Maxwell, Bart. 3 Lombard Street, London. Cherkley, Leatherhead. Carlton. S. of the Rev. W. Aitken, Scotch Minister, Newcastle, New Brunswick. B. 25 May 1879 at Newcastle, New Brunswick; m. 1906, Gladys, d. of Gen. Drury, C.B. Educ. at Newcastle Public School. A Merchant. Knighted 1911. A Unionist. Elected for Ashton-under-Lyne in Dec. 1910 and sat until nominated for the Peerage in Dec. 1916. Created Bart. 3 July 1916. Created Baron Beaverbrook 2 Jan. 1917. PC. 1918. Chancellor of Duchy of Lancaster and Minister of Propaganda/Information from Feb.-Nov. 1918. Acquired the *Daily Express* in 1918 and later the *Evening Standard*; the leading figure in British journalism between the two world wars. Although a consistent supporter of Neville Chamberlain's foreign policy, he was brought into the administration of his old friend Winston Churchill as Minister of Aircraft Production in May 1940. Minister of State May-June 1941. Minister of Supply June 1941-Feb. 1942. Minister of War Production 4-19 Feb. 1942. Lord Privy Seal Sept. 1943-

July 1945. He remained a confidante of the Prime Minister throughout the war, both in and out of office. In 1948 he boasted that he ran his newspaper "purely for propaganda." Chancellor of University of New Brunswick 1947-53. Died 9 June 1964.   [1916]

AKERS-DOUGLAS, Rt. Hon. Aretas. 113 Mount Street, Grosvenor Square, London. Chilston Park, Lenham, Kent. Carlton, Constitutional, and Junior Carlton. Eld. s. of the Rev. Aretas Akers, of Malling Abbey, Kent, by Frances, d. of Francis H. Brandram, Esq., of Tunbridge Wells, Kent. B. 1851; m. 1875, Adeline Mary, d. of Henry Austen Smith, Esq., of Hayes Court, Kent. Educ. at Eton, and at University Coll. Called to the bar at the Inner Temple 1875. Assumed the name of Douglas in addition to his patronymic in 1875. Was Patronage Secretary to the Treasury 1885-86, 1886-92 and for a short time June-July 1895. First Commissioner of Works 1895-1902; PC. 1891; Home Secretary in Mr. Balfour's Ministry from 1902-05. A Unionist. Sat for E. Kent from 1880 to 1885, and for the St. Augustine's division of Kent from 1885 until created Visct. Chilston in 1911. G.B.E. 1920. Died 15 Jan. 1926.   [1911]

ALDEN, Percy. Continued in House after 1918: full entry in Volume III.

ALLAN, Sir William. Scotland House, Sunderland. National Liberal. S. of James Allan, Esq., of Dundee. B. 1837 in Dundee; m. 1870, Jane, d. of Walter Beattie, Esq., of Lockerbie, N.B. Educ. at the Dundee Schools. A Marine-Engine Builder, Chairman of the Albyn Line Limited, and Director of Richardson, Westgarth and Company Limited; J.P. and Dept.-Lieut. for Co. Durham. He successfully adopted the eight-hours system in his factory. Wrote various books including *A Book of Poems, Rough Castings, Songs of Love and War, A Guide to the Marine Engine,* and *The Engine Room.* Knighted 1902. An "advanced Radical", believing "that all old political things should give place to new"; in favour of Home Rule, etc. First elected for Gateshead 1893 and sat until his death 28 Dec. 1903.   [1903]

ALLEN, Arthur Acland. 13 Queen's Gate Gardens, London. 7 Tullybelton House, Perthshire. Reform, Burlington Fine Arts,

4

and National Liberal. S. of Peter Allen, Esq., Publisher of the *Manchester Guardian*, and Sophia Russell, d. of John E. Taylor, Esq., founder of the *Manchester Guardian*. B. 11 Aug. 1868 at Prestwich; m. 1900, Gladys Hope, d. of J. Douglas Walker, Esq., K.C. Educ. at Rugby, and University Coll., Oxford; B.A. Was called to the bar 1893. Member of the London County Council 1899-1913 and was Dept.-Chairman 1908. A Liberal. Unsuccessfully contested the Thornbury division of Gloucestershire in 1895 and E. Dorset in 1900. Sat for Christchurch from 1906 to Jan. 1910, when he was defeated. Elected for Dumbartonshire in Dec. 1910 and sat until defeated in 1918. Died 20 May 1939. [1918]

ALLEN, Charles Francis Egerton. Heywood Cottage, Tenby, Pembrokeshire. Oriental, and Eighty. S. of Charles Allen, Esq., a member of the E.I.C., of Tenby, member of the Legislative Council of India, and Mary, d. of James Allen, Esq., of Freestone Hall, Pembrokeshire. B. 1847 near Agra, India; m. 1891, Georgina, d. of William Wilcox, Esq., of Whitburn, near Sunderland. Educ. at Eton, and St. John's Coll., Cambridge (B.A. 1870, Senior Optime, Mathematical Tripos). A Barrister, called at the Inner Temple 1871; joined the Northern afterwards the North-Eastern Circuit; Calcutta bar 1873, Burma 1877; returned to England 1888. Was a Lecturer in the Presidency Coll., Calcutta, Examiner of Law Students, Judge in the Calcutta Court of Small Causes, Government Advocate, Rangoon, etc. Held Democratic opinions, in favour of Home Rule for Ireland, disestablishment in Wales, Liquor, Land, and Registration law reforms, etc. First returned for Pembroke and Haverfordwest district in July 1892 and sat until defeated in 1895. Borough Magistrate at Tenby 1896-1905. Died 31 Dec. 1927. [1895]

ALLEN, Maj. the Rt. Hon. Charles Peter. 37 Grosvenor Place, London. Reform, and National Liberal. S. of Peter Allen, Esq., Newspaper Proprietor, and his wife, Sophia Russell, d. of John Edward Taylor, Esq. B. at Prestwich 1861; m. 1890, Evelina, d. of Alfred Barker, Esq. Educ. at Rugby School, and University Coll., Oxford. A Barrister-at-Law, called 1888. Appointed a Charity Commissioner (unpaid) 1910, resigned 1917. Dept.-Lieut. for Gloucestershire. PC. 1912. A Maj. in 2/5

Battalion Gloucestershire Regiment; and served in the British Expeditionary Force in France. A Liberal. Unsuccessfully contested Stroud division of Gloucestershire in 1895. First elected there in 1900 and sat until defeated in 1918. Again unsuccessful at Stroud in 1922. Died 18 Sept. 1930. [1918]

ALLEN, Henry George, Q.C. Retired in 1886: full entry in Volume I.

ALLEN, William. Continued in House after 1918: full entry in Volume III.

ALLEN, Maj. William James. Continued in House after 1918: full entries in Volumes III and IV.

ALLEN, William Shepherd. Retired in 1886: full entry in Volume I.

ALLHUSEN, Augustus Henry Eden. Stoke Court, Stoke Poges, Buckinghamshire. Carlton, and White's. Eld. s. of Henry C. Allhusen, Esq., and Alice, d. of Thomas Eden, Esq., of Norton Hall, Gloucestershire, and grand-s. of C. Allhusen, Esq., J.P., Dept.-Lieut. of Newcastle and Stoke Court, Buckinghamshire. B. at Gateshead 1867; m. 1896, Mary Dorothy, younger d. of Lady Jeune, by her 1st husband Col. the Hon. John Stanley. Educ. at Cheltenham Coll., and Trinity Coll., Cambridge; B.A. 1890. A J.P. and Dept.-Lieut. for Buckinghamshire, and Lieut. Royal Buckinghamshire Hussars. A Conservative. Was Member for Salisbury from 1897-1900. Elected for Hackney 1900 and sat until defeated in 1906. High Sheriff for Buckinghamshire 1913. Died 2 May 1925. [1905]

ALLISON, Sir Robert Andrew. Queen Anne's Mansions, London. Scaleby Hall, Carlisle, New University. S. of J. Allison Esq., of Stanwix, Carlisle, by Jane, d. of John Andrew, Esq., of Carlisle. B. at Stanwix 1838; m. 1st 1867, Laura Alicia, d. of J. Milner Atkinson, Esq., of Thorp Arch, Yorkshire (she died 1892); 2ndly, 1897, Sara Eudora, d. of Rev. Canon Slater, of Branksome Park, Bournemouth. Educ. at Rugby, and Trinity Coll., Cambridge. A Magistrate and Dept.-Lieut. for Cumberland, a Director of the Midland Railway Company, and a Vice-President of the United Kingdom Alliance. A Liberal, in favour of Home Rule for Ireland. Sat for

Cumberland N. from 1885 until defeated in 1900. Knighted 1910. Subsequently author of *Essays and Addresses* (1913). Translated various Greek and Latin authors. Died 15 Jan. 1926. [1900]

ALLSOPP, Hon. Alfred Percy. 45 St. James's Place, London. Battenhall Mount, Worcester. Carlton, Junior Carlton, and Arthur's. Youngest s. of 1st Baron Hindlip. B. 1861 at Hindlip Hall, Worcester; m. 1890, Lilian Maud Chesshire, eld. d. of the Rev. John Stanley Chesshire, Rector of Hindlip, Worcestershire. Educ. at Eton, and Trinity Coll., Cambridge. A Director of S. Allsopp and Sons, Limited, Burton-on-Trent; a member of the Worcester Town Council (Mayor 1892-93, 1894-95, and 1909-10), and a Dept.-Lieut. for Staffordshire. A Conservative and Unionist. Returned for Taunton in Apr. 1887 and sat until he retired in 1895. Died 22 Feb. 1929. [1895]

ALLSOPP, Hon. George Higginson. 8 Hereford Gardens, London. 3rd s. of 1st Lord Hindlip, of Hindlip Hall, Worcester. B. 1846; m. 1895, Lady Mildred Georgina, d. of the 8th Earl of Shaftesbury. Educ. at Eton, and Trinity Coll., Cambridge; M.A. 1868. Was twice Mayor of Burton-on-Trent, and J.P. and Dept.-Lieut. for the counties of Derby and Stafford; Chairman of the Burton School Board. A Conservative. Unsuccessfully contested Droitwich in 1880. Sat for Worcester from 1885 until he retired in 1906. Died 9 Sept. 1907. [1905]

ALLSOPP, Hon. Samuel Charles. 33 Hill Street, Berkeley Square, London. Doveridge Hall, Derbyshire. Carlton, and Windham. Eld. s. of Lord Hindlip, by Elizabeth, d. of William Tongue, Esq., of Comberford Hall, Staffordshire. B. at Burton-on-Trent, 1842; m. 1868, Georgiana Millicent, eld. d. of Charles Rowland Palmer-Morewood, Esq., of Alfreton Hall, Derbyshire. Was educ. at Harrow, and at Trinity Coll., Cambridge, where he was junior optime in 1865, and graduated M.A. 1869. A Partner in the firm of Messrs. Samuel Allsopp and Sons, Burton-on-Trent, and Dept. Chairman of the Great Northern Railway. A Magistrate for Derbyshire and Staffordshire, and a Dept.-Lieut. of the latter. A Conservative. Sat for Staffordshire E. from July 1873 to Apr. 1880. when he was an unsuccessful candidate there. Sat for Taunton from 1882 un-

til he succeeded to the Peerage as 2nd Baron Hindlip in 1887. Died 12 July 1897. [1887]

AMBROSE, Daniel. Warren House, Upper Tooting, London. S. of Stephen Ambrose, Esq., of Longhill, Co. Limerick, and his wife, Mary, d. of James Kennedy, Esq., of Adare, Co. Limerick. B. 1843 at Longhill; m. 1867, Anna, only child of James Parker, of Limerick City. Educ. at St. Munchen's Seminary, Limerick, and the Catholic University, Ireland. A M.D. Queen's University, Ireland 1865, also Licentiate Royal Coll. Surgeons, Ireland 1864, and L.M. Royal Coll. Physicians, Ireland 1865. An Irish Nationalist and Home Ruler, of the Anti-Parnellite party. Sat for Louth S. from July 1892 until his death 17 Dec. 1895. [1895 2nd ed.]

AMBROSE, Dr. Robert. The Mount, Shoot-up Hill, Brondesbury, London. National Liberal. S. of M. Ambrose, Esq., of Newcastle West, Co. Limerick. A cousin of Dr. Daniel Ambrose, Member for Louth S. 1892-95. B. 1855. Educ. at Wier's School, Limerick, and Queen's Coll., Cork; B.A. 1876. A Surgeon; L.R.C.P., Edin. and L.M., 1883; a member of the British Medical Association, etc. Practised in the East End of London. A Nationalist, of the Anti-Parnellite party. First elected for W. Mayo in 1893 and sat until he retired in Jan. 1910. Contested Whitechapel for Labour in 1918. Author of *A Plea for Industrial Regeneration of Ireland* (1909). Died 13 June 1940. [1909]

AMBROSE, William. 3 Plowden Buildings, Temple, London. Westover, West Heath Road, Hampstead, London. Carlton, London. Conservative, Manchester. B. at Chester 1832; m. 1866, Georgianna Mary Anne, d. of William Jones, Esq., of Camden Road, London. In 1859 he was called to the bar (Lincoln's Inn, Certificate of Honour, 1st class); in 1874 appointed a Q.C., in 1881 a bencher of the Middle Temple, and in 1895 Attorney-Gen. of the Duchy of Lancaster, and Queen's Attorney and Serjeant for the Co. Palatine of Lancaster. Was a member of the Council of Legal Education from 1889. Also a Co. Alderman for Middlesex from 1888-1900. A Conservative. In 1868 he unsuccessfully contested Stockport. Sat for the Harrow division of Middlesex from

1885 until appointed Master in Lunacy in 1899. Died 18 Jan. 1908.   [1899]

AMERY, Leopold Charles Maurice Stennett. Continued in House after 1918: full entry in Volume III.

AMHERST, William Amhurst Tyssen. 8 Grosvenor Square, London. Didlington Hall, Brandon, Norfolk. Carlton, Travellers', and Athenaeum. Eld. s. of William George Tyssen Tyssen-Amherst, Esq., of Didlington Hall, Norfolk. B. at Narford Hall, Norfolk 1835; m. 1856, Margaret Susan, only d. and heir of Admiral Robert Mitford, of Mitford, Northumberland. Assumed by Royal licence the name of Amherst instead of his patronymic. Educ. at Eton and at Christ Church, Oxford. A Magistrate for Westminster and for Norfolk, and a Magistrate and Dept.-Lieut. for Middlesex. Was High Sheriff of Norfolk in 1866. Patron of 5 livings. A Conservative. Represented Norfolk W. from Mar. 1880 to Nov. 1885 and the S.W. division of Norfolk from Nov. 1885 until he retired in 1892. Created Baron Amherst of Hackney in 1892. Died 16 Jan. 1909.   [1892]

AMHURST-TYSSEN, William Amhurst. See AMHERST, William Amhurst Tyssen.

ANDERSON, Andrew Macbeth. 9 Great King Street, Edinburgh. National Liberal. S. of Charles Enverdale Anderson, Esq., Provost of Coupar Angus, and Jane Lindsay, of Dundee. B. 6 Nov. 1862 at Coupar Angus, N.B. m. 1901, Angus Catherine, d. of George Mackay, of Bellavista, Midlothian. Educ. at Dundee High School, and Edinburgh University; M.A., LL.B., Forensic Prizeman 1888. An advocate of Scottish bar, called 1889; Advocate Depute 1906; K.C. 1908; Standing Counsel to Scottish Liberal Association from 1893. Author of *The Criminal Law of Scotland*. A Liberal. Unsuccessfully contested N. Ayrshire in 1906. Elected for N. Ayrshire in Jan. 1910 and sat until defeated in Dec. 1911 after appointed as Solicitor-Gen. for Scotland. He continued in that post until 1913 when he became a Senator of the Coll. of Justice, Scotland with title of Lord Anderson. Chairman of Scottish Committee on Aliens 1917-18. Died 27 May. 1936.   [1911]

ANDERSON, Charles Henry. 39 Montagu Square, London. Devonshire, and National Liberal. Youngest s. of the Rev. Richard Anderson, of Aiskew House, Bedale, Yorkshire, by Emma, d. of John Weston, Esq. B. at Burnston Vicarage, Yorkshire 1838; m. 1880, Gertrude Emily Ada, eld. d. of Edmund A. Pontifex, Esq., of Cromwell Road, London. Educ. privately. Was called to the bar at the Inner Temple in 1867, and appointed Q.C. in 1885. An "Advanced Liberal", who supported Mr. Gladstone's Home Rule Policy for Ireland. Unsuccessfully contested the united counties of Elgin and Nairn in Nov. 1885. Sat for Elgin and Nairn from July 1886 until his death 25 Aug. 1889. [1889]

ANDERSON, George Knox. 43 St. James Court, London. Bridge Hill House, Nr. Canterbury. S. of John Andrew Anderson, Esq., of Faversham. B. 1854; m. 1883, Mary Ada, d. of John Prall, Esq., of Rochester. A Magistrate and Dept.-Lieut. for Kent. A Conservative. First returned for Canterbury, unopposed, on the death of Maj. F. Bennett-Goldney, 9 Aug. 1918, but retired in Nov. of that year. Member of Central Board for Church Finance 1920-30. Died 19 Mar. 1941.

ANDERSON, William Crawford. 7 Mecklenburg Square, London. S. of Frank Anderson, Esq., Blacksmith. B. 1877 at Gamrie, Banffshire; m. 1911, Mary, d. of J.D. Macarthur, Esq., of Trabboch, Ayrshire. Educ. at elementary school. Was apprenticed to a Manufacturing Chemist 1893; Organiser of Shop Assistants' Union 1903-07; Chairman of Independent Labour Party 1911-13, and of the National Labour Party 1914-15. Wrote many articles and pamphlets on labour questions. A Labour Member. Unsuccessfully contested the Hyde division of Cheshire in Jan. 1910 and the Keighley division of the W. Riding of Yorkshire in 1911. Elected for the Attercliffe division of Sheffield in Dec. 1914 and sat until defeated in 1918. Caught Influenza two months later and died 25 Feb. 1919.   [1918]

ANDREWS, Joseph Ormonde. Beechwood, Boston Spa, Nr. Leeds. S. of John Andrews, Esq., of Liverpool. B. 1873; m. 1904, d. of Richard Fawcett, Esq., of Boston Spa. Called to the bar at the Inner Temple 1898 and practised on the N.E. Circuit. A Liberal. First returned for the Barkston Ash division of the W. Riding of

Yorkshire on the death of Sir R. Gunter, Oct. 1905 and sat until defeated in Jan. 1906. Died 26 Jan. 1909.

ANNAND, James. Ripon. B. in Aberdeenshire 1843, and learned his father's trade as a Blacksmith. Educ. himself and became first a Schoolmaster and then a Journalist. Editor of the *Newcastle Chronicle*, owned by Joseph Cowen 1874-78, but resigned over the Eastern Question. A Liberal. Unsuccessfully contested Tynemouth in 1892 and St. Andrews in 1900. Returned for Aberdeenshire E. in Jan. 1906 and sat until his death 6 Feb. 1906.

ANSON, Rt. Hon. Sir William Reynell, Bart. All Souls College, Oxford. Pusey, Faringdon, Berkshire. 194 Ashley Gardens, London. Brooks's, Travellers', New University, and Athenaeum. Eld. s. of 2nd Bart., of Birch Hall, Manchester, by Elizabeth, d. of Maj.-Gen. Sir Denis Pack, K.C.B. B. 1843 at Avisford, Walberton, Sussex. Educ. at Eton, and Balliol Coll., Oxford. A Fellow All Souls Coll. 1867; Warden there 1881. D.C.L. Called to the bar at the Inner Temple 1869, bencher 1900. Succeeded as 3rd Bart. in 1873. Vinerian Reader in Civil and English Law at Oxford 1874-81. Vice-Chancellor of Oxford University 1898, and resigned in 1899 to become one of its representatives in Parliament; was Parliamentary Secretary of Board of Education 1902-05. Author of works on *Law of Contract, Law and Custom of the Constitution*, etc. Chairman of the Quarter Sessions Oxfordshire. Chancellor of the diocese of Oxford 1899-1912; a Trustee of British Museum and National Portrait Gallery. PC. 1911. A Unionist. In 1880 he unsuccessfully contested W. Staffordshire as a Liberal. First elected for Oxford University in May 1899 and sat until his death 4 June 1914.   [1914]

ANSTRUTHER, Henry Torrens. 6 Chester Street, London. Brooks's, and New Club. 2nd s. of Sir R. Anstruther, Bart., of Balcaskie, Fife (MP for Fife 1864-80, and for the St. Andrew's district 1885-86), by Louisa, d. of the Rev. W. Knox-Marshall, of Wragby, Lincoln. B. in London 1860; m. 1889, Hon. Eva Hanbury-Tracy, eld. d. of the 4th Baron Sudeley. Educ. at Eton, and the University of Edinburgh. J.P. Co. Fife, and Lieut. in the Fife Light Horse Volunteers. Appointed a Junior Lord of the Treasury 1895

and 1900; a Unionist whip. Became a member of the Faculty of Advocates, Edinburgh May 1884. A Liberal Unionist. Sat for the St. Andrews district from July 1886 until appointed Director of Suez Canal Company in 1903. Junior Lord of the Treasury from 1895-1903. Alderman, London County Council 1905-10; Director of North British Railway Company 1900-23. Died 5 Apr. 1926.   [1903]

ANSTRUTHER, Sir Robert, Bart. 1 Eccleston Square, London. Balcaskie, Pittenweem, Fifeshire, Bramore, Caithness. Eld. s. of Sir Ralph Abercrombie Anstruther (4th Bart.), by Jane, eld. d. of Maj.-Gen. Sir Henry Torrens, K.C.B. B. in Edinburgh 1834; m. 1857, Louisa, eld. d. of the Rev. William Knox Marshall, B.D., Rector of Wragby, and Canon of Hereford. Educ. at Harrow. Served in the Grenadier Guards from 1853-62, and received the rank of Capt. and Lieut.-Col. May 1861. A Dept.-Lieut. of Caithness and Lord-Lieut. of the County of Fife. Patron of 1 living. A Liberal. First elected for Fifeshire Apr. 1864. Sat until he retired in 1880. Contested St. Andrews district in Dec. 1885, when the election was tied, and after a scrutiny Sir Robert Anstruther was declared elected on 16 Feb. 1886. Retired in June 1886. Died 21 July 1886.   [1880]

ANSTRUTHER, Robert Hamilton Lloyd-. 18 Wilton Crescent, London. Hintlesham Hall, Ipswich. White's, and Carlton. Eld. s. of Col. Lloyd-Anstruther, of Hintlesham. B. 1841; m. 1st 1871, Gertrude Louisa Georgiana, eld. d. of F. Horatio Fitz-Roy, Esq., of Frogmore Park, Hampshire; 2nd, 1898, Hon. Rachel Calthorpe. Entered the Rifle Brigade in 1858; served during the Indian Mutiny and the Suakin campaign, and received the medals and clasp for his services. He held various staff appointments and retired from the army with the rank of Lieut.-Col. A Magistrate and Dept.-Lieut. for Suffolk. A Conservative. Sat for Suffolk S.E. from July 1886 until defeated in 1892. Died 24 Aug. 1914.   [1892]

ANSTRUTHER-GRAY, Lieut.-Col. **William.** Kilmany, Fife. St. Adrians, Crail, N.B. Carlton, Travellers', and Marlborough. S. of Col. J. Anstruther-Thomson, of Charleton, Fife, and Maria Hamilton Gray, of Carntyne, Glasgow. B. 6 Sept. 1859; m. Clayre, d. of Hon. A. Tennant, of Gleneig, S. Australia. Educ. at Eton. Assumed the name of Gray in lieu of Thomson in 1904. Joined the 13th Hussars 1880, and transferred to Royal Horse Guards 1885; retired with rank of Maj. Was Aide-de-Camp to Earl of Kintore when Gov. of S. Australia 1889-91. Served in S. African War 1901, and was Inspector of Concentration Camps in the Transvaal 1902; commanded 3rd line group Scottish Horse. A J.P. for Fife, Lanark, and Glasgow; F.R.G.S., F.S.A. A Unionist. Unsuccessfully contested St. Andrews Burghs 1903; sat for St. Andrews Burghs from 1906 to Jan. 1910, when he was defeated; re-elected there Dec. 1910 and sat until he retired in 1918. Died 17 Apr. 1938. [1918]

ANSTRUTHER-THOMSON, Lieut.-Col. William. See ANSTRUTHER-GRAY, Lieut.-Col. William.

ARBUTHNOT, Gerald Archibald. 43 Prince's Gardens, London. Carlton, and Bachelors'. S. of Maj.-Gen. William Arbuthnot, C.B., and Selina, d. of Sir Thomas Moncrieff, 7th Bart. B. 19 Dec. 1872; m. 1894, Mary, d. of Charles Oppenheim, Esq. Educ. privately and on H.M.S. *Britannia.* Was a Midshipman in the navy 1886-91, and Private Secretary to the Rt. Hon. W.H. Long, successively as President of the Board of Agriculture 1895-99, President of Local Government Board 1901-02, and Chief Secretary for Ireland 1905. A Unionist. Unsuccessfully contested Burnley in 1906; elected for Burnley in Jan. 1910 and sat until defeated in Dec. 1910. Vice-Chancellor, Primrose League 1912. Engaged in mine sweeping for the first year of the war. Joined Grenadier Guards as 2nd Lieut in Jan. 1916. Killed in action 25 Sept. 1916. [1910]

ARCH, Joseph. Barford, Warwickshire. S. of John Arch, Esq., a Labourer, and Hannah, his wife. B. 1826 at Barford; m. 1847, the d. of Mr. Mills, an Artisan (she died 1894). Educ. at the Barford Schools. As a child he had to earn his living in the fields, and he worked for some years as a Labourer. Becoming connected with the Methodists, he was employed by them as a Preacher. The agitation amongst the Agricultural Labourers brought him to the front of that movement, and having established in 1872 the National Agricultural Labourers' Union he became its President. Lectured for this Union in all

parts of the Kingdom and also in Canada. In 1898 his Autobiography was published, the Countess of Warwick having edited it. A Liberal, favouring Home Rule for Ireland, and the Radical programme generally. Unsuccessfully contested Wilton in Apr. 1880. Was first elected for N.W. Norfolk in 1885, but lost his seat at the general election of 1886. Again elected there 1892 and 1895 and sat until he retired in 1900. Died 12 Feb. 1919. [1900]

ARCHDALE, Edward Mervyn. Continued in House after 1918: full entry in Volume III.

ARCHER-SHEE, Col. Martin. Continued in house after 1918: full entry in Volume III.

ARKWRIGHT, John Stanhope. 56 St. George's Square, Westminster, London. Lyonshall, Herefordshire. Carlton. Only s. of John Hungerford Arkwright, Esq., of Hampton Court, Leominster, Lord-Lieut. of Herefordshire. B. 1872; m. 1906, Stephanie, d. of S. Robinson, Esq. Educ. at Eton, and Christ Church, Oxford; Newdigate Prizeman 1895. A Barrister-at-Law. Was Parliamentary Private Secretary to the Rt. Hon. G. of Balfour, MP. A J.P. and Dept.-Lieut. for Herefordshire. Chief Steward of City of Hereford, F.L.S. A Unionist. Elected for Hereford in 1900 and sat until he accepted Chiltern Hundreds in 1912. Knighted in 1934. Author of *The last muster, The supreme sacrifice,* etc. Died 19 Sept. 1954. [1911]

ARMITAGE, Benjamin. 39 Devonshire Place, London. Chomlea Bank, Pendleton, Lancashire. Devonshire. S. of Sir Elkanah Armitage, of Hope Hall, Pendleton, Lancashire (Mayor of Manchester 1848), by his 1st wife Miss Mary Bowers. B. in Salford 1823; m. 1st. 1845, d. of John Smith, Esq., of Bingley, Yorkshire; 2nd, 1856, d. of George Southam, Esq., of Manchester. Educ. at Barton Hall School, Patricroft, near Manchester. A Manufacturer at Manchester. Elected President of the Manchester Chamber of Commerce 1878-79, 1879-80 and 1880-81; then became one of the directors. A Trustee of the Manchester Grammar School. A Liberal. Sat for Salford from 1880 to 1885 and for Salford W. from 1885 to 1886, when he was defeated standing as a

Gladstonian Liberal. Contested the same seat in 1892. Died 4 Dec. 1899. [1886]

ARMITAGE, Robert. Continued in House after 1918: full entry in Volume III.

ARNOLD, Alfred. Clare Hall, Halifax. Carlton. S. of the Rev. F. Arnold, Rector of Brimington, Derbyshire. B. at Cheltenham 1835; m. 1855, Catherine, d. of Robert Comber, Esq., of The Place, Hadlow, Kent (she died 1891). Educ. at Chesterfield Grammar School and Sidney Sussex Coll., Cambridge. A Barrister, called to the Inner Temple 1878, and a J.P. for the W. Riding of Yorkshire. A Conservative. Contested Halifax July 1892 and again Feb. 1893. First returned for Halifax July 1895 and sat until he retired in 1900. Knighted 1903. Died 31 Oct. 1908. [1900]

ARNOLD, Arthur. 45 Kensington Park Gardens, London. Reform. 3rd s. of Robert Coles Arnold, Esq., of Whartons, Framfield, Sussex, and Heath House, Maidstone, by Sarah, d. of Daniel Pizey, Esq., of the Beeches, Essex. B. 1833; m. 1867, Amelia Elizabeth, d. of Capt. Hyde, of 96th Foot, of Castle Hyde, Co. Cork. Was assistant commissioner to inquire into the condition of the cotton factories under "The Public Works Act" from 1863 to 1866, and on the conclusion of his official duties received the thanks of the Poor Law Board and of a large number of the local authorities. Author of a work entitled *History of the Cotton Famine*, and a volume of travels *From the Levant*, besides several novels, etc. Editor of the *Echo* newspaper on its first establishment. A Liberal, in favour of an amendment of the laws relating to land, so as to facilitate its transfer, etc. Unsuccessfully contested Huntingdon borough in Dec. 1873. Sat for Salford from Apr. 1880 until 1885, when he unsuccessfully contested Salford N. Defeated again at Salford N. as a Gladstonian Liberal in 1886 and Dorset N. 1892. Magistrate for London and Dartmouth. Board of Trade Harbour Commissioner for Dartmouth. President of Free Land League. Knighted 1895. Chairman of London County Council 1895-97. Died 20 May 1902. [1885]

ARNOLD, Sydney. Continued in House after 1918: full entry in Volume III.

ARNOLD-FOSTER, Rt. Hon. Hugh Oakeley. 2 The Abbey Garden, Westminster, London. Athenaeum, and Savile. S. of William Delatield Arnold, Esq., Director of Public Instruction in the Punjaub, and the adopted s. of the Rt. Hon. W.E. Foster. B. 1855 at Dawlish. m. 1885, Mary, 2nd d. of Professor N. Story-Maskelyne, MP for Nl. Wiltshire. Educ. at Rugby, and University Coll., Oxford. Called to the bar at Lincoln's Inn. Was Secretary to the Admiralty 1900-03. PC. 1903. Secretary of State of War 1903-05 in Mr. Balfour's Ministry. He contributed a series of letters to the *Times* on Army Reform, etc., which were republished, and wrote the *Citizen Reader, The Laws of Every Day Life, In a Conning Tower*, and other books. A Liberal Unionist, opposed to Home Rule for Ireland, in favour of shorter hours of labour, licensing reform, and large measures of Naval and Military reform. Was an unsuccessful candidate at Darlington 1886, and at Dewsbury 1888. Sat for W. Belfast from 1892-1906; elected for Croydon in 1906 and sat until his death 12 Mar. 1909. [1908]

ARROL, Sir William. Dennistoun, Glasgow. Seafield, Ayr. S. of Thomas Arrol, Esq., and his wife Agnes, née Hogart. B. 1839 in Glasgow; m. 1864, Miss Elizabeth Pattison. He began work at the age of eight in a cotton mill; was then apprenticed to a Blacksmith, and so became Foreman at Laidlaw and Sons, Boiler and Bridge Makers, Glasgow and Edinburgh. Senior Partner in the firm of Arrol and Company, Engineers and Contractors, who built the Tay and Forth Bridges, and supplied the steel work for the Tower Bridge. A J.P. for Ayrshire and Honorary LL.D. Glasgow. Was Knighted in 1890. A Liberal Unionist. Unsuccessfully contested Ayrshire S. in 1892. First elected for Ayrshire S. in 1895 and sat until he retired in 1906. Died 20 Feb. 1913. [1905]

ASCROFT, Robert. Sonnenberg, East Croydon. Carlton. S. of William Ascroft, Esq., Solicitor, by Eleanor, d. of James Threlfall, Esq., of Lea, near Preston. B. 1847. Educ. at the Royal Grammar School Lancaster. Was a Solicitor from 1869; a J.P. for Oldham, and President of the Oldham Law Association. A Conservative, would promote British Interests, British Commerce, British Labour, and the introduction of bi-metalism, etc. Sat for

Oldham from July 1895 until his death 19 June 1899. [1899]

ASHER, Alexander. 20 Alva Street. Edinburgh. Beechwood, Midlothian. Reform, Brooks's, and Devonshire. S. of the Rev. William Asher, D.D., Minister of Inveravon, by Katherine Forbes, d. of the Rev. John Gordon, Minister of Duffus. B. at Inveravon 1835; m. 1870, Caroline Julia, eld. d. of the Rev. Charles Henry Craufurd Rector of Old Swinford, Worcestershire, and grand-d. of Maj.-Gen. Robert Craufurd, Leader of the Peninsular Light Division. Educ. at Elgin Academy, and King's Coll., Aberdeen; also at Edinburgh University. Was called to the Scottish bar in 1861. Became a Queen's Counsel in 1881, and elected Dean of the Faculty of Advocates 1895. Appointed Solicitor-Gen. for Scotland Aug. 1881-June 1885 again Feb.-July 1886 and a 3rd time Aug. 1892 until he resigned in Aug. 1894. Received the Honorary degree of LL.D. at Aberdeen in 1882; and at Edinburgh in 1891. A Dept.-Lieut. of the city of Edinburgh. A Liberal, in favour of Home Rule. Unsuccessfully contested Glasgow and Aberdeen Universities Apr. 1880. Sat for the Elgin district from July 1881 until his death 5 Aug. 1905. [1905]

ASHLEY, Lieut.-Col. Wilfrid William. Continued in House after 1918: full entry in Volume III.

ASHMEAD-BARTLETT, Sir Ellis. 22a St. James's Street, London. Carlton, Wellington, and St. Stephen's. B. in Brooklyn, U.S.A. in 1849; m. 1874, Frances Christina, eld. d. of H.E. Walsh, Esq., His grandparents on both sides were natural born British subjects. Eld. s. of Ellis Bartlett, Esq., of Plymouth, New England, who graduated at Amherst Coll., Massachusetts, and m. the d. of John King Ashmead, Esq., of Philadelphia. On his father's side was lineally descended from two of the Pilgrim Fathers, viz. Robert Bartlett, of Sussex, who sailed to New England in the ship *Ann* 1623, and m. Mary, d. of Richard Warren, who sailed in the *Mayflower* 1620. Was also descended on the mother's side from Theodore Lehman, who was the companion of William Penn, and received from him a large grant of land in Philadelphia. Was educ. at Torquay, and at Christ Church, Oxford, where he graduated B.A. 1872. Was President of the Oxford University Debating Society. Called to the bar at the Inner Temple June 1877. Held the office of an examiner in the Education Department; resigned 1880. Was Civil Lord of the Admiralty in Lord Salisbury's administration 1885, and again from 1886 to 1892. Knighted 1892. A Conservative, "in favour of strengthening and extending the imperial power and commerce of the United Kingdom." Sat for Eye 1880 to 1885, and from 1885 for the Ecclesall division of Sheffield until his death 18 Jan. 1902. [1901]

ASHTON, Thomas Gair. 39 Prince's Gardens, London. Hyde, Cheshire. Vinehall, Robertsbridge, Sussex, Brooks's, Reform, and New University. Eld. s. of Thomas Ashton, Esq., of Hyde, Cheshire, and Elizabeth Ashton, d. of S.S. Gair, Esq., of Penketh Hall, Liverpool. B. 1855: m. 1886, Eva Margaret, d. of J.H. James, Esq., J.P., of Kingswood, Watford, Hertfordshire. Educ. at Rugby, and University Coll., Oxford; M.A. A J.P. for Lancashire, Cheshire, and Sussex, and County Councillor for Cheshire. A Liberal. Sat for the Hyde division of Cheshire from 1885-86; unsuccessful there in 1886 and 1892. First elected for the Luton division of Bedfordshire in 1895 and sat until created 1st Baron Ashton-of-Hyde 28 June 1911. Died 1 May 1933. [1911]

ASQUITH, Rt. Hon. Herbert Henry. 44 Bedford Square, London. The Wharf, Sutton Courtney. Athenaeum, and Reform. 2nd s. of J. Dixon Asquith, Esq., of Croft House, Morley, Yorkshire, by Emily, d. of W. Willans, Esq., of Huddersfield. B. at Morley 1852; m. 1st, 1877, Helen Kelsall, d. of Frederick Melland, Fsq., of Manchester (she died 1891); 2ndly, 1894, Margaret, d. of Sir Charles Tennant, Bart. Educ. at the City of London School, and Balliol Coll., Oxford, of which he was a scholar and Fellow (B.A.), first class classics, and Craven Scholarship. Called to the bar at Lincoln's Inn 1876; Q.C. 1890; bencher 1894. Was Home Secretary from 1892-95; Chancellor of the Exchequer Dec. 1905 to Apr. 1908, when he was appointed Prime Minister and First Lord of the Treasury; resigned 5 Dec. 1916. Secretary of State for War Apr. to Aug. 1914; Honorary D.C.L. Oxford and Durham; Honorary LL.D. Cambridge, Edinburgh, Glasgow, Leeds, Bristol, St. Andrews and McGill Universities; Lord Rector of

Glasgow University 1906, and Aberdeen University 1909; Honorary Fellow of Balliol Coll. 1908; F.R.S., Eld. Bro. of Trinity House 1909. Awarded special war medals by the King Jan. 1920. A Liberal. MP for E. Fife from 1886 to Dec. 1918 when he was defeated, and for Paisley from Feb. 1920 until he was again defeated in Oct. 1924. Leader of the Liberal Party Apr. 1908-Oct. 1926. K.G. 1925. Created Earl of Oxford and Asquith 1925. Unsuccessful candidate for election as Chancellor of Oxford University 1925. Author of *Memories and Reflections, The Genesis of the War,* and *Fifty Years of Parliament.* Died 15 Feb. 1928. [1924 2nd ed.]

ASTBURY, John Meir. 16 Grenville Place, London. Reform. Eld. s. of F.J. Astbury, Esq., J.P., of Hilton Park, Prestwich. B. 14 June 1860 at Manchester; m. 1888, Evelyn, d. of Paul Susmann, Esq., of Manchester. Educ. at Trinity Coll., Oxford. M.A., B.C.L. Vinerian School 1884. Called to the bar at the Middle Temple 1884; Q.C. 1895; bencher of his Inn 1903. A Liberal. Unsuccessfully contested Manchester S.W. in July 1895 and St. Pancras E. in Oct. 1900. Elected for the Southport division of Lancashire in 1906 and sat until he retired Jan. 1910. Knighted 1913 and appointed Judge in Chancery Division 1913-29. PC. 1929. Died 21 Aug. 1939. [1909]

ASTOR, Hon. Waldorf. Continued in House after 1918: full entry in Volume III.

ATHERLEY-JONES, Llewellyn Archer. 4 Paper Buildings, Temple, London. 25 Pembroke Road, Kensington, London. Kimberscote, Bray, Berkshire. Devonshire. S. of Ernest Jones, Esq., Barrister-at-Law, the wellknown Chartist leader, by Jane, d. of Gibson Atherley, Esq., of Barfield, Cumberland. B. 1851; m. Elizabeth Fannie d. of James Lambert, Esq., of Durham. Educ. at Manchester Grammar School, and Brasenose Coll., Oxford. Was called to the bar at the Inner Temple in 1875; bencher 1907; joined the N.E. Circuit; a Q.C. 1896; Recorder for Newcastle-on-Tyne from 1906. Judge of Burgess and Non-Burgess Courts, Newcastle-on-Tyne 1906. Author of *Commerce in War,* a treatise on International Law, *The Miner's Manual,* a treatise on the law of Mining, *The Law of Children and Young Persons, The Fall of Lord Paddockslea,* a political novel, and other works, including many articles in *The Nine-*

teenth Century and the *Edinburgh Review.* A Liberal, in favour of Disestablishment and partial disendowment with full compensation to the clergy; and of Home Rule in Ireland. Sat for N.W. Durham from 1885 until 1 Jan. 1914 when he resigned on appointment as Judge of the City of London Court and Commissioner at the Central Criminal Court. Died 15 June 1929. [1913]

ATKINSON, Henry John. See FARMER-ATKINSON, Henry John.

ATKINSON, Rt. Hon. John. 68 Fitzwilliam Square, Dublin. Carlton, and Garrick. Kildare Street, Dublin. S. of Edward Atkinson, Esq., of Glenudium, Ballergary, Co. Limerick, and Rosetta, d. of Capt. McCulloch of the 27th Regiment. B. at Drogheda 1844: m. 1874, Rowena, Jane, d. of Richard White, Esq., of Tralee. Educ. at the Royal Belfast Academic Institution, and Queen's University (B.A., LL.B.). Was called to the Irish bar 1865; a Q.C. 1880; bencher of King's Inns 1885; called to the English bar 1890; Solicitor-Gen. for Ireland 1889-92. Attorney-Gen. for Ireland 1892 and 1895-1905. PC. (Ireland) 1892, PC. 1905. A Conservative and Unionist, in favour of progress, justice for all classes, abolition of dual ownership of land in Ireland, etc. Returned for Londonderry N. July 1895 and sat until created Baron Atkinson (Law life peerage) 1905. Lord of Appeal 1905-28. Died 13 Mar. 1932. [1905]

ATTENBOROUGH, Walter Annis. 2 Pump Court, Temple, London. Holbrook, Bedford. St. Stephen's. S. of Robert Attenborough, Esq. B. 27 Nov. 1850. m. 1877, Lizzie, d. of Edward J. Caitler, Esq. Educ. at St. Paul's School, London, and Trinity Coll., Cambridge; M.A., LL.M. A Barrister, called to the bar at the Middle Temple 1874, and practised on the Midland Circuit; a J.P. for Bedford. A Unionist. Elected for Bedford in Jan. 1910 and sat until defeated in Dec. 1910. Died 13 June 1932. [1910]

AUBREY-FLETCHER, Rt. Hon. Sir Henry, Bart., C.B. 1 Upper Belgrave Street, London. Ham Manor, Angmering, Sussex. Dorton House, Nr. Thame. Llantrithyd, Glamorgan. Wreay Hall, Cumberland. Carlton, and Constitutional. Eld. s. of Sir Henry Fletcher, 3rd Bart., by Emily Maria, 2nd d. of George Browne, Esq., of Bombay. B. at Ashley Park, Surrey

1835; m. 1859, Agnes, d. of Sir John Morillyon Wilson, C.B., K.H., of the Royal Hospital, Chelsea. Succeeded as 4th Bart. in 1851. Entered the army as Ensign 69th Foot 1853; Lieut. Grenadier Guards 1855. Was Parliamentary groom-in-waiting 1885-86. A J.P. for Buckinghamshire, Surrey and Sussex, and a Dept.-Lieut. for Sussex. Patron of 7 livings. Was Col. 2nd Sussex Volunteer Infantry Brigade (retired 1904), and in the Westmoreland and Cumberland Yeomanry. C.B. 1900; PC. 1901. Assumed the surname of Aubrey-Fletcher in 1903. A Unionist. Sat for Horsham from Apr. 1880 to Nov. 1885, and for mid-Sussex from Nov. 1885 until his death 19 May 1910.   [1910]

AUSTIN, Sir John, Bart. Red Hill, Castleford. 2nd s. of J. Austin, Esq., Manor House, Kippax. B. 1824; m. 1866, Agnes, d. of S.S. Byron, Esq. Educ. at Kippax Grammar School. A J.P. for the W. Riding, Chairman Visiting Committee of the Co. Justices, York Castle. Was for six years Chairman of the Castleford School Board, and was President of the Osgoldcross Liberal Association. Created Bart. 1894. A Liberal, but opposed to Local Veto. Elected for the Osgoldcross division of the W. Riding of York shire 1886. In June 1899, having disagreed with some of his supporters on the Local Veto question, he resigned, offered himself for re-election. Re-elected as Independent Liberal 5 July 1899 and again in 1900 against the official Liberal candidate, but without Conservative opposition. Sat until he retired in 1906. Died 30 Mar. 1906   [1905]

AUSTIN, Michael. 54 Doddington Grove, Kennington Park, London. S. of John Austin, Esq., of Cork, and Ellin Collins, of Dunmanway, Co. Cork. B. at Cork 1855; m. 1885, Jane, 2nd d. of P. Moriarty, Esq., of The View, Orrey Hill, Cork. Educ. at the Christian Brothers' Schools, Cork. A Compositor, apprenticed 1869. A member of the Royal Commission on Labour, and was identified with the Labour movement in Ireland for many years. A Nationalist and Labour representative, supported the Anti-Parnellite section of the Irish Party. Sat for Limerick W. from July 1892 until he retired in 1900. Died 18 Feb. 1916. [1900]

BADEN-POWELL, Sir George Smyth, K.C.M.G. 114 Eaton Square, London. Athenaeum, Carlton, and R.Y.S. S. of Professor Baden-Powell, of Langton, Kent. B. 1847; m. 1893, Frances, d. of Charles Wilson, Esq., of Glendouran House, Cheltenham. Educ. at Marlborough, and Balliol Coll., Oxford, where he won the Chancellor's English Essay Prize 1876. He travelled much, having been Secretary to Sir George Brown, Governor of Victoria 1877-78, Special Commissioner to examine and report upon the administration and financial affairs of the West Indian Colonies 1882-84; assisted Sir C. Warren in Bechuanaland 1885; was Royal Commissioner to Malta, to arrange for the New Constitution 1887-88; created K.C.M.G. 1888, British Commissioner to Behring Sea June 1891, joint Commissioner at Washington Dec. 1891, and adviser at the Paris Arbitration 1894. LL.D., and wrote *New Homes for the Old Country*, and other works; also many papers and articles on colonial and financial subjects, etc. A Conservative, in favour of Imperial Unity, etc. Sat for the Kirkdale division of Liverpool from Nov. 1885 until his death 20 Nov. 1898   [1898]

BAGGALLAY, Ernest. 73 West Cromwell Road, London. United University, and Carlton. S. of the Rt. Hon. Sir Richard Baggallay, at one time Lord Justice of Appeal, by Marianne, d. of H.C. Lacy, Esq., MP. B. in Russell Square, July 1850; m. 1876, Emily Charlotte Edrica, d. of Sir W.W. Burrell, Bart., MP. Educ. at Marlborough Coll., and Caius Coll., Cambridge. Called to the bar at Lincoln's Inn 1873 and practised on the S.E. Circuit. Appointed Senior Counsel to the Post Office Dec. 1886. A Conservative, was in favour of measures for simplifying the transfer of land, and for establishing representative local government. Sat for the Brixton division of Lambeth from Nov. 1885 until appointed Police Magistrate for West Ham in 1887, which post he held until 1901. Metropolitan Police Magistrate 1901-14. Died 9 Sept. 1931. [1887]

BAGOT, Col. Josceline FitzRoy. Levens Hall, Milnthorp, Westmoreland. Carlton, Guards', and Marlborough. S. of Col. Charles Bagot, Grenadier Guards, and Sophia Louisa, d. of Vice-Admiral the Hon. Josceline Percy, C.B. B. 1854; m. 1885, Theodosia, d. of Sir John Leslie, Bart., of Glaslough, Ireland. Educ. at Eton. Was Parliamentary Private Secretary to

13

Mr. Hanbury, Secretary to the Treasury 1897-98; and to Sir M. Ridley, Home Secretary 1899. He joined the Manchester Regiment in 1873, and Grenadier Guards in 1875; retired as Capt. 1886. Was Lieut.-Col, in the Westmoreland and Cumberland Yeomanry. Aide-de-Camp to the Gov.-Gen. of Canada (Marq. of Lorne) 1882-83, and to Lord Stanley of Preston 1888-89. Served in the South African War 1899-1901, mentioned in despatches. A J.P., County Councillor, and Dept.-Lieut. for Westmoreland. A Unionist. Sat for the Kendal division of Westmoreland from 1892-1906, when he was defeated; re-elected there in Jan. 1910 and sat until his death 1 Mar. 1913. Nominated for Baronetcy in 1913 but died before it was conferred; his S. was then created 1st Bart. [1912]

BAILEY, Sir James. Prince's Gate, London. Lofts Hall, Saffron Walden. Carlton, Junior Carlton, and Constitutional. S. of William Bailey, Esq., of Kensington House, Mattishall, Norfolk. B. at Mattishall 1840; m. 1st, Catherine, d. of J. Smith, Esq., of Wallingford (she died 1892); 2ndly, 1896, Lily, d. of A. Fass, Esq., of Queen's Gate Gardens, London. Educ. at a private school at Dereham. A J.P. for Essex, Dept.-Lieut. for Norfolk, and one of the founders of the Constitutional Club. A Conservative. First elected for the Walworth division of Newington May 1895 and sat until defeated in 1906. Knighted 1905. Died 12 Oct. 1910. [1905]

BAILEY, Sir Joseph Russell, Bart. 11 St. James's Square, London. Glanusk Park, Crickhowell, Brecknockshire. Hay Court, Hereford. Easton Court, Tenbury. Eld. s. of Joseph Bailey, Esq., of Easton Court, Herefordshire, who represented that Co. for many years, by the only d. of William Congreve Russell, Esq., of Leamington. B. at Leamington 1840; m. 1861, d. of Henry Lucas, Esq., M.D. of Glan-yr-afon, Brecknockshire. Educ. at Harrow, and Christ Church, Oxford. He was the 2nd Bart. having succeeded his grandfather in 1858. Lord-Lieut. of Brecknockshire from 1875-1905 and High Sheriff of that Co. 1864. Also J.P. and Dept.-Lieut. for the Counties of Radnor and Hereford, Honorary Col. of the 1st Battalion South Wales Borders Volunteers, and Patron of 6 livings. Chairman of Hereford and Brecon Quarter Sessions 1883-1900. A Conserva-

tive. Sat for Herefordshire from 1865 to 1885 when he successfully contested the S. division at the general election of 1885. Sat for the city of Hereford from July 1886 until defeated in 1892. Created Baron Glanusk in 1899. Died 6 Jan. 1906. [1892]

BAILLIE, James Evan Bruce. 71 South Audley Street, London. Dochfour, Inverness. Carlton. Eld. s. of Evan Montagu Baillie, Esq., of Dochfour, and Lady Francis Bruce, d. of the 7th Earl of Elgin and Kincardine. B. in Paris 1859; m. 1894, Hon. Nellie Bass, d. of the 1st Baron Burton. Educ. at Eton. A J.P. for Co. Inverness, and Commissioner of Supply. A Conservative. Was first elected for Inverness-shire on the resignation of Dr. Macgregor, June 1895 and sat until he retired in 1900. Owner of about 92,600 acres. M.V.O. Died 6 May 1931. [1900]

BAILY, Laurence Richardson. Allerton Hall, Woolton, Lancashire. Windham. S. of John Baily, Esq., of Blandford Square and Gartley House, Kent, by Ann Richardson, d. of William Richardson, Esq., of London and Enfield. B. about 1815 at Stamford Hill, Middlesex. M. 1850, Mary, d. of John Smith, Esq., of Liverpool. Educ. at London and Paris. Was formerly an average adjuster, and was for eight years Government nominee on the Mersey Docks and Harbour Board. A Director of the Great Northern Railway, the Pacific Steam Navigation, and other companies. Wrote works on *Perils of the Sea*, and on *General Average*. A Conservative. Unsuccessfully contested Sunderland July 1874. Sat for the Exchange division of Liverpool from Nov. 1885 until defeated in 1886. Died 18 Apr. 1887. [1886]

BAIN, Sir James. Park Terrace, Glasgow. Crofthead, Harrington, Cumberland. Junior Carlton. S. of Robert Bain, Esq., and his wife, Agnes Dykes Miles, of Glasgow. B. at Glasgow 1818; m. Mary, d. of John Dove, Esq., of Glasgow (she died 1864). Educ. at Glasgow University. An Ironmaster at Harrington, in Cumberland, and lessor from Lord Lonsdale of the extensive Whitehaven Collieries. Was Lord-Provost of Glasgow 1874-77; a Dept.-Lieut. for Lanarkshire, and J.P. for that Co. and Cumberland. Was Knighted in 1877. Wrote papers in the magazines, and also, as a Juror for the Government, a Report on Iron Manufacturers at the

Philadelphia Exhibition of 1876. A Conservative, in favour of an Eight Hours Bill for Miners, and of giving the franchise to women. He was an unsuccessful candidate for Glasgow in 1880. First returned for Whitehaven in Apr. 1891 and sat until defeated in 1892. Died 25 Apr. 1898 [1892]

BAIN, James Robert. Bolton Hall, Gosforth, Cumberland. Carlton, and Junior Carlton. S. of Sir James Bain, of Glasgow, MP for Whitehaven, and Mary, d. of John Dove, Esq., of Glasgow. B. in Glasgow 1851; m. 1886, Lily, d. of Sir George Burton, Chief Justice of Ontario, Canada. Educ. at the University of Glasgow. An Ironmaster. Dept.-Lieut. for the Co. of Cumberland 1900, J.P. 1874; Col. 3rd Battalion Border Regiment (Cumberland Militia). A Conservative. Elected for the Egremont division of Cumberland 1900 and sat until he retired in 1906. Died 28 Feb. 1913. [1905]

BAINBRIDGE, Emerson Muschamp. 4 Whitehall Court, London. Auchnashellach, N.B. Reform, and National Liberal. S. of Emerson Bainbridge, Esq., of Northumberland. B. 1845; m. 1st, 1877, Eliza Armstrong (she died 1892); 2ndly, 1898, Norah Merryweather. A J.P. for Sheffield and Ross-shire; also Chairman of the Lancashire, Derbyshire, and East Coast Railway, and Vice-President of the Gainsborough Liberal Club. A Liberal, in favour of Home Rule. Sat for the Gainsborough division of Lincolnshire July 1895 until defeated in 1900. Endowed several charitable and educational establishments in later years. Died 12 May 1911. [1900]

BAIRD, John. Knodart, Isle-Ornsay. Arthur's, and St. James's. S. of John Baird, Esq., of Lochwood, Lanarkshire, by Margaret, d. of John Findley, Esq., of Springhall. B. 1852; m. 1878, Constance Amelia, d. of J.B. Harford, Esq., of Blaise Castle, Gloucestershire. Educ. at Harrow and Oxford. A Magistrate and Dept.-Lieut. for Inverness-shire. A progressive Conservative, "in favour of granting to Ireland the greatest measure of self-government compatible with maintaining the integrity and the best interests of the Empire"; also of facilitating the transfer of land. Sat for the N.W. division of Lanarkshire from Dec. 1885 until defeated in 1886. Died 8 July 1900. [1886]

BAIRD, John George Alexander. 89 Eaton Square, London. Wellwood, Muirkirk, N.B. Carlton, and Naval & Military. S. of William Baird, Esq., of Gartsherrie, by Janet Johnson. B. at Rosemount, Monkton, N.B. 1854; m. 1880, Susan Georgiana, d. of Sir J. Fergusson, of Kilkerran, Bart. Educ. at Eton, and Christ Church, Oxford. Entered the army in 1876, and retired (Lieut. 16th Lancers) 1882. Lieut.-Col. Ayrshire Yeomanry, Dept.-Lieut. Glasgow, city and Lanarkshire etc. A Conservative. Unsuccessfully contested Central Glasgow in Nov. 1885. First elected for the Central division of Glasgow 1886 and sat until defeated in 1906. Edited the *Private Letters of the Marquis of Dalhousie* (1910). Died 6 Apr. 1917. [1905]

BAIRD, John Lawrence, C.M.G., D.S.O. Continued in House after 1918: full entry in Volume III.

BAKER, Rt. Hon. Harold Trevor. 42 Queen Anne's Gate, London. Lawley Lodge, Clitheroe. Brooks's. S. of Sir John Baker, MP for Portsmouth, and Louisa, d. of R. Crispin, Esq., Paymaster-in-Chief, R.N. B. 22 Jan. 1877 at Portsmouth. Unmarried. Educ. at Winchester, and New Coll., Oxford; Fellow 1900-07. A Barrister, called to the bar at the Inner Temple 1903. Was Parliamentary Private Secretary to Lord Haldane when Secretary for War 1910-11. Financial Secretary to War Office 1912-15. PC. 1915. Inspector and Quarter-Master Gen. Services. Author of *The Territorial Force, a Manual of its Organisation and Administration*. A Liberal. Elected for the Accrington division of N.E. Lancashire in Jan. 1910 and sat until defeated in 1918. Unsuccessfully contested Accrington in 1922. Fellow of Winchester Coll. 1933; Warden 1936-46. Died 12 July 1960. [1918]

BAKER, Sir John. North End House, Portsmouth. 4 Queen's Gardens, Hove. National Liberal. B. 1828 at Portsmouth; m. 1870, Louisa, d. of R. Crispin, Paymaster-in-Chief, R.N. A Woollen Merchant with business houses at Portsmouth, Southampton, and Liverpool. A J.P. and Alderman of Portsmouth; twice Mayor, and 21 years Chairman of the School Board for Portsmouth. Knighted in 1895. A Liberal and Home Ruler. Unsuccessfully contested Portsmouth 1886. Represented

Portsmouth from 1892 until defeated at the general election of 1900. Re-elected there in 1906 and sat until his death 9 Nov. 1909.   [1909]

BAKER, Joseph Allen. Donnington, Harlesden, London. National Liberal. S. of Joseph Baker, Esq. B. 10 Apr. 1852 at Maple Ridge Farm, Trenton, Ontario; m. 1878, Elizabeth, d. of Richard Moscrip, Esq., of Morebattle, Kelso. Educ. at Trenton High School. Chairman of J. Baker and Sons Limited, Engineers, Willesden. A member of the Society of Friends. Member of the London County Council for E. Finsbury from 1895-1907, and was Chairman of the Highways Committee. Was for some years President of the London Adult School Union, and was largely interested in Temperance and Religious Work. A J.P. for Middlesex. An advanced Liberal. Unsuccessfully contested E. Finsbury at the general election of 1900. Represented E. Finsbury from June 1905 until his death 3 July 1918.   [1918]

BAKER, Lawrence James. 28 Queen's Gate. Ottershaw Park, Chertsey. Devonshire, and National Liberal. Eld. S. of John Law Baker, Esq., of Eastcote Lodge, Middlesex, formerly of the Madras Army. B. in London 1827; was twice m., one of his wives being the d. of Richard Taylor, Esq. Spent several years in India; and was once a member of the London Stock Exchange, of which he was also one of the Trustees and Managers. A Liberal, in favour of thorough Reform, "both in the House of Lords, and also in the procedure of the House of Commons." Sat for the Frome division of Somerset from Dec. 1885 until he retired in 1886. Unsuccessfully contested the Chertsey division of Surrey in Mar. 1892 and Feb. 1897. High Sheriff of Surrey 1898. Died 10 June 1921.   [1886]

BAKER, Sir Randolf Littlehales, Bart. 3 Whitehall Court, London. Ranston, Blandford, Dorset. Carlton, Arthur's, and Bath. S. of the Rev. Canon Sir Talbot Baker, 3rd Bart., and Amy, d. of Lieut.-Col. H. Marryat. B. 20 July 1879 at Ranston, near Blandford. Unmarried. Educ. at Winchester, and Magdalen Coll., Oxford; 2nd class History honours. Succeeded as 4th Bart. 1900. A J.P. and County Councillor for Dorset. Maj. Dorset Yeomanry; served in Gallipoli 1915. A Union-

ist. Unsuccessfully contested N. Dorset in 1905 and 1906. Elected for N. Dorset in Jan. 1910 and sat until he retired in 1918. D.S.O. 1918. Died 23 July 1959.   [1918]

BALCARRES, David Alexander Edward Lindsay, Lord. 7 Audley Square, London. Haigh Hall, Wigan. Carlton, and Burlington Fine Arts. Eld s. of the Earl of Crawford, by Emily Florence, d. of Col. the Hon. Edward Bootle Wilbraham. B. 1871; m. 1900, Constance, d. of Sir H. Pelly, MP. Educ. at Eton, and Magdalen Coll., Oxford. Was a Junior Lord of the Treasury Oct. 1903 to Dec. 1905. A Unionist Whip from 1903 and Chief Whip from 1911-13. Was Capt. 1st V.B. Manchester Rifles, and a Trustee of the National Portrait Gallery; Vice-Chairman of the National Trust and Honorary Secretary of the Society for the Protection of Ancient Buildings; LL.D., F.S.A., A.R.I.B.A. A Unionist. Sat for the Chorley division of Lancashire from 7 June 1895 until he succeeded as Earl of Crawford in 1913. President of the Board of Agriculture 1916. PC 1916. Lord Privy Seal 1916-19. Chancellor of Duchy of Lancaster 1919-21. First Commissioner of Works 1921-22. Minister of Transport and Member of Cabinet 1922. Chancellor of Manchester University. Owned 7,000 acres. Author of two books on Italian sculpture and of the article "Museums of Art" in the *Encyclopaedia Britannica* (1911 ed.). Chairman of Royal Fine Art Commission 1924. His active political career ended with the Lloyd George coalition in 1922, but he retained many contacts and an interest in politics. Died 8 Mar. 1940. [1913]

BALDWIN, Alfred. Kensington Palace Mansions, London. Wilden House, Stourport. Carlton, Athenaeum, St. Stephen's, and City of London. S. of George Baldwin, Esq., Ironfounder, of Stourport, and Sarah, d. of the Rev. J. Stanley. B. 1841 at Stourport; m. 1866, Louisa, d. of the Rev. G.B. Macdonald, of Wolverhampton. Educ. at private schools. An Ironmaster, Chairman of Baldwins Limited, the Metropolitan Bank (of England and Wales) Limited, and of the Great Western Railway. A J.P., and Dept.-Lieut. for Worcestershire, and J.P. for Staffordshire. A Progressive Conservative, strongly opposed to Home Rule for Ireland, to disestablishment of the Church, and to the Local Veto measure. Sat for Worcestershire W. from 1892 until his death 13 Feb. 1908. Father of Stanley Baldwin, Prime Minister of the Conservative governments of May 1923-Jan. 1924, and Nov. 1924-June 1929, and the Coalition government, June 1935-May 1937. [1907]

BALDWIN, Rt. Hon. Stanley. 10 Downing Street, London. Astley Hall, Nr. Stourport. Athenaeum, Carlton, United University, and Travellers'. S. of Alfred Baldwin, Esq., of Wilden House, Stourport, for 16 years MP for the Bewdley division of Worcestershire. B. 3 Aug. 1867; m. 12 Sept. 1892, Lucy, O.B.E., d. of E.L.J. Ridsdale, Esq., of Rottingdean. Educ. at Harrow, and Trinity Coll., Cambridge. Parliamentary Private Secretary to Mr. Bonar Law, Chancellor of the Exchequer Dec. 1916; Junior Lord of the Treasury Jan. 1917; Joint Financial Secretary to the Treasury June 1917; President of the Board of Trade 1921 to Oct. 1922; Chancellor of the Exchequer Oct. 1922; Prime Minister and First Lord of the Treasury May 1923 to Jan. 1924, Nov, 1924-June 1929, and from June 1935 to May 1937. Lord President of the Council Aug. 1931-June 1935, and Lord Privy Seal Sept. 1932-Jan. 1934. PC. 1920. Lord Rector of Edinburgh University 1923, and of Glasgow University 1928, Honorary LL.D. Cambridge and St. Andrews and Durham Universities 1923; Honorary D.C.L. Oxford and Durham 1925; F.R.S. 1927; Honorary LL.D. Birmingham and Edinburgh Universities 1927, London and Belfast 1933, Liverpool 1934, Chancellor of St. Andrews University from 1929, and of Cambridge from 1930. Eld. Bro. of Trinity House. Grand Master of Primrose League from 1925. A Trustee of the British Museum 1927. Gov. of Charterhouse 1933. Member of the Institut de France. Honorary Bencher of the Inner Temple 1936. Member of Imperial War Graves Commission 1936. A Conservative. Unsuccessfully contested Kidderminster in 1906. MP for the Bewdley division of Worcestershire from Feb. 1908 to June 1937 when he was created Earl Baldwin of Bewdley. Leader of the Opposition 1924 and 1929-31. Leader of the Conservative Party 1923-37. K.G. 1937. Died 14 Dec. 1947. [1937]

BALFOUR, Rt. Hon. Arthur James, O.M. 4 Carlton Gardens, London. Whittingehame, Prestonkirk, N.B. Carlton, Athenaeum, and Travellers'. S. of James Maitland Balfour, Esq., of Whittingehame, Haddingtonshire, by Lady Blanche Cecil, d. of the 2nd Marq. of Salisbury. B. 1848. Educ. at Eton, and Trinity Coll., Cambridge. Was Private Secretary to the Marq. of Salisbury as Foreign Secretary 1878-80, and during the special mission of Lord Beaconsfield and Lord Salisbury to Berlin 1878; a PC. and President of Local Government Board 1885; Secretary for Scotland 1886-87; Chief Secretary for Ireland 1887-91; First Lord of the Treasury and Leader of the House of Commons from 1891-92 and 1895-1905. Prime Minister from July 1902 to Dec. 1905; Lord Privy Seal 1902-03; First Lord of the Admiralty from May 1915 to Dec. 1916; Secretary of State for Foreign Affairs Dec. 1916 to Oct. 1919; Lord President of the Council from Oct. 1919-Oct. 1922; Member of the Peace Conference, Paris 1919. Undertook a special mission to the United States in 1917. Delegate to Washington Peace Conference 1921. Lord Rector of St. Andrews University 1886, of Glasgow University 1890, Chancellor of the University of Edinburgh from 1891; Chancellor of Cambridge University from Oct. 1919. Leader of the Unionist Party in the House of Commons 1891-1911. Order of Merit 1916. F.R.S., Honorary LL.D. Edinburgh, St. Andrews, Glasgow, Dublin, Manchester, Liverpool, Birmingham, Sheffield, and Bristol. Honorary D.C.L. Oxford, Durham, and Columbia University, New York. President of British Association 1904. Elder Brother of Trinity House, Dept.-Lieut. for E. Lothian. Author of *A Defence of Philosophic Doubt* (1879), *Essays and Addresses* (1883), *The Foundations of Belief* (1895), *Reflections Suggested by the New Theory of Matter, Decadence, Speeches (1880-1905) on Fiscal Reform* (1906), *Criticism and Beauty* (Romanes Lecture) (1910), *Theism and Humanism* (Gifford Lectures) (1914), etc. A Unionist. In the early part of his Parliamentary career he acted with Lord R. Churchill as one of the so-called "Fourth Party." Sat for Hertford from 1874 to 1885, and Manchester E. from 1885-1906 when he was defeated. Elected for the City of London in Feb. 1906 and sat until created 1st Earl of Balfour in May 1922. K.G. 1922. Lord President of the Council Apr. 1925-June 1929. Died 19 Mar. 1930. [1922]

BALFOUR, Charles Barrington. 14 Grosvenor Crescent, London. Newton

Don, Kelso. Guards', Bachelors', Bath, and Carlton. New Club, Edinburgh. S. of Charles Balfour, Esq., of Newton Don and Balgonie, and the Hon. Adelaide, d. of the 5th Visct. Barrington. B. at Newton Don, Kelso 1862; m. 1888, Lady Nina McDonnel, d. of the 10th Earl of Antrim. Educ. at Eton Coll., and the Royal Military Coll., Sandhurst. Lieut. Scots Guards 1881-90; served in Egypt 1882, Tel-el-Kebir medal and clasp and Khedive's star; Capt. Royal Guards Reserve Regiment 1900. J.P. for Roxburghshire, and J.P., Dept.-Lieut. and County Councillor for Berwickshire; Chairman of Finance Committee of County Council; President National Union of Conservative Associations for Scotland 1894-95. A Conservative. Unsuccessfully contested Roxburghshire Nov. 1885, Berwickshire July 1892 Mar. 1894 and July 1895, and the Southport division of Lancashire in May 1899. Elected for the Hornsey division of Middlesex in 1900 and sat until he accepted Chiltern Hundreds in May 1907. Died 31 Aug. 1921.   [1907]

BALFOUR, Sir George, K.C.B. 6 Cleveland Gardens, Hyde Park, London. City Liberal. S. of Capt. George Balfour, by his m. with Miss Susan Hume. B. at Montrose, Scotland, 1809; m. 1848, 3rd d. of Joseph Hume, Esq., MP. Was educ. at the Military Academy, Addiscombe. Entered the Madras Artillery in 1825; became Capt. and Maj. 1844; Col. 1855. Appointed a Maj.-Gen. in 1865; Lieut.-Gen. 1874, and Gen. in 1877. Was Consul at Shanghai from 1843 to the end of 1866. A member of the Madras Military Board from 1849 to 1857, and then Inspector-Gen. of Ordnance. A member of the Military Finance Commission of India in 1859 and 1860, and President of that Commission and Chief of the Military Finance Department from 1860 to 1862. In 1866 and from 1868 to 1870 was on the Royal Commission on Recruiting, and also assistant to the Controller-in-Chief, War Dept. Became C.B. in 1854, and K.C.B. in 1870. Retired 1879. A Liberal, in favour of improvement of laws relating to the tenure of land and of Home Rule for Ireland. Sat for Kincardineshire from Dec. 1872 until he retired in 1892. Died 12 Mar. 1894.   [1892]

BALFOUR, Rt. Hon. Gerald William. 3 Whitehall Court, London. Fishers Hill, Woking,   Surrey.   Carlton,   and Athenaeum. S. of James Maitland Balfour,

Esq., of Whittingehame, Haddingtonshire, by Lady Blanche, d. of the 2nd Marq. of Salisbury. B. at Edinburgh 1853; m. 1887, Lady Betty, eld. d. of the 1st Earl of Lytton. Educ. at Eton, and Trinity Coll., Cambridge, where he took a 1st class in the Classical Tripos of 1875, and became a fellow of his Coll. Was Private Secretary to his brother, the Rt. Hon. Arthur Balfour 1885. P.C. 1895. Was Chief Secretary for Ireland 1895-1900; appointed President of the Board of Trade 1900-05. President of Local Government Board Mar.-Dec. 1905. A Conservative. First elected for the Central division of Leeds 1885 and sat until defeated in 1906. Chairman of Commission on Lighthouse Administration 1908; Chairman of Cambridge Committee of Commission on Oxford and Cambridge Universities. Succeeded brother as 2nd Earl of Balfour in 1930. Died 14 Jan. 1945.   [1905]

BALFOUR, Jabez Spencer. 28 Whitehall Court, London. Burcot, Abingdon. Devonshire, and National Liberal. S. of Mr. James and Mrs. Clara Lucas Balfour, of Reigate, Surrey, the latter a well-known writer and temperance advocate. B. 1843 in London; m. Ellen, youngest d. of James Whittle Mead, Esq., of Westbourne Park. Educ. abroad. Director of various companies, and Chairman of some, including the House and Land Investment Trust, the Lands Allotments Company, the London and General Bank, and the London, Edinburgh, and Glasgow Assurance Company. Was the first Mayor of the borough of Croydon, and a J.P. for London, Surrey and Oxfordshire. A "Radical", and a supporter of Mr. Gladstone's Irish policy. Sat for Tamworth from 1880 to 1885 when he was an unsuccessful candidate at Croydon. Unsuccessfully contested the Walworth division of Newington in 1886 and the Doncaster division of the W. Riding of Yorkshire in Feb. 1888. Sat for Burnley from Feb. 1889 until he accepted Chiltern Hundreds in Dec. 1892. In 1893 he went to Buenos Aires to escape arrest but was eventually extradited and sentenced in 1895 to 14 years penal servitude for conspiracy and fraud in connection with the Liberator Building Society. He was released from prison in 1906. Died 23 Feb. 1910.   [1892 2nd ed.]

BALFOUR, Rt. Hon. John Blair. 67 Jermyn Street, London. 6 Rothesay Terrace,

Edinburgh. Glasclune, North Berwick. Brook's, Reform, Devonshire, National Liberal, and Caledonian. S. of the Rev. Peter Balfour, Minister of Clackmannan, by Jane Ramsay, d. of John Blair, Esq., of Perth. B. at Clackmannan 1937; m. 1st, 1869, Lilias Oswald, eld. d. of Lord Mackenzie, a Lord of Session in Scotland (she died 1872); 2ndly, 1877, Hon. Marianne Eliza, younger d. of the 1st Lord Moncreiff. Educ. at Edinburgh Academy, and at Edinburgh University. Was called to the Scottish bar in 1861; appointed a Queen's Counsel 1880; elected Dean of the Faculty of Advocates July 1885 and again May 1889. Was Solicitor-Gen. for Scotland from Apr. 1880 to Aug. 1881, Lord Advocate of Scotland till July 1885; Lord Advocate again Jan. till July 1886; and a third time Aug. 1892 to July 1895. Appointed member of the Committee of Council on Education for Scotland and a PC. 1883. LL.D. Edinburgh and St. Andrew's. A Dept.-Lieut. for the city of Edinburgh. A Liberal, in favour of Home Rule, etc. Sat for Clackmannan and Kinross from Nov. 1880 until appointed Lord Justice Gen. of Scotland in 1899, with title of Lord Balfour. Created Baron Kinross in 1902. Died 22 Jan. 1905. [1899]

BALFOUR, Kenneth Robert. 11 Lowndes Street, London. Stagsden House, Bournemouth. Naval & Military. 2nd s. of George Edmond Balfour, Esq., of The Manor, Sidmouth, Devon, and Marianna Jowitt, of Denison Hall, Leeds. B. 1863; m. 1st, 1888, Margaret Anne, d. of C. Rogerson, Esq., (she died 1901); 2ndly, 1903, May Eleanor, d. of Col. A. Broadwood. Educ. at Eton. Joined the Royal Dragoons 1885, retired as Capt. 1899; joined the Imperial Yeomanry 1900 as Maj. A J.P. for Dorset. A Conservative. Elected for Christchurch in 1900 and sat until defeated in 1906. Unsuccessfully contested Southampton in Jan. and Dec. 1910. Served in France 1915-18. High Sheriff of Dorset 1924. Member of Church Assembly 1925. Died 7 Sept. 1936. [1905]

BALFOUR, Sir Robert, Bart. Continued in House after 1918: full entry in Volume III.

BALLANTINE, William Henry Walter. 2 Grosvenor Mansions, Victoria Street, London. National Liberal, and Union. S. of William Ballantine, Esq., Serjeant-at-Law, by Eliza, d. of Henry Gyles, Esq. B. 1847, in London; m. 1878, Eleanor, widow of T.A. Mitchell, Esq., MP for Bridport. Educ. at Cheltenham Coll., and Trinity Hall, Cambridge. Called to the bar at the Inner Temple 1871, and joined the S.E. Circuit. An advanced Liberal, in favour of Home Rule for Ireland. Was an unsuccessful candidate at Coventry in 1886; but on Mr. H.W. Eaton's being raised to the peerage in July 1887 he successfully contested the seat, and sat until defeated in 1895. Died 1911. [1895]

BANBURY, Rt. Hon. Sir Frederick George, Bart. Continued in House after 1918: full entry in Volume III.

BANES, George Edward. 37, 38 Mark Lane, London. Red House, Upton, Essex. Eld. s. of G. Dann Banes, Esq., Surveyor of Iron Ship-Building to the Admiralty. B. at Chatham 1829; m. 1850, Mary Ann, eld. d. of M. Place, Esq., of Bromham, Bedfordshire. Educ. at Chatham, and Rochester High School. A Wharfinger and Bonded Warehouseman, trading as Banes, Noel and Company, Mark Lane, and the Colonial Wharves, Wapping. He founded the 3rd Essex Artillery Volunteer Corps in 1859, from which he retired as Maj. in 1876. A J.P. for West Ham, a member of the West Ham School Board from 1874-1901, and an Alderman of the borough. A Conservative, though "not a slavish follower of the party." In favour of "Local Self-Government for Ireland as well as England, Scotland, and Wales, subject to the control of a United Parliament." Did not agree with the Education Act. Believed in Free Trade, but favoured Fiscal Reform as suggested by Mr. Balfour and Mr. Chamberlain. Was MP for West Ham S. from 1886 until defeated 1892; reelected there in 1895 and again in 1900, and sat until he retired in 1906. Died 16 July 1907. [1905]

BANNER, John Sutherland Harmood. See HARMOOD-BANNER, Sir John Sutherland. Continued in House after 1918: full entry in Volume III.

BANNERMAN, Rt. Hon. Henry Campbell. See CAMPBELL-BANNERMAN, Rt. Hon. Sir Henry, G.C.B.

BARBOUR, William Boyle. Newmains Lodge, Camworth. Devonshire, City

19

Liberal, and National Liberal. S. of William Barbour, Esq., formerly Bailie and engaged in business at Paisley, by Janet Boyle, his wife. B. 1828. After assisting his father for some time, he entered the house of Bell and Company, Liverpool. Subsequently became head of the firm of Barbour, Barclay and Company, South American Merchants, Liverpool and Manchester, and spent some time in Buenos Ayres, etc. Retired from business in 1874. An "advanced Liberal", in favour of Home Rule. Sat for Paisley from 1885 until his death 13 May 1891.   [1891]

BARCLAY, James William. 5 Clarendon Place, London. Reform. S. of George Barclay, Esq., of Cults, Aberdeen, by Margaret, d. of James Massie, Esq. B. at Cults 1832; m. 1st, 1863, Jane, d. of John Smith, Esq., (she died 1865); 2ndly, 1882, Lilian Alice, 2nd d. of A.H. Novelli, Esq., of Hyde Park Square (she died 1887). Was educ. at the Grammar School and University of Aberdeen. Was a Town Councillor of Aberdeen from 1862 to 1865, and from 1868 to 1871. A Liberal, in favour of a thorough reform in our system of land tenure, and of a large reduction in our national expenditure. Voted against Mr. Gladstone's Home Rule proposals and thereafter sat as a Unionist. Sat for Forfarshire from Dec. 1872 until defeated in 1892. Died in Nigeria 26 Feb. 1907. [1892]

BARCLAY, Sir Thomas. 13 Old Square, Lincoln's Inn, London. Reform, and National Liberal. S. of George Barclay, Esq., LL.D., of Bonvil, Cupar, N.B., and Louisa, d. of William Giles, Esq., M.D. B. 20 Feb. 1853 at Dunfermline; m. 1877, Marie, d. of R. Teuscher, Esq., M.D. Educ. at Cupar Academy, Johanneum of Hamburg and Universities of London, Paris, and Jena; Ph.D. Jena, LL.B. Paris. A Barrister, called 1881, practised as an International Lawyer in Paris; a member of the Institute of International Law to the University of Oxford 1900; a member of Supreme Council of Congo Free State; Vice-President of Franco-Scottish Society; President and Honorary Secretary of British Chamber of Commerce in Paris; identified with the agitation which led to the entente with France; an officer of the Legion of Honour and a Knight of the Order of Leopold. Wrote *French Companies Law, Problems of International Practice and Diplomacy*, articles on International Law in *Encyclopaedia*

Britannica and *Encyclopaedia of Law of England*, and numerous articles in English and Foreign Magazines and Reviews. Knighted in 1904. A Liberal, specially interested in International Trade Questions, Treatises of Commerce, International Law, Foreign Politics, etc. Unsuccessfully contested Kirkcaldy as a Liberal Unionist in 1886. Elected for Blackburn as a Liberal Jan. 1910 and sat until he retired in Dec. 1910. Gold Medal of Société d'Economie Politique 1927. Died 20 Jan. 1941.   [1910]

BARING, Francis George Baring, Visct. 4 Hamilton Place, London. Eld. s. of the Earl of Northbrook, by Elizabeth Harriet, 3rd d. of Henry Charles Sturt, Esq., of Critchil House, Wimborne, Dorset. B. at Florence 1850. Educ. at Eton. Appointed Ensign Rifle Brigade Apr. 1870; Lieut. Oct. 1871; transferred to the Grenadier Guards June 1876; retired Apr. 1880. Served as Aide-de-Camp to his father while Governor-Gen. of India from 1873 to 1876. A Maj. (retired) 1st Hants. Volunteers and a Magistrate for the Co. A Liberal Unionist. Sat for Winchester from Apr. 1880 to Nov. 1885 but at the ensuing general election he was defeated. Returned for Bedfordshire N. July 1886 and sat until defeated in 1892. Succeeded as 2nd Earl of Northbrook in 1904. Died 12 Apr. 1929.   [1892]

BARING, Sir Godfrey, Bart. Nubia House, Cowes, Isle of Wight. 14 Harrington Gardens, London. National, Brooks's, Bachelors', Royal Yacht Squadron, and Travellers'. S. of Lieut.-Gen. Charles Baring, and Helen, d. of Rt. Hon. Sir James Graham, 2nd Bart., of Netherby. B. 18 Apr. 1871; m. 1898, Eva Hermione, d. of MacKintosh of MacKintosh. Educ. at Eton. A J.P. and Dept.-Lieut. for Hampshire; High Sheriff 1897-98; Chairman of Isle of Wight County Council from 1898-1957; member of Board of Visitors to Parkhurst Prison. Lieut. 3rd Battalion Hampshire Regiment. Parliamentary Private Secretary (unpaid) to Col. Seely when Under Secretary for the Colonies 1908-10, and to Mr. J.A. Pease, President of Board of Education 1911-15; created Bart. 1911. Chairman of the Hampshire and Isle of Wight Appeal Tribunal under the Military Service Act. A Liberal. Unsuccessfully contested Isle of Wight May 1900, Stoke-on-Trent Oct. 1900, and Devonport Dec. 1910. Sat for the Isle of Wight from 1906 to Jan. 1910, when he was defeated. Elected for the Barnstaple division of Devonshire in May 1911 and sat until 1918 when he unsuccessfully contested the Isle of Wight. Unsuccessfully contested Islington E. in 1922. K.B.E. 1952. Died 24 Nov. 1957. [1918]

BARING, Hon. Guy Victor. Biddesden House, Andover. 16 Cadogan Square, London. Carlton, and Guards'. S. of 4th Lord Ashburton. B. 26 Feb. 1873 in London; m. 1903, d. of Hugh C. Smith, Esq. Educ. at Eton, and Royal Military Coll., Sandhurst. Maj. in Coldstream Guards; Maj. Reserve of Officers; Temporary Lieut.-Col. 1915; served in S. Africa 1899-1900; mentioned in despatches; and in Jubaland 1901. A Unionist. Elected for Winchester in 1906 and sat until he was killed in action in Sept. 1916. [1916]

BARING, Thomas Charles. 1 Grafton Street, London. 8 Bishopsgate Within, London. High Beech, Loughton, Essex. University, Travellers', Carlton, and City. Eld. s. of Charles Baring, Esq., D.D., Lord Bishop of Durham, by Mary Ursula, only d. of Col. Charles Sealy, H.E.I.C.S. Nephew of the 1st Lord Northbrook. B. at Adderbury, Oxon 1831; m. 1859, Susan Carter, d. of Robert Browne Minturn, Esq., of New York and Hastings-upon-Hudson. Educ. at Harrow, and Oxford (where he was Scholar of Wadham and afterwards a Fellow of Brasenose Coll.), and graduated B.A. 1852, M.A. 1855. Was for some years a Banker in New York and then a partner in the firm of Messrs. Baring Brothers and Company, London and Liverpool. A J.P. for Essex, Middlesex and Westminster, and Dept.-Lieut. for Essex, and in the Commission of Lieutenancy for London. Author of *Pindar in English Rhyme, The System of Epicurus,* and other works. Sat on the Royal Commission on Loss of Life at sea 1885-87. A staunch Conservative and strong Churchman, but "first of all a Unionist." Sat for Essex S. from Feb. 1874 to Nov. 1885, unsuccessfully contested S.W. Essex in Dec. 1885. First elected for the City of London in July 1887 and sat until his death 2 Apr. 1891. [1890]

BARKER, Sir John, Bart. The Grange, Bishops Stortford. Old Court Mansions, Kensington, London. Devonshire, and National Liberal. Eld. s. of Joseph Barker, Esq., of Loose, near Maidstone. B. 1840. Educ. privately. Head and Founder of John Barker and Company, Kensington. A J.P. for Hertfordshire, and Alderman of the first London County Council; created Bart. 1908. A Liberal. Unsuccessfully contested Maidstone 1888 and 1898; elected there in 1900, but was unseated on petition in Feb. 1901. Elected for Penryn and Falmouth in 1906 and sat until defeated in Jan. 1910. Died 16 Dec. 1914. [1909]

BARLOW, Rt. Hon. Sir Clement Anderson Montague-, Bart., K.B.E. See MONTAGUE-BARLOW, Rt. Hon. Sir Clement Anderson, Bart., K.B.E. Continued in House after 1918: full entry in Volume III.

BARLOW, Sir John Emmott, Bart. Torkington Lodge, Hazel Grove, Cheshire. Bryn Eirias, Colwyn Bay, North Wales. Brooks's, Devonshire, and National Liberal. Eld. s. of Thomas Barlow, Esq., J.P., of Torkington Lodge, Hazel Grove, Cheshire, and Mary Ann, d. of George Emmott, Esq., Civil Engineer, of Disley, Cheshire. B. 1857 at Adswood Grove, near Stockport, Cheshire; m. 1895, Hon. Anna Maria Heywood Denman, sister of Lord Denman. Educ. at Tottenham School, and by private tuition. Was called to the bar at the Inner Temple 1884. Was Senior Partner in the firms of Thomas Barlow and Brother, Manchester and London, and Barlow and Company of Calcutta, Shanghai, Kuala Lumpur, F.M.S., and Singapore. A J.P. for Somerset and Cheshire, and a Co. Alderman for Cheshire; created Bart. 1907. A Liberal. Unsuccessfully contested the Knutsford division of Cheshire in 1885, and Denbigh district in 1886. Sat for the Frome division of Somerset from 1892 to 1895 when he was defeated; re-elected there in 1896 and sat until again defeated in 1918. Died 17 Sept. 1932. [1918]

BARLOW, Percy. Torkington House, Acton, London. 5 Essex Court, Temple, London. National Liberal, Bath, and Royal Automobile. S. of Thomas Barlow, Esq., J.P., of Hazel Grove, Cheshire, and Mary Ann, d. of George Emmott, Esq., of Disley, Cheshire. B. 11 July 1867 at Hazel Grove; m. 1892, Clara Frances, d. of William Staple Lee Midelton, Esq., of Somerset. Educ. privately, and at Pembroke Coll. and Downing Coll., Cambridge; M.A. A Barrister, called to the bar at the Inner Temple 1892; J.P. for Middlesex. A member of the Society of Friends. A Liberal. Unsuccessfully contested Bedford in 1900; elected there in 1906 and sat until defeated in Jan. 1910. Worked as a Recruiting Officer 1915-18. Died 18 June 1931. [1909]

BARNARD, Edmund Broughton. Westminster Palace Hotel, London. Fair Green House, Sawbridgeworth, Hertfordshire. Reform, National Liberal, and Farmers'. S. of William Barnard, Esq., of Harlow Mill, Essex, and Fair Green, Sawbridgeworth. B. 16 Feb. 1856 at Fair Green House; m. 1887, Alice Maude, d. of Charles Richardson, Esq., of Wimbledon Park (she died 1907). Educ. at Brighton Coll., and Downing Coll., Cambridge; M.A. 1880. Vice-Chairman of Hertfordshire County Council, a member from 1888; a member of the Lee and Thames Conservancy Boards, and Chairman of Metropolitan Water Board. Was a member of the Agricultural Board of Studies, Cambridge University. A Radical, in favour of Religious Equality and the Programme of the Trades Union Parliamentary Committee. Advocated an Independent Agricultural Party, and specialised in Local Taxation and Valuation, Water Supply, etc. etc. Unsuccessfully contested Epping division of Essex in 1885, the Maldon division of Essex in 1886, and Kidderminster in 1900. Elected for Kidderminster in 1906 and sat until Jan. 1910 when he unsuccessfully contested Hertfordshire E. Unsuccessfully contested Islington E. as a National Party candidate Oct. 1917, and Hertford as National Party and Farmers candidate in 1918. Knighted 1928. Died 27 Jan. 1930. [1909]

BARNES, Alfred. Ashgate Lodge, Chesterfield. Reform. Youngest s. of John Gorell Barnes, Esq., of Ashgate, Derbyshire, by Elizabeth Taylor, d. of John Clay, Esq., of Northwingfield, Derbyshire. B. at Ashgate 1823; m. 1854, Charlotte, youngest d. of Thomas Wilson, Esq., of Liverpool. Was educ. at a private school at Worksop. An extensive Coal Owner, having Collieries at Grassmoor, near Chesterfield. A Dept.-Lieut. and Magistrate for Derbyshire. A Liberal, but voted against the Home Rule Bill. Sat for Derbyshire 1880-85 and for the Chesterfield division of Derbyshire from 1885 until defeated in 1892. President of Chesterfield and Midland Counties Institution of Engineers in 1893. Died 28 Nov. 1901. [1892]

BARNES, Frederic Gorell. 19 Bramham Gardens, London. Dadmans, Lynsted, Sittingbourne. Carlton, Oxford & Cambridge, and Garrick S. of Charles Barnes, Esq., J.P., of Mossley Hill, Wavertree, Lancashire, and of his wife Marian, eld. d. of the Rev. W. Peach, Vicar of Old Brampton, Derbyshire. B. 1856; m. 1894, Caroline Anne Roper, only d. of Sir Roper Lethbridge, K.C.I.E., MP for N. Kensington. Educ. at the Royal Institution, Liverpool, and Jesus Coll., Cambridge (B.A. 1881, M.A. 1887). Called to the bar at the Inner Temple 1885 and joined the N. Circuit. A J.P. and Dept.-Lieut. for Kent and a Fellow of the Royal Geographical Society. A Conservative, opposed to Home Rule, but in favour of local self-government for Ireland, of the Amendment of the Employers' Liability Act, the Poor Laws, etc., and also of the claims of Agriculture; opposed to disestablishment, etc. Unsuccessfully contested N.E. Derbyshire in 1892. Sat for the Faversham division of Kent from July 1895 until he retired in 1900. Contested Northampton in 1906 and Jan. 1910. Knighted in 1916. Vice-President of Tariff Reform League; various jobs in Ministry of Food 1917-21. Died 17 Mar. 1939. [1900]

BARNES, Rt. Hon. George Nicoll. Continued in House after 1918: full entry in Volume III.

BARNETT, Capt. Richard Whieldon. Continued in House after 1918: full entry in Volume III.

BARNSTON, Harry. Continued in House after 1918: full entry in Volume III.

BARRAN, Sir John, Bart. 24 Queen's Gate, London. Chapel Allerton Hall, Leeds. Reform. S. of John Barran, Esq., of New Wandsworth, Surrey. B. in London 1821; m. 1st, 1842, Ann, d. of Major Hirst, of Leeds (she died 1874); 2ndly, 1878, Eliza, widow of John Bilton, Esq. Educ. privately. A Merchant at Leeds. President of the Leeds Chamber of Commerce, also of the Leeds Liberal Association. A Magistrate for Leeds, and the W. Riding of Yorkshire. Elected Mayor of Leeds in 1870 and again in 1872. Created Bart. Jan. 1895. A Liberal, in favour of Home Rule for Ireland, and "Local Option." Sat for Leeds from Aug. 1876 to Nov. 1885, when he stood unsuccessfully for the Central division of that borough. Elected for the Otley division of the W. Riding of Yorkshire in 1886 and again in 1892 and sat until defeated in 1895. Died 3 May 1905.   [1895]

BARRAN, Sir John Nicholson, Bart. Sawley Hall, Ripon. Reform, Brooks's, and National Liberal. S. of John Barran, Esq., and grand-s. of Sir John Barran, 1st Bart., and Eliza Henrietta, d. of Edward Nicholson, Esq., of Wokingham. B. 16 Aug. 1872 at Leeds; m. 1902, Alice Margarita, d. of Dr. Leighton Parks, Rector St. Bartolomew's New York. Educ. at Winchester, and Trinity Coll., Cambridge. Succeeded as 2nd Bart in 1905. A Director of John Barran and Sons Limited, of Leeds; Parliamentary Private Secretary to Mr. Herbert Samuel 1910-14, Sir Edward Grey 1915, and the Rt. Hon. H.H. Asquith 1915-1917. (Prime Minister 1908-16). First elected for Hawick Burghs in Mar. 1909 and sat until retired in 1918. Unsuccessfully contested Hull N.W. in 1922, 1923 and 1924. Died 8 July 1952.   [1918]

BARRAN, Sir Rowland Hirst. Leathley Hall, Otley, Yorkshire. 24 Queen's Gate, London. Reform, Bath, and Ranelagh. S. of Sir J.B. Barran, MP for Leeds and Otley division of Yorkshire, and Ann, d. of M. Hirst, Esq., of Leeds. B. 1858 at Leeds; m. 1st, 1887, Rose Cardew, d. of the Rev. G. Bradley (whom he divorced in 1899); 2ndly, 1909, Louise, d. of J. Stevenson Brown, Esq., of Montreal. A Director of the firm of John Barran and Sons Limited, Merchants, Leeds. A life Gov. of Yorkshire Coll.; Gov. of Leeds Grammar School; Chairman of Finance Committee, Leeds School Board 1887-1902; member of Leeds City County from 1901; a member of the Court of the University of Leeds. Knighted in 1917. A Liberal and Imperialist. Elected for N. Leeds July 1902 and sat until he retired in 1918. Died 6 Aug. 1949. [1918]

BARRATT, Sir Francis Layland, Bart. See LAYLAND-BARRATT, Sir Francis, Bart.

BARRIE, Charles Coupar. Continued in House after 1918: full entry in Volume III.

BARRIE, Hugh Thom. Continued in House after 1918: full entry in Volume III.

BARROW, Reuben Vincent. Engadine, Croydon. National Liberal, and City

Liberal. S. of John and Mary Barrow. B. 1838 at Exeter; m. 1859, the d. of Edward Aggett, Esq. Educ. by the British and Foreign School Society, Borough Road, London. Entered the Leather Trade in 1854. Became an Alderman of the Borough of Croydon on its incorporation 1885, and Mayor 1885. A J.P. for Croydon, Surrey, and London; a Governor of Whitgift's foundation and F.R.G.S. A Liberal and Radical. Returned for the Bermondsey division of Southwark July 1892 and sat until defeated in 1895. Knighted in 1912. Died 13 Feb. 1918.   [1895]

BARRY, Rt. Hon. Arthur Hugh Smith-. 20 Hill Street, Berkeley Square, London. Fota Island, Co. Cork. Marbury Hall, Northwich, Cheshire. Eld. s. of James Hugh Smith-Barry, Esq., of Fota Island, Co. Cork, and Marbury Hall, Cheshire, by Eliza, eld. d. of Shallcross Jacson, Esq., of Newton Bank, Chester. B. 1843; m. 1st, 1868, Lady Mary Frances, d. of the 3rd Earl of Dunraven (she died 1884); 2ndly, 1889, Mrs. Post, widow of Arthur Post, Esq., of New York. Educ. at Eton, and Christ Church, Oxford. A Magistrate for Cheshire, and was High Sheriff in 1883, a Magistrate and Dept.-Lieut. for Huntingdonshire, and Alderman of Huntingdonshire County Council; also a Magistrate, Dept.-Lieut. and High Sheriff for Co. Cork. Created PC. (I.) 1896. A Conservative, opposed to Home Rule for Ireland. Was Liberal Member for Cork from Feb. 1867 until defeated 1874. Sat for Huntingdonshire S. as a Conservative from July 1886 until he retired in 1900. Created Baron Barrymore in 1902. President of Irish Unionist Alliance. Vice-President of Irish Landowners Convention. Died 22 Feb. 1925.   [1900]

BARRY, Edward. Rathbarry, Rosscarbery, Co. Cork. S. of Garrett Barry, Esq., Farmer. B. 1852 at New Mill, Rosscarbery. Educ. at St. Vincent's Coll., Castleknock, Dublin, and Dr. Knight's Seminary, Cork. A Farmer and a J.P. for Co. Cork. A Nationalist, and Anti-Parnellite. Sat for S. Cork from July 1892 until defeated in Dec. 1910. Died 7 Dec. 1927.   [1910]

BARRY, Sir Francis Tress, Bart. 1 South Audley Street, London. St. Leonards Hill, Windsor. Keiss Castle, Caithness. Eld. s. of Charles Barry, Esq., of The Priory, Orpington, Kent, and Harriet Ades his wife.

B. in London 1825; m. 1851, Sarah Douglas, only d. of Arthur Herron, Esq., of Northiam, Sussex. Educ. privately. Was H.B.M. Vice-Consul for the Province of Biscay, Spain, and for several years Consul-Gen. in England for the Republic of Ecuador. A J.P. and Dept.-Lieut. for Caithness, and J.P. for Berkshire. Created Bart. 1899. A Conservative and Unionist. Sat for Windsor from 2 Apr. 1890 until he retired in 1906. Died 28 Feb. 1907.   [1905]

BARRY, John. 51 and 52 Aldersgate Street, London. Kirkcaldy, Scotland. National Liberal. B. at Bannow, Wexford, Ireland 1845. A Manufacturer (John Barry, Ostlere and Company). An "Irish Nationalist") in favour of the "restoration of legislative independence to Ireland." With Isaac Butt, Esq., he founded the Home Rule Confederation of Great Britain in 1872. Sat for Wexford Co. S. from Apr. 1880 until he accepted Chiltern Hundreds in 1893.   [1893]

BARRY, Rt. Hon. Redmond John. 10 Fitzwilliam Square, Dublin. Reform. S. of P. Barry, Esq., of Cork. B. 14 Sept. 1866 at Cork; m. 1895, Ethel, d. of E. Pyke, Esq., of Merton Bank, Southport. Educ. in Cork, and Royal University of Ireland; B.A. Was called to the Irish bar in 1888. Q.C. 1899. Bencher of King's Inn, Dublin 1906. Solicitor-Gen. for Ireland from Dec. 1905 to Dec. 1909, when he was appointed Attorney-Gen. PC. (I.) 1909. A Liberal. First elected for N. Tyrone in Mar. 1907 and sat until appointed Lord Chancellor of Ireland in Sept. 1911. Died 11 July 1913. [1911]

BARTLETT, Sir Ellis Ashmead-. See ASHMEAD-BARTLETT, Sir Ellis.

BARTLEY, Sir George Christopher Trout, K.C.B. St. Margaret's House, 57 Victoria Street, Westminster, London. Athenaeum, and Constitutional. 2nd s. of Robert Bartley, Esq., of Rectory Place, Hackney, by his wife, Julia Anna Lucas. B. at West Hackney 1842; m. Jan. 1864, Mary Charlotte, 3rd d. of Sir Henry Cole, K.C.B. Educ. at Clapton, and University Coll. School, and was in the Civil Service (Science and Art Department) from 1859 to 1880. Was the founder (1875) of the National Penny Bank Limited, of which he was one of the Managing Committee. Created K.C.B. 1902. Wrote a number of books and pamphlets bearing upon the

questions of thrift and education among the poor: including *Schools for the People, The Parish Net, One Square Mile in the East of London,* and *The Provident Knowledge Papers,* etc. A Conservative, in favour of reforms in local rating, the licensing laws, land-transfers, etc. Unsuccessfully contested Hackney in 1880. Sat for N. Islington from Nov. 1885 until defeated in 1906. Unsuccessfully contested Hull W. 29 Nov. 1907. Died 13 Sept. 1910.   [1905]

BARTLEY-DENNISS, Edmund Robert Bartley. Continued in House after 1918: full entry in Volume III.

BARTON, Sir Andrew William. Continued in House after 1918: full entry in Volume III.

BARTON, Dunbar Plunket. 12 Mandeville Place, London. 13 Clare Street, Dublin. Constitution. Kildare Street and Sackville Street, Dublin. Eld. s. of Thomas Henry Barton, Esq., by his m. with the Hon. Charlotte Plunket, d. of the 3rd Lord Plunket. B. 1853. Educ. at Harrow and Oxford. Was called to the Irish bar 1880, Gray's Inn 1893, and a bencher of Gray's Inn 1898; Q.C. 1889. Private Secretary to the Lord-Lieut. of Ireland, and afterwards to the Lord Chancellor of Ireland (Lord Ashbourne); was Professor of the Law of Personal Property, Practice, Pleading, and Evidence at the King's Inns, Dublin 1885-88, and of the Law of Contract etc., from 1888-91; appointed Solicitor-Gen. Ireland Dec. 1897. A Conservative and Unionist. First elected for Mid Armagh 1891 and sat until appointed Irish High Court Judge in Jan. 1900. Judge of Kings Bench Division 1900-04; Judge of Chancery Division 1904-18. Created 1st Bart. 1918. Member of Irish War Homes Committee 1919; Chairman of the Industrial Court 1920; F.R.H.S.; Author of several works on Bernadotte (King of Sweden), Tim Healy and Shakespeare. PC. (Ireland) 1919. Died 11 Sept. 1937.   [1899]

BARTTELOT, Rt. Hon. Sir Walter Barttelot, Bart., C.B. Stopham, Pulborough, Sussex. Carlton, and Junior United Service. Eld. s. of George Barttelot, Esq., of Stopham House, Pulborough, Sussex, by Emma, youngest d. of James Woodbridge, Esq., of Richmond, Surrey. B. at Richmond 1820; m. 1st, 1852, Harriet, 4th d. of Sir Christopher Musgrave, Bart., of

Edenhall, Cumberland (she died July 1863); 2ndly, 1868, Margaret, only child of Henry Boldero, Esq., of South Lodge, St. Leonard's Forest, Sussex. Educ. at Rugby. Created Bart. 1875. C.B. 1880. Former Capt. 1st Royal Dragoons. Honorary Col. 2nd Volunteer Battalion Royal Sussex Regiment; a Magistrate and Dept.-Lieut. for Sussex; a County Councillor (Pulborough division); a Chairman of Grand Committees, House of Commons 1890; admitted a PC. Jan. 1892. A Conservative, voted against the 3rd reading of the Irish Land Act 1881. Sat for Sussex W. from 1860 to 1885 and for Sussex N.W. from 1885 until his death 2 Feb. 1893.
[1892 2nd ed.]

BASS, Hamar Alfred. 145 Piccadilly, London. Byrkley Lodge, Burton-on-Trent. Brooks's, Devonshire, Windham, and Union. 2nd s. of Michael Thomas Bass, Esq., MP of Rangemore, Burton-on-Trent, by Eliza Jane, eld. d. of Maj. Samuel Arden, of Longcroft Hall, Staffordshire. B. 1842; m. 1879, Hon. Louisa, 2nd d. of the 3rd Baron Bagot. Was educ. at Harrow. A J.P. and Dept.-Lieut. for Staffordshire, and Hon. Col. 4th N. Staffordshire Militia. A Liberal, opposed to Mr. Gladstone's Home Rule proposals. Sat for Tamworth from 1878 to 1885, and for Staffordshire W. from 1885 until his death 8 Apr. 1898.
[1898]

BASS, Sir Michael Arthur, Bart. Retired in 1886: full entry in Volume I.

BATEMAN-HOPE, William Henry. See HOPE, William Henry Bateman.

BATES, Sir Edward, Bart. Manydown Park, Hampshire. Carlton, Conservative, and Junior Carlton. S. of Joseph Bates, Esq., East India Merchant, of Spring Hall, near Halifax, by Rebecca, d. of Thomas Walker, Esq. B. 1816; m. 1st, 1837, Charlotte, d. of C. Smith, Esq. (she died 1841); 2ndly, 1844, Ellen, 2nd d. of Thomas Thompson, Esq., of Hessle, E. Riding, Yorkshire. An East India Merchant and Ship-Owner, also a Magistrate for Lancashire and Hampshire; a Dept.-Lieut. for Lancashire. He was created a Bart. 1880. Patron of 1 living. A Conservative. Sat for Plymouth from 1871 to 1880. He was re-elected there in the latter year, but unseated on petition. Again elected there in 1885 and sat until he retired in 1892. Died 17 Oct. 1896.
[1892]

BATHURST, Hon. Allen Benjamin. 29 Chesham Street, London. Polebrook, Hever, Kent. Carlton. 3rd and youngest s. of 6th Earl of Bathurst, by his 1st wife, the Hon. Meriel Warren, d. of 2nd Baron de Tabley. B. 25 June 1872; m. 1902, Ruby, d. of Lord Edward Spencer-Churchill. Educ. at Eton Coll., and Royal Agricultural Coll., Cirencester. A Maj. (retired) 4th Battalion Gloucester Regiment. Was Parliamentary Private Secretary to Lord Londonderry when Postmaster-Gen. Dept.-Lieut. for Gloucestershire. A Unionist. Sat for the Cirencester division of Gloucestershire from 1895 to 1906, when he was defeated; re-elected there in Jan. 1910 and sat until he retired in 1918. Died 8 Oct. 1947. [1918]

BATHURST, Capt. Sir Charles, K.B.E. Lydney Park, Gloucestershire. 47 Duke Street, St. James's, London. Carlton, Oxford & Cambridge, and Burlington Fine Arts. S. of Charles Bathurst, Esq., of Lydney Park, Gloucestershire. B. 21 Sept. 1867 in London; m. 1898, Hon. Bertha Lopes, d. of 1st Baron Ludlow. Educ. at Sherborne, Eton, and University Coll., Oxford; M.A. A Chancery and Conveyancing Barrister, called to the bar at the Inner Temple 1890. Was a student at the Royal Agricultural Coll., Cirencester 1892-95, and obtained the diploma and gold medal; was later Gov. of the Royal Agricultural Coll., Cirencester, and of the Swanley Horticultural Coll.; a life member (by examination) and silver medallist of the Royal Agricultural Society; a member of the Council of Bath and West and Southern Counties Agricultural Society; Chairman of Central Chamber of Agriculture 1915; an elected Gov. of the Agricultural Organisation Society; member of the committee of the Central Land Association and of the Farmers' Club; was a member of the Agricultural Education Committee, London 1899-1902. A J.P. and Co. Alderman for Gloucestershire, and a Verderer of the Forest of Dean. A Friend of the Chemical Society. Capt. Royal Monmouthshire Royal Engineers (S.R.), Assistant Military Secretary Southern Command and Salisbury Training Centre. Organiser of Government Land Settlement Scheme for ex-Service men 1915-16. Parliamentary Secretary to the Ministry of Food, Dec. 1916 to July 1917. Chairman of Royal Committee on the Sugar Supply from Aug. 1917. A Conservative, and a strong Agriculturalist. Elected for the

Wilton division of Wiltshire in Jan. 1910 and sat until created Baron Bledisloe 15 Oct. 1918. PC. 1926. Parliamentary Secretary at the Ministry of Agriculture 1924-28. Gov.-Gen. of New Zealand 1930-35. Created 1st Visct. Bledisloe 1935. Chairman of Royal Commission on closer union of Southern Rhodesia, Northern Rhodesia and Nyasaland 1938. Director of P. and O. Shipping Company and of Australian Mutual Provident Society (London Board). Chairman National Council of Social Service 1935-38. Died 3 July 1958.   [1918]

BAUMANN, Arthur Anthony. 44 Hyde Park Square, London. 2nd s. of William Baumann, Esq., formerly a Merchant, of Manchester and Glasgow. B. at Glasgow 1856. Educ. at Wellington Coll., and Balliol Coll., Oxford. Was called to the bar at the Inner Temple in 1880. Practised at Parliamentary bar until 1895 and then went into the City. A Conservative, who "preferred experience to experiment, but was anxious to promote social reforms within the lines of existing institutions." Sat for Peckham division of Camberwell from Nov. 1885 until 1892 when he was defeated at Salford N. Unsuccessfully contested Kirkcaldy in Jan. 1910. Author. Died 20 June 1936.   [1892]

BAYLEY, Edward Hodson. Cliff Lodge, Southfields, London. Reform. S. of the Rev. Dr. Bayley, by Lydia Cheek, d. of the Rev. Marcellus Hodson. B. 1841 at Accrington. Educ. at private schools in England, France, and Germany. A J.P. for the Co. of London; Chairman of the W. Metropolitan Tramways Company, and other companies; Master of the Masons Company, and held office in various political and other societies. A Swedenborgian. A Liberal, supported the Home Rule and general policy of Mr. Gladstone. Unsuccessfully contested the N. division of Camberwell in July 1886. First returned for that division in July 1892 and sat until defeated in 1895. Died 17 Mar. 1938. [1895]

BAYLEY, Thomas. Peveral House, Nottingham. Langar Hall, Nottinghamshire. National Liberal, Reform, and Devonshire. Only s. of Thomas Bayley, Esq., of Lenton Abbey, Nottinghamshire, and Harriet his wife. B. 1846 at Lenton; m. 1874, Annie, 2nd d. of Henry Farmer, Esq., (she died 1904). Educ. at Amersham School, and privately. A Colliery Owner.

Sheriff of Nottingham 1881-82; Alderman of the Nottinghamshire County Council from 1889. Greatly interested himself in the Nottinghamshire University Scheme and other educational matters. A Liberal, in favour of Home Rule for Ireland, "one man one vote", etc., reform of the Land Laws, an Eight Hours Bill for Miners, and complete religious equality. Unsuccessfully contested the Barkston Ash division of Yorkshire in 1885 and the Chesterfield division of Derbyshire in 1886. Elected for the Chesterfield division of Derbyshire 1892, re-elected 1895 and 1900, and sat until he retired in Jan. 1906. Died 11 Mar. 1906.   [1905]

BEACH, Rt. Hon. Sir Michael Edward Hicks-, Bart. See HICKS-BEACH, Rt. Hon. Sir Michael Edward, Bart.

BEACH, Hon. Michael Hugh Hicks-. See QUENINGTON, Michael Hugh Hicks-Beach, Visct.

BEACH, Rt. Hon. William Wither Bramston. 17 Suffolk Street, Pall Mall, London. Oakley Hall, Basingstoke, Hampshire. Keevil House, Trowbridge. Carlton. Only s. of William Beach, Esq., of Oakley Hall, Hampshire, and Keevil House, Wiltshire, by Jane Henrietta, d. of John Browne, Esq., of Salperton, Co. Gloucester. B. 1826; m. 1857, Caroline Chichester, youngest d. of Col. Augustus Cleveland, of Tapeley Park, N. Devon. Educ. at Eton, and Christ Church, Oxford, where he graduated B.A. 1849, and M.A. subsequently. A Magistrate, appointed Capt. in the Hampshire Yeomanry Cavalry 1858. Patron of 2 livings. PC. 1900. Father of the House of Commons from 1899-1901. A Conservative, in favour of the reduction of local taxation. Sat for Hampshire N. from Apr. 1857 to Nov. 1885 and for the Andover division of Hampshire from Nov. 1885 until his death on 3 Aug. 1901.   [1901]

BEADEL, William James. 97 Gresham Street, London. Springfield Lyons, Chelmsford. Junior Carlton, St. Stephen's, and Constitutional. Eld. s. of James Beadel, Esq., of Broomfield Lodge, near Chelmsford, by Mary Anne, d. of James Grant, Esq., of Stoke Newington. B. at Witham, Essex 1828. From 1846 was an Estate Agent and Surveyor, and was President of the Surveyors' Institution, and a

J.P. for Essex. A Conservative, "in favour of reform in local taxation, and for increasing the home production of bread." Sat for the mid division of Essex from 1885 until his death 5 Apr. 1892. [1891]

BEALE, Sir William Phipson, Bart. Drumlamford, Barrhill, Ayrshire. 2 Whitehall Court, London. Savile, and Reform. Eld. s. of William John Beale, Esq., Solicitor, of Bryntirion, Dolgelley, Merionethshire, and Martha, d. of William Phipson, Esq., of Westbourne, Edgbaston, Birmingham. B. 1839; m. 1869; Mary, d. of W. Thompson, Esq., of Edgbaston. Educ. at Birmingham, Heidelberg, and Paris. A Barrister; Q.C. 1888; bencher of Lincoln's Inn 1892. Fellow of Chemical and Geological Societies; a Referee of Private Bills; created Bart. 1912. A Liberal. Successfully contested N. Warwickshire in 1885, Central Birmingham 1889, and Aston Manor in 1891. Elected for S. Ayrshire in 1906 and sat until he retired in 1918. Died 13 Apr. 1922. [1918]

BEAUCHAMP, Sir Edward, Bart. Continued in House after 1918: full entry in Volume III.

BEAUFOY, Mark Hanbury. 87 South Lambeth Road, London. Donhead Hall, Coombe House, Nr. Shaftesbury, Dorset. Reform, National Liberal, and Devonshire. Only s. of George Beaufoy, Esq., of South Lambeth, and of Anne Beaufoy. B. 1854 in South Lambeth Road; m. 1884, Mildred Scott, d. of Robert Tait, Esq., of 14 Queen Anne Street, London. Educ. at Eton, and Trinity Hall, Cambridge. A Vinegar and British Wine Maker, head of the firm of Beaufoy and Company. Was elected an Alderman of the London County Council, but later resigned. A J.P. for Surrey and Wiltshire, a Vestryman for Lambeth, and President of the Brixton Liberal Club and the Kennington Liberal and Radical Association. A Liberal, in favour of Home Rule and the Gladstonian programme generally, but was neutral on the Local Veto Bill. In 1886 was an unsuccessful candidate for the Kennington division of Lambeth. First elected there 15 Mar. 1889 and sat until defeated in 1895. Died 10 Nov. 1922. [1895]

BEAUMONT, Henry Frederick. Whitley Beaumont, Huddersfield. Brooks's, Travellers', Turf, and National Liberal. Eld. s. of Henry Ralph Beaumont, Esq., by Catherine, 5th d. of Sir George Cayley, Bart. B. at Scarborough 1833; m. 1857, Maria Johanna, d. of William Garforth, Esq., of Wiganthorp, Yorkshire. Educ. at Eton, and Trinity Coll., Cambridge. A J.P. for the N. and W. Ridings of Yorkshire, and also for Lincolnshire; Honorary Col. 2nd Battalion Duke of Wellington's West Riding Regiment of Volunteers. A Liberal, he voted against Mr. Gladstone's Home Rule proposals. He represented the S. division of the W. Riding of Yorkshire from 1865 until defeated in 1874. He sat for the Colne Valley division of the W. Riding of Yorkshire from 1885 until he retired in 1892. Died 13 Oct. 1913. [1892]

BEAUMONT, Hon. Hubert George. 6 Buckingham Gate, London. Brooks's, Reform, and Garrick. 3rd s. of 1st Lord Allendale (Wentworth B. Beaumont, MP for S. Northumberland 1852-85) and Lady Margaret de Burgh, d. of 1st Marq. of Clanricarde. B. 6 Apr. 1864 in London; m. 1900, Elisa, d. of M.P. Grace, Esq., of Battle Abbey, Sussex. Educ. at Eton, Cheltenham, and Balliol Coll., Oxford; B.A. A Radical, strongly in favour of the abolition of an hereditary second chamber. Unsuccessfully contested King's Lynn 1895, N. Buckinghamshire 1900, and Barnard Castle 1903. Elected for the Eastbourne division of Sussex in 1906 and sat until he retired in Jan. 1910. Died 14 Aug. 1922. [1909]

BEAUMONT, Wentworth Blackett. 144 Piccadilly Terrace, London. Allenheads, Allendale, Northumberland. Bretton Hall, Wakefield. Reform, Travellers', and Brooks's. S. of Thomas Wentworth Beaumont, Esq., (who was MP for Northumberland from 1818 to 1837), by Henrietta Jane Emma, d. of J. Atkinson, Esq., of Maple Hayes, Staffordshire. B. at Hampstead, Middlesex 1829; m. 1st, 1856, Lady Margaret Anne, d. of 1st Marq. of Clanricade (she died 1888); 2ndly, 1891, Lady Colley, widow of Maj.-Gen. Sir G. Pomeroy-Colley, K.C.S.I, and d. of Maj.-Gen. H.M. Hamilton, C.B. Educ. at Harrow and at Trinity Coll., Cambridge. Patron of 9 livings. A Magistrate for Northumberland and appointed Dept.-Lieut. in 1852. A Liberal, in favour of alterations in the laws of entail, etc. and of Mr. Gladstone's Irish Home Rule policy. Sat for Northumberland S. from July 1852

27

to Nov. 1885, and for the Tyneside division of Northumberland from July 1886 until he retired in 1892. Created 1st Baron Allendale in 1906. Died 13 Feb. 1907. [1892]

BEAUMONT, Hon. Wentworth Canning Blackett. 25 St. James's Place, London. Bywell Hall, Stocksfield-on-Tyne. Bretton Park, Wakefield. Brooks's, Travellers', and Turf. Eld. s. of Lord Allendale (W.B. Beaumont) MP for S. Northumberland 1852-85, and Tyneside division 1886-92, by his 1st wife, Margaret Anne, d. of the 1st Marq. of Clanricarde. B. at Bywell Hall 1860; m. 1889, Lady Alexandrina, d. of the 5th Marq. of Londonderry. Educ. at Eton, and Trinity Coll., Cambridge; M.A. 1888. Vice-Chamberlain to H.M. Household and a Liberal Whip, from Dec. 1905-Feb. 1907. Was Capt. 3rd (Militia) Battalion Royal Welsh Fusiliers, and Capt. Yorkshire Hussars from 1886. J.P. and Dept.-Lieut. for Co. Northumberland and the W. Riding of Yorkshire. A Liberal, in favour of measures for promotion of temperance, Free Trade, etc. Contested Wakefield Nov. 1885. First elected for the Hexham division of Northumberland in 1895 and sat until he succeeded as 2nd Baron Allendale 13 Feb. 1907. Created 1st Visct. Allendale in 1911. Capt. of Yeomen of the Guard from 1907-11. Lord-in-Waiting from 1911-16. Died 12 Dec. 1923. [1907]

BECK, Arthur Cecil Tyrrell. Continued in House after 1918: full entry in Volume III.

BECKETT, Ernest William. 11 Connaught Place, London. Kirkstall Grange, Nr. Leeds. Wood Lee, Virginia Water. Carlton, St. James's, Bachelors', and Turf. Eld. s. of William Beckett (formerly Denison), Esq., MP for the Bassetlaw division of Nottinghamshire, by the Hon. Helen, d. of the 2nd Lord Feversham. B. 1856; m. 1883, Lucy Tracy, only child of W.P. Lee, Esq., of New York (she died 1891), Educ. at Eton, and Cambridge. A Partner in the firm of Messrs. Beckett, Bankers, of Leeds, etc., and Lieut.-Col. in the Yorkshire Hussars. Acting-Assistant-Gen. Imperial Yeomanry 1900. Changed his name from Denison to Beckett in 1886. A Conservative. Sat for the Whitby division of the N. Riding of Yorkshire from 1885 until he succeeded his uncle by special remainder as 2nd Baron Grimthorpe on 29 Apr. 1905. Died 9 May 1917. [1905]

BECKETT, William. 138 Piccadilly, London. Nun Appleton, Bolton Percy, Yorkshire. Carlton, White's, Garrick, and Bachelors'. S. of Sir Edmund Beckett, 4th Bart., of Grimthorpe, Yorkshire, by Maria, d. of William Beverley, Esq., of Beverley, and heir presumptive to the Barony of Grimthorpe by special remainder. B. at Doncaster 1826; m. 1855, Hon. Helen Duncombe, d. of 2nd Baron Feversham. Educ. at Rugby, and at Trinity Coll., Cambridge. A Banker, head of the firm of Beckett and Company of York and various towns in Yorkshire and Nottinghamshire, and President of the County Bankers' Association. A Magistrate and Dept.-Lieut. for the W. Riding of Yorkshire. Adopted the surname of Beckett in lieu of Denison in 1886. A Conservative. Sat for E. Retford under the surname of Denison from 1876 to 1880. Elected for the Bassetlaw division of Nottinghamshire in 1885 and sat until his death on 23 Nov. 1890. [1890]

BECKETT, Hon. William Gervase. Continued in House after 1918: full entry in Volume III.

BECTIVE, Thomas Taylour, Earl of. 10 Stratford Place, London. Underley Hall, Kirkby Lonsdale, Westmoreland. Carlton. Eld. s. of the Marq. of Headfort (who sat for Westmoreland from Apr. 1854 until his succession to the Peerage, Dec. 1870), by the only d. and heir of William Thompson, Esq., MP and Alderman of London. B. at Headfort House, Meath 1844; m. 1867, Lady Alice Maria, d. of the 4th Marq. of Downshire. A Conservative, voted against the 3rd reading of the Irish Land Bill 1881. Sat for Westmoreland 1871-85, and for the Kendal division of Westmoreland from 1885 until he retired in 1892. Died during his father's lifetime on 15 Dec. 1893. [1892]

BEGG, Ferdinand Faithfull. 13 Earls Court Square, London. Carlton, and Gresham. S. of James Begg, Esq., D.D., of 50 George Square, Edinburgh, and Maria, d. of the Rev. Ferdinand Faithfull, of Headly Rectory, Epsom. B. at Edinburgh 1847; m. 1873, Jessie Maria Cargill, d. of F.A. Cargill, Esq., of Dunedin, New Zealand. Educ. privately. A Stockbroker from 1873. A Conservative. Unsuccessfully contested the Kennington division of Lambeth in July 1892. Sat for the St. Rollox division of Glasgow from July 1895 until he retired in

1900. Chairman of London Chamber of Commerce 1912-15. Died 4 Dec. 1926. [1900]

BEITH, Gilbert. 15 Belhaven Terrace, Kelvinside, Glasgow. Reform. Eld. s. of the Rev. Dr. Alexander Beith, of the Free Church of Scotland, Stirling. B. 1827 at Kilbrandon, Argyllshire; m. 1st, Miss Flemming, of Clairmont; 2ndly, d. of the Rev. J. Pollock, of Baldernock. Educ. at his father's manse and at the Stirling Academy. Was apprenticed to a Manufacturing firm at Glasgow, and afterwards served with Messrs. Oswald, Stevenson and Company, of that city. In 1856 began business on his own account, and was head of the firm of Beith, Stevenson and Company, Eastern Export Merchants, of Glasgow and Manchester. Also Chairman, Glasgow Chamber of Commerce, etc. An advanced Liberal, advocated Home Rule and the Gladstonian policy generally, including religious equality for Scotland, District Councils, etc. Sat for the Central division of Glasgow from Nov. 1885 until defeated in July 1886. Returned for the Inverness district in July 1892 and sat until he retired in 1895. Died 5 July 1904. [1895]

BELL, Arthur Clive Morrison. See MORRISON-BELL, Arthur Clive. Continued in House after 1918: full entry in Volume III.

BELL, Lieut.-Col. Ernest Fitzroy Morrison. See MORRISON-BELL, Lieut.-Col. Ernest Fitzroy.

BELL, Richard. 72 Acton Street, Gray's Inn Road, London. 115 Brownlow Road, New Southgate, London. B. at Merthyr Tydvil in 1859. Entered the Great Western Railway service 1876. Appointed organizing Secretary of Amalgamated Society of Railway Servants 1893 and Gen. Secretary 1898. Acted as arbitrator before Lord James of Hereford in connection with crisis on N.E. Railway 1897. A Labour representative, independent of political parties. Elected for Derby in 1900 and sat until he retired in Jan. 1910. Joined the Employment Exchange branch of Board of Trade in 1910 and retired in 1920, remaining adviser to Ministry of Labour. Member of Southgate Urban District Council 1922-29. Died 1 May 1930. [1909]

BELLAIRS, Carlyon Wilfroy. Continued in House after 1918: full entry in Volume III.

BELLOC, Joseph Hilaire Peter René. King's Land, Shipley, Horsham. Reform. S. of Louis Swanton Belloc, Esq., and Bessie Rayner Parkes. B. 27 July 1870; m. 1896, Elodie Agnes Hogan, of Napa, California. Educ. at the Oratory School, Edgbaston, and Balliol Coll., Oxford; Brackenbury Scholar, and 1st Class History. A Journalist, and author, wrote *Danton, Robespierre, Paris, Path to Rome, Caliban's Guide to Letters, The Old Road, Bad Child's Book of Beasts, Mr. Burden,* and numerous other works. A Liberal. First elected for S. Salford in 1906 and sat until he retired in Dec. 1910. Mr. Belloc subsequently became one of the leading writers of his time. Died 16 July 1953. [1910]

BEMROSE, Sir Henry Howe. Queen Anne's Mansions, London. Lonsdale Hill, Derby. Carlton, and Constitutional. S. of William Bemrose, Esq., Printer and Publisher, of Derby. B. 1827; m. Miss C. Brindley. Educ. at the Derby Grammar School and King William's Coll., Isle of Man. Chairman of Bemrose and Sons Limited, of Derby and London, Printers and Publishers; also a J.P. for Derby and Derbyshire, an Alderman of Derby (was Mayor 1877), a Director of Parr's Bank, Derby, and of the Linotype Company; a member of the House of Laymen and other Church bodies, etc.; was Capt. 1st Derbyshire Rifle Volunteers; created Kt. 1897. A Conservative and Unionist, opposed to Home Rule and "Disestablishment", in favour of assisting the voluntary schools, and of a good measure of licensing reform. Sat for Derby from July 1895 until defeated in 1900. Died 4 May 1911. [1900]

BENN, Arthur Shirley. Continued in House after 1918: full entry in Volume III.

BENN, Ian Hamilton, D.S.O. Continued in House after 1918: full entry in Volume III.

BENN, Sir John Williams. The Old Knoll, Blackheath, London. National Liberal. S. of Rev. J. Benn, Congregational Minister, and Ann Benn (née Taylor). B. at Hyde, Cheshire 13 Nov. 1850; m. 1874, Elizabeth, d. of J. Pickstone, Esq., of Hyde. Educ. privately. A Journalist and Newspaper Proprietor. A member of the London County Council from 1889; Leader of the Progressive Party; Chairman of General

Purposes and Highways Committees, Vice-Chairman of Council 1895, and Chairman 1904-05. Dept.-Lieut. and J.P. for Co. of London. Knighted 1906. Wrote numerous articles dealing with Social and Municipal Questions. A Liberal. Sat for Tower Hamlets, St. George's division from 1892-95, when he was defeated; unsuccessfully contested Deptford 1897, and Bermondsey 1900. Elected for Devonport in June 1904 and sat until defeated in Jan. 1910. Contested Clapham Dec. 1910. Created Bart. 1914. Died 10 Apr. 1922. [1909]

BENN, Capt. William Wedgwood, D.S.O. Continued in House after 1918: full entry in Volume III.

BENNET, Ernest Nathaniel. Continued in House after 1918: full entry in Volume III.

BENNETT, Joseph. The Cedars, Louth. Reform, National Liberal, and Cobden. S. of William Bennett, Esq., J.P. and Anne Bennett. B. 1829 at Grimsby. Educ. at Wesley Coll., Sheffield. A J.P. for Grimsby, Lindsey and Louth, Lincolnshire. A Liberal, in favour of Home Rule for Ireland. Sat for the W. Lindsey division of Lincolnshire from 1885-86 when he was an unsuccessful candidate. Again returned for the W. Lindsey division of Lincolnshire in July 1892 and sat until he retired in 1895. Died 1 Jan. 1908. [1895]

BENNETT-GOLDNEY, Francis. Abbotts Barton, Canterbury. 3 Devonshire Terrace, Sandgate. Burlington Fine Arts, and Savage. S. of Sebastian Evans, Esq., M.A., LL.D. B. 1865 at Moseley, Birmingham. Educ. privately at Bournemouth, and in Paris. Assumed the name of Goldney in 1892. An Alderman of Canterbury, and was Mayor for six successive years, and a member of Kent Territorial Committee. A Capt. 4th Militia Battalion Middlesex Regiment. Was gazetted Athlone Pursuivant of Arms in 1907, but resigned the office the same year. A Fellow of the Society of Antiquaries and other learned societies, and author of several works on archaeology, art, and antiquities. Honorary Assistant Military Attaché to British Embassy in Paris in 1918. A Conservative, but contested the 1910 elections as an Independent Conservative in opposition to the official Conservative candidate. Unsuccessfully contested Canterbury in Jan. 1910. Elected for Canterbury in Dec. 1910 and sat until his death 27 July 1918. [1918]

BENSON, Godfrey Rathbone. Balliol Coll., Oxford. National Liberal. S. of William Benson, Esq., J.P. of Langton Alresford, Hampshire. B. 1864. Educ. at Winchester Coll., and Balliol Coll., Oxford (B.A., M.A. 1887). Private Secretary (unpaid) to Mr. Herbert Gardner, President of the Board of Agriculture. Lecturer at Balliol Coll., (1888-90). He resigned this office to contest mid Oxfordshire against Mr. G.H. Morrell in Apr. 1891. A Liberal, in favour of Home Rule for Ireland. Sat for the Woodstock division of Oxfordshire from July 1892 until defeated in 1895. Contested S. Pancras W. in 1900 and Worcestershire W. in 1906. Created Baron Charnwood in 1911. Mayor of Lichfield 1909-11; Councillor and then Alderman 1904-38. Died 3 Feb. 1945. [1895]

BENTHAM, George Jackson. Swanland, East Yorkshire. National Liberal. S. of William Jackson, Esq. B. 1 Aug. 1863 at Hull; m. 1886, Ada, d. of Thomas Marshall, Esq. Educ. Privately. Was in business in Hull as a Grocer from 1878. A J.P. for Hull and E. Riding of Yorkshire; a member of the Town Council for Hull. Assumed the additional name of Bentham in 1897. A Liberal. Unsuccessfully contested Hull Central in 1906. Elected for the Gainsborough division of Lincolnshire in Jan. 1910 and sat until defeated in 1918. Died 31 Oct. 1929. [1918]

BENTINCK, Rt. Hon. George Augustus Frederick Cavendish. See CAVENDISH-BENTINCK, Rt. Hon. George Augustus Frederick.

BENTINCK, Lord Henry Cavendish. See CAVENDISH-BENTINCK, Lord Henry. Continued in House after 1918: full entry in Volume III.

BENTINCK, William George Cavendish. See CAVENDISH-BENTINCK, William George.

BERESFORD, Lord Charles William de-la-Poer, G.C.B., G.C.V.O. 1 Great Cumberland Place, London. Carlton, Athenaeum, Turf, United Service, Savage, and Marlborough. 2nd s. of 4th Marq. of Waterford. B. 10 Feb. 1846 in Ireland; m. 1878, Mira, d. of R. Gardner, Esq., MP for

Leicester. Educ. at Bayford School. Entered the navy in 1859. Lieut. 1868; Commander 1875; Capt. 1882; Rear-Admiral 1897; Vice-Admiral 1902; Admiral 1906. Was in command of the Condor at the bombardment of Alexandria, and commanded the Naval Brigade in the Nile Expedition 1884-85; was specially mentioned in despatches. Second in Command Mediterranean Fleet 1900-02, Commanded Channel Squadron 1903-05, Commander-in-Chief Atlantic Fleet 1905, Mediterranean Fleet 1905-07, and Channel Fleet 1907-09. Naval Aide-de-Camp to H.M. Queen Victoria 1896-97; a Junior Lord of the Admiralty 1886-88. C.B. 1885; K.C.B. 1903; G.C.V.O. 1906 and G.C.B. 1911. Wrote *The Break-up of China, Nelson and his Times, Memories* (1916), and numerous essays and articles on naval matters. A Unionist. Sat for Co. Waterford from 1874-80, when he was defeated; sat for Marylebone E. from 1885-89, when he resigned to accept a naval command; sat for York from 1898-Jan. 1900 when he again resigned in order to command the Mediterranean Fleet. Sat for Woolwich from 1902-03, when he accepted the Chiltern Hundreds. Elected for Portsmouth in Jan. 1910 and sat until created 1st Baron Beresford in 1916. Died 6 Sept. 1919. [1915]

BERESFORD-HOPE, Rt. Hon. Alexander James Beresford. Arklow House, 1 Connaught Place, Hyde Park, London. Bedgebury Park, Cranbrook, Kent. Beresford Hall, Ashbourne, Staffordshire. Carlton, Athenaeum, and the University. Youngest s. of Thomas Hope, Esq., of Deepdene, Surrey, author of *Anastasius* by the Hon. Louisa, youngest d. of the 1st Lord Decies, Archbishop of Tuam (she m. 2ndly, Visct. Beresford). B. in London 1820; m. 1842, the Lady Mildred Cecil, eld. d. of 8th Marq. of Salisbury (she died 1881). Gained a scholarship and several prizes at Harrow; in 1840 the English and Latin declamation prizes at Trinity Coll., Cambridge, and in 1841 the Members' B.A. prize for Latin Essay; made LL.D. propter merita at Cambridge, Honorary D.C.L. at Oxford, Honorary LL.D. at Dublin. Assumed the name of Beresford by royal licence in 1854. President of the Institute of British Architects, also a Trustee of the British Museum. Patron of 2 livings. PC. 1880. A Liberal-Conservative, in favour of the maintenance of the Established Church "both as a devine institution, and as an estate of the realm." Sat for Maidstone from June 1841 to July 1852; and from Mar. 1857 till Apr. 1859. Unsuccessfully contested Stoke in 1862, but sat for Stoke from July 1865 to Feb. 1868, from which date he sat for Cambridge University. MP until his death 20 Oct. 1887. [1887]

BERRIDGE, Thomas Henry Devereux. 49 Rutland Gate, London. 11 Old Broad Street, London. Reform, National Liberal, Eighty, and Royal Automobile. S. of the Rev. W. Berridge. B. 1857; married. A Solicitor; Senior Partner in Burn and Berridge, Old Broad Street, Solicitors to the Newfoundland Government. A Liberal. Unsuccessfully contested Warwick and Leamington in 1903; elected there in 1906 and sat until defeated in Jan. 1910. Defeated again at Warwick and Leamington in Dec. 1910. Knighted 1912. Chairman Executive Committee of Royal Flying Corps Hospitals 1916-19. K.B.E. 1920. Died 24 Oct. 1924. [1909]

BERTRAM, Julius. 14 Suffolk Street, Pall Mall, London. Sishes, Stevenage, Hertfordshire. Reform. S. of Julius A. Bertram, Esq., of York Terrace, Regent's Park, and Martha Jane, d. of James Gammell, Esq., of Ardiffery, N.B. B. 8 Nov. 1866; m. 1907, Marjorie, d. of the Hon. Mr. Justice Sutton. Educ. at Repton, and New Coll., Oxford; 3rd Class honours Classics, 2nd Class Modern History, B.A. 1889. A Solicitor, admitted 1893. Wrote *The Case for Free Imports* (1903). A Liberal, in favour of Free Trade, amendment of Education Acts, Trades Union legislation, a strong navy, and encouragement to the volunteers. Opposed to Taxation of Land Values. Elected for N. Hertfordshire in 1906 and sat until he retired in Jan. 1910. Died 5 Nov. 1944. [1909]

BETHELL, George Richard. Sigglesthorne, Hull. Carlton, Naval & Military, and Yorkshire. S. of William Froggatt Bethell, Esq., by his wife, Elizabeth Beckett Bethell. B. Mar. 1849 at Rise, in Holderness. Educ. at Laleham and as a R.N. cadet on H.M.S. *Britannia*. Served on board the *Sutlej, Newport,* and *Shearwater;* served as Lieut. in the *Challenger* during the surveying expedition 1872 to 1876, in the *Warrior* 1877-78, in the *Alert* from 1878 to 1880, and in the *Minotaur* from 1882 to 1884. A Com-

31

mander, and held the Khedive's bronze star and the Egyptian medal. A Conservative. Sat for the Holderness division of the E. Riding of Yorkshire from 1885 until he retired in 1900. Contested same seat in Jan. 1910 as a Free Trade candidate with the support of the local Liberal Association. Died 3 Dec. 1919. [1900]

BETHELL, Sir John Henry, Bart. Continued in House after 1918: full entry in Volume III.

BETHELL, Thomas Robert. 2 Garden Court, Temple, London. The Firs, South Woodford, Essex. National Liberal. S. of George Bethell, Esq., of Woodford, Essex. B. 1867. Educ. at Heversham Grammar School, and King's Coll., London. A Barrister, called to the bar at the Middle Temple, and joined the S.E. Circuit. A Liberal. Elected for the Maldon division of Essex in 1906 and sat until defeated in Jan. 1910. Contested the Eye division of Suffolk E. in 1924. Dept.-Chairman, County of London Electric Supply Company Limited. Knighted 1914. Died 23 Dec. 1957. [1909]

BHOWNAGGREE, Sir Mancherjee Merwanjee. 196 Cromwell Road, London. Carlton, and Constitutional. S. of Merwanjee Bhownaggree, a Parsee Merchant of Bombay, who was also head of the Bombay State Agency for Bhavnagar, and his wife, Cooverbai (she died 1896). B. 15 Aug. 1851; m. a d. of A.E. Chinoy, Esq., Educ. at the University, and Elphinstone Coll., Bombay. A J.P. and a fellow of Bombay University. Became a Journalist in India and in 1872 succeeded his father in the State Agency. Came to England in 1882, and was called to the bar at Lincoln's Inn 1885. Was Judicial Councillor of Bhavnagar, and Commissioner for that state at the Colonial and Indian Exhibition 1886; was awarded the silver medal of the Society of Arts 1885 for his paper on Indian female education, and acted as Secretary to the Rukhmibai Committee which upheld the rights of Indian womanhood. He published a Gujarati translation of Queen Victoria's *Our Life in the Highlands* and *The Constitution of the East India Company*. Was created C.I.E. in 1886 and K.C.I.E. 1897. A member of Council of the Society of Arts and a Life Fellow of the Imperial Institute. A Conservative and Unionist. Was first elected for the N.E. division of Bethnal Green in 1895 and sat until de-

feated in 1906. Died 14 Nov. 1933. [1905]

BICKERSTETH, Robert. 70 Cromwell Road, London. Brooks's, and Windham. Eld. s. of Robert Bickersteth, Esq., D.D., Lord Bishop of Ripon, by Elizabeth, d. of Joseph Garde, Esq., of Co. Cork. B. at Clapham, Surrey, 24 June 1847; m. 1883, Lady Lavinia Bertie, d. of the 5th Earl of Abingdon. Was educ. at Eton, and Corpus Christi Coll., Oxford, and graduated B.A. in Honours (2nd class Law and Modern History) in 1870. Appointed in 1873 one of H.M. Inspectors of Factories. In 1880 became Private Secretary to the Earl of Kimberley, as Secretary for the Colonies and afterwards for India. In 1873 he joined the Sherwood Rangers, and in 1881 he changed to the Middlesex (Duke of Cambridge's Hussars) Yeomanry Cavalry, in which he became Maj. in 1885. A Liberal, in favour of "an enlightened and straightforward foreign policy", "of maintaining the navy and land defences in a state of thorough efficiency", and opposed to any attack on the Church of England. Sat for the N. division of Shropshire from Dec. 1885 until July 1886. When he unsuccessfully contested Leicester as a Liberal Unionist. Died 10 July 1916. [1886]

BICKFORD-SMITH, William. Queen Anne's Mansions, London. Trevarno, Helston, Cornwall. Reform, and Cobden. Eld. s. of George Smith, Esq., LL.D., of Camborne, by Elizabeth, d. of William Bickford, Esq., of Tucking Mill, Cornwall. B. 1827; m. 1st, 1852, Margaret Leaman, only d. of William Venning, Esq., of Broadhempstone, Devon; 2ndly, 1870, Anna Matilda, d. of G. Hickman Bond, Esq., of Radford, Nottinghamshire. Educ. at Saltash and Plymouth. A Patent Safety-Fuse Manufacturer, a Magistrate for Cornwall, a Fellow of the Asiatic and Royal Geographical Societies, and Chairman of the Helston Railway Company. Was one of the founders and Vice-President of the Truro Wesleyan Coll., and a Capt. 16th Cornwall Volunteers. Assumed the additional name of Bickford by Royal Licence 1868. A Liberal and Unionist. Sat for the Truro division of Cornwall from 1885 until he retired in 1892. Died 24 Feb. 1899. [1892]

BIDDULPH, Michael. 19 Ennismore Gardens, London. Ledbury, Herefordshire. Kemble House, Nr. Cirencester. Brooks's.

Eld. s. of Robert Biddulph, Esq., of Ledbury, by Elizabeth, d. of George Palmer, Esq., of Nazing Park, Essex. B. 1834; m. 1st, 1864, Adelaide, d. of Rt. Hon. Gen. and Lady Alice Peel (she died 1872); 2ndly, 1877, Lady Elizabeth Philippa, d. of 4th Earl of Hardwicke, and widow of Henry John Adeane, Esq. Educ. at Harrow. A Partner in the Banking Firm of Messrs. Cocks, Biddulph, and Company, London. A Liberal and Unionist. Sat for Herefordshire 1865-85, and for the S. division of Herefordshire from 1885 until he retired in 1900. Created 1st Baron Biddulph in 1903. Died 6 Apr. 1923. [1900]

BIGGAR, Joseph Gillis. Clifton Park Avenue, Belfast. S. of Joseph Biggar, Esq., Merchant of Belfast, by Isabella, d. of William Houston, Esq., of Ballyearl, Co. Antrim. B. at Belfast 1828. Unmarried. Was educ. at Belfast Academy. Chairman of the Belfast Water Commissioners from Aug. 1869 to Mar. 1872, and Town Councillor of Belfast in Nov. 1871. A Nationalist, in favour of Home Rule for Ireland. Unsuccessfully contested Londonderry city Nov. 1872. Sat for the Co. of Cavan from Feb. 1874 to Nov. 1885, and for the W. division of Co. Cavan from Nov. 1885 until his death 19 Feb. 1890. [1889]

BIGHAM, John Charles. 19 Palace Gate, Kensington, London. S. of John Bigham, Esq., Merchant, of Liverpool, and his wife, Helen East. B. at Liverpool 1840; m. 1871, d. of John Rogers, Esq., of Liverpool. Educ. at the Liverpool Institute. A Barrister of the Middle Temple, called 1870, and became a Q.C. in 1883. Unsuccessfully contested E. Toxteth division of Liverpool as a Liberal in Nov. 1885. Contested the Exchange division of Liverpool as a Liberal Unionist in 1892. Sat for that division from July 1895 until appointed Judge in 1897. Knighted in 1897. Judge of Queens Bench Division 1897-1909; President of Probate, Divorce and Admiralty Division 1909-10; PC. 1909. Created 1st Baron Mersey in 1910; 1st Visct. Mersey in 1916. Died 3 Sept. 1929. [1897]

BIGLAND, Alfred. Continued in House after 1918: full entry in Volume III.

BIGNOLD, Sir Arthur. 2 Curzon Street, London. Loch Rosque Castle, Ross-shire. Strathbran Lodge, Dingwall. Cabnie Lodge, by Achanalt, Ross-shire. Carlton, Junior Carlton, and Constitutional. Youngest s. of Sir Samuel Bignold, MP. B. 1839; m.1st, 1866, Mary, d. of Thomas Lake, Esq., of Armagh (she died 1901); 2ndly, 1906, Emily Florence, d. of Thomas Agar, Esq., of Leicester. Educ. at Trinity Hall, Cambridge; scholar and prizeman; LL.D. A member of the Hon. Society of the Inner Temple. Was President of the Gaelic Society 1900. A founder of the Kennel Club. A J.P. for Ross-shire. Chairman of the Dingwall and Cromartie Railway. Knighted 1904. A Conservative. Elected for Wick in 1900 and sat until defeated in Jan. 1910. Contested same seat in Dec. 1910. Died 23 Mar. 1915. [1909]

BIGWOOD, James. 115 City Road, London. The Lawn, Twickenham. Carlton. S. of James Bigwood, Esq., of 5 Great George Street, Bristol. B. at Clifton 1839; m. 1862, Marian, only d. of Edward Webb, Esq., of Torquay. Educ. at Cotham School, and St. John's Coll., Cambridge; M.A. 1865. A Partner in the firm of Champion and Company, City Road, London. A J.P. for Middlesex and London, and an Alderman and Chairman of the Parliamentary Committee of the Middlesex County Council. Also Chairman of the Parliamentary Committee of the London Justices. A Conservative. He entered Parliament as Member of Finsbury E. at the general election of Nov. 1885 but was defeated there in the contest of July 1886. Was first returned for the Brentford division of Middlesex in Dec. 1886 and sat until defeated in 1906. Died 6 Dec. 1919. [1905]

BILL, Charles. Farley Hall, Cheadle, Staffordshire. Carlton, and United University. S. of John Bill, Esq., J.P., Staffordshire, by Sarah, d. of Abel Humphreys, Esq., of the United States. B. 1843 at Farley Hall, Staffordshire. Educ. at Eton Coll., and University Coll., Oxford. Was called to the bar at Lincoln's Inn 1868. A J.P. Staffordshire and Hon. Col. of the 4th N. Staffordshire Regiment. A Conservative. Sat for the Leek division of Staffordshire from 1892 until defeated in 1906. Died 9 Dec. 1915. [1905]

BILLING, Noel Pemberton-. Continued in House after 1918: full entry in Volume III.

BILLSON, Alfred. 4 Whitehall Court, London. Rowton Castle, Shrewsbury.

Reform, and National Liberal. S. of William Billson, Esq., of Leicester. B. 18 Apr. 1839 at Leicester; m. 1862, Lilla, d. of John Baines, Esq., J.P., of Leicester. Educ. privately. A Solicitor, admitted 1860, and Partner in the firm of Oliver Jones, Billson and Company, of Liverpool; a J.P. for Liverpool and Shropshire. A Liberal. Sat for the Barnstaple division of Devon 1892-95, defeated at the general election of 1895; unsuccessfully contested E. Bradford 1896; elected for Halifax 1897, defeated 1900. Elected for N.W. Staffordshire in 1906 and sat until his death 9 July 1907. He was awarded Knighthood in 1907 but died before it was gazetted. [1907]

BINGHAM, George Charles Bingham, Lord. 5 Portman Square, London. Turf, Carlton, and Naval & Military. Eld. s. of the Earl of Lucan. B. 13 Dec. 1860; m. 1896, Violet, d. of J. Spender Clay, Esq., of Ford Manor, Surrey. Educ. at Harrow and Sandhurst. Was in the Rifle Brigade 1880-96; served in the Bechuanaland Expedition 1884-85. Joined the 1st London Rifle Brigade in 1900 as Maj. and later Lieut.-Col. J.P. and Dept.-Lieut. for Co. Mayo. High Sheriff 1892. A Conservative. Elected for the Chertsey division of Surrey July 1904 and sat until defeated in 1906. Succeeded as 5th Earl of Lucan in 1914. Irish Representative Peer from 1914. Served in the European War 1914-16. Lord-in-Waiting from 1920-24 and 1924-29; Capt. of Gentlemen-at-Arms 1929 and 1931-40. Created 1st Baron Bingham in 1934. PC. 1938. Died 20 Apr. 1949. [1905]

BIRD, Alfred Frederick. Continued in House after 1918: full entry in Volume III.

BIRKBECK, Sir Edward, Bart. 10 Charles Street, Berkeley Square, London. Horstead Hall, Norwich. Carlton, and Marlborough. Youngest s. of Henry Birkbeck, Esq., of Keswick Hall, Norwich, by Elizabeth Lucy, youngest d. of Robert Barclay, Esq., of Clapham, Surrey. B. at Keswick Hall, Norwich 1838; m. 1865, Hon. Mary Augusta, youngest d. of the 1st Lord Hylton. Chairman of the Royal National Lifeboat Institution, and the originator and Chairman of the International Fisheries Exhibition. Created Bart. 1886. A Magistrate and Dept.-Lieut. for Norfolk. A Conservative. Sat for Norfolk N. from 1879 to 1885, and for Norfolk E.

from 1885 until defeated in 1892. Died 2 Sept. 1907. [1892]

BIRKMYRE, William. Victoria Lodge, Innellan, Argyllshire. Reform. S. of William Birkmyre, Esq., of Port Glasgow, and Margaret, d. of Mr. Aitken, of Glasgow. B. 1838; m. 1862, Fanny, 2nd d. of William Marshall, Esq., of Ladyburn, Greenock. Educ. at Port Glasgow, and Glasgow University. A Jute and Linen Manufacture, a Partner in Birkmyre Brothers of Calcutta and Serampore. A Liberal, in favour of Home Rule for Ireland, and the Gladstonian programme generally. Returned for Ayr district in July 1892 and sat until defeated in 1895. Died 19 Apr. 1900. [1895]

BIRRELL, Rt. Hon. Augustine. 70 Elm Park Road, Chelsea, London. The Pightle, Sheringham, Norfolk. Athenaeum, and New University. S. of the Rev. C.M. Birrell, of Liverpool, and Harriet Jane, d. of the Rev. H. Grey, D.D., of Edinburgh. B. 1850 at Wavertree, near Liverpool; m. 1st, 1878, Margaret, d. of Archibald Mirrielees, Esq. (she died 1879); 2ndly, 1888, Eleanor, d. of F. Locker-Lampson, Esq. (she died 1915). Educ. at Amersham Hall School, near Reading, and Trinity Hall, Cambridge. Was called to the bar at the Inner Temple 1875; Q.C. 1895; Bencher 1903; Quain Professor of Law at University Coll., London 1896-99. PC. 1905. Was President of the Board of Education from Dec. 1905 to Feb. 1907, when he was appointed Chief Secretary for Ireland; resigned Apr. 1916. Lord Rector of Glasgow University 1912. Author of *Obiter Dicta, Res Judicatae*, and other works. Unsuccessfully contested Walton division of Liverpool in 1885, and the Widnes division of Lancashire in 1886. Sat for W. Fife from 1889-1900, when he contested Manchester N.E. and was defeated. Elected for N. Bristol in 1906 and sat until he retired in 1918. Died 20 Nov. 1933. [1918]

BLACK, Alexander William. 3 Down Street, London. 5 Learmouth Terrace, Edinburgh. Reform. Scottish Liberal, and University, Edinburgh. S. of the Rev. James Black, Minister of Dunnikeid Free Church, Kirkcaldy, Fifeshire, and Mary Anne, only child of John Sutherland, Esq., of Newton Place, Aberdeen. B. at Kirkcaldy 1859; m. 1888, Ellinor, 2nd d. of Admiral Thomas Wilson, C.B. Educ. at

High School, Kirkcaldy, Stuttgart, Germany, and Edinburgh University. A Writer to the signet, admitted 1885; member of the firm of Menzies, Black and Menzies. An advanced Liberal. Elected for Banffshire in 1900 and sat until his death 29 Dec. 1906. [1906]

BLACK, Sir Arthur William. Springfield, Alexandra Park, Nottingham. National Liberal, and Eighty. S. of William E. Black, Esq., of Nottingham. B. 28 Feb. 1863 at Nottingham; m. 1887, Helen, d. of John Spence Paisley, Esq. Educ. in Nottingham. A Lace Manufacturer. Director of Sceptre Life Association Limited, and Turney Brothers Limited, Leather Works, Nottingham. A member of Nottingham City Council from 1895-1907; Sheriff 1898; Mayor 1902; a J.P. for Nottingham. Knighted 1916. A Liberal, in favour of Licensing Reform, Electoral Reform, etc. Unsuccessfully contested the Doncaster division of Yorkshire in 1900. Elected for N. Bedfordshire in 1906 and sat until defeated in Bedfordshire mid in 1918. Died 13 July 1947. [1918]

BLADES, John Horton. Oakhurst, West Bromwich. S. of Brownlow William Blades, Esq., of West Bromwich, A Blue Brick and Sanitary Pipe Manufacturer, by Sarah, d. of John Horton, Esq., of Tipton, Staffordshire. B. at Great Bridge, West Bromwich, 1841; m. 1865, Sarah, d. of Edmund Collumbell, Esq., of Derby. Educ. at a private school at Oswestry. Joined his father in business in 1862. A Guardian and Town Councillor for W. Bromwich, and was elected Alderman in 1885; was also Secretary to the Great Bridge Wesleyan Day Schools, and Chairman of one of the Board Schools at W. Bromwich. A Radical, in favour of applying the "Elective Principle" to the House of Lords. Sat for W. Bromwich from Nov. 1885 until he retired in 1886. [1886]

BLAINE, Robert Stickney. Summerhill, Bath. Conservative. S. of Benjamin Blaine, Esq., of Hull, by Jane, d. of Robert Stickney, Esq. B. about 1816; m.1st, Constance, d. of George Moger, Esq., of Bath; 2ndly, Letitia, d. of Sir Timothy Vansittart Stonhouse, Bart. A Magistrate for Bath, and was Mayor of that city in 1872 and 1873. A Conservative. Sat for Bath from Nov. 1885 until he retired in 1886. Knighted 30 June 1890. Died 15 Dec. 1897. [1886]

BLAIR, Reginald. Continued in House after 1918: full entry in Volume III.

BLAKE, Hon. Edward. 20 Kensington Gate, London. Humewood, Toronto, Canada. Le Caprice, Murray Bay, Quebec. National Liberal. S. of the Hon. William Hume Blake, Chancellor of Upper Canada (formerly of Wicklow and Galway), and Catherine Hume, of Wicklow. B. 1833 at Adelaide, Co. Middlesex, Upper Canada; m. 1858, Margaret, d. of the Rt. Rev. B. Cronyn, Lord Bishop of Huron, Canada. Educ. at Upper Canada Coll., and University of Toronto. Called to the bar 1856; Q.C. 1864; President and Treasurer of the Law Society of Upper Canada from 1879, he declined both the Chancellorship of Upper Canada and the Chief Justiceship of Canada. Was Chancellor of the University of Toronto from 1876, President Toronto Gen. Trusts Company from 1882; Premier of Ontario 1871-72, member of the Privy Council 1873, Minister of Justice 1875-77; declined K.C.M.G. in 1876; Leader of Canadian Liberal Party 1880-91, when he retired in opposition to the party's policy of "unrestricted reciprocity" with the United States. A Temporary Chairman of Committees. A Canadian Liberal. In general politics a Liberal. A member of the Irish Nationalist party, in favour of Home Rule as meaning "union for the first time in the only true and real sense" of Ireland and Great Britain. Sat for S. Longford from 1892 until he accepted Chiltern Hundreds in 1907. Died 2 Mar. 1912. [1907]

BLAKE, Sir Francis Douglas, Bart. Continued in House after 1918: full entry in Volume III.

BLAKE, John Aloysius. 44 Westland Row, Dublin. Devonshire, and St. James's. Stephen's Green, Dublin. S. of Andrew Blake, Esq., of Waterford (of the family of Blake of Renvyle, Co. Galway, to which the celebrated Admiral belonged), by Mary, d. of Patrick Galway, Esq., of Waterford. B. 1826; m. 1874, Adelaide, d. of Nicholas M. Power, Esq., of Faithlegg, Co. Waterford, and sometime MP for that Co. Educ. at St. John's Coll., Waterford, and the Government Coll., Pau, Basses Pyrenees, France. A Magistrate for the City of Waterford, where he served as Mayor 1855-57, and Chairman of the Fishery Harbours Commission (Ireland, 1884).

Chairman of the Fisheries Committee of 1868 and of the Commission on Sea and Oyster Fisheries of 1869. Author of *Defects in the Moral Treatment of Insanity in Public Asylums, The Sea and Inland Fisheries of Ireland, The Effects of Foreign Agricultural Competition,* etc. A Liberal and Home Ruler. Sat for Waterford City from 1857-69, and for Co. Waterford as a Liberal and Home Ruler from 1880 to 1884. Returned for Carlow Co. without opposition on 29 Jan. 1886 and sat until his death on 22 May 1887. [1887]

BLAKE, Thomas. The Hotel Metropole, London. Lebanon, Ross, Herefordshire. Reform, and Cobden. S. of William Blake, Esq., of Ross, Herefordshire. B. at Ross 1825. Twice married. Educ. locally. Was an Accountant and Estate Agent. Chairman of the Ross School Board for 12 years, and President of the Freehold Land Society, and Trustee and Gov. of the local Savings' Bank, the Cottage Hospital, etc. In 1876 he re-built, at a cost of nearly £4,000, the Baptist Chapel and Schoolrooms at Ross. An "advanced Liberal", in favour of Home Rule, of Sunday closing of public houses, of the reform of the House of Lords, and of the extension of the Franchise to Women Householders. He unsuccessfully contested the Co. of Herefordshire in 1868, and afterwards sat for Leominster from 1876-1880. Sat for the Forest of Dean division of Gloucestershire from 1885 until he accepted Chiltern Hundreds in July 1887. Alderman of Herefordshire County Council from 1889. Died 31 Mar. 1901. [1887]

BLAKISTON-HOUSTON, John. Orangefield and Roddens, Belfast. Carlton. Ulster, Belfast. Eld. s. of Richard Blakiston-Houston, Esq., 5th s. of Sir Matthew Blakiston, 2nd Bart., and Mary J., his wife. B. at Orangefield, Co. Down 1829; m. 1859, Marian, d. of R.S. Streathfield, Esq., of Uckfield, Sussex (she died 1893). A J.P. and Dept.-Lieut., was also Vice-Lieut. Co. Down, and Sheriff of the Co. 1860. A Conservative, and general supporter of the Marq. of Salisbury's ministry, in favour of legislation for Irish agriculture and technical education, and of obtaining for Ireland a share of the money spent for Imperial purposes. Sat for Down N. from Sept. 1898 until he retired in 1900. Died 27 Feb. 1920. [1900]

BLANE, Alexander. Scotch Street, Armagh. B. 1856. Was educ. by the Christian Brothers, and commenced business as a working Tailor. In 1876 he was appointed agent to the Catholic Registration Association, and was President of the Prisoners' Aid Society. An "Irish Nationalist" of the Parnellite party. Sat for S. Armagh from 1885 until defeated in 1892. Unsuccessfully contested N. Westmeath in 1892. [1892]

BLISS, Joseph. Queen Anne's Mansions, St. James's Park, London. Boarbank Hall, Grange-over-Sands, Lancashire. S. of the Rev. Joseph Bliss. B. at Leyland, Lancashire in 1853; m. 1891, Margaret, d. of James McClymont, Esq., of Borgue House, Kirkcudbright. Educ. at Silcoats School, and Edinburgh University. A Banker and Merchant in Turkey and Russia. A Liberal. Contested the N. Lonsdale division of Lancashire twice in 1910. Elected for the Cockermouth division of Cumberland in Mar. 1916 and sat until defeated in the Lonsdale division of Lancashire in 1918. Died 12 Dec. 1939. [1918]

BLUNDELL, Henry Blundell-Hollinshead. 10 Stratton Street, London. Ashurst Lodge, Sunninghill, Berkshire. Deysbrook, Nr. Carlton. Liverpool. Guards', Army & Navy, and United Service. Eld. s. of Richard Benson Blundell-Hollinshead Blundell, Esq., of Deysbrook, by Jane, d. of John Leigh, Esq., of Sandhills, near Liverpool. B. 1831; m. 1863, the Hon. Beatrice, d. of Vice-Admiral the Hon. Henry D. Byng (Maid of Honour to Queen Victoria). Educ. at Eton, and Christ Church, Oxford; B.A. 1854. Entered the Rifle Brigade 1855, and served in the Crimea after the fall of Sebastopol; exchanged into the Grenadier Guards 1863; passed Staff Coll. 1864. Assistant Adjutant-Gen. of the Home District from 1876 to 1881; became Col. 1882; served on the staff in the Nile Expedition 1884-85; retired 1889. A C.B., also a Dept.-Lieut. for Lancashire. A Conservative and Unionist. Sat for the Ince division of Lancashire from Nov. 1885 until defeated July 1892; re-elected there July 1895 and Oct. 1900 and sat until defeated in Jan. 1906. Died 28 Sept. 1906. [1905]

BODKIN, Matthias McDonnell. 9 Great Denmark Street, Dublin. S. of Thomas Bodkin, Esq., F.R.C.S.I., of Castland House, Tuam, by his marriage with Miss

McDonnell, of Cloona, Westport, Co. Mayo. B. at Tuam in 1850; m. 1885, Arabella, d. of Francis Norman, Esq., of Dublin. Educ. at St. Stanislaus Jesuit Coll., Tullamore, and the Catholic University, Dublin. A Barrister-at-Law (called 1887) and Journalist. Wrote books and pamphlets including *The New Departure in Catholic Liberal Education, Poteen Punch*, (a collection of Irish stories), and a novel *Lord Edward Fitzgerald*, the latter put forth as by 'Croor a Boo'. A Nationalist of the Irish Parliamentary (Anti-Parnellite) party, in favour of Home Rule, etc. Returned for the N. division of Roscommon July 1892 and sat until he retired in 1895. Q.C. 1894. County Court Judge in Clare 1907-24. Died 7 June 1933.   [1895]

BOLAND, John Pius. 40 St. George's Square, London. S. of Patrick Boland, Esq., Banker and Miller, of Dublin, and Mary, d. of John Donnelly, Esq., of Dublin. B. in Dublin 1870; m. 1902, Eileen, d. of Dr. P. Moloney, of Melbourne. Educ. at the Oratory School, Edgbaston, London University, B.A., and Christ Church, Oxford, M.A.; semester at Bonn University (Bavaria Verbindung). A Barrister-at-Law, Inner Temple, called 1897; and Vice-President of Irish Industrial Development Association. A Whip to the Irish Party from 1906. A Nationalist. First elected for S. Kerry in 1900 and sat until he retired in 1918. Gen.-Secretary Catholic Truth Society 1926-47; Author of *A Day in the Life of an Irish M.P.* (1944). Died 17 Mar. 1958.   [1918]

BOLES, Lieut.-Col. Dennis Fortescue. Continued in House after 1918: full entry in Volume III.

BOLITHO, Thomas Bedford. Trewidden, Penzance. Greenway House, Brixham. Union. S. of Edward Bolitho, Esq., of Trewidden, Cornwall, by Mary, d. of John Stephens, Esq., of Beerferris, Devon. B. 1835; m. 1893, Frances, 3rd d. of E.C. Wilson, Esq., of Penmount, Truro. Educ. at Harrow School. A Banker, a member of the firm of Bolithos, of Penzance, etc. A J.P. for Cornwall and Devon, and a Dept.-Lieut. for Cornwall; was High Sheriff 1884. A Liberal Unionist. Sat for the St. Ives division of Cornwall from July 1887 until he retired in 1900. Died 22 May 1915.   [1900]

BOLTON, Joseph Cheney. Carbrook, Stirlingshire. Reform, and Devonshire. B. 1819. A Merchant in the East India trade and President of the Glasgow Chamber of Commerce. Was for some years Chairman of the Caledonian Railway Company. A Liberal, in favour of Home Rule. Unsuccessfully contested Glasgow in 1874. Sat for Stirlingshire from Apr. 1880 until he retired in 1892. Died 14 Mar. 1901. [1892]

BOLTON, Thomas Dolling. 3 Temple Gardens, London. Osborne Villas, Windsor. Windham, Devonshire, and City Liberal. S. of James Thomas Bolton, Esq., of Solihull, Warwickshire, by Mary Ratcliffe, d. of the Rev. William Boughey Dolling. B. 1841. Unmarried. Educ. privately. A Solicitor, admitted 1866. A member of Windsor Town Council. Chairman of the Neuchatel Asphalte Company, Isle of Wight, and also of the Newport Junction Railway Company; a Director of the Workshop Waterworks Company. A Liberal, he favoured Mr. Gladstone's Irish Policy. Sat for N.E. Derbyshire from 1886 until his death 6 Dec. 1906.   [1906]

BOLTON, Thomas Henry. 11 Gray's Inn Square, London. South Binns, Heathfield, Sussex. National Liberal, and Garrick. S. of Thomas Bolton, Esq., of Canonbury, by Priscilla Elizabeth, his wife. B. at Clerkenwell, London Feb 1841; m. 18 May 1861, Elizabeth Ann, eld. d. of William Wegg, Esq. Admitted a Solicitor in 1869, and became a member of the firm of Bolton and Mote, of Gray's Inn Square, London. Chairman of the Select Committee on Patent Agents, and held many honorary local positions in Islington, St. Pancras; was Vice-Chairman of the Hailsham Guardians (Sussex). A Liberal Unionist. First returned for N. St. Pancras in Nov. 1885 as a Liberal; voted for the Home Rule Bill of 1886, and for the 2nd reading of the 1893 Bill, but he voted against the 3rd reading and joined the Liberal Unionists. Defeated at the general election of 1886; re-elected for N. St. Pancras in Mar. 1890 and successfully held the seat at the election of 1892 when standing as a Liberal Unionist; sat until he retired in 1895. Died 24 Sept. 1916.   [1895]

BOND, Edward. 1 Suffolk Place, Pall Mall, London. Elm Bank, Hampstead. Athenaeum, Albemarle, and Carlton. S. of Edward Bond, Esq., of Elm Bank,

Hampstead, and his wife, Sarah Jane, the d. of William Pollard, Esq., of Crowtrees, near Bradford. B. 1844. Educ. at Merchant Taylor's School, and St. John's Coll., Oxford, where he obtained a 1st class in final classical school, and was afterwards elected to a fellowship at Queen's Coll. A Barrister, called at Lincoln's Inn 1871, and was Lecturer to the Incorporated Law Society. A member, of the London School Board; resigned on appointment as Assistant Charity Commissioner, which office he held 1884-91. Elected member of the London County Council for Hampstead, 1895 and 1898. A Conservative. Contested Southwark W. 1892. First elected for Nottingham E. 1895 and sat until defeated in 1906. Died 18 Aug. 1920. [1905]

BOND, George Hawkesworth. 37 Bury Street, St. James's, London. Creech Grange, Wareham, Dorset. Carlton, and Junior Carlton. 2nd s. of the Rev. Nathaniel Bond, J.P. of Creech Grange, Dorset, by Mary, d. of J. Hawkesworth Forest, Esq., of Queen's Co. B. 1845 at Holme Priory, Dorset. Educ. at Oriel Coll., Oxford. A J.P. and Dept.-Lieut. for Dorset, and was Lieut. of the Queen's Own Yeomanry. A Conservative. Was an unsuccessful candidate for Dorset E. in 1885. First returned for Dorset E. in July 1886 and sat until his death 5 Nov. 1891. [1891]

BONSOR, Henry Cosmo Orme. 38 Belgrave Square, London. Kingswood Warren, Epsom, Surrey. Carlton, Arthur's, Turf, and Junior Carlton. S. of Joseph Bonsor, Esq., of Polesden, Surrey, and Belgrave Square, London, by Eliza, d. of Maj. Orme. B. at Polesden Sept. 1848; m. 1st, 1872, Emily Gertrude, d. of James Fellowes, Esq., of Kingston House, Dorset (she died 1882); 2ndly, 1886, Mabel, 2nd d. of James Brand, Esq. Educ. at Eton Coll. Chairman of Watney Combe, Reid and Company Limited, Brewers, London; a Director of the Bank of England, Treasurer of Guy's Hospital, Chairman S.E. Railway Company, J.P. and Dept.-Lieut. for Surrey, and a Commissioner of Income Tax for the City of London. Patron of 1 living. A Conservative. Sat for the Wimbledon division of Surrey from 1885 until he retired in 1900. Chairman of Income Tax Commission for the City of London. Created Bart. in 1925. Died 4 Dec. 1929. [1900]

BONTINE - CUNNINGHAME - CUNNINGHAME - GRAHAM, Robert Gallnigad. See GRAHAM, Robert Gallnigad Bontine Cunninghame.

BOORD, Thomas William. 14 Berkeley Square, London. Wakehurst Place, Sussex. Carlton. S. of Joseph Boord, Esq., J.P. of Harefield Grove, Uxbridge, by Mary Anne, d. of Thomas Newstead, Esq., of Dunham, Nottinghamshire. B. in London 1838; m. 1861, Margaret, d. of T.G. Mackinlay, Esq., F.S.A. Was educ. at Harrow and in Germany. A Partner in the firm of Boord and Son, Distillers. A J.P. Sussex. A Conservative, opposed to the overthrow of existing Church establishments, but was in favour of reform in land tenures and increased facilities for its transfer. Sat for Greenwich from Aug. 1873 until he retired in 1895. Created Bart. in 1896. Died 2 May 1912. [1895]

BOOTH, Frederick Handel. Hooton Levett Hall, Maltby. 106 Grosvenor Road, London. National Liberal, and Royal Automobile. S. of John Booth, Esq., Cotton Manufacturer, of Manchester, and Alice Mather Roper. B. 23 July 1867 at Little Hulton, near Bolton; m. 1895, Lucy, d. of Thomas Dreydel, Esq., J.P., of Manchester. Educ. at Bolton-le-Moors High School. Chairman of Yorkshire Coal and Iron Company, Leeds. Was Chairman of Barton Board of Guardians 1895-96, and twice presided at the Annual Conference of Urban District Councils. A Liberal. Unsuccessfully contested King's Lynn in 1900. Elected for Pontefract in Dec. 1910 and sat until defeated in Wentworth in 1918. Died 24 Feb. 1947. [1918]

BOOTH, Rt. Hon. George Sclater. See SCLATER-BOOTH, Rt. Hon. George.

BORLASE, William Copeland, F.S.A. 10 St. James's Place, London. Laregan, Penzance. National Liberal. Only s. of Samuel Borlase, Esq., of Castle Horneck and Pendeen, Cornwall, a Magistrate and Dept.-Lieut. for that Co., by his 2nd wife, Mary Anne, d. or William Copeland, Esq., of Chigwell, Essex. B. at Castle Horneck, 1848; m. 1870, Alice Lucy, eld. d. of Rev. Alfred Kent, Vicar of Coln St. Aldwyns, Gloucestershire. Was educ. at Winchester, and at Trinity Coll., Oxford; graduated B.A. 1870, M.A. 1873. Was President of the Royal Institute of Cornwall from 1868-70.

Appointed Parliamentary Secretary Local Government Board in succession of Mr. Jesse Collings, Apr.-July 1886. Author of *A Work on the Antiquities of Cornwall*, also *Sunways, a Record of Travels in America and the East of Europe*, etc. A Liberal, in favour of Home Rule, of real and personal property being put upon an equality, and of the licensing system being placed under local control. Sat for Cornwall E. 1880-85, and for the St. Austell division of Cornwall from Dec. 1885 until he accepted Chiltern Hundreds in Apr. 1887. Bankrupt 14 June 1887. Died 31 Mar. 1899. [1887]

BORTHWICK, Sir Algernon, Bart. 139 Piccadilly, London. Heath House, Hampstead. Carlton, Garrick, and St. James's. S. of Peter Borthwick, Esq., (for many years MP for Evesham), by Margaret, d. of John Colville, Esq., of Ewart, Northumberland. B. at Cambridge 1830; m. 1870, Alice Beatrice, d. of Thomas Henry Lister, Esq., of Armitage Park, Staffordshire. Educ. at Paris, and King's Coll. School, London. Knighted in 1880. Proprietor of the *Morning Post*, and President of the Newspaper Press Fund. Created a Bart. 1887. A Conservative. Unsuccessfully contested Evesham in 1880. Sat for S. Kensington from Nov. 1885 until created Baron Glenesk in Oct. 1895. Died 22 Nov. 1908. [1895 2nd ed.]

BOSCAWEN, Rt. Hon. Sir Arthur Sackville Trevor Griffith-. See GRIFFITH-BOSCAWEN, Rt. Hon. Sir Arthur Sackville Trevor. Continued in House after 1918: full entry in Volume III.

BOTTOMLEY, Horatio William. Continued in House after 1918: full entry in Volume III.

BOULNOIS, Edmund. 27 Westbourne Terrace, London. Scotlands, Farnham Common, Buckinghamshire. Carlton. B. 1838 in London; m. 1862, Catherine, eld. d. of T.J. Bennett, Esq., of Great Marlow. Educ. at King Edward's School, Bury St. Edmund's, and St. John's Coll., Cambridge (Scholar; B.A. 1861, M.A. 1865). A J.P. and Dept.-Lieut. for the Co. of Middlesex, and Chairman of the Marylebone Bench of Magistrates; was member of the London County Council for Marylebone E. division. Mayor of Marylebone 1900-02. A Conservative. Sat for Marylebone E. from July 1889 until he retired in 1906. Died 7 May 1911. [1905]

BOULTON, Alexander Claude Forster. 5 Kings Bench Walk, Temple, London. 28 Ranelagh Avenue, Barnes, Surrey. Hamingford Grey, St. Ives, Huntingdonshire. Eighty. S. of James Forster Boulton, Esq., Barrister, of Moulton, Lincolnshire, and Ottawa, Canada, and Jane, d. of Col. Graham, 75th Regiment. B. at Port Hope, Canada 1862; m. 1891, Florence, d. of Henry Harms, Esq., of Horsham (she died 1903). Educ. at Trinity Coll. School, and Trinity Coll., Toronto. A Barrister, called to the Canadian bar 1886, and at the Inner Temple 1895. Counsel to the Post Office at the Central Criminal Court. J.P. for Surrey. Author of *Law and Practice of a Case Stated, Liberalism and the Empire, Criminal Appeals*; editor of Canadian editions of *Underhill on Torts*, and other legal textbooks. Lieut. Royal Grenadiers, Canada. A Liberal. Elected or the Ramsey division of Huntingdonshire in 1906 and sat until defeated in Jan. 1910. Unsuccessfully contested the Ramsey division of Huntingdonshire again in Dec. 1910. Contested the New Forest and Christchurch division of Hampshire in 1923 and 1924. Commissioner to local Government Board, Lancashire, 1916. Joint Founder, with Sir W. Besant, of the Atlantic Union, later the English-Speaking Union. Died 12 Mar. 1949. [1909]

BOURKE, Rt. Hon. Robert. 18 Montagu Street, London. Coalstown, Haddington, Scotland. Carlton. 3rd s. of the 5th Earl of Mayo, by Anne Charlotte, only d. and heir of the Hon. John Jocelyn, of Fair Hill, Co. Louth, and grand-d. of 1st Earl of Roden. B. at Hayes, Co. Meath 1827; m. 1863, Lady Susan Georgiana, eld. d. of the Marq. of Dalhousie, the distinguished Gov.-Gen. of India. Educ. at Enniskillen School, at Hall Place, Kent, and at Trinity Coll., Dublin. Called to the bar at the Inner Temple Nov. 1852. Under-Secretary of State for Foreign Affairs from Feb. 1874 to Apr. 1880 and July 1885 to Jan. 1886. Lieut. S. Middlesex Volunteers 1860. Author of *Parliamentary Precedents*, etc. A Conservative. Sat for Lynn Regis from Dec. 1868 until Aug. 1886 when he was appointed Gov. of Madras (until 1890). G.C.I.E. 1887. Created Baron Connemara May 1887. Died 3 Sept. 1902. [1886]

BOUSFIELD, William Robert. 2 Crown Office Row, London. St. Swithin's, Hendon. Carlton. Eld. s. of E.T. Bousfield,

Esq., of Bedford. B. 1854; m. 1879, Florence, d. of George Kelly, Esq., of Shanklin, Isle of Wight. Educ. at Bedford Modern School, and Caius Coll., Cambridge. Was for a time in training as an Engineer at Sir Joseph Whitworth's Works, and afterwards Lecturer on Engineering and Mathematics at University Coll., Bristol. In 1880 was called to the bar at the Inner Temple, and joined the W. Circuit. Became Q.C. in 1891 and a bencher of his inn 1897. An Associate of the Institute of Civil Engineers, and author of a work on Patents, Designs, and Trade Marks. A Conservative. Unsuccessfully contested mid Lanark 1885 and 1888. First elected for Hackney N. May 1892, on the death of Sir Lewis Pelly, and sat until defeated in 1906. F.R.S. 1916. Died 16 July 1943. [1905]

BOWDEN, Lieut.-Col. George Robert Harland. Hazeldene, Harpenden Road, St. Albans. 17 Victoria Street, London. Carlton, and Junior Army & Navy. B. 1873. Maj. 1st Hertfordshire Battery, R.F.A., 4th East Anglian Brigade, and Commanding Officer 17th Battalion Royal Fusiliers. A Unionist. Elected for N.E. Derbyshire in May 1914 and sat until defeated as Independent Conservative candidate against the official Coalition Conservative in 1918. Defeated again at N.E. Derbyshire standing as official Conservative in 1924. Died 10 Oct. 1927. [1918]

BOWERMAN, Rt. Hon. Charles William. Continued in House after 1918: full entry in Volume III.

BOWLES, George Frederic Stewart. 36 Connaught Square, London. Carlton. S. of Thomas Gibson Bowles, Esq., MP for Kings Lynn, and Jessica, d. of Gen. Evans Gordon. B. 1877; m. 1st, 1902. Marion Joan, d. of John Penn, Esq., MP for Lewisham, (divorced 1921); 2ndly, 1922, Madeleine Mary, d. of E.J. Tobin, Esq. Educ. at a private school, and Trinity Coll., Cambridge; M.A. Served in the navy. Was called to the bar at the Inner Temple 1901, but never practised. A Conservative. Elected for the Norwood division of Lambeth in 1906 and sat until he retired in Jan. 1910. Contested Blackburn Jan. 1910, as a Free Trader. Died 1 Jan. 1955. [1909]

BOWLES, Henry Ferryman. Continued in House after 1918: full entry in Volume III.

BOWLES, Thomas Gibson. 25 Lowndes Square, London. Wilbury, Salisbury. B. 1843; m. 1876, Jessica, d. of Gen. Evans Gordon (she died 1887). Educ. privately, and at King's Coll., London. Was a Clerk in the Inland Revenue Department. Was a Correspondent of the *Morning Post*, and wrote *Maritime Welfare, Flotsam and Jetsam, The Declaration of Paris, 1856*, etc. Honorary Lieut. Royal Navy Reserve, and had the Board of Trade certificate as a Master Mariner. A Conservative. Was an unsuccessful candidate at Darlington 1874, Banbury 1880, and S. Salford 1885. Sat for King's Lynn from 1892 to 1906, when he was defeated as a Conservative but because of his free trade views was not readopted by the King's Lynn Conservatives. He contested King's Lynn as an Independent Free Trader in Jan. 1906 and the City of London on 27 Feb. 1906; he subsequently joined the Liberal Party and unsuccessfully contested Glasgow Central on 2 Mar. 1909; elected as Liberal Member for King's Lynn in Jan. 1910 and sat until defeated in Dec. 1910. Unsuccessfully contested Harborough division of Leicestershire on 23 Mar. 1916 as a candidate of the "Leicestershire Attested Married Men's Protest Society." Died 12 Jan. 1922. [1910]

BOYD-KINNEAR, John. See KINNEAR, John Boyd.

BOYLE, Daniel. Castletown Manor, Co. Sligo, via Ballina. S. of Donal Boyle, Esq., Farmer. B. 10 Jan. 1859 at Kilcoo, Co. Fermanagh; m. 1883, Annie, d. of Patrick Gardiner, Esq., of Sligo. Educ. at National Schools. A Journalist, qualified as a Teacher, but never followed that profession. A J.P. for Manchester, and a member of the City Council from 1894, Alderman 1908, and Chairman of Tramways Committee 1898-1906. Was for many years leader of Irish Nationalists in Manchester. A Nationalist. Elected for N. Mayo in Jan. 1910 and sat until he retired in 1918. Unsuccessfully contested Peterborough as a Liberal in 1923 and 1924. Died 1925. [1918]

BOYLE, Sir Edward, Bart. 63 Queen's Gate, London. 1 Kings Bench Walk, Temple, London. Ockham, Hurst Green, Sussex. S. of Edward O. Boyle, Esq., Civil Engineer, and Eliza, d. of William Gurney, Esq., of Norfolk. B. 1849; m. 1874, Constance, d. of William Knight, Esq., J.P., of

Kensington Park Gardens. A Barrister; educ. for the army, but commenced practice as an Architect and was a Fellow of the Surveyors' Institution. Called to the bar at the Inner Temple 1887; Q.C. 1898. A Director of London and India Docks; Dept.-Chairman of Imperial Life Office; created Bart. 1904. Author of *Principles of Rating, Law of Compensation, Lands Clauses Acts,* and *Law of Railway and Canal Traffic.* A Conservative. Unsuccessfully contested Hastings 1900 and the Rye division of Sussex in 1903. Elected for Taunton in 1906 and sat until he accepted Chiltern Hundreds in Feb. 1909 shortly before his death on 19 Mar. 1909.   [1908]

BOYLE, James. Stranorlar, Co. Donegal. S. of Edward Boyle, Esq., Merchant, and Catherine Sweeney. B. at Dungloe, Co. Donegal 1863; m. 1899, Rosaline Mary Theresa, only d. of Edward Allingham, Esq., of Dublin. Educ. at the French Coll., Blackrock, Co. Dublin. A Solicitor; apprenticed 1882, gold medallist, admitted June 1887. Elected "Coroner" W. Donegal, Mar. 1891, after a contest, and held the position from that date. A Nationalist, elected as a United Irish Leaguer. Sat for Donegal W. from Oct. 1900 until he accepted Chiltern Hundreds in 1902. Died Dec. 1936.   [1902]

BOYLE, William Lewis. Tuddenham Lodge. Honingham, Norfolk. Constitutional, Carlton, and Norfolk County. S. of Charles John Boyle, Esq., and Zacyntha, d. of Gen. Sir L. Moore, and grand-s. of Vice-Admiral the Hon. Sir Courtney Boyle. B. 1859; m. 1887, Charlotte Mary, d. of Charles Loyd Norman, Esq. Spent several years in commercial and agricultural pursuits in Canada. A Unionist. Unsuccessfully contested mid Norfolk in 1900 and 1906. Elected for mid Norfolk in Jan. 1910 and sat until his death 2 Oct. 1918.   [1918]

BOYTON, Sir James. 2 Park Square West, Regent's Park, London. Thames Lawn, Marlow, Buckinghamshire. Carlton, and Constitutional. S. of Henry Boyton, Esq. B. 1855; m. 1881, d. of Peter Middleton, Esq. Educ. privately. Senior Partner in the firm of Eliott, Son and Boyton, Auctioneers and Surveyors, Vere Street, London; a member of the Council of the Auctioneers' and Estate Agents Institute (President 1905-06). Was a member of the London County Council from 1907-10. Knighted 1918. A Unionist. Elected for Marylebone E. Jan. 1910 and sat until he retired in 1918. Died 16 May 1926   [1918]

BRACE, Rt. Hon. William. Continued in House after 1918: full entry in Volume III.

BRACKENBURY, Henry Langton. Continued in House after 1918: full entry in Volume III.

BRADLAUGH, Charles. 20 Circus Road, St. John's Wood, London. S. of Charles Bradlaugh, Esq., by Mary, d. of James Trimby, Esq. B. at Hoxton, London 1833; m. 1854, Susannah Lamb, d. of Abraham Hooper, Esq., of Midhurst, Sussex (she died 1877). Was the well-known Radical Lecturer and Proprietor of the periodical *The National Reformer,* also President of the National Secular Society. A Radical, in favour of Home Rule, of the abolition of the system of primogeniture, the separation of Church and State, etc. Unsuccessfully contested Northampton borough Nov. 1868, Feb. 1874, and Oct. 1874. First elected for Northampton borough Apr. 1880, and on its being decided in the Court of Appeal that he was not a person entitled to affirm instead of taking an oath, a fresh election was ordered Apr. 1881, when he was re-elected. Expelled from the House in Feb. 1882, but was again elected, Mar. 1882. On the 11 Feb. 1884 he voted in the House, and on being excluded by resolution he applied for the Chiltern Hundreds, and was elected for a fourth time, but did not take his seat before the dissolution. Was again returned for Northampton in 1885, and took the oath and his seat without opposition. MP until his death 30 Jan. 1891.   [1890]

BRADY, Patrick Joseph. Glena, Booterstown, Dublin. 20 Molesworth Street, Dublin, National Liberal. S. of James Brady, Esq. B. 1868 at Blackrock, Dublin; m. 1900, Evelyn, d. of J.D. Parminter, Esq., Paymaster, R.N. Educ. at St. Vincent's Coll., Castleknock, and University Coll., Dublin. A Solicitor, admitted 1893; a member of the Council of Inc. Law Society of Ireland. A Director of the Midland Great Western Railway of Ireland. A Nationalist. Elected for the St. Stephen's Green division of Dublin in Jan. 1910 and sat until defeated in 1918. Senator, Irish Free State from Jan. 1927-Dec. 1928. Died 20 May 1943.   [1918]

BRAMSDON, Sir Thomas Arthur. Continued in House after 1918: full entry in Volume III.

BRANCH, James. 24 Fountayne Road, Stoke Newington, London. B. 1845 at Bethnal Green. A Boot Manufacturer at Bethnal Green and Northampton; member of the London County Council 1889-1907, and of the Metropolitan Water Board 1906. J.P. for Co. of London. A Liberal, in favour of Nationalization of the Land. Elected for the Enfield division of Middlesex in 1906 and sat until defeated in Jan. 1910. Unsuccessfully contested the Enfield division of Middlesex in Dec. 1910. Died 16 Nov. 1918. [1909]

BRAND, Hon. Arthur George. Huntsland, Crawley Down, Sussex. Reform, Bachelors', and Garrick. 3rd s. of Visct. Hampden (Speaker of the House of Commons). B. in London 1853; m. 1886, Edith, d. of Joseph Ingram, Esq., J.P., of Brooklands, Cheshire (she died 1903). Educ. at Rugby. Was Private Secretary to Arnold Morley, Esq., the Liberal "Whip", during 1883 and 1886, and was also one of the Managers of the Liberal Central Association. In 1893 was Assistant Private Secretary (unpaid) to Mr. Fowler, President, Local Government Board, and from 1894-95 was Treasurer of H.M. Household. J.P. and Dept.-Lieut. for Sussex. A Liberal. Sat for Cambridgeshire N. from July 1891 until defeated 1895; re-elected there 1900 and sat until he retired in 1906. Died 9 Jan. 1917. [1905]

BRAND, Hon. Henry Robert. Temple Dinsley, Hitchin, Hertfordshire. Brooks's, and Travellers'. Eld. s. of the Rt. Hon. Visct. Hampden, G.C.B., former Speaker of the House of Commons, by Eliza, d. of Gen. Robert Ellice. B. at Devonport 1841; m. 1st, 1864, Victoria, eld. d. of His Excellency M. Van-der-Weyer (she died 1865); 2ndly, 1868, Susan, d. of Lord George Cavendish. Educ. at Rugby, and entered the army Dec. 1858. Became Lieut. and Capt. Coldstream Guards May 1863, retired Oct. 1865. Appointed Surveyor Gen. of the Ordnance Jan. 1883. A Liberal. Sat for Hertfordshire from Dec. 1868-Feb. 1874, when he was unsuccessful. Sat for Stroud from July-Dec. 1874, when he was unseated on petition. Was also unsuccessful there in May 1874. Sat for Stroud from 1880 until 1886 when he unsuc-

cessfully contested Cardiff district as a Liberal Unionist. Succeeded as 2nd Visct. Hampden, Mar. 1892. Died 22 Nov. 1906. [1886]

BRASSEY, Albert. 29 Berkeley Square, London. Heythrop, Chipping Norton. Army & Navy, Naval & Military, Carlton, Cavalry, and Oxford & Cambridge. S. of Thomas Brassey, Esq., of Bulkley, and Maria Farrington, d. of Joseph Harrison, Esq. B. 1844 in France; m. Hon. Matilda Maria Helena, eld. d. of the 4th Lord Clanmorris. Educ. at Eton, M.A. of University Coll., Oxford. Was Lieut. 14th Hussars, 1867-71; Col. Queen's Own Oxfordshire Hussars 1892-95. High Sheriff of Oxfordshire 1878; Mayor of Chipping Norton 1898-1901; Master of Heythrop Foxhounds from 1873. A Conservative and Unionist, in favour of Home Legislation. Sat for the Banbury division of Oxfordshire from 1895 until he retired in 1906. Died 7 Jan. 1918. [1905]

BRASSEY, Henry Leonard Campbell. Continued in House after 1918: full entry in Volume III.

BRASSEY, Capt. Robert Bingham. Copse Hill, Lower Slaughter, Gloucestershire. Cavalry, Army & Navy, and Arthur's. S. of Albert Brassey, Esq., MP for Banbury division of Oxfordshire from 1895-1906, and Hon. Matilda Bingham, d. of 4th Bar. Clanmorris. B. 18 Oct. 1875 at Heythrop; m. 1904, Violet Edith, d. of Armar Lowry-Corry. Educ. at Eton. Served in the 17th Lancers 1897-1905, and in the S. African War 1899-1901. Capt. Reserve of Officers. A Unionist. Elected for the Banbury division of Oxfordshire in Jan. 1910 and sat until defeated in Dec. 1910. Died 14 Nov. 1946. [1910]

BRASSEY, Sir Thomas, K.C.B. Retired in 1886: full entry in Volume I.

BRIDGEMAN, Col. Hon. Francis Charles. Carlton, and Wellington. 2nd s. of the Earl of Bradford. B. 1846; m. Gertrude, d. of George Hanbury, Esq., of Blythewood Hall, Buckinghamshire. Educ. at Harrow. Having joined the Scots Fusilier Guards in 1865, he became Lieut. and Capt. in 1869, Lieut.-Col. 1877, Col. 1887, and retired 1889. Served as Aide-de-Camp to H.S.H. Prince Edward of Saxe-

Weimar, the Gen. commanding the home district, during 1875-76, and in the Egyptian War, under Gen. Graham, took part in the action near Suakin when Osman Digma's position was forced, being awarded the Medal and Khedive's Star. A J.P. for Shropshire. A Conservative. Unsuccessfully contested Stafford in 1874, Tamworth Apr. 1878, and Bolton in 1880. Sat for Bolton from 1885 until defeated in 1895. Died 14 Sept. 1917.   [1895]

BRIDGEMAN, William Clive. Continued in House after 1918: full entry in Volume III.

BRIGG, Sir John. Kildwick Hall, Nr. Keighley. National Liberal. 2nd s. of John Brigg, Esq., J.P., of Guard House, Keighley, and Margaret Ann Marriner. B. 1834 at Keighley; m. 1860, Mary, d. of William Anderton, Esq., of Bingley. Educ. at Stubbing Hill, and Dewsbury Moor. Chairman of the Bradford Advisory Board of the United Counties Bank, and a Director of the Leeds and Liverpool Canal Company. A J.P. and Dept.-Lieut. for the W. Riding of Yorkshire; was provisional Mayor of Keighley in 1882, and was a Gov. or member of Council for many institutions in the W. Riding of Yorkshire. A F.G.S. Knighted in 1909. A Liberal, in favour of Home Rule and the Liberal programme generally. Sat for the Keighley division of the W. Riding of Yorkshire from 1895 until his death 30 Sept. 1911.   [1911]

BRIGHT, Allan Heywood. Gorse Hey, West Derby, Liverpool. Brookside, Weston Rhyn, Shropshire. S. of H.A. Bright, Esq., of Liverpool, and Mary Elizabeth, d. of S.H. Thompson, Esq., J.P. B. at Liverpool 24 May 1862; m. 1885, Edith, d. of A. Turner, Esq., J.P., of Liverpool. Educ. at Harrow. A Merchant and Shipowner. J.P. for Liverpool; Chairman of Liverpool Hospital for Women 1900-01. A Liberal, Anti-Imperialist and Free Trader. Unsuccessfully contested Exeter 1899 and 1900, and Oswestry division of Shropshire in 1901. Was elected for the Oswestry division of Shropshire July 1904 and sat until defeated in 1906. Contested Stalybridge Jan. and Dec. 1910. Died 3 Aug. 1941.   [1905]

BRIGHT, Rt. Hon. Jacob. 31 St. James's Place, London. Reform. S. of Jacob Bright, Esq., of Greenbank, near Rochdale. B. at Greenbank 1821; m. 1855, Ursula, d. of Joseph Mellor, Esq., of Liverpool. Brother to the Rt. Hon. John Bright, MP, and a Partner in the firm of John Bright and Brothers, Cotton Spinners and Manufacturers at Rochdale. Educ. at the Friends' School, York. Made a PC. 1894. An advanced Liberal, in favour of Mr. Gladstone's Irish policy. Unsuccessfully contested Manchester in July 1865. Sat for Manchester from Nov. 1867 to Feb. 1874, when he was an unsuccessful candidate. He was re-elected Feb. 1876 and sat up to the dissolution of 1885. Unsuccessfully contested the S.W. division of Manchester in 1885, but elected there in July 1886, and again in 1892 and sat until he retired in 1895. Died 7 Nov. 1899.   [1895]

BRIGHT, Rt. Hon. John. One Ash, Rochdale. Reform, and Athenaeum. S. of Jacob Bright, Esq., of Greenbank, near Rochdale. B. 1811; m. 1st, 1839, Elizabeth, eld. d. of Jonathan Priestman, Esq., of Newcastle-on-Tyne (she died 1841); 2ndly, 1847, Margaret Elizabeth, eld. d. of William Leatham, Esq., of Wakefield, Yorkshire (she died 1878). A Cotton-Spinner and Manufacturer, being a Partner in the firm of John Bright and Brothers, of Rochdale. Was President of the Board of Trade from Dec. 1868-Dec. 1870, and Chancellor of the Duchy of Lancaster from Oct. 1873-Feb. 1874, and from Apr. 1880-July 1882. Elected Lord Rector of Glasgow University Nov. 1880; made D.C.L. of Oxford 1886. Previous to his return to Parliament was chiefly known as an active member of the anti-corn-law league. A Liberal, opposed to Mr. Gladstone's Home Rule Scheme. Unsuccessfully contested Durham City Apr. 1843. Again stood for Durham July 1843, when he was returned and continued to sit for that city until July 1847. Sat for Manchester from July 1847-Apr. 1857, when he was an unsuccessful candidate there. Sat for Birmingham from Aug. 1857 to Nov. 1885 and for Central Brimingham from 1885 until his death on 27 Mar. 1889.   [1888]

BRIGHT, John Albert. One Ash, Rochdale. Reform, and Cobden. Eld. s. of the Rt. Hon. John Bright, MP, and Margaret Elizabeth, d. of William Leatham, Esq., of Wakefield. B. 1848 in London; m. 1883, Edith Eckersley, d. of

William Tuer Shawcross, Esq., of Foxholes, Rochdale. Educ. at Grove House, Tottenham, and University Coll., London. A Director of John Bright and Brothers Limited, Cotton Spinners, of Rochdale, and of the London and North Western Railway Company. A J.P. for Lancashire and Rochdale. A Liberal. Sat for the Central division of Birmingham as a Liberal Unionist from 15 Apr. 1889-95, when he retired. Rejoined the Liberal Party and contested the Montgomery district in Oct. 1900. Elected for Oldham in 1906 and sat until he retired in Jan. 1910. Died 11 Nov. 1924. [1909]

BRIGHT, William Leatham. 37 Queen's Mansions, Victoria Street, London. Reform, and National Liberal. 2nd s. of the Rt. Hon. John Bright, MP, by Margaret Elizabeth, d. of William Leatham, Esq. B. at Rochdale 12 Aug. 1851; m. 28 Mar. 1883, Isabella McIvor, d. of Alfred Taylor, Esq., of Shepley House, Carshalton, Surrey. Was educ. at Grove House School, Tottenham, and was engaged in business as a Colliery Agent and Shipbroker. A Liberal, in favour of Home Rule. Sat for Stoke-upon-Trent from 1885 until he accepted Chiltern Hundreds in 1890. Contested Rochdale in 1895. Died 23 Sept. 1910. [1890]

BRINTON, John. Retired in 1886: full entry in Volume I.

BRISTOWE, Thomas Lynn. 55 Cadogan Square, London. Carlton, and St. Stephen's, London. S. of John Syer Bristowe, Esq., M.R.C.S., of Camberwell, by his wife, Mary Chessyre. B. at Camberwell 1833; m. 1857, Frances Ellen, d. of Joseph Paice Mason, Esq., of Mincing Lane and Champion Park. Was a member of the firm of Bristowe Brothers, and was on the Committee of the Stock Exchange from 1868 to 1885. Was for a time Capt. of the No. 1 Company of the 1st Surrey Rifles, and was Chairman of the Herne Hill and Brixton Conservative Association from its formation in 1880. A Conservative. Sat for the Norwood division of Lambeth from 1885 until his death 6 June 1892. [1892]

BROAD, Harrington Evans. 1 Walbrook, London. Stonewell Park, Edenbridge, Kent. National Liberal, and City Liberal. S. of the Rev. John Broad, Baptist Minister.

B. 1844, at Hitchin, in Hertfordshire; m. 1872, Lillie, d. of Peter Broad, Esq., of Beechwood, Reigate, Surrey. Educ. privately. A member of the firm of Broads, Peterson and Company, Accountants, of London, and connected with several commercial companies in the City. A Liberal, in favour of Home Rule for Ireland and the advanced Liberal programme generally. First elected for the S. division of Derbyshire on the death of Mr. H. Wardle, Mar. 1892 and sat until defeated in 1895. Died 8 Dec. 1927. [1895]

BROADHURST, Henry. 4 Elm Gardens, Brook Green, London. Cromer, Norfolk. Reform, and National Liberal. S. of Thomas Broadhurst, Esq., Journeyman Stonemason. B. at Littlemore, Oxfordshire 1840; m. 1860, d. of Edward Olley, Esq., of Norwich, Journeyman Currier. Worked as a Journeyman Stonemason until 1872. Elected Secretary of the Trades Union Congress Parliamentary Committee 1875; resigned 1890. Parliamentary Secretary to the Home Office Jan. 1886 to June 1886. An Alderman, and J.P. for Norfolk. Sat on the Royal Commissions on Reformatories, on Housing the Working Classes, and on Markets, and was a member of the Royal Commission on Old Age Pensions. An advanced Liberal, in favour of Home Rule, of the reform of the present land laws, thinking they "operated against the free distribution of land", of the abolition of compulsory vaccination, etc. Unsuccessfully contested Wycombe in Feb. 1874. Sat for Stoke-on-Trent from Apr. 1880 until Nov. 1885, for the Bordesley division of Birmingham from Nov. 1885 until June 1886, and for Nottingham W. from July 1886 to July 1892, when he was defeated. Unsuccessfully contested Grimsby in Mar. 1893. First elected for Leicester in 1894 and sat until he accepted Chiltern Hundreds in Mar. 1906, being disappointed at not receiving office in the new Liberal Government. Died 11 Oct. 1911. [1905]

BROCKLEHURST, Col. William Brocklehurst. Butley Hall, Macclesfield. National Liberal. S. of William C. Brocklehurst, Esq., MP. B. 1851 at Macclesfield. Unmarried. Educ. at Cheltenham Coll., and Magdalen Coll., Oxford; B.A. Head of the firm of Brocklehurst and Sons, Silk Manufacturers, Macclesfield. Lieut.-Col. Cheshire Imperial Yeomanry. A J.P.

and County Councillor for Cheshire. A Liberal. Elected for the Macclesfield division of Cheshire in 1906 and sat until he retired in 1918. Died 27 June 1929. [1918]

BROCKLEHURST, William Coare. Butley Hall, Prestbury, Macclesfield. Eld. s. of John Brocklehurst, Esq., of Hurdsfield, MP for Macclesfield from 1832-68. B. 1818; m. 1840, Mary, d. of William Worthington, Esq., of Brocklehurst Hall, Cheshire. Engaged in the Silk Trade. President of the Macclesfield Chamber of Commerce. A Magistrate for Cheshire, and former Capt. in the Earl of Chester's Yeomanry Cavalry. A Liberal. Succeeded his father as MP for Macclesfield in 1868, but in 1880 he was unseated on petition and the borough of Macclesfield was thenceforth disfranchised. Elected for the Macclesfield division of Cheshire in 1885 and sat until he was defeated in 1886 standing as a Gladstonian Liberal. Died 3 June 1900. [1886]

BRODERICK, Hon. St. J.W. See BRODRICK, Rt. Hon. William St. John Fremantle.

BRODIE, Harry Cunningham. 9 Litte Stanhope Street, London. Shrubhurst, Oxted, Surrey. Lorne House, Redhill. Cavalry, Union, National Liberal, and City of London. S. of J.H. Brodie, Esq., of Oxted, and Florence, d. of R.E. Cunningham, Esq., B. 18 Jan. 1875 at Victoria, B.C. Educ. at Winchester, and abroad. A Colonial Merchant, and a Partner in the firm of Findlay, Durham, and Brodie. A Maj. in Middlesex Imperial Yeomanry. Was a member of Toynbee Hall, Whitechapel, and travelled in America, Africa, and the Continent. A Liberal, a supporter of Trades Unionism, and Small Holdings, and believed in giving local authorities greater power for dealing with the Housing and Land questions. Sat for the Reigate division of Surrey from Jan. 1906 until defeated in Jan. 1910. Died 27 Feb. 1956. [1909]

BRODRICK, Hon. William. (Note: MP until 1870 and full entry in Volume I where it is incorrectly listed under Broderick).

BRODRICK, Rt. Hon. William St. John Fremantle. 34 Portland Place, London. Peper Harow, Godalming. Carlton, and Athenaeum. Eld. s. of Visct. Midleton, by Hon. Augusta Mary, 3rd d. of the 1st Baron Cottesloe. B. 1856; m. 1st, 1880, Lady Hilda Charteris, 3rd d. of the Earl of Wemyss (she died 1901); 2ndly, 1903, Madeleine, d. of Col. the Hon. J.C. Stanley. Was educ. at Eton, and Balliol Coll., Oxford, where he graduated B.A. 1879, M.A. 1882. Lieut. 2nd Surrey Militia, Honorary Col. Surrey Yeomanry. Appointed Secretary of State for India Oct. 1903-Dec. 1905. Was Financial Secretary at the War Office 1886-92, Under Secretary of State for War 1895-98, Under Secretary for Foreign Affairs 1898-1900. PC. 1897. Secretary of State for War from 1900-03. Served on the Royal Commission on Irish Prisons 1884. A Conservative. Sat for W. Surrey from 1880-85, and for the Guildford division of Surrey from 1885 until defeated in 1906. Succeeded as 9th Visct. Midleton 1907. Created 1st Earl of Midleton 1920. K.P. 1915. Alderman London County Council 1907-13. Served on Irish convention 1917-18. Hon. LL.D. Trinity Coll., Dublin 1922. High Steward of Kingston-upon-Thames from 1930. Author of *Ireland, Dupe or Heroine* and *Records and Reactions 1856-1939.* Died 13 Feb.1942. Note: incorrectly referred to as Broderick in Volume I). [1905]

BROMLEY-DAVENPORT, William. 1 Belgrave Place, London. Capesthorne Hall, Chelford. Baginton, Coventry. Wootton Hall, Ashbourne. Carlton, White's, and Bachelors'. Eld. s. of William Bromley-Davenport, Esq., MP, by Augusta, eld. d. of John Campbell, Esq., of Islay, N.B. B. 1862. Educ. at Eton, and Balliol Coll., Oxford. Appointed Financial Secretary to the War Office Oct. 1903 to Dec. 1905. A Magistrate for Cheshire, and Patron of 6 livings. A Conservative. Sat for the Macclesfield division of Cheshire from 1886 until defeated in 1906. Contested same seat in Jan. 1910 and the Leek division of Staffordshire in Dec. 1910. Senior Command in Egypt 1916; Assistant Director of Labour, France, 1917; Italian Expeditionary Force Nov. 1917-Apr. 1918. Lord-Lieut. of Cheshire from 1920. K.C.B. in 1924. Died 6 Feb. 1949. [1905]

BROOKE, Francis Richard Charles Guy Greville, Lord. 7 Carlton Gardens. Easton Lodge, Dunmow, Essex. Carlton. Eld. s. of the Earl of Warwick, by Lady Anne, eld. d. of the 8th Earl of Wemyss and March. B. in

Carlton Gardens 1853; m. 1881, Frances Evelyn, eld. d. of the Hon. Charles H. Maynard and the Countess of Rosslyn. Educ. at Oxford. A J.P. for Somerset and Essex, and J.P. and Dept.-Lieut. for Warwickshire; also one of the Governors of Rugby School. Capt. in the Warwickshire Yeomanry. A Conservative. Sat for Somerset E. from 1879 until he retired in 1885; and sat for Colchester from Dec. 1888 until he retired in 1892. Succeeded as 5th Earl of Warwick in 1893. Served in S. Africa 1900. Extra Aide-de-Camp to Lord Milner 1901-02. Reuter's special correspondent during Russo-Japanese War 1904-05. Private Secretary to the C.I.G.S. 1913-14. Aide-de-Camp to Commander-in-Chief, British Army in France 1914-15. Brig.-Gen. with Canadian Infantry. Owned 10,000 acres. Died 15 Jan. 1924.   [1892]

BROOKE, Stopford. William Wentworth. 34 De Vere Gardens, Kensington, London. High Wethersell, Cranleigh, Surrey. St. James's, Bath, and Savile. S. of the Rev. Stopford A. Brooke, LL.D., and Emma Diana, d. of T. Wentworth Beaumont, Esq., MP. B. 1859 in London; m. 1903, Helen. d. of Charles Ellis, Esq., of Boston, U.S.A. Educ. at Winchester, and University Coll., Oxford. Unitarian Minister at Boston, U.S.A. A Liberal. Elected for the Bow and Bromley division of Tower Hamlets in 1906 and sat until defeated in Jan. 1910. Contested Bassetlaw division of Nottinghamshire in Dec. 1910. Died 23 Apr. 1938.   [1909]

BROOKES, Warwick. 8 Hamilton Place, London. B. 1875. A Conservative and Unionist. Unsuccessfully contested W. Newington in Jan. and Dec. 1910. Elected for the Mile End division of Tower Hamlets in Jan. 1916 on the succession of the Hon. Harry Lawson to the peerage and sat until defeated in Preston in 1918. Died Aug. 1935.   [1918]

BROOKFIELD, Arthur Montagu. 8 Victoria Street, London. Leasam House, Rye, Sussex. Carlton. S. of the Rev. W.H. Brookfield, Chaplain to Her Majesty, by Jane Octavia, d. of Sir C. Elton, Bart., of Clevedon Court, Somerset. B. 1853; m. 1877, Olive, only d. of J. Murray Hamilton, Esq., of New Abbey, N.B., and Buffalo, U.S.A. Educ. at Rugby, and Jesus Coll., Cambridge. Lieut. 13th Hussars 1873-80. Col. commanding 1st Cinque Ports Rifle

Volunteers. Served in S. African War. Author of *Post Mortem* and *The Speaker's A.B.C.*; a J.P. for Sussex S. A Conservative, favoured a thoroughly Imperial policy. Sat for the Rye division of Sussex from 1885 until he accepted Chiltern Hundreds in 1903. British Consul for Danzig 1903-10 and Savannah 1910-23. Wrote *Annals of a Chequered Life* (1930). Died 3 Mar. 1940.   [1902]

BROOKS, John. Baguley, Timperley, Cheshire. Junior Carlton. S. of the Rev. John Brooks, Rector of Walton-le-Dale, Lancashire, by Anne, d. of John Jones, Esq., of Shackerly Hall, Shropshire. B. 1856. Educ. at Harrow and Merton Coll., Oxford, in which University he obtained the Newdigate Prize and Honours in History in 1877. In 1881 he was called to the bar at the Inner Temple. A Magistrate for Cheshire and Berkshire. A Conservative. First returned for the Altrincham division of Cheshire Nov. 1885. MP until his death 8 Mar. 1886.   [1886]

BROOKS, Sir William Cunliffe, Bart. 5 Grosvenor Square, London. Barlow Hall, Chorlton-cum-Hardy, Manchester. Forest of Glen Tana, Aboyne, Aberdeenshire. Carlton. S. of Samuel Brooks, Esq., Banker, by Margaret, d. of Thomas Hall, Esq. B. 1819; m. 1st, 1842, Jane Elizabeth, d. of Ralph Orrell, Esq., of Stockport (she died 1863); 2ndly, 1879, Jane, d. of Lieut-Col. Davidson. Educ. at Rugby and at St. John's Coll., Cambridge, where he graduated in Honours 1842 (12th senior optime). Was called to the bar at the Inner Temple 1847, and joined the N. Circuit; relinquished practice, however, on the death of his grandfather and became a Partner in the Banks bearing his name at Manchester, Blackburn, London, etc. A Magistrate and Dept.-Lieut. for Lancashire, also a Magistrate for Cheshire and Manchester. Created Bart. in 1886. Patron of 2 livings. A Conservative, in favour of "import duties on foreign manufacturers which enter in competition with the labour of our own countrymen", and desired "to extend to Ireland so much – but no more – of Home Rule, as is extended to Britain." Sat for Cheshire E. from 1869 to 1885. At the general election of the latter year he unsuccessfully contested Macclesfield division of Cheshire. In Mar. 1886 however, he was returned for the Altrincham division of Cheshire in place of his nephew, Mr. John Brook, and sat until he retired in 1892. Died 9 June 1900. [1892]

BROTHERTON, Edward Allen. Continued in House after 1918: full entry in Volume III.

BROUGHTON, Urban Hanlon. 35 Park Street, Grosvenor Square, London. Carlton, Marlborough, Garrick, Orleans, St. Stephens, Boodle's, Royal Thames Yacht, and Yorkshire. S. of John Broughton, Esq., Railway Manager. B. 12 Apr. 1857 at Worcester; Engineering, Manufacturing, Mining, Financial and Railway work in U.S.A. 1887-1912. m. 1896, Cara Leland, d. of Henry Huttleston Rogers, Esq., of New York. Educ. at Grove Park School, Wrexham, and London University. Student and Miller Prizeman, Inst. C.E. 1877; A.M. Inst. C.E. 1883. Employed on Railway, Drainage and Dock work in U.K. 1878-87, and engaged in Engineering, Manufacturing, Mining, Financial and Railway work in U.S.A. 1887-1912. Was President of Virginian Railway. Utah Consolidated Mining Company and Shone Company; Director and Gen. Manager of United Metals Selling Company; Vice-President of National Copper Bank of New York, and a Director of Anaconda Copper Mining Company, Equitable Trust Company of New York, Guaranty Trust Company of New York, International Smelting and Refining Company, Staten Island Midland Railway, Atlas Tack Company, Boylston Manufacturing Company, Butte Coalition Mining Company, Raritan Copper Works, etc. Lieut. in Volunteer Forces 1883-85. British Juror World's Columbian Exposition 1892. Parliamentary Private Secretary to the Attorney Gen. A Unionist. Elected for Preston in June 1915 and sat until he retired in 1918. Died 30 Jan. 1929. Nominated for Peerage in 1929 but died before it was gazetted and his s. became the 1st Baron Fairhaven. [1918]

BROWN, Sir Alexander Hargreaves, Bart. 12 Grosvenor Gardens, London. Broome Hall, Holmwood, Surrey. Brooks's, and Reform. 3rd s. of Alexander Brown, Esq., of Beilby Grange, Yorkshire, by Sarah Benedict, d. of James Brown, Esq., of New York. Grand-s. of Sir W. Brown, of Liverpool, 1st Bart. B. at Beilby Grange, Yorkshire 1844; m. 1876, Henrietta, d. of R.C. Blandy, Esq. A Cornet 5th Dragoon Guards. Honorary Col. 1st Lancashire Volunteer Artillery. A Partner of Brown, Shipley and Company. J.P. for Surrey and Lancashire. Created Bart. 1902. A Liberal Unionist. Sat for Wenlock from 1868-85, and for the Wellington division of Shropshire from 1885 until he retired in 1906. Died 12 Mar. 1922. [1905]

BROWN, Alexander Laing. Rowantree Butts, Galashiels. S. of William Brown, Esq., Manufacturer, of Gala Hill, Galashiels, by Margery, d. of Mr. Laing of Hawick. B. at Selkirk 1851; m. 1882, Esther, d. of the Rev. George Brown, Free Church Minister, of Castle Douglas. A Manufacturer of Scotch Tweeds and an ex-Town Councillor of Galashiels. A Radical, in favour of Mr. Gladstone's Home Rule proposals. Sat for Hawick district from July 1886 until he retired in 1892. Died 1930. [1892]

BROWN, George Mackenzie. 20 Moray Place, Edinburgh. Royal Societies', and St. James's. S. of Hon. George Brown, Toronto, Canada. B. at Toronto, Canada 1869; m. 1901, Mary, d. of Thomas Nelson, Esq., of Edinburgh. Educ. at Upper Canada Coll., Toronto, Merchiston Castle, Edinburgh, and King's Coll., Cambridge. A Publisher; Managing Trustee of Thomas Nelson and Sons from 1892. A Liberal. Elected for the Central division of Edinburgh in 1900 and sat until he retired in 1906. Died 14 July 1946. [1905]

BRUCE, Gainsford. 2 Harcourt Buildings, Temple, London. Gewhurst, Bromley, Kent. Carlton, and St. Stephen's. S. of the Rev. J. Collingwood Bruce, D.C.L., of Newcastle-on-Tyne, by the d. of T. Gainsford, Esq., of Gerald's Cross, Buckinghamshire. B. 1834; m. 1868, Sophia, d. of Francis Jackson, Esq., of Chertsey. Was educ. at the University of Glasgow. Called to the bar in 1859, became a Q.C. in 1883, and a bencher of the Middle Temple in 1887. Joint author of *Williams and Bruce on Admiralty Practice*, and *Maud and Pollock on the Law of Merchant Shipping*. Was appointed Recorder of Bradford in 1877, and successively, Solicitor-Gen., Attorney-Gen., and Chancellor, for the Co. of Durham in 1879, 1886, and 1887. A Conservative, who held that "continuous Progress is essential to healthy national

47

life." Contested the borough of Gateshead in 1880, and Newcastle-on-Tyne (against Mr. John Morley) in 1883, and contested the Tyneside division of Northumberland against Mr. Albert Grey in 1885 and Barrow-in-Furness against Mr. Caine, at a bye-election in Apr. 1886. First returned for the Holborn division of Finsbury Nov. 1888 and sat until he was appointed Judge and Knighted in July 1892. Retired 1904. PC. 1904. Died 24 Feb. 1912. [1892]

BRUCE, Lord Henry Augustus. See BRUDENELL-BRUCE, Lord Henry Augustus.

BRUCE, John. 2 Elm Court and 3 Pump Court, Temple, London. S. of James Bruce, Esq., of Old Meldrum, Aberdeenshire. B. 1861. A Barrister (Middle Temple) 1889. A Gladstonian Liberal. Originally declared elected for Greenock by 44 votes at the 1892 general election, but a petition was lodged and after a recount he was unseated by 55 votes on 28 July 1892.

BRUCE, Hon. Robert Preston. 22 Eaton Square, London. Broomhall, Dunfermline, Scotland. New University. 2nd s. of the 8th Earl of Elgin, by his 2nd wife, Lady Mary Louisa, 4th d. of the 1st Earl of Durham. B. in Canada 1851. Educ. at Eton, and at Balliol Coll., Oxford. A Dept.-Lieut. and J.P. for Fife. Became Capt. Fife Militia Artillery Sept. 1877 and retired in 1880. A Liberal, not opposed to Home Rule in Ireland and eventual disestablishment in Scotland. Sat for Fifeshire from Apr. 1880 until Nov. 1885 when he was returned for the W. division of Fifeshire and sat until he accepted Chiltern Hundreds in June 1889. Died 8 Dec. 1893. [1889]

BRUDENELL-BRUCE, Lord Henry Augustus. 36 Eaton Place, London. Carlton, Constitutional, and Army & Navy. 3rd s. of 3rd Marq. of Ailesbury, by the Hon. Louisa Elizabeth, 2nd d. of the 2nd Baron Decies. B. 1842; m. 1870, Georgiana Sophia Maria, 2nd d. of G.H. Pinckney, Esq., of Tawstock Court, Barnstaple. Educ. at Eton. Entered the army 1860, the Highland Borderers Militia, and Maj. 3rd Battalion Duke of Edinburgh's (Wiltshire) Regiment, retiring as Lieut.-Col. Auxiliary Forces. An "independent Conservative", would give Ireland "the largest possible share of Local

Government", but opposed to granting a separate Parliament. Unsuccessfully contested Marlborough in Apr. 1880. First returned for Wiltshire N.W. July 1886 and sat until he retired in 1892. Succeeded as 5th Marq. of Ailesbury in 1894. Died 10 Mar. 1911. [1892]

BRUNNER, John Fowler Leece. Continued in House after 1918: full entry in Volume III.

BRUNNER, Rt. Hon. Sir John Tomlinson, Bart. 9 Ennismore Gardens, London. Silverlands, Chertsey. Winnington Old Hall, Northwich. Reform, and National Liberal. S. of the Rev. John Brunner, of Zürich, Switzerland, a successful schoolmaster at Everton, Liverpool, by Catherine, d. of Thomas Curphey, of Balldroma, Isle of Man. B. at Everton 1842; m. 1st, 1864, Salome, d. of James Davies, Esq., of Liverpool; 2ndly, 1875, Jane, d. of Dr. Wyman, of Kettering, Northamptonshire. Educ. by his father. Entered mercantile life at Liverpool in 1857; thence he went to Widnes; and in 1873, in company with the distinguished chemist Ludwig Mond, F.R.S., he established the alkali works at Northwich which became the largest in the world. He gave large sums of money for building and endowing many Schools, Technical Institutions, Free Libraries, and other institutions in Cheshire. A member of the Council and endowed chairs of Economics, Egyptology, and Physical Chemistry at Liverpool University. A member of the Royal Commission for the Paris Exhibition 1900, and Civil List Committee 1901; a member of the Royal Commission on Canals and Waterways 1906. A Dept.-Lieut. for Lancashire, and was created Bart. in 1895, PC. 1906. A Liberal, advocated Home Rule, Local Government, temperance legislation, reform of social evils, religious equality, and international arbitration. Returned for the Northwich division of Cheshire in Nov. 1885. In the following year he was defeated; but in 1887 he was again elected there and sat until he retired in Jan. 1910. Honorary LL.D. and Pro-Chancellor Liverpool University 1909. Died 1 July 1919. [1909]

BRUNSKILL, Gerald Fitzgibbon. 1 Fitzwilliam Place, Dublin. Constitutional. S. of Thomas Richardson Brunskill, Esq. B. 4 Apr. 1866 in Dublin; m. 1896, Annie, d. of

Archibald Robinson, Esq., Taxing Master, High Court of Justice, Ireland. Educ. at Christ's Hospital, Rathmines School, and Trinity Coll., Dublin; M.A. A Barrister, called to the Irish bar 1901. A Director of the City of Dublin Steam Packet Company. Was elected Auditor of the Coll. Historical Society of Trinity Coll., Dublin 1889-90. A Unionist. Elected for mid Tyrone in Jan. 1910 and sat until defeated in Dec. 1910. K.C. 1914. Died 4 Oct. 1918. [1910]

BRYCE, Rt. Hon. James. 54 Portland Place, London. Hindleap, Forest Row, Sussex. Athenaeum. S. of James Bryce, Esq., LL.D., F.G.S., of Glasgow, and Margaret, eld. d. of James Young, Esq., of Abbeyville, Co. Antrim. B. at Belfast 1838; m. 1889, Elizabeth Marion, d. of Thomas Ashton, Esq., of Ford Bank, Manchester. Educ. at the High School, and University of Glasgow, and at Trinity Coll., Oxford, where he graduated B.A. (double 1st class) in 1862, having obtained the Craven and Vinerian scholarships, with other University prizes; Honorary Fellow Oriel and Trinity Colls., Honorary D.Litt., Cambridge, a foreign member of the Institute of France, and of the Royal Academies of Brussels, Naples, Turin, and the Lincei at Rome. President of the Alpine Club. Was called to the bar at Lincoln's Inn 1867. Was Regius Professor of Civil Law at Oxford 1870-93. PC. 1892. Chairman of the Royal Commission on Secondary Education 1894-95. Parliamentary Under Secretary Foreign Affairs 1886, Chancellor of the Duchy of Lancaster, with a seat in the Cabinet 1892, President of the Board of Trade May 1894; resigned with the Rosebery Ministry 1895. Chief Secretary for Ireland, Dec. 1905-Jan. 1907. O.M. 1907. Author of *The Holy Roman Empire, Trans-Caucasia and Ararat, The American Commonwealth, Impressions of South Africa, Studies in History and Jurisprudence, Studies in Contemporary Biography,* etc. A Liberal. Unsuccessfully contested Wick Feb. 1874. Sat for Tower Hamlets from Apr. 1880 till Nov. 1885, and for Aberdeen S. from Nov. 1885 until appointed British Ambassador at Washington 1907-13. Created 1st Visct. Bryce 1914. G.C.V.O. 1918. Died 22 Jan. 1922. [1906]

BRYCE, John Annan. 35 Bryenston Square, London. Savile. S. of James Bryce, Esq., LL.D., of Glasgow, and Margaret, d. of James Young, Esq., of Abbeyville, Co. Antrim. B. 1841; m. Violet, d. of Capt. C. L'Estrange, R.A. Educ. at Glasgow High School and University, Edinburgh University, and Balliol Coll., Oxford; Brackenbury History Scholar, 1st class Final Classical Scholar. Was Secretary, Treasurer, and President of Oxford Union Society. Member of Legislative Council of Burmah and Chairman of Rangoon Chamber of Commerce. A Director of London County and Westminster Bank, Atlas Assurance Company, English, Scottish and Australian Bank, Bombay Baroda Railway Company, and Burma Railways. Twice a member of the Council of the Royal Geographical Society. Member of Royal Commission on Congestion in Ireland 1906-08. A J.P. for Bombay. A Liberal. Elected for Inverness Burghs in 1906 and sat until he retired in 1918. Died 25 June 1923. [1918]

BRYMER, William Ernest. 8 St. James's Street, London. Ilsington House, Puddletown, Nr. Dorchester. Carlton, and Oxford & Cambridge. S. of John Brymer, Esq. B. 1840. Educ. at Harrow, and Trinity Coll., Cambridge. A J.P. for Dorset, and was High Sheriff 1887. Col. of the Dorset Yeomanry. A Conservative. Was MP for Dorchester 1874-85, when the borough was disfranchised. Sat for Dorset S. from 7 May 1891 until defeated in 1906. Died 9 May 1909. [1905]

BUCHANAN, Rt. Hon. Thomas Ryburn. 12 South Street, Park Lane, London. Brooks's, and Reform. S. of John Buchanan, Esq., of Dowanhill, and Jane, d. of J. Young, Esq., of Glasgow. B. at Glasgow 1846; m. 1888, Emily, d. of T.S. Bolitho, Esq., of Trengwainton, Cornwall. Educ. at Glasgow High School, Sherborne School, and Balliol Coll., Oxford; M.A. 1872. A Fellow of All Souls Coll. Called to the bar at the Inner Temple 1873. Financial Secretary of the War Office Dec. 1905 to Apr. 1908, when he was appointed Parliamentary Under Secretary for India Apr. 1908-June 1909. PC. 1908. A Dept.-Lieut. for Edinburgh. A Liberal. Unsuccessfully contested Haddingtonshire in 1880. Sat for Edinburgh City from 1881-85, and the W. division of Edinburgh from 1885. In 1886, whilst still representing Edinburgh W. he joined the Liberal Unionists, but rejoined the Gladstonian Liberals and successfully sought re-election in Edinburgh W. on 18 Feb. 1888 and

49

continued to sit for Edinburgh W. until July 1892 when he was defeated. Successfully contested Aberdeenshire E. on 10 Dec. 1892, which he continued to represent until defeated in 1900. Elected for Perthshire E. in Feb. 1903 and sat until he retired in Jan. 1910. Died 7 Apr. 1911. [1909]

BUCKLEY, Abel. Ryecroft Hall, Audenshaw, Nr. Manchester. Reform, Devonshire, and National Liberal. Younger s. of Abel Buckley, Esq., of Alderdal, Ashton-under-Lyne, by Mary, d. of Mr. Kershaw. B. 1835; m. 1875, Hannah, d. of John Summers, Esq., of Ashton-under-Lyne. Educ. at Mill Hill School and Owen's Coll., Manchester. A Cotton Manufacturer; a J.P. for Lancashire, Cheshire, and the borough of Ashton-under-Lyne and Chairman of the Manchester and Liverpool District Banking Company. A Liberal. Unsuccessfully contested Ashton-under-Lyne in 1874. First returned for the Prestwich division of Lancashire Dec. 1885 and sat until defeated in 1886 standing as a Gladstonian Liberal. Died 23 Dec. 1908. [1886]

BUCKMASTER, Sir Stanley Owen. 1 Porchester Terrace, London. 9 Old Square, Lincoln's Inn, London. Reform, and Garrick. S. of John Charles Buckmaster, Esq., J.P. B. 1861 at Wandsworth; m. 1889, Edith Augusta, d. of S. Lewin, Esq. Educ. at Aldenham School, and Christ Church, Oxford. A Barrister, called to the bar at the Inner Temple 1884; K.C. 1902. Appointed Solicitor-Gen. 1913-15; member of the Council of the Duchy of Lancaster 1912. J.P. for Hertfordshire. A Liberal. Sat for Cambridge from 1906 to Jan. 1910, when he was defeated; unsuccessfully contested Cambridge again in Dec. 1910. Elected for the Keighley division of the W. Riding of Yorkshire in Oct. 1911 and sat until appointed Lord Chancellor 27 May 1915-16 as Baron Buckmaster. Knighted 1913; PC. 1915; G.C.V.O. 1930. Member of Interallied Commission in Finance and Supplies; promoted to a Viscountcy in 1933. Died 5 Dec. 1934. [1915]

BUCKNILL, Sir Thomas Townsend. 10 King's Bench Walk, Temple, London. Hylands House, Epsom. Athenaeum, and Carlton. S. of Sir J.C. Bucknill, M.D., F.R.S., by Mary Anne, d. of Thomas Townsend, Esq., of Hillmorton Hall, Warwickshire. B. 1845; m. Anne, d. of Henry Bell Ford, Esq., of Clifton, Gloucestershire. Educ. at Westminster, and Geneva. Was called to the bar at the Inner Temple 1868; Q.C. 1885; a bencher of his Inn 1891. Recorder of Exeter 1885; Alderman of the Surrey Co. Council 1889-1892. Editor of the last edition of *Abbott on Shipping*. A Conservative. Sat for the Epsom division of Surrey from July 1892 until appointed High Court Judge 1899-1914. Knighted 1899. PC. 1914. Died 4 Oct. 1915. [1898]

BULL, Sir William James. Continued in House after 1918: full entry in Volume III.

BULLARD, Sir Harry. 4 Whitehall Court, London. Hellesden House, Norwich. Carlton, Constitutional, and Junior Carlton. S. of Richard Bullard, Esq., Brewer, of Norwich. B. 1841; m. 1867, Sarah, d. of T. Ringer, Esq., of Rougham, Norfolk. Educ. at the Rev. J. Thompson's School, East Dereham. Entered his father's business at an early age, and was Chairman of Bullard and Sons Limited. A J.P. and Dept.-Lieut. for Norwich and Norfolk; also a Town Councillor for the city of Norwich, of which he was Sheriff and three times Mayor. Knighted in 1887. A Conservative. Sat for Norwich from 1885-86, when he was unseated on petition. Re-elected for Norwich 1895 and sat until his death 26 Dec. 1903. [1903]

BURDETT-COUTTS, William Lehman Ashmead Bartlett-. Continued in House after 1918: full entry in Volume III.

BURGHLEY, Brownlow Henry George Cecil, Rt. Hon. Lord. 32 Eaton Square, London. Burghley House, Stamford. Carlton. Eld. s. of the Marq. of Exeter, by Lady Georgina Sophia, 2nd d. of the 2nd Earl of Longford. B. 1849; m. 1875, Isabella, only d. of Sir Thomas Whichcote, Bart., of Aswarby Park, Lincolnshire. Appointed Lieut. and Capt. Grenadier Guards May 1870; retired Mar. 1877. Lieut.-Col. Commandant in the Northampton and Rutland Militia. Appointed Parliamentary groom-in-waiting 1886-91; and Vice-Chamberlain of H.M. Household 1891-92. PC. 1891. A Conservative, said he would "support cordially the existing union between Church and State." Sat for Northamptonshire N. from Aug. 1877 until he retired in 1895. Succeeded as 5th

Marq. of Exeter on 14 July 1895, 6 days after the dissolution of Parliament. Died 9 Apr. 1898. [1895]

BURGOYNE, Alan Hughes. Continued in House after 1918: full entry in Volume III.

BURKE, Edmund Haviland. See HAVILAND-BURKE, Edmund.

BURN, Col. Charles Rosdew. Continued in House after 1918: full entry in Volume III.

BURNIE, Robert John Dickson. 71 Walter Road, Swansea. National Liberal. S. of John Dickson Burnie, Esq., of Dawlish, S. Devon, and Elizabeth Burnie, née Stamp. B. 1842; m. 1866, Georgianna, d. of Nicholas Elliott, Esq., of Thurlstone, Devon, and the grand-d. of the Rev. B. Beynor, of Cardigan. Educ. at Mr. John Nicholl's Academy, Dawlish. Managing Director of the Swansea Wagon Company Limited, Chairman, Finance Committee of the Swansea Corporation, and of the Towns Harbour Trust; was Mayor of Swansea 1883-84, and as such promoted and laid the first stone of the new Public Library and Science and Art Schools, etc. Author of *Driven Away, Idle Hour Flights*, and several other books. A Liberal, in favour of Home Rule for Ireland, disestablishment, etc. First elected for Swansea Town in July 1892 and sat until defeated in 1895. Died 6 Mar. 1908. [1895]

BURNS, Rt. Hon. John. Alverstoke, Clapham Common, London. National Liberal. S. of Alexander and Barbara Burns. B. 1858; m. 1880, Martha Charlotte, d. of John Gale, Esq., a Working Shipwright. Educ. at the National Schools, Battersea. Was apprenticed as an Engineer at Millbank. When first elected to the London County Council in 1889 (retired 1907) he was working as an ordinary Mechanical Engineer at Hoe's Printing Machine Works. A member of the Council of the Workmen's Peace Society, the Social Democratic Federation, and the executive of the Amalgamated Engineers' trade union. Was a leader in the great docks strike in 1889. President of the Local Government Board Dec. 1905 to Mar. 1914; President of Board of Trade, Mar. to Aug. 1914 when he resigned on the outbreak of war. PC. 1905. Honorary LL.D.

Liverpool 1910, Birmingham and Aberdeen 1911. A Liberal. Unsuccessfully contested W. Nottingham in 1885 as Social Democratic Federation Candidate. Sat for Battersea from 1892 until he retired in 1918. Died 24 Jan. 1943. [1918]

BURNYEAT, William John Dalzell. Millgrove, Moresby. National Liberal, and Reform. S. of William Burnyeat, Esq., J.P., of Whitehaven. B. 13 Mar. 1874 at Whitehaven; m. 1908, Hildeyard, d. of Col. Retzlaff, of Berlin. Educ. at Rugby, and Corpus Christi Coll., Oxford; M.A. A Barrister, called 1899. J.P. for Cumberland. A Liberal. Elected for Whitehaven in 1906 and sat until he retired in Jan. 1910. Died 8 May 1916. [1909]

BURRELL, Sir Percy, Bart. 44 Berkeley Square, London. West Grinstead Castle, Horsham, Sussex. Carlton. 2nd s. of Sir Charles Merrik Burrell, Bart., (who sat for Shoreham from 1806 till his death in 1862), by the d. of the 3rd Earl of Egremont. B. in Grosvenor Place 1812; m. 1856, eld. d. and co-heir of Vice-Admiral Sir George R. Brooke-Pechell, Bart. Appointed Capt. 18th Sussex Rifle Volunteers 1861. Dept.-Lieut. of Sussex. A moderate Conservative, voted against the abolition of church-rates May 1862. First elected for Shoreham in Feb. 1862. MP until his death 19 July 1876. [1876]

BURT, Rt. Hon. Thomas. 20 Burdon Terrace, Newcastle-on-Tyne. Reform, National Liberal, and Eighty. S. of Peter Burt, Esq., Coalminer, of Earsdon, Northumberland, by Rebecca, d. of Thomas Weatherburn, Esq., Engineman, of Cowpen Colliery. B. at Murton Row, Northumberland 1837; m. 1860, Mary, d. of Thomas Weatherburn, Esq., of Seghill, Northumberland. Commenced working in coal-pits at an early age. Was Secretary to the Northumberland Miners' Mutual Confident Association (a trades union consisting of 40,000 Members in Northumberland) 1865 to 1913, when he resigned and was appointed Adviser. Parliamentary Secretary to the Board of Trade in the Gladstone-Rosebery Ministry of 1892-95; PC. 1906. A "Radical." Sat for Morpeth from Feb. 1874 until he retired in 1918. Author of many articles in several journals. President of International Peace League 1882-1914. Father of the House of Commons 1910-18. D.C.L. University of

Durham 1911. Died 13 Apr. 1922. [1918]

BURY, Arnold Allan Cecil Keppel, Visct. 7 St. James's Square, London. Quidenham Park, Thetford, Norfolk. Eld. s. of the 7th Earl of Albemarle, by Sophia Mary, 2nd d. of Sir A. Napier M'Nab, Prime Minister of Canada. B. 1858; m. 1881, the Hon. Gertrude Lucia, only child of the 2nd Baron Egerton of Tatton. A Lieut. Dorset Militia 1876; a Lieut. in the Scots Guards, 1878 to 1883; Maj. 12th Middlesex Rifles from 1884; in command Civil Service Rifles 1892. A J.P. and Dept.-Lieut. for Norfolk. A Conservative and Unionist. Sat for Birkenhead from July 1892 until he succeeded as 8th Earl of Albemarle on 28 Aug. 1894. Served as Lieut.-Col. in S. Africa 1900. (His eld. s. contested Altrincham in 1910). K.C.V.O. 1909; Lord-in-Waiting 1922-24. Died 12 Apr. 1942.
[1894]

BUTCHER, John George. Continued in House after 1918: full entry in Volume III.

BUTCHER, Samuel Henry. 6 Tavistock Square, London. Danesfort, Killarney, Co. Kerry. Athenaeum. S. of Samuel Butcher, Esq., Bishop of Meath, and Mary Leahy, of Southill, Killarney. B. 16 Apr. 1850 at Dublin; m. 1876, Rose Julia, d. of R.C. Trench, Esq., Archbishop of Dublin (she died 1902). Educ. at Marlborough, and Trinity Coll., Cambridge; B.A., M.A., Senior Classic and Chancellor's Medallist 1873. Fellow of Trinity Coll., Cambridge, and Lecturer 1874-76; Fellow of University Coll., Oxford, and Lecturer until 1882. Professor of Greek in the University of Edinburgh 1882-1903; a member of the Scottish Universities Commission 1889-96, the Royal Commission on University Education in Ireland 1901, and of the Royal Commission on Trinity Coll., Dublin 1906; Fellow of the British Academy of Letters 1902; Lecturer at Harvard University 1904. Published *Translation of the Odyssey*, with A. Lang, *Aristotle's Theory of Poetry and Fine Art, Some Aspects of the Greek Subjects, Demosthenes' Critical Text,* Vols. 1 and 2, and other classical works. A J.P. for Co. Kerry. Honorary D.Litt. Oxford; Honorary Litt.D. Cambridge, Dublin, and Manchester; Honorary LL.D. St. Andrew's, Glasgow, and Edinburgh. Honorary Fellow of University Coll., Oxford 1903; Foreign Member (Honorary) American Academy of Arts and Sciences 1905; Trustee of British Museum 1908. President of the British Academy 1909. A Conservative. Elected for Cambridge University in 1906 and sat until his death 29 Dec. 1910. [1910]

BUXTON, Charles Roden. Continued in House after 1918: full entry in Volume III.

BUXTON, Edward North. Knighton, Buckhurst Hill, Essex. Athenaeum, New University, and City Liberal. 3rd s. of Sir Edward North Buxton, Bart., of Cromer, Norfolk, by Catherine, d. of Samuel Gurney, Esq., of Upton, Essex. B. at Upton, 1 Sept. 1840; m. 1882, Emily d. of the Hon. and Rev. Kenelm H. Digby, Rector of Tittleshall, Norfolk. Educ. at Trinity Coll., Cambridge. A member of the firm of Truman, Hanbury, Buxton and Company. A member from the commencement of the London School Board, of which he was Chairman from Jan. 1881 until Dec. 1885. Author of an illustrated work upon *Epping Forest* (of which forest he was a Verderer), *The A.B.C. of Free Trade* (issued by the Cobden Club), and other works. He was, jointly with the Bishop of St. Albans, patron of the living of All Saints', Woodford. A Liberal, in favour of all the points in Mr. Gladstone's "Immediate programme", (1885) of free schools, of legislation against the enclosure of commons, of the enfranchisement of long leaseholds, and of Church Disestablishment in Scotland and Wales. Unsuccessfully contested Essex S. Apr. 1880. Returned for the Walthamstow division of Essex Dec. 1885 and sat until he unsuccessfully contested N.W. Suffolk July 1886. Chairman of Essex Quarter Sessions Alderman of Essex County Council. Died 9 Jan. 1924. [1886]

BUXTON, Noel Edward. Continued in House after 1918: full entry in Volume III.

BUXTON, Rt. Hon. Sydney Charles. 5 Buckingham Gate, London. Newtimber, Hassocks, Sussex. Brooks's, and Athenaeum. S. of Charles Buxton, Esq., of Foxwarren, Cobham, Surrey, (who represented E. Surrey, Maidstone, and Newport), by Emily Mary, d. of Sir Henry Holland, Bart., M.D. B. in London 1853; m. 1st, 1882, Constance, d. of Lord Avebury (she died 1892); 2ndly, 1896, Mildred, d. of Hugh C. Smith, Esq., of Mount Clare, Roehampton. Educ. at Clifton Coll., and

Trinity Coll., Cambridge. Was Under-Secretary of State for the Colonies 1892 to 1895, and Postmaster-Gen. from 1905 to 1910, when he was appointed President of the Board of Trade 1910-14. PC. 1905. Was a member of the London School Board from 1876 to 1882. Honorary Secretary to Mr. Tuke's Irish Emigration Fund 1882-84. Author of the *Handbook to Political Questions, Finance and Politics, An Historical Study, 1783-1885, Mr. Gladstone: as Chancellor of the Exchequer, Fishing and Shooting,* etc. A Liberal, in favour of Home Rule. Unsuccessfully contested Boston in 1880. Sat for Peterborough from June 1883 to Nov. 1885, when he was defeated. Unsuccessfully contested Croydon in Jan. 1886. Sat for the Poplar division of Tower Hamlets from July 1886 until appointed Gov.-Gen. of South Africa in 1914 and created Visct. held this post until 1920. G.C.M.G. 1914. Created 1st Earl Buxton in 1920. Died 15 Oct. 1934. [1913]

BYLES, Sir William Pollard. 8 Chalcot Gardens, Hampstead, London. National Liberal. Eld. s. of William Byles, Esq., Founder of the *Bradford Observer,* and Anna, d. of P.K. Holden, Esq., of Halifax. B. 13 Feb. 1839 at Bradford; m. 1965, Sarah Ann, d. of Stephen Unwin, Esq., of Colchester. Educ. at private schools. A Journalist and chief proprietor of the *Bradford Observer;* a member of Interparliamentary Union for Peace and Arbitration from 1892; studied European and American democratic and social questions; Knighted 1911. And advanced Radical. Sat for the Shipley division of Yorkshire from 1892-95, when he was defeated; unsuccessfully contested E. Leeds in 1900. Elected for N. Salford in 1906 and sat until his death 15 Oct. 1917. [1917]

BYRNE, Alfred. 63 North Strand Road, Dublin. S. of Thomas Byrne, Esq. B. 14 Mar. 1882 in Dublin; m. 1910, Elizabeth, d. of Thomas Heagney, Esq. Educ. at Christian Brothers School, Dublin. An Alderman of Dublin Town Council from 1914; member of Dublin Port and Docks Board. A Nationalist. Elected for the Harbour division of Dublin on 30 Sept. 1915 and sat until defeated in 1918. T.D. (Ind.) for Dublin City N. 1923-28, 1932-56; Senator, Irish Free State 1928-31; 1st Lord Mayor of Greater Dublin. Died 13 Mar. 1956. [1918]

BYRNE, Edmund Widdrington. 33 Lancaster Gate, London. 3 Stone Buildings, Lincoln's Inn, London. Carlton, and Savile. S. of Mr. Byrne, Solicitor, of Whitehall Place, and his wife Mary E. Cowell. B. at Islington 1844; m. 1874, the 4th d. of J. Gulland Newton, Esq., of Wemyss, Fifeshire. Educ. at King's Coll. School, and King's Coll., London. Was called to the bar 1867, appointed Q.C. 1888. A bencher of Lincoln's Inn, a member of the Bar Committee from its foundation, and later of the General Council of the Bar. A Conservative. Sat for the Walthamstow division of Essex from July 1892 until appointed Judge (Chancery division) and Knighted in 1897. Died 4 Apr. 1904. [1896]

BYRNE, Garrett Michael. Outer Temple, Strand, London. 2nd s. of Joseph Byrne, Esq., of Kingstown, Co. Dublin, by Mary Anne, d. of Garrett Byrne, Esq., of Dunganstown, Co. Wicklow. B. at Arklow 1829; m. 1855, Sarah, 2nd d. of James Dillon, Esq., Merchant, of Wicklow, but was left a widower in 1875. Educ. privately, and at Leopardstown Coll. Was an Estate Broker and Surveyor in Liverpool for many years, and at Wicklow he held the post of Principal Officer of Customs and Surveyor to the Board of Trade. He was later a member of the firm of G.M. Byrne and Company, Mortgage Brokers, London. An "Irish Nationalist" of the Parnellite party. Returned for Wexford Co. in 1880, but resigned in 1883 on account of ill-health. Sat for Wicklow W. from 1885 until he retired in 1892. [1892]

CAINE, William Sproston. 42 Grosvenor Road, London. Reform. S. of Nathaniel Caine, J.P. for Cumberland and Lancashire, and Hannah, d. of William Rushton, Esq., of Liverpool. B. at Seacombe, Cheshire 1842; m. 1868, Alice, d. of the Rev. Hugh Stowell Brown. Educ. privately. An Iron Miner. Civil Lord of the Admiralty in Mr. Gladstone's Administration 1884-85; J.P. for the Co. of London and the E. Riding of Yorkshire; author of *Life of Hugh Stowell Brown, A Trip Round the World, Picturesque India, Young India,* and *Local Option: A Handbook.* A Progressive Liberal, strongly interested in Temperance Reform, Indian Questions, and S. Africa. Unsuccessfully contested Liverpool in Feb. 1873 and Feb. 1874. Represented Scarborough 1880-85; unsuccessfully contested the Tottenham division of Middlesex Dec. 1885. Elected for Barrow-in-Furness 6 Apr. 1886 and joined the Liberal Unionists acting as a teller in the Home Rule division on 8 June. Liberal Unionist Chief Whip from 1886 to 1890. Accepted the Chiltern Hundreds in 1890 and offered himself for re-election in Barrow-in-Furness as an Independent Liberal, but was defeated on 2 July 1890. He then rejoined the Gladstonian Liberals and was elected for Bradford E. in 1892 sitting until his defeat in 1895. He sat for Camborne from 1900 until his death on 17 Mar. 1903. [1902]

CAIRNS, Thomas. Dilston Hall, Corbridge, Northumberland. National Liberal. S. of Thomas Cairns, Esq., of Forfarshire. B. 1854 at Sunderland; m. 1880, Isabella, d. of William Dixon, Esq., of Newcastle-on-Tyne. Educ. privately. Head of the firm of Cairns, Noble and Company, Shipowners and Merchants, Newcastle, London, and Cardiff. Member of Newcastle City Council from 1896; and of the School Board 1892-99; Vice-President of Shipowners' International Association; a J.P. for Newcastle-on-Tyne. A Liberal, favour of Housing Reform, Social Legislation, Women Franchise, etc. Elected for Newcastle-on-Tyne in 1906 and sat until his death 3 Sept. 1908. [1908]

CALDWELL, James. 107 Holland Road, Kensington, London. 2 Grosvenor Terrace, Glasgow. National Liberal. S. of Findley Caldwell, Esq., of Glasgow. B. in Kilmarnock 1839. Educ. at the Universities of Glasgow and Edinburgh. Became a member of the Faculty of Procurators in Glasgow in 1864, and practised there, becoming also Lecturer on Law in the Coll. of Science and Arts, Glasgow. He retired from the law, and succeeded his father in the Calico-Printing business of Caldwell and Ritchie at Milton-of-Campsie, later retired from that business. Dept.-Chairman of Ways and Means Feb. 1906-Jan. 1910. PC 1910. A J.P. for Lanarkshire. A Liberal. Was returned for the St. Rollox division of Glasgow as a Liberal Unionist in 1886, but joined the Home Rule party in 1892. At the general election in 1892, he unsuccessfully contested the Tradeston division of Glasgow. First elected for mid Lanarkshire in 1894 and sat until he retired in Jan. 1910. Died 25 Apr. 1925. [1909]

CALLEY, Thomas Charles Pleydell,

C.B., M.V.O. Burderop Park, Swindon. Arthur's, and Naval & Military. S. of Henry Calley, Esq., J.P., Dept.-Lieut., of Burderop Park, Swindon. B. 28 Jan. 1856; m. 1883, Emily, d. of T.P. Chappell, Esq., of Teddington. Educ. at Harrow, and Christ Church, Oxford. Joined 1st Life Guards 1876; Capt. 1886, Maj. 1894, Lieut.-Col. 1898, Col. 1900; served in Egypt and S. Africa 1899-1900; mentioned in despatches; M.V.O. 1901, C.B. 1905. A Unionist. Elected for the Cricklade division of Wiltshire in Jan. 1910 and sat until defeated in Dec. 1910. Died 14 Feb. 1932. [1910]

CAMERON, Sir Charles, Bart. Balclutha, Greenock. Reform, and National Liberal. S. of John Cameron, Newspaper Proprietor, Glasgow and Dublin, and Ellen, d. of Alexander Galloway, Esq., of Edinburgh. B. 1841 in Dublin; m. 1869, Frances Caroline, d. of J.W. Macauley, Esq., M.D. (she died 1899). Educ. at Madras Coll., St. Andrews, and Trinity Coll., Dublin. Studied medicine at Dublin University School; gold medallist Dublin Pathological Society 1862; graduated B.A. as 1st senior moderator and gold medallist in experimental and natural sciences 1862, and took the 1st place in exams. for degrees of M.B. and M. in surgery; also studied at the medical schools of Paris, Berlin, and Vienna. Took the degrees of M.D. and M.A. 1865, and those of LL.B. and LL.D. 1871. Edited the *North British Daily Mail* 1864 to 1874. President Health Section Soc. Science Congress 1881, and of the Public Medicine Sector, British Medical Association Congress 1884; was also Chairman Committee Cattle Transit 1894 and on Habitual Offenders 1894-95, and member Royal Commission on Licencing Laws 1896. A J.P. for the counties of Lanark and Renfrew, J.P. and Dept.-Lieut. for the Co. of the city of Glasgow. Created a Bart. 1893. Brought forward the sixpenny telegrams resolution, the Publicans' Certificates (Scot.) Act 1876, the Marriage Notices (Scot.) Act 1878, the Habitual Drunkards Act 1879, the Statutes (Definition of Time) Act 1880, the Debtors (Scot.) Act 1880, the Municipal Franchise (Scot.) Act 1881, the Bankruptcy and Cessio (Scot.) Act 1881, the Civil Imprisonment (Scot.) Act 1882, etc. Author of various papers on medical, political and scientific subjects. A Radical, in favour of Home Rule, disestablishment, land law reform, and local option. Sat for Glasgow as a

Liberal in 1874 until he retired in 1885. Became a Gladstonian Liberal and sat for the College division of Glasgow 1885 until defeated July 1895 and for the Bridgeton division of Glasgow from 1897 until he retired in 1900. Died 2 Oct. 1924. [1900]

CAMERON, John Macdonald. 25 Stonor Road, West Kensington, London. 52 Lime Street, London. Devonshire, National Liberal, and Savage. Only s. of Lachlan Cameron, Esq., of Saltburn, N.B., by Christina, d. of John Macdonald, Esq., of Brackla, Nairne, N.B. B. at Ballantrae, Ayrshire 1847; m. 1871, Mary Anne Fleming, eld. d. of John Wildman Buttle, Esq., Civil-Engineer, of Inverness. Educ. at a local school, at Sharp's Institution, Perth, and at the Royal School of Mines, London. In 1866 he entered the Inland Revenue service, and was subsequently employed at the Inland Revenue Laboratory, Somerset House (1871-74) as Assistant Chemist. From 1874 to 1879 he was instructor in the Chemical Research Laboratory of the Royal School of Mines. He travelled extensively, and wrote a series of papers on *Quartz Outcrops of Travancore*, on *Copper, Silver, Lead, and Gold Lodes of Huacaino, Mexico, The Bitumenous Deposits of the Camamù Basin, Bahia*, etc. etc., and on *Agricultural Education*. An "advanced Liberal", in favour of Home Rule. Sat for the Wick district from 1885 until defeated in 1892. He subsequently went to Australia and became Master of the Sydney Mint until he resigned on acquiring an interest in the Borneo oilfields. Died 3 Sept. 1912. [1892]

CAMERON, Robert. 26 Queen's Mansions, London. 56 Victoria Street, Westminster, London. S. of the Rev. Duncan Cameron, a Baptist Minister. B. in Perthshire 1825; m. 1881, Alice Anne, eld. d. of John Patton, Esq., of Croft Spa, Co. Durham. Educ. at the parish school of Fortingall, Perthshire, and Borough Road Coll., London. Became a Teacher in 1846. Was Guardian, a member of the School Board (Chairman nine years), Councillor and Alderman for Sunderland; also a J.P., Chairman Free Lib. and Museum Committee, and a Lecturer and writer of magazine articles, etc. A Liberal, in favour of Home Rule, reforms in the Land Laws, Licensing, Registration, and in the House of Lords, and of Religious Equality, etc. Unsuccessfully contested the central division of Sheffield in July 1892. Sat for

Houghton-le-Spring division of Durham from 1895 until his death 13 Feb. 1913. [1912]

CAMPBELL, Sir Archibald Campbell, Bart. 2 Seamore Place, London. Blythswood, Renfrewshire. S. of Archibald Douglas, laird of Mains (who assumed the name and arms of Campbell of Blythswood on succeeding to the estate of his cousin in 1838). B. 1835; m. 1864, Hon. Augusta Carrington, d. of the 2nd Lord Carrington. He was a Vice-Lieut. and Convenor for the Co. of Renfrew, and Lieut.-Col. of the 4th Battalion Argyll and Sutherland Highlanders. He served in the Scots Guards in the Crimea, where he was severely wounded. For his Crimean services he received a medal and clasp, together with the Turkish Order of the Medjidie; he also served in Canada. Retired as Lieut.-Col. Was created Bart. in 1880. A Conservative. Contested Paisley in 1868, and sat for Renfrewshire from Sept. 1873 until defeated in Feb. 1874. Unsuccessfully contested the seat Apr. 1880. First elected for Renfrewshire W. in 1885 and sat until he retired in 1892. Created Baron Blythswood in 1892. Died 8 July 1908. [1892]

CAMPBELL, Lieut.-Col. Duncan Frederick. Wardhead House, Stewarton, Ayrshire. Junior Army & Navy. S. of Archibald Campbell, Esq., Barrister, of Toronto, Canada, and Helen, d. of Col. F.W. Cumberland, of Toronto. B. 28 Apr. 1876 at Toronto; m. 1902, Louise, d. of J.E. O'Reilly, Esq., Master of Supreme Court, Hamilton, Canada. Educ. at Trinity School, Port Hope, and Trinity University, Toronto; B.A. honours in Mental and Moral Philosophy. Joined the Lancashire Fusiliers 1898; served in S. Africa 1899-1901; wounded, and three times mentioned in despatches. D.S.O., transferred to Black Watch 1908. Served with Expeditionary Force in France 1914. A Unionist. Unsuccessfully contested mid Lanark in 1906, Paisley in Jan. 1910, and N. Ayrshire in Dec. 1910. Elected for N. Ayrshire in Dec. 1911 and sat until his death 4 Sept. 1916. [1916]

CAMPBELL, Sir George, K.C.S.I., D.C.L. 17 Southwell Gardens, London. Athenaeum, Brooks's, and Reform. Eld. s. of Sir George Campbell, of Edenwood (eld. bro. of the 1st Lord Campbell), by

Margaret, d. of A. Christie, Esq., of Ferrybank, Fifeshire. B. 1824; m. 1854, Letitia Maria, 2nd d. of T.G. Vibart, Esq., Bengal Civil Service. Was called to the bar at the Inner Temple 1854. Entered the Bengal Civil Service in 1842, and was Judge of the Supreme Court of Calcutta, Commissioner of the Cis-Sutlej States, Chief Commissioner of the Central Provinces; also Lieut.-Gov. of Bengal, and a member of the Council of India, which last-named office he resigned to enter Parliament. A Dept.-Lieut. of Fife. Author of *Modern India, The Irish Land,* and *A Handy Book on the Eastern Question.* D.C.L. University of Oxford, 1870. K.C.S.I. 1874. A Liberal, in favour of Home Rule. Sat for Kirkcaldy from Apr. 1875 until his death 18 Feb. 1892. [1891]

CAMPBELL, Henry. Greenwood Park, Newry, Co. Down. B. 1856; m. 1stly, 1879, Jenny, d. of R. Brewis, Esq., of Newcastle-on-Tyne (she died 1906); 2ndly, Alice Harbottle, d. of Robert Fogan, Esq., of Newcastle-on-Tyne. He was a native of Newry, and was active as a member of the Catholic Young Men's Society, and also as an advocate of temperance. Was Private Secretary to Mr. Parnell, MP, 1880-91. An "Irish Nationalist", of the Parnellite party. Sat for Fermanagh S. from 1885 until he retired in 1892. Town Clerk of Dublin from 1893. Knighted in 1921. Died 6 Mar. 1924. [1892]

CAMPBELL, Henry. See CAMPBELL-BANNERMAN, Rt. Hon. Sir Henry, G.C.B.

CAMPBELL, Rt. Hon. James Alexander. 2 Princes Gardens, London. Stracathro House, Brechin, Scotland. Carlton. S. of Sir James Campbell, Merchant in Glasgow, of Stracathro, Forfarshire, by Janet, d. of Henry Bannerman, Esq., of Manchester. Elder bro. of Sir Henry Campbell-Bannermann, Prime Minister from 1905-08. B. at Glasgow 1825; m. 1854, Anne, d. of Sir Samuel Morton Peto, Bart. (she died 1887). Educ. at the High School, Glasgow, and the University of Glasgow, and was created Honorary LL.D. there. A Merchant in Glasgow; retired 1876. A Dept.-Lieut. for Forfar and Lanark. Was a member of the Scottish Universities Commission 1876, of the Endowed Institutions (Scotland) Commission 1878, of the Educational Endowments (Scotland) Commission 1882, and of the Universities (Scotland) Commission 1889; a PC. 1898. A Conservative, opposed to a separate legislature for Ireland, and opposed to disestablishment. Sat for Glasgow and Aberdeen Universities from Apr. 1880 until he retired in 1906. Died 9 May 1908. [1905]

CAMPBELL, Rt. Hon. James Henry Mussen. 30 Upper Pembroke Street, Dublin. 3 Dr. Johnson's Buildings, Temple, London. Carlton. S. of W.M. Campbell, Esq. B. 1851; m. d. of J. McCullagh, Esq., of Newry. Educ. at Stackpoole's School, Kingstown, and Trinity Coll., Dublin. Called to the Irish bar 1878; English bar 1898; Q.C. (Ireland) 1890; bencher of King's Inns and of Gray's Inn. Was Solicitor-Gen. for Ireland 1901-05, and Attorney-Gen. Dec. 1905. PC. 1905. K.C. (England) 1906. Chancellor of Dioceses of Dublin, Glendalough and Kildare from 1909. A Unionist. Sat for St. Stephen's Green division of Dublin from 1898-1900, when he was defeated. Elected for Dublin University in Mar. 1903 and sat until appointed Lord Chief Justice of Ireland 1917-18. Attorney-Gen. for Ireland in Dec. 1905 and Apr.-Dec. 1916. Created Bart. 1916. Created 1st Baron Glenavy 1921; Lord Chancellor (Ireland) 1918-21; later Chairman of the Irish Free State Senate from 1922-28. Died 22 Mar. 1931. [1916]

CAMPBELL, John. 1 Elm Court, Temple, London. S. of Daniel Campbell, Esq., of Blackwatertown, Co. Armagh. B. 1870. Educ. at St. Patrick's Coll., Armagh, and French Coll., Blackrock. A Barrister-at-Law of the Middle Temple; called 1896; Certificate of Hon. and Campbell-Foster Prize for Criminal Law; LL.B. (1st class honours) University of London. A Nationalist. Elected for Armagh S. in 1900 and sat until he retired in 1906. [1905]

CAMPBELL, Richard Frederick Fotheringham. 17 Cavendish Square, London. Craigie House, Ayr, Scotland. Devonshire, Brooks's, and Junior United Service. S. of James Campbell, Esq., of Craigie, by his 2nd wife, Grace Elizabeth, d. of Gen. Hay. B. at Edinburgh 1831; m. 1869, Arabella Jane, d. of Archibald Argyll Hay, Esq., and widow of Charles Tennent, Esq. Educ. at Rugby. Capt. 8th Madras Cavalry and served on the Staff during the

Indian Mutiny. A Magistrate and Vice-Lieut. of Ayrshire, Lieut.-Col. Ayrshire Yeomanry Cavalry. A Liberal Unionist, in favour of the principle of local control in the licensing laws. Sat for Ayr district from Apr. 1880 until his death on 17 May 1888.
[1888]

CAMPBELL-BANNERMAN, Rt. Hon. Sir Henry, G.C.B. 10 Downing Street, London. Belmont Castle, Meigle, N.B. Brooks's, Reform and Oxford & Cambridge. 2nd s. of Sir James Campbell, of Stracathro, Forfarshire, by the youngest d. of Henry Bannerman, Esq., of Manchester. B. 1836; m. 1860, d. of Maj.-Gen. Sir Charles Bruce, K.C.B. (she died 1906). Educ. at Glasgow University, and Trinity Coll., Cambridge, where he graduated B.A. 1858, M.A. 1861. Assumed Nov. 1872, the name of Bannerman in addition to his patronymic. Was Financial Secretary for War from 1871 to 1874, and again 1880 to 1882; Secretary to the Admiralty 1882 to 1884, when he became Chief Secretary for Ireland 1884-85. PC. 1884. In Mr. Gladstone's 3rd administration Jan. 1886, he became Secretary of State for War, which office he again took under Mr. Gladstone in 1892, and retained when Lord Rosebery became Premier in 1894, till June 1895, when the Ministry resigned; created G.C.B. 1895. Chosen Leader of the Liberal opposition 1899. Was Prime Minister and First Lord of the Treasury, appointed Dec. 1905. Resigned as Prime Minister on 3 Apr. 1908. Elder Brother of Trinity House 1907. A Liberal, in favour of Home Rule. Unsuccessfully contested Stirling district on 30 Apr. 1868. Sat for Stirling district from Dec. 1868 until his death 22 Apr. 1908. Father of the House of Commons 1907-08. [1908]

CAMPION, William Robert. Continued in House after 1918: full entry in Volume III.

CARBUTT, Edward Hamer. Defeated in 1886: full entry in Volume I. (Note: Hamer is incorrectly spelt Homer in Volume I).

CAREW, Charles Robert Sydenham. Continued in House after 1918: full entry in Volume III.

CAREW, James Laurence. 54 Hans Place, London. 12 New Court, Lincoln's Inn, London. Naas, Co. Kildare. Youngest s. of Laurence Carew, Esq., of Kildangan, Co. Meath, by Anne, only d. of Garrett Robinson, Esq., of Kilrainy, Co. Kildare. B. at Kildangan 1853; m. 1896, Helen, widow of H. Coleridge Kennard, Esq., Grenadier Guards. Educ. at Clongowes Coll., Co. Kildare, and Trinity Coll., Dublin (B.A. 1873). A Barrister, called to the bar at the Middle Temple 1878. An "Independent Nationalist". Was a "Whip" of his party. Sat for N. Kildare 1885 to 1892. Defeated there at the general election of 1892 and in 1895. Represented College Green division of Dublin 1896 to 1900. Defeated there at the general election of 1900, but returned unopposed for S. Meath at the same time and was MP until his death 31 Aug. 1903.
[1903]

CAREW, Lieut.-Gen. Sir Reginald Pole. See POLE-CAREW, Lieut.-Gen. Sir Reginald.

CARLILE, Sir Edward Hildred, Bart. Continued in House after 1918: full entry in Volume III.

CARLILE, William Walter. Gayhurst, Newport Pagnell, Buckinghamshire. Carlton, and Junior Carlton. Only s. of J.W. Carlile, Esq., of Ponsbourne Park, Hertford. B. 1862; m. 1885, Blanche Ann, d. of the Rev. E. Cadogan, of Wicken, Northamptonshire. Educ. at Harrow, and Clare Coll., Cambridge. A Dept.-Lieut. and J.P. for the Co. of Buckinghamshire. A Conservative. Unsuccessfully contested Buckinghamshire N. in 1892. Sat for Buckinghamshire N. from 1895 until he retired in 1906. Served in France from 1914 for the "Missing Bureau". Created Bart. 1928. Died 3 Jan. 1950. [1905]

CARMARTHEN, George Godolphin Osborne, Marq. of. 20 De Vere Gardens, London. Carlton, Turf, Marlborough, and Bachelors'. S. of the Duke and Duchess of Leeds. B. in London 1862; m. 1884, Lady Katherine Lambton, d. of the Earl of Durham. Educ. at Eton, and Cambridge. Was Assistant Private Secretary to Sir Henry Holland, Bart., Secretary of State for the Colonies. A Conservative. Unsuccessfully contested Cambridgeshire E. in July 1886. First elected for the Brixton division of Lambeth in July 1887 and sat until he succeeded as 10th Duke of Leeds in Dec. 1895. Treasurer of the Household from

1895-1901. Member of London County Council (City of London) from 1898. Owner of 24,000 acres. Died 10 May 1927. [1895 2nd ed.]

CARMICHAEL, Sir James Morse, Bart. 12 Sussex Place, Regent's Park, London. S. of the 2nd Bart., by Louisa Charlotte, 2nd d. of Sir Thomas Butler, Bart. B. 1844 in London. Educ. at Radley Coll. Was a Clerk in the Admiralty 1862-80; attached to Sir W. Hutt's mission to Vienna 1864; Private Secretary to the Rt. Hon. John Bright as Chancellor of the Duchy of Lancaster 1873, to Mr. Childers as First Lord of the Admiralty and Chancellor of the Exchequer 1882-85, and to Mr. Gladstone when Prime Minister 1885. Served also with the Commission of Liquidation which sat at Cairo in 1880, and was decorated with the Khedive's order of the Medjidieh in consequence. Succeeded as Bart. 1883. A Liberal, in favour of Home Rule, and of the "Newcastle programme" generally. Unsuccessfully contested N. Northamptonshire 1885 and S. Northamptonshire 1886. First returned for the St. Rollox division of Glasgow in July 1892 and sat until defeated in 1895. Died 31 May 1902. [1895]

CARMICHAEL, Sir Thomas David Gibson, Bart. See GIBSON-CARMICHAEL, Sir Thomas David, Bart.

CARNEGIE, Lieut.-Col. the Hon. Douglas George. Fairoak, Petersfield, Hampshire. 6 Hans Crescent, London. S. of the 9th Earl and Dowager Countess of Northesk, d. of Admiral Sir G. Elliot, K.C.B. B. at Edinburgh 1870; m. 1894, Margaret Jean, d. of Arthur Johnstone Douglas, Esq. Maj. (retired) Territorial Reserve Force. A Conservative-Unionist, and Tariff Reformer. Associated with the National Party 1917-18. Elected for Winchester in Oct. 1916 and sat until he retired in 1918. Died 27 Feb. 1937. [1918]

CARR-GOMM, Capt. Hubert William Culling. House of Commons, London. Brooks's, Garrick, and Bath. S. of F.C. Carr-Gomm, Esq., J.P., and Dept.-Lieut., and Emily Blanche, niece of Field-Marshal Sir William Gomm. B. 20 Jan. 1877 in India; m. 1916, Eleanor, d. of Norreys Russell, Esq. Educ. at Eton, and Oriel Coll., Oxford; M.A. Was Honorary Secretary to London Liberal Federation, and Assistant Private Secretary to Sir H. Campbell-Bannerman when Prime Minister (Dec. 1905-Apr. 1906). Capt. 2/22nd Battalion London Regiment (The Queen's), Oct. 1914 to June 1917; served in France 1916, Salonika 1917; later Capt. Territorial Reserve Force. J.P. for Buckinghamshire. A Liberal. Elected for the Rotherhithe division of Southwark in 1906 and sat until defeated in 1918. Again defeated at Rotherhithe in 1922 and at Paddington S. in 1923. Died 21 Jan. 1939 [1918]

CARSON, Rt. Hon. Sir Edward Henry. Continued in House after 1918: full entry in Volume III.

CARVILL, Patrick George Hamilton. 29 Morpeth Mansions, London. 2 Garden Court, Temple, London. Ballyvourney, Co. Cork. Reform, and Ranelagh. S. of Francis Carvill, Esq., of Newry, and Rostrevor, Co. Down, and Margaret, d. of James Hamilton, Esq., of Springfield, Kilkeel. B. 1839; m. 1869, Frances Mary, d. of Thomas McEvoy Gartlan, Esq., of Monalty, Carrickmacross, Co. Monaghan. Educ. at Armagh, and the London University (matriculated). A Barrister, called at the Middle Temple; J.P. for the counties of Down and Armagh, High Sheriff of Armagh 1878; a member of the Court of Referees, House of Commons. A Nationalist. He unsuccessfully contested Newry in the Liberal interest in 1880, but held the seat from 1892 until defeated in 1906 as a Nationalist. Died 10 Jan. 1924. [1905]

CASSEL, Felix. 25 Bryanston Square, London. 5 New Court, Carey Street, London. Carlton, and Alpine. S. of Louis Cassel, Esq. B. 1869; m. 1908, Lady Helen Grimston, d. of Earl of Verulam. Educ. at Elstree, Harrow, and Corpus Christi Coll., Oxford. Called to the bar at Lincoln's Inn 1894, K.C. 1906, a member of the London County Council 1907-10, and was for two years Chairman of Parliamentary Committee. Capt. 19th Battalion London Regiment. A Unionist. Unsuccessfully contested Central Hackney in Jan. 1910. Elected for W. St. Pancras Dec. 1910 and sat until 1916 when he was appointed Judge Advocate General; retired 1934. Created Bart. 1920. PC. 1937. High Sheriff of Hertfordshire 1942-43. Treasurer of Lincoln's Inn 1935. Honorary Fellow Corpus Christi Coll., Oxford. Member of Council of Legal Education. Master of Company of Musicians 1939-44. Chairman of Cassel Educational Trust and of Management Committee of Cassel Hospital for Functional Nervous Disorders, Ham Common. Died 22 Feb. 1953.   [1916]

CASTLEREAGH, Charles Stewart Henry Vane-Tempest-Stewart, Visct. Londonderry House, Park Lane, London. Springfield, Oakham. Carlton. Eld. s. of Marq. of Londonderry and Lady Theresa Talbot, d. of 19th Earl of Shrewsbury. B. 1878; m. 1899, Edith, d. of Rt. Hon. H. Chaplin, MP. Educ. at Eton, and Royal Military Coll., Sandhurst. A Capt. in Royal Horse Guards; M.V.O. 1903. A Unionist. Elected for Maidstone in 1906 and sat until he succeeded as Marq. of Londonderry in 1915. PC. (Ireland) 1918; PC. (Northern Ireland) 1921; PC. 1925. Under-Secretary for Air 1920-21; First Commissioner of Works 1928-29 and 1931. Secretary of State for Air 1931-35. Lord Privy Seal and Leader of the House of Lords 1935. Died 11 Feb. 1949.   [1914]

CATOR, John. Woodbastwick Hall, Norwich. 52 Pont Street, London. Carlton, and Arthur's. S. of Albemarle Cator, Esq., of Woodbastwick Hall, Norwich, and Mary, d. of C.A. Mohun Harris, Esq., of Hayne, Devon. B. 24 Sept. 1862 at Colkirk, Norfolk; m. 1895, Maud, d. of Henry J. Adeane, Esq., of Babraham, Cambridgeshire. Educ. at Eton, and Christ Church, Oxford; B.A. Honorary Maj. Prince of Wales' Own Norfolk Artillery. A member of London School Board. Was Assistant Private Secretary to Mr. H. Chaplin when President of Local Government Board. A Unionist. Unsuccessfully contested N. Norfolk in 1892 and the Huntingdon division of Huntingdonshire in 1906. Elected for the Huntingdon division of Huntingdonshire in Jan. 1910 and sat until he retired in 1918. High Sheriff of Norfolk 1920-21. Died 27 Apr. 1944. [1918]

CAUSTON, Rt. Hon. Richard Knight. 12 Devonshire Place, London. Devonshire, Reform, National Liberal, Gresham, and City Liberal. 2nd s. of Sir Joseph Causton (Alderman of London and Sheriff of London and Middlesex for 1868-70), by Mary Anne, d. of Edward Potter, Esq. B. in London 1843; m. 1871, Selena Mary, eld. d. of Sir Thomas Chambers, Q.C., Recorder of London, and MP for Hertford and Marylebone. A Director of the firm of Sir Joseph Causton and Sons Limited. A Commissioner of Lieutenancy for London, a member of the Executive Committees of the Associated Chambers of Commerce and the London Chamber of Commerce, and a member of the Company of Skinners, of which he served as Master 1877-78. Was a Lord of the Treasury 1892-95. Paymaster Gen. from Dec. 1905-Feb. 1910. A Liberal Whip from 1892-1905. PC. 1906. A Liberal, in favour of "Home Rule for Ireland", and of "the policy of peace abroad, and of a safe and steady progress in those reforms at home so much needed by agriculture and commercial interests". Unsuccessfully contested Colchester in 1874. Sat for Colchester from 1880 until defeated in 1885. Again unsuccessful in 1886. First elected for Southwark W. Feb. 1888 and sat until defeated in Jan. 1910. Created Baron Southwark 1910. President London Chamber of Commerce, 1913. Died 23 Feb. 1929. [1909]

CAUTLEY, Henry Strother. Continued in House after 1918: full entry in Volume III.

CAVAN, Frederick Edward Gould Lambart, Earl of. 6 Arlington Street, St. James's, London. Wheathampstead House, St. Albans. Traigh House, Arisaig, Fort William, N.B. Brooks's, Windham, and Travellers'. Eld. s. of Frederick, 8th Earl of Cavan, by his m. with a d. of Lord Hatherton. Succeeded to the Peerage (Irish) Dec. 1887. B. at Eaglehurst, Hampshire 1839; m. 1863, Mary Sneade, only child of the Rev. John Olive, of Ayot St. Lawrence. Educ. at Harrow. Was in the Royal Navy from 1853 to 1862, and served in the Crimean and Chinese Wars; also accompanied H.R.H. the Prince of Wales to Canada on board H.M.S. *Hero* in 1860. A Dept.-Lieut. for Somerset, and J.P. for Somerset and Hertfordshire. Appointed Vice-Chamberlain of the Household from Feb.-June 1886. PC. 1886. Styled by the courtesy title of Visct. Kilcoursie until he succeeded to the Irish Earldom of Cavan in 1887. A Liberal and Home Ruler. Unsuccessfully contested Taunton in Feb. 1882 and Somerset W. in Feb. 1884. Sat for Somerset S. from 1885 until he retired in 1892. K.P. 1894. Died 14 July 1900. [1892]

CAVE, Rt. Hon. Sir George. 4 Smith Square, Westminster, London. Wardrobe Court, Richmond, Surrey. St. Ann's, Burnham, Somerset. Athenaeum, and Carlton. S. of Thomas Cave, Esq., MP for Barnstaple, and Elizabeth Shallcrass. B. 23 Feb. 1856 in London; m. 1885, Estella, d. of William Mathews, Esq., of Crewkerne, Somerset. Educ. at Merchant Taylors' School, and St. John's Coll., Oxford; 1st class Final Classical School 1878. Honorary Fellow of St. John's Coll. 1916. A Barrister, called to the bar at the Inner Temple; K.C. 1904; a J.P., Dept.-Lieut., and Vice-Lieut. for Surrey; Chairman of Surrey Quarter Sessions 1894-1911; Recorder of Guildford 1904-15. Standing Counsel to Oxford University 1913-15; Attorney-Gen. to Prince of Wales 1914; PC. 1915; Solicitor-Gen. Nov. 1915 to Dec. 1916; Home Secretary from Dec. 1916-Jan. 1919. Knighted 1915. A member of Royal Commission on Land Transfer Acts. A Unionist. Elected for the Kingston division of Surrey in 1906 and sat until created 1st Visct. Cave No. 1918. G.C.M.G. 1920. Lord of Appeal 1919-22. Lord Chancellor 1922-24 and 1924-28. Honorary D.C.L. University of Oxford 1924. Chancellor of Oxford University 1925-28. Died 29 Mar. 1928. [1918]

CAVENDISH, Lord Edward. 378 Piccadilly, London. Devonshire. Youngest s. of the 7th Duke of Devonshire, by Lady Blanche Georgiana, 4th d. of the 6th Earl of Carlisle. Nephew of Lord George H. Cavendish, who represented Derbyshire for 36 years previous to his retirement in 1880. B. in London 1838; m. 1865, Emma Elizabeth, d. of the Hon. William Lascelles (she was an Hon. Lady of the Bedchamber to the Princess Christian). Educ. at Trinity Coll., Cambridge. Appointed a Lieut. Rifle Brigade 1860; Instructor of Musketry 1861, retired 1865. A Magistrate and Dept.-Lieut. for Derbyshire, and Lieut.-Col. 3rd Battalion Derbyshire Regiment. A Liberal Unionist, of which party he was the first "Whip". Sat for Sussex E. from July 1865 to Nov. 1868, when he was defeated. Unsuccessfully contested N.E. Lancashire in 1874 and then sat for Derbyshire N. from Apr. 1880 to Nov. 1885 and for the W. division of Derbyshire from Nov. 1885 until his death 18 May 1891. [1891]

CAVENDISH, Richard Frederick. 6 Carlos Place, London. Ashdown Place,

Forest Row, Sussex. Brooks's. 2nd s. of Lord Edward Cavendish, bro. of the Duke of Devonshire, and Emma Elizabeth, d. of the Rt. Hon. W.S.S. Lascelles. B. 1871 in London; m. 1895, Lady Moyra Beauclerk, d. of the Duke of St. Albans. Educ. at Eton Coll., and Trinity Coll., Cambridge. Lieut. 1st Volunteer Battalion Royal Lancaster Regiment. Was Private Secretary to Lord George Hamilton, Secretary of State for India 1901. A Liberal Unionist. Sat for the Lonsdale division of Lancashire from 1895 until defeated in the 1906 election which he contested as a Liberal after resigning from the Liberal Unionist Party over Free Trade. In 1908 he was granted the precedence of the son of a Duke and was afterwards known as Lord Richard Cavendish. PC. 1912. Served in Europe 1914-15 and was wounded. Died 7 Jan. 1946. [1905]

CAVENDISH, Spencer Compton Cavendish, Lord. See HARRINGTON, Rt. Hon. Spencer Compton Cavendish, Marq. of.

CAVENDISH, Rt. Hon. Victor Christian William. 37 Park Lane, London. Holker Hall, Carnforth, North Lancashire. Brooks's, and White's. Eld. s. of Lord Edward Cavendish, MP for the W. Derbyshire division, by his wife, Elizabeth Emma, d. of the Rt. Hon. W. Seabright Lascelles, MP. B. 1868; m. 1892, Lady Evelyn Fitzmaurice, eld. d. of the Marq. of Landsowne. Educ. at Eton, and Trinity Coll., Cambridge. Maj. Derbyshire Yeomanry and heir presumptive to the Duke of Devonshire. Was Treasurer to H.M. Household 1900-03; Financial Secretary to the Treasury, Oct. 1903 to Dec. 1905; PC. 1905. A Liberal Unionist. First elected for W. Derbyshire in 1891 and sat until he succeeded to the Peerage as 9th Duke of Devonshire in 1908. Civil Lord of Admiralty from 1915-16. Gov.-Gen. of Canada 1916-21. Colonial Secretary from 1922-24. Died 6 May 1938. [1908]

CAVENDISH-BENTINCK, Rt. Hon. George Augustus Frederick. 3 Grafton Street, London. 26 Old Square, Lincoln's Inn, London. Carlton, and Travellers'. S. of Maj.-Gen. Lord Frederick Bentinck, C.B., by Lady Mary, 2nd d. of 1st Earl of Lonsdale. B. in London 1821; m. 1850, Prudence Penelope, 4th d. of Col. Charles Powell Leslie, of Glasslough Castle, Co. Monaghan. Educ. at Westminster School, and Trinity Coll., Cambridge, where he graduated M.A. 1847. Called to the bar at Lincoln's Inn 1846. Was (parliamentary) Secretary to the Board of Trade from Feb. 1874 to Nov. 1875; Judge-Advocate-Gen. from the latter date to Apr. 1880. PC. 1880. A Conservative. Unsuccessfully contested Taunton Apr. 1859, elected for Taunton Aug. following, and sat for Taunton till July 1865, when he was returned for Whitehaven. MP until his death 9 Apr. 1891. [1890]

CAVENDISH-BENTINCK, Lord Henry. Continued in House after 1918: full entry in Volume III.

CAVENDISH-BENTINCK, William George. 6 Richmond Terrace, Whitehall, London. Carlton, and White's. Eld. s. of the Rt. Hon. George Augustus Frederick Cavendish-Bentinck, by Prudence Penelope, sister of Sir John Leslie, Bart., MP for Whitehaven, of Glasslough Castle, Monaghan. B. 1854; m. 1880, Bessie, d. of Maturin Livingston, Esq., of Staatsburgh, Dutchers County, New York, U.S.A. Educ. at Harrow and Jesus Coll., Cambridge (B.A. and M.A.). A J.P. for Dorset, and a Capt. of the Dorset Militia. A progressive Conservative. Unsuccessfully contested Penryn and Falmouth at the general election of 1885. First returned for that division in 1886 and sat until defeated in 1895. Died 22 Aug. 1909. [1895]

CAWLEY, Rt. Hon. Sir Frederick, Bart. Brooklands, Prestwich. Berrington Hall, Leominster. Brooks's, and Reform. S. of Thomas Cawley, Esq., of Priestland. B. 9 Oct. 1850 at Priestland, Cheshire; m. 1876, Elizabeth, d. of John Smith, Esq., of Kynsal Lodge, Audlem, Cheshire. Educ. at Aldersey Grammar School. A J.P. for the counties of Lancaster and Herefordshire. Created Bart. 1906. Member of the Dardanelles Commission 1916; Chancellor of the Duchy of Lancaster from Dec. 1916 until Jan. 1918. PC. 1916. A Liberal. Sat for the Prestwich division of S.E. Lancashire from 1895 until created Baron Cawley 16 Jan. 1918. Died 20 Mar. 1937. [1917]

CAWLEY, Harold Thomas. Berrington Hall, Leominster. 2nd s. of Sir Frederick Cawley, Bart., MP. B. 1878. Educ. at Rossall Prep. School, Rugby School, and New Coll., Oxford. A Barrister, called to the bar at the Inner Temple 1902, and

practised on the N. Circuit; a Lieut. 6th Battalion Manchester Regiment (T.). Parliamentary Private Secretary to Mr. Runciman when President of Board of Education from 1910-11, and to Mr. McKenna, Home Secretary from 1911. A Liberal. Elected for the Heywood division of Lancashire in Jan. 1910 and sat until killed in action in 1915. Died 23 Sept. 1915. [1915]

CAWLEY, Hon. Oswald. Berrington Hall, Leominster. 5th s. of 1st Lord Cawley. B. 1882. Unmarried. Educ. at Rugby, and New Coll., Oxford; B.A. 1905. A Calico Printer. Served with his Regiment in the Expeditionary Force in Palestine. A Liberal, supporter of the Coalition Government. Elected for the Prestwich division of S.E. Lancashire 31 Jan. 1918 and sat until he was killed in action on 22 Aug. 1918. [1918]

CAYZER, Sir Charles William, Bart. 27 Belgrave Square, London. Ralston, Renfrewshire. Gartmore, Perthshire. Newtyle, Forfarshire. Carlton, and City of London. Eld. s. of Charles Cayzer, Esq., of Hatherleigh, Devon. B. 1843; m. 1868, Agnes Elizabeth, only d. of William Trickey, Esq., of Clifton, Bristol. A Shipowner, head of the firm of Cayzer, Irvine and Company, Glasgow, Liverpool, Manchester, and London. Also Honorary Col. 1st Lanarkshire Volunteer Artillery, a J.P. for Stirlingshire, Renfrewshire, and Dumbartonshire. Was created Kt. 1897; Bart. 1904. A Conservative. Sat for Barrow-in-Furness from 1892 until defeated in 1906. Contested Monmouth district in Jan. 1910. Died 28 Sept. 1916. [1905]

CECIL, Rt. Hon. Evelyn. Continued in House after 1918: full entry in Volume III.

CECIL, Rt. Hon. Lord Hugh Richard Heathcote. Continued in House after 1918: full entry in Volume III.

CECIL, Lord John Pakenham. See JOICEY-CECIL, Lord John Pakenham.

CECIL, Rt. Hon. Lord Robert. Continued in House after 1918: full entry in Volume III.

CHALONER, Col. Richard Godolphin Walmesley. Gisboro Hall, Guisborough, Yorkshire. 5 Buckingham Gate, London.

Carlton, Boodle's, and Cavalry. 2nd s. of
R.P. Long, Esq., MP, of Rood Ashton,
Wiltshire, and bro. of the Rt. Hon. W.H.
Long, MP. B. 1856 at Dolforgan,
Montgomeryshire; m. 1882, Margaret, d.
of the Rev. W. Brocklesby Davis, Vicar of
Ramsbury, Wiltshire. Educ. at Winchester.
Entered the army 1878 and served in
Afghanistan and India; commanded the
1st Battalion Imperial Yeomanry in S.
African War 1899-1902, and was Lieut.-
Col. and Honorary Col. 1st Wiltshire
Royal Volunteers 1900-03. Assumed by
Royal License the name of Chaloner in
1888. A J.P. for Wiltshire, and J.P., and
Dept.-Lieut. of the N. Riding of Yorkshire.
A Conservative. Sat for the Westbury div-
ision of Wiltshire from 1895 to 1900, when
he was defeated. Elected for the
Abercromby division of Liverpool in Jan.
1910 and sat until created Baron
Gisborough 23 June 1917. Died 23 Jan.
1938.   [1917]

CHAMBERLAIN, Rt. Hon. Joseph. 40
Prince's Gardens, London. Highbury,
Moor Green, Birmingham. Constitu-
tional. Eld. s. of Joseph Chamberlain, Esq.,
of Moor Green Hall, near Birmingham, by
Caroline, d. of Henry Harben, Esq. B. in
London 1836; m. 1st, 1861, Harriet, d. of
Archibald Kenrick, Esq., of Berrow Court,
Edgbaston (she died 1863); 2ndly, 1868,
Florence, d. of Timothy Kenrick, Esq., of
Maple Bank, Edgbaston (she died 1875);
3rdly, 1888, Mary, only d. of Hon. W.C.
Endicott, Secretary of War, United States,
Cleveland Presidency. Educ. at a private
school and University Coll. School, Lon-
don. Was a Manufacturer in Birmingham;
retired 1874. Three times Mayor of Bir-
mingham 1874-76; Chairman of the Bir-
mingham School Board, and Chairman of
the National Education League. PC. 1880.
Was President of the Board Trade Apr.
1880 to May 1885 and President of the
Local Government Board Jan. to Mar.
1886, in Mr. Gladstone's ministries. Was
Chief Commissioner to settle the North
American Fisheries dispute 1887, Chairman Coal Dust Commission 1891-94, and
Member Aged Poor Commission 1893-95.
Appointed Secretary of State for the Colonies 1895; resigned Sept. 1903. F.R.S.,
Honorary LL.D. Cambridge 1892; Honor-
ary D.C.L. Oxford 1896; Honorary LL.D.
Dublin 1899, Cardiff 1905 and Bir-
mingham 1909. Lord Rector of Glasgow
University 1896. Chancellor of Bir-

mingham University from 1901. Elder
Bro. of Trinity House. A Liberal until Mar.
1886, thereafter a Liberal Unionist. Sat for
Birmingham from June 1876 to 1885, and
for W. Birmingham from 1885 until his
death on 2 July 1914.   [1914]

**CHAMBERLAIN, Rt. Hon. Joseph
Austen.** Continued in House after 1918:
full entry in Volume III.

CHAMBERLAIN, Richard. 39 Cadogan
Square, London. Devonshire. 2nd s. of
Joseph Chamberlain, Esq., of Bir-
mingham, by Caroline, d. of Henry
Harben, Esq., and younger bro. of the Rt.
Hon. Joseph Chamberlain. B. in London
1840; m. 1st, 1872, Emile Agnes, d. of
W.H. Dawes, Esq. (she died 1882); 2ndly,
1887, Râhmih Theodora, d. of Sir John
Swinburne, MP. Educ. at the University
Coll. School, London. Was in business in
Birmingham as a Brass-Founder. Chair-
man of Hampstead Colliery Company.
Director of Ebbw Vale Steel and Iron
Company and of Union Rolling Stock
Company. A J.P. for Warwickshire and
Birmingham, and an Alderman of Bir-
mingham, where he was twice Mayor,
1880-81. He was also for a time Chairman
of the Finance Committee of the town. A
Liberal Unionist. Sat for Islington W. from
Nov. 1885 until he was defeated in 1892.
Chairman of Liberal Unionist Organisa-
tion. Died 2 Apr. 1899.   [1892]

CHAMBERLAYNE, Tankerville. Cran-
bury Park, Winchester. Baddesley Manor,
Romsey. Weston Grove, Southampton.
Carlton, and Junior Carlton. S. of Thomas
Chamberlayne, Esq., of Cranbury Park,
Hampshire, by Amelia, d. of Gen. Denzil
Onslow, of Staughton House, Hampshire.
B. 1843; m. Edith Rachel, d. of S.J. Ashley,
Esq., of Kidlington, Oxford. Educ. at Eton,
and Magdalen Coll., Oxford; B.A. 1865.
Honorary Lieut. in Royal Naval Reserve.
A Conservative. Sat for Southampton
1892-95, when, being re-elected, he was
unseated on petition; re-elected there
1900 and sat until defeated in 1906. Died 17
May 1924.   [1905]

CHAMBERS, James. Grove House, Fox-
rock, Co. Dublin. Carlton, and Constitutional. Ulster, Belfast. Stephen's Green,
and Friendly Brothers, Dublin. S. of Joseph
Chambers, Esq. B. 1863. Educ. at Royal
Academical Institute, and Queen's Coll.,

Belfast. Called to the Irish bar 1886; K.C. 1902, bencher of King's Inns 1905. Solicitor-Gen. for Ireland from Mar.-June 1917. A Unionist. Elected for S. Belfast in Jan. 1910 and sat until his death 11 June 1917.
[1917]

CHANCE, Frederick William. Morton, Carlisle. Reform. S. of Edward Chance, Esq., of Malvern, and Maria, d. of J. Ferguson, Esq., MP for Carlisle 1852-57. B. 26 Dec. 1852 at Malvern; m. 1st, 1880, Mary, d. of G.B. Seton-Karr, Esq., I.C.S. (she died 1905); 2ndly, 1909, Josephine, d. of Sir Wilfrid Lawson, MP. Educ. at Harrow, and Caius Coll., Cambridge. Managing Director of Fergusson Brothers, Cotton Manufacturers, Carlisle; a member of the Council of the Liberal League, and Cumberland County Council; member of Carlisle Town Council (Mayor 1904); Chairman of the Cumberland and Westmoreland Lunacy Commission; J.P. for Carlisle; Dept.-Lieut. and J.P. for Cumberland; a Director of Carlisle and Cumberland Bank. A Liberal. First elected for Carlisle on 14 July 1905 and sat until he retired in Jan. 1910. High Sheriff of Cumberland 1915. K.B.E. 1920. Died 31 Aug. 1932.
[1909]

CHANCE, Patrick Alexander. 72 Warwick Street, London. 15 Westland Row, Dublin. 2nd s. of Albert George Chance, Engineer, by Elizabeth Mary, d. of George Fleming, Esq., of Dublin. B. at Chelsea 1857; m. 1887, Josephine Louisa, d. of Maj. Henry Pix Hill, of Richmond, Surrey. Educ. at the Catholic University School, Dublin, and the Catholic University of Ireland. Was admitted a Solicitor in Trinity term 1882. An "Irish Nationalist" of the Anti-Parnellite section. Sat for Kilkenny S. from 1885 until he accepted Chiltern Hundreds in 1894. Died some time after 1919.
[1894]

CHANCELLOR, Henry George. Hillsborough, Crescent Road, Crouch End, London. National Liberal, and Eighty. S. of John Chancellor, Esq., of Walton, Bridgewater, and Louisa, d. of John Porter, Esq., of Ashcott, Somerset. B. 3 June 1863 at Walton, near Bridgewater; m. 1885, Mary, d. of John Dyer Surl, Esq., of Newent, Gloucestershire. Educ. at Elmfield Coll., York. A Paint Manufacturer and Merchant. A Liberal. Elected for the Haggerston division of Shoreditch in Jan. 1910 and sat until defeated in Shoreditch in 1918. President of English League for Taxation of Land Values in 1910 and 1920. Honorary Secretary International Arbitration League 1938. Died 14 Mar. 1945.
[1918]

CHANNING, Sir Frances Allston, Bart. 40 Eaton Place, London. Oxford & Cambridge, Reform, and National Liberal. Only s. of the Rev. William Henry Channing, of Boston, by Julia, d. of William Allen, Esq., of Fishkill Point, New York. B. 1841; m. Elizabeth, d. of Henry Bryant, Esq., of Boston, U.S.A. Educ. at Liverpool, and at Exeter Coll., Oxford; honours in Classics and Mathematics, Chancellor's English Essay and Arnold Historical Prizes, and became Fellow, Lecturer, and Tutor of University Coll. A Barrister, Lincoln's Inn. A J.P. for Northamptonshire. A member of the Royal Commission on Agriculture 1893 and Small Holdings Committee 1905, and served on many Parliamentary and Departmental Enquiries; Chairman of Standing Committees 1906, was Chairman of the Chambers of Agriculture 1894, and President of the Land Law Reform Association 1894-99. Created Bart. 1906. A Liberal, in favour of Land Law Reforms, a National System of Education, shorter hours of labour, etc. Sat for Northamptonshire E. from 1885 until he retired in Dec. 1910. Created 1st Baron Channing of Wellingborough 1912. Author of *Memories of Midland Politics* (1917). Died 20 Feb. 1926.
[1910]

CHAPLIN, Rt. Hon. Henry. 6 Charles Street, Berkeley Square, London. Hall Farm, Brixworth, Northamptonshire. Carlton, Marlborough, and Turf. S. of the Rev. H. Chaplin, and Caroline Horatia, d. of William Ellice, Esq. B. 22 Dec. 1840; m. 1876, Lady Florence Leveson-Gower, d. of 3rd Duke of Sutherland (she died 1881). Educ. at Harrow, and Christ Church, Oxford; LL.D. Was Chancellor of Duchy of Lancaster 1885-86, President of Board of Agriculture 1889-92, and President of Local Government Board 1895-1900, in Lord Salisbury's Ministries; PC. 1885. A J.P. and Dept.-Lieut. for Lincolnshire. A Unionist. Sat for mid Lincolnshire from 1868-85, and the Sleaford division of Lincolnshire from 1885 until defeated at the general election of 1906. Elected for the Wimbledon division of Surrey in May 1907 and sat until created Visct. Chaplin in 1916. Died 29 May 1923. [1916]

CHAPMAN, Edward. Queen Anne's Mansions, London. Hill End, Mottram-in-Longdendale, Cheshire. Carlton, Constitutional, and Conservative. Union, Manchester. S. of John Chapman, Esq., MP, of Hill End, Mottram, who died 1877, and Anne, d. of George Sidebottom, Esq., of Hill End, Mottram. B. at Hill End, Mottram-in-Longdendale 1839. Educ. at Over Vicarage, and Merton Coll., Oxford, B.A. 1864, M.A. 1866 (1st class Natural Science), Fellow of Magdalen Coll., Public Examiner in Natural Science. Was associated with various boards connected with University extension and teaching. J.P. and Dept.-Lieut. for Cheshire, and J.P. for Lancashire. On roll for High Sheriff 1901. Dept. Chairman of the Great Central Railway, and Director of S.E. Railway. Was for twenty years Chairman of the Mottram District Council, and Chairman of the Hyde Conservative Association. A member of the York House of Laymen. Lord of the Manor of Hattersley, and Freeman of the Turners' Company, London. A Progressive Conservative. Supported the Unionist party as represented by Mr. Balfour and Mr. Chamberlain. In favour of Tariff Reform; opposed to Home Rule. In favour of House of Lords as 2nd chamber; but open to consider improvements in its constitution. Wanted army and navy to be kept efficient. Thought that reorganisation of the army as an efficient war machine should have been the first duty of Parliament. In favour of voluntary schools, and against disestablishment of the Church. Elected for the Hyde division of Cheshire in 1900 and sat until defeated in 1906. Died 26 July 1906. [1905]

CHAPPLE, William Allan. Continued in House after 1918: full entry in Volume III.

CHARLESWORTH, Albany Hawkes. 1 Tilney Street, London. Chapelthorpe Hall, Wakefield. Conservative, and Oxford & Cambridge. Only s. of John C.D. Charlesworth, Esq., MP for Wakefield 1857-59, and his wife Sarah, d. of W. Featherstonhaugh, Esq., of The Hermitage, Durham. B. 1854 at Stanley Hall, Wakefield; m. 1889, Eleanor Charlotte, 2nd d. of Kenneth Bayley, Esq., of Inchicore, Dublin. Educ. at Eton, and Trinity Coll., Cambridge (B.A. 1875, M.A. 1879). A

Colliery Proprietor. A J.P., W. Riding, Yorkshire, and Honorary Col. 1st Volunteer Brigade King's Own Light Infantry. A Conservative. Unsuccessfully contested the Normanton division of the W. Riding of Yorkshire in Dec. 1885 and again in July 1886. First returned for Wakefield in July 1892 and sat until he retired in 1895. Died 12 Sept. 1914. [1895]

CHARRINGTON, Spencer. 19 Carlton House Terrace, London. 1 St. Peter's Road, Mile End. Hunsdon House, Hunsdon, Nr. Ware, Hertfordshire. Conservative. S. of Nicholas Charrington, Esq., of Mile End. B. 1818; m. 1853, Alethe C.P., d. of the Rev. J.G. Calmeyer, Prost., of Hammerfest, Norway. Educ. at Eton. A Partner in the firm of Charrington and Company, Brewers. A Conservative. Sat for the Mile End division of Tower Hamlets from Nov. 1885 until his death 11 Dec. 1904. [1904]

CHEETHAM, John Frederick. Eastwood, Stalybridge. Athenaeum, Brooks's, National Liberal, and Reform. Eld. s. of John Cheetham, Esq., of Eastwood, Stalybridge, MP for S. Lancashire from 1852-59, and for Salford 1865-68. B. 1835; m. 1887, Beatrice Emma, d. of F.D.P. Astley, Esq., Dept.-Lieut. of Dukinfield. Educ. at University Coll., London; B.A. honours. A Cotton Manufacturer at Stalybridge, and a Director of the Manchester and Liverpool District Banking Company. J.P. for Lancashire and Cheshire. Alderman of the Cheshire County Council, and a Governor of Manchester University. Awarded Honorary Freedom of Stalybridge in 1897 on presenting that town with a Jubilee Memorial gift of a free library. A Liberal. Sat for N. Derbyshire from 1880-85. Unsuccessfully contested High Peak division of Derbyshire in 1885 and 1892, Bury 1895, and Stalybridge 1900. First elected for Stalybridge in Jan. 1905 and sat until he retired in Jan. 1910. PC. 1911. Died 25 Feb. 1916. [1909]

CHEETHAM, Joshua Milne. Hotel Metropole, London. Eyford Park, Burton-on-the-Water, Gloucestershire. Hopwood Avenue, Manchester. S. of James and Alice Chetham, of Clough House, Crompton, near Oldham. B. 1835 at Clough House; m. 1862, Sarah, d. of Abram Crompton, of High Crompton. Educ. at the High School, Oldham. A Cotton Manufacturer, member of the firm of James Cheetham and Sons, Manchester, Chairman of the Oldham Joint Stock Bank, and a J.P. for Lancashire. A Liberal, in favour of Home Rule for Ireland and the Gladstonian programme generally. Unsuccessfully contested Oldham in 1886. First returned for Oldham in July 1892 and sat until he retired in 1895. Died 27 Nov. 1902. [1895]

CHELSEA, Henry Arthur Cadogan, Visct. 31 Green Street, Grosvenor Square, London. Crelford House, Bury St. Edmunds. Carlton, and Turf. Eld. s. of the Earl of Cadogan, Lord Lieut. of Ireland, by Lady Beatrix Jane, 4th d. of the 2nd Earl of Craven. B. 1868; m. 1st, 1892, Hon. Mildred Harriet Sturt, 3rd d. of Lord Alington; 2ndly, 1911. Educ. at Eton, and Trinity Coll., Cambridge. Was Lieut. 3rd Battalion Royal Fusiliers. Private Secretary to the Rt. Hon. A.J. Balfour as Chief Secretary for Ireland and 1st Lord of the Treasury. A Conservative. Was an unsuccessful candidate for the Stowmarket division of Suffolk at the general election of July 1892. First returned for Bury St. Edmunds Aug. 1892 and sat until he retired in 1900. Died during his father's lifetime on 2 July 1908. [1900]

CHERRY, Rt. Hon. Richard Robert. 82 St. George's Square, London. 92 St. Stephen's Green, Dublin. National Liberal. S. of Robert W. Cherry, Esq., Solicitor, of Waterford, and Susan, d. of J. Briscoe, Esq., M.D. B. 19 Mar. 1859 at Waterford; m. 1886, Mary Wilhelmina, d. of Robert Cooper, Esq., of Collinstown House, Leixlip. Educ. at a private school, Waterford, and Trinity Coll., Dublin; B.A. 1879, LL.D. 1888. Was called to the Irish bar 1881; Q.C. 1896; bencher of King's Inns, Dublin 1906. Professor of Criminal and Constitutional Law in University of Dublin 1889-94. Attorney-Gen. for Ireland, appointed Dec. 1905 to Nov. 1909. PC. (Ireland) 1905. Author of several textbooks on Irish Land Laws and Criminal Law. A Liberal. Unsuccessfully contested the Kirkdale division of Liverpool in 1900. Elected for the Exchange division of Liverpool in 1906 and sat until appointed Lord Justice of Appeal for Ireland, Nov. 1909-14; Lord Chief Justice of Ireland 1914-16. Died 10 Feb. 1923. [1909]

CHESNEY, Gen. Sir George Tomkyns. K.C.B. 27 Inverness Terrace, London. Athenaeum, and Carlton. S. of Capt. C.C. Chesney of the East India Company's Bengal Artillery. B. 1830; m. 1855, d. of George Palmer, Esq., of Purneah, Bengal. Educ. at Woolwich. Entered the Bengal Engineers 1848; Capt. and Maj. 1858, Lieut.-Col. 1869, Col. 1884, Col.-Commandant 1890, and Gen. 1892. Served in the Indian Mutiny, and was severely wounded at Delhi; also served in Burmah. A member of the Council of the Governor-Gen. of India 1886-91, and President, Royal Indian Engineering Coll. Wrote *The Battle of Dorking, Indian Polity, The Dilemma* (a novel), and other works. A Director of the East India Railway Company, and of the Agra Bank. Created C.S.I. 1883, C.I.E. 1886, C.B. 1887 and K.C.B. 1890. A Conservative. First returned for Oxford in July 1892 and sat until his death 31 Mar. 1895. [1895]

CHESTER-MASTER, Thomas William. See MASTER, Thomas William Chester-.

CHEYNE, Sir William Watson, Bart., K.C.M.G., C.B. Continued in House after 1918: full entry in Volume III.

CHILDERS, Rt. Hon. Hugh Culling Eardley, F.R.S. 6 St. George's Place, Hyde Park Corner, London. Brooks's, and Athenaeum. Only s. of the Rev. Eardley Childers, of Cantley, Yorkshire, by Maria Charlotte, eld. d. of Sir Culling Smith, Bart., of Bedwell Park, Hertfordshire. B. in Brook Street 1827; m. 1st, 1850, Emily, 3rd d. of G.J.A. Walker, Esq., of Norton, Co. Worcester (she died 1875); 2ndly, 1879, Katharine Ann, d. of Rt. Rev. Dr. Gilbert, Bishop of Chichester, and widow of Col. the Hon. Gilbert Elliot. Educ. at Trinity Coll., Cambridge, where he graduated (14th senior optime) B.A. 1850; M.A. 1857. Was a member of the government of Victoria (Australia) from 1851 till 1857, and held a seat in the first Cabinet as Commissioner of Trade and Customs; sat for Portland in the first Legislative Assembly there 1856-57. He returned to England and entered Parliament, and was a Lord of the Admiralty from Apr. 1864 till Aug. 1865, and Financial Secretary to the Treasury from the latter date till July 1866; also First Lord of the Admiralty from Dec. 1868 to Mar. 1871, Chancellor of the Duchy of Lancaster from Aug. 1872 to Sept. 1873, Secretary of State for War from Apr. 1880 to Dec. 1882, when he was appointed

Chancellor of the Exchequer. He held this office till the resignation of Mr. Gladstone's Ministry in 1885, and in Feb. 1886 he joined Mr. Gladstone's third administration as Home Secretary. A Magistrate for the W. Riding of Yorkshire. PC. 1868. A Liberal, in favour of Home Rule. Unsuccessfully contested Pontefract Apr. 1859, but subsequently succeeded in unseating his opponent on petition, and on going to a new election was returned 31 Jan. 1860. He sat for Pontefract from that date to the dissolution of 1885, but at the general election was defeated. His re-election for Pontefract on 15 Aug. 1872, caused by his appointment as Chancellor of Duchy of Lancaster, was the first election in which the Secret Ballot was used. On 29 Jan. 1886, he was returned for Edinburgh S. and and sat until he retired in 1892. Died 29 Jan. 1896. [1892]

CHIOZZA-MONEY, Sir Leo George. See MONEY, Sir Leo George Chiozza.

CHURCHILL, Rt. Hon. Lord Randolph Henry Spencer-. 50 Grosvenor Square, London. Carlton, and Turf. 3rd s. of the 7th Duke of Marlborough, by Lady Frances Anne Emily, eld. d. of the 3rd Marq. of London. B. 1849; m. 1874, Jenny, d. of Leonard Jerome, Esq., of New York. Graduated B.A. at Oxford 1871. A Magistrate and Dept.-Lieut. for Oxfordshire. Appointed Secretary of State for India 1885 to Jan. 1886. Author of *Plain Politics for the Working Classes* (1885). PC. 1885. On the formation of the Marq. of Salisbury's second ministry July 1886 he was appointed Chancellor of the Exchequer, with the leadership of the House of Commons, but on 22 Dec. of that year he resigned. A Conservative. Sat for Woodstock 1874-85. Unsuccessfully contested Birmingham Central against John Bright in 1885. Sat for Paddington S. from 1885 until his death 24 Jan. 1895. [1892]

CHURCHILL, Rt. Hon. Winston Leonard Spencer. Continued in House after 1918: full entries in Volumes III and IV.

CLANCY, John Joseph. 1 Breffni Terrace, Sandycove Road, Co. Dublin. S. of William Clancy, Esq., of Carragh Lodge, Claregalway, Co. Galway. B. 1847; m. 1868, Margaret Louise, d. of P.J. Hickie, Esq., of Limerick (she died Sept. 1912). Educ. at Summer Hill Coll., Athlone, and Queen's Coll., Galway (of which he was Scholar, Exhibitioner, and Prizeman). M.A. National University of Ireland, and was called to the Irish bar in 1887. K.C. 1906. Was on the editorial staff of *The Nation* newspaper from 1870 to 1885. A Nationalist. Sat for the N. division of Co. Dublin from 1885 until defeated in 1918. Author of numerous pamphlets and addresses, also essays in reviews etc. Died 25 Nov. 1928. [1918]

CLARE, Octavius Leigh. See LEIGH-CLARE, Octavius Leigh.

CLARK, Dr. Gavin Brown. National Liberal. 3rd s. of William Clark, Insurance Agent, of Glasgow, by Jessie, d. of John Brown, Esq., of Fenwick, Ayrshire. B. at Kilmarnock, Ayrshire 1846; m. 1st, 1871, Lily, d. of James Scotland, Esq.; 2ndly, Aggie, d. of John Brown, Esq., J.P., Paisley. Educ. at the Universities of Glasgow and Edinburgh, and King's Coll., London. M.D., F.R.C.S., Edinburgh, and L.R.C.P. Edinburgh. Wrote pamphlets on the Land Question, South Africa, India, and some social questions. Was Consul-Gen. of the South African Republic, prior to 1891. A Radical, in favour of federal Home Rule. Sat for Caithness-shire from 1885 until defeated in 1900. (He was not readopted for Caithness-shire in 1900 because of his alleged pro-Boer sympathies and unsuccessfully contested the election as an Independent Liberal.) Unsuccessfully contested the Cathcart division of Glasgow in 1918, as a Labour candidate. Holder of Belgian and Serbian decorations. Died 5 July 1930. [1900]

CLARK, George Smith. Dunlambert, Co. Antrim, Carlton. B. 1861 in Paisley. Educ. at Merchiston Castle School, Edinburgh, and at Cambridge. A Shipbuilder, a founder of the firm of Workman, Clark and Company Limited, Belfast. Dept.-Lieut. for Belfast. A member of Belfast Harbour Board. A Unionist. Elected for N. Belfast in Apr. 1907 and sat until he retired in Jan. 1910. Created Bart. 1917. Chairman Great Northern Railway of Ireland 1926-34. Director of Bank of Ireland. Senator of Northern Ireland Parliament. Died 23 Mar. 1935. [1909]

CLARKE, Charles Goddard. South Lodge, Champion Hill, London. National

Liberal. S. of Richard Clarke, Esq. B. 10 May 1849 in London; m. 1873, Rebecca, d. of Henry Potter, Esq. Educ. at Liverpool. A member of the firm of Potter and Clarke, Wholesale Druggists. A member of the London County Council from 1898; Mayor of Camberwell 1902-03; Alderman 1903; a J.P. for London. A Liberal. Unsuccessfully contested Dulwich 1895 and Mile End 1900. First elected for the Peckham division of Camberwell in 1906 and sat until his death 7 Mar. 1908.   [1907]

CLARKE, Sir Edward George. 2 Essex Court, Temple, London. Thorncote, Staines. Carlton, St. Stephen's, Garrick, and City Carlton. S. of J.G. Clarke, Esq., of King William Street, London. B. 15 Feb. 1841 in London; m. 1st, 1866, Annie, d. of G. Mitchell, Esq., of Lincoln's Inn Fields (she died 1881); 2ndly, 1882, Kathleen, d. of A.W. Bryant, Esq. Educ. at Coll. House, Edmonton, and City of London Coll. Was called to the bar at Lincoln's Inn 1864; Q.C. 1880; bencher 1882. Treasurer of Lincoln's Inn 1906. Tancred Student in Common Law 1861-67; an Associate in Arts of Oxford University; Associate of City of London Coll., and Fellow of King's Coll. London. Was Solicitor-Gen. 1886-92. Knighted 1886. PC. 1908. A Conservative. Sat for Southwark Feb. to Apr. 1880, when he was defeated, and for Plymouth from July 1880-Jan. 1900, when he accepted Chiltern Hundreds. Elected for the City of London in Jan. 1906 and sat until he accepted Chiltern Hundreds in June 1906. Retired from the bar in 1914. Author of *Story of My Life* (1918). Died 26 Apr. 1931.   [1906]

CLAY, Capt. Herbert Henry Spender. See SPENDER-CLAY, Capt. Herbert Henry. Continued in House after 1918: full entry in Volume III.

CLAYTON, Nathaniel George. 2 Belgrave Square, London. Cheston, Humshaugh, Northumberland. Carlton, Oxford & Cambridge, and Wellington. S. of Richard Clayton, Esq., M.A., Master of the Hospital of St. Mary Magdalene, Newcastle-on-Tyne, and Mary Anne, d. of the Rev. Francis Laing. B. 1833, at Lincoln Hill, near Humshaugh, Northumberland; m. Dec. 1860, Isabel, 4th d. of the Rev. Edward Chaloner Ogle, of Kirkley Hall, Northumberland. Educ. at Harrow, and University Coll., Oxford, where he took a second in Final Classical School. Practised as a Solicitor from 1860 to 1890, when he retired on succeeding to the family estates on the death of his uncle, John Clayton, Esq. High Sheriff, Dept.-Lieut. and Magistrate for Northumberland. A Conservative. Sat for the Hexham division of Northumberland from July 1892 until unseated on petition in Nov. 1892. Died 5 Sept. 1895.   [1892 2nd ed]

CLELAND, James William. 32 Doughty Street, London. 4 Harcourt Buildings, Temple, London. National Liberal, and Union. S. of Charles Cleland, Esq., Paper Manufacturer, and Jane Connell. B. 1874 at Glasgow. Unmarried. Educ. at Glasgow Academy, Glasgow University, and Balliol Coll., Oxford. A Barrister, called to the bar at the Middle Temple 1899; a member of the London County Council for Lewisham 1904-07. A Liberal. Unsuccessfully contested Lewisham 1903. Elected for the Bridgeton division of Glasgow in 1906 and sat until he retired in Dec. 1910. Died 21 Oct. 1914.   [1910]

CLIVE, Lieut.-Col. Percy Archer. Whitfield, Allensmore, Hereford. 21 Chester Street, Belgrave Square, London. Carlton, Guards', and Travellers'. S. of C.M.B. Clive, Esq., of Whitfield, Hereford, and Lady Katherine Fielding, d. of 7th Earl of Denbigh. B. 1873 in London; m. 1905, Alice Muriel, d. of Col. G.F. Dallas. Educ. at Eton, and Sandhurst. Entered the Grenadier Guards 1891. Served in W. African Field Force in Nigeria 1898 and S. African War 1899-1902. Rejoined Grenadier Guards on mobilisation, Aug. 1914, and served with Expeditionary Force; received Legion of Honour and was twice wounded. Lieut.-Col. attached 7th Battalion E. Yorkshire Regiment, British Expeditionary Force. Alderman of Herefordshire County Council, and Chairman of Small Holdings Committee. Was Private Secretary to the Chancellor of the Exchequer and other members of the Unionist Government. A Unionist. Sat for the Ross division of Herefordshire from 1900-06 when he was defeated at the general election; re-elected there in Jan. 1908 and sat until he was killed in action on 5 Apr. 1918.   [1918]

CLOUGH, Walter Owen. 89 Gresham Street, London. National Liberal, and Leeds County Liberal. S. of John Clough,

Esq., of Huddersfield. B. 1846; m. 1871, Hannah, 5th d. of George Marshall, Esq., of Newark. Educ. at Huddersfield. Fellow of Institute of Chartered Accountants. Senior Partner in the firm of Clough, Armstrong, and Ford, Chartered Accountants, London, Leeds, Manchester, and Mexico City. A Lieut. of the City of London, and a member (Ward of Cheap) of the Corporation; also a J.P. for Middlesex, Arbitrator of the London Chamber of Arbitration, and a Fellow of the Royal Geographical and Statistical Societies. A Liberal. Sat for Portsmouth from 7 July 1892 until he accepted Chiltern Hundreds in Apr. 1900. Died 17 Apr. 1922. [1900]

CLOUGH, William. The Shroggs, Steeton, Nr. Keighley. S. of Thomas Clough, Esq. B. 13 May 1862 at Steeton; m. 1886, Louisa, d. of William Clapham, Esq., of Keighley. Educ. at Steeton Provident School, Keighley Trade School, and Pannal Coll., Harrogate. A member of W. Riding of Yorkshire County Council. A Liberal. First elected for the Skipton division of the W. Riding of Yorkshire in 1906 and sat until he retired in 1918. Died 11 May 1937. [1918]

CLYDE, Rt. Hon. James Avon. Continued in House after 1918: full entry in Volume III.

CLYNES, John Robert. Continued in House after 1918: full entry in Volume III.

COATES, Sir Edward Feetham, Bart. Continued in House after 1918: full entry in Volume III.

COATS, Sir Stuart Auchincloss, Bart. Continued in House after 1918: full entry in Volume III.

COBB, Henry Peyton. 53 Lincoln's Inn Fields, London. Wealdstone House, Middlesex. Reform, and National Liberal. Youngest s. of Timothy Rhodes Cobb, Esq., Banker of Banbury, by Charlotte, d. of Thomas Pix, Esq., of Northiam, Sussex. B. 1835; m. 1st, 1863, Fanny, d. of John Taylor, Esq., Mining Engineer, of Great Cumberland Place, Hyde Park; 2ndly, 1872, Bessie, d. of William Sharpe, Esq., of Bedford Row and Highbury. Educ. at the Rev. J.P. Malleson's, Brighton, and University Coll. and Hall, London; graduated at the University of London 1856, with honours in mathematics and natural philosophy. A Partner in the firm of Cobb and Son, Banbury, Bankers, and also a Solicitor at 53 Lincoln's Inn Fields (admitted in 1866). A "Radical and Nonconformist", was for many years in favour of Home Rule, not only for Ireland, but for England, Scotland, and Wales. Opposed to coercive legislation, and was one of the few English members who in the Parliament of 1885-86 voted against the Arms Act. Sat for the Rugby division of Warwickshire from 1885 until he retired in 1895. Died 27 Jan. 1910. [1895]

COBBOLD, Felix Thornley. Felixstowe Lodge, Ipswich. 8 Whitehall Court, London. New University, and Reform. S. of John C. Cobbold, Esq., MP, of Ipswich, and Lucy, d. of the Rev. H. Patterson, of Drinkstone, Suffolk. B. 1841 at Ipswich. Educ. at Eton, and King's Coll., Cambridge; 1st class in Classics 1865. Was called to the bar at Lincoln's Inn 1868. Mayor of Ipswich; J.P. for Suffolk. A Liberal. Sat for the Stowmarket division of Suffolk from 1885-86, when he retired. Unsuccessfully contested the Woodbridge division of Suffolk in 1900. Elected for Ipswich and sat until his death 6 Dec. 1909. [1909]

COCHRANE, Cecil Algernon. Oakfield House, Gosforth, Northumberland. Reform, and Royal Automobile. S. of William Cochrane, Esq., and Eliza, d. of W.B. Collis, Esq., Dept.-Lieut., of Wollaston Hall, Stourbridge. B. in 1869; m. 1905, Frances Sibyl, d. of Col. Addison Potter, C.B., of Heaton Hall, Newcastle-on-Tyne. Educ. at Sherborne, and Christ Church, Oxford; M.A. J.P. for Northumberland 1908; Chairman of Cochrane and Company Limited, Middlesbrough; Newbiggin Colliery Company, and Director of other companies. A Liberal. Unsuccessfully contested Durham City in Dec. 1910. Elected for South Shields Mar. 1916 and sat until he accepted Chiltern Hundreds in Oct. 1918. Honorary D.C.L. University of Durham. Knighted in 1933. Died 23 Sept. 1960. [1918]

COCHRANE, Hon. Thomas Horatio Arthur Ernest. Crawford Priory, Cupar, Fife. S. of Thomas, 11th Earl of Dundonald, and Louisa, d. of A. Mackinnon, Esq., MP, of Acryse Park, Kent. B. 1857; m.

1880, Lady Gertrude Boyle, d. of the 6th Earl of Glasgow. Educ. at Eton. Served in the 93rd Highlanders, and in the Scots Guards, and was Honorary Lieut.-Col. 4th Battalion Argyll and Sutherland Highlanders; served in S. Africa 1899-1902. J.P. for Fife, and Dept.-Lieut. for Renfrewshire. Unpaid Private Secretary to Mr. Chamberlain as Colonial Secretary 1895-1901. Was Under-Secretary for the Home Department from 1902-05. A Liberal Unionist, opposed to Home Rule, but in favour of a Local Government scheme for Ireland. Also in favour of reform of the Poor Law, and Land Laws, "one man one vote", equal electorial districts, popular control of the liquor traffics, and readjustment of taxation, etc. Sat for N. Ayrshire from 1892 until defeated in Jan. 1910. Created Baron Cochrane of Cults in 1919. Died 17 Jan. 1951.   [1909]

COCHRANE-BAILLIE, Hon. Charles Wallace Alexander Napier. 26 Wilton Crescent, London. Lamington, Lanarkshire. White's, and Turf. Only s. of Lord Lamington, by Annabella, d. of Andrew Drummond, Esq., of Cadlands, Hampshire. B. 1860. Educ. at Eton, and Christ Church, Oxford. A Lieut. in the Lanarkshire Yeomanry Cavalry, and was a Lieut. in the 3rd Battalion Leicester Regiment. Was appointed Private Secretary to Lord Salisbury when Prime Minister in 1885. A Conservative. Unsuccessfully contested St. Pancras N. at the general election in 1885. First returned for St. Pancras N. in July 1886 and sat until he succeeded as Lord Lamington in 1890. Gov. of Queensland 1895-1901. Gov. of Bombay 1903-07. Capt. of Royal Company of Archers. G.C.M.G. 1900; G.C.I.E. 1903. Died 16 Sept. 1940.   [1890]

CODDINGTON, Sir William, Bart. Wycollar, Blackburn. Carlton, and Junior Carlton. Eld. s. of William Dudley Coddington, Esq., of Wycollar, Blackburn, by Elizabeth, d. of Robert Hopwood, Esq., of Blackburn. B. at Salford 1830; m. 1864, Sarah Katherine, 3rd d. of William Thomas Hall, Esq., of Milnthorpe, near Wakefield. A Magistrate and Dept.-Lieut. for the Co. of Lancaster. Senior Partner in the firm of W.D. Coddington and Sons, Cotton-Spinners. Was created Bart. 1896. A Conservative. Sat for Blackburn from Mar. 1880 until he retired in 1906. Died 15 Feb. 1918.   [1905]

COGAN, Denis Joseph. 115 Thomas Street, Dublin. Laragh, Glendalough, Co. Wicklow. S. of Denis Cogan, Esq., P.L.G., and Mary Cogan. B. at Bray, Co. Wicklow 1859; m. 1886, d. of John Murphy, Esq., P.L.G., of Laragh, Glendalough. Educ. privately. A Provision Merchant. Was town councillor for Dublin Corporation 1885-91, representing Arran Quay Ward; Poor Law Guardian of Rathdrum 1897-1900; County Councillor for Glendalough division, Co. Wicklow, and Chairman of the Finance Committee of Wicklow County Council 1899-1901. A Nationalist. First elected for E. Wicklow in 1900 and sat until he accepted Chiltern Hundreds in June 1907. Unsuccessfully contested Wicklow E. in 1918.   [1907]

COGHILL, Douglas Harry. 14 Stanhope Gardens, London. Carlton, and United University. S. of Harry Coghill, Esq., J.P. Staffordshire and Sussex, and his wife, Mary Jane Fuller. B. 1885. Educ. at Cheltenham Coll., and Corpus Christi Coll., Oxford; B.A. and M.A. 3rd class classical (Hons.) moderations. A Barrister of the Inner Temple, called 1879, and joined the Oxford Circuit. A Liberal Unionist until 1895 when he joined the Conservatives. Sat for Newcastle-under-Lyme 1886-92, defeated there 1892. Sat for Stoke-on-Trent from 1895 until defeated in 1906. Died 13 Dec. 1928.   [1905]

COHEN, Arthur. 6 Holland Park, Notting Hill, London. 2 Paper Buildings, Temple, London. Reform, Devonshire, Oxford & Cambridge, and City Liberal. S. of Benjamin Cohen, Esq., a Merchant in London, of Askgill House, Richmond, Surrey, by Justina, d. of Joseph Montefiore, Esq., of London and sister of Sir Moses Montefiore, Bart. B. at Wyndham Place, Bryanston Square, London 1829; m. 1860, Emmeline, d. of Henry Micholls, Esq., of Manchester. Was educ. at the Gymnasium, Frankfort-on-the-Maine, University Coll., London, and Magdalene Coll., Cambridge; graduated B.A. 1863 as 5th wrangler. Obtained in May 1857 a studentship at the Inner Temple, of which he was a bencher, and was called to the bar Nov. 1857, when he joined the Home or S.E. Circuit. Appointed a Queen's Counsel 1874, and Judge of the Cinque Ports the same year. Elected standing counsel to the University of Cambridge 1876. Was junior counsel on behalf of Great Britain before the Alabama arbitration at Geneva in 1872. A "sincere and earnest" Liberal, in favour of "Home Rule" and of the further reform of the Bankruptcy Laws and the establishment of "a Mercantile Code". Unsuccessfully contested Lewes Feb. 1874. Sat for Southwark from Apr. 1880 to 1885 and again for Southwark from 1885 until he accepted Chiltern Hundreds in 1888. Counsel to Secretary of State for India from 1893; PC. 1905. Judge of Cinque Ports again in 1914. Died 3 Nov. 1914. [1887]

COHEN, Sir Benjamin Louis, Bart. 30 Hyde Park Gardens, London. Highfield, Shoreham, Sevenoaks. Carlton, Junior Carlton, Conservative, and City Carlton. S. of Louis Cohen, Esq., founder of the firm of Louis Cohen and Sons, Stock and Share Dealers, and Floretta Maryanne, d. of Assur Keyser, Esq. B. 1844 at South Street, Finsbury; m. 1870, Louisa Emily, only d. of Benjamin M. Merton. Educ. privately. Entered the Stock Exchange in 1862, and was a Partner in the firm of Louis Cohen and Sons. A Dept.-Lieut. for the City of London, J.P. for the counties of London and Kent, and a member of the London County Council. A Conservative. Sat for Islington E. from 1892 until defeated in 1906. Created Bart. 1905. Died 8 Nov. 1909. [1905]

COHEN, Lionel Louis. 9 Hyde Park Terrace, London. Carlton, City Carlton, and Constitutional. S. of Louis Cohen, Esq., Merchant of Gloucester Place, Portman Square, London, by Floretta, d. of Assur Keyser, Esq., of London. B. in London 1832; m. 1855, Esther, d. of I. Henry Moses, Esq., of Hyde Park Square, London. Educ. privately, partly under James Wigan, Esq., the father of the comedians Alfred and Horace Wigan. A Foreign Banker and member of the Stock Exchange, being Senior Partner of the firm of Louis Cohen and Sons; retired 1885. Among the offices held by Mr. Cohen was that of President of the Jewish Board of Guardians (from 1869), Dept.-Lieut. of London, a Trustee and Manager of the Stock Exchange (from 1870), Vice-President of the Statistical Society (1880-84, re-elected 1886), a member of the Royal Commission on the Depression of Trade, and a member of the Gold and Silver Commission. A Conservative, in favour of free trade and "municipal reform without

centralization", but strongly opposed to disestablishment and disendowment. Sat for N. Paddington from the general election of 1885 until his death 26 June 1887. [1887]

COLDWELLS, Francis Moses. 56 North End, Croydon. St. Helen's, Isle of Wight. National Liberal. B. at Stoke Newington 1832. Educ. at the British School in that place. A Tailor and Outfitter, and an Alderman and J.P. for the borough of Croydon. A Radical, in favour of Home Rule for Ireland, of reforms in respect to the London water supply and the markets of the metropolis, and of enlarging the powers of the London County Council. Sat for Lambeth N. from July 1892 until he retired in July 1895. He was one of five Directors of the Liberator Building Society and was charged with conspiracy in fraud 11 Feb. 1895. He obtained bail in Apr. but was found dead in a Bournemouth Summer House 29 July 1895. [1895]

COLEFAX, Henry Arthur. 85 Onslow Square, London. Savile, United University, and Burlington Fine Arts. S. of J.S. Colefax, Esq. B. 1866. Educ. at Bradford Grammar School, Merton Coll., Oxford, and Strasburg University; M.A. A Barrister. A Unionist. Elected for S.W. Manchester in Jan. 1910 and sat until defeated in Dec. 1910. K.C. 1912; K.B.E. 1920. Subsequently served on many Government Committees and Courts of Enquiry. Died 19 Feb. 1936. [1910]

COLERIDGE, Hon. Bernard John Seymour. 8 Wetherby Place, London. Devonshire. Eld. s. of the Rt. Hon. John Duke, 1st Baron Coleridge, Lord Chief Justice of England, by Jane Fortescue, d. of the Rev. George Turner Seymour, of Farringford, Isle of Wight. B. at Heaths Court, Ottery St. Mary, Devon 1851; m. 1876, Mary Alethea, d. of the Rt. Rev. Dr. Mackarness, Bishop of Oxford. Educ. at Eton, and Trinity Coll., Oxford; graduated M.A. 1877. Was called to the bar at the Middle Temple in 1877, and was a member of the Western Circuit. In 1880 served as Secretary to the Royal Commission of Inquiry into Corrupt Practices at Chester; from 1884 to 1892 was junior counsel to the Post Office on the Western Circuit; appointed Queen's Counsel 1892. An advanced Liberal, in favour of "Home

Rule" opposed to a second legislative chamber, and in favour of all churches being on a footing of perfect equality. Was interested in the legal repression of the practice of vivisection. Sat for the Attercliffe division of Sheffield from 1885 until he succeeded as 2nd Baron Coleridge in 1894. High Court Judge Kings Bench Division 1907-23; Chairman of local Conciliation Board 1912-18. F.R.S.L. 1916. Author. Died 4 Sept. 1927. [1894]

COLLERY, Bernard. Knox Street, and Crigg House, Sligo. B. 1838 at Sligo; m. 1866, Mary Agnes, d. of M. Walsh, Esq., J.P. A Wholesale Wine Merchant in Sligo, also a Landowner, and an Alderman and J.P. for Sligo. Was Mayor 1882 and 1884. A Nationalist of the Anti-Parnellite party. Sat for Sligo N. from Mar. 1891 until he accepted Chiltern Hundreds in Feb. 1900. [1900]

COLLINGS, Rt. Hon. Jesse. Edgbaston, Birmingham. Constitutional. S. of Thomas Collings, Esq., of Littleham, Exmouth, Devon. B. at Exmouth 1831; m. 1859, d. of Edward Oxenbould, Esq. Head of the firm of Messrs. Collings and Wallis, Merchants, at Birmingham; retired from business in 1879. A Common Councilman for Edgbaston Ward from 1868 to 1875, when he was elected an Alderman of Birmingham. A J.P. for Birmingham; Mayor of Birmingham 1878-79, and in that year £10,000 was subscribed as a Mayor's Distress Fund to relieve the want caused by the depression of trade. Was Chairman of the Free Libraries Committee, and was Honorary Secretary and one of the founders of the National Education League. Was a Gov. of King Edward's Grammar School and member of the Council of the Midland Institute. Was President of the National Federation of Liberal Associations. Moved the Small Holdings Resolution, the carrying of which caused the resignation of Lord Salisbury's administration, Jan. 1886. Was founder of the Allotments and Small Holdings Association and President of the Rural Labourers' League. Was Parliamentary Secretary of the Local Gov. Board 1886; PC. Department 1895-1902. A Unionist. Sat as a Radical for Ipswich from 1880-85; returned again for Ipswich Nov. 1885, but unseated on petition Apr. 1886. Elected as a Liberal Unionist for the Bordesley division of Birmingham in July 1886 and sat

until he retired in 1918. Died 20 Nov. 1920. [1918]

COLLINS, Lieut.-Col. Godfrey Pattison, C.M.G. Continued in House after 1918: full entry in Volume III.

COLLINS, Sir Stephen. Elm House, Tring, Hertfordshire. National Liberal, and Reform. S. of William Collins, Esq., of Swanage, and Ann, d. of E. Walpole, Esq., of Kalmarsh, Northamptonshire. B. 9 Oct. 1847 at Swanage; m. 1st, 1872, Frances, d. of H. Webber, Esq., 2ndly, 1901, Jane, d. of William Russell, Esq., of Marsworth, Tring. Educ. at Swanage. Member of the London County Council for Kennington from 1901-07. A member of Lambeth Borough Council. A J.P. for the Co. of London. Knighted 1913. A Liberal, in favour of Temperance Reform, Taxation of Land Values, etc. Elected for the Kennington division of Lambeth in 1906 and sat until he retired in 1918. Died 12 Mar. 1925. [1918]

COLLINS, Sir William Job, M.D., K.C.V.O. 1 Albert Terrace, Regent's Park, London. Meads End, Eastbourne. Reform. S. of Dr. W.J. Collins, Oxford and Regent's Park, and Mary Anne Francisca, d. of Edward Treacher, Esq. B. 1859; m. 1898, Jean Stevenson, d. of John Wilson, Esq., MP for Govan from 1889-1900. Educ. at University Coll. School, St. Bartholomew's Hospital, and London University (scholarship and two gold medals); double 1st class honours at M.B. degree, B.Sc. with Honours, M.S., M.D., D.P.H., F.R.C.S. A Teacher of Anatomy at St. Bartholomew's; Surgeon and Oculist for the Royal Eye Hospital and London Temperance Hospital; member Royal Commission on Vaccination 1889-96, and Vivisection 1906. Life Gov. University Coll., Fellow and Senator London University (Vice-Chancellor 1907-09). Member of London County Council from 1892-1907 (Chairman 1897-98); British Plenipotentiary at International Opium Conference 1912, 1913 and 1914. Chairman of the Conciliation and Arbitration Board for Government Employees 1917. Knighted 1902; K.C.V.O. 1914. Wrote *The Man v. the Microbe, The Crystalline Lens, Physic and Metaphysic, Life and Work of Sir Samuel Romilly, Spinoza, Evolution in Disease*, etc. A Liberal. Unsuccessfully contested St. Pancras W. in 1895 and University of London in Feb. 1900. MP for St. Pancras W. from 1906 un-

71

til defeated Dec. 1910. Elected for Derby in Dec. 1916 and sat until he retired in 1918. Died 12 Dec. 1946. [1918]

COLMAN, Jeremiah James. Belgrave Mansions, London. Carrow House, Norwich. The Clyffe, Corton, Lowestoft. Reform, Devonshire, and City Liberal. S. of James Colman, Esq., of Stoke Holy Cross, near Norwich, by Mary, d. of John Burlingham, Esq. B. at Stoke Holy Cross, near Norwich 1830; m. 1856, Caroline, d. of William Hardy Cozens-Hardy, Esq., of Letheringsett Hall, Norfolk. A Merchant and Manufacturer in Norwich, and head of the firm of Messrs. J. and J. Colman, Mustard and Starch Manufacturers, Cannon Street, London. A Magistrate for Norwich, Norfolk, and Suffolk. Dept.-Lieut. of Norfolk. Alderman of Norwich. Was Sheriff of Norwich for 1862-63, and Mayor for 1867-68. Offered Baronetcy but declined it. A Liberal, in favour of Home Rule. Sat for Norwich from Feb. 1871 until he retired in 1895. Died 18 Sept. 1898. [1895]

COLOMB, Rt. Hon. Sir John Charles Ready, D.C.M.G. 75 Belgrave Road, London. Dromquinna, Kenmare, Co. Kerry. Carlton, United Service, and Bath. S. of Gen. G.T. Colomb, by Mary, d. of Sir A. King, Bart., of Corrard, Co. Fermanagh. B. 1838; m. 1866, Emily Anna, d. of R.S. Palmer, Esq., and widow of Lieut. Charles Augustus Paget, R.N. Educ. privately, and at the Royal Naval Coll. Served in the Royal Marine Artillery from 1854 to 1869, and retired as Capt. Dept.-Lieut. and J.P. for Co. Kerry. Created C.M.G. 1887 and K.C.M.G. 1888. Wrote *The Defence of Great and Greater Britain*, etc. PC. (Ireland) 1903. Fellow of the Royal Geographical Society, of the Royal Statistical Institute and the Royal Colonial Institute. A Conservative and Imperialist, advocated development of new markets for British Trade, and in favour of some special means for recording the votes of sailors. Was an unsuccessful candidate for Bow and Bromley at the general election of 1885, but sat for that division of the Tower Hamlets from 1886 until defeated in 1892. First elected for Great Yarmouth 1895 and sat until he retired in 1906. Died 27 May 1909. [1905]

COLSTON, Charles Edward Hungerford Atholl. 54 Green Street, Grosvenor Square, London. Roundway Park, Devizes. Says Court, Gloucestershire. S. of Edward Colston, Esq., of Roundway Park, and Louisa, d. of the Rev. E. Murray, Vicar of Northolt, Middlesex. B. 1854; m. 1879, Rosalind, d. of Col. Gostling-Murray, of Whitton Park, Hounslow. Educ. at Eton, and Christ Church, Oxford; B.A. 1876. A J.P. and Dept.-Lieut. Wiltshire, and Lieut.-Col. 2nd Wiltshire Rifle Volunteers. A Conservative. Was an unsuccessful candidate at N. Bristol in 1885. Sat for S. Gloucestershire from 1892 until defeated in 1906. Created Baron Roundway in 1916. Died 17 June 1925. [1905]

COLVILLE, John. Cleland House, Motherwell. Reform, and National Liberal. S. of David Colville, Esq., J.P. of Glasgow, and Jessie Colville (Née Barr). B. in Glasgow 1852. An Iron and Steel Manufacturer, established at Motherwell in 1871. A J.P. and County Councillor for Lanarkshire; Chief Magistrate of Motherwell for seven years; and President Lanarkshire Christian Union. A Liberal, in favour of Home Rule, etc. Sat for Lanarkshire N.E. from July 1895 until his death 22 Aug. 1901. [1901]

COLVIN, Brigadier-Gen. Richard Beale. Continued in House after 1918: full entry in Volume III.

COMBE, Charles Harvey. 103 Jermyn Street, London. Cobham Park, Surrey. Carlton, and Windham. S. of Charles Combe, Esq., J.P. and Dept.-Lieut. of Surrey, and Marianne Harriet Catherine, only d. of Capt. Patrick Inglis, R.N. B. at Cobham Park, Surrey 1863. Educ. at Eton. A Director of the firm of Combe and Company (Limited), Brewers, of Castle Street, Long Acre, London. A Conservative, upheld the supremacy of the Imperial Parliament; opposed to the disestablishment of the Church, to changes that may diminish the efficiency of voluntary schools, and to restrictions on the freedom of labour; in favour of Mr. Chaplin's bill for the creation of small holdings, etc. First elected for the Chertsey division of Surrey 3 Mar. 1892 and sat until he accepted Chiltern Hundreds in 1897. High Sheriff of Surrey 1929. Died 14 Aug. 1935. [1896]

COMMERELL, Admiral Sir John Edmund, V.C., G.C.B. 45 Rutland Gate, London. Alverbank, Alverstoke,

Hampshire. Carlton. Youngest s. of John Williams Commerell, Esq., of Stroud Park, Horsham. B. Jan. 1829; m. Matilda Maria, d. of J. Bushby, Esq., of St. Croix. He entered the navy 1842; served in the River Plate 1845-46; was Lieut. of H.M.S. *Vulture* in the Baltic, and served also in the Black Sea and Mediterranean during the Crimean War, for which service he received the Victoria Cross, 1855, etc. Subsequently served in the Chinese War, and in the Ashantee War, where he was severely wounded. Became civil C.B. 1866, military C.B. 1870; was appointed naval Aide-de-Camp to the Queen 1872, groom-in-waiting 1874, and a Junior Lord of the Admiralty Dec. 1879. In 1882 he was appointed Commander-in-Chief on the American and W. Indian stations. Was created K.C.B. 1874, G.C.B. 1887, and was a F.R.G.S., etc. A Conservative. Unsuccessfully contested Southampton in Apr. 1880. Sat for Southampton from 1885 until he accepted Chiltern Hundreds in 1888. Died 21 May 1901.   [1888]

COMMINS, Andrew. The Grange, West Derby. Eldon Chambers, Liverpool. National Liberal. 2nd s. of John Commins, Esq., of Ballybeg, Co. Carlow, by Catherine, d. of Laurence Fogarty, Esq., of Drummond, Co. Carlow. B. at Ballybeg 1832; m. 1885, his cousin, Jane W., d. of J. Neville, Esq., of Liverpool. Educ. successively at St. Patrick's Coll., Carlow, Queen's Coll., Cork, Queen's University, Ireland, where he graduated M.A., and University of London, where he graduated LL.D. Was called to the bar at Lincoln's Inn 1860, and joined the N. Circuit. A Liberal and Nationalist (Anti-Parnellite), in favour of the system of Home Rule for Ireland. Sat for the undivided Co. of Roscommon from 1880 to 1885, and for Roscommon S. from 1885 to 1892 when he was defeated. Sat for S.E. Cork from 28 June 1893 until he retired in 1900. Died 7 Jan. 1916.   [1900]

COMPTON, Lord Alwyne Frederick. 7 Balfour Place, Park Lane, London. Torloisk, Isle of Mull, N.B. Guards, Marlborough, and Turf. 3rd s. of 4th Marq. of Northampton, by Eliza, d. of Admiral the Hon. Sir George Elliot, K.C.B. B. 1855; m. 1886, Mary Evelyn, d. of R.C. De Grey Vyner, Esq., of Newby Hall, Ripon. Educ. at Eton. Joined the Grenadier Guards 1874, and transferred to 19th

Hussars in 1879. Was Aide-de-Camp to the Marq. of Ripon, Viceroy of India 1882-84, and served in the Sudan Expeditions, taking parts in the engagements of El Teb, Tamai, etc. 1884-85. Retired 1887. Raised Compton's Horse and served in the Imperial Yeomanry, S. Africa 1899-1902, and was mentioned in despatches; D.S.O. Lieut.-Col. Bedfordshire Yeomanry. A Dept.-Lieut. for Argyllshire. A Unionist. Sat for N. Bedfordshire from 1895-1906 when he was defeated. Elected for the Brentford division of Middlesex in Jan. 1910 and sat until he accepted Chiltern Hundreds in Mar. 1911. Died 16 Dec. 1911.   [1911]

COMPTON, Francis. 6a Victoria Street, London. Manor House, Minstead, Lyndhurst. Carlton, and United University. 7th s. of Henry Combe Compton, Esq., of Minstead Manor House, Hampshire, by Charlotte, d. of William Mills, Esq., of Bisterne, Hampshire. B. in London 1824. Educ. at Merton Coll., Oxford, and became a Fellow of All Soul's Coll. in 1846 ultimately becoming Senior Fellow. Was called to the bar at Lincoln's Inn and at the Middle Temple, Nov. 1850. A Conservative, opposed to the system called Home Rule as being "an attempt at the disintegration of the Empire", and in favour of land being "relieved from all undue burdens". Sat for Hampshire S. from Apr. 1880-Nov. 1885, and for the New Forest division of Hampshire from Nov. 1885 until he retired in 1892. Died 24 Oct. 1915.   [1892]

COMPTON, Henry Francis. Manor House, Minstead, Lyndhurst, Hampshire. Mapperton House, Beaminster, Dorset. Eld. s. of Henry Compton, Esq., of Minstead, Hampshire. B. 16 Jan. 1872; m. 1895, Dorothy, d. of Sir Richard Musgrave, Bart. A Conservative. Elected for the New Forest division of Hampshire in Dec. 1905 and sat until defeated Jan. 1906. Capt. Hampshire Royal Horse Artillery 1915-19. Died 11 Apr. 1943.

COMPTON, William George Spencer Scott-Compton, Earl. 51 Lennox Gardens, London. Compton Wynyates, Kineton. Travellers', St. James's, and Devonshire. S. of the Marq. of Northampton, and bro. of Lord Alwyne Frederick Compton. B. 23 Apr. 1851; m. 1884, the Hon. Mary Baring, d. of the 2nd Lord

73

Ashburton. Educ. at Eton, and Trinity Coll., Cambridge. He was in the diplomatic service from 1872 to 1880, at Paris, Rome, and St. Petersburg, in succession. In 1881 was attached to the Marq. of Northampton's special mission to Spain. In 1880-82 he acted as a Private Secretary to Earl Cowper when that nobleman was Lord Lieut. of Ireland. A Dept.-Lieut. for Warwickshire and a member of the London County Council until 1891. Afterwards elected an Alderman of the London County Council in place of Lord Hobhouse. A Liberal, in favour of Home Rule, etc. Unsuccessfully contested Warwickshire S. in Nov. 1884. Sat for the Stratford-on-Avon division of Warwickshire 1885-86, but was defeated there in July 1886, and was an unsuccessful candidate for the Holborn division of Finsbury in 1888. Sat for the Barnsley division of the W. Riding of Yorkshire from Mar. 1889 until he succeeded as 5th Marq. of Northampton on 11 Sept. 1897. He was styled as Lord William Compton from his father's succession to the Peerage in 1877 until his brothers death in 1887, and Earl Compton from 1887 until his own succession in 1897. K.G. 1908. Lord-Lieut. of Warwickshire 1912-13. Died 16 June 1913. [1897]

COMPTON-RICKETT, Rt. Hon. Sir Joseph. Continued in House after 1918: full entry in Volume III.

CONDON, Thomas Joseph. New Quay, Clonmel, Tipperary. S. of Jeremiah Condon, Esq., of Clonmel. B. 1850; m. 1875, Alice, d. of J. McGrath, Esq.; 2ndly, 1913, Jenny, d. of Jeremy Maloney, Esq., of Labesheeda. A Cattle Dealer and Victualler in Clonmel, where he was also a Town Commissioner and Poor Law Guardian. Was Mayor of Clonmel 1889 to 1891 and 1900-02, and Alderman from 1887. Member of Tipperary County Council. An "Irish Nationalist". Sat for Tipperary E. from 1885 until defeated in 1918. Unsuccessfully contested N. Roscommon in July 1895 whilst sitting for Tipperary E. [1918]

CONNOLLY, Laurence. Ellerslie, New Brighton, Cheshire. S. of Owen Connolly, Esq., Tenant Farmer, of Hazlehatch, Co. Dublin, by Alice, d. of James O'Brien, Esq., of the same place. B. 1833; m. 1859, d. of Thomas Stafford, Esq., of Wexford. A Fruit Broker and Merchant in Liverpool, as he once was in Dublin. and also proprietor of the aquarium at New Brighton. Was a member of the Liverpool City Council from 1875. An "Irish Nationalist". Sat for Longford S. from 1885 until he accepted Chiltern Hundreds in 1888. Died 4 Mar. 1908. [1888]

CONNOR, Charles Cunningham. 84 Sloane Street, London. Notting Hill House, Belfast. Lea Court, Bangor, Co. Down. Junior Carlton, and Constitutional. S. of Foster Connor, Esq., J.P. Belfast, and Margaret, d. of John Grogan, Esq., Glenbank, Belfast. B. 1842 in Belfast; m. 1873, Ellen, eld. d. of Dr. Bernard Lees. Educ. at the Royal Belfast Academical Institution, and Queen's University of Ireland (B.A. with first class honours). An Alderman and Harbour Commissioner of Belfast, and was Mayor 1889-91. A Fellow of the Chemical Society. A Conservative. Sat for the N. division of Antrim from July 1892 until he retired in 1895. Died some time after 1896. [1895]

CONWAY, Michael. 19 St. Alban's Place, Blackburn, Lancashire. 2nd s. of Edward Conway, Esq., of Tubbercurry, Sligo, by Margaret, d. of William Timlin, Esq., of Crossmolina, Sligo. B. 1844; m. Anne, only d. of Andrew Leonard, Esq., of Aclare, Co. Sligo. At the age of thirteen he became a pupil teacher at St. Anne's, Blackburn. Five years later he entered the St. Mary's Training Coll., Hammersmith, then under the care of the Rev. J.B. Rowe, of the Brompton Oratory. A Schoolmaster; also President of the Blackburn branch of the Irish National League. An "Irish Nationalist" of the Parnellite party. Sat for N. Leitrim from 1885 until he retired in 1892 and unsuccessfully contested Tipperary mid at the same time. [1892]

CONYBEARE, Charles Augustus Vansittart. 47 Halsey Street, London. Tregullow, Scorrier, Cornwall. Savile, and National Liberal. S. of J.C. Conybeare, Esq., of St. Leonard's Grange, Ingatestone, Essex. B. at Kew, June 1853. Educ. at Tonbridge and Christ Church, Oxford, B.A. 1876. Was called to the bar at Gray's Inn 1881, and practised on the S.E. Circuit. A member of the London School Board (Finsbury), and was an Honorary Secretary of the Social and Political Education League. Author of an edition of the Corrupt Practices Acts, and joint author of Conybeare and Andrew's Married Women's Property Acts. A Radical and "Home Ruler". Sat for the Camborne division of Cornwall from 1885 until defeated in 1895. Imprisoned under the Coercion Act for 3 months in 1889. Unsuccessfully contested St. Helens in 1900 and the Horncastle division of Lincolnshire in Jan. 1910. Author of legal treatises. Died 18 Feb. 1919.   [1895]

COOK, Edward Rider. Woodford, Essex. Reform, and City Liberal. S. of Edward Cook, Esq., of Hatfield Peverel, Essex, by Anne, d. of Henry Rider, Esq. B. in London 1836; m. 1st, 1860, Edith, d. of Thomas Piper, Esq., of Bishopgate Street; 2ndly, 1873, Ellen, d. of I. Leonard, Esq., of Bristol. Educ. at the City of London School and University Coll., London, where he took the 1st silver medal for practical, theoretical, and analytical chemistry. Head of the firm of Edward Cook and Company, of Bow, London, Soap-Makers and Chemical Manufacturers. A Fellow of the Chemical Society, J.P. for Middlesex, a member of the Metropolitan Board of Works from 1865, and a conservator of the River Lea. An "advanced Liberal". Sat for West Ham N. from Nov. 1885 until defeated in 1886 standing as a Gladstonian Liberal. Chairman of Annual Charcoal Company 1883-93, and of London Riverside Fish Market Company 1886-98. Magistrate for Essex, Middlesex and London. Died 21 Aug. 1898.   [1886]

COOK, Sir Frederick Lucas, Bart. 24 Hyde Park Gardens, London. Doughty House, Richmond. Montserrat, Cintra, Portugal. Carlton, Princes, Hurlingham, and Ranelagh. Eld. s. of Sir Frances Cook, 1st Bart., and his 1st wife, Emily, d. of Robert Lucas, Esq., of Lisbon. B. in London 1844; m. 1868, Mary Ann Elizabeth, d. of Dr. R. Payne Cotton, of Cavendish Square. Educ. at Harrow. A Partner in the firm of Cook, Son and Company, Warehousemen, of St. Paul's Churchyard; a Commissioner of Lieutenancy for London, F.R.G.S., etc. A Conservative, opposed to any Home Rule measure tending to the disintegration of the Empire, disestablishment of the Church, and the Local Veto Bill; in favour of Social Legislation, etc. Sat for the Kennington division of Lambeth from 1895 until defeated in 1906. Succeeded as Bart. in 1901. Visct.

Monserrate, in Peerage of Portugal. Died 21 May 1920.   [1905]

COOK, William Thomas Gustavus. Ashley House, Birchfields, Birmingham. Liberal. Reform, Birmingham. S. of Anselm Cook, Esq. B. at Kingscourt, Gloucestershire, 1834; m. 1857, d. of Edward Scambler, Esq., of Birmingham. Mr. Cook owed his position to his own ability and exertions: commencing work when eight years of age, he served his apprenticeship to the Pin and Wire trade. He afterwards commenced business on his own account as a Tack and Shoe-Rivet Manufacturer. In 1872 he became a Town Councillor of Birmingham, and he held, in that town the offices of Alderman, J.P., Chairman of the Health Committee, and Chairman of the Hospital Saturday Association, besides having served as Mayor in 1883-84. An advanced Liberal, opposed to the hereditary principle in legislation; in favour of absolutely free education, and of the Disestablishment of the National Church. Returned for the E. division of Birmingham Nov. 1885 and sat until he was defeated in 1886 standing as a Gladstonian Liberal. Unsuccessfully contested the Bordesley division of Birmingham in July 1895. Knighted 1906. Died 26 Jan. 1908.   [1886]

COOKE, Charles Wallwyn Radcliffe. 13 Richmond Road, Bayswater, London. Hellens, Much Marcle, Herefordshire. St. Stephen's. S. of Robert Duffield Cooke, Esq., of Hellens, Herefordshire. B. 1841; m. 1st, 1876, Frances Parnther, d. of the Rev. J.H. Broome, Vicar of Houghton, Norfolk (she died 1891); 2ndly, 1893, Katharine, youngest d. of George Coles, Esq., of Romsey, Hampshire. Educ. at Emmanuel Coll., Cambridge, where he was a scholar of his Coll. and gained the Le Bas and Burney University prizes (twice). Called to the bar at Lincoln's Inn 1872, and joined the Oxford Circuit. Was one of the founders of the Constitutional Union, and gave much attention to questions affecting friendly societies. Author of a work on the Agricultural Holdings Act of 1875, and also of *Four Years in Parliament with Hard Labour*. A J.P. and Dept.-Lieut. for Herefordshire; and President of the Herefordshire Chamber of Agriculture, and for two years Chairman of the Ledbury Highway Board. A Conservative. Sat for W. Newington from 1885 until he

75

retired in 1892. First elected for Hereford Aug. 1893 and sat until he retired in 1900. President and Founder of National Association of English Cider Makers. Died 26 May 1911. [1900]

COOPE, Octavius Edward. MP until his death in 1886: full entry in Volume I.

COOPER, Capt. Bryan Ricco. Mackree Castle, Collooney, Ireland. Carlton. S. of Maj. E.E. Cooper, R.F.A., and Ella, d. of Maj.-Gen. M.M. Prendergast, Indian Army. B. 17 June 1884 at Jutogh, Simla, India. Educ. at Eton, and Royal Military Academy, Woolwich. Was Lieut. Royal Field Artillery 1903-06 and Capt. Sligo Artillery (M.) 1906. A Unionist. Elected for Co. Dublin S. in Jan. 1910 and sat until defeated in Dec. 1910. President Junior Branch Irish Unionist Alliance 1912-14; served at Gallipoli and on Salonika Front; Press Censor in Ireland 1919; returned as Independent to the *Dail Eireann* in 1923, and continued as T.D. until his death 5 July 1930. [1910]

COOPER, George J. 92 Southwark Park Road, London. B. 1844. Educ. at Leeds Grammar School. A Doctor, practised in Bermondsey. Member of the London County Council 1889-1906. Was Chairman of Public Health Committee. A J.P. for London. A Liberal. Elected for the Bermondsey division of Southwark in 1906 and sat until his death 7 Oct. 1909. [1909]

COOPER, Sir Richard Ashmole, Bart. Continued in House after 1918: full entry in Volume III.

COOTE, Capt. Colin Reith. Continued in House after 1918: full entry in Volume III.

COOTE, Thomas. Ambury House, Huntingdon. Devonshire, National Liberal, and Eighty. S. of Thomas Coote, Esq., J.P. of Oaklands St. Ives, Huntingdonshire, and Lisle House, Bournemouth, Hampshire. B. 1850; m. 1878, Elizabeth Pauline, d. of George Newton Day, Esq., of St. Ives, Huntingdon. Educ. privately. A Colliery Factor at St. Ives, Cambridge and other places. A Liberal. Unsuccessfully contested Cambridgeshire in Mar. 1884. Sat for the Huntingdon division of Huntingdonshire from Nov. 1885 until defeated in 1886 standing as a Gladstonian Liberal. [1886]

COOTE, William. Continued in House after 1918: full entry in Volume III.

CORBET, William Joseph. Spring Farm, Delgany, Co. Wicklow. 3rd s. of Robert Corbet, Esq., of Ballykaneen, Queen's Co., by Alice, youngest d. of John Mulhall, Esq., of Clonaslee, Queen's Co. B. at Clonaslee 1825; m. 1st, 1865, Elizabeth, d. of Richard Jennings, Esq. (she died 1870); 2ndly, 1890, Marie, d. of David Fitzhenry, Esq. Educ. privately, and at Broadwood Academy, Lancashire. Published a work entitled *What is Home Rule?*, also poems and articles, statistics of insanity, etc. A Parnellite, in favour of Home Rule for Ireland, perfect equality in education for all religious denominations in Ireland, and such an amendment of the Land Laws as would ultimately establish a "peasant proprietary". Also of the Irish franchise being placed on the same footing as that of England. Sat for the undivided county of Wicklow from 1880 to 1885 and for Wicklow E. from 1885 to 1892, when he was defeated; re-elected there in 1895 and sat until he retired in 1900. Died 1 Dec. 1909. [1900]

CORBETT, Archibald Cameron. 26 Hans Place, London. Rowallan, Kilmaurs, Ayrshire. Brooks's. 2nd s. of Thomas Corbett, Esq., of South Park Cove, Dumbartonshire, and Sarah, d. of A. Cameron, Esq., of Edinburgh. B. 23 May 1856; m. 1887, Alice Mary, d. of John Polson, Esq., of Castle Lovan, near Greenock, N.B. (she died 1902). Educ. by private tuition. A J.P. for Warwickshire and Lanarkshire. A Liberal. Unsuccessfully contested N. Warwickshire in 1884. First returned for the Tradeston division of Glasgow in 1885 and joined the Liberal Unionists in 1886 but resigned the Whip over Free Trade in Aug. 1909 and was re-elected as an Independent Liberal Free Trader in Jan. 1910 defeating the Unionist and Liberal candidates. He rejoined the Liberal Party during the 1910 Parliament and was elected as a Liberal in Dec. 1910 and continued to represent the Tradeston division of Glasgow until created Baron Rowallon on 27 June 1911. Died 19 Mar. 1833. [1911]

CORBETT, Charles Joseph Henry. Woodgate, Danehill, Sussex. 75 Victoria

Street, London. 2 Harcourt Buildings, Temple, London. S. of Charles Joseph Corbett, Esq., and Lizzie, d. of P.H. Byrne, Esq. B. 6 July 1853; m. 1881, Marie, d. of George Gray, Esq. Educ. at Marlborough and New Coll., Oxford; M.A., B.C.L. A Barrister; J.P. for Sussex. A Liberal. Unsuccessfully contested the East Grinstead division of Sussex in 1895 and 1900. Elected for this division in 1906 and sat until defeated in Jan. 1910. Died 20 Nov. 1935.   [1909]

CORBETT, John. 20 Hertford Street, London. Impney, Droitwich. Ynys-y-maengwyn, Towyn, Merionethshire. Reform, and Gresham. Eld. s. of Joseph Corbett, Esq., of Shropshire. B. 1817; m. 1856, Anna Eliza, d. of John O'Meara, Esq., of the Co. of Tipperary. A Proprietor of the Stoke Prior Salt Works, Worcestershire. A Magistrate for the counties of Worcester and Merioneth, and a Dept.-Lieut. for the latter. Patron of 2 livings. An "Independent Liberal" and Unionist, in favour of the re-adjustment of local taxation, so as to reduce the "heavy burdens on land"; also of the amendment of the laws relating to the tenure of land. Unsuccessfully contested Droitwich in 1868. Sat for Droitwich from Feb. 1874 until he retired in 1892. Died 22 Apr. 1901. [1892]

CORBETT, Thomas Lorimer. 57 Warwick Square, London. Carlton, and Constitutional. S. of Thomas Corbett, Esq., of South Park, Cove, Dumbartonshire, and Sarah, d. of A. Cameron, Esq., of Edinburgh. B. in Glasgow 1854; m. d. of John Connell, Esq., of Bushey Down, Tooting Common. Educ. privately. A member of the London County Council; Whip of Moderate party for many years; Dept.-Chairman 1899. A Conservative. Contested Tyrone E. July 1892, and again in July 1895. Unsuccessfully contested Down N. Sept. 1898. Sat for Down N. from 1900 until his death 6 Apr. 1910.   [1909]

CORNWALL, Sir Edwin Andrew. Continued in House after 1918: full entry in Volume III.

CORNWALLIS, Fiennes Stanley Wykeham. Linton Park, Maidstone. Carlton, Junior Carlton, and Bachelors'. Eld. s. of Maj. Fiennes Cornwallis, of the 4th Light Dragoons (s. of Charles Wykeham Martin, Esq., of Leeds Castle),

by Harriet Elizabeth, d. of J.T. Mott, Esq., of Birmingham Hall, Norfolk. B. 1864; m. 1886, Mabel, d. of P.O. Leigh, Esq., of Belmont, Cheshire. Educ. at Eton. In 1883, on the death of Viscountess Holmesdale, he inherited the property of his great-grandfather, the last Earl Cornwallis. Dept.-Lieut. and J.P. for Kent, and Honorary Maj. in the W. Kent Yeomanry, Patron of 2 livings. A Conservative, in favour of a progressive administration of home affairs. Sat for Maidstone from 1888 to 1895, when he retired; re-elected there 1898 and sat until defeated in 1900. President Royal Agricultural Society 1906; Chairman Kent Co. Council 1910-30. Created Baron Cornwallis in 1927. Died 26 Sept. 1935.   [1900]

CORRY, Sir James Porter, Bart. 10 Gledhow Gardens, London. Dunraven, Belfast. Carlton. S. of Robert Corry, Esq., Merchant, by Jane, youngest d. of James Porter, Esq., of Ballyrussell, Co. Down. B. at Newtownards, Co. Down 1826; m. 1849, Margaret, youngest d. of William Service, Esq., Merchant of Glasgow, and was left a widower in 1869. A Ship-Owner and Merchant at Belfast. A Magistrate for Co. Antrim and Belfast, and was created a Bart. in 1885. A Conservative. Sat for Belfast from Feb. 1874 to Nov. 1885. At the general election of 1885 he unsuccessfully contested Belfast E., but on 1 Feb. 1886, on the death of Prof. J. McKane, he was elected for mid Armagh, and sat until his death 28 Nov. 1891.   [1891]

CORY, Sir Clifford John, Bart. Continued in House after 1918: full entry in Volume III.

CORY, James Herbert. Continued in House after 1918: full entry in Volume III.

COSGRAVE, William Thomas. Continued in House after 1918: full entry in Volume III.

COSGROVE, James. A Nationalist. Elected for E. Galway on the death of Mr. Roche, Dec. 1914 and sat until he retired in 1918.   [1918]

COSSHAM, Handel. Weston Park, Bath. Holly Lodge, Bristol. National Liberal. Only s. of Jesse Cossham, Esq., of Bristol. B. Thornbury, near Bristol 1824; m. 1848, Elizabeth, d. of William Wethered, Esq., of

Little Marlow, Buckinghamshire. In 1845 was appointed Manager of the Yate Collieries, and in 1851 became a Colliery Proprietor near Kingswood. Was Mayor of Bath 1882-83, and again 1884-85. Was also a member of the town council of Bristol. A F.G.S., and wrote various pamphlets, etc. A Liberal, in favour of Home Rule. Unsuccessfully contested Nottingham, May 1866, Dewsbury Nov. 1868, and Chippenham in Feb. 1874. Sat for Bristol E. from 1885 until his death 23 Apr. 1890.   [1890]

COTTON, Col. Edward Thomas Davenant. See COTTON-JODRELL, Col. Edward Thomas Davenant.

COTTON, Harry Evan Auguste. c/o National Bank of India, 26 Bishopsgate, London. S. of Sir Henry Cotton, K.C.S.I. B. in Midnapore, Bengal 27 May 1868; m. 1896, Nora, d. of William Henry Grimley, Esq. of the Bengal Civil Service. Educ. at Mont Liban School, Pau, Sherborne, and Jesus Coll., Oxford; open scholar, 2nd class classical moderations, 2nd class history final school, 2nd class jurisprudence. Called to the bar at Lincoln's Inn in 1898, and practised at the Calcutta bar for thirteen years. Secretary and Treasurer in succession, of Oxford Union Society. Acted as special correspondent of the *Manchester Guardian* at Delhi Coronation Durbar 1903 and subsequently as Calcutta correspondent of the *Daily News*; member of the Calcutta Corporation from 1900-06. Member of London County Council (P.) for E. Finsbury from 1910-19. Progressive Whip on the London County Council from 1911-14; Dept.-Chairman of the Council 1914-15; Chairman Hanwell Asylum Management Committee 1915-22; Chairman Establishment Committee 1917-19; member of the London Insurance Committee 1914-22; Chairman Establishment Sub Committee for three years; member of the governing body of London School of Oriental Studies, and Chairman Library Committee 1916-22; Honorary Secretary Indian Reforms Committee; served on Advisory Committee at the India Office in Connection with the Government of India Act 1919; member of Indian Historical Records Commission (Chairman, 1923-25); Vice-President Calcutta Historical Society; Trustee of Victoria Memorial Hall, Calcutta. Author of *The Century in India 1800-1900, Calcutta, Old and New,* a historical and descriptive guide-book to

the city; annotated edition (with J. Macfarlane), of *Hartley House, Calcutta,* a novel of the days of Warren Hastings, *Murray's Handbook to India* (13th and 14th editions), and numerous newspaper articles on political and literary subjects. A Liberal. Unsuccessfully contested the Dulwich division of Camberwell in Jan. 1910. Prospective candidate for the Harrow division of Middlesex from 1912-15. Sat for E. Finsbury from July-Nov. 1918. Unsuccessfully contested Finsbury in Dec. 1918. County Alderman from 1919-22; C.I.E. 1921; President of Bengal Legislature 1922-25; Knighted 1925. Died 7 Mar. 1939.

COTTON, Sir Henry John Stedman. 45 St. John's Wood Park, London. Savile, and National Liberal. S. of J.J. Cotton, Esq., Madras Civil Service. B. 13 Sept. 1845; m. 1867, Mary, d. of James Ryan, Esq., of Limerick. Educ. at Magdalen Coll. School, and King's Coll., London. Entered the Indian Civil Service 1867; Under Secretary to Government 1873; Registrar of High Court 1874; Magistrate and Commissioner 1878-80; Secretary to Board of Revenue 1880-86; Commissioner of Police and Chairman of Calcutta Corporation 1887; Chief Secretary to Government 1891-96; Chief Commissioner of Assam 1896-1902; retired 1902. C.S.I. 1892. K.C.S.I. 1902. Author of *New India,* and other works on Indian affairs. A Liberal. Elected for E. Nottingham in 1906 and sat until defeated Jan. 1910. Died 22 Oct. 1915.   [1909]

COTTON, William Francis. Hollywood, Roebuck, Co. Dublin. Royal Automobile. B. 1841 at Dublin. Educ. in Dublin. Chairman of Alliance Gas Company, and A. Findlater and Company, and a Director of Dublin United Tramways Company, and other companies. An Alderman of Dublin Corporation; Lord Mayor 1911. A Nationalist. Unsuccessfully contested S. Co. Dublin in Jan. 1910. Elected for S. Co. Dublin in Dec. 1910 and sat until his death 8 June 1917.   [1917]

COTTON-JODRELL, Col. Edward Thomas Davenant. Reaseheath Hall, Nantwich, Shallcross Manor, Derbyshire. Carlton. S. of the Rt. Rev. G.E. Lynch Cotton, Bishop of Calcutta, by Sophia Anne, d. of the Rev. H. Tomkinson, of Reaseheath, Nantwich. B. at Rugby 1847; m. 1878, Mary Rennell, d. of William R.

Coleridge, Esq., of Salston, Ottery St. Mary. Educ. at Rugby, Marlborough, and the Royal Military Academy. Entered the Royal Artillery 1868, and retired as Capt. 1881. A J.P. for Cheshire; and Hon. Col. commanding 2nd Cheshire Engineers (Railway) Volunteers. He assumed the additional name of Jodrell by Royal licence in 1890. C.B. 1902. A Conservative. Sat for the Wirral division of Cheshire from 1885 until he retired in 1900. Unsuccessfully contested the Eddisbury division of Cheshire in Jan. 1906. Military Staff Office 1906-12; K.C.B. 1911. Died 13 Oct. 1917. [1900]

COURTHOPE, Maj. George Loyd. Continued in House after 1918: full entry in Volume III.

COURTNEY, Rt. Hon. Leonard Henry. 15 Cheyne Walk, Chelsea, London. Reform, and Athenaeum. S. of John S. Courtney, Esq., of Alverton House, Penzance, by Sarah, d. of John Mortimer, Esq. B. at Penzance 1832; m. 1883, Catherine, d. of R. Potter, Esq., of Standish House, Gloucestershire. Educ. at St. John's Coll., Cambridge, of which he became a Fellow. Called to the bar at Lincoln's Inn 1858; bencher 1889. Was Professor of Political Economy at University Coll., London 1872 to 1875 and Examiner in Constitutional History in the University of London 1873-75. Was Under-Secretary of State for the Home Department Dec. 1880 to Aug. 1881 and Colonial Under Secretary Aug. 1881 to May 1882, when he was appointed Financial Secretary to the Treasury. The latter office he resigned in 1884, in order to advocate Proportional Representation as opposed to the single seat system of the Redistribution Bill. Was Chairman of Committees and Dept. Speaker 1886 to 1892. President Royal Statistical Society, and a large contributor to the periodical press in London. An advanced Liberal, opposed to Mr. Gladstone's Home Rule scheme. Unsuccessfully contested Liskeard in 1874; sat for Liskeard from 1876-85. Sat for the Bodmin division of Cornwall from 1885 until he retired in 1900. He resigned from the Liberal Unionist Party over Boer War Policy in Oct. 1899. Later he rejoined the Liberal Party and unsuccessfully contested Edinburgh W. in 1906. PC. 1889. Frequent contributor to *The Times* and *Nineteenth Century*. Created 1st Baron Courtney of

Penwith in 1906. Died 11 May 1918. [1900]

COWAN, Sir William Henry. Continued in House after 1918: full entry in Volume III.

COWELL-STEPNEY, Sir Emile Algernon Arthur Keppel, Bart. The Dell, Llanelly, South Wales. Travellers'. S. of Sir John Stepney Cowell-Stepney, 1st Bart., who represented the Carmarthen district from 1868 to 1874, and who in 1856 assumed by Royal licence the additional surname of Stepney, by his 2nd wife, Euphemia, d. of Gen. John Murray, of Clonalla, Co. Donegal. B. 1834 at Mannheim, Germany; m. 1875, Hon. Margaret Leicester Warren, youngest d. of the 2nd Baron de Tabley. Educ. at Eton. Was for 20 years a clerk in the Foreign Office, and was attached to the special mission of the Earl of Clarendon to Berlin at the coronation of the King of Prussia, 1861. Succeeded as Bart. 1877. A J.P. for Carmarthenshire, and was High Sheriff of the Co. in 1884. A Liberal. Unsuccessfully contested Carmarthen district in 1874. Elected for Carmarthen district in Aug. 1876, sat until he retired May 1878. When elected was in favour of Mr. Gladstone's Home Rule Bill. Again returned for Carmarthen district July 1886 and sat until he retired in 1892, having joined the Liberal Unionist Party in 1891. Died 3 July 1909. [1892]

COWEN, Joseph. Retired in 1886: full entry in Volume I.

COX, Harold. 6 Raymond Buildings, Grays Inn, London. National Liberal. S. of Homersham Cox, Esq., County Court Judge. B. 1859; m. 1890, Helen, d. of George Clegg, Esq. Educ. at Tonbridge School, and Jesus Coll., Cambridge. A Journalist; Secretary of Cobden Club 1899-1904; Professor of Mathematics at Mahommedan Coll., Aligarh 1885-87; author of a work on Land Nationalization and various political pamphlets. A Liberal. Elected for Preston in 1906, but because of his criticisms of the Liberal Government's social policy the Preston Liberal Association refused to readopt him so he left the Liberal Party and unsuccessfully contested, as a Free Trade candidate, Preston in Jan. 1910 and Cambridge University in Feb. 1911. Alderman London County Council 1910-12; editor of

Edinburgh Review, 1912-19; member of Bryce Commission on German Outrages 1915. Honorary Fellow of Jesus Coll., Cambridge. Died 1 May 1936.   [1909]

COX, Irwin Edward Bainbridge. Moat Mount, Mill Hill, Middlesex. Carlton, and New Oxford & Cambridge. Eld. s. of Mr. E.W. Cox of Moat Mount, Mill Hill, MP for Taunton, Dept. Assistant Judge, Middlesex Sessions, etc., and Sophia, d. of W.H. Harris, Esq., M.D. B. 1838 at Taunton; m. 1865, Katharine, d. of the Rev. B. Nicols, Vicar of Mill Hill (she died 1898). Educ. at Magdalene Coll., Cambridge. Called to the bar at the Middle Temple 1864. Senior Proprietor of the *Field, Queen, Law Times*, and other papers. Dept.-Lieut. for Middlesex, High Sheriff 1898-99, and Chairman Petty Sessional division of Gore, Middlesex; member of Middlesex County Council, Alderman 1901. A Conservative, and strong supporter of Mr. Balfour's Government. Elected for the Harrow division of Middlesex in 1899 and sat until he retired in 1906. Wrote books on angling and shooting. Died 27 Aug. 1922.   [1905]

COX, Joseph Richard. 95 Warwick Street, London. 45 Stephen's Green, Dublin. Hielsgrove Lodge, Kilmore, Co. Roscommon. Catholic Club, O'Connel Street, Dublin. S. of Hugh Cox. Esq., Farmer, of Kilmore, Co. Roscommon, by Anne, d. of Richard Kelly, Esq., J.P. of Leahey, Co. Roscommon. B. at Kilmore, Co. Roscommon 1852. Educ. at St. Mels Coll., Longford. Was Private Secretary to the Lord Mayors of Dublin of 1884 and 1885. An "Irish Nationalist" of the anti-Parnellite party. Sat for Clare E. from the general election of 1885 until defeated in 1892. London Agent of a Wine Company about 1889-92; a Director of the Wine Company from Aug. 1892 to Nov. 1893. Declared bankrupt 18 May 1894. Died 1894.   [1892]

COX, Robert. 14 Grosvenor Crescent, London. 34 Drumsheugh Gardens, Edinburgh. Devonshire, and Royal Societies. University Club, Edinburgh. S. of George Cox, Esq., of Gorgie, Edinburgh, and Isabella, d. of R. Craig, Esq., Surgeon, of Peebles. B. 1845 at Gorgie; m. 1875, Harriet, d. of Professor J. Hughes Bennett. Educ. at Loretto, and the Universities of St. Andrew's and Edinburgh (M.A. St. Andrews). A Manufacturer. A J.P. for Mid-

Lothian and Dept.-Lieut. for the Co. of Edinburgh, Co. Councillor, F.R.S. Edinburgh, F.S.A. Scotland, etc. A Liberal Unionist, also in favour of Imperial Federation, Free Trade with our Colonies etc. Was an unsuccessful candidate in the Kirkcaldy district 11 Mar. 1892. Sat for Edinburgh S. from July 1895 until his death 2 June 1899.   [1899]

COZENS-HARDY, Herbert Hardy. 50 Ladbroke Grove, London. 7 New Square, Lincoln's Inn, London. Letheringsett Hall, Norfolk. Reform. S. of W.H. Cozens-Hardy, Esq., J.P. of Letheringsett Hall, Norfolk, by Sarah, d. of Thomas Theobald, Esq., of Norwich. B. 1838; m. 1866, Maria, d. of Thomas Hepburn, Esq., J.P., of Clapham Common (she died 1886). Educ. at Amersham School, and University Coll., London. Was called to the bar at Lincoln's Inn in 1862, became a Q.C. in 1882, and a bencher of his Inn in 1885. A Fellow of University Coll., and Chairman of the Gen. Council of the bar. A Liberal, in favour of Home Rule, "prepared to extend the Sunday Closing Acts to England", and in favour of "a change in the constitution of the House of Lords." Sat for Norfolk N. from 1885, until appointed Judge in 1899; Knighted in 1899. Judge of Chancery Division 1899-1901. PC. 1901. Lord Justice of Appeal 1901-07. Master of the Rolls 1907-18. Created 1st Baron Cozens-Hardy in 1914. Died 18 June 1920. [1899]

CRAIG, Charles Curtis. Continued in House after 1918: full entry in Volume III.

CRAIG, Ernest. Continued in House after 1918: full entry in Volume III.

CRAIG, Herbert James. 11 Priors Terrace, Tynemouth. Audley House, Margaret Street, London. Reform. S. of James Craig, Esq., MP for Newcastle-on-Tyne, and Kate Sophia Hould, of Wanstead. B. 30 Sept. 1869 at Tynemouth; m. 1909, Elsie, d. of Col. F.M. Rundall, C.B., D.S.O. Educ. at Rugby, and Trinity Coll., Cambridge; LL.B. Called to the bar at the Inner Temple 1892. A Partner of Borries, Craig and Company, Newcastle-on-Tyne. Commander Royal Naval Volunteers, Tyneside Division. J.P. for Northumberland. Member of Royal Commission on Delay in King's Bench Division. A Liberal. Elected for Tynemouth in 1906 and sat until defeated in 1918. Defeated again in Tynemouth in 1922. Commander of Tyne Royal Naval Volunteers 1920-20. Died 18 Mar. 1934. [1918]

CRAIG, James. Tynemouth, Northumberland. S. of Thomas Craig, Esq., Brushmaker, by Elizabeth Jobling. B. 1834; m. 1st, 1858, Annie Eliza, d. of Joseph Jordan, Esq., of Hornsey; 2ndly, 1865, Kate Sophia, d. of James Hould, Esq., of Wanstead. Educ. at St. Thomas's School, Newcastle-on-Tyne. A Merchant in Newcastle-on-Tyne from 1857. A Liberal, strongly supporting Mr. Gladstone's Home Rule policy. First returned for Newcastle-upon-Tyne July 1886 and sat until defeated in 1892. Defeated again at Newcastle-on-Tyne in 1895. Died 28 Aug. 1902. [1892]

CRAIG, Lieut.-Col. Sir James, Bart. Craigavon, Co. Down. Cleve Court, Streatley-on-Thames, Berkshire. 6 Victoria Square, London. Carlton, and Constitutional. S. of James Craig, Esq., of Craigavon, Co. Down. B. 8 Jan. 1871; m. 1905, Cecil Mary Nowell Dering, d. of Sir Daniel Tupper, M.V.O. Served in S. Africa 1900-02; D.L. (Co. Down); Treasurer of the Household Dec. 1916 to Jan. 1918. Parliamentary Secretary to Ministry of Pensions Jan. 1919 to Apr. 1920; Parliamentary and Financial Secretary to the Admiralty Apr. 1920-June 1921. Created Bart. 1918. A Unionist. Unsuccessfully contested Fermanagh N. Mar. 1903. Sat for E. Down 1906-18 and for mid Down from 1918 until he resigned in June 1921. PC. (Ireland) 1921 and PC. (Northern Ireland) 1922. Sat for County Down in the Parliament of Northern Ireland. Honorary LL.D. Queens University Belfast 1922. Honorary D.C.L. Oxford 1926. Created Visct. Craigavon 1927. Prime Minister of Northern Ireland from June 1921 until his death on 24 Nov. 1940. [1921]

CRAIG, Norman Carlyle. 1 Harley Street, London. Fairfield House, St. Peter's, Thanet. 10 King's Bench Walk, Temple, London. Carlton, Royal Thames Yacht, and St. Stephen's. S. of William Simpson Craig, Esq., M.D., of Ham Common, Surrey. B. 15 Nov. 1868; m. 9 Nov. 1918, Dorothy, widow of Lieut. A.W. Stone, R.N.V.R., and d. of Mr. & Mrs. E.S. Eccles, of Hoylake. Educ. at Bedford, and Peterhouse, Cambridge; Classical Scholar and Prizeman, M.A. Was called to the bar

1892; K.C. 1909; bencher of the Inner Temple 1919. Sub-Lieut. R.N.R. Sept. 1914; Lieut. Commander R.N.V.R. Apr. 1915. A Unionist. Elected for the Isle of Thanet division of Kent in Jan. 1910 and sat until his death 14 Oct. 1919. [1919]

CRAIG, Robert Hunter. West Park, Skelmorlie, Ayrshire. Reform. Youngest s. of James Craig and Margaret Brown, of Gowanbank, Partick. B. in Partick 1839; m. 1st, 1864, Jessie, d. of R. Simpson, Esq., of Glasgow (she died 1880); 2ndly, 1884, Sarah Elizabeth, d. of William Foster, Esq., of Goodmanham, Yorkshire. Educ. at Partick and Glasgow Academy. Founder and Chairman of R. Hunter Craig and Company Limited, Produce Importers of Liverpool and London; took a great interest in religious temperance, and philanthropic work in Glasgow and surroundings. A Director of the Scottish Temperance Assurance Company Limited, and of the Glasgow Chamber of Commerce. A J.P. for Ayrshire and Lanarkshire. A Liberal. Elected for the Govan district of Lanarkshire in 1900 and sat until he retired in 1906. Died 12 Aug. 1913. [1905]

CRAIG-SELLAR, Alexander. See SELLAR, Alexander Craig.

CRAIK, Rt. Hon. Sir Henry. Continued in House after 1918: full entry in Volume III.

CRANBORNE, James Edward Hubert Gascoyne Cecil, Visct. 24 Grafton Street, London. Carlton, Athenaeum, and Travellers'. Eld. s. of the Marq. of Salisbury, K.G., by Georgina, d. of Sir Edward Alderson. B. in London 1861; m. 1887, Alice, 2nd d. of the Earl of Arraan. Educ. at Eton, and University Coll., Oxford; B.A. 1884. Lieut.-Col. 4th Battalion Bedfordshire Regiment, and Honorary Col. 1st Battalion Essex Regiment; Vice-Chairman Convocation (House of Laymen). Appointed Under-Secretary for Foreign Affairs 1900-03. A Conservative. Sat for the Darwen division of Lancashire from 1885 to the general election of 1892, when he was defeated. Elected for Rochester on Mr. Alderman Davies being unseated on petition 1893 and sat until he succeeded as Marq. of Salisbury in 1903. PC. 1903. Lord Privy Seal 1903-05; President of the Board of Trade 1905. Achieved debating prominence in opposition to the 1909 Budget.

With Lord Halsbury led the "Die-Hard" opposition to the reform of the House of Lords 1910-11. Served with reserve Battalions in England 1914-18. Chairman of tribunal for concientious objectors 1916. Opposed the Irish Treaty of 1921. A major figure behind the destruction of Lloyd George's coalition in 1922. Chancellor of the Duchy of Lancaster and Lord President 1922-23, and Lord Privy Seal again from 1924-29. Leader of Conservative Party in the House of Lords after Curzon's death in 1925 until resignation in June 1931, to avoid membership of the National Government formed in Aug. by MacDonald. Associated with Churchill in 1930s over India and National Defence. President of National Union of Conservative and Unionist Associations 1942-45. Died 4 Apr. 1947. [1903]

CRAVEN, Joseph. Hotel Metropole, London. Ashfield, Thornton, Nr. Bradford. S. of Joshua Craven, Esq., Spinner and Manufacturer, of Prospect House, Thornton. B. 1825; m. d. of Jonathan Knowles, Esq., of Denholme Brewery. Joined his father in the business of Worsted Spinning etc., but retired in 1875. A Gov. of Thornton Grammar School, of the Crossley Orphanage, and of Airedale Coll. Also a member of the School Board of Thornton, and of the Council of the Chamber of Commerce of Bradford. A Liberal and Home Ruler. Sat for the Shipley division of the W. Riding of Yorkshire from 1885 until he retired in 1892. Died 1914. [1892]

CRAWFORD, Donald. 60 Pall Mall, London. Brooks's, Oxford & Cambridge, and National Liberal. New, and Scottish Liberal, Edinburgh. S. of Alexander Crawford, Esq., of Aros, Argyllshire, by Sibella, d. of Donald Maclean, Writer to the Signet. B. in Edinburgh 1837; m. 1stly, 1881, Virginia, d. of Eustace Smith, Esq., but divorced her in 1886 citing Sir Charles Dilke as co-respondent; 2ndly, 1914, Hon. Lilian, d. of 3rd Lord Moncreiff. Educ. at Edinburgh Academy, the University of Glasgow, Balliol Coll., Oxford, and the University of Heidelberg. Was elected a Fellow of Lincoln Coll., Oxford in 1861 and became an Advocate at the Scottish bar in 1862. From 1880 to 1885 he was Legal Secretary to the Lord Advocate of Scotland, under Mr. Gladstone's Government, a member of the Royal Commis-

sion on the Scottish Universities. A Liberal, in favour of Home Rule. Sat for Lanarkshire N.E. from 1885 until he was appointed Sheriff of Aberdeen, Kincardine, and Banff in June 1895. Retired 1911. Dept. Chairman of Fishery Board for Scotland 1897. K.C. 1903. Died 1 Jan. 1919. [1895]

CRAWFORD, Robert Gordon Sharman. See SHARMAN-CRAWFORD, Robert Gordon. Continued in House after 1918: full entry in Volume III.

CRAWFORD, William. 15 North Road, Durham. S. of William Crawford, Esq., a working Miner. B. at Whitley, Northumberland 1833; m. Sarah Ann, d. of John and Mary Townson, of Tamworth. Educ. at Seaton Sluice School, and for many years worked as a Miner. Was corresponding Secretary of the Durham Miners' Association. Alderman, Durham County Council. A Liberal, in favour of a measure of independent self-government for Ireland. Sat for the mid division of Durham from 1885 until his death 1 July 1890. [1890]

CRAWSHAY-WILLIAMS, Eliot. 5 Aubrey Road, Holland Park, London. Coed-y-Mwstwr, Bridgend, Glamorgan. National Liberal, Brooks's, Eighty, and Junior Naval & Military S. of Arthur J. Williams, MP for S. Glamorgan, and Rose Harriette, d. of Robert Crawshay. B. 4 Sept. 1879 in London; m. 1908 Alice, d. of James Gay Roberts, Esq. Educ. at Eton, and Trinity Coll., Oxford. Was Assistant Private Secretary to Mr. W. Churchill at the Colonial Office 1906-08, and was Parliamentary Private Secretary to Mr. Lloyd George, Chancellor of the Exchequer, from 1910. Joined Royal Field Artillery 1900, resigned commission 1903. Capt. Royal Horse Artillery North Midland Mounted Brigade (T.). Author of *Across Persia, Problems of To-day, Simple Story* (autobiography) (1935), and many other plays and books. A Liberal. Unsuccessfully contested the Chorley division of Lancashire in 1906. Elected for Leicester Jan. 1910 and sat until he accepted Chiltern Hundreds in June 1913. F.R.G.S Served in Middle East 1915-17; attached H.Q. Northern Command 1918-20; Lecturer to H.M. Forces 1943-45. Prolific author up to 1953. Died 11 May 1962. [1913]

CREAN, Eugene. 3 Douglas Street, Cork. B. 1856. A member of Cork Town Council. Secretary to one of the Irish Labour Organisations; was President of the Cork Trades Council, and was Mayor of Cork 1899. A Nationalist. Sat for the Ossory division of Queen's Co. from 1892-1900. First elected for S.E. Cork in 1900 and sat until he retired in 1918. Died 12 Jan. 1939. [1918]

CREMER, Sir William Randal. 11 Lincoln's Inn Fields, London. S. of G.M. Cremer, Esq., of Fareham, Hampshire, a Herald Painter. B. 1838; m. 1st, Charlotte, eld. d. of James Wilson, Esq., of Spalding; 2ndly, Lucy, d. of J. Coombes, Esq., of Oxford, but left a widower for the 2nd time in 1884. Educ. at the National School. Editor and Publisher of the *Arbitrator*, and Secretary to the International Arbitration League; founder of the Amalgamated Society of Carpenters. Four times visited the United States with memorials from British MPs. to Congress in favour of a Treaty of Arbitration. In 1890 the President of the French Republic conferred upon him the Cross of the Legion of Honour. Founded the Inter-Parliamentary Union. Gained the Gold Medal and Nobel Peace Prize 1903, of nearly £8,000, which he gave as an endowment to the International Arbitration League. Knighted 1907. A Liberal and Labour Member. Unsuccessfully contested Warwick 1868 and 1874. Sat for the Haggerston division of Shoreditch from 1885-95 when he was defeated; re-elected there in 1900 and sat until his death 22 July 1908. [1908]

CRICHTON-STUART, Lord Ninian Edward. House of Falkland, Fife, N.B. 43 Bryanston Square, London. Marlborough, and Carlton. 2nd s. of 3rd Marq. of Bute. B. 15 May 1883; m. 1906, Hon. Ismay Preston, d. of 14th Visct. Gormanston. Educ. at Harrow, and Christ Church, Oxford. Lieut.-Col. 6th Battalion Welsh Regiment. A Lieut. Scots Guards. A Unionist. Unsuccessfully contested Cardiff Jan. 1910. Elected for Cardiff in Dec. 1910 and sat until he was killed in action on 6 Sept. 1915. [1915]

CRILLY, Daniel. 173 Abbeville Road, Clapham, London. Claremont, Meath Road, Bray, Co. Wicklow. S. of Daniel Crilly, Esq., of Rostrevor, Co. Down. B. 14 Dec. 1857; m. 1887, Miss Mary E. Colclough. Educ. at the Catholic Institute, Liverpool, and Sedgeley Park Coll., Staffordshire. A Journalist, and was, until his entrance into Parliament, on the staff of the Dublin newspaper, *The Nation*. Was prosecuted in 1887 on the charge of having promoted the agrarian combination known as "The Plan of Campaign", but the jury disagreed, and the case was abandoned. Was Hon. Secretary of the Home Rule Confederation of Great Britain and the Irish National League of of Great Britain. An "Irish Nationalist". Sat for Mayo N. from the general election of 1885 until he retired in 1900. Author of *The Celt at Westminster* (1892) and other works. Died Dec. 1923. [1900]

CRIPPS, Sir Charles Alfred, K.C.V.O. 29 Wilton Crescent, London. Parmoor, Henley-on-Thames. Athenaeum, Carlton, Marlborough, and Oxford & Cambridge. S. of H.W. Cripps, Esq., Q.C., and Julia, d. of Charles Lawrence, Esq. B. 1852; m. Theresa, d. of R. Potter, Esq., of Rusland Hall, Lancashire (she died 1893). Educ. at Winchester and New Coll., Oxford; Fellow of St. John's Coll., and Fellow of Winchester Coll. Gained the Senior Studentship of the Inns of Court 1876. Called to the bar at the Middle Temple 1877; Q.C. 1890. Attorney-Gen. to the Prince of Wales from 1895-1914. Chancellor and Vicar-Gen. of York from 1900-14. Vicar-Gen. of Canterbury 1902-24, K.C.V.O. 1908. PC. 1914. A J.P. for Buckinghamshire and Chairman Quarter Sessions. Author of *Law of Compensation, The Laws of Church and Clergy*, etc. A Unionist. Sat for the Stroud division of Gloucestershire from 1895-1900 when he was defeated; sat for the Stretford division of Lancashire from 1901-06 when he was defeated. Elected for the Wycombe division of Buckinghamshire in Jan. 1910 and sat until created Baron Parmoor in 1914. Joined first Labour government as Lord President of the Council, also having responsibility for League of Nations affairs, in 1924; again Lord President and Leader of the House of Lords from 1929-31. Leader of the Labour Party in the House of Lords in 1924 (jointly with Lord Haldane) and from 1928-31. Honorary Fellow of New Coll., Oxford 1919; Chairman of Buckinghamshire County Council. First Chairman (1920-24) of House of Laity of Church Assembly. Died 30 June 1941. [1913]

CROFT, Henry Page, C.M.G. Continued in House after 1918: full entry in Volume III.

CROMBIE, John William. 91 Onslow Square, London. Balgownie Lodge, Nr. Aberdeen. Reform. S. of John Crombie, Esq., of Balgownie Lodge, Aberdeen, and Jane, d. of John Sang, Esq., Solicitor, of Edinburgh. B. 1858; m. Minna, eld. d. of Eugene Wason, Esq., MP for Clackmannan. Educ. at the Gymnasium, Old Aberdeen, Aberdeen University, M.A., and in France and Germany. A Director of J. and J. Crombie Limited, of Aberdeen, a Dept.-Lieut. for Aberdeenshire, and a Referee of Private Bills. Author of *Some Poets of the People in Foreign Lands*, etc. Contributed articles to the *Edinburgh Review, Macmillan's, Temple Bar*, and other magazines. A Liberal, in favour of Home Rule for Ireland and Mr. Gladstone's programme generally. Sat for Kincardineshire from 1892 until his death 22 Mar. 1908. [1907]

CROMPTON, Charles. 13 Cromwell Place, London. 3 Harcourt Buildings, Temple, London. Eld. s. of Sir Charles Crompton, one of the Judges of the old Court of Queen's Bench, by Caroline, d. of Thomas Fletcher, Esq., of Liverpool. B. 1833; m. 1863, Florence Elizabeth, d. of the Rev. W. Gaskell, of Manchester University. Educ. at University Coll. School and University Coll. London, and Trinity Coll., Cambridge, where he was 4th wrangler 1885. Became a Fellow of his Coll. 1856. Was called to the bar at the Inner Temple 1864, and joined the Northern Circuit. Became Q.C. 1882; and was one of the Commissioners appointed to inquire into the alleged corrupt practices at Knaresborough 1880. A Liberal. Unsuccessfully contested Cheshire W. in Apr. 1880. Returned for the Leek division of Staffordshire Dec. 1885 and sat until defeated in 1886 standing as a Gladstonian Liberal. Bencher of the Inner Temple from Nov. 1887. Died 25 June 1890. [1886]

CROOKS, Rt. Hon. William. Continued in House after 1918: full entry in Volume III.

CROSFIELD, Arthur Henry. Barremman, Hoylake, Cheshire. 39 Hyde Park Gate, London. National Liberal. S. of John Crosfield, Esq. B. 1865; m. 1907, Domini, d. of E.M. Elliadi, Esq., of Southport and Smyrna. Educ. at Uppingham. A Director of Joseph Crosfield and Sons Limited, Soap and Chemical Manufacturers, Warrington. A Liberal. Unsuccessfully contested Warrington in 1900. First elected for Warrington in 1906 and sat until defeated in Dec. 1910. Created Bart. 1915. Chairman National Playing Fields Association. G.B.E. 1929. Died 22 Sept. 1938. [1910]

CROSFIELD, William. Queen Anne's Mansions, London. Annesley, Aigberth, Liverpool. Devonshire, and National Liberal. S. of William Crosfield, Esq., of Liverpool, by Eliza, d. of James Ryley, Esq., of Liverpool. B. 1838; m. 1865, Frances Elizabeth, d. of Thomas B. Job, Esq., Merchant of Liverpool. Educ. at the Royal Institution School, Liverpool. A Dept.-Chairman of the Liverpool Mortgage Insurance Company. One of the Governors of University Coll., Liverpool, and a J.P. for the city. A member of the city council and of the Mersey Docks and Harbour Board. A Liberal, in favour of Home Rule for Ireland. Was an unsuccessful candidate for Warrington 1885, and for Lincoln 1886. First returned for Lincoln in July 1892 and sat until defeated in 1895. Died 17 May 1909. [1895]

CROSLAND, Sir Joseph. Grand Hotel, London. Royds Wood, Huddersfield. 3rd s. of George Crosland, Esq., of Huddersfield, Manufacturer, by Hannah, d. of John Woodhead, Esq., of Newsome, near Huddersfield. B. 1826 at Huddersfield; m. 1864, Mary Ann Linton, d. of John Fox, Esq., of Lindley (she died 1887). Educ. at private schools. A member of the firm of George Crosland and Son, Woollen Manufacturers, Huddersfield. Was an Improvement Commissioner in the borough 1866, a member of the Council of Commerce 1868 (President 1872), Income Tax Commissioner 1874, J.P., etc. and was Chairman of the Huddersfield Joint Stock Bank from 1876. He was Knighted in 1889. A Conservative, in favour of improving the social position of the working classes, and opposed to Home Rule for Ireland. Unsuccessfully contested Huddersfield in 1885, 1886, and 1892. First returned for Huddersfield in Feb. 1893 and sat until defeated in 1895. Died 27 Aug. 1904. [1895]

CROSS, Alexander. 44 Queens Gate Gardens, London. Woodlands Terrace, Glasgow. Marchbank Wood,

Dumfriesshire. Reform. S. of William Cross, Esq., Seed Merchant, of Glasgow, and Marion, d. of Malcolm McLaren, Esq., of Monteith Row, Glasgow. B. 1847; m. 1st, 1876, d. of Sir Peter Coats; 2ndly, 1908, Agnes Jane, d. of J.G. Lawrie, Esq., of Glasgow. Educ. at Glasgow University. A member of the old-established firm of Alexander Cross and Sons, Seed Merchants and Chemical Manufacturers, and a Director of several commercial companies; also Director of the Glasgow Chamber of Commerce, and Scottish Chamber of Agriculture. Chairman of the Glasgow Liberal Association before he became a Liberal Unionist. A Liberal Unionist, in favour of Free Trade, and held advanced views on social questions. Rejoined the Liberal Party in May 1909. Represented the Camlachie division of Glasgow from 1892 until defeated in Jan. 1910 standing as a Liberal candidate. Created Bart. 1912. Author. Died 13 Feb. 1914. [1909]

CROSS, Rt. Hon. Sir Richard Assheton, G.C.B., F.R.S. Retired in 1886: full entry in Volume I.

CROSS, Hon. William Henry. 93 St. George's Road, London. Eccle Riggs. Broughton-in-Furness. Carlton. S. of Visct. Cross, G.C.B. B. 1856 at Appleton Hall, Cheshire; m. 1880, Mary, younger d. of W. Lewthwaite, Esq., J.P. and Dept.-Lieut. of Broadgate, Cumberland. Educ. at Rugby, and University Coll., Oxford. A Barrister, having been called to the bar at the Inner Temple in 1882. A Conservative. Sat for the W. Derby division of Liverpool from Aug. 1888 until his death 11 Dec. 1892. [1892 2nd ed.]

CROSSLEY, Edward. Belgrave Mansions, London. Bermerside, Halifax. National Liberal. S. of Joseph Crossley, Esq., Carpet Manufacturer, of Halifax, by Hannah, d. of Joseph Smith, Esq., of Halifax. B. 1841; m. 20 July 1865, Jane Eleanor, d. of Sir Edward Baines, Dept.-Lieut. of St. Ann's Hill, Leeds. Educ. at private schools at Totteridge and Walthamstow, and at Owen's Coll., Manchester. A Carpet Manufacturer, being Director and Chairman of John Crossley and Sons Limited, of Halifax. An Alderman of Halifax and was Mayor for the three years ending 1875-76 and 1885. Also J.P. for Halifax, and an F.R.A.S. A Liberal, in favour of Home Rule for Ireland. Sat for the Sowerby division of the W. Riding of Yorkshire from 1885 until he retired in 1892. Died 21 Jan. 1905. [1892]

CROSSLEY, Rt. Hon. Sir Savile Brinton, Bart. 12 Carlton House Terrace, London. Somerleyton Hall, Lowestoft. Brooks's, and Marlborough. S. of Sir Francis Crossley, Bart., MP for Halifax, and Martha Eliza, d. of Henry Brunton, Esq. B. 1857; m. Phyllis, d. of Sir Henry de Bathe, Bart. Educ. at Eton, and Balliol Coll., Oxford. Succeeded as Bart. 1872. Paymaster-Gen., appointed 1902-05. M.V.O. 1902. PC. 1902, and one of the Conservative "whips". Held a commission and Honorary Lieut.-Col. in Norfolk Militia Artillery; served in Imperial Yeomanry in S. Africa 1899-1902; was mentioned in despatches. Was High Sheriff of Suffolk in 1896 and a Magistrate for Suffolk and for Norfolk. Took a great interest in hospital work, being one of the Honorary Secretaries of King Edward's Hospital Fund and Chairman of Hospital Saturday Fund. A Liberal Unionist. Sat for the Lowestoft division of Suffolk 1885-92, when he retired from that seat. Unsuccessfully contested Halifax 3 Mar. 1897; elected for Halifax in 1900 and sat until defeated in 1906. Contested Islington W. Jan. 1910. K.C.V.O. 1909. Created Baron Somerleyton in 1916. Lord-in-Waiting and Conservative Whip in House of Lords 1918-24. Died 25 Feb. 1935. [1905]

CROSSLEY, Sir William John, Bart. Glenfield, Altrincham. Pull Woods, Ambleside. Queen Anne's Mansions, Westminster, London. Reform, and National Liberal. S. of Francis Crossley, Esq., and Elizabeth Helen Irwin. B. 22 Apr. 1844 at Glenburn, Dunmuny; m. 1876, Mabel Gordon, d. of Dr. F. Anderson, Inspector-Gen. of Hospitals, Indian Army. Educ. at Royal School, Dungannon, and Bonn, Prussia. Chairman of Crossley Brothers, Engineers, Manchester. A J.P. for Cheshire and Manchester; a Freeman of the city of Manchester. Created Bart. in 1909. A Liberal. Elected for the Altrincham division of Cheshire in 1906 and sat until defeated in Dec. 1910. Died 12 Oct. 1911. [1910]

CROSSMAN, Maj.-Gen. Sir William, K.C.M.G. Cheswick House, Beal, Northumberland. United Service, and National Liberal. S. of Robert Crossman, Esq., J.P., of Cheswick and Holy Island, Northumberland, by Sarah, d. of Edmund Douglas, Esq., of Kingston. B. at Isleworth, Middlesex 1830; m. 1855, Catherine, d. of J.L. Morley, Esq., of Albany, Western Australia. Educ. at the Royal Military Academy, and became Lieut. of the Royal Engineers 1848. Was in charge of various public works in Western Australia, and was a Magistrate in that colony 1852-56. Held various appointments at home including that of Assistant Director of Works for fortifications 1874-75; special Commissioner to Griqualand W. to inquire into the finances of that colony; Royal Commissioner to the West Indies 1882; Col. in command of the Royal Engineers in the Southern District 1822; retired 1885. K.C.M.G. 1884. A Liberal Unionist. Sat for Portsmouth from 1885 until he retired in 1892. Died 19 Apr. 1901. [1892]

CRUDDAS, William Donaldson. The Dene, Elswick, Newcastle-on-Tyne. Haughton Castle, Humshaugh, Newcastle-on-Tyne. Carlton, National, and Constitutional. 2nd s. of George Cruddas, Esq., of The Dene, Elswick, Newcastle-on-Tyne. B. 1831; m. 1861, d. of William Nesham, Esq., of Newcastle-on-Tyne. A J.P. for Northumberland and the city of Newcastle-on-Tyne. A Director of Sir W.G. Armstrong, Mitchell and Company Limited, Elswick Works, and Chairman of the Newcastle and Gateshead Water Company. A Conservative, and supporter of Lord Salisbury's Government. Sat for Newcastle-on-Tyne from July 1895 until he retired in 1900. High Sheriff of Northumberland 1903. Died 8 Feb. 1912. [1900]

CRUMLEY, Patrick. 30 Town Hall Street, Fermanagh. B. 186-. A Cattle Merchant. A Magistrate for the Co. A Nationalist. Elected for S. Fermanagh in Dec. 1910 and sat until defeated in 1918. Died before 1928. [1918]

CUBITT, Rt. Hon. George. 17 Prince's Gate, London. Denbies, Dorking. Carlton. S. of Thomas Cubitt, Esq., of Denbies, by Mary Anne, d. of Samuel Warner, Esq. B. at Clapham Common 1828; m. 1853, Laura, d. of the Rev. James Joyce, Vicar of Dorking. Educ. at Trinity Coll., Cambridge, where he was three times a prizeman of his Coll., and graduated M.A. 1854. Was second Church Estates Commissioner 1874 to 1879. PC. 1880. A Conservative. Sat for Surrey W. from 1860-85, and for the Epsom division of Surrey from 1885 until he retired in 1892. Created Baron Ashcombe in Sept. 1892. Died 26 Feb. 1917. [1892]

CUBITT, Hon. Henry. 20 Prince's Gate, London. Birtley, Bramley, Guildford. Carlton. Only s. of Lord Ashcombe (formerly Rt. Hon. George Cubitt, MP), by Laura, d. of the Rev. James Joyce. B. 1867; m. 1890, Maud Marianne, younger d. of Col. Calvert, of Ockley Court, Dorking. Educ. at Eton, and Trinity Coll., Cambridge; M.A. 1892. A J.P. and Dept.-Lieut. for Surrey, and Lieut.-Col. commanding Surrey Imperial Yeomanry 1901-12. A Conservative and Unionist, strongly approved the policy of Mr. Balfour, domestic as well as Imperial. Sat for the Reigate division of Surrey from 1892 until he retired in 1906. Succeeded as 2nd Baron Ashcombe in 1917. Died 27 Oct. 1947. [1905]

CULLINAN, John. Wolfsdene, Tipperary. S. of Charles Cullinan, Esq., Merchant and Farmer, of Bansha, by Catherine, d. of R.W. Walsh, Esq., of Tourin, Co. Waterford. B. 1857 in Bansha; m. 1913, Rita, d. of Thomas O'Meara, Esq. Educ. at Thurles Lay Coll. A Journalist. A prominent member of the National Movement; Chairman of Poor Law Board, and member of County and District Councils. A Nationalist. Elected for S. Tipperary in 1900 and sat until defeated in 1918. [1918]

CUNNINGHAME-GRAHAM, Robert Gallnigad Bontine. See GRAHAM, Robert Gallnigad Bontine Cunninghame.

CURRAN, Peter Francis. 1 Pretoria Avenue, Walthamstow. S. of James and Mary Curran, working people. B. 28 Mar. 1860 at Glasgow; m. 1st, 1887, May, d. of P. McIntyre, Esq.; 2ndly, 1898, Marian, d. of John Barry, Esq. Educ. at National School. A Trades Union Official. Was a District Secretary of the Gasworkers and General Labourers' Union, Gen. Organiser of this Union from 1889, and President of the General Federation of Trades Unions from 1900. Wrote two pamphlets; *Politics of Labour*, and *Human Documents*. An Independent Labour Member. Unsuccessfully contested Barrow 1895, Barnsley division of Yorkshire 1897, and Jarrow division of Durham 1906. Elected for the latter division in July 1907 and sat until he was defeated in Jan. 1910. Died 14 Feb. 1910. [1909]

CURRAN, Thomas. 68 Cambridge Gardens, Kensington, London. Derryfad House, Letterkenny, Co. Donegal. National Liberal. B. 1840 at Carrick-on-Shannon; m. 1867, Mary, 2nd d. of Dominic Coll, Farmer, of Co. Donegal. Educ. at the National School, Carrick-on-Shannon. Founded a business in Australia. A J.P. in New South Wales and also for Co. Donegal. Was a member of the Royal Commissioners for New South Wales at the Colonial and Indian Exhibitions, and similarly commissioned at the Melbourne Exhibition of 1888. An Irish Nationalist, of the Anti-Parnellite party, to the funds of which he largely contributed. Sat for Sligo S. from July 1892 until he retired in 1900. Died 13 Aug. 1913. [1900]

CURRAN, Thomas Bartholomew. House of Commons, London. S. of Thomas Curran, Esq., MP for Sligo S. B. 1870; m. 1893, Miss Marie Brooke, of Melbourne, Australia. Educ. at the Jesuit Coll., Sydney, Clongowes Wood, Ireland, and Oxford University. He won the gold medal for debating at the Sydney University. A Barrister-at-Law, Middle Temple. A member of the Irish (Anti-Parnellite) Parliamentary party. Sat for Kilkenny City 1892 to 1895. Withdrew to contest N. Donegal in July 1895 and sat until he retired in 1900. Called to the bar 1900 and practised in Australia becoming Dept. Crown Prosecutor of Sydney but returned to England in 1905 and practised at the English bar. Died Oct. 1929. [1900]

CURRIE, Sir Donald, G.C.M.G. 4 Hyde Park Place, London. Garth Castle, Aberfeldy, Perthshire. Reform, and City Liberal. S. of James Currie, Esq., of Greenock, by Elizabeth, d. of Martin Donald, Esq. B. 1825; m. 1851, Margaret, d. of John Miller, Esq., of Liverpool and Ardencraig, Bute, Scotland. Head of the firm of Messrs. Donald Currie and Company, London, who rendered the country signal service in 1879 by supplying with great promptitude steam vessels to proceed to South Africa to convey troops and stores to the seat of war. In 1877 was created a C.M.G. for the assistance rendered to government in the settlement of the Diamond Fields dispute and the boundary question of the Orange River Free States.

Became K.C.M.G. 1881, for services rendered in connection with the relief of Ekowe, and created G.C.M.G. 1897. A Dept.-Lieut. for London. A Liberal and Unionist, in favour of the total abolition of the law of Hypothec. Unsuccessfully contested Greenock in Jan. 1878. Sat for Perthshire from Apr. 1880-85 and for Perthshire W. from 1885 until he retired in 1900. Died 13 Apr. 1909. [1900]

CURRIE, George Welsh. 18 India Street, Edinburgh. Carlton, Caledonian, National, University, and Scottish Conservative. S. of the Rev. J. Currie, LL.D. Principal of Church of Scotland Coll., Edinburgh, and Jane Lyall, d. of George Key, Esq., of Berryfauld, St. Vigeans. B. 9 Feb. 1870 in Edinburgh; m. 1901, Georgina Stuart, d. of Lieut.-Col. C.S. Silver, 15th (Halifax Co.) Nova Scotia Militia. Educ. at Merchant Company's School, and The University, Edinburgh. A Chartered Accountant, member of Council of Society of Accountants in Edinburgh. Was Senior President Diagnostic Society, Edinburgh University, and Secretary of Edinburgh University Boat Club. Honorary Treasurer and Convener of the Literature Committee of Tariff Reform League, Edinburgh. President of Scottish Society of Economists; Central Recruiting Committee 1914; Women's Industrial Employment Committee 1916; Chairman of National Health Investigation Commission; Central War Aims Committee 1917; Munitions Contracts Board 1917; Central Advisory Committee on National Health Insurance 1917. A Unionist. Elected for Leith Burghs in Feb. 1914 and sat until he was defeated in Leith in 1918. Central National Service Commissioner 1917; Adviser and Assistant Comptroller Ministry of Munitions 1918; Government Arsenals Department Inquiry into Workmen's Dwellings (Scotland) 1921. Joined the Labour Party. President, Chelsea Labour Party 1936-39; member of London County Council (Central Wandsworth) 1935-40; Church Commissioner 1948. Died 3 June 1950. [1918]

CURZON, Hon. George Nathaniel. 56 St. Ermin's Mansions, London. Kedleston, Nr. Derby. Carlton, and Bachelors'. Eld. s. of Lord Scarsdale, by Blanche, d. of Joseph Pocklington-Senhouse, Esq., of Netherhall, Cumberland. B. 1859. Educ. at Eton, and Balliol Coll., Oxford, and elected a Fellow of All Souls' Coll., Oxford in 1883. Was Parliamentary Under-Secretary for India Nov. 1891 to Aug. 1892. Wrote Lothian and Arnold History Prize Essays *Russia in Central Asia* and *Persia and the Persian Queen* (1884). Was appointed Private Secretary to Lord Salisbury June 1885. A Magistrate and Dept.-Lieut. for the S. division of the Co. of Derby. A Conservative and Unionist. Unsuccessfully contested the S. division of Derbyshire at the general election of 1885. First elected for the Southport division of S.W. Lancashire in July 1886 and sat until 1898. Under-Secretary for Foreign Affairs 1895-98; PC. 1895. Lord Privy Seal 1915-16; President of the Air Board 1916; Lord President of the Council 1916-19, and member of the inner War Cabinet. Foreign Secretary 1919-23. Lord President again 1924-25. Viceroy of India 1899-1905. Chancellor of Oxford University 1907. Created 1st Baron Curzon of Kedleston (Irish Peerage) 1898 and entered the House of Lords as Irish representative peer in 1908. Created Earl Curzon of Kedleston (U.K. Peerage) in 1911, 1st Marq. 1921. Succeeded as 5th Baron Scarsdale in 1916. Leader of Conservative Party in House of Lords 1916-25. Died 20 Mar. 1925. [1895]

CURZON, Richard George Penn Curzon-Howe, Visct. 20 Curzon Street, London. Woodlands, Uxbridge, Buckinghamshire. Carlton, Travellers', Marlborough, Constitutional, Turf, and Bachelors'. Eld. s. of Earl Howe. B. 1861; m. June 1883, the Lady Georgiana Spencer Churchill, 5th d. of the 7th Duke of Marlborough. Educ. at Eton, and Christ Church, Oxford. Appointed Treasurer of Her Majesty's Household Feb. 1896 to Oct. 1900. A Magistrate for the Co. of Buckinghamshire, and Capt. Prince Albert's Own Leicestershire Yeomanry Cavalry. A Conservative. Sat for the Wycombe division of Buckinghamshire from 1885 until he retired in 1900. Lord-in-Waiting from 1900-03. Succeeded as 4th Earl Howe on 26 Sept. 1900, the day after the dissolution of Parliament. G.C.V.O. 1903. Royal Victorial Chain 1925. Died 10 Jan. 1929. [1900]

CUST, Henry John Cockayne. St. James's Lodge, Chapel Place, Delahay Street, London. Beltham House, Grantham. Carlton, Travellers', and St. James's. Eld. s. of Maj. J.F. Cockayne Cust, MP for Grantham 1874-80, of Cockayne Hatley, Sandy, Bedfordshire, and Sarah Jane, d. of Isaac Cookson, Esq., of Meldon Park, Northumberland, and widow of Maj. Sidney Streatfield. B. 1861; m. 1893, Emmeline Mary Elizabeth, only d. of Sir William Welby-Gregory, Bart. Educ. at Eton, and Trinity Coll., Cambridge. A Magistrate for Bedfordshire, Lord of the Manor of Cockayne Hatley, and a J.P. and Dept.-Lieut. for Lincolnshire. Was a cousin of Earl Brownlow and heir-presumptive to the peerage. Was editor of the *Pall Mall Gazette* 1893-96 and again 1902-06. A Conservative. Sat for the Stamford division of Lincolnshire 1890-95, when he retired. Elected for the Bermondsey division of Southwark in 1900 and sat until defeated in 1906. Member of French bar. Died 2 Mar. 1917. [1905]

DALBIAC, Col. Philip Hugh. 23 Queen's Gate Gardens, London. S. of Henry Aylmer Dalbiac, Esq., J.P. of Durrington, Sussex, by Mary, d. of Sir Harry Mainwaring, Bart., of Peover, Cheshire. B. at Chester Place, Hyde Park Square 1856; m. 1888, Lilian, d. of Sir Charles Seely, Bart., J.P., Dept.-Lieut. of Sherwood, Nottinghamshire, MP for Nottingham. Educ. at Winchester Coll. Joined the army 1875; Capt. 1882, Adjutant 1st Nottinghamshire Rifle Volunteers 1885-90; retired 1890; Col. Commanding 18th Middlesex Rifle Volunteers. A Partner in the Publishing firm of Swan Sonnenschein and Company. A Conservative, opposed to Home Rule, disestablishment, and Local Veto, in favour of Reform of the House of Lords, of the Poor Laws, Registration, etc. Sat for Camberwell N. from July 1895 until he retired in 1900. C.B. 1911. Director of George Allen and Unwin from 1914. Served in France and Salonika 1916-17. Author. Died 28 Apr. 1927. [1900]

DALKEITH, John Charles Montagu-Douglas-Scott, Earl of. Montagu House, Whitehall, London. Eildon Hall, St. Roswell's. Carlton. 2nd s. of the 6th Duke of Buccleuch, by Louisa Jane, d. of the 1st Duke of Abercorn. B. 1864; m. Margaret Alice, d. of Earl of Bradford. Educ. at Christ Church, Oxford. Entered the navy 1877; retired as Lieut. 1886. A Dept.-Lieut. and J.P. for Midlothian, Dumfriesshire, Roxburghshire, and Selkirkshire. A Conservative and Unionist. Sat for Roxburghshire from 1895 until he retired in

1906. Succeeded as 7th Duke of Buccleuch in 1914. Lord-Lieut. of Dumfriesshire from 1915. Died 19 Oct. 1935.   [1905]

DALMENY, Albert Edward Harry Meyer Archibald Primrose, Lord. 38 Berkeley Square, London. Dalmeny, N.B. The Durdans, Epsom. Eld. s. of the Earl of Roseberry. B. 8 Jan. 1882. Educ. at Eton, and Royal Military Coll., Sandhurst. Lieut. Grenadier Guards. A Liberal. Elected for Edinburghshire in 1906 and sat until he retired in Jan. 1910. Served in France 1914-18. Lord-Lieut. of Midlothian 1929-64. Succeeded as 6th Earl of Rosebery in 1929. Regional Commissioner for Civil Defence in Scotland Feb. 1941. Secretary of State for Scotland May-July 1945. PC. 1945. President National Liberal Party 1945-57. Chairman Royal Fine Arts Commission for Scotland 1952. Died 31 May 1974. [1909]

DALRYMPLE, Rt. Hon. Sir Charles, Bart. 20 Onslow Gardens, London. Newhailes, Musselburgh, N.B. Athenaeum. 2nd s. of Sir Charles Dalrymple Fergusson, Bart., of Kilkerran, Ayrshire, by Helen, d. of the Rt. Hon. David Boyle, Lord Justice-Gen. B. at Kilkerran 1839; m. 1874, Alice Mary, d. of Sir Edward Hunter Blair, Bart., of Blairquhan (she died 1884). Educ. at Harrow, and Trinity Coll., Cambridge. Assumed the name of Dalrymple on succeeding to the estates of his great-grandfather, Sir David Dalrymple, Bart. (Lord Hailes) in 1849. Called to the bar at Lincoln's Inn 1865. A J.P. for Midlothian, Dept.-Lieut. for Haddingtonshire, and Honorary Maj. 3rd Battalion Royal Scotch Fusiliers. Was Lord of the Treasury from June 1885 to Jan. 1886; created Bart. 1887; became Chairman of the Select Committee for Public Petitions 1893, and served on the Royal Commissions on Cathedral Estabs., Reformatories, Vaccination, and Universities (Scotland). A Conservative. Sat for Buteshire from 1868 to 1885, with the exception of three months in 1880. In Dec. 1885 he unsuccessfully contested Edinburghshire against Mr. Gladstone, but in Apr. 1886 he was elected for Ipswich and sat until defeated in 1906. PC. 1905. Died 20 June 1916.   [1905]

DALRYMPLE, Hon. Hew Hamilton. Lochinch, Castle Kennedy, Wigtownshire. Brooks's. S. of 10th Earl of Stair. B. 27 Sept. 1857 at Bargany Dailly, Ayrshire. Unmar-

ried. Educ. at Harrow. A Brigadier Royal Company of Archers; Maj. 3rd Battalion Royal Scots Fusiliers. J.P. for the counties of Ayr and Wigtown; Dept.-Lieut. and Convener of Wigtownshire. A Unionist. Unsuccessfully contested Wigtownshire as a Liberal in 1885; elected there in Feb. 1915 and sat until he retired in 1918. Chairman of the Board of Trustees of National Galleries, Scotland. K.C.V.O. 1932. Died 11 July 1945.   [1918]

DALRYMPLE, John James Hamilton Dalrymple, Visct. 17 Eaton Square, London. Lochinch, Castle Kennedy, Wigtownshire. Carlton, and Guards'. Eld. s. of the Earl of Stair. B. 1 Feb. 1879 in London; m. 1904, Violet Evelyn, d. of Col. Harford, Scots Guards. Educ. at Harrow and Sandhurst. A Capt. in Scots Guards; joined 1898; served in South Africa from 1899-1902. A Unionist. Elected for Wigtownshire in 1906 and sat until he succeeded as Earl of Stair in 1914. Served in European War 1914-19. Lord High Commissioner of Church of Scotland 1927-28. Died 4 Nov. 1961.   [1914]

DALRYMPLE-WHITE, Godfrey Dalrymple. Continued in House after 1918: full entry in Volume III.

DALTON, James Joseph. S. of Mr. Dalton of Tipperary. M. 1892, Frances, d. of P. Delaney of Dublin. He was a member of the Irish bar, called Easter term 1888, and up to the time of his election (May 1890) he practised in Australia. An Irish Nationalist of the Parnellite section. Sat for Donegal W. from May 1890 until he retired in 1892 and unsuccessfully contested Meath S. at the same time. Again contested Meath S. 18 Feb. 1893.   [1892]

DALY, James. Esmore Hall, Carrickmacross, South Monaghan. B. 1852. A Merchant at Carrickmacross; also Chairman of the District Council, and a member of the County Council and of the Commissioners Board of Guardians. An Irish Nationalist. Sat for S. Monaghan from July 1895 until he accepted Chiltern Hundreds in Feb. 1902.   [1902]

DALY, John. A Parnellite Nationalist. First returned for Limerick city 13 July 1895 but was shortly afterwards disqualified as a convict, having been sen-

89

tenced to life imprisonment. The election was declared void in Sept. 1895.

DALZIEL, Davison Alexander. Continued in House after 1918: full entry in Volume III.

DALZIEL, Rt. Hon. Sir James Henry. Continued in House after 1918: full entry in Volume III.

DANE, Richard Martin. 19 Warrington Place, Dublin. Carlton, University, Dublin. S. of William Auchinleck Dane, Esq., Solicitor, of Killyreagh, Co. Fermanagh, and Sarah, d. of Lieut. Benjamin F. Foster of the 46th Regiment, and Drumloo Cottage, Monaghan, a descendant (paternally) of Paul Dane, Provost of Enniskillen 1688, and (maternally) of the Rt. Hon. John H. Foster, the last Speaker of the Irish House of Commons. B. 1852 in Dublin; m. 1st, Kate, d. of the Rev. F. Eldon Barnes, M.A., Rector of Kilmaley, Co. Clare, and Head Master of Ennis Coll. (she died 1889); 2ndly, 1895, Annie E. only d. of William Thompson, Esq., J.P. of Rathnally Trim, Co. Meath. Educ. at Portora Royal School and Trinity Coll., Dublin. Was called to the Irish bar 1877, and joined the N.W. Circuit; a Q.C. 1896. A Conservative, strongly opposed to Home Rule, in favour of Fair Rent and Compulsory Sale and Purchase. First elected for Fermanagh N. in 1892 and sat until appointed County Court Judge for Mayo in 1898. Died 22 Mar. 1903.   [1898]

DARLING, Charles John. 36 Grosvenor Road, London. Carlton, and Athenaeum. S. of Charles Darling, Esq., of Langham Hall, Essex, and Sarah Frances, d. of John Tizard, Esq., of Dorchester. B. at Colchester 1849; m. 1885, Mary Caroline, eld. d. of Maj.-Gen. W.H. Greathed, C.B. Educ. privately. Called to the bar at the Inner Temple 1874, and joined the Oxford Circuit. Appointed Q.C. 1885, a bencher of the Inner Temple 1892, and Royal Commissioner of Assize for the Oxford Circuit 1896. Author of *Scintillae Juris Meditations in the Tea Rooms*, and many verses and articles in the *St. James's Gazette*. A Conservative. An unsuccessful candidate at Hackney S. in 1885 and again in 1886. First elected for Deptford Feb. 1888, on the retirement of Mr. W.J. Evelyn, and sat until appointed Judge in 1897; retired 1923. Knighted 1897. PC. 1917. Created Baron Darling in 1924. Died 29 May 1936.   [1897]

DARLING, Moir Tod Stormonth. 10 Great Stuart Street, Edinburgh. Carlton, and Constitutional. S. of James Stormonth Darling, Esq., of Lednathie, Writer to the Signet, and Elizabeth Moir, d. of James Tod, Esq., of Deanston. B. at Edinburgh 1844. Educ. at Kelso Grammar School under Dr. Ferguson, and at the University of Edinburgh; M.A. 1864. Was called to the Scottish bar 1867. Was Lord Rector's Assessor in the University of Edinburgh 1887, and appointed Solicitor-Gen. for Scotland Nov. 1888, and returned to Parliament without opposition immediately after. Made a Q.C. Dec. 1888. A Conservative. Unsuccessfully contested Banffshire at the general election of 1885. Sat for Edinburgh and St. Andrews Universities from Nov. 1888 until appointed Judge of Court of Session with title of Lord Stormonth-Darling in Oct. 1890; retired 1909. Councillor of Royal Company of Archers 1895-1909; Honorary LL.D. of the University of Edinburgh 1895; Railway Commissioner for Scotland 1898-1909. Died 2 June 1912.   [1890]

DARWIN, Maj. Leonard. 18 Wetherby Place, South Kensington, London. Junior United Service. S. of Charles Darwin, Esq., the celebrated naturalist and author, and Emma, d. of J. Wedgwood, Esq., of Maer, Staffordshire. B. 1850; m. 1882, d. of G.R. Fraser, Esq. Educ. at the Royal Military Academy, Woolwich. A Maj. in the Royal Engineers. Served on several scientific expeditions, including those for the observation of the transit of Venus 1874 and 1882. Passed Staff Coll. Was Instructor in chemistry at the School of Military Engineering, Chatham, 1877 to 1882, and on the Head Quarter Staff, Intelligence Department, War Office 1885 to 1890. A Liberal Unionist. Sat for the Lichfield division of Staffordshire from July 1892 until defeated in 1895. Unsuccessfully contested the seat again 26 Feb. 1896. President Royal Geographical Society 1908-11. President Eugenics Education Society 1911-28. Chairman of Bedford Coll., London University 1913-20. Author of *Bimetallism* (1898), *Municipal Trade* (1903) and *The Need for Eugenic Reform* (1926). Died 26 Mar. 1943.   [1895]

DAVENPORT, Harry Tichborne. See HINCKES, Harry Tichborne.

DAVEY, Sir Horace. 8 Old Square, Lincoln's Inn, London. 10 Queen's Gate Gardens, South Kensington, London. Verdley Place, Farnhurst, Sussex. Devonshire, and Oxford & Cambridge. 2nd s. of Peter Davey, Esq., of Horton, Buckinghamshire, and Torquay, by Caroline Emma, d. of the Rev. William Pace, Rector of Rampisham-cum-Wraxall, Dorset. B. 1833; m. 1862, d. of John Donkin, Esq., Barrister, of Ormond House, Old Kent Road. Was educ. at Rugby School, and at University Coll., Oxford, of which he became Scholar and afterwards Fellow; was placed double 1st in moderations and in final school; was also senior mathematical scholar and Eldon law scholar. Called to the bar at Lincoln's Inn Jan. 1861; appointed a Queen's Counsel June 1875; a bencher 1878. Was Solicitor-Gen. in Mr. Gladstone's ministry Feb.-July 1886, and was then Knighted. A Liberal and Home Ruler. Sat for Christchurch from Apr. 1880 to Nov. 1885 when he was defeated. He was defeated at Ipswich in the following Apr. and again at the general election of 1886, when he contested Stockport. Returned for Stockton-on-Tees Dec. 1888 and sat until defeated in 1892. Lord Justice of Appeal 1893-94. PC. 1893. Lord of Appeal in Ordinary 1894-1907. Created (Law Life Peerage) Baron Davey in 1894. Honorary D.C.L. Oxford University 1894. Chairman of Royal Commission appointed to make statutes for London University 1898. F.B.A 1905. Died 20 Feb. 1907.   [1892]

DAVIDSON, John Humphrey. Continued in House after 1918: full entry in Volume III.

DAVIES, Alfred. The Lothians, Fitzjohn's Avenue, Hampstead. Gresham, and National Liberal. S. of the Rev. John Davies, a native of Carmarthenshire, Congregational Minister, Albany Street, London, and Walthamstow, and Mary Kidman Foster, of Houston Mills, Cambridgeshire. B. 1848; m. 1877, Lydia Edith, d. of William Death, Esq., of Burnt Mill, Essex. Educ. at Mill Hill School, and Rickmansworth. An International Carrier and Underwriter. Was on the 1st London County Council. A Radical, with a sound Labour platform. Elected for Carmarthen 1900 and sat until he retired in 1906. Died 27 Sept. 1907.   [1905]

DAVIES, David. Defeated in 1886: full entry in Volume I.

DAVIES, David. Continued in House after 1918: full entry in Volume III.

DAVIES, Ellis William. Continued in House after 1918: full entry in Volume III.

DAVIES, Sir Horatio David, K.C.M.G. 21 Bishopsgate Street Without, London. Carlton, Junior Carlton, and City Carlton. S. of H.D. Davies, Esq., of London. B. in London 1842; m. 1867, Lizzie, d. of Charles John Gordon, Esq., of the City of London. Educ. at Dulwich Coll. A Lieut.-Col. (V.D.) 3rd Middlesex Artillery Volunteers (retired); Lieut. for the City of London, Sheriff of London and Middlesex 1888, Alderman 1889; Lord Mayor of London 1897-98; a Dept.-Lieut. and J.P. for Kent. K.C.M.G 1898. A Conservative. Unsuccessfully contested Rochester 1889; returned for Rochester July 1892, but unseated on petition in Dec. Represented Chatham from 1895 until he retired in 1906. Died 18 Sept. 1912.   [1905]

DAVIES, Matthew Lewis Vaughan. See VAUGHAN-DAVIES, Matthew Lewis. Continued in House after 1918: full entry in Volume III.

DAVIES, Richard. Retired in 1886: full entry in Volume I.

DAVIES, Thomas Hart. See HART-DAVIES, Thomas.

DAVIES, Timothy. 25 Collingham Gardens, London. National Liberal. S. of Henry Davies, Esq., Corn Merchant and Miller. B. 22 Jan. 1857 at Pant-y-Fedwen, near Carmarthen; m. 1893, d. of John Jenkins, Esq. Educ. in Wales. Was in business as a Draper in Fulham from 1885. An Alderman of Fulham Borough Council and Mayor 1901-02, and a member of London County Council from 1901-07. A J.P. for London; Commissioner for Income Tax. A Liberal. Sat for Fulham from 1906 to Jan. 1910, when he unsuccessfully contested the Louth division of Lincolnshire. Elected for the Louth division of Lincolnshire in Dec. 1910 and sat until defeated in 1918. Died 22 Aug. 1951. [1918]

DAVIES, William. 1 Suffolk Place, London. Scoveston, Haverfordwest. Devonshire. S. of Thomas Davies, Esq., B. 1821; m. 1859, Martha Rees, d. of Thomas Morgan, Esq. Was admitted a Solicitor in

DAVIES — DAWSON

1848 and practised at Haverfordwest. A Dept.-Lieut. and J.P. for Pembrokeshire and Haverfordwest. A Liberal, in favour of Home Rule. Unsuccessfully contested Pembrokeshire June 1876. Sat for Pembrokeshire from Apr. 1880 until he retired in 1892. Created Knight 1893. Died 23 Nov. 1895. [1892]

DAVIES, Sir William. See DAVIES, William.

DAVIES, Sir William Howell. Continued in House after 1918: full entry in Volume III.

DAVIES, William Rees Morgan. 17 Pall Mall, London. Scoveston, Milford Haven, Pembrokeshire. Reform. S. of Sir William Davies, Kt., MP for the Co., J.P. and Dept.-Lieut., and Martha Rees, d. of Thomas Morgan, Esq., Haverfordwest. B. 1863 at Spring Gardens, Haverfordwest. Educ. at Eton, and Trinity Hall, Cambridge (B.A. 1885). A Barrister, called at the Inner Temple 1887, and practised on the S. Wales Circuit. A J.P. and Dept.-Lieut. for Pembrokeshire, a J.P. for Haverfordwest, and was Private Secretary (unpaid) to Sir W. Harcourt as Chancellor of the Exchequer. A Liberal, in favour of Home Rule for Ireland, disestablishment of the Church, and of the Newcastle programme generally. Sat for Pembrokeshire from July 1892 until appointed Attorney-Gen. for the Bahamas 1898-1902. King's Advocate for Cyprus 1902-07. K.C. (Hong Kong) 1908. Attornty-Gen. 1907-12, and then Chief Justice 1912-24 for Hong Kong. Knighted 1913. Died 14 Apr. 1939. [1897]

DAVIS, Robert Gent. See GENT-DAVIS, Robert.

DAVITT, Michael. Library, House of Commons, London. S. of Martin Davitt, Esq., of Straide, Co. Mayo, and Scranton, Pa., U.S.A., and Catherine Kielty, d. of Thomas Kielty, Esq., Turlough, Co. Mayo. B. 1846 at Straide. At Haslingden he worked as a factory boy, and lost his right arm through a machine accident. Afterwards he was, successively, Newsboy, "Printer's Devil", and Assistant Postman; joined the Fenian Brotherhood in 1865; in 1870 he was convicted of treason felony, and sentenced to fifteen years penal servitude, but released on "ticket of leave" after eight years imprisonment. Founded the Land League with Mr. Parnell and others 1879. Went to America in 1880, and on returning to Ireland 1881 was arrested and sent back to penal servitude. While at Portland he was elected to Parliament for Meath, on 22 Feb. 1882 but the election was declared invalid. A Journalist. Wrote *Leaves from a Prison Diary, A Defence of the Land League, Life and Progress in Australasia*, etc. "An Irish Nationalist, Land Nationaliser and Republican." Unsuccessfully contested Waterford City in Dec. 1891. Was elected for Meath N. July 1892, but unseated on petition in Dec. 1892. Sat for N.E. Cork from Feb. 1893-May 1893; but resigned on becoming bankrupt through having to pay the costs of an election petition arising out of his return for N. Meath. At the general election of 1895 he was returned for both Kerry E. and Mayo S. (being in Australia at the time), but chose to sit for Mayo S. and was MP until he accepted Chiltern Hundreds in 1899. Travelled in S. Africa during the Boer War and wrote *The Boer Fight for Freedom* (1902); author of works on Irish History and politics. Died 31 May 1906. [1899]

DAWES, James Arthur. Continued in House after 1918: full entry in Volume III.

DAWNAY, Hon. Lewis Payan. 51 Charles Street, Berkeley Square, London. White's, Guards', and Carlton. 2nd s. of the 7th Visct. Downe, by Mary Isabel, 4th d. of the Hon. and Rt. Rev. Richard Bagot, Bishop of Bath and Wells. B. in London 1846; m. 1877, Victoria Alexandrina Elizabeth, d. of Gen. Hon. Charles Gray. Was educ. at Eton. Entered the Coldstream Guards Oct. 1865; retired as Capt. and Lieut.-Col. Dec. 1879. Patron of 1 living. A Conservative, who would "support any measure which would assist the British farmer, so long as it did not interfere with the principles of free trade." Unsuccessfully contested York city Feb. 1874; sat for Thirsk 1880-85; and for Thirks and Malton division of the N. Riding of Yorkshire from 1885 until he retired in 1892. Died 30 July 1910. [1892]

DAWSON, Richard. 47 Scarsdale Villas, Kensington, London. York. S. of Richard Dawson, Esq., J.P. for Co. Clare, Ireland, by Geraldine, d. of the Rev. T. Lloyd, of Fennor, Co. Tipperary. B. at Limerick 1855. Educ. at Hertford Coll., Oxford,

92

DEASY — de LISLE

where he obtained a scholarship. Private Secretary to the Rt. Hon. Henry Chaplin, Chancellor of the Duchy of Lancaster. A Conservative and "a firm supporter of religious denominational education." Sat for Leeds E. from Nov. 1885 until defeated in 1886. [1886]

DEASY, John. 141 Fentiman Road, London. Bishops Town, Cork. S. of M. Deasy, Esq., Civil Engineer, of Cork. B. 1856. Was for some time previous to his election prominently connected with politics as a member of the National League and of the Poor Law Board, Cork. A member of the Anti-Parnellite section of the Irish Nationalist party, and one of its "whips". Returned for Cork city Feb. 1884-85. Sat for Mayo W. from 1885 until he accepted Chiltern Hundreds in July 1893. Died 24 Feb. 1896. [1892]

de COBAIN, Edward Samuel Wesley. Hampton House, Ormond Road, Belfast. Ulster Constitutional. S. of the Rev. Edward de Cobain, Wesleyan Minister, by Harriett Ann Smyth, of Smythborough, Co. Monaghan. B. 1840. Educ. at the Belfast Mercantile Academy. Mr. De Cobain held office under the Belfast Harbour Commission, and as Borough Cashier (Treasurer) to the Belfast Corporation. He was also for five years Grand Master of the Orange Institution of Belfast, and later Dept.-Grand Master for Ireland. A Conservative, "with strong democratic sympathies". Sat for Belfast E. from Nov. 1885 until expelled from the House of Commons on 26 Feb. 1892, for what the 1892 *Journal of the House of Commons* described as "having been charged with having committed ... gross and criminal acts of indecency ... and having fled from justice and failed to obey an order of this house ..." Died 23 Sept. 1908. [1891]

de ERESBY, Lord Willoughby. See WILLOUGHBY de ERESBY, Gilbert Heathcote-Drummond-Willoughby, Lord.

de FOREST, Baron Maurice Arnold. 59 Grosvenor Street, London. Coombe Hurst, Kingston Hill, Surrey. Gaddesby Hall, Nr. Leicester. National Liberal, Royal Automobile, Eighty, and Marlborough. Adopted s. of Baron and Baroness Hirsch. B. 9 Jan. 1879; m. 1904, Hon. Ethel Gerard, d. of 2nd Baron

Gerard. Educ. at Eton, and Christ Church, Oxford. Hereditary Baron of the Austrian Empire, and authorized by Royal Licence to use his title in the United Kingdom. Lieut. Prince of Wales' Own Norfolk Artillery; Honorary Lieut. in the army 1900 and Lieut. Staffordshire Imperial Yeomanry; Lieut.-Commander R.N.V.R. 1914. A member of London County Council from 1910-13. An advanced Radical. Unsuccessfully contested Southport division of S.W. Lancashire in Jan. 1910. Elected for N. West Ham July 1911 and sat until he retired in 1918. Relinquished his Austrian Barony in 1920. Became a naturalised citizen of Lichtenstein in 1932 and was created Count de Bendern in 1936. Died at Biarritz 6 Oct. 1968. [1918]

DELANY, William. Killeigh, Tullamore, Ireland. S. of Denis Delany, Esq., Farmer and Grazier, and Margaret Kinsella, his wife. B. 1855. Unmarried. Educ. privately. A Farmer. Member of Rural District Council, Mountmellick. A Nationalist, favoured Home Rule, Catholic university education, compulsory purchase of land, financial reform, etc. Pledged to sit, vote, and act with the Irish party. First elected for the Ossory division of Queen's Co. in 1900 and sat until his death 7 Mar. 1916. [1915]

de LISLE, Edwin Joseph Lisle March Phillipps. 35 Thurloe Square, London. Carlton. S. of Ambrose Phillipps de Lisle, Esq., of Garendon Park and Gracedieu Manor, Leicestershire, by Laura Mary, d. of the Hon. Thomas Clifford, s. of the 4th Lord Clifford of Chudleigh. B. 1852 at Gracedieu Manor; m. 1889, Agnes, eld. d. of Adrian Hope, Esq. Educ. at Oscott (R. Catholic) Coll., near Birmingham, and at the Universities of Münster, Westphalia, and Innsbrück. Was Private Secretary to Sir Frederick Weld, G.C.M.G., as Governor of the Straits Settlements at Singapore in 1881-82, and to Lord John Manners as Postmaster-Gen. in Lord Salisbury's first administration. A F.S.A., the author of *Parliamentary Oath, Centenary Studies, The Majesty of London*, etc. "A Tory", a Unionist, a scientific Free-and-fair trader, a constructive reformer; supported the legal status of the established churches. Sat for the Loughborough division of Leicestershire from July 1886 until defeated in 1892. Died 5 May 1920. [1892]

93

DENISON, Ernest William. See BECKETT, Ernest William.

DENISON, William Becket. See BECKETT, William.

DENISON, Hon. William Gervase. See BECKETT, Hon. William Gervase. Continued in House after 1918: full entry in Volume III.

DENISON-PENDER, John Cuthbert Denison. Continued in House after 1918: full entry in Volume III.

DENMAN, Hon. Richard Douglas. Continued in House after 1918: full entry in Volume III.

DENNISS, Edmund Robert Bartley. See BARTLEY-DENNISS, Edmund Robert Bartley. Continued in House after 1918: full entry in Volume III.

DENNY, John McAusland. Garmoyle, Dumbarton. Carlton, Oriental, and Constitutional. Imperial Union, and Conservative, Glasgow. S. of Peter Denny, Esq., LL.D., Shipbuilder of Helenslee, Dumbarton, and his wife, Helen Leslie. B. at Dumbarton 1858; m. 1885, Janet Connal, d. of John Tulloch, Esq., Engineer, Dumbarton. Educ. at the Burgh Academy, and Lausanne, Switzerland. A Shipbuilder. Chairman of the Glasgow and Renfrew District Railway; a Director of the Lanarkshire and Dumbartonshire Railway Company, as well as of the India Gen. Navigation and Railway Company, the Union Steam-ship Company, of New Zealand, and the Coast Development Company. Honorary Col. of 1st Dumbarton Rifle Volunteers, a J.P. for Co. Dumbarton, etc. A Conservative. Represented Kilmarnock from 1895 until he retired in 1906. Died 9 Dec. 1922.   [1905]

de ROTHSCHILD, Baron Ferdinand James. See ROTHSCHILD, Baron Ferdinand James de.

de ROTHSCHILD, Lionel Nathan. See ROTHSCHILD, Lionel Nathan de. Continued in House after 1918: full entry in Volume III.

de VALERA, Eamonn. Continued in House after 1918: full entry in Volume III.

DEVLIN, Charles Ramsay. 14 Rathdown Terrace, Dublin. Aylmer, Quebec, Canada. S. of Charles Devlin, Esq., of Co. Roscommon, and Helen Roney, of Aylmer, Quebec. B. at Aylmer 1858; m. 1893, Blanche, d. of Maj. de Montigny. Educ. at Montreal Coll., and Laval University, Quebec. Was for several years connected with the Press, and in Mar. 1903 and sat until he accepted Chiltern Hundreds in Sept. 1906. A member of the Canadian House of Commons 1891-97. Commissioner in Ireland for the Canadian Government 1897-1903. A Nationalist, believed that the treatment extended to Canada should be given to Ireland. Elected for Galway City in Mar. 1903 and sat until he accepted Chiltern Hundreds in Sept. 1906. Returned to Canada in 1906. Minister of Colonisation, also of Mines and Fisheries, and member of Quebec's Executive Council from 1907. Died 1 Mar. 1914.   [1906]

DEVLIN, Joseph. Continued in House after 1918: full entry in Volume III.

DEWAR, Arthur. 8 Drumsheugh Gardens, Edinburgh. Reform. S. of John Dewar, Esq., Distiller. B. 1860 at Perth; m. 1892, Letitia, d. of Robert Bell, Esq., of Clifton Hall. Educ. at Perth, and Edinburgh University; M.A. Admitted a member of the Edinburgh Faculty of Advocates 1885; K.C. 1903. Solicitor-Gen. for Scotland, appointed Feb. 1909. A Liberal. Sat for Edinburgh S. from 1899-1900 when he was defeated; re-elected in 1906 and sat until appointed Senator of College of Justice in Scotland in Apr. 1910 with title of Lord Dewar Died 14 June 1917. [1910]

DEWAR, Sir John Alexander, Bart. Dupplin Castle, Perthshire. 5 Grosvenor Square, London. Brooks's, and Reform. S. of John Dewar, Esq., of Perth. B. at Perth 1856; m. 1st, 1884, d. of William Tod, Esq., of Gospetry, Kinross-shire (she died 1899); 2ndly, 1905, Margaret, d. of Henry Holland, Esq. Educ. at Perth Academy. Chairman of John Dewar and Sons Limited, of Perth. Created Bart. 1907. Was Lord Provost of Perth 1893-99. A J.P. and Dept.-Lieut. for Perthshire. A Liberal. Sat for Inverness-shire from 1900 until created Baron Forteviot in Dec. 1916. Died 23 Nov. 1929.   [1916]

DEWAR, Sir Thomas Robert. 26 Savoy

Hotel Chambers, London. The Grove, Pluckley, Kent. Carlton, Junior Carlton, and Sports. S. of John Dewar, Esq., founder of the firm of John Dewar and Sons, and Janet his wife. B. in Perth 1864. Unmarried. Educ. at Perth and Edinburgh. A Distiller. J.P. for Kent; Lieut. of the City of London; was on the London County Council for W. Marylebone 1892-95; Sheriff of the City of London 1897-98. Author of *A Ramble Round the Globe, Experiences of Prohibition*, etc. Knighted 1902. A Conservative, in favour of better housing of the working classes, and strongly against the unrestricted immigration of pauper aliens. Contested Essex S.W. Feb. 1897. Elected for the St. George's division of Tower Hamlets in 1900 and sat until he retired in 1906. Created Bart in 1917. Created 1st Baron Dewar 1919. Died 11 Apr. 1930.   [1905]

de WORMS, Rt. Hon. Baron Henry. 42 Grosvenor Place, London. Henley Park, Guildford. Carlton, and Junior Carlton. S. of the 1st Baron De Worms, of Park Crescent, Portland Place, London, by Henrietta, d. of S.M. Samuel, Esq., of London. B. in London 1840; m. 1887, Sarah, only d. of Sir B.S. Phillips. Educ. at King's Coll., London, of which he was elected a Fellow in 1868. A F.R.S. Called to the bar at the Inner Temple 1863 and joined the South-Eastern Circuit. A Magistrate and Dept.-Lieut. for Middlesex, and a Royal Commissioner of the Patriotic Fund. President of the Anglo-Jewish Association 1872-86. Published *The Earth and its Mechanism* (1863), *The Austro-Hungarian Empire* (1872), *England's Policy in the East* (1877), and *Memories of Count Beust* (1887). Was Parliamentary Secretary to the Board of Trade 1885-86, and again 1886-88. In 1887 was appointed British Plenipotentiary to, and President of the International Conference on the Sugar Bounties. Was Parliamentary Under-Secretary for the Colonies 1888 to 1892, and became a Privy Councillor in 1889. Hereditary Baron of the Austrian Empire. A Conservative, advocated a strong foreign and colonial policy. Unsuccessfully contested Sandwich in 1868. Sat for Greenwich from 1880-85; was first elected for the E. Toxteth division of Liverpool at the general election of 1885 and sat until created Lord Pirbright in Oct. 1895. Died 6 Jan. 1903.   [1895 2nd ed.]

DIAMOND, Charles. 276 Strand, London. B. 1858 in Co. Derry; m. 1882. Educ. at a National School, and privately. Left Ireland when 20 years of age, and resided in Newcastle-on-Tyne, London, and Glasgow. A Journalist, and Proprietor of several newspapers. A Nationalist and Anti-Parnellite. First returned for the N. division of Monaghan in July 1892 and sat until he retired in 1895. For the Labour Party, he contested Peckham in 1918, Rotherhithe in 1922 and Clapham in 1924. Founder of several London and Provincial weekly newspapers. Died 19 Feb. 1934.   [1895]

DICKINSON, Robert Edmund. The Albany, Piccadilly, London. Combe Cottage, Lyncombe, Bath. Carlton, Conservative, and St. Stephen's. S. of Edmund Henry Dickinson, Esq., J.P., and the Hon. Emily Dulcibella, d. of the 3rd Lord Auckland, Bishop of Bath and Wells. B. 1862. Educ. at Eton Coll., and Trinity Coll., Cambridge. A Director of Stuckey's Somersetshire Bank and National Provident Institution; J.P. for the Co. of Somerset; Capt. N. Somerset Yeomanry and Mayor of Bath 1899. A Conservative. Elected for the Wells division of Somerset in 1899 and sat until defeated in 1906. Contested St. Pancras W. Jan. 1910. Died 16 Nov. 1947.   [1905]

DICKINSON, Rt. Hon. Sir Willoughby Hyett, K.B.E. 4 Egerton Gardens, London. 42 Parliament Street, London. Reform, and National Liberal. S. of S.S. Dickinson, Esq., MP for Stroud, and Frances, d. of W.H. Hyett, Esq., MP, of Painswick House. B. 9 Apr. 1859 at Brown's Hill near Stroud; m. 1891, Minnie Elizabeth, d. of Gen. Sir R. Meade, K.C.S.I. Educ. at Eton, and Trinity Coll., Cambridge; B.A. A Barrister, called 1884. A Temporary Chairman in Committee of the whole House; a member of the Speaker's Conference on Electoral Reform 1916-17. A member of the London County Council 1889-1907; Dept.-Chairman 1892-96; Chairman 1900. Was a member of the London Education Committee; a J.P. and Dept.-Lieut. for London; Chairman of London Liberal Federation; Commissioner (unpaid) on Board of Control for Care of Mentally Defective. PC. 1914. K.B.E. 1918. A Liberal. Unsuccessfully contested Stepney in 1895 and N. St. Pancras in 1900. First elected for N. St. Pancras in 1906 and sat until defeated in 1918. Again defeated at N. St. Pancras in 1922. Joined Labour Party in 1930; joined National Labour 1931; Vice-President of the League of Nations Union 1924; British Delegate (Substitute) to the League of Nations Assembly 1923. Created 1st Baron Dickinson in 1930. Died 31 May 1943.   [1918]

DICKSON, Alexander George. 10 Duke Street, St. James's, London. Glemham Hall, Wickham Market. Carlton, Army & Navy, United Service, and Garrick. S. of George Dickson, Esq., of Belchester, Berwickshire, by Jane, eld. d. of Gen. Sir Martin Hunter, G.C.M.G. of Medomsley, Durham, and Anton's Hill, Berwickshire. B. at Belchester 1834; m. 1861, Charlotte Maria, 3rd d. of the Hon. and Rev. William Eden and widow of Lord North. Educ. at Rugby. Entered the army as Ensign 1853, became Lieut. 1854, afterwards Capt. 6th Dragoon Guards Carabineers, Maj. 13th Hussars 1860; served with the 62nd foot at Sebastopol 1854-55, including the attack on the Quarries on the Redan, for which he had a medal and clasp; was present with the Carabineers at Meerut during the Sepoy mutiny 1857, and at the operations before Delhi, for which he also received a medal and clasp. Chairman of the Crystal Palace Company, and a Director of the London, Chatham, and Dover Railway. A moderate Conservative. Sat for Dover from July 1865 until his death on 4th July 1889.   [1889]

DICKSON, Rt. Hon. Charles Scott. 22 Moray Place, Edinburgh. Carlton, and Constitutional. S. of John Robert Dickson, Esq., M.D., of Glasgow, and Mary Scott. B. in Glasgow 1850; m. 1883, Hester Bagot, d. of W. Banks, Esq., of Edinburgh. Educ. at the High School, Glasgow, and the Universities of Glasgow and Edinburgh; M.A.; LL.D. Glasgow and Aberdeen. Was called to the Scottish bar 1877; advocate depute 1892 and 1895; Q.C. 1896; Solicitor-Gen. for Scotland from 1896-1903; and Lord Advocate 1903-05; PC. 1903. Dean of the Faculty of Advocates. A J.P. and Dept.-Lieut. for Edinburgh. A Unionist. Unsuccessfully contested the Kilmarnock Burghs in 1892, and the Bridgeton division of Glasgow in 1895 and 1897. Sat for the Bridgeton division of Glasgow from 1900-06, when he was defeated. First elected for the Central division of Glasgow in Mar. 1909 and sat until appointed Lord Justice

Clerk in Scotland in 1915, with title of Lord Dickson. Died 5 Aug. 1922.   [1915]

DICKSON, Samuel. Ballysimon. Co. Limerick. Union, London, Limerick and Brighton, Stephen's Green, Dublin. S. of Samuel Dickson, Esq., of Ballysimon, Co. Limerick, by his 2nd wife, d. of John Norris, Esq., of the city of Limerick. B. at Ballysimon, Co. Limerick about 1776. Unmarried. High Sheriff for the Co. of Limerick 1829, and for the city of Limerick in 1845; a Magistrate for the city and Co. of Limerick. A Liberal, in favour of protection to agriculture, and would not support the Repeal of the Union. Unsuccessfully contested Limerick city in 1830 and again in 1832. First returned for Limerick Co. in June 1849, without opposition, when Mr. Smith O'Brien was found guilty of high treason, and sat until he died on 29 Oct. 1850.   [1850]

DICKSON, Thomas Alexander. 78 St. Stephen's Green, Dublin. Miltown House, Dungannon. Reform. S. of James Dickson, Esq., Merchant, of Dungannon. B. 1833; m. 1856, Elizabeth Greer, d. of John McGeagh, Esq., of Cookstown. Educ. at Dungannon School. A Linen Manufacturer and Merchant at Dungannon and Belfast. A J.P. for Tyrone. A Nationalist, supported the Anti-Parnellite party. Sat for Dungannon from Feb. 1874 to July 1880, when he was unseated on petition. Sat for the Co. of Tyrone Sept. 1881 to 1885. In the latter year he was an unsuccessful candidate for Mid-Antrim. Unsuccessfully contested Mid-Armagh in Feb. 1886 and in July 1886 he was defeated at the Govan division of Lanarkshire (standing as a Liberal candidate). Sat for the St. Stephen's Green division of Dublin from May 1888 until he retired in 1892. PC. (Ireland) 1893. Died 17 June 1909.   [1892]

DICKSON-POYNDER, Sir John Poynder, Bart. 8 Chesterfield Gardens, Mayfair, London. Hartham Park, Corsham, Wiltshire. Marlborough, and Reform. S. of Rear-Admiral Bourmaster Dickson, C.B., and Sarah Matilda, 3rd d. of Thomas Poynder, Esq., of Hartham. B. 1866; m. 1896, Anne Beauclerk, d. of Mr. and Hon. Mrs. Henry Dundas. Succeeded as Bart. 1884. Educ. at Harrow, and Christ Church, Oxford. Lieut. 3rd Battalion Royal Scots (M.). Assumed the name of Dickson-Poynder by Royal Licence in

1888. D.S.O. 1900. A member of London County Council and Maj. Royal Wiltshire Yeomanry Cavalry. Was High Sheriff of Wiltshire 1890. First elected as a Conservative, but joined the Liberal Party in Apr. 1904. Represented the Chippenham division of Wiltshire from 1892 until he retired in Jan. 1910. Created Baron Islington in Apr. 1910. Gov. of New Zealand from 1910-12. PC. 1911. Chairman of Royal Commission on Public Services in India 1912-14. Under-Secretary for the Colonies from 1914-15. Under-Secretary for India from 1915-19. Chairman National Savings Committee 1920-26. Died 6 Dec. 1936.   [1909]

DIGBY, John Kenelm Digby Wingfield. See WINGFIELD-DIGBY, John Kenelm Digby.

DILKE, Sir Charles Wentworth, Bart. 76 Sloane Street, London. Reform. S. of Charles Wentworth Dilke, Esq., Proprietor and for many years Editor of the *Athenaeum*, by Maria, d. of Edward Walker, Esq. B. in London 1810; m. 1840, Mary, only d. of Capt. William Chatfield, Madras Cavalry (she died 1853). Educ. at Westminster School, and Trinity Hall, Cambridge. Was a Commisioner of, and well known for his exertions in connection with the Exhibitions of 1851 and 1862. A Commissioner of Lieutenancy of London from 1856. Founder of *Gardener's Chronicle* 1841. Chairman of the Council of Society of Arts. Created Bart. 1862. F.S.A., F.R.G.S. A Liberal. Elected for Wallingford July 1865 and sat until he was defeated in Nov. 1868. English Commissioner to horticultural exhibition in St. Petersburg, where he died on 10 May 1869. [1867]

DILKE, Rt. Hon. Sir Charles Wentworth, Bart. 76 Sloane Street, London. Pyrford Rough, Woking. Dockett Eddy, Shepperton, Middlesex. Reform, National Liberal, and Burlington Fine Arts. Eld. s. of Sir Charles Wentworth Dilke, 1st Bart. (a Royal Commissioner of Exhibitions of 1851 and 1862, and MP for Wallingford from 1865 to 1868), by Mary, d. of Capt. W. Chatfield, Madras Cavalry. B. in Sloane Street 1843; m. 1872, Katherine Mary Eliza, only d. of Arthur Gore Sheil, Esq. (she died 1874); 2ndly, 1885, Emilia Francis Strong, d. of Maj. Strong, of the East India Company, and widow of Mark Pattison,

Esq., of Oxford (she died 1904). Educ. at Trinity Hall, Cambridge; LL.B. 1st, in Law Tripos, LL.M. Was called to the bar at the Middle Temple 1866. Was Under-Secretary of State for Foreign Affairs from Apr. 1880 to Dec. 1882, and President of the Local Government Board 1882-85. PC. 1882. Chairman of several Royal Commissions. Author of *Greater Britain, The Fall of Prince Florestan of Monaco, The Papers of a Critic* (essays by his grandfather, the founder of the *Athenaeum*), *The Present Position of European Politics, The British Army, Problems of Greater Britain*, and joint author of a work on *Imperial Defence*. Proprietor of the *Athenaeum* (Journal), *Notes and Queries*, etc. Succeeded as Bart. in 1869. Cited as co-respondent by Donald Crawford, MP for N.W. Lancashire in the Crawford divorce case 1885-86. An advanced Radical. Sat for Chelsea from 1868 to 1886, when he was defeated; sat for the Forest of Dean division of Gloucestershire from July 1892 until his death 26 Jan. 1911. [1910]

DILLON, John. 2 North Great George's Street, Dublin. S. of John Blake Dillon, Esq., of Dublin, MP for Tipperary, by Adelaide, d. of William Francis Hart, Esq., of Dublin. B. at Dublin 1851; m. 1895, d. of Sir J. Mathew, Judge of the High Court of Justice (she died 1907). Educ. at the Catholic University, Dublin. A Licentiate of the Irish Coll. of Surgeons. Was Leader of the Nationalist Party in succession to Mr. Justin McCarthy 1896-1900. A Nationalist. Sat for Tipperary from 1880-83, when he resigned. Sat for Mayo E. from Nov. 1885 until defeated in 1918. Contested N. Tyrone in Dec. 1885 and S. Roscommon in July 1895 whilst sitting for Mayo E. Chairman of Irish Nationalist Party 1918. Died 4 Aug. 1927. Modern biography by F.S.L. Lyons. [1918]

DILLWYN, Lewis Llewelyn. 10 Kings Bench Walk, London. Hendrefolian, Nr. Swansea. Athenaeum. 2nd s. of Lewis Weston Dillwyn, Esq., of Sketty Hall, (who sat for Glamorganshire from 1832 till 1837, and was well known for his works on Botany and Natural History), by Mary, d. of John Llewelyn, Esq., of Penllergare, Glamorganshire. B. at Swansea 1814; m. 1838, d. and heir of Sir H.T. De La Beche, C.B. (she died 1866). A Magistrate and Dept.-Lieut. for Glamorgan. Honorary Col. 3rd Glamorgan Regt. (Swansea). A Liberal, in favour of Home Rule for Ireland. Sat for Swansea from Feb. 1855 until 1885 and for Swansea Town from 1885 until his death 19 June 1892.   [1892]

DILLWYN-LLEWELYN, Sir John Talbot, Bart. 39 Cornwall Gardens, London. Penllergaer, Swansea. Ynisygerwn, Neath. Athenaeum. S. of John Dillwyn-Llewelyn, Esq., F.R.S., J.P., Dept.-Lieut., etc. and his wife, Emma Thomasina, d. of T. Mansel Talbot, Esq., of Margam Abbey and Penrice Castle. B. 1836 at Penllergaer; m. 1861, Caroline Julia, d. of Sir Michael Hicks-Beach, 8th Bart. Educ. at Eton, and Christ Church, Oxford (M.A.). A J.P. and Dept.-Lieut. for Glamorganshire (High Sheriff 1878); was sometimes Chairman Quarter Sessions; Mayor of Swansea 1890-91, and County Alderman (Glamorganshire). Created Bart. 1890. A Conservative. Unsuccessfully contested Glamorgan S. Dec. 1885, Cardiff District, Feb. 1886, Glamorgan W. Mar. 1888, and Swansea Town July 1892. First returned for Swansea Town July 1895 and sat until defeated in 1900. Died 6 July 1927. [1900]

DILLWYN - VENABLES - LLEWELYN, Charles Leyshon. See VENABLES-LLEWELYN, Charles Leyshon Dillwyn.

DIMSDALE, Rt. Hon. Sir Joseph Cockfield, Bart., K.C.V.O. 29 Sussex Square, London. Goldsmiths, Langdon Hills, Essex. Carlton, Albemarle, and City Carlton. S. of Joseph Cockfield Dimsdale, Esq., and Catharine, d. of T. Stephenson, Esq. B. at 49 Cornhill, London 1849; m. 1873, Beatrice Eliza Bower Holdsworth, d. of R.H. Holdsworth, Esq., 57 Gloucester Gardens, London. Educ. at Eton Coll. Chamberlain of the City of London, appointed 1902. Represented the City of London on the London County Council 1895-1900; Alderman of Cornhill 1891-1902; Sheriff 1893-94; Lord Mayor of London 1901-02; Knighted at Windsor 1894; created Bart., PC., and K.C.V.O. 1902; Knight Commander Star of Ethiopia and Rising Sun of Japan; Master of Grocers' Company 1885-86; Grand Treasurer of Freemasons; Treasurer of, and connected with, many charitable and philanthropic institutions. J.P. for Essex. A Conservative. Elected for the City of London 1900 and sat until he retired in 1906. Died 9 Aug. 1912.   [1905]

DIMSDALE, Baron Robert. 32 Cadogan Terrace, London. Essenden Place, Hatfield, Hertfordshire. Carlton, and Constitutional. Robert Dimsdale, 6th Baron Dimsdale in the Empire of Russia, was the only s. of Baron Charles John Dimsdale, by Jemima, d. of the Rev. Henry A. Pye, prebendary of Worcester. B. 1828; m. 1853, Cecilia Jane, eld. d. of the Rev. Marcus Southwell, Vicar of St. Stephen's, St. Albans, Hertfordshire. Educ. at Eton, and Corpus Christi Coll., Oxford. His ancestor, an eminent physician, received the dignity of a barony of the Russian Empire, with the title of honourable, from the Empress Catharine, for services rendered to her and to her son in 1762. A Conservative, prepared to give a "hearty yet independent support" to Lord Salisbury's administration; in favour of free trade, the revision of local taxation, and the cheapening of the transfer of land. Baron Dimsdale unsuccessfully contested Hertford on 19 Aug. 1859. He sat for Hertford from 1866 until he retired in 1874; he was returned for the Hitchin division of Hertfordshire in 1885 and sat until he retired in 1892. Died 2 May 1898. [1892]

DISRAELI, Coningsby Ralph. 89 Onslow Square, London. Hughenden Manor, High Wycombe. Carlton, and White's. Only s. of Ralph Disraeli, Esq., 15 years Dept.-Clerk of Parliaments, by Katherine, d. of Charles Trevor, Esq. Nephew to the Earl of Beaconsfield, whose property in Buckinghamshire he inherited. B. 1867; m. 1897, Marion, d. of Edward Silva, Esq., of Testcombe, Hampshire. Educ. at the Charterhouse, and at New Coll., Oxford. A J.P., Dept.-Lieut., and Alderman for the County Council of Buckinghamshire. Lieut. Royal Buckinghamshire Hussars. A Conservative, strongly in favour of a reform in our Fiscal System, and of Preferential Tariffs to our Colonies. Sat for the Altrincham division of Cheshire from 1892 until defeated in 1906. Contested Rushcliffe division of Nottinghamshire in Jan. and Dec. 1910. Died 30 Sept. 1936. [1905]

DIXON, Charles Harvey. Continued in House after 1918: full entry in Volume III.

DIXON, Rt. Hon. Sir Daniel, Bart. Ballymenock, Holywood, Co. Down. Ravenside. Co. Louth. Glenville, Cushendale, Co. Antrim. Constitutional. S. of Thomas Dixon, Esq., of Larne, and Sarah,

d. of D. McCambridge, Esq., of Mullarts, Antrim. B. 1844; m. 1st, Lizzie, d. of James Agnew, Esq., of Belfast (she died 1868); 2ndly, 1870, Annie, d. of James Shaw, Esq., of Belfast. Educ. privately, and at Academical Institution, Belfast. A Shipowner and Timber Merchant. Elected member of Belfast Town Council 1871; Alderman 1882; Mayor 1892-93; Lord Mayor 1902-03 and 1905. Knighted 1892. PC. (Ireland) 1902. Created Bart 1903. Chairman of Belfast Harbour Commissioners. J.P., and Dept.-Lieut. for Co. Down, (Sheriff 1896); Dept.-Lieut. for Belfast; J.P. for Co. Antrim. A Conservative. Elected for N. Belfast Sept. 1905 and sat until his death 10 Mar. 1907.   [1906]

DIXON, George. The Dales, 42 Augustus Road, Birmingham. Reform. S. of Abraham Dixon, Esq., of Whitehaven, by Letitia, d. of John Taylor, Esq., of Gomersall, Yorkshire. B. at Gomersall 1820; m. 1855, Mary, d. of James Stansfeld, Esq., County Court Judge of Halifax (she died 1885). Educ. at the Leeds Grammar School. Was Mayor of Birmingham 1867. Became afterwards a prominent member of the National Education League. Was Chairman of the Birmingham School Board 1876-96. A Liberal Unionist. Sat for Birmingham from 1867 to 1876, when he resigned. Represented the Edgbaston division of Birmingham from Nov. 1885 until his death 24 Jan. 1898.   [1897]

DIXON-HARTLAND, Sir Frederick Dixon, Bart. 14 Chesham Place, London. Ashley Manor, Nr. Cheltenham. Carlton, and Garrick. Eld. s. of Nathaniel Hartland, Esq., of The Oaklands, Gloucestershire, by Eliza, d. and co-heir of Thomas Dixon, Esq., of King's Lynn. B. at Evesham 1832; m. 1st, Grace Amy, youngest d. of Col. Wilson, K.H.; 2ndly, 1895, Agnes Chichester, d. of W.L. Christie, Esq., of Glyndebourne, Sussex, MP for Lewes. Was educ. at Cheltenham Coll., and was a F.S.A., F.R.G.S., etc. Created Bart. 1892. J.P. for Middlesex, London, Gloucestershire, Sussex, and Worcestershire, a Lieut. for the City of London, County Alderman for Middlesex, a Governor of Christ's Hospital, and Chairman of the Thames Conservancy Board. Author of Genealogical History of the Royal Houses of Europe, and other works. One of the founders of the Primrose League. A Conservative. Unsuccessfully contested

Hereford in Apr. 1880. Stood for Evesham July 1880, when he was in a minority of 2, but on petition obtained the seat, Dec. 1880, and sat until 1885. Sat for the Uxbridge division of Middlesex from 1885 until his death 15 Nov. 1909.   [1909]

DOBBIE, Joseph. Murrayfield Avenue, Edinburgh. Bentfield, Prestwick, Ayr. National Liberal. S. of James Dobbie, Esq., of Ayr. B. at Ayr, 9 June 1862; m. 1896, Alice, d. of James Sharp, Esq., of Edinburgh. Educ. at Ayr Academy, and Edinburgh University. A Solicitor, Supreme Court of Scotland; head of the firm of Dalgleish and Dobbie, W.S., Edinburgh. Honorary Secretary to Scottish Small Holdings Association; a Member of Scottish Committee of the Cobden Club. A Liberal, in favour of social and industrial reform. Elected for Ayr, Jan. 1904 and sat until defeated in 1906. Unsuccessfully contested Edinburgh Central as Coalition Liberal candidate in 1918. A member of the Departmental Committee on Housing 1908; Chairman Royal Scots Recruiting Committee 1914-16. Knighted 1920. Died 18 May 1943.   [1905]

DOBSON, Thomas William. 124 George Street, Croydon. National Liberal. S. of Thomas Dobson, Esq., of Hackney. B. 9 Nov. 1853 at Hackney; m. 1875, d. of William Potterveld, Esq. Educ. at Congregational School, Hackney. A Coal and Timber Merchant at Croydon and elsewhere; a J.P. for Surrey. A Liberal. Elected for Plymouth in 1906 and sat until he retired in Jan. 1910. Contested E. Nottingham in 1912, Drake division of Plymouth in 1918, and South Croydon in 1922. Died 13 May 1935.   [1909]

DODD, Cyril Joseph Settle. 28 Inverness Terrace, London. National Liberal. S. of the Rev. Joseph Dodd, M.A., Oxon, former Rector of Hampton Poyle, Oxford, by Mary, eld. d. of the Rev. Dr. Sutton, Vicar of Sheffield. B. 1844 at Hampton Poyle, Oxon; m. 1867, Sarah, d. of J. Young, Esq., of Devonport. Educ. at Shrewsbury School, and Merton Coll., Oxford, (B.A. first class mathematics 1866). A Q.C. 1890, called to the bar at the Inner Temple July 1869. One of the Editors of Bullen and Leake's Precedents of Pleading (fourth edition). A Liberal, in favour of Home Rule for Ireland, Parish Councils, Land Law reform, disestablishment, etc.

Unsuccessfully contested the Ecclesall division of Sheffield in 1885 and Cambridge in 1886. First returned for the Maldon division of Essex in July 1892 and sat until defeated in 1895. Died 29 Jan. 1913.   [1895]

DODD, William Huston. 26 Fitzwilliam Square, Dublin. National Liberal. S. of Robert Dodd, Esq., of Rathfriland, and Letty, d. of Dr. J. Huston, of Clough, Co. Down. B. 28 Mar. 1844; m. 1873, Ellen, d. of S. Hunter, Esq., J.P., Coleraine. Educ. at Academical Institution, and Queen's Coll., Belfast; M.A. A Barrister; called 1873; Q.C. 1884; H.M. Third Sergeant at Law in Ireland 1893; Counsel to the Crown for Dublin City and Co., and to the Post Office, N.E. Circuit; President of Statistical Social Inquiry Society of Ireland 1896. A Liberal. Unsuccessfully contested N. Antrim in 1892 and S. Derry 1895. Elected for N. Tyrone in 1906 and sat until appointed Irish High Court Judge 1907-24. PC. (Ireland) 1913. Died 17 Mar. 1930.   [1906]

DODDS, Joseph. 105 Pall Mall East, London.   Ragworth,   Stockton-upon-Tees. Reform. S. of Matthew Dodds, Esq., of Whorley Hill, Co. Durham, by his marriage with Miss Margaret Richardson. B. at Winston, Co. Durham 1819; m. 1847, Anne, only d. of William Smith, Esq., and cousin and co-heiress of Mrs. Elizabeth Starkey, of Stockton-upon-Tees (she died 1876). Admitted a Solicitor Sept. 1850. A Dept.-Lieut. for the Co. of Durham; Mayor of Stockton 1857-58. President of the Stockton Athenaeum, and other local institutions. A Liberal, in favour of Home Rule. Sat for Stockton from Dec. 1868 until he accepted Chiltern Hundreds in Dec. 1888. Name struck off list of Solicitors for embezzlement 18 Feb. 1889. Died 15 Dec. 1891.   [1888]

DOLAN, Charles Joseph. Irish Club. S. of J. Dolan, Esq., J.P., and Brigid Fitzpatrick. B. 18 Aug. 1881 at Manorhamilton. Educ. at St. Patrick's Coll., Cavan, Maynooth Coll., and Wren's London (Gold Medallist in Classics). A School Teacher. A Nationalist. Elected for N. Leitrim in Feb. 1906 and sat until he accepted Chiltern Hundreds on joining Sinn Fein in Jan. 1908. Defeated at a by-election at N. Letrim on 21 Feb. 1908.   [1907]

DONELAN,   Capt.   Anthony   John

Charles. Ballynona, Midleton, Co. Cork. Only s. of Col. Anthony Donelan, 48th Regiment, by Sarah, d. of John Johnson, Esq., of Holbeach, Lincolnshire. B. 1846. Educ. privately, and at Sandhurst. Was Chief Whip to the Irish Party. At one time in the army. A Protestant Home Ruler. Represented E. Cork from 1892-1911, when he was unseated on petition. Elected for E. Wicklow in July 1911 and sat until he retired in 1918. Died Sept. 1924.   [1918]

DONKIN, Richard Sims. Albemarle, Wimbledon Common, London. Carlton, St. Stephen's, Junior Carlton, Orleans, Constitutional, and Union. S. of James Donkin, Esq., Shipowner, by Ann, d. of William Sims, Esq. B. at North Shields 1836; m. 1864, Hannah, d. of John Dryden, Esq., Banker, of Tynemouth. Educ. by the Rev. F. Bewsher, Rector of Birtley. A member of the firm of Nelson, Donkin and Company, Shipowners of Newcastle and London. A J.P. and Dept.-Lieut. for the Co. of Northumberland, and Hon. Col. of the Tynemouth Artillery Volunteers. A Director of the Suez Canal Company. Was one of the signatories to the agreement of the London Shipowners with M. de Lesseps relative to the Suez Canal. A Conservative. Sat for Tynemouth from 1885 until he retired in 1900. Died 5 Feb. 1919.   [1900]

DONNELLY, Patrick. Continued in House after 1918: full entry in Volume III.

DONOVAN, John Thomas. Dunloe, Terenure Road, Dublin. Eld. s. of Daniel Donovan, Esq., of Belfast. B. 1878; m, 1915, Miss Alda Ralph, of Auckland, New Zealand. Educ. at Christian Brothers' School, Belfast, and Royal University of Ireland. A Barrister, called to the Irish bar 1914. Was a Solicitor from 1905-13. Editor of *Belfast Northern Star*. Honorary Secretary of National Volunteers of Ireland. A Nationalist. Elected for W. Wicklow in Aug. 1914 and sat until defeated in S. Donegal in 1918. Died 17 Jan. 1922.   [1918]

DOOGAN, Patrick Charles. Point House, Lisbellaw, Co. Fermanagh. S. of Patrick Doogan, Esq., of Rossavelly, Co. Fermanagh, by Catherine Maguire, d. of Thomas Maguire, Esq., of Gortahurk, Co. Fermanagh. B. 1831. A Farmer. An Irish Nationalist of the Anti-Parnellite Party. Represented E. Tyrone from 1895 until his death 15 June 1906.   [1906]

DORINGTON, Rt. Hon. Sir John Edward, Bart. 30 Queen Anne's Gate, London. Lypiatt Park, Stroud, Gloucestershire. Athenaeum, and Carlton. Eld. s. of J.E. Dorington, Esq., of Lypiatt Park, Stroud, and Queen Anne's Gate, London, by Susan, d. of J. Godman, Esq., of Park Hatch, Surrey. B. 1832; m. 1859, d. of William Speke, Esq., of Jordans, Ilminster. Educ. at Eton, and Trinity Coll., Cambridge. A Commissioner in Lunacy (unpaid), a J.P. and Dept.-Lieut. for Gloucestershire, Chairman of the Gloucestershire County Council, and Chairman of quarter sessions 1878-89. Also Maj. (retired) of the Gloucestershire Yeomanry; a Governor of the Royal Agricultural Coll., Cirencester. Chairman of Committee on Ordnance Survey 1892-93; served on Royal Commission on London Water 1897-99. Created Bart. in Feb. 1886, PC. 1902. A Conservative. Unsuccessfully contested Stroud in Aug. 1867 and Nov. 1868; was elected there at a by-election in Jan. 1874 but defeated at the general election in Feb. This election was declared void and he was elected at the by-election in May and this too was declared void in July. He was defeated again in Stroud in 1880 and in the Cirencester division of Gloucestershire in 1885. First elected for Tewkesbury division of Gloucestershire in 1886 and sat until he retired in 1906. Died 5 Apr. 1911. [1905]

DORIS, William. Altamont Terrace, Westport, Co. Mayo. 37 North Side, Clapham Common, London. S. of Robert Doris, Esq., of Westport. B. 13 Apr. 1860 at Westport; m. 1910, Sarah, d. of Luke Cannon, Esq. Educ. at Christian Brothers' School, Westport. A Journalist. Member of Mayo County Council, of which he was Vice-Chairman 1900-08; Chairman of Westport Urban Council; Vice-Chairman of Castlebar District Asylum, and a member of Westport Board of Guardians and Harbour Board, and of Co. Committees of Agriculture and Technical Instruction. A J.P. for Westport. A Nationalist. Elected for W. Mayo Jan. 1910 and sat until defeated in 1918. Died 13 Sept. 1926. [1918]

DOUGHERTY, Rt. Hon. Sir James Brown. 25 Lytton Grove, London. S. of Archibald Dougherty, Esq., M.R.C.S., and Martha, d. of the Rev. James Brown, M.A. B. 13 Nov. 1844 at Garvagh, Co. Derry; m. 1st, 1880, Mary, d. of T. Donaldson, Esq.,

of The Park Nottingham (she died 1887); 2ndly, 1889, Eliza, d. of H. Todd, Esq., of Oatlands, Co. Dublin. Educ. at Queen's Coll., Belfast. M.A. Queen's University Ireland. Was Assistant Under-Secretary for Ireland 1895-1908 and Permanent Under-Secretary 1908-14. Professor of Logic, Magee Coll., Londonderry 1879-95. Member of Educational Endowments (Ireland) Commission 1885-92. Knighted 1902. PC. (Ireland) 1908; K.C.B. 1910; K.C.V.O. 1911. A Liberal. Unsuccessfully contested N. Tyrone in 1892. Elected for Londonderry city on 30 Nov. 1914 and sat until retired in 1918. Died 3 Jan. 1934. [1918]

DOUGHTY, Sir George. Waltham Hall, Lincolnshire. Carlton. S. of William Doughty, Esq., of Grimsby. B. 1854; m. 1st, 1879, Rebecca Vere (she died 1904); 2ndly, 1907, Eugenia, d. of John Stone, Esq., of Melbourne. Educ. at Wesleyan Higher Grade School, Grimsby. A Merchant and Shipowner. Was twice Mayor of Grimsby. A J.P. for Lincolnshire. Knighted 1904. A Unionist. Was first elected for Grimsby as a Liberal in 1895, but when he joined the Unionist Party (in 1898) he resigned his seat and was re-elected on 2 Aug. 1898 and sat until the general election in Jan. 1910, when he was defeated; re-elected for Grimsby at the general election of Dec. 1910 and sat until his death 27 Apr. 1914. [1914]

DOUGLAS, Rt. Hon. Aretas Akers. See AKERS-DOUGLAS, Rt. Hon. Aretas.

DOUGLAS, Charles Mackinnon. 39 Grosvenor Road, London. Auchlochan, Lesmahagow, Lanarkshire. S. of Dr. Halliday Douglas, Physician of Edinburgh. B. 1865; m. Anne, d. of Robert Tod, Esq. Graduated M.A., D.Sc.; author of *John Stuart Mill, A Study of his Philosophy* (1895), *The Ethics of J.S. Mill* (1898), etc. A Liberal, in favour of Home Rule, Land Reform, Local Control of the Liquor Traffic and an eight-hour day for Miners. Represented N.W. Lanarkshire from 1899 until defeated in 1906. Contested S. division of Lanarkshire as a Liberal Unionist. Dec. 1910. President of the Scottish Agricultural Organ Water Society and sometime member of several similar societies. Died 3 Feb. 1924. [1905]

DOUGLAS-PENNANT, Hon. Edward Sholto. Mortimer House, Halkin Street,

London. Sholebroke Lodge, Towcester. Bachelors'. Eld. s. of Baron Penrhyn, by his 1st wife Pamela, d. of Sir Charles Rushout, 2nd Bart. B. 1864; m. 1887, Blanche Georgina, d. of the 3rd Baron Southampton. Educ. at Eton. A J.P. and Dept.-Lieut. for Carnarvonshire, and a Capt. Buckinghamshire Hussars Yeomanry; Lieut. 1st Life Guards 1885-91. A Conservative and Unionist. Sat for Northamptonshire S. from July 1895 until he retired in 1900. Succeeded as 3rd Baron Penrhyn in 1907. Died 22 Aug. 1927. [1900]

DOUGLAS-SCOTT-MONTAGU, Hon. John Walter Edward. See SCOTT-MONTAGU, Hon. John Walter Edward Douglas.

DOXFORD, Sir William Theodore. Grindon Hall, Sunderland. Carlton, Constitutional, and City of London. S. of William Doxford, Esq., Shipbuilder, and Hannah Pile, his wife. B. 1 Feb. 1841 at Sunderland; m. 1863, Margaret, d. of Richard Wilkinson, Esq. Educ. at Bramham Coll., Yorkshire. A Shipbuilder and Engineer, of the firm of Doxford and Sons Limited, of Sunderland, J.P. for the borough of Sunderland, J.P. and Dept.-Lieut. for Co. Durham, and a River Wear Commissioner. Knighted Jan. 1900. A Conservative. Represented Sunderland from 1895 until he retired in 1906. Died 1 Oct. 1916. [1905]

DRAGE, Geoffrey. 20 Lowndes Square, London. Carlton, Ranelagh, and United University. S. of Charles Drage, Esq., M.D., of Hatfield, and Elinor Margaret Drage. B. 17 Aug. 1860; m. 1896, Ethel, eld. d. of T.H. Ismay, Esq., of Dawpool, Cheshire. Educ. at Eton, Christ Church, Oxford, Berlin, Moscow, and other foreign Universities (B.A. 1883, M.A. 1886). Called as a Barrister at Lincoln's Inn and Middle Temple 1888, but did not practise. Was Secretary to the Royal Commission on Labour 1891-94, and author of *Cyril*, a novel of which eight editions were published, *The Criminal Code, The Labour Problem*, and *The Unemployed*. Travelled much in Europe, the colonies, and America. A Conservative, in favour of self-help in the labour and aged poor questions, also of "a strong foreign and colonial policy", the "support of religious and voluntary schools", and the maintenance of the Established Church. Sat for

Derby from July 1895 until defeated in 1900. Unsuccessfully contested the Cleveland division of the N. Riding of Yorkshire in Nov. 1902, Woolwich in Mar. 1903, and Blackburn in Jan. 1906. Chairman, Training Ship, Exmouth 1901, 1903-06, 1909-14, 1919-22; President Central Poor Law Conference 1906; Vice-President, Royal Statistical Society 1916-18; attached to Military Intelligence Section of War Office 1916; Alderman of the London County Council 1910-19; Director Royal Insurance Company 1898-1939. Died 7 Mar. 1955. [1900]

DRUCKER, Charles Gustavus Adolphus. 39a Curzon Street, London. Carlton, Junior Carlton, and St. Stephen's. S. of Louis Drucker, Esq., Banker, of Amsterdam, and of Theresa Drucker. B. 1868 at Amsterdam. Educ. at the Leyden Gymnasium and University (LL.B. 1891). A student of the Inner Temple; a member of the Loriners' Company, and a Freeman of the City of London. Published a translation of Von Ihering's *Evolution of the Aryan*. A Conservative. Unsuccessfully contested Northampton in 1892. Sat for Northampton from July 1895 until he retired in 1900. Died 10 Dec. 1903. [1900]

DUCKHAM, Thomas. Baysham Court, Ross, Herefordshire. S. of John Duckham, Esq. B. at Shirehampton, near Bristol 1816; m. 1845. Educ. at Hereford and at Prospect Place Academy, Bristol. A Farmer in Herefordshire, which occupation he commenced in 1849. A member of the Council of the Central and Associated Chambers of Agriculture, of which he was the founder; also a member of the Councils of the Bath and West of England and Southern Counties Association, and of the Smithfield Club. A Liberal, in favour of local taxation being re-adjusted, of education rates being levied on the Country at large; also of ratepayers having the control of the county expenditure. Sat for Herefordshire from Apr. 1880 until 1885 and for the Leominster division of Herefordshire from 1885 to 1886 when he unsuccessfully contested the Ross division of Herefordshire. Magistrate and Alderman for Herefordshire. Died 2 Mar. 1902. [1886]

DUCKWORTH, Sir James. Castlefield, Rochdale. 2 Whitehall Court, London. National Liberal. B. 1840. Educ. privately.

Chairman of J. Duckworth Limited, and Belfield Limited, Rochdale; a Director of Boots Limited; J.P. and Alderman for Rochdale; Mayor 1891-92 and 1910-11. President of United Methodist Free Churches 1894; F.R.G.S. Knighted 1908. A Liberal. Unsuccessfully contested Warwick and Leamington in May 1895. Sat for the Middleton division of Lancashire from 1897-1900, when he was defeated. Elected for Stockport in 1906 and sat until he retired in Jan. 1910. Died 1 Jan. 1915. [1909]

DU CROS, Alfred. 4 Addison Road, London. S. of Harvey Du Cros, Esq., and Annie, d. of John Roy, Esq., of Durrow, Queen's Co. B. 10 Dec. 1868; m. 1901, Mrs. Louise Pemberton Hincks of New Orleans (she died 1927); 2ndly, 1933, Mrs. Ethel Maude Hyde. Educ. privately. A Director of companies interested in the cycle and motor car trades. A Unionist. Elected for the Bow and Bromley division of Tower Hamlets in Jan. 1910 and sat until he retired in Dec. 1910. Died 21 Dec. 1946. [1910]

DU CROS, Sir Arthur Philip, Bart. Continued in House after 1918: full entry in Volume III.

DU CROS, William Harvey. Howbery Park, Wallingford, Berkshire. Levetleigh, St. Leonard's-on-Sea. Inniscorrig, Dalkey, Co. Dublin. Carlton, St. Stephen's, and Junior Constitutional. S. of E.P. Du Cros, Esq., of Moone, Co. Kildare, and Maria, d. of John Molloy, Esq., of Dublin. B. 1846 at Dublin; m. 1st, Annie, d. of J. Roy, Esq., of Queen's Co. (she died 1899); 2ndly, Florence, d. of William Gibbings, Esq., of Bow, Devon. Educ. at King's Hospital, Dublin. Chairman of Dunlop Tyre Company; a J.P. for Sussex. A Conservative. Sat for Hastings from 1906 until he accepted Chiltern Hundreds in 1908. Died 21 Dec. 1918. [1907]

DUFF, Robert William. Fetteresso Castle, Stonehaven, N.B. Glassaugh Portsoy, Banffshire. Culter, Aberdeenshire. Brooks's. Only s. of Arthur Duff, Esq., of Fetteresso (who assumed the name of Abercromby on succeeding to the estates of his mother), by Elizabeth, d. of John Innes, Esq., of Cowie, Kincardineshire. B. at Banff 1835; m. 1871, Louisa, youngest d. of Sir William Scott, Bart., of Ancrum.

Educ. at Blackheath school. Entered the navy 1848; attained the rank of Lieut. 1856; retired as Commander 1870. Appointed a Lord of the Treasury June 1882-June 1885, and Civil Lord of the Admiralty Feb.-July 1886. A Dept.-Lieut. of Banff, Aberdeen, and Kincardineshire. Assumed the name of Duff in lieu of Abercromby on succeeding to the estates of his uncle, Dec. 1870. A Liberal, in favour of Home Rule for Ireland, of the reform of the land laws and the maintenance of an efficient navy. Sat for Banffshire from May 1861 until appointed Governor of N.S. Wales 1893. PC. 1892; G.C.M.G. 1893. Died 15 Mar. 1895. [1892 2nd ed.]

DUFFY, William John. Shraidmor, Loughrea, Co. Galway. S. of Lawrence and Mary Duffy (née Higgins). B. at Loughrea Apr. 1865; m. 1908, Ellen, d. of Patrick Hynes, Esq. Educ. at St. Brendan's Coll., Loughrea. A Merchant. Honorary Secretary of the Land League, National League, National Federation, United Irish League, and Co. Galway Gaelic Athletic Association. A Nationalist. First elected for S. Galway in 1900 and sat until defeated in 1918. [1918]

DUGDALE, John Stratford. 7a Mount Street, Grosvenor Square, London. Blyth Hall, Coleshill, Warwickshire. Carlton, and Oxford & Cambridge. S. of W. Stratford Dugdale, Esq., MP for N. Warwickshire, of Merevale Hall and Blythe Hall, Warwickshire. B. 1835; m. 1890, Alice, youngest d. of Gen. H.A. Carleton, C.B., R.A. Educ. at Eton, and Merton Coll, Oxford (B.A. 1857). Called to the bar at the Inner Temple 1862; Q.C. 1882; bencher of his Inn 1888. Was Recorder of Grantham from 1874 to Dec. 1877, when he became Recorder of Birmingham. He was also J.P., Dept.-Lieut. and Chairman of Quarter Sessions and the County Council for Warwickshire, and practised on the Midland Circuit. Chancellor of Dioceses of Worcester and Birmingham. A Conservative, opposed to a separate Parliament for Ireland. He unsuccessfully contested N.E. Warwickshire at the general election of 1885. Returned for N.E. Warwickshire July 1886 and sat until he retired in 1892. Died 27 Oct. 1920. [1892]

DUKE, Rt. Hon. Henry Edward. Maryfield, Exeter. 9 Little College Street, London. Carlton. S. of William Edward

Duke, Esq., Quarry Proprietor, of Merevale, Devon, and Elizabeth, his wife. B. 1855. Educ. privately. A Barrister, called at Gray's inn 1885; Q.C. 1889; Bencher 1899. Was Recorder of Plymouth and Devonport 1897-1900, and of Devonport 1900-14. PC. 1915. Chairman Great Western Railway Conciliation Board 1909; Chairman Royal Commission on Defence of the Realm Losses 1915; Chairman Royal Commission on Liquor Trade Board of Control Losses 1915; Chairman Excess Profits Board of Referees 1916; Attorney-Gen. to H.R.H. Prince of Wales 1915; Chief Secretary for Ireland from 31 July 1916 to Apr, 1918. A Conservative and Unionist. Sat for Plymouth from 1900 to 1906, when he was defeated. Elected for Exeter Jan. 1910. Was declared defeated in Dec. 1910 by four votes, but on a recount the Judges declared him duly elected and he sat until appointed Lord Justice of Appeal Apr. 1918; retired Nov. 1919. President of Probate, Divorce and Admiralty division 1919-33. Kt. 1918; created Baron Merevale Jan. 1925. Died 20 May 1939. [1918]

DUMPHREYS, John Molesworth Thomas. 76 Southwark Park Road, London. S. of Michael Dumphreys, Esq., of Chester. B. 24 Dec. 1844; m. 1865, Hannah, d. of John Wootton, Esq., of Nottingham. As a youth he worked as a Leatherdresser in Bermondsey; subsequently Secretary to Pearks Limited. Represented Deptford on the London County Council. Mayor of Bermondsey. Unsuccessfully contested Birmingham W. in 1885 as a working man's Conservative and Fair Trader. Elected for the Bermondsey division of Southwark 28 Oct. 1909 and sat until defeated in Jan. 1910. Contested the seat again in Dec. 1910. Died 18 Dec. 1925.

DUNCAN, Charles. Continued in House after 1918: full entry in Volume III.

DUNCAN, David. Gayton Hall, Heswall, Cheshire. Reform, and National Liberal. Reform, and Junior Reform, Liverpool. S. of James and Margery Duncan of The Brae, Alyth, Perthshire. B. 1831; m. 1856, Catherine, d. of Archibald Williamson, Esq., of Anstruther, Fife. Educ. at the Dundee High School. A Merchant of Liverpool, Chile, and Peru, a Director of the Royal Insurance, the British and Foreign Marine Assurance, and other companies. A J.P. for Cheshire. A "progressive Liberal". Sat for Barrow-in-Furness from Nov. 1885 until unseated on petition in 1886. Sat for the Exchange division of Liverpool from July 1886 until his death 30 Dec. 1886. [1886]

DUNCAN, Col. Francis, C.B. The Common, Woolwich. Carlton, and United Service. S. of John Duncan, Esq., by Helen Drysdale Douglass, his wife. B. at Aberdeen 1836; m. 1858, Mary Kate, d. of the Rev. W. Cogswell, M.A. Educ. at Aberdeen University. Col. Duncan was M.A. and LL.D. Aberdeen, and also D.C.L. Durham and King's Coll., and University, Canada. Entered the Royal Artillery 1855, became Col. 1885. Author of *A History of the Royal Artillery, The English in Spain, The Royal Province of Nova Scotia, Our Empire in the West*, etc. Commanded the Egyptian Artillery in 1883-85, and served on the staff in many capacities. He was made a C.B. for his military services, and received also the Egyptian War medal and the 3rd class Osmanlieh. A Conservative. Unsuccessfully contested Morpeth in Feb. 1874, Durham City in June 1874, and Finsbury in Apr. 1880. Sat for the Holborn division of Finsbury from Nov. 1885 until his death 16 Nov. 1888. [1888]

DUNCAN, James Archibald. Members' Mansions, Victoria Street, London. Gayton Hall, Heswall, Cheshire. Reform, Savile, and Liverpool Reform. S. of David Duncan, Esq., J.P. of Gayton Hall, Cheshire, and Liverpool (who was elected MP for the Exchange division of Liverpool 1886, and had previously been Member for Barrow-in-Furness), and Catherine, eld. d. of Archibald Williamson, Esq., of Anstruther, Fife. B. 1858 at Valparaiso, Chili. Educ. at Amersham Hall School and Trinity Coll., Cambridge (B.A. and LL.B. 1883, M.A. 1885). A Barrister, called to the Inner Temple 1883, and practised on the Northern Circuit. A Liberal, in favour of Home Rule for Ireland and the "advanced" Liberal programme generally. After the secession of Mr. W.S. Caine from the Liberals supporting Mr. Gladstone's Home Rule policy, Mr. J.A. Duncan was accepted as candidate for Barrow-in-Furness; when in July 1890 Mr. Caine resigned and offered himself for re-election, Mr. Duncan successfully contested the seat and sat until defeated in 1892.

Contested Kircudbright 1895 and Inverness Burghs 1900. Died 13 Feb. 1911. [1892]

DUNCAN, Sir James Hastings. Kineholm, Otley, Yorkshire. National Liberal. S. of James and Elizabeth Duncan. B. at Otley 1855; m. 1879, Janette, d. of Thomas Hunter, Esq., of Newall Close, Otley. Educ. privately. A Worsted Spinner and Manufacturer. Chairman of the School Board; Alderman of the W. Riding County Council; representative on the W. Riding Rivers Board; Knighted 1914. A Liberal. Elected for the Otley division of the W. Riding of Yorkshire in 1900 and sat until he retired in 1918. Died 31 July 1928. [1918]

DUNCAN, Robert. 9 Inverness Terrace, London. Dalchonzie, Comrie, Perthshire. S. of William Duncan and Mary Roberts, of Glasgow. B. 5 Oct. 1850 at Tradeston, Glasgow; m. 1893, Mary, d. of William Jolly, Esq., H.M. Inspector of Schools. Educ. at the High School, the Academy, and the University, Glasgow. An Engineer; Senior Partner of Ross and Duncan, Marine Engineers, of Glasgow. Member of the Institute of Civil Engineering; a J.P. for Lanarkshire. Editor of *Britannia*, National Unity organ, and of *Thoughts on Life*, by Thomas Carlyle. A Conservative. United Empire Loyalist and opponent of the *laissez-faire* school. Unsuccessfully contested the Govan district of Lanarkshire in 1900. Elected there in 1906 and sat until defeated in Jan. 1910. Died 1924/25, probably early 1925. [1909]

DUNCANNON, Vere Brabazon Ponsonby, Visct. Continued in House after 1918: full entry in Volume III.

DUNCOMBE, Arthur. Carlton, and Yorkshire. 2nd s. of Admiral the Hon. Arthur Duncombe (sometime MP for E. Retford), by Delia, d. of John Wilmer Field, Esq., of Heaton Hall, Bradford. B. in London 1840; m. 1869, Katherine, d. of Henry Milbank, Esq., and Lady Margaret Milbank. Educ. at Eton, and University Coll., Oxford; called to the bar at Lincoln's Inn 1867. A Magistrate and Dept.-Lieut. for the N. and E. Ridings of Yorkshire. A Conservative. Unsuccessfully contested Scarborough on 30 July 1880. Sat for the Howdenshire division of the E. Riding of Yorkshire from 1885 until he retired in 1892. Changed his name from

Duncombe to Grey in 1905 in accordance with the will of the 7th Earl of Stamford. Died 12 June 1911. [1892]

DUNCOMBE, Hon. Hubert Ernest Valentine. 19 Belgrave Square, London. Duncombe Park, Helmsley, Yorkshire. 3rd s. of the Earl of Feversham, by Mabel, d. of the Rt. Hon. Sir J.R. Graham, 2nd Bart., of Netherby. B. 1862. Educ. at Harrow, Woolwich, and Cambridge. Maj. 2nd Voluntary Battalion P.W.O. Yorkshire Regiment. A Conservative and Unionist. Sat for Cumberland W. from July 1895 until he retired in 1900. Served in Boer War. D.S.O. 1900. Died 21 Oct. 1918. [1900]

DUNN, Albert Edward. 70 Victoria Street, London. Mount Radford, Exeter. The Battery, Portreath, Cornwall. National Liberal, and Eighty. S. of William Henry Dunn, and Henrietta Dunn (née Collard). B. 13 Feb. 1864 at Exeter. Educ. at Hallam Hall Coll., Clevedon, Somerset. A Solicitor, admitted 1887; a member of Exeter City Council from 1888; Mayor 1900-02; Honorary Town Clerk of Exeter 1905. A Liberal, in favour of Disestablishment, Franchise Reform, etc. Unsuccessfully contested Exeter in 1892. Elected for the Camborne division of Cornwall in 1906 and sat until he retired in Dec. 1910. Joined the Labour Party and contested St. Ives division of Cornwall in 1918 and 1923. Commissioned as Officer in 1914. Died 2 May 1937. [1910]

DUNN, Sir William, Bart. 34 Phillimore Gardens, Kensington, London. The Retreat, Lakenheath, Suffolk. Reform, City of London, and City Liberal. S. of John Dunn, Esq., of Paisley, and Isabella Chalmers. B. 1833; m. 1861, Sarah Elizabeth, d. of James Howse, Esq., of Grahamstown, S. Africa. Senior Partner in the firms of William Dunn and Company, Bankers and Merchants, Broad Street Avenue, London, Mackie, Dunn and Company, Port Elizabeth, W. Dunn and Company, Durban, and Dunn and Company, E. London; a J.P. for Renfrewshire, and for W. Suffolk, and a Director of the Royal Exchange Assurance Corporation, and the Union Discount Company. Created Bart. 1895. A Liberal, in favour of free education, "one man one vote", religious equality, "and consequent union of the Presbyterian churches in Scotland, local option, etc. Contested Renfrewshire

W. July 1886. Elected for Paisley on 1 June 1891 and sat until he retired in 1906. Died 31 Mar. 1912. [1905]

DUNN, Sir William Henry. 9 Gloucester Terrace, Regent's Park, London. Constitutional, City Carlton, and Hurlingham. S. of John Quinn Dunn, Esq., of Clitheroe. B. 1856; m. 1885, Ellen, d. of John Pawle, Esq. Educ. privately. A Land Agent and Surveyor; an Alderman of the City of London 1909-28 (Sheriff 1906-07); a Lieut. of the City of London and a J.P. for the Co. of London; Honorary Col. of 1st London Division Transport and Supply Column; Knighted 1907. Was invested with the following orders: Legion of Honour (France), Knight of St. Olaf (Norway), Knight of the Rising Sun (Japan), Dannebrog (Denmark), and the Order of the Crown (Germany), 2nd class. A Unionist. Elected for W. Southwark in Jan. 1910 and sat until defeated in Dec. 1910. Lord Mayor of London 1916-17; created Bart. 1917. Died 12 June 1926. [1910]

DUNNE, Edward Marten. Gatley Park, Kingsland, Herefordshire. 23 Princes Gate, London. S. of Thomas Dunne, Esq., J.P., Dept.-Lieut., of Bircher Hall, Leominster, and Harriet, d. of Gen. C.G.L. Russell, of Ashford Hall, Ludlow. B. 27 Aug. 1864; m. 1899, Hon. Grace Daphne, d. of Lord Rendel. Educ. at Wellington Coll., and Royal Military Coll., Sandhurst. Entered the army, Border Regiment 1884; retired 1896, but volunteered for active service on outbreak of S. African War, and was on the Staff of Aldershot command; Brigade-Maj. of Bedford Volunteer Infantry Brigade 1896. A J.P. for Herefordshire. A Liberal. Unsuccessfully contested the Kingswinford division of Staffordshire in 1905. Elected for Walsall in 1906 and sat until defeated in Jan. 1910. Contested the Melton division of Leicestershire in Dec. 1910. Staff Officer with rank of Lieut.-Col. in 1915. Died 23 Feb. 1944. [1909]

DUNSANY, John William Plunkett, Baron. Dunstall Priory, Shoreham, Kent. Dunsany Castle, Co. Meath. Carlton, Junior Carlton, St. Stephen's, and Constitutional. An Irish Peer, s. of the 16th Baron Dunsany, by the Hon. Anne Constance Dutton, d. of 2nd Baron Sherborne. B. 1853; m. 1877, Ernle Elizabeth, only d. of Col. F.A. Plunkett Burton. Educ. at Trinity Coll., Cambridge, where he took the degree of M.A. A Lieut. in the Royal Navy Artillery Volunteers. A progressive Conservative. An unsuccessful candidate for the Forest of Dean division of Gloucestershire at the election of 1885. First returned for Gloucestershire S. July 1886 and sat until he retired in 1892. Succeeded to Irish Peerage as 17th Baron Dunsany in 1889. Irish Representative Peer 1893-99. Died 16 Jan. 1899. [1892]

DU PRE, William Baring. Continued in House after 1918: full entry in Volume III.

DURANT, John Charles. 14 Clement's Inn Passage, Strand, London. B. at Fordingbridge, near the New Forest 1846. His father was Christopher Durant, a Tin-Plate Worker, and he was apprenticed to Mr. Titus Mitchell, a Printer. In 1874 he became a Printer on his own account in Charles Street, Hatton Garden, and subsequently established himself in a larger way of business in Clement's Inn Passage, Strand. He was one of the founders of the Land Nationalization Society. A Radical and "Christian Socialist". Sat for the Stepney division of Tower Hamlets from Nov. 1885 until he retired in 1886. Died 14 Dec. 1929. [1886]

DURNING-LAWRENCE, Sir Edwin, Bart. 13 Carlton House Terrace, London. King's Ride, Ascot, Berkshire. Athenaeum, Reform, Devonshire, and Burlington. Youngest s. of William Lawrence, Esq., Alderman of London, and bro. of the Sirs W. and James Clerke Lawrence, former Lord Mayors of London. B. in London 1837; m. 1874, Edith Jane, younger d. and co-heiress of John Benjamin Smith, Esq., MP, of Stockport. Educ. at London University School, and Coll., where he graduated in honours LL.B. Called to the bar at the Middle Temple 1867. A Commissioner of Lieutenancy for London, J.P. for Berkshire, and author of pamphlets on the Progress of the Present Century, etc. Created Bart. 1 Jan. 1898, and assumed by Royal licence the additional name of Durning in same year. A Liberal Unionist, and supporter of Mr. Chamberlain's Social Programme. Unsuccessfully contested E. Berkshire 1885, Haggerston 1886, and Burnley 1892. Represented the Truro division of Cornwall from 1895 until defeated in 1906. Defeated again at Truro in Jan. 1910. Died 21 Apr. 1914. [1905]

DYKE, Rt. Hon. Sir William Hart, Bart.
Lullingstone Castle, Dartford, Kent.
Carlton. S. of Sir Percyvall Hart Dyke,
Bart., by Elizabeth, youngest d. of John
Wells, Esq. of Bickley Park, Kent. B. 1837;
m. 1870, Lady Emily Caroline, eld. d. of
the 7th Earl of Sandwich. Educ. at Harrow,
and at Christ Church, Oxford, where he
graduated M.A. 1864. Succeeded as Bart.
1875. PC. 1880. Was (Patronage) Secretary
to the Treasury from Feb. 1874 to Apr.
1880; Chief Secretary for Ireland June
1885-Jan. 1886 when he resigned; and
Vice-President of the Council Committee
on Education, Jan. 1887 to Aug. 1892.
Chairman of Consultative Committee of
the Board of Education. A Magistrate and
Dept.-Lieut. of Kent. Dept. Chairman of
London, Chatham and Dover Railway. A
Conservative. "A strong supporter of One
Parliament and the maintenance of the
Legislative Union between England and
Ireland as now existing." Sat for W. Kent
from July 1865 to Dec. 1868, for the mid
division of Kent 1868-85, and for the
Dartford division of Kent from 1885 until
defeated in 1906. Conservative Whip from
1868-74; Chief Whip 1874-80. Owned
about 9,000 acres. Died 3 July 1931. [1905]

EATON, Henry William. 16 Princes
Gate, Hyde Park, London. Carlton, Junior
Carlton, St. Stephen's, and Union. B. 1816;
m. 1839, only d. and heir of Thomas
Lender Harman, Esq., of New Orleans (she
died 1877). Educ. at Enfield and at the Coll.
Rollin, Paris. Was largely engaged in the
silk trade in Old Broad Street, London. A
Fellow of the Geographical Society, of the
Horticultural Society, and of the Botanical
Society. A Dept.-Lieut. for Suffolk and for
the Tower Hamlets. A Conservative. Sat
for Coventry from June 1865, when he was
returned just previous to the general election, till Mar. 1880; re-elected Mar. 1881.
Sat until created Lord Cheylesmore, July
1887. Died 2 Oct. 1891. [1887]

EBRINGTON, Hugh Fortescue, Visct. 40
Belgrave Square, London. Brooks's. Eld. s.
of 3rd Earl Fortescue, by Georgiana
Augusta, eld. d. of the Rt. Hon. George
Lionel Dawson Damer. B. 1854; m. 1886,
Hon. Emily Ormsby Gore, 2nd d. of Lord
Harlech. Educ. at Cambridge, where he
was 1st class (bracketed) in law at B.A. ex-
amination. Appointed Capt. N. Devon
Yeomanry Cavalry 1880; Lieut.-Col. 1890.

A Magistrate for Devon. Was Private Secretary to Earl Spencer while Lord President of the Council. A Liberal and
Unionist, in favour of "the authorized
programme." Sat for Tiverton from Nov.
1881 to Nov. 1885 and for the Tavistock
division of Devon from Nov. 1885 until he
retired in 1892. Succeeded as 4th Earl Fortescue 1905. H.M. Lieut. of Devon 1904-28.
K.C.B. 1911. Died 29 Oct. 1932. [1892]

EDGE, Capt. William. Continued in
House after 1918: full entry in Volume III.

EDWARDS, Allen Clement. Continued
in House after 1918: full entry in Volume
III.

EDWARDS, Enoch. Miners' Hall,
Burslem. S. of James Edwards, Esq. B. 10
Apr. 1852 at Talk-o'-th'-hill,
Staffordshire; m. 1875, Elizabeth Alice, d.
of Henry Rathbone, Esq. Educ. at private
school. Began work in a coal mine at the
age of ten, and worked for fifteen years as
a Miner; Secretary of N. Staffordshire
Miners' Federation from 1877; Treasurer
of Miners' Federation of Great Britain
1889-1894; President from 1904; a J.P. and
Alderman for Burslem; Mayor 1899; a
County Councillor of Staffordshire. A
member of the Royal Commission on
Mines. A Labour Member. Unsuccessfully
contested Hanley in 1900; elected there in
1906 and sat until his death 28 June 1912.
[1912]

EDWARDS, Sir Francis, Bart. The Cottage, Knighton, Radnorshire. Reform, and
National Liberal. S. of Edward Edwards,
Esq., of Llangollen. B. 1852; m. 1880,
Catherine, d. of David Davis, Esq., of
Aberdare (she died 1915). Educ. at
Shrewsbury School, and Jesus Coll., Oxford; B.A. J.P. and Dept.-Lieut. for Radnorshire, High Sheriff 1898. Created Bart.
1907. A Liberal. Sat for Radnorshire from
1892-95, when he was defeated; re-elected
there in 1900 and sat until Jan. 1910 when
he was again defeated; re-elected there
once more in Dec. 1910 and sat until he
retired in 1918. Died 10 May 1927. [1918]

**EDWARDS, Sir James Bevan, K.C.M.G.,
C.B.** The Gables, Folkestone. United Ser-
vice, Travellers', and Carlton. S. of S. Price
Edwards, Esq. B. at Womburn,
Staffordshire 1834; m. 1868, d. of Ralph
Brocklebank, Esq., of Childwall Hall, Lan-

cashire. Educ. at the Royal Military Academy, Woolwich. Was 2nd Lieut. Royal Engineers 1852, Maj. 1860, Lieut.-Col. 1871, Col. 1877, Maj.-Gen. 1887, Lieut.-Gen. 1891, retired 1893. Served in the Crimea, during the Indian Mutiny, in China 1864, at Suakin 1885, commanded troops in China 1889-90, and on special service (inspecting local forces) in Australia and New Zealand 1890; C.B. 1877, K.C.M.G. 1891, K.C.B. 1912. A Conservative. Sat for Hythe from July 1895 until he accepted Chiltern Hundreds in 1899. Chairman of the Royal Colonial Institute 1909-15. Died 8 July 1922. [1898]

EDWARDS, John Hugh. Continued in House after 1918: full entry in Volume III.

EDWARDS, Owen Morgan. Lincoln College, Oxford. 3 Clarendon Villas, Oxford. Bryn'r Aber, Llanuwchllyn. S. of Owen Edwards, Esq., of Coedypry, Llanuwchllyn, by Elizabeth, d. of Thomas Jones, Esq., of Plas Deon, Llanuwychllyn, Merionethshire. B. at Coedypry 1858. Educ. at Bala School, University Coll. of Wales and Glasgow, and Balliol Coll., Oxford. A Fellow of Lincoln Coll., Oxford, and Lecturer Modern History 1889. First Warden Guild of Graduates University of Wales; Public Examiner University of Oxford 1898. Author of *Wales, Tro yn yr Eidal* and other works; also Editor and Proprietor of *Cymru,* and *Cymru'r Plant.* A Liberal, in favour of Home Rule, etc. Sat for Merionethshire from May 1899 until he retired in 1900. Chief Inspector of Welsh Department of Board of Education from 1907. Knighted 1916. Died 15 May 1920. [1900]

EDWARDS-HEATHCOTE, Justinian Heathcote. Apedale Hall, Newcastle, Staffordshire. Windham, and Naval & Military. S. of Rev. E.J. Edwards, Vicar of Trentham, Staffordshire, by Elizabeth Anne, d. of R.E. Heathcote, Esq., of Apedale Hall, Staffordshire. B. 1843 at Trentham; m. 1870, Eleanor, d. of Spencer Stone, Esq., of Callingwood, Staffordshire. Educ. at Winchester Coll. Formerly held a commission in the 63rd Regiment, was also Capt. in the Staffordshire Yeomanry from 1875 till 1881, and was a J.P. for Staffordshire. "A Unionist." Unsuccessfully contested the N.W. division of Staffordshire in 1885. First returned for that division in July 1886

and sat until he retired in 1892. Died 21 Jan. 1928. [1892]

EDWARDS-MOSS, Tom Cottingham. 1 Ennismore Gardens, London. Otterspool, Liverpool. Arthur's, Bachelors', and United University. 2nd s. of Sir Thomas Edwards-Moss, Bart., of Otterspool, Lancashire, by Amy Charlotte, only child and heiress of Richard Edwards, Esq., of Roby Hall, Liverpool. B. 1855. Educ. at Eton, and Brasenose Coll., Oxford; B.A. 1878, M.A. 1881. Was Assistant Private Secretary to Sir R.A. Cross, Home Secretary in 1885. A Lieut. in the Lancashire Hussars (Yeomanry), and was President of the Oxford University Boat Club from 1876 to 1878. A Conservative. Sat for the Widnes division of Lancashire from 1885 until he retired in 1892. Died 16 Dec. 1893. [1892]

EGERTON, Hon. Alan de Tatton. 9 Seamore Place, London. Taplow Cottage, Taplow, Buckinghamshire. Rostherne Manor, Knutsford, Cheshire. Carlton. 2nd s. of the 1st Baron Egerton of Tatton, by Lady Charlotte Elizabeth, eld. d. of the 2nd Marq. of Ely. B. 1845; m. 1867, Anna Louisa, d. of Simon Watson Taylor, Esq., of Erlstoke Park, Wiltshire. Maj. Cheshire Yeomanry. A Conservative. Sat for Cheshire 1883-85, and for the Knutsford division of Cheshire from 1885 until defeated in 1906. Succeeded as 3rd Baron Egerton of Tatton in 1909. Vice.-Lieut. of Cheshire. Died 9 Sept. 1920. [1905]

EGERTON, Hon. Alfred John Francis. 4 Upper Grosvenor Street, London. Burwood House, Cobham, Surrey. 2nd s. of the 2nd Earl of Ellesmere, and bro. of the 3rd Earl, his mother having been Lady Mary Louisa Campbell, d. of the Earl of Cawdor. B. 1854; m. 1881, Isabella Corisande Gertrude, d. of Hamilton Gorges, Esq., of Kilbrew, Co. Meath. Was a Lieut. in the Grenadier Guards. A Conservative. Sat for the Eccles division of Lancashire from 1885 until his death 25 Sept. 1890. [1890]

EGERTON, Hon. Francis. Retired in 1886: full entry in Volume I.

ELCHO, Hugo Richard Charteris, Lord. 36 Cadogan Square, London. Stanway, Winchcombe, Gloucestershire. Amisfield House, Haddingtonshire. Carlton, and White's. Eld. s. of the Earl of Wemyss (who sat for Haddingtonshire from 1847 to 1883), by Lady Anne Frederica, 2nd d. of the 1st Earl of Lichfield. B. at Edinburgh 1857; m. 1883, Mary Constance, eld. d. of the Hon. Percy Wyndham, MP. Educ. at Harrow, and Balliol Coll., Oxford. Was for a time Lieut. in the 5th Volunteer Battalion Royal Scots (Lothian Regiment). A Conservative, opposed to Home Rule for Ireland. Sat for Haddingtonshire from Feb. 1883 to Nov. 1885, but was defeated there in the general election of Dec. 1885 by Mr. R.B. Haldane. Was first returned for Ipswich, with Mr. C. Dalrymple, on the unseating of Messrs. H.W. West and Jesse Collings by petition, Apr. 1886 and sat until defeated in 1895. Succeeded as 11th Earl of Wemyss in 1914. Lord-Lieut. of E. Lothian from 1918. Owned 62,000 acres. Died 12 July 1937. [1895]

ELIBANK, Master of. See MURRAY, Rt. Hon. Alexander William Charles Oliphant.

ELLICE, Capt. Edward Charles. 9 Chesham Place, London. Ardochy, Invergarry, Inverness. Travellers'. S. of Robert Ellice, Esq., and d. of Gen. Balfour of Balbirnie. B. 1858; m. 1889, d. of F. Freeman-Thomas, Esq., of Ratton, Sussex. Educ. at Harrow and Sandhurst. Was Capt. in Grenadiers 1886; served with Lord Lovat's Corps in S. African War 1899-1902. A J.P. for Sussex and Invernessshire. A Liberal. Elected for St. Andrews Sept. 1903 and sat until defeated in 1906. Rejoined Grenadiers 1914; Major 1915; commanded an "entrenching" Battalion in France; retired 1918. Died 21 Feb. 1934. [1905]

ELLIOT, Hon. Arthur Ralph Douglas. 27 Rutland Gate, London. Dimbola, Freshwater Bay, Isle of Wight. Brooks's, and Athenaeum. New Club, Edinburgh. 2nd s. of the 3rd Earl of Minto, by Emma Eleanor Elizabeth, only d. of Gen. Sir Thomas Hislop, G.C.B. B. 1846; m. 1888, Madeleine, eld. d. of Sir Charles Lister Ryan, K.C.B. Educ. at Edinburgh University, and Trinity Coll., Cambridge; B.A. 1868, M.A., Honorary D.C.L. Durham. Was called to the bar at the Inner Temple 1870, and joined the N. Circuit. Appointed Financial Secretary to the Treasury, Apr. 1903, resigned Oct. 1903. Author of *The State and the Church*, and *On Criminal Procedure in England and Scotland*, and from Jan.

1895-1912 was Editor of the *Edinburgh Review*. A Liberal Unionist. Sat for Roxburghshire 1880-92, when he was defeated. Unsuccessfully contested Durham city 1895; elected for Durham city 30 June 1898 and sat until defeated in 1906, standing as a Free Trader with Liberal Support. Died 12 Feb. 1923. [1905]

ELLIOT, Sir George, Bart. 1 Park Street, Grosvenor Square, London. Houghton Hall, Durham. Aberaman House, Glamorgan. Bellevue, Newport, Monmouth. Carlton, and St. Stephen's. S. of Ralph Elliot, Esq., of Penshaw, in the Co. of Durham, by Elizabeth, d. of Henry Braithwaite, Esq., of Newcastle-on-Tyne. B. at Gateshead 1815; m. 1836, Margaret, d. of George Green, Esq., of Rainton, Houghton-le-Spring. A Mining Engineer and Colliery Proprietor, President of the Association of Mining Engineers, and head of the firm of Elliot and Company, Wire-Rope Makers, of Great George Street, Westminster. A J.P. for Glamorganshire, and Dept.-Lieut. for Monmouthshire, and wrote *On the Duration of our Coal Supply*, etc. Created Bart. 1874. A Conservative. Sat for Durham N. from Dec. 1868 to Feb. 1874, when he was unsuccessful. He was re-elected there in June 1874, defeated in 1880, but re-elected in 1881, from which date he represented the division until the dissolution of 1885. In Dec. 1885 he unsuccessfully contested Durham S.E. Sat for Monmouth district from July 1886 until defeated in 1892. Died 23 Dec. 1893. [1892]

ELLIOT, Sir George William, Bart. 17 Portland Place, London. Scruton Hall, Bedale. Royal Crescent, Whitby, Yorkshire. Carlton, Garrick, and St. Stephen's. S. of Sir George Elliot, Bart., sometime MP for Monmouth district, by Margaret, d. of George Green, Esq., of Houghton-le-Spring. B. 1844; m. 1866, Sarah, d. of Charles Taylor, Esq., of Sunderland. Educ. at Edinburgh, and Trinity Coll., Cambridge. A Colliery Owner. Dept.-Lieut. for Monmouth, and a J.P. for the N. Riding of Yorkshire. A Conservative. Sat for Northallerton from 1874 to 1885, when he was an unsuccessful candidate for the Richmond division of Yorkshire. First elected for the Richmond division of Yorkshire in 1886 and sat until he retired in July 1895. Succeeded as Bart. 1893. Died 15 Nov. 1895. [1895]

ELLIOT, Hon. Hugh Frederick Hislop. 14 Bruton Street, Berkeley Square, London. Corwar, Newton Stewart, Ayrshire. Brooks's, and Travellers'. 3rd s. of the Earl of Minto. B. in London 1848; m. 1879, Mary Euphemia, 2nd d. of Col. S. Long, of Bromley Hill, Kent. Educ. at Eton, and Cambridge. Was for several years clerk in the House of Commons, and when Sir William Adam was First Commissioner of Works, Mr. Elliot became his Private Secretary. A Dept.-Lieut. for the Co. of Fife and a Magistrate for the Co. of Ayr. A Liberal Unionist, in favour of the Disestablishment of the Church of Scotland. Sat for N. Ayrshire from 1885 until he retired in 1892 and unsuccessfully contested the St. Rollox division of Glasgow at the same time. Unsuccessfully contested N.E. Lanarkshire in 1906. Died 30 Apr. 1932. [1892]

ELLIS, James. Gynsils, Nr. Leicester. National Liberal. S. of Joseph Ellis, Esq., of Glenfield. B. Oct. 1829; m. 1855, Louisa, d. of Thomas Burgess, Esq., of Wigston Grange, Leicestershire. Educ. at the Schools of the Society of Friends. A Quarry Proprietor, a member of the firms of Joseph Ellis and Son, and Ellis and Everard. Chairman of the Leicester School Board, also of the committee of the Industrial School at Desford, and of the Anstey School Board. A Liberal, in favour of Home Rule. Sat for the Bosworth division of Leicestershire from 1885 until he retired in 1892. [1892]

ELLIS, Rt. Hon. John Edward. 37 Prince's Gate, London. Wrea Head, Scalby, Yorkshire. Reform. Eld. s. of Edward Shipley Ellis, Esq., J.P., of The Newarke, Leicester, by Emma, d. of John Burgess, Esq., of Wigston Grange, Leicestershire. B. in Leicester 1841; m. 1867, Maria, d. of John Rowntree, Esq., of Scarborough. Educ. at the Friends' School, Kendal. A J.P. for the Co. and borough of Nottingham and the N. Riding of Yorkshire, and a Dept.-Lieut. for the latter. Was Under-Secretary of State to the India Office 1905-06. PC. 1906. Was one of the "temporary" Chairmen of the House appointed by Mr. Speaker; Chairman of Standing Orders Committee. A Liberal. Sat for the Rushcliffe division of Nottinghamshire from 1885 until his death 5 Dec. 1910. [1910]

ELLIS, Sir John Whittaker, Bart. Petersham Place, Byfleet, Weybridge. 21 Hertford Street, Mayfair, London. Carlton, Garrick, City Carlton, and Constitutional. 5th s. of Joseph Ellis, Esq., of Richmond, Surrey, by Elizabeth Blake, d. of William More, Esq., of Southwark. B. 1829; m. 1859, Mary Ann, d. of John Staples, Esq., of Belmont, Salisbury, Wiltshire. In 1872 he was elected Alderman for Broad Street Ward of the City of London. He served as Sheriff for London and Middlesex 1874-75, and was Lord Mayor in 1881-82. He received the honour of a Baronetcy on the occasion of the Queen's visit to Epping Forest in 1882. A Commissioner of Lieutenancy for London; member of the Court of the Merchant Taylors' Company; Gov. of the Irish Society; J.P. for Londonderry; and Chevalier 2nd class of the Gold Lion of Nassau. A Conservative. Sat for mid Surrey from June 1884 to Nov. 1885, and for the Kingston-on-Thames division of Surrey from Nov. 1885 until he retired in 1892. High Sheriff of Surrey 1899-1900. Died 20 Sept. 1912. [1892]

ELLIS, Thomas Edward. 9 Cowley Street, Westminster, London. Cynlas, Corwen, Merionethshire. S. of Thomas Ellis, Esq., Tenant Farmer, of Cynlas, Llandderfel, Merioneth, by Elizabeth, d. of John Williams, Esq., of Llwynmawr, Bala. B. 1859; m. 1898, Annie, d. of R.J. Davies, Esq., of Cwrt Mawr, Aberystwyth. Educ. at the University Coll. of Wales, Aberystwyth, and New Coll., Oxford. Was a Lord of the Treasury, and Parliamentary Charity Commissioner 1892-94. Was Parliamentary Secretary to the Treasury Mar. 1894 to June 1895, and chief opposition "Whip" 1895-99. Also Warden of the Guild of Graduates of the University of Wales. An advanced Liberal, in favour of Mr. Gladstone's Home Rule policy, and supported the "National demands of Wales." Sat for Merionethshire from 1886 until his death 5 Apr. 1899. [1899]

ELLIS-GRIFFITH, Rt. Hon. Sir Ellis Jones, Bart. Continued in House after 1918: full entry in Volume III.

ELTON, Charles Isaac. 10 Cranley Place, London. Manor House, Whitestaunton, Chard. Carlton, and Union. Eld. s. of F.B. Elton, Esq., Indian Magistrate and Collector, by Mary, d. of Sir Charles Abraham

Elton, of Clevedon Court, Somerset, Bart. B. 1839; m. 1863, Mary Augusta, d. of Richard Strachey, Esq., of Ashwick Grove, Somerset. Educ. at Cheltenham Coll. and Balliol Coll., Oxford; Fellow of Queen's Coll., Oxford 1862. Called to the bar at Lincoln's Inn 1865, and became Q.C. in 1885 and a bencher of his Inn 1887. Author of *Norway, the Road and the Fell, Origins of English History, Tenures of Kent, Law of Copyholds,* and various other law works. A J.P. for Somerset, Dorset, and Devon, and Patron of one living. A Conservative. Was elected for Somerset W. in Feb. 1884. In 1885 he unsuccessfully stood for the Wellington division and was elected for that division in 1886 and sat until he retired in 1892. Died 23 Apr. 1900. [1892]

ELVEDEN, Rupert Edward Cecil Lee Guinness, Visct. Continued in House after 1918: full entry in Volume III.

ELVERSTON, Sir Harold. Fulshow Hall, Nr. Wilmslow, Cheshire. National Liberal. Reform, Manchester. S. of James Booth Elverston, Esq., Merchant. B. 26 Dec. 1866 at Fairfield; m. 1899, Josephine, d. of John Taylor, Esq., of Rusholme. Educ. privately. A Newspaper Proprietor. A J.P. for Cheshire, and was a member of Manchester City Council 1904-10. Honorary Secretary of Lancashire and Cheshire Liberal Federation; a member of Executive Council of the National Liberal Federation 1906-10, and 1921-25. Knighted 1911. Fellow of Chartered Insurance Institute. Member of the Council of Manchester Royal Coll. of Music; Chairman of Essex Union Insurance Company; Director Cuba Bartle Sugar Company. Author of *Municipal Insurance Schemes.* A Liberal. Unsuccessfully contested Worcester in 1908. Elected for Gateshead Jan. 1910 and sat until defeated in 1918. Member of Cheshire County Council and Manchester City Council 1921. Died 10 Aug. 1941. [1918]

EMMOTT, Rt. Hon. Alfred. 30 Ennismore Gardens, London. Brooks's, and Reform. S. of Thomas Emmott, Esq., of Brookfield, Oldham, and Hannah, d. of John Barlow, Esq., of Chorley, Cheshire. B. at Oldham 1858; m. Mary, only d. of J.W. Lees, Esq., of Waterhead. Educ. at Grove House, Tottenham, and London University. Dept.-Speaker and Chairman of Ways and Means, appointed Feb. 1906; retired 1911. Was Mayor of Oldham 1891-92. A J.P. for Oldham and for Co. Lancaster, and President of Oldham Chamber of Commerce. PC. 1908. A Liberal. Represented Oldham from 1899 until created Baron Emmott 2 Nov. 1911. Under-Sec. Colonial office 1911-14. First Commissioner of Works 1914-15. Director of War Trade Department 1915-19. Founder of the Anglo-Belgian Union in 1917. President of World Cotton Congress 1921. President of Royal Statistical Society 1922-24. President of the National Association of Building Societies. G.C.M.G. 1914; G.B.E. 1917. Died 13 Dec. 1926. [1911]

ENGLEDOW, Charles John. Burton Hall, Carlow. Reform. S. of W.H. Engledow, Esq., LL.D., and the only d. of Dr. Boyd, J.P. B. 1860; m. 1883, the only d. of Dr. Hepburn, J.P., of Clonard House, Belfast. Educ. at Cambridge. A J.P. and member Co. Council and District Council for the counties of Carlow and Kildare; High Sheriff for Co. Carlow 1893, Governor Carlow and Kildare District Lunatic Asylum, and the Co. Infirmary, and Chairman of the Carlow Board of Guardians. Aide-de-Camp and Private Secretary to His Excellency Sir R. Harley, K.C.M.G., and also Aide-de-Camp to the Governor-in-Chief of the Windward Islands; a Capt. of Colonial Militia. A Nationalist. Sat for Kildare N. from July 1895 until defeated in 1900. Later Peace Commissioner of Irish State for Co. Cork. Died 1933. [1900]

ERSKINE, David Charles. Linlathen, Broughty Ferry, N.B. Brooks's. S. of James Erskine, Esq., of Linlathen, and Mary Jane MacNabb. B. 1866 at Linlathen. Educ. at Harrow, and in France and Germany. Was on the staff of Earl of Aberdeen, Governor-Gen. of Canada 1893-98. Secretary to Governor-Gen. 1897-98. Chairman of Board of Trustees of Scottish National Galleries. A Liberal. Elected for W. Perthshire in 1906 and sat until he retired in Jan. 1910. Died 26 May 1922. [1909]

ESMONDE, John. Drominagh, Borrisokane, Co. Tipperary. S. of James Esmonde, Esq., Dept.-Lieut., and J.P., of Drominagh Castle, and Caroline, d. of John Sugrine, Esq. B. 27 Jan. 1862 at Tramore, Co. Waterford; m. 1st, Rose, d. of John Maginnis, Esq., of Eltham; 2ndly, Eily, d. of Dr. O'Sullivan, of Kensington.

Educ. at Oscott Coll., Birmingham. A Surgeon from 1885. A Nationalist. Elected for N. Tipperary in Dec. 1910 and sat until his death 17 Apr. 1915.   [1915]

ESMONDE, John Lymbrick. Drominagh, Borrisokane, Co. Tipperary. S. of Dr. J. Esmonde, MP for N. Tipperary. B. 15 Dec. 1893. Capt. 27th Battalion Northumberland Fusiliers. A Nationalist. Elected for N. Tipperary June 1915 and sat until he retired in 1918. Barrister 1921; Senior bar 1942; bencher of King's Inn 1948; T.D. for Wexford 1937-44, and 1948-51. Succeeded as 14th Bart. 1943. Died 6 July 1958. [1918]

ESMONDE, Sir Thomas Henry Grattan, Bart. Ballynastragh, Gorey, Co. Wexford. S. of Sir John Esmonde, the 10th Bart. (created 1628), by Louisa, d. of H. Grattan, Esq., MP, and therefore was great-grand-s. of the Rt. Hon. Henry Grattan. B. at Pau 1862; m. 1891, Alice Barbara, d. of Patrick Donovan, Esq. Was Lieut. 6th Brigade of the S. Irish division of the Royal Artillery (Militia) 1880-86; and was Sheriff of Waterford 1887. A Commissioner of Appeal under the Local Government (Ireland). Papal Chamberlain from 1898; Grand Officer of Order of the Holy Sepulchre and representative of the Order in Ireland. Senior "Whip" of his party. A Nationalist. Sat for the S. division of Dublin Co. from 1885 to 1892, when he was defeated. Sat for Kerry W. from 1892-1900; first elected for N. Wexford in 1900 and sat until defeated in 1918. Succeeded as 11th Bart. 1876. Senator, Irish Free State 1922; Chairman of National Bank Limited; writer of travel books and articles. Died 15 Sept. 1935. [1918]

ESSEX, Sir Richard Walter. Bourton-on-the-Water, Gloucestershire. National Liberal. S. of John Essex, Esq. B. 13 Jan. 1857 in London; m. 1st, 1881, Marie, d. of James Chinchen, Esq., of Wandsworth; 2ndly, 1885, Lizzie, d. of John Benson, Esq., of Newcastle-on-Tyne. Educ. privately. Was a member of Wandsworth Board of Works. J.P. for Gloucestershire. A Liberal. Unsuccessfully contested Kennington in 1900. Sat for Cirencester division of Gloucestershire from 1906 to Jan. 1910, when he was defeated. Elected for Stafford Dec. 1910 and sat as last representative of that borough. Defeated in 1918 contesting the Burslem division of Stoke-on-Trent. Knighted 1913. Died 15 Sept. 1941.   [1918]

ESSLEMONT, George Birnie. Kingsacre, Aberdeen. Reform, and National Liberal. S. of Peter Esslemont, Esq., MP for E. Aberdeenshire from 1885-92, and Anna Birnie. B. 1860 at Aberdeen; m. 1890, d. of Ranald Macdonald, Esq. Educ. privately, and at Aberdeen Grammar School. Was in business as a Manufacturer, Warehouseman and Draper from 1876, in Aberdeen. J.P. for Aberdeen, a member of Town Council, School Board, and Harbour Board. An advanced Liberal. Elected for S. Aberdeen in Feb. 1907 and sat until he accepted Chiltern Hundreds in Mar. 1917. Died 2 Oct. 1917.   [1917]

ESSLEMONT, Peter. 34 Albyn Place, Aberdeen. Cairnballach, Durris, N.B. National Liberal. S. of Peter Esslemont, Esq., Farmer, by his wife, Annie Connon. B. at Udny, East Aberdeenshire June 1834; m. 1st, 1857, Georgia Anna, only d. of George Birnie, Esq., Brewer, of Strichen; 2ndly, 1876, Mary Ann, only d. of the Rev. W. Bradford Sherwood, of U.S.A. Educ. at the parish school of Belhelvie. Senior Partner in the firm of Esslemont and Mackintosh of Aberdeen. Author of a work on the improvement of the hospital system, and a Magistrate of the burgh and Co. of Aberdeen, Lord Provost of Aberdeen, 1880-83, President of the Chamber of Commerce, etc. and a J.P. for Aberdeenshire. An advanced Liberal, who supported Mr. Gladstone's Home Rule measures. Sat for Aberdeenshire E. from 1885 until appointed Chairman of Scottish Fishery Board 12 Nov. 1892, which post he held until his death 8 Aug. 1894.   [1892]

EVANS, Sir Francis Henry, Bart., K.C.M.G. 40 Grosvenor Place, London. Tubbendens, Orpington, Kent. Reform, City, Liberal, and National Liberal. S. of William Evans, Esq., of Manchester, and Mary, d. of M. Nicholson, Esq. B. 1840; m. 1872, Marie de Grasse, d. of the Hon. S. Stevens, Attorney-Gen. of New York. Educ. at Manchester, Neuwied in Germany, and Manchester New Coll., London. Was a pupil of Sir James Brunlees, the eminent Civil Engineer and from 1870 to 1884 was in business as a Banker. A Partner in the firm of Donald Currie and Company, Managers of the Union Castle Steamship Company; a Director of the Thames and Mersey Marine Insurance Company, and the International Sleeping Car Company; a Commissioner of Lieutenancy for London. Created K.C.M.G. 1893; Bart. 1902. A Liberal. Sat for Southampton from 1888 until defeated 1895; re-elected 1896 and sat until defeated at the general election 1900; elected for Maidstone Mar. 1901 and sat until he was defeated in 1906. Died 22 Jan. 1907. [1905]

EVANS, Sir Laming Worthington, Bart. See WORTHINGTON-EVANS, Sir Laming, Bart. Continued in House after 1918: full entry in Volume III.

EVANS, Sir Samuel Thomas. 12 Kings Bench Walk, Temple, London. 3 Whitehall Court, London. Neath, Glamorganshire. National Liberal, Bath, and Reform. S. of John and Margaret Evans, of Skewen, near Neath. B. at Skewen 1859; m. 1st, 1887, Miss Rachel Thomas, of Skewen (she died 1889); 2ndly, Blanche, d. of Charles Rule, Esq., of Cincinnati, U.S.A. Educ. at the Collegiate School, Swansea, and University Coll., Aberystwyth, and the University of London. Was admitted a Solicitor in 1883; called to the bar at the Middle Temple 1891; K.C. 1901; bencher 1908; Solicitor-Gen. Jan. 1908-Mar. 1910; Knighted 1908; Honorary Freeman of Swansea and Neath; a J.P. for Glamorganshire. Recorder of Swansea Sept. 1906 to Jan. 1908. A Liberal and Home Ruler. Sat for the mid division of Glamorganshire from Feb. 1890 until appointed President of the Probate, Divorce and Admiralty Division of the High Court Mar. 1910. PC. 1910. G.C.B. 1916. Died 13 Sept. 1918. [1909]

EVANS-GORDON, Sir William Eden. 4 Chelsea Embankment, London. 33 Stepney Green, London. Naval & Military, Boodle's, and Orleans. S. of Gen. Charles Spalding Evans-Gordon and Catherine Rose, d. of Dr. Rose, of Inverness. B. at Chatham 1857; m. 1892, Julia Charlotte Sophia, d. of Stewart Mackenzie, Esq., of Seaforth. Educ. at Cheltenham Coll., and abroad. Entered the army in 1876; Foreign Department Government of India; retired as Maj. 1896. Was identified with the movement for restriction of Alien Immigration, and author of *The Alien Immigrant, The Cabinet and War*. Received Legion of Honour 1905; Knighted 1905. A Conservative, in favour of Better and Cheaper Housing of the Working Classes, Reform of the Poor Laws, Old Age Pensions, and Army Reform. Unsuccessfully contested the Stepney division of Tower Hamlets in 1898. Elected there in 1900 and sat until he accepted Chiltern Hundreds in Apr. 1907. Died 31 Oct. 1913. [1907]

EVE, Harry Trelawney. 4 New Square, Lincoln's Inn, London. 85 Addison Road, London. Yarner, Bovey Tracey, Devon. Devonshire. S. of Thomas and Elizabeth Eve, of Jamaica. B. in London 1856; m. 1879, Beatrice, d. of Dr. H. Hounsell, of Torquay. Educ. privately, and at Exeter Coll., Oxford; M.A. 1882. Was called to the bar at Lincoln's Inn 1881; Q.C. 1895, and a bencher of his Inn 1899. A Liberal. Elected for the Ashburton division of Devon in Jan. 1904 and sat until appointed High Court Judge 1907-37. Knighted 1907. PC. 1937. Died 10 Dec. 1940. [1907]

EVELYN, William John. Wotton, Dorking. Oxford & Cambridge. Eld. s. of George Evelyn, Esq., of Wotton, of the family of the well-known diarist and author of *Sylvia*, who was b. at Wotton. B. 1822; m. 1873, Frances Harriet, eld. d. of the Rev. G.V. Chichester, Rector of Wotton, Surrey. Educ. at Rugby, and Balliol Coll., Oxford (B.A. 1848). A J.P. and Dept.-Lieut. for Surrey, and in 1860 was High Sheriff of the Co. A Capt. in the 1st Surrey Militia. A F.R.G.S. A Conservative. Sat in Parliament for Surrey W. from 1849 until he retired in 1857. Unsuccessfully contested Guildford in Oct. 1858. Was first returned for Deptford in 1885 and sat until he accepted Chiltern Hundreds in 1888. Died 26 July 1908. [1887]

EVERETT, Robert Lacey. Rushmere, Ipswich. S. of J.D. Everett, Esq., of Rushmere. B. 1833; m. 1863, Elizabeth, d. of O. Nussey, Esq., J.P., of Leeds. Educ. privately. A Yeoman Farmer, J.P. and C.A. for Suffolk; a member of Ipswich Town Council; was on Royal Commission on Agriculture 1893. A Liberal. Unsuccessfully contested E. Suffolk as Farmers' Candidate in 1880. Sat for the Woodbridge division of Suffolk from 1885-86, when he was defeated. Re-elected for the Woodbridge division of Suffolk 1892 but again defeated 1895; re-elected there in 1906 and sat until he retired in Jan. 1910. Died 21 Oct. 1916. [1909]

EVERSHED, Sydney. Westminster Palace Hotel, London. Albury House, Burton-on-

Trent. National Liberal. S. of John and Louisa Evershed, of Albury, near Guildford, Surrey. B. at Albury 1825; m. 1856, Fanny, d. of Henry Whitehead, Esq., of Chelsea. Educ. at the private school of the Rev. E. Kell, Newport, Isle of Wight. A Brewer at Burton from 1853. A Commissioner of Taxes, an Alderman, and was twice Mayor of Burton. Also Feoffee of the town lands, a Governor of the Endowed Schools, J.P. Staffordshire, etc. An earnest Liberal, supported local self-government in Ireland, land and poor-law reform, old age pensions in connection with Friendly Societies, cottage and allotment improvements, etc. Sat for the Burton division of Staffordshire from Aug. 1886; returned without opposition 1892 and 1895 and sat until he retired in 1900. Died 8 Nov. 1903.   [1900]

EWART, Sir William, Bart. Glenmachan House, Strandtown, Belfast. Carlton, and Sackville Street, Dublin. S. of Alderman William Ewart, of Glenbank, Co. Antrim. B. at Belfast 1817; m. 1840, Isabella, d. of Lavens Mathewson, Esq., of Newtown Stewart, Co. Tyrone. Educ. at Belfast Academy. A Merchant and Linen Manufacturer at Belfast. Mayor of Belfast in 1859 and in 1860, and was one of the deputies from Belfast for the arrangement of a treaty of commerce with France in 1864. J.P. for the counties of Antrim and Down and for the borough of Belfast. Baronetcy conferred in 1887. A Conservative. Sat for Belfast from Mar. 1878 and for Belfast N. from 1885 until his death on 1 Aug. 1889.   [1889]

EWING, Sir Archibald Orr, Bart. Lennoxbank, Bonhill, Dumbartonshire. Ballikinrain, Balfron, Stirlingshire. Gollomfield, Fort George, Inverness-shire. Carlton. New, and University, Edinburgh. Western, and New, Glasgow. 7th s. of William Ewing, Esq., of Ardvullan, Dunoon, Argyllshire, by Susan, d. of John Orr, Esq., 1st Provost of Paisley. B. 1819; m. 1847, only d. of James Reid, Esq., of Caldercruix, Lanarkshire. Educ. at the University of Glasgow. A Merchant in Glasgow, where he had been established from 1845. A Dept.-Lieut. of Stirlingshire; also County Councillor of Dumbarton; and a Magistrate for the counties of Dumbarton, Stirling, Lanark, and Inverness. Created Bart. 1886. A Conservative. Sat for Dumbartonshire from Dec. 1868 until he

retired in 1892. Died 27 Nov. 1893. [1892]

EYRE, Col. Henry, C.B. 74 Carlisle Place, Victoria Street, London. Rampton Manor, Nottinghamshire. Carlton. S. of the Rev. C.W. Eyre of Rampton Manor, Nottinghamshire, by a d. of J.R. Foulis, Esq., of Heslerton, Yorkshire. B. at Carlton-in-Lindric, Nottinghamshire 1834; m. 1861, Kathleen, d. of the Rev. R. Machell, Marton Vicarage, Yorkshire. Educ. at Harrow, and Christ Church, Oxford, but did not graduate. Was Lieut. 2nd Battalion Rifle Brigade Jan. 1855; served in the Crimea, for which he had the medal and clasp, as Aide-de-Camp to Sir W. Eyre, K.C.B.; also during the Indian Mutiny 1857-58, for which he held the medal and two clasps. Later served in the Sherwood Rangers Yeomanry Cavalry, and commanded the 2nd Notts. Rifle Volunteers from 1865. A J.P. and Dept.-Lieut. for Nottinghamshire. A C.B. 1887. A Conservative. Was an unsuccessful candidate for Newark in 1874 and for Retford in 1880. First returned for the Gainsborough division of Lincolnshire in July 1886 and sat until defeated in 1892. Contested Mansfield in 1895 and 1900. Died 24 June 1904.   [1892]

EYRES-MONSELL, Bolton Meredith. Continued in House after 1918: full entry in Volume III.

FABER, Edmund Beckett. 19 Park Street, London. Belvedere, Harrogate. Carlton, and Junior Carlton. Eld. s. of Charles W. Faber, Esq., J.P., of Northaw, Hertfordshire, and Mary Beckett, d. of Sir Edmund Beckett, Bart., and sister of Lord Grimthorpe. B. 1847. Educ. at Eton, and Trinity Coll., Cambridge. A Banker, a Partner of Beckett and Company, Leeds Old Bank. Chairman of the County Bankers' Association, and the *Yorkshire Post* newspaper, and a Director of the London and North Western Railway Company, the Sun Insurance Company, and the Aire and Calder Navigation Company. A J.P. and Dept.-Lieut. for the W. Riding of Yorkshire. A Conservative. Unsuccessfully contested the Pudsey division of Yorkshire in 1900. Elected for the Andover division of Hampshire Aug. 1901 and sat until he was created Baron Faber in Dec. 1905. Died 17 Sept. 1920.   [1905]

FABER, George Denison, C.B. 14 Grosvenor Square, London. Rush Court,

Wallingford. Carlton. S. of Charles Wilson Faber, Esq., Dept.-Lieut., and J.P., of Northaw House, Hertfordshire, by Mary, eld. d. of Sir Edmund Beckett, Bart., of Doncaster, and sister of Lord Grimthorpe. Was bro. of Lord Faber. B. 1852; m. 1895, Hilda Georgiana, d. of Sir Frederick Ulric Graham, Bart., of Netherby, Cumberland, and Lady Hermione Graham, eld. d. of 12th Duke of Somerset. Educ. at Marlborough Coll., and University Coll., Oxford; B.A. Called to the bar, Lincoln's Inn 1879. A Partner in Beckett and Company, Bankers, of Leeds. Was Registrar of the Privy Council 1887-96. A J.P. and Dept.-Lieut. for the W. Riding of Yorkshire; a J.P. for Oxfordshire; C.B. 1905. A Unionist. Sat for York from 6 Feb. to Jan. 1910, when he was elected for Clapham and sat until created Baron Wittenham June 1918. Died 1 Feb. 1931. [1918]

FABER, George Henry. Kinloch, Beckenham, Kent. National Liberal, Junior Athenaeum, and Thatched House. S. of George H. Smith, Esq. B. 10 Dec. 1839 at Camberwell; m. 1866, d. of P.T. Pugh, Esq. Educ. at Merchant Taylors' School, and in Paris. An Underwriter, a member of Lloyd's from 1872, a member of the Committee also of the Committee of Management of Lloyd's Register of Shipping. Assumed the name of Faber in lieu of Smith. A Liberal. Elected for Boston in 1906 and sat until he retired in Jan. 1910. Died 6 Apr. 1910. [1909]

FABER, Lieut.-Col. Walter Vavasour. 94 Piccadilly, London. Weyhill, Andover. Naval & Military. S. of Charles W. Faber, Esq., of Northaw, Hertfordshire, and Mary, d. of Sir E. Beckett. Bro. of Lord Faber and Lord Wittenham. B. 11 Feb. 1857 at Barnet; m. 1915, widow of Arthur Byass, Esq. Educ. at Cheam School, and Royal Military Academy, Woolwich. Entered the Royal Artillery 1877; later Lieut.-Col. A Unionist. Elected for the Andover division of Hampshire in 1906 and sat until he retired in 1918. Died 2 Apr. 1928. [1918]

FAIRBAIRN, Sir Andrew. Defeated in 1886: full entry in Volume I.

FALCONER, James. Continued in House after 1918: full entry in Volume III.

FALLE, Sir Bertram Godfrey, Bart. Continued in House after 1918: full entry in Volume III.

FARDELL, Sir Thomas George. 26 Hyde Park Street, London. Carlton, and Conservative. S. of Henry Fardell, Esq., M.A., Canon of Ely and Vicar of Wisbech, and of Eliza, d. of the Bishop of Ely, (B.E. Sparke). B. at The College, Ely 1833; m. 1862, Letitia Anne, only d. of Henry Swann Oldfield, Esq. (she died 1905). Educ. at Eton, and Christ Church, Oxford; B.A. 1856. A Barrister, called to the bar at Lincoln's Inn 1862, joined the Norfolk Circuit, and was appointed Registrar of the Bankruptcy Court of Manchester 1868. Was a member of the London Board of Works 1884-89, instrumental in obtaining appointment of Royal Commission thereon, and was a member of the London County Council from 1889 to 1898; Chairman of Licensing Committee for six years. A J.P. for the Isle of Ely, and some years Chairman of Quarter Sessions. Created Kt. 1897. A Conservative, strongly opposed to Home Rule for Ireland, Disestablishment, and all "revolutionary proposals for the abolition or enfeeblement of the House of Lords"; in favour of adding power to the local governing bodies, and opposed to "centralization". First elected for Paddington S. on 9 Feb. 1895 and sat until he retired in Jan. 1910. Chairman of Metropolitan division of National Union of Conservative Associations 1896-1912. Died 12 Mar. 1917. [1909]

FARMER-ATKINSON, Henry John. Osborne House, Ore, Sussex. Carlton, National, and East Sussex. 2nd s. of George Atkinson, Esq., of Hull. B. 1828; m. 1st 1854, Elizabeth, eld. d. of Thomas Holmes, Esq., of Hull; 2ndly, 1869, Elizabeth, d. of Thomas Farmer, Esq., of Gunnersbury House, Middlesex. Educ. by the Rev. Charles Thompson, of Hull. A Magistrate for Middlesex, Hastings, and Kingston-on-Hull, of which latter town he was a Freeman, having been a member of the Corporation for more than thirty years, and Mayor in 1864-66. Dept.-Lieut. for Lincolnshire, and twice President of the Hull Chamber of Commerce and Shipping; was first President of the Chamber of Shipping of the United Kingdom; a member of the Associated Chamber of Commerce of the United Kingdom, a Director of the City Bank, and Dept.-Chairman of the Star Life Assurance Society. Chairman of the Local Marine Board, Hull, at one time President of the General Shipowners' Society, London. On the Committee of Lloyd's Register of Shipping, and a F.R.S. A Conservative. Unsuccessfully contested Hull in 1868 and 1880; elected for Lincolnshire N. in July 1885 and sat until defeated at the general election of Dec. 1885. Sat for Boston from July 1886 until he retired in 1892. Contested Derby 24 Aug. 1892 as an Independent. F.S.A. Assumed the name of Farmer-Atkinson in 1891. Died 3 Mar. 1913.   [1892]

FARQUHAR, Sir Horace Brand Townsend, Bart. 7 Grosvenor Square, London. Castle Rising, Kings Lynn, Norfolk. Marlborough, and Turf. S. of Sir Walter Minto Townsend-Farquhar, 2nd Bart., MP, by Erica Mackay, d. of the 7th Lord Reay. B. 1844; m. 1895, Emilie Scott, d. of Lieut.-Col. H. Packe, Grenadier Guards, of Twyford Hall, Norfolk, and widow of Sir E.H. Scott, 5th Bart. A J.P. and Dept.-Lieut. for London and Middlesex, and a member of the London County Council for E. Marylebone from its creation in 1889-1901. Was President London Municipal Society, and a Director of the British South Africa Company. Was created Bart. 1892. Heir presumptive to his bro., Sir Robert Farquhar, 6th Bart., of the Mauritius. A Liberal Unionist. Sat for Marylebone W. from July 1895 until created Baron Farquhar in 1898. K.C.V.O. 1901; G.C.V.O. 1902; PC. 1907; Lord in waiting 1907-15; Lord Steward 1915-22; advanced to a Visct. in 1917 and made Earl Farquhar in 1922. G.C.B. 1922. Died 30 Aug. 1923.   [1897]

FARQUHARSON, Henry Richard. Eastbury Park, Blandford, Dorset. Arthur's, Boodle's, St. Stephen's, and Kennel. S. of Henry Farquharson, Esq., of Langton, Blandford. B. at Brighton 1857; m. 1878, d. of J.J. Farquharson, Esq., of Langton. Educ. at Eton, and at Jesus Coll., Cambridge. A Conservative, especially advocated "Fair Trade." Sat for Dorset W. from 1885 until his death 19 Apr. 1895.   [1895]

FARQUHARSON, Robert. 2 Porchester Gardens, London. Finzean, Aboyne, Scotland. Reform, Caledonian, Junior United Service, and National Liberal. S. of Francis Farquharson, Esq., of Finzean, Aberdeenshire, by his m. with Miss Alison Mary

Ainslie. B. at Edinburgh 1837. Educ. at Edinburgh Academy, and at the University of Edinburgh; graduated M.D. 1858. Assistant-Surgeon Coldstream Guards, Medical Officer to Rugby School, and a F.R.C.P. London. Was Assistant-Physician to St. Mary's Hospital, London, and Lecturer on Materia Medica in the Medical School there. Author of numerous medical and scientific works, including *A Guide to Therapeutics, The House of Commons from Within* (1912), and *In and Out of Parliament.* A Liberal. Sat for Aberdeenshire W. from Apr. 1880 until he retired in 1906. PC. 1906. Died 8 June 1918.   [1905]

FARRELL, James Patrick. Market Square, Longford. S. of Patrick Farrell, Esq., of Longford, and his wife Anne, d. of John Lynam, Esq., of Strokestown, Roscommon. B. 1865; m. 1888, Bride, 4th d. of Mathew Fitzgerald, Esq., of Longford. Educ. at St. Mel's Coll., Longford. A Journalist, Editor and Proprietor of the *Longford Leader*, a Nationalist newspaper for the counties of Longford, Westmeath, and Roscommon, and author of a *History of County Longford*, etc. A Nationalist. Unsuccessfully contested Kilkenny City at the general election in 1895. Sat for Cavan W. from 1895-1900. Sat for N. Longford from 1900 until defeated in 1918. Died 11 Dec. 1921.   [1918]

FARRELL, Thomas Joseph. Rectory Lodge, Stoke Newington, London. S. of Mathew Farrell, Esq., and Mary his wife. B. at Waterford 1847; m. 1873, Rebecca Josephine, d. of B. Wall, Esq., H.M. Cavalry. Educ. at St. John's Coll., Waterford. A Merchant. An Irish Nationalist of the Anti-Parnellite section. Unsuccessfully contested Waterford City in July 1895. First elected for Kerry S. in Sept. 1895 and sat until he retired in 1900.   [1900]

FEILDEN, Lieut.-Gen. Randle Joseph, C.M.G. 32 Grosvenor Gardens, London. Wilton Park, Blackburn Carlton, United Service, and Army & Navy. S. of Joseph Feilden, Esq., MP, of Witton (who represented Blackburn from 1865 to 1869), by Frances Mary, d. of the Rev. Streynsham Master, Rector of Croston, Lancashire. B. at Clifton, Bristol 1824; m. 1861, Jean Campbell, d. of James Hozier, Esq., of Maudslie Castle, Lanarkshire. Entered the army Mar. 1843, as 2nd Lieut. 60th Rifles;

became Maj. 1860, and retired on half-pay as Col. 1876; promoted to the rank of Maj.-Gen. 1879; nominated a C.M.G. 1870, for his services on the Red River expedition. A Magistrate for Lancashire. A Conservative. As to the system called "Home Rule" for Ireland, he would "oppose any attempt even to consider the question of a separate legislature" there, but was in favour of all "practicable reduction of public expenditure" consistent with "the complete efficiency of the army and navy." in favour also of the complete repeal of the Indian cotton duties. Sat for Lancashire N. from Apr. 1800 to Nov. 1885 and for the Chorley division of Lancashire N. from Nov. 1885 until his death on 19 May 1895.   [1895]

FELL, Sir Arthur. Continued in House after 1918: full entry in Volume III.

FELLOWES, Rt. Hon. Ailwyn Edward. 3 Belgrave Square, London. Honingham, Norwich. Carlton, and Bachelors'. S. of the 1st Baron De Ramsey, by Mary Julia, eld. d. of the 4th Lord Sondes. B. 1855 at Haverland Hall, Norfolk. Educ. at Eton Coll., and Trinity Hall, Cambridge. Was Vice-Chamberlain 1895-1900. Junior Lord of the Treasury 1900-1905. President of the Board of Agriculture Mar.-Dec. 1905. A J.P. for Norfolk and Huntingdonshire, and Honorary Maj. 3rd Battalion Norfolk Regiment. A progressive Conservative, in favour of allotments, the relief of the occupiers of land, and a measure of County Government. He unsuccessfully contested mid-Norfolk in 1885, and N. Norfolk in 1886. Sat for the Ramsey division of Huntingdonshire from Aug. 1887 until defeated in 1906. K.C.V.O. 1911; K.B.E. 1917; created Baron Ailwyn July 1921. Died 23 Sept. 1924.   [1905]

FELLOWES, Hon. William Henry. 20 Upper Brook Street, London. Abbots Ripton Hall, Huntingdon. Carlton. Eld. s. of Edward Fellowes, Esq., 1st Baron de Ramsey, of Ramsey Abbey, Huntingdonshire (who sat for that Co. from 1837 to 1880), by Hon. Mary Julia, eld. d. of the 4th Lord Sondes. B. in London 1848; m. 1877, Lady Rosamond, 2nd d. of the 6th Duke of Marlborough. Educ. at Eton. Appointed a Sub-Lieut. 1st Life Guards 1867; became Lieut, 1868, Capt. 1872; retired 1877. A Magistrate and Dept.-Lieut. for Huntingdonshire. A Conserva-

tive. Sat for Huntingdonshire from Apr. 1880 until he succeeded as Lord de Ramsey in 1887. Lord-in-Waiting 1890-92. Custos Rotulorum of the Isle of Ely. Died 8 May 1925.   [1887]

FENWICK, Rt. Hon. Charles. 14 Tankerville Terrace, Newcastle-on-Tyne. National Liberal, and Cobden. S. of John Fenwick, Esq., a Working Collier. B. at Camlington village 1850, and after attending the colliery school for a few years he, at the age of nine, went to work on the pit bank, and at the age of ten commenced work underground. Was one of the executive of the Northumberland Miners' Association, and was the Miners' representative at the Trades Union ngress at Aberdeen 1884, Parliamentary Secretary to the Trades Union Congress 1890-94; a Member of the Royal Commission on Secondary Education 1894. A Temporary Chairman of Committees. PC. 1911. A Liberal. First elected for the Wansbeck division of Northumberland in 1885 and sat until he death 20 Apr. 1918.   [1918]

FENWICK, Henry Thomas. 6 Charles Street, London. Southill, Plawsworth, Chester-le-Street, Durham. S. of Henry Fenwick, Esq., of Southill, Co. Durham, MP for Sunderland, by Jane, d. of John Cookson, Esq., of Meldon Park, Northumberland. B. 1863. Entered the Royal Horse Guards 1885, Capt. 1891. A Partner in the firm of Fenwick and Company, Brewers, of Sunderland. A Liberal, in favour of Home Rule and the Gladstonian programme generally. First returned for the Houghton-le-Spring division of Durham Co. in July 1892 and sat until he retired in 1895. Served in S. Africa 1899-1900; D.S.O. 1900; M.V.O. 1901; C.M.G. 1917. Died 30 Aug. 1939.   [1895]

FERENS, Rt. Hon. Thomas Robinson. Holderness House, Hull. 62 Whitehall Court, London. Reform, and National Liberal. S. of George Waller Ferens, Esq., of Bishop Auckland. B. 4 May 1847 at Shildon, C. Durham; m. 1873, Ettie, d. of William Field, Esq., of Hull. Educ. at Belvedere Academy, Bishop Aukland. A Director of Reckitt and Sons Limited, Starch and Glue Manufacturers, Hull, and of the Star Life Assurance Society. Was President of Hull Chamber of Commerce, and took an active part in temperance, religious, and philanthropic affairs. High

Steward of Hull 1912. PC. 1912. A Liberal. Unsuccessfully contested E. Hull in 1900. First elected for E. Hull in 1906 and sat until defeated in 1918. Died 9 May 1930. [1918]

FERGUSON, Robert. Retired in 1886: full entry in Volume I, under FERGUSON, Robert.(II).

FERGUSON, Rt. Hon. Ronald Craufurd Munro. See MUNRO-FERGUSON, Rt. Hon. Ronald Craufurd.

FERGUSSON, Rt. Hon. Sir James, Bart., G.C.S.I., K.C.M.G., C.I.E. 80 Cornwall Gardens, London. Kilkerran, Ayrshire. Carlton. Eld. s. of Sir Charles Dalrymple Fergusson, Bart., by Helen, 2nd s. of the Rt. Hon. David Boyle, Lord Justice Gen. of Scotland. B. at Edinburgh 1832; m. 1st, 1857, Lady Edith Ramsay, 2nd d. of the Marq. of Dalhousie, K.T. (she died 1871); 2ndly, 1873, Olive, d. of John Richman, Esq., of South Australia (she died 1882); 3rdly, 1893, widow of C. Hugh Hoare, Esq., d. of the Rev. T. Twisden, of Charlton, Devon. Educ. at Rugby, and University Coll., Oxford. Served in the Grenadier Guards 1851-55, including the campaign in the Crimea, where he was wounded; also served as Lieut.-Col. Commandant Royal Ayr and Wigton Militia 1858-73. Was Under Secretary of State for India 1866-67; Under Secretary at the Home Office 1867-68; Governor of S. Australia 1868-73; Governor of New Zealand 1873-75; Governor of Bombay 1880-85; Parliamentary Under Secretary at the Foreign Office 1886-91, and Postmaster-Gen. 1891 to Aug. 1892. A Magistrate and Dept.-Lieut. for the Co. of Ayr. A Conservative. Sat for Ayrshire from 1854 until defeated 1857; unsuccessfully contested Sandwich in Apr. and June 1859; re-elected for Ayrshire Oct. 1859 but retired on the division of the Co. 1868. Unsuccessfully contested Frome Nov. 1876 and Greenock Jan. 1878. Sat for Manchester N.E. from 1885 until defeated in 1906. Succeeded as Bart. 1849; PC. 1868; K.C.M.G. 1875; G.C.S.I. 1885; C.I.E. 1884. Died 14 Jan. 1907. [1905]

FETHERSTONHAUGH, Godfrey. 5 Herbert Street, Dublin. Glenmore, Crossmelina, Co. Mayo. Carlton, St. Stephen's, and Junior Constitutional. S. of S.R. Fetherstonhaugh, Esq., of Milltown, Co. Westmeath and Jane, d. of Joseph Boyce, Esq., Dept.-Lieut. B. 1859 in Dublin. Educ. at Chard Grammar School, Somerset, and Trinity Coll., Dublin; M.A. A Barrister, called to the Irish bar 1883, and to the English bar at the Middle Temple 1895; Q.C. 1898; bencher of King's Inn 1900. Member of Senate of Dublin University. A J.P. for counties Mayo, Sligo, Westmeath, and Fermanagh. A Unionist. Elected for N. Fermanagh in 1906, and sat until he accepted Chiltern Hundreds in Oct. 1916. Died Sept. 1928. [1916]

FFRENCH, Peter. Harpoon Town, Co. Wexford. National Liberal. S. of Thomas Ffrench, Esq., Farmer, and Mary Colfer. B. 1844 at Farmhouse, Barmow, Co. Wexford; m. 1870, Anastasia Ellen, d. of Mark Dake, Esq., of Commons, Co. Wexford (she died 1898); 2ndly, Elizabeth, d. of James Power, Esq., of Ballinahask. Educ. privately. A Farmer. A J.P. for Wexford and a Coroner of the Co. A Nationalist. Sat for S. Wexford, unopposed, from 1893 until defeated in 1918. Died 1 Nov. 1929. [1918]

FIELD, Admiral Edward, C.B. The Grove, Alverstoke, Hampshire. Carlton, and United Service. Youngest s. of James Field, Esq., of The Vale, Chesham, Buckinghamshire, by Isabella, d. of John Howe, Esq. B. 1828; m. 1853, Marianne, d. of Capt. E.P. Samuel, of the 2nd Madras Cavalry, and J.P. of Hampshire. Entered the navy in 1845, and obtained his Lieut.'s commission at the Royal Naval Coll., Portsmouth in 1851, that of Commander 1859, and Capt. 1869. Served during the operations in Parana and at Obligato in 1845. He retired in 1876 and was gazetted Rear-Admiral in 1886, Vice-Admiral 1892, and Admiral 1897. A Dept.-Lieut. and J.P. for Hampshire, County Alderman, and Chairman of the Fareham Division of Hampshire. He also served as naval member of the War Office Committee on Guncotton and Explosives from 1870 to 1873. A Conservative, not opposed to "such progress and reform as the circumstances of the time may require." Unsuccessfully contested Newark in 1874 and Brighton in 1880. At Brighton he withdrew his claim as senior candidate on Mr. Marriott's re-election as a Conservative in 1884. Sat for the Eastbourne division of Sussex from 1885 until he retired in 1900. C.B. 1897. Died 26 May 1912. [1900]

FIELD, William. Heath View, Blackrock, Dublin. S. of John and Grace Field. B. at Blackrock, Co. Dublin 1848. Educ. at St. Laurence O'Toole's School, Harcourt Street, and the Catholic University, St. Stephen's Green. President of the Irish Cattle Traders' and Stock Owners' Association; Honorary Secretary Dublin Victuallers' Association; Vice-President National Federation of Meat Trades of the United Kingdom. Member of Dublin Port Docks Board; Gov. Royal Irish Veterinary Coll.; Chairman of Blackrock Technical Instruction Committee, member of Dublin County Council; President All Ireland Town Tenants. Author of works on Government in Ireland, Home Rule, Railway Nationalisation, Treasury Tactics, Town Tenants Texts, etc. A Nationalist and Labour representative, advocated manhood suffrage, international eight hours day, social and economic reforms. Represented the St. Patrick's division of Dublin from 1892 until defeated in 1918. Died 29 Apr. 1935. [1918]

FIELDEN, Edward Brocklehurst. Continued in House after 1918: full entry in Volume III.

FIELDEN, Thomas. Grimston Park, Tadcaster, Yorkshire. Carlton, Boodle's, and St. Stephen's. S. of Joshua Fielden, Esq., of Nutfield Priory, Redhill, former MP for the E. division of the W. Riding of Yorkshire, by Ellen, eld. d. of Thomas Brocklehurst, Esq., of The Fence, Macclesfield. B. at Stamfield Hall, Todmorden 1854; m. 1878, Martha, eld. d. of Thomas Knowles, Esq., MP for Wigan. Educ. at Wellington Coll., and Trinity Coll., Cambridge. A J.P. and Dept.-Lieut. for the W. Riding of Yorkshire. A Conservative and Unionist, but in favour of "any well-considered scheme of local government for Ireland." Unsuccessfully contested the Middleton division of Lancashire at the general election of 1885, but sat for this division from 1886-92 when he was defeated, re-elected 1895 and sat until his death 5 Oct. 1897. [1897]

FIENNES, Hon. Sir Eustace Edward Twisleton-Wykeham-. Bart. Studland Bay, Dorset. 86 Eaton Terrace, London. National Liberal, Orleans, and Cavalry. S. of the 14th Lord Saye and Sele. B. 1864; m. 1894, Florence Agnes, d. of John Rathfelder, Esq., of Constantia, near Wynberg, S.A., and widow of A.W. Fletcher, Esq. Educ. at Malvern Coll. Served in the Biel rebellion in Canada 1885, Suakin Campaign 1888-89 (medal and clasp), Mashonaland 1890 (mentioned in despatches), and S. African War 1900-01 (twice mentioned in despatches, medal, three clasps). Lieut. in the army and Maj. in Oxfordshire Imperial Yeomanry. Temporary Lieut.-Col. Royal Marines. Served in Antwerp and Dardanelles with Royal Naval Division. His eld. s., Capt. John Fiennes, 1st Gordon Highlanders, died of wounds 18 June 1917. A J.P. for Berkshire and Dorset. Parliamentary Private Secretary to Mr. W. Churchill when First Lord of the Admiralty. Created Bart. 1916. A Liberal. Unsuccessfully contested the Banbury division of Oxfordshire in 1900; elected there in Jan. 1906 and sat until Jan. 1910, when he was defeated; re-elected there Dec. 1910 and sat until appointed Gov. of Seychelles Aug. 1918-21. Gov. of Leeward Islands 1921-29. Died 9 Feb. 1943. [1918]

FINCH, Rt. Hon. George Henry. Burley-on-the-Hill, Oakham, Rutland. Carlton. Eld. s. of George Finch, Esq., of Burley-on-the-Hill, Rutland, who represented successively Lymington, Stamford, and Rutland, by his 2nd wife, Lady Louisa, 5th d. of the 6th Duke of Beaufort. B. in London 1835; m. 1st, 1861, Emily Eglantine, d. of John Balfour, Esq., of Balbirnie (she died 1865); 2ndly, 1871, Edith, eld. d. of Alfred Montgomery, Esq., Commissioner of Inland Revenue. Educ. at New Coll., Oxford. A Magistrate and County Councillor for Rutland, a Brevet-Maj. Leicestershire Yeomanry. PC. 1902. A Conservative, in favour of the removal of all burdens on agriculture. Sat for Rutland from Nov. 1867 until his death 22 May 1907. Father of House of Commons 1906-07. [1907]

FINCH-HATTON, Hon. Harold Heneage. 11a Pall Mall, London. Carlton, and St. James's. 4th s. of the 10th Earl of Winchilsea and Nottingham, by Fanny, d. of Edward Royd Rice, Esq., of Eastwell Park. B. 1856. Educ. at Eton, and Balliol Coll., Oxford. Was for nine years resident in Queensland. Author of *Advance Australia!* and an expert with Boomerangs. A Conservative. Unsuccessfully contested

Nottingham E. 1885, 1886, and 1892. Sat for the Newark division of Nottinghamshire from July 1895 until he accepted Chiltern Hundreds May 1898, after disagreement with Government policy. Sheriff of Merionethshire 1903. Died 16 May 1904. [1898]

FINCH-HATTON, Hon. Murray Edward Gordon. Haverholme Priory, Sleaford. 23 Ennismore Gardens, London. White's, and Carlton. 2nd s. of George William, 10th Earl of Winchilsea, by Fanny, d. of Edward Royd Rice, Esq., of Dane Court, Kent. B. 28 Mar. 1851; m. 1875, Edith, only d. of Edward William Harcourt, Esq., of Nuneham Park, Oxon, MP. Educ. at Eton, and Balliol Coll., Oxford, at one time Fellow of Hertford Coll. Served as High Sheriff of Lincolnshire 1879, for which Co. he was a J.P. and Dept.-Lieut. Patron of 2 livings. A Conservative. Unsuccessfully contested Newark in Apr. 1880. Sat for Lincolnshire S. from 1884-85, and for the Holland or Spalding division of Lincolnshire from Dec. 1885 until he succeeded to the Peerage, Earl of Winchilsea 1887. Died 7 Sept. 1898. [1887]

FINDLAY, Alexander. Bellfield House, Motherwell, N.B. Reform, and National Liberal. S. of Alexander and Helen Findlay, of Irvine, Ayrshire. B. 25 Nov. 1844 at Irvine; m. 1874, Isabella, d. of William Cameron, Esq., of Kilmarnock. Educ. at Public Schools, Irvine, and Technical Coll., Glasgow. A Structural Engineer and Steel Bridge Builder, founder and head of the firm of Alexander Findlay and Company, of Motherwell. J.P. for Lanarkshire, Chairman of the Scottish National Council of the Y.M.C.A. and member of the Institute of Engineers and Shipbuilders in Scotland. President of British Iron Trade Association 1908. Provost of Motherwell 1901-04. A Liberal. Elected for Lanarkshire N.E. in Aug. 1904 and sat until he retired in Jan. 1910. Died 2 Feb. 1921. [1909]

FINLAY, Rt. Hon. Sir Robert Bannatyne. 31 Phillimore Gardens, London. Newton Nairn, N.B. Athenaeum, Carlton, Brooks's, and Garrick. Eld. s. of William Finlay, Esq., F.R.C.P.E., of Cherrybank, near Newhaven, Edinburgh. B. 1842 at Newhaven; m. 1874, Mary, d. of Cosmo Innes, Esq., of Edinburgh (she died 1911). Educ. at Edinburgh Academy, and University. Graduated as M.D. Edinburgh in 1863, but left medicine for law, and was called to the bar in the Middle Temple in 1867. He became Q.C. in 1882, and a bencher in 1884. Was Solicitor-Gen. 1895-1900 and Attorney-Gen. 1900-05. Knighted 1895; G.C.M.G. 1904. PC. 1905. Lord Rector of Edinburgh University 1902-03. A Dept.-Lieut. for Nairnshire; Honorary LL.D. Edinburgh, Cambridge and St. Andrews Universities. A Unionist. Unsuccessfully contested Haddingtonshire Feb. 1883. Sat for the Inverness district from 1885-92, when he was defeated; re-elected there in 1895 and sat until 1906 when he was again defeated. Elected for Edinburgh and St. Andrews Universities in Jan. 1910 and sat until appointed Lord Chancellor 11 Dec. 1916. Created Baron 1916 and Visct. Finlay 1919; member of the International Court of Justice 1921. Died 9 Mar. 1929. [1916]

FINLAYSON, James. 9 Edmund Place, Aldersgate, London. Merchiston, Johnstone, Renfrewshire. S. of William Finlayson, Esq., of Merchiston, Johnstone, by Helen, d. of Robert Sharp, Esq., of Fowlis Wester, Perthshire. B. at Dunfermline 1823; m. 1846, Rachel, 2nd d. of Archibald Watson, Esq., of Glasgow. Was Senior Partner in the firm of Finlayson, Bousfield and Company, Flax Spinners and Linen-Thread Manufacturers, Johnstone, near Glasgow, also a Director of the Glasgow and S. Western Railway Company, and two Insurance Companies; a Commissioner of Supply, and a J.P. for Renfrewshire; was Chairman of the Abbey Parish School Board from 1873 to 1882. A Liberal, in favour of the Disestablishment of the Church of Scotland, reform of the House of Lords, etc. Returned for Renfrewshire E. Dec. 1885 and sat until he retired in 1886. Died 17 Feb. 1903. [1886]

FINNEY, Samuel. Continued in House after 1918: full entry in Volume III.

FINUCANE, John. Colle House, Cahreely, Co. Limerick. B. at Herbertstown, Co. Limerick 1842. Educ. for the Priesthood at Thurles Coll. (where he obtained 1st class honours in rhetoric, logic, and metaphysics), and at Maynooth Coll. Instead of entering the Church he became a Farmer, and a leading member of the old Limerick and Clare Farmers' Club, of which he was for many years Honorary Secretary. An "Irish Nationalist" (Anti-Parnellite). Sat for E. Limerick from 1885 until he retired in 1900. Died 23 Mar. 1902. [1900]

FIRBANK, Sir Joseph Thomas. St. Julian's Newport, Monmouthshire. The Coopers, Chislehurst, Kent. Carlton, Junior Carlton, Junior Constitutional, White's, and Union. Eld. s. of Joseph Firbank, Esq., J.P. and Dept.-Lieut. (High Sheriff, Monmouthshire 1886), by his 1st wife, Sarah, widow of John Fryatt, Esq., of Melton Mowbray. B. 1850 at Market Harborough; m. 1883, Harriette, d. of the Rev. J.P. Garrett, of Kilgarron and Kellistown, Co. Carlow, and had, with other issue, Joseph Sydney, b. 1884. Educ. at Cheltenham Coll. A Railway Contractor, J.P., and Dept.-Lieut. for Monmouthshire (High Sheriff 1891); J.P. for Kent; Maj. of the Engineer and Railway Volunteer Staff Corps., and a Director of the Union Assurance Society. Knighted 1902. A Conservative, opposed to Home Rule and the Local Option Bill; in favour of an ammendment of the Employers' Liability Act, Religious Education etc. Unsuccessfully contested the Haggerston division of Shoreditch 1892. Represented Hull E. from 1895 until he retired in 1906. Died 7 Oct. 1910. [1905]

FIRTH, Joseph Firth Bottomley. 2 The Grove, Boltons, South Kensington, London. New Court, Temple, London. Reform, National Liberal, and Cobden. Eld. s. of J. Bottomley-Firth, Esq., of Matlock, Derbyshire. B. near Huddersfield, W. Riding of Yorkshire 1842; m. 1873, Elizabeth, youngest d. of George Tatham, Esq., of Leeds, (Mayor of Leeds 1880-83). Assumed the name of Firth by royal licence in 1873. Graduated LL.B. at London, 1875. Called to the bar at the Middle Temple June 1866, and joined the N.E. Circuit. A member of London School Board for Chelsea 1876-79. President of the Municipal Reform League. Member of London County Council and Dept.-Chairman 1889. A Liberal, in favour of Home Rule for Ireland, "shortening the period of residential qualification for voters", and of making "registration the compulsory duty of a public officer in each borough"; also in favour of a "representative municipal government for London", and of "the reappropriation for

public purposes of the funds of the London Livery Companies." Sat for Chelsea from Apr. 1880 until Nov. 1885 when he was defeated in N. Kensington. Unsuccessfully contested W. Newington in 1886. Elected for Dundee on 16 Feb. 1888 and sat until his death on 3 Sept. 1889. [1889]

FISHER, Rt. Hon. Dr. Herbert Albert Laurens. Continued in House after 1918: full entry in Volume III.

FISHER, Rt. Hon. William Hayes. 13 Buckingham Palace Gardens, London. Carlton. eld. s. of the Rev. Frederick Fisher, Rector of Downham, by Mary, d. of William Hayes, Esq., Conveyancer to the Court of Chancery. B. at Downham Rectory 1853; m. 1895, his cousin, Miss Florence Fisher. Educ. at Haileybury Coll., and University Coll., Oxford. Called to the bar at the Inner Temple 1879. Was Junior Lord of the Treasury, and one of the Conservative "Whips" 1895-1902; Financial Secretary to the Treasury 1902-03; Parliamentary Secretary to Local Government Board from May 1915 to July 1917; President of the Local Government Board from July 1917 to Nov. 1918; Chairman of Royal Patriotic Fund. Was Private Secretary to Sir M. Hicks-Beach and the Rt. Hon. A.J. Balfour. An Alderman of the London County Council 1907-13; Chairman of Finance Committee. Knight of Grace of St. John. A Unionist, in favour of social reform, with the maintenance of imperial interests. Sat for Fulham from 1885 to 1906, when he was defeated; re-elected for Fulham in 1910 and sat until created Baron Downham Nov. 1918. PC. 1911. Chancellor of Duchy of Lancaster Nov. 1918-Jan. 19. Died 2 July 1920. [1918]

FISON, Sir Frederick William, Bart. 64 Pont Street, London. Carlton, and United University. Only s. of William Fison, Esq., J.P., W. Riding, Yorkshire, and Fanny, d. of J. Whitaker, Esq., of Greenholme. B. 1847; m. 1872, Isabel, d. of Joseph Crossley, Esq., of Broomfield, Halifax, J.P. and Dept.-Lieut. for W. Riding. Educ. at Rugby and Christ Church, Oxford (1st Class National Science, M.A.). Senior Partner of W. Fison and Company, of Greenholme, Bradford, and London, a Director of the Great Northern Railway, Fellow of the Chemical Society, etc. A Conservative and Unionist, in favour of legislation for Tariff Reform, the relief of agriculture, amending the Poor Laws, Old Age Pensions, etc. Contested the Otley division of Yorkshire Dec. 1885 and the Buckrose division of Yorkshire July 1892. Sat for Doncaster division of Yorkshire from 1895 until defeated in 1906. Created Bart. 1905. Died 20 Dec. 1927.   [1905]

FITZ-GERALD, James Gubbins. Arundel Lodge, Balham, London. B. 1855 at Mortalstown, near Kilfinane, Co. Limerick. A member of an old Catholic family of that place. A Surgeon, practised at Balham, London. Became L.M. Dublin 1872; a Member of the Royal Coll. of Surgeons, England, 1876; Lic. Apothecaries Hall, Dublin 1877, and F.R.C.S. Edin. 1884. Surgeon to the Balham Orphanage and to Les Dames de la Retraite, Clapham Park. An Irish Nationalist of the Parnellite section. He was returned for S. Longford on the retirement of Mr. Laurence Connolly in June 1888 and sat until he retired in 1892. Unsuccessfully contested Louth S. in 1895.   [1892]

FITZGERALD, Sir Robert Uniacke Penrose, Bart. See PENROSE-FITZGERALD, Sir Robert Uniacke-, Bart.

FITZGIBBON, John. Castlerea, Co. Roscommon. S. of Henry Fitzgibbon, Esq. B. 1 June 1849 at Castlerea; m. 1873; d. of John O'Carroll, Esq., of Beigh Castle, Co. Limerick. Educ. at St. Kyran's, Kilkenny. A Draper. Chairman of Roscommon County Council, and a member of the Congested Districts Board; Vice-Chairman of the General Council of County Council's, and one of the three Trustees of Parliamentary Fund. A Nationalist. Elected for S. Mayo in Dec. 1910 and sat until he retired in 1918. Died 8 Sept. 1919.   [1918]

FITZMAURICE, Lord Edmond George Petty-. Leigh, Bradford-on-Avon, Wiltshire. Brooks's. 2nd s. of the 4th Marq. of Lansdowne, by his 2nd wife, Emily de Flahault, in her own right Baroness Nairne, and bro. of the Marq. B. 1846. Educ. at Eton, and Trinity Coll., Cambridge. In 1871 he was called to the bar at Lincoln's Inn, and became Private Secretary to the Rt. Hon. R. Lowe, when Home Secretary; was H.M. Commissioner for European Turkey under the Berlin Treaty of 1880, a plenipotentiary at the Danubian Conference, London 1882-83,

and Under-Secretary for Foreign Affairs 1883-85. A Boundary Commissioner under the Local Government Act 1887. Chairman of the Wiltshire County Council, and Chairman of Quarter Sessions; member Hist. MSS. Commission, and Trustee of the National Portrait Gallery. Author of *Life of Earl of Shelburne, Life of Sir William Petty,* editor of the *Letters of Gavin Hamilton, Abbé Morellet, Charles, Duke of Brunswick.* A Liberal, in favour of Free Trade, Local Control of the Liquor Traffic, Religious Equality in Education. Sat for Calne from 1868 until he retired 1885. Contested Deptford July 1892 and Cricklade July 1895. Re-entered Parliament as Member for the Cricklade division of Wiltshire Feb. 1898 and sat until he was created Baron Fitzmaurice Jan. 1906. Once more Under-Secretary for Foreign Affairs 1905-08; Chancellor of Duchy of Lancaster 1908-09; PC. 1908; Honorary D.Litt. Bristol University 1912; F.B.A. 1914. Died 21 June 1935.   [1905]

FITZPATRICK, John Lalor. Colt House, Abbeyleix, Queen's Co. S. of Dr. John P. Fitzpatrick, of Naas, Co. Kildare, and Nannie, eld. d. of Richard Lalor, Esq., at one time MP for the Leix division of Queen's Co. B. 1875 at Bolton Lodge, Naas, Co. Kildare; m. 5 July 1916, Kathleen, 3rd d. of William Carroll, Esq., of Cromhill, Kilteely, Co. Limerick. Educ. at St. Patrick's Coll., Mounstrath, Queen's Co. A Farmer in Abbeyleix, Queen's Co. A Nationalist, and supporter of the Irish Parliamentary party. Elected for the Ossory division of Queen's Co. in Apr. 1916 and sat until he retired in 1918.   [1918]

FITZROY, Hon. Edward Algernon. Continued in House after 1918: full entry in Volume III.

FITZWILLIAM, Hon. William Henry Wentworth-. 4 Grosvenor Square, London. The Lodge, Malton, Yorkshire. Brooks's, and Boodle's. 2nd s. of the 6th Earl FitzWilliam, by Lady Frances Harriet, eld. d. of the 18th Earl of Morton. B. 1840; m. 1877, Lady Mary Grace Louisa, d. of the 2nd Marq. of Ormonde. Was educ. at Eton, and at Trinity Coll., Cambridge. Appointed Cornet 1st West York Yeomanry Cavalry 1861, and later became Capt. A Liberal Unionist. Sat for Wicklow Co. from Dec. 1868 to Jan. 1874, when he stood unsuccessfully. Unsuccessfully contested Huntingdonshire June 1877. Sat for the S. division of the W. Riding of Yorkshire from Apr. 1880 to Nov. 1885. Unsuccessfully contested Hallamshire division of the W. Riding of Yorkshire in Dec. 1885. Unsuccessfully contested Doncaster 1886. Elected for the Doncaster division of the W. Riding of Yorkshire from Feb. 1888 until defeated in 1892. Died 10 July 1920. [1892]

FITZWILLIAM, Hon. William John Wentworth-. 4 Grosvenor Square, London. Wentworth Woodhouse, Rotherham. 5th s. of the 6th Earl Fitz-William, by Lady Frances Harriet, eld. d. of the 18th Earl of Morton. B. 1852. Was educ. at Eton, and Magdalene Coll., Cambridge; graduated B.A. 1873. An independent Liberal and Unionist, opposed to the disestablishment of the Church. Sat for Peterborough from Oct. 1878 until his death 11 Sept. 1889. [1889]

FITZWYGRAM, Lieut.-Gen. Sir Frederick Wellington John, Bart. Leigh Park, Havant, Hampshire. Carlton, and Army & Navy. S. of Sir Robert Fitzwygram, by Selina, youngest d. of Sir John M. Hayes. B. 1823; m. 1882, Angela, d. of Thomas Nugent Vaughan, Esq., and Viscountess Forbes. A Magistrate of Hampshire, and Lord of the Manor of Havant. Entered the army in 1843, and was in the Inniskilling Dragoons, and Lieut.-Col. 15th Hussars. He served in the Crimean war. Became Col. 1863; Maj.-Gen. 1869; and Lieut.-Gen. 1883. In 1879 he was appointed Inspector Gen. of Cavalry, and in command of the Cavalry Brigade at Aldershot; Col. 15th (King's) Hussars 1884-89; a member of the Royal Coll. Veterinary Surgeons, President 1875-77. Succeeded his bro. as 4th Bart. 1873. A Conservative. Sat for Hampshire S. from 1884 until he retired in 1900. Died 9 Dec. 1904. [1900]

FLANNERY, Sir James Fortescue, Bart. Continued in House after 1918: full entry in Volume III.

FLAVIN, Martin. Rosemount Villa, Sundays Well, Cork. Eld. s. of Timothy Flavin, Esq. B. in Cork 1841; m. 1881, Arabella, youngest d. of Patrick Flavin, Esq. A Butter Merchant in Cork from 1861. A member of the Cork Town Council and Harbour Board. A Trustee of the Cork Butter Market, a Director of the Cork Railway and of the Munster Permanent Building Society, Manager of the Cork Savings Bank, a member of the Committee Managing the Cork Library, President of the Catholic Club, Treasurer of the Cork Branch of the Irish National Federation, etc. An Irish Nationalist of the Anti-Parnellite party "resolved to win by moral force." Sat for Cork City from Nov. 1891 until he retired in 1892. [1892]

FLAVIN, Michael Joseph. The Rock, Tralee, Co. Kerry. S. of James Flavin, Esq., and his wife, Johanna Mangan. B. 1866 at Ballyduff, Co. Kerry. Educ. at the National Schools and St. Michael's Coll., Listowel, and also privately. A Merchant in Tralee, and President of the Listowel Young Ireland Society; a member of Kerry County Council. A Nationalist. Represented N. Kerry from 1896 until he retired in 1918. Died 3 May 1944. [1918]

FLEMING, Charles James. Avenue House, Alexandra Park, Manchester. S. of Edmond Lionel Fleming, Esq., of Manchester, and Sale, Cheshire, and Anne Rice, d. of Edward Rice Hayward, Esq., of Liverpool. B. 1841 at Sheffield; m. 1869, Georgina, d. of James Brown, Esq., of Eccles, Lancashire. Educ. privately. A Barrister, called at Gray's Inn 1872. Was Chief Assistant to the Accountant Gen. of the Government of Bombay; resigned 1871. In 1869 he compiled a Digest of Rules for Civil Servants in the Bombay Presidency. "A Radical", in favour of Mr. Gladstone's Home Rule and domestic policy generally. Unsuccessfully contested Pontefract 1886. Sat for the Doncaster division of the W. Riding of Yorkshire from July 1892 until he retired in 1895. Unsuccessfully contested Dudley in 1895. Q.C. 1893. Died 25 Dec. 1904. [1895]

FLEMING, Sir John. Dalmuinzie, Murtle, Aberdeen. B. 1847; m. 1870, Elizabeth, d. of John Dow, Esq. Educ. at Dundee. A Dept.-Lieut. for the City of Aberdeen, and Lord Provost of Aberdeen from 1898-1902. LL.D. Knighted 1908. A Timber Merchant. A Liberal. Elected for S. Aberdeen 3 Apr. 1917 and sat until defeated in 1918. Died 25 Feb. 1925. [1918]

FLEMING, Valentine. Pitt House, Hampstead Heath, London. Annisdale, Inverness-shire. Carlton, and Travellers'. S. of Robert Fleming, Esq., High Sheriff of

Oxfordshire 1909-01. B. 17 Feb. 1882 at Newport, Fife, N.B; m. 1906, Evelyn, d. of G.A. St. Croix Rose. Educ. at Eton, and Magdalen Coll., Oxford. A Barrister and a Financier. Maj. Oxfordshire Yeomanry. A Unionist. Elected for the Henley division of Oxfordshire in Jan. 1910 and sat until he was killed in action on 20 May 1917. [1917]

FLETCHER, Bannister. 29 New Bridge Street, Ludgate Circus, London. Anglebay, West Hampstead, London. 2nd s. of Thomas Fletcher, Esq. B. 1833; m. 1863, the only d. of Charles Phillips, Esq. Educ. privately. Was articled to Charles James Richardson, Esq., a well-known Architect, and gained as a student the first prize given by the Royal Institute of British Architects. An Architect and Surveyor, and the District Surveyor of West Newington and part of Lambeth. A Fellow of the Royal Institute of British Architects; and held a commission as Maj. in the Tower Hamlets Rifle Brigade. Wrote text-books on *Delapidations, Light and Air*, Model Houses, and other professional subjects. Professor of Architecture, King's Coll., London. A Liberal. Sat for Chippenham div. of Wiltshire from Dec. 1885 until defeated in 1886 standing as a Gladstonian Liberal. Unsuccessfully contested Christchurch in July 1892. Died 5 July 1899. [1886]

FLETCHER, Rt. Hon. Sir Henry, Bart., C.B. See AUBREY-FLETCHER, Rt. Hon. Sir Henry, Bart., C.B.

FLETCHER, John Robert Kebty. See KEBTY-FLETCHER, John Robert.

FLETCHER, John Samuel. 35 College Cresc, Hampstead, London. Bryony Hill, Nr. Godalming, Surrey. New University, and St. Stephen's. S. of Samuel Fletcher, Esq., of Manchester, and Elizabeth, d. of John Kelsall, Esq., of Ardwick. B. 3 Nov. 1841 at Broomfield, near Manchester; m. 1895, Sara, d. of Jonathan Clark, Esq., of Winchendon. Educ. at Harrow, and Christ Church, Oxford; M.A. A Barrister, called to the bar at Lincoln's Inn 1868. Was a member of the London County Council 1889-1904; Dept-Chairman 1900. Chairman of Hampstead Board of Guardians 1880-98. A J.P. for Middlesex and London. A Unionist. Elected for Hampstead Oct. 1905 and sat until he retired in 1918. Cre-

ated Bart. in 1919. Died 20 May 1924. [1918]

FLOWER, Cyril. Surrey House, 7 Hyde Park Place, London. Aston Clinton, Tring. Buckingham House, Brecon, South Wales. S. of Philip William Flower, Esq., of Furzedown, Streatham, Surrey, by Mary, d. of J. Flower, Esq. B. 1843; m. 1878, Constance, eld. d. of Sir Anthony de Rothschild, Bart. Was educ. at Harrow and at Trinity Coll., Cambridge. Was called to the bar at the Inner Temple Apr. 1870. A Dept.-Lieut. for London and a Lieut. in the Bucks Yeomanry. In 1886 he was appointed a Junior Lord of the Treasury. A Liberal, in favour of Home Rule for Ireland. Sat for Brecknock from Apr. 1880 to Nov. 1885, and for the Luton division of Bedfordshire from Dec. 1885 until created Lord Battersea in Aug. 1892. Died 28 Nov. 1907. [1892]

FLOWER, Sir Ernest Francis Swan. 6 Upper Phillimore Gardens, London. Carlton, Bath, and Junior Carlton. Bradford County Conservative, Bradford. S. of John S. Flower, Esq., and Frances, d. of Edwin Cuthbert, Esq., of Clogh Prior, Co. Tipperary. B. 24 Aug. 1865. Was connected with the People's Palace and philanthropic work in E. London, and in 1897 was elected a Member of the London School Board for the Tower Hamlets. Member of Committee of St. Bartholomews, Metropolitan and Orthopaedic Hospitals. Knighted 1903. A Conservative and Unionist. Unsuccessfully contested Bradford W. in 1892. Represented Bradford W. from 1895 until defeated in 1906. Contested same seat in Jan. and Dec. 1910. Died 30 Apr. 1926. [1905]

FLYNN, James Christopher. York Terrace, Cork. S. of Daniel Flynn, Esq., of Whitechurch, Co. Cork, by Sarah Nicholls, of Northampton. B. in London 1852; became a widower in 1894; m. 2ndly, 1897, Rebecca, widow of T.F. Rice, Esq. Educ. privately, and at the Christian Brothers' Coll., Cork. A Merchant. Honorary Secretary to the United Irish League of Great Britain. A prominent member of the Cork Literary Society, and was Secretary to the Cork Evicted Tenants' Fund. An "Irish Nationalist (Anti-Parnellite); in favour of national and legislative independence for Ireland." Sat for the N. division of Co. Cork from 1885 until he retired in Jan. 1910. Died 15 Nov. 1922. [1909]

FOLEY, Patrick James. 2 Adelaide Buildings, London Bridge, London. National Liberal. S. of Patrick and Mary Foley, of Sligo. B. at Leeds, Yorkshire 1836; m. 1862, d. of John Lawrence, Esq., of Liverpool. Educ. at the Catholic Schools of Prescot and Leeds. Managing Director of the Pearl Assurance Company and was Chairman of the Industrial Assurance Protection Association. An "Irish Nationalist" of the Anti-Parnellite party. Sat for the Connemara division of Galway from 1885 until he retired in 1895. President of Pearl Assurance Company and of National Amalgamated Approval Society. Died 28 June 1914. [1895]

FOLJAMBE, Cecil George Savile. 2 Carlton House Terrace, London. Cockglode, Ollerton, Newark-on-Trent. Brooks's. Eld. s. of George Savile Foljambe, Esq., of Osberton, Nottinghamshire, and Aldwarke, Yorkshire, by his 2nd wife Selina, Viscountess Milton, d. and co-heir of the Earl of Liverpool. B. at Osberton, Nottinghamshire 1846; m. 1869, Louisa Blanche, eld. d. of Frederick John and Lady Fanny Howard (she died 1871); 2ndly, 1877, Susan Louisa, eld. d. of Lieut.-Col. William Henry Frederick and Lady Emily Cavendish. Was educ. at Eton. Entered the navy 1860; became Lieut. 1867, and was on the retired list at that rank. Served in the New Zealand War 1863-64, and was favourably mentioned in despatches. A Magistrate for the N., E., and W. Ridings of Yorkshire and for Nottinghamshire and Northamptonshire, also a Dept.-Lieut. of Nottinghamshire and the E. Riding of Yorkshire. A Liberal, in favour of Home Rule for Ireland. Sat for Nottinghamshire N. from Apr. 1880 to Nov. 1885 and for the Mansfield division of Nottinghamshire from Nov. 1885 until he retired in 1892. Created Baron Hawkebury in 1893 and Earl of Liverpool in 1905 (first holder of revived titles). Lord-in-Waiting 1894-95; Lord Steward 1905-07; PC. 1906. Died 23 Mar. 1907. [1892]

FOLKESTONE, Jacob Pleydell-Bouverie, Visct. 2 Balfour Place, Park Lane, London. Bishopstrow House, Warminster. S. of the 5th Earl of Radnor, and Helen Matilda, d. of the Rev. C. Chaplin, Blankney Hall, Lincolnshire. B. 1868 at Coleshill House, Highworth, Wiltshire; m. 1891, Julia E.A., d. of Charles Balfour, Esq., of Newton Don, Kelso, N.B. Educ. at

Harrow, and Trinity Coll., Cambridge. Was unpaid Private Secretary to the Rt. Hon. H. Chaplin, MP, President of the Board of Agriculture; a J.P. for Wiltshire, and Maj. 1st Wiltshire Rifle Volunteers. A Conservative and Unionist. Sat for Wiltshire S. from July 1892 until he succeeded as 6th Earl of Radnor on 3rd June 1900. Served in S. Africa 1900 and India 1914-17. Chairman of Royal Commission on Care and Control of the Feeble-Minded 1904-08; Director of Agricultural Production; B.E.F. 1918. Died 25 June 1930. [1900]

FOLKESTONE, Rt. Hon. William Pleydell-Bouverie, Visct. 8 Ennismore Gardens, London. Eld. s. of the Earl of Radnor, by Mary Augusta Frederica, 3rd d. of the 1st Earl of Verulam. B. 1841; m. 1866, Helen Matilda, only d. of the Rev. Henry Chaplin, of Ryhall, Rutland. A Magistrate and Dept.-Lieut. for Wiltshire. Treasurer of the Household 1885-86 and 1886-92. A Conservative, voted against the 3rd reading of the Irish Land Bill 1881. Sat for Wiltshire S. from 1874-85 and for the Enfield division of Middlesex from 1885 until he succeeded as Earl of Radnor in 1889. PC. 1885. Died 3 June 1900. [1889]

FOREST, Maurice Arnold, Baron d. See de FOREST, Baron Maurice Arnold.

FORSTER, Sir Charles, Bart. 21 Queen Anne's Gate, London. Lysways Hall, Longdon, Lichfield. Devonshire, and Oxford & Cambridge. Only s. of Charles Smith Forster, Esq., (the first Member for Walsall), by Elizabeth, d. of Richard Emery, Esq., of Burcott House, Shropshire. B. 1815; m. 1840, Frances Catherine, youngest d. of John Surtees, Esq., of Newcastle-upon-Tyne, and niece of Lord Chancellor Eldon. Educ. at Worcester Coll., Oxford, where he graduated B.A. 1840, M.A. 1843. Was called to the bar at the Inner Temple in 1843, and joined the Oxford Circuit. A Magistrate and Dept.-Lieut. for Staffordshire. Created Bart. 1874. A Liberal, in favour of Home Rule. Was an unsuccessful candidate for Walsall in July 1847. Sat for Walsall from July 1852 until his death 26 July 1891. [1891]

FORSTER, Rt. Hon. Henry William. Exbury, Southampton. 41 Hans Place, London. Carlton, Wellington, and R.Y.S. S. of Maj. John Forster, at one time in the 6th Dragoon Guards, and Emily, d. of John

Ashton Case, Esq., of Thingwell Hall, and Ince Hall, Lancashire. B. 1866 at Southend Hall, Kent; m. 1890, the Hon. Rachel Cecily, d. of 1st Lord Montagu of Beaulieu. Educ. at Eton, and New Coll., Oxford. Was a Junior Lord of the Treasury from 1902-05, and one of the Conservative Whips from 1902-11. Financial Secretary to the War Office from May 1915 to Dec. 1919. PC. 1917. A Unionist. Represented the Sevenoaks division of Kent from 1892 to 1918. Elected for the Bromley division of Kent in Dec. 1918 and sat until appointed Gov.-Gen. of Australia 1920-25. Created Baron Forster in Dec. 1919. G.C.M.G. 1920. Gov.-Gen. of Australia 1920-25. Died 15 Jan. 1936. [1919]

FORSTER, Rt. Hon. William Edward. 80 Ecclestone Square, London. Burley, Nr. Leeds, Yorkshire. Reform, and Devonshire. Only s. of William Forster, Esq., (who was for more than 50 years a Minister of the Society of Friends and died on an Anti-Slavery Mission in Tennessee), by Anna, sister of Sir Thomas Fowell Buxton (1st Bart.) B. at Bradpole, Dorset 1818; m. 1850, Jane Martha, eld. d. of the Rev. Thomas Arnold, D.D., Headmaster of Rugby. Created D.C.L. Oxon 1879. A Worsted Manufacturer at Bradford. A Magistrate and Dept.-Lieut. of the W. Riding of Yorkshire, and Capt. 23rd W. Riding Volunteers. Was Under-Secretary for the Colonies from Nov. 1865-July 1866, Vice-President of the Committee of Council on Education, and Fourth Charity Commission Dec. 1868-Feb. 1874. Chief Secretary of Ireland Apr. 1880-May 1882. Presented with the freedom of the city of Edinburgh Nov. 1875. A Liberal. Unsuccessfully contested Leeds Apr. 1859. Sat for Bradford from Feb. 1861 to 1885, and for Bradford Central from 1885 until his death on 5 Apr. 1886. [1886]

FORWOOD, Rt. Hon. Sir Arthur Bower, Bart. The Priory, Gateacre, Liverpool. Carlton, St. Stephen's, and Constitutional. S. of Thomas Brittain Forwood, Esq., J.P. of Thornton Hough, Cheshire, by Charlotte, d. of William Bower, Esq., of Liverpool. B. 1836; m. 1st, 1858, Lucy, d. of Simon Crosfield, Esq., of Liverpool; 2ndly, 1874, Lizzie, d. of Thomas Baines, Esq., F.R.S., of London. Educ. at the High School of Liverpool Coll. A Merchant and Shipowner, being senior Partner in the firms of Leech, Harrison, and Forwood, of Liverpool, Forwood Brothers and Company of London, and Pim, Forwood, and Kellock, of New York; held several important offices in Liverpool including that of Mayor in 1878. Financial Secretary to the Admiralty from 1886 to 1892, and in the latter year became a PC.; created Bart. 1895. A "Conservative of progressive views." Unsuccessfully contested Liverpool Dec. 1882. Sat for the Ormskirk division of Lancashire S.W. from 1885 until his death 27 Sept. 1898. [1898]

FOSTER, Rt. Hon. Sir Balthazar Walter. 30 Grosvenor Road, London. Reform, and National Liberal. S. of B. Foster, Esq., of Drogheda, Ireland, and Beaulieu, Hampshire. B. 1840 at Cambridge; m. Emily Martha, 2nd d. of William Lucas Sargant, Esq., of Edgbaston. Educ. at Drogheda Grammar School, and Dublin. Was a Consulting Physician, F.R.C.P. London; M.D. of the University of Erlangen; D.C.L. Durham; LL.D. Montreal; Gold Medallist for "Distinguished Merit"; Vice-President of the British Medical Association, Emeritus professor of medicine in Queen's Coll., and Consulting Physician to the General Hospital, Birmingham. Knighted in 1886; Parliamentary Secretary to the Local Government Board 1892 to 1895. A J.P. for Warwickshire, Chairman of the Council of the National Liberal Federation 1886-90, and President of the Allotments and Small Holdings Association. Wrote *Method and Medicine, Clinical Medicine, Public Aspects of Medicine*, and other works on Medicine and Sanitary Science. PC. 1906. A Radical. Entered Parliament as Member for Chester City Nov. 1885, but was defeated there July 1886. First elected for the Ilkeston division of Derbyshire in 1887 and sat until he accepted Chiltern Hundreds in Feb. 1910. Created Baron Ilkeston June 1910. Died 31 Jan. 1913. [1909]

FOSTER, Harry Seymour. Continued in House after 1918: full entry in Volume III.

FOSTER, John Kenneth. 49 Pont Street, London. Egton Lodge, Grosmont, Yorkshire. S. of John Foster, Esq., of Coombe Park, Reading, and Bradford. B. 1866; m. 1896, Mary, d. of John Ussher, Esq., of Great Badsworth, Cheshire. Educ. at Eton, and Magdalen Coll., Oxford; M.A. A member of the Metropolitan Water Board and a Director of Queen's Club Gardens Estates. A Unionist. Unsuccessfully contested Coventry in 1906. Elected for Coventry in Jan. 1910 and sat until defeated in Dec. 1910. Army Capt. 1917-19. Died 2 Mar. 1930. [1910]

FOSTER, Sir Michael, K.C.B. Nine Wells, Great Shelford, Cambridgeshire. Athenaeum. S. of M. Foster, Esq., F.R.C.S., of Huntingdon, and Mercy Cooper, of Potton, Bedfordshire. B. 1836; m. 1st, 1863, Georgina, d. of Cyril Edmunds, Esq. (she died 1869); 2ndly, 1872, Margaret, d. of George Rust, Esq., J.P., of Huntingdon. Educ. at Huntingdon Grammar School, and University Coll. School, and University Coll., London. M.R.C.S. 1857, M.D. London 1859. Was Professor of Physiology at University Coll. London 1868-70. In 1870 was elected to the chair of Physiology at Trinity Coll., Cambridge, and in 1883 was elected to the Chair of Physiology at Cambridge, which he resigned in 1903; was a Secretary of the Royal Society 1881-1903. Author of *Textbook of Physiology*, and other works. A Liberal Unionist. Elected for London University Feb. 1900 joined the Liberal Party Apr. 1903 and sat until defeated in 1906. K.C.B. 1899. Died 29 Jan. 1907. [1905]

FOSTER, Philip Staveley. Canwell Hall, Sutton Coldfield. 42 Green Street, Grosvenor Square, London. Carlton, and Junior Carlton. Only s. of A.B. Foster, Esq., J.P., of Canwell Hall, Tamworth, and Rosamond, d. of J. Staveley, Esq., of Withwood Heath, Worcestershire. B. 1865 at Halifax; m. 1890, Louisa Frances, d. of Col. F.C. Wemyss, of H.M. Royal Bodyguard. Educ. at Eton, and Magdalen Coll., Oxford. A J.P. for Staffordshire and Warwickshire, was Honorary Maj. in the Staffordshire Yeomanry. A Unionist. Unsuccessfully contested the Elland division of Yorkshire in 1899. Sat for the Stratford-on-Avon division of Warwickshire from 1901-06, when he was defeated; re-elected there May 1909 and sat until he retired in 1918. High Sheriff of Sussex 1930. Died 5 Mar. 1933. [1918]

FOSTER, Col. William Henry. Queensbury, Yorkshire. Hornby Castle, Lancaster. Carlton, St. Stephen's, and Cavalry. Eld. s. of William Foster, Esq., of Hornby Castle, Lancaster, and Queensbury, Yorkshire. B. 1848; m. 1879, Henrietta, eld. d. of the Rev. Canon J.H. Warnford, of Warnford Place, Wiltshire. Educ. at the Royal Institu-

tion School, Liverpool, and abroad. Lieut.-Col. and Hon. Col. (retired) 2nd West York (Prince of Wales' Own) Yeomanry Cavalry. Lord of the Manors of Hornby, Tatham, and Forest of Merwith (Yorkshire), Master of the Vale of Lune Harriers, and Patron of 3 livings. Also a Director of John Foster and Son Limited, etc. A J.P. and Dept.-Lieut. of Lancashire (High Sheriff 1891), and of Yorkshire, W. Riding. A Conservative. Sat for the Lancaster division of Lancashire N. from July 1895 until defeated in 1900. Unsuccessfully contested the same seat in 1906. Died 27 Mar. 1908. [1900]

FOWLER, Rt. Hon. Sir Henry Hartley, G.C.S.I. Woodthorne, Wolverhampton. Reform, and Athenaeum. S. of the Rev. Joseph Fowler. B. at Sunderland 1830; m. 1857, Ellen C.I., youngest d. of G.B. Thorneycroft, Esq., of Chapel House, Wolverhampton. Was Mayor of Wolverhampton 1863. Under-Secretary of State for the Home Department 1884-85. In 1886 became Financial Secretary to the Treasury, and in June of that year was made a Privy Councillor. Was President Local Government Board, with a seat in the Cabinet, Aug. 1892, and Secretary of State for India 1894-95. Chancellor of Duchy of Lancaster Dec. 1905-Oct. 1908. Dept.-Lieut. for Staffordshire and was created G.C.S.I. 1895. A Liberal. Sat for Wolverhampton E. from Apr. 1880 until created Visct. Wolverhampton in 1908. Lord President of Council Oct. 1908-June 1910. Died 25 Feb. 1911. [1908]

FOWLER, Matthew. Church Street, Durham. National Liberal. S. of James Fowler, Esq., Merchant and Alderman of Durham (five times Mayor). B. 1845 at Durham. A widower. Educ. at a private school. Member of the Durham Town Council, and was Mayor of the city; elected Alderman Oct. 1897. A Liberal, in favour of Home Rule for Ireland, etc. Sat for Durham city from 1892 until his death 13 June 1898. [1898]

FOWLER, Sir Robert Nicholas, Bart. 50 Cornhill, London. Gastard House, Chippenham, Wiltshire. Carlton, Athenaeum, City Carlton, and National. S. of Thomas Fowler, Esq., of Bruce Green, Tottenham, a London Banker, by Lucy, d. of Nicholas Waterhouse, Esq., of Liverpool. B. at Tottenham, Middlesex 1828; m. 1852, Charlotte, 2nd d. of Alfred Fox, Esq. (she died 1876). Educ. at Tottenham High School and University Coll., London. Graduated at London, B.A. 1848, when he was 2nd in mathematical honours and 5th in classics, M.A. 1850. A Banker in London, a Partner in the firm of Messrs. Dimsdale, Fowler, and Company, Cornhill. A Magistrate for Middlesex and Wiltshire and a Commissioner of Lieutenancy for London, Sheriff of London and Middlesex 1880-81. An Alderman of London and a member of the Senate of London University. Elected Lord Mayor of London for 1883-84. Author of *A Tour in Japan, China, and Italy*, was made a Bart. in 1885. A Conservative, was "warmly attached to the Established Church", and anxious to promote religious education. Unsuccessfully contested London in July 1865. Unsuccessfully contested Penryn and Falmouth Oct. 1865. Sat for Penryn and Falmouth from Dec. 1868 until defeated in Jan. 1874. Sat for London from Apr. 1880 until his death 22 May 1891. [1891]

FOX, Henry Wilson. See WILSON-FOX, Henry. Continued in House after 1918: full entry in Volume III.

FOX, Joseph Francis. Wilmount Castle, Queenstown, Co. Cork. National Liberal. B. in Queenstown 1853. Educ. at St. Colman's Coll., Fermoy, and Queen's Coll., Cork. He went to New York, and there became Professor at St. Francis Xavier's Coll., with the degree of Master of Arts. He afterwards took the degree of M.D. at the University of Cincinnati. An F.R.C.P. and surgeon of Kingston, Canada, and practised medicine and surgery at Troy, New York State. Was New York Executive of the National League of America, and founder of the Irish National Federation of America. An "Irish Nationalist", (Anti-Parnellite). Sat for the Tullamore division of King's Co. from 1885 until he retired in 1900. [1900]

FOXCROFT, Charles Talbot. Continued in House after 1918: full entry in Volume III.

FRANCE, Gerald Ashburner. Continued in House after 1918: full entry in Volume III.

FRASER, Lieut.-Gen. Sir Charles Craufurd, K.C.B., V.C. 7 Storey's Gate, London. Bective, Co. Meath, Ireland. Trav-

ellers', Arthur's, Turf, Marlborough, and Bachelors'. 2nd s. of Lieut.-Col. Sir J.J. Fraser, Bart. (a descendant of the 1st Lord Lovat), by his m. with Miss Craufurd, who later became the wife of Sir R. Howard, Bart. His father served in the Peninsula and at Waterloo, where he was wounded; whilst several others of his near relatives were also distinguished officers. B. in Dublin 1829. Educ. at Eton, and in 1847 joined the 7th Hussars, becoming Capt. 1854, and Maj.-Gen. 1877, after having commanded the 11th (Prince Albert's Own) Hussars for 12 years. He served with the greatest distinction during the Indian Mutiny, and was severely wounded in one action. On 31 Dec. 1858 he rescued an officer and men from drowning in the river Raptee by swimming to them under sharp fire and for this "conspicuous and cool gallantry" he received the Victoria Cross. He also gained the Royal Humane Society's 1st class medal. He served in the Abyssinian Expedition 1868, and received the C.B. Was Aide-de-Camp to H.R.H., the Commander-in-Chief, Inspector-Gen. of Cavalry in Ireland and in Great Britain, and for four years Commander of the Curragh; Col. 8th Hussars, 1886, retired 1890. A Conservative. Sat for Lambeth N. from Nov. 1885 until he retired in 1892. K.C.B. 1891. Died 7 June 1895. [1892]

FRASER-MACKINTOSH, Charles. 5 Clarges Street, London. Lochardill, Inverness. Devonshire. S. of Alexander Fraser, Esq., of Dochnalurg, near Inverness, by Marjory, d. of Capt. Alexander Mackintosh. B. at Inverness 1828; m. 1876, Evelyn May, only d. of Richard D. Holland, Esq., of Brooklands, Streatham. Assumed in 1857, by Royal licence, the additional name of Mackintosh, in accordance with the will of his maternal uncle, Eneas Mackintosh, Esq., R.N. Practised as a Solicitor from 1853 to 1867, when he retired. A Magistrate for the Co. of Inverness. Author of *Antiquaruan Notes*, etc. A Liberal Unionist, in favour of limiting the duration of Parliament to quinquennial periods, without power of dissolution. Sat for Inverness district from Feb. 1874 to Nov. 1885, and for Inverness-shire from Nov. 1885 until July 1886 as an Independent Crofter candidate. From July 1886 until July 1892 he maintained the seat as a subsidised Liberal Unionist Crofter candidate. He was defeated at the July 1892 election as a Liberal Unionist, the crofters supporting the Gladstonian Liberal, Dr. MacGregor. Member of Lord Napier's Crofters Commission. Died 25 Jan. 1901. [1892]

FREEMAN-MITFORD, Algernon **Bertram, C.B.** 84 Jermyn Street, London. Batsford Park, Moreton-in-the-Marsh. S. of Henry Reveley Mitford, Esq., of Exbury, Hampshire. B. in London 1837; m. 1874, Lady Clementine Oglivy, 2nd d. of the 7th Earl of Airlie. Educ. at Eton, and Christ Church, Oxford. Entered the Foreign Office in 1858, served as 2nd Secretary of Legation in St. Petersburg, Peking, and Japan. Appointed Secretary of H.M. Office of Works in 1874, resigned 1886. Assumed the name of Freeman-Mitford in 1886. Author of *Tales of Old Japan* (1871) and other works. A Conservative. Sat for the Stratford-on-Avon division of Warwickshire from July 1892 until he retired in 1895. Created C.B. 1882 and Baron Redesdale 1902. Died 17 Aug. 1916. [1895]

FREEMAN-THOMAS, Freeman. 76 Ashley Gardens, London. Ratton, Willingdon, Sussex. Travellers', Brooks's, and Bachelors'. S. of Frederick Freeman-Thomas, Esq., by Mabel, d. of 1st Visct. Hampden. B. 12 Sept. 1866; m. 1892, Hon. Marie Adelaide, d. of Lord Brassey. Educ. at Eton, and Cambridge. A J.P. for Sussex and Maj. in the Sussex Imperial Yeomanry, Capt. in the Sussex Artillery; Aide-de-Camp to Lord Brassey when Gov. of Victoria. A Liberal. Sat for Hastings from 1900 until appointed a Junior Lord of the Treasury Dec. 1905, and defeated at the general election Jan. 1906. Elected for the Bodmin division of Cornwall in July 1906 and sat until he retired in Jan. 1910. Created Baron Willingdon June 1910; Visct. Willingdon 1924; Earl of Willingdon 1931; Marq. of Willingdon 1936. Lord-in-Waiting 1911-13; Governor of Bombay 1913-18; Governor of Madras 1919-24; Governor-Gen. of Canada 1926-30; Viceroy of India 1931-36; Lord Warden of Cinque Ports 1936-41. Died 12 Aug. 1941. [1909]

FREWEN, Moreton. Brede Place, Sussex. Innishannon Co. Cork. S. of Thomas Frewen, Esq., MP for S. Leicestershire. B. 1853; m. Clara, d. of Leonard Jerome, Esq., of New York. Educ. at Trinity Hall, Cambridge. A J.P. for the counties of Cork and Galway. Author of works on economic subjects. A Nationalist. Elected for N.E. Cork in Dec. 1910 and sat until he accepted Chiltern Hundreds in 1911. Died 2 Sept. 1924. [1911]

FRY, Lewis. 13 Arlington Street, London. Goldney House, Clifton Hill, Bristol. Balder Grange, Cotherstone, Yorkshire. Reform, Brooks's, and Devonshire. 4th s. of Joseph Fry, Esq., of Bristol, by Mary Ann, d. of Edward Swayne, Esq., of Henley-on-Thames, and younger bro. of the Rt. Hon. Sir Edward Fry, at one time Lord Justice of Appeal. B. 1832; m. 1859, Elizabeth, d. of Francis Gibson, Esq., of Saffron Walden, Essex (she died 1870). Was admitted a Solicitor in 1854, and was senior member of the firm of Fry, Abbot and Company, Bristol. Was Chairman of the Bristol School Board from 1871 to 1880; also Chairman of the Parliamentary Committee on Town Holdings, 1886-92, and Author of two Reports of same. A Liberal Unionist. Sat for Bristol 1878-85, and for Bristol N. 1885-92 when he was defeated; re-elected there 1895 and sat until he retired in 1900. PC. 1901. Died 10 Sept. 1921. [1900]

FRY, Sir Theodore, Bart. 105 Cromwell Road, London. Woodburn, Darlington. 2nd. s. of Francis Fry, Esq., F.S.A., of Bristol, by Matilda, d. of Daniel Penrose, Esq., of Brittas, Co. Wicklow. Cousin of Hon. Sir E. Fry, and Mr. Lewis Fry, MP. B. at Bristol 1836; m. Sophia, d. of John Pease, Esq., of Darlington. Was educ. at the Public School, Bristol. An Iron Manufacturer, head of the firm of Messrs. Fry, Ianson, and Company, Darlington, of which town he was Mayor in 1877-78. A Magistrate for the Co. of Durham. Created Bart. Jan. 1894. A Liberal, in favour of Home Rule for Ireland, of County Boards, the abolition of the law of intestacy and entail, the power of local option in the licensing system, etc. Sat for Darlington from Apr. 1880 until defeated in 1895. Died 5 Feb. 1912. [1895]

FRYE, Frederick Charlwood. 19 Colville Mansions, North Kensington, London. The Plat, Bourne End, Nr. Maidenhead. National Liberal. S. of John Thomas Frye, Esq., Professor of Music, 64 years organist of the parish church of Saffron Walden, and Cecilia Susan, d. of the Rev. Nicholas Hall, 40 years Vicar of the same parish. B. 1845; m. 1873, Jane Kezia, d. of William

Crosbie, Esq., of Winchester. Educ. at the Saffron Walden Grammar School. A Grocer and Wine Spirit Merchant, Principal of the firm of Leverett and Frye, trading in forty places in England and Ireland. A J.P. for Buckinghamshire. Was a member of the Kensington vestry from 1877; Church-warden of St. Mary Abbots 1888-91; Public Library Commissioner from 1888; a member of the Metropolitan Board of Works 1888, and of the London County Council 1889-92. A Liberal, in favour of Home Rule for Ireland, district councils, registration reform, "one man, one vote", repeal of the Septennial Act, reform of the poor laws, a shortening of the hours of labour, leasehold enfranchisement, etc. Sat for Kensington N. from July 1892 until defeated in 1895. Died in winter of 1913-14.   [1895]

FULFORD, Henry Charles. 32 Cadogan Gardens, London. Augustus Road, Birmingham. National Liberal. S. of Henry and Elizabeth Fulford, of Birmingham. B. 1849 at Birmingham; m. 1879, Agnes, d. of Robert Wood, Esq., of Hodsock Grange, Workshop. Educ. privately. A Brewer in Birmingham. A Liberal, in favour of Home Rule etc., but opposed to the Direct Veto Bill. Unsuccessfully contested Birmingham E. in 1892. Sat for the Lichfield division of Staffordshire from July 1895 until unseated on petition on 19 Dec. 1895. Member of Birmingham city Council until 1894. Chairman of Holt Brewery Limited. Died in Cairo 18 Jan. 1897.   [1895 2nd ed.]

FULLAM, Patrick. Drogheda. S. of Patrick Fullam, Esq., and Catherine, d. of Joseph Andrews, Esq. B. 1847; m. 1877, Bridget, 3rd d. of James Kealy, Esq., of Nivan. Educ. at the Schools of the Christian Brothers, Drogheda. A Farmer at Drogheda, and was Vice-Chairman of the Drogheda Poor Law Union. Was High Sheriff of Drogheda in 1886. A Nationalist of the Anti-Parnellite party. Sat for Meath S. from July 1892 until unseated on petition in Nov. 1892.   [1892 2nd ed.]

FULLER, George Pargiter. 47 Rutland Gate, London. Neston Park, Corsham, Wiltshire. United University, and National Liberal. Eld. s. of John Bird Fuller, Esq., Dept.-Lieut., of Neston, Wiltshire, by Sophia Harriet, 2nd d. of William Hanning, Esq., of Dillington Park, Somerset. B.

1833; m. 1864, Emily, 2nd d. of Sir Michael Hicks-Beach, Bart., of Williamstrip Park, Gloucestershire. Educ. at Winchester, and Christ Church, Oxford. A J.P. and Patron of 2 livings. Was High Sheriff for Wiltshire 1878, Capt. in the Wilts. Royal Yeomanry Cavalry from 1860 to 1883, and Chairman of the Board of County Finance from 1870 to 1878. A Liberal and Home Ruler. Unsuccessfully contested Wiltshire North in 1880. Sat for the Westbury division of Wiltshire from 1885 until defeated in 1895. Died 2 Apr. 1927.   [1895]

FULLER, Sir John Michael Fleetwood, Bart. Jaggards, Corsham. 47 Rutland Gate, London. Brooks's, White's, Pratt's, and Garrick. S. of G.P. Fuller, Esq., of Neston Park, MP for the Westbury division of Wiltshire from 1885-95, by Emily, 2nd d. of Sir M. Hicks-Beach, 8th Bart. B. at Neston Park 1864; m. 1898, Norah, 2nd d. of C.N.P. Phipps, Esq., of Chalcot, Westbury, Wiltshire. Educ. at Winchester, and Christ Church, Oxford; 3rd class honours History 1886. Alderman of Wiltshire County Council from 1888, Major Royal Wiltshire Yeomanry 1901, and Aide-de-Camp to Viceroy of India 1894-95. Was a Junior Lord of the Treasury (unpaid) 1906-07; Vice-Chamberlain of H.M. Household from Feb. 1907 to 1911; and a Liberal Whip. Travelled extensively in the two hemispheres. A Liberal. Unsuccessfully contested Wiltshire N.W. in July 1892, Bath in July 1895, and Salisbury in Jan. 1897. Elected for the Westbury division of Wiltshire in 1900 and sat until he accepted Chiltern Hundreds in 1911. Created Bart. in 1910; K.C.M.G. 1911; Governor of Victoria, Australia 1911-14. Died 5 Sept. 1915.   [1910]

FULLER-ACLAND-HOOD, Rt. Hon. Sir Alexander, Bart. See ACLAND-HOOD, Rt. Hon. Sir Alexander Fuller, Bart.

FULLER-MAITLAND, William. See MAITLAND, William Fuller-.

FULLERTON, Hugh. Brackenhoe, Sale, Cheshire. National Liberal. S. of Samuel Fullerton, Esq. B. 1851 at Manchester; m. Ada, d. of Joseph Copley, Esq., Educ. at public schools. A Merchant. Started as a workman, and built up a successful business of his own. J.P. for Manchester and Cumberland. Member of Manchester

Board of Guardians. Treasurer Discharged Prisoners' Aid Society. A Liberal and Labour Member. Elected for the Egremont division of Cumberland in 1906 and sat until defeated in Jan. 1910. Unsuccessfully contested Royton division of Lancashire in 1918. Died 31 Aug. 1922. [1909]

FULTON, James Forrest. 52 Clarendon Road, Notting Hill, London. Carlton, St. Stephen's, and City Carlton. Youngest s. of Lieut.-Col. Fulton, K.H., by Fanny Goodrich Fulton, 4th d. of J. Sympson Jessopp, Esq., J.P., Barrister-at-Law. B. at Ostend, Belgium 1846; m. 1875, Sophia Browne, eld. d. of John B. Nicholson, Esq., of Eastbourne. Educ. at Norwich Grammar School, and graduated B.A. 1867, LL.B. 1873, at the London University. Was called to the bar at the Middle Temple in 1872. Author of *A Manual of Constitutional History.* Was Counsel to the Post Office at the Central Criminal Court, and also Counsel to the Mint for the Co. of Hertford. A Conservative. Unsuccessfully contested West Ham N. in Nov. 1885. First returned for West Ham N. in July 1886 and sat until defeated in 1892. Knighted 1892; Q.C. 1892; Lieut. for the City of London. Recorder of London 1900-1922. Died 25 June 1925. [1892]

FURNESS, Sir Christopher. 23 Upper Brook Street, London. Grantley Hall, Ripon, Yorkshire. Tunstall Court, West Hartlepool. Reform, and Devonshire. S. of John Furness, Esq., and Averill Wilson, d. of John Wilson, Esq., of Naisbet Hall, Co. Durham. B. at W. Hartlepool 1852; m. 1876, Jane Annette, d. of Henry Suggitt, Esq., of Brierton, Co. Durham. Educ. privately. Head of Furness Line steamers; a Ship and Engine Builder. J.P., and Dept.-Lieut. for the counties of Durham and Yorkshire. A member of the Port of London Authority. Knighted 1895. A Liberal. Elected for Hartlepool in Jan. 1891, and re-elected 1892, but defeated 1895; unsuccessfully contested York 13 Jan. 1898; re-elected for Hartlepool in 1900 and sat until Jan. 1910, when he was elected, but the result was declared void on petition. Created 1st Baron Furness 1910. Owned over 30,000 acres. Died 10 Nov. 1912. [1910]

FURNESS, Sir Stephen Wilson, Bart. Tunstall Grange, West Hartlepool. 60 St. James's Street, London. Reform, and National Liberal. S. of Stephen Furness, Esq.,

of Berwick St. James, Wiltshire, and Mary Anne, d. of Dixon T. Sharper, Esq., of W. Hartlepool. B. 26 May 1872; m. 1899, Eleanor, d. of Matthew Foster, Esq., a Civil Engineer, of Adelaide, South Australia. Educ. at Ashville Coll., Harrogate. Chairman of Furness, Withy and Company Limited, S. Durham Steel and Iron Company, Economic Marine Insurance Company Limited, Gulf Line Limited, etc. Vice-Chairman of Richardsons, Westgarth and Company Limited, Broomhill Collieries, Weardale Steel, Coal and Coke Company Limited, and other shipping and coal and iron companies; Director of Cargo Fleet and Iron Company Limited, Houlder Brothers and Company Limited, London Assurance Corporation, etc. A member of W. Hartlepool Town Council and Durham County Council. Created Bart. 1913. A Liberal. First elected for Hartlepool in June 1910 and sat until his death 6 Aug. 1914. [1914]

FYLER, John Arthur. Woodlands, Windlesham, Surrey. United University. S. of the Rev. F. Fyler, and Charlotte, d. of Col. Fane. B. 2 Dec. 1855 at Ewelme, Oxon; m. 1887, Norah Caroline, d. of A. Hambrough, Esq., of Steephill Castle, Isle of Wight. Educ. at Marlborough and Exeter Coll., Oxford. A Barrister, called 1880. A Conservative. Elected for the Chertsey division of Surrey in Mar. 1903 and sat until he accepted Chiltern Hundreds in June 1904, when bankruptcy proceedings were being brought against him. Died 17 Mar. 1929. [1904]

GALBRAITH, Samuel, O.B.E. Continued in House after 1918: full entry in Volume II.

GALLOWAY, William Johnson. 36 Portman Square, London. The Cottage, Old Trafford, Manchester. Scaife Hall, Blubberhouses, Otley. Carlton, and Wellington. S. of John Galloway, Esq., J.P., of Manchester, by the d. of William Crippin, Esq., of Manchester. B. 1868. Educ. at Wellington Coll., and Cambridge. A Partner in the firm of Galloways (Limited), Engineers, of Manchester. A Conservative. Unsuccessfully contested S.E. Warwickshire at the general election of 1892. Represented S.W. Manchester from 1895 until defeated in 1906. Staff Officer 1914, and thereafter went first to the Ministry of

Munitions (Labour Department), secondly to Ministry of Information as Director of Facilities, and then to the Foreign Office News Department. Died 28 Jan. 1931. [1905]

GANE, John Lawrence. Gloucester House, Upper Tulse Hill. 2 Garden Court, Temple, London. Devonshire, National Liberal, and Leeds. S. of Edward Gane, Esq., by Caroline, youngest d. of Joseph Lawrence, Esq., of Freshford, Somerset. B. 1837; m. Elizabeth, youngest d. of George Dowse, Esq., of Worlon, Wiltshire. Educ. at Taunton, and privately. Was called to the bar at the Middle Temple 1870; became Q.C. 1885. A Liberal, and supporter of Mr. Gladstone's Home Rule policy. Was an unsuccessful candidate for the E. division of Leeds at the general election of 1885. First elected there 1886 and sat until his death at sea on the voyage home from New Zealand in Feb.-Mar. 1895. Travelled abroad 1894-95, with Lord Randolph Churchill, for health reasons. [1895]

GANZONI, Capt. Francis John Childs. Continued in House after 1918: full entry in Volume III.

GARDNER, Alan Coulstoun. Clearwell Castle, Coleford. St. James's, Turf, and White's. B. 1846; m. 1885, d. of Sir James Blyth. A Col. in the army, served in 11th and 14th Hussars, Zulu Campaign 1879; mentioned in despatches, Boer War 1881; Aide-de-Camp to Lord Lieut. of Ireland 1880; Dept.-Lieut. and J.P. for Essex; J.P. for Gloucestershire. A Liberal. Unsuccessfully contested E. Marylebone 1895. Elected for S. Herefordshire in 1906 and sat until his death 25 Dec. 1907. [1907]

GARDNER, Ernest. Continued in House after 1918: full entry in Volume III.

GARDNER, Rt. Hon. Herbert Coulstoun. 48 Charles Street, Berkeley Square, London. Debden Hall, Saffron Walden, Essex. Brooks's, White's, Turf, and St. James's. B. in London 1846. Illegitimate s. of 3rd Baron Gardner. M. 1890, Lady Winifred Byng, eld. d. of the Earl of Carnarvon. Educ. at Harrow, and Trinity Hall, Cambridge, (M.A. 1872). A Dept.-Lieut. for Middlesex. President Board of Agriculture 1892-95. A moderate Liberal, prepared to support Mr. Gladstone's Home Rule scheme. Sat for the Saffron Walden division of Essex from 1885 until he retired in 1895. PC. 1892; created Baron Burghclere 1895. Chairman of Royal Commission on Historical Monuments; an Ecclesiastical Commissioner. Director of Peninsular and Oriental Steamship Company. Author of *The Georgics of Virgil translated into English verse*, 1904. Died 6 May 1921. [1895]

GARDNER, Sir James Tynte Agg. See AGG-GARDNER, Sir James Tynte. Continued in House after 1918: full entry in Volume III.

GARDNER, Robert Richardson. See RICHARDSON-GARDNER, Robert.

GARFIT, William. 7 Chesham Place, London. West Skirbeck House, Boston. Carlton, and Junior Constitutional. S. of William Garfit, Esq., Banker, of Boston, and his wife. Jane, the d. of Richard Hassard Short, Esq., of Edlington Grove. Horncastle. B. 1840 at Boston; m. 1868, d. of Conolly Norman, Esq., of Fahan House, Londonderry. Educ. at Harrow, and Trinity Coll., Cambridge; B.A. 1862. A Director and later Chairman of the Capital and Counties Bank; Capt. 2nd Volunteer Battalion 10th Regiment; J.P., and Dept.-Lieut. of Lincolnshire; Sheriff of Lincolnshire 1892. A Conservative. Represented Boston from 1895 until defeated in 1906. Chairman of Holland division (Lincolnshire) Quarter Sessions 1900-14. Died 29 Oct. 1920. [1905]

GASKELL, Charles George Milnes. Thornes House, Wakefield. Wenlock Abbey, Shropshire. Brooks's, Travellers', and St. James's. Eld. s. of James Milnes Gaskell, Esq., MP for Wenlock 1832-68, and a Lord of the Treasury under Sir Robert Peel, 1841-46, by Mary, 2nd d. of the Rt. Hon. Charles W. Williams Wynn, MP. B. in London 1842; m. 1876, Lady Catherine Henrietta Wallop, eld. d. of the 5th Earl of Portsmouth. Educ. at Eton, and Trinity Coll., Cambridge, B.A. 1863; called to the bar 1866. A Magistrate and Dept.-Lieut. for the W. Riding of Yorkshire. Patron of 1 living. A Liberal and Home Ruler. Unsuccessfully contested Pontefract 1868, Wenlock in 1874 and Knaresborough May 1881. Sat for the Morley division of the W. Riding of Yorkshire from 1885 until he retired in 1892. Chairman of West Riding

County Council 1893-1910; PC. 1908. Died 9 Jan. 1919.   [1892]

GASTRELL, Col. Sir William Henry Houghton. 7 Clarence Terrace, Regent's Park, London. Army Service Corps Barracks, Woolwich. Carlton, Junior Carlton, and Sandown. B. 1852 at Tetbury, Gloucestershire; m. 1878, Jessie, d. of James Houghton, Esq., of Maida Vale; one s. and two d. Educ. at Cheltenham. Col. commanding Army Service Corps Woolwich District; served in European War 1914-17 (mentioned in despatches); Maj. Imperial Yeomanry (Duke of Cambridge's Hussars); raised and commanded Lambeth Battalion National Reserve 1912. A J.P. for London; member of the Territorial Association; served on the Finance and General Purposes Committee, London County Council, S. St. Pancras 1903-06; member of the Grand Council of the Primrose League; Chairman of Finance Committee and Gov. on the Board of Management, Royal Free Hospital; Gov. of the Royal Eye Hospital, also of the Waterloo Hospital; Board of Management of the British Home for Incurables; member of Council of the National Union of Conservative Associations; member of Executive Council, London Municipal Society; Vice-President, Tariff Reform League; Knighted 1917. A Unionist. Contested N. Lambeth in 1906; elected for N. Lambeth in Jan. 1910 and sat until defeated in 1918. Died 11 Apr. 1935.   [1918]

GATHORNE-HARDY, Hon. Alfred Erskine. 22 Charles Street, Berkeley Square, London. Carlton, and Junior Carlton. 3rd s. of the 1st Earl of Cranbrook, by Jane, d. of James Orr, Esq. B. in London 1845; m. 1875, Isabella Louisa, only d. of John Malcolm, Esq., of Poltallock, Argyllshire. Educ. at Eton, and Balliol Coll., Oxford (graduated first class in law and modern history, 1867). Called to the bar at the Inner Temple 1869. A Conservative. Sat for Canterbury from Mar. 1878 to 1880, when he was re-elected, but unseated on petition. Unsuccessfully contested the N. division of the W. Riding of Yorkshire in 1882, and the Doncaster division of the same Co. in 1885. First returned for East Grinstead division of E. Sussex 1886 and sat until he retired in 1895. Author of a number of books on hunting, shooting and fishing and of a memoir of his father. Railway Commis-

sioner 1905-18. Died 11 Nov. 1918. [1895]

GATHORNE-HARDY, Hon. John Stewart. 2 Cadogan Square, London. Brandfold, Goudhurst, Kent. Carlton. Eld. s. of 1st Earl of Cranbrook, by Jane, d. of James Orr, Esq., of Holywood House, Co. Devon. B. 1839; m. 1867, Cecily Marguerite, d. of Joseph Ridgway, Esq., of Fairlawn, Kent, and Wallsoches, Lancashire. Educ. at Eton, and Christ Church, Oxford; was once a Lieut. in the Rifle Brigade. A Magistrate and Dept.-Lieut. for Kent, and Lieut.-Col. of the 2nd Volunteer Battalion Buffs (E. Kent Regiment). A Director of the New River Company. A Conservative. Sat for Rye from 1868 until defeated in 1880, and for Mid-Kent from May 1884 to Nov. 1885. Sat for the Medway division of Kent from 1885 until he retired in 1892. Changed his name from Hardy to Gathorne-Hardy in 1878 and was styled Lord Medway from 1892, when his father was created Earl of Cranbrook, until 1906 when he succeeded to the Earldom. Died 13 July 1911.   [1892]

GEDDES, Rt. Hon. Sir Auckland Campbell, K.C.B. Continued in House after 1918: full entry in Volume III.

GEDDES, Rt. Hon. Sir Eric Campbell, K.C.B., G.B.E. Continued in House after 1918: full entry in Volume III.

GEDGE, Sydney. 54 Victoria Street, London. Carlton, Bath, and Constitutional. S. of the Rev. Sydney Gedge, M.A., by Clara, d. of John Deck, Esq. B. at North Runcton Rectory, Norfolk 1829; m. 1897, Augusta, d. of Robert Herring, Esq., of Cromer. Educ. at King Edward's School, Birmingham, and Corpus Christi Coll., Cambridge (M.A. 1856). Became a Solicitor in 1856, and was Solicitor to the London School Board from 1871 to 1891. Wrote magazine on Church and other subjects. Vice President of Church Missionary Society; Licensed Preacher, Dioceses of London and Southwark. Director of Henley's Telegraph Works Company. A Conservative, opposed to Home Rule for Ireland, and in favour of freedom of trade, freedom of contract, freedom of bequest, and freedom from state and municipal interference. Was Member for Stockport from 1886 until he retired from that seat in 1892. Unsuccessfully contested the Luton division of Bedford 1885, whilst still

133

sitting for Stockport. First returned for Walsall in July 1895 and sat until defeated in 1900. Died 6 Apr. 1923.   [1900]

GELDER, Sir William Alfred. West Parade House, Hull. Reform, and National Liberal. S. of William Gelder, Esq., of Brough, Yorkshire. B. 12 May 1855; m. 1878, Elizabeth, d. of Thomas Parker, Esq., of Hull. Educ. privately. An Architect, F.R.I.B.A., and Fellow of Surveyors' Institute. An Alderman for Hull, of which he was five times Mayor 1899-1903, and carried out extensive street improvements and housing schemes. Knighted 1903. A Liberal. Elected for the Brigg division of Lincolnshire in Jan. 1910 and sat until defeated in 1918. Died 26 Aug. 1941. [1918]

GENT-DAVIS, Robert. 19 Albert Square, London. Carlton, and Constitutional. Only s. of Robert Davis, Esq., of Hampstead. B. 1857; m. 1880. Blanche Ellen, d. of William Dixon, Esq., of the Admiralty. Educ. privately. At the age of 21 entered the business of Sparkes, White and Company, Distillers' Chemists (in which his uncle Mr. John H. Gent was the chief Partner), of St. John Street, London, and in 1880 he became the head of that firm. A Gov. and Auditor of St. Bartholomew's Hospital. A Conservative. Sat for the Kennington division of Lambeth from Nov. 1885 until he accepted Chiltern Hundreds in Mar. 1889. (He had been imprisoned from 29 Nov. 1888 to 11 Jan. 1889 "for non-compliance with an order directing him to pay into Court money come to his hands as a Receiver of the Court.")   [1888]

GIBB, James. 51 Ladbroke Grove, London. National Liberal. S. of James Gibb, Esq., and Margaret Wilson. B. 3 May 1844 in London; m. 1873, Helen, d. of the Rev. David Nimmo, Congregationalist Minister. Educ. privately. An Insurance Broker and Underwriter, a member of Lloyds. A Liberal. Elected for the Harrow division of Middlesex in 1906 and sat until he retired in Jan. 1910. Died 23 June 1910.   [1909]

GIBB, Thomas Eccleston. 16 Lady Margaret Road, London. Bushey, Hertfordshire. S. of James and Jane Gibb, of Liverpool. B. in Liverpool 1838; m. 1863. Educ. at Liverpool Coll. and King's Coll., London; and in early life was con-nected with the *Liverpool Mercury*. In 1864 became connected with the vestry of St. Pancras, and served that parish both as vestry clerk and clerk to the guardians. Wrote pamphlets, etc. on Local Government, Poor Law management, etc. An Associate of King's Coll., a Fellow of the Statistical Society, and also a Fellow of the Society of Antiquaries. A Liberal. Sat for St. Pancras E. from Nov. 1885 until defeated in 1886 standing as a Gladstonian Liberal. Contested St. Pancras E. again in 1892. Chairman, Standing Joint Committee of London Magistrates and County Councillors 1890-92. Alderman of London County Council 1889-92. Died 6 June 1894.   [1886]

GIBBINS, Frederick William. Garthmor, Neath, Glamorgan. Eld. s. of F.J. Gibbins, Esq., of Neath. B. 1861; m. 1898, Sarah, d. of Jenkin Rhys, Esq., of Ysguborfawr. A Magistrate and County Councillor for Glamorgan. High Sheriff of Glamorgan 1908-09. Chairman and Managing Director of Eagle Tin Place Company, Neath. Chairman of Welsh Plate and Sheet Manufacturers' Association. A Liberal. First returned for mid Glamorganshire 31 Mar. 1910 and sat until he retired later that year. Died 30 June 1937.

GIBBONS, John Lloyd. Queen Anne's Mansions, London. Ellowes Hall, Sedgley, Staffordshire. Devonshire, and New Club. S. of Henry Gibbons, Esq., Agricultural Chemist, of Wolverhampton, and his wife Elizabeth, the d. of William Saunders, Esq., of The Newbolds, Wolverhampton. B. 1837; m. 1st, 1885, Emma Eliza, d. of Henry John White, Esq., of Stroud, Gloucestershire (she died 1896); 2ndly, 1898, Eliza Grey, d. of Dr. J.M.N. Ballenden, of Sedgley. Educ. at Rev. G. Cottum's Private School, Wolverhampton. An Engineering Surveyor from 1860. A J.P. for Staffordshire, and was County Councillor, North Bilston, Staffordshire 1891; President, S. Wolverhampton Liberal Unionist Association, Trustee Baldwin and Pugh Church Advowsons, Trustee Bilston Provident Society, and Trustee and Life Governor respectively of the Wolverhampton Women's Hospital and the Wolverhampton Eye Infirmary. A Liberal Unionist. Sat for Wolverhampton S. from Feb. 1898 until retired in 1900. Died 27 Apr. 1919.   [1900]

GIBBS, Hon. Alban George Henry. 82 Portland Place, London. Clifton Hampden, Abingdon. Carlton, City Carlton, Travellers', and Constitutional. Eld. s. of Lord Aldenham, who, as Henry Hucks Gibbs, of Aldenham House, Hertfordshire, was MP for the City of London, by Louisa Anne, d. of W. Adams, Esq., LL.D. B. 1846; m. 1873, Bridget, 6th d. of the Rt. Hon. A.J.B. Beresford-Hope, and Lady Mildred, eld. d. of the Marq. of Salisbury (she died 1896). Educ. at Eton, and Christ Church, Oxford; B.A. 1870, M.A. 1873. A Partner in the firm of Antony Gibbs and Sons, Merchants, of Bishopsgate Street, from 1873. A Conservative, and strong supporter of Mr. Balfour's Foreign and Irish policy; opposed to disestablishment of the church and to any interference with the Corporation of London or the City Guilds. Sat for the City of London from 1892 until he accepted Chiltern Hundreds in Feb. 1906 in order to give A.J. Balfour a safe seat. Succeeded as 2nd Baron Aldenham 13 Sept. 1907. Died 9 May 1936. [1905]

GIBBS, Col. George Abraham. Continued in House after 1918: full entry in Volume III.

GIBBS, Henry Hucks. St. Dunstan's, Regent's Park, London. Aldenham House, Nr. Elstree, Hertfordshire. Carlton, Junior Carlton, City Carlton, and Athenaeum. S. of George Henry Gibbs, Esq., Merchant, of London, and his wife, Caroline, d. of the Rev. Charles Crawley, Rector of Stowe, Northamptonshire. B. in London 1819; m. 1845, Louisa Anne, d. of Dr. William Adams, Advocate, of Thorpe, near Chertsey. Educ. at Rugby and Exeter Coll., Oxford, (M.A. 1844). A Merchant, a Partner in the firm of Antony Gibbs and Sons, of Bishopsgate Street, London, a Director of the Bank of England, 1853-1901; a Member of the House of Commons Standing Committee on Trade, etc. He was Proprietor of the *St. James's Gazette* under Mr. Frederick Greenwood's editorship. Was F.S.A., F.R.G.S., a member of the Philological Society, one of the council of Keble Coll., Oxford, etc. A J.P. for Hertfordshire and Middlesex, and a Lieut. of the City of London. Patron of Aldenham, Hertfordshire, and Clifton Hampden, Oxfordshire. A Conservative. First returned for London City Apr. 1891 and sat until he retired in 1892. A Trustee of National Portrait Gallery. Created Baron Aldenham 1896. Died 13 Sept. 1907. [1892]

GIBBS, Hon. Vicary. St. Dunstan's, Regent's Park, London. Aldenham House, Elstree, Hertfordshire. Athenaeum, and Carlton. 2nd s. of Lord Aldenham, and brother of Hon. Alban George Henry Gibbs, by Louisa Anne, 3rd d. of Dr. William Adams, LL.D., of Thorpe, Surrey. B. 1853 at Frognal, Hampstead. Educ. at Eton, and Christ Church, Oxford, (B.A. 1876). A Barrister, called to the bar at Lincoln's Inn 1880, and a Partner in the house of Antony Gibbs and Sons from 1882. A Conservative. Sat for the St. Albans division of Hertfordshire from July 1892 until he accepted Chiltern Hundreds (Government Contract) in 1904 and lost the subsequent by-election 12 Feb. 1904. Contested Central division of Bradford Jan. 1906. Died 13 Jan. 1932. [1903]

GIBNEY, James. Martinstown, Crossakiel, Co. Meath. S. of Thomas Gibney, Esq., and Mary Cullen. B. 1847 at Beltrasna, Oldcastle, Co. Meath; m. 2ndly, 1897, Catherine Marie, d. of Mr. OBrien, Oldtown, Navan. Educ. at Oldcastle Endowed Schools. A Farmer at Crossakiel, Co. Meath, and a J.P. for Co. Meath. A Home Ruler, supported the Anti-Parnellite section of the Nationalist party. Sat for Meath N. from Feb. 1893 until defeated in 1900. Died 25 May 1908. [1900]

GIBSON, Sir James Puckering, Bart. 33 Regent Terrace, Edinburgh. National Liberal. S. of Thomas Gibson, Esq., J.P., of Edinburgh. B. 14 Aug. 1849 in Edinburgh; m. 1874, d. of Thomas Potter, Esq., of Barton Park, Derby. Educ. at Edinburgh Institution, and Edinburgh University. Head of the firm of R. and T. Gibson, Merchants, Edinburgh. A member of Edinburgh Town Council from 1892; Bailie 1900, and Lord Provost 1906-09; a Dept.-Lieut. for Edinburgh, and J.P. for Midlothian and Edinburgh. Created Bart. 1909. A Liberal. First elected for Edinburgh E. in Apr. 1909 and sat until his death 11 Jan. 1912. [1911]

GIBSON, Rt. Hon. John George. 38 Fitzwilliam Place, Dublin. Carlton, and University, Dublin. Youngest s. of William Gibson, Esq., of Rockforest, Co. Tipperary, taxing master in Chancery, by Louisa,

d. of Joseph Grant, Esq. B. at Dublin 1846; m. 1871, Anna, only d. of the Rev. John Hare, of Tullycorbet, Co. Monaghan. Educ. at Enniskillen Royal School, and Trinity Coll., Dublin, where he took the first two gold medals in classics and history, and political science. In 1870 he was called to the Irish bar, in 1880 he became Serjeant-at-Law, and was appointed Solicitor-Gen. for Ireland in 1885, and again in 1886. He was also Chancellor of the Diocese of Killaloe. Attorney-Gen. for Ireland 1887-88. Q.C. 1880; PC. 1887. A "progressive Conservative." Unsuccessfully contested Co. Wexford 1880. Sat for the Walton division of Liverpool from 1885 until appointed an Irish Judge in 1888, which post he held until 1921. Died 28 June 1923. [1887]

GIBSON-CARMICHAEL, Sir Thomas David, Bart. 81 Duke Street, Grosvenor Square, London. Castle Craig, Dolphinton, N.B. Brooks's, and Athenaeum. S. of the Rev. Sir William Henry Gibson-Carmichael, 10th Bart., by Eleanor Anne, d. of David Anderson, Esq. B. at Edinburgh 1859; m. 1886, Mary, d. of Albert Nugent, Esq. Educ. at St. John's Coll., Cambridge (B.A. 1881, M.A. 1884). Founded Scottish Bee-Keeper's Association in 1891. Succeeded as Bart. in 1891. A Dept.-Lieut. for Peeblesshire, a J.P. and Dept.-Lieut. for Edinburghshire, and was Chairman of the Scottish Board of Lunacy 1894-97. A Liberal. Contested Peebles and Selkirk July 1892. First returned for Edinburghshire in July 1895 and sat until he retired in 1900. K.C.M.G. 1908; G.C.I.E. 1911; G.C.S.I. 1917. Trustee of National Portrait Gallery from 1904-08, of National Gallery from 1906-08 and again 1923-26, and of Wallace Collection. Gov. of Victoria 1908-11, Gov. of Madras 1911-12, and Gov. of Bengal 1912-17. Created Baron Carmichael in 1912. Died 16 Jan. 1926. [1900]

GILBERT, James Daniel. Continued in House after 1918; full entry in Volume III.

GILES, Alfred. 26 Great George Street, Westminster, London. 17 Norfolk Street, Park Lane, London. Cosford, Godalming. Carlton. S. of Francis Giles, Esq., a Civil Engineer, of London, by his m. with Mary Anne Wyer, of Birmingham. B. in London 1816; m. 1838, Jane Emily, youngest d. of John Coppard, Esq., of Hastings. Was Educ. at the Charterhouse. A Civil Engineer and Vice President of the Institute of Civil Engineers in 1889. Chairman of the Union Steamship Company. A Conservative. Sat for Southampton from June 1878 until defeated Apr. 1880; re-elected there Apr. 1883 and sat until defeated in 1892. Awarded the Danish order of Knight of Dannebrog. Died 3 Mar. 1895. [1892]

GILES, Charles Tyrrell. Copse Hill House, Wimbledon, Surrey. 2 Hare Court, Temple, London. Carlton, and St. Stephen's. S. of Alfred Giles, Esq., President of the Institute of Civil Engineers, MP for Southampton, and Jane, d. of J. Coppard, Esq., of Haywards Heath. B. 1850; m. 1891, Isabella Mary, d. of Jeremiah Colman, Esq., of Carshalton Park, Surrey. Educ. at Harrow, and King's Coll., Cambridge. A Barrister, called to the bar at the Inner Temple 1874, and joined the Western Circuit. A J.P. for Surrey, Chairman of the Wimbledon and Putney Commons Conservators, and editor of the 4th edition of Cunningham's *Election Law*. A Conservative. Sat for the Wisbech division of Cambridgeshire from July 1895 until defeated in 1900. Alderman of Surrey County Council 1907-25; K.C. 1908. Contested Southampton Jan. 1910; President Wimbledon Conservative Association from 1919. Knighted 1922. Died 16 Jan. 1940. [1900]

GILHOOLY, James Peter. Bantry, Co. Cork. S. of J. Gilhooly, Esq., an Officer in the Coastguard service. B. 1845. Was in business as a Draper at Bantry. An "Irish Nationalist" and Anti-Parnellite. Sat for the W. division of Cork from 1885 until his death 16 Oct. 1916. [1916]

GILL, Alfred Henry. 61 Hampden Street, Bolton. S. of John Gill, Esq. B. 3 Dec. 1856 at Rochdale; m. d. of John Greenwood, Esq. Educ. at Balderstone School, Rochdale. Was Secretary of Bolton Operative Spinners' Association; member of the United Textile Factory Workers' Association; and the Parliamentary Committee of the Trades Union Congress. A member of Bolton Chamber of Commerce, and the British Cotton Growing Association. A J.P. for Bolton. A Labour Member. Elected for Bolton in 1906 and sat until his death 27 Aug. 1914. [1914]

GILL, Henry Joseph. 50 Upper Sackville

Street, Dublin. Roebuck House, Clouskeagh, Co. Dublin. St. George's. Eld. s. of Michael H. Gill, Esq., by Mary Catherine, d. of Mr. Hart. B. at Dublin 1836; m. 1870, Mary Julia, d. of James Keating, Esq. Educ. at St. Vincent's Coll., Castleknock, and Trinity Coll., Dublin, where he graduated B.A. 1857, and M.A. 1872. A Publisher and Bookseller in Dublin, was elected on the Municipal Council 1877. Wrote various pamphlets and translations from foreign languages. Home Ruler. Sat for Westmeath from Apr. 1880 to Feb. 1883, when he retired. Sat for Limerick from 1885 until he accepted Chiltern Hundreds in Jan. 1888.
[1888]

GILL, Thomas Patrick. 33 Lower Abbey Street, Dublin. Nenagh, Tipperary. Eld. s. of Robert Gill, Esq., a Civil Engineer, of Nenagh, Co. Tipperary, and nephew of Peter Gill, Esq., a candidate for Co. Tipperary in 1868. B. 1858; m. 1882, Annie, d. of John Fennell, Esq., of Dublin. Educ. at Trinity Coll., Dublin. A Journalist. An "Irish Nationalist." Sat for Louth S. from 1885 until he retired in 1892. Chairman of Departmental Committee on Irish Forestry 1907-08; member of committees concerning Irish agricultural production 1914-19. President, Irish Technical Instruction Association 1925-29. Died 19 Jan. 1931.
[1892]

GILLIAT, John Saunders. 18 Prince's Gate, London. Chorley Wood Cedars, Rickmansworth. Carlton, Oxford & Cambridge, and City Carlton. Eld. s. of John Kirton Gilliat, Esq., of Fernhill, Berkshire, head of the firm of John Kirton Gilliat and Company, American Bankers and Merchants, London and Liverpool. B. at Clapham Common 1829; m. 1860, Louisa Ann Fanny, d. of Matthew Babington, Esq., of Rothley Temple, Leicestershire. Educ. at Harrow, and University Coll., Oxford (B.A. 1851, M.A. 1855). After travelling in America, he joined his father's firm, of which he was head from 1856. Became a Director of the Bank of England in 1862, and a Governor in 1883; one of Her Majesty's Lieuts. for the City of London and a J.P. for Hertfordshire. A Conservative, strongly opposed to Mr. Gladstone's Irish policy, and to the disestablishment of the Church. Sat for the Clapham division of Battersea and Clapham 1886-92. Sat for the Widnes

division of Lancashire S.W. from July 1892 until he retired in 1900. Died 13 Feb. 1912.
[1900]

GILMOUR, Lieut.-Col. John. Continued in House after 1918: full entry in Volume III.

GINNELL, Laurence. Continued in House after 1918: full entry in Volume III.

GLADSTONE, Rt. Hon. Herbert John. 9 Buckingham Gate, London. Sandycroft, Littlestone-on-Sea. Reform, Bath, and National Liberal. 4th s. of the Rt. Hon. William Ewart Gladstone, by Catherine, eld. d. of Sir Stephen Richard Glynne, Bart., of Hawarden Castle, Flintshire. B. 1854; m. 1901, Dorothy, d. of the Rt. Hon. Sir R.H. Paget, of Cranmore Hall, Solerset. Educ. at Eton, and at University Coll., Oxford. A Lecturer on History at Keble Coll., Oxford, and Private Secretary (without salary) to his father as Prime Minister in 1880 and later. A Lord of the Treasury, 1881-85, Dept.-Commissioner of the Board of Works 1885, Financial Secretary, War Office Feb.-July 1886, Under Secretary to the Home Office 1892-94, and First Commissioner of Works 1894-95; became PC 1894. Chief "Whip" to the Liberal party 1899-1905. Home Secretary Dec. to Jan. 1910. A Liberal, in favour of Free Trade, Home Rule for Ireland, Temperance Reform, and of the abolition of the veto power of the House of Lords. Unsuccessfully contested Middlesex Apr. 1880. Sat for Leeds from May 1880-85, and for Leeds W. from 1885 until he retired in Jan. 1910. Created Visct. Gladstone 1910; G.C.M.G. 1910; First Governor-Gen. and High Commissioner of South Africa 1910-14; G.C.B. 1914; G.B.E. 1917; Head of War Refugees Association 1914-19; played a major role in the Liberal Party organisation 1919-24; author of *After Thirty Years* (1928). Died 6 Mar. 1930.
[1909]

GLADSTONE, Rt. Hon. William Ewart. 10 Downing Street, London. Hawarden Castle, Chester. United University. 4th s. of Sir John Gladstone (1st Bart.), a Liverpool Merchant. Grand-s. maternally of Andrew Robertson, Esq., Provost of Dingwall. B. at Liverpool 1809; m. 1839, Catherine, eld. d. of Sir Stephen Richard Glynne, Bart., of Hawarden Castle, Flintshire. Was educ. at Eton, and at Christ Church, Oxford, where he obtained a double first class in

137

1831, graduated M.A. 1834, and received the honorary degree of D.C.L. 1848. A Dept.-Lieut. of Wiltshire. Was appointed a Lord of the Treasury in Dec. 1834; was Under-Secretary for the Colonies from Jan. 1835 till Apr. same year; Vice-President of the Board of Trade and Master of the Mint from Sept. 1841 to May 1843, when he became President of that Board, retaining the office of Master of the Mint; resigned both Feb. 1845; was Secretary of State for the Colonies from Dec. 1845 to July 1846, Chancellor of the Exchequer from Dec. 1852 till Feb. 1855, and from June 1859 till July 1866. Leader of the House of Commons 1865-66. Was first Prime Minister from Dec. 1868 to Feb. 1874; from Aug. 1873 was Chancellor of the Exchequer in addition to his other offices. Retired from the leadership of the Liberal Party in 1875 but resumed leadership in 1880. Re-appointed to the Premiership, and in conjunction with that office Chancellor of the Exchequer Apr. 1880. In Dec. 1882 he resigned the latter office to the Rt. Hon. H.C.E. Childers, and in June 1885, on an adverse vote in the House of Commons, the whole Liberal ministry resigned. In Jan. 1886 he returned to office as Prime Minister and Lord Privy Seal in his third administration, but after an adverse vote on his Bill for the Government of Ireland, Parliament was again dissolved and in July 1886 he resigned office. Took office as Premier for the fourth time in Aug. 1892 but retired 3 Mar. 1894 and was succeeded by Lord Rosebery. Went on a special mission to the Ionian Islands as Lord High Commissioner Extraordinary Nov. 1858. Elected Lord Rector of the University of Edinburgh Nov. 1859, and again 1862. Lord Rector of the University of Glasgow 1877. Professor of Ancient History to the Royal Academy Mar. 1876. Author of *The State in its Relations with the Church, Church Principles considered in their Results*, and other works. A Liberal. Sat as a Conservative for Newark from 1832 till his acceptance of office in Dec. 1845, during which time he unsuccessfully contested Manchester 28 July 1837. Sat for the University of Oxford from 1847 till July 1865, when he was returned for Lancashire S., he was unsuccessful at that place Dec. 1868, but obtained a seat for Greenwich, which he held until he was returned Apr. 1880 for Edinburghshire (Midlothian) and Leeds, and elected to sit for the former. On 2 July 1886 he suc-

cessfully contested Edinburghshire (Midlothian) and Leith District and elected to sit for Edinburghshire (Midlothian) which he continued to represent until he retired in 1895. Died May 1898.   [1894]

GLADSTONE, William Glynne Charles. Hawarden Castle, Nr. Chester. 41 Berkeley Square, London. Wellington. S. of W.H. Gladstone, Esq., and Hon. Gertrude Stuart, d. of 12th Baron Blantyre, and grand-s. of the Rt. Hon. W.E. Gladstone, MP. B. 14 July 1885. Unmarried. Educ. at Eton, and New Coll., Oxford; President of Union 1907. Additional Private Secretary to Lord Aberdeen 1909. Was Honorary Attaché to British Embassy at Washington 1910-11. Lord Lieut. of Flintshire from 1911. A Liberal. Elected for Kilmarnock Burghs in Sept. 1911 and sat until he was killed in action on 15 Apr. 1915.   [1915]

GLANVILLE, Harold James. Continued in House after 1918: full entry in Volume III.

GLAZEBROOK, Philip Kirkland. Twemlow Hall, Holmes Chapel, Cheshire. Bath, and 1900. S. of John K. Glazebrook, Esq. B. 1880 at Swinton. Unmarried. Educ. at Eton, and New Coll., Oxford. A Merchant in business in Manchester. Maj. Cheshire Yeomanry. A Unionist. Elected for S. Manchester Mar. 1912 and sat until he was killed in action 11 Mar. 1918. [1918]

GLEN-COATS, Sir Thomas Glen, Bart. 29 Belgrave Square, London. Ferguslie Park, Paisley. Achnamara, Lochgilphead, N.B. Reform, and National Liberal. S. of Thomas Coats, Esq., J.P., of Ferguslie, and Margaret, d. of Thomas Glen, Esq., of Thornhill, Renfrewshire. B. 19 Feb. 1846; m. 1876, Elise Agnes, d. of Alexander Walker, Esq., of Montreal. Educ. at Queenwood Coll., Hampshire. A Director of J. and P. Coats, of Paisley; Honorary Col. (V.D.), commanded 2nd Volunteer Battalion Argyll and Sutherland Highlanders. Vice-Chairman of Council of Scottish Liberal Association; Lord-Lieut. of Co. Renfrew from 1908; Chairman of Paisley School Board 1885-94; created Bart. 1894; assumed the additional surname of Glen in 1894. A Liberal. Unsuccessfully contested W. Renfrewshire in 1900. Elected there in 1906 amd sat until he retired in Jan. 1910. C.B. 1911. Died 12 July 1922.   [1909]

GLENDINNING, Robert Graham. Glengyle, Windsor Avenue, Belfast. National Liberal. S. of William and Martha Glendinning, of Brakagh, Co. Derry. B. 1844 at Brakagh; m. 1st, 1874, Elizabeth, d. of A. Harden, Esq.; 2ndly, Mary, d. of William Hastings, Esq., of Belfast. A member of the firm of Glendinning, McLeish and Company Limited, Linen Manufacturers, Belfast. An Independent Liberal. Elected for N. Antrim in 1906 and sat until he retired in Jan. 1910. PC. (Ireland) 1911. Died 8 June 1928.   [1909]

GLOVER, Thomas. 108 Prescot Road, St. Helens. S. of William Glover, Esq. B. 25 Mar. 1852 at Prescot; m. 1872, d. of William Seddons, Esq., of Aston, Birmingham. Educ. at a Church School, St. Helens. A Miners Agent, and Treasurer of Lancashire and Cheshire Miners Federation; a J.P. Was a member of St. Helen's Board of Guardians. A Labour Member. Elected for St. Helens in 1906 and sat until defeated in Dec. 1910. Died 9 Jan. 1913.   [1910]

GLYN, Hon. Pascoe Charles. 54 Lowndes Square, London. Gaunt's House, Wimborne, Dorset. Brooks's, Arthur's, and National Liberal. 3rd s. of 1st Lord Wolverton, by Marianne, d. of Pascoe Grenfell, Esq. B. in Eaton Place, London, 1833; m. 1861, Caroline Henrietta, d. of Capt. Amherst Hale. Educ. at Harrow, and University Coll., Oxford. A Partner in the firm of Glyn, Mills, and Company from 1864; a Dept.-Lieut. for the City of London, and a J.P. for Middlesex. A moderate Liberal, "in favour of a thorough reform in the Constitution of the House of Lords." Sat for Dorset E. from Dec. 1885 until defeated in 1886 standing as a Gladstonian Liberal. Unsuccessfully contested Dorset E. 27 Nov. 1881. Died 3 Nov. 1904.   [1886]

GLYN-JONES, William Samuel. 26 Old Park Villas, Palmer's Green, London. National Liberal. S. of George Griffiths Jones, Esq., Registrar of Marriages, and Catherine, d. of William Llewellyn, Esq. B. 29 Jan. 1869 at Worcester; m. 1894, Mary, d. of John Evans, Esq., of Llanybyther, Carmarthenshire. Educ. at Merthyr Tydvil Grammar School. A Barrister, called to the bar at the Middle Temple 1904. A Pharmaceutical Chemist. Parliamentary Private Secretary to Dr. Addison, when Minister of Munitions. Parliamentary Secretary of Pharmaceutical Society; Secretary of Proprietary Articles Trade Association; Alderman of Middlesex County Council; and Chairman of Middlesex Insurance Committee. Author of *Law Relating to Poisons and Pharmacy*. A Liberal. Unsuccessfully contested the Stepney division of Tower Hamlets in Jan. 1910. Elected there in Dec. 1910 and sat until he retired in 1918. Knighted 1919. Secretary to the Pharmaceutical Society of Great Britain 1918-26; also Chairman of the Council of the Proprietary Articles Trade Association. Died 9 Sept. 1927.   [1918]

GODDARD, Rt. Hon. Sir Daniel Ford. Oak Hill, Ipswich. Reform, and National Liberal. S. of Ebenezer Goddard, Esq., a Civil Engineer, and a J.P. for Ipswich, and Annie, d. of Thomas Ford, Esq., of Reading. B. 1850 at Ipswich; m. 1st, Lucy, d. of Thomas Harwood, Esq., of Belstead Hall, Surrey; 2ndly, Elizabeth, d. of E. Hitchcock, Esq., of Bramford, Suffolk. Educ. first at Ipswich, then at Hastings, under Dr. Martin Reed. A Civil Engineer, articled 1867. Engineer to the Ipswich Gaslight Company 1872-87. A Municipal Councillor for Ipswich 1886-95; Mayor 1891-92; J.P. for the borough 1892; Alderman 1895; Knighted 1907; PC. 1916. Founded and built the Ipswich Social Settlement in 1896, where he carried on active social and religious work. A Liberal, in favour of Electoral, Poor Law, and Licensing reforms, etc. Was an unsuccessful candidate for Ipswich in 1892. First elected for Ipswich in 1895 and sat until he retired in 1918. Died 6 May 1922.   [1918]

GODSON, Sir Augustus Frederick. 7 Fig Tree Court, Temple, London. 6 Hans Mansions, London. Ashfield, Malvern. Carlton. Eld. s. of Septimus Holmes Godson, Esq., of Gray's Inn, Barrister-at-Law, 14 Rutland Gate, London, and Tenbury, Worcestershire, and nephew to Richard Godson, Esq., Q.C., who was MP for Kidderminster from 1832 to 1894. B. at Tenbury 1835; m. 1869, Jane Charlotte, youngest d. of E. Boughton, Esq., J.P., of Stoke, near Coventry. Educ. at King's Coll., London, and Queen's Coll., Oxford; B.A. 1857, M.A. 1859. Was called to the bar at the Inner Temple in 1859, was for 20 years Honorary Treasurer (Chairman 1866) of the Worcestershire Society, one of the committee of the Herefordshire

Society, and one of the founders of the Knowle Asylum for Persons of Weak Mind, near Birmingham; Grand Master of the Freemasons of Worcestershire, a Loriner and a Patten-Maker, London, etc.; J.P. and Dept.-Lieut. for Worcestershire; Knighted 1898. A Conservative and Unionist. Unsuccessfully contested Warwick at the elections of 1874 and 1880, and Kidderminster in 1885. First elected for Kidderminster in 1886 and sat until he retired in Jan. 1906. Died 11 Oct. 1906. [1905]

GOLD, Charles. 17 Cumberland Terrace, Regent's Park, London. Birchanger, Essex. Devonshire. S. of Michael Gold and Ellen Young, both of Birmingham. B. in London 1837; m. 1859, Fanny Georgiana, youngest sister of Sir Walter Gilbey, Bart. Educ. privately. A Director of the firm of Wine Merchants, W. and A. Gilbey and Company Limited. "A Radical", in favour of Home Rule, etc. Sat for the Saffron Walden division of Essex from July 1895 until he retired in 1900. Knighted 1906. Died 2 Nov. 1924. [1900]

GOLDMAN, Charles Sydney. Trefusis, Falmouth. Walpole House, Chiswick, London. Carlton, and Yorick. B. 1868 in Cape Colony; m. 1899, Hon. Agnes Mary Peel, d. of 1st Visct. Peel. Educ. privately. Was interested in East and South African Mining. Served as special correspondent during S. African War 1899, and afterwards joined the cavalry in that campaign; a member of the Executive of the National Service League, the African Society and S. African Union. Maj. Cornwall Royal Garrison Artillery (T.). Author of *With General French and the Cavalry in South Africa, The Empire and the Century, Cavalry in Future Wars,* and text-books on mining subjects. A Unionist. Elected for Penryn and Falmouth in Jan. 1910 and sat until he retired in 1918. Proprietor of the weekly newspaper *Outlook*; author of several books on South African Mining and its development. Died 7 Apr. 1958. [1918]

GOLDSMID, Rt. Hon. Sir Julian, Bart. 105 Piccadilly, London. Somerhill, Tonbridge, Kent. Brooks's, Athenaeum, St. James's, Turf, and Reform. Eld. s. of Frederick David Goldsmid, Esq., and grand-s. of Sir Isaac Lyon Goldsmid, by Caroline, only d. of Philip Samuel, Esq. B. in London 1838; m. 1868, Virginia, eld. d. of A. Philipson, Esq., of Florence (she died 1892). Educ. at the University of London B.A. (1st in classical honours 1859), and M.A. (1st in classical branch 1861), and in 1895 was elected Vice-Chancellor of the University. Was called to the bar at Lincoln's Inn in 1864. A Dept. Chairman of Committees, and was Chairman of the Standing Committee on Trade; also a Magistrate for Kent, Middlesex, and London, and a Dept.-Lieut. for Kent, Sussex, and Berkshire. Was Honorary Col. of the 1st Sussex Artillery Volunteers from 1881. A Liberal Unionist. Unsuccessfully contested Brighton Feb. 1864 and Cirencester 1865. Sat for Honiton from Mar. 1866 till the disfranchisement of that borough in Nov. 1868. Unsuccessfully contested Mid Surrey 1868. Sat for Rochester from July 1870 to the dissolution of 1880, when he was defeated. Was first returned for St. Pancras S. in Nov. 1885 and sat until his death 7 Jan. 1896. Succeeded as Bart. 1878; PC. 1895. Estate worth over one million pounds. [1895 2nd ed.]

GOLDSMITH, Maj. Francis Benedict Hyam. Cavenham Park, Mildenhall, Suffolk. 14 South Street, London. Carlton, Marlborough, Bachelors', and Garrick. B. 1878. Educ. at Cheltenham and Magdalen Coll., Oxford; M.A. Called to the bar at the Inner Temple 1902. A member of Westminster City Council 1903-07, and of the London County Council (Whip to Municipal Reform Party) 1904-10; Maj. Suffolk Yeomanry. Served in Gallipoli 1915. Alderman W. Suffolk County Council. A Unionist. Elected for the Stowmarket division of Suffolk in Jan. 1910 and sat until he retired in 1918. O.B.E. 1919. He lived in France after the First World War and was a leading figure in the hotel business. Director of Savoy Hotel Company and a founder of the King David Hotel in Jerusalem. Died 4 Feb. 1967. [1918]

GOLDSTONE, Frank Walter. Hamilton House, Mabledon Place, London. 14 Brinkburn Street, Sunderland. S. of Thomas Frederick Goldstone, Esq., Stained Glass Artist. B. 7 Dec. 1870 in Sunderland; m. 1895, Elizabeth Alice, d. of Luke Henderson, Esq., of Whittingham, Northumberland. Educ. at Diamond Hall Council School, Sunderland, and Borough Road Coll., Isleworth. Was a Schoolmaster from 1892-1910, and later an official of the National Union of Teachers; Gen.-Secretary of that Union 1924-31. Was President of National Federation of Assistant Teachers 1902 and first Editor of the *Class Teacher*. Chief Whip to Labour Party 1915-16. A Labour Member. Elected for Sunderland in Dec. 1910 and sat until defeated in 1918. Member of Speaker's Conference on the Franchise and the Royal Commission on the Civil Service 1929-31. Kt. 1931. Died 25 Dec. 1955. [1918]

GOLDSWORTHY, Maj.-Gen. Walter Tuckfield. 22 Hertford Street, Mayfair, London. Yaldham Manor, Wrotham, Kent. Eld. s. of Thomas Goldsworthy, Esq., of Calcutta, and of the Royal Navy, by Sophia, d. of William Tuckfield, Esq., R.N. B. at Purbrook, Hampshire 1837; m. 1879, Mary Emma, only child of Henry Cox, Esq., of Limpsfield, Surrey, and Charton Manor, Kent. He served with the Volunteers in Oude (under Havelock) during the Indian Mutiny, and for his services received a commission as Cornet in the 8th Hussars. He subsequently served in India under Brig. Smith and Sir Hugh Rose, and in the Abyssinian expedition. He retired on half-pay with the rank of Maj.-Gen. in 1885. A Conservative. Sat for Hammersmith from Nov. 1885 until he retired in 1900. C.B. 1907. Died 13 Oct. 1911. [1900]

GOOCH, George Peabody. South Villa, Campden Hill Road, London. National Liberal, and Eighty. S. of C.C. Gooch, Esq., and Mary Blake. B. 1873 in London; m. 1903, Elsa, d. of Julius Schöen, of Berlin. Educ. at King's Coll., London, and Trinity Coll., Cambridge. Lecturer. Was Private Secretary to the Rt. Hon. J. Bryce, when Chief Secretary for Ireland. Author of *English Democratic Ideas in the 17th Century, Annals of Politics and Culture* and other historical works, contributor to *Cambridge Modern History, The Heart of the Empire,* etc. A Liberal. Elected for Bath in 1906 and sat until defeated in Jan. 1910. Unsuccessfully contested Bath in Dec. 1910, and Reading 8 Nov. 1913. President of Historical Association 1922-25; President of National Peace Council 1933-36; F.B.A.; Honorary Fellow of Trinity College, Cambridge. C.H. 1939; O.M. 1963. Died 31 Aug. 1968. [1909]

GOOCH, Henry Cubitt. 17 Oxford Square, London. Carlton, and Constitutional. S. of C.C. Gooch, Esq., and Mary, d. of the Rev. H. Blake. B. 7 Dec. 1871 in London; m. 1897, Maud Mary. d. of the Rev. J.H. Hudleston, of Clayton Hall, S. Stainley, Leeds. Educ. at Eton, and Trinity Coll., Cambridge. Was called to the bar 1894. A member of the London School Board 1897-1904, and of the London County Council 1907-10 and 1914-34 (Vice-Chairman of Education Committee). A J.P. A Unionist. Elected for the Peckham division of Camberwell in Mar. 1908 and sat until defeated in Dec. 1910. Knighted 1928. Alderman of the London County Council from 1914-19; Vice-Chairman of the London County Council from 1922-23; Chairman 1923-24. Vice President of Kings College Hospital. President of Cambridge House, Camberwell. Died 15 Jan. 1959. [1910]

GORDON, Rt. Hon. John. 25 Upper Fitzwilliam Street, Dublin. Constitutional. S. of Samuel Gordon, Esq. B. 1849; m. 1887, Dorothy May, d. of R. Keating Clay, Esq., J.P. Educ. at Royal Academical Institute, Belfast, and Queen's Coll., Galway; M.A. and LL.D. of the Royal University, Ireland. Called to the bar in 1877; Q.C. 1892, and was elected a bencher of the King's Inn 1898. Was one of the leaders of the Irish bar. Attorney-Gen. of Ireland from June 1915 to Apr. 1916. A Unionist. Unsuccessfully contested mid Armagh in Feb. 1900. Elected for S. Londonderry in Oct. 1900 and sat until appointed Judge of High Court of Ireland in Apr. 1916. PC. (Ireland) 1915. Died 26 Sept. 1922. [1916]

GORDON, Hon. John Edward. 44 Albert Court, Prince's Gate, London. 1 Queen's Gardens, Hove, Sussex. Carlton, and Junior Carlton. Eld. s. of Lord Gordon of Drumearn, Lord Advocate 1867-68, and 1874-76, who was created a Life Peer in 1876. B. 5 Feb. 1850 at Edinburgh; m. 1879, Elizabeth Anna, d. of J. Snowdon Henry, Esq., MP. Educ. at Edinburgh Academy and University. A Unionist. Sat for Elgin and Nairn from 1895-1906. Unsuccessfully contested Brighton in 1906. Elected for Brighton June 1911 and sat until he accepted Chiltern Hundreds in June 1914. Died 19 Feb. 1915. [1914]

GORDON, Sir William Eden Evans. See EVANS-GORDON, Sir William Eden.

GORDON-LENNOX, Rt. Hon. Lord Walter Charles. See LENNOX, Rt. Hon. Lord Walter Charles Gordon-.

GORST, Rt. Hon. Sir John Eldon. Queen Anne's Mansions, London. Carlton. S. of Edward Chaddock Lowndes (formerly Gorst), by Elizabeth, d. of John D. Nesham, Esq. B. at Preston 1835; m. 1860, Mary Elizabeth, d. of the Rev. Lorenzo Moorè. Graduated at St. John's Coll., Cambridge; 3rd Wrangler B.A. 1857, M.A. 1860; Fellow of his Coll. Was called to the bar at the Inner Temple 1865; Q.C. 1875. Was Solicitor Gen. 1885-86; Parliamentary Secretary to the India Office 1886-91; and Financial Secretary to the Treasury Nov. 1891 to Aug. 1892; Vice-President Committee of Council 1895-1902. Was Civil Commissioner of Waikato from 1861 to 1863. Author of *The Maori King* (1864). A Conservative. Unsuccessfully contested Hastings 1865. Sat for Cambridge borough from Apr. 1866 until defeated Nov. 1868; for Chatham Feb. 1875 to June 1892, and for Cambridge University from July 1892 until defeated in 1906 as a Free Trader. Contested Preston as a Liberal in Jan. 1910. Knighted 1885; PC. 1890. Died 4 Apr. 1916.   [1905]

GOSCHEN, Rt. Hon. George Joachim. Seacox Heath, Hawkhurst, Kent. Athenaeum, and Carlton. S. of William Henry Goschen, Esq., and Henrietta, his wife. B. 1831; m. 1857, Lucy, d. of John Dalley, Esq. (she died 1898). Educ. at Rugby, and at Oriel Coll., Oxford. Was a member of the firm of Messrs. Fruhling and Goschen, Austinfriars. A Commissioner of Lieutenancy for London; appointed an Ecclesiastical Commissioner Oct. 1882, Lord Rector of Aberdeen University 1887, and Lord Rector of Edinburgh University 1890. Was Vice-President of the Board of Trade, and Paymaster-Gen. from Nov. 1865 till Jan. 1866; PC. 1865; Chancellor of the Duchy of Lancaster from Jan. 1866 till July 1866. President of the Poor Law Board from Dec. 1868 to Mar. 1871, and First Lord of the Admiralty from Mar. 1871 to Feb. 1874. Was engaged on a special mission to Constantinople from May 1880 to Apr. 1881. He accepted the office of Chancellor of the Exchequer in Lord Salisbury's 2nd administration Jan. 1887; retired Aug. 1892. Became First Lord of the Admiralty again June 1895; retired Oct. 1900. Author of *The Theory of the Foreign Exchanges*. A Liberal Unionist. Sat for City of London from 2 June 1863 to Apr. 1880, and for Ripon from 1880 till 1885, when he was elected for Edinburgh E. as an Independent Liberal. In the latter division he was defeated by Dr. Wallace in 1886, and on 26 Jan. 1887 he unsuccessfully contested the Exchange division of Liverpool. Sat for St. George's, Hanover Square from 9 Feb. 1887 until he retired in 1900. Created 1st Visct. Goschen 1900. Died 7 Feb. 1907.   [1900]

GOSCHEN, Hon. George Joachim. 20 Cadogan Gardens, London. Carlton. Eld. s. of Visct. Goschen, formerly First Lord of the Admiralty, etc., by Lucy, d. of John Dallay, Esq. B. 1866 at St. Leonards, Sussex; m. 1892, Lady Margaret Evelyn Gathorne-Hardy, d. of the Earl of Cranbrook. Educ. at Rugby, and Balliol Coll., Oxford. Was a Private Secretary to his father, and served in that capacity to the Earl of Jersey when Governor of New South Wales. Lieut.-Col. commanding 2nd Volunteer Battalion East Kent Regiment, and Aide-de-Camp to Commander-in-Chief (Lord Roberts). A Conservative. Represented the East Grinstead division of Sussex from 1895 until 1906 when he was defeated contesting Bolton. Succeeded as 2nd Visct. Goschen 1907. Joint Parliamentary Secretary to Board of Agriculture Mar.-June 1918. Gov. of Madras 1924-29. Viceroy and Acting Gov.-Gen. of India June-Nov. 1929. PC. 1930. Died 24 July 1952.   [1905]

GOULDING, Sir Edward Alfred, Bart. Continued in House after 1918: full entry in Volume III.

GOURLEY, Sir Edward Temperley. Cleaden, Nr. Sunderland. Devonshire, and Union. S. of John Young Gourley, Esq., Shipowner, by his m. with Miss Mary Temperley. B. at Sunderland 1828. Unmarried. A Merchant and Shipowner at Sunderland. Served ten years as Capt. in the N. Durham Militia; resigned 1864. An Alderman and borough Magistrate for Sunderland, of which he was elected Mayor for the 3rd time 1868. Was for 20 years Commandant of the Sunderland Rifle Volunteers, and afterwards Honorary Col. Knighted 1895. An "advanced Liberal." Sat for Sunderland from Dec. 1868 until he resigned in 1900. Died 15 Apr. 1902.   [1900]

GRAFTON, Frederick William. Retired in 1886: full entry in Volume I.

GRAHAM, Edward John. 44 St. John's Park, London. A Nationalist. Elected for the Tullamore division of King's Co. in Dec. 1914 and sat until his death 26 Mar. 1918. [1918]

GRAHAM, Harry Robert. 8 Marble Arch, London. Athenuem, Carlton, Oxford & Cambridge, and Junior Constitutional. S. of J.B. Graham, Esq., of 15 Warrior Square, St. Leonards-on-Sea, by Louisa, eld. d. of R. Rymill, Esq. B. 1850. Educ. at Exeter Coll., Oxford; B.A. 1873, M.A. 1877. He travelled three times round the world, and visited each of the British colonies. A Conservative, opposed to Home Rule for Ireland, and in favour of a careful revision of the incidence of taxation and a federation of the colonies. Unsuccessfully contested the Handsworth division of Staffordshire 1885, W. St. Pancras 1886, and N. St. Pancras 1890. Represented W. St. Pancras from 1892 until defeated in 1906. Died 11 Jan. 1933. [1905]

GRAHAM, Robert Gallnigad Bontine Cunninghame. Gartmore, in Menteith, Stirling, N.B. Eld. s. of William Cunninghame Bontine, Esq., of Gartmore and Finlaystone, by the Hon. Anne Elizabeth, sister of the 14th Baron Elphinstone, and d. of Admiral Charles Elphinstone-Fleeming, of Cumberland. B. in London 1852; m. Gabrielle, d. of Don Francisco Jose de Labalmondiere. Educ. at Harrow. Until succeeding to the family estates of Gallnigad, Gartmore and Ardoch, was a Cattle-Farmer in South America, the River Plate, and Mexico. J.P. in three counties and a Dept.-Lieut. for Dunbartonshire. A "Socialist, in favour of Legislative Independence for Ireland." Unsuccessfully contested N.W. Lanarkshire as a Liberal/Labour candidate at the general election of 1885. Returned there in July 1886 and sat until he retired in 1892. Unsuccessfully contested the Camlachie division of Glasgow as Scottish Parliamentary Labour Party Candidate 1892. Unsuccessfully contested W. Stirlingshire 1918. Became Honorary President of the Scottish Parliamentary Labour Party when it was formed in 1888; retired 1892. First Chairman of National Party of Scotland 1928. Died 20 Mar. 1936. [1892]

GRANBY, Henry John Brinsley Manners, Marq. of. 23a Bruton Street, London. Carlton, and Turf. S. of the Duke of Rutland, G.C.B., by his wife the d. of Col. Marley, C.B. (died 1854). B. in London 1852; m. 1882, Marian Margaret Violet, d. of Col. the Hon. C.H. Lindsay, C.B. Educ. at Eton, and Trinity Coll., Cambridge. He served in the 3rd Battalion Leicestershire Regiment from 1872 to 1883, became Capt. 1878, and later retired. Was principal Private Secretary to the Marq. of Salisbury as Prime Minister from June 1885 to Feb. 1886, and again from Aug. 1886 to Mar. 1888. A Conservative and Unionist. Sat for the Melton division of Leicestershire from Mar. 1888 until he retired in 1895. Called up the House of Lords as Baron Manners of Haddon in 1896 during his father's lifetime and succeeded his father as Duke of Rutland in 1906. Lord-Lieut. of Leicestershire from 1900. K.G. 1918. Died 8 May 1925. [1895]

GRANT, Corrie Brighton. See GRANT, J. Corrie.

GRANT, Daniel. 12 Cleveland Gardens, Hyde Park, London. Devonshire, and City Liberal. S. of Daniel Grant, Esq., a Master Mariner, of Caithness. B. at South Shields 1826. Educ. at the Upper School, Greenwich Hospital. A partner in the firm of Messrs. Grant and Company, Engravers and Designers, of Clerkenwell. Author of a work on *Home Politics*. Of Liberal opinions, which he "defined as a practical painstaking Liberalism." In favour of a "close and cordial union" being maintained between the "colonies and the mother country", and of an entire repeal of Schedule D in the income-tax, to relieve "from inquisitorial taxation" the precarious results of professional or industrial labour. Unsuccessfully contested Marylebone in Dec. 1868 and again in Feb. 1874. Sat for Marylebone from Apr. 1880 until defeated in Nov. 1885 contesting the E. division of Marylebone. [1885]

GRANT, Sir George Macpherson, Bart. Ballindalloch Castle, Co. Elgin. Invershie House, Co. Inverness. Brooks's. Eld. s. of Sir John Macpherson Grant, 2nd Bart., by Marion Helen, eld. d. of Mungo Nutter Campbell, Esq., of Ballimore, Argyllshire. B. in Inverness-shire 1839; m. 1861, Frances Elizabeth, younger d. of the Rev. Roger Pocklington, Vicar of Walesby, Nottinghamshire. Educ. at Harrow, and Christ Church, Oxford; graduated B.A.

1861. Appointed a Dept.-Lieut. of Banffshire 1860, of Inverness-shire 1861, and of Elginshire 1866. A Liberal. Unsuccessfully contested Inverness-shire 1865. Sat for the united counties of Elgin and Nairn from Sept. 1879 until defeated in 1886. Succeeded as Bart. 1850. Died 5 Dec. 1907. [1886]

GRANT, James Augustus. Continued in House after 1918: full entry in Volume III.

GRANT, J. Corrie. 26 The Avenue, Bedford Park, London. 2 Plowdon Buildings, Temple, London. National Liberal, and Eighty. S. of James Brighton Grant, Esq., of Kettleburgh, Suffolk, Brewer and Maltster, who was imprisoned for the non-payment of Church Rates, and Francis Anne Grant (née Palmer). B. at Kettleburgh, Suffolk in 1850; m. 1885, Anne Mary Adams, of Newnham Coll. and Plymouth, d. of William Adams, Esq., of Plymouth. Educ. at City of London School. A Barrister-at-Law, called to the bar at the Middle Temple Nov. 1877, and joined the N.E. Circuit. K.C. 1906. A Radical. Unsuccessfully contested Woodstock in July 1885, Birmingham W. in July 1892, the Rugby division of Warwickshire July 1895 and the Harrow division of Middlesex Apr. 1899. Elected for Rugby division of Warwickshire in 1900 and sat until he retired in Jan. 1910. Died Dec. 1924. His forenames were Corrie Brighton, despite his usually being cited as J. Corrie. [1909]

GRANTHAM, William. 6 Crown Office Row, Temple, London. 82 St. George's Square, London. Barcombe Place, Nr. Lewes, Sussex. Carlton, and St. Stephen's. S. of George Grantham, Esq., of Barcombe Place, near Lewes, by Sarah, d. of William Verrall, Esq., of Southover, Lewes. B. 1835; m. 1865, Emma, eld. d. of Richard Wilson, Esq., (of the family of Wilson, of Plewlands, Cumberland), of Chiddingley, Sussex, and of Molesworth House, Brighton. Educ. at King's Coll. School, London. Was called to the bar at the Inner Temple 1863, and joined the Home Circuit. Gained in 1863 the Studentship given by the Council of Legal Education for the four Inns of Court. Appointed a Queen's Council 1877, and a bencher of the Inner Temple 1880. A Conservative, in favour of the utmost religious liberty not subversive of the union of Church and State, and not in favour of any measure which would endanger the union of Great Britain and Ireland. Sat for E. Surrey from Feb. 1874 until Nov. 1885 and for Croydon from Nov. 1885 until appointed Judge of Queen's Bench Division in 1886 Knighted 1886-1911. Died 30 Nov. 1911. [1885]

GRAY, Charles Wing. Perces, Halstead, Essex. S. of C. Gray, Esq., Barrister-at-Law. B. 1845; m. Alice Julia, eld. d. of E.H. Bentall, Esq., at one time MP for Maldon. Educ. at Pembroke Coll., Cambridge. A Tenant-Farmer, and a Capt. in the 2nd Volunteer Battalion of the Essex Regiment. A Conservative. Unsuccessfully contested the Maldon division of Essex at the general election of 1885. Returned there in July 1886 and sat until defeated in 1892. Unsuccessfully contested the Saffron Walden division of Essex in 1895, 1900, and 31 May 1901. Died 23 Nov. 1920. [1892]

GRAY, Edmund Dwyer. 32a Weymouth Street, London. 81 Stephen's Green, Dublin. S. of Sir John Gray, of Charlesville House, Co. Dublin (who sat for Kilkenny from 1865 till his death in 1875), by Anna, d. of James Dwyer, Esq. B. in Dublin 1845; m. 1869, Caroline, d. of Maj. Archibald Chisholm (and his wife "Caroline Chisholm the Emigrant's Friend"). A Newspaper Proprietor, Owner of the Dublin *Freeman's Journal* and the Belfast *Morning News*. Lord Mayor of Dublin for 1880, and nominated a second time for 1881, but declined to serve the office. High Sheriff of the city of Dublin for 1882. A "Home Ruler." Unsuccessfully contested Kilkenny city Apr. 1875; sat for Tipperary from May 1877 to Apr. 1880, after which date he sat for Carlow Co. till 1885. Was also elected for Carlow as well as Dublin in the general election of 1885 but he elected to sit for the St. Stephen's Green division of Dublin and was MP until his death 27 Mar. 1888. [1888]

GRAY, Ernest. Continued in House after 1918: full entry in Volume III.

GRAYSON, Albert Victor. Crescent Lodge, Stockwell Park Road, London. S. of William and Elizabeth Grayson. B. 5 Sept. 1882 in Liverpool; m. 1912, Ruth Nightingale (the actress Ruth Norreys) who died in childbirth Feb. 1918. Educ. at Liverpool, and Manchester Universities and Unitarian Home Missionary Coll. A

Journalist, co-Editor of *New Age*. A Socialist, but was not an offical Labour candidate and did not sign the Party Constitution. Elected for the Colne Valley division of the W. Riding of Yorkshire in July 1907 and sat until defeated in Jan. 1910. Unsuccessfully contested the Kennington division of Lambeth in Dec. 1910. He emigrated to New Zealand and after the outbreak of war enlisted in the New Zealand Expeditionary Force. He was wounded at Passchendaele 12 Oct. 1917 and returned to England. He was never positively identified after the Autumn of 1920 and the mystery of his disappearance has never been solved.   [1909]

GREEN, Sir Edward, Bart. Heath Old Hall, Wakefield. Ken Hill, King's Lynn. Carlton. S. of Edward Green, Esq., of Many Gates House. B. at Wakefield 1831; m. 1859, Mary, eld. d. of W.E. Lycett, Esq., of Manchester. Educ. at the West Riding Proprietary School, and in Germany. An Engineer and the patentee of the Fuel Economizer. Was Chairman of the Wakefield School Board from 1871 to 1880. A Director of the Lancashire and Yorkshire Railway, a J.P. for W. Riding of Yorkshire, and for Norfolk; was Lieut. 1st West Yorkshire Yeomanry from 1869 to 1881. Created Bart. 1886. A "progressive Conservative." Was elected for Wakefield in 1874, but was unseated on petition. Contested Pontefract unsuccessfully in 1880; elected at a by-election for Wakefield July 1885 and sat until he retired in 1892. Died 30 Mar. 1923. [1892]

GREEN, Henry. Blackwall Yard, Poplar, London. Cherry Orchard, Old Charlton, Kent. Eld. s. of Henry Green, Esq., of Blackwall and Walthamstow. B. in Blackwall Yard 1838. Educ. at Cheam School, Surrey, and the University of Bonn. Joined the partnership of Messrs. Richard and Henry Green, the well-known Ship-Owners, in 1857, and was at one time Senior Partner of that eminent firm. A Magistrate for Middlesex, and a Director of the E. and W. India Dock Company, and served on the Royal Commission of Inquiry into the Loss of Life and Property at Sea. A Liberal. Sat for the Poplar division of Tower Hamlets from Nov. 1885 until he retired in 1886. Died 7 June 1900. [1886]

GREEN, Walford Davis. Macartney House, Greenwick Park, London. Carlton, and Isthmian. Eld. s. of the Rev. Walford Green, of Blackheath, Kent, ex-President of the Wesleyan Conference. B. 1869; m. 1896, Annie Lillian, d. of C.F. Carpenter, Esq., of Huntley, Bishops Teignton. Educ. at the Leys School, and King's Coll., Cambridge. Chairman of Tamworth Colliery Company, and Lieut. 2nd Volunteer Battalion S. Staffordshire Regiment. Wrote *The Political Career of George Canning*, which gained for him the Members prize for Modern History at Cambridge in 1891, and the *Life of Lord Chatham*. Was called to the bar at the Inner Temple 1895. A Conservative and Unionist. Represented Wednesbury from 1895 until he retired in 1906. Died 17 Nov. 1941.   [1905]

GREENALL, Sir Gilbert, Bart. Walton Hall, Warrington. Carlton, and St. Stephen's. S. of Edward Greenall, Esq., of Wilderspool, Cheshire. B. May 1806; m. 1st, 1836, Mary, d. of David Claughton, Esq. (she died 1861); 2ndly, 1864, Susannah, eld. d. of John Louis Rapp, Esq. A J.P. for Lancashire and Cheshire, and was High Sheriff of Chester in 1873. Patron of 3 livings. A Conservative. Sat for Warrington as a Liberal-Conservative from July 1847 until defeated in Dec. 1868, and again from Feb. 1874 to the dissolution in 1880. Re-elected for Warrington Nov. 1885 and sat until he retired in 1892. Created Bart. 1876. Died 10 July 1894. [1892]

GREENE, Edward. Nether Hall, Bury St. Edmunds. Carlton. S. of Benjamin Greene, Esq., of Russell Square, a West India proprietor, by Catherine, d. of Rev. J. Smith, of Bedford. B. at Bury St. Edmunds 1815; m. 1st, 1840, Emily, 3rd d. of Rev. G. Smythies, Rector of Stanground, Peterborough; 2ndly, 1870, Caroline Dorothea, d. of Charles Prideaux Brune, Esq., and relict of Rear-Admiral Sir William Hoste, Bart. Educ. at the Grammar School, Bury St. Edmunds. Was a Brewer at Bury St. Edmunds from 1836. A Magistrate for Suffolk and also Dept.-Lieut. for the Co. A "progressive Conservative." Sat for Bury St. Edmunds from July 1865 to Nov. 1885, when he retired. Sat for the Stowmarket division of Suffolk from July 1886 until his death on 5 Apr. 1891.   [1891]

GREENE, Sir Edward Walter, Bart. Nether Hall, Bury St. Edmunds. Carlton, R.Y.S., and Cavalry. Only s. of E. Greene,

Esq., MP. B. 1842; m. 1864, d. of Prebendary Royds, Rector of Haughton, Staffordshire. Educ. at Rugby. A J.P. and Dept.-Lieut. for Suffolk, and J.P. for Worcestershire; was High Sheriff for Suffolk 1897, and created a Bart. 1900. Honorary Lieut.-Col. of the Suffolk Yeomanry. A Conservative. Contested Suffolk N.W. May 1891. Elected for Bury St. Edmunds in 1900 and sat until he retired in 1906. Died 27 Feb. 1920.   [1905]

GREENE, Henry David. 13 Connaught Place, Hyde Park, London. 4 Brick Court, Temple, London. Grove, Craven Arms Station, Shropshire. Garrick, New University and Carlton. S. of B.B. Greene, Esq., J.P., of Midgham, Berkshire, at one time Gov. of the Bank of England, and Isabella, d. of T. Blyth, Esq. B. 1843; m. 1879, Harriet Rowland, d. of John Jones, Esq., of Grove, Craven Arms, Shropshire, Chairman of the City Bank. Educ. at Trinity Coll., Cambridge, where he proceeded to the degrees of M.A. and LL.M. Was called to the bar at the Middle Temple 1868 and joined the Oxford Circuit. Became a Q.C. 1885, a bencher of the Middle Temple 1891, and Recorder of Ludlow 1892. A J.P. and Dept.-Lieut. for Shropshire. A Conservative. Sat for Shrewsbury from 1892 until he retired in 1906. Lunacy Commissioner 1908-14. Treasurer of Middle Temple 1910. Died 11 Oct. 1915.   [1905]

GREENE, Walter Raymond. Continued in House after 1918: full entry in Volume III.

GREENWOOD, Sir Granville George. 33 Linden Gardens, London. Eighty, United University, and Wellington. S. of John Greenwood, Esq., Solicitor to the Treasury. B. 1850; m. 1878, d. of Dr. L.T. Cumberbatch. Educ. at Eton, and Trinity Coll., Cambridge. A Barrister, called to the bar 1876, Middle Temple, and joined the W. Circuit. Knighted 1916. A Liberal, advocated a thorough reform of our constitutional machinery, Electoral Reform, Land, Poor, and Labour Law Reform, etc. Unsuccessfully contested Peterborough in 1886, and Central Hull in 1900. First elected for Peterborough in 1906 and sat until defeated in 1918. Author of several works on Shakespeare. Died 27 Oct. 1928.   [1918]

GREENWOOD, Sir Hamar, Bart. Continued in House after 1918: full entry in Volume III.

GREENWOOD, Thomas Hubbard. See GREENWOOD, Sir Hamar, Bart. Continued in House after 1918: full entry in Volume III.

GREER, Harry. Continued in House after 1918: full entry in Volume III.

GREGORY, George Burrow. Retired in 1886: full entry in Volume I.

GREIG, Col. James William, C.B. Continued in House after 1918: full entry in Volume III.

GRENFELL, Cecil Alfred. 4 Great Cumberland Place, London. S. of Pascoe du Pré Grenfell. B. 1864; m. 1898, Lady Lilian Maud Spencer-Churchill, d. of 8th Duke of Marlborough. Educ. at Eton. A member of the Stock Exchange. Maj. Buckinghamshire Yeomanry; served in S. African War 1900. A Liberal. Unsuccessfully contested Rochester in 1895. Elected for the Bodmin division of Cornwall in Jan. 1910 and sat until he retired in Dec. 1910. Served in Europe during the Great War. Died 11 Aug. 1924.   [1910]

GRENFELL, William Henry. 4 St. James's Square, London. Taplow Court, Taplow, Buckinghamshire. Turf, and Travellers'. S. of C.W. Grenfell, Esq., by Georgiana, d. of the Rt. Hon. W. Sebright Lascelles. B. in London 1855; m. 1887, Ethel, d. of the Hon. Julian Fane and Lady Adine (née Cowper). Educ. at Harrow, and Balliol Coll., Oxford. Was in the Harrow eleven 1873-74, and represented the University in athletics and rowing. He twice swam across Niagara. Special Correspondent Suakim Expedition; Private Secretary to Sir William Harcourt at the Exchequer 1885; High Sheriff of Buckinghamshire 1889; Mayor of Maidenhead 1895-97. A J.P. for Buckinghamshire and Berkshire, and Chairman of Thames Conservancy Board. Sat for Salisbury as a Gladstonian Liberal from 1880-Nov. 1882 when he was appointed Parliamentary groom-in-waiting, but was defeated at the resulting by-election. Sat for Salisbury City from Nov. 1885 until defeated in July 1886. Sat for Hereford from 1892 as a Liberal, but resigned in 1893 before the second reading of the Home Rule Bill, and declared himself a Conservative in 1898. Unsuccessfully contested Windsor in 1890. Elected for the Wycombe division of Buckinghamshire in 1900 and sat until created Baron Desborough in Nov. 1905. K.G. 1928. Capt. of Yeomen of Guard 1924-29. President of International Navigation Congress 1923. President of Royal Agricultural Society 1925. President of Amateur Fencing Association from its foundation until 1926. Died 9 Jan. 1945.   [1905]

GRETTON, Col. John. Continued in House after 1918: full entry in Volume III.

GREVILLE, Hon. Ronald Henry Fulke. 11 Charles Street, Berkeley Square, London. Carlton, Turf, and Naval & Military. El. d. s. of Lord and Lady Grenville. B. 1864; m. 1891, Margaret Helen, step-d. of W. McEwan, Esq., at one time MP for Central Edinburgh. Educ. at Rugby. Capt. Yorkshire Dragoons (Yeomanry), Capt. 1st Life Guards, and Lieut. 3rd Argyll and Sutherland Highlanders. A J.P. and Dept.-Lieut. for Co. Westmeath; High Sheriff there in 1899. A Conservative and Free Trader. Unsuccessfully contested the Barnsley division of Yorkshire in 1895. Represented E. Bradford from 1896 until he retired in 1906. Died 5 Apr. 1908. [1905]

GREY, Albert Henry George. Defeated in 1886: full entry in Volume I.

GREY, Arthur. See DUNCOMBE, Arthur.

GREY, Rt. Hon. Sir Edward, Bart., K.G. Falloden, Northumberland. Athenaeum, Brooks's, and Oxford & Cambridge. S. of Lieut.-Col. George Henry Grey, and grand-s. of the Rt. Hon. Sir George Grey, G.C.B., the 2nd Bart., and grand-nephew of the 2nd Earl Grey, the celebrated statesman; by Harriet Jane, d. of Lieut.-Col. Pearson. B. in Chester Square, London 1862; m. 1885, Frances Dorothy, d. of S.F. Widdrington, Esq., of Newton Hall, Northumberland (she died 1906). Educ. at Winchester, and Balliol Coll., Oxford. Was Parliamentary Secretary for Foreign Affairs from 1892-95. PC. 1902. Secretary of State for Foreign Affairs, 1905-16; a Trustee of British Museum. Chairman of the N.E. Railway. Created Knight of the Garter 1912. A Liberal. Sat for the Berwick-on-Tweed division of Northumberland from 1885 until created 1st Visct.

Grey of Fallodon in 1916. Temporary Ambassador to U.S.A. 1919. Author of *Twenty-Five Years* (1925), and *Fallodon Papers* (1926). Succeeded as Bart. 1882. F.R.S. 1914. Leader of Liberal Party in House of Lords in 1916 and from 1921-24. Died 7 Sept. 1933.   [1915]

GRICE-HUTCHINSON,   George William. The Boynes, Upton-on-Severn. Junior Army & Navy, and Carlton. S. of G.R. Hutchinson, Esq., Capt. of the Royal Engineers, and Ellen, d. of W.H. Bevan, Esq., of Glannant, Co. Brecon. B. at Gibraltar 1848; m. 1876, Louisa Elizabeth Mary, only child of the Rev. William Grice, Vicar of Sherborne, Warwickshire. Educ. at Rugby and University Coll., Oxford (B.A. 1870). Assumed the additional surname of Grice in 1885. Entered the army 1871; and served in the Zulu War. Capt. 90th Foot, and of the 3rd Battalion Lancashire Fusiliers. Retired with the rank of Hon. Maj. 1889. A J.P. for Worcestershire. A Conservative. Sat for Ashton Manor from Mar. 1891 until he retired in 1900. Died 18 May 1906.   [1900]

GRIFFITH, Arthur. Continued in House after 1918: full entry in Volume III.

GRIFFITH, Rt. Hon. Sir Ellis Jones Ellis-, Bart. See ELLIS-GRIFFITH, Rt. Hon. Sir Ellis Jones, Bart. Continued in House after 1918: full entry in Volume III.

GRIFFITH-BOSCAWEN, Rt. Hon. Sir Arthur Sackville Trevor. Continued in House after 1918: full entry in Volume III.

GRIFFITHS, Sir John Norton, K.C.B., D.S.O. Continued in House after 1918: full entry in Volume III.

GRIMSTON, James Walter Grimston, Visct. Sopwell, St. Alban's. Carlton, and Bachelors'. Eld. s. of the Earl of Verulam, by Elizabeth J., d. of Maj. Weyland, of Woodeaton, Oxfordshire. B. 1852; m. 1878, Margaret Frances, eld. d. of Sir Frederick Ulric Graham, and widow of Alexander Aeneas Mackintosh, Esq., of Mackintosh. Educ. at Harrow. After serving in the Herts. Militia he entered the army as Cornet in the 1st Life Guards Sept. 1870; became Lieut. Oct. 1871, and retired in 1878. Capt. in the Herts. Yeomanry Cavalry 1879; retired as Maj. 1887. A J.P. for Hertfordshire. In 1886 was elected

147

Chairman of the executive of the Home Counties division of the National Union. A Conservative. Sat for the St. Alban's division of Hertfordshire from 1885 until he retired in 1892. Succeeded as 3rd Earl of Verulam 1895. Member of Hertfordshire County Council, Alderman from 1912. Died 11 Nov. 1924. [1892]

GROSVENOR, Rt. Hon. Lord Richard de Aquila. Retired in 1886: full entry in Volume I.

GROTRIAN, Frederick Brent. West Hill House, Hessle, East Yorkshire. Carlton. Only s. of Frederick L.C. Grotrian, Esq., of London and Brighton, by Amelia, d. of Samuel Brent, Esq., of London and Horndean. B. 1838; m. Elizabeth, d. of John Hunter, Esq., of Gilling, Yorkshire. Educ. privately. A J.P. for Kingston-upon-Hull, Dept.-Chairman of the Humber Conservancy Commissioners, and at one time President of the Hull Chamber of Commerce and Shipping. A Conservative, in favour of Irish Local Self-government, but not of Home Rule with a separate Parliament. Unsuccessfully contested Hull E. at the general election of 1885. First returned for Hull W. July 1886 and sat until defeated in 1892. Died 8 Apr. 1905. [1892]

GROVE, Sir Thomas Fraser, Bart. Ferne House, Salisbury. Army & Navy, National Liberal, and Brooks's. Eld. s. of John Grove, Esq., of Ferne, Wiltshire, by Jean Helen, d. of Sir William Fraser, Bart. B. 27 Nov. 1823; m. 1st, 1847, Katherine Grace, 2nd d. of the Hon. Waller O'Grady, s. of Visct. Guillamore; 2ndly, 1882, Frances Hinton, d. of Henry Northcote, Esq., of Okefield, Devon, relict of the Hon. F. Best, s. of Lord Wynford. Joined the 6th Inniskilling Dragoons 1842, and retired as Capt. 1849. A J.P. for Wiltshire and Dorset, and Lieut.-Col. of the Royal Wiltshire Yeomanry; Dept.-Lieut. and High Sheriff of Wiltshire in 1862. Patron of 1 Living. A Liberal. He voted as a Liberal Unionist in 1886, but later quitted that party. Was MP for Wiltshire S. from 1865 to 1874, when he was defeated and created Bart. Sat for the Wilton division of Wiltshire from 1885 until defeated in 1892. Member of Wiltshire County Council from Apr. 1889 until his death 14 Jan. 1897. [1892]

GROVE, Thomas Newcomen Archibald. Pollard's Park, Chalfont St.

Giles, Buckinghamshire. White's. S. of Capt. E. Grove and Elizabeth, d. of Col. Ponsonby Watts. B. 1855; m. 1889, Kate Sara, d. of Henry J. Sibley, Esq. Educ. privately, and at Oriel Coll., Oxford; Double honours. Studied for the bar at the Inner Temple; Founder, Proprietor, and Editor of the *New Review*; a J.P. for Buckinghamshire and Essex. A Liberal. Unsuccessfully contested Winchester in July 1886. Sat for West Ham N. from 1892-95, when he was defeated. Unsuccessfully contested S. Northamptonshire 1900. Elected for S. Northamptonshire in 1906 and sat until he retired in Jan. 1910. Died 4 June 1920. [1909]

GROVES, James Grimble. Queen Anne's Mansions, London. Oldfield Hall, Altrincham, Cheshire. Carlton. S. of William Peer Grimble Groves, Esq., of Salford, and Elizabeth Groves. B. in Manchester 1854; m. 1878, the younger d. of Robert Marsland, Esq., M.R.C.S.L. Educ. privately in Cheshire, and at Owen's Coll., Manchester. Chairman and Managing Director of the firm of Groves and Whitnall Limited, Brewers, Salford, and Chairman of the Brewers' Society. J.P. for Salford 1892, and Dept.-Lieut. and J.P. for the Co. of Chester 1898; Mayor of Altrincham 1897-98, and 1898-99. A Conservative. Elected for Salford S. in 1900 and sat until defeated in 1906. Died 23 June 1914. [1905]

GUEST, Hon. Christian Henry Charles. Continued in House after 1918: full entry in Volume III.

GUEST, Hon. Frederick Edward, D.S.O. Continued in House after 1918: full entry in Volume III.

GUEST, Hon. Ivor Churchill. Ashby St. Ledger's, Rugby. White's, Marlborough, Reform, and Garrick. Eld. s. of Lord Wimborne, by Lady Cornelia Henrietta Maria, eld. d. of 7th Duke of Marlborough. B. 1873; m. 1902, Alice, d. of Lord Ebury. Educ. at Eton, and Trinity Coll., Cambridge. High Sheriff of Glamorganshire 1900; Capt. Dorset Yeomanry. Chairman of Coast Erosion Commission 1906. Defeated at Plymouth as a Conservative 12 Jan. 1898. Returned for Plymouth in Feb. 1900 and sat until he was elected for Cardiff as a Liberal (which party he joined in Apr. 1904) in Jan. 1906 and sat until he retired in Jan. 1910. Created Baron Ashby St. Ledgers in Mar. 1910. PC. 1910. Paymaster Gen. from 1910-12. Lord-in-waiting from 1913-15. Lord-Lieut. of Ireland from 1915-18. Succeeded as 2nd Baron Wimborne Feb. 1914; created Visct. Wimborne in May 1918. First President of the National Liberal Party 1931. Died 14 June 1939. [1909]

GUINEY, John. Egmont Place, Kanturk, Co. Cork. S. of Timothy Guiney, Esq., Clerk of Kanturk R.D.C. B. 1869 at Newmarket, Co. Cork; m. 1904, Mary, d. of Michael Buckley, Esq., of Duinche, Banteer, Co. Cork. Educ. at St. Vincent's Coll., Castleknock, Dublin, and St. Colman's Coll., Fermoy. A Solicitor, admitted 1892. An Independent Nationalist. Elected for N. Cork Nov. 1913 and sat until he retired in 1918. [1918]

GUINEY, Patrick. Newmarket, Co. Cork. B. 1867 at Newmarket, Co. Cork; m. 1895, Nannette, d. of D.M. O'Connor, Esq., of Ballyclough, Mallow. Educ. at National School, Kanturk and St. Patrick's Monastery, Mountrach. A Farmer, and a member of Cork County Council, and Kanturk Rural District Council. A Nationalist. Unsuccessfully contested E. Kerry in Dec. 1910, whilst representing N. Cork. Elected for N. Cork in Jan. 1910 and sat until his death 12 Oct. 1913. [1913]

GUINNESS, Hon. Rupert Edward Cecil Lee. See ELVEDEN, Rupert Edward Cecil Lee Guinness, Visct. Continued in House after 1918: full entry in Volume III.

GUINNESS, Hon. Walter Edward. Continued in House after 1918: full entry in Volume III.

GULL, Sir William Cameron, Bart. Tapeley Park, Instow, N. Devon. Frilsham House, Newbury, Berkshire. 10 Hyde Park Gardens, London. Reform. S. of Sir W.W. Gull, 1st Bart., and his wife Susan Anne, the d. of Col. Dacre Lacy. B. 1860 in Finsbury Square, London; m. 1886, Annie Clayton, 2nd d. of Sir Nathaniel Lindley, Master of the Rolls. Educ. at Eton, and Christ Church, Oxford. A Barrister-at-Law, called to the bar at Lincoln's Inn 1886; a member of the London School Board from 1891 to 1894. A Liberal Unionist, strongly against Home Rule, and pledged to give immediate attention to British legislation for Agriculture, the Lands Laws, Employers' Liability, etc. Unsuccessfully contested Moray and Nairn shires 1892. Sat for the Barnstaple division of Devonshire from July 1895 until defeated in 1900. High Sheriff of Berkshire 1908. Succeeded as Bart. 1890. O.B.E. 1918. Alderman of Berkshire County Council. Died 15 Dec. 1922. [1900]

GULLAND, Rt. Hon. John William. 23 Summer Place, London. Reform, National Liberal, Glasgow Liberal, and Scottish Liberal. S. of John Gulland, Esq., J.P., of Edinburgh, and Mary Lovell, of Bedford. B. 1864 at Edinburgh; m. 1912, Edith Mary, d. of Walker Allen, Esq., of Whitefield, near Manchester. Educ. at the Royal High School, and the University, Edinburgh. Was a Corn Merchant at Edinburgh. A member of Edinburgh Town Council 1904-06, and of the School Board 1900-06. A Junior Lord of the Treasury and Scottish Liberal Whip 1909-15. Parliamentary Secretary to the Treasury and Chief Liberal Whip, Jan.-May 1915, and Joint Parliamentary Secretary May 1915 to Dec. 1916. PC. 1916. Chief Liberal Whip from Dec. 1916. J.P. for Edinburgh. A Liberal. First elected for Dumfries Burghs in 1906 and sat until defeated in Dumfriesshire in 1918. Died 26 Jan. 1920. [1918]

GULLY, Rt.Hon. William Court. Speaker's House, Palace of Westminster, London. Sutton Place, Seaford, Sussex. Oxford & Cambridge, and Athenaeum. 2nd s. of James Manby Gully, Esq., M.D., by Frances, d. of Thomas Court, Esq. B. in London 1835; m. 1865, Elizabeth Anne Walford, eld. d. of Thomas Selby, Esq., of Whitley, and Wimbush, Essex. Educ. at Trinity Coll., Cambridge; M.A. 1859; Honorary LL.D. 1900, Honorary D.C.L. Oxford; was President of the Cambridge Union. Elected Speaker of the House of Commons Apr. 1895 and again Aug. 1895 and 1900; retired 1905. Was called to the bar at the Inner Temple 1860; became Q.C. 1877, a bencher of his Inn 1879, and was a leader of the N. Circuit. Was Recorder of Wigan 1886-95. A Liberal, who supported Mr. Gladstone's Irish policy. Unsuccessfully contested Whitehaven in 1880 and 1885. Sat for Carlisle from 1886 until created Visct. Selby in 1905. PC. 1895. Died 6 Nov. 1909. [1905]

GUNTER, Sir Robert, Bart. 86 Eaton Square, London. The Grange, Wetherby, Yorkshire. Army & Navy, Hurlingham, and Carlton. Yorkshire Club, York. Eld. s. of Robert Gunter, Esq., of Earls Court, Middlesex, by Fanny, d. of William Thompson, Esq., of Durham. B. 1831; m. 1862, Jane Marguerite, eld. d. of Thomas Benyon, Esq., of Gledhow Hall, Yorkshire. Educ. at Rugby. A Magistrate in the W. Riding of Yorkshire, and Col. 3rd Battalion Yorkshire Regiment. Was in the 4th Dragoon Guards, and served through the Crimean war. Created Bart. 1901. A Conservative. Sat for Knaresborough from Dec. 1884 to Nov. 1885, and for the Barkston Ash division of the W. Riding of Yorkshire from 1885 until his death 17 Sept. 1905. [1905]

GURDON, Robert Thornhagh. 5 Portman Square, London. Letton, Thetford, Norfolk. Grundisburgh, Woodbridge, and Brantham Court, Suffolk. Brooks's, and University. Eld. s. of Brampton Gurdon, Esq., of Letton, Norfolk, by Hon. Henrietta Susannah, eld. d. of Lord Colborne. B. 1829; m. 1st, 1862, Harriet Ellen, 6th d. of Sir William Miles, Bart. (she died 1864); 2ndly, 1874, Emily, d. of the Rev. Robert Boothby Heathcote, of Chingford, Essex. Educ. at Eton, and Trinity Coll., Cambridge, where he graduated M.A. 1852. Was called to the bar of Lincoln's Inn 1856. A Magistrate, and Chairman of Quarter Sessions. Chairman of the Norfolk County Council 1889-1901. Dept.-Lieut. of Norfolk, and Col. of the 4th Volunteer Battalion Norfolk Regiment. A Liberal Unionist. Unsuccessfully contested N. Norfolk 1868, S. Norfolk Apr. 1871, and again Feb. 1874. Sat for S. Norfolk from Apr. 1880 to Nov. 1885, and for mid Norfolk from Nov. 1885 until defeated in July 1892. Re-elected for mid Norfolk in Apr. 1895 and sat until again defeated in July 1895. Created Baron Cranworth Jan. 1899. Died 13 Oct. 1902. [1892]

GURDON, Rt. Hon. Sir William Brampton, K.C.M.G., C.B. Assington Hall, Boxford, Suffolk. 1 Whitehall Gardens, London. Brooks's. Younger s. of Brampton Gurdon, Esq., of Letton Hall, Norfolk, MP for W. Norfolk, and the eld. d. of Lord Colborne. He was also bro. to Lord Cranworth, MP for S. and mid Norfolk. B. in London 1840; m. 1888, Eveline Camilla, d. of the 5th Earl of Portsmouth

(she died 1894). Educ. at Eton, and Trinity Coll., Cambridge. Was a clerk in the Treasury, by competition 1863-85; Private Secretary to Mr. Gladstone as Chancellor of the Exchequer, First Lord, etc. 1865-74; C.B. 1874; K.C.M.G. 1882; PC. 1907. Served on several foreign missions of both Liberal and Conservative ministries, one being M. Leon Say's Paris Monetary Commission of 1878. Was a member of the Transvaal Inquiry Commission 1881; retired from the Treasury 1885. Was Chairman of Committee of Selection; Lord-Lieut. of Suffolk from 1907. A Liberal, in favour of a firm but not aggressive foreign policy, Residential voting, Registration reform, Disestablishment, and Unsectarian Bible Teaching in schools. Opposed to Chinese labour in S. Africa, etc. Unsuccessfully contested Norfolk S.W. in Dec. 1885, Rotherhithe in July 1886, and Colchester in Dec. 1888. Represented Norfolk N. from 1899 until he retired in Jan. 1910. Died 31 May 1910. [1909]

GUTHRIE, David Charles. 64 Grosvenor Street, London. Craigie, Forfarshire. East Haddon Hall, Northamptonshire. Brooks's, Reform, and White's. S. of James Alexander Guthrie, Esq., of Craigie, J.P. and Dept.-Lieut. for Forfarshire, and Elinor, d. of Admiral Sir W. Stirling. B. 1861; m. 1891, Mary, 4th d. of Andrew Low, Esq. Educ. at Eton, and Christ Church, Oxford. Was once Secretary to the Marq. of Ripon. A Liberal and follower of Mr. Gladstone. Unsuccessfully contested Forfarshire in 1886. First returned for Northamptonshire S. in July 1892 and sat until defeated in 1895. Died 12 Jan. 1918. [1895]

GUTHRIE, Walter Murray. 9 Upper Berkeley Street, London. Duart Castle, Isle of Mull, N.B. Carlton, Turf, White's, and Garrick. S. of James Alexander Guthrie, Esq., of Craigie, J.P. and Dept.-Lieut., by his wife Elinor, d. of Admiral Sir James Stirling. B. in London 1869; m. 1894, Olive, youngest d. of Sir John Leslie, Bart. Educ. at Eton, and Trinity Hall, Cambridge. A Director of the National Discount Company and Commercial Union Assurance Company. A Member of the Scottish Archers; Queen's body-guard for Scotland; Alderman of the City of London, and a Merchant Taylor. J.P. and Dept.-Lieut. for Argyll. Manager of Van

Alan Field Hospital in S. Africa 1900. A Conservative. Sat for the Bow and Bromley division of Tower Hamlets from 1899 until he retired in 1906. Died 24 Apr. 1911. [1905]

GWYNN, Stephen Lucius. National Liberal. S. of the Rev. J. Gwynn, D.D., Professor of Divinity, Trinity Coll., Dublin, and Lucy, d. of William Smith O'Brien, Esq. B. 13 Feb. 1864. Educ. at St. Columba's Coll., Rathfarnham, and Brasenose Coll., Oxford; Scholar, 1882, 1st Mods. and Lit.Hum. 1884-86. A Journalist and Author. Was a Teacher of Classics and Literature 1887-96. Wrote *Tennyson, Highways and Byeways in Donegal and Antrim, The Old Knowledge, John Maxwell's Marriage, Masters of English Literature, Fair Hills of Ireland, To-day and To-morrow in Ireland, Fishing Holidays, The Glade in the Forest,* and numerous other works and essays. Enlisted in 7th (S.) Battalion Leinster Regiment 1915; Capt. 6th (S.) Battalion Connaught Rangers; member of the Dardanelles Commission 1916. A Nationalist. Elected for Galway in Nov. 1906 and sat until defeated in 1918. D.Litt. National University of Ireland 1940. D.Litt. Trinity College, Dublin, 1945. Died 11 June 1950. [1918]

GWYNNE, Rupert Sackville. Continued in House after 1918: full entry in Volume III.

HACKETT, John. Thurles, Co. Tipperary. 37 North Side, Clapham Common, London. S. of Thomas Hackett, Esq., Farmer, of Longfordpass, Co. Tipperary. B. 5 Nov. 1865 at Longfordpass. Unmarried. Educ. at Patrician Brothers' Monastery, Mountrath, Queen's Co. A Farmer. Chairman of Thurles Rural District Council from 1900. J.P. for Co. Tipperary. A Nationalist. Elected for mid Tipperary in Jan. 1910 and sat until he retired in 1918. [1918]

HADDOCK, George Bahr. 53 Pall Mall, London. Carlton, and Bath. S. of James Haddock, Esq., and Jane Bahr. B. 1863 at St. Helen's. Educ. at Clifton Coll. A Ship-Owner. Maj. 4th Battalion Loyal N. Lancashire Regiment. A Unionist. Elected for N. Lonsdale division of N. Lancashire in 1906 and sat until he retired in 1918. Died 22 Mar. 1930. [1918]

HAIN, Edward. Treloyhan, St. Ives, Cornwall. Reform, and City of London. S. of Edward and Grace Hain, of St. Ives, Cornwall. B. at St. Ives 1851; m. 1882, Catherine Seward, 2nd d. of James Hughes, Esq., of Whitehaven, Cumberland. Educ. at a private school. A Shipowner of St. Ives, Cornwall, London, and Cardiff. Six times Mayor of St. Ives, Cornwall. Was member of Cornwall County Council; J.P. for Cornwall and the borough of St. Ives. A Liberal Unionist. Elected for the St. Ives division of Cornwall in 1900 and sat until he retired in 1906. In 1904 he became a Liberal on the Free Trade issue. Knighted 1910. President of Chamber of Shipping of U.K. 1910-11; Sheriff of Cornwall 1912. Died 20 Sept. 1917. [1905]

HALDANE, Rt. Hon. Richard Burdon. 28 Queen Anne's Gate, London. 10 Old Square, Lincoln's Inn, London. Cloan, Auchterarder, Perthshire. Brook's, National Liberal, and Athenaeum. Eld. s. of Robert Haldane, Esq., of Cloanden, Perthshire, by Mary Elizabeth, d. of Richard Burdon Saunderson, Esq., of Otterburn, Northumberland. B. at Edinburgh July 1856. Educ. at Edinburgh University; M.A. with 1st class honours in philosophy, Honorary LL.D. 1898, and at Göttingen. Was called to the bar in 1879; Q.C. 1890. PC. 1902. Joint editor and author of *Essays on Philosophical Criticism*; author of *Education and Empire, The Pathway to Reality,* and translator of Schopenhauer's chief works. Secretary of State for War Dec. 1905 to June 1912. Lord Rector of Edinburgh University 1906. Honorary D.C.L. Oxford. A Liberal, in favour of Home Rule. Sat for Haddingtonshire from 1885 until created 1st Visct. Haldane in 1911. Lord High Chancellor 1912-15 and 1924. F.R.S. 1906; K.T. 1913; F.B.A. 1914; O.M. 1915. Leader of Labour Party in House of Lords 1924-28. First President of the Institute of Public Administration 1922. Chancellor of St. Andrews University 1928. Died 19 Aug. 1928. [1910]

HALL, Alexander William. Barton Abbey, Steeple Aston, Oxfordshire. Carlton. Eld. s. of Henry Hall, Esq., of Barton Abbey, Steeple Aston, Oxfordshire, by the Hon. Catherine Louisa, 4th d. of Lord Bridport. B. in London 1838; m. 1863, Emma Gertrude, 2nd d. of Edward Jowett, Esq., of Eltofts, Yorkshire. Educ. at Eton, and Exeter Coll., Oxford. A Brewer at Oxford and a Magistrate and Dept.-Lieut. for Oxfordshire, of which Co. he was High Sheriff in 1867. A Conservative. Sat for Oxford from Mar. 1874 to Apr. 1880, when he was defeated. At a by-election in May 1880 he was re-elected, but unseated on petition. Was again elected for Oxford in 1885 and sat until he retired in 1892. Died 29 Apr. 1919. [1892]

HALL, Rt. Hon. Sir Charles, K.C.M.G. 2 Mount Street, Berkeley Square, London. Recorder's Chambers, Guildhall, London. White's Garrick, Marlborough, and Carlton. 2nd s. of Vice-Chancellor Sir Charles Hall. B. in London 1843. Educ. at Harrow and Trinity Coll., Cambridge (B.A. 1865, M.A. 1868). Was called to the bar at Lincoln's Inn in 1866, and joined the S.E. Circuit; Q.C. 1881; a bencher of the Middle Temple 1884; was Attorney-Gen. to H.R.H. the Prince of Wales and the Duchy of Cornwall 1877-92, and in 1892 was elected Recorder of London. In May 1890 was made a K.C.M.G. PC. 1899. A Conservative. Sat for Cambridgeshire (Chesterton division) 1885-92, when he was defeated. In the following month he was returned for the Holborn division of Finsbury and sat until his death 9 Mar. 1900. [1899]

HALL, Douglas Bernard. Continued in House after 1918: full entry in Volume III.

HALL, Edward Marshall. 3 Temple Gardens, London. 11 Harley House, London. Felder Lodge, Sandwich. Carlton, Garrick, and Beefsteak. S. of Alfred Hall, Esq., F.R.C.P., and Julia Elizabeth, d. of J.W. Sebright, Esq., of Glasgow. B. 16 Sept. 1858 in Brighton; m. 1st, Ethel, d. of Dr. Henry Moon, F.R.C.P. (she died 1890); 2ndly, Henriette, d. of Hans Kroeger. Educ. at St. Andrew's Coll., Chardstock, Rugby, and St. John's Coll., Cambridge; B.A. Was called to the bar at the Inner Temple 1883; Q.C. 1898; bencher 1910. A Unionist. Sat for the Southport division of Lancashire from 1900-06, when he was defeated. Elected for the E. Toxteth division of Liverpool in Jan. 1910 and sat until appointed Recorder of Guildford in 1916. Knighted 1917. Died 24 Feb. 1927. [1916]

HALL, Frederick. Continued in House after 1918: full entry in Volume III.

HALL, Sir Frederick. Continued in House after 1918: full entry in Volume III.

HALLETT, Col. Francis Charles Hughes. See HUGHES-HALLETT, Col. Francis Charles.

HALPIN, James. Newmarket-on-Feyns, Co. Clare. S. of William Halpin, Esq. B. 1843. Educ. at Springfield Coll., Ennis. A Farmer. Came prominently into public life with the movement of Mr. Parnell. A member of Clare County Council and Chairman of the Ennis Board of Guardians from 1880-96. A Nationalist. Elected for W. Clare in 1906 and sat until his death 26 July 1909. [1909]

HALSEY, Rt. Hon. Thomas Frederick. 73 Eaton Place, London. Great Gaddesden Place, Hemel Hempstead, Hertfordshire. Carlton, Constitutional, and United University. S. of Thomas Plumer Halsey, Esq., (who sat for Hertfordshire 1846-54), by Frederica, d. of Frederick Johnston, Esq., of Hilton. B. at Temple Dinsley, Hertfordshire 1839; m. 1865, Mary Julia, youngest d. of F.O. Wells, Esq., of the Bengal Civil Service. Educ. at Eton, and at Christ Church, Oxford; B.A. 1861, M.A. 1864. A J.P. and Vice-Chairman Hertfordshire County Council, Dept. Chairman of Quarter Sessions for the St. Albans division, Honorary Lieut.-Col. Hertfordshire Yeomanry, retired. Patron of 2 livings. PC 1901. Appointed Chairman of Standing Orders and Selection Committees 1899. A Conservative, in favour of re-adjustment of local taxation, and of "steady Conservative progress"; opposed to Home Rule for Ireland, disestablishment, and to "all proposals tending to impair the efficiency of the Voluntary Schools." Sat for Hertfordshire from 1874-85 and for the Watford division of Hertfordshire from 1885 until defeated in 1906. Created Bart. 1920. Died 12 Feb. 1927. [1905]

HAMBRO, Angus Valdimar. Continued in House after 1918: full entry in Volume III.

HAMBRO, Charles Eric. 70 Prince's Gate, London. Travellers', and White's. S. of Everard A. Hambro, Esq., and his wife, Gertrude Mary. B. at Gifford House, Roehampton 1872; m. 1894, Sybil Martin

Smith, 3rd. d. of Martin R. Smith, Esq., of Smith, Payne and Smith, Bankers. Educ. at Eton Coll., and Trinity Coll., Cambridge. A Banker, Partner in the house of C.J. Hambro and Son. A Conservative. Elected for the Wimbledon division of Surrey in 1900 and sat until he accepted Chiltern Hundreds in 1907. K.B.E. 1919. Died 28 Dec. 1947. [1907]

HAMBRO, Charles Joseph Theophilus. 22 Mansfield Street, London. Milton Abbey, Blandford, Dorset. Carlton, White's, Marlborough, Turf, and St. James's. Eld. s. of Charles Joachim, Baron Hambro, of Milton Abbey, Dorset, by Caroline M. Gostenhofer. B. at Copenhagen 2 Oct. 1834; m. 1857, Susan d. of the Hon. and Ven. H.R. Yorke, Archdeacon of Huntingdon. Educ. at Trinity Coll., Cambridge. Was called to the bar at the Inner Temple in 1860. Col. Queen's Own Dorset Yeomanry, a Magistrate, Dept.-Lieut., and Dept. Provincial Grand Master of Freemasons for the Co. Was High Sheriff of Dorset in 1882. He sat as a Liberal-Conservative for Weymouth from 1868 to 1874, was defeated in the latter year, stood for Dorset in 1876, but retired in favour of Col. Digby. Unsuccessfully contested Dorset S. in Nov. 1885 as a Conservative. Returned there in Dec. 1885 and again in July 1886 and sat until his death 11 Apr. 1891. A Baron in the peerage of Denmark. [1891]

HAMERSLEY, Alfred St. George. Ryecote Park, Wheatley, Oxfordshire. Carlton, National, and Union. S. of Hugh Hamersley, Esq., Dept.-Lieut. and J.P., of Pyrton Manor, Oxfordshire, and Margaret, d. of John Shaw Phillips, Esq., of Culham, Oxfordshire. B. 8 Oct. 1848 at Hazeley, Oxford; m. 1876, Isabel Maud, d. of Charles Hastings Snow, Esq., of Wellington, New Zealand. Educ. at Marlborough Coll. Was called to the bar at the Middle Temple 1873; Q.C. 1899. Practised at the Canadian bar and in New Zealand. Commanded a contingent of New Zealand Militia against the Maories. Lieut.-Col. New Zealand Artillery; temporary Maj. Royal Garrison Artillery, raised four Oxfordshire H. Batteries. Capt. of English International Team 1874. A Unionist. Elected for the Woodstock division of Oxfordshire in Jan. 1910 and sat until he retired in 1918. Died 25 Feb. 1929. [1918]

HAMILTON, Charles Edward. 82 Cadogan Square. Carlton, Marlborough, and Constitutional. S. of John Hamilton, Esq., of Liverpool, by Jessy, d. of Peter Kemble, Esq., Capt. 44th Regiment. B. at Liverpool 1845; m. 1867, Mary, d. of George M'Corquodale, Esq., of Newton, Lancashire. Educ. by Dr. Dawson Turner, Liverpool, and at Brussels. Lieut.-Col. (retired) of the 80th Lancashire Rifle Volunteers; a J.P. for Lancashire and the city of Liverpool; and was three times elected on the town council of Liverpool. A "progressive Conservative." Sat for the Rotherhithe division of Southwark from Nov. 1885 until he retired in 1892. Created Bart. 1892. Died 15 Nov. 1928. [1892]

HAMILTON, Rt. Hon. Lord Claud John. 28 Cambridge Square, London. Carlton, Bachelors', St. Stephen's, and Travellers'. 2nd s. of 1st Duke of Abercorn and Lady Louisa Russell, d. of 6th Duke of Bedford. B. 20 Feb. 1843 at Stanmore Priory, Middlesex; m. 1878, Caroline, d. of Edward Chandos Pole, of Radbourne Hall, Derby (she died 1911). Educ. at Harrow. Entered Grenadier Guards 1862; retired 1867. Honorary Col. 5th Battalion Royal Inniskilling Fusiliers, Aide-de-Camp to Queen Victoria 1887. Chairman of Great Eastern Railway, High Steward of Yarmouth, and a Knight of Justice of St. John of Jerusalem. Was a Lord of the Treasury 1868. PC. 1917. A Unionist. Sat for Londonderry City 1865-68 when he was defeated; unsuccessfully contested Brecon Apr. 1869. Sat for King's Lynn 1869-Apr. 1880, when he was defeated, Liverpool Aug. 1880-85, and the W. Derby Division of Liverpool 1885-88, when he retired. Elected for S. Kensington Jan. 1910 and sat until he retired in 1918. Died 26 Jan. 1925. [1918]

HAMILTON, Collingwood George Clements. See HAMILTON, George Clements. Continued in House after 1918: full entry in Volume III.

HAMILTON, Lord Ernest William. Baronscourt, Newton Stewart, Co. Tyrone, Ireland. Naval and Military. 6th and youngest s. of the 1st Duke of Abercorn, by his m. with Lady Jane Russell, 2nd d. of the 6th Duke of Bedford. B. at Tunbridge Wells 1858; m. 1891, Pamela, d. of F.A. Campbell, Esq. Educ. at Harrow, and the Royal Military Coll., Sandhurst.

He entered the army as a Sub-Lieut. in the 11th Hussars in 1878, became Capt. June 1884, and retired in 1885. A Conservative, but "ready to support further measures for the establishment of an independent farming proprietary." Unsuccessfully contested Paisley Feb. 1884. Sat for Tyrone N. from 1885 until he retired in 1892. Author. Died 14 Dec. 1939.   [1892]

HAMILTON, Lord Frederick Spencer. 78 St. Ermin's Mansions, Caxton Street, London. Baron's Court, Newton Stewart, Co. Tyrone. Carlton. 5th s. of the 1st Duke of Abercorn, by Lady Louisa Jane Russell, 2nd d. of the 6th Duke of Bedford. B. 1856. Educ. at Harrow. Was Attaché and Assistant Secretary to the British Embassies at St. Petersburg, Berlin, Lisbon, and Buenos Aires. A Conservative and Unionist. Elected for S.W. Manchester 1885 and sat until defeated in 1886. Returned for Tyrone N. July 1892 and sat until he retired in 1895. Editor of *Pall Mall Magazine* until 1900; produced several novels 1915-21. Died 11 Aug. 1928.   [1895]

HAMILTON, George Clements. Continued in House after 1918: full entry in Volume III.

HAMILTON, Rt. Hon. Lord George Francis, G.C.S.I. 17 Montagu Street, London. Deal Castle. Carlton, and Athenaeum. 3rd s. of the 1st Duke of Abercorn, by Lady Louisa, 2nd d. of the 6th Duke of Bedford. B. 1845; m. 1871, Lady Maud Caroline, youngest d. of 3rd Earl of Harewood. Ensign in the Rifle Brigade 1864; Lieut. Coldstream Guards 1868; retired 1869. Was Under Secretary of State for India 1874 to 1878; Vice-President of the Council 1878 to 1880; First Lord of the Admiralty 1885-86, and again Aug. 1886-92; Secretary of State for India 1895-1903. Governor of Harrow School, and was Chairman London School Board 1894-95. Capt. of Deal Castle 1899. G.C.S.I. 1903. A Conservative. Sat for Middlesex from Dec. 1868 to Nov. 1885, and for the Ealing division of Middlesex from Nov. 1885 until he retired in 1906. PC. 1878. Chairman of Royal Commission on Poor Law and Unemployment 1905-09; Chairman of Mesopotamia Commission 1916-17; wrote two volumes of memoirs (1916 and 1922). Died 22 Sept. 1927. [1905]

HAMILTON, James Albert Edward

Hamilton, Marq. of. Coates House, Fittleworth, Sussex. Carlton. Eld. s. of James, 2nd Duke of Abercorn, by Lady Mary Curzon Howe, d. of Richard, 1st Earl Howe. B. 1869; m. 1894, Lady Rosalind Bingham, only d. of George, 4th Earl of Lucan. Educ. at Eton. Was Treasurer of the Household from 1903-05, and a Unionist Whip; Maj. N. of Ireland Yeomanry, Capt. in the 1st Life Guards; F.Z.S. A Unionist. Elected for Londonderry City in 1900 and sat until he succeeded as 3rd Duke of Abercorn 3 Jan. 1913. Lord-Lieut. of Tyrone from 1917. Senator of Northern Ireland Parliament 1921. Gov. of Northern Ireland 1922-45. PC. (Northern Ireland) 1922; PC. 1945. Died 12 Sept. 1953. [1912]

HAMILTON, John Glencairn Carter. Defeated in 1886: full entry in Volume I.

HAMLEY, Lieut.-Gen. Sir Edward Bruce, K.C.B., K.C.M.G. Palace Chambers, Ryder Street, London. Athenaeum, and Carlton. 4th s. of Admiral William Hamley, by his wife, Barbara Ogilvy. B. at Bodmin, Cornwall 1824. Educ. at the grammar school of William Hicks, the well-known humourist, of Bodmin, and at the Royal Military Academy, Woolwich. He entered the Royal Artillery in 1843; served during the Crimean War on the staff of Sir R. Dacres, and was at the battles of Alma, Balaclava, and Inkermann; successively held the offices of Professor of Military History at Sandhurst 1859-65, Commandant of the Staff Coll., Sandhurst, 1870-77, British Commissioner in Turkey 1879, in Armenia 1880, in Greece 1881, and Commissioner to execute the Treaty of Berlin. He was also Gen. in Command of the 2nd division in the Egyptian campaign of 1882, and led it at Tel-el-Kebir. Retired from the army 1890. Wrote a number of military and biographical works, and also novels, etc., amongst which were *The Campaign of Sebastopol, Wellington's Career, Lady Lee's Widowhood*, etc. etc. A Conservative. Sat for Birkenhead from 1885 until he retired in 1892. C.B. 1867; K.C.M.G. 1880; K.C.B. 1882. Died 12 Aug. 1893.   [1892]

HAMMOND, John. Carlow. National Liberal. B. 1842. A Merchant, having an extensive and long-established business in the town of Carlow. A J.P. for the Co., and member of the Carlow Urban District Council and Carlow County Council.

Chairman of the Carlow Town Commissioners. A Nationalist, of the Anti-Parnellite section. Sat for Carlow from 1891 until his death 17 Nov. 1907.   [1907]

HAMOND, Sir Charles Frederic. Grosvenor Hotel, London. 20 Lovaine Place, Newcastle-on-Tyne. Warkworth, Northumberland. Carlton. S. of G.F. Hamond, Esq., of Blackheath, by Elizabeth, d. of Mr. Surman. B. 1817. Educ. at the Proprietary Coll., Blackheath. Was a Shipowner and Agent for many years in Newcastle-on-Tyne. In 1865 he was called to the bar at the Middle Temple, and joined the Northern Circuit. A J.P. and Dept.-Lieut. for Newcastle; also Town Councillor and Alderman, and was a member of the first Newcastle School Board. Was Knighted 1896. A Conservative. Unsuccessfully contested Newcastle-on-Tyne in Nov. 1868 and again in Jan. 1874. First returned for Newcastle-on-Tyne in Feb. 1874 and sat until defeated in Apr. 1880. Unsuccessfully contested the seat again in 1885 and Feb. 1886. Was once more returned for Newcastle-on-Tyne in 1892 and sat until he retired in 1900. Died 2 Mar. 1905.   [1900]

HANBURY, Rt. Hon. Robert William. Herberthouse, Belgrave Square, London. Ilam Hall, Nr. Ashbourne, Staffordshire. Carlton. S. of Robert Hanbury, Esq., of Bolehall House, Tamworth, by Mary Anne, d. of Maj. Bamford, of Wilnecote Hall, Warwickshire. B. 1845; m. 1884, Ellen, only child of Col. Knott Hamilton. Educ. at Rugby, and Corpus Christi Coll., Oxford. Appointed President of the Board of Agriculture 1900. Was Financial Secretary to the Treasury, and a PC. 1895. Was Capt. in the Staffordshire Yeomanry 1873-80, and Honorary Col. of the 5th Lancashire Artillery Volunteers; a J.P. and Dept.-Lieut. for Staffordshire, Derbyshire, and Warwickshire. Also Lord of the Manors of Norton Canes, Ilam, and Carlton, Staffordshire. A Conservative. Sat for Tamworth from 1872 to 1878, and for N. Staffordshire from 1878 until defeated in 1880. Unsuccessfully contested Wallingford June 1880 and Preston Nov. 1882. First elected for Preston in Nov. 1885 and sat until his death 28 Apr. 1903. [1903]

HANBURY-TRACY, Hon. Frederick Stephen Archibald. 116 Queen's Gate, London. Penybryn Hall, Montgomery. 4th

s. of the 2nd Baron Sudeley, by Emma Elizabeth Alicia, 2nd d. of George Hay Dawkins Pennant, Esq., of Penrhyn Castle. B. 1848; m. 1870, Helena Caroline, d. of Sir Thomas E. Winnington, Bart. Was educ. at Trinity Coll., Cambridge. A Capt. in the Worcestershire Yeomanry Cavalry. A Liberal, in favour of Mr. Gladstone's Irish policy. Sat for the Montgomery district from May 1877 to the dissolution of 1885, when he was defeated by Mr. Pryce Jones. Returned again for Montgomery district in July 1886 and sat until defeated in 1892. Died 9 Aug. 1906.   [1892]

HANCOCK, John George. Continued in House after 1918: full entry in Volume III.

HANKEY, Frederick Alers. 44 Lowndes Square, London. Silverlands, Chertsey, Surrey. Carlton, and Union. Eld. s. of Thomas Alers Hankey, Esq., of Fenchurch Street, London, and Epsom, by Elizabeth, eld. d. of George Green, Esq., of Blackwall. B. in London 1833; m. 1st, 1862, Mary Wickham, d. of P.W. Flower, Esq., of Furzedown, Tooting Common (she died 1863); 2ndly, 1865, Marian Elizabeth, d. of T.J. Miller, Esq., MP. Educ. at Harrow, and Oriel Coll., Oxford (M.A. 1857). A Magistrate for Surrey, Chairman of the Consolidated Bank, and a Director of other companies. Was formerly a Partner in the firm of Hankey and Company, Bankers, Fenchurch Street. A Conservative. Sat for the Chertsey division of Surrey from 1885 until his death 15 Feb. 1892.   [1892]

HANSON, Sir Charles Augustin, Bart. Continued in House after 1918: full entry in Volume III.

HANSON, Sir Reginald, Bart. 4 Bryanston Square, London. Carlton, City Carlton, Constitutional, Junior Carlton, and Garrick. S. of Samuel Hanson, Esq., and Mary Choppin, d. of N.S. Machin, Esq. B. 1840 in the City of London; m. 1866, Constance Hallott, 3rd d. and co-heir of C.B. Bingley, Esq., of Stanhope Park, Middlesex. Educ. at Rugby, and Trinity Coll., Cambridge (LL.D.) Was in business as a Wholesale Grocer (Hanson, Son, and Barter) from 1861, and filled the offices of Common Councillor 1873; Alderman 1880; Sheriff for London and Middlesex 1881; and Lord Mayor 1886. Was also a member of the London School Board 1882-85, Chairman London Chamber of Commerce 1886, and a member of the London County Council 1889-92. Was Knighted in 1882, and created Bart. 1887. Honorary Col. 6th Battalion Royal Fusiliers, Knight Commander of the Redeemer of Greece and of the Crown of Oak of the Netherlands. Almoner of Christ's Hospital, and Treasurer of the Corporation of the Sons of the Clergy. A J.P. and Dept.-Lieut. for Tower Hamlets and Middlesex, J.P. for Westminster and London, one of H.M. Lieuts. for London, Land and Income Tax Commissioner for the City, F.S.A., etc. etc. A Conservative. Sat for City of London from June 1891 until he retired in 1900. Died 18 Apr. 1905. [1900]

HARBISON, Thomas James Stanislaus. Continued in House after 1918: full entry in Volume III.

HARCOURT, Edward William. 6 Prince's Gardens, London. Nuneham Park, Abingdon. Stanton Harcourt, Eynsham, Oxfordshire. Carlton, and Travellers'. Eld. s. of the Rev. William Harcourt, Canon of York, of Nuneham Park, by Matilda Mary, d. of Col. William Gooch; being 4th in descent from the 1st Lord Harcourt, whose estates he inherited. B. at York 1825; m. 1849, Lady Susan Harriet, only d. of the 2nd Earl of Sheffield. Was educ. at Christchurch, Oxford. Was Honorary Col. of the Cinque Ports Artillery from 1862. Patron of 2 livings. A Conservative. Sat for Oxfordshire from Feb. 1878 to 1885 and for S. Oxfordshire from 1885 until he retired in 1886. Died 19 Dec. 1891. [1886]

HARCOURT, Rt. Hon. Lewis Venables Vernon. 14 Berkeley Square, London. Nuneham Park, Oxford. Reform, Devonshire, Bachelors', and National Liberal. Eld. s. of the Rt. Hon. Sir William Harcourt, MP, and Therese, d. of T.H. Lister, Esq., of Armitage Park, Yorkshire. B. in London 1 Feb 1863; m. 1899, Mary Ethel, d. of W.H. Burns, Esq., of North Mymms Park, Hatfield. Educ. at Eton. First Commissioner of Works Dec. 1905 to Nov. 1910, and from May 1915 to Dec. 1916; Secretary for the Colonies 1910-15; Ecclesiastical Commissioner 1913. Was Secretary to his father in his political work. PC. 1905. A Trustee of the British Museum, the Wallace Collection, and the London Museum. Member of Council and Executive of British School at Rome. Honorary D.C.L. Oxford. Honorary F.R.I.B.A. A Radical. Elected for the Rossendale division of Lancashire in Mar. 1904 and sat until created 1st Visct. Harcourt 3 Jan. 1917. Died 24 Feb. 1922. [1916]

HARCOURT, Robert Venables Vernon. 48 Curzon Street, London. Malwood, Lyndhurst, Hampshire. National Liberal, and Bachelors'. 2nd s. of the Rt. Hon. Sir William Harcourt, MP, and Elizabeth, d. of J.L. Motley, Esq., historian, and at one time U.S. Minister in London. B. 7 May 1878 in London; m. 1911, Margorie, d. of William S. Cunard, Esq. Educ. at Eton, and Trinity Coll., Cambridge; honours History Tripos. Was in the Diplomatic Service from 1900 to 1906. Author of the comedies *An Angel Unawares*, and *A Question of Age*. Lieut. R.N.V.R. A Radical. Unsuccessfully contested Hastings Mar. 1908. Elected for Montrose Burghs in May 1908 and sat until he retired in 1918. Pilot Officer R.A.F.V.R. Feb. 1939. Died 8 Sept. 1962. [1918]

HARCOURT, Rt. Hon. Sir William George Granville Venables Vernon-. Malwood, Lyndhurst, Hampshire. Devonshire, Reform, National Liberal, and Oxford & Cambridge. 2nd s. of the Rev. William Vernon-Harcourt, of Nuneham Park, Oxfordshire, Canon of York, by Matilda Mary, d. of Lieut.-Col. William Gooch. B. 1827; m. 1st, 1859, Thérèse, d. of Thomas H. Lister, Esq., 2ndly, 1876, Mrs. Ives, d. of J.L. Motley, Esq., the Historian and United States Minister in London. Educ. at Trinity Coll., Cambridge, where he graduated B.A. 1851. Was called to the bar at the Inner Temple May 1854; Q.C. 1866; wrote a series of letters in the *Times* signed "Historicus", 1860-67. Was Solicitor-Gen. from Nov. 1873 to Feb. 1874, and so Knighted; Secretary of State for the Home Department 1880-85; and Chancellor of the Exchequer Jan. to July 1886, and again 1892 to 1895. On Mr. Gladstone's retirement from Parliament 1894 he became Leader of the House of Commons; retired 1895. Was Professor of International Law at Cambridge University from 1869 to 1887. Honorary Fellow of Trinity College, Cambridge 1902. PC. 1880. Presented with the freedom of the city of Glasgow 1881; and was Dept.-Lieut. Southampton, and Trustee of the British Museum. A Liberal, in favour of Home Rule for Ireland, etc., and leader of the party in the House of Commons from 1894 until he resigned Dec. 1898. Unsuccessfully contested Kirkcaldy Burghs 1859. Sat for the city of Oxford from Dec. 1868 to 8 May 1880, when he stood unsuccessfully on taking office; sat for Derby from 25 May 1880 to July 1895, when he was defeated; returned for Monmouthshire W. July 1895, and sat until his death 1 Oct. 1904.   [1904]

HARCOURT, Rt. Hon. Sir W. Vernon. See HARCOURT, Rt. Hon. Sir William George Granville Venables Vernon-.

HARDCASTLE, Edward. New Lodge, Hawkhurst, Kent. Carlton, and Oxford & Cambridge. S. of Alfred Hardcastle, Esq., of Hatcham House, Surrey, by Eliza, d. of Benjamin Smith, Esq., of Manchester. B. 1826; m. 1851, eld. d. of Samuel Hoare, jun., Esq., Banker of Lombard Street, London, and step-d. of Rear Admiral Sir W.E Parry. Educ. at Trinity Coll., Cambridge, afterwards at Downing Coll., B.A. 1850, M.A. 1853. A Merchant in Manchester, also a Governor of Owens Coll., Manchester, and of Cheetham Hospital and Library, and a trustee of the Grammar School, Manchester. A Magistrate for Lancashire, and a Dept.-Lieut. for Lancashire and Kent. A Conservative. Sat as Member for Lancashire S.E. from 1874 until defeated in 1880. Elected for Salford N. 1885 and sat until he retired in 1892. Died 1 Nov. 1905.   [1892]

HARDCASTLE, Frank. Firwood, Bolton-le-Moors, Lancashire. Carlton, Junior Carlton, and Orleans. S. of James Hardcastle, Esq., J.P., of Firwood, Bolton, and Pen-y-lan, Ruabon, by Hannah Crompton, d. of John Jackson, Esq., of Bolton. B. 1844 at Firwood, Bolton; m. 1885, Ida, eld. d. of Horatio G. Ross, Esq., of Portsmouth. Educ. at Repton School. Was engaged in business as a Bleacher and Colliery Proprietor of Lancashire, and was President of the United Bleachers' Association of Lancashire and Cheshire. A Conservative. Sat for the Westhoughton division of Lancashire S.E. from 1885 until he retired in 1892. High Sheriff of Lancashire 1895-96. Died 6 Nov. 1908.   [1892]

HARDIE, James Keir. 10 Nevill's Court, London. Lochnorris, Cumnock, Ayrshire. S. of David Hardie, Esq., and Mary Keir. B. 1856 in Lanarkshire; m. 1880, Lillie, d. of

Duncan Wilson, Esq. A Working Collier 1866; Miners' Union Secretary 1879; Journalist 1882; Chairman of Independent Labour Party 1893-1900; Founder and Editor of *The Miner*, 1887, and subsequently of the *Labour Leader*. Was Leader of the Labour Party in the House of Commons from 1906-08. Unsuccessfully contested mid Lanarkshire in 1888. Sat for West Ham from 1892-95, when he was defeated. Unsuccessfully contested E. Bradford in 1896, and Preston in Oct. 1900; elected for Merthyr Tydfil in Oct. 1900 and sat until his death 26 Sept. 1915.   [1915]

HARDY, Hon. Alfred Erskine Gathorne. See GATHORNE-HARDY, Hon. Alfred Erskine.

HARDY, George Alexander. Cheshunt House, Champion Hill, London. National Liberal. S. of Edward S. Hardy, Esq. B. 29 Dec. 1852 at Islington; m. 1875, Florence Marian, d. of F.D. Wilson, Esq. Educ. at private schools in London and Manchester. A Merchant and Manufacturer. A member of the London County Council for Dulwich from 1898-1907; President of Free Church Council, S. London 1904. J.P. for London. A Liberal, in favour of Reform of Poor Laws and Land Laws, Old Age Pensions, etc. Elected for the Stowmarket division of Suffolk in 1906 and sat until defeated in Jan. 1910. Contested Bath in Dec. 1910. Died 2 Oct. 1920.   [1909]

HARDY, Hon. John Stewart Gathorne. See GATHORNE-HARDY, Hon. John Stewart.

HARDY, Rt. Hon. Laurence. Sandling Park, Hythe, Kent. 36 Buckingham Gate, London. Carlton, and Wellington. S. of Sir John Hardy, 1st Bart., of Dunstall Hall, Burton-on-Trent, and his wife, Laura, d. of W. Holbech, Esq., of Farnborough Hall, Co. Warwick. B. 1854 at Oldbury Hall, near Atherstone, Warwickshire; m. Evelyn Emily, eld. d. of J. Cathorne Wood, Esq., of Thedden Grange, Alton, Hampshire (she died 1911). Educ. at Eton, and Christ Church, Oxford; M.A. 1st class in History. J.P., Dept.-Lieut., and County Councillor for Kent, J.P. W. Riding, of Yorkshire, and a County Councillor 1889-92. Was one of the Chairman's Panel for Grand Committees 1899-1910, and on the Panel 1917; member of the defences of the Realm Losses Commission 1917. Was Dept.-Chairman of Committees in House of Commons June to Dec. 1905. PC. 1911. A Unionist. Unsuccessfully contested the Shipley division of Yorkshire in 1885. First elected for S. Kent in 1892 and sat until he retired in 1918. Alderman of Kent County Council, Ecclesiastical Commissioner from 1918. Died 21 Jan. 1933.   [1918]

HARE, Sir Thomas Leigh, Bart. Stow Hall, Nr. Downham, Norfolk. Arthur's, Marlborough, and Carlton. S. of Sir Thomas Hare, former Capt. 2nd Life Guards, and A. Grace, his wife. B. 1859; m. 1886, Lady Ida, 2nd d. of the 3rd Earl Cathcart. Educ. at Eton. Entered the 24th Regiment 1879; transferred to the Scots Guards 1880; retired 1885. Served in the Zulu War, and in Egypt, was in the battle of Tel-el-Kebir 1882, and expedition to Suakim 1885, and in S. Africa 1901. Maj. and Honorary Lieut.-Col. Prince of Wales' Own Norfolk Artillery, and a J.P. and Dept.-Lieut. for Norfolk. A Conservative. Represented S.W. Norfolk from 1892 until defeated in 1906. Created Bart. in 1905. M.V.O. 1905. Contested same seat again in Jan. 1910. Died 22 Feb. 1941.   [1905]

HARKER, William. Harefield, Pateley Bridge, Nr. Leeds. 3rd s. of Robert and Nancie Harker, of Pateley Bridge, near Ripon. B. 1819; m. 1863, Annie, eld. d. of George Hodgson, Esq., of Bradford. Educ. at Pateley Bridge and Northallerton Grammar School. Was in business at Bradford as a Worsted Spinner and Manufacturer till 1862, when he retired. A Magistrate for the W. Riding of Yorkshire, and for the city of Ripon, and Chairman of the Bradford Banking Company. A Liberal Unionist, in favour of the Disestablishment, but not the Disendowment, of the Church. Sat for the Ripon division of the Eastern part of the W. Riding of Yorkshire from Dec. 1885 until he retired in 1886. Died 18 Sept. 1905. [1886]

HARLAND, Sir Edward James, Bart. 24 Kensington Palace Gardens, London. Glenfarne Hall, Co. Leitram. Junior Carlton, and St. Stephen's. S. of William Harland, Esq., M.D., of Scarborough, and Anne, d. of Cowan Peirson, Esq., of Goathland, Yorkshire. B. 1831 at Scarborough; m. 1860, Rosa Matilda, d. of Thomas Waun, Esq., of Vermont, Belfast.

Educ. at the Scarborough Grammar School, and the Academy, Edinburgh. A Shipbuilder of the firm of Harland and Wolff, Belfast. A J.P. for the counties of Antrim, Down, and Leitrim; Chairman of the Belfast Harbour Commissioners 1875 to 1886; High Sheriff Co. Down 1887, and Mayor of Belfast 1885 and 1886. He received his Baronetcy upon the occasion of the visit of the Prince and Princess of Wales to Belfast in 1885, when he was Mayor. A Conservative, supported the Unionist policy of the Marq. of Salisbury's government as being of vital importance to Protestantism in Ireland and to religious liberty generally. First elected for Belfast N. Aug. 1889 and sat until his death 24 Dec. 1895.   [1895 2nd ed.]

HARMAN, Rt. Hon. Edward Robert King-. See KING-HARMAN, Rt. Hon. Edward Robert.

HARMOOD-BANNER, Sir John Sutherland. Continued in House after 1918: full entry in Volume III.

HARMSWORTH, Cecil Bisshopp. Continued in House after 1918: full entry in Volume III.

HARMSWORTH, Robert Leicester. Continued in House after 1918: full entry in Volume III.

HARRINGTON, Edward. 51 Tachbrook Street, London. Tralee. S. of Dennis Harrington, Esq., of Castletown, Bere, Co. Cork, by his marriage with Miss Ellen O'Sullivan, and bro. to Timothy Harrington, Esq., at one time MP for the Harbour division of Dublin. B. about 1852. A Barrister, and Editor and Proprietor of the *Kerry Sentinel*. An "Irish Nationalist" of the Parnellite party. Sat for Kerry W. from the general election of 1885 until defeated in 1892.   [1892]

HARRINGTON, Timothy Charles. 70 Harcourt Street, Dublin. S. of Denis Harrington, Esq., of Castletown, Bere, Co. Cork. B. 1851; m. 1892, Elizabeth, 2nd d. of Dr. Edward O'Neill, of Dublin. Educ. at the Catholic University, and Trinity Coll., Dublin. A Barrister. Was Proprietor of *United Ireland*, and of the *Kerry Sentinel*. Lord Mayor of Dublin 1901; re-elected 1902 and 1903. Secretary of the Irish National League, and a Parnellite, but in 1897 he declared himself to be an Independent Nationalist. Sat for Westmeath from Feb. 1883 to Nov. 1885, and for the Harbour division of Dublin from Nov. 1885 until his death 12 Mar. 1910. [1909]

HARRIS, Rt. Hon. Frederick Leverton. 70 Grosvenor Street, London. Camilla Lacey, Dorking. Carlton, and St. James's. S. of Frederick William Harris, Esq., J.P., and Elizabeth, d. of P.M. Wylie, Esq. B. 1864; m. 1886, Gertrude, d. of John G. Richardson, Esq., of Bessbrook and Moyallon, Ireland. Educ. at Winchester Coll., and Caius Coll., Cambridge; M.A. Was Parliamentary Private Secretary to Mr. Arnold-Forster when Secretary of State for War 1904. Member of Tariff Reform Commission 1904. Member of London County Council 1907-10. PC. 1916. Adviser in commerce, War Staff, Admiralty 1915-16. Director of the Restriction of Enemy Supplies Department of the Foreign Office to Dec. 1916. Parliamentary Secretary to the Ministry of Blockade from Dec. 1916 to Jan. 1919. A Unionist. Sat for Tynemouth from 1900-06, when he was defeated; sat for the Stepney division of Tower Hamlets from 1907 to Dec. 1910, when he retired. Elected for E. Worcestershire in July 1914 and sat until he retired in 1918. Died 14 Nov. 1926. [1918]

HARRIS, Frederick Rutherfoord. 101 Mount Street, London. Llangibby Castle, Nr. Newport, Monmouthshire. S. of G.A. Harris, Esq., Judge of the Supreme Court of Madras, and Emma, d. of R. Rutherfoord, Esq. B. 1 May 1856; m. Florence, d. of J. Ling, Esq., of Kimberley. Educ. at Leatherhead Grammar School, Baden, and Edinburgh Universities. Went to S. Africa in 1882 and established a medical practice in Kimberley. He subsequently became Confidential Secretary to Mr. Cecil Rhodes, and 1st Secretary to the Chartered Company. In 1894 was elected Member for Kimberley in the Cape Parliament, and acted as Government Whip 1898. A Conservative. Was returned for Monmouth boroughs at the general election of 1900 but was unseated on petition in 1901. Elected for the Dulwich division of Camberwell in Dec. 1903 and sat until he accepted Chiltern Hundreds in May 1906 in order to travel abroad. Died 1 Sept. 1920. [1906]

HARRIS, Sir Henry Percy, K.B.E. Continued in House after 1918: full entry in Volume III.

HARRIS, Matthew. 46 Great Russell Street, London. Ballinasloe. S. of Peter and Ann Harris. B. 1826 at Roscommon; m. 1860, Miss Nora Bennett. Educ. at local schools. Was originally a working Bricklayer, and later a Builder and Road-Contractor. Found guilty of criminal conspiracy by the "Parnell Commission" in 1889. An "advanced Nationalist, democrat, and social reformer." Sat for Galway E. from the general election of 1885 until his death 14 Apr. 1890. [1890]

HARRIS, Percy Alfred. Continued in House after 1918: full entry in Volume III.

HARRISON, Charles. 29 Lennox Gardens, London. Reform, Devonshire, National Liberal, and City Liberal. S. of Frederick Harrison, Esq., and Jane, d. of Alexander Brice, Esq., of Belfast, formerly of Sutton Place, Guildford, and brother of Frederic Harrison, Esq., the well-known writer. B. at Muswell Hill 1 Aug. 1835; m. 1886, the Lady Harriet, sister of the Earl of Lanesborough. Educ. at King's Coll. School, and by private tutors. A Solicitor; admitted 1858; a Partner in the firm of C. and S. Harrison and Company, 19 Bedford Row, London. An original member of the London County Council, upon which he was made Vice-Chairman in 1895. Also a Director of the Legal and General Life Assurance Society; a Fellow of the Royal Institution, Society Antiquaries, Royal Geographical, and other Societies; a member of the Committee on the taxation of ground values, and an executive member of the Leasehold Enfranchisement Association. Wrote pamphlets on Leasehold Enfranchisement, and other papers. A Liberal, in favour of Home Rule, etc. and of the Unification of London. Unsuccessfully contested the Holborn division of Finsbury in Nov. 1885 and Plymouth July 1892. First returned for Plymouth July 1895 and sat until his death 24 Dec. 1897. [1897]

HARRISON, Sir George. 7 Whitehouse Terrace, Edinburgh. S. of George Harrison, Esq., of Stonehaven, Kincardineshire. B. 1811. Member of Royal Commission on Courts of Law in Scotland 1868-70. Director of North British Railway. Successively Secretary, Dept.-Chairman and Chairman of Edinburgh Chamber of Commerce. Treasurer of Edinburgh City Council 1879-82, Lord Provost of Edinburgh from 1882. Honorary LL.D. Edinburgh University 1884. Knighted in 1884. A Liberal. First returned for Edinburgh S. Nov. 1885 and sat until his death 23 Dec. 1885.

HARRISON, Henry. 9 Chester Place, Regent's Park, London. National Liberal, and Eighty. S. of Henry Harrison, Esq., J.P. of Holywood House, Co. Down, and Letitia Tennent Harrison, d. of Robert James Tennent, Esq., J.P., Dept.-Lieut., of Ardkeen, Co. Down, and Rushbrook Park, Belfast. B. at Holywood House, Co. Down 1867. Educ. at Westminster School, and Balliol Coll., Oxford. A Parnellite, advocating Home Rule for Ireland. Sat for the mid division of Tipperary from May 1890 until he retired in 1892. Unsuccessfully contested Limerick W. in July 1892 and Sligo N. in July 1895. Served in France 1915-18; invalided out 1919. Irish Dominion League 1920-21; Editor and Owner of *Irish Truth*, a weekly journal. Irish correspondent of *The Economist*, 1922-27. Author of several books on Parnell and Anglo-Irish relations. Died 2 Feb. 1954.   [1892]

HARRISON-BROADLEY, Col. Henry Broadley. Welton House, Brough, Yorkshire. Carlton, Conservative, and Bachelors'. B. 1853; m. Belle, d. of J.W. Tracy, Esq. Educ. at Brackenbury's, Wimbledon. Honorary Col. 1st Volunteer Battalion East Yorkshire Regiment; a J.P. for the E. Riding of Yorkshire. Adopted name of Harrison-Broadley in lieu of Harrison in 1896. A Unionist. Elected for the Howdenshire division of the E. Riding of Yorkshire in 1906 and sat until his death 29 Dec. 1914.   [1914]

HART-DAVIES, Thomas. 46 Ravensdale Road, Stamford Hill, London. Reform, East Indian, United Service, Savile, and National Liberal. S. of Ven. Archdeacon T. Hart-Davies and Elizabeth, d. of Thomas Hughes, Esq., Barrister. B. 1849 at Nottingham. Educ. at Marlborough and Lincoln Coll., Oxford. Entered the Indian Civil Service 1869 and later retired. Published translations of Catullus, Relaieff's poems, and Gogol's *Revizor*, and short stories. A Liberal, in favour of Land Reform, Imperial Unity, Women's Suffrage, etc. Unsuccessfully contested Rotherhithe in 1900. Elected for N. Hackney in 1906 and sat until defeated in Jan. 1910. Friend of the Royal Geographical Society. Died 3 Jan. 1920.   [1909]

HARTINGTON, Rt. Hon. Spencer Compton Cavendish, Marq. of. Devonshire House, Piccadilly, London. Holker, Newton-in-Cartmel, Lancashire. Reform, Devonshire, City Liberal, and Brooke's. Eld. s. of the 7th Duke of Devonshire, by the 4th d. of the 6th Earl of Carlisle. B. 1833. Educ. at Trinity Coll., Cambridge, where he graduated M.A. 1854, and was made LL.D. 1862. Was a Lord of the Admiralty for a few weeks Mar. and Apr. 1863. Under-Secretary for War from the latter date till Feb. 1866, and then Secretary for War till July following. Was Postmaster-Gen. from Dec. 1868 to Jan. 1871 and Chief Secretary for Ireland from the latter date to Feb. 1874. Secretary of State for India from Apr. 1880 to Dec. 1882, when he was reappointed Secretary of State for War, which office he held till June 1885. Became Maj. 7th Lancashire Rifle Volunteers, and Dept.-Lieut. of the Co. of Lancaster 1860. Was attached to Earl Granville's special mission to Russia in 1856. Presented with the freedom of the city of Glasgow 1877, and elected Lord Rector of Edinburgh University the same year. A Liberal, but opposed to Mr. Gladstone's Home Rule scheme. Sat for N. Lancashire from Mar. 1857 till Dec. 1868, when he was an unsuccessful candidate there; sat for Radnor district from Feb. 1869 to Apr. 1880, when he was returned for Radnor district and Lancashire N.E., and elected to sit for the latter. Returned for Rossendale division of Lancashire at the general election of 1885 and sat until succeeded as Duke of Devonshire in 1891. PC. 1866; K.G. 1892; G.C.V.O. 1907. Leader of the Liberal Party in the House of Commons from 1875-80. Lord President of Council 1895-1903. President of the Board of Education from 1900-02. Leader of the House of Lords from 1902-03; resigned over the Free Trade issue in 1903. Chairman of the Liberal Unionist Council 1886-1904. Chancellor of Cambridge University from 1892-1908. Lord-Lieut. of Derbyshire from 1892-1908. Styled as Lord Cavendish from 1834-58 and as Marq. of Hartington from 1858-1891. Died 24 Mar. 1908.   [1891]

HARTLAND — HASLETT

HARTLAND, Sir Frederick Dixon Dixon, Bart. See DIXON-HARTLAND, Sir Frederick Dixon, Bart.

HARVEY, Alexander Gordon Cummins. Town House, Littleborough, Lancashire. Reform. S. of Alexander Cummins Harvey, Esq. B. 31 Dec. 1858 at Manchester. Educ. privately, and at Owens Coll., Manchester. A Cotton Manufacturer and Merchant; member of the firm of Harvey and Fothergill, Manchester and Littleborough. A Co. Alderman of Lancashire County Council; was Chairman of Elementary Education Committee. A Liberal. Unsuccessfully contested Rochdale in 1900. Elected for Rochdale in 1906 and sat until he retired in 1918. Died 6 Nov. 1922. [1918]

HARVEY, Thomas Edmund. Continued in House after 1918: full entry in Volume III.

HARVEY, William Edwin. Westminster Palace Hotel, London. 98 Saltergate, Chesterfield. S. of James and Elizabeth Harvey. B. 5 Sept. 1852 at Hasland, near Chesterfield; m. 1873, d. of Joseph Hollingsworth, Esq., of Mansfield. Educ. at Hasland Day School until ten years of age, when he commenced working in the pits. Worked as a Miner until 1881, and was Miners' Agent, and later Gen. Secretary of Derbyshire Miners' Association. A member of Chesterfield Town Council and Education Committee; J.P. for Chesterfield and Derbyshire. Vice-President of Miners' Federation of Great Britain. A Labour Member. Elected for N.E. Derbyshire 30 Jan. 1907 and sat until his death 28 Apr. 1914. [1914]

HARWOOD, George. 70 South Audley Street, London. Brownlow Fold, Bolton. Athenaeum, Reform, and Brasenose. S. of Richard Harwood, Esq., J.P., Mayor of Bolton, and Alice Cunliffe. B. 1845 at Bolton; m. 1st, 1868, Alice, d. of James Marsh, Esq., of Wigan (she died 1894); 2ndly, 1904, Ellen, d. of Sir A. Hopkinson, Vice-Chancellor and Principal of Manchester University. Educ. at Chorlton High School, and Owens Coll., Manchester; M.A. London University. Called to the bar at Lincoln's Inn 1890. Head of the firm of Richard Harwood and Son Limited, Cotton Spinners, of Bolton. Passed the Oxford and Cambridge Examination for Ordination, and as an attempt to extend lay help in the church, served as a Deacon (unpaid) at St. Anne's Church, Manchester from 1886-89, by permission of the Bishop. A member of the Royal Commission on Ecclesiastical Discipline 1904-06. Author of *Disestablishment, The Coming Democracy*, etc. etc. An independent Liberal, in favour of Home Rule, also of the principle of an Established Church, a reformed House of Lords, a diminution of public-houses, but not of Local Veto, etc. Represented Bolton from 1895 until his death 7 Nov. 1912. [1912]

HASLAM, Sir Alfred Seale. Breadsall Priory, Derby. Reform, Devonshire, and City of London. S. of William Haslam, Esq., of Derby, and Ann, d. of J. Smith, Esq., of Branstone, Staffordshire. B. at Derby 1844; m. 1875, d. of Thomas Tatam, Esq., of The Elms, Little Eaton, near Derby. Educ. at Derby, and by private tutor. An Engineer and Ironmaster at Derby, and was Member of Derby Corporation for nineteen years, Mayor 1890-91; Alderman and J.P. for Derbyshire; President of Children's Hospital two years, Deaf and Dumb Institute two years, and Derby Chambers of Commerce three years. Knighted 1891; Mayor of Newcastle-under-Lyme 1901-04. A Liberal Unionist, in favour of re-organisation of the War Office, Poor Law Reform, Fiscal Reform, etc. Contested Derby in July 1892. Elected for Newcastle-under-Lyme 1900 and sat until defeated in 1906. Died 13 Jan. 1927. [1905]

HASLAM, James. 47 Clarence Road, Chesterfield. S. of Thomas Haslam, Esq., and Mary Wholey. B. 1 Apr. 1842 at Clay Cross; m. 1869, Emily, d. of John Gelsthorpe, Esq. Educ. at a Colliery school. Was an Agent of the Derbyshire Miners' Association from 1882. Member of Chesterfield Town Council from 1896-1905; a J.P. for Derbyshire and Chesterfield. A Labour Member. Elected for the Chesterfield division of Derbyshire in 1906 and sat until his death 31 July 1913. [1913]

HASLAM, Lewis. Continued in House after 1918: full entry in Volume III.

HASLETT, Sir James Horner. Prince's Gardens, Belfast. S. of the Rev. Henry

Haslett, Presbyterian Minister, and his wife Mary, the d. of John Wilson Esq., of Drumcroon, Londonderry. B. at Knock, near Belfast 1832; m. 1878, Annie, d. of John Rae, Esq., of Islandreagh, Co. Antrim, and London (she died 1894). Educ. at Knock National School, and the Royal Academical Institution, Belfast. A Chemist and Druggist at Belfast, where he was apprenticed in 1846, and started business in partnership with his bro. 1854. A J.P. and Alderman for Belfast, etc. Was twice Mayor of Belfast, and was Knighted in 1887. A Conservative. Was elected for W. Belfast in Nov. 1885 but defeated by Mr. Sexton June 1886. Elected for the N. division of Belfast on the death of Sir E.J. Harland, Jan. 1896, and sat until his death 18 Aug. 1905. [1905]

HASTINGS, George Woodyatt. Barnard's Green House, Great Malvern. Oxford & Cambridge, and Brooks's. Only s. of Sir Charles Hastings, M.D., D.C.L., of Worcester and Barnard's Green, Malvern, by Hannah, d. of George Woodyatt, Esq., M.D. B. at Worcester 1825; m. 1st, Catherine Anna, d. of the Rev. Samuel Mence, B.D., Rector of Ulcombe, Kent (she died 1871); 2ndly, 1877, Frances Anna, only child of the Rev. William Huntingdon Pillans, Rector of Himley, Staffordshire. Educ. at Bromsgrove Grammar School, and Christ's Coll., Cambridge; graduated LL.B. 1852, LL.M. 1870. Was called to the bar at the Middle Temple May 1850, and joined the Oxford Circuit. A Magistrate for Worcestershire and Hereford, and a Dept.-Lieut. for the latter; Vice-Chairman of Worcester Quarter Sessions from 1872, and Chairman of the County Council. Published several pamphlets on Political Economy, etc. A Liberal and later a Liberal-Unionist. Unsuccessfully contested Beverley as a Conservative in July 1854 and Worcestershire as a Liberal in 1874. Sat for Worcestershire E. from Apr. 1880 until he was expelled from the House of Commons on 21 Mar. 1892 after conviction for fraudulent conversion. Died 21 Oct. 1917. [1892]

HATCH, Ernest Frederic George. 11 Mount Street, Grosvenor Square, London. Carlton, Boodle's, Junior Carlton, and Ranelagh. S. of John William Hatch, Esq., and Matilda Augusta, only d. of Hugh Snell, Esq., Barrister-at-Law, of Callington, Cornwall. B. 1859; m. 1900, Lady Constance Blanche Godolphin, youngest d. of 9th Duke of Leeds. Senior Partner and Founder of Hatch, Mansfield and Company of No. 1 Cockspur Street, London, and a Director of the Fine Arts Insurance Company. Travelled in America, Canada, S. Africa, India, China, and Japan. Took a great interest in Foreign and Colonial affairs, and in the social condition of the people and the development of the Empire. Author of *Far Eastern Impressions*, and other works. A Conservative until Mar. 1905 when he resigned over the Free Trade issue. Contested the Gorton division of Lancashire unsuccessfully in 1889 and 1892. First elected for the Gorton division of Lancashire in 1895 and sat until he retired in Jan. 1906. Created Bart. in 1908; K.B.E. 1920; frequent Chairman of Departmental Committees. Died 17 Aug. 1927. [1905]

HATTON, Hon. Murray Edward Gordon Finch. See FINCH-HATTON, Hon. Murray Edward Gordon.

HAVELOCK, Sir Henry Marshman, Bart., V.C., K.C.B. See HAVELOCK-ALLAN, Sir Henry Marshman, Bart., V.C., K.C.B.

HAVELOCK-ALLAN, Sir Henry Marshman, Bart., V.C., K.C.B. 70 Chester Square, London. Blackwell Hall, Darlington. Reform. Eld. s. of Maj.-Gen. Sir Henry Havelock, K.C.B., the distinguished Gen., by Hannah Shepherd, d. of the Rev. Dr. Marshman, of Serampore, India. B. at Chinsurah, Bengal, 1830; m. 1865, Lady Alice, d. of the 2nd Earl of Ducie. Entered the army 1846; became Capt. 1857; served as Assistant Quartermaster-Gen. in the Persian Campaign of 1857, and as Adjutant-Gen. to Gen. Havelock during the operations in Oude, in the course of which he earned the Victoria Cross at Cawnpore, Aug. 1857, and became Maj., serving to the end of the Mutiny. Was created a Bart. in 1858, with special remainder to the heirs of his father, who died before he received the honours conferred on him in recognition of his pre-eminent and arduous services to the nation during the Indian Mutiny. Maj.-Gen. and Col. Royal Irish Regiment; was Lieut.-Col. 1859; Dept.-Assistant Adjutant-Gen. at Aldershot 1861; served in the New Zealand War (and received the

C.B.) 1863-65; and was Assistant Quarter-master-Gen. in Canada 1867-69. Was from 1869 to 1872 Assistant Adjutant-Gen. in Ireland. Unsuccessfully contested Stroud Jan. 1874. Sat as MP for Sunderland from July 1874 to 1881, when he resigned on appointment to the command of the 2nd Brigade of Foot at Aldershot. K.C.B 1887. A J.P., Dept.-Lieut., and C.A., a J.P. for Yorkshire, N. Riding. In 1880, he assumed the additional surname of Allan. A Liberal Unionist. Sat again in Parliament for Durham S.E. from 1885 until defeated July 1892 re-elected 1895 and sat until his death 30 Dec. 1897.   [1897]

HAVELOCK-ALLAN, Sir Henry Spencer Moreton, Bart. Blackwell Grange, Darlington, Brooks's. S. of Gen. Sir Henry Marshman Havelock-Allen, V.C., K.C.B., 1st Bart., and Lady Alice, d. of 2nd Earl of Ducie. B. 29 Jan. 1872 at Royal Hospital, Dublin; m. 1903, Edith, d. of T.C.J. Sowerby, Esq. Educ. at Eton, and Trinity Coll., Cambridge. A Maj. 4th Battalion Durham Light Infantry; Maj. 17th Battalion Lancashire Fusiliers from Oct. 1915. A J.P. and Dept.-Lieut. for Co. Durham, and a J.P. and the N. Riding of Yorkshire. Was Parliamentary Private Secretary to Mr. J.A. Pease, Chancellor of Duchy of Lancaster 1910, and to Mr. E.S. Montagu, Under-Secretary for India 1911-14. A Liberal. Elected for the Bishop Auckland division of Co. Durham in Jan. 1910 and sat until he retired in 1918. Succeeded as Bart. 1897. Died 28 Oct. 1953. [1918]

HAVILAND-BURKE, Edmund. 70 Waterloo Road, Dublin. Eld. s. (by Jane, 2nd d. of J. Waltham, Esq.) of Edmund Haviland-Burke, Esq., MP for Christchurch, Hampshire, who was the only s. of Thomas William Aston Haviland-Burke, Esq., grand-nephew and heir-at-law of the Rt. Hon. Edmund Burke. B. 1864; m. 1893, Susan, 2nd d. of John Wilson, Esq., of Carn Simpson, Ballycastle, Co. Antrim. Educ. privately, chiefly on the Continent. Acted as a War Correspondent in Epirus to the *Manchester Guardian* during the Turco-Greek war of 1897. A Whip to the Irish Party. A Nationalist. Unsuccessfully contested N. Kerry in 1892, S. Dublin in 1895 and N. Louth in 1900. Elected for the Tullamore division of Kings Co. in Oct. 1900 and sat until his death 12 Oct. 1914.   [1914]

HAWORTH, Sir Arthur Adlington, Bart. Normanby, Altrincham. 12 Kensington Park Gardens, London. Reform, and National Liberal. S. of Abraham Haworth, Esq., J.P., and Elizabeth, d. of John Goodier, Esq. B. 1865 at Eccles; m. 1891, Lily, d. of John Rigby, Esq. Educ. at Rugby School. A Cotton Merchant at Manchester; Chairman of the Manchester Royal Exchange; a Gov. and Treasurer of Manchester Grammar School; a J.P. for Cheshire and Shropshire. A Liberal. Elected for S. Manchester in 1906 and sat until defeated Mar. 1912, after appointment as Junior Lord of Treasury (Feb.-Apr. 1912). Unsuccessfully contested Exchange division of Manchester in 1918. Created Bart. in 1911. Died 31 Aug. 1844. [1911]

HAY, Hon. Claude George Drummond. 5 Connaught Square, London. Turf, Carlton, Bachelors', Garrick, Travellers', and Beefsteak. 5th s. of the 11th Earl of Kinnoull. B. 1862. Educ. at Radley Coll., and abroad. Was Under-Secretary of Lloyds. A J.P. for London. Private Secretary to the Rt. Hon. Edward Stanhope. A Conservative, interested in the housing of the Working Classes, the Municipal Movement in the Metropolis, and in Railway Questions. Unsuccessfully contested the Hoxton division of Shoreditch in 1892 and 1895. Elected for the Hoxton division of Shoreditch in 1900 and sat until defeated in Jan. 1910. Temporary Capt. in army 1915. Died 24 Oct. 1920.   [1909]

HAYDEN, John Patrick. *Westmeath Examiner* Office, Mullingar. S. of Luke and Mary Hayden, of Roscommon, and bro. of Luke Patrick Hayden, MP for S. Leitrim 1885-92 and S. Roscommon 1892-97. B. 1863. Educ. at St. Comans, Roscommon. A Journalist. Editor and Proprietor of the *Westmeath Examiner*. A Nationalist. Represented S. Roscommon from 1897 until defeated in 1918. Member of the Irish Board of Agriculture. Died 3 July 1954. [1918]

HAYDEN, Luke Patrick. 43 Upper Sackville Street, Dublin. Roscommon. S. of Luke Hayden, Esq., of Roscommon. B. 1850. Educ. at Roscommon. Held the Commission of the Peace, Chairman of the Town Commissioners of the borough of Roscommon, and Proprietor of the *Roscommon Messenger*. An "Irish Nationalist" of the Parnellite section. Sat for Leitrim S. 1885 to 1892, and for Roscommon S. from 1892 until his death 23 June 1897. [1897]

HAYNE, Rt. Hon. Charles Hayne Seale-. See SEALE-HAYNE, Rt. Hon. Charles Hayne.

HAYTER, Rt. Hon. Sir Arthur Divett, Bart. 9 Grosvenor Square, London. South Hill Park, Bracknell, Berkshire. Tintagel, Camelford, Cornwall. Brooks's, Travellers', Devonshire, and National Liberal. S. of the Rt. Hon. Sir W.G. Hayter, Bart., MP, Judge Advocate-Gen. 1848, and Secretary of the Treasury 1849-59, and Ann, eld. d. of W. Pulsford, Esq., of Linslade Manor, Leighton Buzzard. B. 1835; m. 1866, Henriette, d. of Adrian J. Hope, Esq., and niece of the Rt. Hon. A. Beresford Hope, MP. Educ. at Eton, and Balliol and Brasenose Colls., Oxford; honours in Classics. Was appointed to Grenadier Guards in 1856; retired as Capt. 1866; Commanded London Rifle Brigade 1872-81; Lord of the Treasury 1880-82; Financial Secretary at War Office 1882-85; Privy Councillor 1894. Chairman of Public Accounts Committee 1901-05. Author of *Essays on Production and its Increase*. Succeeded as Bart. in 1878. A Liberal, in favour of Shorter Parliaments, Registration Reform, Better Housing of the Working Classes, Compensation for injuries in all trades, etc. Unsuccessfully contested Windsor in Nov. 1863. Elected for Wells in 1865 and sat until 1868 when he was defeated in E. Somerset. Unsuccessfully contested Hereford in Feb. 1871 and Bath in June 1873. Sat for Bath from Oct. 1873-1885, when he was defeated. Unsuccessfully contested Bath again in July 1886, and the Torquay division of Devon in July 1892. Elected for Walsall in 1893, defeated in 1895. Re-elected for Walsall in 1900 and sat until he accepted Chiltern Hundreds on being nominated to the Peerage in Dec. 1905. Created Baron Haversham Jan 1906. Died 1 May 1917. [1905]

HAYWARD, Evan. Continued in House after 1918: full entry in Volume III.

HAZEL, Alfred Ernest William. 31 Victoria Street, West Bromwich. Jesus College, Oxford. National Liberal, and Eighty. S. of John Hazel, Esq., of West Bromwich. B. 1869 at Liverpool. Educ. at King Edward's School, Birmingham, and

Jesus Coll., Oxford. A Barrister, called 1898; Fellow and Dean of Jesus Coll., Oxford. Law Lecturer at Oxford; M.A., B.C.L., and LL.D. A Liberal. Elected for W. Bromwich in 1906 and sat until defeated in Jan. 1910. Unsuccessfully contested W. Bromwich again Dec. 1910. Recorder of Burton-on-Trent 1912-38; Reader in Constitutional Land at Inns of Court 1910-26; Dept. Controller, Priority Department Ministry of Munitions 1915-19; C.B.E. 1918; K.C. 1930; Principal of Jesus Coll., Oxford from 1925 until his death 20 Aug. 1944. [1909]

HAZELL, Walter. 9 Russell Square, London. National Liberal, and City Liberal. S. of Jonathan Hazell, Esq., and Martha, d. of the Rev. John Lane. B. in London 1843; m. 1886, Anna, d. of James Tomlin, Esq. Educ. privately. A Printer and Publisher, head of the firm of Hazell, Watson and Viney, Limited, of London and Aylesbury. Also Treasurer of the Peace Society; joint founder of the Self-Help Emigration Society, and the Children's Fresh Air Mission, and was actively interested in other philanthropic enterprises. An advanced Liberal. Sat for Leicester from Aug. 1894 until defeated in 1900. Mayor of Holborn 1911-12; a Commissioner of Income Tax. Died 12 Feb. 1919. [1900]

HAZLETON, Richard. Ivybank, Blackrock, Co. Dublin. 35 North Side, Clapham Common, London. Royal Automobile. S. of Thomas Hazleton, Esq., of Dublin, and Bridget Rose Ryan, of Tipperary. B. 5 Dec. 1880 at Clontarf, Co. Dublin. Educ. at Blackrock Coll., Co. Dublin. A member of Blackrock Urban District Council 1902. Honorary Secretary to Irish Party. Member of Lord Balfour of Burleigh's Committee on Commercial and Industrial Policy 1916. A Nationalist. Unsuccessfully contested Dublin S. Jan. 1906 and N. Louth Jan. 1910. First elected for N. Galway in Feb. 1906, and sat until defeated in 1918. Elected for N. Louth Dec. 1910, whilst sitting for N. Galway, but the election was declared void on petition. Unsuccessfully contested Co. Louth in 1918, and, as a Liberal, the Rotherhithe division of Bermondsey in 1923. Died 26 Jan. 1943. [1918]

HEALY, Maurice. Ashton Lawn, Cork. S. of Maurice Healy, Esq., of Bantry. B. 3 Jan. 1859 at Bantry, Co. Cork; m. 1887, Annie,

d. of A.M. Sullivan, Esq., MP. Educ. at Christian Schools, Lismore. A Solicitor, admitted 1882. A Nationalist. Sat for Cork City from 1885-1900, when he was defeated; re-elected for Cork City 1909 and sat until defeated Jan. 1910. Sat for N.E. Co. Cork, from Mar. to Dec. 1910 when he was again elected for Cork City and sat until he retired in 1918. Died 9 Nov. 1923. [1918]

HEALY, Thomas Joseph. 12 Westmoreland Street, Dublin. Fortview, Wexford. Eld. s. of Maurice Healy, Esq., of Bantry, Co. Cork, and Eliza his wife. B. at Bantry 1854; m. 1879, Kathleen, eld. d. of Matthew F. Shine, Esq., of Dungarvan. Educ. at the National School, Lismore. A Solicitor, admitted 1888. An Irish Nationalist of the Anti-Parnellite section. First returned for Wexford N. without opposition, on the vacation of the seat by Mr. John Redmond, Mar. 1892 and sat until defeated in 1900. Died 1925. [1900]

HEALY, Timothy Michael. Glenaulin, Chapelizod, Co. Dublin. National Liberal. 2nd s. of Maurice Healy, Esq., by his wife Eliza Sullivan. B. at Bantry, Co. Cork 1855; m. 1882, Erina Kate, d. of T.D. Sullivan, Esq. Called to the Irish bar 1884; a Q.C. 1899. Bencher of King's Inn 1905. Called to the English bar 1903. K.C. 1910. Author of *Why there is an Irish Land Question, A Word for Ireland*, etc. etc. A Nationalist. Sat for Wexford borough from Nov. 1880 to 1883, Monaghan 1883-85, when he was elected again for Monaghan, but chose to sit for S. Derry from 1885 until defeated in July 1886. Sat for N. Longford from 1887-92. Sat for Louth N. from 1892 until defeated in Dec. 1910. Elected for N.E. Cork in July 1911 and sat until he retired in 1918. Gov.-Gen. of Irish Free State 1922-28. Died 26 Mar. 1931. [1910]

HEARN, Michael Louis. Dame House, Dame Street, Dublin. "Waterloo", Temple Gardens, Dublin. Collinstown House, Clondalkin, Co. Dublin. S. of Thomas Edmund Hearn, Esq., and Grace Hearn (née Cunningham), both of Cork. B. 1866; m. Sept. 1891, Mary Josephine, younger d. of William Malony, Esq., of Thurles, Co. Tipperary. Educ. at Ratcliffe Coll., Leicester, St. Stanislaus Coll., Tullamore, and the Royal University of Ireland, Dublin. Practiced as a Solicitor in Dublin from Jan. 1889. A member of the Irish Nationalist Party under the leadership of Mr. Red-

mond. Elected for S. Co. Dublin 6 July 1917 and sat until he retired in 1918. [1918]

HEATH, Arthur Howard. 16 Bryanston Square, London. Newbold Revel, Rugby. Carlton, Junior Carlton, and Wellington. S. of Robert Heath, Esq., of Biddulph Grange, Congleton, and Anne, d. of James Beech, Esq., of Tunstall, Staffordshire. B. at Newcastle, Staffordshire 1856; m. 1884, Alice, d. of the Rev. H.R. Peel. Educ. at Clifton Coll., and Brasenose Coll., Oxford. An Ironmaster and Colliery Proprietor. A J.P. for Staffordshire and Col. of Stafford Yeomanry. A Unionist. Unsuccessfully contested Hanley in 1892 and 1895. Sat for Hanley from 1900-06, when he was defeated. Elected for the Leek division of Staffordshire in Jan. 1910 and sat until he retired in Dec. 1910. Died 26 Apr. 1930. [1910]

HEATH, Arthur Raymond. 30 Ennismore Gardens. Thorpe Hall, Louth, Lincolnshire. Carlton. Eld. s. of Admiral Sir L.G. Heath, K.C.B., of Anstie Grange, Holmwood, Surrey, by Mary Emma, 5th d. of Arthur Marsh, Esq., of Eastbury, Hertfordshire. B. at Valetta, Malta 1854; m. 1881, Flora Jean, youngest d. of Edward Baxter, Esq., of Kincaldrum, Forfarshire. Educ. at Marlborough, and Trinity Coll., Cambridge. Was called to the bar at the Inner Temple 1879; and was a J.P. for Oxfordshire. A Conservative, opposed to Home Rule for Ireland. Sat for the Louth division of Lincolnshire from July 1886 until defeated in 1892. Died 8 June 1943. [1892]

HEATH, Sir James, Bart. 81 South Audley Street, London. Ashorne Hill, Leamington. Carlton, and Junior Carlton. S. of Robert Heath, Esq., MP, of Biddulph Grange, Congleton, by Anne, d. of J. Beech, Esq., of Tunstall, Staffordshire. B. 1852 at Kidsgrove; m. 1881, Euphemia Celina, d. of P.G. Vanderbyl, Esq., of Elselnwood, Farnborough, and Cape Town. Educ. at Clifton Coll. An Ironmaster and Colliery Proprietor; was Col. Staffordshire Yeomanry. Created Bart. 1904. A Conservative. Sat for N.W. Staffordshire from 1892 until defeated in 1906. Died 24 Dec. 1942. [1905]

HEATHCOTE, Justinian Heathcote Edwards. See EDWARDS-HEATHCOTE, Justinian Heathcote.

HEATON, John Henniker. 33 Eaton Square, London. Portland, Bath, and Carlton. S. of Lieut.-Col. Heaton, by the d. of John Henniker, Esq. B. at Rochester, Kent 1848; m. 1873, only d. of Samuel Bennett, Esq., of Mundarrah Towers, New South Wales. Educ. at Kent House School, and King's Coll., London. A Landowner in Australia, and also part owner of several Australian Newspapers. Represented the Government of New South Wales at the Amsterdam Exhibition 1883, and in 1884 was deputed by the people of Mauritius to negotiate with the Home Government for a new constitution. Represented the Tasmanian Government at the Berlin International Cable Conference 1885, and was Commissioner for New South Wales at the Indian and Colonial Exhibition 1886. In 1898 he carried his scheme of Imperial Penny Postage, and obtained numerous other postal reforms. Freedom of the City of London in Gold Casket conferred on him in 1900; also Freedom of Canterbury in Silver Casket. Offered, but declined, the title of K.C.M.G. in 1892, 1894, 1898, and 1905. Author of *The Australian Dictionary of Dates and Men of the Time, An Account of a Canonization at Rome*, and a work on the *Australian Aborigines*. A "Progressive Conservative", in favour of "fair trade for English Manufacturers." Sat for Canterbury from 1885 until he retired in Dec. 1910. Created Bart. 1912. Died 8 Sept. 1914.   [1910]

HEATON-ARMSTRONG, William Charles. 30 Portland Place, London. National Liberal, Union, and Automobile. S. of John Heaton-Armstrong, Esq., of Roscrea, MP, and Josephine Theresa, d. of Baron Mayr de Melnhof. B. 1 Sept. 1853; m. 1885, Baroness Bertha Maximilian Zois-Edelstein, of Austria. Educ. privately, and abroad. A Merchant and Banker; Lord of the Manor of Roscrea; Fellow of Royal, Astronomical, Statistical, Botanical, Geological, and Zoological Societies. Published *Calculations of the Sun's Meridian Altitude, Astronomical Tables* etc. A Liberal. Contested the mid division of Tipperary as a Conservative in July 1892. Elected for the Sudbury division of Suffolk in 1906 and sat until retired in Jan. 1910. Died 20 July 1917.   [1909]

HEDDERWICK, Thomas Charles Hunter. 2 Garden Court, Temple, London. The Manor House, Weston Turville,

Wendover. Biggar Park, Lanarkshire. Reform, and Eighty. Scottish Liberal, Edinburgh. S. of Robert Hedderwick, Esq., Queen's Printer and Publisher, Glasgow, by his m. with Anna Mary Walker Hunter, of Dumfries. B. at Glasgow 1850; m. 1884, only d. of James Neilson, Esq., of Biggar Park, Lanarkshire. Educ. at the High School, and University (M.A.) Glasgow, and at Leipsig. Was called to the bar at the Middle Temple 1876, and practised on the N.E. Circuit; a J.P. for Lanarkshire; translated the old puppet play *Doctor Faustus*, and wrote an *Election* and a *Food and Drugs Handbook*. An advanced Liberal. Unsuccessfully contested S. Lanark in 1892 and Wick District 1895. First returned for Wick District in June 1896 and sat until defeated in 1900. Contested the Newbury divison of Berkshire in Jan. 1910. Acting Dept.-Chairman, County of London Sessions 1907-10. Died 6 Feb. 1918.   [1900]

HEDGES, Alfred Paget. Leigh, Nr. Tonbridge, Kent. Reform, and National Liberal. S. of William Hedges, Esq., of Ealing. B. 1867 at Chelsea; m. 1893, Florence, d. of James Hicks, Esq. Educ. privately. A Merchant; Managing Director of Benson and Hedges Limited, London. J.P. for Kent. A Liberal. Elected for the Tonbridge division of Kent in 1906 and sat until defeated in Jan. 1910. Unsuccessfully contested the Tonbridge division of Kent again in Dec. 1910. Died 17 Apr. 1929.   [1909]

HELDER, Augustus. Corkickle, Whitehaven. Carlton, and Constitutional. 2nd s. of George Helder, Esq., of Clement's and Gray's Inns, Solicitor, and Augusta (née Pontet) his wife. B. 1827 at Brixton. Educ. at Pollard's School, Brompton, and at the Coll. of St. Omer, France. Was articled to Richard Armitstead, Solicitor, in Whitehaven in 1843, admitted 1849, but later retired from practice. A Director of various companies including *The Graphic*. A Conservative, offered a hearty support to the Unionist Government, in favour of an Eight Hours Bill for Miners. Represented Whitehaven from 1895 until he retired in Jan. 1906. Died 31 Mar. 1906.   [1905]

HELME, Sir Norval Watson. 2 Whitehall Court, London. Springfield Hall, Lancaster. Reform, and National Liberal. Eld. s. of James Helme, Esq. B. in Lancaster 1849; m. 1877, Mary, eld. d. of Thomas

Wilson, Esq., of Caldbeck, Cumberland. Educ. at Royal Grammar School, Lancaster. Senior Partner in firm of J. Helme and Company, Manufacturers. An Alderman (Mayor 1896-97) of the borough of Lancaster, President of Lancaster and district Chamber of Commerce, Alderman of Lancashire County Council, Chairman of Lancashire Asylums Board, a member of Lancashire Standing, Joint, and Education Committees, President of Non-County Boroughs Association. A J.P. for the Co. of Lancaster. Knighted 1912. A Liberal. First elected for the Lancaster division of N. Lancashire in 1900 and sat until defeated in 1918. Died 6 Mar. 1932.   [1918]

HELMSLEY, Charles William Reginald Duncombe, Visct. Nawton Tower, Nawton, Yorkshire. Carlton, Turf, and Bachelors'. Grand-s. and heir of the Earl of Feversham. B. 8 May 1879; m. 1904, Lady Margaret Greville, d. of the Earl of Warwick. Educ. at Eton, and Christ Church, Oxford; M.A. A Maj. in Yorkshire Imperial Yeomanry. Assistant Private Secretary to Lord Selborne, First Lord of the Admiralty 1902-04. A Unionist. Elected for the Thirsk and Malton division of the N. Riding of Yorkshire in 1906 and sat until he succeeded as Earl of Feversham on 13 Jan. 1915. Killed in action 15 Sept. 1916. [1915]

HEMMERDE, Edward George. Continued in House after 1918: full entry in Volume III.

HEMPHILL, Rt. Hon Charles Hare. 65 Merrion Square, Dublin. Clifton House, Shankill, Co. Dublin. Reform, and National Liberal. S. of John Hemphill, Esq., and Barbara, d. of the Rev. P. Hare. B. 1822 at Cashel; m. 1849, Augusta Mary Stanhope, d. of the Hon. Sir Francis Stanhope, and grand-d. of the 3rd Earl of Harrington (she died 1899). Educ. at the Rev. Dr. Wall's School, Hume Street, Dublin, and Trinity Coll., Dublin (Scholar, 1st Classical Moderator and Auditor of the Coll. Historical Society). A Barrister, and bencher of the King's Inn; Q.C. 1860; at one time H.M. Serjeant-at-Law; was Solicitor-Gen. for Ireland 1892-95, when he became a PC.; also J.P. for the counties of Dublin, Tipperary, and Wicklow. A Liberal, in favour of Home Rule for Ireland, Mr. John Morley's Land Bill, etc. Contested Cashel in 1857 and 1859, the W.

Derby division of Liverpool in July 1886, and Hastings in July 1892. Sat for N. Tyrone from 1895 until he was created Baron Hemphill in Dec. 1905. Died 4 Mar. 1908.   [1905]

HENDERSON, Sir Alexander, Bart. 18 Arlington Street, London. Buscot Park, Faringdon, Berkshire. Glenalmond, Perthshire. Brooks's. S. of George Henderson, Esq., of Langholm, Dumfries. B. 28 Sept. 1850 in London; m. 1874, Jane Ellen, d. of E.W. Davis, Esq. Educ. privately. A Chairman of the Great Central Railway. J.P. for Berkshire, Sheriff 1912. Created Bart. 1902. A Unionist. Sat for W. Staffordshire from 1898-1906, when he was defeated. Elected for St. George's, Hanover Square in July 1913 and sat until created Lord Faringdon in Jan. 1916. C.H. 1917. Died 17 Mar. 1934.   [1915]

HENDERSON, Rt. Hon. Arthur. Continued in House after 1918: full entry in Volume III.

HENDERSON, Lieut.-Col. Hon. Harold Greenwood. Kitemore, Faringdon, Berkshire. Carlton, and Marlborough. Eld. s. of Sir Alexander Henderson, Bart., MP, 1st Baron Faringdon. B. 29 Oct. 1875 at Ealing; m. 1901, Lady Violet Dalzell, d. of 12th Earl of Carnwath. Educ. at Eton. Joined the 1st Life Guards 1897, Capt. and Adjutant 1902-05; served in S. African War 1899-1902; retired from the army in 1906. Lieut.-Col. commanding Foreign Service Unit of Berkshire Yeomanry. A Unionist Whip from 1911. A Unionist, in favour of small ownerships of land. Unsuccessfully contested the Abingdon division of Berkshire in 1906; elected there in Jan. 1910 and sat until he accepted Chiltern Hundreds in 1916. Dept. Assistant Adjutant-Gen. 1916. Died 1 Nov. 1922.   [1915]

HENDERSON, John Macdonald. Cambisgate, Wimbledon, London. The White House, Felixstowe. Reform. S. of William Henderson and Mary Macdonald, both of Aberdeen. B. 1846; m. Kate Mary, d. of Thomas Francis Robins, Esq., of London. Educ. at Gordon's Schools, and Marischal Coll., Aberdeen. A Barrister-at-Law and Fellow of the Institute of Chartered Accountants. Director of Thomas Bolton and Sone Limited, the Great North of Scotland Railway, the Lancashire United Tramways

Company, and other companies. J.P. for Surrey and Suffolk. A Liberal. Unsuccessfully contested Essex E. in Oct. 1900. Elected for W. Aberdeenshire in 1906 and sat until defeated in Aberdeenshire Central in 1918. Died 20 Nov. 1922. [1918]

HENEAGE, Rt. Hon. Edward. Hainton Hall, Lincolnshire. Brooks's. Eld. s. of George Fieschi Heneage, Esq., of Hainton Hall, Lincolnshire (who represented Lincoln for many years), by Frances, d. of Michael Tasburgh, Esq., of Burghwallis, near Doncaster, Co. Yorkshire. B. at Hainton Hall 1840; m. 1864, Lady Eleanor Cecilia, youngest d. of the 2nd Earl of Listowel. Educ. at Eton. Entered the 1st Life Guards Aug. 1857 as Sub-Lieut., and retired July 1863. In Feb. 1886 was appointed Chancellor of the Duchy of Lancaster and Vice-President of the Committee of Council on Agriculture; resigned Apr. 1886. A Magistrate and Dept.-Lieut. for Lincolnshire; also High Steward of Grimsby, and a Board of Trade Commissioner of the Humber Conservancy. Patron of 5 livings. A Liberal Unionist, in favour of complete local self-government by means of Co. Boards, and a thorough reform of the land laws, but opposed to disestablishment. Sat for Lincoln as a Liberal July 1865 to Dec. 1868 when he retired; unsuccessfully contested Great Grimsby 1874 but sat for Great Grimsby from Apr. 1880 to June 1892; became a Liberal Unionist at the election of July 1886. Having been unsuccessful at the general election of 1892 he was re-elected for Great Grimsby in Mar. 1893 and sat until defeated in 1895. PC. 1886. Created 1st Baron Heneage 1896; Chairman of Liberal Unionist Council 1893-98. Owner of 10,800 acres. Died 10 Aug. 1922. [1895]

HENNESSY, Sir John Pope, F.G.S., F.R.A.S., K.C.M.G. 2 Harcourt Buildings, Temple, London. Ballymacmoy House, Kilavullen. S. of John Hennessy, Esq., of Ballyhennessy, Co. Kerry, and Elizabeth, d. of Henry Casey, Esq., of Cork. B. 1834 in Cork. Unmarried. Educ. at St. Vincent's Seminary, Cork, and at Queen's University, Ireland. Called to the bar at the Inner Temple 1861. Gov. of Labuan from 1867-71, of Gold Coast from 1872-73, of the Bahamas from 1873-74, of the Windward Islands from 1875-76, of Hong Kong from 1876-82, and of Mauritius from 1882-89. Created K.C.M.G. in 1880.

Author. A Conservative, and a supporter generally of Lord Derby; said he would support a "practical system of tenant-right"; opposed to every form of "Mixed Education." First elected for King's Co. in May 1859 and sat until he was defeated in 1865. Unsuccessfully contested Co. Wexford in Nov. 1866. Elected as an Anti-Parnellite Nationalist for N. Kilkenny on 22 Dec. 1890 and sat until his death on 7 Oct. 1891. [1865]

HENRY, Sir Charles Solomon, Bart. Continued in House after 1918: full entry in Volume III.

HENRY, Denis Stanislaus. Continued in House after 1918: full entry in Volume III.

HENRY, Mitchell. Strathedon House, Hyde Park, London. Kylemore Castle, Galway. Reform, Devonshire, Kildare Street, Dublin, and County, Galway. S. of Alexander Henry, Esq., (who sat for S. Lancashire before its division), by Elizabeth, d. of Henry Brush, Esq., of Dromore, Co. Down. B. at Ardwick, near Manchester 1826; m. Margaret, d. of George Vaughan, Esq., of Quilly House, Dromore, (she died 1874). Educ. privately, and at University Coll., London. Commenced practice as a Consulting Surgeon in London 1848, and became Surgeon to Middlesex Hospital. A Fellow of the Royal Coll. of Surgeons, England, and of various learned societies; relinquished the medical profession in 1862, and became a Partner in the mercantile firm of Messrs. A. and S. Henry and Company, of Manchester, Huddersfield, etc. A Dept.-Lieut. for Middlesex, and a Magistrate for Middlesex and Westminster, and for Co. Galway. Author of several Medical Papers. A Liberal, voted with the Home Rule party on Mr. Parnell's motion on the Queen's speech, Jan. 1881; in favour of local self-government in all parts of the United Kingdom. Unsuccessfully contested Woodstock in July 1865, and Manchester in Nov. 1867 and again in Nov. 1868. Sat for the Co. of Galway from 1871 until 1885. Sat for the Blackfriars and Hutchesontown division of Glasgow from Nov. 1885 until defeated in 1886 standing as a Liberal Unionist. High Sheriff of Galway from 1888-89. Died 22 Nov. 1910. [1886]

HERBERT, Hon. Aubrey Nigel Henry Molyneux. Continued in House after 1918: full entry in Volume III.

HERBERT, Maj.-Gen. Sir Ivor John Caradoc, Bart. Llanarth Court, Raglan, Monmouthshire. Llanover, Abergavenny, Monmouthshire. 9 Great Stanhope Street, London. Travellers', Marlborough, and National Liberal. S. of J.A.E. Herbert, Esq., Dept.-Lieut. of Llanarth, and Hon. Augusta, d. of 1st Baron Llanover. B. 15 July 1851 at Llanarth Court; m. 1873, Hon. Albertina Denison, d. of 1st Baron Londesborough. Educ. at St. Mary's Coll. (R.C.) Oscott. Entered the Grenadier Guards 1870; Col. 1889; local Maj.-Gen. 1890-95; Brigade-Maj. of Guards 1882-83; Commandant School of Instruction for Auxiliary Forces 1886; Military Attaché at St. Petersburg 1886-90; commanded Canadian local forces 1890-95; Assistant Adjutant-Gen. Home District 1898-99; served in Egypt 1882, Soudan 1884-85, and was Assistant Adjutant-Gen. in S. Africa 1899-1901; retired with rank of Maj.-Gen. 1908. Honorary Maj.-Gen. in Canadian Force and Honorary Col. 3rd Battalion Monmouthshire Regiment; C.B. 1890; C.M.G. 1895. Created Bart. 1907. Had orders of Red Eagle, Crown of Italy, Legion of Honour, and Medjidie. Lord-Lieut. of Monmouthshire from 1913. A Liberal. Elected for S. Monmouthshire in 1906 and sat until created Baron Treowen in June 1917. Died 18 Oct. 1933. [1917]

HERBERT, Hon. Sidney. Herbert House, Belgrave Square, London. Hillingdon Place, Uxbridge. 2nd s. of the Rt. Hon. Sidney Herbert (created Baron Herbert of Lea), by Elizabeth, d. of Maj.-Gen. Charles Ashe à Court, C.B., of Amington Hall, Warwickshire. B. 1853; m. 1877, Lady Beatrix Louisa, d. of the 2nd Earl of Durham. Educ. at Eton and at Oxford, where he graduated B.A. 1875. Was raised to the rank of an Earl's son by royal warrant on the succession of his brother to the Earldom of Pembroke in 1862. A Lord of the Treasury from June 1885 to Jan. 1886, and again from Aug. 1886 to Aug. 1892. A Conservative. Sat for Wilton from Feb. 1877 to the dissolution of 1885. At the general election of 1885 he stood for S. Wiltshire, but was beaten by Sir Thomas F. Grove. Returned for Croydon Jan. 1886 and sat until he succeeded as Earl of Pembroke in May 1895. PC. 1895; G.C.V.O. 1896. Lord Steward 1895-1905. Died 30 Mar. 1913. [1895]

HERBERT, Thomas Arnold. 12 Kensington Park Gardens, London. 5 New Court, Lincoln's Inn, London. Wymers, Marlow. Reform, and National Liberal. S. of Professor T.M. Herbert, of Lancashire Independent Coll., and Maria, d. of Thomas Minshall, Esq., of Oswestry. B. 1 Sept. 1863 at Bowdon, Cheshire. Educ. at the Mill Hill School, Owen's Coll., Manchester, and St. John's Coll., Cambridge; Double 1st in Classics and Law. A Barrister, called 1889, and practised at the Chancery bar. J.P. for Buckinghamshire. Author of *The Law of Prescription.* A Liberal. Elected for the Wycombe division of Buckinghamshire in 1906 and sat until defeated in Jan. 1910. K.C. 1913. Died 22 Nov. 1940. [1909]

HERMON-HODGE, Col. Sir Robert Trotter. Wyfold Court, Reading. White's, Carlton, Pratt's, and Cavalry. S. of George William Hodge, Esq., and Sarah Eliza (née Green). B. at Newcastle-on-Tyne 1851; m. 1877, Frances Caroline, only d. and heiress of Edward Hermon, Esq., MP. Educ. at Clifton Coll., and Worcester Coll., Oxford; M.A. At one time Officer Commanding Queen's Own Oxfordshire Hussars; Co. Alderman and J.P. for Oxfordshire; P.P.J.G.W. Mason; Bart. 1902. Assumed the name of Hermon-Hodge in 1903. A Conservative. Unsuccessfully contested the Accrington division of Lancashire in 1885, elected there in 1886 and sat until 1892 in which year he moved The Address, but was defeated in 1892 and 1893. Elected for the Henley division of Oxfordshire in 1895 and sat until defeated in 1906. Sat for Croydon from 1909 until he retired Dec. 1910. Again elected for the Henley division of Oxfordshire 20 June 1917 and sat until he retired in 1918. Created Baron Wyfold in 1919. Died 3 June 1937. [1918]

HERVEY, Lord Francis. 3 Spring Gardens, London. Cranesden, Mayfield, Sussex. Carlton, United University, and Constitutional. 4th s. of the 2nd Marq. of Bristol, by Katherine Isabella, d. of the 5th Duke of Rutland. B. at Ickworth, Suffolk 1846. Educ. at Eton, and Balliol Coll., Oxford. At Eton he obtained the Newcastle Scholarship, and at Oxford took a 1st class in classical moderations. Was called to the bar at Lincoln's Inn 1872, and became a Fellow of Hertford Coll., Oxford in 1874. On the London School Board for Finsbury 1876-79. A J.P. for Suffolk. A Conservative.

Sat for Bury St. Edmunds from 1874 until defeated in 1880. Re-elected for Bury St. Edmunds 1885 and 1886 and sat until appointed a Civil Service Commissioner in Aug. 1892. Became First Civil Service Commissioner 1907; retired 1909. Died 10 Jan. 1931. [1892]

HERVEY, Capt. Frederick William Fane. 20 Eaton Place, London. Ickworth Lodge, Bury St. Edmunds. Naval & Military, and Marlborough. S. of Lord Augustus H.C. Hervey, and Marianna Hodneth, widow of Ashton Benyon, Esq. B. 8 Nov. 1863 at Dresden; m. 1896, Dora, d. of G.E. Wythers, Esq., of Copped Hall, Epping. Educ. at Tonbridge School, Eastman's Royal Naval Academy, and on H.M.S. *Britannia*. Entered the navy 1877; promoted Capt. 1901. Heir presumptive to the Marq. of Bristol. A Conservative, in favour of Tariff Reform. Elected for Bury St. Edmunds in 1906 and sat until he succeeded his uncle as 4th Marq. of Bristol in 1907. Retired as Rear-Admiral 1911. Chairman West Suffolk County Council 1915-34. President Institute of Naval Architects 1911-16. Owned 32,000 acres. Died 24 Oct. 1951. [1907]

HEWART, Rt. Hon. Sir Gordon. Continued in House after 1918: full entry in Volume III.

HEWINS, William Albert Samuel. 98 St. George's Square, London. Bullingham Manor, Nr. Hereford. Carlton. S. of Samuel Hewins, Esq. B. 11 May 1865 near Wolverhampton; m. Margaret, d. of James Slater, Esq., J.P. of Bescot Hall, Staffordshire. Educ. at Wolverhampton Grammar School, and Pembroke Coll., Oxford; M.A. Was Director of London School of Economics 1895-1903, Teacher of Modern Economic History in University of London 1902-03; Tooke Professor of Economic Science and Statistics at King's Coll. 1897-1903; member of Senate of University of London 1900-03, Secretary of the Tariff Commission 1903-17, Under-Secretary of State for the Colonies 1917-19. Wrote numerous works and articles on Economics and Political Economy including *Trade in Balance* (1924), *Empire Restored* (1927), and *The Apologia of an Imperialist* (1929), also articles on Economics and Protection in the Encyclopeadia Britannica, 1929. A Unionist. Unsuccessfully contested the Shipley division of Yorkshire in Jan.

1910 and the Middleton division of Lancashire S.E. in Dec. 1910 and Aug. 1911. Elected for Hereford in Mar. 1912 and sat until he retired in 1918. Unsuccessfully contested W. Swansea in 1922, 1923 and 1924. Died 17 Nov. 1931. [1918]

HIBBERT, Sir Henry Flemming. Dalegarth, Chorley, Lancashire. Constitutional, and Carlton. S. of Isaac Hibbert, Esq., of Chorley, and Martha, d. of Samuel Flemming, Esq. B. 4 Apr. 1850 at Chorley; m. 1883, Marion, d. of Ernest Reuss, Esq., of Victoria Park, Manchester. Educ. at Hutton and Chorley Grammar Schools. A Flour Merchant. Chairman of Education Committee of Lancashire County Council. Chairman of Education Committees of County Councils Association. Vice-Chairman of Lancashire County Council. Mayor of Chorley 1889-91. Initiated the commerical mission to China sent by Blackburn Chamber of Commerce. One of the founders of the Fair Trade League; member of Senate of Liverpool University and Manchester University. LL.D. (Victoria); member of Consultative Committee of Board of Education; member of Agricultural Education Conference; member of the Committee on Science in the Educational System of Great Britain; Freeman of the City of London. J.P., Dept.-Lieut. and Co. Alderman for Lancashire. F.R.G.S. A Unionist. Elected for the Chorley division of Lancashire in Feb. 1913 and sat until he retired in 1918. Knighted 1903. Created Bart. 1919. Died 15 Nov. 1927. [1918]

HIBBERT, Rt. Hon. Sir John Tomlinson. Treasury, Whitehall, London. Hampsfield, Grange-over-Sands. Reform. S. of Elijah Hibbert, and Elizabeth, d. of A. Hilton, Esq., of Oldham. B. 1824; m. 1st, 1847, Eliza Anne, d. of Andrew Schofield, Esq., 2ndly, 1878, Charlotte H., 4th d. of Admiral Warde, K.H. Educ. at Shrewsbury School, and St. John's Coll., Cambridge (B.A. 1847, M.A. 1851). Was called to the bar at the Inner Temple 1849. A PC. (1886), J.P. and Dept.-Lieut. for Lancashire, and Chairman of the Lancashire County Council. Was Parliamentary Secretary to the Local Government Board from 1872 to 1874, and having been re-appointed in 1880 he held the office till 1883, when he succeeded Earl Rosebery as Under Secretary of State for the Home Department (1883-84). Was Financial Secretary to the

Treasury 1884-85, Secretary to the Admiralty in Mr. Gladstone's short administration of 1886, and again Financial Secretary 1892; retired 1895. Created K.C.B. 1893. A Liberal, in favour of Home Rule for Ireland, the disestablishment of the church in Wales and Scotland, the legal limitation of the hours of labour, and the payment of members of Parliament. Unsuccessfully contested Cambridge 1857 and Oldham 1859. Sat for Oldham from 1862-74 when he was defeated. Unsuccessfully contested Blackburn 1875. Again returned for Oldham 1877 to 1886 when he was defeated; re-elected for Oldham July 1892 and sat until defeated in 1895. Chairman of Lancashire Co. Council and President of Co. Councils Association. Died 7 Nov. 1908.   [1895]

HICKMAN, Sir Alfred, Bart. 22 Kensington Palace Gardens, London. Wightwick, Nr. Wolverhampton. Carlton, and St. Stephen's. S. of George Rushbury Hickman, Esq., Ironmaster, of The Moat, Tipton, Staffordshire, and Mary, his wife. B. 1830 at Tipton; m. 1850, Lucy Owen, d. of William Smith, Esq., Civil Engineer of Portsea. Educ. at King Edward's School, Birmingham. An Ironmaster from 1848. A Dept.-Lieut. and J.P. for Staffordshire. Member of the Advisory Committee of the Board of Trade, the Council of the Mining Association of Great Britain, and of the Iron and Steel Institute; President of the British Iron Trade Association, Chairman of Alfred Hickman Limited, and of the S. Staffordshire Railway and Canal Freighters' Association. Knighted in 1891; created Bart. 1903. A Conservative. Unsuccessfully contested Wolverhampton 1880; was elected for the W. division of Wolverhampton in 1885, lost the seat at the general election 1886; re-elected in 1892 and sat until defeated in 1906. Died 11 Mar. 1910.   [1905]

HICKMAN, Brigadier-Gen. Thomas Edgecombe, C.B. Continued in House after 1918: full entry in Volume III.

HICKS-BEACH, Rt. Hon. Sir Michael Edward, Bart. Coln St. Aldwin's, Fairford, Gloucestershire. Carlton, and Athenaeum. Eld. s. of Sir Michael Hicks-Beach (8th Bart.), who sat for E. Gloucestershire in 1854, by Harriett Vittoria, d. of John Stratton, Esq., of Farthinghoe Lodge, Northamptonshire. B.

in Portugal Street, London 1837; m. 1st, 1864, Caroline Susan, eld. d. of J.H. Elwes, Esq. (she died 1865); 2ndly, 1874, Lady Lucy Catherine, 3rd d. of the 3rd Earl Fortescue. Educ. at Eton, and at Christ Church, Oxford, where he graduated B.A. 1858, M.A. 1861, and was placed in the 1st Class Law and Modern History at the Final examination July 1858. Was Parliamentary Secretary to the Poor Law Board from Feb. till Dec. 1868, with the exception of a few weeks during which he was Under Secretary for the Home Department. Chief Secretary for Ireland from Feb. 1874 to Feb. 1878, and again 1886; retired 1887; Secretary of State for the Colonies 1878 to 1880; President Board of Trade 1888-92. Chancellor of the Exchequer 1885 to 1886, 1895-1902. Was Church Estates Commissioner and a Dept.-Lieut. of Gloucestershire and Lord High Steward of Gloucester. Chairman of the S. Wales and Monmouthshire Coal Conciliation Board. A Conservative. Sat for E. Gloucestershire 1864-85, and for W. Bristol from 1885 until he retired in Jan. 1906. Leader of the House of Commons 1885-86; Father of the House of Commons 1901-06. Succeeded as Bart. 1854; PC. 1874; created Visct. St. Aldwyn 1906 and Earl St. Aldwyn 1915. Died 30 Apr. 1916.   [1905]

HICKS-BEACH, Hon. Michael Hugh. See QUENINGTON, Michael Hugh Hicks-Beach, Visct.

HICKS-BEACH, William Frederick. Witcombe Park, Gloucester. Junior Carlton. S. of Sir M.H. Hicks-Beach, MP, 8th Bart., and Harriet Vittoria, d. of J. Stratton, Esq., of Farthinghoe, Northamptonshire. B. at Williamstrap Park, Gloucestershire 1841; m. 1865, Elizabeth Caroline, d. of T.T. Drake, Esq., of Shardeloes; 2ndly, 1903, Susan, d. of Admiral H. Christian, M.V.O. Educ. at Eton, and Christ Church, Oxford. J.P. for Gloucestershire; Co. Alderman; Chairman of the Cheltenham Board of Guardians and Rural District Council from 1884; Chairman of Co. Public Health Committee, of Insurance Committee, of Diocesan Board of Finance, and of Cheltenham Conservative Association; Vice-President of Tewkesbury Conservative Association. A Conservative. Elected for the Tewkesbury division of Gloucestershire in May 1916 and sat until he retired in 1918. Died 7 Sept. 1923. [1918]

HIGGINBOTTOM, Samuel Wasse. African Chambers, Old Hall Street, Liverpool. Elsinmore, Claughton, Birkenhead. Carlton, and Constitutional. S. of Mr. Higginbottom, of Stalybridge, near Manchester. B. 1853. A Colliery Proprietor and Shipowner, and Director of many companies. Member of the Liverpool City Council, and Chairman of the Electric Lighting and Powers Committees. One of the promoters of the Church Discipline Bill. A Conservative. Sat for the W. Derby division of Liverpool from Sept. 1900 until his death 27 Dec. 1902. [1902]

HIGGINS, Clement. 5 Trebovir Road, South Kensington, London. Reform. S. of William M. Higgins, Esq., of Wrexham, Denbighshire, and Mary, his wife, née Waynman. B. in London 1844; m. 1870, Augusta, d. of Richard Wright, Esq., of West Bank, near Mansfield. Educ. at a private school, and Downing Coll., Cambridge; Foundation Scholar, B.A. 1869, M.A. 1873. Was called to the bar at the Inner Temple 1871, and joined the N. Wales, Chester, and Glamorganshire Circuit; appointed Recorder of Birkenhead 1882; Q.C. in 1886. Author of Higgins *Digest of Patent Cases, On Pollution and Obstruction of Watercourses*, etc. A Fellow of the Chemical Society, and a member of the Physical Society. A Liberal, in favour of Home Rule for Ireland, village councils, etc. Unsuccessfully contested Shropshire N. in July 1886. Sat for mid Norfolk from July 1892 until he accepted Chiltern Hundreds in Apr. 1895. He joined the Liberal Unionists in Mar. 1895. Died 4 Dec. 1916. [1895]

HIGGINS, T. A Nationalist. Returned in 1906 for the N. division of Galway, but died on 26 Jan. 1906 - one hour after midnight on the day after the poll. According to *The Times* obituary on 27 Jan. 1906.

HIGHAM, John Sharp. Birkdale, Southport. National Liberal. S. of Eli Higham, Esq., Cotton Spinner and Manufacturer. B. 14 June 1857 at Sabden, Lancashire; m. 1899, Pollie, d. of Sir W.P. Hartley, of Southport. Educ. privately. A Cotton Spinner and Manufacturer, Head of the firm of Highams Limited, of Accrington, Rochdale, and Manchester. Twelve years a member of the Lancashire County Council; fifteen years a member of Accrington Town Council; Mayor

1898-1900; a J.P. for Accrington. An advanced Liberal. Elected for the Sowerby division of the W. Riding of Yorkshire in July 1904 and sat until defeated in 1918. President of the United Kingdom Commercial Travellers' Association 1926-27. Died 5 Jan. 1932. [1918]

HILL, Rt. Hon. Alexander Staveley. 4 Queen's Gate, London. 13 King's Bench Walk, Temple, London. Oxley Manor, Staffordshire. United University, and Carlton. Only s. of Henry Hill, Esq., of Dunstall, near Wolverhampton, by Anne, d. of Luke Staveley, Esq., of the Co. of Yorkshire. B. at Dunstall 1825; m. 1st, 1864, Katharine Florence, d. of Miles Ponsonby, Esq., of Hale Hall, Cumberland (she died 1868); 2ndly, 1876, Mary Frances, d. of Francis Baird, Esq., of St. Petersburg and Queen's Gate, Kensington (she died 1897). Was educ. at King Edward's School, Birmingham, and Exeter Coll., and at St. John's Coll., Oxford, of which latter Coll. he was for many years a Fellow; a D.C.L. 1855, and Honorary LL.B. Toronto 1892. Was called to the bar at the Inner Temple Nov. 1851; appointed a Queen's Counsel 1868. Was one of the Examiners in the School of Law and Modern History at Oxford 1858, and Dept. High Steward of the University of Oxford 1874. Judge-Advocate of the Fleet and Counsel to the Admiralty Mar. 1875. Created PC 1892. A Conservative. Unsuccessfully contested Wolverhampton June 1861, and Coventry Mar. 1868. Sat for Coventry from Dec. 1868 to Feb. 1874; for Staffordshire W. from Feb. 1874 to Nov. 1885, and for the Kingswinford division of Staffordshire from Nov. 1885 until he retired in 1900. Recorder of Banbury 1866-1903. Died 28 June 1905. [1900]

HILL, Capt. Arthur. Savoy Mansions, Strand, London. The Kennel, Hadley, Barnet. Carlton, and New. Only s. of the Rt. Hon. Lord Arthur William Hill (s. of the 4th Marq. of Downshire), and his wife Annie, only child of Lieut.-Gen. Cookes. B. 1873. Educ. for the army. Entered the Militia, and was Capt. 5th Battalion Royal Irish Rifles. Served in S. Africa 1899-1902. J.P. for Co. Down. A Conservative. Represented W. Down from 1898 until he accepted Chiltern Hundreds in 1905. Died 27 June 1913. [1905]

HILL, Rt. Hon. Lord Arthur William. 53

Eaton Place, London. Carlton, and Junior Carlton. 2nd s. of 4th Marq. of Downshire. B. 1846; m. 1st, 1873, Anne Nisida, d. of Lieut.-Col. George Denham Cookes (she died 1874); 2ndly 1877, Anne, d. of J. Fortescue-Harrison, Esq., MP for Kilmarnock. Was Comptroller of H.M. Household 1885-86, 1886-92 and 1895-98, and a Conservative Whip in Lord Salisbury's Ministries. Lieut, 2nd Life Guards and Lieut.-Col. 2nd Middlesex Artillery; Honorary Col. 5th Battalion Royal Irish Rifles. Dept.-Lieut. and J.P. for Co. Down; J.P. for Berkshire; PC. 1885. A Unionist. Sat for Co. Down 1880-85, and W. Down 1885-98, when he resigned. Contested Belfast S. in Jan. 1906. Elected for Down W. Sept. 1907 and sat until he accepted Chiltern Hundreds Mar. 1908. Died 13 Jan. 1931. [1908]

HILL, Sir Clement Lloyd, K.C.B., K.C.M.G. 13 Chesterfield Street, Mayfair, London. Queen Hoo, Welwyn, Hertfordshire. Travellers', and St. James's. S. of the Rev. J. Hill (bro. of 2nd Visct. Hill), and Charlotte, d. of Hon. Thomas Kenyon. B. 5 May 1845; m. 1st, 1889, Charlotte, d. of Sir G. Denys (she died 1900); 2ndly, 1906, Muriel, d. of Colin G. Campbell, Esq. Educ. at Marlborough. Entered the Foreign Office in 1867; Secretary to Sir Bartle Frere's Mission to Zanzibar and Muscat 1872; Chargé d'Affaires at Munich 1876; member of slave Trade Commission 1881; Special Commissioner to Haiti 1886-87; Superintendent of African Protectorates 1900-05; K.C.M.G. 1887; K.C.B. 1905; F.R.G.S. A Unionist. Elected for Shrewsbury in 1906 and sat until his death 9 Apr. 1913. [1913]

HILL, Sir Edward Stock, K.C.B. Hazel Manor, Compton Martin, Nr. Bristol. Rookwood, Llandaff, Carlton. S. of Charles Hill, Esq., of Bristol. B. at Bedminster 1834; m. 1866, Fanny Ellen, d. of Lieut.-Gen. Tickell, C.B. Educ. at Bishop's Coll., Bristol, and abroad. From 1855 was a member of the firm of Charles Hill and Sons, Shipowners and Shipbuildings, of Bristol. Was Col. Commandant of the Glamorgan Artillery Volunteers from 1864; became President of the Chamber of Shipping of U.K. in 1881; and President of the Associated Chambers of Commerce 1888-91; was High Sheriff of Glamorganshire 1885, and J.P. for Glamorganshire and the borough of Cardiff;

was created C.B. 1881, and K.C.B. 1892; a Knight of the Swedish Order of Wasa. A Conservative Unionist. Unsuccessfully contested Bristol in 1885. Sat for Bristol S. from 1886 until he retired in 1900. Provincial Grand Master of Mask Freemasons for S. Wales from 1899. Died 18 Dec. 1902. [1900]

HILL, Lieut.-Col. Henry Staveley. See STAVELEY-HILL, Lieut.-Col. Henry Staveley.

HILL, Sir James, Bart. Wellwood, Bradford. Craigmore, Morecombe. National Liberal, and Reform. S. of William and Margaret Hill. B. 1849 at Harden, Yorkshire; m. 1875, Alice, d. of Joshua Knight, Esq. Educ. privately at Harden. A Wool Merchant at Bradford from 1891. Member of the Congregational Church, Allerton, Bradford, and for many years an active worker in that church. President of the Bradford Liberal Association from 1906; member of the National Liberal Federation from 1906; Lord Mayor of Bradford 1908-09. Created Bart. 1916. A Liberal. Elected for Bradford central in Jan. 1916 and sat until defeated in 1918. Died 17 Jan. 1936. [1918]

HILLIER, Alfred Peter. 20 Eccleston Square, London. Junior Carlton, and City Carlton. S. of Peter Playne Hillier, Esq., of Shortwood, Gloucestershire. B. 1858 at Shortwood, Gloucestershire; m. 1896, Ethel, d. of F.B. Brown, Esq., of Queenstown, South Africa. Educ. at King William's Coll., and Edinburgh University. Entered the medical profession in 1882, but later retired. M.D., C.M., and B.A. Consulting Physician London Open Air Sanatorium and a member of International Committee for Prevention of Tuberculosis. Was President of South African Medical Congress 1893, and a member of the Reform Committee in Johannesburg 1895-96; a Councillor of the Royal Colonial Institute. Author of *South African Studies, The Commonwealth, A Study of the Federal System of Political Economy*, and other works. A Unionist. Unsuccessfully contested Stockport in 1900, and S. Bedfordshire in 1906. Elected for N. Hertfordshire in Jan. 1910 and sat until his death 24 Oct. 1911. [1911]

HILLS, John Waller. Continued in House after 1918: full entry in Volume III.

HILL-WOOD, Sir Samuel Hill, Bart. Continued in House after 1918: full entry in Volume III.

HINCKES, Harry Tichborne. The Wood House, Tettenhall, Wolverhampton. Carlton. 3rd s. of John Davenport, Esq., of Westwood, Staffordshire, and Foxley, Herefordshire, by Charlotte, d. of George Coltman, Esq., of Hagnaby Priory, Lincolnshire. B. 1833; m. 1868, Georgina Henrietta, d. of Sir William Curtis, Bart., of Caynham Court, Shropshire. Educ. at Harrow, and Christ Church, Oxford. Changed his name to Hinckes 1890. Was called to the bar at the Inner Temple Nov. 1860. A Magistrate for Staffordshire and Chairman of the Wolstanton School Board from 1876. In 1872-73 he was Umpire of the Staffordshire Potteries Board of Arbitration. A Conservative, in favour of the formation of county boards. He was an unsuccessful candidate for Newcastle-under-Lyme in 1874, and at Stoke-upon-Trent 1876. Sat for Satffordshire N. from 1880 to 1885, and unsuccessfully contested the Leek division of Staffordshire in 1885. First returned for that division in July 1886 and sat until he retired in 1892. Died 19 Mar. 1895. [1892]

HINDLE, Frederick George. Thorncliffe, Darwen. National Liberal. S. of John Hindle, Esq., of Darwen. B. 15 Jan. 1848 at Darwen; m. 1876, Helen, d. of Thomas Gillibrand, Esq., of Hollins Grove House, Darwen. Educ. at Queen Elizabeth's Grammar School, Blackburn. A Solicitor, admitted 1870 (Clifford's Inn Prizeman), and Clerk to Darwen Borough Justices. Author of *The Legal Status of Licensed Victuallers.* A Liberal. Unsuccessfully contested the Darwen division of Lancashire in 1906; elected there in Jan. 1910 and sat until defeated in Dec. 1910. Died 1 Mar. 1925. [1910]

HINDS, John. Continued in House after 1918: full entry in Volume III.

HINGLEY, Sir Benjamin, Bart. Grand Hotel, London. Hatherton Lodge, Cradley, Worcestershire. S. of Noah Hingley, Esq., of Hatherton Lodge, Cradley. B. 1830. On his father's death in 1877 he became head of the firm of Messrs. Noah Hingley and Sons, Colliery Proprietors and Ironmasters, of Netherton and elsewhere. A Magistrate for Staffordshire and Dudley, and also Chairman of the S. Staffordshire Ironmasters' Association; Mayor of Dudley 1887-88. Baronetcy conferred 1893. A Liberal, he abstained from voting on Mr. Gladstone's Home Rule measure of 1886, but voted for the Bill of 1893. Unsuccessfully contested Dudley in May 1874. Sat for Worcestershire N. from 1885 until he retired in 1895. Died 13 May 1905. [1895]

HOARE, Edward Brodie. Tenchleys, Limpsfield, Surrey. Carlton, and St. Stephen's. S. of the Rev. Edward Hoare, Hon. Canon of Canterbury, and Vicar of Holy Trinity, Tunbridge Wells, and Maria Eliza, only d. of Sir Benjamin Collins Brodie, Bart. B. at Richmond, Surrey 1841; m. 1868, Katharine, D. of Admiral Sir W.E. Parry. Educ. at Tunbridge School, and Trinity Coll., Cambridge. Was a Partner in Barnett's Bank, and a Director of Lloyds's Bank Limited. Treasurer of the Hampstead Board of Guardians. A Conservative, opposed to the imposition of import duties on the food of the people, or on the raw materials of our manufacturers. Was an unsuccessful candidate for the Attercliffe division of Sheffield in Nov. 1885 and for Central Bradford in Apr. 1886. Sat for Hampstead from Feb. 1888 until he accepted Chiltern Hundreds in 1902. Died 12 Aug. 1911. [1901]

HOARE, Hugh Edward. 117, Piccadilly, London. Reform, and National Liberal. S. of Henry Hoare, Esq., Banker, of 37 Fleet Street, and Staplehurst, Kent, by Lady Mary, 3rd. d. of Charles, 2nd Earl of Romney. B. 1854 in London; m. 1886, eld. d. of James Wolfe Murray, Esq., of Cringletie, Peebles. Educ. at Eton, and Balliol Coll., Oxford. A Brewer, a member of the firm of Hoare and Company, Lower East Smithfield, and a Director of the New England and United States Brewing Companies. A Radical, in favour of Home Rule for Ireland, etc. Sat for W. Cambridgeshire (Chesterton division) from July 1892 until defeated in 1895; defeated again in 1900, and at Chelsea Dec. 1910. Died 15 July 1929. [1895]

HOARE, Sir Samuel, Bart. Sidestrand Hall, Norfolk. Athenaeum, and Carlton. Eld. s. of John Gurney Hoare, Esq., by Caroline, d. of Charles Barclay, Esq., of Bury Hill, Surrey. B. 1841; m. 1866, Katharine Louisa Hart, d. of Richard

Vaughan Davis, Esq. Educ. at Harrow, and Trinity Coll., Cambridge. A Partner in the banking house of Barnetts, Hoare and Company, and was a J.P. for Norfolk and Middlesex, and Lieut. for the City of London. Created Bart. 1899. A Conservative, opposed to Home Rule for Ireland. Was an unsuccessful candidate for Norfolk N. at the general election of 1885, but on Mr. Bullard, the Member for Norwich, being unseated in Mar. 1886 he was returned for the city without opposition on 7 Apr. 1886 and sat until he retired in 1906. Contested the same seat in Jan. 1910. Died 20 Jan. 1915. [1905]

HOARE, Sir Samuel John Gurney, Bart., C.M.G. Continued in House after 1918: full entry in Volume III.

HOBART, Sir Robert Henry. 54 Chester Square, London. Langdown, Hythe, Southampton. Travellers', and National Liberal. S. of Hon and Very Rev. H.L. Hobart, D.D., Dean of Windsor and Wolverhampton (s. of 3rd Earl of Buckinghamshire). B. 1836; m. 1869, Hon. Julia Trollope, d. of 1st Baron Kesteven. Educ. at Charterhouse School, and Trinity Hall, Cambridge; LL.B. In the Civil Service. Was Private Secretary to the Duke of Devonshire when Secretary of State for War, Postmaster-Gen., Chief Secretary for Ireland, and Secretary for India; Chief Secretary to four Secretaries for Scotland and Secretary to the Earl Marshal for the purposes of the Coronation of H.M. King Edward VII and Queen Alexandra; C.B. 1885; K.C.V.O. 1902. Dept.-Lieut. and J.P. for Middlesex; a J.P. for London and Hampshire. Appointed Official Verderer of New Forest 1907. A Liberal. Unsuccessfully contested the New Forest division of Hampshire in Dec. 1905; elected there in Jan. 1906 and sat until defeated in Jan. 1910. Created Bart. 1914. Died 4 Aug. 1928. [1909]

HOBHOUSE, Rt. Hon. Sir Charles Edward Henry, Bart. K2 Albany, Piccadilly, London. Monkton Farleigh, Bradford-on-Avon, Wiltshire. Brooks's. Eld. s. of Sir Charles Parry Hobhouse, Bart., and Lucy, eld. d. of Sir Thomas Turton, Bart. B. in Sussex 1862; m. Georgina Fleetwood, d. of George P. Fuller, Esq., of Neston Park, Corsham, MP for W. Wiltshire from 1885-95. Educ. at Eton, and Christ Church, Oxford, and Royal Military Coll.,

Sandhurst. A Lieut. 60th Rifles 1884, Capt. 7th Battalion King's Royal Rifles (Militia) 1896, Lieut.-Col. 6th Battalion Gloucester Regiment. A J.P. and County Councillor for Wiltshire; member of the Thames Conservancy Board; Church Estates Commissioner 1906-07; was under-Secretary for India 1907-08 and Financial Secretary to the Treasury 1908-11. Chancellor of the Duchy of Lancaster 1911-14. Postmaster-Gen. Feb 1914 to May 1915. Chairman of Select Committee on the wages of Postal Servants, and of the Royal Commission of Decentralization of Government in India. PC. 1909. Succeeded his father as 4th Bart. 30 Dec. 1916. A Liberal, in favour of a complete system of National Education, and of Disestablishment and Disendowment of State churches. Sat for E. Wiltshire from 1892-95, when he was defeated. Elected for E. Bristol in 1900 and sat until defeated in 1918. Unsuccessfully contested Buckingham in 1922. Died 26 June 1941. [1918]

HOBHOUSE, Rt. Hon. Henry. Hadspen House, Castle Cary, Somerset. Athenaeum. S. of Henry Hobhouse, Esq., J.P. (who was the s. of the Rt. Hon. Henry Hobhouse, Under Secretary of State at the Home Office 1817-27), by the Hon. Charlotte, d. of 3rd Lord Talbot De Malahide. B. 1854; m. 1880, Margaret, 7th d. of Richard Potter, Esq., J.P. Educ. at Eton, and Balliol Coll., Oxford; 1st class in Classics 1875, M.A. 1878. Was called to the bar in 1880, and practised as a Parliamentary Draftsman and Counsel. Appointed an Ecclesiastical Commissioner (unpaid) 1890, and a member of Consultative Committee to the Board of Education 1900. PC. 1902. A J.P. for Somerset, and Chairman of Somerset County Council 1904-24. A Liberal Unionist. Sat for E. Somerset from 1885 until he retired in 1906. Died 25 June 1937. [1905]

HODGE, Rt. Hon. John. Continued in House after 1918: full entry in Volume III.

HODGE, Col. Sir Robert Trotter Hermon-. See HERMON-HODGE, Col. Sir Robert Trotter.

HOGAN, James Francis. Montague Mansions, Great Russell Street, London. S. of Roderick Hogan, Esq., of Nenagh, Tipperary, and Mary McGrath, of the same place. B. at Nenagh 1855. While an infant his parents emigrated to Australia and settled near Melbourne. Educ. at St. Patrick's R.C. Coll., Melbourne. Entered the service of the Education Department of Victoria 1875, and in 1881 joined the staff of the *Melbourne Argus*, with which journal he remained connected until his departure for London in 1887. Was a founder and the first President of the Victorian Catholic Young Men's Society, and actively opposed the Victorian state system of secular education. Contributed to the *Melbourne Review*, the *Victorian Review*, the *Contemporary*, and other London reviews, and author of *An Australian Christmas Collection, The Irish in Australia, The Australian in London, The Lost Explorer, The Convict King, Robert Lowe, Viscount Sherbrooke, The Gladstone Colony*, and *The Sister Dominions*. From 1887 he was an extensive contributor to the London press, and wrote principally on colonial subjects. An Anti-Parnellite Home Ruler (Secretary to the Colonial party), and advocate of Imperial Federation. Sat for the mid division of Tipperary from Feb. 1893 until he retired in 1900. Died 9 Nov. 1924. [1900]

HOGAN, Michael H. 70 Doddington Grove, Kennington Park, London. Lisballyard, Rathcabbin, Birr, King's Co. B. 1853. A Tenant Farmer in Co. Tipperary. Vice-Chairman of Birr District Council and Dept.-Vice-Chairman of Board of Guardians. A Nationalist. Elected for N. Tipperary in 1906 and sat until he retired in Dec. 1910. [1910]

HOGG, David Cleghorn. Lissowen, Londonderry. National Liberal. S. of Robert Hogg, Esq. B. 1840 at Melrose; m. 1872, d. of George Cooke, Esq., of Ramelton. A member of the firm of Hogg and Mitchell, Shirtmakers, Londonderry. H.M. Lieut. for Co. of Derry from 1911. A Liberal. Elected for Londonderry city in Jan. 1913 and sat until his death 22 Aug. 1914. [1914]

HOGG, Sir James Macnaghten McGarel-, Bart., K.C.B. See McGAREL-HOGG, Sir James Macnaghten, Bart., K.C.B.

HOGG, Sir Lindsay, Bart. Rotherfield Hall, Sussex. Carlton, and Junior Carlton. S. of William Hogg, Esq., many years Hanseatic Consul at Shanghai, and Eliza S. (née Hickson). B. at Shanghai 1853; m. 1880, Alice, younger d. of John C. Cowley, Esq., of Heathfield, Addington, Surrey. Educ. at

Harrow. A J.P. and County Councillor for Sussex. A Conservative. Elected for the Eastbourne division of Sussex in 1900 and sat until defeated in 1906. Created Bart. 1905. Assumed name of Lindsay Lindsay-Hogg by Royal Licence in 1906. Died 25 Nov. 1923. [1905]

HOGGE, James Myles. Continued in House after 1918: full entry in Volume III.

HOHLER, Gerald Fitzroy. Continued in House after 1918: full entry in Volume III.

HOLBURN, John Goundry. Leith Walk, Edinburgh. B. 1843. A member of the Leith Town Council for several years, and a Tin-Plate Worker. A Liberal, in favour of Home Rule, etc. Sat for the N.W. division of Lanarkshire from July 1895 until his death 23 Jan. 1899. [1898]

HOLDEN, Sir Angus, Bart. Queen Anne's Mansions, St. James's Park, London. Nun Appleton, Bolton Percy, Yorkshire. Reform, and National Liberal. Eld. s. of Sir Isaac Holden, Bart., and Marion, d. of Angus Love, Esq., of Paisley. B. 1833 at Cullingworth, near Bradford; m. Margaret, d. of Daniel Illingworth, Esq., Bradford. Educ. at Wesley Coll., Sheffield, and Edinburgh University. A Manufacturer at Bradford; J.P. for Bradford (Mayor 1878 to 1881 and again in 1887); member of the Bradford School Board. A Liberal, in favour of Home Rule for Ireland, etc. Unsuccessfully contested Knaresborough 1884. Sat for Bradford E. from 1885 until defeated 1886. First elected for the Buckrose division of the E. Riding of Yorkshire 1892 and sat until he retired in 1900. Succeeded as Bart. 1897; created Baron Holden 1908. Died 25 Mar. 1912. [1900]

HOLDEN, Sir Edward Hopkinson, Bart. 5 Threadneedle Street, London. Reform, and National Liberal. B. 1848 near Heywood. Educ. at Wesleyan School, Summerseat and Owen's Coll., Manchester. Started as a Clerk in Manchester and County Bank, Bolton, joined the Birmingham and Midland Bank, became Gen. Manager in London, and later Chairman and Managing Director of the London City and Midland Bank. A Liberal. Unsuccessfully contested the Heywood division of Lancashire in 1900. Elected there in 1906 and sat until he retired in

Jan. 1910. Created Bart. 1909. Died 23 July 1919. [1909]

HOLDEN, Edward Thomas. Glenelg, Great Barr, Nr. Walsall. National Liberal. S. of Edward Holden, Esq., and his wife, Elizabeth Mason. B. at Walsall 1831; m. 1854, Caroline, eld. d. of Robert Glass, Esq., of Edinburgh. Educ. at Aldridge Grammar School and by private tuition. Was in business as a Currier, and was a member of the Walsall Town Council for 60 years, and at one-time Alderman. Served twice as Mayor, and also twice as Chairman of the School Board. A J.P. for Walsall, and for the Co. of Stafford, and Chairman of the local Liberal Association. A Liberal, in favour of Home Rule for Ireland and the other principal items in the "Advanced Liberal" programme. First returned for Walsall Aug. 1891 and sat until defeated in 1892. Knighted 1907. Died 13 Nov. 1926. [1892]

HOLDEN, Sir Isaac, Bart. Oakworth House, Keighley. Reform, and National Liberal. S. of Isaac Holden, Esq., of Greenends, Nent Head, Alston, Cumberland, by Mary, d. of Mr. Forrest, of Alston. B. at Hurlet, near Glasgow 1807; m. 1st, 1832, Marion, 2nd d. of Angus Love, Esq., of Paisley; 2ndly, 1850, Sarah, 2nd d. of John Sugden, Esq., of Dockroyd, near Keighley (she died 1890). A Manufacturer, owned works in Bradford, Yorkshire, and at Rheims and Roubaix, France. A J.P. and Dept.-Lieut. for the W. Riding of Yorkshire. Baronetcy conferred June 1893. A Liberal, and prepared to give a "hearty support" to Mr. Gladstone. Represented Knaresborough from July 1865 until he retired Nov. 1868; unsuccessfully contested the N. division of the W. Riding of Yorkshire Feb. 1872, and the E. division of that Riding at the general elections of 1868 and 1874. Sat for the N. division of the W. Riding of Yorkshire from 1882 to 1885, and for the Keighley division of Yorkshire from 1885 until he retired in 1895. Died 13 Aug. 1897. [1895]

HOLLAND, Rt. Hon. Sir Henry Thurstan, Bart., G.C.M.G. 65 Rutland Gate, London. Pine Wood, Witley, Godalming. Carlton, and Athenaeum. Eld. s. of Sir Henry Holland, 1st Bart. (physician in ordinary to the Queen, etc.), by his 1st wife, Emma Margaret, d. of James Caldwell, Esq., of Linley Wood,

Staffordshire. B. in London 1825; m. 1st, 1852, the youngest d. of Nathaniel Hibbert, Esq., of Munden House, Hertfordshire (she died 1855); 2ndly, 1858, Margaret Jean, eld. d. of Sir Charles E. Trevelyan, Bart., K.C.B. Educ. at Harrow, and Trinity Coll., Cambridge; graduated B.A. 1847. Was called to the bar in 1849 at the Inner Temple, of which he was elected a bencher Jan. 1881. Was legal adviser at the Colonial Office from Jan. 1867 to Feb. 1870. Was Assistant Under-Secretary of State for the Colonies from Mar. 1870 till Aug. 1874, when he resigned to enter Parliament. Succeeded as Bart. 1873. K.C.M.G. 1877; G.C.M.G. 1886; PC. 1885. Was appointed Financial Secretary of the Treasury 1885, and was subsequently Vice-President of the Committee of Council on Education 1885-86. Reappointed to the Vice-Presidency and became 4th Charity Commissioner 1886, and gave up these posts on being appointed Secretary of State for the Colonies, with a seat in the Cabinet, Jan. 1887 which he remained until 1892. In 1887 he was also appointed an Ecclesiastical Commissioner. A Dept.-Lieut. of Middlesex. A Conservative, strongly opposed any Measure tending to affect injuriously the Established Church; voted against the third reading of the Irish Land Bill 1881. Sat for Midhurst from Sept. 1874 to Nov. 1885, and for Hampstead from Nov. 1885 until created Baron Knutsford in 1888, and Visct. Knutsford in 1895. Died 29 Jan. 1914. [1887]

HOLLAND, Hon. Lionel Raleigh. 15 Savile Row, Bond Street, London. Carlton, Bachelors', White's, and Beefsteak. 4th s. of Visct. Knutsford, G.C.M.G., by a d. of Sir Charles Trevelyan, Bart. B. 1865. Educ. at Harrow and King's Coll., Cambridge. Was called to the bar, and a Partner in the publishing house of Edward Arnold. A member of the London Co. Council (Westminster 1895-98), and was Honorary Secretary London Municipal Society. A Conservative, and strong advocate of Social Reforms, such as a full and generous Employers' Liability Bill, Old Age Pensions, facilities for working-classes to purchase their houses, and restrictions to the immigration of destitute aliens. Unsuccessfully contested N.E. Suffolk in July 1892. Sat for the Bow and Bromley division of Tower Hamlets from July 1895 until he accepted Chiltern Hundreds in 1899. Contested Romford division of Essex in 1900 and Edgbaston division of Birmingham in 1906 as a Liberal. Worked for British Red Cross 1914-15. Died 25 May 1936.   [1899]

HOLLAND, Sir William Henry, Bart. 61 Queen's Gate, London. Reform, and National Liberal. Younger s. of William Holland, Esq., J.P., of Manchester. B. 1849 at Manchester; m. 1874, May, eld. d. of James Lund, Esq., Dept.-Lieut. of Malsis Hall, near Bradford. A Cotton and Worsted Spinner at Manchester. Chairman Fine Cotton Spinners Association Limited, Director Williams Deacon's Bank; President Associated Chambers Commerce 1904-07; Commissioner Paris Exhibition 1900; President Manchester Chamber of Commerce 1896-98; member of Indian Currency Committee 1898; of Board of Trade Advisory Committee on Commercial Intelligence from 1900; and of the Joint Stock Companies Committee 1905. Temporary Chairman of Ways and Means. Knighted 1902. Created Bart. 1907. Officer of the Order of Leopold. A Liberal. Sat for Salford N. from 1892-95, when he was defeated. Sat for the Rotherham division of Yorkshire from 1899 until he accepted Chiltern Hundreds in Feb. 1910. Created 1st Baron Rotherham 18 July 1910. Died 26 Dec. 1927.   [1909]

HOLLOWAY, George. 30 Bina Gardens, London. Farm Hill House, Stroud. Carlton. S. of Adam Holloway, Esq., of Stratfield Turgiss, Hampshire. B. 1825; m. 1850, Anne, youngest d. of Charles Strudwick, Esq., of Reading, Berkshire. Educ. at Sherfield Grammar School. A Manufacturer in Stroud. Wrote on *Civilization* (1867), and a prize essay on Benefit Associations (1877). A Conservative. Unsuccessfully contested the borough of Stroud twice in 1874 (Feb. and May), and in 1880, and also unsuccessfully contested the Stroud division of Gloucestershire at the general election of 1885. First returned for that divison in July 1886 and sat until defeated in July 1892. Died 20 Aug. 1892.   [1892]

HOLMES, Daniel Turner. House of Commons, London. National Liberal. S. of James Holmes, Esq. B. 23 Feb. 1863 at Irvine; m. 1896, Margaret, d. of Provost Eadie of Paisley. Educ. at London University; B.A. 1st class honours; Sorbonne, Paris, and University of Geneva. Was engaged in scholastic work up to 1900 and from then in lecturing and literature.

Author of *French Essays on British Poets, Teaching of Modern Languages, Literary Tours in Scotland, A Scot in France and Switzerland*, etc. A Liberal. Elected for the Govan division of Lanarkshire in Dec. 1911 and sat until defeated in the Govan division of Glasgow in 1918. Contested S. Edinburgh 9 Apr. 1920. Died 7 Apr. 1955.   [1918]

HOLMES, Rt. Hon. Hugh. 29 Bury Street, St. James's, London. 3 Fitzwilliam Place, Dublin. Carlton, Garrick, Kildare Street, and University. S. of William Holmes, Esq., of Dungannon, Co. Tyrone. B. 1840; m. 1869, Olivia, d. of J.W. Moule, Esq., of the Hawthorns, Sydenham. Educ. at Trinity Coll., Dublin. Called to the Irish bar in 1865, and became Q.C. in 1877. A J.P. for Co. Tyrone, appointed Law Adviser to the Irish Government in 1877, and was Solicitor-Gen. for Ireland in Lord Beaconsfield's administration from 1878 to 1880. PC. 1885. Attorney-Gen. for Ireland July 1885-Jan. 1886; re-appointed Attorney-Gen. in Aug. 1886; retired June 1887. A Conservative. Sat for Dublin University from June 1885 until appointed Judge of Irish High Court in June 1887. Lord Justice of Appeal (Ireland) 1897-1915. Died 19 Apr. 1916.   [1887]

HOLT, Richard Durning. 54 Ullet Road, Liverpool. 63 Lowndes Square, London. Reform, and National Liberal. S. of Robert D. Holt, Esq., of Liverpool, and Lawrencina, d. of Richard Potter, Esq., of Standish House, Gloucestershire. B. 13 Nov. 1868 in Liverpool; m. 1897, Eliza, d. of John Wells, Esq., of New York. Educ. at Winchester Coll., and New Coll., Oxford. A Shipowner, a Partner in the firm of Alfred Holt and Company. A member of Mersey Docks and Harbour Board, and a J.P. for Lancashire. A Radical. Unsuccessfully contested W. Derby division of Liverpool in 1903 and 1906. First elected for the Hexham division of Northumberland in Mar. 1907 and sat until defeated in Eccles in 1918. Unsuccessfully contested Rossendale in 1922 and Cumberland N. in 1923, 1924, 1926 and 1929. Chairman of Mersey Docks and Harbour Board from 1927; Chairman of Elder Dempster Lines Limited from 1932. Created Bart. 1935. Died 22 Mar. 1941.   [1918]

HOOPER, Arthur George. Selborne, Dudley. National Liberal. S. of G.W.F. Hooper, Esq., of Birmingham. B. 30 Jan.

1857 at Birmingham; m. 1881, Fanny, d. of the Rev. J. Shillito, of Birmingham. Educ. at King Edward's School, Birmingham. A Solicitor in Birmingham; Gov. of Dudley Grammar School, a J.P. for Worcestershire, a Director of London, Liverpool, and Globe Insurance Company. A Liberal. Elected for Dudley in 1906 and sat until defeated in Dec. 1910. Died 28 Apr. 1940.   [1910]

HOOPER, John. 27 Cork Street, Cork. B. in Cork 1846. At the age of fifteen he joined the staff of the *Cork Herald*. Was also connected with the *Freeman's Journal*. In 1883 he was elected Alderman for the S. ward, Cork. An "Irish Nationalist." Sat for S.E. division of the Co. of Cork from the general election of 1885 until he accepted Chiltern Hundreds in May 1889. Editor of the *Cork Herald* and was imprisoned for publishing reports of suppressed branches of the National League. Editor of the *Evening Telegraph* (Dublin) from 1892 until his death 20 Nov. 1897.   [1889]

HOPE, Harry. Continued in House after 1918: full entry in Volume III.

HOPE, James Fitzalan. Continued in House after 1918: full entry in Volume III.

HOPE, Maj. Sir John Augustus, Bart. Continued in House after 1918: full entry in Volume III.

HOPE, John Deans. Continued in House after 1918: full entry in Volume III.

HOPE, Thomas. 26a North Audley Street, London. Bridge Castle, Bathgate, N.B. Carlton, Constitutional, and E.I. United Service. 2nd s. of the Hon. Charles Hope (3rd s. of the 4th Earl of Hopetoun) and Lady Isabella H. Hope (eld. d. of the 5th Earl of Selkirk). B. 1848. Educ. at Eton. Entered the army as Cornet 18th Hussars Mar. 1869; Bombay Staff Corps 1873; Capt. 1881. Held several posts in the Government of India from 1874 to 1886, when he resigned his commission. Later Honorary Lieut.-Col. Volunteers. A Conservative and Unionist. Contested Linlithgowshire 1885, 1886, and again in 1892. First returned for Linlithgowshire in June 1893 and sat until defeated in 1895. Died 28 Mar. 1925.   [1895]

HOPE, William Henry Bateman. East-wood, East Harptree, Bristol. Reform. S. of W.C. Hope, Esq., of Bath, and Emma Byrom. B. 1865 at Bath; m. 1890, Agnes Lucy, d. of J.L. Stothert, Esq., of Bath. Educ. at Eton, and Trinity Coll., Cambridge. Called to the bar 1891. A member of Somerset County Council 1898-1914. A Liberal. Unsuccessfully contested N. Somerset in 1900. Elected there in 1906 and sat until he retired in Jan. 1910. Recorder of Wells 1907-15. Died Dec. 1919.   [1909]

HOPKINSON, Sir Alfred. Continued in House after 1918: full entry in Volume III.

HOPKINSON, Austin. Continued in House after 1918: full entry in Volume III.

HOPWOOD, Charles Henry. 2 St. John's Wood Road, London. Reform, National Liberal, and Albemarle. S. of John Stephen S. Hopwood, Esq., of Montagu Place, and Chancery Lane, Solicitor, by Mary Ann, d. of John Toole, Esq., of Dublin. B. in London 1829. Unmarried. Educ. at Mr. Mullen's private school, Acton, and King's Coll., London. Called to the bar at the Middle Temple June 1853, and joined the Northern Circuit. Made a Queen's Counsel Feb. 1874. Elected a bencher of the Middle Temple Feb. 1876. Issued Registration Cases, Hopwood and Philbrick, etc. Appointed Recorder of Liverpool 1886. An Advanced Liberal, in favour of Home Rule for Ireland, and of short sentences of imprisonment. Sat for Stockport from 1874 until defeated in 1885. Unsuccessfully contested the Middleton division of Lancashire in July 1886. Elected there in July 1892 and sat until defeated in 1895. Died 14 Oct. 1904. [1895]

HORNBY, Sir William Henry, Bart. Pleasington Hall, Blackburn. Carlton. S. of William Henry Hornby, Esq., of Blackburn, and Poole Hall, Nantwich, at one time a Member for Blackburn. B. at Blackburn 1841; m. 1887, Letitia Grace Clayton-Browne, niece of the Bishop of Winchester. Educ. privately. Head of the firm of W.H. Hornby and Company, Cotton Spinners and Manufacturers, and Director of the Lancashire and Yorkshire Railway Company. A J.P. and Dept.-Lieut. for Lancashire. Received the Freedom of Blackburn 1903. Created Bart. 1899. A Conservative. Sat for Blackburn from 1886 until he retired in Jan. 1910. Died 22 Oct. 1928. [1909]

HORNE, Rev. Charles Silvester. 20 Ampthill Square, London. S. of Charles Horne, Esq., M.A., of Newport, Shropshire. B. 1865 at Cuckfield, Sussex; m. 1892, Katharine, d. of Rt. Hon. Sir H. Cozens-Hardy, Master of the Rolls. Educ. at Newport, Shropshire Grammar School, Glasgow University, and Mansfield Coll., Oxford. A Congregational Minister and Superintendent of Whitfield's Central Mission, Tottenham Court Road, from 1903; Chairman of Congregational Union of England and Wales 1910. Author of *Story of the L.M.S.*, *History of the Free Churches*, *Life of David Livingstone*, and other works. A Liberal. Elected for Ipswich Jan. 1910 and sat until his death 2 May 1914. [1914]

HORNE, William Edgar. Continued in House after 1918: full entry in Volume III.

HORNER, Andrew Long. 34 Fitzwilliam Place, Dublin. Carlton, and Constitutional. S. of J.H. Horner, Esq., of Limavady, Co. Londonderry. B. 1864 at Limavady, Co. Londonderry; m. 1901, Annie, d. of John Robb, Esq., J.P., of Lisnabreeny House, Belfast. Educ. at Foyle Coll., Londonderry, and Queen's Coll., Belfast. Was called to the Irish bar 1887; K.C. 1904. Bencher of King's Inns 1912. A Liberal Unionist. Unsuccessfully contested S. Tyrone in 1906; elected for S. Tyrone in Jan. 1910 and sat until his death 26 Jan. 1916. [1915]

HORNER, Frederick William. 2 Charles Street, Berkeley Square, London. Carlton, and Junior Carlton. B. in 1854; m. Aimee, youngest d. of Mr. Isaacson, of Rio de Janeiro, Brazil, and Melbourne, Australia. Educ. privately. Sole Proprietor of the *Whitehall Review*. Member of the Executive and Finance Committees, and of the Council of the National Union of Conservative Associations (Metropolitan division); Chairman of Works Committee and Lighting Committee, St. Martin's-in-the-Fields; Chairman Strand Labour Exchange. Wrote, under the name of Martyn Field, works entitled *The Late Lamented*, *The Bungalow*, *The Other Fellow*, etc. etc. A Conservative. Unsuccessfully contested W. Southwark in 1895. Elected for N. Lambeth in 1900 and sat until defeated in 1906 as an Independent Conservative candidate; he had been refused readoption because of impending bankruptcy proceedings which subsequently proved successful. [1905]

HORNIMAN, Emslie John. 13 Chelsea Embankment, Chelsea, London. Lowicks, Frensham, Surrey. National Liberal, Eighty, and City Liberal. S. of F.J. Horniman, Esq., MP for Falmouth, and Rebekah, d. of John Emslie, Esq., of Dalston. B. 1863 at Forest Hill; m. 1886, Laura Isabel, d. of Col. A.C. Plomer. Educ. privately. Chairman of Horniman and Company, Tea Merchants; a member of the London County Council for Chelsea 1898-1907, and Chelsea Borough Council 1900-06. A J.P. Member of English Royal Commission on Ancient Monuments 1908. A Liberal. Elected for Chelsea in 1906 and sat until defeated in Jan. 1910. Contested W. Walthamstow in 1918. Died 11 July 1932. [1909]

HORNIMAN, Frederick John. Falmouth House, 20 Hyde Park Terrace, London. Surrey Mansion, Brighton. City Liberal. S. of John and Ann Horniman, of Coombe Cliff, Croydon. B. at Bridgewater 8 Oct. 1835; m. 1897, Minnie Louisa, d. of G.W. Bennett, Esq., of Charlton. Educ. at the Friends' Coll., Croydon. A Partner in the firm of W.H. and F.J. Horniman, Tea-Merchants, of Wormwood Street, Bishopsgate, London, and later Chairman. He opened at Forest Hill, presenting it to the public, a collection of objects of art and antiquity called "The Horniman Museum." A Liberal, in favour of Home Rule for Ireland, etc. Returned for Penryn and Falmouth in July 1895 and sat until he retired Jan. 1906. Died 5 Mar. 1906. [1905]

HORRIDGE, Thomas Gardner. 41 Rutland Gate, London. 1 Garden Court, Temple, London. Reform. S. of John Horridge, Esq., of Bolton. B. 1857; m. Evelyne, d. of Mellvill Sandys, Esq., of Lanarth, Cornwall. Educ. at Nassau School, Barnes. Called to the bar 1884 and practised on the N. Circuit. K.C. 1901. A Liberal. Elected for E. Manchester in 1906 and sat until he retired in Jan 1910. Knighted in 1910 and appointed High Court Judge 1910-37. PC. 1937. Died 25 July 1938. [1909]

HOUGHTON-GASTRELL, Col. Sir William Henry. See GASTRELL, Col. Sir William Henry Houghton.

HOULDSWORTH, Sir William Henry, Bart. 35 Grosvenor Place, London. 49 Spring Gardens, Manchester. Coodham, Kilmarnock, N.B. Carlton, and Conservative. S. of Henry Houldsworth, Esq., of Coltness, Scotland, by Helen, d. of James Hamilton, Esq., of Glasgow. B. at Manchester 1834; m. Elizabeth Graham, d. of Walter Crum, Esq., of Thornliebank, Renfrewshire. Educ. at St. Andrew's University. Was in business as a Cotton-Spinner in Manchester. Was the delegate of Great Britain at the Monetary Conference, Brussels 1892. Created Bart. 1887. A Conservative, would support a Sunday closing bill for England, and would resist every attempt to destroy religious establishments. Unsuccessfully contested Manchester in 1880; elected there Oct. 1883 and sat until he retired in 1906. Died 18 Apr. 1917. [1905]

HOULT, Joseph. The Rocklands, Thornton Hough, Cheshire. S. of John Hoult, Esq., of Liverpool, and Alice, d. of Joseph Welsby, Esq., of Norton. B. at Liverpool 1847; m. 1872, Julia Anne, 2nd d. of James Murray, Esq., of Edinburgh (she died 1901). Educ. at Wavertree Coll. A J.P. for Liverpool and Cheshire. A Conservative. Elected for the Wirral division of Cheshire in 1900 and sat until defeated in 1906. Died 19 Oct. 1917. [1905]

HOUSTON, Robert Paterson. Continued in House after 1918: full entry in Volume III.

HOWARD, Edward Stafford. Thornbury Castle, Thornbury, Gloucestershire. Travellers'. 2nd s. of Henry Howard, Esq., of Greystoke Castle, Cumberland, by Charlotte, eld. d. of Henry L. Long, Esq., of Hampton, Surrey. B. at Greystoke Castle 1851; m. 1876, Lady Rachel Anne Georgina, d. of the 2nd Earl Cawdor. Was educ. at Harrow, and at Trinity Coll., Cambridge. Called to the bar at the Inner Temple 1875. A Liberal. Sat for E. Cumberland from Apr. 1876 to Nov. 1885, and for the Thornbury div. of Gloucestershire from Dec. 1885 until defeated in 1886 standing as a Gladstonian Liberal. Under Secretary for India 1886. Commissioner of Woods and Forests and of Land Revenues 1893-1912; Ecclesiastical Commissioner from 1914. K.C.B. 1909. Died 8 Apr. 1916. [1886]

HOWARD, Hon. Geoffrey William Algernon. Continued in House after 1918: full entry in Volume III.

HOWARD, Henry Charles. Greystoke Castle, Penrith. Travellers', and Arthur's. Eld. s. of Henry Howard, Esq., of Greystoke, by Charlotte Caroline Georgina, d. of Henry Lawes Long, Esq., of Hampton Lodge, Surrey. B. 1850; m. 1878, Lady Mabel McDonnell, 2nd d. of the Earl of Antrim. Educ. at Harrow, and Trinity Coll., Cambridge. A Magistrate and Dept.-Lieut. for the counties of Westmoreland and Cumberland. A Liberal. Sat for the Penrith division of Cumberland from Dec. 1885 until he retired in 1886. Unsuccessfully contested the Eskdale division of Cumberland as a Liberal Unionist in 1892 and 1895. Chairman of Cumberland County Council. Died 4 Aug. 1914. [1886]

HOWARD, John. Sibton Park, Lyminge, Kent. Carlton, and Cavalry. S. of W. Howard, Esq., of Ersham, Kent. B. 1863; m. 1896, Hon. Mrs. Pawson, widow of W. Hargrave Pawson, Esq., and d. of 3rd Visct. St. Vincent. J.P. for Kent 1895; Maj. Royal E. Kent Yeomanry. Served in S. Africa with Imperial Yeomanry 1899-1902. A Conservative. Elected for N.E. Kent in 1900 and sat until defeated in 1906. Contested Canterbury in Dec. 1910 but defeated by an Independent Conservative candidate. Died 5 Sept. 1911. [1905]

HOWARD, John Morgan. 22 Gloucester Street, Warwick Square, London. 6 Pump Court, Temple, London. Carlton, Junior Carlton, and Constitutional. S. of John Howard, Esq., of Swansea, by Martha, d. of Maj. Howell. B. 1837; m. 1857, Ann, d. of George Bowes, Esq., of Homerton, Middlesex. Was called to the bar at the Middle Temple, 1858; became Q.C. 1874, and a bencher of his inn 1877. Recorder of Guildford, and was H.M. Chief Commissioner in the Norwich election inquiry 1875. A Magistrate for Middlesex and Westminster, Chairman of the County Law and Parliamentary Committee, one of the Council of Legal Education for the Inns of Court, F.R.G.S., etc. etc. A Conservative. Contested the borough of Lambeth unsuccessfully in 1868, 1874 and 1880. Sat for the Dulwich division of Camberwell from 1885 until appointed County

Court Judge in Nov. 1887. Died 10 Apr. 1891. [1887]

HOWARD, Joseph. 18 Kensington Court, London. 2nd s. of John Eliot Howard, Esq., F.R.S., of Tottenham, by Maria, d. of William Dillworth Crewdson, Esq., of Kendal, Banker. B. at Tottenham 1834; m. 1859, Ellen, d. of Henry Waterhouse, Esq., of Manchester. Educ. at University Coll. London. Was called to the bar in 1856, but was later engaged in the Iron Tube trade. A J.P. and C.A. for Middlesex, and a Lieut. of the City of London. A Conservative. Sat for the Tottenham division of Middlesex from 1885 until he retired in 1906. Died 2 Mar. 1923. [1905]

HOWELL, George. Hampden House, Ellingham Road, Shepherd's Bush, London. Cobden. S. of Edwin John and Mary Howell. B. at Wrington, Somerset 1833; m. 1857, Dorcas, d. of George Taviner, Esq. Went to London when twenty-one years of age and worked as a Bricklayer. He then became a member of the Bricklayers' Society, and subsequently was appointed Secretary to the London Trades Council. He also served as Parliamentary Secretary of the Trades Union Congress 1871-75, Secretary of the Reform League 1864-69, Secretary of the Plimsoll Committee 1871-74, and on the executives of many other associations, such as the Land Tenure Reform Association and National Education League. Honorary member of the Cobden Club and a Fellow of the Statistical Society, and wrote *The Conflicts of Capital and Labour*, *A Handy-Book of the Labour Laws*, Trade Unionism, New and Old, *The Employers' Liability Act*, and numerous pamphlets, articles in the magazines, etc. An "advanced Liberal", in favour of Home Rule. Unsuccessfully contested Aylesbury in 1868 and 1874, and Stafford in 1881. Sat for N.E. Bethnal Green from 1885 until defeated in 1895. Died 16 Sept. 1910. [1895]

HOWELL, William Tudor. 7 King's Bench Walk, Temple, London. Deanery, St. David's. S. of the Very Rev. David Howell, Dean of St. David's, by Ann, d. of David Powell, Esq., of Pencoed, Glamorganshire. B. 1862 at Pwllheli, Carnarvonshire. Educ. at Wrexham Grammar School, Shrewsbury School, and New Coll., Oxford. A Barrister, called to the bar 1887, at the Inner Temple, and joined the S. Wales Circuit. A Conservative. Sat for Denbigh district from July 1895 until he retired in 1900. [1900]

HOWORTH, Sir Henry Hoyle, K.C.I.E. 30 Collingham Place, London. Bentcliffe, Eccles, Manchester. Carlton. S. of Henry Howorth, Esq., Merchant of Lisbon. B. 1842. Educ. at Rossall School. Called to the bar at the Inner Temple 1867 and joined the N. Circuit. A F.R.S., F.S.A., and D.C.L. Durham; Vice-President of the Manchester Conservative Association, a Governor of Owens Coll., and a Trustee respectively of the British Museum, of Chetham Coll., and of Henshaw's Asylum. Wrote a *History of the Mongols*, a *History of Chinghiz Khan and his Ancestors*, *The Mammouth and the Flood* (1887), a book against *The Glacial Theory* in geology, and edited for the Chetham Society a *History of the Vicars of Rochdale*. Also author of a large numer of papers contributed to various scientific societies, and of a series of letters to *The Times* on fiscal and political subjects. Created K.C.I.E. 1892. A Conservative. Sat for Salford S. from 1886 until he retired in 1900. Died 15 July 1923. [1900]

HOYLE, Isaac. The How, Prestwich, Nr. Manchester. Reform, and National Liberal. 4th s. of Joshua Hoyle, Esq., of Bacup, by a d. of James Bentley, Esq. B. 1828; m. 1st, 1854, Elizabeth, d. of James Smallpage, Esq., of Burnley (she died 1870); 2ndly, 1872, Mary Hamer, d. of John Robinson Kay, Esq., of Walmersley, Bury. Educ. privately. A Cotton-Spinner, a Director of the firm of Joshua Hoyle and Sons Limited, which was transformed into a company in order to promote co-operation between the employers and employed. Magistrate for Manchester, a Director of the Manchester Chamber of Commerce. A Liberal and Home Ruler. Sat for the Heywood division of Lancashire from 1885 until he retired in 1892. Died 2 Sept. 1911. [1892]

HOZIER, Hon. James Henry Cecil. 36 Grosvenor Square, London. Mauldslie Castle, Carluke, Lanarkshire. St. James's, Carlton, Garrick, Pratt's, White's, Automobile, and Bachelors'. Only s. of Lord Newlands, 1st Baron, of Mauldslie Castle, Lanarkshire, and his wife Fanny, d. of John O'Hara, Esq., of Raheen, Co. Galway. B. at Tannochside, Lanarkshire 1851; m. 1880, Lady Mary Cecil, 2nd d. of the 3rd

Marq. of Exeter. Educ. at Eton, and Balliol Coll., Oxford. Served in the Foreign Office 1874-78, and was Diplomatic Secretary on Lord Salisbury's special embassy to the Constantinople Conference of 1876-77, Private Secretary to Lord Salisbury as Foreign Minister from 1878 to 1880, and again when he became Prime Minister 1885-86. Was Grand Master Mason of Scotland 1899-1903; Public Works Loan Commissioner from 1900. A Conservative Unionist. Unsuccessfully contested S. Lanarkshire in 1885. Represented S. Lanarkshire from the general election of 1886 until he retired in 1906. Succeeded as 2nd Baron Newlands in 1906. Lord-Lieut. of Lanarkshire. Died 5 Sept. 1929. [1905]

HUBBARD, Hon. Egerton. 23 Cadogan Place, London. Addington Manor, Winslow, Buckinghamshire. Eld. s. of Lord Addington, by Hon. Maria Margaret, eld. d. of the 8th Lord Napier, of Thirlestane. B. in London 1842; m. 1880, Mary Adelaide, 3rd d. of Wyndham Spencer Portal, Esq., of Malshanger, Basingstoke. Educ. at Radley, and Christ Church, Oxford (graduated B.A. 1865, M.A. 1866). A Partner in the firm of John Hubbard and Company, Russian Merchants, a Director of the Royal Exchange Assurance Company and of the Surrey Commercial Docks Company; also a Magistrate for the borough and Co. of Buckingham, and was in the Buckinghamshire Yeomanry (Lieut. 1st Buckinghamshire Rifle Volunteers). A Conservative. Sat for Buckingham borough from Feb. 1847 until defeated in Apr. 1880, and then for the Buckingham division of Buckinghamshire from July 1886 until he succeeded as Lord Addington in 1889. Died 14 June 1915. [1889]

HUBBARD, Hon. Evelyn. 38 Lennox Gardens, London. The Rookery, Downe, Kent. Carlton, and Wellington. Youngest s. of Lord Addington (1st Peer), MP for Buckingham, and the City of London, by Maria, d. of the 8th Lord Napier. B. 1852; m. 1881, Eveline Maude, d. of W.S. Portal, Esq., of Malshanger, Hampshire. Educ. at Radley Coll. and Christ Church, Oxford (M.A. 1878). A Partner in the firm of John Hubbard and Company, London, Russia Merchants, and of Eberton, Hubbard and Company, St. Petersburg. A Lieut. for the City of London, a Director of the Bank of England 1890-1909, a Commissioner of Public Works Loans, etc. Chairman of Guardian Assurance Co. 1900-30. A Conservative, strongly opposed to Home Rule and disestablishment. Was an unsuccessful candidate in N. Buckinghamshire 1889 and 1891, and at Plymouth 1895. Sat for the Brixton division of Lambeth on the Marq. of Carmarthen becoming Duke of Leeds, Jan. 1896. MP until he accepted Chiltern Hundreds in Mar. 1900. Died 24 Aug. 1934. [1899]

HUBBARD, Rt. Hon. John Gellibrand. 24 Prince's Gate, Hyde Park, London. Addington Manor, Winslow, Buckinghamshire. Carlton. S. of John Hubbard, Esq., of Stratford Grove, Essex, by Mariana, d. of John Morgan, Esq., of Bramfield Place, Hertfordshire. B. at Stratford, Essex, 1805; m. 1837, Hon. Maria Margaret, eld. d. of 8th Lord Napier. A Banker and Merchant, a Director of the Bank of England, and was Chairman of Public Works Loan Commission from 1853-1874. A Commissioner of Lieutenancy for London. Published in 1843 *The Currency of the Country*, and in 1853 *How should the Income Tax be Levied*, and *Reform or Repeal the Income Tax*, besides other pamphlets on commercial and financial policy. PC 1874. A Conservative. Sat for the borough of Buckingham from May 1859 to Dec. 1868. Sat for London from Feb. 1874 until created Baron Addington 22 July 1887. Died 28 Aug. 1889. [1887]

HUDSON, George Bickersteth. 15 Gloucester Square, Hyde Park, London. Frogmore Hall, Hertford. Carlton. S. of the Rev. Thomas Dawson Hudson, and his wife Isabella Mary, d. of the Rev. W. Leigh Bennett. B. 1845; m. 1885, Lucy Rebecca, d. of George Ley, Esq., of Coburg, Ontario. Educ. at Rugby and Exeter Coll., Oxford; B.A. 1868, M.A. 1872. A Barrister, called at the Inner Temple June 1872, of the S.E. Circuit; J.P. and Dept.-Lieut. and County Councillor for Hertfordshire. A Conservative. Represented N. Hertfordshire from 1892 until he retired in 1906. Died 29 Feb. 1912. [1905]

HUDSON, Walter, O.B.E. Elswick House, Atherfold Road, Stockwell, London. S. of Henry C. Hudson, Esq., Employee of the North Eastern Railway Company. B. 25 Jan. 1852 at Richmond Station, Yorkshire; m. 1875, d. of William Harker, Esq. Educ. at Richmond National School. Was Presi-

dent of Amalgamated Society of Railway Servants 1891-99; Irish Secretary 1898-1906; member of Royal Commission on Accidents to Railway Men; President of Irish Trade Congress 1903, and of Labour Congress at Hull 1908. O.B.E. 1917. A Labour Member. Elected for Newcastle-on-Tyne in 1906 and sat until defeated in Newcastle E. in 1918. Retired from Trade Union activity in 1923. Died 18 Mar. 1935.
[1918]

HUGHES, Col. Sir Edwin. Effingham House, Arundel Street, Strand, London. 32 Green's End, Woolwich, London. Oak Lands, Plumstead Common. Carlton, and Constitutional. B. at Droitwich 1832; m. Mary Adele Elliott, d. of G.M. Gibbs, Esq. Educ. at King Edward VI's Grammar School, Birmingham. Was admitted a Solicitor in 1860. A Conservative agent for the City of London, Kent, and Greenwich; a member of the London School Board, London County Council and Technical Education Board. Honorary Col. of the 2nd Kent Artillery Volunteers. Was Mayor of Woolwich 1900. Succeeded in getting pensioners' grievances adjusted for old sailors at Greenwich Hospital, and Government workmen at Woolwich. A Conservative. Sat for Woolwich from Nov. 1885 until he accepted Chiltern Hundreds in 1902. Knighted 1902. Died 15 Sept. 1904.
[1902]

HUGHES, Spencer Leigh. Continued in House after 1918: full entry in Volume III.

HUGHES-HALLETT, Col. Francis Charles. 108 Cromwell Road, London. United Service, Junior United Service, and Carlton. S. of Charles Hughes-Hallett, Esq., Judge in the East India Company's service (and grand-s. of the Rev. Charles Hughes-Hallett, of Higham Park, Canterbury, Kent), by Emma Mary, d. of Charles Roberts, Esq., also Judge in the East India Company's service. The name Hallett was assumed by the above-named Rev. Charles Hughes-Hallett in accordance with the will of Mr. Hallett, of Little Dunmow, Essex, from whom the property held by the celebrated "Flitch of Bacon" tenure, with the Lordship of the Manor, came into the family. B. 1838; m. 1st, Lady Selwyn, widow of Lord Justice Selwyn (she died 1875); 2ndly, Emilie, d. of Col. Von Schaumburg, of Philadelphia, U.S.A. Educ. at Brighton Coll., and the Royal

Military Academy, Woolwich. Served in the Royal Artillery and Royal Horse Artillery, and retired in 1872. In 1881 was appointed to the command of the 2nd Brigade North Irish Division of the Royal Artillery, and this he exchanged in 1884 for the command of the 2nd Brigade Southern Division of the Royal Artillery. "A firm but independent supporter of Lord Salisbury's Government." Unsuccessfully contested Sandwich in 1874. First elected for Rochester in 1885 and sat until he accepted Chiltern Hundreds in Mar. 1889. Died 1903.
[1889]

HULSE, Edward Henry. 26 Upper Brook Street, London. Breamore House, Salisbury. Carlton, Bachelors', Marlborough, and Turf. Eld. s. of Sir Edward Hulse (5th Bart.), by Katharine, d. of Dean Hamilton, of Salisbury. B. at Breamore, near Salisbury 1859; m. 1888, Edith Maud Webster, d. of E.L. Lawson, Esq., of Hall Barn, Beaconsfield. Educ. at Eton, and Brasenose Coll., Oxford. A J.P. for Wiltshire and Hampshire, and Dept.-Lieut. for Wiltshire; also Capt. of the Salisbury Troop Royal Wilts Yeomanry Cavalry. A Conservative and Unionist. First elected for Salisbury 1886 and sat until he accepted Chiltern Hundreds in 1897. Succeeded as 6th Bart. in 1899. Served in S. Africa 1900. Died 29 May 1903.
[1896]

HUME-WILLIAMS, William Ellis. Continued in House after 1918: full entry in Volume III.

HUMPHREYS-OWEN, Arthur Charles. Glansevern, Berriew, Montgomeryshire. Athenaeum, Bath, Oxford & Cambridge, and National Liberal. S. of Erskine Humphreys, Esq., of Lincoln's Inn, Barrister-at-Law, and Eliza, youngest d. of Edward Jones, Esq., M.D., of Garthmyl. B. at Garthmyl, Montgomeryshire 1836; m. 1874 Maria, eld. d. of James Russell, Esq., Q.C. Educ. at Harrow, and Trinity Coll., Cambridge. A Barrister of Lincoln's Inn; called to the bar Apr. 1864. A Landowner in his native Co., and Chairman of the County Council and Dept.-Chairman of Quarter Sessions there. Also Chairman of the Cambrian railway, a Governor of the University Colls., at Aberystwyth and Bangor, Chairman to the Central Board under the Welsh Intermediate Education Act 1889, and member of Consultative Committee of the Board of Education. On succeeding to the property of Mrs. Owen, of Glansevern, he assumed, by Royal licence, the name of Owen. A Liberal, in favour of Home Rule for Ireland, Welsh disestablishment, reform of the land laws, Local Control of the Liquor Traffic, unsectarian elementary schools, etc. Represented Montgomeryshire from 1894 until he retired in 1906. Died 9 Dec. 1905. [1905]

HUNT, Sir Frederick Seager, Bart. 7 Cromwell Road, South Kensington, London. Carlton, Conservative, and Union. S. of James Hunt, Esq., an eminent Railway Contractor, by Eliza, d. of James Lys Seager, Esq. B. at Chippenham, Wiltshire 1838; m. 1867, Alice Harriet, d. of Alfred Hunt, Esq. Educ. at Westminster. Head of the firm of Seager, Evans, and Company, and Chairman of Earl's Shipbuilding Company. A Dept.-Lieut. of the Co. of London; Chairman of the United Westminster Almshouses, and Governor of the Westminster Blue Coat School. Patron of the living of Charmouth, Dorset. Created Bart. 1892. A Conservative. Unsuccessfully contested Marylebone in 1880. Sat for Marylebone W. from Nov. 1885 to June 1895. Sat for Maidstone from July 1895 until he accepted Chiltern Hundreds in 1898. Died 21 Jan. 1904. [1897]

HUNT, Rowland. Carlton, and United University. S. of Rowland Hunt, Esq., and Florence, d. of R. Humfrey, Esq., of Stoke Albany. B. 1858; m. 1890, Veronica, d. of D.H.R. Davidson, Esq., of Tulloch. Educ. at Eton, and Magdalene Coll., Cambridge. A J.P. for Shropshire. Master of Foxhounds for twelve years. Served with Lovat's Scouts in S. African War 1899-1902. Maj. City of London Yeomanry. A Unionist. Elected for the Ludlow division of Shropshire in Dec. 1903 and sat until he retired in 1918. Associated with National Party 1917-18. Died 30 Nov. 1943. [1918]

HUNTER, Sir Charles Roderick, Bart. Mortimer Hill, Reading. Naval & Military, and Travellers'. S. of Sir C. Hunter, 2nd Bart. B. 1858; m. 1887, Agnes, d. of A.S. Kennard, Esq., of Crawley Court, Hampshire. Educ. at Eton. Capt. in Rifle Brigade, Maj. London Rifle Brigade, and Inspector of Musketry Gen. Staff 1914; served in S. African War 1900. A Unionist. Elected for Bath Jan. 1910 and sat until he

retired in 1918. Succeeded as Bart. 1890. Died 24 June 1924. [1918]

HUNTER, William. 3 Randolph Crescent, Edinburgh. Reform, and National Liberal. B. at Ayr 1865. Unmarried. Educ. at Ayr Academy, and Edinburgh University. An advocate of the Scottish bar, admitted 1889, K.C. 1905. Appointed Solicitor-Gen. for Scotland Apr. 1910. A Liberal. Elected for the Govan district of Lanarkshire in Jan. 1910 and sat until appointed Senator, Coll. of Justice in Scotland with the title of Lord Hunter 1911-36. Died 10 Apr. 1957. [1911]

HUNTER, William Alexander. Fountain Court, Temple, London. Reform, and National Liberal. S. of James Hunter, Esq., Granite Manufacturer, Aberdeen, by his wife, Margaret Boddie. B. 1844. Educ. at Aberdeen Grammar School and University. Held the degrees M.A. and LL.D. Was called to the bar at the Middle Temple 1867. Was Professor of Jurisprudence, Roman Law, the Principles of Legislation and International Law at University Coll., London. Author of *Roman Law in the Order of a Code*, and *Introduction to Roman Law*. A Liberal and Home Ruler, opposed to a second legislative chamber, in favour of the disestablishment and disendowment of the Church, and of legislation to secure old age pensions. Sat for Aberdeen N. from Nov. 1885 until he accepted Chiltern Hundreds in 1896. Died 21 July 1898. [1895]

HUNTER, Sir William Guyer, K.C.M.G. 21 Norfolk Crescent, Hyde Park, London. East India United Service, Carlton, and Travellers'. Eld. s. of Thomas Hunter, Esq., of Catterick, Yorkshire, and Norwood, Surrey. B. 1829; m. 1st, d. of Rev. C. Packe; 2ndly, a d. of J. Stainburn, Esq. Educ. privately, and at King's Coll. Studied medicine at Charing Cross Hospital, and at Aberdeen University, where he took the degree of M.D. Also F.R.C.P. amd F.R.C.S. of both London and Edinburgh. In 1850 he joined the Indian Medical Service, and served through the Burmese War and Sepoy Mutiny. In 1867 was appointed Principal of the Grant Medical Coll., in 1877 Surgeon-Gen., and in 1879, Vice-Chancellor of the University of Bombay; retired 1880, and was appointed Honorary Surgeon to the Queen. In 1883 was appointed Consulting Physician to Charing

Cross Hospital, and on the outbreak of cholera in Egypt was sent by the Government on a special mission to that country, for his services on which occasion he was created K.C.M.G. in 1884. Appointed June 1885 British delegate to the International Sanitary Conference at Rome, and in Sept. Honorary Commandant of the Volunteer Medical Staff Corps. Was a member of the London School Board. A Conservative. Sat for Hackney Central from Nov. 1885 until he retired in 1892. Died 14 Mar. 1902. [1892]

HUNTER-WESTON, Sir Aylmer Gould. Continued in House after 1918: full entry in Volume III.

HUNTINGTON, Charles Philip. 8 Chelsea Embankment, London. Astley Bank, Darwen, Lancashire. Reform. S. of James Huntington, Esq., of Mitcham, Surrey, and his wife (the d. of Mr. Philip Balla). B. 1833 at Mitcham; m. 1876, Jane Hudson, d. of Walter Sparkes, Esq., of Holloway. Educ. privately. A Paper Maker, of the firm of J.G. Potter and Company, and a J.P. for the Co. of Lancaster from 1879. A Liberal, in favour of Home Rule for Ireland, and Mr. Gladstone's policy generally. Sat for the Darwen division of N.E. Lancashire from July 1892 until defeated in 1895. Contested seat again Oct. 1900. Created 1st Bart. 1906. Died 23 Dec. 1906. [1895]

HUNTINGTON-WHITELEY, Sir Herbert James, Bart. See WHITELEY, Sir Herbert James, Bart.

HUSBAND, John. Moreton Lodge, Upper Clapton, London. National Liberal, and Hackney Reform. B. at Hackney 1839; m. 1866, the only d. of Edward Hinkley, Esq., of Brighton. Educ. privately. A Corn Merchant, and President of the South Hackney Liberal and Radical Association. An Advanced Liberal, in favour of Home Rule for Ireland and the "Newcastle programme" generally. Sat for Cricklade division of Wiltshire from July 1892 until he retired in 1895. [1895]

HUTCHINSON, Charles Frederick. Knowle, Mayfield, Sussex. Reform. S. of R.R. Hutchinson, Esq., M.D., and Frances Hadden. B. at Nottingham 1850; m. 1880, Ellen, d. of S. Horner-Soames, Esq. Educ. at Elstree, Uppingham, and Edinburgh

University, also at Berlin, Vienna, and Paris. M.D. Edinburgh 1874; retired from practice 1898. A J.P. for Sussex. A Liberal. Unsuccessfully contested Rye in 1900. Elected for the Rye division of Sussex Mar. 1903 and sat until defeated in 1906. Knighted 1906. Died 15 Nov. 1907. [1905]

HUTTON, Alfred Eddison. Crow Trees, Rawdon, Yorkshire. 15 Arlington Street, London. Brooks's, and Devonshire. S. of John and Eliza Hutton. B. 1865 at Eccleshill, near Bradford. Educ. at Mill Hill School, Hendon, and Trinity Coll., Cambridge. A Manufacturer. A Temporary Chairman of Committees, 1907-1909. A Liberal, in favour of Home Rule, etc. First elected for the Morley division of Yorkshire in 1892 and sat until he retired in Jan. 1910. Died 30 May 1947. [1909]

HUTTON, James Frederick. Victoria Park, Manchester. S. of William M. Hutton, Esq., by his marriage with Miss Elizabeth Chapman. B. in London 1826; m. 1855, Catherine, eld. d. of J. Roger Jones Esq., of Pen-y-pylle, Flintshire. Educ. at Clapham, and King's Coll.,London. An African Merchant and Manufacturer of Cotton goods. On the invitation of the King of the Belgians, he became a member of the International Association for opening up the Congo territory. A J.P. for Lancashire, President of the Manchester Chamber of Commerce, F.R.G.S., etc. A moderate and independent Conservative. Sat for Manchester N. from Nov. 1885 until defeated in 1886. Belgian Consul in Manchester from 1887. Died 1 Mar. 1890. [1886]

HUTTON, John. Solberge, Northallerton, Yorkshire. Carlton. S. of John Hutton, Esq., and Caroline, d. of Thomas Robson, Esq., of Holtby Hall, Yorkshire. B. 1847 at Solberge, Northallerton; m. 1870, Hon. Caroline Shore, eld. d. of the 2nd Lord Teignmouth. Educ. at Eton, and Christ Church, Oxford. A J.P., Dept.-Lieut., Chairman of the N. Riding Quarter Sessions 1892 to 1899, and of the County Council 1895-1915. Author of Yorkshire Coroners Act 1897, and Cottage Homes Bill. A Conservative. Was MP for Northallerton from 1868-74, when he retired. Sat for the Richmond division of Yorkshire from 1895 until he retired in 1906. Died 19 Dec. 1921. [1905]

HYDE, Clarendon Golding. 75 Gloucester Terrace, Hyde Park, London. Lyndhurst, Wednesbury. Reform, Union, and National Liberal. S. of Henry Barry Hyde, Esq., and Mary Anne, d. of Golding Bird, Esq., of Derry. B. 5 Feb. 1858 in London; m. 1886, Laura Adrie, d. of the Rev. Canon Palmer, Rector of Newington, London. Educ. at Royal Institutional School, Liverpool, and King's Coll., London. Was called to the bar at the Middle Temple 1881. Vice-President of S. Pearson and Son Limited, the well-known Contractors; a Fellow of Statistical Society; author of several treatises on company law. A Liberal, in favour of labour legislation, etc. Unsuccessfully contested Southampton in 1900. Elected for Wednesbury in 1906 and sat until defeated in Jan. 1910. Knighted 1910. Contested Cardiff in Dec. 1910. Member and Chairman of a large number of Government Committees 1909-23. Died 24 June 1934. [1909]

HYLTON-JOLLIFFE, Hon. Hylton George. See JOLLIFFE, Hon. Hylton George Hylton.

IBBETSON, Rt. Hon. Sir Henry John Selwin, Bart. See SELWIN-IBBETSON, Rt. Hon. Sir Henry John, Bart.

IDRIS, Thomas Howell Williams. Millfield, West Hill, Highgate, London. Dolycae, Cader Idris, Corris, Merionethshire. S. of Benjamin and Catherine Williams. B. 5 Aug. 1842 at Vallen Farm, Pembroke; m. 1873, Emeline, d. of John Trevena, Esq., of Pembroke Dock. Educ. at Tavernspite National School. Assumed the name of Idris in addition to Williams. Chairman of Idris and Company, Mineral Water Manufacturers; a member of the London County Council from its foundation in 1889 (except for a brief period) until 1907; a Director of the Garden City, a J.P. for London and Merioneth; an Alderman of St. Pancras; Mayor 1903. Author of *Notes on Essential Oils*, and several chemical papers. A Liberal. Unsuccessfully contested Denbigh in 1892 and Chester in 1900. Elected for Flint in 1906 and sat until he retired in Jan. 1910. Died 10 Feb. 1925. [1909]

ILLINGWORTH, Rt. Hon. Albert Holden. Continued in House after 1918: full entry in Volume III.

ILLINGWORTH, Alfred. Daisy Bank, Bradford. Reform, and National Liberal. Eld. s. of Daniel Illingworth, Esq., of Bradford, by Elizabeth, d. of Michael Hill, Esq., of Bradford. B. at Bradford 25 Sept. 1827; m. 1866, Margaret, d. of Sir Isaac Holden, Bart., of Oakworth, Yorkshire, a Dept.-Lieut. for that Co. and MP for the Keighley division of Yorkshire. Educ. at Huddersfield Coll. A Worsted Spinner at Bradford, and was one of the Dept. Chairmen of "Ways and Means." A Liberal and Home Ruler, in favour of a reform of the Land Laws. the disestablishment of the Church, "an effective control of the people over the licensing system", or "Parliament being relieved from legislating upon matters of local importance", etc. Sat for Knaresborough from Dec. 1868 until he retired Feb. 1874. Sat for Bradford from Apr. 1880 to 1885 and for Bradford W. from 1885 until he retired in 1895. Died 2 Jan. 1907. [1895]

ILLINGWORTH, Percy Holden. 102 Lancaster Gate, London. Westwood, Clayton Heights, Bradford. Reform, Union, and National Liberal. Youngest s. of Henry Illingworth, Esq., of Ladye Royde Hall, Bradford, and Mary, d. of Sir Isaac Holden, Bart., MP. B. 1869 at Bradford; m. 1907, Mary, d. of George Coats, Esq., of Staneley, Paisley. Educ. at Jesus Coll., Cambridge; M.A., LL.B. Was called to the bar 1895. Served in S. Africa with Yorkshire Yeomanry 1900; Capt. Westminster Dragoons Imperial Yeomanry. Was Private Secretary (unpaid) to Mr. Birrell, Chief Secretary for Ireland; a Junior Lord of the Treasury and a Liberal Whip 1910-12. Appointed Parliamentary Secretary to the Treasury and Chief Liberal Whip 1912. Chairman of Yorkshire Liberal Federation. A Liberal. Unsuccessfully contested the Shipley division of the W. Riding of Yorkshire in 1900; elected there in 1906 and sat until his death 3 Jan. 1915. Nominated for the Privy Council in Jan. 1915 but died before he could be sworn in. [1914]

INCE, Henry Bret. Defeated in 1886: full entry in Volume I.

INGLEBY, Holcombe. Sedgeford Hall, Norfolk. 31 Grosvenor Place, London. Athenaeum, Boodle's, and Carlton. S. of Clement Mansfield Ingleby, Esq., LL.D. and Sarah Oakes, of Valentines, Essex. B.

18 Mar. 1854 at Edgbaston, Birmingham; m. 1886, Harriet Jane, d. of Charles F.N. Rolfe, Esq., of Heacham Hall, Norfolk. Educ. at Malvern, and Corpus Christi, Oxford; M.A. Entered Inner Temple 1876 where he read and kept his terms. Was a Solicitor from 1883-86. A J.P. for Norfolk and Mayor of King's Lynn 1910. Author of *Poems and Plays*, and other works. A Unionist. Elected for King's Lynn in Dec. 1910 and sat until he retired in 1918. Died 6 Aug. 1926.   [1918]

INGRAM, Sir William James, Bart. 198 Strand, London. Swineshead Abbey, Spalding, Lincolnshire. The Bungalow, Westgate-on-Sea. 2nd s. of Herbert Ingram, Esq., the founder of the *Illustrated London News* and MP for Boston 1856-60, by his marriage with Miss Anne Little, of Eye, Northamptonshire, (later Lady Watkin). B. 1847; m. 1874, Mary Eliza Collingwood, eld. d. of Edward Stirling, Esq., of Queen's Gardens, Hyde Park, and Adelaide, Australia. Educ. at Winchester, and Trinity Coll., Cambridge. Was called to the bar at the Middle Temple in 1872. One of the proprietors of the *Illustrated London News*, and a J.P. for Surrey and the Cinque Ports. Created Bart. June 1893. A Liberal, in favour of Home Rule and the Gladstonian programme generally. First returned for Boston Feb. 1874 and sat until 1880. Returned again at the election of Apr. 1880, but on petition the election was declared void. At the next election for Boston, in Nov. 1885, he was re-elected and sat until defeated July 1886. Once more returned for Boston 1892 and sat until defeated July 1895. Died 18 Dec. 1924.   [1895]

ISAACS, Lewis Henry. 3 Pembridge Square, Bayswater, London. 3 Verulam Buildings, Gray's Inn, London. Carlton, Whitehall, Constitutional, and Royal London Yacht. Youngest s. of Isaac Isaacs, Esq., of Devonshire Square, Gentleman, by Sarah, d. of Lewis Henry, Esq., Merchant, of Liverpool. B. at Manchester 1830. Educ. at the Royal Lancaster Grammar School, and University Coll., London. An Architect, and Surveyor to the Holborn Board of Works, and the Honorary Society of Gray's Inn, 1868-99. He was the Architect of the Holborn Town Hall, the Northumberland Avenue Hotel, and other buildings. An Associate of the Institute of Civil Engineers and F.R.I.B.A.

Wrote *A Treatise on Sewerage and Drainage,* and many papers, etc., on subjects connected with his profession. A "progressive Conservative." Sat for the Walworth division of Newington from Nov. 1885 until defeated in 1892. Mayor of Kensington 1902-04. Died 17 Oct. 1908.   [1892]

ISAACS, Rt. Hon. Sir Rufus Daniel, K.C.V.O. 32 Curzon Street, London. Foxhill, Reading, Berkshire. Reform and National Liberal. S. of J.M. Isaacs, Esq., Merchant and Shipbroker, of London. B. 10 Oct. 1860 in London; m. 1st, 1887, Alice Edith, d. of A. Cohen, Esq., of London (she died 1930) 2ndly, 1931, Stella, d. of Charles Charnand, Esq., she was created Baroness Swanborough in 1958 and died in 1971. Educ. at Brussels, Hanover, and University Coll. School, London. A Barrister, called to the bar at the Middle Temple 1887, Q.C. 1898. Was Solicitor-Gen. Mar. to Oct. 1910, when he was appointed Attorney-Gen. and a member of the Cabinet 1912. Knighted 1910. K.C.V.O. 1911. PC. 1911. A Liberal. Unsuccessfully contested N. Kensington in 1900. Elected for Reading in July 1904 and sat until appointed Lord Chief Justice of England in Oct. 1913. Created Baron Reading in Jan. 1914, Visct. Reading 1916, Earl of Reading 1917 and Marq. of Reading 1926. G.C.B. 1915; G.C.I.E. 1921; G.C.S.I. 1921; G.C.V.O. 1922. Ambassador in Washington from 1918-19, remaining Lord Chief Justice until 1921. Viceroy of India 1921-26. Foreign Secretary in the National Government Aug.-Nov. 1931. Capt. of Deal Castle from 1926, Lord Warden of Cinque Ports 1934-35. Died 30 Dec. 1935.   [1913]

ISAACSON, Frederick Wootton. 18 Upper Grosvenor Street, London. Carlton, and Orleans. Eld. s. of Frederick Isaacson, Esq., of Mildenhall, Suffolk. B. 1836; m. 1857, Elizabeth Marie Louise, only d. of Herr Stephen Jäger, Banker, of Frankfurt. A J.P. and Dept.-Lieut. for the Tower Hamlets, J.P. Monmouthshire, F.R.G.S., M.R.S.L., etc. A "progressive Conservative." Was an unsuccessful candidate for Wednesbury 1880, and for the Stepney division of Tower Hamlets at the general election of 1885, a petition which alleged that sixteen aliens had voted for him having been successfully presented. Sat for the Stepney division of Tower Hamlets from 1886 until his death 22 Feb. 1898.   [1898]

188

JACKS, William. Queen Anne's Mansions, London. 9 Claremont Terrace, Glasgow. S. of Richard and Margaret Jacks, née Lamb. B. 1841, at Cornhill, near Coldstream; m. 1878, Matilda Ferguson, d. of John Stiven, Esq., Manufacturer and Merchant of Glasgow. Educ. at the village school of Swinton, Berwickshire. He was apprenticed to a Shipbuilder of West Hartlepool; afterwards engaged in the shipyard of Messrs. Pile and Company, of Sunderland; subsequently became Manager of the Sunderland and Seaham Engine Works and Foundry. Later he set up an Iron and Steel business of his own, known as William Jacks and Company, Glasgow. A J.P. for Lanark. Wrote lectures on social, economic, and literary subjects, some of which were published. An advanced Liberal, in favour of Home Rule for Ireland. Sat for Leith district 1885-July 1886, when he retired in favour of Mr. Gladstone, but failed re-election in Aug. 1886 as a Liberal Unionist. Voted against Home Rule in 1886, but later changed his opinions and réjoined the Gladstonian Liberals. First returned as a Gladstonian Liberal for Stirlingshire in July 1892 and sat until defeated in 1895. Author of several historical works. Died 9 Aug. 1907. [1895]

JACKSON, Hon. Francis Stanley. Continued in House after 1918: full entry in Volume III.

JACKSON, Sir John, C.V.O. 48 Belgrave Square, London. Henley Park, Oxfordshire. Carlton, Royal Societies, Royal Yacht Squadron, and Royal Automobile. S. of Edward Jackson, Esq., of York. B. 4 Feb. 1851 at York; m. 1876, Ellen Julia, d. of George Myers, Esq. Educ. at St. Martin's School, York, and Edinburgh University. A Civil Engineer and Contractor for Public Works; constructed part of Manchester Ship Canal, foundations of Tower Bridge, Dover Harbour, Keyham Docks, Singapore Harbour, Railway over Andes from Chili to Bolivia, Euphrates-Tigris Irrigation Works and other large works in all parts of the world. Was a member of Royal Commission to inquire into the War in S. Africa; C.V.O. 1911; LL.D., F.R.S. Edin., J.P. for Devon. Knighted 1895. A Unionist. Unsuccessfully contested Devonport in 1904 and 1906. Elected for Devonport in Jan. 1910 and sat until he retired in 1918. Died 14 Dec. 1919. [1918]

JACKSON, John Arthur. Moresby Hall, Whitehaven. B. 30 Nov. 1862. Educ. at St. Peter's School, York. A member of the firm of J. and W. Jackson, Timber Merchants, Whitehaven, Vice-Chairman of Whitehaven Hematite Iron and Steel Company, and a Director of various Iron Ore Mining Companies. A member of Cumberland County Council, and Whitehaven Harbour Board. Lieut.-Col. 5th Battalion Border Regiment. Magistrate and Dept.-Lieut for Cumberland. A Unionist. Elected for Whitehaven in Jan. 1910 and sat until defeated in Dec. 1910. Died 25 Nov. 1937. [1910]

JACKSON, Richard Stephens. Stobcross Lodge, Crooms Hill, Greenwich. National Liberal. S. of John Jackson, Esq., of Sittingbourne, and Harriett, d. of William Tress, Esq., of Upchurch, Kent. B. 7 May 1850 at Newington, Kent; m. 1878, Mary Ann, d. of John Bell, Esq., M.A., of Blackheath. Educ. at Elm House School, Sittingbourne. A Solicitor, admitted 1872, and practised in London and Greenwich; a member of the London County Council from 1889-95, and 1898-1907. Mayor of Greenwich 1900. J.P. for London. Wrote a pamphlet on the Law of Distress. A Liberal. Unsuccessfully contested Greenwich in 1900. Elected for Greenwich in 1906 and sat until defeated in Jan. 1910. Died 10 June 1938. [1909]

JACKSON, Rt. Hon. William Lawies. 27 Cadogan Square, London. Allerton Hall, Chapel Allerton, Leeds. Carlton, and Athenaeum. Eld. s. of William Jackson, Esq., of Leeds. B. at Otley, Yorkshire 1840; m. 1860, Grace, d. of George Tempest, Esq. (she died 1901). Was Financial Secretary to the Treasury 1885 to Jan. 1886; and again from Aug.; and succeeded Mr. Balfour as Chief Secretary for Ireland Nov. 1891, when he also became a member of the Cabinet. Resigned with the ministry 1892. Admitted PC. May 1890, and a PC. Ireland Nov. 1891. F.R.S. 1891. Chairman of the S. African Committee 1896. A J.P. for the W. Riding of Yorkshire and for Leeds, and was elected Mayor of Leeds 1895. Chairman of the Great Northern Railway Company 1895-1908. A Conservative. Unsuccessfully contested Leeds Aug. 1876. Sat for Leeds from 1880-85 and for Leeds N. from 1885 until created Lord Allerton in 1902. Chairman of the Royal Commission on the coal resources of the

U.K. from 1901-05. Died 4 Apr. 1917. [1902]

JACOBSEN, Thomas Owen. The Holmes, Stradella Road, Herne Hill, London. Hyde, Cheshire. National Liberal, London Magistrates, and Hyde Reform. S. of Rudolph Bernard Jacobsen, Esq., of Liverpool, and Elizabeth Victoria, née Owen of Dublin. B. at Liverpool 1864; m. 1890, Pauline, d. of Marius Veillard, Banker. Educ. at the Liverpool Institute. Commenced business as a Manufacturing Stationer in 1893; Chairman of Jacobsen, Welch and Company Limited, London, Hyde, and Glasgow. J.P. for the Co. of London 1910; President of the Brixton Liberal Association 1906-07; President of the N. Lambeth Liberal Association 1916; Vice-President of the Hyde division of the Liberal Association from 1906. Travelled extensively (seven times round the world); F.R.G.S. A Liberal. Elected for the Hyde division of Cheshire in Mar. 1916 and sat until defeated in 1918. Unsuccessfully contested S.E. Southwark as a Coalition Liberal candidate 14 Dec. 1921 and, as a Liberal, Lambeth Kennington in 1923 and City of London in 1929. President of the Stationers' Association of Great Britain and Ireland 1929-31. Contested City of London in 1929. Died 15 June 1941. [1918]

JACOBY, Sir James Alfred. 34 Eaton Place, London. Oakhill, Nottingham. Reform, and Ranelagh. 2nd s. of Moritz Jacoby, Esq., of Nottingham. B. 1852; m. 1883, Miss F. Liepmann, of Glasgow. Educ. privately. A Town Councillor of Nottingham from 1876 and Sheriff 1877-78. President of the Nottingham Chamber of Commerce, Chairman of the Technical Schools Committee (which he took an active part in promoting), and of the Nottingham Liberal Club, and a Fellow of the Statistical Society. Knighted 1906. A Liberal and Home Ruler, in favour of "Local Option", of reform in the House of Lords, etc. Sat for mid Derbyshire from 1885 until his death 23 June 1909. [1909]

JAMES, Charles Herbert. Inns of Court Hotel, London. Brynteg, Merthyr Tydvil. Devonshire. B. 1817. A Solicitor at Merthyr Tydvil, where he practised for many years. A Liberal and Home Ruler. Sat for Merthyr Tydvil from Apr. 1880 until he accepted Chiltern Hundreds in 1888. Died 3 Oct. 1890. [1887]

JAMES, Frank. Aldridge, Nr. Walsall. National Conservative. S. of John James, Esq., of Walsall, and Mary James, née Green. B. 1821 at Walsall; m. 1st, Ann Wells, eld. d. of Thomas Wells Ingram, Esq., of Birmingham; 2ndly, 1859, Emma, youngest d. of W.H. Holland, Esq., of St. George's Square, London. Educ. at Handsworth by the Rev. D.W. Walton, and at King's Coll. School, London. A Manufacturer of Walsall. A J.P. and Dept.-Lieut. for the Co. of Stafford 1873; Vice-Chairman Staffordshire County Council; Chairman South Staffordshire Water Works Company. A Conservative. Unsuccessfully contested Walsall in 1885 and 1891. First returned there in July 1892 and sat until unseated on petition in Oct. 1892. [1892 2nd ed.]

JAMES, Rt. Hon. Sir Henry. 41 Cadogan Square, London. 1 New Court, Temple, London. Devonshire, and Garrick. S. of Philip Turner James, Esq., of Hereford, by Frances Gertrude, 3rd d. of John Bodenham, Esq., of The Grove, Presteign. B. at Hereford 1828. Unmarried. Educ. at Cheltenham Coll. Was Lecturer's Prizeman at the Inner Temple 1850 and 1851. Called to the bar at the Middle Temple Jan. 1852. Appointed a Queen's Counsel 1869, and to the ancient office of Postman of the Court of Exchequer 1867. Was Solicitor-Gen. Oct. 1873, and Attorney-Gen. from Nov. 1873 to Feb. 1874; re-appointed Apr. 1880, and held office till Mr. Gladstone's ministry resigned in June 1885. Appointed Attorney-Gen. to H.R.H. the Prince of Wales and Duchy of Cornwall 1892. President of the Council of Cheltenham Coll. A Liberal, opposed to Mr. Gladstone's Home Rule scheme. Sat for Taunton from Mar. 1869 (when he obtained the seat on petition) till 1885. Sat for Bury from Nov. 1885 until he retired in 1895. Knighted 1873. PC. 1885. Created 1st Baron James of Hereford 1895; Chancellor of Duchy of Lancaster 1895-1902. Died 18 Aug. 1911. [1895]

JAMES, Hon. Walter Henry. 6 Whitehall Gardens, London. Updown, Sandwich. Reform, and Travellers'. Eld. s. of the 1st Baron Northbourne, by Sarah Caroline, younger d. of Cuthbert Ellison, Esq., of Hebburn Hall, Co. Durham. B. at Whitehall Place, London 1846; m. 1868, Edith, d. of J.N. Lane, Esq., and Hon. Mrs. Newton Lane, of King's Bromley, near

Lichfield. Was educ. at St. Peter's Coll., Radley, and at Christ Church, Oxford. A Liberal, and a supporter of Mr. Gladstone's Home Rule and Land Bills of 1885. Sat for Gateshead from Feb. 1874 until succeeded to peerage as Lord Northbourne in 1893. Died 27 Jan. 1923. [1892 2nd ed.]

JAMESON, John Eustace. 43 Courtfield Gardens, London. Tenby House, Dundrum, Dublin. Reform, Hurlingham, and Naval & Military. S. of James Jameson, Esq., of Airfield, Co. Dublin, a Partner in the Distillery firm of W. Jameson and Company of Dublin. B. 1852; m. Mary, d. of J. Bond Cabbell, Esq., of Cromer Hall, Norfolk. Educ. at Wimbledon, and Sandhurst Coll. A J.P. for Co. Dublin. Was in the 18th Royal Irish, 20th Hussars, and Queen's Own Worcestershire Hussars. Retired as Maj. Was also one of the Government Inspectors of Factories, and Manager of his father's business. Unsuccessfully contested Bury St. Edmunds as a Liberal in 1892. Elected as a Nationalist for W. Clare in 1895 and sat until 1906, joining the Conservatives in 1904. Unsuccessfully contested Chatham as a Conservative in 1906. During the Great War he held Military posts in London, Dublin, and Flanders. Died 22 Dec. 1919. [1905]

JARDINE, Ernest. The Park, Nottingham. The Abbey, Glastonbury, Somerset. Carlton, and Constitutional. B. 23 Sept. 1859; m. 1884. Educ. at private school, Nottingham, and at St. Omer, France. A Textile Machine Builder at Nottingham. A J.P. for Nottingham. A Liberal Unionist. Elected for E. Somerset in Jan. 1910 and sat until he retired in 1918. Created Bart. 1919. Died 26 Apr. 1947. [1918]

JARDINE, Sir John, Bart., K.C.I.E. Applegarth, Godalming. Reform, and Scottish Liberal. S. of William Jardine, Esq., J.P., of Dunstable, and Jane, d. of Robert Sharpe, Esq., of Closeburn. B. 27 Sept. 1844 at Dunstable. Educ. at Christ's Coll., Cambridge. Chancellor's Medal for English Poem 1864. Entered the Bombay Civil Service 1864; served in revenue, judicial, and political offices; Secretary for trial of Gaekwar of Baroda 1875; Law Officer to Government of India 1877; Judicial Commissioner of Burma 1878-85; Chief Secretary to Bombay Government 1885; Judge of Bombay High Court 1885-97; acting Chief Justice 1895; Vice-Chancellor of Bombay University; K.C.I.E. 1897; created Bart. 1916. Author of *Notes on Buddhist Law, Customary Law of Chin Tribe*, etc. A J.P. for Godalming and Surrey. LL.D. Aberdeen. A Liberal, interested in India and Colonial Questions, Temperance Reform, Army Questions, and Small Holdings. Unsuccessfully contested Roxburghshire in 1900. First elected there in 1906 and sat until he retired in 1918. Died 26 Apr. 1919. [1918]

JARDINE, Sir Robert, Bart. 24 St. James's Place, London. Castle Milk, Lockerbie, and Laurick Castle, Doune, N.B. Brooks's, Devonshire, and Reform. Youngest s. of David Jardine, Esq., of Muirhousehead, Co. Dumfriesshire. B. at Muirhousehead 1825; m. 1867, Margaret Seton, d. of John Buchanan Hamilton, Esq., of Leny and Bardowie, Perthshire (she died 1868). Was educ. at Edinburgh. Head of the firm of Jardines Matheson and Company, Merchants in China. A J.P. and Dept.-Lieut. for the Co. of Dumfries. A Liberal, in favour of the abolition of the Law of Entail, and a revision of the Land Laws; opposed to any measure of Home Rule for Ireland "which would tend to impair the integrity of the United Kingdom". Sat for Ashburton from July 1865 to Dec. 1868, and for Dumfries district from the latter date to Feb. 1874, when he was an unsuccessful candidate for Dumfriesshire, for which Co. he sat from Apr. 1880 until he retired in 1892. Created Bart. 1885. Died 17 Feb. 1905. [1892]

JARVIS, Alexander Weston. 3 Little St. James's Street, London. Middleton Towers, King's Lynn. Carlton, and Bachelors'. S. of Sir Lewis Whincop Jarvis, by Emma, d. of Alexander Bowker, Esq., of King's Lynn. B. 1855, at King's Lynn. Unmarried. Educ. at Harrow. Was a Banker from 1875, and a J.P. for the Co. of Norfolk from 1879. A Conservative. Sat for Lynn Regis from Aug. 1886, when he succeeded the Hon. R. Bourke on the latter being appointed Governor-Gen. of Madras. MP until he retired in 1892. Served in the Matabele War 1896; Lieut.-Col. in Boer War; active service at Dardanelles 1915; Staff Officer in France 1917-19. Chairman of Royal Empire Society 1930-32. Knighted 1931. Died 31 Oct. 1939. [1892]

JEBB, Sir Richard Claverhouse.

Springfield, Newnham, Cambridge. Athenaeum, and Albermarle. S. of Robert Jebb, Esq., Barrister-at-Law, and his wife, Emily Harriet, d. of Dr. Horsley, Dean of Brechin. B. at Dundee 1841; m. 1874, Caroline Lane, d. of the Rev. J. Reynolds, D.D., and widow of Gen. A.L. Slemmer, U.S.A army. Educ. at St. Columba's Coll., Charterhouse, and Trinity Coll., Cambridge. A Fellow of Trinity Coll. 1863 (Lecturer 1863-75); Public Orator of the University 1869-76; Greek Professor, University of Glasgow 1875-89; Regius Professor of Greek at Cambridge 1889. Litt. D. Cambridge, Honorary D.C.L. Oxon; Honorary LL.D. Harvard, Edinburgh, Dublin, and Glasgow; Honorary Doctor of Philosophy, Bologna; Com. of the Order of the Saviour, Greece; also F.S.A.; and President Society Promotion of Hellenic Studies; a member of the Royal Commission on Secondary Education 1894; London University Commission 1898; Royal Commission on Irish University Education 1901; and Consultant Committee of Board of Education 1900; Chairman Parliamentary Committee Burial Laws 1897-98. Honorary Professor Ancient History in Royal Academy. A Trustee of the British Museum. Knighted 1900. A Conservative, strongly opposed to legislative interference with the Established Church and its endowments, and in favour of maintaining the independence and integrity of the Colls. of the University. Sat for Cambridge University from 1891 until his death 10 Dec. 1905. [1905]

JEFFREYS, Rt. Hon. Arthur Frederick. Burkham House, Nr. Alton, Hampshire. Carlton. S. of Arthur Jeffreys, Esq., R.N. B. 1848; m. 1877, Amy Constantia, d. of George J. Fenwick, Esq., Dept.-Lieut. Pelton, Co. Durham. Educ. at Christ Church, Oxford; B.A. honours Mathematics. Was called to the bar at the Inner Temple 1872 but never practised; a Dept.-Lieut., J.P., and County Councillor for Hampshire. Dept. Chairman of Ways and Means 1902-05, PC. 1902. Parliamentary Secretary, Local Government Board, June-Dec. 1905. A Conservative, in favour of War Office Reform, and improving the condition of British soldiers; would relieve agriculture by reducing the burdens on agricultural land, and by giving greater facilities for the carriage of farm produce. Sat for Hampshire N. from 1887 until his death 14 Feb. 1906. [1905]

JENKINS, David James. Defeated in 1886: full entry in Volume I.

JENKINS, John Hagan. Grangetown, Cardiff. B. 1852 at Pembroke Dock. Was apprenticed to Ship-Building. President of Cardiff Shipbuilding Society; President of Trades Union Congress 1893; Mayor of Cardiff 1903; a J.P. for Cardiff. A Labour Member. Elected for Chatham in 1906 and sat until defeated in Jan. 1910. [1909]

JENKINS, Sir John Jones. 43 Pall Mall, London. The Grange, Swansea. Reform. S. of Jenkin Jenkins, Esq., of Morriston, Glamorganshire, by Sarah, d. of John Jones, Esq., of Clydach. B. at Clydach, Swansea, 10 May 1835; m. 1st, 1854, Margaret, d. of Josiah Rees, Esq., of Morriston (she died 1863); 2ndly, 1864, Katherine, d. of Edward Daniel, Esq., a Civil Engineer, of Morriston. A J.P. and Dept.-Lieut. for Glamorganshire (High Sheriff 1889). County Councillor for the Oystermouth division of Glamorganshire, J.P. for Carmarthenshire and Swansea, and Mayor of Carmarthenshire 1869-70, 1879-80, and 1880-81. Honorary Lieut. R.N.A.V., member of the Governing Body Intermediate and Technical Education, Swansea, President Royal Institution of South Wales 1889-90; member (resigned Chairmanship 1898) Swansea Harbour Trust and Chairman Swansea Royal Metal Exchange. In 1895 he received the Honorary Freedom of Swansea in recognition of 30 years' public service. A Liberal Unionist, in favour of local self-government, legislation in aid of British Trade, Taxation of Royalties and Ground Rents, Old Age Pensions, etc. Unsuccessfully contested Carmarthen district in Apr. 1880. Elected there in Jan. 1882 and sat until defeated in July 1886. Unsuccessfully contested the constituency in July 1892. Returned there in July 1895 and sat until defeated in 1900. Knighted 1881. Created Baron Glantawe June 1906. Died 27 July 1915. [1900]

JENNINGS, Louis John. 73 Elm Park Gardens, London. Athenaeum, and Carlton. B. in London 1837; m. 1867, Madeline Louise, d. of David M. Henriques, Esq., of New York. Resided in India and the United States. Author of *Republican Government in the United States, Field Paths, Rambles among the Hills, The Millionaire, Mr. Gladstone: a Study,* and editor of *The Croker Papers.* Was one of the five members appointed by the Speaker to act as Dept.-Chairman of Committees of the House of Commons. A Conservative. First returned for Stockport Nov. 1885 and sat until his death 9 Feb. 1893.   [1892 2nd ed.]

JESSEL, Col. Sir Herbert Merton, Bart. 24 South Street, Park Lane, London. Carlton, Army & Navy, White's, Beefsteak, and Garrick. Youngest s. of the Rt. Hon. Sir George Jessel, Master of the Rolls. B. 1866 at Brighton; m. 1894, Maud, d. of the Rt. Hon. Sir Julian Goldsmid, MP. Educ. at Rugby, where he gained an entrance scholarship, and New Coll., Oxford. Capt. 17th Lancers and Berkshire Yeomanry; served in India 1887-90; retired from the army 1896. Honorary Col. 1st Royal Fusiliers (City of London Regiment). Rejoined army Oct. 1914, Assistant Commandant Dec. 1914 and Commandant (Army Remount Service) with rank of Lieut.-Col. Jan. 1915; mentioned in despatches 1917. Trustee of London Municipal Society, Chairman 1903 to 1915, and Alderman for the City of Westminster, Mayor 1903. A Dept.-Lieut. and J.P. for the Co. of London. Member of advisory committee on Prevention and Relief of Distress Aug. 1914. He carried through the House of Commons "Municipal Elections Acts" 1911, "Old Age Pensions Act" 1911, and "Affiliation Orders Act" 1914. Member of Public Accounts Committee from 1910. Created Bart. 1917. A Unionist. Sat for S. St. Pancras from 1896 to 1906, when he was defeated; re-elected there Jan. 1910 and sat until he retired in 1918. Contested St. Georges, Westminster June 1921; created 1st Baron Jessel 1924; member of Crown Lands Advisory Committee 1924; London Whip, Unionist Central Office 1920-27. Died 1 Nov. 1950.   [1918]

JODRELL, Neville Paul. Continued in House after 1918: full entry in Volume III.

JOHN, Edward Thomas. Llanidan Hall, Llanfair P.G., Anglesey. 63 Warwick Square, London. National Liberal. S. of John and Margaret John. B. 14 Mar. 1857 at Pontypridd, Glamorgan; m. 1881, Margaret, d. of William Rees, Esq., of Caerwiga, Pendoylan, Glamorgan. Educ. at Wesleyan Day School, Pontypridd. Managing Director of Smelting and Mining Companies. J.P. for Middlesborough. A Welsh Nationalist. Elected for E. Denbighshire in Dec. 1910 as a Liberal, but joined Labour Party in July 1918, and sat until defeated in Denbigh in 1918. Unsuccessfully contested Brecon and Radnor in 1922 and 1924 and Anglesey in Apr. 1923. President National Union of Welsh Societies 1916-26; President Celtic Congress 1918-27. Author of several works concerning Wales. Died 16 Feb. 1931.   [1918]

JOHNS, Jasper Wilson. 16 Grenville Place, Cromwell Road, London. Reform. Only s. of Thomas Evans Johns, Esq., of Cardiganshire, by Elizabeth Tudor, d. of T. Avis, Esq., of Suffolk. B. at Dublin 1824; m. 1854, Emily Theresa, eld. d. of James Bird, Esq., M.R.C.S. London. Educ. privately. Educ. as a Civil Engineer, and practised his profession up to 1854, when he joined the firm of William Bird and Company, Iron Merchants of London. Was an active promoter of railways, etc. in Wales, and for many years Dept.-Chairman of some of the companies. A J.P. and Dept.-Lieut. for Merionethshire, and J.P. for Montgomeryshire. A Liberal, advocated an elective House of Lords. Unsuccessfully contested Northallerton in July 1865 and again in Nov. 1868. Sat for the Nuneaton division of Warwickshire from Dec. 1885 until defeated in 1886 standing as a Gladstonian Liberal. Died 26 July 1891.   [1886]

JOHNSON, John. 20 The Avenue, Durham. S. of Thomas and Martha Johnson. B. 1 Oct. 1850 at Wapping, Northumberland; m. d. of T. Errington, Esq. Educ. at an Old Dame School. Commenced work in the pits before reaching the age of ten. Financial Secretary to the Durham Miners' Association. Was a member of the Durham County Council. Attended several International Congresses of Miners. A Liberal and Labour Member. Elected for Gateshead in Jan. 1904 and sat until defeated in Jan. 1910. Died 29 Dec. 1910.   [1909]

JOHNSON, William. Miners' Office, Bedworth, Warwickshire. S. of John and Susan Johnson, of Chilvers Coton. B. 1849 at Chilvers Coton; m. 1st, d. of S. Davenport, Esq.; 2ndly, 1908, Mrs. Anne Copson, of Leicester. Educ. at Collycroft School. Started work in a factory and a coal mine. Was Gen. Secretary and Agent of Warwickshire Miners' Association 1885-1916. Was Miners' Agent for Warwickshire. Alderman of Warwickshire County Council and of the Co. Education Committee; a member of Foleshill District Council and Board of Guardians; Chairman of Bedworth Parish Council. A J.P. for Warwickshire. A Labour member until Apr. 1914 when the Labour whip was withdrawn and he became a Liberal. Unsuccessfully contested Warwickshire N. in 1892 and Nuneaton in 1900. Elected for the Nuneaton division of Warwickshire in 1906 and sat until he retired in 1918. M.B.E. 1918. Died 20 July 1919.   [1918]

JOHNSON-FERGUSON, Jabez Edward. 55 Cadogan Square, London. Springkell, Ecclefechan, N.B. Reform. Only s. of Jabez Johnson, Esq., J.P., of Kenyon Hall, near Manchester, by Mary, d. of John Johnson, Esq., of Broughton, Manchester. B. 1849; m. 1874, the d. of W.A. Cunningham, Esq., of Manchester. Educ. at St. John's Coll., Cambridge (32nd wrangler 1872, M.A. 1875). Was called to the bar, but did not practise. Assumed the name of Johnson-Ferguson in 1881. A Liberal. Sat for the Loughborough division of Leicestershire from 1885 until he was defeated in July 1886. Re-elected there 1892 and sat until defeated in the Burton division of Staffordshire Oct. 1900. Created 1st Bart. 1906. Died 10 Dec. 1929.   [1900]

JOHNSTON, Christopher Nicholson. 4 Heriot Row, Edinburgh. Constitutional, and New Conservative, Edinburgh. Conservative, Glasgow. County Perth. B. 18 Oct. 1857; m. Agnes Warren, 2nd d. of James E. Dunn, Esq., of Dunmullin, Strathblane. Educ. at Madras Coll., St. Andrews, and the Universities of St. Andrews, Edinburgh; M.A., and Heidelberg. Advocate 1880. Sub-Commissioner on Educational Endowments; Counsel for the Board of Trade, Woods and Forests, Admiralty, and War Office. Advocate Depute; Sheriff of Caithness, Orkney and Shetland 1899-1900; Sheriff of Inverness, Elgin and Nairn 1901-05. K.C. 1902. Author of Manuals on Agricultural and Crofter Legislation, *Handbook of Church Defence, Ecclesiastic Law in Scotland, St. Paul and his Mission to the Roman Empire, Major Owen and Other Tales, John Blaw of Castlehill,* etc. A Conservative. Unsuccessfully contested Paisley in 1892. Elected for Edinburgh and St. Andrews Universities in Dec. 1916 and sat until appointed Judge of Court of Session with title of Lord Sands in July 1917. Kt. 1917. Died 26 Feb. 1934.   [1917]

JOHNSTON, William. Ballykilbeg, Co. Down. Eld. s. of John Brett Johnston, Esq., of Ballykilbeg,Co. Down, by Thomasina Anne Brunette, d. of Thomas Scott, Esq., Surgeon, Royal Horse Guards. B. at Downpatrick 1829; m. 1st, 1853, Harriet, d. of Robert Allen, Esq.; 2ndly, 1861, Arminella Frances, d. of the Rev. Thomas Drew, D.D.; and 3rdly, 1863, Georgiana Barbara, d. of Sir John Hay, Bart., of Park. Educ. at Trinity Coll., Dublin, where he took the M.A. degree. Was called to the Irish bar in 1872. Author of several works of fiction, viz *Nightshade, Under which King,* etc. A Protestant Conservative. Sat for Belfast from 1868 until 1878 when he was appointed Inspector of Irish Fisheries, and for Belfast S. from 1885 until his death 17 July 1902.   [1902]

JOHNSTONE, John Heywood. Bignor Park, Pulborough, Sussex. Trewithen, Grampound Road, Cornwall. Carlton, and University. S. of the Rev. George D. Johnstone, Rector of Creed, Cornwall, and Mary Anne, d. of John Hawkins, Esq., of Bignor Park. B. 1850 at Stonegate, Sussex; m. 1878, Josephine, d. of J.J. Wells, Esq., of Bickley, Kent. Educ. at Trinity Coll., Cambridge. A Barrister, called to the bar at the Inner Temple Nov. 1874. A J.P. and member of the County Council for W. Sussex. A Conservative. Was an unsuccessful candidate at the St. Austell election in 1885. Sat for the Horsham division of Sussex from Feb. 1893 until his death 10 Oct. 1904.   [1904]

JOICEY, Sir James, Bart. 58 Cadogan Square, London. Longhirst, Northumberland. Gregynog, Newtown, Montgomeryshire. Reform, Devonshire, and National Liberal. S. of George Joicey, Esq., Mining Engineer, of Newcastle-on-Tyne, by Dorothy his wife. B. at Tanfield, Durham 1846; m. 1st, 1879, Amy, d. of Joseph Robinson, Esq., J.P., of North Shields; 2ndly, 1884, Margaret, d. of Col. Drever, Bengal Cavalry, of the East India Company. Educ. at Gainford School, near Darlington. A large Coal-Owner of the firm of Joicey and Company, and the Lambton Collieries Limited. A Dept.-Lieut. for Co. Durham, J.P. for Northumberland, Durham, Montgomeryshire, and Newcastle-on-Tyne. Created Bart. June 1893. An "advanced Liberal" and Home Ruler. Sat for the Chester-le-Street division of Durham from 1885 until created

1st Baron Joicey 1905. Joined Conservative Party in 1931. Died 21 Nov. 1936. [1905]

JOICEY-CECIL, Lord John Pakenham. Newton Hall, Stockfield-on-Tyne, Northumberland. 5a Mount Street, London. S. of 3rd Marq. of Exeter. B. 1867; m. 1896, Isabella Maud, d. of Col. Joicey, MP, of Newton Hall, Northumberland, when he assumed the additional name of Joicey. Col. of 4th Battalion (M.) Lincolnshire Regiment. In the Grenadier Guards. A J.P. for Peterborough. A Conservative. Elected for the Stamford division of Lincolnshire in 1906 and sat until he retired in Jan. 1910. Died 25 June 1942. [1909]

JOLLIFFE, Hon. Hylton George Hylton. 1 West Halkin Street, London. Carlton, Travellers', and Bachelors'. Only s. of Lord Hylton, 2nd Baron, by his 1st wife, Agnes Mary, eld. d. of the 2nd Earl of Strafford. B. 1862; m. 1896, Alice, d. of Marq. of Bristol. Educ. at Eton, and Oriel Coll., Oxford (B.A. 1885, M.A. 1891). Was attaché in the Diplomatic Service 1888, third Secretary in same service 1890, and second Secretary 1894. A J.P. for Somerset, and a Capt. N. Somerset Yeomanry. A Conservative. Sat for the Wells division of Somerset from July 1895 until he succeeded as Lord Hylton in 1899. Lord-in-Waiting 1915-18. Edited *The Paget Brothers 1790-1848* (1918). Captain of Yeomen of Guard 1918-24. Died 26 May 1945. [1899]

JONES, Rt. Hon. Sir David Brynmor. 27 Bryanston Square, London. 12 King's Bench Walk, Temple, London. Reform, National Liberal, Ranelagh, and Devonshire. Eld. s. of the Rev. Thomas Jones, of Rhayader House, Swansea (Chairman of the Congregational Union of England and Wales). B. 1852 at Pertrepoeth, near Swansea; m. 1892, Florence, widow of Mr. A de M. Mocatta, d. of Maj. Lionel B. Cohen. Educ. privately, and at University Coll. School, and University Coll., London; LL.B. University of London. Was Hume Scholar at University Coll. 1873; obtained the studentship of the Council of Legal Education 1875; called to the bar, Middle Temple 1876; Q.C. 1893; a bencher 1899. Practised as a Barrister in London and on the S. Wales and Chester Circuit. Recorder of Merthyr-Tydvil from 1910 to 1914. Was Co. Court Judge Mid Wales and Gloucestershire from 1885; resigned 1892. Member of the Court of University of Wales, also Junior Dept. Chancellor and Honorary Counsel; a Vice-President of the Cymmrodorion Society, member of the Welsh Land Commission 1894-96, Welsh Church Commission 1907, and Venereal Diseases Commission 1913. A J.P. for Glamorgan. Chairman of Co. Court Dept. Committees 1893 and 1899; Chairman of Metropolitan Police Commission 1906. Knighted 1906. Chairman of the Welsh Liberal Parliamentary Party 1912. A Referee of Private Bills. PC. 1912. Wrote *Home Rule and Imperial Sovereignty, Welsh History and Recent Research,* and *The Welsh People* (jointly with J. Rhys); edited *The Divine Order, and other Sermons* (by his father), with an introduction by Robert Browning, the poet. A Liberal. Sat for the Stroud division of Gloucestershire from 1892-95, and for Swansea district from 1895 until appointed Master of Lunacy in 1914. Recorder of Cardiff 1914-15. Died 6 Aug. 1921. [1914]

JONES, Sir Edgar Rees. Continued in House after 1918: full entry in Volume III.

JONES, Maj. Evan Rowland. 12 Cumberland Terrace, Regent's Park, London. Savage, and National Liberal. S. of William Jones and Mary Rowlands. B. 1840 at Tregaron, Cardiganshire; m. 1867, Kate Alice, d. of William and Jane Evans, of Llanpaglan, Carnarvonshire. Educ. at Llangeithe and Tregaron Schools. A Journalist, Editor and Proprietor of the *Shipping World.* Served in the United States Army, in which he was Capt. and Maj. was United States Consul at Newcastle for twenty-three years; a member of the Council of the University Coll. of North Wales and Monmouthshire, President of the Cymmrodorion Society of Cardiff. Wrote *Four Years in the Army of the Potomac, Historical Sketches,* a life of his friend Joseph Cowen, MP, and other books. An advanced Liberal, in favour of Home Rule for Ireland, etc. First returned for Carmarthen district in July 1892 and sat until defeated in 1895. Died 16 Jan. 1920. [1895]

JONES, Henry Haydn. Continued in House after 1918: full entry in Volume III.

JONES, Rev. Josiah Towyn. Continued in House after 1918: full entry in Volume III.

JONES, Rt. Hon. Leifchild Stratten. Continued in House after 1918: full entry in Volume III.

JONES, Sir Pryce. See PRYCE-JONES, Sir Pryce.

JONES, William. 24 Gordon Street, London. B. in Anglesey 1860. Educ. at Bangor Normal Coll., Aberystwyth University Coll., and at Oxford. Served as Schoolmaster in Wales, and under the London School Board. Was a Private Tutor at Oxford. Appointed a Junior Lord of the Treasury and a Liberal Whip 1911. A Liberal, and Home Ruler. Represented N. Carnarvonshire from 1895 until his death 9 May 1915. [1915]

JONES, William Kennedy. Continued in House after 1918: full entry in Volume III.

JONES-PARRY, Thomas Duncombe Love. Defeated in 1886: full entry in Volume I. (Note: Love is incorrectly spelt Lone in Volume I.)

JORDAN, Jeremiah. 12 and 13 High Street, Enniskillen. S. of Samuel Jordan, Esq., Farmer, of Brookborough, Co. Fermanagh. B. 1830. Educ. at a National School, and the Royal School, Enniskillen. A Provision Merchant, and a Tenant Farmer, and several times Chairman of the Enniskillen Town Commissioners; a member of Fermanagh County Council and of Enniskillen Urban Council and Board of Guardians. A Nationalist. Sat for W. Clare from 1885-92. Unsuccessfully contested N. Fermanagh in 1892. Sat for S. Meath from 1893-95, when he was elected for S. Fermanagh; sat for S. Fermanagh until he retired in Dec. 1910. Died 21 Dec. 1911. [1910]

JOSSE, Henri. 128 Leadenhall Street, London. Becklands, Barnold-by-le-beck, Great Grimsby. National Liberal. B. in France about 1828, where he received his education; studied law and practised in a Solicitor's Office in Caen. Having taken an active part in politics, in the year 1848 he resisted Louis Napoleon's coup d'état, and in 1851 he was arrested; after six weeks' imprisonment, he was expelled from France. He was subsequently naturalized as a British subject, and entered the service of Mr. Hyppolite Worms, who had establishments for the export of coal at Newcastle and Cardiff. In this capacity Mr. Josse took an important part in the development of the town and the foreign trade of Grimsby, and ultimately became a Partner in the firm known as Worms, Josse and Company, Coal Exporters, who had houses in numerous parts of Europe, Asia, Africa, and America. A J.P., and President of the Grimsby Liberal Association from its foundation. A follower of Mr. Gladstone. First returned for Great Grimsby July 1892 and sat until he accepted Chiltern Hundreds Feb. 1893. Died 23 July 1893. [1892 2nd ed.]

JOWETT, Frederick William. Continued in House after 1918: full entry in Volume III.

JOYCE, Michael. The Moorings, O'Connel Avenue, Limerick. Irish. S. of Richard Joyce, Esq., Pilot. B. 1854 in Limerick. Educ. at Christian Brothers School, Limerick. Was Mayor of Limerick 1905-06 and Alderman from 1899. Was a Pilot from 1876 to 1900. A Nationalist. First elected for Limerick city in 1900 and sat until he retired in 1918. [1918]

JOYNSON-HICKS, William. Continued in House after 1918: full entry in Volume III.

KAVANAGH, Walter MacMorrough. Borris, Co. Carlow. S. of the Rt. Hon. A.M. Kavanagh, MP for Co. Wexford from 1866-68 and Co. Carlow 1869-80. B. 1856. Educ. at Eton, and Christ Church, Oxford. Dept.-Lieut. and J.P. for Co. Carlow, High Sheriff 1884. J.P. for Co. Kilkenny. High Sheriff for Co. Wexford 1893. Held a commission in 5th Battalion Royal Irish Rifles. A Nationalist. Unsuccessfully contested, as a Unionist, N. Kilkenny in 1892 and S. Armagh in 1895. Elected as a Nationalist for Co. Carlow in Feb. 1908 and sat until he retired in Jan. 1910. PC. Ireland 1916. Died 18 July 1922. [1909]

KAY-SHUTTLEWORTH, Rt. Hon. Sir Ughtred James, Bart. 28 Prince's Gardens, Lincoln. Gawthorpe Hall, Burnley, Lancashire. Barbon Manor, Kirkby Lonsdale. Athenaeum, National Liberal, and Reform. Eld. s. of Sir James Phillips Kay-Shuttleworth, Bart., D.C.L., by Janet, d. of Robert Shuttleworth, Esq., of Gawthorpe Hall. B. in Westminster 1844; m. 1871, Blanche Marion, youngest d. of Sir Woodbine Parish, K.C.H. Educ. at Harrow, and the University of London. Succeeded as Bart. 1877. Author of *The First Principles of Modern Chemistry*. Sat on the London School Board from 1880 to 1882, and in the latter year was appointed a member of the Royal Commission on Reformatory and Industrial Schools. PC. 1886. In 1886 he became Parliamentary Under-Secretary for India, and then Chancellor of the Duchy of Lancaster which office he held until July 1886; from 1892 to 1895 was Secretary to the Admiralty. A J.P. for Westmoreland and Lancashire, and Dept.-Lieut. for Westmoreland. A Liberal, and an Educational Reformer. In the House of Commons in 1874 he moved a resolution on the Improvement of the Dwellings of the Working Classes, and in 1878 a resolution on the Reform of London Government. Unsuccessfully contested Lancashire N.E. Nov. 1868. Sat for Hastings from 1869 until defeated 1880. Contested Coventry 1881. Sat for the Clitheroe division of Lancashire from 1885 until created Lord Shuttleworth in 1902. Chairman of Royal Commission on Canals 1906-11. Lord-Lieut. of Lancashire 1908-28. Died 20 Dec. 1939.   [1902]

KEARLEY, Rt. Hon. Sir Hudson Ewbanke, Bart. 41 Grosvenor Place, London. Wittington, Marlow. Gwylfa Hiraethog, Denbigh, North Wales. Reform. S. of George Ewbanke Kearley, Esq., of Uxbridge, and Mary Anne, d. of Charles Hudson, Esq., of Devonshire Square, London. B. 1856 at Uxbridge; m. 1888, Selina, d. of Edward Chester, Esq., of Blisworth, Northamptonshire. Educ. at Cranleigh School. A Partner in the firm of Kearley and Tonge. Parliamentary Secretary to the Board of Trade from Dec. 1905 to Jan. 1909. A Bart. 1908. PC. 1909. A Liberal. Represented Devonport from 1892 until he retired in Jan. 1910. Created Baron Devonport June 1910; created Visct. Devonport in June 1917; Chairman of Port of London Authority 1910-25; Food Controller 1916-17; Chairman of Royal Commission on Sugar Supplies 1916-17. Died 5 Sept. 1934.   [1909]

KEATING, Matthew. National Liberal. S. of Cornelius Keating, Esq., of Caherciveen, Co. Kerry. B. 23 May 1869 at Mountain Ash, S. Wales. Unmarried. Educ. at Duffyn School, Mountain Ash, and privately. A Manufacturer's Agent in London. A Nationalist. First elected for S. Kilkenny in Aug. 1909 and sat until defeated in 1918. Subsequently Director of Irish Shell Limited. Died 25 May 1937.   [1918]

KEAY, John Seymour. 90 Ladbroke Grove, London. Orleans, and National Liberal. S. of the Rev. John Keay, a Minister of the Church of Scotland, and of Agnes Keay, née Straiton. B. at Bathgate, in Linlithgowshire 1839; m. 1878, Nina, 2nd d. of William Carne Vivian, Esq. Educ. at Madras Coll., St. Andrews. Entered upon his business as a Banker in Scotland 1856, and in 1862 established himself in India. On his return to England he interested himself in Afghan and Egyptian questions, and wrote *The Spoliation of India, Spoiling the Egyptians, Landlord, Tenant, and Taxpayer,* and a pamphlet on the Central Asian question entitled *The Great Imperial Danger.* A Radical, in favour of Home Rule, one vote for every citizen, shorter Parliaments, payment of MPs, " Disestablishment", "Local Option", a radical reform of the land laws, free education, the abolition of hereditary legislators, etc. Contested W. Newington unsuccessfully in 1885. First elected for Elgin and Nairn Oct. 1889 and sat until defeated in 1895. Contested the Tamworth division of Warwickshire in 1906. Died 27 June 1909.   [1895]

KEBTY-FLETCHER, John Robert. The Paddock, Hootton, Cheshire. Only s. of George Fletcher, Esq., of Liverpool. B. 1868. Educ. at Liverpool and on the Continent. A Partner in the firm of George Fletcher and Company, Provision Merchants, Liverpool, and a Director and President of Liverpool Produce Exchange. A member of Liverpool Town Council; acted as Correspondent for *Liverpool Daily Post* during South African War. A Unionist. Unsuccessfully contested Rossendale division of Lancashire in 1906 and Jan. 1910. Elected for the Altrincham division of Cheshire in Dec. 1910 and sat until he accepted Chiltern Hundreds in 1913. Died 12 July 1918.   [1913]

KEKEWICH, Sir George William. St. Alban's, Feltham, Middlesex. Reform, and National Liberal. S. of S.T. Kekewich, Esq., MP for S. Devon, and Louisa, d. of L.W. Buck, Esq., MP. B. 1 Apr. 1841; married. Educ. at Eton, and Balliol Coll., Oxford. Was Examiner in Education Department 1867; Senior Examiner 1871; Secretary to Education Department 1890-1900, to Science and Art Department 1899-1900, and to the Board of Education 1900-03. K.C.B. 1895; Honorary D.C.L. Durham; a

J.P. for Middlesex. A Liberal. Elected for Exeter in 1906 and sat until he retired in Jan. 1910. Died 5 July 1921.   [1909]

KELLAWAY, Frederick George. Continued in House after 1918: full entry in Volume III.

KELLEY, George Davy. 63 Upper Brook Street, Manchester. S. of Thomas and Sarah Frances Kelley. B. 1848 at Ruskington, Lincolnshire. Educ. at the village school. A Lithographic Printer and Gen. Secretary of Amalgamated Society of Lithographic Printers, and National Printing and Kindred Trades Federation. A J.P. and Councillor for Manchester. A Labour Member. Elected for S.W. Manchester in 1906 and sat until he retired in Jan. 1910. Died 18 Dec. 1911.   [1909]

KELLY, Bernard. Ballyshannon, Co. Donegal. S. of Peter Kelly, Esq., of Ballyshannon, who was engaged in trade as a Grocer, and an Owner of Potteries and was Chairman of the Town Commissioners. He was in business with his father, and was also Secretary to the local branch of the National League. An "Irish Nationalist." Sat for Donegal S. from Dec. 1885 until his death 1 Jan. 1887.   [1886]

KELLY, Edward Joseph. Continued in House after 1918: full entry in Volume III.

KELLY, John Richards. 25 Upper Phillimore Gardens, Kensington, London. S. of Frederick Festus Kelly, Esq., at one time Inspector-Gen. of Letter-Carriers in the Post Office, by Harriet, d. of John Richards, Esq., of Maida Vale, London. B. in London 1844; m. 1879, his cousin, Fanny Lydia, only d. of Edward Robert Kelly, Esq., of Shepherd's Bush. Educ. at Eton, and Trinity Hall, Cambridge. A Barrister-at-Law, having been called at the Inner Temple in 1879. A "moderate Conservative", in favour of reasonable reforms in the House of Lords, and of the "principles of Fair Trade", though opposed to taxing articles of food, and strongly opposed to Mr. Gladstone's Home Rule policy. Sat for Camberwell N. from July 1886 until defeated in 1892. Died 20 July 1922. [1892]

KEMP, Sir George. Beechwood, Rochdale. Lingholm, Keswick. White's, and Arthur's. S. of George Tawke Kemp, Esq., of Beechwood, Rochdale, and Emily

Lydia, d. of Henry Kelsall, Esq., of The Butts, Rochdale. B. 1866 at Beechwood; m. 1896, Lady Beatrice Egerton, d. of the Earl of Ellesmere. Educ. at Shrewsbury School, and Trinity Coll., Cambridge; B.A. Classical Tripos. Managing Director of Kelsall and Kemp, Flannel Manufacturers. Was a Maj. in the Duke of Lancaster's Own Yeomanry and Honorary Lieut.-Col. in the Army. Served in South Africa 1900-02, mentioned in despatches. A Unionist until he joined the Liberal Party over the Free Trade issue in Aug. 1904. Sat for the Heywood division of Lancashire from 1895 to 1906, when he retired. Elected for N.W. Manchester in Jan. 1910 and sat until he accepted Chiltern Hundreds in July 1912. Knighted 1909. Created Baron Rochdale in Jan. 1913. Lord-Lieut. of Middlesex from 1929. Died 24 Mar. 1945.   [1912]

KENNAWAY, Rt. Hon. Sir John Henry, Bart., C.B. Escott, Ottery St. Mary, Devon. 1 Whitehall Gardens, London. Athenaeum, and National Liberal. Eld. s. of Sir John Kennaway, Bart., by the d. of Thomas Kingscote, Esq., of Kingscote, Gloucestershire. B. at Park Crescent 1837; m. 1866, Frances, eld. d. of Archibald F. Arthbuthnot, Esq., of Hyde Park Gardens, London, and grand-d. of the 1st Visct. Gough. Was educ. at Harrow, and Balliol Coll., Oxford, where he was 1st class in the law and modern history school. Called to the bar at the Inner Temple 1864; sworn a Privy Councillor 1897. C.B. 1902. Honorary Col. 4th Battalion Devon Regiment. President Church Missionary Society, and of the London Society for Promoting Christianity among the Jews. A J.P. for Devon. Author of a work entitled *On Sherman's Track*. A Conservative. Sat for E. Devon from 1870-85, and for the Honition division of Devon from 1885 until he retired in Jan. 1910. Succeeded as Bart. in 1873. Father of the House of Commons 1908-10. Died 6 Sept. 1919.   [1909]

KENNEDY, Edward Joseph. 38 Claverton Street, London. 5 Charlemont Terrace, Kingstown. S. of Edward Kennedy, Esq., of Cavan, by his marriage with Miss C. Brady. B. 1851; m. 1886, d. of Alderman O'Connor, MP, at one time Lord Mayor of Dublin. Educ. at Cavan Coll. A Tobacco Manufacturer in Dublin, and served as High Sheriff of that city in 1885, of which he was a Town Councillor and Justice of the Peace. A Nationalist. Sat for Sligo S. from Feb. 1887 until he accepted Chiltern Hundreds in May 1888. [1888]

KENNEDY, Patrick James. Rathcore House, Enfield Co. Meath. National Liberal. S. of Bryan Kennedy, Esq., of Rathcore House, Enfield Co. Meath, by his wife Brigid Bourke. B. at Rathcore House 1864; m. 1888, Cornelia, 3rd d. of Professor P.A. Duncan, of the University of Vienna. Educ. at St. Vincent's Coll., Castleknock, Co. Dublin. A Landowner and Gentleman Farmer; elected Chairman of the 1st County Council, established in Apr. 1899, by the Local Government Act 1898, for his native Co. of Meath. Was Chairman of the Meath County Council 1900-02. A J.P. for Co. Meath, and served on all local bodies; a member of the Council of Agriculture. An Irish Nationalist, strongly in favour of a scheme of compulsory purchase of land for Ireland and of the establishment of an Irish University for Catholics, both to be accomplished by Imperial financial aid, as a set-off to the financial grievances of Ireland. Sat for N. Kildare from 1892-95, when he retired. Sat for Westmeath N. from Oct. 1900 until he retired in 1906. Died 10 Mar. 1947. [1905]

KENNEDY, Vincent Paul. Heath Lodge, Cavan. National Liberal, and Leinster. S. of H.P. Kennedy, Esq., Crown Solicitor, of Cavan, and Catherine R. Maginnis, of London. B. 15 Feb. 1876 at Cavan; m. 1912, Cecillia Beatrice, d. of Adolph Boursot, Esq. Educ. at Clongowes Wood Coll. A Solicitor, admitted July 1900, practised in Cavan and the surrounding counties. A Nationalist. Elected for W. Cavan June 1904 and sat until he retired in 1918. Continued to practise as an Irish Solicitor. 18 Nov. 1943. [1918]

KENNY, Courtney Stanhope. 9 Bridge Street, London. Downing College, Cambridge. Reform. Eld. s. of William Fenton Kenny, Esq., of Halifax and Ripon, Solicitor and J.P., by Agnes, d. of John Rhodes Ralph, Esq., J.P., of Halifax. B. 1847; m. 1876, Emily Gertrude, d. of W.W. Wiseman, Esq., M.R.C.S. Educ. at Heath Grammar School, and Downing Coll., Cambridge (senior in the Law and History Tripos 1874, Chancellor's Legal Medallist and Winchester Prizeman 1875, and thrice Yorke Prizeman of the University, 1877-79,

LL.D. 1886). Was admitted a Solicitor in 1869 (obtaining on admission the Clifford's Inn Prize, and Broderip Gold Medal); called to the bar 1881. Lecturer in Law and Moral Science at Downing Coll., and Lecturer on Law at Trinity Coll., Cambridge. Author of works on the Law of Primogeniture, the Law of Married Women's Property, and *Endowed Charities*. A Liberal and Home Ruler, desirous of promoting the codification of the law, and in favour of "an entire reconstruction of the House of Lords". Sat for the Barnsley division of the W. Riding of Yorkshire from 1885 until he accepted Chiltern Hundreds in Feb. 1889. Appointed Reader in English Law (1888) and then Professor of the Laws of England (1907-18) at Cambridge University. Alderman of Cambridgeshire County Council 1901-20. Chairman of Cambridgeshire Quarter Sessions 1912-22. F.B.A. 1909. Died 18 Mar. 1930. [1888]

KENNY, Joseph Edward. 15 Rutland Square East, Dublin. S. of the Manager of a Lead Mine near Palmerston, Co. Dublin, where he was b. in 1845. Educ. at Dublin, and admitted a licentiate of both the Royal Colls. of Physician and Surgeons at Edinburgh in 1870. Also received the degree of L.A.H. Dublin, from the Catholic University. Was visiting Surgeon to the N. Dublin Union Hospital, and held other medical appointments under the Local Government Board, from which he was dismissed on his arrest as a "suspect" in 1883; but on disputing the legality of his dismissal, he was reinstated and received a public testimonial. Was elected Coroner for the city of Dublin July 1891. An "Irish Nationalist" of the Parnellite party. Sat for Cork Co. S. division from 1885 to 1892. Sat for the Coll. Green division of Dublin City from July 1892 until he accepted Chiltern Hundreds in 1896. Died 9 Apr. 1900. [1895]

KENNY, Matthew Joseph. 16 Warrington Place, Dublin. Freagh Castle, Miltown, Malbay, Co. Clare. S. of Michael Kenny, Esq., Solicitor, of Miltown Malbay, Co. Clare, by his m. with Miss Bridget Frost, of Ballymorris House, Cratloe, Ireland. B. at Freagh Castle, Miltown Malbay, Co. Clare 1861. Educ. at Ennis Coll., and Queen's Coll., Ireland. Called to the bar at Gray's Inn May 1886. Also called to the Irish bar, where he practised on the N.W. Circuit. A Nationalist, in favour of the settlement of the Irish question on the lines laid down in the Home Rule Bill of 1886. Sat for Ennis from 1882 to 1885, and for mid Tyrone from 1885 until he retired in 1895. King's Counsel 1914. Senior Crown Prosecutor for Co. Kerry 1916; Circuit Court Judge for Cork 1925-33. Died 8 Dec. 1942. [1895]

KENNY, William. 35 Fitzwilliam Place, Dublin. Brooks's. S. of Edward Kenny, Esq., Solicitor, and Catherine his wife. B. 1846 in Dublin; m. 1873, Mary, eld. d. of David Coffey, Esq., Master in Chancery. Educ. privately, and at Trinity Coll., Dublin. A Barrister, called in Ireland 1868; appointed Q.C. 1885, and Solicitor-Gen. for Ireland 1895. M.A. Trinity Coll., Dublin, member of the Senate of Dublin University; a bencher of the King's Inn, Dublin 1890. Was one of the Secretaries of the Liberal Union of Ireland, which association he was largely instrumental in establishing in 1887. A Liberal Unionist, believed that the maintenance in its integrity of the Legislative Union, gave to Ireland the only guarantee for order, freedom and progress. Sat for the St. Stephen's Green division of Dublin from July 1892 until appointed High Court Judge (Ireland) in 1897. PC. 1902. Died 4 Feb. 1921. [1897]

KENRICK, William. 71 St. Ermin's Mansions, London. The Grove, Harborne, Birmingham. 2nd s. of Archibald Kenrick, Esq., of West Bromwich, Manufacturer, and J.P. for the counties of Stafford and Worcester, by Anne, d. of W. Paget, Esq., of Loughborough. B. 1831; m. 1862, Mary, d. of Joseph Chamberlain, Esq., and sister of the Rt. Hon. Joseph Chamberlain, MP. Educ. by the Rev. J.P. Malleson, of Hove, Brighton; afterwards obtained a gold medal for chemistry at University Coll., London. An Ironfounder. In 1870 he entered the town council of Birmingham; in 1877 became Alderman and served as Mayor. J.P. for Birmingham, Chairman of the Museum and School of Art Committee of the town council; was Governor of King Edward VI's Grammar School, and was Vice-President of the Midland Institute from 1864 to 1866. A Liberal Unionist. Sat for Birmingham N. from 1885 until he accepted Chiltern Hundreds in 1899. PC. 1899. Died 31 July 1919. [1898]

KENYON, Barnet. Continued in House after 1918: full entry in Volume III.

KENYON, Hon. George Thomas. Llanerch Panna, Flintshire. Carlton. S. of the 3rd Baron Kenyon, by the Hon. Georgina de Gray, d. of the 4th Baron Walsingham. B. at Harley Street, London in 1840; m. 1875, Florence, d. of John Harleston Leche, Esq., of Carden Park, Chester. Educ. at Harrow, and at Christ Church, Oxford; graduated B.A. 2nd class Law and History 1864, M.A. 1870. Called to the bar at the Middle Temple 1869. A J.P. for Shropshire, Denbighshire, and Flintshire, and a Dept.-Lieut. for Flintshire; junior Dept. Chancellor University of Wales 1898; Capt. in Shropshire Yeomanry Cavalry 1873-78. Wrote the *Life of Lord Kenyon, Lord Chief Justice of England.* A Conservative, in favour of completion of the educational system, especially technical and secondary, reform of Poor Laws, better housing for the working classes, etc. Unsuccessfully contested Denbigh district in 1874 and 1880. Sat for Denbigh district from 1885-95, when he retired, and in Sept. 1897 unsuccessfully contested E. Denbighshire. Elected again for Denbigh in 1900 and sat until defeated in 1906. Died 26 Jan. 1908. [1905]

KENYON, James. Walshaw Hall, Bury, Lancashire. Conservative, Carlton, and Constitutional. S. of James Kenyon, Esq., and his wife Margaret (née Watson). B. 1846 at Bury; m. 1874, Elise, 2nd d. of F. Genth, Esq., of Burnage, near Manchester. Educ. at Bury Grammar School, and the Liverpool Collegiate Institution. A Woollen and Cotton Manufacturer at Bury, and a J.P. for Lancashire. A Conservative and Unionist. Was an unsuccessful candidate for the Heywood division of Lancashire in 1885. First elected for Bury 1895 and sat until he accepted Chiltern Hundreds in 1902. Died 25 Feb. 1924. [1902]

KENYON-SLANEY, Col. the Rt. Hon. William Slaney. Hatton Grange, Shifnal, Shropshire. Wellington, and Carlton. S. of Col. William Kenyon-Slaney (who was a grand-s. of the 1st Lord Kenyon), by Frances Catherine, d. and co-heiress of R.A. Slaney, Esq., MP, of Hatton Grange. B. at Rajkote, Bombay 1847; m. 1887, Mabel Selina, eld. d. of the Earl of Bradford. Educ. at Eton, and Christ Church, Oxford. Entered the Grenadier Guards in 1867, and became Maj. and Col. in 1883; served in Egypt 1882. A J.P. and Dept.-

Lieut. for Shropshire. PC. 1904. A Conservative, desired to treat Ireland "in a spirit of generous justice", but opposed to Home Rule with a separate Parliament. Unsuccessfully contested the Wellington division of Shropshire in 1885. Represented Shropshire N. from 1886 until his death 24 Apr. 1908.   [1908]

KER, Richard William Blackwood. Montalto and Portavo, Nr. Ballinahinch, Co. Down. Carlton, Boodle's, and Naval and Military. S. of David Stewart Ker, Esq., of Montalto, sometime MP for Co. Down, by the Hon. Anne Dorothea Blackwood, d. of Hans, 3rd Lord Dufferin and Clandeboye. B. 1850 and inherited the Montalto and Portavo estates on the death of his elder bro., 1877; m. 1878, Edith Louisa, d. of W.G. Rose, Esq., of Walston Heath, Warwick. A Magistrate for Co. Down, where he served as High Sheriff in 1880. A Conservative. Elected for Co. Down in 1884, and represented the E. division of Co. Down from 1885 until he accepted Chiltern Hundreds in 1890. Died 19 June 1942.   [1890]

KERANS, Frederick Harold. Hesseworth House, 1 Lancaster Gate, London. Carlton. S. of Lyons Kerans, Esq., by Emily, d. of R.J.D. Ashworth, Esq., Barrister and Commissioner in Bankruptcy, of Strawberry Hill, Manchester, and Clough House, Huddersfield. B. at Hooton Levett Hall, near Rotherham 1849; m. 1882, Marian, only child of J.C.W. Heyn, M.D. London. Educ. at Rugby. Called to the bar in 1873 but ceased to practise before becoming an MP. A "Liberal Conservative". Unsuccessfully contested the city of Lincoln at the general election of 1885. First returned for Lincoln July 1886 and sat until defeated in 1892. Dept.-Lieut. for Lincolnshire. Died 17 Apr. 1894. [1892]

KERR, John. Gaddesden Place, Hemel Hempstead, Hertfordshire. Junior Carlton. S. of John Kerr, Esq. B. 1852. Educ. at St. Andrews and Glasgow Universities. An Engineer, Chairman of Dick, Kerr and Company Limited, of Kilmarnock and Preston. A J.P. for E. Lothian. A Conservative. Unsuccessfully contested Haddingtonshire in 1900. Elected for Preston May 1903 and sat until defeated in 1906.   [1905]

KERR-SMILEY, Peter. Continued in House after 1918: full entry in Volume III.

KERRY, Henry William Edmond Petty-Fitz-maurice, Earl of. 20 Mansfield Street, London. Sheen Falls, Kenmare, Co. Kerry. Guards', Turf, and Brooks's. Eld. s. of Marq. of Lansdowne. B. 1872; m. 1904, Elizabeth Caroline, d. of Sir Edward Hope, K.C.B. Educ. at Eton, and Balliol Coll., Oxford; M.A. 1895. Entered the Grenadier Guards 1895; transferred to Irish Guards 1900; retired as Maj. 1906; Lieut.-Col. 1915; served in S. African War 1899-1900. D.S.O. 1900, M.V.O. 1905. A member of the London County Council for W. Marylebone 1907-10. A Unionist. Unsuccessfully contested the Appleby division of Westmorland in 1906. Elected for W. Derbyshire Apr. 1908 and sat until defeated in 1918. Senator, Irish Free State 1922-29; succeeded as 6th Marq. of Lansdowne 3 June 1927. Died 5 Mar. 1936.   [1918]

KESWICK, Henry. Cowhill Tower, Dumfries. 3 Lombard Street, London. Carlton, and Oriental. Eld. s. of William Keswick, Esq., MP for Epsom division of Surrey. B. 20 Oct. 1870 at Shanghai; m. 1900, Ida Winifred, d. of J.W. Johnston, Esq., Chartered Surveyor, of Cowhill Tower, Dumfries. Educ. at Eton, and Trinity Coll., Cambridge; B.A. A member of the firm of Jardine, Matheson and Company Limited, Merchants, Hong Kong, China and Japan. A member of Hong Kong Legislative Council and Shanghai Municipal Council. Served in S. African War 1900. A member of the Royal Company of Scottish Archers, King's Body Guard. A Unionist. Elected for the Epsom division of Surrey in Mar. 1912 and sat until he retired in 1918. Unsuccessfully contested Dumfriesshire in 1922. President of Dumfriesshire Unionist Association. Died 29 Nov. 1928.   [1918]

KESWICK, William. 3 Lombard Street, London. Eastwick Park, Leatherhead. B. 1835. A member of the firm of Jardine and Company, China Merchants. A Dept.-Lieut. and J.P. for Surrey, High Sheriff 1898. A member of the Legislative Council of Hong Kong. Director of Indo-China Steam Navigation Company. A Unionist. Sat for the Epsom division of Surrey from Jan. 1899 until his death 9 Mar. 1912. [1912]

KETTLE, Thomas Michael. Newtown, St. Margaret's Co. Dublin. S. of A.J. Kettle, Esq., Farmer, and Margaret, d. of L. McCourt, Esq., of St. Margaret's, Co. Dublin. B. 2 Feb. 1880; m. 1909, Mary, d. of D.

Sheehan, Esq., MP. Educ. at Dublin University; B.A. A Barrister-at-Law, called to the bar in May 1906, and Professor of National Economics of Ireland in National University of Ireland from 1910. Author of *The Philosophy of Politics, Handbook on Old Age Pensions Act, 1908,* English edition of L.P. Dubois' *Contemporary Ireland,* etc. A member of the Gaelic League. A Nationalist. Elected for E. Tyrone in July 1906 and sat until he retired in Dec. 1910. Served as Lieut. in Leinster Regiment and then in Royal Dublin Fusiliers. Killed in action on 9 Sept. 1916. [1910]

KILBRIDE, Denis. Luggacurren, Stradbally, Queen's Co. S. of Thomas Kilbride, Esq., and Maria Ryan. B. 1848 at Luggacurren. Unmarried. Educ. at Clongowes Wood Coll., Clane. A Tenant Farmer. A Nationalist. Sat for S. Kerry from 1887-95. Returned unopposed for S. Kerry and N. Galway in 1895, but elected to sit for N. Galway, which he represented from 1895-1900, when he retired. Elected for S. Kildare May 1903 and sat until defeated in 1918. Died Oct. 1924. [1918]

KILCOURSIE, Frederick Edward Gould Lambart, Visct. See CAVAN, Frederick Edward Gould Lambert, Earl of.

KILEY, James Daniel. Continued in House after 1918: full entry in Volume III.

KIMBER, Sir Henry, Bart. Albany Chambers, York Street, London. Lansdowne Lodge, East Putney, London. Carlton, City Carlton, St. Stephen's, and Royal Automobile. S. of Joseph Kimber, Esq., of Canonbury. B. in London July 1834; m. 1860, Mary Adelaide, d. of Gen. Charles Dixon, of the Royal Engineers, of Rectory Grove, Clapham (she died 1901). Was admitted a Solicitor in 1858, having previously taken 1st prize of Incorporated Law Society, and a 2nd Honour in Law at University Coll., London. Retired from practice in 1890. Chairman of the South Indian Railway Company and the Natal Land and Colonization Company, and Director of the Capital and Counties Bank. Also a member of the Royal Colonial Institute; created Bart. in 1904. A "Progressive Conservative", in favour of Imperial Federation, Reform of Representation, etc. Sat for Wandsworth from 1885 until he accepted Chiltern Hundreds in 1913. Died 18 Dec. 1923. [1913]

KINCAID-SMITH, Thomas Malcolm Harvey. Wellesbourne, Warwick. 17 Queen's Street, Mayfair, London. Army & Navy, Bachelors', and Cavalry. S. of Maj. Kincaid-Smith, of Polmont, and Mrs. Kincaid-Smith, of Aldingbourne House, Chichester. B. 6 July 1874 in London. Educ. at Eton, and Royal Military Coll., Sandhurst. Received a commission in 9th Lancers 1894. Served in S. African War 1901; retired as Capt. A Liberal. Elected for the Stratford-on-Avon division of Warwickshire 1906, and sat until he accepted Chiltern Hundreds in Mar. 1909, so that he could leave the Liberal Party. Stood again as an Independent 4 May 1909, advocating compulsory military training for young men, but was defeated by a large margin. Unsuccessfully contested Frome in 1918, as a National Party candidate. Died 31 Dec. 1938. [1909]

KING, Alfred John. Rock Bank, Bollington, Nr. Macclesfield. 2 Whitehall Court, London. National Liberal. S. of Alderman John King, of Manchester, and Frances Fell, of Warrington. B. 14 Feb. 1859 in Manchester; m. 1888, Julia Constance, d. of Thomas Oliver, Esq., of Bollington. Educ. at Oliver's Mount School, Scarborough, and Owen's Coll., Manchester; B.Sc. A Bleacher and Finisher; a member of the Cheshire County Council; President of Manchester Branch of Peace Society; a member of the Society of Friends. Fellow of the Chemical Society. A Liberal. Elected for the Knutsford division of Cheshire in 1906 and sat until defeated in Jan. 1910. Died 16 Mar. 1920. [1909]

KING, Sir Henry Seymour. 25 Cornwall Gardens, London. Carlton, Conservative, St. Stephen's, Savile, Royal Automobile, and Alpine. Eld. s. of Henry Samuel King, Esq., J.P., of Manor House, Chigwell. B. 1852; m. 1875, Julia Mary, d. of the Rev. Dr. Jenkins, of Montreal. Educ. at Charterhouse, and Balliol Coll., Oxford; M.A. Head of the firm of Henry S. King and Company, Bankers and East Indian Agents, of Cornhill and Pall Mall, London, and Calcutta and Bombay, India. Created K.C.I.E. 1892, and was a Lieut. of the City of London; was the 1st Mayor of Kensington 1900; re-elected 1901. F.R.G.S. A Unionist. Sat for Hull central from 1885 until 1911 when the election was declared void on petition. Chairman of Income Tax

Commission for City of London 1925; created Bart. in 1932. Died 14 Nov. 1933. [1911]

KING, Joseph. Witley, Surrey. 20 St. Thomas' Mansions, London. Reform, Eighty, and National Liberal. S. of Joseph King, Esq., M.R.C.S., of Liverpool, and Phoebe, d. of Joseph Powell, Esq. B. 31 Mar. 1860 at Liverpool; m. 1887, Maud Egerton, d. of H.G. Hine, Esq., V.P.R.I. Educ. at Uppingham School, and Trinity Coll., Oxford; M.A. A Barrister, called to the bar at the Inner Temple 1889. Author of *Electoral Reform, Our Electoral System,* and various other works on political and foreign affairs. A Liberal. Unsuccessfully contested the New Forest division of Hampshire in 1892, and the Isle of Thanet division of Kent in 1904 and 1906. Elected for N. Somerset in Jan. 1910 and sat until he retired in 1918. Joined Labour Party and contested Ilford in Sept. 1920 and York in 1923. Died 25 Aug. 1943. [1918]

KING-HARMAN, Rt. Hon. Edward Robert. Rockingham, Boyle, Co. Roscommon. Newcastle, Ballymahon, Co. Longford. Carlton, Arts, and Wellington. Eld. s. of the Hon. Lawrence Harman King-Harman, of Rockingham (youngest s. of the 1st Visct. Lorton), by Mary Cecilia, d. of James Raymond Johnstone, Esq., of Alva, Stirlingshire. B. 1838; m. 1861, Emma Frances, youngest d. of Sir William Worsley, Bart. Educ. at Eton. A Lieut. 60th Foot, retired (5th Battalion Connaught Rangers). Appointed Parliamentary Under Secretary for Ireland Apr. 1887. A Privy Councillor for Ireland (1885), Lord-Lieut. of Co. Roscommon, a Magistrate for the counties of Longford, Sligo, and Westmeath, and Honorary Col. of the Roscommon Militia. A Conservative. Unsuccessfully contested Longford in May 1870 and Dublin city in Aug. 1870. Sat for Co. Sligo from Jan. 1877 to Apr. 1880 when he was defeated. Sat for Dublin Co. from 1883-85; and for the Isle of Thanet division of Kent from 1885 until his death 10 June 1888. [1888]

KINLOCH, Sir John George Smyth, Bart. Kinloch, Meigle, Perthshire. Glen Isla House, by Alyth, Forfarshire. Devonshire, Reform. New Club, Edinburgh. Eld. s. of Sir George Kinloch, Bart., and Margaret, only child of George Canning, Esq., of Arbroath, Forfarshire. B. 1849 at Kinloch, Meigle, N.B.; m. 1878, Jessie Montgomerie, eld. d. of George Lumsden, Esq., of Edinburgh. Educ. at Cheltenham Coll., and Trinity Coll., Cambridge (B.A. 1872). J.P. for the counties of Perth and Forfar, and a Dept.-Lieut. of Perth. Succeeded as Bart. in 1881. A "Radical", in favour of Home Rule for Ireland. Sat for Perthshire E. from Feb. 1889 until he accepted Chiltern Hundreds in 1903. Died 20 May 1910. [1902]

KINLOCH-COOKE, Sir Clement. Continued in House after 1918: full entry in Volume III.

KINNEAR, John Boyd. 9 Old Square, Lincoln's Inn, London. Kinloch, Ladybank, Fifeshire. Eld. s. of Charles Kinnear, Esq., of Kinloch, Co. Fife, by Christiana, only child of John Boyd Grenshelds, Esq., Advocate. B. at Kinloch 1828; m. 1st, 1852, Sarah Harriet, only child of George Firth, Esq., of Worksop (she died 1866); 2ndly, 1868, Teresa, d. of Clementi Bassano, of Venice. Educ. at the Universities of St. Andrews and Edinburgh; and was called to the bar both of Scotland (1850) and England (1856). Wrote *A Treatise on the Law of Bankruptcy in Scotland, A Digest of Decisions of the House of Lords on Appeal, Principles of Reform, Political and Legal, Principles of Property in Land,* and several pamphlets on the Eastern Question, Ireland, etc. A Radical. Unsuccessfully contested Fifeshire in Nov. 1868. First returned for E. Fifeshire in Dec. 1885 and sat until defeated in 1886 standing as a Liberal Unionist. Died 10 Nov. 1920. [1886]

KIRKWOOD, John Hendley Morrison. Yeo Vale, Fairy Cross, North Devon. 62 Sloane Street, London. S. of Maj. J. Morrison Kirkwood, of Yeo Vale, N. Devon, and Isabel, d. of the Rev. Tatton Brockman, of Beachborough, Kent. B. 11 May 1877; m. 1902, Gertrude, d. of Robert Park Lyle, Esq. Lieut. 7th Dragoon Guards, and later Capt. Royal N. Devon Yeomanry; served in South African War 1899-1902. A J.P. for Devon. A Unionist. Elected for S.E. Essex in Jan. 1910 and sat until he accepted Chiltern Hundreds in 1912. D.S.O. 1917. Died 7 Feb. 1924. [1911]

KITCHING, Albert George. Florence House, Enfield. Rydal Lodge, Clacton-on-Sea. Only s. of Dr. George Kitching, M.D., of Enfield. B. 1840. Educ. privately under the Rev. Arthur Abbott, at Hitchin. A member of the London Stock Exchange, a Magistrate for Middlesex, and a F.G.S. A Liberal. Unsuccessfully contested Malmesbury in 1880. Sat for the Maldon division of Essex from Dec. 1885 until he retired in 1886. He was a Liberal Unionist in 1886, but rejoined the Liberals and unsuccessfully contested Norfolk S. in 1892. Died Nov. 1919.   [1886]

KITSON, Rt. Hon. Sir James, Bart. 105 Pall Mall, London. Gledhow Hall, Leeds. Reform. S. of James Kitson, Esq., Engineer, of Elmete Hall, Leeds. B. at Leeds 1835; m. 1st, 1860, Emily, d. of J. Cliffe, Esq., of Wortley, Leeds; 2ndly, 1881, Laura, d. of E. Fisher Smith, Esq., of The Priory, Dudley. Educ. at Wakefield Proprietary School, and University Coll., London. An Iron and Steel Manufacturer; President of the Leeds Chamber of Commerce, and a Director of the N.E. Railway. Created Bart. 1886; PC. 1906. Mayor, later Lord Mayor of Leeds 1896-97. Chairman of the Yorkshire Banking Company. A Liberal. Contested the Central division of Leeds in July 1886. First elected for the Colne Valley division of the W. Riding of Yorkshire in 1892 and sat until created Lord Airedale in 1907. Died 16 Mar. 1911.   [1907]

KNATCHBULL-HUGESSEN, Hon. Edward. 5 Mandeville Place, Manchester Square, London. Brooks's, and Guards'. Eld. s. of Lord and Lady Brabourne. B. 1857 at Great Malvern; m. 1880, Amy Virginia, d. of W.B. Beaumont, Esq., MP, of Bretton Park, Yorkshire. Educ. at Eton, and Magdalen Coll., Oxford. Held a commission in the Coldstream Guards from 1879 to 1881. A J.P. and Dept.-Lieut. for the Co. of Kent. A Liberal, in favour of Home Rule for Ireland. On the death of Col. King-Harman he was an unsuccessful candidate for the representation of the Isle of Thanet division of Kent, in June 1888. Returned for Rochester city in Apr. 1889 and sat until he retired in 1892. Succeeded as 2nd Baron Brabourne 1893. Died 29 Dec. 1909.   [1892]

KNATCHBULL-HUGESSEN, Herbert Thomas. 19 Ryder Street, St. James's Street, London. Lynsted, Sittingbourne, Kent. Carlton, and Junior Carlton. Youngest s. of the Rt. Hon. E. Knatchbull, Bart., of Mersham Hatch, Ashford, Kent

(who represented E. Kent for many years), by Fanny Catherine, d. of Edward Knight, Esq., of Godmersham Park, Kent, and Chawton House, Hampshire. B. 1835. Educ. at Eton, and Trinity Coll., Oxford; B.A. 1856, M.A. 1859. Called to the bar at Lincoln's Inn 1860. An "independent Conservative". Sat for N.E. Kent from 1885 until he retired in 1895. Died 15 May 1922.   [1895]

KNIGHT, Maj. Eric Ayshford. Continued in House after 1918: full entry in Volume III.

KNIGHTLEY, Sir Rainald, Bart. Fawsley Park, Daventry, Northamptonshire. Carlton, and White's. Only s. of Sir Charles Knightley, 2nd Bart. (who sat for Northamptonshire from 1834-1852), by Selina Mary, eld. d. of Felton Lionel Hervey, Esq., of Englefield Green, Surrey. B. in Upper Brook Street 1819; m. 1869, Louisa Mary, only d. of Gen. Sir Edward Bowater. A Magistrate and a Dept.-Lieut. of Northamptonshire. A Conservative, but not pledged to any party. Sat for Northamptonshire S. from July 1852 until he retired in 1892. Succeeded as Bart. in 1864. Created Baron Knightley in 1892. Alderman for Northamptonshire County Council. Died 19 Dec. 1895.   [1892]

KNOTT, James. Close House, Wylam-on-Tyne. B. 31 Jan. 1855. Educ. privately. Founder and Head of Prince Line of steamers, Newcastle-on-Tyne, and was interested in Collieries and other industries. Was called to the bar. A Unionist. Unsuccessfully contested the Tyneside division of Northumberland in 1906. Elected for Sunderland in Jan. 1910 and sat until he retired in Dec. 1910. Created Bart. 1917. Died 8 June 1934.   [1910]

KNOWLES, Sir Lees, Bart. 46 Park Street, London. 4 New Square, Lincoln's Inn, London. Westwood, Pendlebury. Turton Tower. Carlton, and Junior Carlton. Union and Conservative, Manchester. Eld. s. of John Knowles, Esq., J.P. and Dept.-Lieut. (High Sheriff of Lancashire 1892-93), of Westwood, Pendlebury, by Elizabeth, d. of James Lees, Esq., of Green Bank, Oldham. B. 1857. Educ. at Rugby, and Trinity Coll., Cambridge, where he took the degrees M.A. and LL.M. Was President of the Cambridge University Athletic Club 1878; called to the bar at Lincoln's Inn

1882; joined the N. Circuit 1883; was unpaid Private Secretary to Mr. Ritchie (President Local Government Board) 1887, (President Board of Trade) 1895. Was Honorary Secretary of the Guinness Trust; a member of the Select Committee on Town Holdings, and Chairman of the Select Committee on the Plumbers' Registration Bill. Was successful in passing five Acts of Parliament, dealing chiefly with sanitation. Lieut.-Col. 3rd Volunteer Battalion Lancashire Fusiliers; a Dept.-Lieut. for Lancashire; 2nd Church Estates Commissioner (unpaid) from 1895 to 1900, a Trustee of the London Parochial Charities, a Member of Merchant Taylors' Company, Member of the Council of Rossall School, a Trustee of 3 livings. Knight of St. John of Jerusalem, and Honorary Secretary to the Lancashire Conservative MPs. Association; created Bart. 1903. O.B.E. 1920. A Conservative. Unsuccessfully contested the Leigh division of Lancashire 1885. First elected for Salford W. 1886 and sat until defeated in 1906. 2nd Church Estates Commissioner (unpaid) 1896-1906. Author of several works of a military nature. The Lees Knowles Lectures in Military Science are delivered in his memory at Trinity Coll., Cambridge. Lieut.-Col. in Territorials, retired 1918. Died 7 Oct. 1928. [1905]

KNOX, Edmund Francis Vesey. 5 Paper Buildings, Temple, London. National Liberal. S. of Vesey Edmund Knox, Esq., (52nd Regiment) of Shimnah, Newcastle, Co. Down, and of Margaret Clarissa, d. of the Rev. J.P. Garrett. B. at Newcastle, Co. Down 1865. Educ. at St. Columba's Coll., Co. Dublin, Keble Coll., Oxford (B.A. 1st in Modern History 1886), Fellow of All Souls' Coll. 1886, M.A. 1890. A Barrister, called to the bar at Gray's Inn 1889; bencher 1906; treasurer 1913. An Irish Nationalist. Succeeded Mr. Biggar as Member for Cavan W. Mar. 1890. Elected there in 1895 as well as for Londonderry city, but decided to sit for the latter. MP until he accepted Chiltern Hundreds on 13 Dec. 1898. K.C. 1906. Died 15 May 1921. [1898]

KYFFIN-TAYLOR, Col. Gerald. Lingcroft, Tower Road North, Heswall, Cheshire. Junior Army & Navy, and 1900. S. of Ven. W.F. Taylor, D.D., Archdeacon of Liverpool, and Anne, d. of the Rev. H. Evans. B. 1863 in Liverpool; m. 1892, Bessie, d. of Thomas Cope, Esq., J.P., of Huyton. Educ. at Liverpool Coll. A Solicitor, admitted 1884; Partner in the firm of Lamb, Kyffin-Taylor, and Walker, of Liverpool. A member of Liverpool City Council from 1904; Chairman of Northern Council of Church Association; a member of Committee of Church of England Schools Society, and of Liverpool School of Public Health; a Life Gov. of Liverpool Coll., Chairman of Liverpool Insurance Committee. Lieut.-Col. and Honorary Col. 1st W. Lancashire Brigade Royal Field Artillery (Territorials) V.D., and member of W. Lancashire Territorial Force Association. A Unionist. Sat for the Kirkdale division of Liverpool from July 1910 until he accepted Chiltern Hundreds in Feb. 1915. Died 11 Dec. 1949. [1914]

KYNOCH, George. Hamstead Hall, Handsworth, Staffordshire. Carlton, and St. George's. S. of John Kynoch, Esq., of Peterhead, by Margaret Ballantine, of Edinburgh. B. 1834; m. 1863, Helen Birley, d. of Samuel Birley, Esq. of Birmingham. Educ. at the parish school of Peterhead, Aberdeenshire. An Ammunition Manufacturer at Witton, Birmingham. A Conservative, strongly opposed to Home Rule for Ireland. Returned for Aston Manor July 1886 and sat until his death 28 Feb. 1891. [1890]

LABOUCHERE, Henry Du Pré. 10 Carteret Street, Queen Anne's Gate, London. Reform, Union, National Liberal, and St. James's. S. of John Labouchere, Esq., of Broome Hall, Dorking, Surrey, by Mary, 2nd d. of James Du Pré, Esq., MP, of Wilton Park, Buckinghamshire. B. in London 1831; m. 1868, Henrietta, d. of James Hodson, Esq., of Dublin. Educ. at Eton. A nephew of Lord Taunton, Chief Secretary for Ireland and Secretary of State for the Colonies. Entered the Diplomatic Service 1854, retired 1864. Proprietor of *Truth*, which journal he established. An advanced Liberal, in favour of the disendowment and disestablishment of the Church of England, and Home Rule for Ireland. Sat for Windsor from July 1865 to Apr. 1866, when he was unseated on petition; sat for Middlesex from Apr. 1867 to Dec. 1868, when he was an unsuccessful candidate there. Unsuccessfully contested Nottingham in 1874. Sat for Northampton from Apr. 1880 until he retired in 1906. PC. 1906. Died 15 Jan. 1912. [1905]

LACAITA, Charles Carmichael. 11 Upper Brook Street, London. Rowbarns, Leatherhead. New University, Reform, and Brooks's. S. of Sir James P. Lacaita, K.C.M.G., by Maria Clavering, d. of Sir Thomas Gibson Carmichael, Bart. B. at Edinburgh 1853; m. 1885, Mary Annabel, d. of Sir Francis Hastings Doyle, Bart. Educ. at Eton, and Balliol Coll., Oxford; B.A. 1875, M.A. 1878. Was called to the bar at Lincoln's Inn 1879, and was Assistant Private Secretary to Lord Granville until June 1885. A Liberal, and Home Ruler. Sat for Dundee from 1885 until he accepted Chiltern Hundreds in 1887. Died 17 July 1933. [1887]

LAFONE, Alfred. Hanworth Park, Middlesex. Carlton. S. of Samuel Lafone, Esq., of West Derby, Liverpool, By Sarah, d. of Francis Hurry, Esq., of Great Yarmouth. B. at Park Lodge, Toxteth Park, Liverpool 1821; m. 1852, Jane, d. of William Boutcher, Esq., of Grately House, Hampshire (she died 1885). Educ. privately. He represented Southwark on the first two School Boards for London, and was a J.P. for Middlesex. A Conservative and Unionist. Unsuccessfully contested Bermondsey in 1885. MP for the Bermondsey division of Southwark 1886-92, when he was defeated; re-elected there 1895 and sat until he retired in 1900. Died 26 Apr. 1911. [1900]

LAIDLAW, Sir Robert. 44 Princes Gardens, London. Reform, Cobden, National Liberal, and City Liberal. S. of William Laidlaw, Esq., Farmer, of Bonchester, Roxburgh, and Agnes Purdom. B. 15 Jan. 1856 at Bonchester; m. 1879, Mary Eliza, d. of Capt. W.B. Collins. Educ. at Kirkton, and Denholm Parish Schools. Chairman of Whiteaway, Laidlaw and Company Limited, of London, India, and China; a Proprietor of tea estates in Darjeeling; and rubber estates in Malay States; travelled three times round the world; F.R.G.S. A Liberal, in favour of Temperance Reform, Taxation of Land Values, etc. Elected for E. Renfrewshire in 1906 and sat until defeated in Jan. 1910. Knighted 1909. Died 3 Nov. 1915. [1909]

LALOR, Richard G. 4 Norfolk Street, Strand, London. Tenakill, Mountrath, Queen's Co. S. of Patrick Lalor, Esq., of Tenakill, Queen's Co. (who represented Queen's Co. in 1833-34), by Anne, d. of Patrick Dillon, Esq., of Sheane, Queen's Co. B. at Tenakill 1823; m. 1852, Margaret, d. of Michael Dunne, Esq., of Mountrath, Queen's Co. A Civil Engineer; also engaged in farming. A Magistrate for Queen's Co. An "Irish Nationalist" of the Parnellite party. Sat for Queen's Co. from Apr. 1880 to 1885 and for the Leix division of Queen's Co. from 1885 until he retired in 1892. Died 13 Nov. 1893. [1892]

LAMB, Edmund George. Borden Wood, Liphook, Hampshire. Oxford & Cambridge Union, and Bath. S. of Richard W. Lamb, Esq., of West Denton, Northumberland. B. 1863; m. 1893, Mabel, d. of Stephen Winkworth, Esq., of Campden Hill, London. Educ. at Oratory School, University Coll., London, and Merton Coll., Oxford. A Colliery Proprietor in Northumberland and a Sussex Landowner; Fellow of the Chemical Society. A Liberal, in favour of Poor law reform, electoral reform, and an efficient army and navy, etc. Elected for the Leominster division of Herefordshire in 1906 and sat until defeated in Jan. 1910. Unsuccessfully contested the Leominster division of Herefordshire again in 1918. Died 3 Jan. 1925. [1909]

LAMB, Sir Ernest Henry, C.M.G. Kingswood Chase, Surrey. National Liberal, and Eighty. S. of Benjamin Lamb, Esq., of Lightwater, Bagshot. B. 4 Sept. 1876 at Hornsea, Yorkshire; m. 1913, Rosa Dorothea, d. of W.J. Hurst, Esq., J.P., of Drumaness. Educ. at Dulwich and Wycliff Coll., Stonehouse, Gloucestershire. Chairman and Governing Director of Foster's Parcels and Goods Express Limited. A member of Common Council of City of London from 1903. A Vice-President of Home Counties Liberal Federation and of the Land Law Reform Association; a J.P. for Surrey. C.M.G. 1907. Knighted 1914. A Liberal. Sat for Rochester from 1906 to Jan. 1910, when he was defeated; re-elected there in Dec. 1910 and sat until he retired in 1918. Created Baron Rochester in Jan. 1931; Paymaster Gen. 1931-35. Supported the Labour Party in House of Lords 1931, then joined National Labour. Vice President of Methodist Conference 1941-42 and of British Council of churches 1942-44. Died 13 Jan. 1955. [1918]

LAMBERT, Rt. Hon. George. Continued in House after 1918: full entry in Volume III.

LAMBERT, Isaac Cowley. 23 Albert Gate, London. Little Tangley, Nr. Guildford. New University, and Carlton. S. of Thomas Lambert, Esq., of Telham Court, Battle. B. at Stockwell, Surrey 1850; m. 1879, Margaret Annie, d. of Robert Chamberlin, Esq., of Catton House, Norfolk. Educ. at Rugby, and Trinity Coll., Cambridge; B.A. 1872, M.A. 1876. Called to the bar at the Middle Temple 1874, and joined the Midland Circuit for a short time. A F.R.G.S. and wrote *A Trip to Cashmere and Ladak*, a sporting account of a years travel in the East. A "progressive Conservative", in favour of "local self-government for Great Britain and Ireland", with "the supremacy of the Imperial Parliament," Unsuccessfully contested E. Islington at the general election of 1885. First returned there in July 1886 and sat until he retired in 1892. Died 16 Oct. 1918. [1892]

LAMBERT, Richard Cornthwaite. 100 Abbey Road Mansions, London. National Liberal, and Eighty. Eld. s. of the Rev. R.U. Lambert, Vicar of Christ Church, Bradford-on-Avon, and Agnes, d. of the Ven. T. Stanton, Archdeacon of Wiltshire. B. 5 May 1868; m. 1893, Lilian, d. of R.H. Burman, Esq., of Sutton Coldfield. Educ. at Shrewsbury School, and Trinity Coll., Cambridge; B.A. honours History. Was called to the bar at the Inner Temple 1893, and practised on the Midland Circuit; a member of Kingston-on-Thames Town Council 1894-96. A member of London County Council and of Executive Committee of the Eighty Club; a J.P. for London. A Radical, who believed in pushing forward rather than hanging back. Unsuccessfully contested the Ecclesall division of Sheffield 1906, Attercliffe division of Sheffield 1909, and Portsmouth Jan. 1910. Elected for the Cricklade division of Wiltshire in Dec. 1910 and sat until he retired in 1918. Librarian of Athenaeum Club, 1922-35. Died 5 Nov. 1939. [1918]

LAMBTON, Hon. Frederick William. 72 Upper Berkeley Street, London. Fenton, Wooler, Northumberland. Turf, and Travellers'. 2nd s. of 2nd Earl of Durham, and twin bro. of the Earl. B. 1855; m. 1879, Beatrix, d. of John Bulteel, Esq., of Pamflete, Devon. Educ. at Eton. Served from 1874 to 1880 in the Coldstream Guards. Dept.-Lieut. for Northumberland. A Liberal Unionist. Sat for S. Durham from 1880-85, when he retired. Unsuccessfully contested Berwick-upon-Tweed division of Northumberland in 1886, Sunderland in 1892, and S.E. Durham Feb. 1898. Elected for S.E. Durham in 1900 and sat until defeated in Jan. 1910. Succeeded his twin bro. as Earl of Durham in 1928. Died 31 Jan. 1929. [1909]

LAMBTON, Hon. Hedworth. See MEUX, Admiral of the Fleet Hon. Sir Hedworth.

LAMONT, Norman. 4 Queen Street, Mayfair, London. Knockdow, Toward, Argyllshire. Palmiste, Trinidad, British West Indies. Travellers', St. James's, and Bachelors'. S. of James Lamont, Esq., of Knockdow, MP for Buteshire from 1865-68, and Adelaide, d. of Sir George Denys, Bart., of Draycott, Yorkshire. B. 7 Dec. 1869 at Knockdow. Unmarried. Educ. at Winchester and Downton Agricultural Coll. (certificate 1890). Was largely interested in the West Indies. A J.P., Dept-Lieut., of Argyllshire; a member of Argyll County Council 1901-07. Assistant Private Secretary (unpaid) to the Prime Minister (Sir H. Campbell-Bannerman) 1906-08. F.S.A. (Scotland). Chairman of Dept. Committee on Labour Exchanges 1909. A Liberal. Unsuccessfully contested Buteshire in 1900. Elected there in Mar. 1905 and sat until defeated in Jan. 1910. Succeeded father as 2nd Bart. 1913; Member of Legislative Council of Trinidad 1915-23; subsequently Chairman of West India Association of Glasgow; author of several books on the West Indies. Died 3 Sept. 1949. [1909]

LANE, William John. 7 North Mall, Cork. S. of John Lane, Esq., Merchant, of Cork, by a d. of M. O'Keefe, Esq., of Cork. B. at North Mall, Cork Aug. 1849; m. 1891, Miss Armstrong, of Brooklyn, U.S.A. Educ. at the Vincentian Coll., Cork. A Butter Merchant. On the town council of Cork from 1881, and was a member of the Council of the Cork Chamber of Commerce; was on the Committee of Merchants, and on the Council of the Literary and Scientific Society of the city; also a Trustee of the Cork Savings' Bank, and was one of the originators of the Irish National Industrial Exhibition, Dublin 1882. An "Irish Nationalist" (Anti-Parnellite). Sat for E. Cork from 1885 until he retired in 1892. [1892]

LANE-FOX, George Richard. Continued in House after 1918: full entry in Volume III.

LANGLEY, J. Batty. Queen's Park, Bournemouth. National Liberal. S. of Thomas and Jemima Langley. B. 1834 at Uppingham, Rutland. Educ. at Uppingham. A Timber Merchant in a large way of business in Sheffield. Was for many years a prominent Non-conformist member of Sheffield City Council; a J.P. for Sheffield and Yorkshire, an Alderman, Overseer; Chairman of the Burial Board, member of the School Board; President of the Sheffield Sunday School Union and of the Liberal Association, etc. Was Mayor of Sheffield in 1893 and as such promoted the Sheffield Conference for settling the great coal strike of 1893. During his Mayoralty the town was made a city. An advanced Liberal. First elected for the Attercliffe division of Sheffield in June 1894 and sat until he accepted Chiltern Hundreds in Apr. 1909. Died 19 Feb. 1914.   [1909]

LANSBURY, George. Continued in House after 1918: full entry in Volume III.

LARDNER, James Carrige Rushe. Swan Park, Monaghan. 4 Leinster Street, Merrion Square, Dublin. Stephen's Green. S. of Hugh W. Lardner, Esq., of Swan Park, Monaghan, and Anne, d. of John Loughran, Esq. B. 1879 at Monaghan. Educ. at Christian Brothers School, and St. McCarten's Coll., Monaghan, and Clongowes Wood Coll., Sallins, Co. Kildare. A Solicitor, 1900; a Barrister 1913. A Nationalist. Elected for N. Monaghan June 1907 and sat until he retired in 1918. K.C. 1921. Died 3 May 1925.   [1918]

LARMOR, Sir Joseph. Continued in House after 1918: full entry in Volume III.

LATHAM, George William. Bradwall Hall, Sandbach, Cheshire. National Liberal. 2nd s. of John Latham, Esq., of Bradwall Hall, Cheshire, by Elizabeth Anne, d. of Sir Henry Dampier, Judge of the King's Bench. B. 1827; m. 1856, Elizabeth Sarah, d. of the Rev. Henry Luttman Johnson, of Binderton House, Sussex. Educ. at Brasenose Coll., Oxford; B.A. 1849, M.A. 1852. Was called to the bar at the Inner Temple 1852, and practised on the N. Wales and Chester Circuit. A Magistrate for Cheshire, was one of the founders of the Farmers' Alliance, and one of its Vice-Presidents, and a Manager of the Bradwall Reformatory School. An "advanced Radical", did not consider a second legislative chamber necessary. Unsuccessfully contested the mid division of Cheshire in Mar. 1873, Apr. 1880, and again in Mar. 1883 when the Hon. W. Egerton succeeded to the Peerage. Sat for the Crewe division of Cheshire from Nov. 1885 until he retired in June 1886. Died 4 Oct. 1886.   [1886]

LAURIE, Lieut.-Gen. John Wimburn, C.B. 47 Porchester Terrace, London. Oakfield, Nova Scotia. Carlton. Eld. s. of John Laurie, Esq., of Marshalls, Essex, MP for Barnstaple, and Eliza Helen, d. of Kenrick Collett, Esq., Master in Chancery. B. in London 1835; m. 1863, Frances, d. of the Hon. Enos Collins (Halifax, N.S.). Educ. at Harrow, Dresden, and the Royal Military Coll., Sandhurst. Entered the 2nd Queen's Royals 1853; Maj. on special service in Canada Dec. 1861, Maj.-Gen. 1882, Lieut.-Gen. 1887. Served in the Crimea 1854-56, the Indian Mutiny Campaign, the repulse of Fenian raids 1866, the expedition to the Transvaal 1881, and was 2nd in command in the Canadian N.W. Rebellion Campaign, 1885. Was Red Cross Commissioner in Servia 1886, and made a K.C. of the Order of St. Sava, etc. Honorary Col. Royal Munster Fusiliers and 63rd Halifax Rifles of Canada. Was Inspecting Field Officer when in Nova Scotia 1862-81, President of the Central Board Agriculture, Nova Scotia, Warden of the Halifax Council 1880-81, and a Canadian MP 1887-91. Borough Councillor for Paddington 1891 and 1900; a Governor, City and Guilds Institute, Northampton Institute, City Polytechnic, and Imperial Institute. A Grand Master of Freemasons in S. Wales 1897. Master Sadlers' Company 1892, etc. etc. C.B. 1902. A Conservative and Unionist. Unsuccessfully contested Pembroke and Haverfordwest district in 1892, first elected in 1895 and sat until he retired in 1906. Died 20 May 1912. [1905]

LAURIE, Robert Peter. 55 Eaton Place, London. Hardres Court, Canterbury. Carlton, and Conservative. S. of Robert Peter Laurie, Esq., of Harley Street, London, by Elizabeth, d. of Charles Sparkes, Esq., of Harley Street. B. in Harley Street 1835; m. 1867, Amy Forbes, d. of Sir James Ranald Martin, C.B. Educ. at Tonbridge

School. A J.P. for the counties of London and Kent, and Col.-Commandant 3rd London Rifle Volunteers. A Conservative. Elected for Canterbury in May 1879, and was re-elected in 1880, but unseated on petition. Unsuccessfully contested Bath in 1885. First returned for Bath July 1886 and sat until he retired in 1892. C.B. 1887. Died 29 July 1905.   [1892]

LAW, Rt. Hon. Andrew Bonar. 10 Downing Street, London. Carlton. S. of the Rev. James Law, M.A., of New Brunswick, Canada, and Eliza Anne Kidston. B. 1858 in New Brunswick; m. 1891, Annie Pitcairn, d. of Harrington Robley, Esq., of Glasgow (she died 1909). Educ. in Canada, and Glasgow High School. At one time an Iron Merchant in Glasgow, and Chairman of Scottish Iron Trade Association. J.P. for Dunbartonshire; PC. 1911. Leader of the Unionist Party in the House of Commons from Nov. 1911-Mar. 1921 and Oct. 1922-May 1923. Parliamentary Secretary to the Board of Trade from 1902-05. Secretary of State for the Colonies and Member of War Committee May 1915 to Dec. 1916. Member of Mr. Lloyd George's War Cabinet. Chancellor of the Exchequer and Leader of the House of Commons Dec. 1916-Jan. 1919. Plenipotentiary Peace Conference 1919; Lord Privy Seal and Leader of House of Commons Jan. 1919 to Mar. 1921. Prime Minister and First Lord of the Treasury 23 Oct. 1922-20 May 1923. Honorary LL.D. Cambridge 1920. Honorary LL.D. Glasgow. Lord Rector Glasgow University 1919. A Conservative. Sat for Glasgow Blackfriars from 1900 to Jan. 1906 when he was defeated, and for Dulwich from May 1906 to Dec. 1910 when he unsuccessfully contested N.W. Manchester. Sat for Bootle from Mar. 1911 to 1918 and for Glasgow Central from 1918 until his death on 30 Oct. 1923.   [1923]

LAW, Hugh Alexander. Marble Hill, Ballymore, Co. Donegal. S. of the Rt. Hon. H. Law, Lord Chancellor of Ireland, and Helen Mary, d. of William White, Esq., of Shrubs, Co. Dublin. B. at Dublin 1872; m. 1893, Charlotte, d. of the Rev. A.G. Stuart, of Bogay House, Londonderry. Educ. at Rugby, and University Coll., Oxford. A J.P. for Co. Donegal. A Nationalist. Elected for W. Donegal in 1902 and sat until he retired in 1918. Served on Advisory Council to Ministry of Reconstruction in 1918; member of the *Dail Eireann* 1927-32. Died 2 Apr. 1943.   [1918]

LAWRANCE, John Compton. 3 Onslow Square, South Kensington, London. 3 Paper Buildings, Temple, London. Dunsby Hall, Bourne, Lincolnshire. Junior Carlton, and Garrick. Only s. of Thomas M. Lawrance, Esq., by Louisa, d. of John Compton, Esq., of Waternewton, Huntingdonshire. B. at Dunsby Hall, Lincolnshire 1832; m. 1861, Charlotte Georgina, d. of Maj. Smart of Tumby Lawn, Lincolnshire. Was called to the bar at Lincoln's Inn June 1859. Appointed a Queen's Counsel 1877. Recorder of Derby Feb. 1880. A Conservative, in favour of a readjustment of local taxation, so as to relieve land from some of its present burdens; also of the establishment of County Financial Boards. Unsuccessfully contested Peterborough in Oct. 1878. Sat for Lincolnshire S. from Apr. 1880 to Nov. 1885, and for the Stamford division of Lincolnshire from Nov. 1885 until appointed Judge in 1890, and Knighted. Sat in High Court until 1912. PC. 1912. Died 5 Dec. 1912.   [1889]

LAWRENCE, Sir Edwin, Bart. See DURNING-LAWRENCE, Sir Edwin, Bart.

LAWRENCE, Sir James Clarke, Bart. 75 Lancaster Gate, Hyde Park, London. Reform, Devonshire, and City Liberal. 2nd s. of William Lawrence, Esq., an Alderman of London, and Sheriff of London and Middlesex 1849-50, by Jane, d. of James Clarke, Esq. B. in London 1820. Unmarried. A Builder in London, and was a partner in the firm of Messrs. William Lawrence and Sons. Elected an Alderman of London 1860; Sheriff of London and Middlesex 1862-63; Lord Mayor of London 1868-69. President of Bridewell and Bethlehem Hospitals; a Magistrate for Middlesex and Westminster; a Commissioner of Lieutenancy for London; a member of the Courts of Justice Commission. A Liberal, in favour of the removal of all restrictions upon trade. Sat for Lambeth from May 1865 to July following, when he was defeated there. Regained his seat for Lambeth in Dec. 1868 and sat until Nov. 1885 when he was defeated contesting the N. division of Lambeth. Died 21 May 1897.   [1885]

LAWRENCE, Sir James John Trevor, Bart. 57 Prince's Gate, London. Burford Lodge, Dorking, Surrey. S. of Sir William Lawrence, Bart. (Serjeant-Surgeon to the

Queen, and for many years a celebrated Surgeon in London), by Louisa, d. of James Trevor, Esq., of Broughton House, Aylesbury, Buckinghamshire. B. in London 30 Dec. 1831; m. 1869, Bessie, only d. of John Matthew, Esq., of Burford Lodge, Dorking, and Park Street, Park Lane, London. Educ. at Winchester Coll. Was in the Medical Service of the army in India. President of the Royal Horticultural Society; and a Magistrate for Surrey. Succeeded as Bart. in 1867. A Conservative. Unsuccessfully contested the city of Gloucester Feb. 1874. Sat for Mid-Surrey from Nov. 1875 to Nov. 1885, and for the Reigate division of Surrey from Nov. 1885 until he retired in 1892. K.C.V.O. 1902. Died 22 Dec. 1913. [1892]

LAWRENCE, Sir Joseph. 9 Buckingham Palace Gardens, London. Oaklands, Kenley, Surrey. Carlton, Constitutional, and City Carlton. S. of Philip Lawrence, Esq., of Ionian Islands. B. 1848 at Zante; m. 1873, Margaret Alice, d. of Joseph Jackson, Esq., of Southport. Educ. privately, and at Owen's Coll., Manchester. Chairman of the Linotype and Machinery Limited, Edison Ore Milling Syndicate, Dept. Chairman Dunderland Iron Ore Company, and Director of British Westinghouse Electric Company; a member of Surrey County Council and J.P. for Surrey. Was Capt. in 40th Lancashire Volunteers 1873-78. Lieut. for the City of London, and Sheriff 1901. Was one of the pioneers of the Manchester Ship Canal. Knighted 1902. A Conservative and an Imperialist. Unsuccessfully contested Cardiff at the general election of 1900. Elected for Monmouth May 1901 and sat until he retired in 1906. Created Bart. 1918. Died 24 Oct. 1919. [1905]

LAWRENCE, William Frederic. 27 Eaton Square, London. Cowesfield House, Whiteparish, Salisbury. Athenaeum, New University, and Carlton. S. of the Rev. Charles W. Lawrence, incumbent of St. Luke's, Liverpool, by Lucia, d. of Sir Samuel Young, Bart., of Formosa, Berkshire. B. 1844. Educ. at Eton, and Christ Church, Oxford, where he graduated B.A. 1867 and M.A. Was called to the bar at Lincoln's Inn 1871; J.P. for Wiltshire, 2nd Chairman of Wiltshire Quarter Sessions at Salisbury, and joint-patron of the living of St. Luke's, Liverpool. A Conservative. Sat for the

Abercromby division of Liverpool from Nov. 1885 until defeated in 1906. Died 15 Jan. 1935. [1905]

LAWSON, Hon. Harry Lawson Webster. 37 Grosvenor Square, London. Orkney Cottage, Taplow. Athenaeum, Marlborough, and Oxford & Cambridge. Eld. s. of Lord Burnham and Harriette Georgiana, d. of B. Webster, Esq. B. in London 1862; m. 1884, Olive, d. of Gen. Sir H. de Bathe, 4th Bart. Educ. at Eton, and Balliol Coll., Oxford; M.A. Called to the bar at the Inner Temple 1891. A J.P. and Dept.-Lieut. for Buckinghamshire, Lieut. of the City of London, and Honorary Col. Bucks Yeomanry. A member of the London County Council 1889-92 and 1897-1904, and Mayor of Stepney 1907-09. A Liberal Unionist. Sat as a Liberal for W. St. Pancras from 1885-92. Contested E. Gloucestershire in 1892, but was defeated by three votes. On petition, the judges declared a tie, and in 1839 he was elected, and sat until defeated in 1895. Unsuccessfully contested N.E. Bethnal Green as a Liberal in Oct. 1900, and Bury in 1902 as a Liberal Unionist. Sat for the Mile End division of Tower Hamlets from 1905-06, when he was defeated; re-elected for the Mile End division of Tower Hamlets in Jan. 1910 and sat until he succeeded his father as Baron Burnham in Jan. 1916. Companion of Honour 1917. Created 1st Visct. Burnham in 1919. Chairman of the Standing Joint Committee representing teachers and local education authorities which in 1920 formulated the 'Burnham Scales.' Chairman of 3rd, 4th and 9th International Labour Conferences at Geneva 1921, 1922 and 1926. G.C.M.G. 1927. Managing Proprietor of the *Daily Telegraph* 1903-28. Chairman of Newspaper Proprietors Association, President of Institute of Journalists, President of Imperial Press Conferences Ottawa 1920 and Melbourne 1925. Died 20 July 1933. [1915]

LAWSON, Sir John Grant, Bart. 65 Grosvenor Street, London. Knavesmire Lodge, York. Nuttall Hall, Lancashire. Carlton, Bachelors', and White's. S. of Andrew S. Lawson, Esq., J.P. and Dept.-Lieut. of Aldborough Manor, Yorkshire, and Isabella, d. of John Grant, Esq., J.P. and Dept.-Lieut. of Nuttall Hall, Lancashire. B. 1856; m. 1902, Silvia, d. of Charles Hunter, Esq., of Selaby, Darlington. Educ. at Harrow, and Christ

Church, Oxford, where he took honours in Law; B.A. 1879, M.A. 1882. Parliamentary Secretary to the Local Government Board from 1900 until June 1905. Was Dept. Chairman of "Ways and Means" from June 1905 to Jan. 1906, a Charity Commissioner (unpaid) 1895-1900, a J.P. for the N. and W. Ridings, and Dept.-Lieut. for the N. Ridings of Yorkshire. Was called to the bar at the Inner Temple. A Progressive Conservative. Stood unsuccessfully for Bury 1885, and for the Heywood division of Lancashire in 1886. Represented the Thirsk and Malton division of the N. Riding of Yorkshire from 1892 until he retired in 1906. Created Bart. in 1905. Died 27 May 1919.   [1905]

LAWSON, Sir Wilfrid, Bart. (I) Brayton, Cumberland. Reform. Eld. s. of Sir W. Lawson, 1st Bart., of Brayton, Cumberland, by Caroline, 3rd d. of Sir J. Graham, Bart. B. at Brayton 1829; m. 1860, Mary, 3rd d. of J. Pocklington-Senhouse, Esq., of Netherhall, Cumberland. Educ. privately. Succeeded his father as Bart. 1867. President of the United Kingdom Alliance for the Suppression of the Liquor Traffic, etc. A Radical, in favour of Home Rule for Ireland; introduced "Direct Veto" Bill. Unsuccessfully contested W. Cumberland in 1857. Sat for Carlisle 1859-65, when he was defeated, and 1868-85, when he was defeated in Cockermouth; sat for the Cockermouth division of Cumberland from 1886 until defeated in 1900. Sat for the Camborne division of Cornwall from 1903-1906. Re-elected for the Cockermouth division of Cumberland in Jan. 1906 and sat until his death 1 July 1906.   [1906]

LAWSON, Sir Wilfrid, Bart. (II) Isel Hall, Cockermouth. Wellington. Eld. s. of Sir William Lawson, 2nd Bart., MP, and Mary, d. of Joseph Pocklington-Senhouse, Esq., of Netherhall, Cumberland. B. 1862 at Arkleby Hall, Cumberland; m. 1891, Mary Camilla, d. of Turner A. Macan, Esq., of Elstow, Bedfordshire, and Cariff, Co. Armagh. Educ. at Harrow, and Trinity Coll., Oxford. A Dept.-Lieut. for Cumberland. A Liberal. Unsuccessfully contested Penrith division of Cumberland in 1886 and the Cockermouth division of Cumberland in Jan. 1910. Elected for the Cockermouth division of Cumberland in Dec. 1910 and sat until he accepted Chiltern Hundreds in 1916. Succeeded as

Bart. 1906. Died 28 Aug. 1937.   [1915]

LAYLAND-BARRATT, Sir Francis, Bart. 68 Cadogan Square, London. Manor House, Torquay. Tregarne Lodge, Cornwall. Reform, Devonshire, and National Liberal. Only s. of Francis Barratt, Esq., of St. Austell, Cornwall, and Anna Mitchell, d. of J.P. Bennetts, Esq., J.P., of Falmouth. B. 1860 at St. Austell; m. 1884, Frances, eld. d. of Thomas Layland, Esq., of Stonehouse, Wallasey. Educ. at Trinity Hall, Cambridge; M.A., LL.B. A Dept.-Lieut., J.P., and Co. Alderman for Cornwall. J.P. for Devon. Member of Cornwall County Council from 1889. High Sheriff 1897. Assumed by Royal Licence the additional name of Layland in 1895. Created Bart. 1908. A Liberal. Unsuccessfully contested the Torquay division of Devonshire in 1895; sat there from 1900 to Dec. 1910, when he was defeated. Elected for the St. Austell division of Cornwall in Nov. 1915 and sat until he retired in 1918. Died 12 Sept. 1933.   [1918]

LEA, Hugh Cecil. 60 Cadogan Place, London. Junior Athenaeum, and Reform. S. of Carl Adolph Lea, Esq. B. 27 May 1869; m. 1896, Jessie, d. of Charles Fish, Esq. Educ. abroad. A Newspaper Proprietor. Served in British and American armies. A Liberal. Elected for E. St. Pancras in 1906 and sat until he retired in Jan. 1910. Member of London County Council 1910-13. Died 29 Jan. 1926.   [1909]

LEA, Sir Thomas, Bart. 49 Roland Gardens, Kensington, London. The Larches, Kidderminster. Sea Grove, Dawlish, Devon. Reform, and City Liberal. S. of George B. Lea, Esq., of The Larches, Kidderminster, by Emma, d. of G. Harris, Esq., of Oaklands, Dursley, Gloucestershire. B. at Kidderminster 1841; m. 1864, Louisa, d. of W. Birch, Esq., of Barton-under-Needwood, Burton-on-Trent. Educ. privately. A Magistrate for Worcestershire. Created Bart. Aug. 1892. A Liberal, opposed to Home Rule for Ireland. Sat for Kidderminster from Dec. 1868 to Feb. 1874, when he was an unsuccessful candidate; he stood unsuccessfully for Donegal in Aug. 1876, but was successful for Donegal in 1879, and again in 1880 and sat till 1885. In the latter year he was unsuccessful in Donegal E. First elected for Londonderry S. 1886 and sat until he retired in 1900. Died 9 Jan. 1902.   [1900]

LEACH, Charles. Springfield, Canonbury Park South, London. S. of Harry Leach, Esq. B. 1 Mar. 1847 at Illingworth, near Halifax; m. 1867, Mary, d. of Charles Fox, Esq. Educ. privately, and at Ranmoor Theological Coll., Sheffield. Was for thirty years a Congregational Minister in Sheffield, Birmingham, Manchester, and London. A member of Chelsea Vestry. A Founder and Vice-Chairman of the Abstainers and General Insurance Company, and a member of London Chamber of Commerce. Founder of Queen's Park Coll., London. Author of *Old, Yet Ever New*, *Is My Bible True?*, *Sermons to Working Men*, and numerous other books and stories. A Liberal, in favour of Progressive Social and Political Reform. Elected for the Colne Valley division of the W. Riding of Yorkshire in Jan. 1910 and sat until the seat was declared vacant in 1916 under the Lunacy (Vacating of Seats) Act, 1886. Died 24 Nov. 1919. [1916]

LEAHY, James. Moat Lodge, Athy, Co. Kildare. S. of Daniel Leahy, Esq., a Farmer of Co, Tipperary, Ireland. B. at Summerhill, Templemore, Co. Tipperary 1822; m. 1850, Julia, eld. d. of John Mulhall, Esq., of Boyle, Co. Roscommon. A Tenant Farmer. A Parnellite, in favour of the system called Home Rule for Ireland. Sat for Co. Kildare from Apr. 1880 to Nov. 1885, and for the S. division of Kildare from Nov. 1885 until defeated in 1892. [1892]

LEAKE, Robert. The Dales, Whitefield, Manchester. Reform. Eld. s. of Robert Leake, Esq., of Manchester, by Mary, eld. d. of William Lockett, Esq., of Richmond Hill, Salford, the 1st Mayor of that town. B. at Manchester 1824; m. 1st, 1859, Mabelle Sara, youngest d. of Richard Nolan, Esq., of Dublin, and Sea View, Wicklow (she died 1863); 2ndly, 1865, Louisa Maria, 2nd d. of Mr. Wright Turner, of Pendleton, Manchester. President of the Salford Liberal Association 1870, also of the Manchester Liberal Association and other local Liberal bodies. A J.P. for Lancashire. A Liberal and Home Ruler. Sat for S.E. Lancashire from Apr. 1880 until 1885 and for the Radcliffe cum Farnworth division of Lancashire from 1885 until he retired in 1895. Died 1 May 1901. [1895]

LEAMY, Edmund. 60 Edith Road, West Kensington, London. S. of James Leamy, Esq., of Waterford. B. at Waterford 1848; m. 1889, Margaret, d. of Edward Hanly, Esq., Kilmurray Grove, Bray, Co. Wicklow. Educ. at Tullabeg, and University High School, Waterford. Admitted a Solicitor in Ireland 1878; called to the Irish bar 1885. Published some volumes of *Fairy Tales*. An Irish Nationalist. Stood by Mr. Parnell at the time of the division in the ranks of the Irish Parliamentary Party. He first entered Parliament as one of the two members for Waterford City in 1880. Elected without opposition for N.E. Cork Nov. 1885 and again in July 1886; sat until he accepted the Chiltern Hundreds in May 1887. Whilst sitting for N.E. Cork he unsuccessfully contested another seat, mid Armagh, in Dec. 1885. Returned for S. Sligo July 1888 and sat until 1892, when he retired from the seat to contest E. Waterford as a Parnellite. Contested Galway City 1895 and 1900. Sat for Kildare N. from Oct. 1900 until his death 10 Dec. 1904. [1904]

LEATHAM, Edward Aldam. Retired in 1886: full entry in Volume I.

LECHMERE, Sir Edmund Anthony Harley, Bart. 61 Curzon Street, London. The Rhydd Court, Hanley Castle, Worcester. Whitwell Hall, York. Carlton. Only s. of Sir Edmund Hungerford Lechmere, 2nd Bart., by Maria Clara, 2nd d. of the Hon. David Murray, who was bro. to the 7th Lord Elibank. B. at Great Malvern 1826; m. 1858, Louisa Rosamund, only d. of John Haigh, Esq., of Whitwell Hall, North Riding of Yorkshire. Educ. at Charterhouse, and Christ Church, Oxford. Chancellor of the English branch of the Order of St. John of Jerusalem. Served in the Turko-Servian War and received the Servian order of the Takova. Had also the Grand Cordon of the Medjedieh. Appointed a Dept.-Lieut. of Worcestershire 1852; High Sheriff of that Co. 1862. Succeeded as Bart. 1856. Patron of 4 livings. A progressive Conservative, in favour of a re-adjustment of local taxation and the relief of ratepayers and tenant-farmers, allotments, etc. Sat for Tewkesbury from Mar. 1866 to Dec. 1868, when he was defeated. Unsuccessfully contested Tewkesbury again Jan. 1874. Sat for W. Worcestershire from June 1876 to Nov. 1885; for the Bewdley division of Worcestershire from 1885 to the general election of 1892, when he was chosen for the Evesham division of Worcestershire and was MP until his death 18 Dec. 1894. [1894]

LECKY, Rt. Hon. William Edward Hartpole. 38 Onslow Gardens, London. Athenaeum. University Club, Dublin. S. of John Hartpole Lecky, Esq., of Longford Terrace, Monkstown, Co. Dublin, J.P. of Queen's Co., and Mary Anne, d. of W.E. Tallents, Esq., of Newark-on-Trent. B. 1838 at Newtown Park, Co. Dublin; m. 1871, Elisabeth Baroness de Dedem, d. of Baron de Dedem, Lieut.-Gen. in the Dutch Service. Educ. at Cheltenham Coll., and Trinity Coll., Dublin, B.A. 1859, M.A. 1863. Honorary LL.D., Dublin, Glasgow and St. Andrew's, Litt.D. Cambridge, and Honorary D.C.L. Oxford; also a corresponding member of the Institute of France. Created PC. 1897. Wrote *The Leaders of Public Opinion in Ireland* (1861), *A History of the Rise and Influence of Rationalism in Europe* (1865), *History of European Morals from Augustus to Charlemagne* (1869), *History of England in the XVIIIth Century* (1878-90), *Democracy and Liberty* (1896), *The Map of Life; Conduct and Character* (1899), and other works. A Unionist. Sat for Dublin University from Dec. 1895 until he accepted Chiltern Hundreds in 1903. O.M. 1902. Died 22 Oct. 1903. [1902]

LEE, Col. Sir Arthur Hamilton, G.B.E., K.C.B. 2 The Abbey Garden, Westminster, London. Chequers, Princes Risborough, Buckinghamshire. Carlton, United Services, and Beefsteak. S. of the Rev. Melville L. Lee, Rector of Bridport, Dorset. B. at Bridport 1868; m. 1899, Ruth, d. of J.G. Moore, Esq., of New York. Educ. at Cheltenham Coll., and the Royal Military Academy, Woolwich. Was Brevet-Maj. Royal Artillery, retired 1900; Adjutant Hong Kong Volunteers 1889-90; Adjutant Royal Artillery Isle of Wight 1891-93; Professor of Strategy and Tactics Royal Military Coll., Canada 1893-98; British Military Attaché with U.S. Army, Spanish-American War 1898; Military Attaché with rank of Lieut.-Col. at British Embassy, Washington 1899-1900. Chairman of inter-Departmental Committee on Humane Slaughtering of Animals 1904. Introduced and piloted through Parliament Criminal Law Amendment (White Slave Traffic) Act 1912. Chairman of Parliamentary Aerial Defence Committee 1910-15. Alderman of Hampshire County Council 1906-10. Life President of the Council of Cheltenham Coll. Was Civil Lord of the Admiralty 1903-05. Rejoined army 1914, with temporary rank of Col. and selected for Special Service with Expeditionary Force (twice mentioned in despatches). Parliamentary Military Secretary to the Munitions Department Oct. 1915 to July 1916. Personal Military Secretary to Secretary of State of War July to Dec. 1916. K.C.B. 1916. Appointed Director-Gen. on Food Production Feb. 1917; G.B.E. Jan. 1918; Honorary Col. in army 1917. J.P. for Buckinghamshire. A Unionist. Elected for S. Hampshire in 1900 and sat until created Baron Lee of Fareham 9 July 1918. P.C. 1919. Minister of Agriculture and Fisheries (in Cabinet) Aug. 1919-Feb. 1921; First Lord of Admiralty from Feb. 1921 until Nov. 1922; gave the Chequers estate to the nation in 1921; thereafter frequently Chairman of Royal Commissions; Trustee of the National Gallery. Created 1st Visct. Lee of Fareham in 1922. G.C.S.I. 1925; G.C.B. 1929. Died 21 July 1947. [1918]

LEES, Sir Elliott, Bart. 14 Queen Anne's Gate, London. 61 Hamilton Square, Birkenhead. South Lytchet Manor, Poole, Dorset. Conservative, Carlton, and Garrick. S. of T.E. Lees, Esq., J.P., and Dept.-Lieut. of Woodfield, Oldham, and Hyde Park Square, by Bernarda, d. of Elliott Bay Turnbull, Esq. B. at Hathershaw, Oldham 1860; m. 1882, Florence, d. of P. Keith, Esq. Educ. at Eton, and Christ Church, Oxford, where he took the M.A. degree. A J.P. for Dorset, and Capt. in the Dorset Yeomanry. Served in S. Africa 1899-1902, and was twice mentioned in despatches; D.S.O. Created Bart. 1897. A Conservative and Unionist. Unsuccessfully contested Rochdale in 1885. Sat for Oldham from 1886 to 1892, when he was defeated. In June 1893 he unsuccessfully contested Pontefract. Represented Birkenhead from Oct. 1894 until defeated in 1906. A Director of *The People* newspaper. Died 16 Oct. 1908. [1905]

LEESE, Sir Joseph Francis, Bart. Sutton Park Cottage, Guildford. Reform. S. of Joseph and Frances Susan Leese. B. 1845 at Manchester; m. 1867, Mary Constance, only child of William Hargreaves, Esq., of Send, Woking, Surrey. Educ. privately, and at London University (B.A.) and Cambridge. A Barrister, called to the bar at the Inner Temple 1868; Q.C. 1891; a bencher there 1899. Knighted 1895. Created Bart. 1908. An Advanced Liberal, advocated Home Rule for Ireland, Electoral, Land Law, and Financial reforms, disestablishment of the Scotch and Welsh Churches, the "Direct Veto" as regarded licensing, an Eight Hours day for Miners, District Councils, etc. Unsuccessfully contested Preston in 1868. Unsuccessfully contested the Accrington division of Lancashire 1886. Elected there 1892, and again 1893, when he vacated his seat because he was appointed Recorder of Manchester, and at the elections of 1895, 1900, and 1906. Retired Jan. 1910. Died 29 July 1914. [1909]

LEES-SMITH, Hastings Bertrand. Continued in House after 1918: full entry in Volume III.

LEFEVRE, Rt. Hon. George John Shaw. See SHAW-LEFEVRE, Rt. Hon. George John.

LEGGE, Hon. Heneage. 90 Piccadilly, London. Carlton, and Wellington. S. of William, 4th Earl of Dartmouth, and the Hon. Frances Barrington, 2nd d. of George, 5th Visct. Barrington. B. at Sandwell Park, West Bromwich 1845. Educ. at Eton. Coldstream Guards 1863-73, Col. 9th Lancers 1873-90. Commanded H.M. Reserve Regiment of Lancers 1900-01. Vestryman, St. George's, Hanover Square 1894-1900; Councillor on the London County Council 1896-1901; Councillor on Westminster City Council 1900-01. A Conservative. Contested the Holmfirth division of the W. Riding of Yorkshire Dec. 1885. Elected for St. George's, Hanover Square in 1900 and sat until he accepted Chiltern Hundreds in June 1906. Died 1 Nov. 1911. [1906]

LEGH, Hon. Thomas Wodehouse. 7 Upper Belgrave Street, London. Lyme Park, Disley, Cheshire. Carlton, and St. James's. Eld. s. of Lord Newton (who was many years MP successively for S. Lancashire and E. Cheshire), by his marriage with Emily Jane, d. of Canon Wodehouse, of Norwich. B. 1857; m. 1880, Evelyn, d. of W. Bromley-Davenport, Esq., MP. Educ. at Eton, and Christ Church, Oxford. Entered the diplomatic service in 1880; was appointed to the British Embassy at Paris 1881; 3rd Secretary in 1882; retired 1886. A Conservative. Sat for the Newton div-

ision of S.W. Lancashire from Aug. 1886 until he succeeded as Lord Newton on 15 Dec. 1898. PC. 1915. Paymaster Gen. 1915-16; Assistant Under-Secretary at the Foreign Office 1916-19. Author of biographies of Lord Lyons and the 5th Marq. of Lansdowne, and of a volume of memoirs entitled *Retrospection*. Died 21 Mar. 1942. [1898]

LEGH, William John. 20 Belgrave Square, London. Lyme Park, Cheshire. Goldbourne Park, Warrington, Lancashire. Carlton, and Army & Navy. S. of William Legh, Esq., and Mary Anne his wife. B. at Ratcliffe Hall, Leicestershire 1828; m. 1856, Emily Jane, d. of the Rev. Charles Nourse Wodehouse, Canon of Norwich, and Lady Jane Wodehouse. Educ. at Rugby. Entered the army Dec. 1848. Appointed Dept.-Lieut. of Chester, and of the Co. Palatine of Lancaster 1860. A Conservative. Sat for S. Lancashire from 1859 to 1865, when he was defeated, and for E. Cheshire from 1868 to 1885, when he was defeated contesting the Hyde division of Cheshire. Created Baron Newton Aug. 1892. Died 15 Dec. 1898. [1885]

LEHMANN, Rudolf Chambers. 59 Ashley Gardens, London. Fieldhead, Bourne End, Buckinghamshire. Reform, and Athenaeum. S. of Frederick Lehmann, Esq., and Nina, d. of Robert Chambers, Esq., of Edinburgh. B. 3 Jan. 1856 near Sheffield; m. 1898, Alice Marie, d. of Harrison Davis, Esq. Educ. at Highgate School, and Trinity Coll., Cambridge; M.A. Called to the bar at the Inner Temple 1880. A Journalist; Chairman of Liberal Publication Department; a member of the staff of *Punch*; Editor of *Daily News* 1901. A J.P. for Buckinghamshire; High Sheriff 1901. Author of *Digest of Overruled Cases, Punch's Prize Novels, Rowing, Isthmian Library, Anni Fugaces, Crumbs of Pity*, and other works. A Liberal, in favour of Home Rule. Unsuccessfully contested Cheltenham in 1885, Central Hull in 1886, and Cambridge in 1892. Elected for the Harborough division of Leicestershire in 1906 and sat until he retired in Dec. 1910. Died 22 Jan. 1929. [1910]

LEICESTER, Joseph Lynn. The Crescent, Belvedere Road, Lambeth. Central City. S. of Thomas Leicester, Esq., Glass-Blower, of Warrington. B. 1825; m. 1st, Charlotte, d. of John and Eliza Coote, of Southwark;

2ndly, Clara, d. of William and Maryann Mitchel, of Southwark. Educ. at the National Schools, Warrington. He worked as a Glass-Blower from his tenth year, and for many years at Messrs. Powell's Glassworks in Whitefriars. Secretary of the Glass-Blowers' Friendly Society, and a prominent temperance advocate. Served on several juries and commissions, and contributed numerous articles to the Glassmakers' Magazine. In 1870 the Society of Flint-Glassmakers presented him with a purse of £100, in recognition of his services to the trade. A Radical, an advocate of "Local Option" and the closing of public houses on Sunday. Sat for West Ham S. from Nov. 1885 until defeated in 1886 standing as a Gladstonian Liberal. Died 13 Oct. 1903.   [1886]

LEIGH, Sir Joseph. The Towers, Didsbury, Manchester. Reform. S. of Thomas Leigh, Cotton Spinner, Stockport. B. 1841; m. 1868, Alice A., eld. child of Daniel Adamson, first Chairman of the Manchester Ship Canal. Educ. at Stockport Grammar School, and privately. A J.P. for Stockport and Cheshire. Was four times Mayor of Stockport; Honorary Freeman of the borough of Stockport; Chevalier of the Legion of Honour, France. A Liberal, in favour of such measures of domestic reform as Old Age Pensions, the Housing of the Poor, the Rating of Land Values, the Temperance Question, and administrative reform in the War Office. Was an unsuccessful candidate for Stockport in 1885 and 1886. Elected for Stockport in 1892 and sat until defeated in 1895. Re-elected there in 1900 and sat until he retired in 1906. Knighted 1894. Died 22 Sept. 1908. [1905]

LEIGH-BENNETT, Henry Currie. 61 Elm Park Gardens, London. Thorpe Place, Chertsey. United University, and Carlton. S. of the Rev. Henry Leigh-Bennett, of Thorpe Place, Surrey, by Caroline, 2nd d. of George Henry Crutchley, Esq., of Sunninghill Park, Berkshire. B. at Thorpe Place 1852; m. 1878, Florence Nightingale, 3rd d. of T.M. Mackay, Esq., of Earl's Court Square, London. Educ. at Winchester, and New Coll. A Barrister (called 1878, Inner Temple), of the Oxford Circuit, but did not practise; also a J.P. and Dept.-Lieut. for Surrey, senior Dept. Chairman Quarter Sessions, member Surrey County Council (for Chertsey and Thorpe), Chairman Chertsey Rural District Council, and Chairman Thorpe Parish Council. Director of the L. and S.W. Railway Company. A Conservative. Sat for the Chertsey division of Surrey from Feb. 1897 until his death 7 Mar. 1903.   [1903]

LEIGH-CLARE, Octavius Leigh. 11 New Court, Carey Street, London. Hindley Cottage, East Sheen. Carlton, New University, and St. Stephen's. Manchester Conservative. S. of William Clare and Elizabeth Leigh. B. at Walton Breck, Liverpool 1841; m. 1st, 1868, Harriet, d. of William Huson, Esq., of Liverpool; 2ndly, 1889, Jane Maria, d. of James Wigan, Esq., of Mortlake. Educ. at Rossall School, and St. John's Coll., Cambridge. A Barrister, called 1866. A bencher of the Inner Temple, and a member of the Gen. Council of the Bar. A Conservative. Was an unsuccessful candidate in the Eccles division of Lancashire in 1892. Elected for that division in 1895 and sat until he retired in 1906. Died 16 July 1912.   [1905]

LEIGHTON, Sir Baldwin, Bart. Loton Park, Nr. Shrewsbury. S. of the late Sir Baldwin Leighton, 6th bart., by his 2nd wife, sister of 1st Lord Stanley of Alderley. B. at Sunderland, 1805; m. 1832, Mary, d. of Thomas Netherton Parker, Esq., of Sweeney Hall, Shropshire (she died Mar. 1864). Educ. at Rugby. Appointed a Dept.-Lieut. of Shropshire, 1846. Elected Chairman of Quarter Sessions of Salop, 1855. Patron of 1 living. Of moderate Conservative opinions. First for South Shropshire, Sept. 1859, and sat until defeated July 1865. Died 26 Feb. 1871.   [1865]

LEIGHTON, Stanley. 70 Chester Square, London. Sweeney Hall, Oswestry. Carlton, and Athenaeum. 2nd s. of Sir Baldwin Leighton (7th Bart.), MP for S. Shropshire, by Mary, d. and heiress of Thomas Netherton Parker, Esq., of Sweeney Hall, Oswestry. B. at Loton Park 1837; m. 1873, Jessie Maria, d. and co-heiress of Henry B.W. Williams-Wynn, Esq., of Nant-y-meiched, Montgomeryshire, and Howberry Park, Oxfordshire. Was educ. at Harrow, and at Balliol Coll., Oxford; graduated M.A. 1860. Was called to the bar at the Inner Temple 1861, and joined the Oxford Circuit; Honorary Commissioner for S. Australia at the Paris Exhibition 1878. F.S.A., and author of *Records of Oswestry* and several papers on social and archaeological subjects. A J.P. for Shropshire and

Montgomeryshire, a Dept.-Lieut. for Shropshire, member of the House of Laymen, Governor of Shrewsbury School, and Director of the Clergy Pensions Institution. A Conservative. Unsuccessfully contested Bewdley in 1874. Sat for N. Shropshire 1876-85, and for the Oswestry division of Shropshire from 1885 until his death 4 May 1901. [1901]

LE-MARCHANT, Sir Denis, Bart. 7 Harley Street, London. Cobham Place, Surrey. S. of Gen. Le-Marchant, by the d. of John Carey, Esq., of Guernsey. B. 1795; m. 1835, the 4th d. of Charles Smith, Esq., of Suttons, Essex. Was called to the bar in 1822. Appointed principal secretary to the Lord Chancellor in 1830; clerk of the Crown in Chancery 1834, but resigned the same year; was Secretary to the Board of Trade from 1836 to June 1841, when he was appointed Secretary to the Treasury; resigned the last office in Sept. 1841. Editor of the *Memoirs of the Reign of George III*, by Horace Walpole, Earl of Orford. A Liberal. First returned for Worcester City in July 1846 and sat until he retired in July 1847. Under Secretary for the Home Department 1847-48 and again Secretary to Board of Trade 1848-50. Chief Clerk to House of Commons 1850-71. Died 30 Oct. 1874. [1847]

LENG, Sir John. 186 Fleet Street, London. Kinbrae, Newport, Fife. National Liberal, and Eastern Club, Dundee. S. of Adam Leng, Esq., of Hull, and Mary, d. of Christopher Luccock, Esq., Land Surveyor, of Malton, Yorkshire. B. 1828 at Hull; m. 1st, 1851, Emily, d. of W. Cook, Esq., of Beverley (she died 1894); 2ndly, 1897, Mary, d. of W. Low, Esq., of Kirriemuir. A Journalist. In 1847 he was Sub-Editor of the *Hull Advertiser*, and in 1851 he became Editor and Managing Proprietor of the *Dundee Advertiser*. He established several popular journals in Scotland, including the *People's Journal*. Author of *America in 1876*, *Scotch Banking Reform*, *American Competition*, *Practical Politics*, *The Best Methods of dealing with the Unemployed*, *Home Rule All Round*, *Letters from India and Ceylon*, etc. J.P. for the counties of Forfar and Fife, and Dept.-Lieut. for Angus and the city of Dundee. Knighted 1893. A Liberal, considered the most urgent subjects demanding legislation were Temperance Reform, Taxation of Land Value, and Registration Reform. First returned for Dundee on the

death of Mr. Firth, 1889 and sat until he retired in Jan. 1906. Died 13 Dec. 1906. [1905]

LENNOX, Rt. Hon. Lord Walter Charles Gordon. 46 Lower Sloane Street, London. Goodwood, Chichester. Carlton, and Wellington. 4th s. of the Duke of Richmond and Gordon. B. 1865. Educ. at Eton. Was Private Secretary to the Marq. of Salisbury when Prime Minister 1887-1888. Was Lord Treasurer of the Queen's Household 1891-92. A Conservative. Returned for Chichester division of Sussex on the retirement of his brother, the Earl of March, Mar. 1888, and re-elected without opposition on his appointment as Lord Treasurer 1891. He sat until he accepted Chiltern Hundreds in 1894. PC. 1891. Died 21 Oct. 1922. [1894]

LEON, Herbert Samuel. 98 Mount Street, Berkeley Square, London. Bletchley Park, Buckinghamshire. S. of George Leon, Esq., of the London Stock Exchange. B. in London 1850; m. 1st, 1873, Esther, 2nd d. of E.H. Beddington, Esq., of Lancaster Gate (she died 1875); 2ndly, 1880, Fanny, 3rd d. of David Hyam, Esq., of Tavistock Square. Educ. privately. A member of the London Stock Exchange from 1868; and a member of the Buckinghamshire County Council. A Liberal, in favour of Home Rule for Ireland. First elected for Buckinghamshire N. May 1891 and sat until defeated in 1895. Unsuccessfully contested the Handsworth division of Staffordshire in Jan. 1906. Created Bart. 1911. Chairman of Buckinghamshire County Council Finance Committee. Died 23 July 1926. [1895]

LETHBRIDGE, Sir Roper, K.C.I.E., 19 Clanricarde Gardens, London. Lynsted Lodge, Nr. Sittingbourne, Kent. Carlton, National Conservative, and Junior Constitutional. Eld. s. of E. Lethbridge, Esq., of Ste. Adresse, France, by Caroline Elizabeth, d. of Leonard Cridland, Esq., of Plymouth. B. at Plymouth 1840; m. Eliza, d. of W. Finlay, Esq., of Ste. Adresse, and grand-niece of Lord Teynham. Educ. at Exeter Coll., Oxford, where he held a scholarship, and took honours in classics and mathematics (B.A. 1863). In 1868 was appointed Professor of Political Economy to the State Colleges of Calcutta University; in 1874 Principal of Krishnaghur Coll., Bengal; and in 1878 Press Commissioner of India and an Indian Political Agent of the first class. Was called to the bar at the Inner Temple 1880. Wrote *A History of India*, *A History of Bengal*, *High Education in India*, and many other educational and political works. A "progressive Conservative", advocated "reforms in the administration of India, and an Imperial federation between the United Kingdom, India, and the Colonies." Sat for Kensington N. from Nov. 1885 until he retired in 1892. Knighted 1885. K.C.I.E. 1890. Vice-President of Tariff Reform League. Died 15 Feb. 1919.   [1892]

LEUTY, Thomas Richmond. Headingly Lodge, Leeds. S. of Thomas Leuty, Esq., Linen Manufacturer, of Leeds, formerly of Rawcliffe, by Elizabeth, d. of Richard Brown, Esq., of Sawley, Ripon. B. at Leeds 1853; m. 1880, Annie Ellen, d. of John Arthington, Esq., of Leeds. Educ. at Bramham Coll., Tadcaster. A Linen Manufacturer, Castleton Mills, Leeds. Was elected Town Councillor of Leeds in 1882 (New Wortley ward), Mayor 1893-94. A Liberal, in favour of Home Rule for Ireland and the "Newcastle Programme", also of the limitation of the powers of the House of Lords, "Eight Hours" for Miners, etc. Unsuccessfully contested Leeds N. in 1892. First elected for Leeds E. 30 Apr. 1895 and sat until he retired in 1900. Died 15 Apr. 1911.   [1900]

LEVER, Arthur Levy. Continued in House after 1918: full entry in Volume III.

LEVER, William Hesketh. The Hill, Hampstead, London. Thornton Manor, Thornton Hough, Cheshire. Reform, Automobile, Devonshire, and National Liberal. S. of James Lever and Eliza Lever, née Hesketh. B. 19 Sept. 1851 at Bolton; m. 1874, Elizabeth Helen Hulme. Educ. at Church Institute, Bolton. Was in business as a Grocer 1867-86; later head of the firm of Lever Brothers, Soap Makers, Port Sunlight. A Liberal. Unsuccessfully contested Birkenhead in 1892, 1894, and 1895, and the Wirral division of Cheshire in 1900; elected for the Wirral division of Cheshire in 1906 and sat until he retired in Jan. 1910. Unsuccessfully contested the Ormskirk division of Lancashire 1910. Created Bart. 1911. High Sheriff of Lancashire 1917; Mayor of Bolton 1918-19; Created Baron Leverhulme in 1917 and advanced to Viscountcy 1922. Died 7 May 1925.   [1909]

LEVESON-GOWER, Frederick Neville Sutherland. Berkeley House, Hay Hill, London. Travellers', and St. James's. Only s. of Lord Albert Sutherland Leveson-Gower. B. 1874. Educ. at Eton, and Christ Church, Oxford. A Liberal Unionist. Elected for Sutherlandshire in 1900 and sat until defeated in 1906. Died 9 Apr. 1959.   [1905]

LEVESON-GOWER, George Granville. 14 South Audley Street, London. Holmbury, Dorking, Surrey. Brooks's, National Liberal, and St. James's. Only s. of the Hon. E.F. Leveson-Gower, at one time MP for Bodmin, by Lady Margaret, d. of the 2nd Marq. of Northampton. B. in London 1858. Educ. at Eton, and Balliol Coll., Oxford; graduated in honours 1880. Was Assistant Private Secretary to the Prime Minister, the Rt. Hon. W.E. Gladstone, from June 1880 to Aug. 1885. Was a Junior Lord of the Treasury in 1886; appointed Controller of the Household 1892 and held office until 1895. Also a Church Estates Commissioner. A Liberal, in favour of Home Rule for Ireland. Sat for Staffordshire N.W. from Nov. 1885 to June 1886, when he was defeated. In 1889 he unsuccessfully contested E. Marylebone. First elected for Stoke-upon-Trent in Mar. 1890 and sat until defeated in 1895. Commissioner of Woods and Forests 1908-24; member of London School Board 1897-99; European Editor of North American Review in England 1899-1908; Chairman Home Counties Liberal Federation 1905-08; Chairman of two local London Railway Companies 1925; Chairman of the Lilleshall Company. Author of several works of a historical nature. K.B.E. 1921. Died 18 July 1951.   [1895]

LEVY, Sir Maurice, Bart. Humberstone Hall, Leicester. Reform, National Liberal, Hurlingham, and Royal Automobile. S. of Joseph Levy, Esq. B. at Leicester 1859; m. 1885, Elise, d. of Max Zossenheim, Esq. Educ. privately, and at University School, London. Chairman of Messrs. Hart and Levy Limited, of Leicester and London. A J.P. for Leicestershire. Knighted 1907. Created Bart. 1913. A Liberal. Elected for mid Leicestershire in 1900 and sat until he retired in 1918. High Sheriff of Leicestershire 1926-27. Died 26 Aug. 1933.   [1918]

LEVY-LAWSON, Hon. Harry Lawson

Webster. See LAWSON, Hon. Harry Lawson Webster.

LEVY-LEVER, Arthur. See LEVER, Arthur Levy. Continued in House after 1918: full entry in Volume III.

LEWIS, Sir Charles Edward, Bart. 36 Hyde Park Gate, London. 23 Brunswick Terrace, Brighton. Carlton, Conservative, and St. Stephen's. 3rd s. of the Rev. George William Lewis, M.A., of Magdalen Hall, Oxford. B. at Wakefield, Yorkshire 1825; m. 1850, Isabella, d. of Richard Annesley Ellison, Esq., of Bristol. Educ. privately, and at St. Saviour's Grammar School, Southwark. Was a Solicitor (admitted 1847), a member of the firm of Lewis, Munns, and Longdean. A Magistrate for the Co. of Londonderry. Author of several legal hand-books. Held "Conservative principles, but considered that the maintenance of the union in its integrity stood before all party combinations." Sat for Londonderry city from Nov. 1872 till Oct. 1886, when he was unseated on petition. Elected for Antrim N. in Feb. 1887 and sat until he retired in 1892. Created Bart. 1887. Author of *The Four Reformed Parliaments*, and other works. Died 10 Feb. 1893. [1892]

LEWIS, John Harvey. 24 Grosvenor Street, London. Union. S. of William Lewis, Esq., of Harlech, Co. Dublin, and Dora, his wife. B. in Dublin 1814; m. 1st, Emily, only child of George Ball, Esq. (she died 1850); 2ndly, Jane Isabella, d. of William Browne, Esq. Educ. at Trinity Coll., Dublin, where he graduated M.A. Was called to the bar in Ireland 1838; relinquished practice 1850. A Magistrate for Middlesex and Westminster, and Dept.-Lieut. of Middlesex and of the Tower Hamlets. High Sheriff of Kildare 1857. A Liberal, "paired" in favour of the disestablishment of the Irish Church 1869; in favour of strict economy, especially in the Admiralty department. Unsuccessfully contested Bodmin in 1857, and Hull in Apr. and Aug. 1859. First elected for Marylebone in Apr. 1861 and sat until he retired in 1874. Died 23 Oct. 1888. [1873]

LEWIS, Rt. Hon. John Herbert. Continued in House after 1918: full entry in Volume III.

LEWIS, Thomas P. 14 Craven Street, Strand, London. Bryn Ogwen, Bangor. S. of Thomas Lewis, Esq., a Tenant Farmer, of Cemaes, Anglesey. B. 1821; m. 1846, Laura, d. of Henry Hughes, Esq., of Pantdu, Llanllyfni. Educ. at the Llanfechell National School, Anglesey. Was in business as a Corn and Flour Merchant. A frequent contributor to Welsh periodicals. A Liberal, in favour of Mr. Gladstone's Home Rule policy, and advocated a Land Bill for Wales, etc. Sat for Anglesey from 1886 until he retired in 1895. Died 2 Dec. 1897. [1895]

LEWISHAM, Rt. Hon. William Heneage Legge, Visct. 55 Manchester Street, London. Woodsome, Huddersfield. Carlton, Junior Carlton, and St. Stephen's. Eld. s. of the Earl of Dartmouth, by Lady Augusta, eld. d. of the 5th Earl of Aylesford. B. in Hill Street, London 1851; m. 1879, Lady Mary, youngest d. of the 2nd Earl of Leicester. Educ. at Eton, and Christ Church, Oxford. Appointed Vice-Chamberlain of H.M. Household 1885, and again 1886, holding office until 1891. A Conservative, and "would resist to the utmost any attempt to undermine the ancient relation between Church and State." Sat for Kent W. from May 1878 to Nov. 1885, and for Lewisham from Nov. 1885 until he succeeded as Earl of Dartmouth in 1891. Lord-Lieut. of Staffordshire 1891-1927. Owned 20,000 acres. Died 11 Mar. 1936. [1891]

LEWISHAM, William Legge, Visct. 37 Charles Street, Berkeley Square, London. Cambridge House, West Bromwich. Carlton. Eld. s. of Earl of Dartmouth. B. 22 Feb. 1881 in London; m. 1905, Lady Ruperta Carrington, d. of Marq. of Lincolnshire. Educ. at Eton, and Christ Church, Oxford. A J.P. for Staffordshire and Maj. in Staffordshire Yeomanry. Was a member of the London County Council for Lewisham 1907-10. A Unionist. Unsuccessfully contested West Bromwich in 1906; elected there in Jan. 1910 and sat until defeated in 1918. G.C.V.O. 1934. Succeeded as Earl of Dartmouth in 1936. Lord Great Chamberlain 1928-36. President of M.C.C. 1933-34. Died 28 Feb. 1958. [1918]

LIDDELL, Harry. Lynwood, Addison Crescent, London. Carlton, Constitutional, and Automobile. S. of William Liddell, Esq., J.P., of Donacloney. B. 1866. A Director of William Liddell and Company

Limited, Linen Manufacturers. A Unionist. Elected for W. Down in July 1905 and sat until he accepted Chiltern Hundreds in 1907. Died 8 July 1931. [1907]

LINCOLN, Ignatius Timothy Tribich. Park View, Darlington. National Liberal. S. of Nathan Tribich. B. 4 Apr. 1879 at Budapest, Hungary; m. 1910, Miss Margarethe Kahlor, of Hamburg. Educ. at Presburg Coll., Germany, Budapest, and Montreal, Canada. A Curate of the Church of England. Assisted Mr. B. Seebohm Rowntree in the production of *Land and Labour, Lessons from Belgium.* A Liberal. Elected for Darlington in Jan. 1910 and retired in Dec. 1910. Worked as a Censor of Hungarian and Rumanian letters for the Post Office Aug.-Sept. 1914. Arrested in New York for forgery, Aug. 1915, eventually extradited to London and sentenced to 3 years penal servitude. British citizenship revoked; deported on 11 Aug. 1919. Participated in the Kapp Putsch in Germany in Mar. 1920. Acted as political adviser to Gen. Yang-sen in China and spent most of the rest of his life in the Far East. Worked with the Japanese in Shanghai after their invasion of China and died there 9 Oct. 1943. [1910]

LINDSAY, William Arthur. Continued in House after 1918: full entry in Volume III.

LINDSAY-HOGG, Sir Lindsay, Bart. See HOGG, Sir Lindsay, Bart.

LITTLE, Thomas Shepherd. 8 Harcourt Buildings, Temple, London. 13 Union Court, Castle Street, Liverpool. S. of Thomas Little, Esq., of Kilkenny. B. 1845. Educ. at Trinity Coll., Cambridge. A Barrister, called to the bar at the Inner Temple 1874, and a member of the Northern Circuit. Editor of the English Law part of Lord Mackenzie's work on Roman Law. A Liberal, in favour of Home Rule for Ireland, the direct popular veto, as regards the liquor traffic, registration reform, etc. Sat for Whitehaven from July 1892 until defeated in 1895. Stipendiary Magistrate for Liverpool 1908-10. Died 28 June 1910. [1895]

LLEWELLYN, Evan Henry. 1c King Street, St. James's, London. Langford Court, Somerset. Carlton. S. of Llewellyn Llewellyn, Esq., of Buckland, Filliegh, N.

Devon, and Eliza, d. of John Strick, Esq. B. 1847 at Ynispenllwch, Glamorgan; m. 1868, Mary Blanche, d. of Thomas Somers, Esq., of Mendip Lodge, Somerset. Educ. at Rugby. A Landowner; J.P., and Alderman for Co. Somerset, and Maj. and Honorary Lieut.-Col. 4th Battalion Somersetshire Regiment. A Conservative. Sat for N. Somerset from 1885 to 1892, when he was defeated, and from 1895 until he retired in 1906. Died 27 Feb. 1914. [1905]

LLEWELYN, Charles Leyshon Dillwyn Venables. See VENABLES-LLEWELYN, Charles Leyshon Dillwyn.

LLEWELYN, Sir John Talbot Dillwyn, Bart. See DILLWYN-LLEWELYN, Sir John Talbot, Bart.

LLOYD, George Ambrose. Continued in House after 1918: full entry in Volume III.

LLOYD, George Butler. Continued in House after 1918: full entry in Volume III.

LLOYD, Wilson. Burlington Hotel, London. Myvod House, Wood Green, Wednesbury. Carlton, Junior Carlton, and Grosvenor. S. of Samuel Lloyd, Esq., of the firm of Lloyds, Bankers, Birmingham, and Mary his wife, who was d. of Joseph Hurychurch, of Falmouth, Cornwall. B. 1835 at Wednesbury; m. 1883, the d. of Thomas Underhill, Esq., M.D., and J.P., Staffordshire. Educ. at the Friends' School, York. An Ironmaster and Mine Owner in Wednesbury. A J.P. for Staffordshire, and Chairman of the Wednesbury School Board, Mayor of Wednesbury 1888-90, etc. A Conservative, opposed to Home Rule for Ireland, "disestablishment", and hostile foreign tariffs, but did not advocate a duty on foreign raw materials; in favour of an eight hours bill for Miners, and in favour of a federation of our colonies. First elected for Wednesbury 1885, but lost the seat at the general election in the following year. Returned again for Wednesbury in July 1892 and sat until he retired in 1895. Died 4 Sept. 1908. [1895]

LLOYD-ANSTRUTHER, Robert Hamilton. See ANSTRUTHER, Robert Hamilton Lloyd-.

LLOYD GEORGE, Rt. Hon. David. Bron-y-de, Court, Farnham. Ty Newydd, Llanystumdwy, North Wales. Reform, and

National Liberal. S. of William George, a former master of the Hope Street Unitarian Schools, Liverpool, and Elizabeth, d. of David Lloyd, Baptist Minister, of Llanystumdwy, Carnarvonshire. B. 1863; m. 1st 1888, Margaret, d. of Richard Owen, Esq., of Nynydd Ednyfed, Criccieth (she died 1941); 2ndly, 23 Oct. 1943, Frances Louise, C.B.E., d. of John Stevenson, Esq., of Worthing. Educ. at Llanystumdwy Church Schools and privately. Admitted a Solicitor, June 1884. President of the Board of Trade Dec. 1905 to Apr. 1908; Chancellor of the Exchequer 1908-15; Minister of Munitions 1915-16; Secretary of State for War July-Dec. 1916; First Lord of the Treasury and Prime Minister 7 Dec. 1916 to 23 Oct. 1922. PC. 1905. Awarded special war medals by the King Jan. 1920; Grand Cordon of the Legion of Honour 1920; Lord Rector of Edinburgh University 1920. Constable of Carnarvon Castle 1908. Chancellor for Wales of the Welsh Priory of St. J., 1918; Prior of the Priory from 1943. Honorary D.L. University of Wales; Honorary D.C.L. Oxford. O.M. 1919. A Liberal. MP for Carnarvon district from Apr. 1890 to Jan. 1945 when he was created Earl Lloyd George of Dwyfor. Leader of the Liberal Party 1926-31, and of Independent Liberal Group 1931-35. Father of the House of Commons 1929-45. Died 26 Mar. 1945. [1945]

LOCKER-LAMPSON, Godfrey Lampson Tennyson. Continued in House after 1918: full entry in Volume III.

LOCKER-LAMPSON, Oliver Stillingfleet, C.M.G. Continued in House after 1918: full entry in Volume III.

LOCKIE, John. Stone Hall, Stonehouse. Buston Hall, Lesbury, Northumberland. Royal Societies. S. of J. Lockie, Esq., of Glasgow, and Elizabeth Laidlaw Smyth. B. 1863 at Glasgow; m. 1892, Annie, d. of John Farrell, Esq. Educ. at George Watson's Coll., Edinburgh. A Shipowner at Newcastle-on-Tyne. Established the Tyne Tube Company at Jarrow. Chairman and Founder of the National Industrial Association, and took a leading part in despatching a commission to inquire into trade prospects in S. Africa 1902. A Conservative. Unsuccessfully contested Devonport at the general election 1900. Elected for Devonport Oct. 1902 and sat until he ac-

cepted Chiltern Hundreds in 1904, when bankruptcy proceedings were being brought against him. Died 26 Jan. 1906. [1904]

LOCKWOOD, Rt. Hon. Amelius Richard Mark, C.V.O. 5 Audley Square, London. Bishop's Hall, Romford, Essex. Carlton, Arthur's, and Pratt's. S. of Gen. Mark Wood (formerly Lockwood) and his wife, the d. of Sir Robert Williams, Bart. B. in London 1847; m. 1876, Isabella, d. of Sir John R. Milbanke, Bart. Educ. at Eton. Entered the Coldstream Guards 1866; retired with the rank of Lieut.-Col. 1883. Assumed the surname of Lockwood in 1876. PC. and C.V.O. 1905. A Unionist. Represented W. Essex from 1892 until created Baron Lambourne 19 June 1917. President of Royal Horticultural Society. Director of London and North Western Railway Company. Lord-Lieut. of Essex from 1919. G.C.V.O. 1927. Died 26 Dec. 1928. [1917]

LOCKWOOD, Sir Frank. 26 Lennox Gardens, London. Cober Hill, Cloughton, Nr. Scarborough. Brooks's, and Garrick. S. of Charles Day Lockwood, Esq., of Doncaster. B. 1846; m. 1874, Julia, d. of Salis Schwabe, Esq., of Glyn Garth, Anglesey. Educ. at the Manchester Grammar School, and Caius Coll., Cambridge (B.A. 1868). Was called to the bar at Lincoln's Inn 1872, became Q.C. in 1882, and a bencher in 1887. Was Recorder of Sheffield and in 1880 acted as Royal Commissioner to inquire into corrupt practices at the Chester election. Was Solicitor-Gen. 1894-95. Created Kt. 1894. A J.P. and Dept.-Lieut. N. Riding of Yorkshire. A Liberal and Home Ruler. Unsuccessfully contested Kings Lynn in 1880 and York in Nov. 1883. Sat for York city from Nov. 1885 until his death 19 Dec. 1897. [1897]

LODER, Gerald Walter Erskine. Abinger House, Brighton. Wakehurst Place, Ardingly, Sussex. Carlton, Athenaeum, St. Stephen's, and St. James's. 4th s. of Sir Robert Loder, Bart., MP for Shoreham 1880 to 1885, and Maria, d. of Hans Busk, Esq. B. 1861; m. Oct. 1890, Lady Louise de Vere, eld. d. of the Duke of St. Albans. Educ. at Eton, and Trinity Coll., Cambridge; M.A. and LL.B. (Law Tripos), 1884. Was called to the bar at the Inner Temple 1888. Was Private Secretary to the Rt. Hon. C.T. Ritchie, as President to the

Local Government Board 1888-92, and to the Rt. Hon. Lord George Hamilton, Secretary of State for India 1896-1901. A J.P. and Dept.-Lieut. for Sussex. A Conservative, and supported the idea of a Liberal Unionist alliance with the Conservative Party. First elected for Brighton in 1889 and sat until appointed Junior Lord of the Treasury in Mar. 1905, but failed to secure re-election at a by-election on 5 Apr. 1905. President of Royal Horticultural Society 1929-31. Director of London, Brighton and South Coast Railway, and then Southern Railway; Chairman from 1932. Created Baron Wakehurst in 1934. Died 30 Apr. 1936.   [1905]

LOGAN, John William. East Langton Grange, Market Harborough. National Liberal, Reform, and Cobden. S. of John Logan, Esq., of The Maindee, Newport, Monmouthshire. B. 1845 at Newport; m. 1874, Maud Ansdall, d. of the Rev. B.E. Watkins, of Treeton Rectory, Rotherham. Educ. at Gloucester Collegiate School. A Railway Contractor. A J.P. for Leicestershire and an associate member of the Institute of Civil Engineers. A Liberal. Sat for the Harborough division of Leicestershire from 1891-1904, when he retired; re-elected there in Dec. 1910 and sat until he accepted Chiltern Hundreds in 1916. Died 25 May 1925.   [1916]

LONG, Charles Wigram. Severn Bank, Severn Stoke, Worcestershire. Naval & Military. 2nd s. of the Ven. Charles Maitland Long, Archdeacon of the E. Riding of Yorkshire, by Anna Maria, d. of Sir Robert Wigram. B. 1842; m. Constance Mary, d. of Lieut.-Col. R. Vansittart, Coldstream Guards. A Lieut.-Col. Royal Artillery, retired 1886. A J.P. and Dept.-Lieut. for Worcestershire, and Chairman of the Severn Stoke Parish Council. A Conservative and Unionist. Col. Long passed the Market Gardeners' Compensation Bill, 1895. First elected for the Evesham division of Worcestershire in Jan. 1895 and sat until he retired in Jan. 1910. Died 13 Dec. 1911.   [1909]

LONG, Rt. Hon. Walter Hume. Continued in House after 1918: full entry in Volume III.

LONSDALE, James Rolston. Continued in House after 1918: full entry in Volume III.

LONSDALE, Sir John Brownlee, Bart. 13 Prince's Gardens, London. The Dunes, Sandwich. Carlton, Bachelors', and White's. S. of James Lonsdale, Esq., J.P., Dept-Lieut. of Armagh, by Jane, d. of William Brownlee, Esq. B. 23 Mar. 1850; m. Florence, d. of William Rumney, Esq., of Stubbins House, Lancashire. A J.P. and Dept.-Lieut. for Co. Armagh; High Sheriff 1895. Honorary Secretary and Whip to the Irish Unionist Party. Created Bart. 1911. A Conservative. Sat for mid Armagh from Feb. 1900 until created Baron Armaghdale Jan. 1918. Died 8 June 1924.   [1917]

LOPES, Henry Yarde Buller. 45 Lennox Gardens, London. Carlton, and Wellington. S. of the Rt. Hon. Sir Massey Lopes and Bertha, d. of the 1st Baron Churston, and nephew to 1st Baron Ludlow. B. 1859 at Meriston, Roborough, S. Devon; m. 1891, Lady Albertha Edgcumbe, 2nd d. of the Earl of Mount Edgcumbe. Educ. at Eton, and Balliol Coll., Oxford. A J.P. and County Councillor for Devon. Served in the Royal 1st Devon Yeomanry. Called to the bar at the Inner Temple 1888. Served for a short time as Secretary to the Rt. Hon. W.H. Smith and to Visct. Cross. Travelled much in the East. A Conservative. Unsuccessfully contested the Totnes division of Devon in Dec. 1885. Sat for Grantham from July 1892 until defeated in 1900. Unsuccessfully contested the Torquay division of Devon in Jan. 1906 and again in Jan. 1910. Succeeded as Bart. 1908. High Sheriff of Devon 1914. Chairman of Devon County Council 1916-38. Created Baron Roborough Jan. 1938. Died 14 Apr. 1938.   [1900]

LORNE, the Rt. Hon. John Douglas Sutherland Campbell, Marq. of. Kensington Palace, London. Rosneath, Dunbartonshire. Eld. s. of the Duke of Argyll, by his 1st wife, Elizabeth, d. of the 2nd Duke of Sutherland. B. 1845; m. 1871, H.R.H. Princess Louise. Educ. at Eton, and Trinity Coll., Cambridge. Served as Private Secretary to his father when Secretary of State for India 1868-71; was Governor-Gen. of Canada and Governor of Prince Edward's Island 1878-83; and in 1892 was appointed Governor and Constable of Windsor Castle. Was Lieut.-Col. Commander 1st Argyll and Bute Artillery Volunteers 1866 to 1884, Hon. Col. of the 5th Volunteer Battalion Highland Light

221

Infantry 1871 to 1890, and Honorary Col. Royal (15th Battalion) Canadian Militia. K.T. 1871; PC. 1875; LL.D.; G.C.M.G. 1876, and Dept.-Lieut. for Co. Dunbarton. A Liberal Unionist, in favour of Imperial Federation, etc. Was MP for Argyllshire Mar. 1868-78 when he accepted the post of Gov.-Gen. of Canada, etc. An Unsuccessful candidate for Hampstead 1885 and Central Bradford 1892. First returned for Manchester S. July 1895 and sat until he succeeded as Duke of Argyll in Apr. 1900. G.C.V.O. 1901; Royal Victorian Chain 1902; K.G. 1911. Author of books on Canada, biography of Palmerston, verse, fiction, and two volumes of memoirs. Died 2 May 1914. [1900]

LOUGH, Rt. Hon. Thomas. 97 Ashley Gardens, Westminster, London. Drom Mullac, Killeshandra, Co. Cavan, Ireland. Reform, National Liberal, and Eighty. Stephens Green, Dublin. Royal Irish Yacht. S. of Matthew Lough, Esq., of Killynebber House, Cavan, and Martha, d. of William Steel, Esq. B. 1850 at Cavan; m. 1880, Edith Helen, d. of the Rev. John Mills. Educ. at the Royal School, Cavan, and the Wesley Coll., Dublin. A Wholesale Tea Merchant. Was Parliamentary Secretary to the Board of Education Dec. 1905 to Apr. 1908. H.M. Lieut. of Co. Cavan from 1907. A member of the Royal Archaeological Society of Ireland and of the Statistical Society, and author of *England's Wealth, Ireland's Poverty*, etc. PC. 1908. A Liberal, advocated the "Newcastle" and "London Liberal" programmes, with Labour Reform, etc. Unsuccessfully contested the Truro division of Cornwall in July 1886. Represented W. Islington from 1892 until defeated in 1918. Died 11 Jan. 1922. [1918]

LOW, Sir Frederick. 51 Sloane Gardens, London. 3 Hare Court, Temple, London. Reform, National Liberal, and Ranelagh. S. of Stephen Philpot Low, Esq., Dept.-Lieut., J.P. B. 1856; m. 1882, Katherine, d. of Charles Thompson, Esq. Educ. at Westminster, and privately. Was admitted a Solicitor 1878, and called to the bar at the Middle Temple 1890. K.C. 1902. Was Recorder of Ipswich from 1906. A Liberal. Unsuccessfully contested Salisbury in 1900 and Clapham in 1906. Elected for Norwich in Jan. 1910 and sat until appointed Judge of the High Court of Justice 1915. Knighted 1909. Died 4 Sept. 1917. [1914]

LOW, William Malcolm. 22 Roland Gardens, London. Clatto, Fifeshire. Union, and Carlton, and New Club, Edinburgh. Eld. s. of Gen. Sir John Low, G.C.S.I., K.C.B., of Clatto, Fifeshire, by Augusta, d. of John Talbot Shakespear, Esq. B. 1835 at Lucknow, India; m. 1872, the Lady Ida Fleming, d. of the 7th Earl of Denbigh. Educ. by Private Tutors, and at Haileybury Coll. Entered the Bengal Civil Service 1856; was Commissioner of the Nerbudda Province from 1869 to 1876; and received the special thanks of the Queen for services as a Political Officer with the forces during the Indian Mutiny, in which he was severely wounded. A J.P. and Dept.-Lieut. for Fifeshire. A "progressive Conservative", strongly opposed to "the degradation of Ireland by withdrawing from her her share in the councils of the Empire, and by the establishment of semi-independent legislative authority in Ireland." He stood unsuccessfully for the Ayr district at the election of 1885. First returned for Grantham July 1886 and sat until he retired in 1892. Died 14 June 1923. [1892]

LOWE, Sir Francis William, Bart. Continued in House after 1918: full entry in Volume III.

LOWLES, John. 12 Russell Square, London. S. of George Lowles, Esq., of Frant, Sussex, and Jane Westoby, of Beverley, Yorkshire. B. 1850 in London; m. 1871, his cousin Agnes, d. of J. Westoby, Esq. Was largely interested in the colonies and was Commissioner to Australia of the United Empire Trade League in 1896. He travelled much and was an ardent Imperial Federationist. Member of London County Council 1889 to 1892; a Fellow of the Royal Statistical Society, Colonial Institute, etc. A Conservative, opposed to Home Rule, and in favour of Social Legislation, State Aided Emigration, etc. Sat for the Haggerston division of Shoreditch from July 1895 until defeated in 1900. Died 1903. [1900]

LOWTHER, Claude William Henry. Continued in House after 1918: full entry in Volume III.

LOWTHER, Brigadier-Gen. Sir Henry Cecil. Continued in House after 1918: full entry in Volume III.

LOWTHER, Rt. Hon. James. 59

Grosvenor Street, London. Wilton Castle, Redcar, Yorkshire. Younger s. of Sir Charles Hugh Lowther, Bart., by Isabella, eld. d. of the Rev. Robert Morehead, D.D., Rector of Easington-cum-Liverton, Yorkshire. B. at Swillington House, Leeds 1840. Educ. at Westminster School, and at Trinity Coll., Cambridge; graduated B.A. 1862, M.A. 1866. Called to the bar at the Inner Temple 1864. A J.P., Dept.-Lieut., and Alderman for the N. Riding of Yorkshire. Was Parliamentary Secretary to the Poor Law Board from Aug. to Dec. 1868. Under-Secretary for the Colonies from Feb. 1874 to Feb. 1878; and Chief Secretary for Ireland from Feb. 1878 to Apr. 1880. PC. 1878. A Conservative. Sat for the city of York from July 1865 to Mar. 1880, when he was defeated; unsuccessfully contested E. Cumberland Feb. 1881; sat for N. Lincolnshire from 1 Sept. 1881 to Nov. 1885. In 1885 he unsuccessfully contested the Louth division of Lincolnshire, and in 1886 the Eskdale division of Cumberland. Was first elected for the Isle of Thanet division of Kent June 1888 and sat until his death 12 Sept. 1904.
[1904]

LOWTHER, Rt. Hon. James William. Continued in House after 1918: full entry in Volume III.

LOWTHER, Hon. William. Lowther Lodge, Kensington Gore, London. Campsea Ashe, Wickham Market, Suffolk. Carlton, and Travellers'. 3rd s. of Col. the Hon. Henry Cecil Lowther (2nd s. of the 1st Earl of Lonsdale), by Lady Eleanor, eld. d. of the 5th Earl of Harborough (extinct). B. at Cottesmore, Rutland 1821; m. 1853, Hon. Charlotte Alice, d. of Lord Wensleydale. Educ. at Magdalene Coll., Cambridge. Proceeded to Berlin 1841 as attaché; to Naples as Secretary of Legation July 1852; to the same office at St. Petersburg Apr. 1858; transferred to Berlin 1859; became Secretary of Embassy there 1862; minister plenipotentiary to the Argentine Republic Oct. 1867; resigned Jan. 1868. Was Mayor of Appleby 1868. A Magistrate for Westmoreland, Cumberland, and Suffolk. Was raised to the rank of an Earl's s. 1872. A Conservative. Sat from Jan. 1868 to Nov. 1885 for the Co. of Westmoreland, which had been represented by his father from 1812 till his death in 1867. Sat for the Appleby division of Westmoreland from 1885 until he

retired in 1892. Died 23 Jan. 1912. [1892]

LOYD, Archie Kirkman. 21 Cadogan Square, London. Downs House, Steventon, Berkshire. Carlton, Windham, Union, British Empire. 3rd s. of Thomas Kirkman Loyd, Esq., B.C.S., and Annie, d. of James Haig, Esq. B. 1847; m. 1885, Henrietta Louisa, d. of E.L. Clutterbuck, Esq., of Hardenhuish Park, Chippenham, Wiltshire. Called to the bar at the Middle Temple 1868 and joined the Norfolk and Midland Circuits. Q.C. 1892; bencher 1894, retired July 1895 on being elected MP for N. Berkshire. A J.P. and Dept.-Lieut. for Berkshire, and an Alderman of Berkshire County Council. A Conservative. Sat for N. Berkshire from July 1895 to Jan. 1906, when he retired. Was returned unopposed for N. Berkshire Aug. 1916 and sat until he retired in 1918. Died 1 Dec. 1922. [1918]

LOYD, Col. Lewis Vivian. 8 Rutland Gate, London. Charlecote Park, Warwickshire. 12 Esplanade, Scarborough. Guards', and Carlton. Eld. s. of William Jones Loyd, Esq., of Langleybury, Hertfordshire, by Caroline Gertrude, 2nd d. of John Henry Vivian, Esq., MP, of Singleton, near Swansea. B. 1852; m. 1879, Lady Mary Sophia, d. of the 4th Earl of Donoughmore. Educ. at Eton. Was a Lieut. Grenadier Guards 1872-83, and Col. 2nd Battalion Royal Warwickshire Regiment. J.P. and Dept.-Lieut. for Warwickshire, J.P. for Tipperary, and a Director of the London and North Western Railway Company. A Conservative. Sat for Chatham from July 1892 until he retired in 1895. Died 21 Sept. 1908. [1895]

LUBBOCK, Rt. Hon. Sir John, Bart., F.R.S. 2 St. James's Square, London. 15 Lombard Street, London. High Elms, Down, Kent. Athenaeum, National Liberal, and City Liberal. Eld. s. of Sir John William Lubbock, Bart., who was Vice-President of the Royal Society, and a distinguished scientific author, by Harriet, d. of Lieut.-Col. George Hotham, of York. B. in Eaton Place 1834; m. 1st, 1856, Ellen Frances, only d. of Rev. Peter Hordern, of Chorlton-cum-Hardy, Lancashire (she died 1879); 2ndly, 1884, Alice, d. of Gen. and the Hon. Mrs. Fox-Pitt-Rivers. Educ. at Eton; a D.C.L. Oxon 1875, LL.D. Cambridge 1883, LL.D. of Dublin and Edinburgh and M.D. Wurzburg. A Banker and Chairman of the London Bankers; also Chairman Central Association of Bankers. Was Vice-Chancellor of the University of London 1874-80, when he resigned to represent the University in Parliament. Chairman and Vice-Chairman and later Alderman of the London County Council. A J.P. and Dept.-Lieut. for Kent, a Commissioner of Lieutenancy for London, and a Trustee of the British Museum. President of the Linnean Society; Fellow of the Royal and various other scientific societies, and author of *Prehistoric Times, The Origin of Civilization and the Primitive Condition of Man, The Origin and Metamorphoses of Insects, British Wild Flowers considered in relation to Insects, Fifty Years of Science, Ants, Bees, and Wasps, On Representation, The Senses of Animals, Fruits, Flowers and Leaves, The Pleasures of Life, On Seedlings, The Use of Life, The Scenery of Switzerland, The Beauties of Nature,* etc., and numerous scientific memoirs. Succeeded as Bart. 1865. Chairman of Public Accounts Committee 1888-89. PC. 1890. A Liberal Unionist. Unsuccessfully contested W. Kent in 1865 and 1868. Sat for Maidstone from Feb. 1870 to Apr. 1880, when he was an unsuccessful candidate there; sat for London University from June 1880 until created Lord Avebury in Jan. 1900. Rector of St. Andrews University 1908. Died 28 May 1913. [1899]

LUCAS, Francis Alfred. Stornoway House, Cleveland Row, St. James's, London. Easton Park, Wickham Market, Suffolk. Athenaeum, Carlton, and St. James's. S. of Sampson Lucas, Esq., of Gloucester Square, London, and Lydia, d. of M. Davidson, Esq. B. at Gloucester Square in 1850; m. 1887, Alice, younger d. of Visct. de Stern. Educ. privately, and afterwards at University Coll., London. Was for some years a Partner in the firm of Lucas, Micholls and Company, of London, Manchester, and Stockport. An enthusiastic volunteer, for thirty-five years in the Artists' Corps, mostly as an officer, and was appointed to the command of the Harwich Volunteer Infantry Brigade 1900; a Governor of Christ's Hospital, Guy's Hospital, and of several other philanthropic institutions. A Director of the Alliance Insurance Company, and one of the members representing the Eastern Counties on the National Union of Conservative Associations; also a J.P. for the Co. of Suffolk. A Conservative. Contested the Louth division of Lincolnshire July

1895. Elected for the Lowestoft division of Suffolk in 1900 and sat until defeated in 1906. Contested Kennington in Jan. and Dec. 1910. Died 11 Dec. 1918. [1905]

LUCAS, Reginald Jaffray. Queen Anne's Mansions, London. Carlton, Turf, Marlborough, and Bachelors'. S. of Sir Thomas Lucas, Bart. B. in London 1865. Unmarried. Educ. at Eton, and Trinity Coll., Cambridge. Private Secretary to the Rt. Hon. A. Akers-Douglas, Chief Unionist Whip 1886-92; to the Rt. Hon. Sir W.H. Walrond, Chief Unionist Whip 1895-1900. Wrote *Felix Dorrien* and other novels. Was Lieut. London Rifle Brigade, Aide-de-Camp to Brigadier commanding Fourth London Volunteer Brigade, later Capt. 3rd Battalion (M.) Hampshire Regiment. A Conservative, and a loyal supporter of the Church of England, strongly opposed to lawlessness and illegal innovations in church practice. Earnestly desired legislation for better housing of the working classes in London and other great towns. Elected for Portsmouth in 1900 and sat until he retired in Jan. 1906, and unsuccessfully contested Bury at the same time. Died 9 May 1914. [1905]

LUCAS-SHADWELL, William. 1 Curzon Street, London. The Hall, Fairlight, Hastings. Carlton, New University, and Constitutional. Only s. of W.D. Lucas-Shadwell, Esq., Dept.-Lieut. and J.P. for Sussex, of The Hall, Fairlight, near Hastings, and Florentia M., only child and heiress of the Rev. H. Wynch, Rector of Pett, Sussex. B. 1852 at Fairlight; m. 1878, Beatrice Margaret, d. of J. Buckley Rutherford, Esq. Educ. at Pembroke Coll., Cambridge. A J.P. and Dept.-Lieut. for Sussex. A Conservative and strong Churchman. A Unionist, in favour of a strong Foreign Policy, Religious Education, care of the Voluntary Schools, Old Age Pensions, and Social Reform; opposed to disestablishment and to the late Local Option Bill. He unsuccessfully contested Finsbury E. in 1892. First returned for Hastings in July 1895 and sat until he retired in 1900. Died 31 May 1915. [1900]

LUNDON, Thomas. Kilteely, Co. Limerick. 35 North Side, Clapham Common, London. S. of W. Lundon, Esq., MP for E. Limerick. B. 21 June 1883 at Kilteely, Co. Limerick. Unmarried. Educ. at Kilteely National and Classical Schools.

Was Secretary of Kilteely branch of United Irish League from its formation. Was Secretary to National Federation and to the E. Limerick Executive of United Irish League during the movement of the Coercion Act. A Nationalist. Elected for E. Limerick in 1909 and sat until defeated in 1918. Died 28 Oct. 1951. [1918]

LUNDON, William. Kilteely, Co. Limerick. S. of M. Lundon, Esq., Farmer, and Alice Lundon, (née Malony). B. 1839 in Kilteely; m. 1879, Anne, d. of Hugh Torpey, Esq., Farmer. Educ. at Kilteely Classical Academy. A Professor of languages. A Teacher of considerable repute. A Nationalist. A prominent politician on the side of the Irish Nationalist Party for 40 years. Elected for E. Limerick in 1900 and sat until his death on 24 Mar. 1909. [1909]

LUPTON, Arnold. 7 Victoria Street, London. Grantham Road, Sleaford. National Liberal. S. of Arthur Lupton, Esq., M.A., of Leeds, and Elizabeth Wicksteed, of Shrewsbury. B. 1846 at Whitby; m. Jessie, d. of J.W. Ramsden, Esq. Educ. privately. A Civil and Mining Engineer, M.I.C.E., M.Inst. Mech.E., M.I.E.E., F.G.S., etc. Professor of Mining at Yorkshire Coll., Leeds; a member of Leeds Town Council 1886-89, and Rural District Council of Blackwell, Derbyshire 1897-1900. Author of several text-books on engineering and kindred subjects. A Liberal, in favour of small holdings, old age pensions, the increase of the Volunteer Force, reduction of standing army, and was a strenuous anti-vaccinator. Elected for the Sleaford division of Lincolnshire in 1906 and sat until defeated in Jan. 1910. Unsuccessfully contested the Plaistow division of West Ham as an Independent Liberal in 1918, and the Abbey division of Westminster on 25 Aug. 1921 as an Independent Liberal Anti War Waste candidate. Died 23 May 1930. [1909]

LUTTRELL, Hugh Courtenay Fownes, Ward House, Bere Alston, Devon. S. of George Fownes Luttrell, Esq., of Dunster Castle, Somerset, and Anne, d. of Sir Alexander Hood, Bart. B. 1857 at Woodlands, Somerset; m. 1904, Dorothy Hope, d. of Sir W. Wedderburn, Bart. Educ. at Cheltenham Coll. A Capt. in Rifle Brigade; Capt. and Honorary Maj. in Cornwall Light Infantry; Aide-de-Camp to

Lord Cowper, and Lord Spencer when Viceroys of Ireland, and Sir J. Adye when Gov. of Gibraltar 1892-1900. A Liberal. Sat for the Tavistock division of Devon from 1892 until he retired 1900; re-elected there in 1906 and sat until defeated in Dec. 1910. Died 14 Jan. 1918. [1910]

LYELL, Hon. Charles Henry. 1 Cadogan Gardens, London. Kinnordy, Kirriemuir, N.B. Reform. Only s. of Lord Lyell. B. 18 May 1875; m. 1911, Rosalind Margaret, d. of Vernon Watney, Esq., of Cornbury Park, Oxfordshire. Educ. at Eton, and New Coll., Oxford. Was Parliamentary Private Secretary (unpaid) to Mr. Asquith when Prime Minister (1908-15); and a temporary Chairman of Committees; a J.P. for Forfarshire and Vice-Chairman of Forfarshire Co. Territorial Association. Capt. Highland (Fife) Royal Garrison Artillery 1914, Maj. 1915. Severely wounded at the Front Nov. 1916. A Liberal. Sat for E. Dorset from 1904 to Jan. 1910, when he unsuccessfully contested W. Edinburgh. First elected for S. Edinburgh Apr. 1910 and sat until he accepted Chiltern Hundreds in 1917. Died 18 Oct. 1918 [1917]

LYELL, Sir Leonard, Bart. 48 Eaton Place, London. Kinnordy, Kirriemuir, N.B. Reform, and Athenaeum. New Club, Edinburgh. Eld. s. of Lieut.-Col. Henry Lyell (a bro. of Sir Charles Lyell, the Geologist), by his m. with Katharine, d. of Leonard Horner, Esq., F.R.S. B. in London 1850; m. 1874, Mary, d. of the Rev. John Mayne Stirling. Educ. privately and at the Berlin and London Universities. Sir Leonard was for a time Professor of Natural Science at the University Coll. of Wales. Succeeded to the family estate of Kinnordy on the death of his uncle, Sir Charles Lyell, Bart. A Magistrate for Forfarshire. Created Bart. Jan. 1894. A Liberal. First elected for Orkney and Shetland in 1885 and sat until defeated in 1900. Created 1st Baron Lyell 1914. Died 18 Sept. 1926. [1900]

LYMINGTON, Newton Wallop, Visct. 25 Cavendish Square, London. Hurstbourne Park, Micheldever, Hampshire. Brooks's. Eld. s. of the Earl of Portsmouth, by Lady Eveline Alicia Juliana, eld. d. of the 3rd Earl of Carnarvon. B. at Hurstbourne Park, Hampshire 1856; m. Feb. 1885, Beatrice Mary, only child of E. Pease, Esq., of Greencroft,

Darlington, and the Summer House, Bewdley, Worcestershire. Asquith was employed as his tutor, to coach him before going up to Oxford, for a few months in 1874. Educ. at Balliol Coll., Oxford (honours in classics and in modern history, and M.A.). A Liberal Unionist. Sat for Barnstaple from Feb. 1880-85 and for the S. Molton division of Devon from 1885 until he succeeded as Earl of Portsmouth in 1891. He rejoined the Liberal Party in 1905 and served in the Campbell-Bannerman administration as Under Secretary for War from 1905 to 1908. Died 4 Dec. 1917. [1891]

LYNCH, Arthur Alfred. 80 Antrim Mansions, Haverstock Hill, London. B. 1861 at Smythesdale, Victoria. Educ. at Melbourne University; M.A., C.E., Berlin University, Paris, Hôpital Beaujon, and St. Mary's Hospital Medical School; held diploma of Ecole Sup. de l'Electricité (Paris). A Physician, L.R.C.P., M.R.C.S., a Civil Engineer. Was Col. of the 2nd Irish Brigade on the Boer side in S. African War 1899-1902. Author of *Approaches: the Poor Scholar's Quest of a Mecca, Our Poets, Human Documents, Modern Authors, Religio Athletae, A Koran of Love, Une Question de Representation Geometrique, Prince Azreel, Pyschology: A New System, Progress and Evolution, Sonnets of the Banner and the Star, Ireland's Vital Hour, Poppy Meadows, Roman psychologique* (in French), *l'Ethique Nouvelle, l'Evolution dans ses rapports avec l'Ethique,* and other works. A Nationalist. Unsuccessfully contested Galway City Feb. 1886 and 1892; elected for this constituency in 1901; in 1903 was convicted of high treason, disqualified from membership of the House and condemned to death, which sentence was commuted to penal servitude for life. In 1904 he was released on licence and received a free pardon from the Crown in 1907. Elected for W. Clare in 1909 and sat until he retired in 1918 and unsuccessfully contested Battersea S. as a Labour candidate at the same time. In 1922 he unsuccessfully contested Hackney central. Col. in Army June 1918. Author of *My Life Story* (1924). Died 25 Mar. 1934. [1918]

LYNCH, Henry Finnis Blosse. 33 Pont Street, London. Wardington House, Banbury. Athenaeum. S. of Thomas Kerr Lynch, Esq., of Partry House, Co. Mayo, and Harriet, d. of Col. Robert Taylor, of the Indian Political Service. B. 18 Apr. 1862. Educ. at Eton, and Trinity Coll.,

Cambridge; M.A. A Merchant. Author of *Armenia: Travels and Studies,* 2 vols., and various articles in proceedings of learned societies. A Liberal, in favour of Licensing reform, small holdings, Land Law reform, etc. Elected for the Ripon division of Yorkshire in 1906 and sat until defeated in Jan. 1910. Contested Gloucester in Dec. 1910. Died 24 Nov. 1913. [1909]

LYTTELTON, Rt. Hon. Alfred. 16 Great College Street, London. 3 Paper Buildings, Temple, London. Wittersham House, Wittersham, Kent. Athenaeum, Carlton, and Brooks's. S. of the 4th Baron Lyttelton and Mary, d. of Sir Stephen Glynne, 8th Bart. B. in St. James's Square, London 1857; m. 1st, 1885, Laura Octavia, d. of Sir C. Tennant, Bart. (she died 1886); 2ndly, 1892, Edith, d. of Archibald Balfour, Esq. Educ. at Eton, and Trinity Coll., Cambridge; honours in History and the Oration Prize. Was called to the bar, Inner Temple 1881; bencher 1899. Recorder of Hereford 1893, and Recorder of Oxford 1894-1903. Q.C. 1900. Was Secretary of State for the Colonies 1903-05; a member of the Council of the Bar. PC. 1903. A member of the Royal Commissions on the Port of London, and Alien Emigration. Chairman of Transvaal Concessions Commission. Chancellor of Diocese of Rochester 1903. A Unionist. Sat for Warwick and Leamington from May 1895 until defeated at the general election of Jan. 1906. Elected for St. George's, Hanover Square in June 1906 and sat until his death 4 July 1913. [1913]

LYTTELTON, Hon. John Cavendish. Hagley Hall, Stourbridge. 70 South Audley Street, London. Brooks's. Eld. s. of Visct. Cobham. B. 23 Oct. 1881; m. 1908, Violet, d. of Charles Leonard, Esq. Educ. at Eton. A Lieut. in Rifle Brigade; served in S. African War 1902. Was Aide-de-Camp and Assistant Private Secretary to High Commissioner in S. Africa 1905-08. A J.P. for Worcester and Capt. in Worcestershire Yeomanry. A Unionist. Elected for the Droitwich division of Worcestershire in Jan. 1910 and sat until he accepted Chiltern Hundreds in Feb. 1916. Succeeded as 9th Visct. Cobham 9 June 1922. Served in Worcestershire Yeomanry 1914-17 (Gallipoli, Egypt, Palestine). Lord-Lieut. County and City of Worcester from 1923. Col. in Territorial Army 1925-31. Owned 6,000 acres. Under Secretary for

War 1939-40. K.C.B. 1942. Died 31 July 1949. [1915]

MacALEESE, Daniel. Monaghan. B. about 1834 in the N. of Ireland. For the most part a self-educated man. A Journalist, having risen through the grades of Clerk, Printers' Reader, Reporter, etc. Was Editor of the *Belfast Morning News* under E. Dwyer Gray, Esq., MP, and was also Editor of the *Ulster Examiner*. Later Editor and Proprietor of the Monaghan paper, the *People's Advocate*, and a Town Commissioner and a Poor Law Guardian. A Home Ruler of the Anti-Parnellite section. Sat for Monaghan N. from July 1895 until his death 1 Dec. 1900. [1900]

McARTHUR, Alexander. 79 Holland Park, London. Reform, City Liberal, and National Liberal. S. of the Rev. J. McArthur, Wesleyan Minister, of Londonderry. B. 1814; m. 1853, Maria, 2nd d. of the Rev. W.B. Boyce, of Australia. Resided many years in Australia; was a member of the Legislative Assembly of New South Wales during two Parliaments. In 1861 was nominated a member of the Legislative Council, and was a Magistrate of the Territory. Returned to Engand in 1863. A Partner in the firm of Messrs. W. and A. McArthur, Australian Merchants, and a Director of the Land Mortgate Bank of Victoria. Was a member of the first School Board for London (Lambeth division); a J.P. for Surrey and a Dept.-Lieut. for the City of London. A Liberal, voted for Mr. Gladstone's Home Rule measure, and said he would vote for the abolition of the laws of primogeniture and entail. Sat for Leicester from Feb. 1874 until he retired in 1892. Died 1 Aug. 1909. [1892]

McARTHUR, Charles. 13a Exchange Buildings, Liverpool. Villa Marina, New Brighton, Cheshire. 13 St. Mary Axe, London. 25 Army and Navy Mansions, Victoria Street, London. S. of Charles McArthur, Esq., of Port Glasgow. B. 1844 at Kingsdown, Bristol; m. Jessie, d. of John Makin, Esq., of Liverpool. Educ. at Bristol Grammar School. An Average-Adjuster; Chairman of the Association of Average-Adjusters. Was President of the Liverpool Chamber of Commerce 1892-96, a member of the Lord Chancellor's Committee for Codifying the Marine Insurance Laws, and Chairman of the Bill of Lading Committee. Author of works on Marine Insurance, *The Evidences of Natural Religion*, etc. A Unionist. Sat for the Exchange division of Liverpool from 1897 until defeated at the general election of 1906; elected for the Kirkdale division of Liverpool in Sept. 1907 and sat until his death 3 July 1910. [1910]

McARTHUR, William Alexander. 12 Buckingham Gate, London. Reform, Devonshire, National Liberal, and City Liberal. Eld. s. of A. McArthur, Esq., MP for Leicester, by Maria, 2nd d. of the Rev. W.B. Boyce, of Australia. B. at Sydney, New South Wales 1857; m. 1890, Florence, d. of J.C. Clarke, Esq., MP for Abingdon. Educ. privately. A Partner in the firm of W. and A. McArthur, Colonial Merchants, and a Director of the Bank of Australasia. A Dept.-Lieut. of the City of London, and was a Commissioner for New South Wales to the Indian and Colonial Exhibition. Was a Lord of the Treasury 1892-95 and one of the "Whips" to the Liberal party. A Radical, in favour of a separate legislative body empowered to deal with purely Irish affairs. In July 1886 was a successful candidate for the Buckrose division of the E. Riding of Yorkshire, but on petition and scrutiny the seat was awarded, on 11 Dec. to his opponent, Mr. C. Sykes. Elected for the St. Austell division of Cornwall in May 1887 and sat until he accepted Chiltern Hundreds in 1908. Later returned to Australia and died in Sydney on 7 June 1923. [1907]

MACARTNEY, Rt. Hon. William Grey Ellison. 98 St. George's Square, London. Clogher Park, Co. Tyrone. Carlton, and St. Stephen's. Ulster Club, Belfast. Kildare Street Club, Dublin. Eld. s. of John William Ellison Macartney, Esq., Dept.-Lieut. and J.P., who was MP for Tyrone from 1874 to 1885, by Elizabeth Phoebe, eld. d. of the Rev. John Grey Porter. B. in Dublin 1852; m. 1897, Ettie, eld. d. of J.E. Scott, Esq., of Outlands, Devonport. Educ. at Eton, and Exeter Coll., Oxford. Called to the bar at the Inner Temple 1878. Was Financial Secretary to the Admiralty 1895-1900. PC. 1900. A Conservative. Sat for Antrim S. from 1885 until appointed Dept. Master of the Mint 1903-13. Whilst sitting for Antrim S. he unsuccessfully contested the Scotland division of Liverpool in July 1895. High Sheriff of Co. Antrim 1908. K.C.M.G. 1913. Gov. of Tasmania 1913-17; Western Australia 1917-20. Died 4 Dec. 1924. [1902]

McCALLUM, Sir John Mills. Continued in House after 1918: full entry in Volume III.

McCALMONT, Harry Leslie Blundell. 11 St. James's Square, London. Cheveley Park, Newmarket. Carlton, Guards', Marlborough, and Turf. Only s. of H.B.B. McCalmont, Esq., Barrister, of Lincoln's Inn. B. 1861; m. 1st, 1885, Amy, d. of Gen. John Miller, 3rd Dragoon Guards (she died 1889); 2ndly, 1897, Winifred, d. of Gen. Sir H. de Bathe, Bart. Educ. at Eton. Entered the army, 6th Foot, 1881; exchanged to the Scots Guards 1885; retired 1889. A J.P. and Dept.-Lieut. for Cambridgeshire, and Col. 6th Battalion Royal Warwickshire Regiment. Was well-known owner of racehorses. A Conservative and Unionist. Sat for the Newmarket division of Cambridgeshire from July 1895 until his death 8 Dec. 1902.   [1902]

McCALMONT, Maj.-Gen. Hugh, C.B. Abbeylands, Co. Antrim. Carlton, Army & Navy, and Bachelors'. S. of James McCalmont, Esq., J.P., of Abbeylands, Co. Antrim, and Emily, d. of James Martin, Esq., J.P. and Dept.-Lieut., of Ross, Co. Galway. B. 1845 in Dublin; m. 1885, Hon. Rose Elizabeth, d. of 4th Baron Clanmorris. Educ. at Eton. Joined the 9th Lancers 1865, 7th Hussars 1870, commanded the 4th Dragoons 1888-92; Col. 1885, Maj.-Gen. 1896. A Conservative, in favour of a Liberal extension of the Land Purchase Act, and of a Redistribution of Seats Bill. Unsuccessfully contested Londonderry S. in 1885. Sat for Antrim N. from July 1895 until he accepted Chiltern Hundreds in 1899. Commanded in Cork district 1898-1903. C.B. 1885; K.C.B. 1900; C.V.O. 1903. Died 2 May 1924.   [1898]

McCALMONT, Col. James Martin. Magheramorne, Co. Antrim. Carlton. S. of James McCalmont, Esq., of Abbeylands, Belfast, by Emily, d. of James Martin, Esq., J.P. and Dept.-Lieut. of Ross, Galway. B. 1847; m. 1880, Mary, d. of Col. Romer, of Bryncemlyn, Dolgelly. Educ. at Eton. Joined the 8th Hussars as Cornet 1866, and retired as Capt. 1874. Afterwards held a Commission as Capt. in the Denbighshire Hussars, and served as Aide-de-Camp to both the Duke of Marlborough and Earl Cowper during their tenure of the Viceroyalty of Ireland. A J.P. for Co. Antrim. Honorary Col. Royal Antrim Artillery, and Dept. Grand Master of the Orangemen of Ireland. A Unionist. Sat for Antrim E. from 1885 until his death 2 Feb. 1913.   [1913]

McCALMONT, Lieut.-Col. Robert Chaine Alexander. Continued in House after 1918: full entry in Volume III.

McCANN, James. 29 Anglesea Street, Dublin. Simmons Court Castle, Donnybrook, Co. Dublin. Teltown, Co. Meath. B. 1840 at Chammrock, Louth, Co. Louth. A Stockbroker in Dublin, and Chairman of the Grand Canal Company. A Magistrate for the counties of Dublin and Meath. He spoke and wrote on inland navigation in Ireland in which he took a great interest, and believed much could be done for Ireland by the proper utilization of her canals, navigable rivers and canalized rivers. Delivered an address on "Economics of the Irish Problem" before the Bankers' Institute in Ireland 1901. A Nationalist and Independent Home Ruler, strongly in favour of a Catholic University. Sat for the St. Stephen's Green division of Dublin city from Oct. 1900 until his death 14 Feb. 1904.   [1903]

M'CARTAN, Michael. 2 Hopefield Avenue, Antrim Road, Belfast. Liberal. S. of John M'Cartan, of Castlewellan, by his m. with Miss Mary M'Veigh, of Mullertown, Kilkeel, Co. Down. B. 1851. Educ. at St. Malachy's Coll., Belfast, and the French Coll., Blackrock, Dublin. A Solicitor, entered 1882. An Irish Nationalist of the Anti-Parnellite party. Sat for Down S. from 1886 until he accepted Chiltern Hundreds Jan. 1902. Died 30 Sept. 1902.   [1901]

McCARTAN, Dr. Patrick. Continued in House after 1918: full entry in Volume III.

McCARTHY, John W. [John F. in *Dod*] 42½ Great Brunswick Street, Dublin. S. of Michael McCarthy, Esq. B. 1862. Educ. at a local private school. A Provision Merchant. A Nationalist of the Anti-Parnellite section. Sat for mid Tipperary from July 1892 until his death 8 Feb. 1893.   [1892 2nd ed.]

McCARTHY, Justin. Westgate-on-Sea. S. of Michael Francis McCarthy, Esq., of Cork, by his marriage with Miss Ellen FitzGerald-Canty, of Cork. B. in Cork

1830; m. 1855, Charlotte, d. of W.G. Allman, Esq., of Bandon, Co. Cork (she died 1879). A Journalist, Editor of the *Morning Star*, etc. Author of *A History of our own Times*, *A History of the Four Georges*, and also of *Dear Lady Disdain*, *Miss Misanthrope*, *Donna Quixote*, *Maid of Athens*, and other novels. A "Nationalist" and "Home Ruler", supported a reform of the University system in Ireland, the enlargement of the Irish Franchise, etc. On the deposition of Mr. Parnell as Leader of the Irish Nationalist Party 1890, Mr. McCarthy was elected in his stead; resigned 1896. Sat for Longford Co. from Apr. 1879 to Nov. 1885 and for N. Longford from Nov. 1885 to Oct. 1886, when having been also returned for Londonderry city he chose that seat. In 1892 was defeated at Londonderry, but elected for Longford N. and retained the seat until he retired in 1900. Died 24 Apr. 1912. [1900]

McCARTHY, Justin Huntly. 20 Cheyne Gardens, Chelsea Embankment, London. Arts, Savile, and Junior Travellers'. S. of Justin McCarthy, Esq., MP, and Miss Charlotte Allman, of Bandon, Co. Cork. B. 1859. A Journalist and the author of an *Outline of Irish History*, *England under Gladstone*, *The Candidate*, *a Comedy*, *Hafiz in London*, etc., etc. An "Irish Nationalist" of the Anti-Parnellite party. Sat for Athlone from June 1884 to Nov. 1885 and for Newry from Nov. 1885 until he retired in 1892. Died 20 Mar. 1936. [1892]

MacCAW, William John MacGeagh. 103 Eaton Square, London. Rooksnest Park, Godstone, Surrey. Carlton, Constitutional, Oriental, St. Stephen's, and City of London. S. of the Rev. William MacCaw, D.D., and Sarah, d. of John MacGeagh, Esq., J.P., of Co. Tyrone. B. 1850; m. Eleanor Elizabeth, d. of Walter Hardy, Esq., Solicitor. Had large business interests in India and the Far East. Fellow of Royal Colonial Institute; F.R.G.S.; member of Royal Society of Arts. A Unionist. Unsuccessfully contested E. Tyrone Jan. and July 1906. First elected for W. Down Mar. 1908 and sat until he retired in 1918. Died 3 Mar. 1928. [1918]

McCrae, George. Continued in House after 1918: full entry in Volume III.

McCULLOCH, John. Glenhead, Stranraer, N.B. Liberal. S. of John Mc-Culloch, Esq., Farmer, of Killiemore, Wigtownshire, by Margaret, d. of William Mitchel, Esq., of Woodhead, Kirkcudbrightshire. B. 1842. Educ. at Kirkcowan and Glenluce Schools. Was well known as a successful Farmer at Denbie Mains, Dumfriesshire; he made important contributions to the literature of his profession, being author of a report on the *Agricultural Lease*, and six times a medallist of the Highland Society. In 1880 went out, in the interest of two Scottish companies, as Inspector and Reporter on American land and securities; and was largely employed as a land valuator in both America and Europe. A Liberal, in favour of immediate reform in the land system, and the establishment of a Land Court; of reform of the House of Lords, and of a more independent government for Ireland. Sat for the St. Rollox division of Glasgow from Nov. 1885 until he retired in 1886. Unsuccessfully contested Buteshire 9 Oct. 1891, and the Camlachie division of Glasgow in 1892. [1886]

McCURDY, Charles Albert. Continued in House after 1918: full entry in Volume III.

McDERMOTT, Patrick. Mill House, Clifton Hill, St. John's Wood. Whitegate, Co. Galway. S. of John McDermott, Esq., Miller and Farmer, and his wife Margaret, d. of Mr. Holland. B. 1860 at Derrygoolen Mills, Woodford, Co. Galway. Educ. At Deroober School, Co. Galway. He took a prominent part in the opposition of the tenants on the Woodford estate to their landlord, Lord Clanricarde, and was imprisoned several times in consequence. An Irish Nationalist. First returned for N. Kilkenny in Oct. 1891 and sat until he accepted the Chiltern Hundreds in 1902. Died Sept. 1942. [1902]

MACDONA, John Cumming. Hilbre House, West Kirby, Cheshire. Carlton, and Bath. S. of G. de Landre Macdona, Esq., F.R.G.S., of Hilbre House, West Kirby, Cheshire, and Eliza Bowen, d. of John Cummins, Esq., of Exeter. B. 1836; m. 1864, Esther, only child of James Milne, Esq., of Heyside, Shaw, Lancashire. Educ. at Trinity Coll., Dublin, and Oxford. A Barrister-at-Law. Was Parliamentary Secretary to Mr. Hanbury, Secretary to the Treasury 1895. Was Rector of Cheadle, Cheshire, from 1874 to 1882, and restored the parish church at an outlay of £10,000. He travelled much, and wrote *Across the Atlantic*, *Days in Florida*, *Life in Texas*, *Across the Andes*, *Sweden and Norway*, etc. He introduced and passed the Floating Derelict Bill, and the Lancashire Electric Power Supply Bill which was made the Test Bill for all other Electric Power Bills. A Progressive Conservative, supported the ancient rights and privileges of the Thames Lightermen and Watermen, the interests of sailors, etc. Contested the Chesterfield division of Derbyshire in Dec. 1885. Represented the Rotherhithe division of Southwark from 1892 until defeated in 1906. Died 4 May 1907.   [1905]

MACDONALD, Rt. Hon. James Ramsay. Upper Frognal Lodge, Hampstead, London. Athenaeum. S. of John MacDonald, Esq., Farm Servant, and Anne Ramsay. B. 12 Oct. 1866 at Lossiemouth; m. 1896, Margaret d. of Professor J. Hall Gladstone, F.R.S. (she died 1911). Educ. at Drainie Board School; Honorary LL.D. Glasgow, Edinburgh, Wales, Toronto and McGill Universities. F.R.S. 1930; Eld. Bro. of Trinity House 1930. A Journalist. Secretary to the Labour Party 1900-12; Chairman 1912-14; Member of London County Council 1901-04. Editor of *The Socialist Review*. Leader of the Labour Party 1922-31. Leader of the National Labour Party 1931-37. A Trustee of the Treasury and Foreign Secretary Jan.-Oct. 1924. Prime Minister, First Lord of Treasury and Foreign Secretary Jan.-Oct. 1924. Leader of the Opposition 1922-24 and 1924-29. Prime Minister and First Lord of the Treasury June 1929-35; Lord President of the Council June 1935-May 1937; PC. 1924. A National Labour Candidate. Unsuccessfully contested Southampton 1895 and Leicester 1900. MP for Leicester from 1900 to 1918, when he was defeated contesting Leicester W. Unsuccessfully contested Woolwich E. Mar. 1921. MP for Aberavon from Nov. 1922 to May 1929, for Seaham from May 1929 to Oct. 1935, when he was defeated, and for Scottish Universities from Jan. 1936 until his death on 9 Nov. 1937.   [1938]

MACDONALD, Rt. Hon. John Archibald Murray. Continued in House after 1918: full entry in Volume III.

MACDONALD, Rt. Hon. John Hay Athole, C.B., 15 Abercromby Place, Edin-burgh. Carlton. University, New, and Conservative, Edinburgh. S. of Matthew Norman Macdonald-Hume, Esq., of Ninewells, W.S., by Grace, d. of Sir John Hay, Bart., of Smithfield and Haystoune. B. in Edinburgh 1836. Educ. at the Edinburgh Academy, and the Universities of Basle and Edinburgh, LL.D. 1884. Was called to the Scottish bar 1859, and appointed Q.C. 1880. Was Sheriff of Ross and Cromarty, and Sutherland 1874-76, Solicitor-Gen. for Scotland 1876-80, Sheriff of Perthshire 1880-85, when he became Lord Advocate of Scotland, in the Marq. of Salisbury's administration, and a Privy Councillor. Again Lord Advocate, Aug. 1886 to 1888. Was Dean of the Faculty of Advocates 1882-85, and a member of the Committee of Council for Education in Scotland. Was no less distinguished in Science than in Law, and was a member of the Society of Telegraphic Engineers and Electricians and a F.R.S. Edinburgh. A J.P. and Dept.-Lieut. for the county of the city of Edinburgh, Col. Commandant of the Queen's Edinburgh Rifle Volunteers, a member of the Council of the National Rifle Association, etc. etc. A Conservative, strongly in favour of an extension of scientific education, and of raising the necessary qualification of licensed practitioners of medicine. Unsuccessfully contested Edinburgh 1874 and 1880, and the Haddington Burghs 1879. Sat for the Edinburgh and St. Andrew's Universities from 1885 until appointed Lord Justice Clerk of Scotland (Lord Kingsburgh) in 1888, which post he held until 1915. K.C.B. 1900; G.C.B. 1916. Died 9 May 1919.   [1888]

McDONALD, Peter. 11 Clarinda Park West, Kingstown, Dublin. S. of Randal McDonald, Esq., by his wife, Maria Frizelle. B. at Kilfinane, Co. Limerick 1836; m. 1859, Catherine, eld. d. of Michael Carmody, Esq. Educ. at Blackrock Coll. A Partner in the firm of Cantwell and McDonald, Dublin, Wine Merchants and Rectifying Distillers. An "Irish Nationalist and Parnellite." Sat for Sligo N. from the general election of 1885 until his death 12 Mar. 1891.   [1891]

MACDONALD, Dr. Roderick. 131 Camden Road, London. Kilmuir, Dunvegan, Skye. S. of Angus Macdonald, Esq., Joiner, by Elizabeth, d. of R. Macneil, Esq., Merchant, of Stein, Skye. B. at Fairy Bridge, Skye 1840; m. Jan. 1890, Frances E.

Maryon, d. of Spencer Perceval, Esq., and grand-d. of the Rt. Hon. Spencer Perceval. Educ. at Glasgow Normal School and University. A Physician and Surgeon, L.R.C.P. and Surgeon Edin. 1867, F.R.C.S. Edin. 1883, M.D. Durham 1883. Coroner for N.E. Middlesex, and Treasurer to the London Crofters' Aid and Defence Fund. An advanced Liberal and (Anti-Parnellite) Home Ruler, "would support a sweeping measure of reform for the House of Lords." Unsuccessfully contested Ross and Cromarty as a Radical in Aug. 1884. Sat for Ross and Cromarty from 1885 until he retired in 1892. Died 9 Mar. 1894. [1892]

MACDONALD, William Archibald. 9 Bridge Street, Westminster. S. of Archibald Macdonald, Esq., of Dublin, by Anne, only d. of George Kennan, Esq., of Newtown Cottage, Co. Wicklow. B. at Enniskerry, Co. Wicklow 1841; m. 1875, Harriett, d. of Edward Liveing, Esq., of Nayland, Suffolk, and sister of Professor Liveing, of Cambridge. Educ. at the school of the Rev. W.J. Dundas, D.D., and Trinity Coll., Dublin, where, not withstanding his having lost his sight at the age of 13, he obtained a sizarship in 1861, a scholarship in 1865, and gained high classical honours in 1866. Author of pamphlets on various subjects. An Irish Nationalist of the Parnellite section. Having unsuccessfully contested Islington W. against Mr. Richard Chamberlain on 6 July 1886, he was nominated for the Ossory division of Queen's Co., and was elected there without opposition 9 July 1886, and sat until he retired in 1892. Unsuccessfully contested the same seat in July 1895. [1892]

MACDONNELL, Mark Antony. 14 Ridgway Place, Wimbledon. S. of M.G. MacDonnell, Esq., of Palmfield House, and Shraigh, Co. Mayo. B. 1854; m. 1884, the d. of James Hyndman, Esq., M.D., of Boston, U.S.A. Educ. at St. Ignatius Jesuit Coll., Queen's University, Ireland, and Richmond Hospital, Dublin. M.D., M. Ch., and L.M. 1876. Was a Surgeon to the Liverpool Cancer and Skin Hospital, and Consulting Medical Officer to the Toxteth Infirmary. A Nationalist. Sat for the Leix division of Queen's Co. from July 1892 until he retired in Jan. 1906. Died 9 July 1906 [1905]

M'EWAN, William. 16 Charles Street, Berkeley Square, London. Devonshire, and Reform. S. of John M'Ewan, Esq., Shipowner, of Alloa, by Anne, d. of Peter Jeffrey, Esq., of Thirsk. B. 1827; m. 1885, Helen, d. of Thomas Anderson, Esq. Educ. at the Alloa Academy, and privately. A member of the firm of M'Ewan and Company, Brewers, of Edinburgh, and a Dept.-Lieut. for the city of Edinburgh. A Liberal, in favour of Home Rule for Ireland. First sat for the central division of Edinburgh from July 1886 until he retired in 1900. PC. 1907. Died 12 May 1913. [1900]

McFADDEN, Edward. Letterkenny and Drumnahough House, Letterkenny. National Liberal. S. of M. McFadden, Esq., J.P., M.C.C., of Drumnahough House, Breenagh, Letterkenny, and B. McGahan, his wife. B. at Drumnahough House 1862. Unmarried. Educ. at St. Eunan's Seminary, Letterkenny, and the Catholic University, Dublin. A Solicitor, admitted Trinity term 1886; Chairman Donegal County Council from 1899; Chairman Letterkenny Urban Council from 1899. A Nationalist. Sat for Donegal E. from Oct. 1900 until he retired in 1906. [1905]

MACFARLANE, Sir Donald Horne. 46 Portman Square, London. Dorset Cottage, Fulham, London. Costessy Hall, Norwich. Reform, and National Liberal. Youngest s. of Allan Macfarlane, Esq., of Caithness, a Magistrate for that Co., by Margaret, d. of James Horne, Esq., of Stirkoke, near Wick, a Magistrate and Dept.-Lieut. B. 1830 at Caithness; m. 1st, 1857, Mary Isabella, d. of Henry R. Bagshawe, Esq., Q.C.; 2ndly, 1888, Fanny, d. of James Robson, Esq., of Pontefract. Educ. privately. An East India Merchant. Was Knighted 1 Jan. 1894. A Liberal, in favour of Home Rule for Ireland, reforms in favour of the Crofters, etc. MP for Carlow from Apr. 1880 to 1885, and for Argyllshire 1885-86, but was an unsuccessful candidate in 1886. Returned again for Argyllshire in July 1892 and sat until defeated in 1895. Died 2 June 1904. [1895]

McGAREL-HOGG, Sir James Macnaghten, Bart., K.C.B. 17 Grosvenor Gardens, London. Carlton, and Travellers'. Eld. s. of Sir James Weir Hogg, Bart., Member of Council for India, who sat many years for Beverley and Honiton, by Mary, 2nd d. of Samuel Swinton, Esq., of Swinton, Co. Berwick. B. at Calcutta 1823; m. 1857, Hon. Caroline Elizabeth Emma, eld. d. of 1st Lord Penrhyn. Educ. at Eton, and Christ Church, Oxford. Joined the 1st Life Guards 1843; became Maj. and Lieut.-Col. 1855; retired 1859. Chairman of the Metropolitan Board of Works from Nov. 1870 (salary £2,000). K.C.B. 1874. Succeeded as Bart. 1876. A Conservative, but not opposed to progress. Sat for Bath from July 1865 to July 1868; for Truro from Sept. 1871 to Nov. 1885 and for the Hornsey division of Middlesex from Nov. 1885 until created 1st Baron Magheremorne July 1887. Died 27 June 1890. [1887]

McGHEE, Richard. 69 North Street, Lurgan. S. of Richard McGhee, Esq., of Lurgan. B. 1851 at Lurgan; m. 1880, Mary, d. of George Campbell, Esq., of Glasgow. Educ. at St. Peter's School, Lurgan. A Merchant and Commission Agent. A Nationalist. Sat for S. Louth from 1896 to 1900, when he was defeated. Elected for mid Tyrone Dec. 1910 and sat until he retired in 1918. [1918]

McGILLIGAN, Patrick. 4 Hanover Place, Coleraine. The Villa, Castlerock. National Liberal. S. of Michael McGilligan, Esq., and Jane McGilligan, née Doherty. B. 1847 at Coleraine; m. 1886, Catherine, d. of John O'Farrel, Esq. Educ. at the Coleraine Academy and National School. A Nationalist of the Anti-Parnellite section. Sat for the S. division of Fermanagh from July 1892 until he retired in 1895. [1895]

McGOVERN, Thomas. Gortmore, Dernacrieve, Belturbet. S. of Brian McGovern, Esq., Farmer and Contractor, and Anne Hassard. B. at Gortmore, Bawnbery, Co. Cavan 1851. Educ. privately. An Auctioneer and Farmer; J.P. for Co. Cavan from 1895; President of the League of Governors of Bawnbery Union 1890; member of Cavan County Council, elected Apr. 1899; represented Co. Cavan on the Council of Agriculture, under the Agricultural and Technical Instruction Act; a Director of Cavan and Leitrim Railway Company. A Nationalist. Sat for Cavan W. from Oct. 1900 until his death 6 Apr. 1904. [1904]

MACGREGOR, Dr. Donald. Westminster Palace Hotel, London. Ardross, Inverness. National Liberal. S. of Robert MacGregor, Esq., of Rannoch, Perthshire. B. 1839; m. Harriette d. of E.

Reddin, Esq., of Albury House, Clapham Rise. Educ. at Rannoch, and Edinburgh (L.M. 1864). Became a licentiate of the Royal Colls. of Physicians and Surgeons, Edinburgh 1864, practised at Penrith, Cumberland, and London, but later retired. Was Public Vaccinator Penrith, Resident Physician at the Peebles Hydropathic Institute, Medical Superintendent Barnhill Hospital and Asylum, Glasgow, and wrote in the *Lancet, Glasgow Medical Journal,* and other journals. A Liberal, accepted the Gladstonian programme generally. Sat for Inverness-shire from July 1892 until he accepted Chiltern Hundreds in 1895 after a disagreement with the Government's Highland land policy. Died 20 July 1911. [1895]

McGUINNESS, Joseph. Continued in House after 1918: full entry in Volume III.

M'HUGH, Edward. Albert Hotel, Belfast. National Liberal. S. of Edward M'Hugh, Esq. B. 1846. A Director of B. and E. M'Hugh and Company Limited, Linen Manufacturers. A Nationalist of the Anti-Parnellite party. Sat for Armagh S. from July 1892 until his death on 28 Aug. 1900. [1900]

M'HUGH, Patrick Aloysius. "Champion" Office, Wine Street, Sligo. S. of Peter M'Hugh, Esq., Tenant Farmer, of Leitrim, and Anne M'Hugh (née M'Dermott). B. 1858 at Annagh, Glenfarne, Leitrim; m. 1882, Mary, d. of J. Harte, Esq., of Sligo (she died 1894). Educ. for the R.C. ministry, but declining orders he taught science and classics in the Athlone and Sligo Intermediate Schools. Became Owner of the *Sligo Champion* in 1885. Elected to the Sligo County Council in 1899, Chairman 1899. Mayor of Sligo 1888, and again 1895-98 and 1900. Was imprisoned for publishing in his paper a seditious libel on Jury Packing in Sligo. An Irish Nationalist. Unsuccessfully contested Clare E. in July 1895. Sat for N. Leitrim from 1892-1906; elected for N. Leitrim and N. Sligo in 1906 but chose the latter constituency and sat until his death 30 May 1909. [1909]

MACINNES, Miles. 6 Bryanston Street, London. Rickerby, Carlisle. Oxford & Cambridge. Eld. s. of Gen. MacInnes, of Fern Lodge, Hampstead, by Anna Sophia, d. of Jacob Foster Reynolds, Esq., of Carshalton. B. in London 1830; m. 1859,

Euphemia, d. of Andrew Johnston, Esq., of Holton Hall, Suffolk, and grand-d. of Sir T. Fowell Buxton. Educ. at Rugby, and Balliol Coll., Oxford. A J.P., Dept.-Lieut., and County Alderman for Cumberland, a J.P. for Middlesex, and a Director of the London and North West Railway Company. A Liberal and Home Ruler. Sat for the Hexham division of Northumberland from 1885 to the general election of 1892, when he was defeated by Mr. N.G. Clayton. The latter being unseated on petition in Feb. 1893, he again contested the seat with Mr. Clayton's brother, and was successful. MP until he retired in 1895. Died 28 Sept. 1909.   [1895]

MacIVER, David. 52 Lime Street, London. Manor Hill, Birkenhead. Wanless How, Ambleside. Carlton, and St. Stephen's. Eld. s. of Charles MacIver, Esq., of Calderstone, Allerton, near Liverpool, and Mary Anne, youngest d. of D. Morison, Esq., of Glasgow. B. in Liverpool 1840; m. 1st, 1863, Annie, d. of Robert Rankin, Esq., of Bromborough; 2ndly, 1873, Edith Eleanor, d. of A.T. Squarey, Esq., of Bebington. Educ. at the Royal Institutional School, Liverpool. A Steamship Owner, and Senior Partner of the firm of David MacIver and Company, whose vessels were regular traders between Liverpool and the River Plate. A Director of the Great Western Railway, and of the Fishguard and Rosslare Railways and Harbours Company, Chairman of Bala and Festiniog Railway. A J.P. for the city of Liverpool. A Conservative, in favour of Tariff Reform. Sat for Birkenhead from Nov. 1874 to 1885, when he retired. First elected for the Kirkdale division of Liverpool in 1898 and sat until his death 1 Sept. 1907.   [1907]

McIVER, Sir Lewis, Bart. 25 Upper Brook Street, London. Sarisbury, Southampton. Brooks's, St. James's and White's. Eld. s. of John McIver, Esq., of Dingwall, and of Madras. B. 1846; m. Charlotte Rosalind, d. of N. Montefiore, Esq. Educ. at Kensington Grammar School, and the University of Bonn. Entered the Indian Civil Service and held several offices in India and Burma during seventeen years prior to 1884. Was called to the bar at the Middle Temple 1878. Author of Census Reports on British Burma (1872) and Madras (1882), and of the Madras section of the Imperial Gazetteer of India; Honorary Col. Edin-

burgh Volunteer Artillery. Created Bart. 1896. A Liberal Unionist. Was elected as an Advanced Liberal for the Torquay division of Devon in 1885, but was defeated there as a Liberal Unionist in 1886. Unsuccessfully contested Edinburgh S. in 1892. Sat for Edinburgh W. from May 1895 until he accepted Chiltern Hundreds in 1909. Died 9 Aug. 1920.   [1909]

McKANE, Professor John. Lower Leeson St., Dublin. S. of a Linen Manufacturer in Ballymena. Educ. at Queen's University, Belfast, and took degree of LL.D. Called to the bar in 1864 and practised on the N.E. Circuit. Professor of Civil Law at Queen's University until 1885. A Conservative. Returned for the mid division of Armagh Co. Dec. 1885 and sat until his death 11 Jan. 1886.

MACKARNESS, Frederick Michael Coleridge. 21 Montpelier Square, London. Reform. S. of the Rt. Rev. J.F. Mackarness, Bishop of Oxford, and Alettea Buchanan, d. of Sir J.T. Coleridge. B. 31 Aug. 1854 at Tardebigge, Worcestershire; m. 1882, Amy, d. of the Rev. R. Chermside. Educ. at Marlborough, and Keble Coll., Oxford. A Barrister, called at the Middle Temple 1879; advocate of Cape Supreme Court 1882; revising Barrister for London 1889-1903; Recorder of Newbury 1894-1903; Professor of Roman Dutch Law at the University of London 1905-06. A Liberal. Elected for the Newbury division of Berkshire in 1906 and sat until he retired in Jan. 1910. A County Court Judge from 1911. Died 23 Dec. 1920.   [1909]

McKEAN, John. Ardnagreina, Kingstown, Co. Dublin. B. 1868 at Castleblayney. Educ. at St. Macarten's Seminary, Monaghan; Inter. Exhib. and Medallist. A Barrister-at-Law, called 1900. Was an occasional contributor to the press. A Nationalist. Elected for S. Monaghan in 1902 and sat until he retired in 1918.   [1918]

McKENNA, Sir Joseph Neale. 67 Lancaster Gate, London. Ardo House, Ardmore, Youghal. Eld. s. of Michael McKenna, Esq., of Dublin, by Mary, eld. d. of Oliver Plunket Gregan, Esq., of Dublin. B. in Dublin 1819; m. 1st, 1842, Esther Louisa, youngest d. of Edmund Howe, Esq., of Dublin (she died 1871); 2ndly, 1880, Amelia Anne, only d. of George

Keats Brooks, Esq., and widow of Richard Warner Hole, Esq., of Shelthorpe House, Loughborough, and Quorndon, Leicestershire. Was educ. at Trinity Coll., Dublin. Called to the bar in Ireland 1848. A Dept.-Lieut. for the Co. of Cork and a Magistrate for the counties of Cork and Waterford. Knighted in 1867. A Liberal, an Irish Nationalist of the Parnellite party, and in favour of denominational education. Unsuccessfully contested New Ross Apr. 1859, and again June 1863; also Tralee Feb. 1865. Sat for Youghal from July 1865 until defeated in Dec. 1868, and again sat for Youghal from Feb. 1874 to Nov. 1885. First elected for Monaghan S. Dec. 1885 and sat until he retired in 1892. Died 15 Aug. 1906. [1892]

McKENNA, Rt. Hon. Reginald. 36 Smith Square, Westminster, London. Brooks's, and Reform. S. of William Columban McKenna, Esq., and Emma, d. of Charles Hanby, Esq. B. 1863; m. 1908, Pamela, d. of Sir H. Jekyll. Educ. privately, and at Trinity Hall, Cambridge; B.A. Was Financial Secretary to the Treasury 1905-07; President of the Board of Education Feb. 1907 to Apr. 1908; First Lord of the Admiralty 1908-11; Home Secretary Oct. 1911-15; Chancellor of the Exchequer May 1915 to Dec. 1916. PC. 1907. Director of the London City and Midland Bank May 1917. A Liberal. Unsuccessfully contested Clapham 1892. Represented N. Monmouthshire from 1895 until defeated in Pontypool in 1918. Chairman of Midland Bank from 1919; offered Chancellorship of the Exchequer by Bonar Law in 1922 but declined it; author of *Post-War Banking Policy* (1928). Died 6 Sept. 1943. [1918]

McKILLOP, James. Polmont Park, Stirlingshire. Conservative, and Imperial Union. Eld. s. of James McKillop, Esq., Coalmaster, of Drumclair, Slamannan. B. 1844; m. 1873, Jesse, eld. d. of Adam Nimmo, Esq., of St. Andrews. Educ. at Slamannan and the Andersonian University, Glasgow. Was in Mine-Engineering and kindred subjects. Was largely engaged in Coal-Mining and Mechanical Engineering in Stirlingshire and Lanarkshire, and was a J.P. and Dept.-Lieut. for Co. Stirling. A Conservative. Represented Stirlingshire from 1895 until he retired in 1906. Died 5 Nov. 1913. [1905]

McKILLOP, William. Laurieville, Queen's Drive, Glasgow. National Liberal. B. 1860. Was a Refreshment Contractor and Restaurant Proprietor, later dealing in wine. Took a prominent part in Irish political organizations. A Nationalist. Sat for N. Sligo from 1900-06. Elected for S. Armagh in 1906 and sat until his death 25 Aug. 1909. [1909]

MACKINDER, Halford John. Continued in House after 1918: full entry in Volume III.

MACKINTOSH, Charles Fraser. See FRASER-MACKINTOSH, Charles.

McLAGAN, Peter. Pumpherston, Midcalder, Scotland. Junior Athenaeum, and Windham. S. of Peter McLagan, Esq., of Pumpherston, Midcalder, Scotland. B. 1823 at Demerara; m. 1876, Elizabeth Anne, d. of George Taylor, Esq., of Headingley, Leeds (she died 1882). Was educ. at Tillycoultry School, and at the University of Edinburgh. A member of Council of the University of Edinburgh. Appointed a Royal Commissioner in 1864 to inquire into the law relating to the "Landlords' right of Hypothec in Scotland", and in 1877 to inquire into the laws regulating "Grocers' Licences." A J.P. for the counties of Edinburgh and Linlithgow, and Vice-Lieut. for the latter. A Liberal and Home Ruler. Sat for Linlithgowshire from July 1865 until he accepted Chiltern Hundreds in 1893. Died 31 Aug. 1900. [1893]

McLAREN, Rt. Hon. Sir Charles Benjamin Bright, Bart. 43 Belgrave Square, London. Bodnant, Tal-y-cafn, Denbighshire. Hilders, Haslemere, Surrey. Reform, National Liberal, Royal Automobile, and Savile. S. of Duncan McLaren, Esq., MP, of Edinburgh, and Priscilla, d. of Jacob Bright, Esq., of Rochdale, and sister of the Rt. Hon. John Bright. B. at Edinburgh 1850; m. 1877, Laura, only d. of H.D. Pochin, Esq., of Bodnant, Denbighshire. Educ. at the University of Edinburgh; M.A. First Class Honours 1870, and at the Universities of Bonn and Heidelberg. A Barrister of Lincoln's Inn (called 1874), and practised at the Chancery Bar; Q.C. 1897. A Landowner in N. Wales; J.P. for Denbighshire, Flintshire, and Surrey; Chairman of the Metropolitan Railway Company, Tredegar Coal and Iron Company, and John

Brown and Company, of Sheffield and Clydebank; and a Director of the Sheepbridge Coal and Iron Company; Chairman of British Iron Trade Association; Association of Institute of Naval Architects. Author of *The Basic Industries of Great Britain*. Created Bart. 1902; PC. 1908. Had the Third Class of the Order of Sacred Treasure. A Radical. Sat for Stafford from 1880-86, when he was defeated. First elected for the Bosworth division of Leicestershire in 1892 and sat until he retired in Dec. 1910. Created Baron Aberconway in June 1911. Died 23 Jan. 1934. [1910]

McLAREN, Hon. Francis Walter Stafford. 8 Little College Street, Westminster, London. Bodnant Hall, Tal-y-cafn, N. Wales. Bachelors', and St. James's. 2nd s. of Lord Aberconway, Q.C., J.P., MP. B. 6 June 1886; m. 1911, Barbara, d. of Col. Sir Herbert Jekyll. Educ. at Eton, and Balliol Coll., Oxford. Was Parliamentary Private Secretary (unpaid) to Mr. Lewis Harcourt. Received a Commission Sept. 1914 in R.N.V.R. for service with armoured motor-car section. Transferred to Royal Flying Corps, 2nd Lieut. Jan. 1916. A Liberal. Elected for the Spalding division of Lincolnshire in Jan. 1910 and sat until he was killed in action on 30 Aug. 1917. [1917]

McLAREN, Hon. Henry Duncan. Continued in House after 1918: full entry in Volume III.

McLAREN, Walter Stowe Bright. 56 Ashley Gardens, London. Great Comp Cottage, Borough Green, Kent. National Liberal. S. of Duncan McLaren, Esq., MP for Edinburgh, and Priscilla, d. of Jacob Bright, Esq., of Rochdale, and sister of the Rt. Hon. John Bright. B. 1853 in Edinburgh; m. 1883, Eva, d. of William Muller, Esq., of Valparaiso and Shenley, Hertfordshire. Educ. at Craigmount School, Edinburgh, and Edinburgh University; M.A. A Director of Bolckow, Vaughan and Company, and other large Coal and Iron companies. An independent Liberal, strongly in favour of Disestablishment, Woman's Suffrage, Free Trade, etc. Unsuccessfully contested Inverness district in Nov. 1885. Sat for the Crewe division of Cheshire from 1886 to 1895, when he was defeated; re-elected for the Crewe division of Cheshire in Apr.

1910 and sat until his death 29 June 1912. [1912]

MACLEAN, Rt. Hon. Sir Donald, K.B.E. Continued in House after 1918: full entry in Volume III.

MACLEAN, Francis William. 9 Southwell Gardens, London. Rougham House, Bury St. Edmunds. United University, and Garrick. S. of Alexander Maclean, Esq., of Barrow Hedges, Carshalton, Surrey. B. 1844; m. 1869, Mattie, d. of John Sowerby, Esq., of Benwell Tower, Northumberland. Was educ. at Westminster, and Trinity Coll., Cambridge. Called to the bar at the Inner Temple 1868, and created a Q.C. in 1886. A Liberal Unionist. Sat for the Woodstock division of Oxfordshire from 1885 until appointed Master of Lunacy in 1891. Chief Justice of Bengal 1896-1909. Died 11 Nov. 1913. [1891]

MACLEAN, James Mackenzie. 40 Nevern Square, Earl's Court, London. Carlton. S. of Alexander Maclean, Esq., of Liberton, Edinburgh, by Mary, d. of Mr. Mackenzie Baigrie. B. 1835; m. 1867, Anna, d. of Philip Whitehead, Esq. (she died 1897). A Journalist and Newspaper Proprietor, and a Fellow of Bombay University. Was Proprietor and Editor of the *Bombay Gazette*; also Chairman of the Bombay Town Council. A Proprietor of the *Western Mail*, Cardiff. Was President of the Institute of Journalists 1896-97, etc., and author of books and papers on India. A Conservative and Unionist. An unsuccessful candidate in the Elgin Burghs 1880. Sat for Oldham 1885-92, when he was defeated. Sat for Cardiff district from July 1895 until he retired in 1900. Died 22 Apr. 1906. [1900]

MACLEOD, John. 103 West End Lane, Hampstead, London. Queen's House, Queensgate, Inverness. Gartymore, Helmsdale, N.B. S. of John Macleod, Esq., Fish-Curer, of Helmsdale, Sutherlandshire. B. at Helmsdale 1863. Educ. at Glasgow. Studied gold assaying; helped in working a gold mine in N. Wales. He subsequently went to Inverness, and established the *Highland News*, of which he was Proprietor. Was a member of the Royal Commission on Deer Forests, etc., and was Secretary to the Highland Land League. An Advanced Liberal, in favour of Home Rule, etc. First returned for Sutherlandshire in Oct. 1894 and sat until defeated in Oct. 1900. [1900]

MacLEOD, John Mackintosh. Continued in House after 1918: full entry in Volume III.

MACLURE, Sir John William, Bart. Whalley Range, Nr. Manchester. Carlton, Conservative, and Junior Carlton. S. of John Maclure, Esq., Merchant, of Manchester, by Elizabeth, d. of William Kearsley, Esq., Merchant, of Manchester. B. at Manchester 1835; m. 1859, Eleanor, 2nd d. of Thomas Nettleship, Esq., of East Sheen, Surrey. Educ. at the Grammar School, Manchester. A Director of various railway and other companies, and a Knight of St. John of Jerusalem. Was Honorary Secretary to the Committee of the Lancashire Cotton Famine Fund 1862-65, which distributed over £1,750,000 amongst the distressed working classes; was Maj. 40th Lancashire Volunteers, and a J.P. and Dept.-Lieut. for the Co. of Lancaster; a J.P. for Manchester, Dept. Chairman of the Manchester Royal Infirmary, and Trustee of other public charities in S.E. Lancashire, etc. Created Bart. 1 Jan. 1898. A Conservative, in favour of Free Trade, and opposed to Home Rule for Ireland. Unsuccessfully contested the Stretford division of Lancashire at the general election of 1885, but was elected there in 1886 and MP until his death 28 Jan. 1901. [1900]

MACMASTER, Donald. Continued in House after 1918: full entry in Volume III.

McMICKING, Maj. Gilbert, C.M.G. Continued in House after 1918: full entry in Volume III.

McMORDIE, Robert James. Cabin Hill, Knock, Belfast. Carlton, and Constitutional. S. of the Rev. J.A. McMordie, Presbyterian Minister of Seaforde, Co. Down. B. 31 Jan. 1849 at Cumran, Co. Down; m. 1885, Julia, d. of Sir William Gray, of West Hartlepool. Educ. at Royal Academical Institution, Belfast, and Queen's Coll., Belfast; M.A. Queen's University. Was admitted a Solicitor 1874, and retired from practise in 1899. A member of Belfast Corporation from 1907. Lord Mayor 1910-14. President of Irish Industrial Development Association, Belfast. A Unionist. Elected for E. Belfast in Dec. 1910 and sat until his death 25 Mar. 1914. [1914]

MACNAGHTEN, Edward, Q.C. 198 Queen's Gate, London. Runkerry, Bushmills, Co. Antrim. United University. 2nd s. of Sir Edmund C. Workman Macnaghten, 2nd Bart., who for some years sat for Antrim, by Mary, only d. of Edward Gwatkin, Esq. B. 1830; m. 1858, Frances Arabella, d. of the Rt. Hon. Sir Samuel Martin, one of the Barons of the Exchequer. Educ. at Cambridge; graduated B.A. 1852, M.A. 1855, and became a Fellow of Trinity Coll. Called to the bar at Lincoln's Inn Jan. 1857. Appointed a Queen's Counsel 1880. A Conservative, said he would "uphold in its integrity the ancient custom of Ulster Tenant right", in favour of "the amendment of the Grand Jury Laws, so as to give the tax-payer a greater control over the imposition of taxation." Sat for Antrim from Apr. 1880 to Nov. 1885 and for N. Antrim from Nov. 1885 until he was created Baron Macnaghten (Law life peerage) and appointed Lord of Appeal-in-Ordinary in 1887. PC. 1887. G.C.M.G. 1903. G.C.B. 1911. Succeeded as Bart. 1911. Died 17 Feb. 1913. [1886]

MACNAMARA, Rt. Hon. Thomas James. Continued in House after 1918: full entry in Volume III.

MacNEILL, John Gordon Swift. 17 Pembroke Road, Dublin. National Liberal. Only s. of the Rev. John Gordon Swift MacNeill, Chaplain of the Richmond Bridewell, Dublin (a descendant of Godwin Swift, the uncle and guardian of Jonathan Swift, Dean of St. Patrick's), and Susan, d. of the Rev. H. Tweedy, M.A. Was a lineal descendant of John MacNeill, Laird of Barra, and of William Lenthall, Speaker of the Long Parliament. B. 1849 in Dublin. Educ. at Trinity Coll., Dublin, and Christ Church, Oxford; M.A. Was called to the Irish bar in 1876; Q.C. 1893. Examiner Law School, Trinity Coll., Dublin 1880. Professor of Constitutional and Criminal Law, King's Inns, Dublin 1882-88; Dean of Faculty of Law, Professor of Constitutional Law, and Clerk of Convocation in the National University of Ireland; Member of Committee of Privileges 1908. Author of *The Irish Parliament, what it was, and what it did, How the Union was Carried, Titled Corruption*, and other works. A Nationalist. Sat for Donegal S. from 1887 until he retired in 1918. Died 24 Aug. 1926. [1918]

MACNEILL, Ronald John. Continued in

House after 1918: full entry in Volume III.

MACONOCHIE, Archibald White. 22 Westbourne Street, Hyde Park, London. B. 1855 of Scottish parentage; m. 1890. Educ. at Shrewsbury and Stratford he was intended for the army, and had a nomination for Sandhurst. Managing Director of Maconochie Brothers Limited, of London, Fraserburgh, and Lowestoft, Preserved Provision Merchants. He travelled over most of the globe. A Liberal Unionist. Elected for E. Aberdeenshire in 1900 and sat until defeated in 1906. Contested the Partick division of Lanarkshire in 1910 and the Wednesbury division of Staffordshire in 1918. Died 3 Feb. 1926.   [1905]

MACPHERSON, Rt. Hon. James Ian. Continued in House after 1918: full entry in Volume III.

MACPHERSON, John Thomas. 12 Bellingham Avenue, Norton, Stockton-on-Tees. B. 1872 in London; m. 1899, Catherine Ann, d. of R.D. MacArthur, Esq., Master Mariner. Educ. at elementary schools, and Ruskin Coll., Oxford. Was at one time a Sailor and then became a Steel Smelter at Middlesbrough. Was later Organizing Secretary to British Steel Smelters' Trade Union, appointed 1899. A Labour Member. Elected for Preston in 1906 and sat until defeated in Jan. 1910.   [1909]

MACTAGGART-STEWART, Sir Mark John, Bart. Southwick, Dumfries. Ardwell, Wigtownshire. 1 Whitehall Gardens, London. Carlton, and Athenaeum. S. of Mark Hathorn Stewart, Esq., of Southwick. B. 1834; m. 1866, Marianne Susanna, only child of John Orde Ommanney, Esq. Educ. at Winchester, and Christ Church, Oxford; M.A. Called to the bar at the Inner Temple in 1862. A J.P. and Dept.-Lieut. for the Stewartry of Kirkcudbright, and Dept.-Lieut. and J.P. for Wigtownshire. Honorary Col. 1st Ayr and Galloway Artillery Volunteers (V.D.) Chairman of the School Board of Stonykirk. Created Bart. in 1892. Assumed the additional name of MacTaggart in 1895. A Unionist. Elected for Wigtown Burghs Feb. 1874, but election declared void on petition and seat awarded to the Rt. Hon. George Young May 1874. Mr. Young appointed Judge of the Court of Session June 1874 and Mr. Stewart won the resultant election. Sat un-

til defeated Apr. 1880. Returned for Wigtown Burghs May 1880 but election declared void on petition in July 1880. Sat for Kirkcudbrightshire from 1885-1906, when he was defeated; re-elected for Kirkcudbrightshire in Jan. 1910 and sat until he retired in Dec. 1910. Died 26 Sept. 1923.   [1910]

McVEAGH, Jeremiah. Continued in House after 1918: full entry in Volume III.

McVEIGH, Charles. Letterkenny, Co. Donegal. B. 1849 at Gortnavern. Emigrated to Australia in 1867 and amassed a fortune in the gold fields. A J.P. for Donegal. A Nationalist. Elected for E. Donegal in 1906 and sat until he retired in Jan. 1910.   [1909]

MADDEN, Rt. Hon. Dodgson Hamilton. 41 Fitzwilliam Square, Dublin. Carlton, and University. Kildare Street, Dublin. S. of the Rev. Hugh Hamilton Madden, Chancellor of Cashel and Rector of Templemore, by Isabella, d. of Henry J. Monck Mason, Esq. B. 1840 at Loughgall, Co. Armagh; m. 1868, Minnie, eld. d. of Lewis Moore, Esq., Dept.-Lieut. of Cremorgan, Queen's Co. Educ. privately, and at Dublin University; a classical scholar and medallist, gold medallist in Ethics and Logics, B.A. 1862. Was called to the Irish bar 1864, appointed Q.C. 1880, one of her Majesty's Serjeants 1887, Solicitor-Gen. for Ireland Jan. 1888 to 1889, and Attorney-Gen. for Ireland 1889-92. Wrote a treatise on the *Registration of Deeds and Judgment Mortgages* (1863), and *The Law and Practice of the Landed Estates Court* (1870). A Conservative. First returned for Dublin University July 1887 and sat until he retired in 1892. PC. 1889. Irish High Court Judge (Queen's Bench Division) 1892-1919. Vice Chancellor of Dublin University 1895-1919. Died 6 Mar. 1928.   [1892]

MADDISON, Fred. 12 Acris Street, Wandsworth, London. National Liberal. S. of Richard Maddison, Esq., of Horncastle, and Mary Yates, of Wainfleet, Lincolnshire. B. 17 Aug. 1856 at Boston; m. 1877, Jane Ann, d. of Richard Weatherill, Esq., of Hull. Educ. at Adelaide Street, Wesleyan School, Hull. A Compositor; Chairman of Trades Union Congress 1886; first Workman member of Hull Corporation 1887-89; a member of Tottenham School Board 1891-97. Was offered a post in the Labour Department of the Board of Trade 1892. Secretary of the International Arbitration League. A Radical, in favour of Taxation of Land Values, Reform of the House of Lords, etc. Unsuccessfully contested Central Hull in 1892 and 1895; sat for the Brightside division of Sheffield from 1897-1900, when he was defeated. Elected for Burnley in 1906 and sat until defeated in Jan. 1910. Contested Darlington in Dec. 1910 the Holderness division of the E. Riding of Yorkshire in 1918, S. Dorset in 1922 and Reading in 1923. [1909]

MADEN, Sir John Henry. Rockcliffe House, Nr. Bacup, Lancashire. Reform, Devonshire, and National Liberal. Eld. s. of Henry Maden, Esq. B. 11 Sept. 1862; m. 1891, Alice d. of Joshua Meller, Esq., of Lytham. Educ. at the Grammar School, Manchester. Chairman of the firm of John Maden and Son Limited, of Springholme, Throstle, and Lee Mills, Bacup, and 18a, Mosley Street, Manchester. A J.P. for the Co. of Lancaster; Mayor of Bacup 13 times between 1896 and 1917 and first Freeman of Bacup; also President of the Bacup Liberal Council and of the Bacup Liberal Club, and was an active promoter of many other local institutions and movements in the division. High Sheriff, County Councillor and Magistrate for Lancashire. A Liberal, in favour of Home Rule for Ireland, disestablishment of the Church, local option, and the other leading items in the advanced Liberal programme. First elected for the Rossendale division of N.E. Lancashire in succession to Lord Hartington in Jan. 1892 and sat until he accepted Chiltern Hundreds in Jan. 1900. Re-elected for the Rossendale division of N.E. Lancashire on 13 Feb. 1917, and sat until he was defeated in 1918. Knighted 1915. Died 18 Feb. 1920. [1900]

MAGNIAC, Charles. Defeated in 1886: full entry in Volume I.

MAGNUS, Sir Philip, Bart. Continued in House after 1918: full entry in Volume III.

MAGUIRE, James Rochfort. 10 Park Lane, London. S. of the Rev. John M. Maguire, Rector of Kilkeedy, Co. Limerick, and A.J. Maguire, née Humphreys, the d. of Major Humphreys, of Milltown House, Strabane. B. 1856; m. 1895, Julia, d. of 1st Visct. Peel. Educ. at Cheltenham Coll.,

and Merton Coll., Oxford. A Fellow of All Souls Coll., Oxford, and a Barrister-at-Law; called to the Inner Temple 1883. An Irish Nationalist of the Parnellite party. Sat for Donegal N. June 1890 to July 1892. First returned for Clare W. July 1892 and sat until defeated in 1895. Unsuccessfully contested E. Leeds as a Liberal in 1900, Chairman of Rhodesian Railways; C.B.E. 1918; Chairman of British South Africa Co. from 1923. Died 18 Apr. 1925. [1895]

MAHON, Charles James Patrick O'Gorman, 'The O'Gorman Mahon'. Ennis, Co. Clare, Ireland. Eld. s. of Patrick Mahon, Esq., by Barbara, only d. of The O'Gorman. B. 17 Mar. 1800 in the Co. of Clare; m. Christina Maria, eld. d. and co-heir of John O'Brien, Esq., of FitzWilliam Square, Dublin (she died 1877). Graduated M.A. at Trinity Coll., Dublin. Was called to the bar in Ireland 1834, but never practised. A Magistrate and Dept.-Lieut. for Clare, and formerly Capt. in the Clare Co. Militia. A Liberal, in favour of Home Rule for Ireland, etc. Sat for Clare for a short time in 1830 but he was unseated on petition and defeated in 1831. Sat for Ennis from Aug. 1847 to July 1852, when he was an unsuccessful candidate. Unsuccessfully contested Clare in Aug. 1877. Sat for Clare from May 1879 to Nov. 1885. At the two general elections of 1885 and 1886 he was not a candidate, but on the death of Mr. J.A. Blake he was elected for Carlow in Aug. 1887 and sat until his death on 15 June 1891. [1891] (Note: Volume I makes no mention of his first name Charles. He was born 17 Mar. 1800 and not 1803 as stated in Dod).

MAHONY, Pierce Charles de Lacy. Kilmorna, Co. Kerry. S. of Pierce Kenifec Mahony, Esq., of Kilmorna, Co. Kerry, by Jane, d. of Robert Gun Cuninghame, Esq., Dept.-Lieut., of Mount Kennedy, Co. Wicklow. B. in Dublin 1850; m. 1877, Helen Louise, only d. of Maurice Collis, Esq. Educ. at Rugby, Magdalen Coll., Oxford and the Royal Agricultural Coll., Cirencester (where he took the Haygarth gold medal in 1875). A J.P. for the counties of Kerry and Limerick, and a member of the Irish Piers and Roads Commission, also one of the Royal Commissioners of Market Rights and Tolls. Assistant Land Commissioner from 1881 to 1884. A Parnellite. First returned for Meath N. in July 1886 and sat until defeated in 1892. Unsuccessfully contested Meath N. in Feb. 1893, the St. Stephen's Green division of Dublin in Sept. 1895 and W. Wicklow in 1918. C.B.E. 1920. Died 31 Oct 1930. [1892]

MAINS, John. Eastbourne, Coleraine, Co. Londonderry. S. of Patrick Mains, Esq., J.P. Manure Manufacturer, of Coleraine, and Mary, d. of John Millen, Esq., Builder and Contractor, of the same place. B. 1851 at Glasgow; m. 1882, Margaret Josephine, d. of James Byrne, Esq., of San Francisco, U.S.A., formerly of Ballymena, Co. Antrim. Educ. at the Coleraine Academical Institution. A J.P. for the counties of Londonderry and Antrim; elected several times S.C. for Coleraine from 1875; an ex-officio member of the Coleraine Board of Guardians from 1885; a member of the Coleraine, Portrush, and Bushmills Dispensary Committees, and of the Portrush Water and Sanitary Committees; also a member of the Royal Society of Antiquarians, Ireland. An Anti-Parnellite. Sat for Donegal N. from July 1892 until he retired in 1895. [1895]

MAINWARING, Hon. William Frederick Barton Massey. See MASSEY-MAINWARING, Hon. William Frederick Barton.

MAITLAND, William Fuller-. 8 Hertford Street, London. Garth House, Builth, Brecknockshire. Stansted, Bishop Stortford, Essex. Brook's, and Oxford & Cambridge. S. of William Fuller-Maitland, Esq., of Stansted, Essex, and Garth, Brecknockshire, by Lydia, only d. of Lieut.-Col. Prescott, 5th Dragoon Guards. B. at Stansted, Essex 1844. Educ. at Harrow, and at Christ Church, Oxford. A Liberal, in favour of Home Rule. Unsuccessfully contested Brecknockshire in 1874. Sat for Brecknockshire from May 1875 until he retired in 1895. Died 15 Nov. 1932. [1895]

MAJENDIE, James Henry Alexander. Hedingham Castle, Essex. Carlton, and Marlborough. Royal Naval, and Royal Albert, Portsmouth. S. of Lewis Ashurst Majendie, Esq., MP, and Lady Margaret, d. of 25th Earl Crawford and Balcarres. B. at 9 Grosvenor Square 1871; m. 1893, Beatrice Cecilia, d. of James Mitchon, Esq., Dept.-Lieut. and J.P., of Holbrook Hall. Educ. at Winchester. A Dept.-Lieut. and Magistrate for Essex and Suffolk; Lieut.

3rd Royal Scots. A Conservative, in favour of Mr. Chamberlain's proposals. Unsuccessfully contested Portsmouth in May 1900. Elected for Portsmouth in Oct. 1900 and sat until he retired in 1906. Died 11 Jan. 1939. [1905]

MAKINS, William Thomas. 1 Lowther Gardens, London. Rotherfield Court, Henley-on-Thames. Carlton. Eld. s. of Charles Makins, Esq., of Craven Hill, London, by Frances, d. of Thomas Kirkby, Esq., Banker of Leeds. B. at Woodhouse, Leeds 1840; m. 1861, Elizabeth, 2nd d. of Lightly Simpson, Esq., of Gower Street, London. Was educ. at Harrow, and at Trinity Coll., Cambridge; graduated B.A. 1861, M.A. 1865. Was called to the bar at the Middle Temple 1862. J.P. for Essex and Oxfordshire, Dept.-Lieut. for Essex, and a member of the Court of Lieutenancy, City of London; also Honorary Col. commanding 2nd Volunteer (Essex) Brigade, Eastern division, Royal Artillery 1874, and passed the Woolwich examination for the latter. Governor of the Gas Light and Coke Company, and a Director and Dept. Chairman of the Great Eastern Railway. A Conservative, and said he would offer "an uncompromising opposition" to the disestablishment of the national Church. Unsuccessfully contested Kidderminster in 1868. Sat for Essex S. from Feb. 1874 to Nov. 1885, and for the S.E. division from 1885 to June 1886. Sat for the S.W. division of Essex from 1886 until he retired in 1892. Created Bart. in 1902. Died 2 Feb. 1906. [1892]

MALCOLM Ian Zachery. Continued in House after 1918: full entry in Volume III.

MALCOLM, John Wingfield. Achnamara, Lochgilphead, Argyllshire. Carlton, and Junior Carlton. S. of John Malcolm, Esq., of Poltalloch, Argyllshire, by Isabella Harriet, d. of the Hon. John Wingfield Stratford, of Addington Place, Kent (who assumed the name of Stratford). B. in London 1833; m. 1861, Hon. Alice Frederica, youngest d. of the 4th Lord Boston. Educ. at Eton, and Christ Church, Oxford. A Magistrate for Argyllshire and Kent, and a Dept.-Lieut. for Argyllshire; Lieut.-Col. Argyllshire Highland Rifle Volunteers, and Capt. in the Kent Artillery Militia. A Conservative, opposed to Home Rule for Ireland. Sat for Boston from Oct. 1860 to Feb. 1874. In the election of Feb. 1874 he was unsuccessful at the poll, but secured the seat on petition in June 1874; Remained Member till Aug. 1878 when he accepted the Chiltern Hundreds to contest Argyllshire. Unsuccessfully contested the latter seat again Apr. 1880. First returned for Argyllshire July 1886 and sat until defeated in 1892. C.B. 1892. Created 1st Baron Malcolm of Poltalloch 1896. Owned over 85,000 acres. Died 6 Mar. 1902.   [1892]

MALLABY-DEELEY, Harry Mallaby. Continued in House after 1918: full entry in Volume III.

MALLALIEU, Frederick William. Continued in House after 1918: full entry in Volume III.

MALLET, Charles Edward. The Green, Wimbledon Common, London. Milford Corner, Lymington, Hampshire. Athenaeum. S. of Charles Mallet, Esq., and Louisa, d. of George Udny, Esq. B. 2 Dec. 1862 in London; m. 1895, Margaret, d. of the Rt. Hon. Sir Henry Roscoe. Educ. at Harrow, and Balliol Coll., Oxford. Was called to the bar 1889. Appointed Financial Secretary to the War Office 1910-11. Author of a work on the French Revolution and other historical writings, and author of several works on elder statesmen. A Liberal. Unsuccessfully contested W. Salford 1900. Elected for Plymouth in 1906 and sat until defeated in Dec. 1910. Secretary for Indian Students at the India Office 1912-16; Knighted in 1917. Contested N. Salford in 1917 and S. Aberdeen in 1922 and 1923. Died 21 Nov. 1947. [1910]

MALLOCK, Richard. Cockington Court, Nr. Torquay. Carlton. S. of Charles Herbert Mallock, Esq., of Cockington Court, Devon, by Maria, youngest d. of Arthur Champernowne, Esq., MP, of Dartington, Devon. B. 1843; m. 1st, 1876, Mary Jones, d. of T.A.H. Dickson, Esq., of Liverpool (she died 1878); 2ndly, 1880, Elizabeth Emily, d. of George Maconchy, Esq., of Co. Longford. Educ. at Harrow, and the Royal Military Academy, Woolwich. Was Lieut. in the Royal Artillery from 1865 to 1876, and a J.P. for Devonshire; Patron of the livings of Cockington, Devon, and St. John's, Torquay, A Conservative. Was an unsuccessful candidate for the Torquay division of Devon at the general election of 1885. First elected there 1886 and sat until

he retired in 1895. Died 28 June 1900.   [1895]

MANDEVILLE, Francis, ('Frank'). Ballydine Castle, Kilsheelan, and Orchardstown, Co. Tipperary. S. of James H. Mandeville, Esq., of Ballyquirkeen House, Co. Tipperary, and his wife, Jane O'Mahoney. B. 1850 at Lochanna, Kilbenny, Co. Limerick. Educ. at the Lay Coll., Carlow, and in France. Was a bro. of John Mandeville, Esq., of Michelstown, who died after his imprisonment in Tullamore Gaol under the Crimes Act. He was an active member of the National League, but later joined the Irish National Federation. An Anti-Parnellite. First returned for Tipperary S. in July 1892 and sat until he retired in 1900. Died 2 Jan. 1905.   [1900]

MANFIELD, Harry. Moulton Grange, Northampton. 240 St. James's Court, London. Reform, Bath, and National Liberal. Eld. s. of Sir Philip Manfield. B. 1 Feb. 1855 at Northampton; m. 1909, Louisa, d. of Sir J. Barran, Bart. Educ. privately. Senior Partner of Manfield and Sons, Boot Manufacturers, Northampton. J.P. and Co. Alderman for Northamptonshire. A Liberal. Elected for mid Northamptonshire in 1906 and sat until he retired in 1918. Died 9 Feb. 1923.   [1918]

MANFIELD, Sir Moses Philip. Blomfield House, London. Northampton. National Liberal. B. 1819 a native of Bristol; m. a d. of Mr. Milne, Borough Surveyor. After working as a Journeyman in his trade he went to Northampton to manage a small business. He was one of the largest Shoe-Manufacturers in the town. Was in the Town Council from 1866; an Alderman and J.P., and was Mayor. Was Knighted in 1894. An advanced Radical and supporter of Mr. Gladstone's Home Rule policy for Ireland. Was one of the earliest supporters of Mr. Bradlaugh and Mr. Labouchere in their candidatures for Northampton. First elected for Northampton Feb. 1891 and sat until he retired in 1895. Died 31 July 1899.   [1895]

MANNERS, Lord Cecil Reginald John. 8 Hanover Square, London. Belvoir Castle, Leicestershire. Carlton, and Bachelors'. 3rd s. of the 7th Duke of Rutland, by Janetta, d. of Thomas Hughan, Esq., of Airds, Kirkcudbrightshire. B. 1868. Unmarried. Educ. at Charterhouse, and Trinity Hall,

Cambridge. Was Assistant Private Secretary to the Secretary of State for India (Visct. Cross). A Conservative. Elected for the Melton or Eastern division of Leicestershire in 1900 and sat until he retired in 1906. Died 8 Sept. 1945. [1905]

MANNERS, Lord Edward William John. 207 Piccadilly, London. Naval & Military, and Turf. 2nd s. of the Duke and Duchess of Rutland. B. in London 1864. Educ. at Wellington Coll. Entered the Rifle Brigade Feb. 1885, retired 1895. Maj. of Militia. A Conservative. Sat for Leicestershire E. from July 1895 until he retired in 1900. Died 26 Feb. 1903. [1900]

MANNERS, Rt. Hon. Lord John James Robert, G.C.B. 3 Cambridge Gate, Regent's Park, London. Belvoir Castle, Grantham, Lincolnshire. St. Mary's Tower, Birnam, Scotland. Carlton. 2nd s. of 5th Duke of Rutland, by the d. of 5th Earl of Carlisle. B. at Belvoir Castle 1818; m. 1st, 1851, Catherine, only d. of Col. Marlay, C.B. (she died 1854); 2ndly, 1862, Janetta, eld. d. of Thomas Hughan, Esq. Educ. at Eton, and Trinity Coll., Cambridge. Created D.C.L. at Oxford 1876. Was Commissioner of Works and Buildings from Mar. till Dec. 1852, with a seat in the Cabinet, and again from Mar. 1858 till June 1859, and a third time from July 1866 to Dec. 1868; also Postmaster-Gen. from 1874 to 1880, and again in 1885, and Chancellor of the Duchy of Lancaster, Aug. 1886-Aug. 1892. Author of a *Plea for National Holidays*, etc. A Tory. Represented Newark from 1841 till July 1847. Unsuccessfully contested London in 1849. Sat for Colchester from Feb. 1850 to Feb. 1857, for Leicestershire N. from that date to Nov. 1885, and for the Melton division of Leicestershire from Nov. 1885 until he succeeded his bro. as 7th Duke of Rutland in Mar. 1888. PC. 1852. G.C.B. 1880. K.G. 1891. Created Baron Roos of Belvoir in his own right in 1896. Died 4 Aug. 1906. [1888]

MANSFIELD, Horace Rendall. Church Gresley, Nr. Burton-on-Trent. Broom Leys, Coalville, Nr. Leicester. National Liberal. S. of Cornelius and Harriett Mansfield, of Stratford, London. B. at Stratford 1863; m. 1st, 1885, Annie, d. of the Rev. W. Rose, of Retford, Nottinghamshire (she died 1905); 2ndly, 1908, Sarah Elizabeth, d. of William Winterton, Esq., J.P., of Leicester. Educ. privately at

Portsmouth, and London. A Manufacturer and J.P. for the County of Derby 1892. A Liberal. Elected for the Spalding division of Lincolnshire in 1900 and sat until he retired in Jan. 1910. Died 9 Feb. 1914. [1909]

MAPLE, Sir John Blundell, Bart. Clarence House, Regent's Park, London. Falmouth House, Newmarket. Childwickbury, St. Alban's, Hertfordshire. Carlton, Constitutional, Junior Constitutional, and St. Stephen's. S. of John Maple, Esq., of Hampstead, London. B. 1845; m. 1874, Emily H., d. of M. Merryweather, Esq., of Clapham. Educ. at Cranford Coll., Maidenhead, and King's Coll., London. Governor of Messrs. Maple and Company Limited, of Tottenham Court Road, London; was a member of the London County Council 1895-1901; created Bart. 1897 upon the occasion of Queen Victoria's Golden Jubilee. Knighted Aug. 1892. A Conservative, an earnest supporter of Mr. Balfour's policy, opposed to Church disestablishment, and to excessive expenditure. Contested St. Pancras S. Nov. 1885. Sat for the Dulwich division of Camberwell from 1 Dec. 1887 until his death 24 Nov. 1903. [1903]

MAPPIN, Sir Frederick Thorpe, Bart. 38 Prince's Gate, London. Thornbury, Sheffield. Reform, and National Liberal. S. of Joseph Mappin, Esq., of Sheffield, by Mary Ann, d. of Thomas Thorpe, Esq., of Haines, Bedfordshire. B. 1821; m. 1845, Mary Crossley, d. of John Wilson, Esq., of Sheffield. Chairman in the firm of Thomas Turton and Sons Limited, Sheaf and Spring Works, Sheffield, and served the office of Master Cutler in 1855-56. A J.P. and Dept.-Lieut. for the W. Riding of Yorkshire. For Sheffield, was Chairman of Town Trustees, and Mayor in 1877-78. Chairman of the Sheffield Technical School, and also Chairman of the Sheffield Gas Company. Freedom of Sheffield was conferred on him in 1900. Was one of the Jurors at the Paris International Exhibition of 1878, and appointed to the Legion of Honour at its close. Created Bart. July 1886. A Liberal. Sat for E. Retford from Apr. 1880 to Nov. 1885, and for the Hallamshire division of the W. Riding of Yorkshire from 1885 until he retired in 1906. Died 19 Mar. 1910. [1905]

MARCH, Charles Henry Gordon-Len-

nox, Earl of. Goodwood Park, Chichester, Sussex. Carlton. Eld. s. of the Duke of Richmond, by Frances Harriet, eld. d. of Algernon Frederick Greville, Esq. B. in Portland Place 1845; m. 1st, 1868, Amy Mary, eld. d. of Percy Ricardo, Esq. (she died 1879); 2ndly, 1882, Isabel, d. of W.G. Craven, Esq. (she died 1887). Educ. at Eton. Appointed Lieut. Grenadier Guards 1868; retired 1869. A Conservative. Sat for W. Sussex from 1869-85, and for the Chichester division of Sussex from 1885 until he accepted Chiltern Hundreds in 1888. Succeeded as 7th Duke of Richmond in 1903. C.B. 1902. G.C.V.O. 1904. K.G. 1905. Chancellor of Aberdeen University from 1917. Died 18 Jan. 1928.   [1888]

MARJORIBANKS, Rt. Hon. Edward. 134 Piccadilly, London. Ninewells, Chirnside, Berwickshire. Brooks's. New Club, Edinburgh. Eld. s. of the 1st Baron Tweedmouth, by Isabella, d. of the Rt. Hon. Sir James Weir Hogg, Bart. B. 1849; m. 1873, Lady Fanny Octavia Louisa, 3rd d. of the 6th Duke of Marlborough. Was educ. at Harrow, and Christ Church, Oxford. Called to the bar at the Inner Temple Nov. 1874. A Magistrate for the Counties of Berwick and Inverness. PC. 1886. Appointed Comptroller of H.M. Household, Jan.-July 1886. Patronage Secretary to the Treasury, and Government chief "Whip", Aug. 1892-Mar. 1894. A Liberal and Home Ruler, in favour of the assimilation of the laws regarding landed and personal property, and a large measure of local government in counties. Unsuccessfully contested W. Kent in 1874. Sat for the Co. of Berwick from Apr. 1880 until he succeeded as Lord Tweedmouth in 1894. Lord Privy Seal and Chancellor of Duchy of Lancaster 1894-95. First Lord of the Admiralty from Dec. 1905-Apr. 1908. Lord President of Council Apr.-Sept. 1908. K.T. 1908. Died 15 Sept. 1909.   [1893]

MARKHAM, Sir Arthur Basil, Bart. 47 Portland Place, London. Beachborough Park, Shorncliffe. Newstead Abbey, Nottingham. Reform. 2nd s. of Charles Markham, Esq., J.P., of Tapton House, Chesterfield, and a grand-s. on his mother's side of Sir Joseph Paxton. B. 1866; m. 1898, Lucy, only d. of Capt. A.B. Cunningham, R.A. Educ. at Rugby. Chairman of Bullcroft Main Collieries, Oxcroft, Oakdale Navigation Collieries, Wagon Finance Corporation Limited, and

was a Managing Director of other Coal and Iron companies. A J.P. for Leicestershire and Derbyshire, and was a Capt. in the 3rd Sherwood Foresters. Created Bart. 1911. A Liberal. Elected for the Mansfield division of Nottinghamshire in 1900 and sat until his death 7 Aug. 1916.   [1916]

MARKS, Sir George Croydon, C.B.E. Continued in House after 1918: full entry in Volume III.

MARKS, Harry Hananel. 6 Cavendish Square, London. Callis Court, St. Peter's, Thanet. Carlton. S. of the Rev. Professor D.W. Marks and Cecilia, d. of M. Wolff, Esq., of Liverpool. B. 9 Apr. 1855 in London; m. 1884, Annie Estelle, d. of W. Benjamin, Esq., of Montreal. Educ. at University Coll., London, and L'Athenee Royale, Brussels. A Journalist; Editor, and Founder of *The Financial News*. A J.P. for Kent. Maj. commanding 1st C.B. The Buffs (E. Kent Regiment). A member of London County Council from 1889-98. A Conservative, a strong advocate of Tariff reform and colonial preference, in favour of restriction of alien immigration, social legislation, etc. Unsuccessfully contested N.E. Bethnal Green in 1892; sat for the St.-George's division of the Tower Hamlets from 1895 until he retired 1900. Elected for the Thanet division of Kent in Oct. 1904 and sat until he retired in Jan. 1910. Died 22 Dec. 1916.   [1909]

MARNHAM, Francis John. Crouch Oak, Addlestone, Surrey. National Liberal. B. 1853 at Blackheath; m. 1881, d. of R. Drury Lown, Esq. Educ. at private schools. A member of the Stock Exchange; for six years Chairman of Chertsey Urban Council. J.P. for Surrey. Governor of Royal Holloway Coll., Egham. A Liberal. Elected for the Chertsey division of Surrey in 1906 and sat until he retired in Jan. 1910. Mayor of Torquay 1926-27. A Baptist. Died 18 Jan. 1941.   [1909]

MARRIOTT, John Arthur Ransome. Continued in House after 1918: full entry in Volume III.

MARRIOTT, Rt. Hon. Sir William Thackeray. 56 Ennismore Gardens, London. 6 Crown Office Row, Temple, London. 3rd s. of Christopher Marriott, Esq., of Crumpsal, near Manchester, by Jane

Dorothea, youngest d. of John Poole, Esq., of Cornbrook Hall, Manchester. B. 1834; m. Charlotte Louisa, eld. d. of Capt. Tennant, R.N. of Needwood, Staffordshire. Graduated at Cambridge (St. John's Coll.) 1858. Was called to the bar at Lincoln's Inn 1864, and joined the S.E. Circuit. Was appointed a Queen's Counsel in 1877, and elected a bencher of Lincoln's Inn 1879. A Commissioner of the Lieutenancy of London. Judge-Advocate-Gen. June 1885 to Jan 1886 and again Aug. 1886 to Aug. 1892. Was made a Knight 1888. A Unionist. First elected for Brighton as a Liberal Apr. 1880. In Feb. 1884, in consequence of his dissatisfaction with Mr. Gladstone's Foreign and Egyptian policy, he took the Chiltern Hundreds. Was reelected for Brighton as a Conservative by a large majority in Mar. 1884 in opposition to Mr. R. Romer, the Liberal candidate, and sat until he accepted Chiltern Hundreds in 1893. PC. 1885. Died 27 July 1903. [1892]

MARSHALL, Sir Arthur Harold, K.B.E. Continued in House after 1918: full entry in Volume III.

MARSHALL-HALL, Edward. See HALL, Edward Marshall.

MARTIN, Joseph. Vancouver, British Columbia, Canada. S. of Edward Martin, Esq., of Canada. B. 24 Sept. 1852 at Milton, Ontario; m. Elizabeth J. Eaton, of Ottawa (she died 1913). Educ. at Public Schools of Ontario and Michigan, and Toronto University. A Canadian Barrister and Solicitor; Q.C. 1899. Was Attorney-Gen. of Manitoba 1888-91, and of British Columbia 1898-1900, Premier of British Columbia 1900, and was a Member of the Canadian House of Commons. A Liberal until he joined the Labour Party in July 1918. Unsuccessfully contested Stratford-on-Avon division of Warwickshire in 1909. Elected for E. St. Pancras in Jan. 1910 and sat until he retired in 1918. Died 2 Mar. 1923. [1918]

MARTIN, Sir Richard Biddulph, Bart. 10 Hill Street, London. Overbury Court, Tewkesbury. Windham, Athenaeum, and Ranelagh. Eld. s. of Robert Martin, Esq., of Overbury Court, Worcestershire, by Mary Anne, d. of John Biddulph, Esq. B. at Eaton Square, London 1838; m. 1864, Mary Frances, d. of Admiral Richard Crozier, K.T.S., of West Hill, Isle of Wight. Educ. at Harrow, and Exeter Coll., Oxford. A Banker, Chairman of Martin's Bank Limited. A Liberal Unionist. Unsuccessfully contested London City Apr. 1880; sat for Tewkesbury July 1880-85; unsuccessful in the Chelmsford division of Essex in 1885 and in the Ashburton division of Devonshire 1886. Sat for the Droitwich division of Worcestershire from 1892 until he retired in 1906. Created Bart. in 1905. Died 23 Aug. 1916. [1905]

MARTON, George Blucher Heneage. Capernwray, Lancashire. Carlton, Arthur's, and St. James's. S. of George Marton, Esq., (who once represented the borough of Lancaster), by Lucy Sarah, d. of Chief-Justice Sir Robert Dallas. B. at Capernwray, near Lancaster, 1839; m. 1866, the Hon. Gertrude Flower, d. of Visct. Ashbrook. Graduated as a senior optime Trinity Coll., Cambridge. A Maj. in the 3rd Battalion Royal Lancaster Regiment, and J.P. and Dept.-Lieut. for Lancashire and Westmoreland. Was High Sheriff for Lancashire in 1877 and an Alderman of Lancashire County Council. A Patron of 2 livings. A Conservative. Sat for the Lancaster div. of Lancashire from Dec. 1885 until defeated in 1886. Died 18 Aug. 1905. [1886]

MARUM, Edward Purcell Mulhallen. Aharney House, Ballyragget, Co. Kilkenny. St. George's. Eld. s. of Richard C. Marum, Esq. of Aharney House, Queen's Co., by Elizabeth Mary Anne, d. of John Purcell Mulhallen, Esq., of Malcolmville, Kilkenny. B. 1827; m. 1861, Maryanne Josephine, d. of John Brennan, Esq., J.P. of Woodview, Co. Kilkenny. Was educ. at Carlow Coll., and at the University of London, where he graduated M.A., and subsequently LL.B. Was called to the bar in Ireland 1846. A Magistrate for Kilkenny Co., and Queen's Co. Author of *Protestant Ascendancy in Ireland; its Cause and Cure, The Right of Irish Tenants under the British Constitution to Fixity of Tenure vindicated.* An Irish Nationalist. Unsuccessfully contested Kilkenny City in Apr. 1875. Sat for Kilkenny Co. 1880-85 and for the N. division of Kilkenny Co. from 1885 until his death on 21 Sept. 1890. [1890]

MASKELYNE, Mervin Herbert Nevil Story, F.R.S. See STORY-MASKELYNE, Mervin Herbert Nevil, F.R.S.

MASON, Alfred Edward Woodley. 17 Stratton Street, London. Garrick. S. of W.W. Mason, Esq., of Dulwich. B. 7 May 1865. Educ. at Dulwich Coll., and Trinity Coll., Oxford; B.A. A Novelist; author of *Courtship of Maurice Buckler, Philanderers, Parson Kelly* (with Andrew Lang), *Miranda of the Balcony, The Four Feathers, The Broken Road,* and several other well-known novels. A Liberal. Elected for Coventry in 1906 and sat until he retired in Jan. 1910. Declined a Knighthood. Died 22 Nov 1948.   [1909]

MASON, David Marshall. Continued in House after 1918: full entry in Volume III.

MASON, James Francis. 1 Chesterfield Gardens, London. Eynsham Hall, Witney, Oxfordshire. Carlton, Marlborough, Arthur's, and Travellers'. S. of James Mason, Esq., of Eynsham Hall, Oxfordshire. B. 1861; m. 1895, Lady Evelyn Lindsay, d. of Earl of Crawford. Educ. at Eton. Chairman of Mason and Barry, and a Director of Dorman, Long and Company, Middlesbrough. Was a Maj. in Oxfordshire Yeomanry. A Unionist. Elected for Windsor in 1906 and sat until he retired in 1918. Unsuccessfully contested W. Leyton on 1 Mar. 1919. Director of Great Western Railway. Died 2 Apr. 1929.   [1918]

MASON, Robert. Continued in House after 1918: full entry in Volume III.

MASON, Stephen. 24 Belhaven Terrace, Glasgow. National Liberal, and Cobden. S. of David Mason, Esq., by his wife Christian Hogg. B. 1832 at Kennoway, in the "kingdom" of Fife; m. Martha, d. of John Marshall, Esq., of Machan, Lanarkshire. Educ. at Kennoway, and privately. A Merchant at Glasgow, and a J.P. for Lanarkshire. Also a Director of the Glasgow Chamber of Commerce, and at one time its President. Wrote pamphlets on the monetary and land questions, the French Treaty of 1860, Scotch banking, etc. A Liberal, and Home Ruler. Sat for the mid division of Lanarkshire from 1885 until he accepted Chiltern Hundreds in 1888. Died 21 Apr. 1890.   [1887]

MASSEY-MAINWARING,   Hon. William Frederick Barton. 30 Grosvenor Place, London. Carlton, Junior Carlton, and Burlington Fine Arts. S. of the 3rd Baron Clarina, by Susan, d. of Hugh Barton, Esq., of Straffan, Co. Kildare. B. 1845; m. 1872, Isabella Ann, only child of Charles B. Lee Mainwaring, Esq., of Richmond, and widow of Maj.-Gen. Milman. On his marriage he assumed the name of Mainwaring, in addition to his patronymic. Educ. at Trinity Coll., Dublin, where he was distinguished in science; B.A. and LL.B. 1866. A Barrister, of the Inner Temple (1868) and joined the Home Circuit. Was well-known for his taste and liberality as a collector and owner of pictures and works of art. A Dept.-Lieut. for Lincolnshire and a Director of several companies. A Conservative and Unionist, in favour of the Sunday opening of Museums, etc. Unsuccessfully contested Norwich in 1880. Represented Finsbury central from 1895 until he retired in 1906. Died 12 Mar. 1907.   [1905]

MASSIE, John. 101 Banbury Road, Oxford. Reform, and National Liberal. S. of the Rev. Robert Massie, Congregational Minister, and May Souttar. B. 3 Dec. 1842 at Newton-le-Willows; m. 1876, d. of Alexander Ogilvie, Esq., of Great George Street, Westminster, and Sizewell House, Suffolk. Educ. at Atherstone Grammar School, and St. John's Coll., Cambridge. M.A. Oxford and Cambridge; Honorary D.D. Yale. Was Professor at Spring Hill Coll., Birmingham 1869-86, and Yates Professor of New Testament Exegesis, Mansfield Coll., Oxford 1886-1903. A Councillor and Alderman of Leamington 1878-87. Assistant Commissioner to the Royal Commission on Secondary Education 1894; Treasurer to National Liberal Federation 1903-06. Contributed to Hastings' *Dictionary of the Bible,* Cheyne's *Encyclopedia Biblica,* and other theological publications. A Liberal. Sat for Wiltshire N. from Jan. 1906 until defeated in Jan. 1910. Member of the Executive of the National Liberal Federation 1894-1906 and from 1910; President, Oxford Free Church Council 1896-1921. Died 11 Nov. 1925.   [1909]

MASTER, Thomas William Chester-, jun. Stratton House, Cirencester. Carlton. Eld. s. of Thomas William Chester-Master, Esq., of The Abbey, Cirencester, and Knole Park, Bristol, by Catherine Elizabeth, eld. d. of Sir George Cornewall, Bart., of Moccas Court, Herefordshire. B. in London 1841; m. 1866, Georgina Emily, 5th d. of John Etherington Welch Rolls,

Esq., of the Hendre, Monmouthshire. Educ. at Harrow, and Christ Church, Oxford. Maj. Royal North Gloucester Militia. A Magistrate for Gloucester and Monmouth. A Conservative. Sat for Cirencester from Mar. 1878 until he retired in 1885. Unsuccessfully contested the Cirencester division of Gloucestershire in July 1892; elected there at a by-election on 13 Oct. 1892 but on petition this election was declared void and he was defeated at a second by-election on 23 February 1893. Died 14 Nov. 1914.   [1885]

MASTERMAN, Rt. Hon. Charles Frederick Gurney. Continued in House after 1918: full entry in Volume III.

MATHER, Sir William. 16 Kensington Palace Gardens, London. Caradoc Court, Ross, Herefordshire. Salford Ironworks, Manchester. Reform, Brooks's, and Devonshire. S. of William Mather, Esq., of Manchester, by Amelia, d. of James Tidswell, Esq., of Manchester. B. 1838; m. 1863, Emma, d. of Thomas Watson, Esq., of Highbury. Educ. at private schools and in Germany. Chairman of Mather and Platt Limited, Salford Ironworks, and a member of the Institute of Civil Engineers, a Governor and member of the council of Owen's Coll. and of the Victoria University. Knight of Francis Joseph Order of Austria 1873. Investigated and reported on Technical Education in America and Russia for the Royal Commission on Technical Instruction in 1883. Was engaged for some years in promoting Technical Education. Chairman of the Froebal Educational Institute of London. Member of Committee on re-organization of the War Office 1902. Knighted 1902. A Liberal. Sat for the S. division of Salford from 1885 until defeated 1886; sat for the Gorton division of Lancashire from 1889 until defeated in 1895. First elected for the Rossendale division of Lancashire Feb. 1900 and sat until he accepted Chiltern Hundreds in 1904. PC. 1910. Died 18 Sept. 1920.   [1903]

MATHIAS, Richard. Valndre Hall, St. Mellons, Monmouthshire. National Liberal, and Royal Societies. S. of John Mathias, Esq., Shipowner, of Aberystwith. B. 1863 at Aberystwith; m. 1899, Annie, d. of Evan Hughes, Esq., of Cardiff. Educ. at Towyn Academy, and Ardwyn School, Aberystwith. A member of the firm of J.

Mathias and Sons, Shipowners, of Cardiff, a Director of Cambrian Steam Navigation Company, and of London Steam Ship Owners Association. A member of Cardiff Chamber of Commerce and a Gov. of University Coll. of S. Wales and Monmouthshire. A Liberal. Unsuccessfully contested Cheltenham in Jan. 1910. Elected for Cheltenham in Dec. 1910 and sat until 1911 when the election was declared void on petition. Contested Merthyr division of Merthyr Tydfil in 1922 as an Independent with National Liberal and Conservative support. Knighted 1913. Created Bart. 1917. Life member of Institute of Directors. Died 26 Oct. 1942.   [1911]

MATTHEWS, Rt. Hon. Henry. 6 Carlton Gardens, London. Carlton, Windham, Athenaeum, and Orleans. S. of the Hon. Henry Matthews, Puisne Justice of Ceylon, by Emma, d. of William Blount, Esq., of Orleton, Herefordshire. B. in Ceylon 1826. Unmarried. Educ. at the University of Paris (Bachelier-ès-lettres 1844), and the University of London (B.A. 1847, LL.B. 1849). Was called to the bar at Lincoln's Inn 1850, was appointed Q.C. and bencher of his Inn in 1868, and a member of the senate of the University of London in 1885. PC. 1886. Was Home Secretary from Aug. 1886 to Aug. 1892. A Conservative. MP for Dungarvan 1868-74, when he was defeated; unsuccessfully contested Dungarvan Jan. 1877; unsuccessfully contested N. Birmingham Nov. 1885. First elected for E. Birmingham 1886, re-elected July 1892 and sat until he retired in 1895. He was the first Roman Catholic Cabinet Minister since the passing of the Catholic Emancipation Act in 1829. Created Visct. Llandaff in 1895. Chairman of Royal Commission on London's Water Supply. Died 3 Apr. 1913.   [1895]

MATTINSON, Miles Walker. 1 Garden Court, Temple, London. Ivanhoe, Keswick Road, Putney, London. Only s. of Thomas Mattinson, Esq., of Newcastle-on-Tyne. B. 1854. Entered Gray's Inn 1874; took the Bacon scholarship there, and was called to the bar in 1877. Joined the Northern Circuit, and was appointed recorder of Blackburn 1886-1922. Joint author of a work on the *Law of Corrupt Practices at Elections*, and of *A Select Collection of Precedents for Pleading.* A Conservative. Unsuccessfully contested Carlisle in 1880 and Dumfries

Burghs in 1885 and 1886. First returned for the Walton division of Liverpool Feb. 1888 and sat until he retired in 1892. Unsuccessfully contested Bolton in Jan. 1910. Q.C. 1897. Knighted 1922. Died 29 Feb. 1944. [1892]

MAXWELL, Rt. Hon. Sir Herbert Eustace, Bart. 49 Lennox Gardens, London. Monreith, Whauphill, Wigtownshire. Carlton. S. of Sir William Maxwell, 6th Bart., of Monreith, Wigtownshire, by Helenora, youngest d. of Sir Michael Shaw Stewart, Bart. B. at Abercromby Place, Edinburgh 1845; m. 1869, Mary, eld. d. of Henry Fletcher Campbell, Esq., of Boquhan, Stirlingshire. Educ. at Eton, and at Christ Church, Oxford. Was a Lord of the Treasury 1886 to 1892; served on the Royal Commission on Aged Poor 1893-94, Chairman of Royal Commission on Tuberculosis 1896-97; Vice-Chairman of Society for Suppression of Consumption; created P.C. 1897. Lord-Lieut. for Wigtownshire, 1903-35. Lieut.-Col. 3rd Battalion Royal Scots Fusilliers; F.R.S., President Society Scottish Antiquaries, Honorary LL.D., Glasgow, and author of numerous works in history, archaeology, fiction and natural history. Succeeded as Bart. in 1877. A Conservative. Sat for Wigtownshire from Apr. 1880 until he retired in 1906. Chairman, National Library of Scotland 1928-35. K.T. 1933. Died 30 Oct. 1937. [1905]

MAXWELL, Sir John Maxwell Stirling-, Bart. See STIRLING-MAXWELL, Sir John Maxwell, Bart.

MAXWELL, William Jardine Herries. Munches, Dalbeattie, and Terraughtie, Dumfries. Brooks's. S. of Wellwood Herries Maxwell, Esq., of Munches, and Jane Home, eld. d. of Sir William Jardine, Bart., of Applegarth. B. at Munches, Dalbeattie 1852; m. 1877, Dorothea, 2nd d. of C.L. Maitland Kirwan, Esq., of Dalgan Park, Co. Mayo, and Gelston Castle, Castle Douglas. Educ. at Edinburgh Academy, and Exeter Coll., Oxford. Convenor of the Stewartry of Kirkcudbright from 1899. Was called to the Scottish bar in 1876. A Liberal Unionist. Elected for Dumfriesshire July 1892, defeated July 1895. Re-elected 1900 and sat until he retired in 1906. Died 31 July 1933. [1905]

MAYNE, Rear-Admiral Richard

Charles, C.B. 101 Queen's Gate, London. United Service, Army & Navy, and Marlborough. S. of Sir Richard Mayne, K.C.B., Chief Commissioner of the Metropolitan Police from 1829 to 1869, by Georgiana, d. of T. Carrick, Esq., of Wyke. B. 1835; m. 1870, Sabine, d. of Thomas Dent, Esq., of Hyde Park Gardens. Educ. at Eton Coll. Entered the navy 1847; served in the Baltic, Black Sea, and Sea of Azof 1854-55; was seriously wounded in New Zealand 1863; commanded in the survey of the Straits of Magellan, 1866-69; retired with the rank of Rear-Admiral 1879. A C.B., Kt. of the Legion of Honour, and had the Order of the Medjidie, and the Crimean, Baltic, and New Zealand medals. Also a Fellow of the Geographical Society, J.P. for Middlesex, Westminster, and Haverfordwest, a Director of several companies, and author of *Four Years in British Columbia and Vancouver Island*, and *Practical Notes on Marine Surveying and Nautical Astronomy*. A Conservative, in favour of a measure of Local Government for Ireland. Unsuccessfully contested the Pembroke and Haverfordwest district at the general election of 1885. First returned for that district July 1886 and sat until he died on 29 May 1892. [1892]

MAYNE, Thomas. 33 Castle Street, Dublin. Queensborough Road, Bray, Co. Wicklow. S. of John Mayne, Esq., of High Street, Dublin, by Jane, d. of Arthur Ward, Esq., of Enniscorthy, Co. Wexford. B. in Dublin 1832; m. 1860, Susannah, d. of Patrick Rooney, Esq., of Dolphin's Barn, Dublin. Educ. at the Royal Coll. of Science, Dublin, also at the Catholic University, Dublin. A Warehouseman in Dublin, and Town Councillor, Chairman of the Finance Committee, and a member of the Port and Docks Board of that city, and was Chairman of the Bray Township Commissioners. A "Home Rule Nationalist." Unsuccessfully contested Portarlington in Feb. 1883. Sat for Tipperary from Mar. 1883 to Nov. 1885, and for the mid division of Tipperary from Nov. 1885 until he accepted Chiltern Hundreds in 1890. [1890]

MEAGHER, Michael. Chestnut Villa, Tullaroan, Co. Kilkenny. S. of Patrick Meagher, Esq., of Tullaroan, and Mary Josephine O'Dwyer, of Grastown Castle, Co. Tipperary. B. 27 Feb. 1846 at Tullaroan, Co. Kilkenny; m. 1881, Johanna, only d. of William Corcoran, Esq., of

Ballingarry. Educ. at Mountrath Coll., Queen's Co. A Farmer. Joined the Fenian movement and took part in the rising in 1867. A Nationalist. First elected for N. Kilkenny in Mar. 1906 and sat until he retired in 1918. Died Dec. 1927.   [1918]

MEDWAY, John Stewart Gathorne-Hardy, Lord. See GATHORNE-HARDY, Hon. John Stewart.

MEEHAN, Francis Edward. Manorhamilton, Co. Leitrim. S. of Laurence Meehan, Esq. B. 17 Sept. 1868 at Manorhamilton; m. 1908, Mollie, d. of W. Hamilton, Esq. Educ. at Manorhamilton Intermediate Classical School. Member of Leitrim County Council, and President of N. Leitrim Executive of United Irish League. A Nationalist. Elected for N. Leitrim in Feb. 1908 and sat until he retired in 1918. Died 22 Dec. 1946. [1918]

MEEHAN, Patrick Aloysius. Maryborough, Queen's Co. B. 1852. Educ. privately, and at Christian Brothers' Schools. A Farmer. Chairman of Queen's Co. County Council; a Treasurer of the Irish Nationalist party. A Nationalist. Elected for the Leix division of Queen's Co. in 1906 and sat until his death 10 May 1913. [1913]

MEEHAN, Patrick Joseph. Church Street, Maryborough, Queen's Co. National Liberal. S. of Patrick A. Meehan, Esq., MP for the Leix division of Queen's Co. from 1906-13. B. 28 Mar. 1877 at Maryborough; m. 1905, Margaret, d. of Terence Byrne, Esq., of Monasterevan, Co. Kildare. Educ. at Christian Brothers School, Maryborough, and St. Vincent's Coll., Castleknock, Dublin. A Solicitor, admitted 1900. A Nationalist. Elected for the Leix division of Queen's Co. in June 1913 and sat until defeated in the Queen's County in 1918. [1918]

MELLOR, John James. Queen Anne's Mansions, London. The Woodlands, Whitefield, Manchester. Carlton, Junior Carlton, and St. Stephen's. Youngest s. of Jonathan Mellor, Esq., J.P., of Hope House, Oldham. B. 1830; m. 1865, Jeanette, only child of R. Clegg, Esq., of Clayton-le-Moors, Lancashire. Educ. privately. A Cotton Manufacturer; a J.P. and Dept.-Lieut. for Lancashire, a Director of the Metropolitan and of the S.E. Railway,

and a Fellow of the Royal Astronomical Society; Honorary Col. 1st Volunteer Battalion Lancashire Fusiliers; retired after 27 years service. A Liberal Conservative. Was an unsuccessful candidate for the Radcliffe cum Farnworth division of Lancashire at the general election of 1892. First returned for the Radcliffe division of Lancashire in July 1895 and sat until he retired in 1900. Died 12 Jan. 1916. [1900]

MELLOR, Rt. Hon. John William. 68 St. George's Square, London. Culmhead, Pitminster, Taunton. Brooks's. Eld. s. of the Rt. Hon. Sir John Mellor, Justice of the Court of Queen's Bench (who sat successively for Yarmouth and Nottingham from 1857 to 1861), by Elizabeth Cook, only d. of William Moseley, Esq., of Peckham Rye, Surrey. B. in London 1835; m. 1860, Caroline, d. of Charles Paget, Esq.. MP, of Ruddington Grange (she died 1900). Educ. at Trinity Hall, Cambridge; graduated B.A. 1857, 8th senior optime; M.A. 1860. Was called to the bar at the Inner Temple June 1860; Leader of the Midland Circuit 1882. Honorary member of the New York State Bar Association. Appointed a Queen's Counsel 1875, and elected a bencher of the Inner Temple 1877. Was Recorder of Grantham; resigned 1874; Judge Advocate Gen. and PC. 1886 Royal Commissioner Tweed and Solway Inquiry 1896, and Water Supply to London 1897. A J.P. for Somerset and Devon, and Dept.-Lieut. for Somerset. Was Dept. Speaker and Chairman of Ways and Means 1893-95. A Liberal, in favour of the abolition of the Bishops' Veto, and the defence of Protestantism within the Church. Contested Grantham 1874. Sat for Grantham 1880 to 1886, when he was defeated; unsuccessfully contested Bassetlaw division of Nottinghamshire 1890. First elected for the Sowerby division of Yorkshire 1892 and sat until he accepted Chiltern Hundreds in 1904. Died 13 Oct. 1911. [1904]

MELVILLE, Beresford Valentine. 32 Grosvenor Gardens, London. Capo di Monte, Cannes. Arthur's, Carlton, and Junior Constitutional. S. of the Rev. David Melville, Canon Residentiary of Worcester, and Emma, d. of Capt. Hill, R.N., of Bryansford, Co. Down. B. 1857 at Shelsley, Worcestershire; m. 1888, Sydney, d. of the Rev. J. Garrett, of Kilgarrone Park, and widow of J. Spender Clay, Esq.

Educ. at Marlborough Coll., and Brasenose Coll., Oxford. A J.P. for Kent, Surrey, and London. A Conservative. Unsuccessfully contested Derbyshire S. in Mar. 1892. Represented Stockport from 1895 until he retired in 1906. O.B.E. 1919. Died 1 Oct. 1931. [1905]

MENDL, Sigismund Ferdinand. 14 Devonshire Street, Portland Place, London. Reform, New University, and National Liberal. Eld. s. of Ferdinand Mendl, Esq., of Broad Street, London, and 39 Holland Park, London. B. 1866 at Paddington, London; m. 1888, Frances, d. of A.H. Moses, Esq., of London. Educ. at Harrow, and University Coll., Oxford. Called to the bar at the Inner Temple 1888, but did not practise. A member of the firm of Ferdinand Mendl and Company, Grain Importers and Shipowners, and a Director of the Metropolitan Life Assurance Society. A Liberal, in favour of Home Rule and the Advanced Liberal Programme generally. Stood unsuccessfully for the Isle of Wight 1892, and for Plymouth 1895. First returned for Plymouth Jan. 1898 and sat until defeated in 1900. Unsuccessfully contested Stockton 1906. President, London Corn Trade Association 1909-12 and 1915-19; member of War Office Advisory Committee on Army Contracts 1915-18. K.B.E. 1918. Died 17 July 1945. [1900]

MENZIES, Robert Stewart. 32 Queen's Gate, London. Hallyburton, Forfarshire, and Pitcur, Perthshire. Brooks's, and Oxford & Cambridge. Eld. s. of Graham Menzies, Esq., of Hallyburton, Forfarshire, Dept.-Lieut. for the county of Edinburgh, and J.P. for Perthshire, by Beatrice, d. of William Dudgeon, Esq. B. 1856. Educ. at Harrow, and Christ Church, Oxford, graduating B.A. 1880 with 2nd class honours in modern history. Was called to the bar at Lincoln's Inn in 1882; and was a Magistrate for Forfarshire and Perthshire. A Liberal, and Home Ruler. Sat for Perthshire E. from 1885 until his death on 25 Jan. 1889. [1888]

MENZIES, Sir Walter. 34 Gordon Square, London. Culcreuch, Fintry, Stirlingshire. Reform. S. of James Menzies, Esq., of Eastpark, Rutherglen, and Mary Ferguson. B. 24 July 1856; m. 1886, Margaret Henrietta, d. of Capt. J. Baker. Educ. at Glasgow High School. Was head of the Phoenix Tube Works, Glasgow;

retired in 1898. Secretary to the Scottish Liberal members. Knighted 1909. A Liberal. Unsuccessfully contested the central division of Glasgow in 1892 and S. Lanarkshire in 1900. Sat for S. Lanarkshire from 1906 until his death 26 Oct. 1913. [1913]

MEUX, Admiral of the Fleet Hon. Sir Hedworth. Theobald's Park, Waltham Cross. 18 Portman Square, London. S. of the 2nd Earl of Durham. B. 1856; m. 1901, Viscountess Chelsea, d. of the 1st Baron Alington and widow of the 2nd s. of the 5th Earl Cadogan. In 1911 he assumed the name of Meux, by Royal Licence, in lieu of Lambton. Served in Egypt 1882; commanded the Naval Brigade in S. Africa 1899-1900. Commander-in-Chief of the China Squadron. Commander-in-Chief at Portsmouth 1912-16. Was Private Secretary to two First Lords of the Admiralty, an Aide-de-Camp to King Edward, and commander of the Royal Yacht. A Unionist. Unsuccessfully contested Newcastle on Tyne in 1900. Elected for Portsmouth Jan. 1916 and sat until he retired in 1918. C.B. 1900; C.V.O. 1901; K.C.V.O. 1906; K.C.B. 1908; G.C.B. 1913. Died 20 Sept. 1929. [1918]

MEYSEY-THOMPSON, Ernest Claude. Continued in House after 1918: full entry in Volume III.

MEYSEY-THOMPSON, Sir Henry Meysey, Bart. Kirby Hall, York. Brooks's, Turf, Marlborough, and Bachelors'. S. of Sir Henry Stephen Meysey-Thompson, Bart., MP, for Whitby 1859-65, and his wife, d. of Sir John Croft, Bart., of Doddington Hall, Kent. B. 1845 at Moat Hall, Yorkshire; m. 1885, Ethel Adeline, d. of Sir Henry Pottinger, Bart. Educ. at Eton, and Trinity Coll., Cambridge. Maj. Yorkshire Hussar Yeomanry. J.P. and Dept.-Lieut. for the W. Riding of Yorkshire, a Director of the N.E. Railway and a Director of the Barrow Hematite Steel Company. Succeeded as Bart. in 1874. A Liberal Unionist. Was elected for Knaresborough 1880, but unseated on petition; unsuccessfully contested N. Lincolnshire July 1885. Sat for the Brigg division of Lincolnshire 1885-86, when he retired. First elected for the Handsworth division of Staffordshire in 1892 and sat until he was created Baron Knaresborough in Dec. 1905. Died 3 Mar. 1929. [1905]

MICKLEM, Nathaniel. 6 New Court, Carey Street, London. Northridge, Boxmoor, Hertfordshire. National Liberal. S. of Thomas Micklem, Esq., of Hoddesden. B. 1853. Educ. at Mill Hill School, and New Coll., Oxford. A Barrister, called to the bar at Lincoln's Inn 1881; bencher 1906; Q.C. 1900. A J.P. for Middlesex and Hertfordshire. A Liberal. Elected for the Watford division of Hertfordshire in 1906 and sat until defeated in Jan. 1910. Defeated again in Dec. 1910. Retired from Barristers practice in 1923; member of Royal Commission on Lunacy and Mental Disorder 1924; Treasurer of Lincoln's Inn 1930. Died 19 Mar. 1954.   [1909]

MIDDLEBROOK, Sir William. Continued in House after 1918: full entry in Volume III.

MIDDLEMORE, John Throgmorton. Forelands, Bromsgrove. Carlton. S. of William Middlemore, Esq., Manufacturer, of Birmingham, and one of the Middlemores, former Lords of the Manor of Edgbaston. B. at Edgbaston 1844; m. 1881, Mary, d. of the Rev. Thomas Price, of Selly Oak, Birmingham. Educ. at Edgbaston Proprietory School, and Bowdoin Coll., Brunswick, U.S. Was educ. for the medical profession, but ill-health prevented his becoming a Practitioner. A J.P. for Birmingham and Worcestershire, a member of the Birmingham City Council, and a munificent contributor of works of art, etc., to the city Art Gallery, etc. He also founded and managed for some forty years, the Middlemore Children's Emigration Homes, for the training in agriculture of destitute children in Canada. A Unionist, an Imperialist, and Tariff Reformer, he was in favour of, as an urgent necessity, better Primary, Secondary, and military service. Elected for N. Birmingham in 1899 and sat until he retired in 1918. Created Bart. 1919. Died 17 Oct. 1925.   [1918]

MILBANK, Sir Frederick Acclom. Retired in 1886: full entry in Volume I.

MILBANK, Sir Powlett Charles John, Bart. Norton Manor, Norton. Thorp Perrow, Bedale. Barningham Park, Barnard Castle. Carlton, Arthur's, and Boodle's. Only s. of Sir Frederick, 1st Bart., MP for Yorkshire N. Riding, by Alexina, d. of Sir Alexander Don, 6th Bart. B. 1 May 1852;

m. 1875, Edith Mary, d. of Sir R. Green Price, Bart. Educ. at Eton Coll. A J.P. and Dept.-Lieut. for the N. Riding of Yorkshire, and J.P. and Lord Lieut. for Radnorshire. A Conservative. Sat for Radnorshire from July 1895 until he retired in 1900. Succeeded as Bart. in 1898. Died 30 Jan. 1918.   [1900]

MILDMAY, Rt. Hon. Francis Bingham. Continued in House after 1918: full entry in Volume III.

MILLAR, James Duncan. Continued in House after 1918: full entry in Volume III.

MILLS, Hon. Arthur Robert. Vernon House, St. James's London. 3rd s. and heir of Lord Hillingdon. B. 1891 in London; m. 1916, d. of Visct. Chelsea. Educ. at Eton, and Magdalen Coll., Oxford. Lieut. W. Kent Yeomanry. A Unionist. Elected for the Uxbridge division of Middlesex in Nov. 1915 and sat until he retired in 1918. Succeeded as 3rd Baron Hillingdon 6 Apr. 1919. Chairman of the Marine Insurance Company. Died 5 Dec. 1952.   [1918]

MILLS, Hon. Charles Thomas. Vernon House, Park Place. St. James's, London. Hillingdon Court, Uxbridge. Carlton, and Turf. Eld. s. of Lord Hillingdon. B. 13 Mar. 1887 in London. Educ. at Eton, and Magdalen Coll., Oxford; B.A. A Partner in Glyn Mills and Company, Bankers. A Lieut. W. Kent Yeomanry. J.P. and Co. Alderman for Middlesex. A Unionist. Elected for the Uxbridge division of Middlesex in Jan. 1910 and sat until he was killed in action on 6 Oct. 1915.   [1915]

MILLS, Charles William. Camelford House, Park Lane, London. Wildernesse Park, Sevenoaks. Eld. s. of Sir Charles Henry Mills, Bart., 1st Baron Hillingdon. Banker, who was MP for Kent W. from 1868 to 1880, and previously for Northallerton, by Lady Louisa Isabella, eld. d. of the 3rd Earl of Harewood. B. 1855. Educ. at Eton. A Partner in the eminent Banking firm of Glyn, Mills, and Company. A Conservative. Sat for the Sevenoaks division of Kent from 1885 until he retired in 1892. Succeeded as 2nd Baron Hillingdon in 1898. Died 6 Apr. 1919.   [1892]

MILNER, Rt. Hon. Sir Frederick George, Bart. 11 Hereford Gardens, London. Carlton, and Bachelors'. 2nd s. of Sir

William Mordaunt Edward Milner (5th Bart.), MP for Yorkshire, and Lady Anne Georgina, sister of the 9th Earl of Scarborough. B. at Nun-Appleton 1849; m. 1880, Adeline Gertrude, d. of W. Beckett, Esq., (formerly Denison), the Member for Nottinghamshire (she died 1902). Educ. at Eton, and Christ Church, Oxford. A J.P. and Dept.-Lieut. for the W. Riding of Yorkshire. Succeeded as Bart. in 1880. A Conservative, "a strong supporter of Tariff Reform, and of the Unionist Government, a determined opponent of Home Rule for Ireland, Wales, and Scotland"; in favour of Boards of Conciliation for the settlement of labour disputes, and of a stringent reform of the poor laws. Was MP for York city from Nov. 1883 to Nov. 1885; unsuccessfully contested York city at the general election in Nov. 1885, Sowerby division of the W. Riding of Yorkshire Dec. 1885, and the Radcliffe-cum-Farnworth division of S.E. Lancashire July 1886. Sat for the Bassetlaw division of Nottinghamshire from Dec. 1890 until defeated in 1906. PC. 1900; G.C.V.O. 1930. Died 8 June 1931.   [1905]

MILNES-GASKELL, Charles George. See GASKELL, Charles George Milnes.

MILTON, William Charles de Meuron Wentworth-Fitzwilliam, Visct. Wentworth Woodhouse, Rotherham. Carnew Castle, Carnew, Wicklow. Bachelors', and Pratt's. Eld. s. of Visct. Milton (and grands. of Earl Fitzwilliam), by Laura Maria, eld. d. of Lord Charles Beauclerk. B. 1872; m. 1896, Maud Frederica, d. of the Marq. of Zetland. Educ. at Eton, and Trinity Coll., Cambridge. Was Aide-de-Camp to the Marq. of Lansdowne as Viceroy of India, and Capt. 4th Battalion Oxford Light Infantry. Served in S. Africa 1900. A J.P. for the W. Riding of Yorkshire and J.P. and County Councillor for Co. Wicklow. A Liberal Unionist. Sat for Wakefield from July 1895 until he succeeded as Earl Fitzwilliam in 1902. Served in Army 1914-15. Travelled greatly in Europe and India. Died 15 Feb. 1943.   [1901]

MILVAIN, Thomas. 17 Rutland Gate, London. 3 Plowden Buildings, Temple, London. Carlton, St. Stephen's, New University, and Hurlingham. S. of Henry Milvain, Esq., of Newcastle-on-Tyne, and Jane Aitken, d. of E. Davidson, Esq., of Newcastle-on-Tyne. B. 1844 at Newcastle-

on-Tyne; m. 1875, Mary Alice, d. of John Henderson, Esq., of Durham. Educ. at Durham Grammar School, and Trinity Hall, Cambridge; LL.B. 1866, LL.M. 1871. A Barrister-at-Law, called 1869; Q.C. 1888. Bencher of Middle Temple 1893; Chancellor of the Co. Palatine of Durham and Recorder of Bradford from 1892. Was Chairman of the S. African Compensation Commission 1901. A Conservative. Sat for Durham from 1885-92, when he was defeated. Unsuccessfully contested the Cockermouth division of Cumberland in 1895 and Maidstone in 1901. Elected for Hampstead in Jan. 1902 and sat until he accepted Chiltern Hundreds on appointment as Judge Advocate Gen. in Aug. 1905. C.B. 1912; Kt. 1913. Died 23 Sept. 1916.   [1905]

MILWARD, Col. Victor. Wellesbourn Hall, Warwick. Carlton, and Constitutional. S. of Henry Milward, Esq., J.P. of The Poplars, Redditch, and Catherine, d. of John Gosling, Esq. B. 1840 at The Poplars, Redditch; m. 1867, Eliza, d. of James Tomson, Esq., of Barnt Green. Educ. privately. A Director of Henry Milward and Sons Limited, and of the Metropolitan Assurance Society; J.P. and Dept.-Lieut. for the Co. of Worcester (High Sheriff 1886); a J.P. Co. Warwick, Lieut.-Col., and Honorary Col. 2nd Volunteer Battalion Worcestershire Regiment 1887-95, and had the Volunteer Decoration. A Conservative. Sat for the Stratford-on-Avon division of Warwickshire from July 1895 until his death 31 May 1901.   [1901]

MINCH, Matthew Joseph. Rockfield House, Athy, Co. Kildare. B. 1857. Educ. at French Coll., Blackrock, Dublin. A Merchant and a Town Commissioner and Chairman of the Board of Guardians, Athy; also J.P. for Kildare and Queen's counties. An Irish Nationalist, and Anti-Parnellite. Sat for Kildare S. from 1892 until he accepted Chiltern Hundreds in May 1903.   [1903]

MITCHELL, Edward. Derryvullen. Enniskillen. S. of William and Jane Mitchell. B. at Dovederney, Co. Fermanagh 1859; m. 1887, d. of Mr. Wadsworth, of Fermanagh. Educ. at Fivemiletown School, and privately. A Gentleman Farmer, Grazier, and Stockbreeder, owning over 1,000 acres in the counties of Meath and Fermanagh. A Liberal Unionist, in favour of Compulsory Land Purchase, but joined the Liberals in Feb. 1904. Elected as an Independent Conservative for N. Fermanagh in Mar. 1903 but joined the Liberals in Feb. 1904. Defeated in 1906. [1905]

MITCHELL, William. Fern Hill, Stacksteads, Rossendale. Carlton. Eld. s. of John Mitchell, Esq., of Waterfoot, Lancashire. B. 1838; m. 1876, d. of Robert Munn, Esq., of Heathhill, Lancashire. Educ. at the Burnley Grammar School, and at Upper School of the Liverpool Collegiate Institution. J.P. for Lancashire. A Conservative. Unsuccessfully contested the Accrington division of Lancashire in 1895 and the Middleton division of Lancashire in 1897. Elected for Burnley in 1900 and sat until he retired in 1906. Died 5 Mar. 1914. [1905]

MITCHELL, William Foot. Continued in House after 1918: full entry in Volume III.

MITCHELL-THOMSON, Sir William, Bart., K.B.E. Continued in House after 1918: full entry in Volume III.

MOLESWORTH, Sir Lewis William, Bart. 3 Great Cumberland Place, Hyde Park, London. Trewarthenick, Grampound Road, Cornwall. Turf, Brooks's, and Reform. S. of Sir Paul William Molesworth, 10th Bart., and Jane Frances, eld. d. of Gordon William Francis Gregor, Esq., of Trewarthenick, Grampound Road, Cornwall. B. 1853 at Trewarthenick; m. 1875, Jane Graham, 2nd d. of Brig.-Gen. D.M. Frost, U.S. Army. Educ. privately. Succeeded as Bart. in 1889. A J.P. and Dept.-Lieut. for Cornwall; High Sheriff 1899. A Liberal Unionist. Unsuccessfully contested Cornwall N.E. in July 1892. Elected for the Bodmin division of Cornwall in 1900 and sat until he retired in 1906. Died 29 May 1912. [1905]

MOLLOY, Bernard Charles. Queen Anne's Mansions, London. 4 Paper Buildings, Temple, London. National Liberal. S. of Kedo Molloy, Esq., of Cornolaur, King's Co., by Maria Theresa, d. of James Tracy Lynam, Esq. B. 1842. Educ. at St. Edmund's Coll., Hertfordshire, and in Germany and France. Was called to the bar at the Middle Temple 1872. Held a Capt's. commission, and was Aide-de-Camp in the French army, and Private Chamberlain at the Court of the Vatican. A Liberal, in favour of "Home Rule" for Ireland. Unsuccessfully contested King's Co. in Feb. 1874 and Co. Louth in Apr. 1874. Returned for King's Co. in 1880 and sat until 1885; he was then elected for the Birr division of King's Co. and sat until defeated in 1900. Died 26 June 1916. [1900]

MOLLOY, Michael. Carlow, Ireland. B. 1850 at Straboe, Co. Carlow; m. 1880, d. of J. Lalor, Esq. Educ. at Grange School, Carlow, and privately. Was in business in Carlow. Was eight times elected Chairman of Carlow Urban District Council; a J.P., County Councillor, and member of Poor Law Board of Guardians, Carlow. A Nationalist. First elected for Carlow in Jan. 1910 and sat until he retired in 1918. [1918]

MOLTENO, Percy Alport. 10 Palace Court, London. Parklands, Shere, Guildford. Glenlyon, Fortingal, Perthshire. Reform, National Liberal, Royal Automobile, and City of London. S. of Sir John Charles Molteno, 1st Premier of Cape Colony, and Elizabeth Maria, d. of H.C. Jarvis, Esq., M.C.L. B. 1861 at Edinburgh; m. Elizabeth Martin, d. of Sir Donald Currie. Educ. at Cape University, and Trinity Coll., Cambridge: M.A., LL.M. Called to the bar at the Inner Temple 1886. Author of *Life and Times of Sir J.C. Molteno*, and *A Federal South Africa*. A Liberal. Elected for Dumfriesshire in 1906 and sat until defeated in 1918. Unsuccessfully contested Kinross and W. Perthshire in 1923. One of the founders of The Royal Institute of International Affairs. Died 19 Sept. 1937. [1918]

MONCKTON, Edward Philip. Queen Anne's Mansions, London. Lamb Buildings, Temple, London. Fineshade Abbey, Nr. Stamford. Laundimer House, Oundle. Carlton, and Junior Carlton. S. of E.H.C. Monckton, Esq., of the East India Company, and Maria Catherine, d. of H. Tydd, Esq. B. 1840 at Bareilly, India; m. 1866, Christabel, d. of the Rev. C.D. Francis (she died 1899). Educ. at private schools, and Trinity Coll., Cambridge. A Barrister called to the bar at the Inner Temple 1868, and joined the Midland Circuit. Recorder of Northampton. A J.P. and County Councillor for Northamptonshire, a J.P. for Rutland (Sheriff 1883-84) and Liberty of Peterborough, and wrote handbooks on legal subjects. A Conservative and Unionist. Sat for Northamptonshire N. from July 1895 until he retired in 1900. Chairman of Peterborough Quarter Sessions. Recorder of Northampton 1900-16. F.S.A. Died 17 Apr. 1916.   [1900]

MOND, Rt. Hon. Sir Alfred Moritz, Bart. Continued in House after 1918: full entry in Volume III.

MONEY, Sir Leo George Chiozza. The Grey House, Hampstead Lane, London. S. of Joseph Chiozza, Esq., and Fawnia, d. of Edward Allwright, Esq. B. 1870 at Genoa; m. 1892, Gwendolen, d. of George Elliott Stevenson, Esq. Educ. privately. An author and contributer to the leading newspapers and reviews on economical, social, scientific, and political questions; a Fellow of the Royal Statistical Society. Knighted 1915. Member of the Home Work Committee 1907-08. Parliamentary Private Secretary (unpaid) to Mr. Lloyd George when Minister of Munitions 1915. Lieut. R.N.V.R.; member of Restriction of Enemy Supplies Committee 1914-15; Retrenchment Committee 1915; War Trade Advisory Committee from 1915; Parliamentary Secretary to the Ministry of Shipping from Dec. 1916 to Jan. 1919. Author of *British Trade and the Zollverein Issue, Elements of the Fiscal Problem, Riches and Poverty, Things that Matter, Money's Fiscal Dictionary, Insurance v. Poverty, The Future of Work, The Nation's Wealth,* etc. Changed his name in 1903 from Leone Giorgio Chiozza to Leo George Chiozza Money. A Liberal and Collectivist. Sat for N. Paddington from 1906 to Jan. 1910, when he was defeated. Elected for E. Northamptonshire in Dec. 1910 and sat until defeated in 1918 standing as Labour candidate for S. Tottenham. Unsuccessfully contested Stockport 27 Mar. 1920, also as a Labour candidate. Member of Royal Commission on Coal Industry 1919; one of the Editors of 14th (1929) edition of *Encyclopaedia Britannica.* Died 25 Sept. 1944.   [1918]

MONK, Charles James. 5 Buckingham Gate, London. Bedwell Park, Hatfield, Hertfordshire. Travellers', and Turf. S. of the Rt. Rev. J.H. Monk, D.D. Bishop of Gloucester and Bristol 1830-36, by Jane, only d. of the Rev. Hugh Hughes, of Nuneaton, Warwickshire. B. 1824 at Peterborough; m. 1853, Julia, d. of P.S. Ralli, Esq., Consul-Gen. of Greece (she died

1870). Educ. at Eton, and Trinity Coll., Cambridge (Sir W. Browne's medallist 1845, Members' Prizeman 1846 and 1847, B.A. with honours 1847, M.A. 1850). Called to the bar, Lincoln's Inn 1850; a J.P. and Dept.-Lieut. for Gloucestershire; Director Suez Canal from 1884; Chancellor of Bristol 1855-84, of Gloucester 1859-84; President Associated Chambers of Commerce 1881-84. A Liberal Unionist, offered a hearty support to the Government of Lord Salisbury. Contested Cricklade unsuccessfully in 1857. Was MP for Gloucester from Apr. 1859, but unseated on petition in Aug. 1859. Sat again 1865-85, then retired. Was an unsuccessful candidate in 1892. Returned again for Gloucester in July 1895 and sat until he retired in Oct. 1900. Died 10 Nov. 1900.   [1900]

MONTAGU, Rt. Hon. Edwin Samuel. Continued in House after 1918: full entry in Volume III.

MONTAGU, George Charles. Ladyham, Burford, Oxfordshire. Carlton, and Automobile. S. of Admiral the Hon. Victor Montagu (bro. to the Earl of Sandwich) and of Lady Agneta, d. of the 4th Earl of Hardwicke. B. in London 1874. Educ. at Winchester Coll., and Magdalen Coll., Oxford; took his degree in 1897. Was Private Secretary to the President of the Board of Agriculture 1898-1900, and to President of Local Government Board 1900-03. A Conservative. Elected for S. Huntingdonshire in 1900 and sat until he retired in 1906. Succeeded as 9th Earl of Sandwich 26 June 1916. Lord-Lieut. of Huntingdonshire 1922-46; Alderman and Chairman of the County Council 1933-46; Director Exchange Telegraph Company 1902-61; Chairman Central Prisoners of War Committee 1917-18. Trustee of Tate Gallery 1934-41; member of Committee of the British Council from 1946. Author. Died 15 June 1962.   [1905]

MONTAGU, Hon. John Walter Edward Douglas Scott-. See SCOTT-MONTAGU, Hon. John Walter Edward Douglas.

MONTAGU, Sir Samuel, Bart. 12 Kensington Palace Gardens, London. South Stoneham House, Hampshire. Reform, and National Liberal. S. of Louis Samuel, Esq., a Watchmaker and Silversmith of Liverpool, by his marriage with Miss

Henrietta Israel. B. 1832; m. 1862, Ellen, d. of Louis Cohen, Esq., of the London Stock Exchange. Educ. at the High School of the Liverpool Institute, and by private tuition. Assumed by Royal License the surname of Montagu, which had been conferred on him by his father, in lieu of his patronymic. In 1853 entered on the business of a Foreign Banker in London, and was head of the firm Samuel Montagu and Company, of Old Broad Street. Was made a Bart. in 1894 and assumed the name of Montagu Samuel-Montagu. Was intimately connected with the establishment of various synagogues and Jewish benevolent institutions, and in 1875 visited Jerusalem and afterwards various parts of Europe and America for philanthropic purposes. An advanced Liberal, in favour of "a truly representative second chamber", of manhood suffrage, of the extension of the Parliamentary franchise to women, and of self-government in Ireland. Sat for the Whitechapel division of Tower Hamlets from Nov. 1885 until he retired in 1900 and unsuccessfully contested Leeds central at the same time. Created Baron Swaythling in June 1907. Died 12 Jan. 1911.   [1900]

MONTAGUE-BARLOW, Rt. Hon. Sir Clement Anderson, Bart., K.B.E. Continued in House after 1918: full entry in Volume III.

MONTGOMERY, Henry Greville. 2 Edinburgh Mansions, London. Bacton Lodge, Nr. North Walsham. National Liberal, and Savage. S. of Hugh Montgomery, Esq., and Elizabeth Longhurst. B. 15 Dec. 1863 in London; m. 1st, Florence, d. of C.M. Shepherd, Esq.; 2ndly, Emily, d. of D. Lewis, Esq. Educ. privately. A Newspaper Proprietor, Founder of the *British Clayworker*. Patron of 1 living. A Liberal, in favour of Nationalization of Railways and Canals, Electoral Reform, etc. Elected for the Bridgewater division of Somerset in 1906 and sat until he retired in Jan. 1910. Died 2 Dec. 1951.   [1909]

MOON, Edward Robert Pacy. 6 Onslow Gardens, London. Athenaeum, and Carlton. S. of Robert Moon, Esq., Barrister, of the Inner Temple and Princes Gardens, London, and Mary Jane, d. of Robert Pacy, Esq. B. 1858 in London; m. 1900. Frideswide, d. of the Hon. Mr. Justice

Kekewich. Educ. at Winchester Coll. (head of the school 1876-77), and New Coll., Oxford; M.A. 1884. Called to the bar at the Inner Temple 1884, and practised at the Chancery bar, also joined the N. Circuit. He travelled extensively, and specially studied the questions of the Near East and the Far East. Fellow of the Royal Colonial Institute and the Statistical Society, and a member of London Chamber of Commerce. A Progressive Conservative and Unionist. Unsuccessfully contested N. St. Pancras in 1892. First elected for this division in 1895 and sat until defeated in 1906. Poor Law Guardian for Kensington 1907-19; Kensington Borough Council 1913-31. Died 11 Sept. 1949.   [1905]

MOONEY, John Joseph. 11 Allen House, Allen Street, Kensington, London. National Liberal. S. of J.G. Mooney, Esq., Merchant, of Dublin. B. in Dublin 1874. Educ. at Ushaw Coll., Durham, and Trinity Coll., Dublin. Called to the Irish bar 1895, and English bar (Middle Temple) 1900. A Referee of Private Bills. A J.P. for Dublin Co. Treasurer of the Irish Party. A Nationalist. Sat for Dublin Co. S. from 1900-1906. Elected for Newry in 1906 and sat until he retired in 1918. Died 12 Apr. 1934.   [1918]

MOORE, Count Arthur John. 19 Grafton Street, Piccadilly, London. Aberlow Castle, Tipperary. S. of Charles Moore, Esq., of Mooresfort, Co. Tipperary, and MP for Tipperary from 1865 till his death in 1869, by Marian Elizabeth, d. of John Story, Esq., of Dublin. B. 1849; m. 1877, Mary Lucy, only d. of Sir Charles Clifford, of Hatherton, Staffordshire. Was a Chamberlain to the Pope previous to 1878, when he was High Sheriff, Tipperary. In 1879 created Count of the Holy Roman Empire. A Nationalist, in favour of Home Rule, etc. Was one of the original Home Rulers who brought forward the proposition with Mr. Isaac Butt in 1874. Sat for Clonmel 1874-85, when he retired. Contested Tipperary S. July 1895. Sat for Londonerry city from Feb. 1899 until defeated in 1900. Died 5 Jan. 1904.   [1900]

MOORE, Sir Newton James. Continued in House after 1918: full entry in Volume III.

MOORE, William. Moore Lodge, Kilrea, Co. Antrim. 3 Lower Merrion Street,

Dublin. Carlton. Eld. s. of William Moore, Esq., of Moore Lodge, Co. Antrim, J.P. B. 1864; m. 1888, Helen, 4th d. of Joseph Wilson, Esq., Dept.-Lieut., Co. Armagh. Educ. at Marlborough Coll., and Trinity Coll., Dublin; M.A., Vice-Chancellor's Prizeman, etc. A Dept.-Lieut. and J.P. for Co. Antrim. Was Private Secretary (unpaid) to Chief Secretary for Ireland 1903-04; was one of the founders of the Ulster Council. A member of the General Synod of the Disestablished Irish Church, and of Dio. Court, Down, Connor, and Dromore. Called to the Irish bar 1887, and at Lincoln's Inn 1899; a Q.C. (Ireland) 1899, bencher of King's Inns. Senior Crown Prosecutor, Belfast. A Unionist. Sat for N. Antrim from 1899-1906; when he was defeated at the general election. Elected for N. Armagh in Nov. 1906 and sat until appointed Irish High Court Judge 1917-21; PC. (Ireland) 1921; PC. (N. Ireland) 1922; Appeal Court of Northern Ireland 1921-25; Lord Chief Justice of Northern Ireland 1925-37; created Bart. 1932. Died 28 Nov. 1944. [1917]

MOORSOM, James Marshall. 14 Essex Villas, Phillimore Gardens, Kensington, London. Oxford & Cambridge. S. of Vice-Admiral C.R. Moorsom, eld. s. of Admiral Sir Robert Moorsom, K.C.B., who commanded the *Revenge* at Trafalgar, and Mary, eld. d. of Jacob Maude, Esq., of Selaby Park, Durham. B. 1837 at Edgbaston, Warwickshire: m. 1877, Emma Catherine, eld. d. of William Browne, Esq., of Tallantire Hall, Cumberland. Brought up at King Edward's School, Birmingham, and Trinity Coll., Cambridge. Called to the bar 1863; a Q.C. 1885; elected a bencher, Inner Temple 1892. A Liberal, in favour of Home Rule for Ireland, reform in the land of liquor laws, and of the House of Lords, etc., and of "absolute religious equality and enlightened political freedom." Sat for Great Yarmouth from July 1892 until defeated in 1895. Died 26 Mar. 1918. [1895]

MORE, Robert Jasper. 19 Gerald Road, London. Linley, Bishop's Castle, Shropshire. Larden Cottage, Much Wenlock. Brooks's, and Oxford & Cambridge. Only s. of the Rev. T.F. More, J.P., of Linley Hall, Shropshire, by Harriott Mary More, of Larden. B. at Corsley 1836; m. 1871, Evaline Frances, d. of the Rev. Canon Carr, of St. Helen's. Educ. at

Shrewsbury, and Balliol Coll., Oxford (M.A. and B.C.L. 1862). Was called to the bar at Lincoln's Inn 1863. A Magistrate and Dept.-Lieut., and in 1881 was High Sheriff, of Shropshire; a Magistrate for Montgomeryshire and the borough of Wenlock, and Lord of the Manor of Linley. Author of *Under the Balkans*, and of numerous pamphlets. Patron of 3 livings. A Liberal Unionist. Was MP for S. Shropshire from 1865 until defeated in 1868. Unsuccessfully contested S. Shropshire again in 1880. Sat for the Ludlow division of Shropshire from 1885 until his death 25 Nov. 1903. [1903]

MORGAN, David John. Bentley Mill, Brentwood. Carlton, and City of London. S. of David Thomas Morgan, of Whipp's Cross, and Mary, d. of Col. Ridge. B. at Leytonstone in 1844; m. 1867, Emily, d. of A. Bigland, Esq. Educ. at Forest School, Walthamstow, and Vevey, Switzerland. A Russian Merchant, Chairman of Surrey Commercial Docks and Northampton Brewery Company; a J.P. for Essex, and Alderman of the County Council for Essex, a Dept.-Lieut. for the City of London, Chairman of City of London Club, and Verderer of Epping Forest. A Conservative. Elected for the Walthamstow division of Essex in 1900 and sat until he retired in 1906. Died 28 Feb. 1918. [1905]

MORGAN, Hon. Frederic Courtenay. Ruperra Castle, Newport, Monmouthshire. Carlton, and Army & Navy. 3rd s. of the 1st Baron Tredegar, by Rosamond, d. of Gen. Godfrey Basil Mundy. B. at Brighton 1834; m. 1858, Charlotte Anne, d. of Charles A. Williamson, Esq., and sister of David Williamson, Esq., of Lawers, Perthshire. Educ. at Winchester. Capt. Rifle Brigade; served through the Crimean War, and had a medal and four clasps; also Medjidieh Turkish Medal; Honorary Col. 2nd Battalion S. Wales Borderers. A Conservative. Sat for Monmouthshire from 1874 to 1885, and for the S. division from 1885 until he retired in 1906. Died 8 Jan. 1909. [1905]

MORGAN, George Hay. 15 Hamilton Terrace, St. John's Wood, London. 4 Harcourt Buildings, Temple, London. Reform. S. of Walter Morgan, Esq., of Hay, Brecon. B. 1866; m. Margaret, d. of Henry Lewis, Esq., J.P., of Pontnewynydd, Monmouthshire. Educ. at University Coll.,

Cardiff, and University Coll., London; B.Sc. 1894. A Barrister, called to the bar at the Inner Temple 1899. K.C. 1913. A Liberal. Unsuccessfully contested Tottenham in 1900. Elected for the Truro division of Cornwall in 1906 and sat until defeated in Ipswich in 1918. Unsuccessfully contested Abertillery division of Monmouthshire as a Coalition Liberal in Dec. 1920, Penryn and Falmouth as a Lloyd George Liberal in 1922 and W. Salford as a Liberal in 1923. Died 24 Jan. 1931. [1918]

MORGAN, Rt. Hon. Sir George Osborne, Bart. 24 Draycott Place, London. Athenaeum, and Devonshire. Eld. s. of the Rev. Morgan Morgan, Vicar of Conway, Carnarvonshire. B. 1826; m. 1856, Emily, 2nd d. of Leopold Reiss, Esq., of Broom House, Eccles. Educ. at Friar's School, Bangor, afterwards at Shrewsbury School, and at Balliol Coll., Oxford, graduated 1st class in classics, obtained the Newdigate prize for English Verse and the Chancellor's prize for English Essay, gained the Craven University Scholarship while still at school, and afterwards the Eldon Law Scholarship, and Stowell Civil Law Fellowship. Called to the bar in 1853 at Lincoln's Inn, of which he was a bencher, and in 1890 was Treasurer; made a Queen's Counsel 1869, and a PC. 1880. Judge Advocate-Gen. Apr. 1880 to June 1885, and Parliamentary Secretary to the Colonial Office Jan. to July 1886. Created Bart. Aug. 1892. A J.P. for Denbighshire; was the first Vice-President of the University Coll. of N. Wales; and was Chairman of the Standing Committee on Bills on Law, Trade, from 1888 to 1895. Elected Chairman of the Parliamentary Association of Welsh Liberals in 1894. Author of a work on *Chancery Practice*, and other legal books, as well as several political pamphlets. A Liberal and Home Ruler. Amongst other measures he carried through the House of Commons the Burials Bill of 1880, the Married Women's Property Bill 1882, and the Act for Abolishing Corporal Punishment in the Army. Sat for Denbighshire from Dec. 1868 to 1885, and for the E. division from 1885 until his death 25 Aug. 1897. [1897]

MORGAN, John Lloyd. 105 Pall Mall, London. 4 Harcourt Buildings, Temple, London. Reform, and Oxford & Cambridge. S. of the Rev. William Morgan, Professor of Theology, Presby-

terian Coll., Carmarthen, and Margaret, d. of Thomas Rees, Esq. B. 1861 at Carmarthen. Educ. at Tettenhall Coll., Wolverhampton, and Trinity Hall, Cambridge; B.A. A Barrister-at-Law, called to the bar at the Inner Temple 1884; K.C. 1906. Recorder of Swansea from 1908. A Liberal. First elected for Carmarthenshire W. in July 1889 and sat until appointed County Court Judge for Carmarthen Nov. 1910-26. Died 17 May 1944. [1910]

MORGAN, Octavius Vaughan. Church Street, Battersea. Ross House, 13 The Boltons, South Kensington, London. Albermarle, Devonshire, and Junior Athenaeum. S. of Thomas Morgan, Esq., of Glasbury, Breconshire, by Marianne, d. of William Vaughan, Esq., of Brecon. B. 1837; m. 1867, Katharine Ann, d. of Henry Simkin, Esq., of Highbury. Educ. at Abergavenny. At 21 he became a Partner with his brothers in the firm of Morgan Brothers, Merchants and Bankers, of Cannon Street, and subsequently in the Crucible Company of Battersea. An extensive traveller, having visited various portions of Europe, Asia, Australia, and the continent of America. Was one of the founders of the *European Mail*. A J.P. for London and Surrey; a Fellow of the Statistical Society, of the Royal Colonial Institute and a member of the Imperial Federation League, and of the Municipal Reform League. A Liberal and Home Ruler, in favour of the substitution of a chamber chiefly elective for the House of Lords, of imperial federation, and of continuity of action in foreign affairs; also of Municipal Reform and "Local Option." Sat for the Battersea division of Battersea and Clapham from Nov. 1885 until he unsuccessfully contested Ashton-under-Lyne in July 1892. Died 26 Feb. 1896. [1892]

MORGAN, William Pritchard. 1 Queen Victoria Street, London. National Liberal. B. 1844 in South Wales. Entered his profession as a Solicitor in Newport, Monmouthshire about 1865. Went to Queensland in 1867 and there interested himself in Mining, in addition to practising his profession. He returned home in 1885, and discovering gold at Dolgelly in N. Wales, formed a company for turning this discovery to account. Also interested in gold mining in China. A "Liberal to the backbone", in favour of an extended system of Local Government or Home Rule not only for Ireland, but Scotland and Wales, disestablishment, etc. First elected for Merthyr Tydvil Oct. 1888 and sat until defeated in 1900. Died 5 July 1924. [1900]

MORISON, Hector. National Liberal. S. of John Morison, Esq., Calico Printer. B. 1850 at Alexandria, Dumbartonshire; m. 1876, Josephine, d. of Joseph Ashton, Esq., of Manchester. Educ. at the Academy, and University, Glasgow. A member of the Stock Exchange. J.P. for Surrey. A Liberal. Unsuccessfully contested the Lewes division of Sussex in 1906, and Eastbourne division of Sussex in Jan. and Dec. 1910. Elected for S. Hackney in May 1912 and sat until he retired in 1918. Died 4 June 1939. [1918]

MORISON, Thomas Brash. Continued in House after 1918: full entry in Volume III.

MORLEY, Rt. Hon. Arnold. 7 Stratton Street, Piccadilly, London. Brooks's, and Reform. S. of Samuel Morley, Esq., former MP for Bristol, etc., of Hall Place, Tunbridge, Kent, by Rebecca Maria, d. of Samuel Hope, Esq., of Liverpool. B. 1849. Educ. at Trinity Coll., Cambridge, where he graduated B.A. 1871, M.A. 1874. Called to the bar at the Inner Temple Nov. 1873. Appointed Patronage Secretary to the Treasury (an office to which was attached that of chief "Whip") Jan. 1886; Opposition Chief Whip 1886-92; Postmaster-Gen. 1892-95 and PC. 1892. A Liberal and Home Ruler. Sat for Nottingham from May 1880 to Nov. 1885, and for Nottingham E. from Nov. 1885 until defeated in 1895. Chairman of Dominions Commission 1912. Died 16 Jan. 1916. [1895]

MORLEY, Charles. 46 Bryanston Square, London. Shockerwick House, Bath. Brooks's, Reform, Travellers', and Athenaeum. 3rd s. of Samuel Morley, Esq., for many years MP for Bristol, by Rebecca Maria, d. of Samuel Hope, Esq., of Liverpool. Bro. of the Rt. Hon. Arnold Morley, at one time Postmaster-Gen. B. 1847. Educ. at Trinity Coll., Cambridge; B.A. 1870, M.A. 1874. A Director of the Holborn Viaduct Land Company, and Honorary Secretary of the Royal Coll. of Music. A Liberal. Was an unsuccessful candidate for E. Somerset in 1892. Sat for Breconshire from 1895 until he retired in 1906. Died 27 Oct. 1917. [1905]

MORLEY, Rt. Hon. John. Flowermead, Wimbledon Park, London. Athenaeum. S. of J. Morley, Esq., Sugeon, of Blackburn. B. at Blackburn 1838. Educ. at Cheltenham Coll., and Lincoln Coll., Oxford; graduated M.A. 1873. Called to the bar at Lincoln's Inn in 1873, but never practised. Was elected a bencher of his Inn 1893. F.R.S., Honorary D.C.L., Oxford, Honorary LL.D. of Cambridge, Edinburgh, St. Andrews, and Glasgow Universities, and a Trustee of the British Museum. Member of Royal Historical MSS Commission, and Honorary Professor of Ancient Literature in Royal Academy of Arts. Author of various works, including: *Life of Gladstone, Life of Cobden, Edmund Burke, Voltaire,* and *Oliver Cromwell.* PC. 1886. In Mr. Gladstone's 3rd administration, Jan. 1886, he was appointed Chief Secretary for Ireland, which post he held to July 1886; re-appointed Aug. 1892, but resigned with the Rosebery Ministry, June 1895. Secretary of State for India, Dec. 1905 to Nov. 1910. Received the Order of Merit 1902; Honorary Fellow of All Souls Coll., Oxford 1903. A Liberal, in favour of Home Rule in Ireland, etc. Unsuccessfully contested Blackburn in Mar. 1869 and Westminster in 1880; sat for Newcastle-on-Tyne from 1883 to 1895, when he was defeated. Elected for the Montrose district in 1896 and sat until created Visct. Morley of Blackburn in 1908. Chancellor of Manchester University from 1908. Lord President of the Council Nov. 1910-14; resigned from the Cabinet as a result of the declaration of War in Aug. 1914. Died 23 Sept. 1923. [1908]

MORPETH, Charles James Stanley Howard, Visct. Calthwaite Hall, Carlisle. 105 Eaton Place, London. Brooks's, and Travellers'. Eld. s. of the Earl of Carlisle and Rosalind, d. of 2nd Lord Stanley of Alderley. B. 8 Mar. 1867; m. 1894, Rhoda Ankaret, d. of Col. Paget L'Estrange. Educ. at Rugby, and Balliol Coll., Oxford. Capt. 3rd Battalion (M.) Border Regiment, and Capt. 5th Battalion Rifle Brigade. Served in South African War 1902. A J.P., Dept.-Lieut. and Co. Alderman for Cumberland; a member of the London School Board. A Unionist. Unsuccessfully contested Chester-le-Street in 1895, Hexham in 1900, and Gateshead in Jan. 1904. Elected for S. Birmingham in Feb. 1904 and sat until he succeeded as Earl of Carlisle 16 Apr. 1911. One of the Unionist

Whips in the House of Commons until 1911. Died 20 Jan. 1912. [1911]

MORRELL, George Herbert. Headington Hill Hall, Oxford. Streatley House, Nr. Reading. Carlton, Junior Carlton, and New University. S. of the Rev. George Kidd Morrell, D.C.L., Vicar of Moulsford, Berkshire, and his wife, Anna Letitia, d. of David Powell, Esq., of Loughton, Essex. B. 1845 at Adderbury, Oxfordshire; m. 1874, Emily Alicia, only child of James Morrell, Esq., of Headington Hill. Educ. at Rugby, and Exeter Coll., Oxford; M.A. and B.C.L., 2nd class Natural Science 1867. Called to the bar at the Inner Temple 1871, and was a member of the Oxford Circuit. A J.P. for Berkshire and Oxfordshire; Dept.-Lieut. for Oxfordshire; High Sheriff 1885, and Alderman for the County Council, Oxfordshire, and Lieut.-Col. and Honorary Col. V.D. Oxford University Volunteers 1879-97, (retired). Wrote *A Manual of Comparative Anatomy and Guide to Dissection.* A Conservative, opposed to a separate Parliament for Ireland, but in favour of a "a measure of local self-government for that island." In favour also of social legislation, cheap and easy transfer of land, Old Age Pensions, etc., and opposed to disestablishment, etc. Sat for the Woodstock division of Oxfordshire from 1891-92, when he was defeated; re-elected there in 1895 and sat until defeated in Jan. 1906. Died 30 Sept. 1906. [1905]

MORRELL, Philip Edward. 44 Bedford Square, London. Garsington Manor, Nr. Oxford. Savile. S. of Frederick Parker Morrell, Esq., of Black Hall, Oxford, and Harriette Anne, d. of Philip Wynter, Esq., President of St. John's Coll., Oxford. B. 4 June 1870 at Oxford: m. 1902, Lady Ottoline Cavendish-Bentinck, sister of the Duke of Portland. Educ. at Eton, and Balliol Coll., Oxford; M.A. 1894. A member of the firm of Philpot and Morrell, Solicitors, London and Oxford. A Liberal. Sat for the Henley division of Oxfordshire from 1906 to Jan. 1910, when he was defeated. Elected for Burnley Dec. 1910 and sat until he retired in 1918. Died 5 Feb. 1943. [1918]

MORRIS, Hon. Martin Henry Fitzpatrick. 34 Grosvenor Place, London. Spiddal, Co. Galway. Wellington. Eld. s. of Michael Morris (Baron Morris and 1st Baron Killanin), by Anna, d. of the Hon. George Henry Hughes. B. 1867. Educ. at Trinity Coll., Dublin, where he obtained the gold medal for Composition given by the University Philosophical Society. Called to the English bar 1892; 1899 elected a County Councillor for Galway. A J.P. for Cavan and Galway, and was High Sheriff of Galway 1897. Author of *Transatlantic Traits*, etc. A Conservative. Unsuccessfully contested Galway city 1895. Returned for Galway city Oct. 1900 and sat until he succeeded as 2nd Baron Kilannin 8 Sept. 1901. Galway County Councillor 1899-1920. Member of Irish Agricultural Wages Board 1917-19. PC. 1920. Contributor to the *Nineteenth Century* and other magazines. Died 11 Aug. 1927. [1901]

MORRIS, Samuel. Newrath House, Waterford. National Liberal. S. of George Morris, Esq., Merchant, of Fiddown, Co. Kilkenny, and Catharine, d. of James Aylward, Esq. B. 1846 at Templeorum, Co. Kilkenny; m. Catharine, d. of James Feehan, Esq. Educ. at O'Shea's Grammar School, Carrick-on-Suir, and Dublin. A Merchant and Shipowner. J.P. for the counties of Tipperary and Waterford, and for the city of Waterford. An Anti-Parnellite. Elected for Kilkenny S. without opposition in 1894 and sat until he retired in 1900. Died Aug. 1920. [1900]

MORRISON, Hugh. Continued in House after 1918: full entry in Volume III.

MORRISON, Capt. James Archibald. Basildon Park, Reading. Carlton, White's, and Marlborough. S. of Alfred Morrison, Esq., of Hindon, Wiltshire. B. 18 Sept. 1873; m. 1901, Hon. Mary Trevor, d. of 1st Baron Trevor. Joined the Grenadier Guards in 1896, retired as Capt. Served in the Soudan 1898, and in South Africa 1900. A Unionist. Sat for the Wilton division of Wiltshire from July 1900 to 1906, when he was defeated. Elected for E. Nottingham in Jan. 1910 and sat until he accepted Chiltern Hundreds in 1912. Served in Europe 1914-16 (wounded). D.S.O. 1916. Died 27 Oct. 1934. [1912]

MORRISON, Walter. 77 Cromwell Road, London. Malham Tarn, Langcliffe, Settle. 5th s. of James Morrison, Esq., MP, of the City firm of Morrison, Dillon and Company, and Basildon Park, Berkshire, by Mary Anne, d. of John Todd, Esq., of

Todd, Morrison and Company. B. in London 1836. Educ. at Eton, and Balliol Coll., Oxford. A Magistrate for the W. Riding of Yorkshire; filled the office of Sheriff in 1883. Was Capt. of the 15th W. Riding Rifle Volunteers, and Lieut.-Col. commanding the 2nd Administrative W. Riding Volunteer Rifles. A Liberal Unionist, opposed to disestablishment, the late Local Veto Bill, and the abolition of the House of Lords. Sat for Plymouth from 1861 to 1874, when he was an unsuccessful candidate; also unsuccessful in the City of London 1880. Sat for the Skipton division of Yorkshire 1886-92, when he was defeated; again elected there 1895, and sat until defeated in 1900. Died 18 Dec. 1921.   [1900]

MORRISON-BELL, Arthur Clive. Continued in House after 1918: full entry in Volume III.

MORRISON-BELL, Lieut.-Col. Ernest Fitzroy. Pitt House, Chudleigh, Devon. 5 Cambridge Gate, Regent's Park, London. Carlton, Cavalry, and Royal Automobile. 3rd s. of Sir Charles Morrison-Bell, Bart. B. 19 Apr. 1871 in Durham; m. 1902, Maud Evelyn, d. of Col. F. Henry, of Elmestree, Tetbury. Educ. at Eton. Joined the 9th Lancers 1891, and retired as Capt. 1906; served in S. African War 1900, and was mentioned in despatches. Magistrate and Dept.-Lieut. for Gloucestershire. A Unionist. Unsuccessfully contested the Ashburton division of Devon in 1906; sat for the Ashburton division of Devon from Jan. 1908 to Jan. 1910, when he was defeated; re-elected there Dec. 1910, and sat until he retired in 1918. Served in Army Aug. 1914-July 1919. O.B.E. 1919. Died 20 Oct. 1960.   [1918]

MORROGH, John. 7 Pelham Place, South Kensington, London. Lee Villa, Sundays Well, Cork, National Liberal. S. of Dominick and Mary Morrogh. B. at Cork 1849; m. 1st 1878, Kate, d. of M. Kennedy, Esq., of Kimberley, South Africa (she died 1884); 2ndly, 1886, at Cork, Kate, d. of Joseph Griffin, Esq. Educ. at the School of the Christian Brothers, Cork. Mr. Morrogh was an early participator in the working of the famous Kimberley Diamond Mines, South Africa, and later a Director of the Consolidated Mines, De Beers, etc., of Kimberley. He was also engaged in Woollen Manufacture at Cork.

An Irish Nationalist (Anti-Parnellite). Sat for the S.E. division of Cork from June 1889 until he accepted Chiltern Hundreds in 1893. Died in 1901.   [1892]

MORSE, Levi Lapper. The Croft, Swindon. National Liberal, and Reform. S. of Charles Morse, Esq., of Stratton St. Margaret, Wiltshire. B. 1853 at Stratton St. Margaret; m. 1875, Winifred, d. of Isaac Humphries, Esq., of Broad Hinton, Wiltshire. Educ. at Swindon High School. A member of Swindon Town Council, a J.P. and C.A. for Wiltshire. A Liberal. Elected for the Wilton division of Wiltshire in 1906 and sat until he retired in Jan. 1910. Died 10 Sept. 1913.   [1909]

MORTON, Sir Alpheus Cleophas. 47 Gauden Road, Clapham, London. 124, Chancery Lane, London. National Liberal, and Scottish Liberal. S. of Francis Morton, Esq. B. 1840. Educ. privately in Canada. An Architect and Surveyor; a member of the Corporation of the City of London from 1882 (Dept. Alderman), of the City of London Board of Guardians, and of the City and Guilds of London Institute; a Lieut. of the City of London. Gov. of St. Bartholomew's Hospital, Chairman of Metropolitan Paving Committee. Knighted 1918. A Liberal, in favour of Land Law Reform, "One man, one vote", etc. Unsuccessfully contested Hythe in 1885, Christchurch in 1886, and Bath in 1900. Sat for Peterborough from 1889-95, when he was defeated. Elected for Sutherlandshire in 1906 and sat until he retired in 1918. Died 26 Apr. 1923. [1918]

MORTON, Arthur Henry Aylmer. 80 Eaton Place, London. Carlton, Athenaeum, Wellington, St. Stephen's, and Ranelagh. 2nd s. of Edward Morton, Esq., of Hyde Park Gate, Kensington Gore, by Harriet, d. of William Sainsbury, Esq., of Bath. B. in London 1836; m. 1903, Evelyn, d. of Sir W.H. Wilson-Todd, Bart., MP. Educ. at Eton, and was a Fellow of King's Coll., Cambridge, where he served as Senior Dean and Bursar. In 1895 he was elected on the London County Council, where he was Vice-Chairman of the Housing of the Working Classes Committee, and a member of the Technical Education Board. An Ecclesiastical Commissioner, appointed 1904. A Conservative, who would support measures calculated to ameliorate the conditions of life among the industrial classes. Unsuccessfully contested E. Leeds in 1892, and N. Manchester 1895. Sat for Deptford from 1897 until defeated in 1906. Died 15 June 1913. [1905]

MORTON, Edward John Chalmers. National Liberal. S. of John Chalmers Morton, Esq. B. 1856 at Moulsey, Surrey. Educ. at Harrow School, and St. John's Coll., Cambridge (B.A. 1880, M.A. 1883). A Barrister, called to the bar at the Inner Temple 1885, and a member of the N.E. Circuit. One of the University Extension Lecturers on Astronomy. Was one of the founders of the Home Rule Union, and was its Honorary Secretary. A Liberal, in favour of Home Rule, and the advanced Liberal programme generally. Sat for Devonport from July 1892 until his death 3 Oct. 1902. [1902]

MOSS, Richard. 49 George's Road, London. North Gate, Winchester. S. of Richard Moss, Esq., of London. B. 1823. A Brewer at Winchester, and Secretary to the Brewers' Association there. A Conservative. Sat for the city of Winchester from Apr. 1880 to 1885. He did not offer himself at the general election in the latter year, but was re-elected on the death of Col. Tottenham, Jan. 1888 and sat until he retired in 1892. High Steward of Winchester 1905. Died 2 Mar. 1905 [1892]

MOSS, Samuel. 3 (North) King's Bench Walk, Temple, London. 29 Eastgate Row, London. 50 Hough Green, Chester. National Liberal. 2nd s. of Enoch Moss, Esq., of Broad Oak, Rossett, N. Wales. B. 1858; m. 1895, Eleanor, d. of E.B. Samuel, Esq., of The Darland, near Wrexham. Educ. privately, and at Worcester Coll., Oxford; B.A. 2nd in Law 1878, B.C.L., 2nd in honours and M.A. 1880. A Barrister, called to the bar at Lincoln's Inn 1880, and joined the Chester and N. Wales Circuit. Author of *The English Land Laws* (1886). Was Assistant Boundary Commissioner in Wales under Lord E. Fitzmaurice in 1887; a member of the Denbighshire County Council, its Vice-Chairman for the first four years, afterwards Chairman for three years; a member of the Town Council of Chester. A Liberal, in favour of Home Rule, perfect religious equality, including disestablishment of the State Church, an Eight Hours Bill, "One Man One Vote", and reform of the House of Lords. Represented E. Denbighshire from 1897 until

appointed County Court Judge in July 1906. Died 14 May 1918. [1906]

MOULTON, Sir John Fletcher. 57 Onslow Square, London. Reform, and Garrick. S. of the Rev. James Egan Moulton, Wesleyan Minister, by Catherine, d. of S. Fiddian, Esq., of Birmingham, and bro. of Dr. Moulton, of Cambridge. B. at Madeley, Shropshire 1844; m. 1st, 1875, Clara, relict of R.W. Thompson, Esq., of Edinburgh (she died 1888); 2ndly, d. of Maj. Henry Davis, of Syracuse, New York. Educ. at New Kingswood School, Bath, and St. John's Coll., Cambridge; Matriculated at London University 1863; M.A. 1868. At Cambridge he became senior-wrangler and 1st Smith's prizeman, and subsequently a Fellow and Lecturer of Christ's Coll., Lecturer at Jesus Coll., and also President of the Union. Was called to the bar at the Middle Temple 1874, and obtained a large practice: became Q.C. in 1885. Member of Senate of London University 1898. For his researches in electrical science he was appointed F.R.S. Officer de la Légion d'Honneur. Wrote in advocacy of the Taxation of Ground Values, Old Age Pensions, etc. A Liberal, in favour of revision of taxation, including "betterment", the unification of London, restriction of the House of Lords, Technical Education, Local Option, etc. Sat for Clapham 1885, but was defeated there in the general election of 1886. Contested Nottingham S. in July 1892. Sat for S. Hackney from 1894-95, when he was defeated. First elected for the Launceston division of Cornwall in Aug. 1898 and sat until he retired in 1906. PC. 1906; Knighted 1906. Judge of Court of Appeal from 1906 to 1912. Created Baron Moulton (a Life Peerage) in 1912. Lord of Appeal in Ordinary 1912-21. K.C.B. 1915; G.B.E. 1917. Died 9 Mar. 1921. [1905]

MOUNT, William Arthur, C.B.E. Continued in House after 1918: full entry in Volume III.

MOUNT, William George. Wasing Place, Berkshire. Carlton. S. of W. Mount, Esq., J.P. and Dept.-Lieut. for Berkshire, and MP for Newport, Isle of Wight, by Charlotte, d. of G. Talbot, Esq., of Temple Guiting, Gloucestershire. B. 1824; m. 1862, Marianne Emily, d. of R. Clutterbuck, Esq., of Watford House, Hertfordshire. Educ. at Eton, and Balliol

Coll., Oxford. Chairman Standing Orders and Selection Committees; also Dept.-Lieut. for Berkshire, Chairman of the County Council for Berkshire, and Chairman of the Berkshire Quarter Sessions, having been a Magistrate for the Co. for 46 years. Patron of 1 living. A Conservative. Sat for the Newbury division of Berkshire from 1885 until he retired in 1900. Died 14 Jan. 1906.   [1900]

MOWBRAY, Rt. Hon. Sir John Robert, Bart. 47 Onslow Gardens, London. Warennes Wood, Mortimer, Reading. Carlton, and Oxford & Cambridge. S. of Robert Stribling Cornish, Esq., of Exeter. B. at Exeter 1815; m. 1847, Elizabeth Gray, only child of George Isaac Mowbray, Esq., of Bishopwearmouth, Co. Durham, and Mortimer, Berkshire, on which occasion he assumed the name of Mowbray in lieu of his patronymic. Educ. at Westminster and at Christ Church, Oxford, of which he was Honorary student; graduated M.A. 1839, and was created Honorary D.C.L. 1869. Called to the Bar at the Inner Temple 1841, and joined the W. Circuit. A Magistrate and Dept.-Lieut. of Durham, and a Magistrate and Co. Alderman of Berkshire. PC. 1858. Was Judge-Advocate-Gen. from Mar. 1858 till June 1859, and from July 1866 to Dec. 1868; and was Church Estates Commissioner from Aug. 1866 to Dec. 1868, and again from 1871 to 1892. Was Chairman Standing Orders and Selection Committees from 1874. Created Bart. in 1880. A Conservative. Sat for Durham city from June 1853 to Dec. 1868, and for the University of Oxford from Dec. 1868 until his death 22 Apr. 1899. Father of the House of Commons 1898-99.   [1899]

MOWBRAY, Sir Robert Gray Cornish, Bart. 10 Little Stanhope Street, Mayfair, London. Warennes Wood, Mortimer, Berkshire. Carlton, and Athenaeum. S. of the Rt. Hon. Sir J.R. Mowbray, Bart., MP for Oxford University, by Elizabeth, d. of G.I. Mowbray, Esq., of Bishopwearmouth, Co. Durham. B. in London 1850. Educ. at Eton, and Balliol Coll., Oxford; 1st class in classics 1872, and Fellow of All Souls 1873. Was called to the bar at the Inner Temple 1876, and joined the Oxford Circuit. A J.P. and Dept.-Lieut., and Vice-Chairman of Quarter Sessions for Berkshire. Was Secretary of the Royal Commission on the Stock Exchange 1876-77; Parliamentary Private

Secretary to Chancellor of the Exchequer 1887-92; Member of the Royal Commissions on Opium 1893-94, and Indian Expenditure 1896-1900. Succeeded as Bart. in 1899. A Conservative and Unionist. Unsuccessfully contested Whitby in 1880. Unsuccessfully contested the Prestwich division of Lancashire Dec. 1885. Sat for Prestwich division of Lancashire from 1886-95, when he was defeated. Elected for the Brixton division of Lambeth in Mar. 1900 and sat until he retired in 1906. Died 23 July 1916.   [1905]

MULDOON, John. 49 Jeffrey's Road, Clapham, London. Dunedin, Orwell Park, Dublin. S. of James Muldoon, Esq. B. 1865 at Dromore, Co. Tyrone; m. 1903, Olive, d. of James Whamond, Esq., of Westport. Educ. at local school, and Queen's Coll., Galway. A Barrister-at-Law, King's Inns, Dublin 1894. K.C. 1913. A Nationalist. Sat for N. Donegal from June to Jan. 1906, when he retired. Sat for E. Wicklow from 1907 to July 1911, when he was elected for E. Cork and sat until he retired in 1918. Died 20 Nov. 1938.   [1918]

MULHOLLAND, Hon. Henry Lyle. 7 Eaton Square, London. Ballywalter Park, Co. Down. Eld. s. of Lord Dunleath, by his m. with Frances Louisa, d. of Hugh Lyle, Esq. B. 1854; m. 1881, Norah Louisa Fanny, d. of the Hon. S.R.H. Ward, s. of the 3rd Visct. Bangor. Educ. at Eton, Royal Military Academy, Woolwich, and Balliol Coll., Oxford (B.A. with honours, 2nd class Modern History). Was Lieut. Royal Engineers 1873-78. A Conservative. Sat for Londonderry N. from 1885 until he retired in 1895. Succeeded as Baron Dunleath in 1895. Magistrate and Dept.-Lieut. for Co. Down. Died 22 Mar. 1931.   [1895]

MUNCASTER, Lord. 5 Carlton Gardens. Muncaster Castle, Ravenglass, Cumberland. Carlton, Army & Navy, and Marlborough. Josslyn Francis Pennington, 5th Baron Muncaster in the peerage of Ireland, and a Bart. of England (1676), was the 2nd s. of the 3rd Baron, by Frances, youngest d. of Sir John Ramsden, Bart. B. in London Dec. 1834; m. 1863, Constance Ann, 2nd d. of Edmund L'Estrange, of Tynte Lodge, Co. Antrim. Educ. at Hatfield School, and Eton. A Capt. in the Rifle Brigade, and the 90th Light Infantry; served in the Crimea, at the storming of the Redan, etc., and had the medal and clasp. Lord-Lieut. of Cumberland, and the Honorary Col. of the Cumberland Volunteers. Patron of 2 livings. Succeeded to Irish Peerage in 1862. A Conservative. Sat for Cumberland W. from 1872 to 1880, when he was defeated, and for the Egremont division of Cumberland from 1885 until defeated in 1892. Baron in U.K. peerage 1898. Died 30 Mar. 1917. [1892]

MUNDELLA, Rt. Hon. Anthony John. Elvaston Place, London. Reform, Savile, and Atheneaum. S. of Antonio Mundella, Esq., an Italian refugee, by Rebecca, d. of T. Alsopp, Esq., of Leicester. B. at Leicester 1825; m. 1844, Mary, d. of William Smith, Esq., of Kibworth-Beauchamp, Leicestershire (she died 1890). Was a Manufacturer at Nottingham, in which town he served the offices of Sheriff, Alderman, and J.P. Was J.P. for Middlesex; F.R.S. and F.S.S. Vice-President of the Committee of Council on Education from Apr. 1880 until June 1885; also a Charity Commissioner for England and Wales. PC. 1880. In Jan. 1886 he became President of the Board of Trade, with a seat in the Cabinet until July 1886; again appointed 1892; resigned May 1894. An advanced Liberal, in favour of Home Rule. Sat for Sheffield from Dec. 1868 to Nov. 1885, and for the Brightside division of Sheffield from Nov. 1885 until his death 21 July 1897. [1897]

MUNRO, Rt. Hon. Robert. Continued in House after 1918: full entry in Volume III.

MUNRO-FERGUSON, Rt. Hon. Ronald Craufurd. 46 Cadogan Square, London. Raith, Kirkcaldy. Novar, Ross-shire. Brooks's. Eld. s. of Col. Robert Munro Ferguson (at one time MP for Kirkcaldy), by Emma, d. of James Mandeville, Esq., of Merton, Surrey. B. 1860; m. 1889, Lady Helen Hermione Blackwood, d. of 1st Marq. of Dufferin and Ava. Educ. at Sandhurst. Was Private Secretary to Lord Rosebery 1886 and 1894. Vice-Lieut. of Fifeshire: Lieut. in the Grenadier Guards. A Lord of the Treasury and one of the Liberal "Whips" 1894-95. A Referee of Private Bills. Provost of Kirkcaldy from 1906; a Director of the North British and Mercantile Insurance Company. PC. 1910. A Liberal, in favour of Devolution. Sat for Ross and Cromatry from 1884 to Nov. 1885, when he was defeated. Unsuccessfully contested Dumbartonshire in July

1886. First elected for Leith Burghs Aug. 1886 and sat until appointed Gov.-Gen. of Australia 1914. G.C.M.G. 1914. Gov.-Gen. of Australia 1914-20. Created Visct. Novar in Nov. 1920. Secretary for Scotland in Conservative administrations 1922-24. Chairman of Political Honours Sorting Committee from 1925. K.T. 1926. Died 30 Mar. 1934. [1914]

MUNTZ, Sir Philip Albert, Bart. Dunsmore, Nr. Rugby. Carlton. S. of G.F. Muntz, Esq., of Umberslade, Warwickshire (who died 1857), by Eliza, d. of the Rev. John Pryce, of Dolforwyn Hall, Montgomery. B. 1839; m. 1859, Rosalie, d. of Philip Henry Muntz, Esq., MP, of Edstone Hall, Warwickshire. Dept.-Lieut. and J.P. for Warwickshire. Created Bart. 1902. A Conservative. Sat for N. Warwickshire from 1884-85, and for the Tamworth division of Warwickshire from 1885 until his death 21 Dec. 1908. [1908]

MUNTZ, Philip Henry. 34 Eaton Square, London. Somerset House, Leamington. Reform. S. of Philip Muntz, Esq., a French gentleman, who settled in Birmingham in 1793, by Catherine, d. of Robert Purdan, Esq., of Radford Hall, Warwickshire. Was bro. to George F. Muntz, Esq., who sat for Birmingham from 1840 till his death in 1857, and was a well-known politician in that town. B. at Selly Hall, Worcestershire 1811; m. 1831, Wilhelmine, d. of J. D'Olhofen, Esq., Counseiller de finance, Carlsruhe. Educ. at Shrewsbury and Heidelberg. A General Import and Export Merchant at Birmingham from 1832. Was Mayor of Birmingham 1839-41. A Magistrate for Warwickshire from 1845. A Radical, in favour of religious equality and the abolition of the law of primogeniture. Sat for Birmingham from Nov. 1868 until he retired in 1885. [1885]

MURDOCH, Charles Townshend. 12 Cadogan Gardens, London. Buckhurst, Wokingham. Carlton, and Junior United Service. S. of James Gordon Murdoch and Caroline Penelope Murdoch. B. 1837 at Frognal, Hampstead; m. Sophia, d. of William Speke, Esq., of Jordans, Ilminster. Educ. at Eton. Served in the Rifle Brigade, and a Partner in the Banking Firm of Barclay, Ransom and Company; a J.P. and Dept.-Lieut. for Buckinghamshire. Director of the Great Western Railway, Imperial Fire Insurance Company, London

Life Assurance, etc., and Chairman Great Northern Hospital. A Conservative. Sat for Reading from 1885 to 1892 when he was defeated. Re-elected July 1895 and sat until his death 8 July 1898.   [1898]

MURNAGHAN, George. Lisanelly House, Omagh, Co. Tyrone. S. of a Farmer of Omagh. B. 1847; m. 1877. Resided for some time in America but returned to Omagh to start a dairy and livestock farm. A Landowner, engaged in Agriculture and Dairying, and J.P. for Co. Tyrone. A member of the Poor Law Reform Commission in Ireland; also Chairman of the Omagh Union Board of Guardians, and of the Omagh Rural District Council. Vice-Chairman of Tyrone County Council. A Nationalist. Elected for the mid division of Tyrone in 1895 and sat until defeated as an Independent Nationalist in Jan. 1910. Member of Omagh Rural District Council 1899-1924. Died 13 Jan. 1929.   [1909]

MURPHY, John. Park Place, Killarney. S. of John Murphy, Esq., Sawyer, and Johanna, his wife. B. 1870; m. 1894, Annie, d. of Edward McCarthy, Esq., of Killarney. Educ. at the Presentation Monastery, Killarney. A member of the Kerry County Council, Killarney Urban Council and Asylum Committee. A Nationalist. Represented E. Kerry from 1900 until defeated in Jan. 1910. Died 17 Apr. 1930.   [1909]

MURPHY, Martin Joseph. Tramore, Co. Waterford. B. 1862. Educ. at St. Kieren's Coll., Kilkenny. Proprietor of Waterford and Tramore Race Course and Golf Links and Grand Hotel. High Sheriff of the City of Waterford 1889-90. J.P. for Co. Waterford. A Nationalist. Elected for E. Waterford in Feb. 1913 and sat until he retired in 1918. Died 4 Sept. 1919.   [1918]

MURPHY, Nicholas Joseph. Ballyhole, Co. Kilkenny. B. 1880. Educ. at St. Kieran's Coll., Kilkenny. A Merchant. A Nationalist. Elected for S. Kilkenny in July 1907 and sat until adjudicated a bankrupt 25 July 1908 and the seat declared vacant 15 July 1909. Unsuccessfully contested Kilkenny S. Dec. 1910. Died 27 Apr. 1913.   [1909]

MURPHY, William Martin. Dartry, Upper Rathmines, Co. Dublin. Bantry, Co. Cork. National Liberal. Leinster, Dublin.

Only s. of Denis William Murphy, Esq., of Bantry, Co. Cork. B. 1844; m. 1870, Mary Julia, only d. of James F. Lombard, Esq., J.P. of South Hill, Co. Dublin. Educ. at the Jesuits' Coll., Belvedere House, Dublin, and studied civil engineering with J.J. Lyons, of Dublin. Was largely engaged as a Contractor in the construction of railways and tramways. An Associate of the Institute of Civil Engineers in Dublin, and a J.P. for Co. Cork. A Director of the Waterford and Limerick Railway Company, and of the Belfast Tramways Company. An Anti-Parnellite Nationalist. Sat for the St. Patrick's division of Dublin from Nov. 1885 until defeated in 1892. Unsuccessfully contested Kerry S. in Sept. 1895 and Mayo N. in Oct. 1900. Presiding Dublin Chamber of Commerce 1912-13; Chairman of the Dublin United Tramways Company; and prominent in opposition to the strike of 1913 in Dublin. Founded in 1905 the *Irish Independent*, the country's cheapest daily morning newspaper. Died 26 June 1919.   [1892]

MURRAY, Rt. Hon. Alexander William Charles Oliphant (Master of Elibank). Elibank, Walkerburn, N.B. Brooks's, Bachelors', Marlborough, and Garrick. Eld. s. of Visct. Elibank, and Blanche Alice, eld. d. of E.J. Scott, Esq., of Southsea. B. 12 Apr. 1870; m. 1894, Hilda, youngest d. of James Wolfe Murray, Esq. Educ. at Cheltenham Coll. Styled Master of Elibank from 1871. A Lieut. Lothian Yeomanry. A J.P. and Dept.-Lieut. for Peeblesshire. Was Assistant Private Secretary to the Colonial Office 1892-95. Comptroller to H.M. Household and Scottish Liberal Whip, Dec. 1905 to June 1909, and Under-Secretary of State for India June 1909 to Feb. 1910, when he was appointed Parliamentary (Patronage) Secretary to the Treasury and Chief Liberal Whip; retired in Aug. 1912. PC. 1911. A Liberal. Unsuccessfully contested W. Edinburgh in May 1895, Peebles and Selkirk in July 1895, and York City in Feb. 1900. Sat for Midlothian from 1900-06, and Peebles and Selkirk from 1906 to Jan. 1910, when he was elected again for Midlothian. Sat there until he was created 1st Baron Murray of Elibank in 1912. Died 13 Sept. 1920.   [1912]

MURRAY, Rt. Hon. Andrew Graham. 10 Hanover Square, London. 7 Rothsay Terrace, Edinburgh. Stenton, Dunkeld. Carlton, and Wellington. S. of Thomas

Graham Murray, Esq., Writer to the Signet, of Stenton, Dunkeld, and Caroline Jane, d. of John Tod, Esq., of Kirkhill, Midlothian. B. 1849 in Edinburgh; m. 1874, Mary Clementina, d. of Admiral Sir William Edmonstone, Bart., of Duntreath, Stirlingshire. Educ. at Harrow, and Trinity Coll., Cambridge (scholar of Coll., B.A. 1872, M.A. 1874). Was called to the Scotch bar in 1874; Sheriff of Perthshire 1890-91; Q.C. 1891; Solicitor-Gen. for Scotland 1891-92, again 1895-96; Lord Advocate 1896-1903; a PC. 1896; appointed Secretary for Scotland Oct. 1903. A Conservative. Contested Perthshire E. Dec. 1885. Sat for Buteshire from Oct. 1891 until appointed Lord President of the Court of Session Feb. 1905, holding this office until 1913. Lord Appeal in Ordinary 1913-32. Created Baron Dunedin in 1905 and Visct. Dunedin in 1926. K.C.V.O. 1908; G.C.V.O. 1923. Died 21 Aug. 1942. [1904]

MURRAY, Hon. Arthur Cecil, D.S.O. Continued in House after 1918: full entry in Volume III.

MURRAY, Charles James. 41 Belgrave Square, London. Loch Carron, Ross-shire. Carlton, and St. James's. S. of the Rt. Hon. Sir Charles Murray, K.C.B., 2nd s. of the 5th Earl of Dunmore, and Elizabeth, d. of James Wadsworth, of Genesco, New York. B. 1851; m. 1875, Lady Anne Finch, only d. of the 6th Earl of Aylesford. Educ. at Eton. Entered the Diplomatic Service in 1872; served in the Foreign Office, was attaché at Rome 1873-75, and at St. Petersburg 1875-76, when he retired. A Dept.-Lieut. of Ross-shire, and Maj. Highland Artillery Volunteers. A Conservative and Unionist, in favour of legislation to extend commerce, develop new markets, etc., and to reform the Poor Laws, provide Old Age Pensions, etc. Sat for Hastings from 1880 until he retired 1883. Was an unsuccessful candidate at Coventry in 1892; elected there in 1895 and sat until he retired in 1906. Served in France (Temp. Maj.) 1917-18. Died 25 Sept. 1929. [1905]

MURRAY, Charles Wyndham, C.B. 10 Rutland Gate, London. Froyle Place, Alton, Hampshire. Carlton, and Army & Navy. S. of the Rev. T.B. Murray, Prebendary of St. Paul's by Helen, d. of Gen. Sir William Douglas, K.C.H., of Timpendean, Roxburghshire. B. 1844; m. 1890, Emma

Cecilia, d. of Mr. Edward Walker. Educ. at Marlborough Coll., entered the army in 1862. Was Dept. Assistant Quartermaster-Gen. Intelligence Branch, Dublin 1876-77, Brigade Maj. at Aldershot 1878-79, during which period he was employed with the Boundary Commission, and as Military Attaché in Turkey, and served in the Zulu War of 1879 as Dept. Assistant Adjutant-Gen., Intelligence Branch of the division (Brevet of Maj. and medal with clasp), served in the Afghan War with the 72nd Highlanders (medal) 1880, in the Mari expedition 1881, as Dept. Assistant Adjutant-Gen. with the expeditionary force in Egypt (Brevet of Lieut.-Col., medal with clasp for Tel-el-Kebir, etc.), 1882, and in the Bechuanaland expedition under Sir Charles Warren as Assistant Adjutant-Gen. and Quartermaster-Gen. 1885. Retired from the service 1890, and in 1891 was appointed one of H.M. Honorary Corps of Gentlemen at Arms. A Knight of St. John of Jerusalem. C.B. 1902. A Conservative. Sat for Bath from 1892 until defeated in 1906. Kt. 1905; K.C.B. 1917. Died 1 Nov. 1928. [1905]

MURRAY, James. Buckingham Gate, London. Glenburnie, Aberdeen. Reform, and Arts. S. of William Murray, Esq., of Mastrick, Aberdeenshire, and Mary, d. of John Stephen, Esq., of Aberdeen. B. 19 Sept. 1850 at Woodside, Aberdeen; m. 1st, 1874, Martha, d. of William Benton, Esq., of Crookmore, Alford (died); 2ndly, 1876, Charlotte, d. of Charles Keith, Esq., of Newcastle-on-Tyne. Educ. at Woodside School, and Aberdeen University. A Merchant in business at Aberdeen. Dept.-Lieut. and J.P. for the County and City of Aberdeen. A member of the Board of Trustees of the National Galleries of Scotland. A Liberal. Elected for E. Aberdeenshire in Feb. 1906 and sat until he retired in Jan. 1910. Knighted 1915. Died 12 Apr. 1932. [1909]

MUSPRATT, Max. The Grange, Fulwood Park, Liverpool. National Liberal. S. of Dr. E.K. Muspratt, Pro-Chancellor of Liverpool University. B. 1872 at Seaforth Hall, near Liverpool; m. 1896, Helena, d. of T.W. Ainsworth, Esq., of Blackburn. Educ. at Clifton Coll., and Zurich. A Director of United Alkali Company, Strelite Explosives Company, and Albion Products Company, and Chairman of Liverpool Rubber Company. A member of Liverpool City Council, and of the Council of Liverpool University, and Chairman of School of Russian Studies. A Liberal. Elected for the Exchange division of Liverpool in Jan. 1910 and sat until defeated in Dec. 1910. Contested Bootle in Mar. 1911. Chairman of United Alkali Company 1914; Director of Imperial Chemical Industries. Lord Mayor of Liverpool 1917. Created 1st Bart. 1922. President of Federation of British Industries 1926; withdrew from the Liberal Party in 1926. Died 20 Apr. 1934.   [1910]

MYER, Horatio. 64 Maida Vale, London. National Liberal. S. of H. Myer, Esq., of Hereford. B. 1850 at Hereford. Educ. privately. Head of the firm of Myer and Company Limited, Bedstead Manufacturers and Ironfounders, of Lambeth. A member of the London County Council for Kennington 1889-1904. A J.P. A Liberal, in favour of Taxation of Ground Values, Local Option, Home Rule, etc. etc. Elected for N. Lambeth in 1906 and sat until defeated in Jan. 1910. Died 1 Jan. 1916. [1909]

MYERS, William Henry. Swanmore House, Bishops Waltham, Hampshire. Carlton, Oxford & Cambridge, and Wellington. Eld. s. of Charles Myers, Esq., of Swanmore House, and Henrietta, 5th d. of Henry Ashton, Esq., of Woolton, Lancashire. B. 1854; m. 1888, Frances Mary, d. of E.A. Prideaux Brune, Esq. Educ. at Eton, and Balliol Coll., Oxford. A Barrister, called at the Inner Temple 1881. Joined the W. Circuit. A J.P. and Dept.-Lieut. for Co. Southampton, and a County Councillor for the Droxford division of that Co. A Conservative. Was unsuccessful as a candidate for the Leigh division of Lancashire in 1886. Elected for Winchester in 1892 and sat until he retired in 1906. Died 21 Dec. 1933.   [1905]

NANNETTI, Joseph Patrick. 47 Whitworth Road, Drumcondra, Dublin. S. of Joseph Nannetti, Esq. B. in Dublin 1851; m. Mary, d. of Edward Egan, Esq., of Dublin. Educ. at Baggot Street Convent, and Christian Brothers' Schools, North Richmond Street, Dublin. A Foreman Printer for *Freeman's Journal.* Lord Mayor of Dublin 1906 and 1907. A member of the Catholic Cemeteries Committee, and a J.P. for Dublin City. A Nationalist and Labour Member. Sat for the College Green division of Dublin from Oct. 1900 until his death 26 Apr. 1915.   [1915]

NAOROJI, Dadabhai. Northbrook Indian Club, National Liberal, and Press. S. of Mr. Naoroji, A Parsee Priest, his mother's name being Manekbai. B. 1825 at Bombay; m. 1838, d. of Mr. Sorabje, a Priest. Educ. at the Elphinstone Institute School and Coll. Was Head Native Teacher at Elphinstone Coll. 1845, and Professor Mathematics and Natural Philosophy there 1855-81. Prime Minister to the Dewan of Baroda 1874; a member of the Bombay Corporation 1876, and of the Legislative Council of Bombay 1885-88. Also a Merchant, a member of the firm of Cama and Company, of London, Liverpool, Bombay, and Calcutta, from 1855. In 1867 he helped in establishing the East India Association, and became Honorary Secretary. Wrote much upon Political and Economical Indian questions. A Liberal, in favour of Home Rule for Ireland, Indian reforms, and the Advanced Liberal programme generally. Was an unsuccessful candidate for the Holborn division of Finsbury 1886. First returned for the Central division of Finsbury July, 1892 and sat until defeated in 1895. Unsuccessfully contested N. Lambeth in 1906 as an Independent Liberal nominated by the London Liberal and Radical Union. President of Indian National Congress 1886, 1893, and 1906. Member of Royal Commission on Indian Expenditure 1895; author of *Poverty and Un-British Rule in India* (1901), *The Rights of Labour* (1906), and many other works. Died 2 July 1917.   [1895]

NAPIER, Hon. Mark Francis. 3 Paper Buildings, Temple, London. Little Mulgrave House, Fulham, London. 4th s. of the 9th Baron Napier, of Ettrick, by Anne Jane Charlotte, only d. of R.M. Lockwood, Esq., of Dun-y-Greig, Glamorganshire. B. 1852; m. 1878, Emily, d. of the 7th Visct. Ranelagh. Educ. at Cambridge. Called to the bar at the Inner Temple 1876. Was Junior Counsel to Arabi Pasha on his trial at Cairo 1882. A Liberal, favouring the Gladstonian programme of reforms. Was an unsuccessful candidate for Roxburghshire in 1886. First returned for Roxburghshire in July 1892 and sat until defeated in 1895. Died 19 Aug. 1919.   [1895]

NAPIER, Thomas Bateman. 25 Hendon Lane, Finchley, London. 7 New Square, Lincoln's Inn, London. Reform, and Eighty. S. of R.C. Napier, Esq., of Preston, and Sarah, d. of Thomas Bateman, Esq., of Salford. B. 1854 at Preston. Educ. at Rugby, and London University; LL.D. A Barrister, called 1883; a Fellow and member of the Senate of London University; a member of London County Council 1893-1907; Chairman of Parliamentary Committee; a J.P. for Middlesex; author of several legal works. A Liberal. Unsuccessfully contested N. Islington in 1895. Elected for the Faversham division of Kent in 1906 and sat until defeated in Jan. 1910. Judge of Derbyshire County Courts 1912. Co-opted member of London Education Committee 1915. Gov. of Rugby School 1927. Author of several legal works. Died 6 Nov. 1933.   [1909]

NAYLOR-LEYLAND, Sir Herbert Scarisbrick, Bart. Hyde Park House, 3 Albert Gate, London. Lexden Park, Colchester. Turf, Marlborough, and White's. S. of Col. Tom Naylor-Leyland, of Nantclywd, Denbighshire, and Mary, only d. of Charles Scarisbrick, Esq., of Scarisbrick, Lancashire. B. 1864; m. 1889, Jane, 2nd d. of H.S. Chamberlain, Esq., of Cleveland, U.S.A. Educ. at the Royal Military Coll., Sandhurst. Entered 2nd Life Guards 1882; became Capt. Jan. 1891; resigned 1895. A Fellow of the Royal Geographical and Zoological Societies. A Liberal, in favour of Home Rule, Land Law Reforms, and other advanced Liberal measures. Sat as a Conservative for Colchester 1892 to Feb. 1895, when, having changed his opinions on the Home Rule question, he joined the Liberal party and resigned his seat. In the same year he was created Bart. Contested the Southport division of Lancashire in July 1895. First returned for the Southport division in Aug. 1898 and sat until his death 7 May 1899.   [1899]

NEEDHAM, Christopher Thomas. Ranighar, Lancaster Road, Didsbury, Lancashire. Reform. S. of John Needham, Esq., of Eccles, Lancashire. B. 30 Aug. 1866 at Salford; m. 1902, Florence White (she died 1905). Educ. at the Grammar School, and University, Manchester; B.A. 1887. Senior Partner in the firm of John Needham and Sons, Iron and Steel Merchants, of Manchester. Director of Manchester and Liverpool District Bank; Director of Manchester Ship Canal Company; Director of Kellner Partington Pulp Company Limited; member of the Coun-

cil and Court of Governors of the University of Manchester; Chairman of Convocation of Manchester University 1911. Director of Manchester Chamber of Commerce; Honorary Secretary Association Chambers of Commerce 1913. J.P. for Lancashire. A Liberal. Unsuccessfully contested S.W. Manchester in Jan. 1910; elected there in Dec. 1910 and sat until defeated in the Hulme division of Manchester in 1918. Was on Advising Council of Ministry of Reconstruction 1918. Knighted 1919. A member of the Royal Commission on the Civil Service 1929-31; Chairman of District Bank Limited 1922-36; many other business interests. Died 29 Apr. 1944.   [1918]

NEILSON, Francis. 4 Westminster Mansions, London. Gee Cross, Hyde, Cheshire. S. of Francis Butters, Esq., and Isabel Neilson. B. 1867 in Birkenhead; m. 1893, Catherine Eva, d. of James O'Gorman, Esq., of U.S.A. Educ. at Liverpool Institute High School, and privately. Assumed the name of Neilson by deed poll in 1902. An author and Journalist and Editor of *Democratic Monthly*. Author of *Madame Bohemia*, *The Bath Road*, *Manabozo*, and many plays, libretti, and short stories, and numerous pamphlets on Taxation of Land Values, Free Trade, Socialism, etc. Travelled extensively in Europe, Canada, and U.S.A., and made land system a special study. President of English League for Taxation of Land Values. A Liberal. Unsuccessfully contested the Newport division of Shropshire in 1906 and 1908. Elected for the Hyde division of Cheshire in Jan. 1910 and sat until accepted Chiltern Hundreds in Mar. 1916. Became U.S. citizen in 1921. Died 13 Apr. 1961.   [1916]

NEVILLE, Ralph. 42 Cadogan Terrace, London. Addlestone, Surrey. National Liberal, and Liverpool Reform. S. of Henry Neville, Esq., M.D., of Esher, Surrey, and Mary his wife. B. at Esher 1848; m. 1872, Edith Cranstoun, eld. d. of H.T.J. Macnamara, one of Her Majesty's Railway Commissioners. Educ. at Tonbridge School, and Emmanuel Coll., Cambridge. A Barrister, called at Lincoln's Inn 1872. One of the Editors of Neville and Macnamara's *Railway and Canal Traffic Cases*. An ardent Liberal, supported Mr. Gladstone's proposals for the self-government of Ireland. Unsuccessfully contested Kirkdale division of Liverpool in 1886, but was returned for the Exchange division of Liverpool on the death of Mr. David Duncan, Jan. 1887 and sat until he retired in 1895. Q.C. 1888. Appointed High Court Judge of the Chancery division in 1906. Knighted 1906. Died 13 Oct. 1918.   [1895]

NEVILLE, Reginald James Neville. Continued in House after 1918: full entry in Volume III.

NEWARK, Charles William Sydney Pierrepont, Visct. 5 Cadogan Square, London. Holme Pierrepont, Nottinghamshire. Carlton, White's, and Guards'. Eld. s. of the 3rd Earl Manvers, by Georgine, d. of Duc de Coigny, of France. B. in London 1854; m. 1880, Helen, d. of Sir Michael and Lady Octavia Shaw Stewart. Educ. at Eton. Entered the Grenadier Guards 1872, and retired 1880. Brigadier-Gen. in command of the N. Midlands Infantry Volunteers and was for some time Capt. in the S. Nottinghamshire Yeomanry Cavalry. A J.P. for Nottinghamshire. A Conservative. Sat for the Newark division of Nottinghamshire from 1885 to 1895, when he retired. Re-elected without opposition in 1898 and sat until he succeeded as Earl Manvers in Jan. 1900. Died 17 July 1926.
[1899]

NEWDIGATE, Francis Alexander. See NEWDIGATE-NEWDEGATE, Francis Alexander.

NEWDIGATE-NEWDEGATE, Francis Alexander. Arbury, Nuneaton. 36 Grosvenor Place, London. Carlton, and Bachelors'. Only s. of Lieut.-Col. Francis William Newdigate, Coldstream Guards, and Charlotte, d. of Field-Marshal Sir Alexander Woodford, G.C.B. B. 1862 at Royal Hospital, Chelsea; m. 1888, Hon. Elizabeth, youngest d. of the 3rd Baron Bagot. Educ. at Eton, and Royal Military Coll., Sandhurst. Assumed the name of Newdigate in addition to Newdigate in 1902. Was in the Coldstream Guards 1883-85. A Co. Alderman, J.P., and Dept.-Lieut. for Warwickshire; a Dept.-Lieut. for Derbyshire. Gov. of Rugby School. A Unionist. Sat for the Nuneaton division of Warwickshire from 1892 to 1906, when he was defeated. First elected for the Tamworth division of Warwickshire in 1909 and sat until appointed Gov. of Tasmania in 1917-20. K.C.M.G. 1917; G.C.M.G.

1925. Gov. of Western Australia 1920-24; later Chairman of Coventry and District Employment Committee. Died 2 Jan. 1936.   [1916]

NEWMAN, John Robert Pretyman. Continued in House after 1918: full entry in Volume III.

NEWMAN, Sir Robert Hunt Stapylton Dudley Lydston, Bart. Continued in House after 1918: full entry in Volume III.

NEWNES, Frank Hillyard. 4 Whitehall Court, London. Hollerday, Lynton, Devon. Devonshire. S. of Sir George Newnes, Bart., MP. B. 28 Sept. 1876 at Manchester. Educ. at Clare Coll., Cambridge; M.A., LL.B. Called to the bar at the Inner Temple. A Newspaper Proprietor; a Director from 1908-21 of The Westminster Gazette, George Newnes Limited, and Country Life. A Liberal. Elected for the Bassetlaw division of Nottinghamshire in 1906 and sat until defeated in Jan. 1910. Succeeded as Bart. in 1910. Involved with several Insurance and Investment Companies and other commercial concerns. C.B.E. 1954. Died 10 July 1955.   [1909]

NEWNES, Sir George, Bart. Wildcroft, Putney Heath, London. Hollerday, Lynton, Devon. S. of the Rev. T. Mold Newnes, Nonconformist Minister, of Matlock and d. of Daniel Urquhart, Esq., of Dundee. B. 1851; m. 1875, Priscilla, d. of the Rev. J. Hillyard, of Leicester. Educ. at Silcoates Hall, Wakefield, Shireland Hall, Warwickshire, and the City of London School. In 1867 he entered upon a commercial career, but decided to turn to publishing. Became the Proprietor of several serial publications, including Tit-Bits, which attained an enormous circulation, and The Strand Magazine. Founder and Managing Director of George Newnes Limited, and Proprietor of the Westminster Gazette. Created a Bart. 1895. A Liberal, and Home Ruler. Sat for the Newmarket division of Cambridgeshire from 1885 until he was defeated 1895. Elected for Swansea Town in 1900 and sat until he retired in Jan. 1910. Died 9 June 1910.
[1909]

NEWTON, Harry Kottingham. Continued in House after 1918: full entry in Volume III.

NICHOLLS, George. Kimberley Lodge, 162 Lincoln Road, Peterborough. B. 25 June 1864 at Whittlesea, Cambridgeshire; m. 1888. Self-educated. Started work on a farm when eight years old; was a Navvy, Market Gardener, and a Congregational Lay Pastor; a member of the Urban District Council and Education Committee. A Labour Member, specially interested in agricultural legislation. Elected for N. Northamptonshire in 1906 and sat until defeated in Jan. 1910. Contested Faversham division of Kent in Dec. 1910, the Newmarket division of Cambridgeshire in May 1913, Camborne division of Cornwall as Labour candidate in 1918; thereafter he was the unsuccessful Liberal candidate in Peterborough 1922, Warwick and Leamington 1923 and 1924, Bury St. Edmunds Dec. 1925 and Harborough in 1929. Elected to Peterborough Town Council in 1912; Mayor 1916-18; member of Agricultural Wages Board. Died 30 Nov. 1943. [1909]

NICHOLSON, Sir Charles Norris, Bart. 35 Harrington Gardens, London. Oxford & Cambridge. S. of W.N. Nicholson, Esq., Master in Lunacy, and Emily, d. of J.S. Daniel, Esq., of Ramsgate. B. 30 July 1857 in London; m. 1882, Amy Letitia, d. of George Crosfield, Esq., of Warrington. Educ. at Charterhouse, and Trinity Coll., Cambridge; M.A., LL.B. Called to the bar 1878; was for many years Chairman of Shoreditch Board of Guardians and Poor Law Schools Committee. Appointed Second Church Estates Commissioner 1910. Created Bart. 1912. Chairman of the Board of Control of Regimental Institutes 1915. A Liberal. Elected for the Doncaster division of the W. Riding of Yorkshire in 1906 and sat until he retired in 1918. He died on 29 Nov. 1918, 4 days after the dissolution of Parliament. [1918]

NICHOLSON, William Graham. Continued in House after 1918: full entry in Volume III.

NICOL, Donald Ninian. 80 Harley Street, London. Ardmarnoch, Tighna Bruaich, Argyllshire. Carlton. New Club, Edinburgh. 3rd s. of John Nicol, Esq., J.P., of Ardmarnoch, by Margaret, d. of Ninian Duncan, Esq. B. 1843; m. 1874, Anne Millicent, d. of Sir Edward Bates, Bart., of Manydown Park, Hampshire. Educ. in Edinburgh, Glasgow University, and

Queen's Coll., Oxford; M.A. Called to the bar in 1870, but did not practise. A J.P. and Dept.-Lieut. for Co. Argyll, and Convener of Argyll County Council. A Conservative and Unionist, in favour of the application of the Irish Land Purchase Act to the Crofter grievance. Sat for Argyllshire from July 1895 until his death 27 July 1903. [1903]

NIELD, Sir Herbert. Continued in House after 1918: full entry in Volume III.

NOBLE, Wilson. 52 Sloane Street, London. Warrior Square, St. Leonards. Carlton. S. of John Noble, Esq., J.P. and Dept.-Lieut. of Park Place, Henley-on-Thames, by Lily, d. of Capt. Ellis, of the Bengal Artillery. B. 1854; m. 1879, Marian, d. of W.P. Dana, Esq., an Artist, of Boston, U.S. Educ. at Eton, and Cambridge. Was called to the bar at the Inner Temple in June 1880. A Conservative. Was an unsuccessful candidate for Hastings at the general election of 1885. First returned for Hastings July 1886 and sat until he retired in 1895. Died 1 Nov. 1917. [1895]

NOEL, Ernest. Defeated in 1886: full entry in Volume I.

NOLAN, John Philip. Ballinderry, Tuam. Army & Navy. S. of John Nolan, Esq., J.P., Barrister, of Ballinderry, by Mary, d. of Walter Nolan, Esq., of Loughboy, Mayo. B. in Dublin 1838. Unmarried. Educ. at Stoneyhurst, Trinity Coll., Dublin, and Staff and Artillery Coll. Entered the Royal Artillery in 1857 and served throughout the Abyssinian campaign, and retired from the army with the rank of Lieut.-Col. in 1881. A Nationalist. Sat for Co. Galway for a short time from Feb.-June 1872, when he was unseated on petition; represented Co. Galway from 1874 to 1885, and the N. division from 1885 to 1895, being defeated in the latter year by the Anti-Parnellite. Contested Louth S. in Mar. 1896. Re-elected for Galway N. in Oct. 1900 and sat until defeated in 1906. Died 30 Jan. 1912. [1905]

NOLAN, Joseph. 404 Clapham Road, London. A native of Louth. B. 1846; m. 1884. Was a Teacher in Ireland and at a Reformatory School in Liverpool. Later employed as Manager of the Aquarium and Casino at New Brighton, near Liverpool, but resigned on election in 1885. An

"Irish Nationalist". At one time represented the Northern division of Louth, from which, as Mr. Parnell's nominee, he drove Mr. Philip Callan in 1885. He took the side of Mr. Parnell in his efforts to retain the leadership of the Parliamentary party, and standing in 1892 for the Southern division, lost his seat. Defeated in N. Louth in July 1895 and Limerick city in Sept. 1895. Represented S. Louth from 1900 until he retired in 1918.   [1918]

NORMAN, Rt. Hon. Sir Henry, Bart. Continued in House after 1918: full entry in Volume III.

NORRIS, Edward Samuel. 24 Chester Terrace, Regent's Park, London. Hurst Dene, Hastings, Sussex. Junior Carlton, City of London, and Constitutional. S. of Samuel Edward Norris, Esq., of Upper Clapton, Middlesex, and of an old Northamptonshire family. B. 1832 in London; was twice married. Educ. privately. Once member of the firm of Norris and Company, Merchants and Manufacturers. Treasurer of the Merchant Seamen's Orphan Asylum, Snaresbrook, and of the East London Hospital for Children; Dept.-Chairman of the Southampton Dock Company; Capt. Commandant in the Sussex Volunteer Artillery. A J.P. for Middlesex, the Liberty of the Tower of London, and a Dept.-Lieut. of the Tower Hamlets. Wrote several political pamphlets. A "progressive Conservative". Sat for the Limehouse division of Tower Hamlets from Nov. 1885 until he retired in 1892. Contested Colchester 1895. Died 22 Feb. 1908.   [1892]

NORTHCOTE, Hon. Sir Henry Stafford, Bart., C.B. 25 St. James's Place, London. Carlton, and Athenaeum. 2nd s. of the 1st Earl of Iddesleigh, by Cecilia Frances, d. of Thomas Farrer, Esq., of Lincoln's Inn. B. 1846; m. 1873, Alice, adopted d. of Lord Mount-Stephen, of Montreal, Canada. Educ. at Eton, and at Merton Coll., Oxford. Appointed to a Clerkship in the Foreign Office 1868, till Feb. 1871, when he proceeded to Washington, being attached to Earl De Grey's special mission to arrange the Treaty of Washington; subsequently acted as Secretary to Mr. Russell Gurney in connection with the details of the same Treaty. Was Private Secretary to the Marq. of Salisbury's Special Embassy to Constantinople, and appointed Acting Third Secretary in the Diplomatic Service

Nov. 1876. Was Private Secretary to the Chancellor of the Exchequer from 1877 to 1880; Financial Secretary to the War Office 1885-86, and Surveyor-Gen. of Ordnance 1886. Created Bart. 1887, on the abolition of the Surveyorship of Ordnance, and was a Charity Commissioner (unpaid) 1891-92. C.B. 1880. A Conservative. Sat for Exeter from Apr. 1880 until appointed Gov. of Bombay in 1899. Created 1st Baron Northcote in 1900, and Gov.-Gen. of Australia 1903-08. G.C.I.E. 1900; G.C.M.G. 1904; PC. 1909. Died 29 Sept. 1911.   [1899]

NORTON, Capt. Cecil William. 2 Onslow Gardens, London. Reform, and National Liberal. S. of the Rev. W. Norton, M.A., Rector of Baltinglass, Ireland, by Caroline, d. of George Riddick, Esq., of Triton Lodge, Co. Louth. B. 23 June 1850; m. 1st, Cecilia L., d. of James Kennedy, Esq.; 2ndly, Marguerite, d. of Sir C.P. Huntingdon, Bart., MP for Drawen, Lancashire. Educ. at Trinity Coll., Dublin, (Double Prizeman), the Royal Military Coll., and the Staff Coll. Served in the 5th (Royal Irish) Lancers; was Brigade-Maj. of Cavalry at Aldershot. Was a junior Lord of the Treasury and a Liberal Whip from 1905 to 1910, when he was appointed Assistant Postmaster-Gen.; he held this office until the formation of the Coalition Government in May 1915. An advanced Liberal. Unsuccessfully contested Great Yarmouth in 1885 and 1886. First elected for W. Newington in 1892 and sat until created Lord Rathcreedan in Jan. 1916. Additional Parliamentary Secretary to the Ministry of Munitions and to Ministry of Supply 1919-21. Author of *Memories of a Long Life* (1931). Died 7 Dec. 1930. [1915]

NORTON, Robert. Downs House, Yalding, Maidstone. Carlton, and Union. S. of William Norton, Esq., of Barcott House, Northamptonshire. B. 1838; m. 1867, d. of the Rev. John Duncombe Shafto, of Durham. Educ. privately. Was called to the bar at the Middle Temple in 1866, and served ten years in the War Office. Took a prominent part in questions relative to the Poor Laws and the management of hospitals and educational establishments in Kent, of which Co. he was a J.P. A Conservative. Sat for the Tunbridge division of Kent from 1885 until he retired in 1892. High Sheriff of Kent 1910. Died 7 June 1926.   [1892]

NORTON-GRIFFITHS, Sir John. Continued in House after 1918: full entry in Volume III.

NUGENT, John Dillon. 272 North Circular Road, Dublin. B. 1869 at Keady, Co. Armagh; m. 1896. Educ. at National Schools, Keady, Was National Secretary of the Ancient Order of Hibernians (Board of Erin) from 1904; member of Dublin Town Council from 1912; and of N. Dublin Board of Guardians. A Nationalist. Elected for the College Green division of Dublin in June 1915 and sat until defeated in the St. Michan's division of Dublin in 1918. Member of Northern Ireland Parliament 1921-25. Died 1 Mar. 1940.   [1918]

NUGENT, Sir Walter Richard, Bart. Donore, Multifarnham, Co. Westmeath. Reform, National Liberal, and United Service. S. of Sir W.G. Nugent, 2nd Bart., and bro. of 3rd, and Maria More, d. of the Rt. Hon. M.R. O'Ferrall, MP. B. 12 Dec. 1865; m. June 1916, Aileen Gladys, younger d. of Middleton-More O'Malley, Esq., J.P., of Ross, Lewport, Co. Mayo. Educ. at Downside Coll., and University Coll. Dept.-Chairman of the Midlands and Great Western Railway of Ireland. A J.P. and Dept.-Lieut. for Westmeath. Succeeded as Bart. in 1896. A Nationalist. Elected for S. Westmeath in Apr. 1907 and sat until defeated in Co. Westmeath in 1918 standing as an Independent opposed by both Nationalist and Sinn Fein candidates. Continued career as Director of Irish Railway Companies and Harbour Boards; Director of Bank of Ireland 1920; Dept.-Gov. 1924. High Sheriff of Co. Westmeath 1922 and 1923. Senator of Irish Free State 1928. Died 12 Nov. 1955. [1918]

NUSSEY, Sir Thomas Willans, Bart. Rushwood, Tanfield, Bedale, Yorkshire. Brooks's, and Eighty. Only s. of Thomas Nussey, Esq., of Bramley Grange, Thorner, near Leeds and Helen, d. of J. Dodgson, Esq., of Leeds. B. 1868 at Leeds; m. 1897, Edith, only d. of Dr. E.M. Daniel, of Fleetwood, Lancashire. Educ. at Leamington School, and Trinity Hall, Cambridge; B.A. 1890. Called to the bar at the Inner Temple in 1893. A J.P. and Dept.-Lieut. for the N. Riding of Yorkshire. Created Bart. in 1909. A Liberal, in favour of Home Rule. Unsuccessfully contested Maidstone in 1892. Sat for Pontefract from June 1893 until he retired in Dec. 1910. Died 12 Oct. 1947.   [1910]

NUTTALL, Harry. Briarfield, Walton-on-the-Hill, Surrey. Bank of England Chambers, Manchester. Reform, and National Liberal. S. of Joseph Nuttall, Esq., of Manchester. B. 1849 at Manchester; m. 1886, Edith Mary, d. of William Smith, Esq., of Bolton-le-Moors. Educ. privately, and at Owens Coll., Manchester. An Import and Export Merchant at Manchester. President of Manchester Geographical Society; President of Manchester Chamber of Commerce 1905; a J.P. for Cheshire and Manchester. F.R.G.S. A Liberal, in favour of Electoral Reform, Rating of Land Values, etc. Unsuccessfully contested the Stretford division of S.E. Lancashire in 1900; elected there in 1906 and sat until he retired in 1918. Died 25 Sept. 1924. [1918]

O'BRIEN, James Francis Xavier. 39 Gauden Road, Clapham, London. B. 1831. Gen. Secretary to the United Irish League of Great Britain. Was tried in 1867 for high treason and sentenced to be hanged, "drawn and quartered", the sentence was commuted to penal servitude for life, and afterwards he was released. Was a Tea and Wine Merchant in Dublin. An "Irish Nationalist." Sat for Mayo S. from 1885 until June 1895, when he resigned in order to stand for Cork City. Sat for Cork City from June 1895 until his death 23 May 1905.   [1905]

O'BRIEN, Kendal Edmund. Golden Hills, Golden, Cashel, Co. Tipperary. S. of Richard O'Brien, Esq., Solicitor, of Cullen, Tipperary, and Ballina House, Clara, King's Co., by Kate, d. of James Byrne, Esq., J.P., Dept.-Lieut., of Lysterfield House, Co. Roscommon. B. 1849 at Cullen; m. 1895, Anne Frances, eld. d. of Cuthbert Clayton, Esq., of Golden Hills House, Cashel, Co. Tipperary. Educ. at Prospect House, Sandymount, Co. Dublin, and Carmelite Monastery, Clondalkin, Co. Dublin. A Farmer, took a prominent part in land agitation, also in organizing labour. Wrote articles advocating National Proprietary in land, or what was known as Land Nationalization, in several prominent Irish Journals. J.P. for Co. Tipperary. A Nationalist. Represented mid Tipperary from 1900 until his death 21 Nov. 1909.   [1909]

O'BRIEN, Patrick. House of Commons, London. National Liberal, Automobile, and Leinster. 2nd s. of James O'Brien, Esq., and Catherine, d. of P. Byrne, Esq. B. 1853 at Tullamore, King's Co. An Engineer. A Nationalist, and "Whip" to the Irish Party. "Remained faithful to Mr. Parnell in the divisions of No. 15 Committee-Room, although in prison under the Coercion Act at the time." Sat for N. Monaghan from Feb. 1886 to 1892. Unsuccessfully contested Limerick City in July 1892. Represented Kilkenny City from 1895 until his death 12 July 1917. [1917]

O'BRIEN, Patrick Joseph. 22 Castle Street, Nenagh, Tipperary. Only s. of James O'Brien, Esq., of Nenagh, by Bridget, d. of John Gunning Regan, Esq., of R.N. B. at Nenagh 1835; m. 1878, Bridget, d. of Denis Hayes, Esq., of Ballintoher, Nenagh. Educ. at local schools. A Hotel Proprietor. Was Chairman of the Nenagh Town Commissioners 1880-87, 1890-91; was Chairman of the Board of Guardians 1885-99; County Councillor, and Chairman of the District Council 1899-1900. "An Irish Nationalist." Sat for N. Tipperary from 1885 until he retired in 1906. Died 10 Jan. 1911. [1905]

O'BRIEN, William. Bellevue, Mallow, Co. Cork. S. of James O'Brien, Esq., of Mallow, by Kate, d. of James Nagle, Esq., of Mallow. B. 2 Oct. 1852; m. 1890, Sophie, d. of Hermann Raffalovich, Esq., of Paris. Educ. at Cloyne Diocesan Coll., and Queen's Coll., Cork. A Journalist and founder of the *United Ireland* and *Irish People* newspapers; author of *When We were Boys* (1890), *Irish Ideas* (1893), *A Queen of Men* (1896), *Recollections* (1905), *An Olive Branch in Ireland and its History* (1910). In 1898 founded The United Irish League. Was a member of the Land Conference from whose recommendations the Land Purchase Act 1903 sprung; retired from the Irish Party when they repudiated the Policy of Conciliation embodied in that Act. He continued to advocate that policy through the All-for-Ireland movement. A Nationalist. Sat for Mallow from 1883-85; sat for S. Tyrone from 1885-86, when he was defeated; sat for N.E. Cork from May 1887 until July 1892 when he was returned for N.E. Cork and for Cork City and chose to represent the City. Sat for Cork City from 1892-June 1895, when he resigned returned again for Cork City 1900, but

resigned 1909. Elected in Jan. 1910 for both Cork City and N.E. Cork, and elected to sit for Cork City, which he represented until he retired in 1918. Unsuccessfully contested E. Cork and W. Mayo Dec. 1910, whilst sitting for Cork City. Author of *Evening Memories* (1920), *The Irish Revolution and How it Came About* (1923), *Edmund Burke as an Irishman* (1924), and *The Parnell of Real Life* (1926). Died 25 Feb. 1928. [1918]

O'CONNOR, Arthur. 5 Essex Court, Temple, London. Eld. s. of William O'Connor, Esq., M.D., of Dingle, Kerry. B. 1844; m. Ellen, eld. d. of W. Connolly, Esq. Educ. at St. Cuthbert's Coll., Ushaw, Durham. Dept.-Chairman of Committee of "Ways and Means." Was a Secretary of the Irish Parliamentary party. Appointed Q.C. England 1899. An Irish Nationalist. Sat for Queen's Co. from Apr. 1880 to Nov. 1885, when he was elected for the Ossory division of Queen's Co. and for E. Donegal. He chose to represent the latter and sat for E. Donegal from Nov. 1885 until he unsuccessfully contested N. Donegal in Oct. 1900. Chairman of Public Accounts Committee 1895-1900. Appointed County Court Judge in 1900 for Durham, and for Dorset 1911-20. Died 30 Mar. 1923. [1900]

O'CONNOR, James. House of Commons, London. S. of Patrick O'Connor, Esq., of Glen Imaal, Co. Wicklow, and of Anne Kearney, of Donard, Cd. Wicklow. B. Feb. 1836. Was on the staff of the *Irish People*, a Fenian organ. In 1865 he, with Luby, O'Leary, and Charles Kickham, of the *Irish People*, was convicted of treason felony, and was sentenced to 7 years penal servitude. Was liberated before the term had expired, and was then connected with the editorial staffs of several journals and magazines. A Nationalist. Represented W. Wicklow from 1892 until his death 12 Mar. 1910. [1910]

O'CONNOR, John, (I). Abbey View, Dalkey, Dublin. Catholic Club, O'Connell Street, Dublin. S. of Edward O'Connor, Esq., Farmer, of Mulgeeth House, by Maria Flanagan, of Brookestown, Co. Kildare. B. about 1835; m. 1st, 1866, Marianne, only d. of Denis Byrne, Esq., of Dublin; 2ndly, 1873, Mary Margaret, d. of James White, Esq., of Clontarf, Dublin. Was educ. at a school in Kildare. Elected to the town council of Dublin in 1880, became Alderman in 1883, and served as

Lord Mayor during 1885. Was Owner of seven public-houses. An "Irish Nationalist and Home Ruler." Sat for Kerry S. from 1885 until accepted Chiltern Hundreds in 1887. Died 12 Jan. 1891.   [1887]

O'CONNOR, John, II. 4 Paper Buildings, Temple, London. National Liberal. S. of W. O'Connor, Esq., and Julia, d. of John Corbet, Esq., of Mallow. B. 10 Oct. 1850 at Mallow. Unmarried. Educ. at the Christian Brothers School, Cork, and privately. A Barrister, called 1893. Was a member of the Royal Commission for the British Section of the Chicago Exhibition 1893, and a member of the Council of the Society of Arts. A Nationalist. Sat for Tipperary from Jan.-Nov. 1885 and for S. Tipperary from Dec. 1885-92. Unsuccessfully contested Kilkenny city and S. Tipperary in July 1892. Elected for N. Kildare in Feb. 1905 and sat until defeated in 1918. K.C. 1919. Died 27 Oct. 1928.   [1918]

O'CONNOR, Thomas Power. Continued in House after 1918: full entry in Volume III.

ODDY, John James. Moorville, Birkenshaw, Nr. Bradford. Carlton. S. of James Oddy, Esq., of Bradford. B. 24 Feb. 1867 at Bradford; m. 1892, d. of John Ambler, Esq., of Bradford. Educ. at Ley's School, Cambridge. A Spinner and Manufacturer at Moorland's Mills, Birkenshaw. A Conservative. Elected for the Pudsey division of the W. Riding of Yorkshire in June 1908 and sat until defeated in Jan. 1910. Defeated again in Dec. 1910. Knighted 1916. Died 20 Feb. 1921.   [1909]

O'DOHERTY, James Edward. 5 East Wall, Londonderry. Milburn, Buncrana. S. of B.P. O'Doherty, Esq., a Merchant, of Buncrana. B. 1848. Educ. at Castleknock, Armagh, and at Maynooth Coll., and after obtaining the gold medal of the Incorporated Law Society and the first place at all its examinations, he was admitted a Solicitor in 1871. An "Irish Nationalist." Sat for Donegal N. from 1885 until he accepted Chiltern Hundreds in 1890.   [1890]

O'DOHERTY, Kevin Izod. S. of William Izod O'Doherty, Esq., and Anne McEvoy. B. in Dublin 7 Sept. 1823; m. 1855, Mary Anne Kelly, the Irish poetess. Educ. for the medical profession, but, before he had

graduated, he assisted in starting the *Irish Tribune*, as a successor to the suppressed *United Irishman*. The new paper was speedily suppressed, and Mr. O'Doherty, after three trials, was sentenced to ten years' transportation for his writings in it. He was afterwards set free on the condition that he should reside abroad, and he then resumed his studies in Paris. In 1856 he received a free pardon, and returned to Dublin, where he was admitted a F.R.C.S. and Licentiate of the King and Queen's Coll. of Physicians. He practised in Dublin, and then went to Queensland, where he became a member of the Legislative Assembly and Council, and had not returned at the opening of Parliament. An "Irish Nationalist." Sat for Meath N. from Nov. 1885 until he retired in 1886. He returned to Brisbane in 1888 and died on 15 July 1905.   [1886]

O'DOHERTY, Philip. 11 East Wall, Londonderry. S. of Owen O'Doherty, Esq., and Margaret O'Doherty. B. 1871 at Clonmany. Educ. at St. Columb's Coll., Londonderry. A Solicitor, admitted 1895; a member of Londonderry Town Council, and Chamber of Commerce. A Nationalist. Elected for N. Donegal in 1906 and sat until defeated in 1918. Died 6 Feb. 1926.   [1918]

O'DOHERTY, William. 12 Clarence Avenue, Londonderry. Carndonagh, Co. Donegal. Reform, and National Liberal. S. of Owen O'Doherty, Esq., a Merchant, Carndonagh, Co. Donegal, and Julia, d. of B. McGorrisk, Esq. B. at Carndonagh 1868; m. 1894, Margaret, d. of William Mitchell, Esq., Shipowner, Derry, and grand-d. of Sir Robert McVicker. Educ. at St. Columb's Coll., Londonderry. A Solicitor, admitted 1893 (medallist of final exam.); elected Coroner Feb. 1894 for Donegal Co. Was elected Member Londonderry Corporation 1896; Chairman of Public Health Committee; Governor of Londonderry Infirmary. A Nationalist. Sat for the N. division of Donegal Co. from Oct. 1900 until his death 18 May 1905.   [1905]

O'DONNELL, Charles James O'Cahan. 24 Park Side, Albert Gate, London. Great Copse House, Eversley, Hampshire. Wellington. S. of Capt. Bernard O'Donnell, of Carndonogh, Donegal. B. 28 May 1850 at Port Louis, Mauritius; m.

Constance, niece of E.R. Langworthy, MP for Salford. Educ. at St. Ignatius Coll., and Queen's University, Ireland; M.A. Was in the Indian Civil Service 1872-1900. Author of *Ruin of an Indian Province, Failure of Lord Curzon, Causes of Present Discontent in India*, etc. A Liberal, pledged to support radical reform in social and labour conditions, and condemned over-taxation of the land in India. Elected for the Walworth division of Newington in 1906 and sat until he retired in Jan. 1910. Died 3 Dec. 1934. [1909]

O'DONNELL, John. Westport, Co. Mayo. Williamsgate Street, Galway. S. of Patrick and Bridget O'Donnell. B. 1870 at Westport. Educ. at National Schools. A Journalist and founder of the *Connaught Champion* newspaper and general printing works. Was first organizer of the United Irish League, and Gen. Secretary for five years. At one time a member of Co. Mayo Asylums Committee, and Westport Rural District Council. A Nationalist. First elected for S. Mayo in Feb. 1900 and sat until he retired in Dec. 1910. [1910]

O'DONNELL, Thomas. Killorglin, Co. Kerry. S. of Michael O'Donnell, Esq., Farmer, and his wife Ellen Rohan. B. at Liscarney, Co. Kerry 1872; m. 1897, Nora, youngest d. of Michael Ryan, Esq., of Killorglin. Educ. at National School, and Marlborough Street Training Coll., M.A. Royal University Ireland. A Barrister, called to the Irish bar June 1905. Chairman of Tralee and Dingle Railway. A Nationalist. Represented W. Kerry from 1900 until he retired in 1918. Appointed Irish Judge in 1941. Died 11 June 1943. [1918]

O'DOWD, John. Dathi House, Bunninadden, Co. Sligo. S. of John O'Dowd, Esq., Farmer, and Catherine, his wife. B. 1856 at Goldfield, Co. Sligo. Educ. at National Schools, and at Albany, U.S.A. A Merchant and Farmer. Chairman Tubbercurry, S. Sligo Board of Guardians 1888-98, Chairman to Sligo County Council. Author of *Lays of South Sligo* and a book of national poems. Was imprisoned in Dundalk and Sligo gaols under the Forster-Coercion Act; prosecuted by Liberal and Unionist Governments for his participation in the Agrarian movement. A Nationalist. Was returned for N. Sligo unopposed on 7 Mar. 1900 and sat until he was elected for S. Sligo at the general elec-

tion in 1900. MP until defeated in 1918. [1918]

O'DRISCOLL, Florence. 18 Gower Street, London. National Liberal, and Savage. S. of William O'Driscoll, Esq., of Sundays Well, Co. Cork, and Alice Honoria, only d. of Charles W. Blakeney, Holywell, Co. Roscommon. B. 1858 at Mountmellick, Queen's Co. Educ. chiefly in Australia. A Railway Official in Queensland, was in the Chief Engineers' Department 1874-86. Later a Civil Engineer in private practice in London, and a writer on scientific and technical subjects in the engineering journals. An Associate Member of the Institution of Civil Engineers 1887. A Nationalist and Home Ruler of the Anti-Parnellite section. Sat for the S. division of Monaghan from July 1892 until he retired in 1895. Unsuccessfully contested the mid division of Tipperary in Oct. 1900. Chief Correspondent of the *Times* in South America 1910-13. Died 6 Jan. 1939. [1895]

O'FLYNN, James Christopher. See FLYNN, James Christopher.

OGDEN, Frederick. Woodlands, Pudsey. National Liberal. S. of Jonas Ogden, Esq. B. 11 May 1871 at Glossop; m. 1899, Laura Emelia Webster, of Pudsey. Educ. at Halifax High School, and Yorkshire Coll., Leeds. A Boot Manufacturer. A member of Leeds Town Council; Chairman of Waterworks Committee 1904-06; and Vice-Chairman of Education Committee 1903-04. A Liberal. Unsuccessfully contested the Pudsey division of the W. Riding of Yorkshire in June 1908. Elected there in Jan. 1910 and sat until he retired in 1918. Unsuccessfully contested S. Bradford in 1929. Died 24 Apr. 1933. [1918]

O'GORMAN MAHON, Charles James Patrick Mahon, The. See MAHON, Charles James Patrick O'Gorman.

O'GRADY, James. Continued in House after 1918: full entry in Volume III.

O'HANLON, Thomas. Londonderry. A native of Newry, and a Wholesale Licensed Grocer at Derry. A member of the Newry Board of Guardians, and also of the Derry Town Council. An "Irish Nationalist" (Parnellite). Sat for Cavan E. from 1885 until he retired in 1892. [1892]

O'HARE, Patrick. 25 Circus Drive, Dennistoun, Glasgow. B. 1849. In business in Glasgow, and a Baillie of that city; took a leading part in the Irish movement in Scotland. A Nationalist. First elected for N. Monaghan in 1906 and sat until he accepted Chiltern Hundreds in 1907. Died Nov. 1917.   [1907]

O'HEA, Patrick. Cork. 17 Bachelors' Walk, Dublin. S. of Dr. O'Hea, of Clonakilty. B. 1848. Educ. at the Gayfield (Dublin) branch of the Catholic University. A Solicitor (admitted 1875) and practised in Cork, and was a member of the Cork Town Council. An "Irish Nationalist." Sat for Donegal W. from the general election of 1885 until he accepted Chiltern Hundreds in 1890.   [1890]

O'KEEFE, Francis Arthur. The Crescent, Limerick. S. of Laurence O'Keefe, Esq., High Sheriff of Limerick in 1886. B. 4 Oct. 1856 at Limerick. Educ. at the Jesuit School, Limerick, Clongowes Wood Coll., and Trinity Coll., Dublin. A Solicitor, admitted 1877; and was elected Mayor of Limerick 1887, 1888, and 1889. An Irish Nationalist (Anti-Parnellite). Sat for Limerick city 1888 to July 1895. Unsuccessfully contested Wicklow E. July 1895. Re-elected for Limerick city Sept. 1895 and sat until he retired in 1900. Died 21 Apr. 1909.   [1900]

O'KELLY, Conor. Claremorris, Co. Mayo. S. of William O'Kelly, and Jane (née Mullen) his wife. B. at Claremorris in 1873. Educ. locally, and at Dublin. Elected member of the Mayo County Council for the Co. district of Claremorris Apr. 1899; Chairman of the Mayo County Council 1899-1908; member of the Royal Commission on Congestion in Ireland 1906-08. A Nationalist. Represented N. Mayo from 1900 until he retired in Jan. 1910 and unsuccessfully contested Mayo S. at the same time.   [1909]

O'KELLY, Edward Peter. St. Kevins, Baltinglass, Co. Wicklow. S. of William Kelly, Esq. B. 4 July 1846 at Baltinglass; m. 1882, Judith, d. of Myles Whelan, Esq., of Athy. Educ. at Montrath, and Carlow Coll. A Merchant and Land Agent. A J.P. for Co. Wicklow, and Chairman of Wicklow County Council. A Nationalist. Sat for E. Wicklow from Apr.-July 1895 when he retired. First elected for W. Wicklow in Mar. 1910 and sat until his death 22 July 1914.   [1914]

O'KELLY, James Joseph. 17 Brewster Gardens, London. S. of John O'Kelly, Esq., of Roscommon, by Bridget, d. of John Lalor, Esq., of Queen's Co. B. 1845. Educ. at the University of Dublin, and at the Sorbonne, Paris. An Officer in the French army, which he quitted soon after the fall of Paris. Adopted the occupation of a Journalist in 1870, and was one of the editors of the *New York Herald*. Was London Editor of the *Irish Daily Independent*. Published a work entitled *The Mambi Land, a History of Personal Adventures with President Cespides in the Cuban Insurrection*. A Nationalist. Sat for Roscommon from 1880-85; sat for the N. division of Roscommon from 1885-92, when he was defeated; re-elected 1895 and sat until his death 22 Dec. 1916.   [1916]

OLDROYD, Mark. 38 Hyde Park Gate, London. Hyrstlands, Dewsbury. S. of Mark Oldroyd, Esq., of Dewsbury, by Rachel, d. of Marmaduke Fox, Esq., of Soothill. B. at Dewsbury 1843; m. 1871, Maria Tew, 3rd d. of W. Mewburn, Esq., J.P., and Dept.-Lieut., of Wykham Park, Banbury, Oxfordshire. Educ. by private tuition, and at New Coll., St. John's Wood. A Woollen Manufacturer and Merchant. An Alderman of Dewsbury, and was Mayor 1887-88. An Advanced Liberal, in favour of Home Rule, undenominational education, "Disestablishment", reform of the land laws, etc. Sat for Dewsbury from 1888 until he accepted Chiltern Hundreds in Jan. 1902. Kt. 1909. Died 5 July 1927. [1901]

O'LEARY, Daniel. Friendly Cove House, Durrus, Co. Cork. S. of F. and Mary O'Leary. B. May 1875 at Glandart House, Bantry, Co. Cork; m. 26 June 1913, d. of Patrick Laide, Esq., of Rock Street, Tralee. Educ. at private schools. Was by profession a Barrister-at-Law. A Nationalist. Unsuccessfully contested W. Cork in Jan. and Dec. 1910. Elected for W. Cork Nov. 1916 and sat until he retired in 1918. Died 23 Dec. 1954.   [1918]

O'MAHONY, Pierce Charles de Lacy. See MAHONY, Pierce Charles de Lacy.

O'MALLEY, William. 92 South Side, Clapham Common, London. S. of Michael and Honoria O'Malley. B. in Connemara 1857; m. 1886, the youngest d. of Thomas

O'Connor, Esq., of Athlone, a sister of Mr. T.P. O'Connor, MP. Educ. at the Model School, Galway, and St. Mary's Coll., London. At one time was a Schoolmaster in London, but ceased that profession to become a Journalist. An Irish Nationalist and Anti-Parnellite. Represented the Connemara division of Galway from 1895 until defeated in 1918. Died Sept. 1939. [1918]

O'MARA, James. Continued in House after 1918: full entry in Volume III.

O'MARA, Stephen. An "Irish Nationalist". First returned for the Ossory division of Queen's County Feb. 1886 but retired shortly afterwards at the July 1886 election.

O'NEILL, Hon. Arthur Edward Bruce. 29 Ennismore Gardens, London. Carlton, and Bachelors'. Eld. s. of Lord O'Neill. B. 19 Sept. 1876; m. Lady Annabel Crewe-Milnes, d. of the Marq. of Crewe. Educ. at Eton. Joined the 2nd Life Guards 1897; Capt. 1902. Served in S. African War 1899-1900. J.P. and Dept.-Lieut. for Co. Antrim. A Unionist. Elected for mid Antrim in Jan. 1910 and sat until he was killed in action on 4 Nov. 1914. [1914]

O'NEILL, Charles. Glenravel House, Coatbridge, N.B. National Liberal, and Irish. S. of Hugh O'Neill, Esq., of Glenravee, Co. Antrim. B. 1849 in Co. Armagh; m. 1874, Margaret, d. of Michael McKillop, Esq., of Airdrie. Educ. at Glasgow University; M.B.C.M. 1892. A Physician and Surgeon in practice at Coatbridge. Appointed Assistant Professor of Botany 1897; a member of Coatbridge Town Council, Old Monkland School Board, and Airdrie and Coatbridge Water Trust. A member of Lanark County Council, and Senior Magistrate of Coatbridge. J.P. for Lanarkshire. Was associated with Mr. Isaac Butt at the inception of the Home Rule movement. A Nationalist. Unsuccessfully contested S. Armagh in 1900; first elected for S. Armagh in 1909 and sat until his death 14 Jan. 1918. [1917]

O'NEILL, Hon. Robert Torrens. 3 Regent Street, London. Derrynogd, Draperstown, Co. Londonderry. Rullymore Lodge, Ballymena, Co. Antrim. 2nd s. of the 1st Baron O'Neill, by his 1st wife, Henrietta, d. of the Hon. Robert Torrens,

Judge of the Court of Common Pleas in Ireland. B. in Co. Armagh 1845. Educ. at Harrow, and Brasenose Coll., Oxford; M.A. 1870. A Maj. in the 4th Battalion Royal Inniskilling Fusiliers. A J.P. and Dept.-Lieut. for Co. Londonderry, and was High Sheriff of the Co. on 1871. A J.P. for Co. Antrim. A Conservative. Unsuccessfully contested Antrim in May 1885. First elected for mid Antrim at the general election of 1885 and sat until he retired in Jan. 1910. Died 25 July 1910. [1909]

O'NEILL, Hon. Robert William Hugh. Continued in House after 1918: full entries in Volumes III and IV.

ORDE-POWLETT, Hon. William George Algar. Wensley Hall, Leyburn, Yorkshire. Carlton, and Wellington. Eld. s. of Lord Bolton. B. 21 Aug. 1869 at Bolton Hall, Yorkshire; m. 1893, Hon. Elizabeth Mary Gibson, d. of 1st Lord Ashbourne. Educ. at Eton, and Sandhurst. A Lieut. 60th Rifles and Yorkshire Yeomanry. Maj. 4th Battalion (T.) Yorkshire Regiment, later Lieut.-Col. Territorial Force Reserves. A Unionist. Elected for the Richmond division of the N. Riding of Yorkshire in Jan. 1910 and sat until he retired in 1918. Succeeded as 5th Baron Bolton 14 Aug. 1922. Died 11 Dec. 1944. [1918]

ORMSBY-GORE, Hon. George Ralph Charles. 37 Chesham Place, London. The Lodge, Malpas, Cheshire. Guards', and Travellers'. S. of Lord Harlech, 2nd Baron, and Lady Emily Charlotte, d. of Admiral Sir George Seymour. B. 1855 in London. Educ. at Eton, and Sandhurst. Was Lieut. in the Coldstream Guards 1875-83. Lieut.-Col. commanding the Shropshire Yeomanry; a J.P. and Dept.-Lieut. for Shropshire and Merionethshire, and also for Co. Leitrim, of which Co. he was High Sheriff in 1885. A Conservative. Elected for the Oswestry division of Shropshire May 1901 and sat until he succeeded as Baron Harlech in 1904. K.C.B. 1936. Died 8 May 1938. [1904]

ORMSBY-GORE, Hon. Seymour Fitzroy. 27 Lowdnes Street, London. Turf. 3rd s. of the 2nd Lord Harlech, and Lady Emily Charlotte, d. of Sir George Seymour. B. at 18 Chesham Place in 1863. Educ. at Eton, and Brasenose Coll., Oxford; M.A. A Stockbroker, Senior Partner of Gore and Company, Stockbrokers. Lieut. 4th Battalion Oxford Light Infantry, later Capt. 3rd Kent Volunteer Artillery. A frequent contributor to magazines, chiefly on Irish political subjects. Author of fictional works under the *nom de plume* of Simon Carne. A Conservative and Imperialist, a supporter of the Tory Democracy. Elected for the Gainsborough division of Lincolnshire in 1900 and sat until he retired in 1906. Assistant Cable Censor 1914; Staff Officer from 1915. Died 19 Nov. 1950.   [1905]

ORMSBY-GORE, Hon. William George Arthur. Continued in House after 1918: full entry in Volume III.

ORR-EWING, Sir Archibald, Bart. See EWING, Sir Archibald Orr, Bart.

ORR-EWING, Charles Lindsay. 25 Cranley Gardens, London. Red House, Ayr. Dunskey, Portpatrick. Carlton, and Bachelors'. Youngest s. of Sir Archibald Orr-Ewing, Bart., MP for Dumbartonshire 1868-92, and Elizabeth, d. of James Reid, Esq., of Caldercruix. B. 1860; m. 1898, Lady Augusta, eld. d. of the Earl of Glasgow. Educ. at Harrow 1875-80. Capt. 3rd Argyll and Sutherland Highlanders. Member of Wigtonshire County Council. A Conservative. Sat for Ayr Burghs from 1895 until his death 24 Dec. 1903.   [1903]

O'SHAUGHNESSY, Patrick Joseph. Rathkeale, Co. Limerick. S. of David O'Shaughnessy, Esq., Merchant, Auctioneer, and Farmer, of Rathkeale, and Norah, d. of John W. Power, Esq., Merchant of Rathkeale. B. at Rathkeale 1872. Educ. at the Classical Academy, Rathkeale, and French Coll., Blackrock, Co. Dublin; obtained gold medal and special certificate at Preliminary Law Exam., 2nd place in 1st class Intermediate Law Exam., and was a member of the United Irish League. A Nationalist. Represented W. Limerick from 1900 until he retired in 1918. Died 29 Dec. 1920. [1918]

O'SHEA, William Henry. Retired in 1886: full entry in Volume I.

O'SHEE, James John. Bellevue Place, Clonmel. S. of John Shee, Esq., and Marianne Britton. B. 1866 at Newton, Carrick-on-Suir, Co. Tipperary. Educ. at the local National School, Rockwell Coll.,

Cashel, and University Coll., Dublin. A Solicitor from 1890. Was Honorary Secretary of the Irish Land and Labour Association. Assumed the surname of O'Shee in 1900. An Irish Nationalist, Anti-Parnellite, in favour of radical land and labour reforms. Represented W. Waterford from Sept. 1895 until defeated in Co. Waterford in 1918. Died 1 Jan. 1946.   [1918]

OSMOND-WILLIAMS, Sir Arthur. Castell Dendraeth and Borthwen, Merionethshire. Reform. S. of David Williams, Esq., MP for Merioneth 1868, of Castle Dendraeth, Merionethshire, and Annie Ll., d. of William Williams, Esq., of Peniarthucha, Merioneth. B. 1849 at Castle Dendraeth, Merionethshire; m. 1880, Frances Evelyn, 4th d. of S.W. Greaves, Esq., of Bericote, Warwickshire, and sister to the Lord-Lieut. of Carnarvonshire. Educ. at Eton. Was Chairman of Merioneth County Council for three years; Alderman of that body, Dept.-Chairman of Quarter Sessions, and J.P., and Dept.-Lieut. for Merionethshire and Carnarvonshire. A Liberal. Elected for Merionethshire in 1900 and sat until he retired in Jan. 1910. Created Bart. in 1909. Died 28 Jan. 1927.   [1909]

O'SULLIVAN, Eugene. House of Commons, London. Firies Castle, Farranfore, Co. Kerry. B. 1879. A Farmer in Co. Kerry. A member of the Central Council of Land and Labour Association. A Nationalist. Unsuccessfully contested Kerry E. in Jan. 1906; first elected there in Jan. 1910 and sat until he was unseated on petition in June 1910. Died 19 May 1942.   [1910]

O'SULLIVAN, Timothy. Main Street, Killarney. S. of Michael O'Sullivan, Esq., J.P. B. 7 Jan. 1879; m. 1906, d. of John Crothy, Esq., J.P., of Lismore. Educ. at St. Brendon's Seminary, Killarney. A Merchant. J.P. for Co. Kerry. A Nationalist. Elected for E. Kerry in Dec. 1910 and sat until he retired in 1918. Died 15 Aug. 1950.   [1918]

OSWALD, James Francis. 111 Harley Street, London. 6 New Square, London. Carlton. S. of W. Oswald, Esq., of Highbury New Park, and Elizabeth, d. of P. Laing, Esq., of J.P. of Deptford, Sunderland. B. 1838 at Limehouse; m. 1887, Isabella, d. of John Turrill, Esq. Educ. at Stepney Grammar and Islington Proprietary Schools, and St. Edmund Hall, Oxford. Was admitted a Solicitor in 1861, and called to the bar (Middle Temple) 1869; a Q.C. 1893, a bencher of Gray's Inn 1893. Was a member of the Bar Committee, and one of the Gen. Council of the Bar, and also of the Council of Law Reporting, and author of a book upon *Contempt of Court*; was a Vestryman and Churchwarden, etc., of Islington, and served 12 years in Field Battalion of Hon. Artillery Company. A Conservative. Sat for Oldham from July 1895 until he accepted Chiltern Hundreds in 1899. Died 14 Sept. 1908.   [1899]

OTTER, Francis. Ranby Hall, Wragby. National Liberal, and New University. S. of Francis Otter, Esq., by Elizabeth, d. of Samuel Younge, Esq. B. at Gainsborough 1831; m. 1875, Emily Helen, d. of W. Cross, Esq., of London and Glasgow, and sister-in-law of George Eliot, Esq. Educ. at Rugby, and Corpus Christi Coll., Oxford, of which he subsequently became a Fellow. Was called to the bar at Lincoln's Inn 1860, but was chiefly distinguished for his success as a private tutor at Oxford. J.P. for Lindsey. Patron of 1 living. An "advanced Liberal," in favour of "Local Option" and "Sunday Closing" in the liquor traffic. Sat for the Louth division of Lincolnshire from Nov. 1885 until he retired in 1886. Unsuccessfully contested the Sleaford division of Lincolnshire in Sept. 1889, and the Horncastle division of Lincolnshire in July 1892. Died 29 May 1895.   [1886]

OUTHWAITE, Robert Leonard. 30 Arundel Gardens, Notting Hill, London. National Liberal. S. of Robert Outhwaite, Esq., Pastoralist, Australia. B. 1869 in Tasmania; m. 1898, d. of James Anderson, Esq., Barrister, New Zealand. Educ. at Church of England Grammar School, Melbourne. A Journalist. Spent several years in country life in Australia and New Zealand. Was interested in the Land Reform movement. Author of works on political subjects. A Liberal. Unsuccessfully contested W. Birmingham 1906 and the Horsham division of Sussex Jan. 1910. Elected for Hanley July 1912 and sat until defeated as an Independent Liberal in the Hanley division of Stoke on Trent in 1918. Died 6 Nov. 1930.   [1918]

OWEN, Arthur Charles Humphreys-. See HUMPHREYS-OWEN, Arthur Charles.

OWEN, Thomas. 5 Whitehall Gardens, London. Henley Grove, Westbury-on-Trym, Bristol. National Liberal, and Devonshire. S. of Owen Owen, Esq., Yeoman. B. 1840 at Cwmyrhaiadr; m. 1868; Elizabeth, d. of Charles Todd, Esq., of Shawforth, Lancashire. Educ. privately. Chairman of Thomas Owen and Company (Limited), Cardiff. A Liberal. Sat for the Launceston division of Cornwall from July 1892 until his death 10 July 1898. [1898]

PAGE CROFT, Henry, C.M.G. See CROFT, Henry Page, C.M.G. Continued in House after 1918: full entry in Volume III.

PAGET, Almeric Hugh. 39 Berkeley Square, London. Panshanger, Hertford. Carlton, Turf, Garrick, Orleans, and Royal Thames Yacht. S. of Gen. Lord Alfred Paget, C.B., and Cecilla, d. of George T. Wyndham. B. 14 Mar. 1861 in London; m. 1895, Pauline, d. of Hon. William C. Whitney, at one time Secretary of United States Navy (she died 1916). Educ. at Harrow. Parliamentary Provincial Whip for the Eastern and Home Counties, and President for the Eastern Division of National Unionist Association. Member of the Executive Committee of the Tariff Reform League. J.P. for Suffolk, High Sheriff 1909. Gov. Guy's Hospital. Vice-Commodore of Royal Thames Yacht Club. A Unionist, a strong supporter of Fiscal Reform, and the extension of Land Ownership. Unsuccessfully contested Cambridge 1906; elected there in Jan. 1910 and sat until he accepted Chiltern Hundreds in 1917. Created Baron Queenborough 1918. President National Union of Conservative and Unionist Associations 1928-29, 1940 and 1941. Director of several finance Companies. Died 22 Sept. 1949.   [1917]

PAGET, Sir Richard Horner, Bart. 58 Queen Anne Street, London. Cranmore Hall, Shepton Mallet. Carlton. S. of John Moore Paget, Esq., of Cranmore, Somerset, by Elizabeth Jane, d. of the Rev. J.F. Doveton, Rector of Mells, Somerset. B. 1832; m. 1866, Caroline Isabel, 2nd d. of H.E. Surtees, Esq., MP, of Redworth, Co. Durham, and Dane End, Hertfordshire. Educ. at Sandhurst. Entered the army 1848, and served in the 66th Foot till 1863. Was Capt. North Somerset Yeomanry, and Lieut.-Col. 3rd Somerset Battalion

Rifle Volunteers. A Magistrate, Dept.-Lieut. and Chairman of Quarter Sessions for Somerset; also Chairman of the Somerset Co. Council. A Conservative. Sat for Somerset E. from July 1865 to Dec. 1868, when he was elected for the Mid division and sat for it till Nov. 1885. Sat for the Wells division of Somerset from Nov. 1885 until he retired in 1895. Created Bart. in 1886. PC. 1895. Died 3 Feb. 1908.   [1895]

PAGET, Thomas Tertius. Retired in 1886: full entry in Volume I.

PALMER, Sir Charles Mark, Bart. 37 Curzon Street, London. Grinkle Park, Loftus, Yorkshire. Brooks's, and Reform. Eld. s. of George Palmer, Esq., Merchant and Shipowner. B. at South Shields 1822; m. 1st, 1846, Jane, d. of Ebenezer Robson, Esq., of Newcastle (she died 1865); 2ndly, Augusta Mary, d. of Alfred Lambert, Esq., of Paris (she died 1875); 3rdly, 1877, Gertrude, 2nd d. of James Montgomery, Esq., of Hartland, Cranford, Middlesex. An Owner of Collieries situated in Northumberland and Durham. The founder of the Jarrow Shipbuilding Yard, Rolling Mills, Furnaces, and Engine Works. A Magistrate and Dept.-Lieut. for Durham and the N. Riding of Yorkshire. Honorary Col. of the 1st Durham Engineer Volunteers. Created Bart. in 1886. A Liberal. Unsuccessfully contested South Shields in 1868. Sat for N. Durham from Feb. 1874 to Nov. 1885 and for the Jarrow division of Durham from Nov. 1885 until his death 3 June 1907.   [1907]

PALMER, George William. 36 Queen Anne's Gate, London. Marlston House, Nr. Newbury, Berkshire. Reform, Devonshire, and National Liberal. S. of George Palmer, Esq., who was MP for Reading 1878-85, and Sarah Elizabeth, eld. d. of Robert Meatyard, Esq., of Basingstoke. B. at Reading 1851; m. 1879, the eld. d. of Henry Barrett, Esq., of Surbiton, Surrey, and grand-d. of Jonathan Dymond, Esq., of Exeter, the essayist. Educ. at Grove House, Tottenham. A Biscuit Manufacturer, Director of Huntley and Palmers Limited, Reading. A J.P. for Reading and the Co. of Berkshire, and was a member of the Town Council from 1882, of which he was Mayor 1888-89. A Liberal. Sat for Reading from 1892 until defeated July 1895; unsuccessfully contested Wokingham division of Berkshire

Mar. 1898; re-elected for Reading July 1898 and sat until he accepted Chiltern Hundreds in 1904. PC. 1906. Died 8 Oct. 1913.   [1904]

PALMER, Godfrey Mark. Continued in House after 1918: full entry in Volume III.

PALMER, James Dampier. 7 Park Place, St. James's, London. 31 Brunswick Terrace, Brighton. Heronden Hall, Tenterden, Kent. Carlton, Junior Carlton, and Coaching. Eld. s. of William Palmer, Esq., of Romford, Essex. B. 1851 at Woodford, Essex; m. 1874, Isabella Elizabeth, eld. d. of W. Curteis Whelan, Esq., of Heronden Hall, Tenterden, Kent. Educ. at Felstead School. Chairman of Messrs. Palmer and Company Limited, Stratford, London. J.P. for Kent and West Ham, and Honorary Col. 1st Kent Artillery Volunteers, Eastern Division, Royal Artillery. A progressive Conservative. Sat for Gravesend from July 1892 until he accepted Chiltern Hundreds in June 1898. Died 16 Oct. 1899.   [1898]

PALMER, Sir Walter, Bart. 50 Grosvenor Square, London. Sunninghill, Berkshire. Carlton, Junior Carlton, and St. James's. S. of George Palmer, Esq., MP for Reading 1878-85. B. at Reading in 1858; m. Jean, d. of W.Y. Craig, Esq., MP for N. Staffordshire 1880-85. Educ. at University Coll., London, Sorbonne University, Paris; B.Sc. degree of London University. A Director of Huntley and Palmers, Limited; J.P., and Dept.-Lieut. for Berkshire. Created Bart. 1904. A Conservative. Elected for Salisbury in 1900 and sat until defeated in 1906. Died 16 Apr. 1910.   [1905]

PARKER, Charles Stuart. 15 Great Queen Street, Westminster, London. Fairlie, Ayrshire. Athenaeum. Eld. s. of Charles S. Parker, Esq., of Fairlie, Ayrshire, and Aigburth, Liverpool, by Anne, eld. d. of Samuel Sandbach, Esq., of Woodlands, near Liverpool, and Hafodunos, Denbighshire. B. 1829. Educ. at Eton, thence elected Scholar, and afterwards Fellow of University Coll., Oxford, where he graduated with 1st class honours, B.A. 1852, M.A. 1856. Was Public Examiner in 1859, 1860, 1863, and 1868. Was named as a Special Commissioner in the Public Schools Act 1868. Was Maj. in the Oxford University R.V., and a member of the Royal Commissions on Military Education 1869-70, and on Educational

Endowments (Scotland) from 1872 to 1875. Was Private Secretary to Mr. Cardwell at the Colonial Office from 1864 to 1866. Appointed Chairman of Referees on Private Bills 1886. Wrote on "Popular Education" in *Questions for a Reformed Parliament* (1866), and on *The History of Classical Education,* and *The Early Political Life of Sir Robert Peel.* A Liberal, and Home Ruler. Sat for Perthshire from Dec. 1868 to Feb. 1874 when he was an unsuccessful candidate there. Sat for the city of Perth from Feb. 1878 until defeated in 1892. Unsuccessfully contested W. Perthshire in 1900. PC. 1907. Died 18 June 1910.   [1892]

PARKER, Hon. Francis. Wilton House, Hobart Place, London. Carlton. 4th s. of the 6th Earl of Macclesfield, by his 2nd wife Lady Mary Frances Grosvenor, d. of the 2nd Marq. of Westminster. B. in London 1851; m. 1882, Henrietta, 3rd d. of Henry Lomax Gaskell, Esq., of Kiddington Hall, Woodstock. Educ. at Eton, and Christ Church, Oxford. Was called to the bar at the Inner Temple in 1875. A Conservative. Sat for the Henley division of Oxfordshire from 1886 until he retired in 1895. Died 22 Oct. 1931.   [1895]

PARKER, Rt. Hon. Sir Horatio Gilbert George, Bart. 20 Carlton House Terrace, London. Athenaeum, Carlton, and Garrick. S. of Capt. J. Parker, R.A. B. in Canada 1862; m. 1895, d. of Ashley Van Tine, of New York. Educ. at Trinity University, Toronto. Author of *Pierre and his People, The Trail of the Sword, When Valmond Came to Pontiac, The Seats of the Mighty, The Battle of the Strong, The Lane that had no Turning, The Right of Way, The Weavers, Northern Lights, The Pomp of the Lavilettes, The Judgment House, The World for Sale, The Money Master, You Never Know Your Luck,* etc., and of a war book called *The World in the Crucible,* an historical description called *Old Quebec,* and of three plays. Was Honorary Col. Royal Garrison Volunteer Artillery; Honorary D.C.L., Litt.D., and LL.D. Knighted 1902; created Bart. 1915; PC. 1916. Organised the first Conference of the Universities of the Empire 1903. Chairman of the Imperial South African Association for seven years. Controller of American publicity until 1917. A Unionist. Elected for Gravesend in 1900 and sat until he accepted Chiltern Hundreds in May 1918. Died 6 Sept. 1932.   [1918]

PARKER, James. Continued in House after 1918: full entry in Volume III.

PARKES, Sir Edward Ebenezer. Hermitage Road, Edgbaston, Birmingham. Constitutional. S. of Israel Parkes, Esq., of Harborne Road, Edgbaston. B. 1848. Educ. at the Wesley Coll., Sheffield. An Ironmaster. A J.P. for Birmingham; was a member of the City Council. At one time Chairman of the local Liberal Unionist Association. Knighted 1917. A Unionist. Represented central Birmingham from 1895 until he retired in 1918. Died 29 June 1919.   [1918]

PARNELL, Charles Stewart. Euston Hotel, London. Avondale, Rathdrum, Ireland. National Liberal. Eld. s. of John Henry Parnell, Esq., of Avondale, Co. Wicklow (and High Sheriff there in 1836), by Delia Tudor, only d. of Admiral Charles Stewart, of the United States Navy. B. 1846; m. June 1891, Katharine, d. of Sir John Page Wood and divorced wife of W.H. O'Shea, Esq., former MP for Clare and Galway City. Educ. privately at Chipping Norton, and at Magdalene Coll., Cambridge. Was presented with the freedom of the city of Cork 1880, and that of Edinburgh 1889. A J.P. for Wicklow, of which he was High Sheriff in 1874. Leader of the Irish Nationalist party, in favour of "Home Rule" for Ireland. Unsuccessfully contested Co. Dublin in Mar. 1874. Sat for Meath from Apr. 1875 to Apr. 1880, when he was returned simultaneously for Meath, Mayo, and Cork city, but elected to sit for Cork city, and was MP until his death on 6 Oct. 1891. Mr. Parnell was Leader of the Irish Nationalist Party from May 1880 until 6 Dec. 1890 when he was deposed in the aftermath of the O'Shea divorce case. 26 Members remained loyal to him and the Parnellite Party continued to exist, under the leadership of John Redmond, until 1900.   [1891]

PARNELL, John Howard. Avondale, Rathdrum, Co. Wicklow. Eld. s. of John Henry Parnell, Esq., of Avondale, by Delia Tudor, d. of Commodore Charles Stuart, of the United States Navy, and brother of Charles Stewart Parnell, Esq., MP, sometime leader of the Irish Home Rule party. B. 1843. He lived in Alabama, U.S.A. until the death of his brother, Mr. C.S. Parnell. In 1898 he was elected by the Dublin Corporation to the Office of City Marshall. A

Parnellite Home Ruler. Was an unsuccessful candidate for Co. Wicklow in 1874 and for W. Wicklow in 1892. Sat for Meath S. from July 1895 until he retired in 1900. Contested the seat at a by-election 1903. Died 3 May 1923.   [1900]

PARROTT, Sir James Edward. 12 Cumin Place, Edinburgh. National Liberal. S. of E.B. Parrott, Esq., of Wavertree, Liverpool, and Margaret, d. of John Johns, Esq., of St. Clears, Carmarthenshire. B. at Skegness 1 June 1863; m. Elizabeth Sophia, youngest d. of John Shirley, Esq., of Derby. Educ. at St. Paul's Coll., Cheltenham, and Trinity Coll., Dublin; M.A., and LL.D. of Trinity Coll. Editor to the publishing house of Thomas Nelson and Sons Limited from 1898. President for thirteen years of the South Edinburgh Liberal Association, and for eight years of the Edinburgh United Liberal Committee 1908-19. J.P. for the City of the Co. of Edinburgh. Author of *A Pageant of British History, A Pageant of English Literature, Allies, Foes and Neutrals, Britain Overseas,* and numerous school books. Editor of Funk and Wagnall's *Standard Encyclopaedia,* etc. Was Knighted in 1910. A Liberal. Elected for S. Edinburgh in May 1917 and sat until defeated in W. Edinburgh in 1918. Died 5 Apr. 1921.   [1918]

PARROTT, William. Parma House, Huddersfield Road, Barnsley. S. of James and Susannah, Parrott. B. at Row Green, Somerset 18 Dec. 1843; m. 1868, Eliza, d. of T. Thompson, Esq., of Methley, Yorkshire. General and Corresponding Secretary of the Yorkshire Miners Association, a member of the Coal Trade Conciliation Board, member of the Barnsley Town Council. A Labour and Liberal Member, in favour of free trade. Sat for the Normanton division of the W. Riding of Yorkshire from Mar. 1904 until his death 9 Nov. 1905.   [1905]

PARRY, Thomas Duncombe Love Jones. See JONES-PARRY, Thomas Duncombe Love. Defeated in 1886: full entry in Volume I. (Note: Love is incorrectly spelt Lone in Volume I.)

PARRY, Thomas Henry, D.S.O. Continued in House after 1918: full entry in Volume III.

PARTINGTON, Hon. Oswald. Bolney House, Ennismore Gardens, London. Red Court, Glossop, Derbyshire. Reform, Marlborough, Brooks's, and Bachelors'. S. of Edward Partington, J.P., the 1st Lord Doverdale. B. 4 May 1872; m. 1902, Hon. Clara Isabel Murray, d. of Visct. Elibank. Educ. at Rossall School. A Capt. 4th Volunteer Battalion Cheshire Regiment; J.P. for Derbyshire. Was a Junior Lord of the Treasury and a Liberal Whip 1909-10; Alderman London County Council 1913. Member of the Royal Commission on Paper 1916. A Liberal. Sat for the High Peak division of Derbyshire from 1900 to Dec. 1910, when he was defeated. Elected for the Shipley division of the W. Riding of Yorkshire in Feb. 1915, and sat until he retired in 1918. Succeeded as 2nd Baron Doverdale 5 Jan. 1925. Died 23 Mar. 1935.
                    [1918]

PAUL, Herbert Woodfield. 13 Tite Street, London. Cherry Orchard, Forest Row, Sussex. Reform. S. of the Rev. Canon Paul, of Finedon, Northamptonshire, and Jessie, d. of Capt. Mackworth, R.N. B. 16 Jan. 1853 at Finedon; m. 1883, Elinor, d. of the Hon. W. Ritchie, Advocate Gen., Calcutta. Educ. at Eton, and Corpus Christi Coll., Oxford; 1st class Lit. Hum., President of the Union. Called to the bar at Lincoln's Inn 1878; a political leader-writer for the *Daily News* until 1901; author of *History of Modern England,* 5 vols., *Men and Letters, Life of Froude,* and other works. A Liberal. Sat for S. Edinburgh from 1892-95, when he was defeated. Elected for Northampton in 1906 and sat until he retired in Jan. 1910. 2nd Civil Service Commissioner 1909-18. Died 4 Aug. 1935.   [1909]

PAULTON, James Mellor. 2 Delahay Street, London. Boughton Hall, Send, Surrey. Brooks's. Only s. of A.W. Paulton, Esq., of Bolton, a well-known Free Trader, by Martha, d. of James Mellor, Esq., of Liverpool. B. in London 1857. Educ. at the International Coll., Spring Grove, and Trinity Hall, Cambridge, taking honours in the Historical Tripos in 1879. Was Private Secretary to Mr. J. Bryce, MP for Aberdeen S., also to Mr. H. Childers, as Home Secretary in 1886. In 1893 was Private Secretary (unpaid) to Mr. Asquith, Home Secretary. A Referee of Private Bills. A Liberal. Sat for the Bishop Auckland division of Durham from 1885 until he retired in Jan. 1910. Assistant Paymaster Gen. Supreme Court 1909-21. Died 6 Dec. 1923.   [1909]

PEACOCK, Richard. Gorton Hall, Lancashire. Reform, Whitehall, and Cobden. Union, and Reform, Manchester. S. of Ralph Peacock, Esq., of Bank House, Swaledale, Yorkshire, by Dorothy, d. of John Robinson, Esq. B. 1820. Educ. at the Grammar School, Leeds. A Civil Engineer. In 1854 he retired from the post of Chief Locomotive Engineer of the Manchester, Sheffield, and Lincolnshire Railway, and became Partner with Charles Beyer, Esq., in the Gorton Foundry, Manchester. A J.P. for the Co. of Lancashire. An advanced Liberal, in favour of Home Rule, of the Reform of the House of Lords, the disestablishment and disendowment of the Church, and the establishment of local self-government. Sat for the Gorton division of Lancashire from 1885 until his death on 2 Mar. 1889.   [1889]

PEARCE, Sir Robert. 9 Downside Crescent, Haverstock Hill, London. 116 Fore Street, London. National Liberal, and City Liberal. S. of Joseph Pearce, Esq., of Ipswich. B. 15 Jan. 1840 at Ipswich; m. 1st, 1880, Elizabeth, d. of Edward Deane, Esq., of Streatham (she died 1910); 2ndly, 1914, Margaret, d. of the Rev. R.B. Exton. Educ. privately, and at Ipswich Grammar School. A Solicitor, admitted 1865, a Partner in Baylis, Pearce and Company, 116 Fore Street, London, and clerk to the Cripplegate Charities, and a member of the Carmen's Company, F.R.A.S. Knighted 1916. A Liberal. Unsuccessfully contested the Leek division of Staffordshire in 1895 and 1900; sat for the Leek division of Staffordshire from 1906 to Jan. 1910, when he was defeated; re-elected there in Dec. 1910 and sat until he retired in 1918. Died 29 Sept. 1922. [1918]

PEARCE, Sir William, Bart. 10 Park Terrace, Glasgow. Cardell House, Wemyss Bay, Scotland. Carlton, and St. Stephen's. Only s. of Joseph George Pearce, Esq., of the Admiralty, by Louisa, d. of W. Lee, Esq. B. at Brompton, Kent 8 Jan. 1833. Educ. as a naval architect and engineer. In 1870 he became a Partner in the firm of John Elder and Company. Chairman of the Guion Line Company and of the Scottish Oriental Steam Shipping Company, and has served on the Royal Commissions on Tonnage, on Loss of Life at Sea, and on the Depression of Trade. A Magistrate for Lanarkshire, and was created a Bart. in 1887. A Conservative. Unsuccessfully contested Glasgow in Apr. 1880. Sat for the Govan district of Lanarkshire from 1885 until his death on 18 Dec. 1888.   [1888]

PEARCE, Sir William. Continued in House after 1918: full entry in Volume III.

PEARCE, Sir William George, Bart. 1 Hyde Park Gardens, London. Chilton Lodge, Hungerford, Berkshire. Cardwell, Wemyss Bay, Renfrewshire. Carlton. Only s. of Sir W. Pearce, MP for the Govan division of Lanarkshire 1885-88, by Dinah Elizabeth, d. of R. Sowter, Esq. B. 1860. Educ. at Rugby, and Trinity Coll., Cambridge; B.A., LL.B. 1884, M.A. 1887. Was called to the bar at the Inner Temple 1885. A J.P. for Berkshire, and Chairman of the Fairfield Shipbuilding and Engineering Company, and of the Guion and the Oriental Steamship Company. Succeeded as Bart. in 1888. A Unionist. Sat for Plymouth from July 1892 until he retired in 1895. Died 2 Nov. 1907. [1895]

PEARSON, Rt. Hon. Sir Charles John, Kt. 54 Chester Square, London. 7 Drumsheugh Gardens, Edinburgh. Carlton, and Scottish Conservative. 2nd s. of Charles Pearson, Esq., C.A., Edinburgh, and Margaret Dalziel, d. of John Dalziel, Esq., of Earlston, Berwickshire. B. 1843; m. 1873, Elizabeth, d. of M.G. Hewat, Esq., of Norwood. Educ. at Edinburgh Academy. St. Andrews and Edinburgh Universities, and Corpus Christi Coll., Oxford (M.A.) Called to the bar of the Inner Temple June 1870; a member of the Faculty of Advocates in Scotland July 1870; Sheriff of Chancery, Scotland 1885-88, of the Counties of Renfrew and Bute 1888-89, and of Perthshire 1889-90; Procurator of the Church of Scotland 1886-90; Knighted 1887; appointed Solicitor Gen. for Scotland and a Q.C. 1890; PC. Oct. 1891. Dept.-Lieut. for Edinburgh, City and Co. Lord Advocate 1891-92 and 1895-96. Dean of Faculty of Advocates 1892-95. A Conservative. Sat for Edinburgh and St. Andrews Universities from Nov. 1890 until Apr. 1896 when he was appointed Judge of the Court of Session, with the title of Lord Pearson. Retired 1909. Died 15 Aug. 1910.
[1896]

PEARSON, Sir Weetman Dickinson, Bart. 16 Carlton House Terrace, London. Paddockhurst, Worth, Sussex. Reform. S. of George Pearson, Esq., of Brickendonbury, Hertford. B. 1856; m. 1881, Annie, 2nd d. of Sir John Cass. of Bradford, Yorkshire. Educ. at Harrogate. Head of the firm of S. Pearson and Son Limited, Contractors, of Westminster. Created Bart. in 1894. An advanced Liberal. Unsuccessfully contested Colchester in 1892; first elected there in Feb. 1895 and sat until he retired in Jan. 1910. Created Baron Cowdray in June 1910; Visct. Cowdray Dec. 1916; PC. 1917. President of the Air Board Jan.-Nov. 1917. G.C.V.O. 1925. Died 1 May 1927.   [1909]

PEARSON, Hon. Weetman Harold Miller. 6 Richmond Terrace, London. Capron House, Midhurst. Marlborough. Eld. s. of Lord Cowdray. B. 18 Apr. 1882; m. 1905, Beryl, d. of Lord Edward Spencer Churchill. Educ. at Rugby, and Christ Church, Oxford. A Maj. Sussex Yeomanry. A Liberal. Unsuccessfully contested Rutland at the general election in Jan. 1906. Elected for the Eye division of Suffolk in Apr. 1906 and sat until he retired in 1918. Succeeded as 2nd Visct. Cowdray 1 May 1927. Died 5 Oct. 1933.
[1918]

PEASE, Alfred Edward. Pinchinthorpe House, Guisborough, Yorkshire. Brooks's, and National Liberal. Eld. s. of Sir Joseph W. Pease, Bart., MP for the Barnard Castle division of Durham, by Mary, d. of Alfred Fox, Esq., of Falmouth (she died 1892). B. 1857; m. 1880, Helen, 3rd d. of Sir Robert N. Fowler, Bart., MP. Educ. at Grove House, Tottenham, and Trinity Coll., Cambridge (M.A. 1883). A Director of Pease and Partners Limited, and of the National Provident Institution; a J.P. and Dept.-Lieut. for the N. Riding of Yorkshire, a Dept.-Lieut. for London, a member of the Council of the Royal Agricultural Society and of the Royal Commission on horse breeding. A Liberal and Home Ruler, a Free Trader, and in favour of measures for the promotion of Temperance, including Sunday closing. Sat for York 1885-92 when he was defeated. Defeated again in 1895. Elected for the Cleveland division of the N. Riding of Yorkshire while away in Somaliland Jan. 1897 and sat until he accepted Chiltern Hundreds in 1902. Succeeded as Bart in 1903. Resident Magistrate Transvaal 1903-05; Alderman of N. Riding 1889-1937; published *The Diaries of Edward Pease* (1907), *Elections and Recollections* (1932), and several other works. Died 27 Apr. 1939.   [1902]

PEASE, Arthur. 2 Prince's Gardens, London. Cliff House, Marske-by-the-Sea, Yorkshire. Reform. S. of Joseph Pease, Esq., MP for S. Durham from 1832 to 1841. B. at Darlington 1837; m. 1864, Mary, d. of Ebenezer Pike, Esq., of Besborough, Co. Cork. An Alderman and the Chairman of the Co. Council of Durham, an Alderman of Darlington, of which borough he was Mayor in 1873-74, and Dept.-Lieut. for Yorkshire, N. Riding. A Liberal Unionist. Sat as MP for Whitby 1880-85 when he was defeated. Contested Darlington July 1892. First returned for Darlington July 1895 and sat until his death 27 Aug. 1898. [1898]

PEASE, Henry Fell. Brinkburn, Darlington. Stanhope Castle, Durham. Reform. S. of Henry Pease, Esq., MP for S. Durham from 1857 to 1865, by Anna, only d. of Richard Fell, Esq., of Belmont, Uxbridge. B. at Middleton St. George, near Darlington 1838; m. 1863, Elizabeth, eld. d. of John Beaumont Pease, Esq., of Darlington. In business as a Coal-Owner, being a member of the firm of Pease and Partners, Limited. Also a Director of Water and Engineering Companies, a J.P. for Durham, and a Dept.-Lieut. for the N. Riding of Yorkshire. Was Mayor of Darlington 1874-75, during the Railway Jubilee, and President of the National Liberal Federation 1881-83. A Liberal, in favour of Home Rule, more extended local self-government, and the Sunday closing of Public Houses. Sat for the Cleveland division of Yorkshire from 1885 until his death on 6 Dec. 1896.   [1896]

PEASE, Rt. Hon. Herbert Pike. Continued in House after 1918: full entry in Volume III.

PEASE, Rt. Hon. Joseph Albert. 8 Hertford Street, London. Headlam Hall, Gainford. Brooks's, National Liberal, and Turf. S. of Sir Joseph W. Pease, Bart., MP, and Mary, d. of Alfred Fox, Esq., of Falmouth. B. 1860 at Darlington; m. 1886, Ethel, d. of Maj.-Gen. Sir Henry Havelock-Allan, Bart., V.C., MP. Educ. at Tottenham School, and Trinity Coll., Cambridge; M.A. A Director of Pease and Partners, Limited and other colliery companies. A J.P. and Dept.-Lieut. for Co. Durham, and a J.P. for the N. Riding of Yorkshire. A member of Guisborough School Board from 1882-85, of Durham County Council and Education Commit-

tee 1889-1903, and of Darlington Town Council from 1882-90 (Mayor 1889-90). Private Secretary (unpaid) to Mr. John Morley as Chief Secretary for Ireland 1892-95, a Junior Lord of the Treasury 1905-08, Patronage Secretary and Chief Liberal Whip 1908-10, Chancellor of the Duchy of Lancaster 1910-11, President of Board of Education 1911-15, and Postmaster General Jan.-Dec. 1916. PC. 1908. A Liberal. Sat for the Tyneside division of Northumberland from 1892-1900, when he was defeated at the general election. Sat for the Saffron Walden division of Essex from 1901 to Jan. 1910, when he was again defeated at a general election. Elected for the Rotherham division of the W. Riding of Yorkshire in Mar. 1910 and sat until created Baron Gainford 3 Jan. 1917. Chairman of British Broadcasting Company Limited 1922-26; Vice-Chairman 1926-32; President Federation of British Industries 1927-28. Died 15 Feb. 1943.
[1916]

PEASE, Joseph Walker. Hesslewood House, Yorkshire. S. of Joseph Robinson Pease, Esq., and Harriet Walker. B. at Hull 1820; m. 1843, Barbara, d. of the Rev. H. Palmer, of Withcote Hall, Leicestershire. Educ. at Rugby. A Banker in Hull. Lieut.-Col. East York Volunteers. Magistrate and Dept.-Lieut. for the E. Riding of Yorkshire. A Conservative. Elected for Hull 24 Oct. 1873 and sat until defeated in Feb. 1874. Died 22 Nov. 1882.

PEASE, Sir Joseph Whitwell, Bart. 44 Grosvenor Gardens, London. Hutton Hall, Guisborough, Yorkshire. Reform, Brooks's, Devonshire, and City Liberal. S. of Joseph Pease, Esq., of Darlington, Merchant, who sat for S. Durham 1832-41, by Emma, d. of Joseph Gurney, Esq., of Lakenham Grove, Norwich. B. at Southend, Darlington 1828; m. 1854, Mary, d. of Alfred Fox, Esq., of Falmouth (she died 1892). A J.P. and Dept.-Lieut. for Durham and the N. Riding of Yorkshire; Chairman of Pease and Partners Limited, and Chairman of the N. Eastern Railway. Created Bart. in 1882. A Liberal. Sat for Durham S. 1865-85, and for the Barnard Castle division of Durham from 1885 until his death 26 June 1903.   [1903]

PEDDIE, John Dick. 132 Buckingham Palace Road, London. 33 Buckingham Terrace, Edinburgh. Reform. University, and Scottish Liberal, Edinburgh. S. of

James Peddie, Esq., Writer to the Signet, Edinburgh, by Margaret Coventry, d. of the Rev. Professor John Dick, D.D., of Glasgow. B. at Edinburgh 1824; m. 1851, Euphemia Lockhart, d. of James Stephens More, Esq., of Edinburgh. An Architect, which profession he entered in 1848, and retired 1878. He erected numerous public and private buildings in Scotland. Elected an Associate of the Royal Scottish Academy 1868, and academician of that body 1870. Wrote various papers in the *Transactions of the Architectural Institute in Scotland.* A Liberal. Sat for Kilmarnock from Apr. 1880 until defeated in Dec. 1885.
[1885]

PEEL, Hon. Arthur George Villiers. 61 Catherine Street, Buckingham Gate, London. Mancetter Manor, Atherstone. Brooks's, Reform, and Beefsteak. S. of 1st Visct. Peel, former Speaker of the House of Commons, and grand-s. of Sir Robert Peel, former Prime Minister (Dec. 1834-Mar. 1835, and Sept. 1841-July 1846), and Adelaide, d. of W.S. Dugdale, Esq., of Merevale Hall, Atherstone. B. in London 27 Feb. 1868; m. 1906, Lady Agnes Lygon, d. of the 6th Earl Beauchamp. Educ. at Harrow, and New Coll., Oxford. Clerk in the Treasury 1893-95; Secretary of Gold Standard Association 1895-98; Director of the Eastern Extension Telegraph Company; Arbitrator under the Board of Trade in the Somerset Mining Area 1912; J.P. for Warwickshire 1911; Dept.-Lieut. 1917. Author of *Enemies of England, Friends of England, Future of England* (1911), *The Tariff Reformers* (1913), *The Reign of Sir Edward Carson* (1914), *The Private Letters of Sir Robert Peel* (1921) and several works on French economic policy. A Liberal. Elected for the Spalding division of Lincolnshire 25 Oct. 1917 and sat until defeated in the Holland-with-Boston division of Lincolnshire in 1918. Unsuccessfully contested Rugby in 1922. Head of War Trade Department, Egypt 1917. Died 25 Apr. 1956.   [1918]

PEEL, Rt. Hon. Arthur Wellesley. House of Commons. The Lodge, Sandy, Bedfordshire. United University. Youngest s. of Sir Robert Peel, 2nd Bart., the well-known Minister, by Julia, youngest d. of Gen. Sir John Floyd, Bart. B. 1829; m. 1862, Adelaide, eld. d. of William Stratford Dugdale, Esq., of Merevale, Warwickshire (she died 1890). Educ. at Eton, and Balliol Coll., Oxford (Honorary D.C.L. 1887). Was

Secretary to the Poor Law Board from Dec. 1868 to Jan. 1871, Parliamentary Secretary to the Board of Trade from the latter date to Aug. 1873, and (patronage) Secretary to the Treasury and Liberal Chief Whip from Aug. 1873 to Feb. 1874; also Under-Secretary of State for the Home Department from Apr. to Dec. 1880. Was first elected Speaker of the House of Commons Feb. 1884, and three times re-elected (Jan. and Aug. 1886 and Aug. 1892), upon all four occasions without opposition. He retired in Apr. 1895. Patron of 1 living. PC. 1884. A Liberal. Unsuccessfully contested Coventry in Oct. 1863. Sat for Warwick July 1865 to Nov. 1885, and for Warwick and Leamington from Nov. 1885 until created Visct. Peel in Apr. 1895. Trustee of British Museum 1898-1907. Died 24 Oct. 1912.   [1895]

PEEL, Rt. Hon. Sir Robert, Bart., G.C.B. 9 Spring Gardens. Drayton Manor, Nr. Tamworth, Staffordshire. Carlton, St. James's, Piccadilly, and Constitutional. Eld. s. of the Rt. Hon. Sir Robert Peel, who was Premier 1834-35, and again 1841-46, by Julia, d. of Gen. Sir John Floyd. B. 1822; m. 1856, Lady Emily Hay, d. of George, 8th Marq. of Tweeddale, K.T. Educ. at Harrow, and Christ Church, Oxford. Succeeded his father as 3rd Bart., 1850. A Magistrate and Dept.-Lieut. of Staffordshire. Was in Spain and Switzerland in the diplomatic service 1844-50; Secretary to the Special Embassy to Russia on the Coronation of Alexander II. Junior Lord of Admiralty from 1855-57; PC. 1861. Was Chief Secretary for Ireland from 1861-65, in Lord Palmerston's administration. G.C.B. 1866. Patron of 1 living. Elected as a Peelite Liberal-Conservative in 1850 and moved over to the Liberals after 1859; in 1874 he again called himself a Liberal-Conservative and was effectively a Conservative from 1878 to 1886 when as a Home Ruler he rejoined the Liberals. Sat as Member for Tamworth from 1850 until Apr. 1880 when he retired. Unsuccessfully contested Gravesend July 1880. Sat for Huntingdon from Mar. 1884 to Nov. 1885. Sat for Blackburn from Nov. 1885 until he retired in July 1886. Unsuccessfully contested the Inverness district in July 1886 and Brighton in Oct. 1889.   [1886]

PEEL, Lieut.-Col. Robert Francis. Continued in House after 1918: full entry in Volume III.

PEEL, Hon. William Robert Wellesley. 52 Grosvenor Street, London. Carlton, Brooks's, and White's. Eld. s. of Visct. Peel (former Speaker of the House of Commons). B. 1867 in London; m. 1899, Hon. Ella Williamson, d. of Lord Ashton. Educ. at Harrow, and Balliol Coll., Oxford. A Barrister, called to the bar at the Inner Temple 1893. A member of the London County Council from 1900-04 and 1907-10. Leader of the Municipal Reform Party from 1908-10. A J.P. for Bedfordshire, a Gov. of Manchester University, and Maj. Bedfordshire Yeomanry. Was a member of Royal Commission for the Port of London. A Unionist. Sat for S. Manchester from May 1900 to 1906, when he unsuccessfully contested the Harrow division of Middlesex. First elected for Taunton in 1909 and sat until he succeeded as 2nd Visct. Peel in Oct. 1912. Member of London County Council for Kennington from 1913-19; Chairman of London County Council 1914-16; Joint Parliamentary Secretary to National Service Department 1917-19. G.B.E. 1919. PC. 1920. Under-Secretary of State for War 1919-21; Chancellor of Duchy of Lancaster, and Minister of Transport 1921-22; Secretary of State for India 1922-24 and 1928-29; First Commissioner of Works 1924-28; Lord Privy Seal 1931; advanced to an Earldom in 1929; Chairman of several Royal Commissions and member of the Round Table Conferences in India and Burma; a Director of Barclays Bank. G.C.S.I. 1932. Died 28 Sept. 1937.   [1912]

PELLY, Sir Lewis, K.C.B., K.C.S.I. 21 Eaton Square, London. Athenaeum, Carlton, United Service, and Windham. S. of John Hinde Pelly, Esq., of the Indian Civil Service, and of Hyde House, Cotswold Hills, Gloucestershire, by Elizabeth Lewis, of Brinscombe, Gloucestershire. B. at Hyde House 1825; m. 1878, Amy H. d. of the Rev. John Lowder. Educ. at Rugby. A Lieut.-Gen. on the Indian Staff Corps, a F.R.G.S., a F.R.A.S., and held many diplomatic and administrative offices in India. K.C.S.I. 1874; K.C.B. 1877. Wrote works on the *North-West Frontier of India,* and *Views and Opinions of General John Jacob,* and an edition of a Persian play *Hussan and Hussein.* A Conservative and "Constitutionalist", prepared to support a practicable and well considered scheme whereby the Colonies and British India should be represented at

London in a central consultative body co-operating with the Imperial Parliament. Sat for Hackney N. from Nov. 1885 until his death 22 Apr. 1892. Promoted Gen. in *Gazette* of 22 Apr. 1892, the day of his death. [1892]

PEMBERTON, John Stapylton Grey. 16 Park Lane, London. Belmont, Durham. Hawthorn Tower, Seaham Harbour. Carlton, Wellington, and Constitutional. S. of Richard Laurence Pemberton, Esq., of Hawthorn Tower and The Barnes, Co. Durham, and Jane Emma, d. of the Rev. Martin Stapylton. B. at The Barnes, Sunderland 1860; m. 1st, 1890, Janet Maud, 2nd d. of Col. T.H. Marshall, C.B., of Hartford, Cheshire; 2ndly, 1895, Nira, younger d. of Hercules G. Ross, Bengal Civil Service. Educ. at Eton, and New Coll., Oxford. A Barrister-at-Law, called to the bar 1889. Fellow of All Souls' 1885, M.A.; J.P. for Co. Durham, and Assistant Secretary to Opium Commission 1894. A Progressive Conservative. Unsuccessfully contested Sunderland in 1892. Elected for Sunderland in 1900 and sat until defeated in 1906. Vice-Chairman of Co. Durham Quarter Sessions 1907-31; and Chairman 1931-38; a member of Durham County Council for 22 years. Died 22 Feb. 1940. [1905]

PEMBERTON-BILLING, Noel. See BILLING, Noel Pemberton-. Continued in House after 1918: full entry in Volume III.

PENDER, Sir James, Bart. 2 Mount Street, Berkeley Square, London. Thornby Hall, Northamptonshire. Carlton, Naval & Military, and Turf. Eld. s. of Sir John Pender, G.C.M.G., MP, and Marion, d. of James Cairns, Esq. B. 1841 at Bonhill, Dumbartonshire; m. Mary Rose, 3rd d. of Edward John Gregge Hopwood, Esq., of Hopwood Hall, Lancashire. Educ. at University Coll. School and Coll., London. A Lieut. King's Own Scottish Borderers; retired 1869; a J.P. for Northamptonshire and Linlithgow; created Bart. 1897. A Conservative. Unsuccessfully contested Mid Northamptonshire in 1892. Sat for the mid division of Northamptonshire from July 1895 until defeated in 1900. Died 20 May 1921. [1900]

PENDER, Sir John. 18 Arlington Street, London. Foots Cray Place, Kent. Brooks's, Reform, and Garrick. Western Club,

Glasgow. Union, Manchester. 2nd s. of James Pender, Esq., of the Vale of Leven, Dumbartonshire. B. 1816; m. 1st, 1840, Marion, d. of James Cearns, Esq.; 2ndly, Emma, d. of Henry Denison, Esq., of Daybrook, Nottinghamshire. Educ. at the High School, Glasgow. Many years a Merchant in Manchester. A leading promoter of schemes of Ocean Telegraphy, particularly of the original Atlantic cable. A J.P. and Dept.-Lieut.; Fellow of the Royal, Geographical and other societies, and author of *The Statistics of Trade.* Was created K.C.M.G. in 1888, and G.C.M.G. 1892. A Liberal Unionist, in favour of a large measure of local self-government for Ireland, as well as for the rest of the kingdom. Sat for Totnes from Dec. 1862 until 1866 when he was unseated on petition. Unsuccessfully contested Linlithgowshire in 1868. Sat for the Wick district from 1872-85 when he was defeated. Unsuccessfully contested Stirling district in 1886, and the Govan division of Lanarkshire in 1889. Returned again for the Wick district in July 1892 and sat until he accepted Chiltern Hundreds in May 1896. Died 7 July 1896. [1896]

PENN, John. 22 Carlton House Terrace, London. North Berwick. Carlton, Marlborough, Turf, and Windham. S. of John Penn, Esq., F.R.S., of Lee, and his wife Ellen English. B. 1848 at Lewisham; m. 1876, a d. of Sir Thomas Lucas. Educ. at Harrow, and Cambridge. Was a Marine Engineer of the firm of John Penn and Sons, Greenwich and Deptford, and later Chairman. A Conservative. Sat for Lewisham from Aug. 1891 until his death 21 Nov. 1903. [1903]

PENNEFATHER, John de Foblanque. Continued in House after 1918: full entry in Volume III.

PENROSE-FITZGERALD, Sir Robert Uniacke-, Bart. 35 Grosvenor Road, London. Corkbeg Island, Whitegate, Co. Cork. Carlton, and Kildare Street. S. of Robert Uniacke-Penrose-Fitz-Gerald, Esq., by Frances Matilda, d. of the Rev. R. Austen, D.D., Rector of Midleton, Co. Cork. B. at Corkbeg Island, Whitegate, Co. Cork 1839; m. Sept. 1867, Jane Emily, d. of Gen. Sir William Codrington, G.C.B. Educ. at Westminster, and Trinity Hall, Cambridge; graduated M.A. 1863. A J.P. and Dept.-Lieut. for Co. Cork, and was for some time a Member of the Cork Marine Board. Created Bart. 1896. An independent Conservative, in favour of extending the franchise to women who were otherwise legally qualified. In 1874 he unsuccessfully contested Youghal, when he was defeated by Sir J.N. M'Kenna. Sat for Cambridge from 1885 until he retired in 1906. Died 10 July 1919.   [1905]

PENTON, Frederick Thomas. Sutton Park, Sandy, Bedfordshire. Carlton, and Army & Navy. Eld. s. of Col. Henry Penton, J.P. and Dept.-Lieut., of Pentonville, Middlesex, by Eliza Maria, d. of Maj. Langley, of Brittas Castle, Co. Tipperary. B. 1851, at Boulogne; m. 1883, Caroline Helen Mary, d. of Alex J.R. Stewart, Esq., of Ards, Co. Donegal, and Lady Isabella Stewart, d. of the 2nd Earl of Norbury. Educ. at Harrow, and Christ Church, Oxford. Was appointed to the 4th Dragoon Guards 1873. Served in the Egyptian campaign, for which he had the medal and the Khedive's star, and retired as Capt. 1884. A Landowner in Pentonville, a J.P. and Dept.-Lieut. for Middlesex, and Honorary Col. of the 21st King's Royal (Finsbury) Rifle Corps. A Conservative. First returned for the Central division of Finsbury from July 1886 until defeated in 1892. High Sheriff of Buckinghamshire 1896. Died 12 June 1929.   [1892]

PERCY, Lord Algernon Malcolm Arthur. 2 Grosvenor Place, London. 2nd s. of the 6th Duke of Northumberland, by Louisa, eld. d. and co-heir of Henry Drummond, Esq., of Albury Park, Surrey. B. 1851; m. 1880, Lady Victoria Frederica Caroline, eld. d. of the 4th Earl of Mount Edgcumbe. Educ. at Christ Church Coll., Oxford, and graduated M.A. 1871. Became a Sub-Lieut. Grenadier Guards 1872; Lieut. and Adjutant 1877; retired 1880. Appointed Maj. 3rd Battalion Berkshire Militia 1881. A Conservative. Sat for Westminster from 1882-85, and for St. George's, Hanover Square, from Nov. 1885 until he accepted Chiltern Hundreds in 1887. Maj. 3rd Battalion Northumberland Fusiliers 1886-95; Lieut.-Col. 1895-1910. Aide-de-Camp to the King 1902-20. Died 28 Dec. 1933.   [1886]

PERCY, Henry Algernon George Percy, Earl. 64 Curzon Street, London. Alnwick Castle, Northumberland. Carlton, Travellers', and Junior Carlton. Eld. s. of the Duke of Northumberland, by Edith, d. of the 8th Duke of Argyll. B. in London 1871. Educ. at Eton, and Christ Church, Oxford; 1st class in Classical Moderations, and a 1st class in the final *Lit. Humaniores*; also won the Newdigate prize for English poetry. Was Under-Secretary for India 1902-03; Under-Secretary for Foreign Affairs, Oct. 1903 to Dec. 1905. A J.P. and Dept.-Lieut. for Northumberland. Trustee of the National Portrait Gallery. A Conservative. Contested Berwick division of Northumberland in July 1895. Was Lord Warkworth when elected for Kensington S. in Nov. 1895 and sat until his death 22 Dec. 1909. Styled Lord Warkworth until 1899 when he became Earl Percy on his father's succession to the Dukedom of Northumberland.   [1909]

PERKINS, Walter Frank. Continued in House after 1918: full entry in Volume III.

PERKS, Sir Robert William, Bart. 11 Kensington Palace Gardens, London. 15 Great George Street, Westminster, London. Wykham Park, Banbury, Littlestone, Kent. National Liberal, and City Liberal. S. of the Rev. George T. Perks, M.A. B. 1849 at Kensington; m. 1878, Edith, youngest d. of William Mewburn, Esq., Dept.-Lieut., of Wykham Park, Banbury. Educ. at New Kingswood School, Bath, and King's Coll., London. Practised from 1876-1900 as a Solicitor in partnership with Lord Wolverhampton (Sir H.H. Fowler, MP), having special business in Railways, Docks, and Public Works. Was associated with the construction of the Barry Docks and Railways, Preston Docks, Manchester Ship Canal, the Buenos Aires Harbour Works, and Rio Harbour Works, Brazil; interested in Georgian Bay and Montreal Canal. An Associate of the Institute of Civil Engineers, and a Director and Partner in C.H. Walker and Company Limited, Contractors. Chairman of the Metropolitan District Railway. Honorary Treasurer Free Church Congress, and Honorary Treasurer of the Liberal League; J.P. for Oxfordshire and Kent. A Bart. 1908. A Liberal. Represented the Louth division of Lincolnshire from 1892 until he retired in Jan. 1910. Retired from C.H. Walker and Company Limited in 1912; First Vice-President Methodist Church 1932-33. Died 30 Nov. 1934. [1909]

PETO, Basil Edward. Continued in

House after 1918: full entry in Volume III.

PHILIPPS, Maj.-Gen. Sir Ivor, K.C.B., D.S.O. Continued in House after 1918: full entry in Volume III.

PHILIPPS, John Wynford. Lydstep Haven, Penally, and Roch Castle, Pembrokeshire. Devonshire, Wellington, and National Liberal. Eld. s. of the Rev. Sir James Erasmus Philipps, 12th Bart. (created 1621), and Vicar of Warminster, by Mary Margaret, eld. d. of the Hon. and Rev. Samuel Best, Rector of Abbots Ann. B. at Warminster, Wiltshire 1860; m. 1888, Nora, younger d. of I. Gerstenberg, Esq., of London. Educ. at Felsted School, and Keble Coll., Oxford. Was called to the bar at the Middle Temple July 1886. A Liberal, in favour of Home Rule for Ireland, Land Law Reform, a Progressive Income Tax, Local Option, etc. In 1886 he unsuccessfully contested the Devizes division of Wiltshire. Sat for mid Lanarkshire from 1888 to 1894, when he resigned on account of ill-health. Elected for Pembrokeshire in 1898 and sat until he accepted Chiltern Hundreds on elevation to the Peerage as Baron St. Davids in 1908. Created Visct. St. Davids in 1918. PC. 1914. Lord-Lieut. of Pembrokeshire. Chairman of Unemployment Grants Committee 1920-32. Died 28 Mar. 1938.   [1908]

PHILIPPS, Sir Owen Cosby, G.C.M.G. Continued in House after 1918: full entry in Volume III.

PHILLIPS, John. Corboy House, Edgworthstown, Ireland. B. about 1839. Educ. at Queen's Coll., Galway. Chairman of Longford County Council. A J.P. for Longford. A Nationalist. Elected for S. Longford in Sept. 1907 and sat until his death 2 Apr. 1917.   [1917]

PHILLPOTTS, Arthur Stephens. Phillpottstown, Navan. Chelston Cross, Torquay. Carlton, United Service, and Hurlingham. S. of Henry Phillpotts, Esq., J.P., and grand-s. of the Bishop of Exeter. B. 1844 at Bishopstowe, Torquay; m. 1883, Camilla, d. of the Rt. Hon. Sir Bernhard Samuelson, Bart. Educ. at Chudleigh Grammar School, and the Royal Academy, Gosport. Entered the navy 1858; Lieut. 1866; Commander 1880; Capt. (retired) 1895; served with the Abyssinian Relief Force 1867, and was mentioned in despatches. Served as divisional officer in the Coastguard 1882-88. A Conservative. Sat for the Torquay division of Devon from July 1895 until he retired in 1900. Died 12 Aug. 1920.   [1900]

PICKARD, Benjamin. 2 Huddersfield Road, Barnsley. National Liberal, and Cobden. S. of Thomas Pickard, Esq., Miner. B. at the mining village of Kippax, near Leeds 1842; m. 1864, d. of John Freeman, Esq. Educ. up to twelve years of age at Kippax Grammar School. When he left school it was to work in the pit as a "hurrier". Up to 1873 he worked for one firm in various pits near Kippax. Became Secretary to the Yorkshire Miners' Association, Barnsley 1881; also President of the Miners' Federation of Great Britain, and was a member of the Wakefield School Board, and Alderman W. Riding County Council. An advanced Liberal, in favour of Home Rule, of shorter Parliaments, payment of members, an Affirmation Bill, the abolition of the House of Lords, and other radical measures. Sat for the Normanton division of the W. Riding of Yorkshire from 1885 until his death 3 Feb. 1904.   [1903]

PICKERSGILL, Edward Hare. 2 Essex Court, Temple, London. S. of T. Pickersgill, Esq., of York, and Ann, d. of Robert Hare, Esq., of Northallerton. B. 1850; m. 1907, Elizabeth, d. of William Zimmerman, Esq. (she died 1910). Educ. at St. Peter's School, York, and London University; B.A. At one time in the Civil Service. Called to the bar at the Inner Temple 1884; a member of London County Council 1892-95, and of Metropolitan Water Board 1903-07. A Liberal. Sat for S.W. Bethnal Green from 1885-1900 when he was defeated; re-elected there in 1906 and sat until appointed Metropolitan Police Magistrate in July 1911. Died 13 Oct. 1911.   [1911]

PICTON, James Allanson. 80 Regent's Park Road, London. S. of Sir James Allanson Picton, Kt., F.S.A., of Sandyknowe, near Liverpool. Author of *The Memorials of Liverpool*, etc. B. 1832; m. 1st, Margaret, d. of J. Beaumont, Esq.; 2ndly, 1866, Jessie, d. of S. Williams, Esq. Appointed a Royal Commissioner of the Market Rights and Tolls enquiry Jan. 1888. Author of a *Life of Oliver Cromwell*, etc. A Liberal and Home Ruler. Sat for Leicester from June 1884 until he accepted Chiltern Hundreds in 1894. Died 4 Feb. 1910. [1894]

PIERPOINT, Robert. 8a Bickenhall Mansions, London. St. Austin's, Warrington. Carlton, and Windham. S. of Benjamin Pierpoint, Esq., J.P., of St. Austin's, Warrington, and Frances, d. of Thomas Green, Esq., of Warrington. B. 1845; m. 1902, Marie Eugéne, widow of J. Wills, Esq., of Leeds. Educ. at Eton, and Christ Church, Oxford; B.A. 1869, M.A. 1871. Called to the bar at the Inner Temple 1873 and joined the N. Circuit. A J.P. for Cheshire. A Conservative. Represented Warrington from 1892 until defeated in 1906. Unsuccessfully contested Warrington in Jan. 1910. Died 22 Jan. 1932. [1905]

PILKINGTON, Sir George Augustus. Swinthwaite Hall, Bedale. Belle Vue, Southport. Reform, and National Liberal. S. of R. Gorton Coombe, Esq. B. 1848 at Upwell, Cambridgeshire; m. 1876, Mary, d. of James Pilkington, Esq., MP, and assumed that surname 1882. Educ. privately, and at Guy's Hospital. Settled for practice in Southport; and was Mayor there 1884-85 and 1891-92. A J.P. for Lancashire and the N. Riding of Yorkshire, and also Co. Alderman for Lancashire. Created Kt. 1893. A Liberal, in favour of Home Rule, etc. Sat for the Southport division of Lancashire from 1885-86 when he was defeated. Returned again for Southport May 1899 and sat until defeated in 1900. Died 28 Jan. 1916. [1900]

PILKINGTON, Richard. Rainford Hall, St. Helens, Lancashire. Carlton, and Devonshire. 2nd s. of Richard Pilkington, Esq., of Windle Hall, Lancashire, and Anne, d. of Richard Evans, Esq., of Haydock Grange, Lancashire. B. 1841; m. 1868, Louisa, d. of Arthur Sinclair, Esq., of St. Helens. A Manufacturer at St. Helens; also Col. commanding 2nd Volunteer Battalion Prince of Wales South Lancashire Regiment. Was four times Mayor of St. Helens. A Conservative and Unionist, and a strong supporter of the Foreign, Colonial and Domestic policy of the Balfour administration. Elected for the Newton division of S.W. Lancashire in 1899 and sat until defeated in 1906. Died 12 Mar. 1908. [1905]

PINKERTON, John. Secon, Ballymoney, Co. Antrim. S. of John Pinkerton, Esq., of Ballymoney, Co. Antrim. B. at Secon, Ballymoney 1845; m. 1873, Isabella, d. of Robert Pinkerton, Esq., of Ballaghmore, Co. Antrim. Educ. at the private school of the Rev. J. M'Fadden, Unitarian Minister. A Tenant Farmer, and Magistrate for Co. Antrim. A member of the Irish Parliamentary (Anti-Parnellite) party. Unsuccessfully contested N. Antrim in 1885. Was first returned, unopposed, for Galway City in 1886 and sat until he retired in 1900. Died 4 Nov. 1908. [1900]

PIRIE, Duncan Vernon. Stoneywood, Aberdeenshire. 26 Ebury Street, London. Bachelors', and National Liberal. S. of Gordon Pirie, Esq., of Chateau de Varennes, France, and Valentine, d. of Comte Rousseau de Labrosse. B. 1858; m. 1894, Evelyn, 2nd d. of the 17th Baron Sempill. Educ. at Glenalmond. Entered the army 1879, retired as Capt. 3rd Hussars, 1898; served in the Egyptian 1882, Soudan 1884, and Nile 1884-85, campaigns, mentioned twice in despatches, and had the medal with four clasps etc. Was Aide-de-Camp to the Gov. of Ceylon 1890-93. A Director of Alexander Pirie and Sons Limited, of Aberdeen. Dept.-Lieut. and J.P. for Aberdeenshire. F.R.S.G.S. Organised the relief of wounded in Greece during the Greco-Turkish war 1897. Served in S. Africa 1899-1900 (medal with two clasps) and with the British Expeditionary Force 1914. Maj. 1916. A member of the Council of Inter-Parliamentary Union from 1908. A Liberal, in favour of Devolution. Unsuccessfully contested W. Renfrewshire in 1895. First elected for N. Aberdeen in 1896 and sat until defeated in 1918. Died 11 Jan. 1931. [1918]

PITT-LEWIS, George. 12 Airlie Gardens, Campden Hill, Kensington, London. 4 Paper Buildings, Temple, London. Reform, National Liberal, and Devon & Exeter. Eld. s. of the Rev. George Tucker Lewis, of the Limes, Exminster, Devon, by Jane Frances, d. of the Rev. William Palmer, D.D., J.P., for Devon, Dorset, and Somerset, and grand-d. of Stephen Pitt, Esq., of Campden House, Kensington, and Cricket-Malherbie, Somerset. B. at the Grammar School, Honiton 1845; m. 1881, Mai, d. of Maj.-Gen. J.G. Palmer, of Paris. Educ. privately. He assumed the additional surname of Pitt by Royal Licence in 1876. Obtained Inns of Court studentship, and was called to the bar at the Middle Temple

1870; became Recorder of Poole 1885-1904, and Q.C. 1885; a bencher of his Inn 1891-1904. Author of *Complete Practice of the County Courts* (1880). A Liberal Unionist of "broad principles", in favour of reforms in the transfer of land, in national expenditure, and in church preferment; also advocated international arbitration, and various restrictions on the liquor traffic, etc. Sat for the Barnstaple division of Devon from 1885 until he retired in 1892. Died 30 Dec. 1906.   [1892]

PLATT-HIGGINS, Frederick. Queen Anne's Mansions, London. Carlton. S. of James Higgins, Esq., J.P. B. 1840 at Salford; m. Mary Emilie, d. of James Mottram, Esq., of Manchester. Educ. at Cheltenham Coll., and Berlin. In 1889 he obtained a Royal warrant authorizing him to take the name of Platt in addition to that of Higgins. A J.P. for Co. Chester. A Conservative and Unionist. Represented N. Salford from 1895 until defeated in 1906. Died 6 Nov. 1910.   [1905]

PLAYFAIR, Rt. Hon. Sir Lyon, K.C.B., F.R.S., LL.D. 68 Onslow Gardens, South Kensington, London. Athenaeum. University Club, Edinburgh. S. of Dr. George Playfair, Inspector-Gen. of Hospitals, Bengal, by his m. with Miss Jessie Ross. B. at Meerut, Bengal 1819; m. 1st, 1845, Margaret Eliza, d. of James Oakes, Esq.; 2ndly 1857, Jean Ann, d. of Crowley Millington, Esq.; 3rdly, 1878, Edith, eld. d. of Samuel H. Russell, Esq., of Boston, America. Educ. at St. Andrews, at Edinburgh, and afterwards proceeded to Giessen, in Hesse Darmstadt, to study under Liebig. Appointed Professor of Chemistry at the Royal Institution, Manchester 1843. Was from 1853 till 1858 Government Inspector-Gen. of Schools and Museums of Science and Art. Professor of Chemistry, University of Edinburgh from 1858 till 1869. Was Special Commissioner in charge of the departments of Juries at the Great Exhibition of 1851, after which he was created C.B. PC. 1873. Was Postmaster-Gen. from Nov. 1873 to Feb. 1874; also Chairman of Ways and Means and Dept.-Speaker of the House of Commons from Apr. 1880 to Apr. 1883, and in 1886 he was appointed Vice President of the Committee of Council. K.C.B. 1883. In 1888 appointed member of the Council of H.R.H. the Prince of Wales. Was Commander of the Legion of Honour, Commander of the Austrian Order "Francis Joseph", and Knight of various foreign orders. Author of several works on chemical subjects, and on Public Health and Political Economy. A Liberal, and Home Ruler, in favour of technical instruction for the manufacturing classes. Sat for the Universities of Edinburgh and St. Andrews 1868-85, and for Leeds S. from 1885 until created Lord Playfair in Aug. 1892. Lord-in-Waiting from 1892-95. G.C.B. 1895. Died 29 May 1898.
                    [1892 2nd ed.]

PLOWDEN, Sir William Chichele, K.C.S.I. 5 Park Crescent, Portland Place, London. Devonshire, National Liberal, and Oriental. S. of W.H. Chichele Plowden, Esq., of Ewhurst Park, Hampshire, former MP for Newport, Isle of Wight, by Annette, d. of Edward Campbell, Esq., and niece of Sir Robert Campbell, Bart. B. 1832; m. 1862, Emily, eld. d. of M.T. Bass, Esq., MP, and sister of the 1st Baron Burton. Educ. at Harrow, and Haileybury Coll. Was a member of the Bengal Civil Service from 1852 to 1885, serving on the Viceroy's Legislative Council, the Board of Revenue for the N.W. Provinces, the Imperial Census Commission, etc. etc., and was specially mentioned for his services during the Indian Mutiny. Author of various reports on the Census of the Indian Empire 1881, and of the N.W. Provinces 1865 and 1872. A J.P. for Middlesex and Dorset. K.C.S.I. 1886. A Liberal, in favour of Mr. Gladstone's Irish policy. Unsuccessfully contested Wolverhampton W. at the general election of 1885. First returned for Wolverhampton W. in July 1886 and sat until defeated in 1892. Died 4 Sept. 1915.
                    [1892]

PLUMMER, Sir Walter Richard. 4 Queen's Square, Newcastle-on-Tyne. Carlton, and Constitutional. S. of Alderman Benjamin Plummer, J.P., and Grace, d. of Thomas Fell, Esq., of St. Laurence House, Newcastle-on-Tyne. B. at Newcastle 1858. Unmarried. Educ. privately at Newcastle. A Merchant and was for fifteen years a member of the Newcastle School Board, and four years Chairman; for fourteen years in city Council, also a city Magistrate. Knighted 1904. A Conservative, advocated Army Reform, Redistribution of Seats, etc. Elected for Newcastle-on-Tyne in 1900 and sat until defeated in

1906. Contested same seat in Jan. 1910. Died 10 Dec. 1917. [1905]

PLUNKET, Rt. Hon. David Robert. 12 Mandeville Place, London. Carlton. 3rd s. of the 3rd Baron Plunket, by Charlotte, 3rd d. of the Rt. Hon. Charles Kendal Bushe, Chief Justice of the Queen's Bench in Ireland. B. 1838. Educ. at Trinity Coll., Dublin. Was called to the bar in Ireland 1862 and made a Queen's Counsel there in 1868. Was Law Adviser to the Crown in Ireland for a short time in 1868. Also Solicitor-Gen. for Ireland from Jan. 1875 to Mar. 1877. Paymaster-Gen. for a few weeks Mar. 1880. PC. 1880. First Commissioner of Works 1885-Jan. 1886, and again Aug. 1886-92. A Conservative. Unsuccessfully contested City of Dublin in 1868. Sat for the University of Dublin from Feb. 1870 until created Lord in Oct. 1895. Died 22 Aug. 1919. [1895]

PLUNKETT, George Noble Plunkett, Count. Continued in House after 1918: full entry in Volume III.

PLUNKETT, Rt. Hon. Horace Curzon. 105 Mount Street, London. Carlton, and Wellington. Kildare Street Club, Dublin. 3rd s. of the 16th Baron Dunsany, by the Hon. Anne Dutton, d. of the 2nd Baron Sherborne. B. 1854. Educ. at Eton, and University Coll., Oxford. Vice-President Agriculture and other Technical Industries and a Commissioner of the Congested Districts Board of Ireland 1891-1918; and also a Commissioner of the Colonization Board of Scotland and Ireland. Created PC. (Ireland) 1897. He founded and was Chairman of the Recess Committee and of the Irish Agricultural Organisation Society. A Conservative. Sat for the S. division of Dublin Co. from July 1892 until defeated in 1900. Contested Galway Town Nov. 1901. Vice-President of Department of Agriculture and Technical Instruction for Ireland from 1899-1907. K.C.V.O. 1903. Chairman, Irish Convention 1917-18; Senator, Irish Free State 1922-23. Author of several works on Irish matters including *A Better Way: an Appeal to Ulster not to desert Ireland* (1914). Died 26 Mar. 1932. Falsely reported dead on 1 Jan. 1920 giving rise to some premature obituaries. [1900]

PLUNKETT, Hon. John William. See DUNSANY, John William Plunkett, Baron.

POINTER, Joseph. 84 Stafford Road, Sheffield. 21 Stockwell Park Road, London. S. of John Pointer, Esq., a native of Norfolk. B. 12 June 1875 at Sheffield; m. 1902, Jane Annie, d. of William Tweddle, Esq., Sub-Postmaster, Middlesbrough. Educ. at Board School, and Central Higher Grade School, Sheffield, and Ruskin Hall, Oxford. Was apprenticed as an Engineer's Patternmaker 1890; joined the United Patternmakers' Association in 1895 and filled most of the offices in this Union. A member of Sheffield City Council 1908-11. A Whip to the Labour Party 1912. A Labour Member. Elected for the Attercliffe division of Sheffield in 1909 and sat until his death 19 Nov. 1914. [1914]

POLE-CAREW, Lieut.-Gen. Sir Reginald. Antony, Cornwall. Carlton, Marlborough, Turf, Travellers', and Pratt's. S. of W.H. Pole-Carew, Esq., of Antony, Cornwall. B. 1 May 1849 at Antony; m. 1901, Lady Beatrice Butler, d. of Marq. of Ormonde. Educ. at Eton, and Christ Church, Oxford. Joined the Coldstream Guards 1869, Col. 1895, served in Afghan War 1879, South Africa 1881, Egypt 1882, Burma 1886, and S. African War 1899-1900, when he commanded the Guards Brigade, and subsequently 11th Division; was mentioned in despatches and promoted to Maj.-Gen. K.C.B. 1900, C.V.O. 1901. Was Military Secretary to Sir Frederick (Earl) Roberts when Commander-in-Chief in India. Retired from the army 1906. Dept.-Lieut. for Cornwall. A Unionist. Unsuccessfully contested Pembroke district in 1906 and the Bodmin division of Cornwall in Jan. 1910. Elected for the Bodmin division of Cornwall in Dec. 1910 and sat until he accepted Chiltern Hundreds in Aug. 1916. Died 19 Sept. 1924. [1916]

POLLARD, Sir George Herbert. Sundown, Southport. Reform, and Royal Automobile. S. of James Pollard, Esq., of Southport. B. 1864 at Burnley; m. 1888, Charlotte, d. of Thomas Butterworth, Esq., J.P., of Burnley. Educ. at Edinburgh, and Oxford Universities. A Barrister, called 1893; also M.D. and C.M. A member of Lancashire County Council; Mayor of Southport 1896-97. Knighted 1909. A Liberal. Unsuccessfully contested the Southport division of Lancashire in 1892, and the Radcliffe division of Lancashire in 1895. First elected for the Eccles division of

S.E. Lancashire in 1906 and sat until he retired in 1918. Died 27 Aug. 1937. [1918]

POLLOCK, Sir Ernest Murray, K.B.E. Continued in House after 1918: full entry in Volume III.

POLLOCK, Harry Frederick. 1 Cumberland Place, Regent's Park, London. Reform, City of London, and Hurlingham. S. of G.F. Pollock, Esq., the Queen's Remembrancer, by Frances Diana, eld. d. of the Rev. Henry Herbert. B. 9 Feb. 1855; m. 1880, Phyllis, d. of Maj.-Gen. Broome, C.S.I. Educ. at Winchester Coll. A Solicitor from 1878. A Liberal Unionist. Unsuccessfully contested the Spalding division of Lincolnshire in 1892. First returned for that division in July 1895 and sat until he retired in 1900. Died 2 May 1901. [1900]

POMFRET, William Pomfret. Godinton Park, Ashford. Carlton, Union, Constitutional, and Empire. Eld. s. of William Burra, Esq., Banker, by Mary Catherine, d. of John Butler Pomfret, Esq., of Tenterden. He assumed the name of Pomfret by Royal Licence in 1882. B. 1828; m. 1st, 1853, d. of G. Nottidge, Esq., of Tunbridge; 2ndly, eld. d. of C.F. Hore, Esq., of Beckenham. Educ. at Shrewsbury, and Tunbridge Grammar Schools. J.P. for Kent and Senior Partner in the Ashford Bank. A Conservative, "a Fair-trader and Imperial Federationist." Sat for the Ashford division of Kent from the general election of 1885 until he retired in 1892. Died 11 Aug. 1902. [1892]

PONSONBY, Arthur Augustus William Harry. Continued in House after 1918: full entry in Volume III.

POPE-HENNESSY, Sir John, K.C.M.G. See HENNESSY, Sir John Pope, K.C.M.G.

PORTMAN, Hon. Edwin Berkeley. 12 Ashley Place, Victoria Street, London. St. James's, Devonshire, and United University. 2nd s. of the 1st Visct. Portman. B. at Bryanston, Blandford 1830. Educ. at Rugby, and Balliol Coll., Oxford. Was a Fellow of All Souls' Coll., and was called to the bar at the Inner Temple 1852. A Liberal and Home Ruler. Sat for Dorset N. from 1885 until he retired in 1892. Died 27 Apr. 1921. [1892]

POTTER, Thomas Bayley. 31 Courtfield Gardens, South Kensington, London. Reform. S. of Sir Thomas Potter, of Buile Hill, Manchester, (bro. of Sir John Potter, MP for Manchester), by Esther, d. of Thomas Bayley, Esq., of Booth Hall, near Manchester. B. at Manchester 1817; m. 1st, 1846, Mary, d. of Samuel Ashton, Esq., of Pole Bank, Gee Cross, Hyde (she died 1885); 2ndly, 1887, Helena, d. of John Hicks, Esq., of Bodmin, Cornwall. Educ. at Rugby, and at University Coll., London. Was a Merchant. A Magistrate and Dept.-Lieut. of the Co. Palatine of Lancaster, and a Magistrate for Manchester. Was President of the Union and Emancipation Society during the war in the United States. Honorary Secretary of the Cobden Club. A "Radical Reformer", in favour of Home Rule, of "religious equality", and a thorough revision of the land laws. Sat for Rochdale from the death of Mr. Cobden, Apr. 1865 until he retired in 1895. Died 6 Nov. 1898. [1895]

POWELL, Sir Francis Sharp, Bart. 1 Cambridge Square, Hyde Park, London. Horton Old Hall, Bradford. S. of the Rev. Benjamin Powell, by Anne, d. of the Rev. T. Wade. B. at Wigan 1827; m. 1858, Annie, d. of Matthew Gregson, Esq., of Toxteth Park, Liverpool. Educ. at St. John's Coll., Cambridge where he took classical and mathematical honours in 1850, and was elected a Fellow in 1851. Called to the bar at the Inner Temple 1853. Treasurer of the Committee for Church Defence, and of the University of Leeds. Served on the Royal Sanitary Commission; J.P. for Lancashire and the W. Riding of Yorkshire; an Honorary Freeman of the boroughs of Wigan and Bradford. Patron of 1 living. Chairman of the Governors of Sedbergh Grammar School, member of the Council of Selwyn Coll., and Church of England Training Colls., Vice-President of the Royal Statistical Society, and of the Sanitary Institute. Created a Bart. in 1892. Honorary LL.D. Leeds University. A Conservative and a Free Trader, a promoter of sanitary, educational, and church extension measures, and an opponent of all proposals which would injure the usefulness of the Church. Unsuccessfully contested Wigan in 1852 and Oct. 1854. Was MP for Wigan from 1857 until defeated in 1859. Sat for Cambridge from 1863 until defeated in 1868. Unsuccessfully contested Stalybridge in Mar. 1871. Sat for the N.

division of the W. Riding of Yorkshire from Feb. 1872 until defeated in 1874. Unsuccessfully contested Manchester in Feb. 1875 and the N. division of the W. Riding of Yorkshire in 1880. Returned for Wigan again in 1881, but was unseated on petition; re-elected for Wigan in 1885 and sat until he retired in Jan. 1910. Died 24 Dec. 1911.   [1909]

POWELL, Walter Rice Howell. Maesgwynne, Whitland, Carmarthenshire. Eld. s. of Walter Rice Howell Powell, Esq., of Maesgwynne, Carmarthenshire, by Mary, d. of Joshua Powell, Esq., of Brislington, Somerset. B. 1819; m. 1st, 1840, Emily Anne, 2nd d. of Henry Skrine, Esq., of Stubbings, Berkshire and Warleigh Manor, Bath (she died 1846); 2ndly, 1851, Catherine Anne, 2nd d. of Grismond Philipps, Esq., of Cwmgwilly, Carmarthenshire. Graduated at Oxford (Christ Church). A Magistrate and Dept.-Lieut. for Pembrokeshire and Carmarthenshire, and was High Sheriff of the latter in 1849. A Liberal, in favour of Home Rule, Local Option, Sunday closing, the establishment of a system of Local Government in counties, and the disestablishment and disendowment of the Church of England in Wales. Unsuccessfully contested Carmarthenshire in 1874. Sat for Carmarthenshire from Apr. 1880 to Nov. 1885, and for the W. division of Carmarthenshire from Nov. 1885 until his death 26 June 1889.   [1889]

POWER, Patrick Joseph. 13 Templeton Place, London. Newtown House, Tramore, Co. Waterford. S. of Pierse Power, Esq., and Eliza, d. of Patrick Hayden, Esq., of Carrickbeg, Co. Waterford. B. 1850. Educ. at Stonyhurst Coll., Lancashire. A Magistrate for Co. Waterford and Chairman of the Waterford Board of Guardians; a temporary Chairman of Committees. A Nationalist. Sat for Waterford Co. from 1884-85, and for the E. division of Waterford Co. from 1885 until his death 8 Jan. 1913.   [1912]

POWER, Richard. Pembrokestown House, Tramore, Waterford. Garrick. S. of Patrick William Power, Esq., J.P. (s. of P. Power, Esq., J.P. and Dept.-Lieut. of Bellevue, Co. Kilkenny), by Ellen, d. of Edmund Power, Esq., Dept.-Lieut. of Gurteen, Co. Waterford. B. at Tramore, Co. Waterford 1851. Educ. at Carlow, and Old

Hall, Hertfordshire. A Nationalist, in favour of the system called "Home Rule" for Ireland. Sat for the city of Waterford from Feb. 1874 until his death 29 Nov. 1891.   [1891]

POYNDER, Sir John Poynder Dickson, Bart. See DICKSON-POYNDER, Sir John Poynder, Bart.

PRATT, John William. Continued in House after 1918: full entry in Volume III.

PRETYMAN, Rt. Hon. Ernest George. Continued in House after 1918: full entry in Volume III.

PRICE, Charles Edward. 133 Harley Street, London. 10 Atholl Crescent, Edinburgh. Reform, and National Liberal. Scottish Liberal, Edinburgh. B. 1857. A Partner in McVitie and Price, Biscuit Manufacturers, Edinburgh and London; retired 1901. A J.P. A Liberal. Elected for Central Edinburgh in 1906 and sat until he retired in 1918. Died 7 July 1934.   [1918]

PRICE, Capt. George Edward. 39 Onslow Gardens, London. S. of George Price, Esq., (and grand-s. of Sir Rose Price, Bart. of Trengwainton, Cornwall), by the Hon. Emily, d. of the 14th Lord Dunsany. B. at Dinan, France 1842; m. 1873, Gertrude, d. of J. Lawrence, Esq. Entered the navy Mar. 1855; attained the rank of Lieut. Aug. 1862, Commander Oct. 1873. A Conservative, in favour of the maintenance of the connection between Church and State. Sat for Devonport from Feb. 1874 until defeated in 1892. Died 29 June 1926.   [1892]

PRICE, Sir Robert John. 6 Sussex Mansions, London. The Thatched House, Wroxham, Norfolk. Bank, Lyndhurst, Hampshire. National Liberal. S. of Edward Price, Esq., of Belle Vue House, Highgate, Railway Contractor. B. 1854 at Highgate; m. 1881, Eva Montgomery Johns, d. of Jasper W. Johns, Esq., MP for the Nuneaton division of Warwickshire. Educ. at Cholmeley School, Highgate, and University Coll., London. M.R.C.S. 1876. Was called to the bar at the Middle Temple 1883. Knighted 1908. A Liberal. Represented E. Norfolk from 1892 until he retired in 1918. Died 18 Apr. 1926. [1918]

PRICE, Thomas Phillips. 135 Sloane

Street, London. Triley Court, Abergavenny. Dines Hall, Halstead. Union, and Devonshire. Only s. of the Rev. William Price, Vicar of Llanarth. B. 1844; m. 1882, Frances Ann, d. of the Rev. C.J. Rowlatt. Educ. at Winchester, and University Coll., Oxford; graduated 2nd class classics, June 1867. Was called to the bar at the Inner Temple in 1869. A J.P. for Monmouthshire and Essex, and was High Sheriff of Monmouthshire in 1882. Was Capt. Monmouthshire Royal Militia. "An advanced Liberal and Home Ruler". Sat for N. Monmouthshire from 1885 until he retired in 1895. Died 28 June 1932.   [1895]

PRIESTLEY, Sir Arthur. Hungerton Hall, Nr. Grantham. Bath. S. of Briggs Priestley, Esq., MP for the Pudsey division of Yorkshire, and Grace, his wife. Younger bro. of Sir W.E.B. Priestley, MP for E. Bradford. B. 1864. Unmarried. Educ. privately. A Magistrate for Grantham and S. Kesteven, Lincolnshire. Knighted 1911. Mayor of Grantham 1915, 1916, and 1917. A Liberal, in favour of army reform, reform of the Land Laws, revision of the Registration laws, removal of all taxes on the necessaries of life, Licensing Reform, etc. Unsuccessfully contested the Stamford division of Lincolnshire 1890, 1892, and 1895. Elected for Grantham in 1900 and sat until he retired in 1918. Died Apr. 1933.   [1918]

PRIESTLEY, Briggs. 2 Queen Anne's Mansions, London. Apperley Bridge, Nr. Leeds. B. 1831. A Worsted Manufacturer, a member of the firm of Briggs, Priestley and Company, of Bradford. A Liberal and Home Ruler. Sat for the Pudsey division of the W. Riding of Yorkshire from the general election of 1885 until he retired in 1900. Died 21 Oct. 1907.   [1900]

PRIESTLEY, Sir William Edwin Briggs. Rosemount House, Bradford. Littledale Hall, Caton, Nr. Lancaster. Queen Anne's Mansions, London. Reform, National Liberal, Ranelagh, and Royal Automobile. S. of Briggs Priestley, Esq., MP for the Pudsey division of Yorkshire. Bro. of Sir Arthur Priestley, MP for Grantham. B. 12 Apr. 1859 at Thronton, Bradford; m. 1883, Ruth, d. of J. Craven, Esq., MP for the Shipley division of Yorkshire. Educ. privately. Chairman of Priestleys Limited, Stuff Manufacturers, Bradford. A J.P. for Bradford, Mayor 1904-05. Knighted 1909.

A Liberal. Unsuccessfully contested E. Bradford in 1900. First elected there in 1906 and sat until defeated in 1918. Died 25 Mar. 1932.   [1918]

PRIESTLEY, Sir William Overend, M.D. 17 Hertford Street, Mayfair, London. Westbrook Hall, Horsham. Athenaeum. S. of Joseph Priestley, Esq., of Morley Hall, Leeds, by Mary, d. of James Overend, Esq., of Morley. B. 1829 at Churwell, near Leeds; m. 1856, Eliza, d. of Dr. Robert Chambers, of Edinburgh, author of *Traditions of Edinburgh,* etc. Educ. at Edinburgh, King's Coll. London, and Paris. Was Professor of Obstetrics in King's Coll., London and later Fellow; member of Council and Consulting Physician to King's Coll. Hospital. Was examiner for diplomas and degrees for the Royal Coll. Physicians and Royal Coll. Surgeons of England, Universities of London and Cambridge and the Victoria University. Was Physician Accoucheur to Princess Alice and Princess Christian. Fellow of many learned societies; Honorary LL.D. Edinburgh; author of various works in Science and Medicine; he was Knighted in 1893. A Conservative and Unionist. Sat for Edinburgh and St. Andrews Universities from May 1896 until his death 12 Apr. 1900.   [1900]

PRIMROSE, Rt. Hon. Neil James Archibald. 5 Great Stanhope Street, London. Brooks's. Youngest s. of Earl of Rosebery. B. 14 Dec. 1882 at Dalmeny; m. 1915, Lady Victoria Stanley, d. of Earl of Derby. Educ. at Eton, and New Coll., Oxford. Parliamentary Under-Secretary to the Foreign Office Feb. to May 1915; Parliamentary Military Secretary to the Ministry of Munitions Sept.-Dec. 1916; Joint Parliamentary Secretary to the Treasury from Dec. 1916-Mar. 1917. Capt. Royal Buckinghamshire Yeomanry. PC. 1917. A Liberal. Elected for the Wisbech division of Cambridgeshire in Jan. 1910 and sat until he died of wounds received in action on 17 Nov. 1917.   [1917]

PRINGLE, William Mather Rutherford. Continued in House after 1918: full entry in Volume III.

PRITCHARD-MORGAN, William. See MORGAN, William Pritchard.

PROBY, Col. Douglas James. Little

Walden Hall, Saffron Walden. Elton Hall, Peterborough. Guards', and Travellers'. Only s. of the Rt. Hon. Lord Claud Hamilton, bro. of 1st Duke of Abercorn, and Lady Elizabeth Emma Proby, d. of 3rd Earl of Carysfort. B. 23 Sept. 1856; m. 1882, Lady Margaret Frances Hely-Hutchinson, d. of 4th Earl of Donoughmore. Educ. at Eton, and Christ Church, Oxford; B.A. Joined the Coldstream Guards 1880, served in Egyptian Campaign 1882 and Suakin Expedition 1885; exchanged into Royal Fusiliers as Capt. 1891. Maj. 1898; transferred to Irish Guards in 1900, retired with rank of Brevet-Col. 1908. Assumed the surname of Proby in lieu of Hamilton by Royal Licence in 1904. A Unionist. Elected for the Saffron Walden division of Essex in Jan. 1910 and sat until defeated in Dec. 1910. Member of Huntingdonshire County Council from 1913; Col. commanding Irish Guards Regiment 1914-17. Died 18 Nov. 1931. [1910]

PROTHERO, Rt. Hon. Rowland Edmund, M.V.O. Continued in House after 1918: full entry in Volume III.

PROVAND, Andrew Dryburgh. 2 Whitehall Court, London. Reform. S. of George Provand, a Glasgow Merchant, by Ann Reid, d. of the Rev. David Dryburgh. B. at Glasgow 1838. Unmarried. Educ. at private schools. A Manchester Merchant, and wrote much on economic and commercial subjects in the columns of the *Manchester Guardian* and elsewhere. A Liberal. Sat for the Blackfriars and Hutchesontown division of Glasgow from 1886 until defeated in 1900. Unsuccessfully contested the seat again in 1906. Died 18 July 1915. [1900]

PRYCE-JONES, Col. Edward. Milford Hall, Newtown, North Wales. Carlton, Constitutional, and Phyllis Court. Eld. s. of Sir Pryce Pryce-Jones, MP for the Montgomery district from 1885-86 and 1892-95. B. 1861 at Newtown, N. Wales; m. 1886, Beatrice, d. of Herbert Hardie, Esq., of Orford House, Cheshire. Educ. at Liverpool Coll., and Jesus Coll., Cambridge; M.A. Was called to the bar at the Inner Temple 1892. Was Managing Director of Pryce-Jones Limited, Merchants and Manufacturers, Newtown. J.P., Dept.-Lieut. and County Councillor for Montgomeryshire; Dept. Junior Chan-

cellor of University of Wales 1911-13. Raised 5th Volunteer Battalion S. Wales Borderers and was its first commanding officer 1895-1905; Capt. Montgomery Yeomanry 1883-95, retired as Honorary Maj. and was Honorary Col. 7th Royal Welsh Fusiliers. Joint Honorary Treasurer of the International Parliamentary Union. Joint Honorary Secretary of the Commercial Committee of the House of Commons; Joint Honorary Secretary and Treasurer of the Parliamentary Commercial Committee of the Allied Powers. A Unionist. Sat for the Montgomery district from 1895-1906, when he was defeated; unsuccessfully contested Montgomery district Jan. 1910; re-elected there in Dec. 1910 and sat until he retired in 1918. Created Bart. in 1918. Died 22 May 1926. [1918]

PRYCE-JONES, Sir Pryce. Dolerw, Newtown, North Wales. St. Stephen's. 2nd s. of William Jones, Esq., Solicitor, of Newtown, Montgomeryshire. B. 1834 at Newtown; m. 1859, Eleanor, d. of Edward Rowley Morris, Esq. Educ. privately. A Merchant and Manufacturer of woollen and other fabrics at Newtown, Montgomeryshire; a Director of the Welshpool and Llanfair Railway Company, and a J.P. for Montgomeryshire (High Sheriff 1891-92). Knighted in 1887, when he assumed the additional name of Pryce. A moderate and progressive Conservative, opposed to Home Rule for Ireland, but said he would give that nation a system of Local Government as liberal as that enjoyed by the rest of the Kingdom. Was unsuccessful as a candidate for Montgomery district 1880, was elected there 1885, and lost the seat in 1886. Again returned for Montgomery district July 1892 and sat until he retired in 1895. Died 11 Jan. 1920. [1895]

PUGH, David. Hotel Metropole, London. Manoravon, Carmarthenshire. Oxford & Cambridge. Eld. s. of D.H. Pugh, Esq., of Manoravon, J.P. and Dept.-Lieut. (High Sheriff of Carmarthenshire 1820), by Elizabeth, d. of William Beynon, Esq., of Trewern, Pembrokeshire. B. at Manoravon 1806. Unmarried. Educ. at Rugby, and Balliol Coll., Oxford (graduated B.A. 1828). Was called to the bar at the Inner Temple in 1837. A J.P. for Carmarthenshire, was Chairman of Quarter Sessions from 1843 to 1852, and High Sheriff of the county in 1874. Also J.P. and

Dept.-Lieut. for Cardiganshire. A Liberal, in favour of Home Rule, and of reforms in local taxation, the Land Laws, the House of Lords, the procedure of the House of Commons, and of the disestablishment and disendowment of the Church. Was Conservative MP for Carmarthenshire from June 1857 to 1868, when he was defeated, and sat for the E. division of Carmarthenshire from 1885 until his death on 12 July 1890.   [1890]

PUGH, David. Llanerchydol, and Rhiwargor, Montgomeryshire. Carlton. S. of Charles Pugh, Esq., of Perry Hill, Kent, by the 3rd d. of William Lloyd, Esq., of Montgomery, descended from the Masons of Wrockley, formerly representatives of Montgomery. B. at Perry Hill, 1789; m. 1814, Anne, only child and heir of the late Evan Vaughan, Esq., of Beguildy, Radnorshire. Educ. at Trinity Coll., Oxford. A Dept.-Lieut. and Magistrate of Montgomeryshire; Recorder of Welshpool; and late a Major in the Montgomeryshire Yeomanry. Was High Sheriff of that county in 1823. A Liberal-Conservative. First returned for Montgomery in 1832; unseated on petition in 1833. Re-elected there in 1847 and sat until his death 20 April 1861.   [1861]

PULESTON, Sir John Henry. 4 Whitehall Yard, London. Ffynogion, Ruthin, North Wales. Carlton, and Conservative. Eld. s. of John Puleston, Esq., of Ruthin, by Mary, d. of John Jones, Esq., of Tryddyn. B. at Llanfair, North Wales 1830; m. 1857, Margaret, d. of the Rev. Edward Lloyd, of Llanfyllin, North Wales. Was educ. at Ruthin Grammar School, and King's Coll., London. Was Knighted in 1887, in recognition of his services as Chairman of the General Committee of the Welsh Eisteddfod. Appointed Constable of Carnarvon Castle 1890. A Conservative, in favour of a reduction of local taxation. Sat for Devonport from Feb. 1874 until he retired in 1892 having withdrawn from Devonport to contest Carnarvon Boroughs, where he was defeated by Mr. Lloyd George. Died 19 Oct. 1908.   [1892]

PULLAR, Sir Robert. 18 Chenies Street, London. Tayside, Perth. Reform, and National Liberal. S. of John Pullar, Esq., who was for six years Lord Provost of Perth. B. 18 Feb. 1828; m. 1859, Ellen, d. of Charles Daniell, Esq., of Wantage, Berkshire (she

died 1904). Educ. at Perth Schools. A Proprietor of Pullar's Dye Works, Perth. J.P. for Perth, F.R.S.E., LL.D. St. Andrews. Knighted in 1895. A Liberal. Elected for Perth in Feb. 1907 and sat until he retired in Jan. 1910. Died 9 Sept. 1912.   [1909]

PULLEY, Charles Thornton. Continued in House after 1918: full entry in Volume III.

PULLEY, Joseph. Defeated in 1886: full entry in Volume I.

PURVIS, Sir Robert. 11 King's Bench Walk, Temple, London. 43 Ashley Gardens, London. Oxford & Cambridge. B. in Roxburghshire 1844; m. 1874, a d. of W.H. Peat, Esq., of Mincing Lane, London. Educ. at Marlborough School, and Downing Coll., Cambridge, where he took the degrees of M.A. and LL.D. Was called to the bar at the Inner Temple in 1873. A Liberal Unionist. Unsuccessfully contested the Abingdon division of Berkshire in 1885, S. Edinburgh in 1886 and Peterborough in 1892. Sat for Peterborough from 1895 until defeated in 1906. Knighted in 1905. Contested Peterborough again in Jan. 1910. Died 23 June 1920.   [1905]

PYM, Charles Guy. 35 Cranley Gardens, London. Caesar's Camp, Sandy, Bedfordshire. Carlton, and Junior Carlton. Youngest s. of the Rev. W.W. Pym, Rector of Willian All Saints, Hertfordshire, by Sophia, d. of S. Gambier, Esq., Commissioner of the navy, and grand-s. of Francis Pym, Esq., MP, of Hazels Hall, Bedfordshire. B. at Willian Rectory 1841; m. 1885, Mildred, d. of H.S. Thornton, Esq., of Battersea Rise House. Educ. at Rossall Hall. Entered the War Office 1859; retired 1873. Director and Chairman of the W. End Board of the N. British Mercantile Insurance Company, and a J.P. and Dept.-Lieut. for Bedfordshire. A Conservative, in favour of improvement of the dwelling of the poor, just temperance reforms, arbitration tribunals, reform of the Poor Laws, the prevention of alien immigration, national systems of Fire Brigades, etc. Unsuccessfully contested Bedford in 1892. Sat for Bedford from 1895 until defeated in 1906. High Sheriff of Co. of London 1911. Died 12 Nov. 1918.   [1905]

PYNE, Jasper Douglas. Lisfarny Castle, Waterford. S. of the Rev. William Masters

Pyne, Rector of Oxted, Surrey. B. 1847; m. his 1st cousin, a d. of Jasper Pyne, Esq., of Ballyvolane and Castle Martyr, Co. Cork. A large Tenant Farmer in Waterford, under the Duke of Devonshire. An "Irish Nationalist". Sat for Waterford W. from 1885 until 14 Nov. 1888 when he was missing presumed drowned.   [1888]

QUENINGTON, Michael Hugh Hicks-Beach, Visct. 81 Eaton Place, London. Mill House, Coln St. Aldwyns, Gloucestershire. Carlton, and Bachelors'. Eld. s. of Earl St. Aldwyn (Rt. Hon. Sir M. Hicks-Beach, MP), and Lady Lucy Catherine, d. of 3rd Earl Fortescue. B. 1877; m. 1909, Marjorie, d. of H.D. Brocklehurst, Esq., of Sudeley Castle, Gloucestershire. Educ. at Eton, and Christ Church, Oxford; M.A. A J.P. for Gloucestershire, 2nd Lieut. Royal Gloucestershire Hussars Yeomanry, Capt. 4th (M.) Battalion Gloucestershire Regiment. Director of Lloyds Bank and Bank of Australasia. Styled Visct. Quenington after 1915 on his father's elevation as Earl St. Aldwyn. A Unionist. Elected for the Tewkesbury division of Gloucestershire in 1906 and sat until he died of wounds received in action on 23 Apr. 1916. [1916]

QUILTER, Sir William Cuthbert, Bart. 74 South Audley Street, London. Bawdsey Manor, Suffolk. Eld. s. of William Quilter, Esq., by Elizabeth Hariot, 2nd d. of Thomas Cuthbert, Esq. B. in London 1841; m. 1867, Mary, d. of John Wheeley Bevington, Esq., of Brighton. Educ. privately. A Dept.-Lieut. and J.P. for Suffolk; President Suffolk Horse Society, and Vice-Com. Royal Harwich Yacht Club. Created Bart. 1897. A Liberal Unionist. Sat for the Sudbury division of Suffolk from 1885 until defeated in 1906. Died 18 Nov. 1911.   [1905]

QUILTER, Sir William Eley Cuthbert, Bart. Methersgate Hall, Woodbridge, Suffolk. 12 Hertford Street, London. Carlton, and Boodle's. S. of Sir Cuthbert Quilter, 1st Bart., MP for the Sudbury division of Suffolk from 1885-1906. B. 17 July 1873; m. 1899, Hon. Gwynedd Douglas-Pennant, d. of 2nd Baron Penrhyn. Educ. at Harrow, and Trinity Coll., Cambridge. A Capt. Suffolk Yeomanry. Succeeded as Bart. in 1911. A Unionist. Elected for the Sudbury division of Suffolk in Jan. 1910 and sat until he retired in 1918. Died 18 Sept. 1952.   [1918]

QUINN, Thomas. Annally House, Cadogan Square, Chelsea, London. S. of Matthew Quinn, Esq. B. at Longford 1838; m. 1863, Mary, d. of Michael Canian, Esq. Educ. at Longford, and Mullingar. An Irish Nationalist of the Anti-Parnellite party. Was chosen at Longford to stand in the election of 1885, but being then a Government Contractor was prevented from offering himself for election. First returned for Kilkenny July 1886 and sat until he retired in 1892. Died 3 Nov. 1897.   [1892]

RADFORD, Sir George Heynes. 27 Chancery Lane, London. Chiswick House, Ditton Hill, Surrey. National Liberal, Reform, and Eighty. S. of G.D. Radford, Esq., of Plymouth, and Catherine Agnes Heynes. B. 1851 at Plymouth; m. 1882, Emma Louisa, d. of Daniel Radford, Esq., J.P., of Mount Tavy, Tavistock. Educ. at Amersham Hall, and University Coll., London; LL.B. A Solicitor, admitted 1872. A member of London County Council for W. Islington from 1895-1907; Chairman of the National Liberal Club Buildings Company Limited. A J.P. for Surrey. Knighted 1916. Author of *Falstaff in "Obiter Dicta", Occasional Verses, Shylock and others*, etc. A Liberal. Elected for E. Islington in 1906 and sat until his death 5 Oct. 1917.   [1917]

RAFFAN, Peter Wilson. Continued in House after 1918: full entry in Volume III.

RAIKES, Rt. Hon. Henry Cecil. Llwynegrin, Mold, North Wales. Carlton, United University, and St. Stephen's. Eld. s. of Henry Raikes, Esq., of Llwynegrin, Flintshire, by Lucy Charlotte, youngest d. of Ven. Francis Wrangham, F.R.S., Archdeacon of the E. Riding of Yorkshire. Was grand-s. of the Rev. Henry Raikes, for many years Chancellor of the Diocese of Chester. B. at the Deanery, Chester 1838; m. 1861, Charlotte Blanche, 4th d. of C.B. Trevor-Roper, Esq., of Plas-Teg. Educ. at Shrewsbury School, and Trinity Coll., Cambridge, of which he was elected scholar 1859, graduated (2nd class in classics) 1860, M.A. 1863. Was called to the bar at the Middle Temple 1863, and elected a bencher 1880. Appointed Postmaster-Gen. Aug. 1886. Was Chairman of Ways and Means and Dept.-Speaker of the House of Commons from Mar. 1874 to Apr. 1880. Was Chairman of the Council of the Conservative and Constitutional Associations from 1867 to 1875. President of the Central Council of Diocesan Conferences. PC. 1880. A "constitutional reformer" and opposed to any encroachment upon the union of Church and State. Unsuccessfully contested Derby in 1859, Chester Aug. 1865, and Devonport May 1866. Sat for Chester from Nov. 1868 until defeated Apr. 1880; sat for Preston from Feb. to Nov. 1882, and represented Cambridge University from Nov. 1882 until his death on 24 Aug. 1891.   [1891]

RAINY, Adam Rolland. 29 Lower Seymour Street, London. 3 Tantallon Terrace, North Berwick. Reform, Union, and National Liberal. S. of the Rev. Dr. Rainy, Principal of New Coll., Edinburgh, and Susan, d. of Adam Rolland, Esq., of Gask, Fife. B. 3 Apr. 1862 at Glasgow; m. 1887, 2nd d. of Hugh M. Matheson, Esq., J.P., and Dept.-Lieut. of Lombard Street. Educ. at Edinburgh Academy, and Edinburgh, Vienna, and Berlin Universities; M.A., M.B., and C.M. Was a Surgeon-Oculist in London from 1887 till entering on political work. President of Edinburgh Speculative Society and Edinburgh University Diagnostic Society. A member of Ophthalmological Society, London. Elder of Presbyterian Church of England. Member of British and Foreign Bible Society. A Liberal. Unsuccessfully contested Kilmarnock in 1900; elected for Kilmarnock in 1906 and sat until his death 26 Aug. 1911.   [1911]

RAMSAY, Hon. Charles Maule. 48 Grosvenor Street, London. Brechin Castle, N.B. Carlton, and Junior United Service. S. of George, 12th Earl of Dalhousie, Admiral, and Sarah Frances, his wife. B. 1859 at Pembroke; m. 1885, Estelle, 2nd d. of W.R. Garrison, Esq., of New York. Educ. at the Royal Military Academy, Woolwich. A Lieut. Royal Artillery Jan. 1877, resigned 1883; Maj. Forfar and Kincardine Artillery 4 Oct. 1890. A strong Unionist, "opposed to any measure aiming at the disestablishment and disendowment of the Church of Scotland until the people of Scotland have have an opportunity of expressing their opinion on this question put before them as a distinct issue." Sat for Forfarshire from Nov. 1894 until defeated in 1895. Unsuccessfully contested Forfarshire again in Jan. 1897 and 1900. Died 7 Apr. 1936.   [1895]

RAMSAY, John. Retired in 1886: full entry in Volume I.

RAMSDEN, Sir John William, Bart. Defeated in 1886: full entry in Volume I.

RANDELL, DAVID. 223 Camden Road, London. Llanelly, South Wales. S. of John Randell, Esq., Merchant, Llanelly. B. 1854 at Llanelly; m. 1880, Sarah Ann, d. of Richard Geroge, Esq., Manufacturer, Llanidloes, N. Wales. Educ. at Rev. Thomas James's School, Llanelly, and Dr. Condor's School, New Wandsworth. A Solicitor, admitted 1878, and was much employed in trade unionist actions at law. Was Solicitor of the Llanelly Urban District Council, and also of the Harbour Commissioners. A Radical, an ardent Welsh Nationalist and Home Ruler, opposed to Church establishments, etc. Was first returned for the W. or Gower division of Glamorgan on the death of Mr. F.A. Yeo, Mar. 1888 and sat until he retired in 1900. Died 5 June 1912.   [1900]

RANDLES, Sir John Scurrah. Continued in House after 1918: full entry in Volume III.

RANKIN, Sir James, Bart. Bryngwyn, Hereford. Carlton, and New University. Only s. of Robert Rankin, Esq., of Bromborough Hall, Cheshire, by Ann, d. of John Strang, Esq., of St. Andrew's, Canada. B. at Liverpool 1842; m. 1865, Annie Laura, 2nd d. of Christopher Bushell, Esq., of Hinderton, Cheshire. Educ. at Trinity Coll., Cambridge; B.A. 1st class Natural Science Tripos, 1865. A J.P. and Dept.-Lieut. of Herefordshire, a J.P. for Hereford, and Chief Steward of Hereford 1878. Was High Sheriff of Herefordshire in 1873. Wrote various papers on scientific subjects. Created Bart. in 1898. A Unionist. Sat for Leominster division of Herefordshire from 1880 to 1885, when he was defeated; re-elected 1886, and sat until 1906 when he was once more defeated; again re-elected for the Leominster division of Herefordshire in Jan. 1910 and sat until he accepted Chiltern Hundreds in 1912. Died 17 Apr. 1915.   [1911]

RANKIN, Capt. James Stuart. Continued in House after 1918: full entry in Volume III.

RAPHAEL, Sir Herbert Henry, Bart. Hockley Sole, Nr. Folkestone. Reform, Portland, and Automobile. S. of H.L. Raphael, Esq. B. 23 Dec. 1859; m. Rosalie, d. of G.F. Coster, Esq., Educ. abroad, and at Trinity Hall, Cambridge; LL.B., B.A. A member of London School Board, London County Council and Essex County Council; a J.P. for Essex and Derbyshire. A Trustee of the National Portrait Gallery. Created Bart. 1911. Raised 18th and 23rd K.R.R.C., in which he was successively second in command. A Liberal. Unsuccessfully contested S. Essex in 1892 and 1897, St. Pancras N. in 1895 and S. Derbyshire in 1900. Elected for S. Derbyshire in 1906 and sat until he retired in 1918. Died 24 Sept. 1924. [1918]

RASCH, Sir Frederic Carne, Bart. Woodhill, Danbury, Chelmsford, Essex. Naval & Military, and Windham. S. of F.C. Rasch, Esq., J.P., Dept.-Lieut., of Woodhill, by Catherine James, d. of James Edwards, Esq., of The Grove, Harrow. B. 1847; m. 1878, Katherine Anne, d. of Henry Lysons Griffinhoofe, Esq., of Arkesden, Essex. Educ. at Eton, and Trinity Coll., Cambridge. He entered the 6th Dragoon Guards (Carbineers) in 1867; a Maj. in the 4th Essex Regiment; a J.P., and also a Dept.-Lieut. for Essex; created Bart. 1903. A Conservative. Unsuccessfully contested the Elland division of the W. Riding of Yorkshire in 1885. Sat for S.E. Essex from July 1886-1900. Elected for mid Essex Oct. 1900 and sat until he accepted Chiltern Hundreds in 1908. Died 26 Sept. 1914. [1908]

RATCLIFF, Maj. Robert Frederick, C.M.G. Newton Park, Burton-on-Trent. Brooks's, and Devonshire. S. of Robert Ratcliff, Esq., and Emily, his wife (née Payne). B. 1867 at Burton-on-Trent. Educ. at Rossall School, and Jesus Coll., Cambridge; B.A. A Director of Bass's Limited. Lieut.-Col. 6th Battalion N. Staffordshire Regiment; later on Territorial Reserve. C.M.G. 1917. A Unionist. Elected for the Burton division of Staffordshire in 1900 and sat until he retired in 1918. Died 19 Jan. 1943. [1918]

RATHBONE, William. 18 Prince's Gardens, London. Greenbank, Liverpool. Athenaeum, Devonshire, and Reform. S. of William Rathbone, Esq., of Greenbank, Liverpool, by Elizabeth, d. of Samuel Creg, Esq., of Quarry Bank, Cheshire. B. at Liverpool 1819; m. 1st, 1847, Lucretia, d. of S.S. Gair, Esq., of Liverpool; 2ndly, 1862, Emily, d. of Acheson Lyle, Esq., of The Oaks, Londonderry. A Merchant at Liverpool. A Dept.-Lieut. and J.P. for Lancashire. A "decided Liberal", in favour of complete religious equality, would give a general support to Mr. Gladstone. Sat for Liverpool from Dec. 1868 to Apr. 1880, when he was an unsuccessful candidate for Lancashire S.W. Sat for Carnarvonshire from Nov. 1880 to Nov. 1885 and for the Arfon division of Carnarvonshire from Nov. 1885 until he retired in 1895. Honorary LL.D., Victoria University, 1895. Died 6 Mar. 1902. [1895]

RATTIGAN, Sir William Henry. Lanarkslea, Cornwall Gardens, London. Ranelagh. S. of Bartholemew Rattigan, Esq., of Athy, Co. Kildare, and Sarah Abbott, of Deptford. B. 1842 at Delhi; m. 1878 (2nd wife), Evelyn, d. of Col. A. Higgins, C.I.E. Educ. at the High School, Agra, and King's Coll., London; LL.D., University of Göttingen. Called to the bar at Lincoln's Inn 1873, and practised chiefly in India; Q.C. 1897; created bencher of his Inn 1903. Four times Judge at the Chief Court of Punjaub. Was Vice-Chancellor of the Punjaub University 1887-95. Additional member of the Supreme Legislative Council of India 1892-99. Member of the Punjaub Legislative Council 1898-99. Honorary LL.D. of Glasgow and Punjaub Universities. Knighted 1895. A member of the Royal Asiatic Society and of the Council of the East India Association. Author of *Science of Jurisprudence, Private International Law*, and numerous other works on Law. A Liberal Unionist. Unsuccessfully contested N.E. Lanarkshire at the general election 1900, but was elected for the same constituency at a by-election Sept. 1901 and sat until his death 4 July 1904. [1904]

RAWLINSON, John Frederick Peel. Continued in House after 1918: full entry in Volume III.

RAWSON, Col. Richard Hamilton. 64 Cadogan Square, London. Gravenhurst, Hayward's Heath, Sussex. Carlton, Arthur's, and Bachelors'. Eld. s. of Phillip Rawson, Esq., J.P., and Dept.-Lieut. of Woodhurst, Sussex, and Octavia, d. of P. Gilmour, Esq., J.P., of The Grove, Londonderry. B. 21 Feb. 1863 at Aigburth,

Lancashire; m. 1890, Lady Beatrice Anson, d. of 2nd Earl of Lichfield. Educ. at Eton, and Brasenose Coll., Oxford. A Capt. 1st Life Guards and Col. commanding Sussex Yeomanry 1908-14. A J.P. and Dept.-Lieut. for Sussex, High Sheriff 1899. A Unionist, but associated with the National Party 1917-18. Unsuccessfully contested the Reigate division of Surrey in 1906. Elected there in Jan. 1910 and sat until his death 18 Oct. 1918. [1918]

RAWSON-SHAW, William. See SHAW, William Rawson.

REA, Rt. Hon. Russell. Dean Stanley Street, Westminster, London. Tanhurst, Nr. Dorking. Reform, and National Liberal. S. of Daniel K. Rea, Esq., of Eskdale, Cumberland, and Elizabeth, d. of Joseph Russell, Esq., Shipbuilder, of Liverpool. B. 11 Dec. 1846 in Manchester; m. 1872, Jane Philip, d. of P.L. MacTaggart, Esq., of Liverpool. Educ. privately. Founder and Senior Partner of R. and J.H. Rea, Shipowners and Merchants, and Dept.-Chairman of Taff Vale Railway Company. Was Chairman of Dept. Committee to inquire into economic effect of an Eight Hours Day for Miners 1906, the Joint Committee on the Port of London Bill, and the Dept. Committee on Railway Amalgamation 1909. PC. 1909. Wrote various articles and pamphlets on economic subjects. A Liberal. Unsuccessfully contested the Exchange division of Liverpool in Nov. 1897. Sat for Gloucester from 1900 to Jan. 1910, when he was defeated. First elected for South Shields in Oct. 1910 and sat until his death 5 Feb. 1916. [1915]

REA, Walter Russell. Continued in House after 1918: full entry in Volume III.

RECKITT, Harold James. 1 Wilton Terrace, London. Winestead Hall, Hull. Reform, Bath, and National Liberal. Eld. s. of Sir James Reckitt, Bart. B. 1868 at Brough, E. Yorkshire; m. 1899, Christine, d. of Alexander Howden, Esq., of Holland Park, London. Educ. at Oliver's Mount School, Scarborough, and King's Coll., Cambridge. Called to the bar at the Inner Temple 1891. Appointed J.P. for the E. Riding of Yorkshire in 1892. A Liberal, in favour of Home Rule, Etc. Unsuccessfully contested the Thirsk and Malton division of the N. Riding of Yorkshire in July 1892. Elected MP for Pontefract Feb. 1893, but

unseated on petition in June 1893. Unsuccessfully contested the Brigg division of Lincolnshire in Dec. 1894. Sat for the Brigg division of Lincolnshire from 1895 until he accepted Chiltern Hundreds in 1907. Contested Shoreditch in 1924 and 1929. Succeeded as 2nd Bart. 1924. Died 29 Dec. 1930. [1906]

REDDY, Michael. Shannonbridge, King's Co. A Farmer and Chairman of the Birr Rural District Council. A J.P. for King's Co. and a member of the United Irish League. A Nationalist. Represented the Birr division of King's Co. from 1900 until he retired in 1918. Died 30 July 1919.[1918]

REDMOND, John Edward. 18 Wynnstay Gardens, Kensington, London. Aughavanagh, Aughrim, Co. Wicklow. Eld. s. of William Archer Redmond, Esq., MP for the Wexford borough from 1872-1880, by Mary, d. of Maj. R. Hoey, 61st Foot, of Hoeyfield, Co. Wicklow. B. at Dublin 1856; m. 1883, d. of James Dalton, Esq., of New South Wales. Educ. at Clongowes Wood Coll., and at Trinity Coll., Dublin. Entered as a Law Student at Gray's Inn Nov. 1880, called to the bar at Gray's Inn 1866, Irish bar 1887. Leader of the Parnellite Nationalists from 1891-1900 and of the reunited Nationalist Party 1900-18. A Nationalist. Sat for New Ross from Jan. 1881 to Nov. 1885. Unsuccessfully contested the Kirkdale division of Liverpool in Nov. 1885. Sat for N. Wexford from Dec. 1885-1891. On the death of Mr. Parnell in 1891 he resigned to contest Cork city, but was beaten by Mr. Flavin on 6 Nov. 1891. In Dec. 1891, he was returned for Waterford city, which he continued to represent until his death 6 Mar. 1918. [1918]

REDMOND, William Archer. Continued in House after 1918: full entry in Volume III.

REDMOND, William Hoey Kearney. Glenbrook, Delgany, Co. Wicklow. S. of W.A. Redmond, Esq., MP. B. 1861; m. 1886, Eleanor, d. of James Dalton, Esq., of Orange, New South Wales. Educ. at Clongowes Coll.; took the B.L. degree at Dublin University 1891. Capt. 6th Battalion Royal Irish Regiment. A Nationalist. Sat for Wexford borough from July 1883 to Nov. 1885, for N. Fermanagh from 1885 and 1892. Returned for Clare E. in 1892 and whilst still sitting for Clare E., unsuc-

298

cessfully contested Cork city in Dec. 1910. Sat for Clare E., from 1892 until he was killed in action on 9 June 1917.   [1917]

REED, Sir Edward James, K.C.B. 19 Fitzgeorge Avenue, Kensington, London. The Lodge, Ascot. National Liberal. S. of John Reed, Esq., of Sheerness, by Elizabeth, d. of Mr. Arney. B. 1830; m. 1851, Rosetta, eld. d. of Nathaniel Barnaby, Esq., of Sheerness. Educ. at the School of Mathematics and Naval Construction, Portsmouth. Was Chief Constructor of the navy from 1863 till 1870. A Fellow of the Royal Society, Vice-President of the Institute of Naval Architects, member of the Institute of Civil Engineers, member of the Institute of Mechanical Engineers, J.P. for Pembrokeshire and Glamorganshire, and Knight of Stanislaus of Russia, of the Rising Sun of Japan, and of the Medjidie, and Commander of the Order of Francis Joseph of Austria. Wrote largely upon naval construction, and was a Lord of the Treasury from Feb. to July 1886. Advocated the construction of a tubular railway across the bed of the English Channel as an alternative to Sir E. Watkin's scheme. K.C.B. 1880. A Liberal until Mar. 1905 when he joined the Liberal Unionists. Unsuccessfully contested Hull in 1873. Sat for Pembroke district from 1874-80. Sat for Cardiff district from 1880 until defeated 1895; re-elected there in 1900 and sat until he retired in Jan. 1906. Died 30 Nov. 1906.   [1905]

REED, Henry Byron. 4 Collingham Place, London. Carlton, and St. Stephen's. S. of Henry Draper Reed, Esq. B. in the city of London 1855; m. Hannah, d. of Matthew Alkin, Esq., of Sheffield. A J.P. for Darlington, a member of the School Board of that town 1880-86, and Chairman of the National Union of Conservative Associations at the Birmingham Conference 1891. Was well known as a Lecturer and Speaker on Church and political subjects throughout England and Wales. A Conservative, in favour of Fair Trade, Old Age Pensions in co-operation with the friendly societies, an eight hours system for dangerous trades, freehold houses for the working classes, and temperance reforms, but not the Local Veto. Unsuccessfully contested Bradford W. in 1885. Sat as MP for Bradford E. from 1886 until defeated in July 1892, and from July 1895 until his death on 5 Oct. 1896.   [1896]

REES, Griffith Caradoc. 5 Elm Court, Temple, London. 92 Ashley Gardens, Victoria Street, London. S. of Griffith Rees, Esq., of Cilgerran, S. Wales. B. 1868 at Birkenhead. Unmarried. Educ. at Liverpool Institute. A Barrister, called 1903; was a Solicitor 1893-1903; Parliamentary Private Secretary to Sir John Simon, Home Secretary 1915. A Liberal. Unsuccessfully contested Denbigh Boroughs Dec. 1910. Elected for N. Carnarvonshire July 1915 and sat until he retired in 1918. Died 20 Sept. 1924.   [1918]

REES, Sir John David, K.C.I.E., C.V.O. Continued in House after 1918: full entry in Volume III.

REID, Rt. Hon. Sir George Houston, G.C.M.G., G.C.B., D.C.L. 1 Melbury Road, London. Athenaeum, British Empire, Cobden, and Royal Societies'. S. of the Rev. John Reid, of the Church of Scotland, and Marion, d. of William Crybbace, Esq., J.P., of Edinburgh. B. 25 Feb. 1845 at Johnstone, Renfrewshire; m. 1891, Flora, d. of John Bromby, Esq., of Thornton, Cressy, Tasmania. Educ. at Scot's Coll., Melbourne, and private tuition, Sydney. A Barrister, 1879. K.C. 1902. Was elected to the New South Wales Legislative Assembly in 1880 and, with an interval in 1884-85, remained MP for E. Sydney till 1901. Was Prime Minister and Colonial Treasurer of New South Wales 1894-99, and during that period as Senior Prime Minister carried the Federal movement to a successful issue. After Federation, was Member for E. Sydney 1901-09; Leader of Federal Opposition for some time; and was in 1904-05 Prime Minister of Australia. Published *Five Free Trade Essays, New South Wales, the Mother Colony of Australia*, etc. Gold Medallist of the Cobden Club. PC. 1897; K.C.M.G. 1909; G.C.M.G. 1911; G.C.B. 1916. An Independent Imperialist. Was returned, on the invitation of both the Conservative and Liberal parties, in Jan. 1916 for the St. George's division of Hanover Square, and sat until his death 12 Sept. 1918.   [1918]

REID, Hugh Gilzean. Warley Hall, Nr. Birmingham. Middlesborough-on-Tees. National Liberal. S. of Hugh Reid, Esq., by Christian Gilzean, both descendants of Highland crofters. B. at Cruden, Aberdeenshire, 1836; m. 1863, Anne, eld. d. of John and Margaret Craig, of Peterhead, N.B. Was partly self-educ. and attended lectures at Aberdeen and Edinburgh, being designed for the Baptist ministry, but became a writer for the press in Aberdeen, Banff, and Peterhead, and ultimately became Editor of a popular weekly newspaper at Edinburgh. Established and owned several newspapers in Middlesborough and other places in the N. of England and in Scotland. Also wrote *Past and Present; or Social and Religious Life in the North, Co-operation Applied to the Dwellings of the People, Old Oscar, the Faithful Dog, The Life of the Rev. John Skinner*, and several other works, besides articles in the *Fortnightly, Westminster*, and other reviews, etc. President of several Liberal and other associations in the N. of England and in the Midlands. An "advanced Liberal", especially interested in the housing of the poor, and in all social, industrial, and co-operative movements; would give to all classes "the largest extension of individual liberty and self-government, compatible with the rights of citizenship and the integrity and supremacy of the Empire." Sat for Aston Manor from Nov. 1885 until defeated in 1886 standing as a Gladstonian Liberal. Unsuccessfully contested the Handsworth division of Staffordshire in July 1892. President of Society of Newspaper Proprietors 1898-99; Chief founder and (1888-90) first President of the Institute of Journalists; connected with Iron and Steel industry. Resided much in Belgium; interested in missionary work in the Congo. Knighted 1893. Died 5 Nov. 1911.   [1886]

REID, James. 1 Whitehall Gardens, London. Monfode, Greenock. Carlton, and Conservative. S. of Henry Reid, Esq., Merchant, of Belfast, and Catherine Barnett, d. of John Barnett, Esq., of Belfast. B. in Belfast 1839; m. 1872, Jessie Ryburn Galbreath, d. of John Galbreath, of Greenock, a widower, (1899). Educ. at the Academy, and Queen's Coll., Belfast. Dept.-Chairman of Fleming, Reid and Company Limited, Worsted Spinners and Hosiery Manufacturers, Greenock. J.P. 1882 and Dept.-Lieut. 1894 for Co. Renfrew. A Conservative. Elected for Greenock in 1900 and sat until defeated in 1906. Died 29 June 1908.   [1905]

REID, Sir Robert Threshie. 1 Temple Gardens, London. Kingsdown House, Nr. Dover. Brooks's, and National Liberal. 2nd s. of Sir James John Reid, of Mouswald Place, Dumfriesshire, Chief Justice of the

Ionian Islands, by Mary Dalzell, d. of Robert Threshie, Esq., of Barnbarroch, near Dalbeattie, Kirkcudbrightshire. B. at Corfu 1846; m. 1871, Emily, d. of A.C. Fleming, Esq. (she died 1904). Educ. at Cheltenham Coll., and at Balliol Coll., Oxford; 1st class in classics at moderations 1866, B.A. 1st class in classics 1868, when he was also Ireland scholar. Called to the bar at the Inner Temple June 1871, and joined the Oxford Circuit. Appointed a Q.C. Dec. 1882, a bencher of his Inn 1890, Solicitor Gen. May 1894 (with knightage), and was Attorney Gen. from Oct. 1894 to June 1895. Became G.C.M.G. in 1899 for services in the Venezuela boundary arbitration case. A Liberal. Sat for Hereford from 1880 to 1885, and was unsuccessful in the ensuing election as a candidate for Dumbartonshire. Elected for Dumfries district in 1886 and sat until appointed Lord Chancellor Dec. 1905. Created Baron Loreburn Jan. 1906; Earl Loreburn June 1911; PC. 1905; Lord Chancellor 1905-12. Author of *Capture at Sea* (1913). Died 30 Nov. 1923.   [1905]

REMNANT, Sir James Farquharson, Bart. Continued in House after 1918: full entry in Volume III.

RENDALL, Athelstan. Continued in House after 1918: full entry in Volume III.

RENDEL, Stuart. 1 Carlton House Gardens, London. Hatchlands Place, Nr. Guildford. Athenaeum, Brooks's, and Garrick. S. of James Meadows Rendel, Esq., F.R.S., the well-known Civil Engineer. B. 1834; m. 1857, d. of William Egerton Hubbard, Esq., of Leonardslee, Horsham, Sussex. Was educ. at Eton, and Oriel Coll., Oxford. Graduated B.A. 1856. Was called to the bar at the Inner Temple June 1861, but did not practise. President of the North Wales Liberal Federation from Dec. 1886, President of the National Council of Wales from 1887, and Chairman of the Parliamentary Association of Welsh Liberals from 1888. A Liberal and Home Ruler. Sat for Montgomeryshire from Apr. 1880 until created Lord Rendel in 1894. Died 4 June 1913.   [1894]

RENSHAW, Sir Charles Bine, Bart. 82 Cadogan Square, London. Barochan, Houston, N.B. Garvocks, Greenock. Carlton, and Garrick. S. of Thomas Charles Renshaw, Esq., Q.C., of Lincoln's

Inn, and Sandrocks, Sussex, by Elizabeth Blaker, of Patcham, Sussex. B. 1848; m. 1872, Mary, 3rd. of A.F. Stoddard, Esq., of Broadfield, Renfrewshire. Educ. at St. Clere, Kent, and in Germany. A Manufacturer; J.P. and Dept.-Lieut. for Co. of Renfrew, a F.R.G.S., etc. Created Bart. 1902. A Conservative, strongly opposed to the establishment of a separate Parliament in Ireland. Represented W. Renfrewshire from 1892 until he retired in 1906. Died 6 Mar. 1918. [1905]

RENTON, Alexander Leslie. Naseby Hall, Northamptonshire. Brooks's, Naval & Military, and Cavalry. S. of James H. Renton, Esq. B. 6 July 1868 in London; m. 1895, Kathleen, d. of Charles Taylor, Esq., of Horton Manor, Buckinghamshire. Educ. at Harrow, and Royal Military Coll., Sandhurst. Joined the Royal Scots Greys in 1888, served in S. African War 1900, mentioned in despatches; a Maj. Northampton Imperial Yeomanry. J.P. for Northamptonshire. A Liberal until Nov. 1907 when he joined the Liberal Unionists. Unsuccessfully contested S. Dorset in 1900. Elected for the Gainsborough division of Lincolnshire in 1906 and sat until he retired in Jan. 1910. Contested Reading in Jan. 1910, as a Liberal Unionist. Served in European War 1914-18. Died 6 May 1947. [1909]

RENTOUL, James Alexander. 1 Pump Court, Temple, London. 23 Old Queen Street, Westminster, London. Carlton. Eld. s. of the Rev. Alexander Rentoul, D.D., M.D., of Ray, Co. Donegal, and Erminda, eld. d. of James Chittick, Esq., of Manor Cunningham, Co. Donegal. B. 1854; m. 1882, Florence Isabella, youngest d. of D.W. Young, Esq., of Wallington Lodge, Surrey, and London. Educ. at Cookstown Academy, Queen's Coll., Galway, Queen's University, Ireland, Royal University, Berlin, and in Brussels; and graduated B.A. and LL.B. both with honours and first University Exhibition, and LL.D. with first place by examination. A Barrister of the Inner Temple 1884, first place at bar final examination; on S.E. Circuit; held the Inner Temple equity scholarship of one hundred guineas, and became Q.C. 1895. A member of the London County Council for Woolwich, and Chairman of the Woolwich Conservative Association; a member of the Belfast Chamber of Commerce. A Conservative,

opposed to Home Rule. Sat for Down E. from 1890 until appointed Judge of the City of London Court in 1901. Died 12 Aug. 1919. [1901]

RENWICK, George. Continued in House after 1918: full entry in Volume III.

REYNOLDS, William James. Howard Terrace, Dungannon, Co. Tyrone. National Liberal. S. of David Reynolds, Esq., of Dublin, by his m. with Miss Ellen Campbell, of Dungannon. B. at Dungannon 1856; m. 1881, Minnie Teresa, d. of M. Montague, Esq., of Dungannon. Educ. at the Royal School. Was admitted a Solicitor 1879. An "Irish Nationalist" (Anti-Parnellite). Sat for Tyrone E. from 1885 until he retired in 1895. Died 23 May 1934. [1895]

RHYS-WILLIAMS, Sir Rhys, Bart. Continued in House after 1918: full entry in Volume III.

RICE, Hon. Walter FitzUryan. 15 Lower Berkeley Street, London. Carlton, and Bachelors'. Only s. of Lord Dynevor. B. 17 Aug. 1873 at Dursley, Gloucestershire; m. 1898, Lady Margaret Villiers, d. of Earl of Jersey. Educ. at Eton, and Christ Church, Oxford. Was Assistant Private Secretary to Lord George Hamilton when Secretary of State for India 1899-1903, and to Lord Selborne, when First Lord of the Admiralty 1904-05. A Dept.-Lieut. for Carmarthen, Capt. Carmarthen Artillery. A Unionist. Elected for Brighton in Jan. 1910 and sat until succeeded as Baron Dynevor 8 June 1911. Changed surname from Rice to Rhys in 1916. Member of Carmarthenshire County Council from 1919-35. Lord-Lieut. of Carmarthenshire from 1928-48. Chairman of Land Union 1920-37. Died 8 June 1956. [1911]

RICHARD, Henry. 22 Bolton Gardens, South Kensington, London. Devonshire. S. of the Rev. Ebenezer Richard, a Calvinistic Methodist Minister, of Tregaron, Cardiganshire, by Mary, d. of William Williams, Esq., of the same place. B. at Tregaron 1812; m. 1866, Augusta Matilda, 3rd d. of John Farley, Esq., of Kennington Park Road, near London. Educ. at a private school in Wales, and subsequently at Highbury Congregational Coll. Was for several years Minister of Marlborough (Independent) Chapel, Southwark. Secretary of the London Peace Society from 1848 to

1885. Author of *Memoirs of Joseph Sturge, Social and Political Condition of the Principality of Wales, The Present and Future of India,* etc. An "advanced Liberal", in favour of Home Rule, and of the total severance of Church and State. Sat for Merthyr Tydvil from Dec. 1868. MP until his death 20 Aug. 1888.

[1888]

RICHARDS, Henry Charles. 2 Mitre Court Buildings, Temple, London. Caerhayes, St. Leonards-on-Sea. Carlton, Junior Carlton, and Constitutional. S. of Frederick Richards, Esq., J.P., of West Hill, St. Leonards-on-Sea, and Anne Georgiana, only d. of Mr Field, of London and Plymouth. B. 1851 at Hackney. Educ. at the Proprietary School at Gravesend, and the City of London School, under Dr. Mortimer. Called to the bar as Bacon Scholar 1879, Gray's Inn 1881; Q.C., and a bencher of Gray's Inn 1898. Senior Counsel for the Post Office at the Central Criminal Court; also F.S.A., F.R.H.S., and author of legal works on Parish Councils, Railway Rates, Compensation, the Candidates and Agents Corrupt Practices Act, Education Acts, Licensing Law, etc. "A Democratic Tory", in favour of social reforms, the union of Church and State, denominational schools, old age pensions, redistribution of seats, and better housing of the working classes. Contested Northampton in Feb. 1884, Nov. 1885 and July 1892. Sat for E. Finsbury from 1895 until his death 1 June 1905. [1905]

RICHARDS, Rt. Hon. Thomas. Continued in House after 1918: full entry in Volume III.

RICHARDS, Thomas Frederick. 115 Knollys Road, Streatham, London. B. 1863 at Wednesbury; m. 1882, Emma, d. of John Mee, Esq. Educ. at elementary schools. Commenced work at twelve in a licensed house; became an assistant to Boiler Maker, then worked in the Boot Trade at Leicester; joined the Union in 1885; Vice-President 1894; President 1898-1906. A member of the Management Committee of the Federation of Trades Unions; a member of the Leicester Town Council 1894-1903. A Labour Member and Socialist. Elected for Wolverhampton W. in 1906 and sat until defeated in Jan. 1910. Contested Northamptonshire E. as an Independent Labour candidate in Dec. 1910. General President, National Union

of Boot and Shoe Operators 1910-29. Member of the Leicester City Council 1929-39. Died 4 Oct. 1942. [1909]

RICHARDSON, Albion Henry Herbert. Continued in House after 1918: full entry in Volume III.

RICHARDSON, Alexander. Continued in House after 1918: full entry in Volume III.

RICHARDSON, Arthur. 6 Friar Yard, Nottingham. S. of William and Eliza Richardson, of E. Bridgford, Nottinghamshire. B. 1860 at E. Bridgford; m. 1886, Frances, d. of John Whitby, Esq., of Nottingham. Educ. at the local National School, and Magnus Grammar School, Newark. Apprenticed as a Grocer in 1877, became Wholesale Representative in 1880, and took over a business in Nottingham. A J.P. for Nottingham. Represented S. Nottingham as a Liberal-Labour Member from 1906-Jan. 1910, when he was defeated. Again defeated at S. Nottingham in Dec. 1910. Elected as a Liberal for the Rotherham division of the W. Riding of Yorkshire in Feb. 1917 and sat until defeated in W. Nottingham in 1918. Unsuccessfully contested the Melton division of Leicestershire in 1922, 1923 and 1924. Died 27 June 1936. [1918]

RICHARDSON, John Maunsell. Healing Manor, Nr. Grimsby. Younger s. of William Richardson, Esq., of Limber, near Brigg. B. at Great Limber 1846; m. 1881, Victoria, widow of the 3rd Earl of Yarborough. Educ. at Harrow, and Cambridge, for which University he played in the cricket eleven. On Lord Yarborough's death in 1875, the management of the famous Brocklesby hounds devolved upon Mr. Richardson. A Dept.-Lieut. and J.P. for Lincolnshire, and member of the Lincolnshire County Council; an officer in the Light Horse Volunteers. A Conservative. Unsuccessfully contested the Brigg division of Lincolnshire in 1886 and 1892. First returned for that division Dec. 1894 and sat until defeated in 1895. Died 22 Jan. 1912. [1895]

RICHARDSON, Joseph. Potto Hall, Northallerton. Reform, and National Liberal. S. of Caleb Richardson, Esq., of Sunderland, Merchant. B. 1830 at Sunderland; m. 1st, 1856, Anne Eliza, only d. of F.

Blackhouse, Esq., Banker, of Stockton-on-Tees (she died 1886); 2ndly, 1892, Flora, youngest d. of James MacDonald, Esq., of Birkenhead (she died 1897). Educ. at The Friends' School, York. An Iron Ship-builder, of the firm of Richardson, Duck and Company, Stockton-on-Tees. Was Mayor of Stockton 1870, 1877, 1878, and 1886; Alderman of the County Council for Durham, and of the borough of Stockton; J.P. and Dept.-Lieut. for Durham; J.P. for the N. Riding of Yorkshire, and Stockton; High Sheriff of Durham 1885-86. A Liberal, in favour of Registration, Land Law, and Temperance reforms, reform of the House of Lords, etc. Sat for the S.E. division of Durham, 1892-95, when he was defeated; re-elected there Feb. 1898 and sat until defeated in 1900. Died 25 Sept. 1902.   [1900]

RICHARDSON,   Thomas,   (I).
Kirklevington, Yarm, Yorkshire. Reform. Eld. s. of Thomas Richardson, Esq., a Coal-Owner and Iron-Founder at Castle Eden, Co. Durham. B. at Castle Eden 1821; m. 1843, Maria, d. of Richard Greenwell, Esq., of Sunderland. A Magistrate and Dept.-Lieut. for the Co. of Durham, and a Magistrate for the N. Riding of the Co. of Yorkshire, and was head of the Marine Engine-Building firm of T. Richardson and Sons, of Hartlepool. A Liberal, and Unionist.   Unsuccessfully   contested Hartlepool   in   Dec.   1868.   Sat   for Hartlepool from Feb. 1874 to July 1875, when he retired, and from Apr. 1880 until his death on 29 Dec. 1890.   [1889]

RICHARDSON,   Sir   Thomas.
Kirklevington Grange, Yarm, Yorkshire. Reform, and Northumberland. Eld. s. of T. Richardson, Esq., MP for Hartlepool, and Maria, d. of R. Greenwell, Esq., of Sunderland. B. Dec. 1846 at Castle Eden, in the Co. of Durham; m. 1878, Anna Constance, d. of the Rev. John C. Faber, Rector of Cricklade, Wiltshire. Educ. at Rossall, and Magdalene Coll., Cambridge. A member of the firm of T. Richardson and Sons, Marine Engine Builders, Hartlepool. A J.P. and Dept.-Lieut. for Co. Durham, an Alderman of Hartlepool (was Mayor of the borough 1886-88), and was Knighted 1897. A Liberal Unionist. Contested Hartlepool July 1892. First returned for Hartlepool July 1895 and sat until defeated in 1900. Died 22 May 1906.   [1900]

RICHARDSON,   Thomas,   (II).
Tyneholme, Thyra Grove, North Finchley, London. S. of Robert Richardson, Esq., Miner. B. 6 June 1868 at Usworth, Co. Durham; m. 1888, Mary, d. of John Purvis, Esq. Educ. at Usworth Board School. A member of the Executive of Durham Miners' Association and the Durham Coal Conciliation Board; Vice-President of the Northumberland Miners' Permanent Relief Fund; a member of Durham County Council for nine years and Vice-Chairman of the Education Sub-Committee. A Labour Member. Elected for Whitehaven Dec. 1910 and sat until defeated in the Bosworth division of Leicestershire in 1918. Stood as a Labour candidate in Yale, British Columbia in 1920. Died 22 Oct. 1928.   [1918]

RICHARDSON-GARDNER, Robert. 46 Grosvenor Square, London. Bythsia Villa, Boscombe, Hampshire. Chateau Louis XIII, Cannes. Carlton, Constitutional, and Lyric. S. of John Richardson, Esq., (a Magistrate), of Swansea, Glamorganshire, and Elizabeth his wife. B. 1827; m. 1854, Maria Louisa, only d. and heir of Henry Gardner, Esq., whose surname he assumed by royal sign manual in 1864 (she died 1889). Was called to the bar at the Middle Temple 1853. Was one of the first volunteers in Hampshire, where he assisted in raising a corps, to which he was gazetted Capt.-Commandant 1859; retired after 10 years service as Honorary Col. of N.E. London Rifles. A Dept.-Lieut. of the Tower Hamlets, and Commander of the Royal Order of the Crown of Italy, and Officer of the Royal Order of Leopold of Belgium, conferred upon him by the Kings of Italy and Belgium respectively in appreciation of his efforts for the amelioration of the condition of the blind in all countries. A Conservative. Unsuccessfully contested Windsor Dec. 1868, for which borough he sat for from Feb. 1874 until he accepted Chiltern Hundreds in 1890. Died 4 Jan. 1898.   [1890]

RICKETT, Rt. Hon. Sir Joseph Compton. See COMPTON-RICKETT, Rt. Hon. Sir Joseph. Continued in House after 1918: full entry in Volume III.

RIDLEY, Rt. Hon. Sir Matthew White, Bart. 10 Carlton House Terrace, London. Blagdon Cramlington, Northumberland.

Athenaeum, Carlton, and Travellers'. Eld. s. of Sir Matthew White Ridley, 5th Bart., of Blagdon, by Cecilia Anne, d. of Lord Wensleydale. B. in London 1842; m. 1873, Hon. Mary Georgiana, eld. d. of the 1st Baron Tweedmouth (she died 1899). Educ. at Harrow, and at Balliol Coll., Oxford, of which he was a Scholar; graduated B.A., 1st class in classics 1865; became Fellow of All Souls and M.A. 1867. Succeeded as Bart. in 1877. Appointed Home Secretary June 1895, and held office until Nov. 1900. Was Chairman of the Northumberland County Council until he took office as Home Secretary. Lieut.-Col. of the Northumberland Yeomanry; resigned 1895. Was Under-Secretary of State for the Home Department 1878-80, Financial Secretary to the Treasury from 1885-86 and admitted a PC. Aug. 1892. A Conservative. Sat for N. Northumberland from 1868-85. Contested the Hexham division of Northumberland Dec. 1885 and Newcastle-on-Tyne July 1886. Sat for the Blackpool division of Lancashire from Aug. 1886 until he resigned in Dec. 1900. He was defeated candidate for the Speakership of the House in 1895. Created Visct. Ridley Dec. 1900. Died 28 Nov. 1904.   [1900]

RIDLEY, Hon. Matthew White. 36 Portland Place, London. Carlton, and Turf. Eld. s. of Visct. Ridley and Mary Georgina, d. of the 1st Baron Tweedmouth. B. in London 1874; m. 1899, Rosamund, 4th d. of 1st Baron Wimborne. Educ. at Eton, and Balliol Coll., Oxford (B.A. with honours). Capt. in Northumberland Hussars; Secretary to Lord Aberdeen, Governor-Gen. of Canada; and to Mr. Ritchie at the Home Office. A Conservative. Sat for Stalybridge from Oct. 1900 until he succeeded as 2nd Visct. Ridley in Nov. 1904. Died 14 Feb. 1916.   [1904]

RIDLEY, Samuel Forde. 19 Cadogan Place, London. Carlton. S. of S.E. Ridley, Esq., of St. Helen's, Isle of Wight, and Nona Jackson, d. of Francis Kent, Esq., of Hampton. B. in London 1864; m. 1896, Muriel Paget, only d. of Sir W. Paget Bowman, Bart., of Joldwynds, near Dorking. Educ. at Clifton Coll. An Officer in 3rd Middlesex Artillery Volunteers. A Unionist. Sat for S.W. Bethnal Green from 1900 to 1906 when he was defeated. Elected for Rochester in Jan. 1910 and sat until defeated in Dec. 1910. Died 17 Nov. 1944.   [1910]

RIDSDALE, Edward Aurelian. 7 Queen's Gate Gardens, London. Waterwynch, Tenby, South Wales. Reform, and National Liberal. S. of E.L.J. Ridsdale, Esq., of the Royal Mint, and Esther Lucy Thacker. B. 23 Feb. 1864 in London; m. 1900, Susan Stirling, d. of J.R. Findlay, Esq., of Edinburgh. Educ. at University Coll. School, and Royal School of Mines. A member of the Stock Exchange, for several years on the Committee, retired 1904. Fellow Geological Society. Author of *Cosmic Evolution*. A Liberal. Elected for Brighton in 1906 and sat until he retired in Jan. 1910. Chairman of British Red Cross Society 1912-14, and Dept. Chairman from 1914-1919; Special Commissioner in Salonika and Mesopotamia 1915-16; Acting Red Cross Commissioner in France 1916. G.B.E. 1920. Died 6 Sept. 1923. [1909]

RIGBY, Sir John. 76 Jermyn Street, London. Glenturret, Crieff, N.B. Reform, and National Liberal. 2nd s. of Thomas Rigby, Esq., of Hatton, in the Co. of Chester, and Elizabeth, d. of Joseph Kendall, Esq., of Liverpool. B. 1834 at Runcorn, Cheshire. Educ. at Liverpool Collegiate Institution, and Trinity Coll., Cambridge. Graduated 2nd wrangler and 2nd Smith's Prizeman in 1856, and 2nd class in the classical tripos, and was elected a Fellow of his Coll. Called to the bar at Lincoln's Inn 1860; junior equity counsel to the Treasury 1875 to 1881; Q.C. 1881; a bencher of his Inn 1884. Appointed Solicitor-Gen. and Knighted 1892. Attorney Gen. May-Oct. 1894. PC. 1894. An advanced Liberal and Radical, in favour of Home Rule, and the Liberal programme generally. Sat for the Wisbech division of Cambridgeshire 1885-86; unsuccessful candidate there 1886. Sat for Forfarshire from July 1892 until appointed Lord Justice of Appeal in 1894; resigned 1901. Died 26 July 1903.
                                        [1894]

RIGG, Richard. 4 Brick Court, Temple, London. Applegarth, Windermere. Reform, Eighty, and National Liberal. S. of John Rigg, Esq., Co. Alderman for Westmoreland, and Sarah Anne, d. of J. Sutton, Esq., of Dairy, Galloway, N.B. B. at Windermere 1877; m. 1904, Gertrude Anderson. Educ. at Hawkshead Grammar School, and Caius Coll., Cambridge (B.A. 1900). Barrister-at-Law of the Inner Temple 1899, and King's Inn, Dublin 1902. A J.P. for the N. Riding of Yorkshire,

Westmoreland, and Durham; Capt. in 2nd Voluntary Battalion of the Border Regiment; conservator of the Kent Fishery District, and a member of the Sea Fisheries Committee. A Liberal (Imperialist), but resigned the whip in Nov. 1904. Sat for the Appleby division of Westmoreland from Oct. 1900 until he accepted Chiltern Hundreds in Dec. 1904. High Sheriff of Westmoreland 1909-10; O.B.E. 1918; Grand Deacon of English Freemasons; member of many hospital boards. Mayor of city of Westminster 1939-40; Vice-Chairman of Abbey division of Westminster Constitutional Assocication. Died 29 Aug. 1942.   [1904]

RITCHIE, Rt. Hon. Charles Thomson. 37 Princes Gate, London. Welders, Gerrard's Cross, Buckinghamshire. Carlton, and Athenaeum. S. of William Ritchie, Esq., of Rockhill, Forfarshire, by Elizabeth, d. of J. Thomson, Esq. B. at Dundee 1838; m. 1858, Margaret, d. of Thomas Ower, Esq., of Perth. A J.P. for Middlesex, and Honorary Col. 1st Volunteer Battalion Queen's Royal West Surrey Regiment; Secretary to the Admiralty 1885-86, President of the Local Government Board 1886-92, President Board of Trade 1895-1900, Home Secretary 1900-02, Chancellor of the Exchequer 1902-03. PC. 1886. In 1888 he introduced the Bill establishing County Councils. In 1894 he was elected Alderman of the London County Council, resigned 1895. Lord Rector of Aberdeen University 1903. A Conservative, in favour of the readjustment of local taxation, etc. Sat for the Tower Hamlets from Feb. 1874 to Nov. 1885, and for the St. George's-in-the-East division of the Tower Hamlets 1885-92, when he was defeated. Contested Walsall Feb. 1893. First elected for Croydon in May 1895 and sat until created 1st Baron Ritchie of Dundee in Dec. 1905. Died 9 Jan. 1906.   [1905]

ROBERTS, Charles Henry. Continued in House after 1918: full entry in Volume III.

ROBERTS, C.H. Crompton. A Conservative. Elected for Sandwich at a by-election in May 1880, but was unseated on petition in Aug. of the same year.

ROBERTS, Rt. Hon. George Henry. Continued in House after 1918: full entry in Volume III.

ROBERTS, John. Bryngwenallt, Abergele, North Wales. S. of David Robert, Esq., of Tanyrallt, Denbighshire. B. at Liverpool 1835; m. 1861, Catherine Tudor, d. of Rev. John Hughes (she died 1880). A Timber Merchant. A Magistrate for Liverpool and for Denbighshire. A Liberal, and Gladstonian. Sat for Flint district from 5 July 1878 until he retired in 1892. Died 24 Feb. 1894.   [1892]

ROBERTS, John Bryn. 17 Orchard Street, London. Brynn Adda, Bangor. Reform. Eld. s. of Daniel Roberts, Esq., of Bryn Adda, Bangor, by Anne, d. of Griffith Jones, Esq., of Plas Gwanas, near Dolgelley. B. at Bryn Adda 1843. Educ. at Cheltenham Grammar School. Was a Solicitor, admitted in 1868. In 1889 was called to the bar at Lincoln's Inn; a J.P. and Dept-Lieut. for Carnarvonshire, and Dept.-Chairman Quarter Sessions. A Radical and Home Ruler, was "irreconcilably opposed to Liberal Imperialism." Sat for the Eifion division of Carnarvonshire from 1885 until appointed a County Court Judge in Apr. 1906. Died 14 Apr. 1931.   [1906]

ROBERTS, Sir John Herbert, Bart. Bryngwenallt, Abergele. 32 Queen's Gate Gardens, London. Reform. S. of John Roberts, Esq., at one time MP for the Flint district, and Catherine Tudor, d. of the Rev. J. Hughes, of Liverpool. B. 1863; m. 1893, Hannah Rushton, d. of W.S. Caine, Esq., at one time MP for Camborne. Educ. privately, and at Trinity Coll., Cambridge; History honours. A J.P. for Denbighshire. Travelled in the Colonies and India 1884-85, and wrote a *World Tour*. President of Anglo-Indian Temperance Association; Chairman of Welsh Liberals 1915. Created Bart. 1908. A Liberal. Represented W. Denbighshire from 1892 until he retired in 1918. Created Baron Clwyd Apr. 1919. Died 19 Dec. 1955.   [1918]

ROBERTS, Sir Samuel. Continued in House after 1918: full entry in Volume III.

ROBERTSON, Rt. Hon. Edmund, K.C. 95 Croxted Road, Dulwich, London. The Admiralty, London. Reform. S. of Edmund Robertson, Esq., Schoolmaster at Kinnaird, near Dundee. B. 28 Oct. 1845. Educ. at St. Andrew's University, and at Oxford, where he was senior scholar of Lincoln Coll., a University prizeman, and

Vinerian scholar. Took a first class in classics (moderations and final), became Fellow of Corpus Christi Coll., and was subsequently Public Examiner in Law, both at Oxford and the Inns of Court. Called to the bar at Lincoln's Inn 1872, a bencher 1898, and joined the N.Circuit. Was Civil Lord of the Admiralty Aug. 1892-95. Q.C. 1895. Parliamentary Secretary to the Admiralty from Dec. 1905 to Apr. 1908. PC. 1906. A Liberal, in favour of Mr. Gladstone's Home Rule policy. Sat for Dundee from 1885 until created Lord Lochee in 1908. Died 13 Sept. 1911. [1908]

ROBERTSON, Sir George Scott, K.C.S.I. 14 Cheyne Walk, Chelsea, London. Athenaeum, National Liberal, Savile, and Burlington Fine Arts. S. of T.J. Robertson, Esq., of Rousay, Orkney, and Robina Corston, d. of Robert Scott, Esq., of Kirkwall. B. 22 Oct. 1852 in London; m. 1st, 1882, Catherine, d. of Col. A.J.C. Birch; 2ndly, Mary, d. of Samuel Laurence, Esq., the painter. Educ. privately, and at Westminster Hospital Medical School. Entered the Indian Medical Service in 1878; served in the Afghan campaign 1879. Employed in the Indian Foreign Office 1888-98. British Agent at Gilgit 1895. Retired as Lieut.-Col. 1898; K.C.S.I. 1895; Honorary D.C.L. Toronto University. Author of *Kafiristan, Chitral, the story of a Minor Siege*. A Liberal. Unsuccessfully contested Stirlingshire in 1900. Elected for Central Bradford in 1906 and sat until his death 3 Jan. 1916. [1915]

ROBERTSON, Henry. Retired in 1886: full entry in Volume I.

ROBERTSON, Rt. Hon. James Patrick Bannerman. 19 Drumsheugh Gardens, Edinburgh. Muchalls Castle, Kincardineshire. Carlton. Conservative, Edinburgh. S. of the Rev. R. Robertson, of Forteviot, Perthshire, by Helen, d. of the Rev. J. Bannerman, of Cargill, Perthshire. B. at Forteviot 1845; m. 1872, Philadelphia Mary Lucy, d. of W.N. Fraser, Esq., of Tornaveen, Aberdeenshire. Educ. at the University of Edinburgh; M.A. 1864. Was called to the Scottish bar 1867, made Q.C. 1885, and was Solicitor-Gen. for Scotland from 1885-Jan. 1886; reappointed to the latter post Aug. 1886, and appointed Lord Advocate for Scotland 1888. A Conservative. Unsuccessfully contested Linlithgowshire in 1880. Sat for Buteshire

from 1885 until appointed Lord Justice General, with the title of Lord Robertson, in 1891-99. PC. 1888. Lord Rector of Edinburgh University 1893-96; Chairman of Royal Commission on British University Education 1901. Created Baron Robertson (life peerage) in 1899. Lord of Appeal in Ordinary 1899-1909. Died 1 Feb. 1909. [1891]

ROBERTSON, Rt. Hon. John MacKinnon. Knight's Place, Pembury, Tunbridge Wells. National Liberal. S. of John Robertson, Esq., of Perthshire, and Susan, d. of John MacKinnon, Esq., of Brodick, Arran. B. 14 Nov. 1856 at Brodick; m. 1893, Maude, d. of Charles Mosher, Esq., of Iowa, U.S.A. Educ. at Stirling. A Journalist, Lecturer, and author, began as a Leader-Writer on *Edinburgh Evening News*, 1878. Author of *Modern Humanists, Essays towards a Critical Method, Buckle and his Critics, History of Free Thought, Pagan Christs, Trade and Tariffs*, and numerous other works on ethical, political, literary and historical subjects, especially *The Political Economy of Free Trade* (1928). Parliamentary Secretary to Board of Trade 1911-15. PC. 1915. An advanced Liberal. Unsuccessfully contested Northampton as an Independent Liberal in 1895. Elected for the Tyneside division of Northumberland in 1906 and sat until defeated in Wallsend in 1918. Unsuccessfully contested Hendon in 1923. Died 5 Jan. 1933. [1918]

ROBERTSON, Thomas Herbert. The Cedars, South Hackney. Huntington Castle, Clonegal, Co. Carlow. Athenaeum, Carlton, and Savile. S. of Thomas Storm Robertson, Esq., M.D., and Maria Louisa, only d. of Robert Manning, Esq., of Clapham. B. in London 1849; m. 1880, Helen Alexandrina Melian, eld. d. of Alexander Durdin, Esq., of Huntington Castle, Co. Carlow. Educ. at Magdalen Coll., Oxford, where he took the degree of M.A. Called to the bar at Lincoln's Inn 1873. A J.P. for the counties of London and Carlow, and High Sheriff for Co. Carlow 1899. A Conservative, in favour of the better housing of the working classes, increase of allotment grounds, of old age pensions, and of improvements in the registration of voters and the distribution of seats. Unsuccessfully contested S. Hackney in 1892 and 1894. Represented S. Hackney from 1895 until defeated in 1906. Died 11 July 1916. [1905]

ROBERTSON, Sir William Tindal. Gray's Inn, London. 9 Belgrave Terrace, Brighton. Royden, Essex. St. Stephen's and Constitutional. S. of Frederick Fowler Robertson, Esq., of Bath, and Anne Tindal, of Grantham. B. at Grantham 1825; m. 1855, the youngest d. of John Leavers, Esq., of Nottingham. Educ. at the Universities of Edinburgh and Paris. Became a Physician in 1846, and a F.R.C.P. 1874. A Town Councillor of Brighton. Was Chairman of the Brighton Conservative Association 1882, and Vice Chairman of the Conservative Home Counties Union 1886. Wrote works on scientific and medical subjects, and edited Reports of Proceedings of the British Association for the Advancement of Science, etc. etc. He was Knighted 1 Jan. 1888. Sir W.T. Robertson, like Mr. Fawcett, a former member for Brighton, was blind, and was a member of the Royal Commission for Inquiring into the Condition of the Blind. A Conservative. He was elected for Brighton, without opposition, on the death of Alderman David Smith, 29 Nov. 1886 and sat until he committed suicide on 6 Oct. 1889. [1889]

ROBINSON, Brooke. 26 Chapel Street, London. Barford House, Warwickshire. Carlton, and Junior Carlton. S. of William Robinson, Esq., Solicitor, of Dudley, by Harriet, d. of John Johnson, Esq., of Leverington, Isle of Ely. B. at Dudley 1836; m. 1870, Eugenia Frederica Louisa, d. of George Richmond Collis, Esq., of Stourton Castle, Stourbridge (she died 1891). Educ. at Rugby. Was a Solicitor in Dudley, but later retired. Was also an officer in the Worcestershire Yeomanry. A Conservative. Unsuccessfully contested Dudley in 1885. Represented Dudley from 1886 until he retired in 1906. Died 20 Oct. 1911. [1905]

ROBINSON, Sidney. Continued in House after 1918: full entry in Volume III.

ROBINSON, Sir Thomas. Maisemore Park, Nr. Gloucester. Reform, and National Liberal. B. Jan. 1827; m. 1852, Harriet, d. of John Goodwin, Esq., J.P., of Worcester. Educ. at private schools. Was engaged in business as a Corn Merchant from 1849, and was a member of the town council of Gloucester from 1857 to Nov. 1886. A J.P. and was four times Mayor of Gloucester (1865, 1866, 1872 and 1874). Knighted in 1894. A Liberal and Home Ruler, in favour of reform of the land laws, reform of the House of Lords, shortening the hours in which public-houses opened on Sunday, local option, and opposed to compulsory vaccination. Elected for Gloucester in Apr. 1880 but was unseated on petition in June 1880. Sat for Gloucester from 1885 until he retired in 1895. Died 26 Oct. 1897. [1895]

ROBSON, Sir William Snowdon. 26 Eaton Square, London. 3 Paper Buildings, Temple, London. Reform. 3rd s. of Robert Robson, Esq., J.P., of Newcastle-on-Tyne. B. at Newcastle 1852; m. 1887, Catherine, d. of Charles Burge, Esq., of Park Crescent, London. Educ. privately, and at Caius Coll., Cambridge. Called to the bar at the Inner Temple 1880, joined the N.E. Circuit; Q.C. 1892, Recorder of Newcastle-on-Tyne 1895-1905, a Bencher of his Inn 1899. Was Solicitor-Gen. from Dec. 1905 to Jan. 1908, when he was appointed Attorney-Gen. Knighted 1905. Honorary D.C.L. Durham University 1906. A Liberal. Sat for the Bow and Bromley division of Tower Hamlets from 1885-86, when he was defeated. Unsuccessfully contested Middlesbrough 1892. Represented South Shields from 1895 until appointed Lord of Appeal and created Lord Robson (law life peerage) in Oct. 1910. Retired as former in 1912. PC. 1910. G.C.M.G. 1912. Died 11 Sept. 1918. [1910]

ROBY, Henry John. Hope Hall, Pendleton, Manchester. Oxford & Cambridge. S. of Henry Wood Roby, Solicitor of Tamworth, and Elizabeth, d. of J.E. Robins, Esq., of Golden Square, London. B. at Tamworth 1830; m. 1861, Matilda, d. of Peter A. Ermen, Esq., of Dawlish, formerly of Manchester (she died 1889). Educ. at Bridgnorth Grammar School, and St. John's Coll., Cambridge; was senior classic in 1853, and elected Fellow of his Coll. 1854 (Honorary Fellow 1886). Was a Coll. Lecturer and Private Tutor at Cambridge 1853-61; Under-Master of Dulwich Coll. 1861-65; Secretary to the Schools' Inquiry and Endowed Schools' Commissions 1865-72; a Commissioner of Endowed Schools 1872-74; Professor of Jurisprudence, University Coll. 1866-68; Partner in the firm of Ermen and Roby, Sewing Cotton Manufacturers, Manchester from 1875. Honorary LL.D. Cambridge and Edinburgh; a Governor of Owens' Coll., and of the Grammar School and Hulme's

Charity, Manchester, and a J.P. for Manchester. Also a Dept.-Chairman of Committees, House of Commons. Author of *Remarks on College Reform* (1858), a *Grammar of the Latin Language*, 2 vols. (1871-74), *Introduction to Justinian's Digest* (1884). A Liberal, in favour of Home Rule for Ireland, Local Option, an Eight Hours' Day Bill for Miners, Reform of the House of Lords, simplification of Registration, "One man one vote", District Councils for Local Government, an extension of Religious but not denominational education, "Disestablishment" for Wales, and (if the Scotch desired it) for Scotland, and also favoured much reform in the administration of the army and navy. Sat for the Eccles division of Lancashire from Oct. 1890 until defeated in 1895. Author of several works on Roman Law, including chapter 3 in Vol. II of the *Cambridge Mediaeval History* (1913). Died 2 Jan. 1915. [1894]

ROCH, Walter Francis. Plas-y-Bridell, Kilgerran, Pembrokeshire. 24 Sloane Court, Chelsea, London. Reform. S. of William F. Roch, Esq., of Butter Hill, Pembrokeshire, and Emily Catherine, d. of W.R.H. Powell, Esq., for many years MP for W. Carmarthenshire. B. 20 Jan. 1880; m. 1911, Fflorens, d. of Maj.-Gen. Sir Ivor Herbert, Bart., MP. (1st Baron Treowen). Educ. at Harrow. A Barrister, called to the bar at the Middle Temple 1913. A Liberal. Elected for Pembrokeshire in July 1908 and sat until he retired in 1918. Died 3 May 1965. [1918]

ROCHE, Hon. James Boothby Burke. 60 St. James Street, London. Brooks's, and Hurlingham. 2nd s. of the 1st Lord Fermoy (MP for Marylebone), by Elizabeth, d. of J.B. Boothby, Esq., of Twyford Abbey. B. 1852; m. 1880, Frances, d. of Frank Work, Esq., of New York. Educ. at Trinity Coll., Cambridge; B.A. 1873, M.A. 1876. A Nationalist. Sat for E. Kerry from Mar. 1896 until he retired in 1900. Succeeded as 3rd Baron Fermoy 1 Sept. 1920. Died 30 Oct. 1920. [1900]

ROCHE, John. The Mills, Woodford, Co. Galway. National Liberal. S. of William Roche, Esq. B. 1848; m. 1878, Theresa, d. of Thomas Donnelly, Esq., of Douras, Co. Galway. A Miller and Corn Merchant. Once imprisoned for opposing the eviction proceedings of Lord Clanricarde whilst himself a tenant on the Woodford estate of Sir Henry Burke. A Nationalist, and Anti-Parnellite advocate of Home Rule. First elected for E. Galway in 1890, without opposition, and sat until his death 27 Aug. 1914. [1914]

ROCHE, Michael Augustine. King Street, Cork. S. of Michael Roche, Esq. B. about 1856 at Cork. Unmarried. Educ. at private schools. A Wholesale Wine-Merchant. Was Mayor of Cork 1893-94, High Sheriff 1902, and Lord Mayor 1904. A Nationalist. Unsuccessfully contested Cork city in June and July 1895. Sat for Cork city from 1905 to Dec. 1910, when he was defeated. Elected for N. Louth in Mar. 1911 and sat until his death 7 Dec. 1915. [1915]

ROE, Sir Thomas. Litchurch, Derby. Reform, and National Liberal. S. of Thomas Roe, Esq., J.P., Alderman and Mayor of Derby from 1863-65, and Deborah, d. of Absolam Oakley, Esq., of Derby. B. at Derby 1832; m. 1903, Emily, d. of Matthew Kirtley, Esq., of Derby (she died 1909). Educ. at local schools. A J.P. and Alderman for the borough of Derby, of which he was Mayor in 1867-68, 1896-97 and 1910-11; and a J.P. for Derbyshire. Knighted in 1894. A Liberal, in favour of Eight Hours' Day for all workers in hazardous trades, Electoral Reform, Payment of Official Election Expenses, Temperence Reform, Taxation of Land Values, Unsectarian Education (under popular control), etc. Represented Derby from 1883 to 1895, when he was defeated, and from 1900 until nominated for Peerage in Dec. 1916. Created Baron Rae in Jan. 1917. Died 7 June 1923. [1916]

ROGERS, Francis Edward Newman. Rainscomb, Pewsey, Wiltshire. 48 Iverna Gardens, London. Brooks's. S. of W.L. Rogers, Esq., J.P., of Rainscomb, Pewsey, and Hermione Lucy, sister of Sir E.A. Hamilton, Bart. B. 26 Dec. 1868 in London; m. 1893, Louisa Annie, d. of Edward Jennings, Esq. Educ. at Eton, and Balliol Coll., Oxford. A J.P. for Wiltshire; Vice-Chairman of Wiltshire County Council and of Education Committee; a Governor of Marlborough Grammar School; a Guardian for Pewsey Union. A Liberal. Unsuccessfully contested the Devizes division of Wiltshire in 1900; elected there in 1906 and sat until defeated in Jan. 1910. Unsuccessfully contested the Wilton division of Wiltshire in Dec. 1910. Commissioner, Board of Agriculture from 1911. Died 28 Mar. 1925. [1909]

ROGERS, James Edwin Thorold. Beaumont Street, Oxford. S. of George Vining Rogers, Esq., of Westmeon, Hampshire, by his marriage with Miss Mary Ann Blyth. B. at Westmeon 1823; m. Ann Susannah, 2nd d. of Henry R. Reynolds, Esq., Solicitor to the Treasury. Educ. at King's Coll., London, and Magdalen Hall, Oxford. Graduated B.A. 1st class in classics 1846, and M.A. 1849. Appointed Master of the Schools at Oxford University 1853, and Classical Examiner for 1857-58; also Tooke Professor of Economic Science at King's Coll., London 1859, and was Professor of Political Economy at Oxford from 1862 to 1868. A Clergyman of the Church of England, but relinquished orders to enter Parliament. Author of numerous works including *The Protests of the Lords, with Historical Introductions, A Manual of Political Economy, Six Centuries of Work and Wages,* and *A History of Agriculture and Prices.* An advanced Liberal, but was not decided as to the questions of Home Rule. Was an unsuccessful candidate for Scarborough Feb. 1874. Sat for Southwark from Apr. 1880 to 1885 and for the Bermondsey division of Southwark from 1885 until defeated in 1886 standing as a Gladstonian Liberal. Re-elected Professor of Political Economy at Oxford 1888. Died 14 Oct. 1890. [1886]

ROLLESTON, Sir John Fowke Lancelot. 54 Curzon Street, London. Glen Parva Grange, Leicester. Carlton, and Junior Carlton. S. of the Rev. William Lancelot Rolleston, and Mary Sophia, d. of Sir Frederick Fowke, Bart. B. at Great Dalby 1848; m. 1892, Eliza, d. of Capt. George Morant, Grenadier Guards. Educ. at Repton, and Applied Science Department, King's Coll., London. A Surveyor from 1868 in Leicester and London; President of Surveyors' Institution 1901. A J.P., and Dept.-Lieut. for Leicestershire. A Director of Law Union and Rock Assurance Company, Dept.-Chairman of Investment Registry Limited. Knighted in 1897. Knight of Grace of St. John. A Unionist. Unsuccessfully contested Leicester in 1894 and 1895. Sat for Leicester from 1900-06, when he was defeated at the general election, and again at by-election Mar. 1906. First elected for Hertford division of Hertfordshire in Jan. 1910 and sat until he

accepted the Chiltern Hundreds in 1916. Died 9 Apr. 1919. [1915]

ROLLIT, Sir Albert Kaye. 45 Belgrave Square, London. The Willows, Nr. Windsor. Manor House, Inverurie, N.B. 18 Avenue d'Antin, Paris. Carlton, and Junior Naval & Military. S. of John Rollit, Esq., Solicitor, by Eliza, d. of Joseph Kaye, Esq., of Huddersfield, Architect. B. at Hull 1842; m. 1st, 1872, Eleanor Anne, 2nd d. of William Bailey, Esq., J.P., of Winstead Hall, Holderness (she died 1885); 2ndly, 1896, Mary, Duchess of Sutherland, d. of the Rev. Dr. Michell. Educ. at King's Coll., and the University of London, of which he was a Fellow and member of the Senate; B.A. 1st class honours 1863, LL.B. 1st class honours Principles of Legislation, etc. 1864, LL.D. first and University gold medallist 1866, D.C.L. Durham 1891. A Solicitor in London and at Hull, a prizeman of the Incorporated Law Society 1863, and Vice-President of the Society. Also a Shipowner at Hull, Newcastle, and London. Sheriff of Hull 1875-76, and Mayor 1883-85; Honorary Freeman of Hull and Huddersfield; Elder Bro. Trinity House, Hull; President of the Associated Chambers of Commerce; President Municipal Corporations Association; Chairman of Savings Bank Inspection Committee; member of Commercial Intelligence Committee of Board of Trade; Lieut.-Col. Engineer Militia. J.P. for Co. of London, and Dept.-Lieut. London and Yorkshire. Was knighted in 1885. A "progressive and independent Conservative", in favour of wide local government for both England and Ireland. Contested Hull W. Nov. 1885. Represented S. Islington from 1886 until defeated in 1906 as an Independent Free Trader. Contested Epsom division of Surrey in Jan. 1910 as a Liberal. Consul-Gen. for Romania in London from 1911. Died 12 Aug. 1922. [1905]

RONALDSHAY, Lawrence John Lumley Dundas, **Earl of.** 38 Grosvenor Street, London. Carlton, Turf, and Travellers'. Eld. s. of Marq. of Zetland. B. 1876; m. 1907, Ciceley, d. of Col. M. Archdale. Educ. at Harrow, and Trinity Coll., Cambridge. Capt. in 1st N. Riding Volunteer Artillery and Aide-de-Camp to Lord Curzon, when Viceroy of India. Chairman of Central Asian Society, member of Grand Council of Primrose League, and the Council of the National Union;

member of Royal Commission on Public Services in India 1912. Temporary Maj. 3/4th Battalion Yorkshire Regiment. Author of *Sport and Politics under an Eastern Sky*, *A Wandering Student in the Far East*, *On the Outskirts of Empire in Asia*, *An Eastern Miscellany*, biographies of Curzon (1928), and Cromer (1932), of *Steps Toward Indian Home Rule* (1935), and several other works on India. A Unionist. Unsuccessfully contested the Richmond division of Yorkshire at the general election of 1906. Elected for the Hornsey division of Middlesex in June 1907 and sat until appointed Gov. of Bengal in 1916-22. PC. 1922. Succeeded as 2nd Marq. of Zetland in 1929. Secretary of State for India 1935-40. President of Society for the Study of Religions 1930-51. Chairman of National Trust 1931-45. A Steward of the Jockey Club 1928-31. Died 6 Feb. 1961. [1916]

ROPNER, Sir Emil Hugh Oscar, Robert, Bart. Preston Hall, Stockton-on-Tees. Skutterskelfe Hall, Cleveland. Carlton, and Constitutional. S. of John Henry Ropner, Esq., (Officer). B. at Magdeburg, Germany 1838; m. in 1858, d. of John Craik, Esq. Educ. at the Grammar School, Helmstedt. A large Shipowner and Shipbuilder, and was Mayor of Stockton 1892-93. Dept.-Lieut. for the Co. of Durham; High Sheriff 1896; J.P. for the Co. of Durham and the N. Riding of Yorkshire. Knighted 1902; created Bart. 1904. Chairman of the House of Commons Shipping Committee. A Conservative. Unsuccessfully contested the Cleveland division of the N. Riding of Yorkshire in 1895 and 1897. Elected for Stockton in 1900 and sat until he retired in Jan. 1910. Died 26 Feb. 1924. [1909]

ROSCOE, Sir Henry Enfield, F.R.S. 10 Braham Gardens, London. Athenaeum. Reform, Manchester. S. of Henry Roscoe, Esq., Barrister (author of the *Laws of Evidence* etc.), and grand-s. of William Roscoe, the Historian, by Maria, d. of Thomas Fletcher, Esq., Merchant of Liverpool. B. in London 1833; m. 1863, Lucy, d. of Edmund Potter, Esq., F.R.S. Educ. at University Coll., London, and at Heidelberg University. He took up the study of chemistry at an early age, and graduated B.A. at London University, taking the prize for that science. Also received the Honorary degree of LL.D. from the Universities of Cambridge, Dublin, Heidelberg, and Montreal, and the Honorary D.C.L. from the University of Oxford. In 1857 was appointed Professor of Chemistry at Victoria University (Owens Coll.), Manchester (resigned in 1886), and in 1880 was elected President of the Chemical Society of London. In 1881 was appointed by Royal Commission to inquire into the technical education of the working classes, and in 1884 was Knighted in acknowledgment of his eminence as a scientific instructor. Wrote *Elementary Chemistry*, *Lectures on Spectrum Analysis*, *A Treatise on Chemistry*, and other works, some of which were translated into various European and Oriental languages. Also a member of the Senate, London University, and of the Royal Commission on the Scottish Universities, and in 1887 was President of the British Association meeting in Manchester. A Liberal and Home Ruler, opposed to the maintenance of a State Church. Sat for Manchester S. from Nov. 1885 until defeated in 1895. Vice-Chancellor of London University 1896-1902. PC. 1909. Died 18 Dec. 1915. [1895]

ROSE, Sir Charles Day, Bart. Hardwick House, Whitchurch, Oxfordshire. Suffolk House, Newmarket. 31 St. James's Place, London. Reform, Brooks's, and Turf. 2nd s. of the Rt. Hon. Sir John Rose, Bart., of Montreal. B. 23 Aug. 1847 at Montreal; m. 1871, Lily, d. of J.R. MacLean, Esq., MP. Educ. at Rugby School. A Partner in the American banking firm of Morton, Rose and Company. Was a Capt. in the Montreal Garrison Artillery and Assisted to quell the Fenian Rebellion in Canada in 1866. A member of the Jockey Club and a breeder and owner of racehorses. Created Bart. in 1909. A Liberal. Unsuccessfully contested the Newmarket division of Cambridgeshire in 1900; sat for the Newmarket division of Cambridgeshire from Jan. 1903 to Jan. 1910, when he was defeated; re-elected there in Dec. 1910 and sat until his death 20 Apr. 1913. [1913]

ROSS, Alexander Henry. 9 Upper Berkeley Street, London. Carlton. S. of Charles Ross, Esq., (who represented St. Germans from 1826 to 1832, and Northampton from 1832 to 1837), by Lady Mary, d. of Marq. Cornwallis. B. in London 1829; m. 1859, Juliana, d. of William Moseley, Esq., of Leaton Hall, Staffordshire. Was educ. at Eton, and at Christ Church, Oxford; graduated M.A. 1851. Called to the bar at the Inner Temple June 1854. A Conservative. Unsuccessfully contested Maidstone Feb. 1874, but was returned for Maidstone in Apr. 1880 and sat until his death on 3 Dec. 1888.   [1888]

ROSS, John. 66 Fitzwilliam Square, Dublin. S. of the Rev. Robert Ross, D.D., Ex-Moderator of the Gen. Assembly of the Presbyterian Church in Ireland, and Margaret, d. of J. Christie, Esq., London-derry. B. 1853 at Londonderry; m. 1882, Katherine Mary, d. of Col. Deane Mann, J.P., of Dunmoyle, Co. Tyrone. Educ. at Foyle Coll., Londonderry, and Trinity Coll., Dublin. A Barrister, called to the Irish bar, Michaelmas 1879; Q.C. 1891. A Conservative and Unionist. Sat for Lon-donderry city from July 1892 until de-feated in 1895. Judge of Irish High Court, Chancery Division, 1896-1921; PC. (Ire-land) 1902; Commissioner of National Education 1905; created Bart. 1919; Lord Chancellor of Ireland 1921-22. Died 17 Aug. 1935.   [1895]

ROTHSCHILD, Baron Ferdinand James de. 143 Piccadilly, London. Waddesdon Manor, Nr. Aylesbury. 2nd s. of Baron Anselm de Rothschild, of Vienna. B. at Paris 1839; m. 1865, his cousin, Evelina, the youngest sister of Lord Rothschild, but was left a widower the following year. A Trustee of the British Museum, and a J.P. and Dept.-Lieut. for Buckinghamshire, of which Co. he was High Sheriff in 1883. Founder of the Evelina Hospital, in South-wark Bridge Road. A Liberal Unionist. Elected for Aylesbury July 1885 on the vacation of the seat by Lord Rothschild's elevation to the peerage, and from the general election of the same year sat for the Aylesbury division of Bucking-hamshire until his death 17 Dec. 1898.   [1898]

ROTHSCHILD, Lionel Nathan de, O.B.E. Continued in House after 1918: full entry in Volume III.

ROTHSCHILD, Hon. Lionel Walter. 148 Piccadilly, London. Tring Park, Buckinghamshire. Bachelors', and Royal Societies'. Eld. s. of Nathan Mayer Lord Rothschild, and his wife Emma Louisa. B. in London 1868. Educ. privately, and at Magdalene Coll., Cambridge, and Bonn, Germany. A Partner in the firm of N. and M. Rothschild and Company. Was Treas-urer of Middlesex Hospital. A Lieut. of the City of London and a Trustee of the British Museum. Maj. Royal Buckinghamshire Yeomanry. Joint editor of *Novitates Zoologicae*, etc. A Liberal Unionist, and staunch supporter of Mr. Balfour's and Lord Salisbury's foreign policies. Elected for the Aylesbury division of Buckinghamshire in 1899 and sat until he retired in Jan. 1910. Succeeded as 2nd Baron Rothschild in 1915. Died 27 Aug. 1937.   [1909]

ROUND, Rt. Hon. James. 31 De Vere Gardens, London. Birch Hall, Essex. Carlton. Eld. s. of the Rev. James Thomas Round, B.D., Rector of All Saints, Col-chester, and Hon. Prebendary of St. Paul's, by Louisa, 2nd d. of the Rev. G.F. Barlow, Rector of Burgh, Suffolk. Nephew of Charles Gray Round, Esq., of Birch Hall, who sat for N. Essex from 1837 till 1847, and whose family were connected with Charles Gray, Esq., who sat for Colchester in five Parliaments in the nineteenth cen-tury. B. at Colchester 1842; m. 1870, his cousin, Sybilla Joanna, 4th d. of the Rev. Henry Freeland, Rector of Hasketon, Suffolk. Educ. at Eton, and Christ Church, Oxford; graduated B.A. 1864, M.A. 1872. Called to the bar at the Inner Temple 1868. A Magistrate and Dept.-Lieut. for Essex, and an Alderman Essex County Council; was Maj. W. Essex Militia. Patron of 4 livings, and was a member of the House of Laymen. PC. 1902. A Conserva-tive. Sat for E. Essex from 1868 to 1885, when he was returned for the Harwich division of Essex and sat until he retired in 1906. Died 25 Dec. 1916.   [1905]

ROUNDELL, Charles Savile. 16 Curzon Street, Mayfair, London. Dorfold Hall, Cheshire. S. of the Rev. D.R. Roundell, of Screven and Gledstone, Yorkshire, and Hannah, eld. d. of Sir W. Foulis, Bart., of Ingleby Manor, Yorkshire. B. 1827 at York; m. 1873, Julia, d. of Wilbraham Tollemache, Esq., of Dorfold Hall, Cheshire. Educ. at Harrow, and Balliol Coll., Oxford, and became a Fellow of Merton. Was called to the bar at Lincoln's Inn 1857, but in 1865 was appointed Secre-tary to the Royal Commission on the dis-turbances in Jamaica under Governor Eyre. In 1869 he went to Ireland as Private Secretary to the Lord-Lieut., Earl Spencer. In 1871 he was appointed a member of the Royal Commission on Friendly and

Benefit Building Societies, and in the following year he served as Secretary to the Royal Commission on the revenues of Oxford and Cambridge. A J.P., a Governor of Owen's Coll., Harrow School, and Dulwich Coll., a member of the Council of the Girls' Public Day School Company, etc. A Liberal and Home Ruler, in favour of the disestablishment of the Church in Scotland and Wales. In 1868 he stood unsuccessfully as Parliamentary candidate for Clitheroe. Was MP for Grantham 1880-85 when he retired. Sat for the Skipton division of the W. Riding of Yorkshire from July 1892 until he retired in 1895. Died 3 Mar. 1906. [1895]

ROWLANDS, James. 119 Mercer's Road, Tufnell Park, London. 8 Buckingham Street, Strand, London. National Liberal. S. of William Bull Rowlands, Esq. B. 1 Oct. 1851 in Finsbury; m. 1879, Kate, d. of Joseph Boyden, Esq. (she died 1905). Educ. at Working Men's Coll, Great Ormond Street, London, and also attended lectures at the School of Mines, and at the Shoreditch Town Hall. Was apprenticed to Watch Case making, and was a Freeman of the Goldsmith's Company. A member of the London School Board. Honorary Secretary of the Land Law Reform Association. A Liberal, Radical, and Home Ruler. Unsuccessfully contested E. Finsbury in 1885. Sat for E. Finsbury from 1886 to 1895, when he was defeated. Sat for the Dartford division of Kent from 1906 to Jan. 1910 where he was again defeated. Re-elected in Dec. 1910 and sat until his death 1 Mar. 1920. [1918]

ROWLANDS, William Bowen. 33 Belsize Park, London. 3 King's Bench Walk, Temple, London. Glenmare, Broad Haven, Co. Pembroke. National Liberal. S. of Thomas Rowlands, Esq., J.P. of Glenover, Co. Pembroke, by Anne, do of John Bowen, Esq., of Dygoed, Co. Pembroke. B. at Haverfordwest 1837; m. 1864, Adeline Wogan, only child of J.D. Brown, Esq., of Kensington House, Haverfordwest. Educ. at Gough House, Chelsea, and Jesus Coll., Oxford. Gained a 1st class certificate of honour at the General Examination for the bar in 1870, and was called to the bar at Gray's Inn in 1871; became Q.C. in 1882, and a bencher of Gray's Inn in the same year. A J.P. for Pembrokeshire, Cardiganshire, and Haverfordwest, and a Dept.-Lieut. for Cardiganshire. Also a

member of the Council of Legal Education, and of the Bar Library Committee, and a Treasurer of Gray's Inn. Appointed Recorder of Swansea June 1893. A Liberal, in favour of Mr. Gladstone's Irish policy. Sat for Cardiganshire from 1886 until he retired in 1895. County Court Judge from 1900; episcopally nominated Lay member of Catholic Education Council. Died 4 Sept. 1906. [1895]

ROWNTREE, Arnold Stephenson. Chalfonts, York. Reform, and National Liberal. S. of John Stephenson Rowntree, Esq., of York. B. 1872 in York; m. 1906, Mary Katharine, d. of William Harvey, Esq., of Leeds. Educ. at Bootham Friends' School, York. A Director of Rowntree and Company Limited, Cocoa Manufacturers, York, and Honorary Secretary of the National Adult School Union. A Liberal. Elected for York in Jan. 1910 and sat until defeated in 1918. Director of Westminster Press and Associated Papers. Died 21 May 1951. [1918]

ROWNTREE, Joshua. 40 Pont Street, London. Scarborough. S. of John Rowntree, Esq., of Scarborough, by Jane, d. of Joshua Priestman, Esq., of Thornton, near Pickering. B. in Scarborough 1844; m. 1880, Isabella Ann, d. of Robert Tindall, Esq., of Kirkby Misperton Hall and Scarborough. Educ. at the Friends' School, York. A Solicitor; admitted in 1865. He entered the Scarborough Town Council in 1880. Was elected Mayor in Nov. 1885, but resigned on becoming a candidate for the representation of Scarborough in Parliament. A Magistrate for Scarborough. An "earnest Liberal", and supporter of Mr. Gladstone's Irish policy. First returned for Scarborough in July 1886 and sat until defeated in 1892. Chairman of Scarborough Harbour Commissioners. Died 10 Feb. 1915. [1892]

ROYDEN, Thomas Bland. Holmfield House, Aigburth, Nr. Liverpool. Carlton, St. Stephen's, and Constitutional. S. of Thomas Royden, Esq., of Frankly Hall, Cheshire. B. at Toxteth Park, Liverpool 1832; m. 1865, Alice Elizabeth, d. of T. Dowdall, Esq. Educ. at Liverpool Coll. A Shipbuilder, a member of the Liverpool city Council, and a Magistrate for the city, of which he was Mayor in the year 1878-79. Served in the Royal Commission on Tonnage, on the Load-line Committee, and on Mr. Chamberlain's Commission on Unseaworthy Ships. A Conservative. Sat for the W. Toxteth division of Liverpool from Nov. 1885 until he retired in 1892. Created Bart. 1905. Dept.-Chairman Cunard Steamship Company, Director of Lancashire and Yorkshire Railway, and London, City and Midland Bank. Died 29 Aug. 1917.   [1892]

ROYDS, Col. Clement Molyneux, C.B. Greenhill, Nr. Rochdale. Carlton, and United Service. S. of William E. Royds, Esq., of Greenhill, Lancashire, and Danehill Park, Sussex, and Mary Ann, eld. d. of Anthony Molyneux, Esq., of Newsham House, Lancashire. B. at Rochdale 1842; m. 1882, Annette Nora, 2nd d. of T. Littledale, Esq., of Highfield, Lancashire. Educ. abroad. A J.P. and Dept.-Lieut.; Col. Commanding the Duke of Lancaster's Own Yeomanry, and Honorary Col. 2nd Volunteer Battalion Lancashire Fusiliers. Created C.B. 1902; Knight of the Order of St. John of Jerusalem. In 1889 was High Sheriff of the Co. Palatine of Lancaster. Chairman of the Rochdale Canal Company, and of the Williams Deacons Bank. A Unionist, in favour of Reform of the Poor Laws, Old Age Pensions, Land Reform, Licensing Reform with regard to existing interests, and the enfranchisement of duly qualified women. Unsuccessfully contested Rochdale in 1892. Represented Rochdale from 1895 until defeated in 1906. Knighted in 1906. Died 28 Jan. 1916.   [1905]

ROYDS, Edmund. Continued in House after 1918: full entry in Volume III.

RUNCIMAN, Rt. Hon. Walter, (Visct. Runciman of Doxford). Continued in House after 1918: full entry in Volume III.

RUNCIMAN, Sir Walter, Bart. Fernwood House, Newcastle-on-Tyne. Shoreston Hall, Chathill, Northumberland. Reform, National Liberal, and Royal Thames Yacht. S. of Walter Runciman, Esq., of Dunbar. B. 6 July 1847 at Dunbar; m. 1868, Ann Margaret, d. of John Lawson, Esq., of Blakemoor, Northumberland. Educ. at Church School, and privately. Joined a sailing vessel as cabin boy when 12 years old, commanded a clipper barque when under 22, and a steamer at 26. A Shipowner and Ship and Insurance Broker, Senior Partner of Walter Runci-

man and Company, of Newcastle and London, head of the Moor Line of steamships, Director of many shipping organisations. Chairman of Several Insurance companies. Member of Dept. Committee on Boy Seamen 1906-07. Member of Advisory Committee of Marine Department of Board of Trade. President of Chamber of Shipping of United Kingdom 1911-12. Chairman of Northern Liberal Federation and other political organisations. J.P. for Newcastle-on-Tyne, Durham and Northumberland. Author of *Windjammers and Sea Tramps, The Shellback's Progress in the 19th Century, Looking Seaward Again, The Tragedy of St. Helena*, etc. Created Bart. in 1906. A Liberal. Elected for Hartlepool Sept. 1914 and sat until he retired in 1918. Created 1st Baron Runciman in 1933. Died 13 Aug. 1937.   [1918]

RUSSELL, Sir Charles Arthur. 86 Harley Street, London. 10 New Court, Lincoln's Inn, London. Tadworth Court, Nr. Epsom, Surrey. Reform, National Liberal, Turf, and Portland. S. of Arthur Russell, Esq., of Newry and Seafield House, Rosstrevor, by Margaret, widow of John Hamill, Esq., of Belfast. B. at Newry 1833; m. 1858, Ellen, eld. d. of J.S. Mulholland, Esq., M.D., of Belfast. Was educ. at Castle Knock Coll., Dublin, and Trinity Coll., Dublin. Was called to the bar May 1859 at Lincoln's Inn, of which he was a bencher; appointed a Queen's Counsel 1872. Became Attorney Gen. in 1886, and was then Knighted; again Attorney Gen. 1892 to 1894. Created G.C.M.G. in connection with the Behring Sea Arbitration, 1893. A J.P. for Surrey. A Liberal and Home Ruler. Unsuccessfully contested Dundalk in 1868 and 1874. Sat for Dundalk 1880-85, and for Hackney S. from 1885 until appointed Lord of Appeal (Lord Russell of Killowen) in May 1894. PC. 1894. Lord Chief Justice of England from June 1894 until his death on 10 Aug. 1900.   [1894]

RUSSELL, Edward Richard. 6 Abercromby Square, Liverpool. Reform, and National Liberal. Reform, Liverpool. S. of Edward Haslingden Russell, Esq., by his marriage with Miss Mary Ann Crook. B. at Barbican, city of London, 1834; m. 1858, Eliza Sophia, d. of Stephen Bradley, Esq., of Bridge, Canterbury. Educ. at private schools. Became assistant editor of the *Liverpool Daily Post* in 1860. From 1866 to 1869 was a leader writer for the London

Morning Star (which became merged in the *Daily News*). In 1869 became editor of the *Liverpool Daily Post*. Beside his newspaper writings he wrote pamphlets, chiefly literary and critical, some being upon Shakesperian questions. Was the first Chairman of the Liverpool Reform Club, was President of the Literary and Philosophical Society of that city from 1879 to 1881, and was a life Gov. of University Coll. there. An "advanced Liberal" and Home Ruler, considered that "the hereditary principle in the composition of the Upper House was doomed." Sat for the Bridgeton division of Glasgow from 1885 until he accepted Chiltern Hundreds in 1887. Knighted 1893. Author of works on literary and philosophical subjects and of a volume of reminiscences entitled *That Reminds Me*. Created 1st Baron Russell of Liverpool in 1919. Died 20 Feb. 1920.   [1887]

RUSSELL, Lord Edward. 8 Park Lane, London. Reform. S. of 6th Duke of Bedford. B. 24 Apr. 1805 at Stable Yard, St. James', London; m. Mary Ann, d. of Aaron Taylor, Esq., of Kensington. Educ. at Westminster 1816-18. Entered navy 13 Jan. 1819, Lieut. of the Philomel Brigade 18 Oct. 1826; served at battle of Navarino 20 Oct. 1827; Capt. 19 Nov. 1833; commanded the *Actaeon* in South America 1834-38. A Liberal. First returned for Tavistock in 1841 and sat until he retired in 1847. Naval Aide-de-Camp to the Queen 1846-50. Kept race horses, his horse Sting was the best two-year old of his year 1845. Capt. of the *Vengeance* in the Mediterranean 13 Jan. 1851 to about May 1855. Took part in the attack on Sebastopol 17 Oct. 1854. C.B. 5 July 1855; admiral 20 Mar. 1867, retired 1 Apr. 1870. Died 21 May 1887 at Royal Yacht Squadron Castle, Cowes.   [1847]

RUSSELL, Francis Shirley. 34 Dover Street, London. Aden House, Aberdeenshire. Carlton, and Arthur's. S. of James Russell, Esq., J.P. and Dept.-Lieut., of Aden, Aberdeenshire. B. 1840; m. 1888, Philippa, d. of the Rt. Hon. Henry Baillie, MP, of Redcastle, Inverness-shire, by a d. of the 7th Visct. Strangford. Educ. at Radley Coll., and Balliol Coll., Oxford (B.A. with honours 1862). Entered the 14th Hussars 1863; Aide-de-Camp in Ireland 1869-70; in Ashantee campaign 1873-74; Inspector in Tactics, Royal Military Coll.,

1875-76; in Intelligence Department 1878-79; served in the Zulu War 1879, and in the Boer War 1880-81; Commander 1st Royal Dragoons 1885-87; a military attaché at Berlin 1889-91. Became Col. in the army 1885, Maj.-Gen. 1897; created C.M.G. 1891; Brig.-Gen. of Aberdeen Defence Brigade 1892. A Conservative. Unsuccessfully contested E. Aberdeenshire July and Dec. 1892. First returned for Cheltenham July 1895 and sat until he retired in 1900. Died 18 Mar. 1912. [1900]

RUSSELL, Sir George, Bart. Swallowfield Park, Reading. Carlton. Youngest s. of Sir Henry Russell, by Marie Clotilde, d. of Baron Benoit Mottet de la Fontaine. B. 1828; m. 1867, Constance, d. of Lord Arthur Lennox, niece of the 5th Duke of Richmond. Educ. at Eton, and Exeter Coll., Oxford. Was called to the bar at Lincoln's Inn 1853 and joined the Oxford Circuit. Was a Co. Court Judge. Succeeded to the Baronetcy on the death of his eld. bro., Sir Charles Russell, 1883. A Conservative. Sat for the Wokingham division of Berkshire from July 1885 until his death 7 Mar. 1898. [1897]

RUSSELL, George William Erskine. 18 Wilton Street, London. Woburn, Bedfordshire. Reform, and Eighty. Younger s. of Lieut.-Col. Lord Charles James Fox Russell, s. of the 6th Duke of Bedford, and MP for Bedfordshire from 1832 to 1841, and again in 1847, by Isabella Clarissa, d. of William Davies, Esq., of Penylan, Carmarthenshire, and niece and adopted d. of Col. Henry Seymour, of Woburn. B. at 16 Mansfield Street, London 1853. Educ. at Harrow, and University Coll., Oxford, of which he was scholar and prizeman (graduated B.A. 1876, M.A. 1880). Was Parliamentary Secretary to the Local Government Board 1883-85; appointed Under-Secretary of State for India 1892, and was Under-Secretary of State, Home Department 1894-95. Was elected Alderman of the London County Council 1889; and was President of the Liberal Churchmen's Union. A Radical, and a strong advocate of social reforms. Sat for Aylesbury from 1880 until he retired 1885. Unsuccessfully contested Fulham in Nov. 1885 and again in July 1886. Sat for Bedfordshire N. from July 1892 until defeated in 1895. Author of *Politics and Personalities* (1917), an autobiography and several other works. Died 17 Mar. 1919. [1895]

RUSSELL, Rt. Hon. Sir Thomas Wallace, Bart. Olney, Terenure, Co. Dublin. National Liberal. S. of David Russell, Esq. B. 28 Feb. 1841 at Cupar, Fife; m. 1st, 1865, Harriet Wentworth, d. of Thomas Agnew, Esq., of Dungannon (she died 1894); 2ndly, 1896, Martha, d. of Lieut.-Col. Keown, 15th Hussars. Educ. at Madras Academy, Cupar, Fife. Vice-President of the Department of Agriculture and Technical Instruction for Ireland from 1907 until 1918. Was Parliamentary Secretary to Local Government Board 1895-1900. PC. (Ireland) 1908. Created Bart. 1917. A Liberal and a Unionist until Feb. 1904 when he rejoined the Liberals. Unsuccessfully contested Preston 1885. Sat for S. Tyrone from 1886 to Jan. 1910, when he was defeated. Elected for N. Tyrone Oct. 1911 and sat until he retired in 1918. Died 2 May 1920. [1918]

RUSTON, Joseph. Retired in 1886: full entry in Volume I.

RUTHERFORD, Sir John, Bart. Continued in House after 1918: full entry in Volume III.

RUTHERFORD, Vickerman Henzell. 6 Cambridge Terrace, Regent's Park, London. Eighty, and National Liberal. S. of Dr. J.H. Rutherford, of Newcastle-on-Tyne, and Margaret Walton. B. 6 Dec. 1860 at Newcastle; m. 1893, Alice, d. of Paul Henwood, Esq., of Bromley, Kent. Educ. at Royal High School, Edinburgh, and Sidney Sussex Coll., Cambridge; M.A., M.B. A Specialist in diseases of the skin; Assistant Physician, St. John's Hospital, London. An advanced Radical, in favour of self-government for Ireland, Temperance, Social and Labour Reforms. Unsuccessfully contested the Osgoldcross division of the W. Riding of Yorkshire in 1900. Elected for the Brentford division of Middlesex in 1906 and sat until defeated in Jan. 1910. Contested Bishop Auckland as a Liberal candidate in 1918 and Sunderland as a Labour candidate in 1920 and 1922. Died 25 Apr. 1934. [1909]

RUTHERFORD, Sir William Watson. Continued in House after 1918: full entry in Volume III.

RYDER, John Herbert Dudley. 9 Grosvenor Gardens, London. Carlton, and Travellers'. Eld. s. of the Hon. Henry Dudley Ryder (4th Earl of Harrowby) and Susan Juliana, d. of V. Dent, Esq., of Barton Court, Lymington. B. 1864; m. 1887, Hon. Mabel Smith, youngest d. of the Rt. Hon. W.H. Smith, MP, and Viscountess Hambleden. Educ. at Trinity Coll., Cambridge. A Partner in the Banking Firm of Coutts and Company, Strand; a J.P. for London and Dept.-Lieut. for Staffordshire; Lieut. Staffordshire Y.C. A Conservative. Sat for Gravesend from July 1898 until he retired in Oct. 1900. Styled Visct. Sandon from Mar. 1900, when his father succeeded as 4th Earl of Harrowby, until Dec. 1900 when he succeeded as 5th Earl of Harrowby. Lord-Lieut. of Staffordshire 1927-48. Died 30 Mar. 1956. [1900]

RYLANDS, Peter. 78 St. George's Square, London. Massey Hall, Thelwall, Warrington. Reform. S. of John Rylands, Esq., of Bewsey House, Warrington, by Martha, d. of the Rev. James Glazebrook, Vicar of Belton, Leicestershire. B. at Warrington 1820; m. 1861, Caroline, d. of William Reynolds, Esq., of Penketh House, Warrington. Educ. at Boteler's Grammar School, Warrington. An Iron Master and Director of Pearson and Knowles' Coal and Iron Company (Limited), also of the Manchester and Liverpool District Banking Company. A Magistrate for Lancashire, Cheshire, and for Warrington; elected Mayor of the latter 1853-54. A Liberal, in favour of the decentralization of Government departments, and a great reduction in the national expenditure. Sat for Warrington from Dec. 1868 to Feb. 1874, when he was an unsuccessful candidate there, as also for S.E. Lancashire. Sat for Burnley from Feb. 1876. MP until his death 8 Feb. 1887. [1886]

SACKVILLE, Col. Sackville George Stopford. See STOPFORD-SACKVILLE, Col. Sackville George.

SADLER, Sir Samuel Alexander. Whitehall Court, London. Southlands, Eaglescliffe, Co. Durham. Carlton, Cleveland, and Junior Carlton. S. of James Sadler, Esq., of Langley Hall, Oldbury, and his wife, the d. of Thomas Millership, Esq., Colliery Owner, West Bromwich. B. at Oldbury in 1842; m. 1874, d. of John Field, Esq., Ironmaster, of Oldbury. Educ. privately, and at University Coll. A Manufacturing Chemist, Coalowner, etc.; founded the firm of Sadler and Company Limited, Middlesbrough. Was three times Mayor of Middlesbrough, Chairman of Bearpark Coal Company, Durham, and Malton and Etherley Collieries, member of the Town Council, Chairman of River Tees Port Authority, and a J.P. for Middlesbrough, N. Riding of Yorkshire, and Co. Durham; Lieut.-Col. and Honorary Col. 1st Volunteer Battalion Durham Light Infantry from 1875, commanded Regiment twenty-two years. A Conservative. Unsuccessfully contested Middlesbrough in 1878, 1880, and 1895. Elected for Middlesbrough in 1900 and sat until defeated in 1906. Knighted 1905. Died 29 Sept. 1911. [1905]

ST. AUBYN, Sir John, Bart. 5 Lowndes Street, London. St. Michael's Mount, Cornwall. Brooks's, Travellers', and Boodle's. Eld. s. of Sir Edward St. Aubyn, Bart., by Emma, d. of Gen. Knollys. B. at Clowance, Cornwall 1829; m. 1856, Lady Elizabeth Clementine, 2nd d. of the 4th Marq. Townshend. Educ. at Eton, and Trinity Coll., Cambridge, where he graduated B.A. 1852. A Magistrate and Dept.-Lieut. for Cornwall from 1854. Col. (retired) 3rd Battalion Duke of Cornwall's Light Infantry. A Dept. Special Warden of the Stannaries of Devon and Cornwall. A Liberal Unionist. Sat for Cornwall W. from July 1858 until created Baron St. Levan, 1887. Succeeded as Bart. 1872. Mayor of Devonport 1891-93. Died 14 May 1908. [1886 2nd ed.]

ST. MAUR, Richard Harold. Stover, Teigngrace, Newton Abbot, Devon. S. of Lord Ferdinand St. Maur, s. of the Duke of Somerset. B. 1869; m. 1891, Elisabeth, d. of W.H.F. Palmer. Educ. at Wellington Coll. Author of *Annals of the Seymours*. A Liberal. Unsuccessfully contested Exeter in Jan. 1910. First returned there at the general election of Dec. 1910 beating his opponent H.E. Duke by 4 votes, but on petition was unseated by 1 vote. Awarded Legion of Honour and Croix de Guerre in the Great War. Died in Kenya 1927.

SALIS-SCHWABE, Col. George. 8 Clarges Street, Piccadilly, London. Rhodes, Middleton, Manchester. United Service, and National Liberal. 2nd s. of Salis Schwabe, Esq., of Rhodes, Middleton, and Glyn-y-Garth, Anglesea, J.P., Dept.-Lieut., and Calico-Printer, of Rhodes and Manchester, by his marriage with Julie Salis Schwabe, well known for her efforts to advance education in Italy, etc. B. at Manchester 1843; m. 1870, May Jaqueline, only d. of Sir W. Milbourne James, Lord Justice of Appeal. Educ. at University Coll., London, (B.A. 1862). Entered the army in 1863, and became Lieut.-Col. and Brevet-Col. in command of 16th Lancers. Was Brigade-Maj. of cavalry at Aldershot and the Curragh 1873-77. Was employed on special service during the latter part of the Zulu War, for which he had the S. African War medal and clasp. Also a Partner in the firm of Salis Schwabe and Company, Calico-Printers, of Rhodes, near Middleton, and Manchester. A Liberal, in favour of "a thorough reform in the House of Lords", of the Disestablishment of the Church, and of a scheme for free education that would not injure voluntary schools, but opposed to Home Rule for Ireland. Sat for the Middleton division of S.E. Lancashire from Dec. 1885 until he retired in 1886. Commanded in Gloucester district 1890-95; Maj.-Gen. 1897; Gen. Officer commanding Mauritius 1896-98; Lieut.-Gov. Royal Hospital, Chelsea 1898-1905. C.B. 1902. Died 13 June 1907. [1886]

SALT, Thomas. 85 St. George's Square, London. Weeping Cross, Stafford. Carlton, St. Stephen's, and United University. S. of Thomas Salt, Esq., of Weeping Cross, Stafford, by Harriet Letitia, d. of Rev. John Hayes Petit, of Lichfield. B. 1830; m. 1861, Helen, youngest d. of J.L. Anderdon, Esq., of Chislehurst. Educ. at Rugby, and at Balliol Coll., Oxford; graduated B.A. 1853. Was a Banker from 1855 to 1865, in the firm of Stevenson, Salt and Company, Stafford, and subsequently sleeping Partner in the firm of Messrs. Bosanquet, Salt and Company, Lombard Street. President, Institute of Bankers, 1891. Appointed Capt. 2nd Stafford Militia 1853, and a Dept.-Lieut. of Staffordshire 1859. Was Parliamentary Secretary to the Local Government Board from Jan. 1876 to Apr. 1880. Appointed a second Church Estates Commissioner 1879, an Ecclesiastical Commissioner 1880, and an Honorary Commissioner in Lunacy (without salary) Jan. 1883. Also permanent Chairman of the latter Commission, and a Chairman of Standing Committees in the House of Commons. A moderate Conservative. Sat for Stafford from Apr. 1859 to July 1865, when he retired, and from June 1869 to

Apr. 1880, when he was an unsuccessful candidate there; regained his seat Nov. 1881; was unsuccessful at the general election of 1885, but again returned for Stafford in 1886 and sat until he retired in 1892. Created Bart. 1899. Died 8 Apr. 1904. [1892]

SALTER, Arthur Clavell. 26 Montagu Square, London. 2 Mitre Court Buildings, Temple, London. Basingfield, Basingstoke. Athenaeum, Garrick, and Carlton. S. of Henry Hyde Salter, Esq., M.D., F.R.S., and Henrietta Salter (née Blunt). B. 30 Oct. 1859 in London; m. 1894, Mary Dorothea, d. of Maj. J.H. Lloyd, R.A. Educ. at King's Coll., London; B.A., LL.B., London University. Was called to the bar at the Middle Temple 1885. K.C. 1904. Recorder of Poole from 1904. A Unionist. Unsuccessfully contested W. Southwark at the general election of Jan. 1906. First elected for Basingstoke division of Hampshire in Mar. 1906 and sat until appointed High Court Judge and Knighted in 1917. Died 30 Nov. 1928. [1917]

SAMUEL, Rt. Hon. Sir Harry Simon. Continued in House after 1918: full entry in Volume III.

SAMUEL, Rt. Hon. Herbert Louis. Continued in House after 1918: full entry in Volume III.

SAMUEL, Jonathan. 23 Lorne Terrace, Stockton-on-Tees. National Liberal. S. of Thomas Samuel, Esq., of Tredegar, Monmouthshire, and Jane Clara, d. of E. Davies, Esq., of Bassellag, Monmouthshire. B. 1853 at Victoria, Ebbw Vale; m. 1892, Hannah, d. of Joshua Mellor, Esq., of Huddersfield. Educ. at a public school, Ebbw Vale. A member of Stockton Town Council from 1882-1904, Alderman 1896, Mayor 1894-95, and 1902, Honorary Freeman of the borough 1904. A member of Tees Conservancy Board 1893-1904. A member of Durham County Council from 1889, Alderman from 1903, and member of Co. Education Committee. Member of Tees Conservancy Commissioners. A J.P. for Stockton. A Liberal. Sat for Stockton-on-Tees from 1895 to 1900, when he was defeated; re-elected there in Jan. 1910 and sat until his death 22 Feb. 1917. [1916]

SAMUEL, Montagu. See MONTAGU, Sir Samuel, Bart.

SAMUEL, Samuel. Continued in House after 1918: full entry in Volume III.

SAMUEL, Sir Stuart Montagu, Bart. 12 Hill Street, Mayfair, London. Chelwood Vetchery, Nutley, Sussex. S. of Edwin Louis Samuel, Esq., Banker, of Liverpool, and Clara Yates, d. of Ellis Samuel Yates, Esq. B. at Liverpool 1856; m. 1893, Ida, d. of Alphonse Mayer, Esq. Educ. at Liverpool Institute, and University Coll. School, London. A Banker. J.P. for the Co. of London. Created Bart. in 1912. A Radical. Elected for the Whitechapel division of Tower Hamlets in 1900 and sat until he was disqualified for holding a contract with the Secretary of State for India. Another election was held at which he was returned on 30 Apr. 1913 and continued to represent the Whitechapel division of Tower Hamlets until he accepted Chiltern Hundreds in 1916. Died 13 May 1926. [1916]

SAMUEL-MONTAGU, Sir Montagu, Bart. See MONTAGU, Sir Samuel, Bart.

SAMUELS, Rt. Hon. Arthur Warren. Continued in House after 1918: full entry in Volume III.

SAMUELSON, Rt. Hon. Sir Bernhard, Bart. 56 Prince's Gate, London. Bodicote Grange, Banbury. Reform. S. of Samuel Henry Samuelson, Esq., a Liverpool Merchant, by Sarah his wife. B. 1820; m. 1st, 1844, Caroline, d. of Henry Blundell, Esq., of Hull (she died 1886); 2ndly, Lelia Mathilde, d. of the Chevalier Leon Serena. A Fellow of the Royal Society, a member of the Institution of Civil Engineers, President of the Iron and Steel Institute, and also of the British Iron Trade Association, Chairman of the Royal Commission on Technical Education, an Alderman, and Chairman of the Technical Committee of Oxfordshire, J.P. for Oxfordshire, etc. A Liberal, voted for Mr. Gladstone's Government of Ireland Bill. Sat for Banbury from Feb. till Apr. 1859, and from July 1865 to Nov. 1885. Sat for the Banbury division of Oxfordshire from Nov. 1885 until he retired in 1895. Created Bart. 1884. PC. 1895. Died 10 May 1905. [1894]

SAMUELSON, Godfrey Blundell. 56 Prince's Gate, London. Isthmian, Devonshire, and Eighty. 3rd s. of Sir Bernhard Samuelson, Bart., MP for the

Banbury division of Oxfordshire, by his wife, Caroline, d. of T. Blundell, Esq., of Hull. B. 1863, at Banbury, Oxfordshire; m. Sept. 1887, Anne, 3rd d. of the Rev. Brocklesby Davis, of Apsley House, Torquay. Educ. at Rugby, and Balliol Coll., Oxford. Was Private Secretary to the Rt. Hon. A.J. Mundella, President of the Board of Trade. A Liberal, in favour of Union with Ireland through Home Rule, of Land Law and Local Government reform, free elementary education, and absolute Religious Equality. Unsuccessfully contested Tewkesbury division of Gloucestershire Nov. 1885, and the Frome division of Somerset in June 1886. First returned for the Forest of Dean division of Gloucestershire in July 1887 and sat until he was defeated in the Tewkesbury division of Gloucestershire in 1892. Died 3 Nov. 1941. [1892]

SAMUELSON, Henry Bernhard. 56 Princes Gate, London. Chelston Cross, Torquay. Reform Eld. s. of Sir B. Samuelson, Bart., of Bodicote Grange, (MP for Banbury), by Caroline, d. of Henry Blundell, Esq., of Hull. B. at Hull 1845; m. 1874, Emily Maria, eld. d. of John Goodden, Esq., of Over Compton, Dorset. Educ. at Rugby, and Trinity Coll., Oxford. A Magistrate for Somerset and Devon, and Capt. (retired) 3rd Battalion Gloucestershire Regiment. A Liberal. Sat for Cheltenham from Dec. 1868 to Jan. 1874, when he was defeated there. Sat for Frome from Nov. 1876 until he retired in 1885. [1885]

SANDERS, Robert Arthur. Continued in House after 1918: full entry in Volume III.

SANDERSON, Lancelot. 62 Palace Gardens Terrace, London. 2 Mitre Court Buildings, Temple, London. Ward House, Nr. Lancaster. Carlton. S. of John Sanderson, Esq., of Ward House, near Lancaster, and Alice, d. of John Tunstall, Esq., of Lancaster. B. 24 Oct. 1863 at Lancaster; m. 1891, Edith Mabel, d. of Alfred Fletcher, Esq., Dept.-Lieut. of Allerton, near Liverpool. Educ. at Elstree, Harrow, and Trinity Coll., Cambridge; M.A., LL.B. Was called to the bar at the Inner Temple 1886; K.C. 1903, bencher 1912. Was Recorder of Wigan from 1901. A Unionist. Unsuccessfully contested Carlisle in 1905. Elected for the Appleby division of Westmoreland in Jan. 1910 and sat until Knighted and appointed Chief Justice of Bengal 1915-26; thereafter Chairman of Lancashire and Westmoreland Quarter Sessions and member of the Judicial Committee of the Privy Council. PC. 1926. Died 9 Mar. 1944. [1915]

SANDON, John Herbert Dudley Ryder, Visct. See RYDER, John Herbert Dudley.

SANDYS, Capt. George John. 37 Eaton Square, London. Hatherleigh House, Weston-super-Mare. Carlton, Marlborough, and White's. Only s. of James Sandys, Esq., of Slade House, Stroud, Gloucestershire. B. 23 Sept. 1875; m. 1905, Mildred Helen, d. of Duncan Cameron, Esq., of Canterbury, New Zealand. Educ. at Clifton Coll., and Pembroke Coll., Oxford; M.A. Lieut. 2nd Life Guards, and Capt. Glamorgan Yeomanry, later Capt. Res. Regiment 2nd Life Guards; served in S. African War 1899-1902, and with the British Expeditionary Force in France 1914 (wounded). A Unionist. Unsuccessfully contested the Launceston division of Cornwall at the general election of 1906, and the Bodmin division of Cornwall July 1906. Elected for the Wells division of Somerset in Jan. 1910 and sat until he retired in 1918. Honorary Attaché British Legion in Berne 1921-22; Paris 1922-25. Died 3 Sept. 1937. [1918]

SANDYS, Col. Thomas Myles. 87 Jermyn Street, St. James, London. Graythwaite Hall, Ulverston, Lancashire. Carlton, Naval & Military, and United Service. Only s. of Capt. Thomas Sandys, R.N., of the East India Company. B. at Blackheath 1837. Educ. at Shrewsbury School. Entered the service of the East India Company. Served in Bengal throughout the Sepoy Mutiny in 1857-58, and afterwards served in the Punjab Frontier Force. Exchanged to the 7th Royal Fusiliers, from which he sold out as Capt. with twenty years service. Lieut.-Col. of 3rd Royal Lancashire Militia (later 3rd Battalion Royal North Lancashire Regiment); retired 1897 as Honorary Col. Dept.-Lieut. for Lancashire. A Conservative. Sat for the Bootle division of Lancashire from 1885 until he accepted Chiltern Hundreds in Mar. 1911. Died 18 Oct. 1911. [1910]

SASSOON, Sir Edward Albert, Bart. 25 Park Lane, London. Trent Park, New Barnet, Hertfordshire. Shorncliffe Lodge,

Sandgate, Kent. S. of Sir Albert David Sassoon, 1st Bart., by Hannah, d. of E. Moise, Esq. B. 1856; m. 1887, Aline, d. of Baron Gustave de Rothschild (she died 1909). Succeeded as Bart. 1896. President of the Folkestone Chamber of Commerce. Capt. Middlesex Yeomanry. A Liberal Unionist. Elected for Hythe in 1899 and sat until his death 24 May 1912. [1912]

SASSOON, Sir Philip Albert Gustave David, Bart. Continued in House after 1918: full entry in Volume III.

SAUNDERS, William. Mount View, Streatham, London. National Liberal. S. of A.E. Saunders, Esq., of Market Lavington, Wiltshire, and his wife Mary Box. B. 1823 at Market Lavington; m. 1852, Caroline, eld. d. of L.C. Spender, Esq., of Bath. Educ. at Devizes Grammar School. A Journalist (retired in 1887). Vice-President of the United Kingdom Alliance, a member of the London County Council, and wrote a *History of the First London County Council*, the *Land Struggle in London*, *Through the Light Continent*, and other books. Established the *Western Morning News* and the *Eastern Morning News*, also the Central News Agency. A Radical, in favour of Federal Home Rule, the taxation of ground values, Local Option, the legal eight hours day, improvement by betterment, etc. Sat for Hull E. in the Parliament of 1885 until defeated in 1886 standing as a Gladstonian Liberal. Sat for the Walworth division of Newington from July 1892 until his death on 1 May 1895. [1895]

SAUNDERSON, Rt. Hon. Edward James. 5 Deanery Street, London. Castle Saunderson, Belturbet, Co. Cavan. Carlton. S. of Col. Saunderson, by the Hon. Sarah Juliana, eld. d. of Henry, 6th Lord Farnham. B. at Castle Saunderson 1837; m. 1865, the Hon. Helena Emily, youngest d. of Thomas, 3rd Lord Ventry. Col. 4th Battalion Royal Irish Fusiliers; a J.P. and Lord-Lieut. of Cavan, and was High Sheriff of Co. Cavan in 1859; created PC. 1899. Chairman of the Irish Unionist Party. A Conservative. Sat as a Liberal for Cavan Co. 1865-74, when he was defeated. First elected for N. Armagh in 1885 and sat until his death 21 Oct. 1906. [1906]

SAVORY, Sir Joseph, Bart. 33 Upper Brook Street, London. Buckhurst Park, Ascot. Carlton, National, and City Carlton. S. of Joseph Savory, Esq., of Buckhurst Park, Ascot, and Mary Caroline, d. of Isaac Braithwaite, Esq., of Kendal. B. at Upper Clapton 1843; m. 1888, Helen Pemberton, only d. of Lieut.-Col. Sir George A. Leach, K.C.B., of the Royal Engineers. Educ. at Harrow. Was Sheriff of London and Middlesex 1882-83, and Lord Mayor of London 1890-91. J.P. and Dept.-Lieut. for the City of London and the counties of Berkshire and Westmoreland; Chairman of Christ's Hospital, a Governor of St. Bartholomew's and St. Thomas's Hospitals, of Queen Anne's Bounty, and the Royal Holloway Coll., and was a member of the School Board for London. A Conservative. Sat for Appleby division of Westmoreland from July 1892 until defeated in 1900. Died 1 Oct. 1921. [1900]

SCANLAN, Thomas. 110 Ashley Gardens, London. 3 Brick Court, Temple, London. Devonshire. S. of Matthew Scanlan, Esq., Farmer. B. 21 May 1874 at Sligo; m. 1905, Mary Helen, d. of John Mullen, Esq. Educ. at Summerhill Coll., Sligo, and St. Andrews University. A Barrister; one of the Secretaries of the Irish Party. A Nationalist. Elected for N. Sligo Aug. 1909 and sat until defeated in 1918. Metropolitan Police Magistrate 1924-27. Died 9 Jan. 1930. [1918]

SCARISBRICK, Sir Tom Talbot Leyland, Bart. 3 Mount Street, Grosvenor Square, London. Greaves Hall, Nr. Southport, Lancashire. Only s. of Sir Charles Scarisbrick. B. 1874 in Germany; m. 1895, Josephine, d. of W.S. Chamberlain, Esq., of Cleveland, U.S.A. Educ. privately. A J.P. for Lancashire and Dorset; Mayor of Southport 1902-03. A Liberal. Elected for S. Dorset in 1906 and sat until defeated in Jan. 1910. Created Bart. 1909. Died 18 May 1933. [1909]

SCHOLEFIELD, Joshua. Edgbaston Grove, Warwickshire. Reform. B. 1775; m. 1st, 1804, 2nd d. of C. Cottrell; 2ndly, 1824, youngest d. of C. Cottrell; 3rdly, Mary Anne, d. of T. Rose Swaine of London. A Banker and Merchant at Birmingham. Was Vice President of the Political Union, Director of the National Provincial Bank of England, and of Metropolitan Life Assurance Society. A radical Reformer, in favour of free trade, the ballot, the repeal of the Corn Laws, etc. In 1832 pledged

319

himself to resign his seat whenever a majority of constituents expressed themselves dissatisfied with his general parliamentary conduct. Sat for Birmingham from 1832 until his death 4 July 1844. (An incorrect entry is given in Volume I). [1844]

SCHWANN, Charles Duncan. 4 Prince's Gardens, London. Reform, New Oxford & Cambridge, and Ranelagh. S. of Sir Charles E. Schwann, Bart., MP for Manchester N. B. at Didsbury 27 Jan. 1879. Educ. at Eton, and Balliol Coll., Oxford; M.A. Called to the bar at the Inner Temple 1904. A Journalist, author of *The Spirit of Parliament*, and other works. A Liberal, in favour of Electoral Reform and Taxation of Land Values; but a strong opponent of Women's Suffrage. Elected for the Hyde division of Cheshire in 1906 and sat until he retired in Jan. 1910. Changed his name to Swann in 1913. Succeeded as Bart. 1929. Died 10 Mar. 1962. [1909]

SCHWANN, Rt. Hon. Sir Charles Ernest, Bart. See SWANN, Rt. Hon. Sir Charles Ernest, Bart.

SCLATER-BOOTH, Rt. Hon. George. 74 St. George's Square, London. The Priory, and Hoddington House, Odiham, Hampshire. Carlton, and Athenaeum. Eld. s. of William Lutley Sclater, Esq., of Hoddington House, Hampshire, by Anne Maria, d. of William Bowyer, Esq. B. in London 1826; m. 1857, Lydia Caroline, only d. of Maj. George Birch, of Clare Park, Hampshire, of the East India Company (she died 1881). Educ. at Winchester, where he obtained the gold medal for Latin verse 1844, and at Balliol Coll., Oxford, where he was 2nd class in Classics 1847, and graduated M.A. 1848. Called to the bar at the Inner Temple 1851. Assumed the name of Booth by Royal licence in 1857, in addition to his patronymic. Was Parliamentary Secretary to the Poor Law Board from Mar. 1867 to Feb. 1868, when he became Financial Secretary to the Treasury; resigned Dec. 1868. Was also President of the Local Government Board from Feb. 1874 to Apr. 1880. Official Verderer of the New Forest 1877. A Magistrate for Hampshire, one of the Public Works Loan Commissioners, and a Gov. and Fellow of Winchester Coll. A Conservative, in favour of the further mitigation of local burdens. Sat for Hampshire N. from Apr. 1857 until created Lord Basing in 1887. PC. 1874. Died 22 Oct. 1894. [1887]

SCOBLE, Sir Andrew Richard, K.C.S.I. Chivelston, Wimbledon Common. Athenaeum, and Carlton. S. of John and Marianne Scoble, of Kingsbridge, Devon. B. in London 1831; m. 1863, Augusta Harriette, only d. of Joseph Nicholson, Esq. Educ. at the City of London School. Was called to the bar at Lincoln's Inn 1856, appointed Q.C. 1876, a bencher of Lincoln's Inn 1879, and Treasurer 1899. Was Advocate-Gen. and member of the Legislative Council at Bombay 1872-77, and legal member of the Council of Governor-Gen. of India 1886-91. Created C.S.I. 1889, and K.C.S.I. 1890. A Conservative. Contested Shrewsbury 1880, Newcastle-under-Lyme Nov. 1855 and S. Hackney Feb. 1886. Sat for the Central division of Hackney from July 1892 until he retired in 1900. Member of Judicial Committee of Privy Council 1901. PC. 1901. Died 17 Jan. 1916. [1900]

SCOTT, Alexander MacCallum. Continued in House after 1918: full entry in Volume III.

SCOTT, Alfred Henry. 108 Westbourne Terrace, London. s. of Charles Henry Scott, Esq., of Bridgwater, and Mary Ann Birks, of Stockport. B. 1868 at Manchester; m. Amelia Jane, d. of the Rev. J.T. Shawcross (she died 1904); 2ndly, 1907, Katherine Duncan Lewis, d. of Col. Blauton Duncan, of Kentucky, U.S.A. Educ. at Tideswell, and Lichfield Grammar School. A Director of Burgons Limited, Wholesale Provision Dealers, of Manchester. Member of Manchester City Council 1897-1906; J.P.; Vice-President of Association of Municipal Corporations. A Liberal, in favour of Nationalization of Land and Railways, Home Rule, Abolition of House of Lords, etc. Unsuccessfully contested E. Manchester in 1900. Elected for Ashton-under-Lyne in 1906 and sat until defeated in Dec. 1910. Unsuccessfully contested Darlington in 1918, the Stratford division of West Ham in 1922 and Finsbury in 1923. Alderman of London County Council 1913-22; Alderman for Margate Borough Council. Died 17 July 1939. [1910]

SCOTT, Charles Prestwich. The Firs, Fallowfield, Manchester. Reform, and National Liberal. Youngest s. of Russell Scott, Esq., of London, by Isabella, d. of Joseph

Prestwich, Esq. B. 1846; m. 1874, Rachel, d. of Rev. Professor John Cook, D.D., of St. Andrew's. Educ. privately, and at Corpus Christi Coll., Oxford; 1st class in classics. Editor of the *Manchester Guardian* 1872-1929, a J.P. for Manchester, President of the Manchester Liberal Union, and a member of the governing bodies of the Victoria University of Manchester, the University of Liverpool, the Manchester Grammar School, and the Hulme Trust. A Liberal and Home Ruler. Contested Manchester N.E. in July 1886, Oct. 1891, and July 1892. Returned for the Leigh division of Lancashire in 1895 and sat until he retired in 1906. Died 1 Jan. 1932.   [1905]

SCOTT, Leslie Frederic. Continued in House after 1918: full entry in Volume III.

SCOTT, Sir Samuel Edward, Bart. Continued in House after 1918: full entry in Volume III.

SCOTT-MONTAGU, Hon. John Walter Edward Douglas. 3 Tilney Street, Park Lane, London. 29 Cornhill, London. The Lodge, Beaulieu, Brockenhurst, Hampshire. Carlton, Automobile, Bachelors', and Beefsteak. Eld. s. of 1st Lord Montagu of Beaulieu, and the Hon. Cecily Susan, sister of the Earl of Wharncliffe. B. 1866 at Beaulieu, Southampton; m. 1889, Lady Cecil Victoria, eld. d. of the 9th Marq. of Lothian. Educ. at Eton, and New Coll., Oxford. A Maj. 4th Volunteer Battalion Hampshire Regiment. Was distinguished in athletics and science at Eton and Oxford. A J.P. and member of the County Council for Hampshire. Editor of *The Car*. A progressive Conservative. Sat for the New Forest division of Hampshire from July 1892 until he succeeded as Lord Montagu of Beaulieu 1905. C.S.I. 1916; K.C.I.E. 1919. Adviser on Mechanical Transport Services to Government of India 1915-19. Member of the Road Board 1909-19; Vice-President of R.A.C. Died 30 Mar. 1929.   [1904]

SEALE-HAYNE, Rt. Hon. Charles Hayne. 6 Upper Belgrave Street, London. Kingswear Castle, and Pill House, Devon. Reform, and National Liberal. S. of Charles Hayne Seale-Hayne, Esq., (a s. of Sir J. Seale, MP for Dartmouth), by Louisa, d. of R. Jennings, Esq., of Ridge House, Hertfordshire, and 21 Portland Place, London. B. 1833. Educ. at Eton, and called to the bar at Lincoln's Inn in 1857. Chairman of the Texas Land and Mortgage Company. Was Paymaster-Gen. from 1892-95; a PC. 1892. J.P. for Devon, Middlesex, and the borough of Dartmouth. Col. of the 3rd Battalion Devon Regiment, a Vice-President of the Devon County Agricultural Association, Treasurer of the Cobden Club, etc. Wrote *Politics for Working Men, Farmers, and Landlords*, and other works. A Liberal, in favour of Home Rule, registered manhood suffrage, and a revision of the constitution of the House of Lords. He contested Dartmouth unsuccessfully in 1857 and 1860. Sat for the Ashburton division of Devon from 1885 until his death 22 Nov. 1903. By the terms of his will the residue of his property formed a trust to endow the Seale-Hayne Agricultural Coll., Newton Abbot.   [1903]

SEARS, John Edward. Rydal Mount, Holders Hill, Hendon, London. National Liberal. S. of the Rev. J. Sears, Baptist Minister, and Harriet Tresidder. B. 1857 in London; m. Selina, d. of Hugh H. Read, Esq., of Streatham. Educ. privately, and at University Coll., London. An Architect; F.R.I.B.A. A member of London County Council 1901-07; Chairman of Bridges Committee 1903-04; and Chairman of Housing Committee 1905-06. A member of Hendon School Board 1898-1901. A Liberal. Elected for Cheltenham in 1906 and sat until he retired in Jan. 1910. Unsuccessfully contested S.W. St. Pancras as a Labour candidate in 1935. Died 20 Jan. 1941.   [1909]

SEAVERNS, Joel Herbert. 16 Eastcheap, London. 25 Grosvenor Road, London. National Liberal. S. of Dr. Joel Seaverns, of Boston, U.S.A. B. 13 Nov. 1860 at Boston, U.S.A.; m. 1892, Helen, d. of H.B. Brown, Esq., of Portland, Maine. Educ. at Harvard University. A member of the firm of Henry W. Peabody and Company, Colonial Merchants, London. A Liberal. Elected for the Brixton division of Lambeth in 1906 and sat until defeated in Jan. 1910. Unsuccessfully contested the Brixton division of Lambeth again in Dec. 1910, and the Gainsborough division of Lincolnshire in 1922. Died 11 Nov. 1923.   [1909]

SEDDON, James Andrew. Continued in House after 1918: full entry in Volume III.

SEELY, Charles. Furzedown Park, Tooting, London. Brooke House, Isle of Wight. Reform, Devonshire, and City Liberal. S. of Charles Seely, Esq., of Lincoln, by Anne, d. of J. Wilkinson, Esq. B. at Lincoln 1803; m. 1831, Mary, youngest d. of J. Hilton, Esq., of Newcastle-on-Tyne. Educ. at Lincoln. Was High Sheriff of Hampshire 1860; a Magistrate for the Isle of Wight, Lincolnshire, Surrey and the city of Lincoln; also a Dept.-Lieut. for the Isle of Wight, and for Lincolnshire. A Liberal. Unsuccessfully contested Lincoln in 1841. Sat for Lincoln from Aug. 1847 till Mar. 1848, when he was unseated on petition. Re-elected for Lincoln in Oct. 1861 and sat until he retired in 1885. Died 21 Oct. 1887. (Omitted from Volume I). [1885]

SEELY, Col. Charles. 1 Carlton House Terrace, London. Sherwood Lodge, Nottinghamshire. Brook House, Isle of Wight. Brooks's, and Reform. Only s. of Charles Seely, Esq., MP for Lincoln, of Brook House, Isle of Wight, and Mary, d. of Jonathan Hilton, Esq., of Newcastle-on-Tyne. B. 1833 at Lincoln; m. 1857, Emily, d. of William Evans, Esq., of Manchester. Educ. privately. A Coal-Owner, J.P. for Nottinghamshire, Derbyshire, and Hampshire; Dept.-Lieut. for Nottinghamshire. Was Col. of the Robin Hood Rifle Volunteers. A Liberal Unionist. Unsuccessfully contested Nottingham 1868. Sat for Nottingham 1869-74, when he was defeated. Re-elected for Nottingham 1880 and sat until 1885 when he was elected for Nottingham W.; sat until defeated 1886. Re-elected for Nottingham W. July 1892 and sat until he retired in 1895. Created Bart. 1896. Died 16 Apr. 1915. [1895]

SEELY, Sir Charles. See SEELY, Col. Charles.

SEELY, Sir Charles Hilton, Bart. Sherwood Lodge, Arnold, Nottinghamshire. Gatcombe House, Newport, Isle of Wight. Brooks's, Union and Athenaeum. S. of Sir Charles Seely, Bart., of Sherwood Lodge, Nottingham, MP for Nottingham and Emily, d. of William Evans, Esq. B. at Brookhill Hall, Pinxton, Nottinghamshire 1859; m. 1891, Hilda Lucy, d. of R.T.A. Grant, of West Cowes, Isle of Wight. Educ. at Cheam, Harrow, and Trinity Coll., Cambridge (M.A. 1884). A Colliery Owner; J.P. for Nottinghamshire and Hampshire, and Maj. of the 5th Volunteer Battalion of the Hampshire Regiment. Formerly Capt. of the 1st Nottinghamshire Rifle Volunteers (Robin Hoods). A Liberal Unionist until 1905 when he became a Free Trader and contested the general election of 1906 and Jan. 1910 against both Conservative and Liberal opposition; subsequently joined the Liberal Party. Unsuccessfully contested the mid division of Derbyshire in 1886 and the Rushcliffe division of Nottinghamshire in 1892. Sat for Lincoln from 1895 to 1906 when he was defeated; defeated there again in Jan. 1910. Elected for the Mansfield division of Nottinghamshire as a Liberal in Sept. 1916 and sat until 1918 when he was defeated in the Broxtowe division of Nottinghamshire. Succeeded as Bart. in 1915. Died 26 Feb. 1926. [1918]

SEELY, Rt. Hon. John Edward Bernard, C.B., D.S.O. Continued in House after 1918: full entry in Volume III.

SELLAR, Alexander Craig. 75 Cromwell Road, South Kensington, London. Athenaeum, Oxford & Cambridge, Brooks's, and Reform. S. of Patrick Sellar, Esq., of Westfield, Morayshire, by Ann, d. of Thomas Craig, Esq., of Barmackety, Morayshire. B. at Morvich, Sutherlandshire 1835; m. 1870, Gertrude, d. of Octavius Smith, Esq., of Ardtornish, Argyllshire. Educ. at Rugby, and Balliol Coll., Oxford; graduated 1st class in classics 1858. Was called to the Scottish bar in 1862. A Magistrate and Dept.-Lieut. for Argyllshire; and one of the Dept.-Chairman of "Ways and Means." Appointed Assistant Commissioner to Education (Scotland) Commission in 1864; was Legal Secretary to the Lord Advocate of Scotland from 1870 to 1874; served in the Parliamentary Commission to inquire into the operation of the Truck Acts in 1870, and in the Royal Commission on Endowed Institutions (Scotland) 1873. A Liberal Unionist. Unsuccessfully contested Devonport in 1880; sat for the Haddington district from Aug. 1882 to Nov. 1885, and for the Partick division of Lanarkshire from Nov. 1885 until his death 16 Jan. 1890. [1889]

SELWIN-IBBETSON, Rt. Hon. Sir Henry John, Bart. 16 James Street, Pimlico, London. Down Hall, Harlow, Essex. Carlton. Only s. of Sir John Thomas Ibbetson-Selwin, 6th Bart., by Isabella, d. of Gen. John Leveson-Gower, of Bill Hill, Berkshire. B. 1826; m. 1st, 1850, Hon. Sarah Elizabeth, eld. d. of Lord Lyndhurst (she died 1865); 2ndly, 1867, Eden, widow of Sir Charles Ibbetson, Bart. Educ. at St. John's Coll., Cambridge. Assumed the name of Ibbetson (which his father had formerly borne) in addition to that of Selwin in 1867. Succeeded as Bart. in 1869. Was Under-Secretary for the Home Department from Feb. 1874 to Apr. 1878, and Financial Secretary to the Treasury from Apr. 1878 to Apr. 1880. Was second Church Estates Commissioner 1885-86 and 1886-92. PC. 1885. A Conservative, said he would lighten some of the burdens of local taxation; would resist the dismemberment of our empire, and the severing of Ireland from Great Britain. Unsuccessfully contested Ipswich in 1857 and 1859. Sat for Essex S. from July 1865 to Dec. 1868 and for the W. division of Essex from that date to Nov. 1885, and for the Epping division of Essex from Nov. 1885 until he was created Baron Rookwood in June 1892. Died 15 Jan. 1902.   [1892]

SELWYN, Capt. Charles William. 21 Lowndes Square, London. Turf, Marlborough, White's, Naval & Military, and Junior Carlton, etc. Eld. s. of the Rt. Hon. Sir Charles Jasper Selwyn, Lord Justice of the Court of Appeal in Chancery, by his 1st wife, Hester, 5th d. of J.G. Ravenshaw, Esq., and widow of Dr. Thomas Dowler. B. 1858; m. 1884, Isabella Constance, 2nd d. of F.G. Dalgety, Esq., J.P. of Lockerly Hall, Romsey. Educ. at Eton, and Trinity Coll., Cambridge. A Capt. in the Royal Horse Guards, and served in the Egyptian Campaign 1882. A Conservative. Unsuccessfully contested the Wisbech division of Cambridgeshire at the general election of 1885. First returned for the Wisbech division of Cambridgeshire in July 1886 and sat until he accepted Chiltern Hundreds in 1891. Died in Auckland, New Zealand on 1 Mar. 1893. [1891]

SETON-KARR, Sir Henry, C.M.G. 47 Chester Square, London. Kippilaw, St. Boswell's, N.B. Carlton. New Club, Edinburgh. S. of George Berkeley Seton-Karr, Esq., of the Indian Civil Service, by Eleanor, 2nd d. of H. Usborne, Esq., of Branches Park, Suffolk. B. in India 1853; m. 1880, the d. of W. Pilkington, Esq., of Roby Hall, Liverpool (she died 1884);

2ndly, 1886, the d. of W. Thorborn, Esq., of Edinburgh. Educ. at Harrow School, and Corpus Christi Coll., Oxford. Was called to the bar in 1879, and practised two years on the N. Circuit. A J.P. and Dept.-Lieut. for Roxburghshire. Knighted and C.M.G. 1902. A Conservative. Sat for St. Helen's from 1885 until defeated in 1906. Contested Berwickshire in Jan. 1910. Died 29 May 1914.   [1905]

SEXTON, Thomas. 6 Gloucester Walk, Kensington, London. 20 North Frederick Street, Dublin. Eld. s. of John Sexton, Esq., of Waterford. B. at Waterford 1848. Joined the editorial staff of the *Nation* newspaper in 1869. High Sheriff of Dublin 1887; and Lord Mayor 1888 and 1889. A member of the independent Irish Parliamentary Party (Anti-Parnellite), and in favour of "Home Rule", the creation of a "peasant proprietary", and of a system of "elective county government" for Ireland. Sat for Sligo Co. from Apr. 1880 to Nov. 1885, and for the S. division of Sligo from Nov. 1885 to July 1886, when being returned for S. Sligo and for Belfast W. he chose to sit for the latter. At the general election of 1892 he offered himself for both Belfast W. and Kerry N., and having been beaten at Belfast W., and elected at Kerry N., he sat for the latter until he accepted the Chiltern Hundreds in 1896. Chairman of Freemans Journal Limited 1892-1912; member of Viceregal Commission on Irish Railways 1906-10. Died 1 Nov. 1932.   [1895 2nd ed.]

SHACKLETON, David James. 350 Great Western Street, Rusholme, Manchester. S. of William and Margaret Shackleton. B. 1863 at Cloughfold, Lancashire. Educ. at the elementary schools at Rawtenstall, and Haslingden. He had much influence among textile workers; Secretary of the Darwen Weavers' Association; member of Blackburn Chamber of Commerce. A J.P. for Accrington and Lancashire; member of Parliamentary Committee of Trade Union Congress; Chairman of the N. Counties Amalgamated Weavers' Association. A Labour Member, in favour of Home Rule, Universal Suffrage, Free Trade, etc. Elected for the Clitheroe division of Lancashire in Aug. 1902 and sat until appointed Senior Labour Adviser to the Home Office Nov. 1910-11. Permanent Secretary, Minister of Labour 1916-21; K.C.B. 1917; Chief Labour Adviser 1921-25. Died 1 Aug. 1938.   [1910]

SHARMAN-CRAWFORD, Robert Gordon. Continued in House after 1918: full entry in Volume III.

SHARPE, William Edward Thompson. 11 Ladbroke Square, London. S. of Christopher Sharpe, Esq., of Birr, King's Co., and his wife, Margaret, d. of William Edward Thompson, Esq., of Queen's Co. B. at Birr 1833; m. 1873, Frances Sophia, youngest d. of the Rev. P. Guillebaud, of Clifton, at one time Rector of Nailsea, Somerset. M.A. and at one time Scholar of Trinity Coll., Dublin. Entered the Ceylon Civil Service in 1857 and became Government Agent of the N.W., S., and Central provinces, and a member of the Legislative Council; retired 1889. A Barrister of the Inner Temple 1880. A Conservative. Represented N. Kensington from 1895 until he retired in 1906. Died 5 Nov. 1909. [1905]

SHAW, Hon. Alexander. Continued in House after 1918: full entry in Volume III.

SHAW, Sir Theodore Frederick Charles Edward, Bart. Tettenhall, Wolverhampton. Reform, Bath, and Eighty. Eld. d. of E.D. Shaw, Esq., of Oaklands, Wolverhampton. B. 1859. Educ. at Tettenhall Coll., Wolverhampton, and Balliol Coll., Oxford. Studied for the bar. In 1875 he entered the firm of John Shaw and Sons Limited, Merchants, of Wolverhampton. He travelled extensively; was Capt. 3rd Volunteer Battalion S. Staffordshire Regiment, and twice a member of the Wolverhampton Town Council. Created Bart. 1908. A Liberal, in favour of registration reform, disestablishment, land-law reform, popular control of the liquor traffic, "one man one vote", all elections on one day, etc. First elected for Stafford in 1892 and sat until he retired in Dec. 1910. Died 17 Apr. 1942. [1910]

SHAW, Thomas. Westminster Palace Hotel, London. Allangate, Halifax. Oakes House, Stainland, Yorkshire. Reform. 3rd s. of Joseph Shaw, Esq., of Green Bank, Stainland, Halifax. B. at Green Bank, Stainland 1823; m. 1854, Elizabeth, 3rd d. of William Rawson, Esq., J.P. of Wilton Polygon, Manchester. Educ. at Huddersfield Coll. Honorary Treasurer of the Anti-Corn Law League. A Woollen Manufacturer and Merchant of Brookroyd Mills, Halifax. A Magistrate for Halifax, a Dept.-Lieut. and Magistrate for the W. Riding of Yorkshire. Was Mayor of Halifax for two years from 1866 to 1868, and for three years President of the Chamber of Commerce of that town from 1874 to 1876. Was President of the Halifax Mechanics' Institute from 1872. An "advanced" Liberal, in favour of Mr. Gladstone's policy, especially in Ireland. Sat for Halifax from Aug. 1882 until his death on 15 Jan. 1893. [1892 2nd ed.]

SHAW, Rt. Hon. Thomas. 17 Abercromby Place, Edinburgh. Reform, and National Liberal. S. of Alexander Shaw, Esq., of Dunfermline, N.B., and Isabella Wishart. B. 1850; m. 1879, Elsie Stephen, d. of George Forrest, Esq., of Ludquharn, Aberdeenshire. Educ. at the High School, Dunfermline, and Edinburgh University. M.A., L.L.B., Q.C., (1894), LL.D. St. Andrews (1902), and LL.D. Aberdeen (1906). Passed Advocate 1875, was Lord Rector's Historical Prizeman, and Hamilton Fellow in Mental Philosophy, Edinburgh University. Dept.-Lieut. for Edinburgh. Solicitor-Gen. for Scotland 1894-95. Lord Advocate, appointed Dec. 1905. PC. 1905. A Liberal, in favour of Home Rule for Ireland and also for Scotland, reform in the land laws, the "local veto", disestablishment, free secondary, technical, and University education, payment of Members of Parliament, etc. Represented Hawick from 1892 until appointed Lord of Appeal and created Life Peer (Baron Shaw of Dunfermline) Feb. 1909; retired from the former office in 1929. Created Baron Craigmyle 1929. Died 28 June 1937. [1908]

SHAW, William Rawson. Stonygate, Halifax. Oakes House, Nr. Halifax. Reform, and Union. S. of Thomas Shaw, Esq., Dept.-Lieut., J.P. and MP for Halifax by Elisabeth, d. of William Rawson, Esq., J.P., of Wilton, Polygon, Manchester, Hon. Treasurer of the Anti-Corn-Law League. B. 1860 at Stainland; m. 1888, Mary Josephine, only d. of Joseph Crook, Esq., MP for Bolton. Educ. at Rugby, and Trinity Coll., Cambridge, where he took the M.A. degree. Was a Lieut. 2nd West Yorkshire Yeomanry Cavalry (Prince of Wales' Own), and passed in the School of Auxiliary Cavalry at Aldershot. Was for three years Honorary Private Secretary to Professor Stuart, MP. Was President of the Stainland Liberal Association from its commencement. A Liberal, a supporter of the Rosebery administration. Sat for Halifax from Feb. 1893 until he accepted Chiltern Hundreds in 1897. Magistrate for Sussex and the W. Riding of Yorkshire. Member of W. Sussex County Council. Died 14 Apr. 1932.   [1896]

SHAW-LEFEVRE, Rt. Hon. George John. 18 Bryanston Square, London. Oldbury Place, Ightham, Kent. Athenaeum, and Brooks's. S. of Sir John George Shaw-Lefevre, K.C.B., by Rachel Emily, d. of Ichabod Wright, Esq., of Mapperley Hall, Nottingham. B. 12 June 1831; m. 1874, Lady Constance Emily, d. of the 3rd Earl of Ducie. Educ. at Eton, and Trinity Coll., Cambridge. Was called to the bar 1856 at the Inner Temple, of which he was elected a bencher in 1882. Was a Lord of the Admiralty from May to July 1866, Parliamentary Secretary to the Board of Trade from Dec. 1868 to Jan.1871, Under-Secretary for the Home Department from Jan. 1871 to Mar. 1871, Secretary to the Admiralty from Mar. 1871 to Feb. 1874, and again from Apr. 1880, to Nov. 1880, when he was appointed First Commissioner of Works and Buildings. PC. 1880. Was Postmaster-Gen. (When he took a seat in the Cabinet) 1884-85, and a second time First Commissioner of Works from 1892-94. President of the Local Government Board Mar. 1894 to June 1895. In 1886 he was appointed Chairman of the Royal Commission on the Loss of Life at Sea. Author of a collection of essays on questions relating to land in England and Ireland, *English Commons and Forests*, etc. A Liberal, and Home Ruler. Sat for Reading from Oct. 1863 to Nov. 1885, but was defeated there in the ensuing general election. On the death of Mr. Forster (Apr. 1886), he was elected for Central Bradford and sat until defeated in 1895. Member of London County Council 1897. Created Baron Eversley June 1906. Author of *The Partitions of Poland* (1915) and *The Turkish Empire* (1917). Died 19 Apr. 1928.   [1895]

SHAW-STEWART, Sir Michael Hugh, Bart. 20 Mansfield Street, Cavendish Square, London. Ardgowan, Greenock, N.B. Carlton, and Travellers'. Eld. s. of Sir Michael R. Shaw-Stewart, Bart., of Ardgowan, Renfrewshire, by Lady Octavia Grosvenor, d. of the 2nd Marq. of Westminster. B. 1854; m. 1883, Lady Alice Emma Thynne, eld. d. of the 4th Marq. of Bath. Educ. at Eton, and Christ Church, Oxford. A J.P. and Dept.-Lieut. for the counties of Stirling and Renfrew. Capt. 4th Battalion (Princess Louise's) Argyll and Sutherland Highlands; and was a member of the Royal Commission on Physical Education (Scotland) 1902. A Conservative, in favour of Free Trade. Unsuccessfully contested Stirlingshire in 1885; first elected for E. Renfrewshire in 1886 and sat until defeated in 1906. Succeeded as Bart. in 1903. C.B. 1916. Lord-Lieut. for Renfrewshire from 1922. K.C.B. 1933. Died 29 June 1942.   [1905]

SHEE, James John. See O'SHEE, James John.

SHEEHAN, Daniel Desmond. Rockhurst, Victoria Road, Cork. S. of Daniel Sheehan, Esq., evicted Tenant, and Ellen, née Fitzgerald. B. 1874 at Knockardrahan Kanturk, Co. Cork; m. 1894, Mary, d. of Martin O'Connor, Esq., of Tralee. Educ. at National Schools, and privately. A Barrister, called to the bar at King's Inns 1911. Was for nearly two years acting Editor of the *Catholic News*, and subsequently for five years Editor of the Cork *Southern Star*. Honorary Secretary of All-for-Ireland League. President of Irish Land and Labour Association. Honorary Secretary of Cork Advisory Committee of the United Irish League. Law Exhibitioner and Prizeman, University Coll., Cork 1908-09. Honoursman, King's Inns, Dublin 1910. Capt. 9th (S.) Battalion Royal Munster Fusiliers, served with Expeditionary Force 1915 and 1916. A Nationalist, in favour of the policy of conciliation as applied to Irish Politics. Returned unopposed, as a Nationalist, for mid Cork in May 1901 and Jan. 1906, and sat until he accepted Chiltern Hundreds in Dec. 1906. Re-elected for mid Cork in Dec. 1906 but in Jan. 1907, resigned his seat as a protest against his exclusion from the Nationalist Party. Was re-elected for mid Cork, without opposition, as an Independent Nationalist, and sat until he retired in 1918. Unsuccessfully contested W. Limerick in Dec. 1910 while sitting for mid Cork. [1918]

SHEEHAN, Jeremiah Daniel. Innisfallen Hotel, Killarney. B. 1847. A native of Killarney, and Vice-Chairman of the Board of Guardians of that town. An Hotel Proprietor at Killarney, and was President of the local branch of the Irish

National League. An "Irish Nationalist" (Anti-Parnellite). Sat for Kerry E. from 1885 until he retired in 1895. [1895]

SHEEHY, David. Windsor House, Rathmines, Dublin. 2nd s. of Richard Sheehy, Esq., of Holly Bank, Dublin. B. at Broadford, Co. Limerick 1844; m. 1876, Elizabeth, 2nd d. of Richard McCoy, Esq., of Loughill (she died 1918). Educ. at the Jesuit Seminary, and Irish Coll., Paris. Joined his father in business in Mallow in 1867. One of the staff officials of the United Irish League. A Nationalist. Sat for S. Galway from 1885 to 1900, when he retired. Unsuccessfully contested Waterford city in 1892, whilst sitting for S. Galway. Elected for S. Meath in Oct. 1903 and sat until he retired in 1918. Died 17 Dec. 1932. [1918]

SHEFFIELD, Sir Berkeley Digby George, Bart. Continued in House after 1918: full entry in Volume III.

SHEIL, Edward. 29 Thurlow Square, South Kensington, London. Garrick, and Arthur's. Stephen's Green, Dublin. S. of Gen. Sir Justin Sheil, K.C.B. (bro. of the Rt. Hon. Richard Lalor Sheil, MP), by Mary Leonora, d. of the Rt. Hon. Stephen Woulfe, MP, afterwards Chief Baron of the Exchequer, Ireland. B. 1851. Educ. at Dr. Newman's Oratory School, near Birmingham, and Christ Church, Oxford. A Parnellite, advocated "Home Rule" for Ireland. Sat for Athlone from Apr. 1874 until defeated Apr. 1880. Sat for Meath from Apr. 1882 to Nov. 1885, and for the S. division of Meath from Nov. 1885 until he retired in 1892. Died 3 July 1915. [1892]

SHEPHERD-CROSS, Herbert. 19 Queen's Gate Gardens, London. Mortfield, Bolton. Hamels Park, Buntingford. Carlton. S. of Thomas Cross, Esq., J.P., Banker and Cotton-Spinner, of Mortfield, Bolton. B. at Mortfield, Bolton 1847; m. 1st, 1870, Lucy Mary Shepherd, d. of the Rev. J. Shepherd Birley (she died 1891); 2ndly, 1895, Penelope, d. of James Hortor, Esq., of Edinburgh. Educ. at Harrow, and Exeter Coll., Oxford. Assumed the name of Shepherd in 1884 by Royal Licence. Was Maj. in the Duke of Lancaster's Own Regiment of Yeomanry, J.P. for the counties of Lancaster and Hereford, and served for eight years on the Bolton School Board. A Conservative. Sat for Bolton

from 1885 until he retired in 1906. Died 9 Jan. 1916 [1905]

SHERIDAN, Henry Brinsley. 6 Colville Gardens, London. 5 Essex Court, Temple, London. Devonshire, and City Liberal. S. of Garrett Sheridan, Esq., of Cavan, Ireland, by Jane Juliana Darnley, d. of Sir Richard Perrott. B. in London 1820; m. 1850, Elizabeth Frances, d. of the Rev. J. Wood. Called to the bar at the Inner Temple in 1851. Appointed a Capt. in the 6th Cinque Ports Authority Volunteers 1861. A Magistrate for Middlesex and Kent. A Liberal. Sat for Dudley from Apr. 1857 until defeated in 1886 standing as a Gladstonian Liberal. Died 19 Apr. 1906. [1886]

SHERWELL, Arthur James. 4 Harley Gardens, South Kensington, London. Rockcliffe, Dalbeattie, Kirkcudbrightshire. Reform, National Liberal, and 1917. 2nd s. of John Viney Sherwell, Esq., of S. Devon, and London. B. 1863 in London; m. 1909, Amy, d. of J.H. Whadcoat, Esq., of Bodiam, Sussex. Educ. at Tredegar School, North London Grammar School, and at Handsworth Coll., Birmingham. An author. Wrote *Life in West London*, and joint author of *The Temperance Problem and Social Reform, Taxation of the Liquor Trade, State Prohibition and Local Option, Public Control of the Liquor Traffic*, etc., etc. also author of numerous pamphlets and articles on economic and political questions. He travelled extensively, and was familiar with the Colonies and the U.S.A. A Liberal. Elected for Huddersfield Nov. 1906 and sat until he retired in 1918. Died 13 Jan. 1942. [1918]

SHIPMAN, John Greenwood. Templemore, Dallington, Northampton. S. of John Shipman, Esq., Wine Merchant, of Northampton, and Ruth, d. of Thomas Sheffield, Esq., of Wigton, Cumberland. B. at Hulme, Manchester 1848; m. 1st, 28 May 1885, Ann Elizabeth, d. of David Hobbs, Esq., of London (she died 11 July 1885); 2ndly, 1906, Clara Alice, d. of Sydney Gent, Esq., of Northampton. Educ. at Northampton, Hurstpierpoint and New Coll., Oxford. A Barrister-at-Law, called 15 May 1878, and joined the Midland Circuit; B.C.L., M.A. (Oxford) 1879, LL.D. (London) 1895. Oxford Vinerian Law Scholar 1878, Inns of Court Studentship 1877, J.P. for Northamptonshire. Honorary Secretary of the Parliamentary "Three

Dozen" Liberal Club. A Radical and Home Ruler. Unsuccessfully contested Gravesend in 1892. Elected for Northampton in Oct. 1900 and sat until he retired in Jan. 1910. Died 20 Oct. 1918.
[1909]

SHIRLEY, Walter Shirley. 2 Dr. Johnson's Buildings, Temple, London. Only s. of W.E. Shirley, Esq., twice Mayor, and for many years town clerk of Doncaster, by his marriage with Jane Winteringham, d. of John Shirley, Esq., of Attercliffe, Sheffield. B. 1851. Educ. at Rugby, and Balliol Coll., Oxford, where he graduated with honours 1875. Was called to the bar at the Inner Temple 1876, and practised on the N.E. Circuit, and at the W. Riding Sessions. Author of several law books and a pamphlet, entitled *Politics made Easy*, which had a large sale. An "advanced Liberal," in favour of Land Law reform, a democratic system of local self-government in the counties, and the Disestablishment of the Church of England in Wales, reform of the House of Lords, Sunday closing of public-houses. legalizing marriage with a deceased wife's sister, etc. Sat for the Doncaster division of W. Riding of Yorkshire from 1885 until he accepted Chiltern Hundreds in Feb. 1888. Died 1 May 1888. [1887]

SHORTT, Rt. Hon. Edward. Continued in House after 1918: full entry in Volume III.

SHUTTLEWORTH, Rt. Hon. Sir Ughtred James Kay, Bart. See KAY-SHUTTLEWORTH, Rt. Hon. Sir Ughtred James, Bart.

SIDEBOTHAM, Joseph Watson. 83 Elizabeth Street, London. Merle Bank, Bowdon, Cheshire. Carlton, and Brasenose. Conservative, Manchester. S. of Joseph Sidebotham, Esq., J.P., F.S.A, of Erlesdene, Bowdon, Cheshire, by Anne, only d. of Edward Coward, Esq., of Bowdon, Cheshire. B. 1857 at Ashton-on-Mersey, Cheshire; m. 1886, Marian, younger d. of Edward Dowling, Esq., Vicar of Timperley, Cheshire. Educ. at a private school, and Owen's Coll., Manchester. A Mus. B. of Oxford, and a Vice-President of Trinity Coll., London; also a joint patron of the living of St. Anne's, Haughton, Lancashire, and J.P. for the Co. of Chester. A Conservative and Unionist. Sat for the

Hyde division of Cheshire from 1886 until he retired in 1900. Died 10 June 1925.
[1900]

SIDEBOTTOM, Tom Harrop. Westminster Palace Hotel, London. Etherow House, Hollingworth, Cheshire. Carlton, Junior Carlton, and Constitutional. Eld. s. of William Sidebottom, Esq., J.P., of Etherow House, Hollingworth, Cheshire, by Agnes, d. of Jonah Harrop, Esq., of Bardsley House, Ashton-under-Lyne. B. 1826; m. 1886, Edith, eld. d. of James Murgatroyd, Esq., of Warley, Didsbury. Educ. at the Manchester Grammar School, and at private schools. A J.P. for Cheshire and Derbyshire, and a Dept.-Lieut. for Derbyshire; received the freedom of the borough of Stalybridge 1897. A Conservative. Was MP for Stalybridge from Feb. 1874 to the dissolution of 1880, when he was defeated; re-elected there 1885, and sat until he retired in 1900. Died 25 May 1908. [1900]

SIDEBOTTOM, William. Harewood Lodge, Broadbottom. Carlton, St. Stephen's and Constitutional. Conservative, Manchester. S. of William Sidebottom, Esq., of Etherow House, Hadfield, by Agnes, d. of Jonah Harrop, Esq., of Bardsley House, Lancashire. B. 1841. Was Mayor of Glossop 1873-74, and a Magistrate for the Co. of Chester and the borough of Glossop; a Lieut.-Col. in the 4th Cheshire Rifle Volunteers. A "moderate Conservative", in favour of reforms in the House of Lords, with the creation of life peerages. Unsuccessfully contested N. Derbyshire in 1880. Sat for the High Peak division of Derbyshire from 1885 until he retired in 1900. Dept. Chairman of Cammell Laird and Company Limited. Died 3 Jan. 1933. [1895]

SILCOCK, Thomas Ball. Walden, Bath. Eighty, and National Liberal. S. of T.B. Silcock, Esq., of Bradford-on-Avon. B. 1854 at Bradford-on-Avon; m. 1881, Mary Frances, d. of the Rev. H. Tarrant. Educ. at Bristol Grammar School, and London University; B.Sc. A Partner in Silcock and Reay, Architects and Surveyors, Bath and London. Was a member of Bath Town Council (Mayor 1900-01). A Liberal. Elected for the Wells division of Somerset in 1906 and sat until defeated in Jan. 1910. Died 1 Apr. 1924. [1909]

SIMEON, Sir John Stephen Barrington, Bart. 19 Wilton Crescent, London. Swainston, Newport, Isle of Wight. Brooks's and Travellers'. Eld. s. of Sir John Simeon, 3rd Bart., by his 1st wife, Jane Maria, only d. of Sir F.F. Baker, 2nd Bart. B. 1850 at Swainston, Isle of Wight; m. 1872, Isabella Mary, only d. of the Hon. Ralph H. Dutton, of Timsbury Manor, Romsey, Hampshire. Educ. at the Oratory School, Edgbaston. Was an Ensign in the 2nd Battalion Rifle Brigade 1868-70; and was Private Secretary to the Rt. Hon. John Bright, MP, 1880-83. A J.P. for Hampshire, a Dept.-Lieut. and County Alderman for the Isle of Wight, and a Director of the London and South Western Railway Company. Succeeded as Bart. in 1870. A Liberal Unionist. Sat for Southampton from 1895 until he retired in 1906. Died 26 Apr. 1909. [1905]

SIMON, Sir John. 36 Tavistock Square, London. 1 Dr. Johnson's Buildings, Temple, London. Reform, and Cobden. S. of Isaac Simon, Esq., of Luss, Mount Pisgah, and of Montego Bay in Jamaica, by Rebecca, only d. of Jacob Orobio Furtado, Esq., of Montego Bay, Jamaica. B. at Montego Bay, 9 Dec. 1818; m. 1843, Rachel, 5th d. of S.K. Salaman, Esq., of Baker Street, Portman Square, London. Educ. at University Coll., and graduated LL.B. 1841 at the University of London. Was called to the bar at the Middle Temple, Nov. 1842; created a Serjeant-at-Law Feb. 1864, and received a patent of precedence Jan. 1868. Knighted Aug. 1886. A Liberal Reformer, in favour of the abolition of primogeniture and entail, and a reform of "the settlement of land, so as to prevent tying it up for generations." Sat for Dewsbury from Dec. 1868 until he accepted Chiltern Hundreds in 1888. Died 24 June 1897. [1887]

SIMON, Rt. Hon. Sir John Allsebrook. Continued in House after 1918: full entry in Volume III.

SINCLAIR, Rev. John. Grangemouth, N.B. National Liberal. S. of the Rev. John Sinclair (Minister, first of the Church of Scotland, then, in 1843, of the Free Church, Bruan, Caithness, N.B.) and his wife Dorothea, d. of William Wilson, Esq., Banker, of Thurso. B. at Bruan 1842; m. 1871, Elizabeth Greig, d. of G.G. Mackay, Esq., Ship-Owner, of Grangemouth, N.B.

Educ. at Moray House, the High School, and University, Edinburgh, and New Coll. A retired clergyman of the Free Church of Scotland, ordained at Grangemouth, N.B. 1869; transferred to St. Bernard's, Edinburgh 1880; resigned his charge 1884. Wrote *Heather Bells*, a modern Highland story, and *Sabbath Lessons from Westminster*, and was editor and part author of *The Church on the Sea*. An advanced Liberal, strongly in favour of Mr. Gladstone's policy of Home Rule and a National Parliament (for purely Irish affairs) for Ireland, in favour also of Religious Equality, Free Education, Reform of the Land Laws and of the House of Lords. Sat for Ayr district from June 1888 until he accepted Chiltern Hundreds in 1890. Died 7 Jan. 1892. [1889]

SINCLAIR, Rt. Hon. John. 2 Cambridge Square, London. Brooks's, Army & Navy, and National Liberal. S. of Capt. George Sinclair, 3rd s. of Sir John Sinclair, Bart., of Dunbeath, by Agnes, only d. of John Learmonth, Esq., of Dean. B. 1860; m. 1904, Lady Marjorie Gordon, only d. of the Earl of Aberdeen. Educ. at the Edinburgh Academy, and at Wellington Coll. Entered the 5th Royal Irish Lancers 1879, and became Capt. Served in the Suakim Expedition 1885, and had the medal with clasp; Aide-de-Camp to the Earl of Aberdeen when Lord-Lieut. of Ireland; and retired from the army 1887. Secretary for Scotland from Dec. 1905 until Feb. 1912; one of the Liberal Whips 1900-06. PC. 1905. Sat for E. Finsbury on the London County Council 1889-91. In 1896-97 he served as Governor General's Secretary to the Earl of Aberdeen, Governor Gen. of Canada. A Liberal. Unsuccessfully contested the Ayr district 1886. In 1892 he was elected for Dunbartonshire, and sat till the general election of 1895, when he was defeated. First elected for Forfarshire 1897 and sat until created 1st Baron Pentland in 1909. Governor of Madras 1912-19. G.C.I.E. 1912; G.C.S.I. 1918. Died 11 Jan. 1925. [1908]

SINCLAIR, Louis. Daydawn, Netherhall Gardens, Hampstead, London. 28 Castle Hill Avenue, Folkestone. Carlton, and Constitutional. B. 1861 at Paris; m. 1886, Nina, d. of Daniel de Pass, Esq., of London and Cape Town. Educ. at University Coll. School, London. Was on the staff of the *Melbourne Argus*. Subsequently chose a commercial career in Australia. Joint Honorary Secretary of the House of Commons Commercial Committee. A Conservative. Sat for the Romford division of Essex from 1897 until defeated in 1906. Reformed the Commercial Committee of the House of Commons in 1913; similarly involved with other European Parliamentary bodies; served in R.A.C. War Transport Services; wrote several political works. Died 4 Jan. 1928.   [1905]

SINCLAIR, William Pirrie. 36 Eaton Square, London. Rivelyn, Princes Park, Liverpool. Reform, and Devonshire. Ulster Liberal, Belfast. Reform, Liverpool. S. of John Sinclair, Esq., of The Grove, Co. Antrim, by Eliza, d. of William Pirrie, Esq., of Conlig, Co. Down. B. at Belfast 1837; m. 1865, Agnes, d. of Rev. Hugh Critchton, D.D. of Liverpool. Educ. at the Royal Academical Institution, and Queen's Coll., Belfast and at Heidelberg. A Merchant and Ship-Owner at Liverpool, and elsewhere, and a member of the Mersey Docks and Harbour Board; J.P. for the city of Liverpool. A "moderate Liberal, in favour of the introduction of Local County Government into Ireland", and of "an entire change in the 'Castle' system of administration", but was "opposed to Home Rule." Elected for Co. Antrim in May 1885, but defeated for Antrim N. in Dec. 1885. First elected for Falkirk district in July 1886 and sat until defeated in 1892. Died 1 Nov. 1900.   [1892]

SITWELL, Sir George Reresby, Bart. 3 Arlington Street, London. Renshaw Hall, Chesterfield, Derbyshire. Carlton. Only s. of Sir Sitwell Reresby Sitwell, by Louisa, 4th d. of Col. the Hon. Hely-Hutchinson, of Weston Hall, Northamptonshire. B. 1860; m. 1885, Lady Ida, d. of the 1st Earl of Londesborough. Educ. at Eton, and Christ Church, Oxford. A J.P. for Derbyshire, Lord of the Manor of Renshaw, and a Lieut. in the W. Yorks. Yeomanry Cavalry. Succeeded as Bart. in 1862. A moderate Conservative. Unsuccessfully contested Scarborough 3 Nov. 1884 and again 25 Nov. 1884. Sat for Scarborough from 1885-86, when he was defeated. Returned again for Scarborough July 1892 and sat until defeated in 1895. Unsuccessfully contested Scarborough again in Oct. 1900. Lieut.-Col. 1904-08. Died 8 July 1943.   [1895]

SKEWES-COX, Sir Thomas. 8 Lancaster Place, Strand, London. Heron House, Richmond, Surrey. Carlton. S. of William Nicholas Cox, Esq., of Richmond. B. 1849; m. 1882, Jessie, d. of Edmund Warne, Esq. Educ. privately. Assumed the additional surname of Skewes in 1874. A Solicitor, admitted 1881, and a member of the firm of Skewes-Cox, Nash, and Company; a J.P., and an Alderman of Richmond (Mayor 1892), and of the Surrey County Council. A Conservative, and Unionist. Represented the Kingston division of Surrey from 1895 until he retired in 1906. Knighted 1905. Died 15 Oct. 1913. [1905]

SLACK, John Bamford. 10 Woburn Square, London. Green Hill House, Ripley, Derbyshire. Reform, City Liberal, Eighty, and Alpine. S. of Thomas Slack, Esq., of Ripley, Derbyshire, and Mary Ann Slack (née Bamford). B. 11 July 1857 at Ripley; m. 1888, Alice Maude Mary, d. of E. Bretherton, Esq., of Clifton. Educ. at Wesley Coll., Sheffield; B.A. London University 1876. A Solicitor, admitted 1880; head of the firm of Slack, Monro and Atkins, Queen Victoria Street, London. Was a member of the Derbyshire County Council 1889-1902. A Liberal and Free Trader. Elected for the St. Albans division of Hertfordshire in Feb. 1904 and sat until defeated in 1906. Kt. 1906. Died 11 Feb. 1909.   [1905]

SLAGG, John. Hopefield, Pendleton, Manchester. Reform, National Liberal, and Savile. Eld. s. of John Slagg, Esq., a Magistrate of Manchester, by Jane, D. of William Crighton, Esq. B. at Manchester 1841; m. 1866, Katherine Parker, d. of Maj. German, of Maywood, Sevenoaks, Kent. A Merchant of Manchester. Was President of the Manchester Chamber of Commerce, one of the Royal Commissioners on Technical Education, and an Administrator of the Suez Canal. A Liberal, supported Mr. Gladstone's Irish policy. Sat for Manchester from Apr. 1880 to Nov. 1885, when he was defeated in N.W. Manchester. Was an unsuccessful candidate at the general election of July 1886 when he stood for the Darwen division of Lancashire. Returned for Burnley in Feb. 1887 and sat until he accepted Chiltern Hundreds in Feb. 1889. Died 7 May 1889.   [1888]

SLOAN, Thomas Henry. House of Commons, London. B. 1870. A sub-contractor to Harland and Wolff, Shipbuilders, Belfast, and a member of the National Amalgamated Union of Labour. A strong Temperance Reformer and President of the Belfast Protestant Association. An Independent Conservative and Free Trader. Elected for S. Belfast in 1902 and sat until defeated in Jan. 1910. Unsuccessfully contested S. Belfast in Dec. 1910.   [1909]

SMALL, John Francis. Hill Street, Newry, Co. Down. Only s. of Arthur John Small, Esq., Town Councillor of Newry, by Mary, d. of Patrick O'Callaghan, Esq., of Dublin. B. at Newry 1853. Unmarried. Admitted a Solicitor in Ireland 1875. A Town Councillor of Newry, and Coroner for the Co. of Armagh. Wrote a *History of Newry*. A Nationalist. Sat for Wexford Co. from June 1883 to Nov. 1885. Returned for Down S. Dec. 1885 and sat until he retired in 1886.   [1886]

SMALLWOOD, Edward. Lyndhurst, Lordship Park, Stoke Newington. National Liberal. S. of James and Mary Smallwood. B. at Birchwood 29 Aug. 1861; m. 1886, d. of Henry Fenemore, Esq., of Steeple Aston, Oxfordshire. Educ. at Doncaster Grammar School. J.P. for London from 1908; member of the London County Council for E. Islington. A Liberal and Radical. Elected MP for E. Islington 23 Oct. 1917 and sat until defeated in 1918. Unsuccessfully contested East Ham South in 1922 and 1923. First President of the Coal Merchants' Federation of Great Britain 1918-21; President of the London Brotherhood Movement 1925-26; National President 1928-29; Chairman of Society of Coal Merchants (London) 1934. Died 26 Feb. 1939.   [1918]

SMEATON, Donald Mackenzie, C.S.I. Reform. S. of D.J. Smeaton, Esq., of Leatham, Fife, and Elizabeth Charlotte Mackenzie. B. 9 Sept. 1848; m. 1st, 1873, Annette Louisa, d. of Sir H. Lushington, Bart. (she died 1880); 2ndly, 1894, Marion, d. of Maj. Ansell, 4th King's Own. Educ. at private school, and St. Andrew's University; M.A. Was in the Indian Civil Service, N.W. Provinces, 1868-87, Burma 1887-98; member of Viceroy's Legislative Council 1899-1902; C.S.I. 1895; K.I.H. 1900. Author of *Monograph on the Indian Currency*, *Karens of Burma*, and other works. Vice-President of Hampshire Liberal Federa-

tion. A Liberal. Elected for Stirlingshire in 1906 and sat until he retired in Jan. 1910. Died 19 Apr. 1910.   [1909]

SMILEY, Peter Kerr-. See KERR-SMILEY, Peter. Continued in House after 1918: full entry in Volume III.

SMITH, Abel. 35 Chesham Place, London. Woodhall Park, Hertford. Carlton, and Travellers'. S. of Abel Smith, Esq., of Woodhall Park, Hertfordshire (who sat for Hertfordshire from 1835 till 1847), by his 2nd wife, Frances Anne, d. of Sir Harry Calvert, Bart. Cousin to Lord Carrington. B. in Portland Place, London 1829; m. 1st, 1853, Lady Susan, 2nd d. of 3rd Earl of Chichester (she died 1875); 2ndly, 1877, Frances Julia, eld. d. of Sir Percival Hart Dyke, Bart. Educ. at Harrow, and at Trinity Coll., Cambridge, where he graduated B.A. A Conservative, in favour of local taxation being relieved out of the Imperial funds, and held that "the burdens now on land are very unjust." Sat for Hertfordshire from May 1854 till Apr. 1857, when he retired, and from May 1859 till July 1865, when he was unsuccessful; re-elected July 1866. On the Co. being divided 1885, he was elected to represent the E. division of Hertfordshire, and was MP until his death 31 May 1898.   [1898]

SMITH, Abel Henry. Woodhall Park, Hertford. Carlton, and Travellers'. Eld. s. of Abel Smith, Esq., MP for the Hertford division of Hertfordshire, by Lady Susan, d. of the 3rd Earl of Chichester. B. 1862; m. 1889, the Hon. Isabella, d. of the 2nd Lord Lurgan. Educ. at Eton, and Trinity Coll., Cambridge; B.A. 1884, M.A. 1888. Private Secretary (unpaid) to the Rt. Hon. Walter Long, President of the Board of Agriculture 1895-1900. A J.P. for Hertfordshire, and Maj. Hertfordshire Yeomanry from 1890. A Conservative. Sat for Christchurch from 1892-1900. Elected for the Hertford division of Hertfordshire in Oct. 1900 and sat until he retired in Jan. 1910. Alderman of Hertfordshire County Council. Died 10 Nov. 1930.   [1909]

SMITH, Albert. Continued in House after 1918: full entry in Volume III.

SMITH, Sir Clarence. 4 Queen Victoria Street, London. Chislehurst. Devonshire, City Liberal, and National Liberal. S. of the Rev. Gervase Smith, D.D. B. 1849 at

Wakefield; m. 1875, Mary, d. of William Webster, Esq., of Highbury. Educ. at Kingswood School. A member of the London Stock Exchange. Was Sheriff of London and Middlesex 1883; a Dept.-Lieut. for London and J.P. for Kent. A Liberal, in favour of Mr. Gladstone's scheme of Home Rule for Ireland, registration and electoral reform, shorter Parliaments, disestablishment for Wales and Scotland, etc. Unsuccessfully contested the W. division of Cambridgeshire 7 July 1886. Sat for the E. division of Hull from July 1892 until defeated in 1895. Unsuccessfully contested Bristol N. 4 Oct. 1900. Knighted in 1895. Afterwards Chairman of Eltham (Kent) Petty Sessions. Chairman of Star Life Insurance Society. Director of Ocean Accident Insurance Corporation. Died 10 June 1941.   [1895]

SMITH, David. Buckingham Palace Hotel, London. 11 Arundel Terrace, Brighton. Conservative, and Constitutional. Union, Brighton. S. of Alexander Smith, Esq., of Manor House, Camberwell, by Mary, d. of David Richardson, Esq., of London. B. in London 1826. Educ. in Scotland. Entered upon a mercantile career at an early age. Was in business for many years as a Colonial Merchant, and was first elected to the Town Council of Brighton in 1872. In 1877, he became Alderman, and was Mayor of the town in 1880-81. A J.P. for Brighton, and a Dept.-Lieut. for Sussex and the City of London. A Conservative. Sat for Brighton from Nov. 1885 until his death on 3 Nov. 1886.   [1886]

SMITH, Rt. Hon. Sir Frederick Edwin, Bart. Continued in House after 1918: full entry in Volume III.

SMITH, Harold. Continued in House after 1918: full entry in Volume III.

SMITH, Harry. Somerset House, Guildford. Reform. S. of Alexander Smith, Esq., of Glenmillan, Aberdeenshire, and Elizabeth, d. of William Lamond, Esq. B. about 1829; m. 1861, Julia Medina, d. of Col. Rice Jones, of the Royal Engineers, and K.H. Educ. at the University of Aberdeen, where he took the M.A. degree. Admitted an Advocate of the Scottish bar 1857. Was Sheriff Substitute for Renfrewshire, but resigned on becoming a Parliamentary candidate in 1885. An ad-

vanced Liberal and Home Ruler. Unsuccessfully contested W. Renfrewshire in 1885, and the Falkirk district in 1886. First returned for Falkirk district in July 1892 and sat until defeated in 1895. Died 29 Sept. 1910.   [1895]

SMITH, Hastings Bertrand Lees. See LEES-SMITH, Hastings Bertrand. Continued in House after 1918: full entry in Volume III.

SMITH, Hugh Crawford. 6 Osborne Terrace, Newcastle-on-Tyne. Northumberland, and Northern Counties'. S. of George Smith, Esq., of Glasgow, and Rosina, d. of Matthew Strang, Esq., of Kilmarnock. B. at Glasgow 1846; m. 1878, Hannah Ralston, 2nd d. of Robert Lockhart, Esq., of Newcastle. Educ. at the High School, Glasgow. A Director of Public Companies, J.P. for Northumberland and Newcastle-on-Tyne. A Liberal Unionist. Elected for the Tyneside division of Northumberland in 1900 and sat until he retired in 1906. Died 10 Sept. 1907.   [1905]

SMITH, Rt. Hon. James Parker. 20 Draycott Place, London. Jordanhill, Glasgow. Reform. New Club, Edinburgh, and Western Club, Glasgow. S. of Archibald Smith, Esq., F.R.S., and Susan Emma, d. of Vice-Chancellor Sir James Parker. B. 1854; m. 1882, Mary Louisa, d. of William Hamilton, Esq., of Minard and Partickhill. Educ. at Winchester, and Trinity Coll., Cambridge; 4th Wrangler, and 2nd Smith's Prizeman 1877; a Fellow of Winchester and Trinity Coll. Was called to the bar at Lincoln's Inn 1881, and joined the Oxford Circuit. A J.P., and Dept.-Lieut. for Renfrewshire, and the Co. of the city of Glasgow, J.P. for Lanarkshire, and Director of the Union Bank of Scotland. Was Parliamentary Private Secretary to Mr. J. Chamberlain, Colonial Secretary 1901. PC. 1904. A Liberal Unionist, opposed to the disestablishment of the Church. In 1886 he unsuccessfully contested Paisley. First elected for the Partick division of Lanarkshire in Feb. 1890 and sat until defeated in 1906. Contested Greenock in Jan. 1910. Died 30 Apr. 1929.   [1905]

SMITH, Samuel. Carleton, Prince's Park, Liverpool. Orchill, Braco, Perthshire. Eld. s. of James Smith, Esq., of South Carleton,

331

Borgue, Kircudbrightshire (a Magistrate for that Co.) B. at Roberton, Borgue, Kircudbrightshire 1836; m. 1864, Melville, d. of the Rev. John Christison, D.D., of Biggar, Lanarkshire (she died Mar. 1893). Educ. at Borgue Academy, and at the University of Edinburgh. A Merchant and Cotton Broker at Liverpool, where he commenced business in 1860, and founded the firm of Messrs. Smith, Edwards and Company, and in 1864 opened the firm of Messrs. James Finlay and Company in that city, and retired from it in 1883. Was President of the Liverpool Chamber of Commerce in 1876-77, and during four years a member of the Liverpool City Council. A Magistrate for Liverpool and for Kircudbrightshire. Published various essays on political and economical subjects, also a work on *The Credibility of the Christian Religion*. A Liberal, and a strong Protestant. Sat for the whole of Liverpool from 1882 to 1885. At the general election in 1885 he was defeated in the Abercromby division of Liverpool, but in Mar. 1886, whilst in India, he was returned for Flintshire and sat until he retired in Jan. 1906. Died 29 Dec. 1906. [1905]

SMITH, Sir Swire. Steeton Manor, Nr. Keighley. National Liberal. S. of George Smith, Esq., of Keighley. B. 4 Mar. 1842 at Keighley. Unmarried. Educ. privately, and at Wesley Coll., Sheffield. Member of Royal Commission on Technical Instruction 1881-84; Vice-Chairman Royal Commission on International Exhibitions 1909-12; Honorary Freeman, Clothworkers Company, London 1886; Warden 1914-15. J.P. for Yorkshire W. Riding, and Keighley. Honorary LL.D. Leeds 1912. Knighted 1898. Wrote pamphlets and articles on Technical Education, Free Trade, etc. A Liberal. Elected for the Keighley division of the W. Riding of Yorkshire in June 1915 and sat until his death 16 Mar. 1918. [1918]

SMITH, Thomas Malcolm Harvey Kincaid-. See KINCAID-SMITH, Thomas Malcolm Harvey.

SMITH, William. Cable Street, Lancaster. National Liberal. S. of Joseph and Mary Anne Smith. B. at Lancaster 1849; m. 1872, Ellen, d. of Henry Verity, Esq., of Lancaster. Educ. at Appleton Academy, near Warrington, and St. Joseph's Coll. A Corn Merchant and Miller, and a Port

Commissioner of Lancaster. President of the Lancashire Agricultural Society, and was Mayor of Lancaster 1891-92. A Radical, in favour of reform of the Land Laws, and of the House of Lords, the disestablishment of the Church in Wales and Scotland, payment to members of Parliament, etc. Sat for the N. Lonsdale division of Lancashire from July 1892 until he retired in 1895. Died 30 Oct. 1913. [1895]

SMITH, Hon. William Frederick Danvers. 3 Grosvenor Place, London. Greenlands, Henley-on-Thames. Carlton, and Wellington. S. of the Rt. Hon. W.H. Smith, MP, First Lord of the Treasury, and his wife, Emily Smith, d. of F. Dawes Danvers, Esq. (The dignity of a peerage was conferred upon Mrs. Smith, with the title Viscountess Hambleden, immediately after the death of the Rt. Hon. W.H. Smith). B. 1868 at Filey, Yorkshire; m. 1894, Esther, d. of the Earl of Arran. Educ. at Eton, and New Coll., Oxford. Was a Partner in the firm of W.H. Smith and Sons, Newsagents, etc., of the Strand from 1 Jan. 1890. A Dept.-Leiut. for Devon, and was Maj. Royal 1st Devon Imperial Yeomanry. A Conservative. First elected for Strand in Oct. 1891 and sat until he retired in Jan. 1910. Succeeded as Visct. Hambleden in 1913. Died 16 June 1928. [1909]

SMITH, Rt. Hon. William Henry. 3 Grosvenor Place, London. Greenlands, Henley-on-Thames. Carlton. S. of William Henry Smith, Esq., and Mary Ann, his wife. B. in Duke Street, Grosvenor Square, London 1825; m. 1858, Emily, eld. d. of Frederick Dawes Danvers, Esq. Head of the firm of Messrs. William Henry Smith and Son, the well-known newspaper agents, etc. Was Financial Secretary to the Treasury from Feb. 1874 to Aug. 1877, First Lord of the Admiralty from the latter date to Apr. 1880, Secretary of State for War 1885 to Jan. 1886, and again Aug. 1886. Chief Secretary for Ireland for a few days in Jan. 1886. In Jan. 1887 took the office of First Lord of the Treasury, in lieu of Secretary of War, and became also Leader of the House of Commons. A Magistrate for Hertfordshire, Liberty of St. Alban's, and a member of Council of King's Coll., London. Created D.C.L. at Oxford 1879. PC. 1877. A Liberal-Conservative, in favour of the amendment of taxation so as to lighten local rates, opposed to any plan for giving a separate Parliament to Ireland. Unsuccessfully contested Westminster July 1865. Sat for that city from Dec. 1868 to Nov. 1885 and for Strand from Nov. 1885 until his death on 6 Oct. 1891. Was Lord Warden of the Cinque Ports from May 1891.   [1891]

SMITH-BARRY, Rt. Hon. Arthur Hugh. See BARRY, Rt. Hon. Arthur Hugh Smith-.

SMITHWICK, John Francis. Retired in 1886: full entry in Volume I.

SMYTH, Thomas Francis. Mohill, Co. Leitrim. S. of William F. Smyth, Esq., Farmer. B. 8 May 1875 at Longford. Educ. at Longford and Clooneogh National Schools, and at St. Mel's Coll., Longford. An Auctioneer and Gen. Insurance Agent. A Nationalist. Elected for S. Leitrim in 1906 and sat until he retired in 1918. Died in Buenos Aires Dec. 1937.   [1918]

SNAPE, Thomas. The Gables, Croxteth Road, Liverpool. National Liberal. S. of Henry and Elizabeth Snape. B. 1835 at Salford; m. 1860, Sarah, younger d. of William and Sarah Lloyd, of Chirk, Denbighshire. Educ. privately at Salford. An Alkali Manufacturer. A member of the Lancashire Co. Council (Widnes) from its formation, Alderman in 1892; Chairman of the Technical Instruction Committee in the same council; Chairman House Committee Lancashire County Asylum; President Liverpool Peace Society; a Governor of University Coll., Liverpool, etc. Author of essays on *The Poetry of Mr. Swinburne*, *The Growth of Democratic Power*, etc. "A radical Liberal", in favour of Home Rule, disestablishment, the "Direct Veto", of Education, and reforms in Registration, Taxation, and the House of Lords. Sat for the Heywood division of Lancashire from July 1892 until defeated in 1895. Unsuccessfully contested S.E. Cornwall in Oct. 1900 and Wakefield in Jan. 1906. Magistrate for Lancashire. Died 9 Aug. 1912.
                                                    [1895]

SNOWDEN, Philip. Continued in House after 1918: full entry in Volume III.

SOAMES, Arthur Wellesley. 18 Park Crescent, London. Reform, and United University. S. of William Aldwin Soames, Esq., of Brighton. B. 1852; m. 1876, Eveline, d. of T. Horsman Coles, Esq., of Ore, Sussex. A Liberal, in favour of Home Rule, and other items in the advanced Liberal programme. Unsuccessfully contested Ipswich 1892 and 1895. Elected for S. Norfolk in 1898 and sat until he retired in 1918. Died 2 Nov. 1934.   [1918]

SOARES, Ernest Joseph. Upcott, Barnstaple, North Devon. Oxford & Cambridge, and National Liberal. S. of J.L.X. Soares, Esq., a Merchant in Liverpool, and Hannah, d. of John Hollingsworth, Esq., of Liverpool. B. 1864; m. 1893, Kate Carolyn, d. of Samuel Lord, Esq., of Oakleigh, Ashton-on-Mersey. Educ. privately, and at St. John's Coll., Cambridge; Exhibitioner and 1st Class Prizeman, B.A. and LL.B. with honours in law, and subsequently proceeding M.A. and LL.D. Admitted a Solicitor in 1888, and belonged to a leading firm of Solicitors, from which he retired. Was Parliamentary Private Secretary (unpaid) to Mr. H. Gladstone when Home Secretary. A Junior Lord of the Treasury (unpaid) and a Liberal Whip, appointed Feb. 1910. Represented Charity Commission in House of Commons 1908-10. A Liberal. Elected for the Barnstaple division of Devon in 1900 and sat until appointed Assistant Comptroller National Debt Office 1911-16. Knighted 1911. Died 15 Mar. 1926.   [1911]

SOMERVELL, James. Sorn Castle, Ayrshire. Conservative. New Club, Edinburgh, and Conservative, Glasgow. S. of Graham Somervell, Esq., of Sorn, and Henrietta Jane, d. of William Stirling, Esq. B. 1845. Educ. at Harrow and Oxford. Was called to the bar at the Inner Temple Nov. 1870. Capt. and Honorary Maj. Ayrshire Yeomanry 1868. A Conservative. Unsuccessfully contested Tradeston division of Glasgow in 1885. First returned for Ayr district Mar. 1890 and sat until defeated in 1892. Died 10 Feb. 1924.   [1892]

SOMERVELL, William Henry. Brantfield, Kendal, Westmoreland. S. of John Somervell of Kendal. B. 5 Apr. 1860 in Kendal; m. 1889, Florence, d. of Theodore Howard. Educ. at Grove House School, Tottenham. A J.P. for Westmoreland and Kendal. Director of Somervell Brothers (Kendal) Limited. A Liberal. Unsuccessfully contested the Kendal division of Westmoreland Dec. 1910 and Mar. 1913. Returned for the Keighley division of

333

the W. Riding of Yorkshire at a by-election in Apr. 1918 and sat until defeated in Dec. 1918. Died 26 Sept. 1934.

SOUTTAR, Robinson. 24 Penywern Road, London. Reform. S. of William Souttar, Esq., of Edenville, Aberdeen, and Mary Souttar. B. 23 Oct. 1848 at Aberdeen; m. 1873, d. of Philip Dixon Hardy, Esq., member of the Royal Irish Academy, Dublin. Educ. at the Gymnasium Aberdeen, and Oxford University, Non. Coll. (M.A., B.C.L.) A Civil Engineer, apprenticed 1862; retired 1884. Vice-President of the National Council of the Y.M.C.A. A Liberal, in favour of Home Rule, etc. In 1892 he unsuccessfully contested Oxford against Gen. Sir George Chesney. Sat for Dumfriesshire from July 1895 until defeated in 1900. Author of *Glimpses of our Empire, Alcohol, its Place and Power in Legislation* (1904), etc. Died 4 Apr. 1912. [1900]

SPEAR, Sir John Ward. St. Stephens, Westminster, and Venn, Tavistock, Devon. S. of John Spear, Esq., Yeoman, of Eastcott, Milton Abbott. B. 1848 at Eastcott, Tavistock; m. 1877, d. of John Willcock, Esq., of Kingsbridge, Devon. Educ. at Milton Abbott, and in Bodmin, Cornwall. A Tenant Farmer and Yeoman. Chairman of Tavistock District Council and a member of the Board of Guardians; an Alderman of Devon County Council and a J.P. for Devonshire. President of the Poor Law Union Association of England and Wales. Knighted 1911. A Unionist. Sat for the Tavistock division of Devon from 1900 to 1906, when he was defeated; unsuccessfully contested that constituency in Jan. 1910; re-elected there Dec. 1910 and sat until he retired in 1918. Died 27 Apr. 1921. [1918]

SPENCER, Rt. Hon. Charles Robert. 28 St. James's Place, London. Dallington House, Northampton. Turf, Brooks's, and Marlborough. S. of Frederick, 4th Earl Spencer, and Adelaide Horatia Elizabeth, d. of Sir Horace Seymour, K.C.H. B. at Spencer House, St. James's 1857; m. 1887, Hon. Margaret, 2nd d. of Edward Charles, 1st Lord Revelstoke. Educ. at Harrow, and Trinity Coll., Cambridge; M.A. 1883. J.P., and Dept.-Lieut. for Northamptonshire; Honorary Maj. 1st Volunteer Battalion of Northamptonshire Regiment from 1896. Was Heir Presumptive to Earl Spencer. Was Parliamentary Groom-in-Waiting 1886; Vice-Chamberlain 1892-95; Privy Councillor 1892. A Liberal. A Liberal Whip 1900-05. Sat as Member for N. Northamptonshire 1880-85, and for mid Northamptonshire 1885-95, when he was defeated; unsuccessfully contested E. Hertfordshire 1898. Elected again for mid Northamptonshire in 1900 and sat until created Visct. Althorp in 1905. Lord Chamberlain 1905-12. Grand Cross, Danebrog 1906 (a Danish award). Lord-Lieut. of Northamptonshire from 1908. Succeeded half-bro. as 6th Earl Spencer in 1910 G.C.V.O. 1911; K.G. 1913. Died 26 Sept. 1922. [1905]

SPENCER, Sir James Ernest. 1 Dr. Johnson's Buildings, Temple, London. 10 St. James's Place, London. Warren Mount, Oxshott, Surrey. Carlton. S. of John Spencer, Esq., of West Bromwich. B. 1848 at Phoenix House, West Bromwich; m. Helen, only child of Thomas Williamson, Esq., of the Bombay Civil Service. Educ. privately. In 1885 was called to the bar at the Middle Temple, and joined the Oxford Circuit. Was Counsel to the Austrian Consulate. J.P. and Dept.-Lieut. of Staffordshire. Knighted 1901. A Conservative-Unionist. Unsuccessfully contested West Bromwich in 1885. First elected for West Bromwich in 1886 and sat until he retired in 1906. Died 29 June 1937. [1905]

SPENDER-CLAY, Capt. Herbert Henry. Continued in House after 1918: full entry in Volume III.

SPENSLEY, Howard. 12 Earl's Court Square, South Kensington, London. Harecourt, Temple, London. Eld. s. of William Spensley, Esq., of London. B. 1834; m. 1868. At an early age he went to Australia. Here, while studying for the bar, he became a writer for the press. In 1864 he was called to the bar in Victoria. In 1871 he was elected to the Legislative Assembly of Victoria, and shortly afterwards was appointed Solicitor-Gen. in Mr. (later Sir) Charles Gavan Duffy's administration. In 1873 he returned to England, and was appointed representative of the Colony of Victoria at the Exhibition of 1873. In 1876 he was called to the English bar at the Middle Temple. Acted as representative of Victoria at the Geographical Congress of Venice (1881), and at the Exhibition of Amsterdam (1883). In connection with the first of these posts he was made a Knight of the Order of the Cross of Italy, by King Humbert. A F.R.G.S., and a Fellow of the Statistical Society. An "advanced Liberal." Sat for the Central division of Finsbury from Nov. 1885 until he was defeated in 1886 standing as a Gladstonian Liberal. Unsuccessfully contested Dudley in July 1892. Died 8 Aug. 1902.   [1886]

SPICER, Rt. Hon. Sir Albert, Bart. 10 Lancaster Gate, London. Reform, City Liberal, British Empire, and National Liberal. S. of J. Spicer, Esq., J.P., and Dept.-Lieut. of Woodford. B. 1847 at Brixton; m. 1879, Jessie, d. of D. Stewart Dykes, Esq., of Grove Hill, Surrey. Educ. at Mill Hill School, and in Germany. Chairman of James Spicer and Sons Limited, Paper Warehousemen and Manufacturers. President of London Chamber of Commerce 1907-10; a member of Commercial Intelligence Advisory Committee of the Board of Trade; Chairman of Court of Governors of Mill Hill School; member of Advisory Committee on Spiritual and Moral Welfare of the army, and on the care of Recruits and Time-expired Men; Treasurer of London Missionary Society 1885-1910; First Lay Chairman of Congregational Union of England and Wales; Vice-Chairman of State Children's Association 1907 to 1917. A J.P. for Essex. Created Bart. 1906; PC. 1912. A Liberal. Unsuccessfully contested Walthamstow 1886; sat for Monmouth Boroughs from 1892-1900 when he was defeated; unsuccessfully contested Monmouth Boroughs May 1901; elected for Central Hackney in 1906 and sat until he retired in 1918. Retired from the Papermaking business (Spicer Brothers Limited) at the end of 1924 after a career of 60 years in the City. Died 20 Dec. 1934.   [1918]

SPICER, Henry. 14 Aberdeen Park, Highbury, London. New Bridge Street, Blackfriars, London. S. of Henry Spicer, Esq., one of the founders of a well-known Wholesale Stationers. B. at Barnsbury 1837; m. d. of the Rev. Dr. Mullens of the London Missionary Society. Educ. at Mill Hill Grammar School, and New Coll., St. John's Wood, graduating as B.A. at the London University. A member of the firm of Spicer Brothers, Wholesale Stationers. A member of the School Board from 1879, and Chairman of its Industrial Schools Committee. A member of the

Fishmongers' Company, also a Fellow of the Geographical and Zoological Societies, and a Magistrate for Middlesex. A Liberal. Sat for Islington S. from Nov. 1885 until defeated in 1886 standing as a Gladstonian Liberal. Died 18 Oct. 1915.   [1886]

STACK, John. Listowel, Co. Kerry. A native of Listowel, a Farmer, and also in business as a Draper. Educ. privately. President of the Listowel Branch of the National League. An "Irish Nationalist" (Anti-Parnellite). Sat for Kerry N. from the general election of 1885 until he retired in 1892. Died 5 Mar. 1897.   [1892]

STAFFORD, Cromartie Sutherland-Leveson-Gower, Marq. of. Retired in 1886: full entry in Volume I, under STAFFORD, Marq. of. (II).

STANGER, Henry Yorke. New Court, Temple, London. Hill Brow, Northwood, Middlesex. Reform. S. of George Eaton Stanger, Esq., Surgeon, of Nottingham. B. 11 Nov. 1849 at Nottingham; m. 1880, Henrietta Sophia, d. of the Rev. J.W. Green, Rector of March. Educ. privately, and at Lincoln Coll., Oxford; Sen. Class. Sch. 1868; 1st Cl. Final Class. Sch. 1872. Was called to the bar at Lincoln's Inn 1874 and joined the Midland Circuit; Q.C. 1895; bencher 1898; a revising Barrister for Warwickshire 1892-95; a member of Council of the bar 1902-05. A Liberal. Unsuccessfully contested S. Nottingham in Oct. 1900 and the Newark division of Nottinghamshire in Feb. 1900. Elected for N. Kensington in 1906 and sat until he retired in Jan. 1910. County Court Judge 1910-22. Died 19 Apr. 1929.   [1909]

STANHOPE, Rt. Hon. Edward. 111 Eaton Square, London. Revesby Abbey, Boston, Lincolnshire. Carlton, and Athenaeum. 2nd s. of the 5th Earl Stanhope, by Emily Harriet, 2nd d. of Sir Edward Kerrison, Bart. B. in London 1840; m. 1870, Lucy Constance, youngest d. of the Rev. Thomas Egerton, and niece of Lord Egerton, of Tatton. Was educ. at Harrow, and Christ Church, Oxford; obtained a first class in mathematics at the 1st public examination Dec. 1861; graduated B.A. 1862, M.A. 1865; elected Fellow of All Souls' Coll. 1862. Was called to the bar at the Inner Temple 1865 and joined the Home Circuit. Was one of the Assistant-Commissioners of the Employment

of Women and Children in Agriculture 1867. Was (Parliamentary) Secretary to the Board of Trade from Nov. 1875 to Apr. 1878, and Under-Secretary of State for India from the latter date to Apr. 1880. He was Vice-President of the Committee of Council on Education from June to Aug. 1885, President of the Board of Trade from the latter date to Jan. 1886, Colonial Secretary Aug. 1886, and Secretary of State for War Jan. 1887 to 1892. PC. 1885. A Conservative. Sat for Mid Lincolnshire from Feb. 1874 to Nov. 1885, and for the Horncastle division of Lincolnshire from Nov. 1885 until his death on 21 Dec. 1893.
[1893]

STANHOPE, Hon. Philip James. 3 Carlton Gardens, London. National Liberal, Turf, St. James's, and Devonshire. 4th s. of the 5th Earl of Stanhope. B. in London 8 Dec. 1847; m. 1877, Alexandra, d. of Count Cancrine and widow of Count Tolstoy. Educ. privately. Served in the navy 1862-67. Chairman of National Reform Union and of British Group of Inter-Parliamentary Union. An advanced Liberal. Unsuccessfully contested Dover in 1880 and Wednesbury Nov. 1885. Sat for Wednesbury 1886-92, when he was defeated, and for Burnley 1893-1900, when he was again defeated. Elected for the Market Harborough division of Leicestershire in June 1904 and sat until he was nominated for a Peerage in Dec. 1905. Created Baron Weardale in Jan. 1906. Died 1 Mar. 1923.
[1905]

STANIER, Sir Beville, Bart. Continued in House after 1918: full entry in Volume III.

STANLEY, Albert. Woods Eaves, Hednesford, Staffordshire. National Liberal. B. 1862 at Dark Lane, Salop; m. 1882. Educ. at National School. A Miners' Agent for Cannock Chase Miners' Association from 1886, Secretary of the Midland Miners' Federation, and a member of the Joint Conciliation Board of Coalowners and Miners. A member of Staffordshire County Council from its formation. J.P. for Staffordshire. A Labour Member. Elected for N.W. Staffordshire on 31 July 1907 and sat until his death on 17 Dec. 1915. [1915]

STANLEY, Rt. Hon. Sir Albert Henry. Continued in House after 1918: full entry in Volume III.

STANLEY, Hon. Sir Arthur, C.B., G.B.E., M.V.O. Treasurer's House, St. Thomas's Hospital, London. 50 Upper Brook Street, London. Carlton, Royal Automobile, and Turf. S. of 16th Earl of Derby, and bro. of Lord Stanley, MP for the W. Houghton division of Lancashire. B. 1869. Educ. at Wellington Coll. Was in the Diplomatic Service, also a Clerk in the Foreign Office, and Private Secretary to the Rt. Hon. A.J. Balfour, when First Lord of the Treasury. M.V.O. 1905. Knight of Justice of St. John of Jerusalem. In the Diplomatic Service under Lord Cromer at Cairo 1895-1898, when he was elected MP. A Conservative and Unionist, and strongly supported both the domestic and foreign policies of Mr. Balfour. Elected for the Ormskirk division of S.W. Lancashire in 1898 and sat until he retired in 1918. C.B. 1916; G.B.E. 1917. Chairman of the R.A.C. 1905-07 and 1912-36; Chairman of the Executive Committee of the British Red Cross 1914-43. G.C.V.O. 1944. Died 4 Nov. 1947. [1918]

STANLEY, Hon. Arthur Lyulph. 26 St. Leonard's Terrace, Chelsea, London. Brooks's, and Travellers'. Eld. s. of Lord Stanley of Alderly. B. 14 Sept. 1875 in London; m. 1905, Margaret, d. of H. Evans Gordon, Esq. Educ. at Eton, and Balliol Coll., Oxford. A Barrister, called to the bar at the Inner Temple 1902. A member of London County Council for Lewisham 1904-07. Served in S. Africa 1900. Parliamentary Private Secretary (unpaid) to Mr. S. Buxton, Postmaster-Gen. A Liberal. Elected for the Eddisbury division of Cheshire in 1906 and sat until defeated in Jan. 1910. Contested the Eddisbury division of Cheshire again in Dec. 1910, Oldham in Nov. 1911 and the Knutsford division of Cheshire in 1923. K.C.M.G. 1914. Succeeded as 5th Baron Sheffield and 5th Baron Stanley of Alderly in 1925. Died 22 Aug. 1931. [1909]

STANLEY, Hon. Edward George Villiers. See STANLEY, Rt. Hon. Edward George Villiers Stanley, Lord.

STANLEY, Rt. Hon. Edward George Villiers Stanley, Lord. 36 Great Cumberland Place, London. Coworth Park, Sunningdale. Turf, Carlton, Guards', and Marlborough. Eld. s. of the 16th Earl of Derby, by Lady Constance, d. of the Earl of Clarendon. B. in London 1865: m. 1889,

Lady Alice Montagu, youngest d. of the 7th Duke of Manchester. Educ. at Wellington Coll. Was Junior Lord of the Treasury 1895-1900; Financial Secretary to the War Office 1900-03; Postmaster-Gen. Oct. 1903-Dec. 1905; Lieut. Grenadier Guards 1885-95; Aide-de-Camp to his father as Governor-Gen. of Canada, Aug. 1889 to July 1891. Served in S. African War, first as Chief Press Censor, afterwards as Private Secretary to Lord Roberts. PC. 1903. Styled Lord Stanley from his father's succession to the Earldom in 1893 until his own succession in 1908. A Conservative. Sat for the Westhoughton division of Lancashire S.E. from 1892 until defeated in 1906. Succeeded as 17th Earl of Derby in 1908; Director-Gen. of Recruiting 1915-16; Under Secretary for War 1916: Secretary of States for War 1916-18 and 1922-24; Ambassador to France 1918-20. C.B. 1900; K.C.V.O. 1905; G.C.V.O. 1908; K.G. 1914: G.C.B. 1920. Died 4 Feb. 1948.   [1905]

STANLEY, Edward James. Quantock Lodge, Bridgwater. Carlton, and Travellers'. Eld. s. of Edward Stanley, Esq., of Crosshall, Lancashire, by Lady Mary, 2nd d. of the 8th Earl of Lauderdale. B. at Geneva, Switzerland 1826; m. 1872, Hon. Mary, eld. d. of Baron Taunton. Educ. at Eton, and at Christ Church, Oxford; graduated B.A. 1849 and subsequently M.A. A Dept.-Lieut. for Lancashire and Somerset, and a Magistrate for Somerset, and served the office of High Sheriff of the latter in 1880. A Conservative, in favour of great change being made in our system of local taxation. Sat for W. Somerset from Apr. 1882 to Nov. 1885, and for the Bridgwater division of Somerset from Nov. 1885 until he retired in 1906. Died 29 Sept. 1907.   [1905]

STANLEY, Edward Montagu Cavendish Stanley, Lord. Continued in House after 1918: full entry in Volume III.

STANLEY, Rt. Hon. Sir Frederick Arthur, G.C.B. Retired in 1886: full entry in Volume I.

STANLEY, Hon. George Frederick, C.M.G. Continued in House after 1918: full entry in Volume III.

STANLEY, Sir Henry Morton, G.C.B. 2 Richmond Terrace, Whitehall, London. Cadoxton Lodge, Neath, Glamorganshire. S. of Mr. Rowlands, of Denbigh, Wales. B. 1841; m. 1890, Miss Dorothy Tennant. At an early age he emigrated to New Orleans, where he was adopted by Mr. Stanley, a Merchant, whose name he adopted. He joined the Confederates in the Civil War, and was taken prisoner; and he then served in the Federal army, and also in the navy. In 1868 he was a "special correspondent", reporting Hancock and Sherman's campaigns. In 1868 he served in the same way with the British army in Abyssinia. After this war the *New York Herald* sent him on an expedition through Spain, Crete, Turkey, Egypt, and Persia. In 1871 he started on his search for Dr. Livingstone, whom he "found", describing the fact in the first of his famous books, *How I found Livingstone*. In 1873 he reported the Ashantee war for the *New York Herald*, and from 1874 to 1878 was engaged in his great expedition to the African Lakes. Journeys through the Congo State and another for the relief of Emin Pasha followed. In 1885 he represented America at the Berlin Conference on African affairs. He received gold medals for his discoveries from the leading learned societies; was an Honorary D.C.L. Oxford and LL.D. Cambridge. Was created G.C.B. 1899. A Liberal Unionist. Unsuccessfully contested Lambeth N. in 1892. Sat for Lambeth N. from July 1895 until he retired in 1900. Died 10 May 1904.   [1900]

STANSFELD, Rt. Hon. Sir James. Stoke Lodge, Hyde Park Gate, London. Castle Hill, Rotherfield, Sussex. Athenaeum, Reform, and Devonshire. S. of James Stansfeld, Esq., a Solicitor, and afterwards Judge of the County Court at Halifax, by Emma, d. of the Rev. John Ralph, of Halifax. B. at Halifax 1820; m. 1st, 1844, Caroline, d. of William Henry Ashurst, Esq., of London, Solicitor; 2ndly, 1887, Frances, widow of H.A. Severn, Esq., of Sydney, New South Wales. Educ. at University Coll., London. Called to the bar at the Inner Temple 1849. Was a Lord of the Admiralty from Apr. 1863 till Apr. 1864, Under-Secretary for India from Feb. till July 1866, a Lord of the Treasury from Dec. 1868 to Nov. 1869, President of the Poor Law Board from Mar. 1871 to Aug. following, when he became President of the Local Government Board, resigned Feb. 1874. Was again appointed to the latter office upon the resignation of Mr.

Chamberlain, Mar. 1886, and held office until July 1886. A Radical and Home Ruler. Sat for Halifax from Apr. 1859 until he retired in 1895. PC. 1869. G.C.B. 1895. Died 17 Feb. 1898.   [1895]

STANTON, Charles Butt. Continued in House after 1918: full entry in Volume III.

STARKEY, John Ralph. Continued in House after 1918: full entry in Volume III.

STAVELEY-HILL, Lieut.-Col. Henry Staveley. Oxley Manor, Nr. Wolverhampton. Carlton, Junior Carlton, and Junior Constitutional. S. of the Rt. Hon. Alexander Staveley-Hill, MP, and Katherine, d. of Miles Ponsonby, Esq., Dept.-Lieut. of Hale Hall, Cumberland. B. 22 May 1865; m. 1901, Eileen de Grey, d. of de Burgh d'Arcy. Educ. at Westminster, and St. John's Coll., Oxford. Assumed by Royal Licence the additional surname of Staveley, 1906. A Barrister, called to the bar at the Inner Temple 1891, and joined the Oxford Circuit; a J.P. and Dept.-Lieut. for Staffordshire. Capt. Staffordshire Yeomanry; later Lieut.-Col. commanding 2/1st Staffordshire Yeomanry (mentioned in despatches). Recorder of Banbury from 1903; member of the Cannock Rural District Council and Board of Guardians. Travelled in Canada, Australasia, and Europe. A Referee of Private Bills. Chairman of United Club 1910-12. Member of Dept. Committee on Agricultural Education 1907. A Conservative, interested in all questions connected with the administration of the Poor Law and Licensing. Elected for the Kingswinford division of Staffordshire in July 1905 and sat until he retired in 1918. County Court Judge 1922-28. County Councillor for Staffordshire. Died 25 Mar. 1946.   [1918]

STEADMAN, William Charles. 69 Thornton Avenue, Turnham Green, London. New Reform. S. of William and Jane Steadman. B. 12 July 1851 at Poplar; m. 1875, Jessie, d. of William Wall, Esq. Educ. at Poplar National School, and evening classes at Battersea. Was apprenticed in 1866 to the Barge-Building trade and became Secretary to the Barge-Builders' Union; Secretary to the Parliamentary Committee of Trades Union Congress; a member of the London County Council for Stepney 1892-1907. J.P. for the Co. of London. A Liberal and Labour Member.

Unsuccessfully contested mid-Kent 1892 and Hammersmith 1895. Sat for the Stepney division of Tower Hamlets from 1898-1900, when he was defeated. Elected for central Finsbury in 1906 and sat until defeated in Jan. 1910. Died 21 July 1911.   [1909]

STEEL-MAITLAND, Sir Arthur Herbert Drummond Ramsay, Bart. Continued in House after 1918: full entry in Volume III.

STEPHENS, Henry Charles. 7 Buckingham Gate, London. Avenue House, Church End, Finchley, London. Cholderton, Wiltshire. Carlton, and Junior Carlton. S. of Henry Stephens, Esq., Surgeon, by Anne, d. of Michael O'Reilly, Esq. B. in London 1841; m. 1863, Agnes, d. of George Wilson Mackreth, Esq. Educ. at University Coll., London. Was Proprietor of the well-known Stephen's Writing Inks, Aldersgate Street, London. A Fellow of the Chemical, Linnaean, and Geographical Societies. Alderman of the County Council for Middlesex, and J.P. for Middlesex and Wiltshire. Author of *Parochial Self-Government in Rural Districts*. A Conservative, a firm supporter of the Union of the Empire and of Church and State. Sat for the Hornsey division of Middlesex from 19 July 1887 until he retired in 1900. Died July 1918.   [1900]

STEPNEY, Sir Emile Algernon Arthur Keppel Cowell, Bart. See COWELL-STEPNEY, Sir Emile Algernon Arthur Keppel, Bart.

STERN, Sydney James. 10 Great Stanhope Street, London. Hengrave Hall, Bury St. Edmunds. Reform, St. James's, and Bachelors'. Eld. s. of Visct. de Stern, of London, by Sophia, d. of A.A. Goldsmid, Esq., of Cavendish Square, and niece of Sir Issac Lyon Goldsmid, Bart. B. 1844. Educ. at Magdalene Coll., Cambridge. Honorary Col. of the 4th Volunteer Battalion E. Surrey Regiment, and a Magistrate for the counties of Surrey and London. A Liberal, in favour of Home Rule for Ireland. Contested Mid Surrey in 1880 and 1884, Tiverton in 1885, and Ipswich in 1886. First elected for Suffolk N.W. on 5 May 1891 and and sat until he retired in 1895. Created Baron Wandsworth in 1895. Visct. de Stern in the peerage of Portugal. Died 10 Feb. 1912.   [1895]

STEVENSON, Francis Seymour. 5 Ennismore Gardens, London. Playford Mount, Nr. Woodbridge, Suffolk. Athenaeum, Reform, and Devonshire. S. of Sir William Stevenson, K.C.B., Governor of Mauritius, by Caroline Octavia, d. of Joseph Seymour Biscoe, Esq., and afterwards wife of the Rev. F. Barham Zincke. B. 1862; m. 1889, Mary Kate, d. of Edward Joicey, Esq., J.P., of Blenkinsopp Hall, Northumberland. Educ. at Wherstead, Lausanne, Harrow, and Balliol Coll., Oxford, where he took a 1st class in classics. A J.P. for Suffolk, and Alderman E. Suffolk County Council, also Dept.-Lieut. for the Co. Was Parliamentary Charity Commissioner 1894-95. Served on the King's Civil List Committee 1901. President of the Anglo-Armenian Association. Author of *Historic Personality*, the *Life of Grosseteste, Bishop of Lincoln*, and *History of Montenegro* (1912). An advanced Liberal. Sat for the Eye division of Suffolk from 1885 until he accepted Chiltern Hundreds in Mar. 1906. Died 9 Apr. 1938.   [1905]

STEVENSON, James Cochran. 33 Devonshire Place, London. Westoe, South Shields. Reform. S. of James Stevenson, Esq., Merchant, of Glasgow (Senior Partner in the Jarrow Chemical Company, South Shields), by Jane Stewart, d. of Alexander Shannan, Esq., Merchant, of Greenock. B. at Glasgow 1825; m. 1855, Elisa Ramsay, d. of the Rev. James Anderson, D.D., of Morpeth. Educ. at the High School, and at the University of Glasgow. A Vice-Chairman of the United Alkali Company Limited; one of the Life Commissioners appointed by the Tyne Improvement Act of 1850, and Chairman of the Board; also one of the Tyne Pilotage Commissioners; Lieut.-Col. Commandant 3rd Durham Artillery Volunteers; a member of the General Council of the University of Glasgow, and a member of the Institute of Chemistry. A Liberal and Home Ruler. Sat for South Shields from Dec. 1868 until he retired in 1895. Died 11 Jan. 1905.   [1895]

STEWART, Gershom. Continued in House after 1918: full entry in Volume III.

STEWART, Halley. The Red House, Harpenden, Hertfordshire. National, and New Reform. S. of the Rev. A. Stewart, Congregational Minister, Barnet. B. 1838; m. 1865, Jane Elizabeth, d. of Joseph Atkinson, Esq., of Norwood. Educ. at his father's school. Chairman of B.J. Forder and Son Limited, Cement Manufacturers. Founder and first editor of *Hastings and St. Leonards Times*. Chairman of Mansfield House University Settlement, Canning Town. J.P. for Sussex. An advanced Liberal. Advocated adult suffrage for both sexes, religious equality, the land for the people, and abolition of hereditary legislators. Unsuccessfully contested the Spalding division of Lincolnshire in 1885, 1886, 1895, and Peterborough in 1900. Sat for the Spalding division of Lincolnshire from 1887 until defeated 1895. Elected for Greenock in 1906 and sat until he retired in Jan. 1910. Knighted 1932. Died 26 Jan. 1937.   [1909]

STEWART, Sir Mark John, Bart. See MACTAGGART-STEWART, Sir Mark John, Bart.

STEWART-SMITH, Dudley. 31 Norfolk Square, Hyde Park, London. 3 New Square, Lincoln's Inn, London. Reform, and Junior Athenaeum. S. of Alexander Stewart-Smith, Esq., of London and Hong Kong, and Susanna, d. of James Laming, Esq., of Birchington Hall, Kent. B. 1857 in London; m. 1892, Katherine, d. of Henry Cautley, Esq., of Burton Pidsea, Yorkshire. Educ. at Isleworth Coll., London, University Coll., and London University; LL.B. Admitted a Solicitor in 1879; called to the bar 1886; K.C. 1902; author of a treatise on the Companies' Acts. A member of the Royal Commission on Land Transfer. A Liberal. Elected for the Kendal division of Westmoreland in 1906 and sat until defeated in Jan. 1910. Contested E. Nottingham in Dec. 1910. Knighted 1917. Died 9 May 1919.   [1909]

STIRLING, Lieut.-Col. Archibald. Keir Dunblane, Scotland. Cawdor, Bishopbriggs, Nr. Glasgow. Guards', Turf, and Travellers'. 2nd s. of Sir William Stirling Maxwell, 9th Bart., and Lady Anna Maria, 2nd d. of the 10th Earl of Leven and Melville. B. 1867 at Keir, Dunblane, Scotland; m. Hon. Margaret Fraser, d. of the 15th Lord Lovat. Educ. at Eton, and Cambridge. A member of Scots Guards 1889; served in Egyptian Army 1899-1900 (medal with clasps, Soudan); South Africa 1900-02, (S. African medal, three clasps; King's medal, two clasps); Capt. Reserve of Officers, from 1903; commanded 2nd Lovat Scouts; commanded Highland

Mounted Brigade; served in Gallipoli and Egypt 1915-16, mentioned in despatches. A Unionist. Elected for W. Perthshire 21 Feb. 1917 and sat until he unsuccessfully contested Kinross and W. Perthshire in 1918. Died 18 Feb. 1931.   [1918]

STIRLING-MAXWELL, Sir John Maxwell, Bart. 48 Belgrave Square, London. Pollok House, Pollokshaws, N.B. Carlton, White's, and Bachelors'. Was the 10th Bart., eld s. of Sir Willing Stirling-Maxwell, K.T., 9th Bart., by his 1st wife, Lady Anna, d. of David, 10th Earl of Leven and Melville. B. 1866 at Park Street, London; m. 1901, Christian, d. of the Rt. Hon. Sir Herbert Maxwell. Educ. at Eton, and Trinity Coll., Cambridge. Was Private Secretary to Lord Knutsford as Colonial Secretary 1887-92, and was Honorary Col. 3rd Lanarkshire Volunteers. A Dept.-Lieut. for the counties of Inverness, Renfrew, Glasgow, and Lanark. Succeeded as Bart. in 1878. A Conservative and Unionist, opposed to Home Rule, the Disestablishment of the Church, and the Local Veto Bill; in favour of legislation on Employers' Liability, Control of Licenses, Old Age Pensions, etc. Unsuccessfully contested the Coll. division of Glasgow in 1892. Represented the Coll. division of Glasgow from 1895 until defeated in 1906, standing as Conservative Free Trader. Unsuccessfully contested that seat again in Jan. 1910. K.T. 1929. Chairman of Royal Fine Art Commission for Scotland. Chairman of Ancient Monuments Board for Scotland. Chairman of Forestry Commission 1929-32. Died 30 May 1956.   [1905]

STOCK, James Henry. 16 Basil Mansions, London. White Hall, Tarporley, Cheshire. Knolle Park, Woolton, Lancashire. Glenapp Castle, Ballantrae, N.B. Arthur's, Carlton, Hurlingham, and Wellington. S. of John Stock, Esq., of Knolle Park, Woolton, Co. Lancaster, by Lydia, d. of Peter Wedd, Esq., of Boston, Lincolnshire. B. Dec. 1855 at Westdale, Wavertree, Co. Lancaster; m. 1880, May Sabina, 2nd d. of the Rt. Hon. Arthur MacMurrough Kavanagh, Lord-Lieut. Co. Carlow, MP from 1868-80. Educ., owing to delicate health, by a private tutor, and afterwards at Christ Church, Oxford; B.A. and M.A. 1882. A Barrister, called to the bar 1882; J.P. for Cheshire: Maj. Lancashire Hussars. A Conservative, strongly supported the Unionist policy of Mr. Balfour. Rep-

resented the Walton division of Liverpool from 1892 until he retired in 1906. Died 14 June 1907.   [1905]

STOKER, Robert Burdon. Continued in House after 1918: full entry in Volume III.

STOKES, Sir George Gabriel, Bart. Lensfield Cottage, Cambridge. Athenaeum. S. of the Rev. Gabriel Stokes, Rector of Skreen, Co. Sligo, and Elizabeth, d. of the Rev. John Haughton, Rector of Kilrea, Co. Derry. B. 1819 at Skreen; m. 1857, Mary Susanna, d. of the Rev. T. Romney Robinson, D.D., of the Observatory, Armagh. Educ. at Dr. Wall's School, Dublin, Bristol Coll., and Pembroke Coll., Cambridge. Was elected Lucasian Professor of Mathematics, Cambridge 1849; Fellow of Pembroke Coll., 1841-57, and from 1868. Was Secretary of the Royal Society 1854 to 1885 and President from 1885. Was President of the British Association 1869. Author of *Memoirs in Transactions Cambridge Philosophical Soc., Royal Soc.*, etc. was made a Bart. May 1889. A Conservative, but aimed at representing the University rather than any party; "opposed to Home Rule for Ireland; in favour of Church Reform, but against disestablishment." First returned for Cambridge University Nov. 1887 and sat until he retired in 1892. Elected Master of Pembroke Coll. in 1902. Died 1 Feb. 1903.   [1892]

STONE, Sir John Benjamin. The Grange, Erdington, Warwickshire. Midland Grand Hotel, St. Pancras, London. Carlton. S. of Benjamin Stone, Esq., of Aston Manor, by Rebecca, d. of Richard Matthews, Esq., of Cookley, Co. Worcester. B. at Birmingham 1838; m. 1867, Jane, d. of Peter Parker, Esq., of Lothersdale, Yorkshire. Educ. at King Edward VI's Grammar School. Was for a long time a prominent public man in Birmingham and the Chairman of the Conservative party there. High Steward of Sutton Coldfield, a J.P., and Mayor of Sutton Coldfield. Knighted 1892. Travelled in Europe, Asia, Africa, and South America, and published several books, including a *History of Lichfield Cathedral*. A Commissioner for St. Louis Exhibition, 1904. Also a Fellow of the Geological Society, F.L.S., etc. A Conservative. Represented Birmingham E. from 1895 until he retired in Jan. 1910. Official Photographer for 1911 Coronation. Died 2 July 1914.   [1909]

STOPFORD-SACKVILLE, Col. Sackville George. Drayton House, Thrapston, Carlton, and Travellers'. Eld. s. of William Bruce Stopford-Sackville and Caroline Harriet, d. of the Hon. George Germain. B. in London 1840; m. 1875, Edith Frances, only child of William Rashleigh, Esq., of Menabilly, Cornwall, and grand-d. of the 11th Baron Blantyre. Educ. at Eton, and Christ Church, Oxford; B.A. 1862, M.A. 1865. He entered the Diplomatic Service in 1865 and was employed in the Foreign Office and as an Attaché at Lisbon, resigned in 1867. A J.P. and Dept.-Lieut. for Northamptonshire, Chairman of Quarter Sessions 1891-1904: Chairman of the County Council from 1893; held a commission for nearly forty years in the 3rd Battalion (Militia) of the Northamptonshire Regiment, of which he was Honorary Col. A Conservative. He unsuccessfully contested Northampton 1865; returned for N. Northamptonshire at a by-election in 1867 and continued to represent the constituency till 1880, when he was an unsuccessful candidate; in 1885 unsuccessfully contested the Bosworth division of Leicestershire; unsuccessfully contested by-election in 1894 for N. Cambridgeshire. Re-elected for N. Northamptonshire in 1900 and sat until defeated in 1906. Died 6 Oct. 1926. [1905]

STOREY, Samuel. Southill, Chester-le-Street. S. of Robert Storey, Esq., of Whitburn. B. 13 Jan. 1840 at Sherburn, Co. Durham; m. 1864, eld. d. of J. Addison, Esq., of Sunderland (she died 1877). A Newspaper Proprietor and Manufacturer. A J.P. and Dept.-Lieut. for Co. Durham; a J.P. for Berwickshire. Mayor of Sunderland 1876-77 and 1880. An Independent Tariff Reformer. Sat for Sunderland as a Home Ruler and Radical from 1881-95, when he was defeated. Unsuccessfully contested Newcastle-on-Tyne in 1900. Elected for Sunderland again in Jan. 1910 as an Independent Unionist Free Trader, and sat until he retired in Dec. 1910. Died 18 Jan. 1925. [1910]

STORMONTH-DARLING, Moir Tod. See DARLING, Moir Tod Stormonth.

STORY-MASKELYNE, Mervin Herbert Nevil, F.R.S. Basset Down House, Swindon. Salthrop, Wroughton, Swindon. Athenaeum, and Brooks's. Eld. s. of A.M. Reeve Story Maskelyne, Esq., F.R.S., of Basset Down House, Swindon, by Margaret, only child of Dr. Nevil Maskelyne, Astronomer-Royal. B. at Basset Down House, Swindon 1823; m. Theresa Mary, d. of J.D. Llewelyn, Esq., of Penllergare, Glamorgan. Educ. at (Wadham Coll.) Oxford, where he graduated M.A. 1849 and became an Honorary Fellow. Appointed Professor of Mineralogy in the University of Oxford 1856-95; a Fellow of the Institute of Chemistry; and was Keeper of the Mineral Department in the British Museum from 1857 to 1880. A Dept.-Lieut. for Brecknockshire, and a Magistrate for Gloucestershire and Wiltshire. Published works on Mineralogy, Chemistry, and Crystallography. A Liberal Unionist. Sat for Cricklade from 1880 to 1885, and for the Cricklade division of Wiltshire from 1885 until defeated in 1892. Died 20 May 1911. [1892]

STRACHEY, Sir Edward, Bart. 27 Cadogan Gardens, London. Sutton Court, Pensford, Somerset. Brooks's, Travellers', and National Liberal. Eld. s. of Sir Edward Strachey, 3rd Bart., of Sutton Court, Somerset, and Mary Isabella, d. of John Addington Symonds, Esq., M.D. B. 1858 at Clifton, Bristol; m. 1880, Constance, d. of C.B. Braham, Esq. Educ. at Christ Church, Oxford. Was Treasurer of H.M. Household, and a Liberal Whip Dec. 1905 to Dec. 1909, when he was appointed Parliamentary Secretary to the Board of Agriculture, which post he held until Oct. 1911; a J.P., Dept.-Lieut. and a County Councillor for Somerset. Was Lieut. 4th Battalion Somerset Regiment 1878-82. He carried the Outdoor Relief Friendly Societies Act 1894, the Post Office Amendment Act 1895, and the Post Office Guarantee Amendment Act 1898. Chairman of Central Chamber of Agriculture. Member of Court of Bristol University from 1910. A Liberal, in favour of Home Rule for Ireland for purely Irish affairs. Specially identified himself with Agricultural and Friendly Societies' interests in Parliament. He was an unsuccessful candidate for Somerset N. in 1885, and at Plymouth in 1886. Elected for S. Somerset in 1892 and sat until created 1st Baron Strachey 3 Nov. 1911. Succeeded as Bart. in 1901. PC. 1912. Paymaster-Gen. 1912-15. Died 25 July 1936. [1911]

STRAUS, Bertram Stuart. 8 Hyde Park

Mansions, London. National Liberal, and Eighty. S. of Henry S. Straus, Esq., Vice-Consul for the Netherlands at Manchester. B. 17 Mar. 1867 at Prestwich, Lancashire. Educ. at Harrow. A Partner in Hale and Son, Colonial Brokers, Mincing Lane, retired 1898. A member of London County Council for Mile End 1898-1907; Chairman of several Committees, President of League of Mercy for Mile End. J.P. for the Co. of London. A Liberal, in favour of Land Law Reform, One Man One Vote, etc. Unsuccessfully contested W. Marylebone in 1895, the St. George's division of Tower Hamlets 1900, and the Mile End division of Tower Hamlets in 1905. Elected for the Mile End division of Tower Hamlets in 1906 and sat until defeated in Jan. 1910. Unsuccessfully contested the seat again Dec. 1910. Died 26 Aug. 1933. [1909]

STRAUSS, Arthur. 1 Kensington Palace Gardens, London. 16 Rood Lane, London. Carlton. S. of S. Strauss, Esq., of Mayence. B. 28 Apr. 1847; m. 1893, Minna, d. of S. Cohen, Esq. Was educ. at a German University. A Metal Merchant. A Partner in the firm of A. Strauss and Company, Merchants, and Owner of several Smelting Works. A Unionist, in favour of Enfranchisement of Leaseholds. Unsuccessfully contested Camborne division of Cornwall in 1892; sat for that constituency from 1895-1900, when he was defeated; unsuccessfully contested that seat again at a by-election in 1903. Contested N. Paddington 1906; elected there in Jan. 1910 and sat until defeated in 1918, as an Independent Labour candidate. Died 30 Nov. 1920. [1918]

STRAUSS, Edward Anthony. Continued in House after 1918: full entry in Volume III.

STRONG, Richard. Helstonleigh, Champion Park, Denmark Hill, London. National Liberal, and City Liberal. S. of Richard Strong, Esq., of Mark Lane. B. in London 1833; m. 1st, 1857, d. of William Howard, Esq.; 2ndly, 1870, d. of John Mersh, Esq. Educ. at private schools. A Magistrate for Surrey, Chairman of the Camberwell Board of Guardians, of the Board of Managers of the S. Metropolitan District Schools, and of the estates Governors of Dulwich Coll. President of the Lambeth Liberal Association, and a member of the council of the London Municipal Reform League. A Liberal. Sat for Camberwell N. from Nov. 1885 until he retired in 1886. Alderman and Vice-Chairman of London County Council. Died 30 Jan. 1915. [1886]

STROYAN, John. Saxon Hall, Palace Court, London. Ochtertyre, Crieff, N.B. Kirkchrist, Kirkcowan, Wigtownshire. S. of John Stroyan, Esq., of Kirkchrist, Wigtownshire. B. 1856; m. 1889, Edith, d. of T.E. Dean, Esq. Educ. at the Dumfries Academy. Had large financial interests in South Africa. A Unionist. Elected for W. Perthshire in 1900 and sat until defeated in 1906. Contested Stockton Jan. 1910. Died 5 Dec. 1941. [1905]

STRUTT, Hon. Charles Hedley. 2 Chelsea Embankment, London. Blunts Hall, Witham, Essex. Carlton. 4th s. of the 2nd Baron Rayleigh, by Clara, d. of Capt. Vicars, of the Royal Engineers. B. 1849. Educ. at Winchester, and Trinity Coll., Cambridge; 1st class Moral Science Tripos 1871. An Alderman of the Essex County Council 1888-1925, Chairman of the Witham Bench of Magistrates, and Chairman Quarter Sessions 1904-21. A Conservative and Unionist, in favour of legislation for the relief of agriculture, etc. Was MP for E. Essex from 1883-85, and an unsuccessful candidate for the Saffron Walden division of Essex 1885. Elected for the Maldon division of Essex in 1895 and sat until defeated in 1906. Died 19 Dec. 1926. [1905]

STUART, James. 24 Grosvenor Road, London. Carrow Abbey, Norwich. Reform, and National Liberal. S. of Joseph Gordon Stuart, Esq., of Markinch, Fife, and Catherine, d. of D. Booth, Esq., of Newburgh, Fife. B. 1843 at Markinch: m. 1890, Laura Elizabeth, d. of J.J. Colman, Esq., MP for Norwich. Educ. at Madras School, and the University, St. Andrew's, and Trinity Coll., Cambridge. LL.D. St. Andrews. A Fellow of Trinity Coll., Professor of Mechanism and Applied Mechanics at Cambridge University 1875-89. Associate member of the Institute of Civil Engineers. Lord Rector of St. Andrew's University 1899-1901. Founder of the system of University Extension Teaching. A member of the London County Council. Author of various books and pamphlets on scientific and educational subjects. A Liberal. Unsuccessfully contested Cambridge University in 1882. Sat for Hackney from 1884-85; sat for the Hoxton division of Shoreditch 1885-1900, when he was defeated. Elected for Sunderland in 1906 and sat until defeated in Jan. 1910. PC. 1909. Published a volume of Reminiscences in 1912. Died 12 Oct. 1913. [1909]

STUART-WORTLEY, Rt. Hon. Charles Beilby. 7 Cheyne Walk, Chelsea, London. Carlton, and Marlborough. Grand-s. of the 1st Baron Wharncliffe, and s. of the Rt. Hon. James Stuart-Wortley, Q.C., MP for Halifax and Buteshire, Recorder of London, and Solicitor-Gen., by the Hon. Jane Lawlay, only d. of 1st Lord Wenlock. B. at Escrick Park, York 1851; m. 1st, 1880, Beatrice, d. of T. Adolphus Trollope, Esq. (she died 1881); 2ndly, 1886, Alice Caroline, d. of Sir J.E. Millais, Bart., P.R.A. Educ. at Rugby, and at Balliol Coll., Oxford; M.A. Called to the bar at the Inner Temple Jan. 1876 and joined the N.E. Circuit; Q.C. 1892. From 1895 was one of the "Temporary" Chairmen in Committee of the whole House, as well as a member of the Chairmen's Panel for Standing Committees. Parliamentary Under-Secretary of State for the Home Department in the Ministry of Lord Salisbury, June 1885, to Jan. 1886, and again Aug. 1886 to 1892. Was chief delegate of the Government at the International Conference on Industrial Property at Madrid 1890, and at Brussels 1897 and 1900. In 1895 he became a Church Estates Commissioner, and in 1896 a PC. A Unionist. Unsuccessfully contested Sheffield in 1879. Sat for the undivided borough of Sheffield from 1880-85, and for the Hallam division of Sheffield from 1885 until nominated for a peerage Dec. 1916. Created 1st Baron Stuart of Wortley in 1917. A Director of the Underground Electric Railway Company. Died 24 Apr. 1926. [1916]

STURGIS, Henry Parkman. 4 Great Cumberland Place, Hyde Park, London. St. James's. S. of Russell Sturgis, Esq., of 17 Carlton House Terrace, and Leatherhead, Surrey. B. at Boston, U.S.A., 1847; m. 1st, 1872, Mary, 4th d. of Visct. Hampden, G.C.B., at one time Speaker of the House of Commons, (she died 1886); 2ndly, 1894, Marie, d. of George Meredith, the famous author. Educ. at Eton, and Christ Church, Oxford. From 1869 to 1884 Mr. Sturgis was engaged in business as a Merchant in con-

nection with the house of Messrs. Baring Brothers and Company. A Liberal, in favour of reform in the House of Lords, of Local Option and of Sunday closing in public houses; considered it of the greatest importance that the navy should be kept in the highest state of efficiency. Sat for Dorset S. from Dec. 1885 until he was defeated in 1886 standing as a Gladstonian Liberal. Chairman of Union Bank of Australia 1911-29. Died 1 Mar. 1929. [1886]

STURROCK, Peter. London Road, Kilmarnock. Scottish Conservative, Edinburgh, and Glasgow. S. of David Sturrock, Esq., Farmer, of Struthers, Kilmarnock, by his marriage with Helen Woodburn, of Aird. B. 1820; m. 1850, Helen Hutchison Gurthrie, d. of John Guthrie-Holms, Esq., of Kilmarnock. Educ. at Kilmarnock Academy, and in Glasgow. Was a Civil Engineer, and from 1847 a Colliery-Owner at Hurlford, Ayrshire. In 1856 was appointed Town Treasurer of Kilmarnock, in 1871 Dean of Guild, and from 1874 to 1886 he was Provost of the town. A Magistrate for the Co. of Ayr. A Conservative. Sat for Kilmarnock district from Dec. 1885 until defeated in 1886. Died 7 Mar. 1904. [1886]

STURT, Hon. Humphrey Napier. 38 Portman Square, London. Crichel, Wimborne, Dorset. Carlton, White's, and Marlborough. Eld. s. of Lord Alington and his wife, Lady Augusta Bingham. B. 1859; m. 1883, Lady Fiodorowna Yorke, d. of the Earl and Countess of Hardwicke. Educ. at Eton, and Christ Church, Oxford. A Lieut. Dorset Yeomanry, a Dept.-Lieut. for Dorset and a member of the County Council for the Handley division of Dorset. A Conservative. Unsuccessfully contested Dorset N. in 1885. Sat for Dorset E. from Nov. 1891 until he succeeded as Lord Alington in 1904. C.V.O. 1905; K.C.V.O. 1908. Died 30 July 1919. [1903]

SULLIVAN, Donal. 1 Belvidere Place, Mountjoy Square, Dublin. National Liberal. B. 1838. S. of Daniel Sullivan, Esq., and bro. of T.D. Sullivan, Esq., Lord Mayor of Dublin 1886, MP for the College Green division of Dublin and W. Donegal. Was Manager of the publishing department of *The Nation* newspaper, of which his bro. was Proprietor. "An Irish Nationalist." Secretary to the Irish Parliamentary party 1893-

1898. Sat for Westmeath S. from the general election of 1885 until his death 3 Mar. 1907. [1907]

SULLIVAN, McDonnell. See SULLIVAN, Donal.

SULLIVAN, Timothy Daniel. 1 Belvedere Place, Dublin. National Liberal. Eld. s. of Daniel Sullivan, Esq., of Amiens Street, Dublin, by his m. with Miss Catherine Baylor. B. at Bantry, Co. Cork 1827; m. 1856, Catherine, d. of Thomas Healy, Esq., of Bantry (she died 1899). Educ. privately, and at the Bantry Schools. Was Editor and Proprietor of *That Nation*, the *Dublin Weekly News*, and *Young Ireland*, and was imprisoned under the Crimes Act for reporting meetings of the National League in these papers, Dec. 1887. Author of several volumes of Irish national poems, and other works. Was elected Lord Mayor of Dublin for 1886 and again for 1887. An "Irish Nationalist" (Anti-Parnellite), in favour of the system called Home Rule for Ireland, being "convinced that without self-government there could never be peace, prosperity, or contentment in Ireland." Sat for Westmeath Co. 1880-85, for the College Green division of Dublin 1885-92, and for Donegal W. from 1892 until he retired in 1900. Died 31 Mar. 1914. [1900]

SUMMERBELL, Thomas. 14 St. Vincent Street, Sunderland. B. 1861. Educ. at National School, Seaham Harbour. A Printer, and a member of the Typographical Association. Secretary of Trades Council, a Town Councillor for Sunderland, Chairman of Tramways Committee, and a Founder of the Labourers' Union of Great Britain. A Labour Member. Elected for Sunderland in 1906 and sat until defeated in Jan. 1910. Died 10 Feb. 1910. [1909]

SUMMERS, James Woolley. Emral Park, Worthenburg, Flintshire. S. of John Summers, Esq., of Sunnyside, Ashton-under-Lyne, and Mary, d. of John Woolley, Esq., of Stalybridge. B. 24 Mar. 1849 at Dukinfield; m. 1883, Edith, d. of Hugh Mason, Esq., MP for Ashton-under-Lyne. Chairman of John Summers and Sons Limited, Ironworks, Shotton. Chairman of Flintshire County Council from 1904-10, on the Roll for High Sheriff 1910. A J.P. for Lancashire, Denbighshire, and Flintshire. A Liberal, in favour of disestablishment of the Church in Wales, Self-Government for Ireland in regard to purely Irish affairs, subject to supreme authority of Imperial Parliament. Elected for Flint district in Jan. 1910 and sat until his death 1 Jan. 1913. [1912]

SUMMERS, William. Ryecroft Hall, Audenshaw, Manchester. Reform. 2nd s. of John Summers, Esq., (an Iron Merchant at Stalybridge), of Sunnyside, Ashton-under-Lyne, by Mary, d. of Samuel Woolley, Esq. B. at Stalybridge 1853. Educ. at Owens Coll., Manchester, and University Coll., Oxford. Graduated M.A. at London and B.A. at Oxford; gained a gold medal in classics and an exhibition in English at London University, besides various scholarships and prizes at Owens Coll. Was called to the bar at Lincoln's Inn 1881. A Governor of Victoria University, Manchester. A Liberal, in favour of "an active and orderly progress", and of Home Rule for Ireland. Sat for Stalybridge from Apr. 1880 until defeated Nov. 1885. First elected for Huddersfield 1886 and sat until his death of smallpox in Allahabad on 1 Jan. 1893. [1892 2nd ed.]

SUTHERLAND, Angus. 69 Agincourt Road, Hampstead, London. Helmsdale, Sutherlandshire. S. of a Crofter whose family were settled for generations in the Strath of Kildonan. B. at Helmsdale, Sutherlandshire 1848. Educ. at the Free Kirk School of the parish, where he became pupil teacher in 1863. In 1868 he entered the Edinburgh Training Coll., and in 1872 went to Glasgow University. In 1876 he became one of the mathematical masters at the Glasgow Academy. A Liberal, in favour of reforms in croftertenures, and of Mr. Gladstone's scheme of Home Rule for Ireland, and the Newcastle programme. At the general election of 1885 he was an unsuccessful candidate for the representation of Sutherlandshire. First elected for Sutherlandshire 1886 and sat until appointed Chairman of Scotch Fishery Board in 1894. Member of Royal Commission on Congested Districts in Ireland 1906. C.B. 1907. Died 16 Jan. 1922. [1894]

SUTHERLAND, John Ebenezer. Durn House, Portsoy, N.B. Reform, and National Liberal. B. 1854 at Lossiemouth. Was educ. at Aberdeen University. A Partner of P. and J. Sutherland, of Portsoy.

J.P. for Banffshire; for several years Chairman of Fordyce School Board; Chairman of Scottish Temperance and Social Reform Association; Chairman of Committee on Scottish Sea Fisheries 1917. A member of Banffshire County Council. A Liberal. Elected for Elgin Burghs Sept. 1905 and sat until his death 17 Aug. 1918.   [1918]

SUTHERLAND, Sir Thomas, G.C.M.G. 4 Buckingham Gate, London. Coldharbour Wood, Liss, Hampshire. Reform. S. of R. Sutherland, Esq., of Aberdeen, by Christian, d. of T. Webster, Esq. B. 1834: m. 1880, Alice, d. of the Rev. J. Macnaught, Vicar of W. Kensington. Was educ. at the Grammar School, and University of Aberdeen, in which University he held the honorary degreee of LL.D. Chairman of the Peninsular and Oriental Steam Navigation Company, and also a Director of the Suez Canal Company. Was for some years a member of the Legislative Council of Hongkong. A Commissioner of Lieutenancy for London; became K.C.M.G. 1891, and G.C.M.G. 1897; also a Chevalier of the Legion of Honour. A Liberal and Unionist, not indifferent to the national defences, and the efficient maintenance of the navy. Sat for Greenock from Nov. 1884. At the election there in 1892 the polling figures as first reported put Sir Thomas in a minority. On scrutiny, however, a contrary decision was arrived at and he was MP for Greenock until he retired in 1900. Director, London, City and Midland Bank; Vice-President of the Suez Canal Company; Chairman of Peninsular and Oriental Company until 1914. Died 1 Jan. 1922.   [1900]

SUTHERLAND - LEVESON - GOWER, Frederick Neville. See LEVESON-GOWER, Frederick Neville Sutherland.

SUTTON, John Edward. Continued in House after 1918: full entry in Volume III.

SWANN, Charles Duncan. See SCHWANN, Charles Duncan.

SWANN, Rt. Hon. Sir Charles Ernest, Bart. 4 Princes Gardens, London. Reform. 5th s. of Frederick Schwann, Esq., Merchant, of 23 Gloucester Square, Hyde Park, and Henrietta, d. of the Rev. Edmund Kell, of Birmingham. B. at Huddersfield 1844; m. 1876, Elizabeth, 3rd d. of David Duncan, Esq., of Manchester (she

died 1914). Educ. at Huddersfield Coll., and University Coll., London. Started business as a Merchant in Manchester in 1864. Chairman of the Manchester Liberal Association and vice-president of the National Reform Union. Director of Manchester Chamber of Commerce. Created Bart. 1906. PC. 1911. Assumed by Royal License the name of Swann in 1913. An advanced Liberal, in favour of Land Reform, Temperance Reform, Disestablishment, Free Trade, etc. Unsuccessfully contested N. Manchester in 1885. Sat for N. Manchester from 1886 until he retired in 1918. Died 13 July 1929.   [1918]

SWEETMAN, John. 54 South Street, Park Lane, London. Drumbaragh, Kells, Co. Meath. Reform. St. Stephen's Green, Dublin. S. of John Sweetman, Esq., Brewer, of Dublin, and his wife Honoria (she died 1879), only child of Malachy O'Connor, Esq., Merchant, of Dublin. B. 9 Aug. 1844 in Co. Dublin. Educ. at Downside Coll., Somersetshire. A principal shareholder in the *National Press* newspaper. An ardent supporter of the Nationalist cause, and a member of the Anti-Parnellite section of the Irish party. Sat for Wicklow E. from July 1892 until he accepted Chiltern Hundreds in 1895, as a result of his joining the Parnellite group. Contested the Wicklow E. by-election of 26 Apr. 1895 but was defeated by Mr. E.P. O'Kelly, the Anti-Parnellite candidate. Unsuccessfully contested N. Meath as a Parnellite in July 1895.   [1895]

SWETENHAM, Edmund. 73 Eccleston Square, London. 3 Plowden Buildings, Temple, London. Cam-yr-alyn, Rossett, Wrexham. Carlton, and County Club, Chester. S. of Clement Swetenham, Esq., of Somerford Booths, Cheshire, by Eleanor, d. of John Buchanan, Esq., of Hales, Shropshire. B. at Somerford Booths 1822; m. 1st, 1851, Elizabeth Jane, 2nd d. of Wilson Jones, Esq., of Hartsheath Park, Flintshire; 2ndly, 1867, Gertrude, 2nd d. of Ellis Cunliffe, Esq., and grand-d. of Sir Foster Cunliffe, of Acton Park, Denbighshire. Educ. at Macclesfield Grammar School, and Brasenose Coll., Oxford. Was called to the bar at Lincoln's Inn in 1848, and became a Q.C. in 1880. A J.P. for Denbighshire. A "Progressive Conservative", and Unionist. Unsuccessfully contested the Carnarvon district in Nov. 1885. Returned for Carnarvon district July 1886 and sat until his death on 19 Mar. 1890.   [1889]

SWIFT, Rigby Philip Watson. 17 Kidderpore Avenue, Hampstead, London. 1 Garden Court, Temple, London. S. of Thomas Swift, Esq., Barrister. B. 7 June 1874 at St. Helens; m. 1902, Beatrice, d. of John Banks Walmsley, Esq., of Liverpool. Educ. at Parkfield School, Liverpool. LL.B. London University. A Barrister, called at Lincoln's Inn 1895, and practised on the Northern Circuit. K.C. 1912. Recorder of Wigan from 1915-20. Bencher of Lincoln's Inn Nov. 1916. A Unionist. Unsuccessfully contested St. Helens in Jan. 1910. Elected for St. Helens in Dec. 1910 and sat until he was defeated in 1918. Knighted in 1920. Judge of Kings Bench Division from 1920-37. Died 19 Oct. 1937.   [1918]

SWINBURNE, Sir John, Bart. Victoria Mansions, 28 Victoria Street, London. Capheaton, Newcastle-on-Tyne. Brooks's. 3rd s. of Edward Swinburne, Esq., of Calgarth, and grand-s. of Sir John E. Swinburne, whom he succeeded in the Baronetcy 1860. B. 1831; m. 1863, Emily Elizabeth, d. of Rear-Admiral Henry Broadhead, and niece of Sir Theordore Brinckman. He entered the navy at an early age, and served in the Burmese War 1852, and in the Baltic during the Russian War of 1854. Retired in 1880 with the rank of Capt. A Magistrate for Northumberland, of which Co. he was High Sheriff in 1866. Lord of the manor of Capheaton and was a F.R.G.S. A Liberal, and Home Ruler. Unsuccessfully contested Lichfield in Apr. and July 1880. Sat for the Lichfield division of Staffordshire from 1885 until defeated in 1892. Unsuccessfully contested the Newbury division of Berkshire in 1895 and the Widnes division of Lancashire in 1906. Died 15 July 1914.   [1892]

SYKES, Col. Sir Allan John, Bart. Continued in House after 1918: full entry in Volume III.

SYKES, Christopher. 11 Hill Street, Mayfair, London. Brantinghamthorpe Brough, Yorkshire. White's, and Carlton. 2nd s. of Sir Tatton Sykes, 4th Bart., of Sledmere, by Mary Ann, d. of Sir William Foulis, Bart. B. at Sledmere 1831. Educ. at Rugby, and Trinity Coll., Cambridge. A Conservative, would support the constitution of England in Church and State. Sat for Beverley from July 1865 to

Dec. 1868, and for the E. Riding of Yorkshire from that date to 1885. In 1885 he was returned for the Buckrose division of the E. Riding of Yorkshire and in Dec. 1886, after being defeated by one vote, was returned on petition, in July, and sat until he retired in 1892. Died 15 Dec. 1898.   [1892]

TALBOT, Christopher Rice Mansel. 3 Cavendish Square, London. Penrice Castle, Swansea. Margam, Port Talbot, Glamorgan. Travellers'. S. of Thomas Mansel Talbot, Esq., of Margan, by Lady Mary Lucy, d. of 2nd Earl of Ilchester. B. 1803; m. 1835, Lady Charlotte, 2nd d. of 1st Earl of Glengall (she died 1846). Patron of 5 livings. Lord-Lieut. of Glamorganshire, and Honorary Col. Glamorgan Rifles; also F.R.S. and F.S.L. A Liberal, voted against Home Rule for Ireland but otherwise supported Mr. Gladstone and did not act as a Liberal Unionist. Father of the House of Commons. Sat for mid Glamorganshire uninterruptedly from 1830 until his death on 17 Jan. 1890.   [1889]

SYKES, Sir Mark, Bart. Continued in House after 1918: full entry in Volume III.

TALBOT, Rt. Hon. Lord Edmund Bernard. Continued in House after 1918: full entry in Volume III.

TALBOT, Rt. Hon. John Gilbert. 10 Great George Street, London. Falconhurst, Edenbridge, Kent. Carlton, and Travellers'. S. of the Hon. John Chetwynd Talbot, Q.C., by Hon. Caroline Jane, d. of the 1st Baron Wharncliffe. B. in London 1835; m. 1860, Hon. Meriel Sarah, eld d. of the 4th Baron Lyttelton. Educ. at the Charterhouse, and at Christ Church, Oxford; M.A. 1860, Honorary D.C.L. 1878. Chairman of the W. Kent Quarter Sessions from 1867, and a member of the Kent County Council from 1889. Elected Alderman 1904. An Ecclesiastical Commissioner; was (Parliamentary) Secretary to the Board of Trade from Apr. 1878 to Apr. 1880, and created PC. 1897. A Conservative. Unsuccessfully contested Kidderminster in 1862 and Malmesbury in 1865. Sat for W. Kent from Dec. 1868 to May 1878, when he was first elected for the University of Oxford and sat until he retired in Jan. 1910. Died 1 Feb. 1910.   [1909]

TANNER, Dr. Charles Kearns Deane. 2 Coleherne Mansions, Bolton Gardens, London. Lapps Island, Cork. S. of Dr. Tanner, an eminent Physician of Cork. B. in Cork 20 Sept. 1849; m. 1888, Elizabeth Audriah, only child of Capt. J. McDonnel Webb, 4th Dragoon Guards, of Rosanna, Co. Cork. Educ. in Paris, at Winchester, at Queen's Coll., Cork, and at the Universities of Leipzig and Berlin. A graduate in Arts (B.A.), M.D. and M.Ch. of the Queen's University in Ireland; L.R.C.S. Ireland, etc., and Physician to several hospitals in the city of Cork. Was elected Mayor of Cork in 1890. An "Irish Nationalist" (Anti-Parnellite), and a "whip" of his party. Unsuccessfully contested the N. division of Galway in July 1892. Sat for Cork mid from the general election of 1885 until his death 21 Apr. 1901. [1901]

TALING, Thomas Keay, Kingswood, Dulwich, London. Balkissock, Ballantrae, Ayrshire. Carlton, and Garrick. S. of Thomas Tapling, Esq., of Kingswood, Dulwich, and Gresham Street, London, by his m. with Miss Elizabeth Annie Keay. B. 1855. Unmarried. Educ. at Harrow, and Trinity Coll., Cambridge (M.A. and LL.D.) In 1881 he was called to the bar at the Inner Temple, but afterwards he became head of the firm of Tapling and Company, Wholesale Carpet Retailers and Manchester Warehousemen. A Conservative. Unsuccessfully contested Leicestershire S. in Dec. 1885. First returned for Leicestershire S. July 1886 and sat until his death on 11 Apr. 1891. [1891]

TAYLOR, Austin. 30 Eccleston Square, London. S. of the Ven. W.F. Taylor, D.D., Archdeacon of Liverpool, and Anne, d. of the Rev. H. Evans. B. Jan. 1858 at Liverpool; m. 1886, Lucia, d. of Edward Whitaker, Esq., of Liverpool (she died 1906); 2ndly, 1909, Gertrude Evans. Educ. at Liverpool Coll., and Cambridge University; B.A. 1880. A Steamship Owner, head of the firm of Hugh Evans and Company, Liverpool. Was a member of the Liverpool City Council. Elected for the E. Toxteth division of Liverpool in Nov. 1902 as a Conservative; re-elected in Jan. 1906 as a Conservative but joined the Liberals in Feb. 1906. MP until he retired in Jan. 1910. Contested the Buckrose division of the E. Riding of Yorkshire as a Liberal in 1918. Retired from the shipping business in

1912. Chairman of Westminster Hospital from 1925 to 1928. Died 27 Apr. 1955. [1909]

TAYLOR, Francis. 54 Victoria Street, London. Diss, Norfolk. Royal Thames Yacht Club. 3rd s. of Thomas Lombe Taylor, Esq., of Starston, Norfolk, by Mary, d. of David Cooper, Esq. B. at Starston 1845; m. 1873, Susan, d. of Edward Rigby, Esq., M.D., of Berkeley Square, London. Educ. at Hove House School, Brighton, University Coll School, and University Coll. London. A J.P. for Norfolk. A Liberal Unionist. Sat for Norfolk S. from 1885 until he accepted Chiltern Hundreds in 1898. Died 1 Sept. 1915. [1898]

TAYLOR, Col. Gerald Kyffin. See KYFFIN-TAYLOR, Col. Gerald.

TAYLOR, John Wilkinson. The Avenue, Durham. B. 11 Aug. 1855; m. d. of J. Mason, Esq. Started work when nine years old, was apprenticed to a Blacksmith at 12, and afterwards worked in Dipton Colliery. Was Secretary of Durham Colliery Mechanics' Association and member of County Durham Mining Federated Board. President of Durham Aged Mineworkers' Homes Association. J.P. for Co. Durham. A Labour Member. Elected for the Chester-le-Street division of Durham in 1906 and sat until he resigned in 1919. Died 26 June 1934. [1918]

TAYLOR, Theodore Cooke. Sunny Bank, Batley. National Liberal. S. of Joshua Taylor, Esq., Woollen Manufacturer, of Batley, by Alice, d. of Samuel Cooke, Esq., Carpet Manufacturer, of Liversedge. B. at Batley 1850; m. 1874, d. of W.J.P. Ingraham, Esq., of Philadelphia, U.S.A.; 2ndly, 1920, Mary McVean. Educ. at Batley Grammar School, and Silcoates Northern Congregational School. A Woollen Manufacturer, head of the firm of J., T. and J. Taylor Limited, under whose profit-sharing scheme over £200,000 went to employees. J.P. for Batley; member of County Council, W. Riding of Yorkshire 1889-92; served as member on the board of Trade Textiles Committee. A Liberal, a strong advocate of profit-sharing; took a leading part in the Anti-Opium Movement, largely in which interest he visited India, the Far East, and British Colonies. Sat for the Radcliffe cum Farnworth div-

347

ision of Lancashire from 1900 until he retired in 1918. Died 19 Oct. 1952. [1918]

TAYLOR, Thomas. Tudor House, Heaton, Bolton. National Liberal. S. of William Taylor, Esq., of Bolton. B. 31 Jan. 1851 in Bolton; m. 1875, Mary, d. of Robert Lomax, Esq., of Bolton. Educ. at Church Institute, Bolton. A Cotton Manufacturer; Founder of the firm of T. Taylor Limited, Bolton. Was Examiner in Cotton Weaving to the City and Guilds of London Institute 1888-94. Member of Bolton School Board 1899-1902; J.P. for Bolton and Lancashire. A Liberal. Elected for Bolton in Nov. 1912 and sat until he accepted Chiltern Hundred in Feb. 1916. Died 17 Dec. 1916. [1915]

TEMPLE, Sir Richard, Bart., G.C.S.I. Heath Brow, Hampstead, London. The Nash, Kempsey, Nr. Worcester. Athenaeum, and Carlton. S. of Richard Temple, Esq., J.P. Worcestershire, by Louisa, sister of Sir James Rivett-Carnac. B. at Kempsey, near Worcester 1826; m. 1st, 1849, Charlotte, d. of B. Martindale, Esq.; 2ndly, 1871, Mary Augusta, d. of C.R. Lindsay, Esq. Educ. at Rugby, and Haileybury Coll. Entered the Bengal Civil Service 1847 in which he eventually attained high distinction, and filled in succession the offices of Chief Commissioner of the Central Provinces of India, Foreign Secretary, Prime Minister in the Government of India 1868-73, Lieut.-Governor of Bengal 1874-77, and Governor of Bombay 1877-80. C.S.I. 1866; K.C.S.I.. 1867. Was created a Bart. 1876, and G.C.S.I. and C.I.E. 1877. Was Vice-Chairman of the School Board for London, of which he was a member for some time, and was President of the Social Science Association. A Magistrate for Worcestershire, and had the honorary degrees of D.C.L. Oxford, and LL.D. Cambridge and Montreal. His chief contributions to literature were *India in 1880*, *Men and Events of my Time*, *Cosmopolitan Essays*, *Oriental Experience*, and *Palestine* illustrated. A Conservative. Said he would promote the registration of secondary teachers and the superannuation of elementary teachers; also would support the Conservative proposals regarding reform of electoral registration and of the Poor Law, the enfranchisement of duly qualified women, and all moderate measures of social progress. Unsuccessfully contested E. Worcestershire in

1880. Sat for the Evesham division of Worcestershire 1885 to June 1892, and for the Kingston-upon-Thames division of Surrey from June 1892 until he retired in 1895. PC. 1896. F.R.S. 1896. Died 15 Mar. 1902. [1895]

TENNANT, Sir Charles, Bart. Defeated in 1886: full entry in Volume I.

TENNANT, Sir Edward Priaulx, Bart. 34 Queen Anne's Gate, London. Wilsford Manor, Salisbury. Glen, Innerleithen, N.B. Brooks's. Eld. s. of Sir Charles Tennant, 1st Bart. B. 1859; m. 1895, d. of Hon. Percy Wyndham. Educ. at Eton, and Trinity Coll., Cambridge; M.A. Read for the bar at the Inner Temple. Private Secretary to Sir George Trevelyan when Secretary for Scotland. A J.P. and County Councillor for Wiltshire. A Liberal, in favour of Temperance Reform. Unsuccessfully contested the Partick division of Lanarkshire in 1892 and Peebles and Selkirk in 1900. Elected for Salisbury in 1906 and sat until defeated in Jan. 1910. Succeeded as Bart. in 1906. Created Baron Glenconner Mar. 1911; Lord High Commissioner to General Assembly of Church of Scotland 1911-14. Lord-Lieut. of Peeblesshire 1908-20. Died 21 Nov. 1920. [1909]

TENNANT, Rt. Hon. Harold John. 33 Bruton Street, London. Great Maytham, Rolvenden, Kent. Edinglassie, Strathdon, N.B. Brooks's, Reform, and National Liberal. Youngest s. of Sir Charles Tennant, Bart. B. at The Glen, Innerleithen, N.B. 1865; m. 1st, 1889, Helen, d. of Maj. Gordon Duff, of Drummuir (she died 1892); 2ndly, 1896, Margaret Edith, d. of George Whitley Abraham, Esq., of Rathgar, Co. Dublin. Educ. at Eton, and Trinity Coll., Cambridge. Was Assistant Private Secretary to Mr. Asquith as Home Secretary. Was Parliamentary Secretary to Board of Trade 1909-11, and Financial Secretary to the War Office 1911-12; Under Secretary of State for War 1912-16; Secretary for Scotland July to Dec. 1916. A J.P. for Kent, and Dept.-Lieut. for Aberdeenshire. PC. 1914. A Liberal. Represented Berwickshire from 1894 until defeated in Berwick and Haddington in 1918. Unsuccessfully contested Glasgow Central in 1923. Died 9 Nov. 1935. [1918]

TERRELL, George. Continued in House after 1918: full entry in Volume III.

TERRELL, Henry. 11 New Square, Lincoln's Inn, London. S. of Thomas Hull Terrell, Esq., County Court Judge, and Isabella, d. of Capt. R. Spry, of the East India Company. B. 9 May 1856 at Versailles; m. 1885, Georgina, d. of G. Poole, Esq. Educ. at Christ's Coll., Brecon, and St. John's Coll., Cambridge. Was called to the bar at the Middle Temple 1882; Q.C. 1897; bencher 1904. Maj. 11th Gloucester Regiment Oct. 1914. A Unionist. Unsuccessfully contested the Forest of Dean division of Gloucestershire in 1900 and Gloucester in 1906. First elected for Gloucester in Jan. 1910 and sat until he retired in 1918. Appointed County Court Judge 1920, retired 1929. Died 9 Sept. 1944.
[1918]

THEOBALD, James. 125 Victoria Street, London. Bedfords, Havering-atte-Bower, Essex. Carlton, City Carlton, Junior Carlton, and Orleans. S. of James Theobald, Esq., J.P., of Hyde Abbey, Winchester, by Sarah, d. of the Rev. C. Richards, Canon of Winchester. B. at the Close, Winchester 1829; m. Mabel Laura, d. of W. Eaton, Esq., of Cheshire. Educ. at Trinity Coll., Oxford. A Dept.-Lieut. for Essex, Lord of the Manor of Grays Thurrock, and a large landowner in the Co. A Conservative, opposed to Home Rule as unjust to Ireland. Contested the Romford division of Essex Dec. 1885. Sat for the Romford division of Essex from July 1886 until his death on 10 Mar. 1894. [1893]

THOMAS, Abel. 85 Cornwall Gardens, South Kensington, London. 7 King's Bench Walk, Temple, London. Reform, National Liberal, and Bath. S. of the Rev. Theophilus Evan Thomas, J.P., and of Mary John, of Trahale, Co. Pembroke. B. at Trahale 1848; m. 1875, Bessie, d. of Samuel Polak, Esq. (she died 1890). Educ. at Clifton Coll., and University of London; B.A. Was called to the bar at the Middle Temple 1875, and practised on the S. Wales and Chester Circuits; a Q.C. 1892, and a bencher of the Middle Temple. A J.P. for Pembrokeshire and Chairman of the Pembrokeshire Quarter Sessions. A Liberal, in favour of a measure of Welsh Home Rule, as well as of Irish Home Rule, Disestablishment, Land and Leasehold Reform, etc. Sat for Carmarthenshire E. from Aug. 1890 until his death 23 July 1912. [1912]

THOMAS, Sir Abraham Garrod. 167 Ashley Gardens, London. Bron-y-gaer, Newport, Monmouthshire. National Liberal, and Royal Automobile. S. of Lewis Thomas, Esq., of Panteryrod, Aberayron, Cardiganshire. B. at Panteryrod 5 Oct. 1853; m. 11 Nov. 1879, the only child of R.H. Richards, Esq., of Newport, Monmouthshire. Educ. at Milford Haven, Edinburgh University, Berlin, and Vienna. M.D. Edinburgh 1878 (M.B. 1876). High Sheriff of Cardiganshire 1900-01; Dept.-Lieut. of Monmouthshire 1897; Chairman of *South Wales Argus.* Knighted 1912. A Liberal. Elected for S. Monmouthshire 13 July 1917 and sat until he retired in 1918. Died 30 Jan. 1931. [1918]

THOMAS, Sir Alfred. Bronwydd, Cardiff. Devonshire, Reform, and National Liberal. S. of Daniel Thomas, Esq. B. 1840 A Merchant of Cardiff, of which town he was Mayor in 1882. Received the Freedom of Cardiff 1887. At one time President of the South Wales University Coll., and President of National Museum for Wales. A J.P. for Cardiff, and J.P. and Dept.-Lieut. for Glamorgan. Chairman of the Welsh Liberal Parliamentary Party from 1898. Knighted 1902. A Liberal and Home Ruler. Sat for E. Glamorganshire from 1885 until he retired in Dec. 1910. Created Baron Pontypridd Jan. 1912. Died 14 Dec. 1927. [1910]

THOMAS, David Alfred. 122 Ashley Gardens, London. Llanwern, Newport, Monmouthshire. Reform, National Liberal, and Devonshire. S. of Samuel Thomas, Esq., Colliery Owner. B. 1856 at Aberdare; m. 1882, Sybil Margaret, d. of George Augustus Haig, Esq., of Penithon, Radnorshire. Educ. at Gonville, and Caius Coll., Cambridge; B.A. Mathematical tripos 1880, M.A. 1883. Senior Partner in the firm of Thomas and Davey, Coal Shippers, Cardiff. A J.P. and Dept.-Lieut. for Glamorganshire, and J.P. for Monmouthshire. A Liberal. Sat for Merthyr Tydvil from 1888 to Jan. 1910, when he transferred to Cardiff which he represented until he retired in Dec. 1910. Created Baron Rhondda Jan. 1916; created Visct. Rhondda June 1918; President of Local Government Board 1916-17; Food Controller 1917-18; PC. 1916. Died 3 July 1918. [1910]

THOMAS, Rt. Hon. James Henry. Continued in House after 1918: full entry in Volume III.

THOMAS, John Aeron. 18 York Street, Swansea. S. of Lewis Thomas, Esq., of Panterywd. B. 1850; m. 1880, Eleanor, eld d. of John Lewis, Esq., J.P., of Nantgwynne, Carmarthenshire. Educ. at Llwyn-rhydowen Grammar School, and Milford Grammar School. Admitted a Solicitor 1874, and began to practise in Swansea; Senior Partner in the firm of Aeron Thomas and Company; Alderman of the borough of Swansea from 1888, and was Mayor 1887-88; representative of the Duke of Beaufort on the Swansea Harbour Trust, and interested in many Colliery undertakings. A Liberal. Elected for the Gower division of Glamorganshire in 1900 and sat until he retired in 1906. Died 1 Feb. 1935.   [1905]

THOMASSON, Franklin. 36 Gloucester Square, London. Hallsteads, Nr. Penrith. Reform, Ranelagh, and Automobile. S. of J.P. Thomasson, Esq., at one time MP for Bolton, and Katherine Thomasson (niece of the Rt. Hon. John Bright). B. 1873 at Alderley Edge, Cheshire; m. 1895, Elizabeth Lawton, d. of Caleb Coffin, Esq., of U.S.A. Educ. privately. A member of the firm of John Thomasson and Son Limited, Cotton Spinners, Bolton. A J.P. for Bolton and Lancashire. A Maj. 5th Loyal N. Lancashire Regiment. A Liberal. Unsuccessfully contested Westhoughton in 1900 and Stretford 1901. Elected for Leicester in Mar. 1906 and sat until he retired in Jan. 1910. Died 29 Oct. 1941.   [1909]

THOMAS-STANFORD, Charles. Continued in House after 1918: full entry in Volume III.

THOMPSON, Maj. A. Green. A Conservative. Elected for Cockermouth in Apr. 1868 and sat until Nov. 1868 when he did not seek re-election when the constituency was reduced to one Member. (Omitted from Volume I).

THOMPSON, Edward Charles. Camorven House, Omagh, Co. Tyrone. S. of Henry Thompson, Esq., F.R.C.S.I., of Omagh, Co. Tyrone, and Nannie, d. of Edward Blake, Esq., Dept.-Lieut. of Castlegrove, Co. Mayo. B. 1851 at Omagh; m. 1st, Diana, d. of Col. F. Ellis, Feccarry,

Omagh; 2ndly, Dorothea Selina, eld. d. of Col. G.P. McClintock. Educ. at the Royal School, Raphoe, and Dublin University. A Physician and Surgeon. Was a Surgeon in the navy from 1872-74, a Surgeon at Tyrone County Hospital, and visiting and consulting Physician for Tyrone and Fermanagh Asylum. Presented with Albert Medal for saving life on land. Wrote pamphlets on Hygiene, Vaccination, and Medical Education, *The Trial of the Maguires*, and contributed articles to the medical journals. Was once a Liberal Unionist, but elected as a Nationalist and Imperialist. Unsuccessfully contested mid Tyrone as a Unionist in 1892 and 1895, N. Fermanagh as an Independent Unionist in Nov. 1898 and S. Tyrone as a Nationalist in 1900. Elected for N. Monaghan Dec. 1900 and sat until he retired in Jan. 1906. Died 20 Jan. 1933.   [1905]

THOMPSON, Ernest Claude Meysey. See MEYSEY-THOMPSON, Ernest Claude. Continued in House after 1918: full entry in Volume III.

THOMPSON, Sir Henry Meysey, Bart. See MEYSEY-THOMPSON, Sir Henry Meysey, Bart.

THOMPSON, John William Howard. 2 Southwick Crescent, Hyde Park, London. Boodle's, Eighty, and National Liberal. S. of Gustavus Thompson, Esq., Solicitor, of London, and Harriet Marion, d. of John R. Scott, Esq. B. 1861; m. 1894, Antionette Ebden, d. of Theophilus Joseph Keene, Esq., of Seaborough Court, Somerset. Educ. at Dr. Barrett's School, Carshalton, Surrey, and "Whitgift", Croydon, Surrey. A Solicitor, at one time Solicitor to the Conservative Land Society, and Honorary Solicitor to the National Footpaths Preservation Society; Director of W.P. Griggs and Company Limited, and South Essex Recorders Limited, both of Ilford, Essex. A Liberal. Elected for E. Somerset in 1906 and sat until defeated in Jan. 1910. Unsuccessfully contested E. Somerset in Dec. 1910 and Ilford 25 Sept. 1920, and 1922, also the Wells division of Somerset in 1931. Maj. 1916. Died 17 Oct. 1959.   [1909]

THOMPSON, Rt. Hon. Robert. Drum House, Co. Down. Bertha House, Belfast. Carlton, and Constitutional. S. of Robert Thompson, Esq. B. 1838 at Ballylesson; m. 1861, Susanna, d. of Edward Thomas, Esq.

Educ. at Purdysburn Schools, and Wellington Academy, Belfast. Chairman of Lindsay, Thompson and Company Limited, Flax Spinners and Linen Manufacturers, Belfast; a Director of Belfast and Co. Down Railway; Chairman of Belfast Harbour Board; President of Ulster Flax Spinners' Association; President of Belfast Chamber of Commerce; a member of the Advisory Committee and of the Conciliation Board for the settlement of Disputes of the Board of Trade; Chairman of the Board of Governors, Campbell Coll., Belfast. A J.P. for Co. Down and Dept.-Lieut. for Belfast. PC. 1916. A Unionist. Elected for N. Belfast in Jan. 1910 and sat until his death 3 Aug. 1918. [1918]

THOMSON, Frederick Whitley. 4 Chelsea Court, London. Savile Heath, Halifax. Reform. S. of Jonathan Thomson, Esq., Merchant of Glasgow, and Emma Whitley, of Halifax. B. at Glasgow 1851; m. 1888, Bertha Florence, d. of Matthew Smith, Esq., of Halifax. Educ. at Glasgow Academy, and Andersonian University, Glasgow. A Cardmaker, head of the old-established firm of John Whitley and Sons, Halifax. Vice-President of the Halifax Liberal Association and Elland division Liberal Association; member of the Council of the Halifax Chamber of Commerce. Alderman of Halifax County Borough Council; Mayor 1908-11. A Liberal. Elected for the Skipton division of the W. Riding of Yorkshire in 1900 and sat until he retired in 1906. Unsuccessfully contested the Ross division of Herefordshire 31 Jan. 1908 and Colchester Jan. 1910. Changed his name to Whitley-Thomson in 1914. Kt. 1916. Died 21 June 1925. [1905]

THOMSON, William Mitchell-. See MITCHELL-THOMSON, William. Continued in House after 1918: full entry in Volume III.

THORBURN, Sir Walter. Kerfield, Peebles, N.B. Devonshire. New Club, Edinburgh. S. of Walter Thorburn, Esq., Banker, of Peebles, by Jane Grieve, d. of Robert Grieve, Esq., of Kiclator, Perthshire. B. at Peebles 1842; m. 1871, Elizabeth Jackson, eld. d. of David Scott, Esq., of Meadowfield, Edinburgh. Educ. at the Grammar School, Musselburgh, and privately. A Woollen Manufacturer. J.P.

and Dept.-Lieut. for the Co. of Peebles. Knighted in 1900. A Unionist. Sat for Selkirk and Peebles from 1886 until defeated in 1906. Died 10 Nov. 1908. [1905]

THORNE, George Rennie. Continued in House after 1918: full entry in Volume III.

THORNE, William James. Continued in House after 1918: full entry in Volume III.

THORNTON, Percy Melville. 30 Evelyn Gardens, South Kensington, London. Carlton, and United University. S. of Rear-Admiral Samuel Thornton and Emily, d. of the Rev. J. Rice. B. 1841; m. 1877, Florence Emily, d. of H. Sykes Thornton, Esq. Educ. at Harrow, and Jesus Coll., Cambridge; LL.B. 1864. Wrote *The Recovered Thread of England's Foreign Policy, Foreign Secretaries of the Nineteenth Century, Harrow School and its Surroundings, The Stuart Dynasty, Some Things We Have Remembered* (1912), and other books. A Conservative. Sat for the Clapham division of Battersea and Clapham from 1892 until he retired in Jan. 1910. Died 8 Jan. 1918. [1909]

THYNNE, Lord Alexander George. 15 Manchester Square, London. Norton Hall, Daventry, Northamptonshire. Carlton, and Turf. S. of 4th Marq. of Bath. B. 17 Feb. 1873. Unmarried. Educ. at Eton, and Balliol Coll., Oxford. Was in S. African Civil Service 1902-05; a member of London County Council 1899-1900, and from 1907 Chairman of Improvements Committee. Served in S. African War 1900-02 and Somaliland Campaign 1903-04; served in the Expeditionary Force; wounded in action 1916. A Unionist. Unsuccessfully contested the Frome division of Somerset in 1896 and Bath in 1906. Elected for Bath in Jan. 1910 and sat until he was killed in action on 16 Sept. 1918. [1918]

TICKLER, Thomas George. Continued in House after 1918: full entry in Volume III.

TILLETT, Benjamin. Continued in House after 1918: full entry in Volume III.

TILLETT, Louis John. Catton, Norfolk. S. of William H. Tillett, Esq., Solicitor, and Janette Elizabeth Tillett (née Turner). B. at Sprowston, Norfolk 13 June 1865; m. 1896, May, d. of J. Reeve, Esq., (she died 1905).

Educ. privately. A Solicitor, admitted 1889. A Member of Norwich Town Council from 1890, and J.P. for Norfolk. A Liberal. Elected for Norwich in Jan. 1904 and sat until he retired in Jan. 1910. Died 24 Nov. 1929. [1909]

TINDAL-ROBERTSON, Sir William. See ROBERTSON, Sir William Tindal.

TIPPING, William. Retired in 1886: full entry in Volume I.

TOBIN, Alfred Aspinall. 2 Plowden Buildings, Temple, London. Carlton, and Junior Carlton. S. of James Aspinall Tobin, Esq., of Eastham House, Cheshire, and Olivia, d. of Lister Ellis, Esq., of Crofthead, Cumberland. B. 26 Dec. 1855 at Eastham House. Unmarried. Educ. at Rugby, and University Coll., Oxford; B.A. 1st class Honours, Scholar of Jurisprudence. Was called to the bar at the Middle Temple 1880; bencher 1912; K.C. 1903. Recorder of Salford from 1904-1915. A Unionist. Unsuccessfully contested the Scotland division of Liverpool in 1906. First elected for Preston in Jan. 1910 and sat until appointed Judge of County Court in 1915. Knighted in 1919. Retired 1935. Died 30 Nov. 1939. [1915]

TOLLEMACHE, Henry James. 2 Cheyne Walk, London. Dorfold Hall, Nantwich. Carlton, and Arthur's. Eld. s. of Wilbraham Spencer Tollemache, Esq., of Dorfold Hall, Cheshire, by Anne, eld. d. of James Tomkinson, Esq. B. at Dorfold Hall 1846; m. 1904, Katherine, widow of E.C. Streatfield, Esq. Educ. at Eton, and Christ Church, Oxford; graduated B.A. 1870. A Magistrate and Dept.-Lieut. for Cheshire. A Conservative. MP for Cheshire W. from Apr. 1881 to Nov. 1885, and for the Eddisbury division of Cheshire from Nov. 1885 until he retired in 1906. Died 2 Apr. 1939. [1905]

TOMKINSON, Rt. Hon. James. Willington Hall, Tarporley. Brunswick House, Cromer. 17 Bolton Street, London. Brooks's, Bath, and National Liberal. S. of Lieut.-Col. William Tomkinson, and Susan, d. of Thomas Tarleton, Esq., of Bolesworth Castle, Cheshire, by Frances, d. of Sir Philip Grey Egerton, Bart. B. at Willington, Tarporley 1840; m. 1871, Emily Frances, only d. of Sir George Hudson Palmer, 3rd Bart., of Wanlip Hall,

Leicester (she died 1905). Educ. at Rugby School, and Balliol Coll., Oxford; B.A. 1863. A Director of Lloyd's Bank. High Sheriff of Cheshire 1887, Chairman of Petty Sessional Bench of Magistrates, Alderman of County Council and 1st Vice-Chairman of same, J.P. and Dept.-Lieut. for the Co. of Chester. Maj. and Honorary Lieut.-Col. Earl of Chester's Imperial Yeomanry, retired 1906. Appointed 2nd Church Estates Commissioner 1907. Edited his father's journal as the *Diary of a Cavalry Officer*, (1809-15). PC. 1909. A Liberal. Contested W. Cheshire in Apr. 1881, the Wirral division of Cheshire in Dec. 1885, Eddisbury division of Cheshire in July 1886 and July 1892, and N.E. Warwickshire in July 1895. Elected for the Crewe division of Cheshire in 1900 and sat until his death 10 Apr. 1910 [1909]

TOMLINSON, Sir William Edward Murray, Bart. 3 Richmond Terrace, Whitehall, London. Heysham House, Lancashire. Athenaeum, Carlton, and St. Stephen's. Eld. s. of Thomas Tomlinson, Esq., of 3 Richmond Terrace, Whitehall, London, and Heysham House, Lancashire, (one of the benchers of the Inner Temple), by Sarah, d. of the Rev. Roger Mashiter, Incumbent of St. Paul's Church, Manchester, and of Bolton-le-Sands, Lancashire. B. at Heysham House, Lancashire 1838. Educ. at Westminster School, and Christ Church, Oxford; graduated M.A. 1862. Called to the bar at the Inner Temple 1865. A Dept.-Lieut. and J.P. for Lancashire, and retired Maj. and Honorary Lieut.-Col. 11th Volunteer Battalion N. Lancashire Regiment. Created Bart. 1902. A Conservative. Sat for Preston from Nov. 1882 until defeated in 1906. Died 17 Dec. 1912. [1905]

TOOTILL, Robert. Continued in House after 1918: full entry in Volume III.

TORRANCE, Sir Andrew Mitchell. 16 Highbury Quadrant, London. National Liberal, and City Liberal. S. of John Torrance, Esq., Weaving Agent, and Jane Mitchell. B. 13 Feb. 1845 at Old Cumnack, Ayrshire; m. 1870, Flora Weir, d. of John Drummond, Esq. Educ. at Parish School, Old Cumnack. A Partner in Miller, Son and Torrance, Muslin and Lace Manufacturers, London, Belfast, and Glasgow. A member of London County Council 1889-1907; Dept.-Chairman 1897, Vice-

Chairman 1900, and Chairman 1901. Was a member of the Common Council of London 1882-92; Mayor of Islington 1903-04. Knighted 1906. A Liberal. Unsuccessfully contested E. Islington 1900. Elected for Glasgow Central in 1906 and sat until his death 4 Feb. 1909.   [1908]

TOTTENHAM, Arthur Loftus. Glenfarne Hall, Enniskillen, Ireland. Kildare Street Club, Dublin, and Carlton. Eld. s. of Nicholas Loftus Tottenham, Esq., of Glenfarne, by Anna Maria, eld. d. of Sir Francis Hopkins, Bart. B. at Dublin 1838; m. 1859, Sarah Anne, d. of George Addenbroke Gore, Esq., of Barrowmount, Co. Kilkenny. Educ. at Eton. Entered the Rifle Brigade 1854; became Capt. 1858; retired 1861. A Magistrate for Cavan, Fermanagh, and Leitrim, and a Dept.-Lieut. for the latter, of which he was also High Sheriff in 1866. A Conservative, opposed to "the disturbance of the present Imperial relations of Great Britain." Sat from 1880 to 1885 for Leitrim, which he contested unsuccessfully in July 1876. Sat for Winchester from 1885 until his death 4 Dec. 1887.
                                                              [1887]

TOUCHE, Sir George Alexander. 125 Victoria Street, London. Broomfield, Westcott, Dorking. Carlton, City Carlton, Pilgrims, and Royal Automobile. University, Edinburgh. Union, Brighton. S. of Anthony Murray Touche, Esq., of Inverleithfield, Edinburgh, and Margaret, d. of Alexander Guild, Esq., of Edinburgh. B. 24 May 1861 in Edinburgh; m. 1887, Jessie, d. of Isaac Brown, Esq., of Hampstead. Educ. at Edinburgh Institution, and Edinburgh University. Senior Partner in G.A. Touche and Company, Chartered Accountants, London, with branches in U.S.A., Canada, and S. America; Chairman of Industrial and General Trust Limited, The Trustees Corporation, and other companies. Order of St. Sava (Serbia); Lieut. for the City of London; Alderman of the City of London from 1915. Sheriff 1915-16. Knighted 1917. Gov. of Royal Hospitals and of Queen Anne's Bounty. A Unionist. Unsuccessfully contested N.E. Lanarkshire 1904, and N. Islington Jan. 1910. Elected for N. Islington Dec. 1910 and sat until he retired in 1918. Created Bart. 1920. Died 7 July 1935.   [1918]

TOULMIN, Sir George. 127 Fishergate,

Preston. Priors Oak, Penwortham, Preston. Reform, National Liberal, and Eighty. S. of George Toulmin, Esq., J.P., of Preston. B. 1857 at Bolton; m. 1882, Mary Elizabeth, d. of T. Edelston, Esq., Official Receiver of Preston. Educ. at Preston Grammar School. A Newspaper Proprietor; Governing Director of *Preston Guardian* and *Lancashire Daily Post*. A J.P. for Lancashire and Preston; Vice-Chairman of Preston Board of Guardians. President of Newspaper Society 1912-13. Knighted 1911. A Liberal. Elected for Bury May 1902 and sat until defeated in 1918. Died 21 Jan. 1923.   [1918]

TOWNSEND, Charles. St. Mary's, Stoke Bishop, Bristol. Devonshire, and National Liberal. S. of John Henry Townsend, Esq., of Bristol, and Hannah, d. of William Barton, Esq., of Doncaster. B. 1832 at Edgbaston; m. 1859, Anna Maria, d. of Adam Holden, Esq., of Bristol. Educ. at private schools in Leeds and Bristol. A Wholesale and Export Druggist, head of the firm of Ferris and Company, Bristol; a J.P. for the city and Co. of Bristol, member of the Bristol Town Council from 1872. President Bristol Liberal Federation, and a member of the general purposes committee of the National Liberal Federation. A Liberal, in favour of Home Rule for Ireland, disestablishment, an Eight Hours' Bill for Miners, Registration reform, Local Option, Parish Councils, Land Law reform, etc. Sat for Bristol N. from July 1892 until defeated in 1895. President of Bristol Baptist Association. Died 4 Nov. 1908.   [1895]

TOWNSEND, Frederick. Honington Hall, Warwickshire. Arthur's, and Carlton. S. of the Rev. Edward James Townsend (who was 3rd s. of Gore Townsend, Esq., and the Lady Elizabeth Townsend), by Mary Catharine, only d. of John Hambrough, Esq., of Marchwood, Hampshire. B. 1823; m. 1863, Mary Elizabeth, only child of the Rev. Robert Butler, Vicar of St. John's, Kilkenny, who was great-grandson of the 1st Visct. Lanesborough. Educ. at Harrow, and Trinity Coll., Cambridge. A Fellow of the Linnean Society, and author of the *Flora of Hampshire*, pamphlets on Provident Medical Clubs and Dispensaries (1878), and various papers in the *Journal of Botany*. A J.P. and Dept.-Lieut. for the Co. of Warwick and J.P. for Worcester. Patron of 1

353

living and Lord of the Manor of Honington. A Conservative. Sat for the Stratford-on-Avon district of Warwickshire from July 1886 until he retired in 1892. Died 16 Dec. 1905.   [1892]

TOWNSEND-FARQUHAR, Sir Horace Brand, Bart. See FARQUHAR, Sir Horace Brand Townsend, Bart.

TRACY, Hon. Frederick Stephen Archibald Hanbury-. See HANBURY-TRACY, Hon. Frederick Stephen Archibald.

TREVELYAN, Charles Philips. Continued in House after 1918: full entry in Volume III.

TREVELYAN, Rt. Hon. Sir George Otto, Bart. 8 Grosvenor Crescent, London. Wallington, Cambo, Northumberland. Reform, Athenaeum, and Brooks's. S. of Sir Charles Edward Trevelyan, Bart., by Hannah Moore, d. of Zachary Macaulay, Esq. B. at Rothley Temple, Leicestershire 1838; m. 1869, Caroline, eld. d. of R.N. Philips, Esq., MP of Welcombe, Stratford-on-Avon, and The Park, Manchester. Educ. at Harrow, and Trinity Coll., Cambridge, where he was 2nd in the first class of the classical tripos; created LL.D. of Edinburgh 1883, and D.C.L. of Oxford 1885. Was a Lord of the Admiralty from Dec. 1868 to June 1870. Secretary to the Admiralty from Nov. 1880 to May 1882, when he was appointed Chief Secretary for Ireland; became Chancellor of the Duchy of Lancaster in Oct. 1884, with a seat in the Cabinet, and left office in June 1885. He was Secretary for Scotland from Jan. to Mar. 1886 when he resigned with Joseph Chamberlain over the Home Rule issue, and again 1892 to 1895. Author of *The Competition Wallah, Cawnpore, The Life and Letters of Lord Macaulay, The Early Life of Charles James Fox,* etc. PC. 1882. Succeeded as Bart. 1886. A Liberal, in favour of Home Rule, etc. Sat for Tynemouth from 1865 to 1868, for Hawick district from 1868 to 1886. Having opposed the Home Rule Bill of 1886, he was defeated at the ensuing general election. But having become satisfied with Mr. Gladstone's Irish policy he was elected by the Bridgeton division of Glasgow on 2 Aug. 1887 and sat until he accepted Chiltern Hundreds 30 Jan. 1897. Author of *The American Revolution,* 4 vols. (1909), and works on George III and

Charles Fox (1912 and 1914). O.M. 1911. Died 17 Aug. 1928.   [1896]

TRIBICH-LINCOLN, Ignatius Timothy. See LINCOLN, Ignatius Timothy Tribich.

TRITTON, Sir Charles Ernest, Bart. 5 Cadogan Square, London. Bloomfield, Norwood. New University, and Carlton. S. of Joseph Tritton, Esq., and Amelia, his wife. B. 1845 at Battersea; m. 1872, Edith, 2nd d. of Frederick Green, Esq. Educ. at Rugby, and Trinity Hall, Cambridge; B.A. 1868. A Partner in Brightwen and Company, Billbrokers, admitted 1869; a member of the London Chamber of Commerce, Treasurer of the Church of England Temperance Society, and a member of the London City Mission Committee. A Conservative, in favour of fair and equitable Temperance legislation, but strongly opposed to the Direct Veto. Sat for the Norwood division of Lambeth from 1892 until he retired in 1906. Died 28 Dec. 1918.   [1905]

TROTTER, Henry John. 2 Harcourt Buildings, Temple, London. 35 Clarges Street, London. Langton Grange, Gainford, Darlington. St. James's, Carlton, and Constitutional. New Club, Edinburgh. S. of Lieut.-Col. William Trotter, by Henrietta, d. of Maj. A.P. Skene, and Grand-s. of Col. John Trotter, Dept.-Lieut. and J.P. of the county of Durham. B. 1836. Unmarried. Was educ. at Oriel Coll., Oxford, where he was a successful essayist (M.A. 1863). Was called to the bar at the Inner Temple 1864. Was Lieut. 2nd W. Yorkshire Yeomanry (Prince of Wales' Hussars), and was appointed Lieut.-Col. commanding the 2nd Battalion Durham Rifle Volunteers Jan. 1887. A Dept.-Lieut. and J.P. for Durham Co. and a F.S.A., also a Director of the Great Eastern and N. British Railway Companies. An "Independent Conservative." Contested Tynemouth 1868 and 1880, and Berwick on Tweed 1881. Sat for Colchester from Nov. 1885 until his death on 6 Dec. 1888.   [1888]

TRYON, Maj. George Clement. Continued in House after 1918: full entry in Volume III.

TUFF, Charles. The Friars, Rochester. Cliff House, Tankerton, Whitstable.

Carlton, and Constitutional. S. of Henry Tuff, Esq., of Rochester. B. at Plumstead 1855; m. 1879, Marian, d. of G.W. Gill, Esq., of Rochester (she died 1897). Educ. at Sandwich School. A Merchant and Contractor in Rochester, a member of the Town Council 1900-04, Mayor 1900-02; a J.P. for Rochester, a Governor of Mathematical and Girl's Grammar Schools in Rochester. A Conservative. Elected for Rochester Sept. 1903 and sat until defeated in 1906. Died 27 Jan. 1929. [1905]

TUFNELL, Edward. 46 Eaton Square, London. The Grove, Wimbledon Park, London. Carlton, Junior United Service, and St. James's. S. of Edward Carleton Tufnell, Esq., Poor Law Commissioner, and Honoria Mary, only d. and heiress of Col. Macadam, K.H. B. at 26 Lowndes Square, London 1848; m. 1891, Ellen Bertha, d. of the Rev. R.S. Gubbins, Rector of Upham, Hampshire. Educ. at Eton Coll. Entered the army as Ensign in 39th Regiment, May 1867; exchanged to 18th Royal Irish Nov. 1870; Capt. 1879, Maj. 1882. In 1884-85 served in the Nile expedition, for which he received the medal with clasp and the Khedive's Star. Retired from the army in Nov. 1889, with the rank of Lieut.-Col.; in Mar. 1894 was appointed one of the Royal Bodyguard of Hon. Corps of Gentlemen-at-Arms. A Knight of Grace of the Order of St. John of Jerusalem 1900. A Conservative. Elected for S.E. Essex in 1900 and sat until he retired in 1906. Died 15 Aug. 1909. [1905]

TUITE, James. Greville Street, Mullingar, Co. Westmeath. S. of John Tuite, Esq., Watchmaker, by Margaret, d. of Christopher Downes, Esq., both of Mullingar. B. 1849. Educ. at St. Mary's Coll., Mullingar. Was elected Chairman of the Mullingar Town Commissioners Oct. 1881, and was re-elected to that post four times. An Irish Nationalist (Anti-Parnellite), and a "Whip" to his party. Sat for Westmeath N. from 1885 until he retired in 1900. Died 6 Oct. 1916. [1900]

TUKE, Sir John Batty. Balgreen, Gorgie, Edinburgh. 20 Charlotte Square, Edinburgh. Carlton, and Royal Societies. S. of John Batty Tuke, Esq., of Beverley, Yorkshire, and Mary, d. of Robert Stour, Esq., of Hull. B. 1835; m. 1856, Lydia Jane, d. of the Rev. John Magee, Rector of Drogheda, and sister of the Rt. Rev. W.C.

Magee, at one time Archbishop of York. Educ. at Edinburgh Academy, and the University of Edinburgh. M.D., F.R.S.E., F.R.C.P.E., and representative of the latter body on the General Medical Council; LL.D. Edinburgh, D.Sc. (Honours) Dublin; at one time Morrisonian Lecturer on Insanity, and was the author of several works upon the subject. Knighted 1898. A Conservative. Elected for Edinburgh and St. Andrew's Universities in May 1900 and sat until he retired in Jan. 1910. Died 13 Oct. 1913. [1909]

TULLIBARDINE, John George Stewart-Murray, Marq. of. 84 Eaton Place, London. Dunkeld House, Dunkeld, N.B. Carlton, Marlborough, Bachelors', Naval & Military, Royal Aero, and Caledonian. New Club, Edinburgh. Eld. s. of Duke of Atholl. B. 15 Dec. 1871 at Blair Atholl; m. 1899, Katharine Marjory, (later MP for Kinross and W. Perthshire), d. of Sir James H. Ramsay, Bart., of Banff. Educ. at Eton. Joined Royal Horse Guards 1892; Capt. and Brevet Maj. 1900; served with Egyptian Cavalry in the Soudan 1898 (D.S.O.), and was mentioned twice in despatches; served in the S. African War 1899-1902, first attached to Royal Dragoons and later as Lieut.-Col. commanding Scottish Horse (2 Regiments), which corps he raised for service in S. Africa 1900; was mentioned three times in despatches; M.V.O. 1902. Brig-Gen. Scottish Horse Brigade Imperial Yeomanry. Chairman of Perthshire Territorial Association from 1908. A J.P., Dept.-Lieut. and County Councillor for Perthshire; J.P. for Glasgow. Grand Master Mason of Scotland 1908-13; Chairman Royal Aero Club 1913. A Unionist. Unsuccessfully contested E. Perthshire in 1906. Elected for W. Perthshire in Jan. 1910 and sat until he succeeded as Duke of Atholl 20 Jan. 1917. C.B. 1917. Lord-Lieut. of Perthshire 1917-42. K.T. 1918. Lord High Commissioner of the Church of Scotland 1918-20. PC. 1921. Lord Chamberlain 1921-22. G.C.V.O. 1923. Died 15 Mar. 1942. [1916]

TULLY, Jasper. Boyle, Co. Roscommon. S. of G.M. Tully, Esq., Proprietor of the *Roscommon Herald*, and Honoria J. Costello, of Tuam. B. at Boyle 1859; m. 1891, Marie, d. of John Mason, Esq., of Boyle. Educ. at Summerhill Coll., Athlone. A Journalist, Editor of the *Roscommon Herald*, etc. Proprietor of the *Westmeath Nationalist* as well as of the *Roscommon Herald*. A Nationalist. Sat for the S. division of Leitrim from July 1892 until he retired in 1906. Died 16 Sept. 1938. [1905]

TURNOUR, Edward Turnour, Visct. See WINTERTON, Edward Turnour, Earl. Continued in House after 1918: full entries in Volumes III and IV.

TURTON, Edmund Russborough. Continued in House after 1918: full entry in Volume III.

TWISLETON - WYKEHAM - FIENNES, Hon. Sir Eustace Edward, Bart. See FIENNES, Hon. Sir Eustace Edward Twisleton-Wykeham-, Bart.

TWIST, Henry. Continued in House after 1918: full entry in Volume III.

TYLER, Sir Henry Whatley. Pymmes Park, Edmonton, Middlesex. Army & Navy, and Carlton. Eld. s. of John Chatfield Tyler, Esq. B. at Chesterfield Street, London 1827; m. 1852, Margaret, d. of Gen. Sir Charles Pasley, K.C.B., R.E. Was educ. at the Royal Military Academy, Woolwich. Entered the Royal Engineers as Lieut. Dec. 1844, became Capt. 1853, retired 1867. Was appointed Inspector of Railways (Board of Trade) Apr. 1853; Chief Inspector of Railways from 1871 to 1877, when he retired. Knighted 1877. A Conservative. Sat for Harwich from 1880 to 1885 and for Great Yarmouth from 1885 until defeated in 1892. Dept.-Chairman, Great Eastern Railway. Died 30 Jan. 1908. [1892]

TYSSEN-AMHERST, William Amhurst. See AMHERST, William Amhurst Tyssen.

TYSSEN-AMHURST, William Amhurst. See AMHERST, William Amhurst Tyssen.

UNIACKE - PENROSE - FITZGERALD, Sir Robert, Bart. See PENROSE-FITZGERALD, Sir Robert Uniacke-, Bart.

URE, Rt. Hon. Alexander. 31 Heriot Row, Edinburgh. National Liberal, Ranelagh, Royal Automobile, and Bath. S. of John Ure, Esq., a Merchant of Cairndhu, Helensburgh, at one time Lord Provost of Glasgow, by Isabella née Gibb. B. 1853 at Glasgow; m. Margaret Mac-Dowall, d. of Thomas Steven, Esq., of Glasgow. Educ. at Larchfield Academy, Helensburgh, and Glasgow University; M.A., LL.B. An Advocate, called to the bar in 1878; was Lecturer on Constitutional Law and History at Glasgow University from 1878 to 1888, Q.C. 1897, and Solicitor-Gen. for Scotland Dec. 1905 to Feb. 1909, when he was appointed Lord Advocate; PC. 1909. A Liberal, in favour of Home Rule, etc. Unsuccessfully contested W. Perthshire in 1892 and Linlithgowshire in June 1893. Elected for Linlithgowshire in 1895 and sat until appointed Lord Justice Gen. and Lord President of Court of Session with title of Lord Strathclyde in Oct. 1913; retired 1920. Created Baron Strathclyde Jan. 1914; G.B.E. 1917. Died 2 Oct. 1928. [1913]

USBORNE, Thomas. Writtle, Nr. Chelmsford. Carlton, and City. S. of Thomas Masters Usborne, Esq., and Margaret Usborne. B. 1840 at Limerick; m. 1863, d. of Joseph Alfred Hardcastle, Esq., MP for Bury St. Edmunds. Educ. at Harrow, and Trinity Coll., Cambridge. A J.P. for Essex, and Chairman of the Anglo-Egyptian Bank; also Chairman of the Writtle Brewery Company. A Conservative. Sat for the Chelmsford division of Essex from Apr. 1892 until he retired in 1900. Died 7 June 1915. [1900]

VALENTIA, Arthur Annesley, Visct. Bletchington Park, Oxford. Carlton, Cavalry, and Turf. Grand-s. of the 10th Visct. B. 1843 at Inveresk, near Edinburgh; m. 1878, Laura Sarah, d. of D. Hale Webb, Esq., and widow of Sir A.W. Peyton, 4th Bart. Educ. at the Royal Military Academy, Woolwich. A Lieut. 10th Royal Hussars. A J.P. Oxfordshire (High Sheriff 1874), Honorary Col. Oxfordshire Yeomanry; Chairman of Oxfordshire County Council. Succeeded as the 11th Visct. and also Baron Mountnorris in the peerage of Ireland, and a Bart. in 1863. Was Comptroller in H.M. Household Oct. 1898 to Dec. 1905, and a Unionist Whip 1898-1911. A Lord-in-Waiting from June 1915 to Jan. 1924. A Conservative. Unsuccessfully contested mid Oxfordshire in 1885. First elected for Oxford City in Apr. 1895 and sat until created Baron Annesley in the U.K. peerage in 1917. C.B. 1900; M.V.O. 1901; K.C.V.O. 1923. Died 20 Jan. 1927. [1917]

VALENTINE, Charles James. Bankfield,

Workington. Constitutional. S. of James Valentine, Esq., of Stockport, by Mary, d. of C.A. Bradbury, Esq., of the same town. B. at Stockport, Sept. 1837; m. 1861, Anne, d. of Peter Kirk, Esq., of Chapel-en-le-Frith. Educ. privately. An Ironmaster in business at Workington, Cumberland. Managing Director of the Moss Bay Hematite Iron and Steel Company, Director of the Cleator and Workington Junction Railway Company, etc. A Magistrate for Cumberland, Chairman of the Workington Local Board, etc. F.R.G.S. A Conservative, but "favourable to advanced temperance legislation". Sat for the Cockermouth division of Cumberland from Dec. 1885 until he retired in 1886. [1886]

VANDERBYL, Philip. Defeated in 1886: full entry in Volume I.

VAUGHAN-DAVIES, Matthew Lewis. Continued in House after 1918: full entry in Volume III.

VENABLES - LLEWELYN, Charles Leyshon Dillwyn. Llysdinam, Newbridge-on-Wye, Radnorshire. Carlton, and Arthur's. Only s. of Sir John Dillwyn-Llewelyn, Bart., and Julia, sister of Lord St. Aldwyn. B. 1870; m. 1893, Katharine Minna, d. of the Rev. R.L. Venables, and then assumed the additional surname of Venables. A J.P. and Dept.-Lieut. for Brecon, a J.P. for Radnor and Glamorgan, and Maj. Glamorgan Yeomanry. A Unionist. Unsuccessfully contested Radnorshire in 1900 and 1906. Elected there in Jan. 1910 and sat until defeated in Dec. 1910. Succeeded as 2nd Bart. 1927; Lord-Lieut. Radnorshire 1929-49. Died 24 June 1951. [1910]

VERDIN, Robert. The Brockhurst, Northwich, Cheshire. Reform. S. of Joseph Verdin, Esq., of Highfield House, Winsford, by Margaret, d. of Wharton Sadler, Esq., of Northwich. B. at Northwich 1835. Unmarried. Educ. privately. Senior Partner in the firm of Joseph Verdin and Sons, Salt Proprietors, of Northwich, Winsford, etc. and of Verdin Brothers, Merchants, of Liverpool. Also a Magistrate for the Co., Commissioner for the Upper Mersey, and President of the Salt Chamber of Commerce, of the White Salt Trade Association, and Chairman of the Winsford Local Board. A Liberal, opposed to Home Rule for Ireland. Sat for the Northwich division of Cheshire from July 1886 until his death 25 July 1887. [1887]

VERNEY, Capt. Edmund Hope. 92 Onslow Gardens, London. Rhianva, Anglesey. Travellers', United Service, and National Liberal. Eld. s. of the Rt. Hon. Harry Verney, Bart., and Eliza, d. of Admiral Sir George Johnstone Hope, K.C.B., and grand-d. maternally of the 7th Lord Kinnaird. B. 1838 at Westminster; m. 1868, Margaret Maria, eld. d. of Sir John and Lady Sarah Hay Williams. Educ. at Harrow School. Entered the navy in 1851; served in the Crimea and in the Indian Mutiny Campaign; became Capt. 1877; retired 1884. Chairman of Quarter Sessions for Anglesey, J.P. and Dept.-Lieut. for Anglesey and Buckinghamshire, and a member of the Anglesey County Council and of the London County Council (Lambeth, Brixton division). Author of *The Shannon's Brigade in India, The Last Four Days of the Eurydice, Village Sketches,* and *Four Years of Protest in The Transvaal.* A Liberal, in favour of Home Rule, Local Option, Land Law reforms, and reform of municipal government. Unsuccessfully contested Marlow in 1868, Beaumaris district in 1874 and Portsmouth in 1880. Sat for Buckinghamshire N. from Dec. 1885 until July 1886 when he was defeated standing as a Gladstonian Liberal. Returned again for Buckinghamshire N. in Oct. 1889 and sat until he was expelled in May 1891 for being convicted at the Central Criminal Court for conspiring to procure a girl under 21 years of age for an immoral purpose. Succeeded as Bart. in 1894. Died 8 May 1910. [1891]

VERNEY, Frederick William. 12 Connaught Place, London. Brooks's, Travellers', and National Liberal. S. of the Rt. Hon. Sir Harry Verney, Bart., MP. B. 1846 at Claydon House, Winslow; m. 1870, Maude Sarah, d. of Sir John Hay Williams. Educ. at Harrow, and Christ Church, Oxford. A Barrister, called 1873. Secretary to Siamese Legation 1883, and subsequently Councillor; a member of Buckinghamshire County Council from 1889 and London County Council 1898-1907. A Liberal. Unsuccessfully contested S.W. Kent in 1885, Bath in 1886, Norwich in 1895, and the Exchange division of Liverpool in 1900. Elected for N. Buckinghamshire in 1906 and sat until he retired in Dec. 1910; unsuccessfully contested Christchurch at the same time. Died 26 Apr. 1913.   [1910]

VERNEY, Sir Harry Calvert Williams, Bart. Claydon House, Steeple Claydon, Buckinghamshire. Brooks's. S. of Sir Edmund Verney, 3rd Bart., and Margaret, d. of Sir John Hay Williams, 2nd Bart. B. 7 June 1881 at Rhianva, Menai Bridge; m. 1911, Lady Rachel Bruce, d. of Earl of Elgin. Educ. at Harrow, and Balliol Coll., Oxford; M.A. Was Assistant Private Secretary to Lord Elgin and Lord Crewe at the Colonial Office 1907-10. Parliamentary Private Secretary to Mr. A. Birrell, Chief Secretary for Ireland 1911-14. Parliamentary Secretary to the Board of Agriculture and Fisheries 1914-15. Lieut.-Col.; Assistant Director of Labour with the British Expeditionary Force in France from 1916. A J.P. and County Councillor for Buckinghamshire. A Liberal. Unsuccessfully contested the Basingstoke division of Hampshire in Jan. and Mar. 1906, and S. Wiltshire in Jan. 1910. Elected for N. Buckinghamshire Dec. 1910 and sat until defeated 1918. Contested Basingstoke by-election 1920, Skipton 1922, 1923, Banbury 1924, Buckrose by-election 1926. Member of Anglesey County Council from 1949-55. Editor of *The Verneys of Claydon* (1969); author of *Florence Nightingale at Harley Street* (1971). Died 23 Dec. 1974.   [1918]

VERNEY, Hon. Richard Greville. 35 Harley Street, London. Kineton, Warwickshire. Carlton, and Pratt's. Eld. s. of Henry, 18th Baron Willoughby-de-Broke, by Geraldine, d. of J.H. Smith-Barry, Esq., of Marbury Hall, Co. Chester. B. 1869; m. 1895, Marie, youngest d. of Charles Hanbury, Esq. Educ. at Eton, and New Coll., Oxford. A J.P. and Dept.-Lieut. for Warwickshire and Lieut. Warwickshire Yeomanry Cavalry. A Conservative. Sat for the Rugby division of Warwickshire from July 1895 until he retired in 1900. Succeeded as 19th Baron Willoughby-de-Broke in 1902. Died 16 Dec. 1923.   [1900]

VERNON, Hon. Greville Richard. 23 Cadogan Street, London. Auchan's House, Kilmarnock. Travellers', and Wellington. Youngest s. of Lord Lyveden. B. in London 1835; m. 1858, Susan Cockerell, 2nd d. of Richard Cockerell, Esq., by his wife Theresa, afterwards Countess of Eglinton and Winton. Educ. at

Harrow. Was in the Foreign Office from 1855 to 1859, and was attached to Sir Henry Bulwer's special mission to the Danubian provinces 1856-57. A J.P. for Ayrshire and Lieut.-Col. of the Ayrshire Artillery Volunteers. A Liberal Unionist. First returned for the S. division of Ayrshire July 1886 and sat until he retired in 1892. Died 19 Feb. 1909.   [1892]

VERNON-HARCOURT, Rt. Hon. Sir William George Granville Venables. See HARCOURT, Rt. Hon. Sir William George Granville Venables Vernon-.

VERNON-WENTWORTH, Bruce Canning. See WENTWORTH, Bruce Canning Vernon-.

VERRALL, George Henry. 2 Whitehall Court, London. Sussex Lodge, Newmarket. Carlton, and Constitutional. S. of John Verrall, Esq., of Lewes. B. 7 Feb. 1848 at Lewes; m. Sophia Agnes, d. of John Francis Clark, Esq., of Newmarket. Educ. at Lewes Grammar School. An Auctioneer, Accountant, and Racecourse Manager. Vice-Chairman of Cambridgeshire County Council from 1907, and an Alderman from 1889. A J.P. for Suffolk and Cambridgeshire. Author of *British Flies,* 2 volumes. A Unionist. Unsuccessfully contested the Newmarket division of Cambridgeshire in 1906. Elected there in Jan. 1910 and sat until defeated in Dec. 1910. Died 16 Sept. 1911.   [1910]

VILLIERS, Rt. Hon. Charles Pelham. 50 Cadogan Place, London. Brooks's, Athenaeum, Travellers', and Reform. 3rd s. of the Hon. George Villiers (s. of the 1st Earl of Clarendon), by the only d. of 1st Lord Boringdon. B. 1802. Graduated at Cambridge M.A. 1827; was called to the bar at Lincoln's Inn 1827; was one of the Examiners of witnesses in the Court of Chancery from 1833 till Dec. 1852, Judge Advocate Gen. from Dec. 1852 till Mar. 1858, and President of the Poor Law Board from July 1859 till July 1866. Also one of the Commissioners of Inquiry into the operations of the Poor Laws. A Dept.-Lieut. for Hertford; in 1879 his statue was erected in Wolverhampton. Created the status of an Earl's younger son in 1839. PC. 1853. A Liberal Unionist, well known before 1846 for his frequent motions against the Corn Laws. Sat for

Wolverhampton from 1835 to 1847; was returned for that borough at the general election in the latter year, and was at the same time chosen for Lancashire S. He chose to sit for Wolverhampton, which he represented until his death 16 Jan. 1898, sitting for S. Wolverhampton from 1885 onwards. Both in age and in continuous length of service, he was the father of the House of Commons from 1890 to his death. [1897]

VILLIERS, Ernest Amherst. 22 Adelaide Crescent, Brighton. Arthur's, and St. James's. S. of the Rev. Charles Villiers and Florence Tyssen-Amherst, sister of Lord Amherst of Hackney. B. 14 Nov. 1863; m. 1898, the Hon. Elaine Guest, d. of Lord Wimborne. Educ. at Uppingham School, and Peterhouse Coll., Cambridge. Was ordained in 1893 and was Vicar of Haverlands and Rector of Brandiston in Norfolk, which livings he resigned in 1900, when he availed himself of the Clerical Disabilities Act and gave up orders. A Liberal. Elected for Brighton in Apr. 1905 and sat until he retired in Jan. 1910. Unsuccessfully contested the Clapham division of Wandsworth in 1922. Died 26 Sept. 1923. [1909]

VINCENT, Col. Sir Charles Edward Howard, K.C.M.G., C.B. 1 Grosvenor Square, London. Villa Flora, Cannes. Carlton, Naval & Military, Athenaeum, Royal Societies', and Marlborough. S. of the Rev. Sir Frederick Vincent (11th Bart.), Canon of Chichester, by Maria Copley, d. of R. Herries Young, Esq., of Auchenskrugh, Dumfriesshire. B. at Slinfold, Sussex 1849; m. 1882, Ethel Gwendoline, d. of George Moffatt, Esq., MP, of Goodrich Court, Herefordshire. Educ. at Westminster, and the Royal Military Coll., Sandhurst. Joined the Royal Welsh Fusiliers 1868, and retired as Lieut. in 1873, when appointed Capt. in the Royal Berkshire Militia; resigned 1875 for the Lieut.-Colonelcy of the Central London Rangers. Director of Criminal Investigations in the Metropolitan Police 1878-84. Called to the bar, Inner Temple 1876, and practised two years on the S.E. Circuit and in the Probate, Divorce, and Admiralty Division of the High Court. He also entered 1877 at the Paris Faculté de Droit. Col. of the Queen's Westminster Volunteers, and Aide-de-Camp to the King (S. African Medal and Volunteer Decoration).

Was British representative at the Anti-Anarchist Conference at Rome 1898. Vice-Chairman of Commercial Committee, Chairman of Alien Immigration Parliamentary Committee, Chairman of National Union 1895, and from then Chairman of Publication Committee. Member of Grand Council of Primrose League from 1884. Knight of St. John of Jerusalem in England, Commander of the German Crown, the Crown of Italy, and the Legion of Honour. Senior Dept.-Lieut. of London, a J.P. for Middlesex, Westminster, and Berkshire, and was a member of the Metropolitan Board of Works 1886-88, and of the London County Council 1888-96. Founder and honorary Secretary of the United Empire Trade League 1891. Wrote *Elementary Military Geography, The Law of Criticism and Libel, The Improvement of the Volunteer Force, A Police Code and Manual of the Criminal Law,* etc. C.B. 1885. Knighted 1896. K.C.M.G. 1899. A Conservative and Fair Trader, an advocate of Imperial Federation, and of preferential trading relations between all parts of the British Empire, etc. Sat for Central Sheffield from 1885 until his death 7 Apr. 1908. [1908]

VINCENT, Sir Edgar. Esher Place, Esher, Surrey. Carlton, Guards', and St. James's. Youngest s. of the Rev. Sir F. Vincent, 11th Bart., and bro. of Sir Charles Edward Howard Vincent, Bart., K.C.M.G. B. 1857; m. 1890, Helen, d. of 1st Earl of Feversham. Educ. at Eton, and thence passed as student dragoman in Constantinople and joined the Coldstream Guards, Lieut. 1877, retired 1882. In 1880 he became Military Attaché to the British Embassy, Constantinople, and acted as Private Secretary to Lord E. Fitzmaurice, MP, as Commissioner on E. Roumelian affairs; in 1881 was Assistant Commissioner for cession of Thessaly by Turkey to Greece; in 1882 English, Belgian, and Dutch representative on Ottoman Public Debt; from 1883-89 Financial Adviser to Government of Egypt; and 1889-97 Gov. Ottoman Bank at Constantinople. Created K.C.M.G. 1887. Had the Grand Cordon of the Medjidie, Osmanieh, and Imtiaz. A Conservative. Elected for Exeter in 1899 and sat until defeated in 1906. Contested Colchester as a Liberal in Dec. 1910. Created Baron D'Abernon 1914, Visct. D'Abernon 1926. Chairman Dominions Royal Trade Commission 1912-17. Chairman Central Control Board (Liquor

Traffic) 1915-20. PC. 1920. Ambassador to Germany 1920-26. Head of British Economic Mission to the Argentine and Brazil 1929. Chairman Medical Research Council 1929-33. F.R.S. 1934. Succeeded as 16th Bart. 1936. Author of memoirs (two volumes) and other works. Died 1 Nov. 1941.   [1905]

VIVIAN, Henry Harvey. Continued in House after 1918: full entry in Volume III.

VIVIAN, Sir Henry Hussey, Bart. 27 Belgrave Square, London. Singleton, Swansea, Glamorganshire. Arthur's, Brooks's, and Athenaeum. Eld. s. of John Henry Vivian, Esq., (MP for Swansea from 1832 till 1855) by Sarah, eld. d. of Arthur Jones, Esq., of Reigate. B. at Singleton 1921; m. 1st, 1847, Jesse Dalrymple, d. of Ambrose Goddard, Esq., of Swindon (she died 1848); 2ndly, 1853, Caroline, d. of Sir Montagu J. Cholmeley, Bart., MP (she died 1868); 3rdly, 1870. Averil, d. of Capt. R. Beaumont, R.N., of Rutland Gate. Educ. at Eton, and Trinity Coll., Cambridge. A Dept.-Lieut. and Chairman of Glamorgan County Council; Col. of the 4th Glamorgan Rifles. Created Bart. 1882. In 1886 a statue of him was erected in Swansea. An Independent Liberal, opposed to the Home Rule Bill of 1886, but later supported Mr. Gladstone's Irish policy. Sat for Truro from July 1852 till Apr. 1857. Sat for Glamorganshire from Apr. 1857 to Nov. 1885; sat for Swansea district from Nov. 1885 until created Lord Swansea in June 1893. Died 28 Nov. 1894.
                                                    [1893]

WADDY, Samuel Danks. 27 Maresfield Gardens, Hampstead, London. National Liberal. S. of the Rev. Samuel D. Waddy, D.D., Principal of Wesley Coll., Sheffield, and President of the Wesleyan Conference, by Elizabeth, d. of Thomas Danks, Esq., of Wednesbury. B. at Gateshead 1830; m. 1860, Emma, d. of S.A. Garbutt, Esq., of Hull. Educ. at Wesley Coll., Sheffield; graduated B.A. at London University 1850. Called to the bar in 1858 at the Inner Temple, of which he was elected a bencher 1876. Became a Queen's Counsel 1874. A Liberal, in favour of Mr. Gladstone's Irish policy. Sat for Barnstaple from Feb. 1874 to Dec. 1879, and for Sheffield from the latter date to Apr. 1880, when he was an unsuccessful candidate there. Sat for Edinburgh from Nov. 1882

to the dissolution of 1885, when he unsuccessfully contested Islington N. First returned for the N. Lindsey division of Lincolnshire from 1886 until appointed Recorder of Sheffield in 1894. Unsuccessfully contested Grantham in 1895. Appointed County Court Judge 1896. Died 30 Dec. 1902.   [1894]

WADSWORTH, John. 2 Huddersfield Road, Barnsley. B. 1850 at West Melton, near Rotherham; m. 1872, Annie Eliza Bell, of Newbegin, near Sheffield. Educ. at Brompton School. Commenced work at an early age in a coal-mine; appointed checkweighman 1883, was Secretary and President of Wharncliffe Branch of the Yorkshire Miners' Association. Later the Gen. and Corresponding Secretary of Yorkshire Miners' Association; President 1904. A Labour Member. Elected for the Hallamshire division of the W. Riding of Yorkshire in 1906 and sat until he retired in 1918. Died 10 July 1921.   [1918]

WALDRON, Laurence Ambrose. 10 Anglesea Street, Dublin. Marino, Ballybrack, Co. Dublin. Reform, National Liberal, and Burlington Fine Arts'. S. of Laurence Waldron, Esq., MP for Tipperary, and Anne, d. of Francis White, Esq., President College of Surgeons (I.) B. 14 Nov. 1858 at Ballybrack, Co. Dublin. Unmarried. Educ. at Bellvedere Coll., Dublin, and Oratory School, Birmingham. A Stockbroker, a member of Dublin Stock Exchange, and one of the Stockbrokers to the Court of Chancery, Landed Estates Court, and Land Commission in Ireland. Chairman of the Grand Canal Company; a Governor of the National Gallery, Ireland. An Independent Nationalist. Elected for the St. Stephen's Green division of Dublin in Mar. 1904 and sat until he retired in Jan. 1910. PC. (Ireland) 1911. Died 27 Dec. 1923.   [1909]

WALKER, Henry de Rosenbach. Melton Lodge, Swanage, Dorset. 28 Hornton Court, Kensington, London. St. James's, and National Liberal. S. of R.F. Walker, Esq., of Shooter's Hill, Kent, and Marie von Rosenbach, of Karritz, Esthonia, Russia. B. 30 May 1867 at Ealing; m. 1900, Maud Eleanor, d. of the Rev. D.W. Chute, Rector of Sherborne, Basingstoke. Educ. at Winchester, and Trinity Coll., Cambridge. Was a Clerk in the Foreign Office from 1889-92. Author of *Australasian Democracy*,

West Indies and the Empire. A Liberal. Unsuc-
cessfully contested Stowmarket division of
Suffolk in 1895 and Plymouth in 1900.
Elected for the Melton division of
Leicestershire in 1906 and sat until de-
feated in Dec. 1910. London County
Council member for E. St. Pancras 1913.
Alderman 1919. Died 31 July 1923. [1910]

WALKER, Col. William Hall. Continued
in House after 1918: full entry in Volume
III.

WALLACE, John Stewart. Copthall
House, London. Cliftonville Avenue,
Belfast. National Liberal, and City Liberal.
S. of John Wallace, Esq., Contractor and
Brick Manufacturer, and Mary Sarah
Stewart. B. 1840 at Edenderry Lodge,
Belfast; m. 1866, Jane Miller, eld. d. of the
Rev. James Hodgens of Belfast. Educ. at
the Belfast Royal Academy. A Timber
Merchant, invented and patented many
inventions; travelled much in the colonies,
etc. visited the United States over twenty
times, and was interested in gold mines
there. A member of the International Arbitration Society, Vice-President Irish Protestant Home Rule Association, member
of the London Chamber of Commerce,
Fellow of the Chemical Society, etc. An advanced Liberal, in favour of Mr.
Gladstone's Scheme of Home Rule for Ireland, and the "Newcastle programme"
generally. Sat for the Limehouse division
of Tower Hamlets from July 1892 until he
retired in 1895. [1895]

WALLACE, Professor Robert. 9 Edith
Villas, London. 1a Middle Temple Lane,
London. Reform. S. of Jasper Wallace,
Esq., of Culross, Perthshire. B. at St.
Andrews, Fifeshire 1831. Educ. at the
Geddes Institution, Culross, the High
School, Edinburgh, and the Universities of
St. Andrews and Edinburgh. Was a
Minister at the Greyfriars and other
churches in Edinburgh and was for some
time Editor of the *Scotsman.* The latter post
he quitted in 1880. A D.D. of the Univer-
sity of Glasgow, Examiner in Philosophy
at St. Andrews, and a Professor of Church
History at the University of Edinburgh. In
Nov. 1883 he was called to the bar at the
Middle Temple. An advanced Liberal, in
favour of Home Rule, etc. Sat for Edinburgh E. from July 1886 until his death 6
June 1899. [1899]

WALLACE, Robert. 32 Clarence Gate
Gardens, London. 2 Garden Court, Temple, London. S. of the Rev. Robert
Wallace, of St. Stephen's Green, Dublin. B.
in Dublin 1850. Educ. at Wesley Coll., and
Queen's University, Dublin; B.A. 1871,
LL.B. 1873. A Barrister, called to the bar at
the Middle Temple 1874, and joined the
N.E. Circuit; became Q.C. in 1894, and
was Examiner in the Supreme Court, and
a Revising Barrister for Middlesex. A
Liberal, in favour of Home Rule, etc. Unsuccessfully contested Wandsworth 1885,
W. Edinburgh 1886, and W. Renfrewshire
1892. First elected for Perth in 1895 and sat
until appointed Chairman of the County
of London Sessions 1907-1931. Knighted
1916. Died 19 Mar. 1939. [1906]

**WALROND, Rt. Hon. Sir William Hood,
Bart.** 9 Wilbraham Place, Sloane Street,
London. Carlton. Eld. s. of Sir John
Walrond Walrond, Bart., of Bradfield,
Devon (who sat for Tiverton from July
1865 to Nov. 1868), by Hon. Frances
Caroline, younger d. of 2nd Lord Brid-
port. B. at Exeter 1849; m. 1871, Elizabeth
Katharine, only d. and heir of James S. Pit-
man, Esq., of Dunchideock House, Devon.
Was educ. at Eton. Entered the Grenadier
Guards as Ensign and Lieut. Feb. 1869;
became Lieut. and Capt. 1871, and retired
1872. Was Lieut.-Col. 1st Devon Royal
Volunteers, and was a J.P. and Dept.-
Lieut. for Devon. Succeeded as Bart. in
1889. Chancellor of Duchy of Lancaster
1902-05. Was Patronage Secretary to the
Treasury 1895-1902; and a Lord of the
Treasury 1885-Jan. 1886 and Aug. 1886-92.
PC. 1899. Chief Conservative Whip
1895-1902. A Conservative. Sat for E.
Devon from 1880 to 1885, and for the
Tiverton division of Devon from 1885 until he was created Baron Waleran in Dec.
1905. Died 17 May 1925. [1905]

**WALROND, Hon. William Lionel
Charles.** Bradfield, Cullompton, Devon.
11 Hill Street, London. Carlton,
Bachelors', and Garrick. Eld. s. of Sir
William Walrond, MP, 1st Lord Waleran.
B. 1876; m. 1904, Lottie, d. of George
Coats, Esq., of Belleisle, Ayr. Educ. pri-
vately. Private Secretary to two chief Con-
servative Whips (Sir W. Walrond and Sir
A. Acland-Hood). A Conservative and
Unionist. Elected for the Tiverton division
of Devon in 1906 and sat until his death on
active service on 2 Nov. 1915. [1915]

WALSH, Hon. Arthur Henry John. 16 Pont Street, London. Eywood, Titley, Herefordshire. Carlton, Turf, Marlborough, and White's. Eld. s. of Lord Ormathwaite, by the d. of the 7th Duke of Beaufort. B. 1859; m. 1890, Lady Clementine Frances, only d. of the 3rd Marq. of Camden. Educ. at Eton. A Dept.-Lieut. for Radnorshire and Lieut. in the 1st Life Guards (retired Apr. 1886). Also a Magistrate for Radnorshire. A "moderate Conservative". Sat for Radnorshire from 1885 until he retired in 1892. Lord-Lieut. of Radnorshire. K.C.V.O. 1912; G.C.V.O. 1920. Succeeded as Baron Ormathwaite in 1920. Died 13 Mar. 1937. [1892]

WALSH, John. Eversleigh, Bandon, Co. Cork. B. 1850. Head of the firm of J. Walsh and Company, Bandon; Chairman of Beamish and Crawford Bottling Company Limited, Bandon. A J.P. and County Councillor for Cork. A Nationalist. Elected for S. Cork in Dec. 1910 and sat until he retired in 1918. Died 25 Aug. 1925. [1918]

WALSH, Stephen. Continued in House after 1918: full entry in Volume III.

WALTERS, Sir John Tudor. Continued in House after 1918: full entry in Volume III.

WALTON, Sir John Lawson. 40 Great Cumberland Place, London. Coombe Hill, Butler's Cross, Buckinghamshire. Brooks's, and Reform. S. of the Rev. John Walton, M.A., President of the Wesleyan Conference, and Emma Walton, d. of the Rev. Thomas Harris. B. 1852 in Ceylon; m. 1882, Joanna M'Neilage, d. of Robert Hedderwick, Esq., of the *Glasgow Citizen*. Educ. at the Merchant Taylors' School, Great Crosby, Lancashire, and London University. Was called to the bar at the Inner Temple; (First Prizeman, Common Law) June 1877; elected bencher 1897; Q.C. 1890. Attorney-Gen., appointed Dec. 1905; Knighted 1905. A Liberal. Contested Central Leeds unsuccessfully July 1892. First elected for S. Leeds Sept. 1892 and sat until his death 19 Jan. 1908. [1907]

WALTON, Sir Joseph, Bart. Continued in House after 1918: full entry in Volume III.

WANKLYN, James Leslie. 75 Chester Square, London. Marlborough, and New. Eld. s. of the Rev. James Hibbert Wanklyn, of Trinity Coll., Oxford, and of Radley Coll., by a d. of John Leslie, Esq. B. 1860 at Bournemouth; m. 1898, Laura, widow of Col. H. Bacon, and d. of Martin Stapylton, Esq. Educ. privately. Chairman of the La Plata and Ensenada Tramways Company; Director of the Natal and Nova Cruz (Brazilian) Railway; Chairman of the Aragon and Catalonia Railway, etc. A Liberal Unionist, reprobated attacks on Constitution as affecting the credit of the Country. Represented the central division of Bradford from 1895 until he retired in 1906. Died 6 July 1919. [1905]

WARD, Arnold Sandwith. 25 Grosvenor Place, London. Stocks, Tring. S. of T. Humphry Ward, Esq., and Mrs. Humphry Ward. B. 8 Nov. 1876 at Oxford. Unmarried. Educ. at Eton, and Balliol Coll., Oxford; Craven Scholar and Chancellor's Prizeman. A Barrister, called to the bar 1903. Lieut. Hertfordshire Yeomanry, and served with the Expeditionary Force. A Unionist. Unsuccessfully contested the Cricklade division of Wiltshire in 1906. Elected for the Watford division of Hertfordshire in Jan. 1910 and sat until he retired in 1918. Died 1 Jan. 1950. [1918]

WARD, John. Continued in House after 1918: full entry in Volume III.

WARD, Hon. Robert Arthur. 42 Grosvenor Square, London. Cape, South Africa. Carlton, Marlborough, Turf, and Bachelors'. S. of the 1st Earl of Dudley, by his 2nd wife, Georgina Elizabeth, d. of Sir Thomas Moncreiffe, 7th Bart. B. 1871 at Witley Court, Worcester. Educ. at Sunningdale School, Berkshire, at Eton, and at Trinity Hall, Cambridge. Lieut. Queen's Own Worcestershire Yeomanry Cavalry and in 1895 was appointed an Assistant Private Secretary (unpaid) to Mr. Chaplin, President of the Local Government Board. A Conservative and Unionist, opposed to Home Rule, "Local Option" without compensation, and the abolition of the House of Lords; in favour of Employers' Liability, with liberty for "private arrangements", and legislation on agricultural depression, the unemployed, old age pensions, etc. Sat for the Crewe division of Cheshire from July 1895 until he retired in 1900. O.B.E. 1919. Died 14 June 1942. [1900]

WARD, William Dudley. Continued in House after 1918: full entry in Volume III.

WARDE, Col. Charles Edward. Barham Court, Maidstone. Carlton, Royal Automobile, and Naval & Military. S. of Gen. Sir Edward Warde. B. 1845 at Limerick; m. 1890, Helen, d. of Visct. de Stern. Educ. privately. A Lieut.-Col. (retired) 4th Hussars; served also in the 19th Hussars; Aide-de-Camp to the Gov. of Gibraltar 1873-76; Aide-de-Camp to Gen. Commanding N. Dist. Ireland 1884-86. A Dept.-Lieut. and J.P. for Kent, Col. commanding W. Kent Yeomanry, etc. A Unionist. Represented mid Kent from 1892 until he retired in 1918. Created Bart. 1919. Died 12 Apr. 1937.   [1918]

WARDLE, George James. Continued in House after 1918: full entry in Volume III.

WARDLE, Henry. Highfield, Burton-on-Trent. Reform, City Liberal, National Liberal, and National. S. of Francis Wardle, Esq., by his marriage with Elizabeth Billinge. B. at Twyford, Berkshire, 1832; m. Mary Ellen, d. of T.F. Salt, Esq. Educ. at a private school. A Brewer, being Senior Partner in the firm of Salt and Company of Burton-on-Trent. An Alderman of Burton-on-Trent, a J.P. for Derbyshire, and a J.P. and Dept.-Lieut. for Staffordshire. Was Chairman of the Burton School Board up to 1885. A Liberal, and Home Ruler, in favour of an Affirmation Bill. Sat for Derbyshire S. from 1885 until his death on 16 Feb. 1892.   [1892]

WARING, Col. Thomas. Waringstown, Lurgan, Co. Down. Carlton, and Ulster. Eld. s. of Maj. H. Waring, of Waringstown, Lurgan, Co. Down, by Frances Grace, 3rd d. of the Very Rev. Holt Waring, Dean of Dromore. B. in Dublin 1828; m. 1st, 1858, Esther, d. of Ross T. Smyth, Esq.; 2ndly, 1874, Fanny, d. of Admiral Tucker, of Trematon Castle, Cornwall; and 3rdly, 1885, Geraldine, d. of Alex. Stewart, Esq., of Ballyedmond, Co. Down. Educ. privately and at Trinity Coll., Dublin. Was called to the Irish bar 1852. In 1855 he was appointed Capt. of the Royal South Down Militia, later the 5th Battalion of the Royal Irish Rifles, retired as Col. in 1889. Served as High Sheriff of Co. Down 1868-69, and was Grand Master of the Loyal Orange Institute of England from 1892. A "Constitutionalist and Imperialist". Sat for Down N.

from 1885 until his death 12 Aug. 1898.   [1898]

WARING, Maj. Walter. Continued in House after 1918: full entry in Volume III.

WARKWORTH, Henry Algernon George Percy, Lord. See PERCY, Henry Algernon George Percy, Earl.

WARMINGTON, Cornelius Marshall. 43 Courtfield Gardens, London. 7 New Square, Lincoln's Inn, London. S. of Edward Warmington, Esq., of Colchester. B. 1842; m. 1871, Anne, d. of Edward Winch, Esq., of Chatham. Educ. privately and at University Coll., London. He became a Solicitor; but obtaining an Inns of Court studentship joined the other branch of the legal profession. Was called to the bar at the Middle Temple 1869, and joined the Oxford Circuit. Was appointed a Q.C. 1882, and a bencher of the Middle Temple 1885. A Liberal and Home Ruler. Unsuccessfully contested Monmouthshire in Apr. 1880. Sat for Monmouthshire W. from 1885 until he retired in 1895. Created Bart. 1908. Died 12 Dec. 1908.   [1895]

WARNER, Sir Thomas Courtenay Theydon, Bart., C.B. Continued in House after 1918: full entry in Volume III.

WARR, Augustus Frederick. 43 Campden House Court, Kensington, London. 5 Alexandra Drive, Liverpool. Carlton, and Savile. S. of the Rev. Canon Warr, of Childwall Vicarage, near Liverpool. B. in Liverpool 1847; m. 1878, Henrietta Georgiana, d. of Henry Barnes, Esq., of Liverpool, and sister of the Hon. Mr. Justice Gorell Barnes. Educ. at the Liverpool Royal Institution School. A Solicitor, a member of the firm of Batesons, Warr and Wimshurst, Liverpool, admitted 1870. A Conservative. First elected for the E. Toxteth division of Liverpool Nov. 1895 and sat until he accepted Chiltern Hundreds in 1902. Died 24 Mar. 1908.   [1902]

WASON, Rt. Hon. Eugene. 8 Sussex Gardens, Hyde Park, London. Blair, Dailly Ayrshire. Reform. S. of Rigby Wason, Esq., MP for Ipswich. B. 1846 at Corwar, Ayrshire; m. 1870, Eleanor Mary, d. of Charles Reynolds Williams, Esq., of Dolmelynllyn, Dolgelly. Educ. at Rugby, and Wadham Coll., Oxford; M.A. Was called to the bar at the Middle Temple in 1870, and was Assistant Examiner to Incorporated Law Society for four years. Chairman of Scottish Liberal members and Chairman of the Committee on Food Production in Scotland. A Dept.-Lieut., and J.P. for Ayrshire. PC. 1907. A Liberal, and Home Ruler, in favour of Reform in the House of Lords, placing the control of the Liquor Traffic in the hands of the people, One Man One Vote, Free Trade, etc. Sat for S. Ayrshire from 1885-86, when he was defeated. Re-elected for S. Ayrshire in 1892 and sat until again defeated 1895. First elected for Clackmannan and Kinross in 1899 and sat until he retired in 1918. Died 19 Apr. 1927.   [1918]

WASON, John Cathcart. Continued in House after 1918: full entry in Volume III.

WATERLOW, David Sydney. 38 Cornwall Gardens, London. Reform, National Liberal, and Automobile. S. of Sir Sydney Waterlow, Bart. B. 1857 at Highgate; m. 1883, d. of Mrs. F. Maitland, member of London School Board. Educ. at Northampton, and Switzerland. Was a Director of Waterlow and Sons, Printers; retired in 1898. A Director of Improved Industrial Dwellings Company Limited. A member of London County Council from 1898. A Liberal. Elected for N. Islington in 1906 and sat until defeated in Dec. 1910. Chairman of Waterlow and Sons in 1922. Governor of Great Northern Hospital. Chairman of Governors, United Westminster Schools. Died 25 Aug. 1924.   [1910]

WATKIN, Sir Edward William, Bart. Charing Cross Hotel, London. Rose Hill, Northenden, Cheshire. The Chalet, Beddgelert. Reform. S. of Absalom Watkin, Esq., of Rose Hill, Northenden, Cheshire, by Elizabeth, his wife. B. at Salford 1819; m. 1st, 1845, Mary, d. of Jonathan Mellor, Esq., of Hope House, Oldham (she died 1888); 2ndly, 1892, Mrs. Ingram, widow of Mr. Herbert Ingram, founder of the *Illustrated London News*, and d. of Mr. W. Little. Chairman of the S.E. Metropolitan and many other railway companies. High Sheriff of Cheshire for 1874. Knighted 1868. Created Bart. in 1880. Published various political pamphlets, also *India, Alderman Cobden, of Manchester, Recollections of Canada and the United States 1851-86.* An independent Liberal and Unionist, and an ardent advocate of a Channel Tunnel. Elected for Great Yarmouth in Mar. 1857 but on petition the election was declared void. Unsuccessfully contested Great Yarmouth in Apr. 1859. Sat for Stockport from May 1864 until defeated Nov. 1868. Contested E. Cheshire in 1869 and Exeter in 1873. Sat for Hythe from Feb. 1874 until he retired in 1895. Died 14 Apr. 1901.   [1895]

WATSON, James. Berwick, Nr. Shrewsbury. Carlton, and Conservative. Only s. of James Watson, Esq., of Edgbaston, near Birmingham, by Mary, d. of R. Spreadborough, Esq., of Aston, Warwickshire. B. 1817; m. 1856, Jane, d. of Leonard Willan, Esq., of Lancaster and Silverdale, Lancashire. A Magistrate for Staffordshire, Shropshire, and Worcestershire. Patron of the living of Berwick, Shropshire. A Conservative. First returned for Shrewsbury in 1885 and sat until he retired in 1892. Died 5 July 1895.   [1892]

WATSON, Capt. John Bertrand. Continued in House after 1918: full entry in Volume III.

WATSON, Thomas. Horse Carrs, Rochdale. B. at Galgate, Lancashire, 1823. Was originally a working Silk-Weaver. Went to Rochdale about 1845, and there founded, with the assistance of partners, a business which greatly extended and became entirely his own. Later became a Silk-Spinner and Hat Clothmaker, and was the inventor of a successful imitation of sealskin. Chairman of the Rochdale School Board, a Magistrate for the borough, and Treasurer of the Free Church. The Rochdale Infirmary was built at his expense. A Liberal. Sat for the Ilkeston division of Derbyshire from Dec. 1885 until his death on 7 Mar. 1887.   [1886]

WATSON, Hon. William. Continued in House after 1918: full entry in Volume III.

WATT, Henry Anderson. Ardenslate House, Hunter's Quay, Argyllshire. Dempsterton, Dunscore, Dumfriesshire. Woodhouse, Newton Blossomville, Buckinghamshire. National Liberal. S. of George Henry Watt, Esq., of Glasgow, and Elizabeth, d. of James Anderson, Esq., of Glasgow. B. 28 Feb. 1863 at Govan; m. 1894, Caroline, d. of James Frackelton,

Esq., of Dunmury. Educ. at Glasgow High School, Bellahouston Academy, and Glasgow University; M.A. Was called to the bar at Gray's Inn 1896. Was in business in Glasgow. A J.P. for Argyllshire. A Liberal. Elected for the College division of Glasgow in 1906 and sat until defeated in Glasgow Maryhill in 1918. Unsuccessfully contested Argyllshire in 1922 and Glasgow Govan in 1923. Died 2 Dec. 1929.   [1918]

WATT, Hugh. 119 St. George's Road, London. S. of John Watt, Esq., honorary Sheriff-substitute and J.P. for Ayrshire, by Jane, d. of Capt. Thomas Baird. B. at Kilmarnock 1848; m. 1st, 1880, Julia, d. of C.M. Welstead, Esq., of Home Place, near Battle; 2ndly, 1906, Lady Violet Jocelyn, d. of the 5th Earl of Roden. Educ. at Kilmarnock Academy, and the University of Geneva. A member of the firm of Hugh Watt and Company, Merchants, London; also Chairman of the Maxim Weston Electric Company (Limited). In 1886 he had conferred upon him the Grand Cross of the Order of Simon Bolivar, for distinguished commercial services in connection with Venezuela. A Liberal, and Home Ruler. Sat for the Camlachie division of Glasgow from 1885 until defeated in 1892, standing as an Independent Liberal. Died Mar. 1921.   [1892]

WAYMAN, Thomas. Oaklands, Clapham Park, London. Reform, and National Liberal. S. of William Henry Wayman, Esq., Cardmaker, of Halifax. B. 1833; m. 1856, Sarah, d. of James Ellis, Esq., Cardmaker, of Halifax. Educ. at private schools in Halifax. Retired from business 30 May 1892. Was Mayor of Halifax from Nov. 1872 to Nov. 1874. A J.P. for Halifax and Governor of the Crossley Orphanage. A Liberal Home Ruler, said he would maintain the constitution as represented by Queen, Lords, and Commons, subject to necessary reforms, which in the House of Lords he thought immediate and pressing. Sat for the Elland division of the W. Riding of Yorkshire from 1885 until he accepted Chiltern Hundreds in 1899. Died 8 Feb. 1901.   [1898]

WEBB, Alfred John. 31 South Street, Thurloe Square, London. 74 Abbey Street, Dublin. Dublin Friends' Institute. S. of Richard Davis Webb, Esq., of Dublin, and Hannah, d. of Thomas Waring, Esq., of Waterford. B. in Dublin 1834; m. 1861, Elizabeth, d. of George Shackleton, Esq., of Ballytore, Co. Kildare. Educ. at private schools. A Master Printer, who carried on business in Dublin. Wrote *A Compendium of Irish Biography* (Dublin 1878) and sundry political pamphlets. An Anti-Parnellite. Was one of the few Protestant survivors of those who joined the Home Rule movement at its inception in 1870. First returned for Waterford W. in Feb. 1890 and sat until he accepted Chiltern Hundreds in Aug. 1895. Died 1908. [1895]

WEBB, Lieut.-Col. Sir Henry, Bart. Continued in House after 1918: full entry in Volume III.

WEBB, William George. 25 De Vere Gardens, Kensington, London. Wordesley, Staffordshire. Carlton, Junior Carlton, St. Stephen's, and Junior Constitutional. Eld. s. of Edward Webb, Esq., of Wordesley, Staffordshire, and Eliza, his wife. B. 1843 at Wordesley, Stourbridge; m. 1874, Ada, d. of Capt. W. Broughton-Pryce. A Magistrate for the Co. of Staffordshire. Was Col. of S. Staffordshire Militia. A Conservative. Elected for the Kingswinford division of Staffordshire in 1900 and sat until his death 14 June 1905.   [1905]

WEBSTER, Sir Richard Everard, Bart., G.C.M.G. 2 Pump Court, Temple, London. Hornton Lodge, Kensington, London. Winterfold, Cranleigh, Surrey. Athenaeum, Carlton, St. Stephen's, and United University. 2nd s. of Thomas Webster, Esq., Q.C., by Elizabeth, d. of Richard Calthrop, Esq., of Swineshead Abbey, Lincoln. B. 1842; m. 1872, Louisa Mary, only d. of William Calthrop, Esq., of Withern, Lincolnshire (she died 1877). Educ. at King's Coll. School, Charterhouse, and Trinity Coll., Cambridge, where he obtained a scholarship. He graduated as 35th wrangler and with a 3rd class in the Classical Tripos. Was called to the bar at Lincoln's Inn in 1868, and became Tubman and Postman in the old Court of Exchequer. Q.C. in 1878, Attorney-Gen. 1885 before his election to Parliament for Launceston, and was Knighted. In 1893 he was made G.C.M.G. in connection with the Behring Sea Arbitration; was again Attorney-Gen. 1886-92, and for the 3rd time 1895-1900. In 1899 he received a Baronetcy for services in the Venezuela Arbitration. A Conservative. Unsuccessfully contested

Bewdley in 1880. Sat for Launceston from July-Nov. 1885 and for the Isle of Wight division of Hampshire from Nov. 1885 until appointed Master of the Rolls in May 1900. Created Baron Alverstone June 1900 and Visct. Alverstone in 1913. Lord Chief Justice Oct. 1900 to 1913. Died 15 Dec. 1915.   [1900]

WEBSTER, Robert Grant. 83 Belgrave Road, London. Carlton, and Conservative. S. of Robert Webster, Esq., Advocate, Edinburgh, by Louisa, d. of the Rev. John Dodgson, of Comley Bank, Perth, N.B. B. in Marylebone, Middlesex 1845; m. Emily, d. of Boswell Middleton Jalland, Esq., J.P., Dept.-Lieut., of Holderness House, near Hull, Yorkshire. Educ. at St. Peter's Coll., Radley, and Trinity Coll., Cambridge (1st class in Political Economy, LL.B. 1868). A Barrister-at-Law; also a Magistrate for Middlesex. Served for sixteen years in the 3rd Battalion S. Lancashire Regiment. Author of *Shoulder to Shoulder* (1873), *The Trade of the World* (1880), *The Law relating to Canals*, etc. A Conservative, in favour of Imperial Federation and of "such useful measures as altered circumstances render necessary", and opposed to Home Rule for Ireland. Contested Cockermouth 1880 and St. Pancras E. in 1885. Sat for the E. division of St. Pancras from 1886 until he accepted Chiltern Hundreds in 1899. Died 14 Jan. 1925.   [1899]

WEDDERBURN, Sir William, Bart. 84 Palace Chambers, Westminster, London. Meredith, Gloucester. Reform, and National Liberal. S. of Sir John Wedderburn, 2nd Bart., by a d. of William Milburn, Esq., of Bombay. B. 1838 in Edinburgh; m. 1878, Mary Blanche, d. of H.W. Hoskyns, Esq., of North Perrot Manor, Somerset. Educ. at Loretto House, and the University, Edinburgh. Entered the Bombay Civil Service in 1860; and succeeded his brother, the 3rd Bart. in 1882. Was Judge at Poona, and Agent for the Sirdars of the Deccan. In 1885 he became acting Judge of the High Court of Bombay, and in 1886 Chief Secretary to the Bombay Government. He retired in 1887. In 1889 and 1910 he presided over the Indian National Congress at Bombay. A Radical, in favour of Home Rule and the Newcastle programme generally, also of reforms in the government of India, of measures to benefit the fishing industry, and an extension of the Crofters' Act. At the general

election of 1892 he was an unsuccessful candidate for N. Ayrshire. First elected for Banffshire Mar. 1893 and sat until he retired in 1900. Died 25 Jan. 1918.   [1900]

WEDGWOOD, Josiah Clement. Continued in House after 1918: full entry in Volume III.

WEIGALL, Lieut.-Col. William Ernest George Archibald. Continued in House after 1918: full entry in Volume III.

WEIR, James Galloway. 4 Frognal, Hampstead, London. National Liberal. S. of James Ross Weir, Esq., and Margaret McLaren, of Perthshire. B. 1839; m. 1st, 1863, Mary Anne, d. of George Dash, Esq. (she died 1896); 2ndly, 1898, Marion Jolly. Educ. at the Dollar Academy, and in London. Was engaged in businesses; retired in 1880. A member of the Committee of the Scottish Corporation, and of the London County Council 1892-95. A J.P. for the Co. of London. A Liberal and Home Ruler, in favour of the Gladstonian programme generally, but put in the forefront amendment of the Crofter Act. Unsuccessfully contested the Falkirk district in 1885. Represented Ross and Cromarty from 1892 until his death 18 Apr. 1911.   [1911]

WELBY, Alfred Cholmeley Earle. 26 Sloane Court, London. Carlton, and Garrick. 7th s. of Sir G.E. Welby-Gregory, 3rd Bart., of Denton Hall, by Frances, d. of Sir Montague Cholmeley, Bart. B. at Denton, Lincolnshire 1849; m. 1898, Alice Desiree, 2nd d. of A. Copland-Griffiths, Esq. Lieut.-Col. Royal Scots Greys, and twice represented the Regiment in Russia; had the Order of St. Anne of Russia, 2nd class (jewelled). A Conservative. Contested Grantham Nov. 1885, the Poplar division of Tower Hamlets in July 1886 and again in July 1892. Sat for Taunton from 1895 until he retired in Jan. 1906 and contested Finsbury E. unsuccessfully. Member of the London County Council, (Finsbury E.) from 1907-10. K.B.E. 1918. Died 18 May 1937.   [1905]

WELBY, Sir Charles Glynne Earle, Bart., C.B. Denton Manor, Grantham. Carlton, Travellers', Wellington, and Beefsteak. S. of Sir William Earle Welby-Gregory, 4th Bart., by Hon. Victoria, d. of Hon. Charles Stuart-Wortley. B. 1865; m. 1887, Maria, d. of Lord Augustus Hervey, MP. Educ. at

Eton, and Christ Church, Oxford. Was Private Secretary to the Rt. Hon. E. Stanhope and Marq. of Lansdowne, when Secretary of State for War. Assistant Under-Secretary for War 1900-02. A J.P., Dept.-Lieut., and Alderman of Kesteven, Lincolnshire County Council. Created C.B. 1897. Succeeded as Bart. 1898. A Conservative. Elected for the Newark division of Nottinghamshire in Feb. 1900 and sat until he retired in 1906. Died 19 Mar. 1938.
[1905]

WENTWORTH, Bruce Canning Vernon-. Wentworth Castle, Barnsley, Yorkshire. Dall Rannoch, N.B. Carlton, White's, Guards', and Wellington. S. of Thomas F.C. Vernon-Wentworth, Esq., (of Wentworth Castle, Yorkshire, and Blackheath, Saxmundham, Suffolk), by Lady Harriet de Burgh, d. of the 1st Marq. of Clanricarde. A great-grand-s. of the Rt. Hon. George Canning. B. 1862 at Edinburgh. Educ. at Harrow, and Sandhurst Coll. Entered the army Nov. 1883, and was later Capt. Grenadier Guards. A J.P. for the W. Riding of Yorkshire. A Conservative. Unsuccessfully contested the Barnsley division of Yorkshire in 1885, 1886 and 1889. On the retirement of Sir W. Marriott in 1893, he was elected for Brighton without opposition and sat until he retired in 1906. Died 12 Nov. 1951.   [1905]

WENTWORTH-FITZWILLIAM, Hon. William Henry. See FITZWILLIAM, Hon. William Henry Wentworth-.

WENTWORTH-FITZWILLIAM, Hon. William John. See FITZWILLIAM, Hon. William John Wentworth-.

WEST, Henry Wyndham. Defeated in 1886: full entry in Volume I.

WEST, Col. William Cornwallis. Ruthin Castle, North Wales. Newlands Manor, Lymington, Hampshire. Travellers', Devonshire, and Windham. 2nd s. of Frederic West, Esq., MP (grand-s. of John, 2nd Earl De La Warr), by Theresa, d. of Capt. John Whitby. B. 1835; m. 1872, Mary, d. of Mr. and Lady Olivia Fitz-Patrick, and grand-d. of the 2nd Marq. of Headfort. Educ. at Eton and called to the bar, but never practised. Lord-Lieut. of Denbighshire, and Lieut.-Col. of the 1st Volunteer Battalion Royal Welsh Fusiliers. Mayor of Ruthin 1886 and 1887. A Liberal and Unionist, in favour of reform of the House of Lords and in the procedure of the House of Commons, reform of the Land Laws, etc. Voted against the Home Rule Bill in 1886 and was from then on classified as a Liberal Unionist. Unsuccessfully contested Lymington in 1874 and W. Cheshire in 1880. Sat for Denbighshire W. from 1885 until defeated in 1892. Assumed the additional surname of Cornwallis in 1895. Died 4 July 1917.   [1892]

WESTLAKE, John. The River House, 3 Chelsea Embankment, London. Tregarthen Cottage, Zennor, St. Ives, Cornwall. Athenaeum. S. of John Westlake, Esq., of Lostwithiel, Cornwall, and afterwards of Cambridge, by Eleanora, d. of the Rev. George Burgess, Rector of Atherington, Devonshire. B. 1828 at Lostwithiel; m. 1864, Alice, d. of Thomas Hare, Esq., author of a *Treatise of Representation*, etc. Educ. privately, and at Trinity Coll., Cambridge, of which he became a Fellow, after having been placed as 6th wrangler (bracketed) in the Mathematical Tripos of 1850. Was called to the bar at Lincoln's Inn in 1854, became Q.C. in 1874, bencher of his inn in 1875, and retired from practice in 1882. Wrote a *Treatise on Private International Law*, and many papers in reviews, etc.; one of the founders and editors of the *Revue de Droit International*, of Brussels, and Vice-President of the Institute of International Law. Was President of the Jurisprudence Department of the National Association for the Promotion of Social Science, 1884-85, and was Foreign Secretary to the same association from 1862. Also an Honorary LL.D. of Edinburgh. A Liberal, in favour of the Disestablishment and Disendowment of the Church, and of allowing Members of Parliament to take their seats without any oath or affirmation; believed that in the present state of this country an hereditary House of Lords ought no longer to exist. Sat for the Romford division of Essex from Dec. 1885 until defeated in 1886 standing as a Liberal Unionist. Unsuccessfully contested mid Cornwall in July 1892. Professor of International Law at Cambridge University 1888-1908. Author of several legal treatises. Died 14 Apr. 1913.   [1886]

WESTON, Col. John Wakefield. Continued in House after 1918: full entry in Volume III.

WESTON, Sir Joseph Dodge. 21 Warwick Square, London. Dorset House, Clifton Down, Bristol. Reform. Youngest s. of Thomas Weston, Esq., Merchant of Bristol. B. 1822; m. 1888, Harriet A., youngest d. of W.C.P. Beloe, Esq., of Clifton. Educ. at the Bishop's Coll., Clifton. Joined his father in business and for many years carried on extensive Iron works at West Bromwich and Cym Bryn, Newport, Monmouthshire. Chairman of the Patent Nut and Bolt Company, of the Bristol Waggon Works Company, and of the Great Western Cotton Works, Bristol. A Magistrate for Bristol, and Mayor of the city during the four years 1880-84. A Liberal of advanced views, in favour of Home Rule, etc. In 1884 he was selected to succeed Mr. Samuel Morley in the representation of Bristol, and the following year was returned for Bristol, S. division; but at the general election of 1886 he lost this seat. In the same year he was Knighted. In 1890, on the death of Mr. Handel Cossham, he was first returned for Bristol E. and sat until his death on 5 Mar. 1895.   [1894]

WEYMOUTH, Thomas Henry Thynne, Visct. 48 Berkeley Square, London. Widcombe House, Bath. Carlton, and Marlborough. Eld. s. of John Alexander, Esq., the 4th Marq. of Bath, by Hon. Frances Isabella Catherine, eld. d. of the 3rd Visct. de Vesci. B. 1862; m. 1890, Violet Caroline, eld. d. of Sir Charles Mordaunt, Bart. Educ. at Eton, and Balliol Coll., Oxford, where he took honours in history in 1884. Appointed Lieut. in the Wiltshire Yeomanry Cavalry in 1882; and an Assistant Secretary to Lord Iddesleigh as Foreign Secretary in Aug. 1886. A Conservative. Unsuccessfully contested the Frome division of Somerset in 1885. Returned for this division in 1886 but defeated 1892. Re-elected there in 1895 and sat until he succeeded as Marq. of Bath in 1896. Under-Secretary of State for India Jan.-Dec. 1905. K.G. 1917. PC. 1922. Master of the Horse 1922-24. Died 9 June 1946.   [1896]

WHARTON, Rt. Hon. John Lloyd. 1c King Street, St. James's, London. Bramham, Boston Spa. Carlton, and Oxford & Cambridge. Only s. of John Thomas Wharton, Esq., of Dryburn, Durham, and Aberford, Yorkshire (who was s. of the Rev. R. Wharton, Chancellor of Lincoln), by Mary, 2nd d. of the Rev. J.H. Jacob, of The Close, Salisbury. B. at Aberford 1837; m. 1870, Susan Frances, eld. d. of the Rev. A. Duncombe Shafto, Rector of Brancepeth, Durham (she died 1872). Educ. at Eton, and Trinity Coll., Cambridge. Was called to the bar at the Inner Temple 1862. A Magistrate for the W. Riding of Yorkshire, a Magistrate, Dept.-Lieut. and Chairman of Quarter Sessions for the Co. of Durham, and was elected Chairman of the County Council 1889. Created PC. 1897. A Conservative. He unsuccessfully contested the city of Durham in 1868, but afterwards sat for Durham from 1871 to 1874; was again unsuccessful in 1874, and in 1880, and unsuccessful in the Ripon division of the W. Riding of Yorkshire in 1885; returned for the Ripon division of the W. Riding of Yorkshire 1886 and sat until he was defeated in 1906. Died 11 July 1912.   [1905]

WHELER, Granville Charles Hastings. Continued in House after 1918: full entry in Volume III.

WHITBREAD, Samuel. 10 Ennismore Gardens, Prince's Gate, London. Southill, Biggleswade, Bedfordshire. Brooks's, and Reform. S. of Samuel Charles Whitbread, Esq., of Cardington, Bedfordshire, who was MP for Middlesex from 1820 to 1830. Grand-s. of the well-known politician whose name he bore. B. at Cardington 1830; m. 1855, Lady Isabella, 3rd d. of 3rd Earl of Chichester. Educ. at Rugby, and Cambridge. Appointed Dept.-Lieut. of Bedfordshire 1852; was a Lord of the Admiralty from June 1859 till Mar. 1863, and was a member of the House of Commons Committee of Selection from 1866. A Liberal and Home Ruler, in favour of a measure of licensing reform. Sat for Bedford from July 1852 until he retired in 1895. Died 25 Dec. 1915.   [1895]

WHITBREAD, Samuel Howard. 11 Mansfield Street, London. Brooks's, and Travellers'. S. of S. Whitbread, Esq., MP for Bedford from 1852-95, and Lady Isabella Pelham, d. of 3rd Earl of Chichester. B. 8 Jan. 1858 in London; m. 1904, Madeline, d. of the Hon. Edward Bourke. Educ. at Eton, and Trinity Coll., Cambridge; M.A. Vice-Chairman of Bedfordshire Quarter Sessions, County Council, and Territorial Forces Association. Chairman of Education and Licensing

Committees. Was Assistant Private Secretary to 1st Earl of Northbrook 1880-82, and Sir. U. Kay-Shuttleworth 1886 at the Admiralty. Unsuccessfully contested Bootle 1885, and S. Huntingdonshire 1892. Sat for S. Bedfordshire from Sept. 1892-95. Unsuccessfully contested Bedford 1895. Elected for S. Huntingdonshire in 1906 and sat until he retired in Jan. 1910. Alderman of the Bedfordshire County Council; Chairman Bedfordshire Quarter Sessions. Died 29 July 1944. [1909]

WHITE, Sir George. The Grange, Eaton, Norwich. National Liberal, and Reform. S. of Thomas and Mary White, of Bourne, Lincolnshire. B. 1840; m. 1863, Anne, d. of Henry Ransome, Esq., of Norwich. Educ. at the Grammar School, Bourne. A Boot Manufacturer; Alderman, J.P., and Honorary Freeman of Norwich; Chairman of the Education Committee; Sheriff from 1888-89. Knighted 1907. An advanced Liberal. Elected for N.W. Norfolk in 1900 and sat until his death 11 May 1912. [1912]

WHITE, Lieut.-Col. Godfrey Dalrymple. See DALRYMPLE-WHITE, Godfrey Dalrymple. Continued in House after 1918: full entry in Volume III.

WHITE, James Dundas. 43 Burton Court, London. Goldsmith Building, Temple, London. Reform, National Liberal, and Eighty. S. of James Orr White, Esq., of Norwood, and Fanny, d. of James White, Esq., of Overtoun, and sister of Lord Overtoun. B. 10 July 1866 at Rutherglen; m. 1894, Lydia Grace, d. of the Rev. R. Haythornthwaite, Vicar of Cleator Moor. Educ. at Rugby, and Trinity Coll., Cambridge; M.A., LL.D. A Barrister, called to the bar at the Inner Temple 1891. Parliamentary Private Secretary (unpaid) to Lord Pentland, Secretary for Scotland 1910-12, to Mr. T. McKinnon Wood, Secretary for Scotland 1912-July 1916, and to Mr. T. McKinnon Wood, Chancellor of the Duchy of Lancaster and Financial Secretary to the Treasury July-Dec. 1916. Chairman of one and member of several other Departmental Committees during the European War. Author of works on the Merchant Shipping Acts and Marine Insurance Act, *Economic Ideals, The A B C of the Land Question, A Scheme for Land Value Taxation, Land Value Taxation and Feu Duties, Steering by the Stars for Night Flying, Night*

Marching, etc. and numerous papers on economic, legal, and nautical subjects. A Liberal. Sat for Dunbartonshire from 1906 to Dec. 1910, when he retired. Elected for the Tradeston division of Glasgow in July 1911 and sat until defeated in 1918. Joined the Independent Labour Party in 1919. Contested W. Middlesborough 1923 and central Glasgow 1924 as the Labour candidate but subsequently left the party. Published last of many works on land value reform in 1948. Died 30 Apr. 1951. [1918]

WHITE, James Martin. Balruddery, Nr. Dundee, Forfarshire. National Liberal. S. of J.F. White, Esq., of Balruddery, by Elizabeth, d. of W. Grundy, Esq., of Parr, Lancashire. B. 1857. Educ. at the Dundee Institution, Cassel, and Edinburgh University. Was head of the firm of J.F. White and Company, of New York, Importers of Textiles, etc. Also a J.P. of Forfar and Dundee; member of the Council of University Coll., Dundee; Chairman of the Technical Institute, and President of the Dundee Technical Association, etc. A Liberal, in favour of Home Rule, etc. Was an unsuccessful candidate for the St. Andrew's Burghs in 1892. First returned for Forfarshire July 1895 and sat until he accepted Chiltern Hundreds in 1896. Unsuccessfully contested the S. division of Wiltshire in Oct. 1900 and Great Yarmouth in Jan. 1906. Died 7 July 1928. [1896]

WHITE, John Bazley. Wilmington, Dartford, Kent. Carlton, Junior Carlton, and Wellington. 2nd s. of John Bazley White, Esq., of Swanscombe, Dartford, by his m. with Mary, only child of W. Leatham, Esq., of Andover, Hampshire. B. 1847; m. 1876, Lady Grace, d. of the Countess of Rothes, by her m. with Capt. Haworth, who assumed by Royal licence the name of Leslie. Educ. at Blackheath Proprietary School. A Director of John Bazley White and Brothers, Limited, Portland Cement Manufacturers. A Conservative. First elected for Gravesend at the general election of 1885 and sat until he retired in 1892. [1892]

WHITE, Sir Luke. Driffield, East Yorkshire. National Liberal. S. of James White, Esq., of Deighton, near York. B. 1845 at Deighton; m. 1869, d. of A. Wood, Esq., of York (she died Dec. 1916). Educ. at Foss Bridge School, York. Admitted a Sol-

icitor in 1874 and was one of H.M. Coroners for Yorkshire, E. Riding district. A J.P. and Dept.-Lieut. for the E. Riding of Yorkshire. Knighted 1908. A Liberal. Elected for the Buckrose division of the E. Riding of Yorkshire in 1900 and sat until he retired in 1918. Died 17 Aug. 1920.
[1918]

WHITE, Patrick. Clonalvy, Balbriggan. S. of Thomas and Mary White. B. 1860 at Clonalvy. Owned a Dublin Drapery establishment. A Farmer in Co. Meath. A member of the Dublin Corporation. A Parnellite, but later a prominent member of the United Irish League. Represented N. Meath from 1900 until he retired in 1918.
[1918]

WHITEHEAD, Sir James, Bart. 9 Cambridge Gate, Regent's Park, London. Reform, and City Liberal. S. of James Whitehead, Esq., of Appleby, Westmoreland, and his wife Agnes, d. of Robert Atkinson, Esq., of Hay Close, Hutton-in-the-Hay, Westmorland. B. 1834 at Bramhall, near Sedbergh, Yorkshire; m. 1860, Mercy Matilda, 4th d. of Thomas Hinds, Esq., Bank House, St. Neots, Huntingdon. Educ. at Appleby School, Westmoreland. A Bradford Merchant in London 1860 to 1882, when he retired. A J.P. and Dept.-Lieut. for Westmoreland, J.P. for Kent and the Co. of London, High Sheriff of London and Middlesex 1884-85, Lord Mayor there 1888-89, when he arbitrated in the great dock strike; a Lieut. for London, Commander of the Legion of Honour, and Knight of many foreign orders, F.S.A., F.R.Hist.S., etc. Created Bart. 1889. An advanced Liberal and Home Ruler, in favour of registration reform, shorter Parliaments, reform of the House of Lords, disestablishment, district and parish councils, leasehold enfranchisement, the "direct veto", etc. Unsuccessfully contested the Appleby division of Westmoreland in 1885 and 1886. First returned for Leicester July 1892, and sat until he accepted Chiltern Hundreds in 1894. Thereafter active in charitable work, hospitals, prisons, etc. Died 20 Oct. 1917.
[1894]

WHITEHEAD, Rowland Edward. 8 Grove End Road, St. John's Wood, London. S. of Sir James Whitehead, Bart. B. 1 Sept. 1863 in London; m. 1893, Ethel, d. of Philip H. Rathbone, Esq., of Liverpool.

Educ. at Clifton Coll., and University Coll., Oxford. A Barrister, called 1888. A Lieut. of the City of London; member of the Council of Clifton Coll. Parliamentary Secretary (unpaid) to Rt. Hon. H.L. Samuel, Under-Secretary of State for the Home Department. A Liberal. Unsuccessfully contested S.E. Essex in 1900; elected there in 1906 and sat until defeated in Jan. 1910. K.C. 1910. Private Secretary to Attorney-Gen. 1909-10; member of Committee of Work of National Importance 1916-19. Succeeded bro. as 3rd Bart. in 1931. Died 9 Oct. 1942.
[1909]

WHITEHOUSE, John Howard. 13 Hammersmith Terrace, London. National Liberal, and Eighty. B. 1873. Unmarried. Educ. at Mason Coll., and Midland Institute, Birmingham. Was the 1st Secretary of the Carnegie Dunfermline Trust 1902; Secretary of Toynbee Hall 1904-07 and Warden of Manchester Univeristy Settlement 1909-10. A member of Dept. Committees on the Employment of Children's Act, on Night Labour for Young Persons 1911, and on Reformatory and Industrial Schools 1912. Founder of the Ruskin Society; Editor of *Saint George* 1898-1911. Parliamentary Private Secretary to Mr. Lloyd George 1913-15, Honorary Warden and Founder of Secondary Schoolboys Camp and Honorary Secretary of the National League of Workers with Boys. Author of *Problems of a Scottish Provincial Town, The Boys' Club, its Place in Social Progress, Problems of Boy Life, National System of Education, Essays on Social and Political Questions, Belgium in War, Educational and Social Experiments*, and other works. A Liberal. Elected for mid Lanarkshire in Jan. 1910 and sat until defeated as an Independent Liberal in the Hamilton division of Lanarkshire in 1918. Unsuccessfully contested the Hanley division of Stoke on Trent in 1922, Hereford in 1923 and 1924, Southampton in 1929, the Thornbury division of Gloucestershire in 1931 and Stoke Newington in 1935. Founded Bembridge School in 1919; Headmaster 1919-54; President of the Ruskin Society in 1932. F.R.G.S. and F.R.S.A. Died 28 Sept. 1955.
[1918]

WHITELAW, Graeme Alexander Lockhart. 21 Hans Place, London. Colzium, Kilsyth, N.B. Conservative. 2nd s. of Alexander Whitelaw (former MP), of Gartshore, Dunbartonshire, and

Woodhall, Lanarkshire, by Barbara Forbes, d. of Robert Lockhart, Esq., of Castlehill, Lanarkshire. B. 1863; m. 1885, Elizabeth, 2nd d. of Col. Reid Stewart. Educ. at Harrow, and Trinity Coll., Cambridge. A Capt. in the 3rd Battalion Argyll and Sutherland Highlanders. A Conservative and Unionist. Sat for the N.W. division of Lanarkshire from July 1892 until defeated in 1895. Unsuccessfully contested the seat again in Feb. 1899. Died 23 July 1928. [1895]

WHITELAW, William. 28 Wilton Crescent, London. Bredisholm, Baillieston, N.B. Huntingtower, Perth. Conservative. S. of Alex. Whitelaw, Esq., of Gartshore, Dunbartonshire, and Barbara Forbes Lockhart, of Castlehill, Lanarkshire. B. 1868; m. 1890, Gertrude, d. of T.C. Thompson of Milton Hall, Cumberland. Educ. at Harrow and Trinity Coll., Cambridge (B.A. 1890). A Lieut. in the Lanarkshire Yeomanry Cavalry. A Conservative. Sat for Perth city from July 1892 until defeated in 1895. Unsuccessfully contested Perth city again in 1900, Banffshire in Feb. 1907 and Stirling district in May 1908. Died 19 Jan. 1946. [1895]

WHITELEY, Rt. Hon. George. 31 Princes Gate, London. Hawkstone Park, Shropshire. St. Anthony's, Milnthorpe. S. of George Whiteley, Esq., of Halifax, and Margaret, d. of Dr. Pickop, of Blackburn. B. at Witton, near Blackburn 1855; m. 1881, d. of William Tattersall, Esq., J.P. and County Councillor of Quarry Bank, Blackburn, and St. Anthony's, Milnthorpe. Educ. at foreign schools, and Zurich University. Patronage Secretary to the Treasury and Chief Liberal Whip from Dec. 1905 to June 1908. PC. 1907. A J.P. for Hampshire. Mayor of Blackburn. A Conservative until 1900 when he joined the Liberal Party, renounced his candidature for Stockport and was adopted as Liberal candidate for Pudsey. Contested the Northwich division of Cheshire July 1892. Sat for Stockport 1893-1900. Elected for the Pudsey division of the W. Riding of Yorkshire in 1900 and sat until created 1st Baron Marchamley 1908. Died 21 Oct. 1925. [1908]

WHITELEY, Sir Herbert James, Bart. Thorngrove, Worcester. Carlton, and Constitutional. S. of George Whiteley, Esq., of Halifax, and Margaret Pickop, of Blackburn. B. at Blackburn 1857; m. 1895, Florence Kate, eld. d. of W. Balle Huntington, Esq., Dept.-Lieut. for Darwen, Lancashire. Educ. in Herefordshire, Germany, and France. Was Mayor of Blackburn in 1892 and High Sheriff of Worcestershire in 1913. Created Bart. 1918. A Unionist. MP for Ashton-under-Lyne from 1895-1906, when he was defeated. Unsuccessfully contested Ashton-under-Lyne Jan. 1910. Elected for mid Worcestershire in Feb. 1916 and sat until he retired in 1918. Assumed the additional name of Huntington in 1918; his s. and heir, Herbert Maurice, m. Stanley Baldwin's 3rd d. in 1919. Died 22 Jan. 1936. [1918]

WHITLEY, Edward. 185 Piccadilly, London. The Grange, Halewood, Nr. Liverpool. Carlton, St. Stephen's, and Conservative, Liverpool. S. of John Whitley, Esq., of Liverpool, Solicitor, by Isabella, d. of Edward Greenall, Esq., of Willderspool, Cheshire. B. at Liverpool 1825: m. 1878, Elizabeth Eleanor, d. of Henry Walker, Esq., of Whitehaven. Educ. at Rugby. Became a Solicitor in 1849. Was a member of the Town Council of Liverpool from 1866, and a Magistrate from 1868, in which year he was Mayor of that town; was also President of the Liverpool Law Society from 1877 to 1878. A Conservative, voted against the 3rd reading of the Irish Land Bill 1881. Sat for Liverpool from Feb. 1880 to 1885, and was elected for the Everton division of Liverpool Nov. 1885 and sat until his death on 14 Jan. 1892. [1891]

WHITLEY, Rt. Hon. John Henry. Continued in House after 1918: full entry in Volume III.

WHITMORE, Charles Algernon. 75 Cadogan Place, London. Manor House, Lower Slaughter, Bourton-on-the-Water, Gloucestershire. Wellington, Oxford & Cambridge, and Carlton. Eld. s. of C. Shepland Whitmore, Esq., Q.C., Recorder of Gloucester and Judge of the Southwark County Court. B. in London 1851. Educ. at Eton, and Balliol Coll., Oxford; first class and elected to a Fellowship at All Souls in 1874. He was called to the bar at the Inner Temple in 1876, and joined the Oxford Circuit. Was Assistant-Private Secretary to the Home Secretary (Mr. Matthews) Aug. 1886-92. Elected Alderman of London County Council in 1895; and was a

Church Estates Commissioner. A Conservative. Unsuccessfully contested Chelsea at the general election of 1885. First elected for Chelsea in 1886 and sat until defeated in 1906. Died 10 Sept. 1908. [1905]

WHITTAKER, Rt. Hon. Sir Thomas Palmer. Continued in House after 1918: full entry in Volume III.

WHITTY, Patrick Joseph. 22 Cross Avenue, Co. Dublin. 35 North Side, Clapham Common, London. 3rd s. of Dr. P.J. Whitty, of Lady Lane, Waterford, and Mrs. Whitty (née Hazleton, sister of Mr. Hazleton, MP). B. at Waterford 1894. Educ. at St. Vincent's Coll., Castleknock, Co. Dublin. An Accountant by profession. A Nationalist. Elected for N. Louth in Feb. 1916 and sat until he retired in 1918. [1918]

WHYTE, Alexander Frederick. 3 Barton Street, Westminster, London. S. of the Rev. Alexander Whyte, D.D., Principal of New Coll., Edinburgh, and Jane Elizabeth, d. of G.F. Barbour, Esq., of Bonskeid. B. 30 Sept. 1883 in Edinburgh; m. 1912, Margaret, d. of the Rev. William Fairweather, D.D., one d. Educ. at Edinburgh Academy, Abbotsholme, Jena University, and Edinburgh University; M.A. 1st class honours Modern Languages. President of Edinburgh University Union 1904; Lecteur Adjoint at the Collége de la Sorbonne, Paris 1905; and Warden of Edinburgh University Settlement 1907-08. Parliamentary Private Secretary (unpaid) to Mr. Churchill 1910-15; Lieut. R.N.V.R. for special duty Dec. 1914. Editor of *The New Europe* from May 1917. A Liberal. Elected for Perth in Jan. 1910 and sat until he retired in 1918. Travelled in U.S.A. 1919-20. President of Legislative Assembly, India 1920-25. Political Adviser to National Government of China 1929-32. Knighted in 1922. Director-Gen. of English Speaking Union 1938. Director of the American division, Ministry of Information 1939-40. Author of several works on international affairs. Died 30 July 1970. [1918]

WICKHAM, William. Binsted-Wyck, Alton, Hampshire. Athenaeum, and Carlton. S. of Henry Louis Wickham, Esq., of Binsted-Wyck, Hampshire, by Lucy, youngest d. of William Markham, Esq., of Becca Hall, Yorkshire. B. in London 1831; m. 1860, Sophia Emma, youngest d. of Henry F. Shaw-Lefevre, Esq. Educ. on the foundation of Westminster School, and a M.A. of Balliol Coll., Oxford. Called to the bar at the Inner Temple 1857. A J.P. for Hampshire 1866; Dept.-Lieut. 1891; High Sheriff, Hampshire 1888; a Director of the Sun Fire and Life Assurance Company, and editor of the *Correspondence of the Rt. Hon. William Wickham* (1870). A Conservative, in favour of wise and prudent reforms, and opposed to Home Rule. Sat for the Petersfield division of Hampshire from July 1892 until his death 16 May 1897. [1897]

WIGGIN, Henry. Metchley Grange, Harborne, Staffordshire. Reform. S. of William Wiggin, Esq., of Cheadle, Staffordshire, by Elizabeth, d. of William Milner, Esq., of Tean, Staffordshire. B. at Cheadle 1824; m. 1851, Mary Elizabeth, 2nd. d. of David Malins, Esq., of Edgbaston, near Birmingham. A J.P. and Dept.-Lieut. for Staffordshire and a J.P. for Worcestershire and Birmingham, of which town he was Mayor in 1865. A Director of the Midland Railway and South Staffordshire Water Works Company. A Liberal and Unionist, and prepared "to support all measures of Liberal progress." In favour of an amendment of the Land Laws, the establishment of a system of local government in counties, etc. Sat for Staffordshire, E. from Apr. 1880 to Nov. 1885 and for the Handsworth division of Staffordshire from Nov. 1885 until he retired in 1892. Created Bart. 1892. Died 12 Nov. 1905. [1892]

WIGRAM, Alfred Money. 101 Eaton Square, London. Havering-atte-Bower, Essex. Carlton, and Junior Carlton. S. of Money Wigram, Esq., of Esher, who was a grand-s. of Sir Robert Wigram, 1st Bart., of Wexford, and cousin of Lieut.-Gen. Sir F.W. Fitzwygram, the 4th Bart., and one time MP for Hampshire S. B. 1856; m. 1882, Venetia Mary, d. of the Rev. John Whitaker Maitland, Rector of Loughton, and his wife, a d. of Sir Digby Neave, of Dagnam, the 3rd Bart. Educ. at Winchester School. Chairman of Reid's Brewery Company Limited, Liquorpond Street, Gray's Inn Lane. A Conservative. Sat for Essex S. from Apr. 1894 until he accepted Chiltern Hundreds in 1897. Died 13 Oct. 1899. [1896]

WILES, Rt. Hon. Thomas. 168 Ashley

Gardens, London. Satwell Spinneys, Rotherfields Greys, Oxfordshire. Reform, and National Liberal. S. of Joseph Wiles, Esq., of St. Albans. B. 19 June 1861 at St. Albans; m. 1890, Winifred Alice, d. of the Rev. H. Crassweller, of Highbury. Educ. at Amersham Hall School. Senior Partner of Joseph Wiles and Son Limited, Grain Merchants, Mark Lane, and a member of the London Corn Exchange and Baltic Exchange. A member of London County Council 1899-1907. Was Parliamentary Private Secretary (unpaid) to Mr. McKinnon Wood, when Financial Secretary to the Treasury. PC. 1916. Honorary Secretary to London Liberal members and Chairman of Finance Committee of London Liberal Federation. A J.P. for Co. of London and Oxfordshire. A Liberal. Elected for S. Islington in 1906 and sat until defeated in 1918. Unsuccessfully contested S. Islington in 1922 and Eastbourne in 1923. Member of the Port of London Authority from 1923 and Chairman 1941-46. Chairman of Anglo-Portuguese Colonial and Overseas Bank. Died 18 May 1951. [1918]

WILKIE, Alexander. Continued in House after 1918: full entry in Volume III.

WILL, John Shiress. 13 West Cromwell Road, London. 2 Garden Court. Temple, London. Ardovie, Brechin, N.B. Reform, Devonshire, and National Liberal. Only s. of John Will, Esq., of Hanover, Jamaica (originally of Dundee, N.B.), by Mary, d. of John Chambers, Esq. B. 1840; m. 1873, Mary, d. of William Shiress, Esq., of Brechin, Forfarshire. Educ. at Brechin Grammar School, University of Edinburgh, and King's Coll., London. Called to the bar at the Middle Temple 1864; appointed a Queen's Counsel 1883; and a bencher of his Inn 1888. Wrote and edited several legal works. A Liberal, and Home Ruler. Sat for the Montrose district from 1885 until he accepted Chiltern Hundreds in 1896. Appointed County Court Judge from 1906. Died 24 May 1910. [1895 2nd ed.]

WILLIAMS, Aneurin. Continued in House after 1918: full entry in Volume III.

WILLIAMS, Arthur John. Morva, Eastbourne. Windham, Reform, National Liberal, and Savile. S. of John Morgan Williams, Esq., Surgeon, of Bridgend, Glamorgan, by Caroline Augusta, d. of T. Whitesmith, Esq., of Bawtry, Yorkshire. B. 1836; m. 1877, Rose Harriette, eld. d. of Robert Thompson Crawshay, Esq., of Cyfarthfa Castle, Glamorgan. Educ. privately. Was called to the bar at the Inner Temple 1867. For many years Hon. Secretary to the Law Amendment Society in succession to the Rt. Hon. G.J. Shaw-Lefevre. Also Honorary Secretary to the Legal Education Association, which under Lord Selborne's Presidency was formed to found a University of Law. Also Secretary to the Accidents in Mines Commission. Was one of the founders of the National Liberal Club, and a member of the Liberation Society; wrote *The Appropriation of the Railways by the State, Hints to Honest Citizens on Going to Law,* and other works. A J.P. for Glamorgan. A Radical and Home Ruler. Unsuccessfully contested Birkenhead 1880. Sat for Glamorgan S. from 1885 until defeated in 1895. Died 12 Sept. 1911. [1895]

WILLIAMS, Sir Arthur Osmond. See OSMOND-WILLIAMS, Sir Arthur.

WILLIAMS, Eliot Crawshay. See CRAWSHAY-WILLIAMS, Eliot.

WILLIAMS, John. Continued in House after 1918: full entry in Volume III.

WILLIAMS, John Carvell. 2 Serjeant's Inn, Fleet Street, London. Hornsey Rise Gardens, London. National Liberal. S. of John Allen and Mary Williams. B. 1821 at Stepney; m. 1849, Anne, d. of Richard Goodman, Esq., of Hornsey. Educ. privately. Was in the Legal profession. Parliamentary Chairman of the Liberation Society (the Society for the Liberation of Religion from State-Patronage and Control) from 1877, and Chairman of the Executive Committee. Also Chairman of the Congregational Union of England and Wales. Author of several publications on Disestablishment and the Burial Laws. An advanced Liberal, in favour of Home Rule, disestablishment, unsectarian education, temperance legislation, and international arbitration. Sat for Nottingham S. 1885-86, when he was defeated, and for the Mansfield division of Nottinghamshire from 1892 until he retired in 1900. Died 8 Oct. 1907. [1900]

WILLIAMS, John Charles. Caerhays

Castle, St. Austell, Cornwall. Werrington Park, Launceston. Brooks's. S. of John Michael Williams, Esq., of Caerhays Castle, and Gnaton Hall, Devonshire, by Elizabeth Maria, d. of Stephen Davey, Esq., of Bochym House, Cornwall. B. 1861; m. 1884, Mary, 2nd d. of Sir F.M. Williams, Bart., MP. Educ. at Rugby and Trinity Hall, Cambridge. Was High Sheriff of Cornwall in 1888. A Liberal Unionist. Sat for the Truro division of Cornwall from July 1892 until he retired in 1895. Lord-Lieut. of Cornwall 1918-36. Died 29 Mar. 1939. [1895]

WILLIAMS, Rt. Hon. Joseph Powell. 6 Great George Street, London. St. David's, Beckenham. Devonshire. S. of Joseph Williams, Esq., of Worcester. B. 1840; m. a d. of Mr. Bindley, F.R.C.S., of Birmingham. Educ. at the Proprietary School, Edgbaston. In 1877 became a member of the town council of Birmingham; appointed Chairman of the Finance Committee 1879, and was elected Alderman 1883. Was Financial Secretary to the War Office 1895-1900. Was Hon. Secretary to the National Liberal Federation, and a J.P. for the Co. of Worcester and city of Birmingham. Chairman of Management Committee of Liberal Unionist Association. PC. 1900. A Liberal Unionist. Sat for Birmingham S. from Nov. 1885 until his death 7 Feb. 1904. [1903]

WILLIAMS, Penry. Continued in House after 1918: full entry in Volume III.

WILLIAMS, Sir Rhys Rhys-., Bart. See RHYS-WILLIAMS, Sir Rhys, Bart. Continued in House after 1918: full entry in Volume III.

WILLIAMS, Sir Robert, Bart. Continued in House after 1918: full entry in Volume III.

WILLIAMS, Thomas Howell. See IDRIS, Thomas Howell Williams.

WILLIAMS, Thomas Jeremiah. Continued in House after 1918: full entry in Volume III.

WILLIAMS, William. 4 Victoria Street, London. Maes-y-gwernen Hall, Swansea Valley. National Liberal. S. of William Williams, Esq., of Morriston. B. 1840. Was one of the largest Tin-Plate Manufacturers in the world. He was employed, when a boy, in the Forest Steel and Tin-Plate Works, of Morriston, and was later Proprietor of those works. He also owned the Worcester and the Morlais Tin-Plate Works. A J.P. for Swansea (of which town he was Mayor), and for Glamorganshire, and was a County Councillor for Glamorgan and a Dept.-Chairman of the Glamorganshire Banking Company. He also held office in the Congregational body. An advanced Liberal, in favour of Home Rule, Disestablishment, etc. Elected for the Swansea district in June 1893 and sat until he retired in 1895. Died 21 Apr. 1904. [1895]

WILLIAMS, William Llewelyn. 111 Ashley Gardens, Westminster, London. National Liberal, Reform, and Eighty. S. of Morgan Williams, Esq., of Brownhill, Carmarthen, and Sarah, d. of T. Davies, Esq., of Bankylan, Carmarthen. B. 10 Mar. 1867 at Brownhill; m. Elinor, d. of James Jenkins, Esq., of Llangadock. Educ. at Llandovery Coll., and Brasenose Coll., Oxford; M.A., B.C.L. A Barrister, called 1897, and practised on the S. Wales and Chester Circuit. K.C. 1912. Bencher of Lincoln's Inn 1917. Recorder of Swansea 1912-15 and of Cardiff from 1915. Author of *Welsh Catholics on the Continent*, several essays on Welsh History and Literature, and two Welsh novels. A Liberal. Elected for Carmarthen Boroughs in 1906 and sat until he retired in 1918. Unsuccessfully contested in Cardiganshire in Feb. 1921. Died 22 Apr. 1922. [1918]

WILLIAMSON, Sir Archibald, Bart. Continued in House after 1918: full entry in Volume III.

WILLIAMSON, George Henry. Curriehill, Wimbledon, London. Constitutional. S. of G. Williamson, Esq., of Worcester. B. 1845 in London. Educ. at Worcester. Managing Director of a Tin-Plate works at Worcester; Mayor of Worcester 1893-94; and was twice High Sheriff of Worcestershire; a J.P. for Worcester. A Conservative and Tariff Reformer. Elected for Worcester in Jan. 1906 and sat until unseated on petition May 1906. Unsuccessfully contested the Romford division of Essex in Jan. 1910. Died Mar. 1918. [1906]

WILLIAMSON, James. Ryelands, Lancaster. Devonshire, and National Liberal. County Club, Lancaster. S. of James Williamson, Esq., J.P. of Parkfield, Lancaster, by his wife Eleanor Miller. B. in Lancaster 31 Dec. 1842; m. 1880, the 2nd d. of James Stewart, Esq., of Clapham, Yorkshire. Educ. at the Lancaster Royal Grammar School and at a private school in Cheshire. A Manufacturer. A J.P. for the borough, and J.P. and Dept.-Lieut. for the Co. of Lancaster; was High Sheriff of Lancashire in 1885. A Liberal, in favour of Mr. Gladstone's Irish policy. First elected for the Lancaster division of Lancashire N. in 1886 and sat until he retired in 1895. Created 1st Baron Ashton in 1895. Died 27 May 1930. [1895]

WILLIAMSON, Stephen. 8 Eaton Square, London. Copley, Neston, Cheshire. Glenogil, Forfarshire. Eld. s. of Archibald Williamson, Esq., of Anstruther, Fifeshire, a Shipowner. B. at Kilrenny 1827; m. 1859, Annie, d. of the Rev. Thomas Gurthrie, D.D., of Edinburgh. A Merchant and Shipowner and Partner in the firm of Messrs. Balfour, Williamson and Company at Liverpool. A Magistrate for Cheshire, and a Vice-President of the Liverpool Chamber of Commerce. Published several pamphlets in connection with the currency question, Socialism, and the Disestablishment question, etc. A "decided Liberal", in favour of Home Rule for Ireland. Sat for the St. Andrew's district from Apr. 1880 to 1885. At the general election of that year he was defeated on a scrutiny following the declaration of a "tie". First elected for the Kilmarnock district 1886 and sat until defeated in 1895. Died 16 June 1903. [1895]

WILLOUGHBY, Hon. Claude Heathcote-Drummond-. Continued in House after 1918: full entry in Volume III.

WILLOUGHBY, Hon. Gilbert Heathcote-Drummond-. See WILLOUGHBY de ERESBY, Gilbert Heathcote-Drummond-Willoughby, Lord.

WILLOUGHBY de ERESBY, Gilbert Heathcote - Drummond - Willoughby, Lord. 6 Audley Square, London. Normanton Park, Stamford. Carlton. Eld. s. of the Earl of Ancaster and Lady Evelyn Elizabeth Gordon, d. of the 10th Marq. of Huntly. B. 1867; m. 1905 Eloise, d. of W.L. Breese, Esq., of New York. Educ. at Eton, and Trinity Coll., Cambridge. A J.P. for the Kesteven division of Lincolnshire and for Rutland. Honorary Lieut.-Col. in the Lincolnshire Yeomanry, and Chancellor of the Primrose League 1903. A Unionist. In 1892 he unsuccessfully contested Boston. Elected for the Horncastle division of Lincolnshire in 1894 and sat until he succeeded as 2nd Earl of Ancaster 24 Dec. 1910. Styled Lord Willoughby de Eresby from 1892, when his father was created Earl of Ancaster, until he succeeded to the Earldom in 1910. Chairman of Quarter Sessions, Kesteven, Lincolnshire 1911-36. Parliamentary Secretary to the Minister of Agriculture 1921-24. Lord-Lieut. of Rutland 1921-51. Lord Great Chamberlain of England 1937-50. Died 29 Sept. 1951. [1910]

WILLOX, Sir John Archibald. Queen Anne's Mansions, London. 9 Abercromby Square, Liverpool. Parkside House, Huyton, Lancashire. Carlton, Constitutional, and Savage. S. of John Willox, Esq., and Katharine his wife. B. 1842 at Edinburgh; m. 1888, Sara, widow of Thomas Cope, Esq., J.P. and Tobacco Manufacturer, of Liverpool. Educ. privately. Was for many years Editor and Proprietor of the *Liverpool Courier*, and in that character took an active part in the political affairs of Lancashire and Cheshire. Was Chairman of the Press Association, President of the Institute of Journalists, Trustee Journalists' Orphans' Fund, etc. Was created Kt. 1897. A Conservative. First returned for the Everton division of Liverpool (without opposition) on the death of Mr. E. Whitley, 15 Feb. 1892 and sat until he accepted Chiltern Hundreds in Feb. 1905. Died 9 June 1905. [1904]

WILLS, Arthur Walters. Colebrook, The Grange, Wimbledon. Reform, Flyfishers, Epée, and Sword. S. of George Wills, Esq., of Pepperdon, Devon, and Lucy, d. of D. Walters, Esq., of London. B. 1868. Educ. at Harrow, and Trinity Coll., Cambridge. A Barrister, called to the bar at the Inner Temple 1894. A Liberal, he favoured land system reform and readjustment of the rating system, including taxation of land values, free trade, etc. First elected for N. Dorset in Jan. 1905 and sat until defeated in Jan. 1910. Defeated again in N. Dorset in Dec. 1910. Died 17 Nov. 1948. [1909]

WILLS, Sir Frederick, Bart. 9 Kensington

Palace Gardens, London. Northmoor, Nr. Dulverton, and Manor Heath, Bournemouth. Reform, Gresham, and Royal Thames Yacht. S. of Henry Overton Wills, Esq., of Bristol, and Isabella, d. of William Board, Esq., of Bristol. B. 1838 at Bristol; m. 1867, Anne, d. of the Rev. James Hamilton, D.D. Educ. at Independent Coll., Taunton, and Amersham School, Buckinghamshire. Director of W.D. and H.O. Wills Limited, Tobacco Merchants and Manufacturers; J.P. for the Co. of Somerset. Received the dignity of a Baronetcy 1897. A Liberal Unionist. Unsuccessfully contested Launceston division of Cornwall 1895 and 1898. Elected for N. Bristol in 1900 and sat until he retired in 1906. Died 18 Feb. 1909.   [1905]

WILLS, Sir Gilbert Alan Hamilton, Bart. Continued in House after 1918: full entry in Volume III.

WILLS, Sir William Henry, Bart. 25 Hyde Park Gardens, London. Blagdon, Somerset. East Court, St. Laurence-on-Sea, Thanet. Reform, Royal Thames Yacht, and National Liberal. S. of William Day Wills, Esq., of Bristol, by Mary, 3rd d. of Robert Steven, Esq., of Camberwell, Surrey (one of the founders of the London Missionary and Bible Societies). B. at Bristol 1830; m. Elisabeth, youngest d. of John Stancomb, Esq., of Trowbridge, Wiltshire (she died 1896). Educ. at Mill Hill School, and University Coll., London. Chairman of W.D. and H.O. Wills Limited; a J.P. and Dept.-Lieut. for Somerset, High Sheriff of Bristol 1877-78, and Chairman of the Bristol Chamber of Commerce. A Director of the Great Western Railway, and of the Bristol Water Works Company; also Chairman of the Provincial Water Companies Association, a Trustee of the Bristol Municipal Charities, a Governor of the Bristol Grammar School, a Governor of Sion Hospital, and a Fellow of the Royal Geographical Society. Created Bart. 1893. A Liberal, in favour of Home Rule for Ireland, etc. Sat for Coventry 1880-85. Unsuccessfully contested S.E. Essex in 1885 and again in 1886, and Bristol S. in 1892. First elected for Bristol E. in Mar. 1895 and sat until he retired in 1900. High Sheriff of Somerset 1905-06. Created Baron Winterstoke in Feb. 1906. Pro-Chancellor of Bristol University. Died 29 Jan. 1911.   [1900]

WILSON, Arthur Stanley. Continued in House after 1918: full entry in Volume III.

WILSON, Charles Henry. 41 Grosvenor Square, London. The Bungalow, Cottingham. Warter Priory, Yorkshire. Villa Pastorell, St. Helene, Nice. Reform. S. of Thomas Wilson, Esq., of Cottingham, and Hull, Yorkshire. B. at Hull 1833; m. 1871, Florence Jane Helen, d. of Col. Wellesley. Educ. at Kingston Coll., Hull. A Merchant and Steamship Owner, and Honorary Brother of the Hull Trinity House. Received the Freedom of the city of Hull in 1899. A Liberal, and Home Ruler, in favour of "local option", Sunday closing, and facilities for the transfer of land. Sat for Hull from Feb. 1874 to 1885, and for the W. division of Hull from 1885 until he was created 1st Baron Nunburnholme in Dec. 1905. Died 27 Oct. 1907.   [1905]

WILSON, Hon. Charles Henry Wellesley. Ferriby Hall, Hull. Eld. s. of Lord Nunburnholme. B. 1875; m. 1901, Lady Marjorie Wynn-Carrington, d. of Earl Carrington. A Maj. in 2nd Volunteer Battalion E. Yorkshire Regiment; served in S. Africa 1900 with C.I.V.; D.S.O. 1900. A Liberal. Elected for W. Hull in 1906 and sat until he succeeded as 2nd Baron Nunburnholme on 27 Oct. 1907. Lord-Lieut. of the E. Riding of Yorkshire. Died 15 Aug. 1924.   [1907]

WILSON, Frederick William. Artillery Mansions, Victoria Street, London. The Dale, Searning, Norfolk. High Row, Felixstowe. Reform. 2nd s. of William Wilson, Esq., of the Manor House, Scarning, Norfolk. B. at Scarning 1844; m. Elizabeth, d. of Edward Capps, Esq., of Forest Hill, author of Our National Debt, etc. Educ. at King Edward the Sixth School, Wymondham, Norfolk. A Journalist; was indentured to J.H. Tillett, MP for Norwich, Editor of the Norfolk News. A J.P. for Suffolk, and President of the Newspaper Society of the United Kingdom 1894. A Liberal. Was an unsuccessful candidate for mid Norfolk in Apr. 1895; first returned there at the general election in July 1895 and sat until he retired in 1906. Knighted 1907. Died 26 May 1924.   [1905]

WILSON, Lieut.-Col. Hon. Guy Greville. Park House, Cottingham, East Yorkshire. 1 Portman Square, London. Brooks's, and Bachelors'. 2nd s. of 1st

Lord Nunburnholme. B. 1877; m. 1904, Lady Isabel Innes-Ker, d. of 7th Duke of Roxburgh (she died 1905); 2ndly, 1911, Avery, d. of Mr. Geoffrey Buxton, of Dunston Hall, Norwich. Three children. Educ. at Eton. Entered the army in 11th Hussars 1898; Lieut. 1900; retired 1903. Served in S. African War with Damant's Horse 1902, when he received the D.S.O. Lieut.-Col. E. Riding Imperial Yeomanry; a Director of Earl's Shipbuilding and Engineering Company, Hull; J.P. and Dept.-Lieut. of E. Yorkshire. Parliamentary Private Secretary to Mr. McKenna when First Lord of the Admiralty. A Liberal. Sat for W. Hull from Nov. 1907 until defeated in 1918. Died 1 Feb. 1943.   [1918]

WILSON, Henry Joseph. Osgathorpe Hills, Sheffield. National Liberal, and New Reform. S. of William Wilson, Esq., of Sherwood Hall, Mansfield, and Eliza, d. of Joseph Read, Esq., of Sheffield. B. at Nottingham 1833; m. 1859, Charlotte, d. of Charles Cowan, Esq., MP for Edinburgh. Educ. at the West of England Dissenters' Proprietary School, Taunton and University Coll., London. Largely interested in the Sheffield Smelting Company. A J.P. for the W. Riding of Yorkshire and Sheffield. Was a member of the Sheffield School Board for fifteen years, the India Office Committee on Regulation of Prostitution in India, and the Royal Commission on Opium 1893-95. A Radical, opposed to Agressive Foreign Policy, Militarism, Protection, etc. Sat for the Holmfirth division of Yorkshire from 1885 until he accepted Chiltern Hundreds in 1912. Died 29 June 1914.   [1912]

WILSON, Isaac. Nunthorpe Hall, Yorkshire. Reform. S. of Isaac Wilson, Esq., of Kendal, Westmoreland, by Mary. d. of John Jowitt, Esq., of Leeds. B. at Kendal 1822; m. 1847, Anne Dorothy, d. of Robert Benson, Esq., of Parkside, Kendal. Educ. at Tottenham School. An Ironmaster. A Magistrate for Durham and for the N. Riding of Yorkshire. A Liberal. Sat for Middlesborough from July 1878 until he retired in 1892. Died 22 Sept. 1899.   [1892]

WILSON, John, (I). Hillhead House, Glasgow. National Liberal. S. of James Wilson, Esq., Grocer, of Ferguslie, Paisley, and his wife Jean Stevensen. B. 1828; m. 1861, d. of Mathew Gemmill, Esq., of Fen-

wick. Educ. at Paisley High School. Was a large employer of labour in the district, being head of the firm of John Wilson and Son, Iron Tube Manufacturers, Oxford Street, Glasgow, and Govan. A Dept.-Lieut. and J.P. for Lanarkshire, and a J.P. for Lanark. "A Radical", and supported Home Rule for Ireland, "and for Scotland also"; in favour of popular control of the liquor traffic, religious equality, taxation of feu duties and ground rents, and free education, compulsorily administered, if necessary. Sat for the Govan division of Lanarkshire from 18 Jan. 1889 until he retired in 1900. Died 29 Dec. 1905. [1900]

WILSON, John, (II). 23 Royal Terrace, Edinburgh. S. of John Wilson, Esq., Merchant, of Edinburgh, by Margaret, d. of David Paton, Esq., of Edinburgh. B. 1830; m. 1880, Ann, only d. of Robert Saunderson, Esq., of Dalkeith. Educ. at the High School, Edinburgh. A Partner in the firm of Honeyman and Wilson, Merchants, of Edinburgh from 1856. A Magistrate for Edinburgh from 1872, became Town Councillor and Treasurer of the city 1876; Dept.-Chairman of the Chamber of Commerce, and Commissioner of Leith Harbour 1881, and held various other appointments. Chairman of the Liberal Association. A Liberal. Sat for the Central division of Edinburgh from Nov. 1885 until defeated in 1886 standing as a Gladstonian Liberal.   [1886]

WILSON, John, (III). 97 Kennington Road, London. North Road, Durham. Miners' Institute, Durham. S. of Christopher Wilson, Esq., of Greatham, Durham, and Hannah Sponton, of Hamsterley, Durham. B. 1837 at Greatham; m. 1862, Margaret, d. of George Firth, Esq., Coal Miner, of Sherburn Hill, Durham. He began work at Stanhope Quarries at the age of ten, and went down the pit at Ludworth Colliery, Durham when he was thirteen. At nineteen he went to sea for a few years; and then worked in the Haswell Colliery. In 1863-67 he worked in Pennsylvania, and Illinois, U.S.A. He helped to establish the Durham Miners' Association in 1869 and in 1876 became Secretary of the Miners' Franchise Association. In 1882 he was elected Treasurer of the Miners' Association, in 1890 he became its financial Secretary, and in 1896 corresponding Secretary. Was Primitive Methodist local preacher. Honorary D.C.L. Durham 1910. An advanced Liberal. In 1885 he was returned to Parliament as Member for the Houghton-le-Spring division of Durham, but he lost his seat at the general election of 1886. Sat for Durham mid from July 1890 until his death 24 Mar. 1915 [1915]

WILSON, John, (IV). Finnish Malise, Drymen, N.B. New, and Imperial Union, Glasgow. S. of James Wilson, Esq., Merchant, of Glasgow, by his wife, Margaret Gibbs. B. 1837; m. 1883, Margaret, d. of John Hewetson, Esq., of Ellergill, Westmorland. Educ. at Glasgow. A Governor of the Glasgow and W. of Scotland Technical Coll., a member of Stirling County Council, Dept.-Lieut. and J.P. for Stirlingshire. A Liberal Unionist. Elected for the St. Rollox division of Glasgow in 1900 and sat until defeated in 1906. Died 5 Jan. 1928. [1905]

WILSON, John, (V). Airdrie House, Airdrie. Kippen Tower, Dunning, Perthshire. Reform, and Bath. New Club, Glasgow, and Liberal, Edinburgh. S. of James Wilson, Esq., Coalmaster, of Airdrie, and Agnes Motherwell, of Airdrie. B. 1844. Educ. at the Airdrie and Glasgow Academies. A Coalowner; a J.P. and Dept.-Lieut. for the Co. of Lanark and city of Glasgow. A Liberal Unionist from the introduction of the Home Rule Bill of 1886. Withdrew his support from Unionist Government from the introduction of Fiscal Policy, and joined the Liberals in Feb. 1904. Sat for Falkirk from 1895 until he retired in 1906. Created Bart. (Sir John Wilson of Airdrie) in 1906. Died 28 July 1918. [1905]

WILSON, Rt. Hon. John William. Continued in House after 1918: full entry in Volume III.

WILSON, Joseph Havelock. Continued in House after 1918: full entry in Volume III.

WILSON, Lieut.-Col. Leslie Orme. Continued in House after 1918: full entry in Volume III.

WILSON, Sir Mathew, Bart. Defeated in 1886: full entry in Volume I.

WILSON, Maj. Sir Mathew Richard Henry, Bart., C.S.I. Continued in House after 1918: full entry in Volume III.

WILSON, Philip Whitwell. 16 Percy Circus, London. National Liberal. S. of Isaac Whitwell Wilson, Esq., J.P., of Kendal, and Anne, d. of Jonathan Bagster, Esq., Bible Publisher. B. 21 May 1875 at Kendal; m. 1899, Alice, d. of Henry Collins, Esq., of Pawtucket, U.S.A. Educ. at Kendal Grammar School, and Clare Coll., Cambridge. A Journalist; Parliamentary Correspondent of the Daily News: author of Why we believe, Liberty and Religion, etc. A Liberal. Elected for St. Pancras S. in 1906 and sat until defeated in Jan. 1910. Contested Appleby division of Westmorland in Dec. 1910. Member of the Press Gallery for 12 years, later the American Correspondent of the Daily News. Died 6 June 1956. [1909]

WILSON, Sir Samuel. 10 Grosvenor Square, London. Hughenden Manor, Buckinghamshire. Ercildoune, Victoria. Carlton, Conservative, Constitutional, and Bachelors'. 6th s. of Samuel Wilson, Esq., of Ballycloughan, Co. Antrim. B. 1832, at Ballycloughan; m. 1861, in Melbourne, Jean, d. of the Hon. W.M.L.C. Campbell. Was twice elected to the Legislative Assembly and twice to the Upper House of Victoria. He built the Wilson Hall of the Melbourne University at a cost of about £40,000, in recognition of which he was Knighted in 1875; in 1877 introduced salmon to Australian waters; and rendered other valuable services in the cause of acclimatization in the Australian colonies. Was Royal Commissioner for the Fisheries Exhibition, and Vice-President of the Melbourne International Exhibition of 1881. A F.R.G.S., F.L.S., and Dept.-Lieut for Middlesex. Author of Salmon at the Antipodes, The Angora, and other works. A Conservative Unionist, in favour of Imperial Federation. Unsuccessfully contested Co. Londonderry in 1881 and Buckinghamshire N. in 1885. First returned for Portsmouth in July 1886 and sat until he retired in 1892. Died 11 June 1895. [1892]

WILSON, Thomas Fleming. Felmington House, Uddingston, N.B. National Liberal. S. of John Wilson, Esq., Builder and Contractor, of Glasgow. B. 2 June 1862 in Glasgow; m. 1888, Helen, d. of William Barr, Esq., J.P., of Loanhead, Uddingston. Educ. at Glasgow High School, and Glasgow University. A Solicitor, a Partner in the firm of Wilson, Chalmers, and Hendry, Glasgow, from 1886, a Director of

London and Lancashire Life Office (Scottish Board), and a Gov. of Marshall (Educational) Trust; a member of Lanarkshire County Council for fifteen years, and Chairman of Public Health Committee. A Liberal. Elected for N.E. Lanarkshire in Jan. 1910 and sat until he accepted Chiltern Hundreds in 1911. K.B.E. in 1918. Died 2 Apr. 1929. [1910]

WILSON, William Tyson. Continued in House after 1918: full entry in Volume III.

WILSON-FOX, Henry. Continued in House after 1918: full entry in Volume III.

WILSON-TODD, Sir William Henry, Bart. Halnaby Hall, Croft, Darlington. Tranby Park, Hessle, Yorkshire. Carlton, and Army & Navy. S. of Col. J.J. Wilson, 74th Regiment, of Roseville, Co. Wexford, and Frances, d. of the Hon. John Robinson. B. 1828; m. 1855, Jane Marian Rutherford Todd, only child of John Todd, Esq., of Halnaby Hall, Yorkshire, and Tranby Park, Yorkshire. Assumed the additional surname of Todd in 1855. Educ. at Sandhurst. A Capt. in the 39th Regiment; served in the Crimean War and had the medal. A J.P. and Dept.-Lieut. for the N. Riding of Yorkshire, and thrice elected (unopposed) on the County Council, Croft division. Created Bart. 1903. A Conservative and Unionist. Unsuccessful candidate for Darlington 1885. Sat for the Howdenshire division of the E. Riding of Yorkshire from 1892 until he retired in 1906. Died 10 Apr. 1910. [1905]

WINFREY, Sir Richard. Continued in House after 1918: full entry in Volume III.

WING, Thomas Edward. 5 Woodland Crescent, Muswell Hill Road, London. National Liberal. S. of Edward Wing, Esq. B. 12 Aug. 1853 at Hull; m. 1897, Louisa, widow of S.J. Dobson, Esq., of Grimsby. Was Parliamentary Agent of the United Kingdom Commercial Travellers' Association for fifteen years. Member of Grimsby Town Council from 1903-09. A Liberal. Sat for Grimsby from Jan. to Dec. 1910, when he was defeated. Elected for the Houghton-le-Spring division of Durham in Mar. 1913 and sat until he was defeated in 1918. Unsuccessfully contested the Dartford division of Kent in 1920, the Spannymoor division of Durham in 1922, and Grimsby in 1924. Died 12 May 1935. [1918]

WINGFIELD-DIGBY, John Kenelm Digby. 1 Whitehall Gardens, London. Sherborne Castle, Dorset. Coleshill Park, Warwickshire. Carlton. Eld. s. of John Digby Wingfield-Digby, Esq., of Sherborne Castle, Dorset, and Coleshill Park, Warwickshire, by his m. with Maria, eld. d. of Capt. Frederick Madan. B. 1859; m. 1st, 1883, the Hon. Georgina Rosamond Hewitt, 5th d. of Visct. Lifford; 2ndly, Charlotte, 2nd d. of William Digby, Esq., of Moat Lodge, Co. Galway. Educ. at Harrow, and Christ Church, Oxford. In 1881 became Lieut. in the Dorset (Queen's Own) Yeomanry, in 1884 Capt., and in 1897 Maj. A J.P. for Dorset, Warwick, and Somerset. Unsuccessful candidate for Somerset mid Mar.-Nov. 1885. Unsuccessful candidate for Somerset S. 1885. Sat for Dorset N. from July 1892 until his death on 25 Dec. 1904. [1904]

WINN, Hon. Rowland. 11 Grosvenor Gardens, London. Nostell Priory Wakefield. Carlton, Guards', and Marlborough. Eld. s. of Lord St. Oswald, by Harriet Maria, d. of Col. Henry Dumaresq, and niece of the 5th Lord of Lanesborough. B. 1857. Educ. at Eton. A Capt. in the Coldstream Guards, and served with his regiment in the Soudan War 1884. A Conservative. Sat for Pontefract from the general election of 1885, when he defeated Mr. Childers, until he succeeded as Lord St. Oswald in 1893. Died 13 Apr. 1919. [1892 2nd ed.]

WINTERBOTHAM, Arthur Brend. Norman Hill, Dursley, Gloucestershire. National Liberal, Reform, and Devonshire. S. of Lindsey Winterbotham, Esq., Banker, of Stroud, by his m. with Miss Sarah Selfe Page. B. at Tewkesbury 1838; m. 1863, Elizabeth, d. of J.G. Strachan, Esq., J.P. of Farmhill Park, Stroud. Educ. at Amersham School, Buckinghamshire. A Woollen Cloth Manufacturer, being Partner in the firm of Hunt and Winterbotham, Dursley. A Magistrate for Gloucestershire. A Liberal, voted against the Home Rule Bill of 1886, but later declared for Mr. Gladstone's modified Irish policy. Sat for the Cirencester division of Gloucestershire from 1885 until his death on 8 Sept. 1892. [1892]

WINTERTON, Edward Turnour, Earl. Continued in House after 1918: full entries in Volumes III and IV.

WODEHOUSE, Hon. Armine, C.B. 21 Sloane Gardens, London. Brooks's. S. of the Earl of Kimberley, by Lady Florence Fitz-Gibbon, d. of 3rd Earl of Clare. B. 1860; m. 1889, Eleanor, d. of Matthew Arnold, Esq. Educ. privately. Private Secretary to Lord Kimberley 1886, 1892-95. C.B. 1895. A Commissioner of Chelsea Public Libraries. A Liberal, in favour of Army Reform, Graduated Income Tax, and Reform of the Laws connected with land and agriculture. Unsuccessfully contested the Isle of Wight 1895. Sat for the Saffron Walden division of Essex from Oct. 1900 until his death 1 May 1901. [1901]

WODEHOUSE, Rt. Hon. Edmond Robert. 56 Chester Square, London. Travellers', Oxford & Cambridge, and Brooks's. Only s. of Sir Philip E. Wodehouse, G.C.S.I., K.C.B., by Catherine Mary, eld. d. of F.J. Templer, Esq. B. 1835; m. 1876, Adela, 2nd d. of the Rev. Charles W. Bagot, Rector of Castle Rising, Norfolk. Educ. at Eton, and Balliol Coll., Oxford, where he was 1st class in moderations and in final classical schools. Was called to the bar at Lincoln's Inn 1861. Was Private Secretary to the Earl of Kimberley when Lord-Lieut. of Ireland from 1864 to 1866, and again from 1868 to 1874 in the Privy Seal and Colonial offices; created PC. 1898. A Liberal Unionist. Unsuccessfully contested N. Norfolk Nov. 1868, and Lynn Regis Feb. 1874. Sat for Bath from Apr. 1880 until he retired in 1906. Died 14 Dec. 1914. [1905]

WODEHOUSE, John Wodehouse, Lord. Witton Park, North Walsham, Norfolk. Eld. s. of 2nd Earl of Kimberley. B. 11 Nov. 1883. Educ. at Eton, and Trinity Coll., Cambridge. A Liberal. Elected for mid Norfolk in 1906 and sat until he retired in Jan. 1910. Served in France 1914-17 and Italy 1918-19. Owned 11,000 acres. Succeeded as 3rd Earl of Kimberley in 1932. Died 16 Apr. 1941. [1909]

WOLFF, Gustav Wilhelm. 42 Park Street, London. The Den, Strandtown, Belfast. Carlton, Junior Carlton and Garrick. S. of F.M. Wolff, Esq., a German Merchant, and Fanny Schwabe his wife. B. at Hamburg 1834. Educ. at private schools, Hamburg, and the Collegiate Schools, Liverpool. Was an iron Shipbuilder and Engineer and a member of the Belfast firm of Harland and Wolff. Chairman of the Belfast Rope-works Company, and Director of the Union Castle Steamship Company. A Conservative. First elected for Belfast E. on the expulsion of Mr. De Cobain, Mar. 1892 and sat until he retired in Dec. 1910. Died 17 Apr. 1913. [1909]

WOLMER, Roundell Cecil Palmer, Visct. Continued in House after 1918: full entry in Volume III.

WOLMER, William Waldegrave Palmer, Visct. 9 John Street, Berkeley Square, London. Blackmoor, Petersfield, Hampshire. Brooks's. Eld. s. of the Earl of Selborne, Lord Chancellor in Mr. Gladstone's 2nd administration, by Lady Laura Waldegrave, 2nd d. of the 8th Earl Waldegrave. B. in Portland Place, London 1859; m. 1883, Lady Maud Cecil, eld. d. of the Marq. of Salisbury. Educ. at Winchester and University Coll., Oxford. At Oxford he took a first class in Modern History 1881. Was Private Secretary to the Rt. Hon. H.C.E. Childers, at the War Office 1882-83, and at the Treasury 1883-84; from 1884-85 was Private Secretary to Lord Selborne as Lord-Chancellor. A Capt. in the 3rd Battalion Hampshire Regiment, and a Magistrate for Hampshire. A Liberal Unionist, said he would retain the present state of the law in respect to voluntary schools; would reform the procedure of the House of Commons and the constitution of the House of Lords; and in favour of maintaining the army and navy in the highest state of efficiency. Sat for the Petersfield division of Hampshire 1885 to 1892. Sat for Edinburgh W. from July 1892 until he succeeded as Earl of Selborne on 4 May 1895. Under-Secretary for the Colonies 1895-1900; First Lord of the Admiralty 1900-05; High Commissioner for South Africa 1905-10; President of Board of Agriculture 1915-16; PC. 1900; Director of Lloyds Bank. Chairman of House of Laity in the Church Assembly from 1924. Died 26 Feb. 1942. [1895]

WOOD, Hon. Edward Frederick Lindley. Continued in House after 1918: full entry in Volume III.

WOOD, James. 30 Rosemary Street, Belfast. Mount Salem, Dundonald. Co. Down. National Liberal. S. of James and Anna Wood, of Belfast. B. 1865 at Clones, Co. Monaghan; m. 1891, Sara, d. of J. Mc-

Connell, Esq., of Belfast. Educ. privately. A Solicitor. A Liberal, opposed to Home Rule, in favour of Compulsory Land Purchase. Elected as a Liberal Unionist for E. Down in Feb. 1902 but joined the Liberals in Feb. 1904, and stood unsuccessfully for E. Down as a Liberal in 1906, and again in Jan. 1910. Died 31 Oct. 1936. [1905]

WOOD, Lieut.-Col. Sir John, Bart. Continued in House after 1918: full entry in Volume III.

WOOD, Nicholas. 7 Tilney Street, Park Lane, London. R.Y.S., Cowes. Carlton, Boodle's, Garrick, and Yorkshire. S. of Nicholas Wood, Esq., J.P. of Hetton, Durham, by Maria, d. of Collingwood Lindsay, Esq. B. at Killingworth, Northumberland 1832; m. 1881, Edith Florence, d. of J. St. Vincent Jervis, Esq., of Chatkeill, Staffordshire. Educ. at Repton School. A J.P. and Dept.-Lieut. for the Co. of Durham. A Conservative. Unsuccessfully contested the Houghton-le-Spring division of Durham Nov. 1885. First returned for that division July 1886 and sat until defeated in July 1892. Died 24 Dec. 1892. [1892]

WOOD, Samuel Hill-. See HILL-WOOD, Sir Samuel Hill, Bart. Continued in House after 1918: full entry in Volume III.

WOOD, Rt. Hon. Thomas McKinnon. 16 Portland Place, London. Starfield, Crowborough, Sussex. Reform, National Liberal, Scottish Liberal, and Glasgow Liberal. S. of Hugh Wood, Esq., and Jessie, d. of the Rev. T. McKinnon. B. 1855 in London; m. Isabella, d. of Alexander Sandison, Esq., J.P. Educ. at Mill Hill School, and University Coll., London. Was Parliamentary Secretary to the Board of Education, Apr. to Oct. 1908, Under-Secretary for Foreign Affairs 1908-11, and Financial Secretary to the Treasury 1911-12. Secretary for Scotland 1912-16. Chancellor of Duchy of Lancaster and Financial Secretary to the Treasury July to Dec. 1916; member of London County Council 1892-1909; Leader of Progressive Party; Chairman 1898-99; Alderman 1907. A Dept.-Lieut. for London; LL.D. for St. Andrews; PC. 1911. Wrote articles in *Encyclopaedia Britannica* and reviews. A Liberal. Unsuccessfully contested E. Islington 1895, the St. Rollox division of

Glasgow in 1900, and Orkney and Shetland in 1902. Sat for the St. Rollox division of Glasgow from 1906 until defeated in 1918. Unsuccessfully contested Hackney Central in 1922. Died 26 Mar. 1927. [1918]

WOODALL, William. Queen Anne's Mansions, London. Bleak House, Burslem. Reform, and Savage. B. at Shrewsbury 1832; m. 1862, Evelyn, d. of James MacIntyre, Esq., of Burslem (she died 1870). Senior Partner in the firm of James MacIntyre and Company, Potters, Burslem. A J.P. for Staffordshire, Chairman of the Sneyd Colliery Company, and the Wedgwood Institute Committee. He served on the Royal Commission on Technical Instruction, and on the Commission for Inquiring into the Condition of the Blind, Deaf and Dumb. Was President of the Municipal Corporations Association, and of the N. Staffordshire Association of Mining and Mechanical Engineers, and a Chevalier of the Legion of Honour. Was Surveyor-Gen. of Ordnance, Feb.-June 1886. Was Financial Secretary at the War Office 1892-95. A Liberal and Home Ruler, in favour of conferring the Parliamentary franchise on duly qualified women, of "disestablishment", and of a veto by inhabitants on victuallers' licences. Sat for Stoke-on-Trent from 1880 to 1885, and for Hanley from 1885 until he retired in 1900. Died 8 Apr. 1901. [1900]

WOODHEAD, Joseph. 14 Craven Street, London. Huddersfield. S. of Godfrey Woodhead, Esq., Leather Merchant, of Holmfirth. B. 1824. A Woollen Manufacturer, but later a Newspaper Proprietor and Editor. Also Town Councillor and Alderman of Huddersfield and twice Mayor of that town. A Liberal, and Home Ruler. Sat for the Spen Valley division of the W. Riding of Yorkshire from 1885 until he retired in 1892. Unsuccessfully contested Huddersfield in Feb. 1893. Freeman of Borough of Huddersfield from 1898. Died 21 May 1913. [1892]

WOODHOUSE, Sir James Thomas. Brough Hall, Brough, Yorkshire. Reform, Bath, and National Liberal. Eld. s. of James Woodhouse, Esq. B. 1852; m. 1876, Jessie, d. of W.J. Reed, Esq., of Skidby, Yorkshire. Educ. at the Hull Coll., and University Coll., London; LL.B. London. A Solicitor, admitted 1873, senior member of the firm of Woodhouse, Aske, and Ferrins, of Hull.

An Alderman of Hull (Mayor 1891), a J.P. for the city, and Dept.-Lieut. for the E. Riding of Yorkshire; Maj. 1st Volunteer Battalion E. Yorkshire Regiment; Chairman of Governors Hymer's Coll., and of the Hull Public Libraries, a Trustee of the Hull Municipal Charities, and a Director of the Hull and Barnsley Railway Company and London City and Midland Bank. Vice-President of Association of Municipal Corporations. Knighted in 1895. A Liberal. Unsuccessfully contested the Howdenshire division of the E. Riding of Yorkshire in July 1892. Sat for Huddersfield from 1895 until appointed Railway Commissioner in Nov. 1906. Created Baron Terrington 1918. Died 8 Feb. 1921. [1906]

WOODS, Samuel. 19 Buckingham Street, Strand, London. Rose Villa, Brynn, Nr. Wigan. S. of Thomas Woods, Esq., Miner, of St. Helens, and Margaret Rothwell who also worked in the mine up to 1840. B. 1846 at Parr, St. Helens; m. 1867, Sarah Lea, d. of a Miner of St. Helens. Educ. at a night school by the Rev. F.J. Greening, Baptist Minister. Was a Miner from his youth. In 1878 he established the Lancashire Miners' Federation, and was made its first President; also Vice-President of the Miners' National Federation, and Secretary to Parliamentary Committee Trades Union Congress from 1894 to 1905. He served as a member of the Ashton Local Board from 1884 to 1887, and in 1895 was elected a member of the District Council. "A representative of Labour", supported the Liberal party generally; advocated a Miners' eight hours bill, compulsory employers' liability bill, Home Rule for Ireland, local option, payment of members, nationalization of Royalty rents, etc. Sat as MP for the Ince division of Lancashire from 1892-95, but was defeated at the general election in the latter year. Sat for the Walthamstow division of Essex from Feb. 1897 until defeated in 1900. Died 23 Nov. 1915. [1900]

WORSLEY-TAYLOR, Henry Wilson. Moreton Hall, Whalley, Lancashire. Carlton, Conservative, and Ranelagh. S. of James Worsley, Esq., J.P., of the Laund, Accrington. B. 1847 at Accrington; m. 1871, Harriette Sayer, only d. of Sir E.W. Watkin, Bart. Educ. at Harrow, and Exeter Coll., Oxford. Called to the bar at the Middle Temple 1871, Q.C. 1891, bencher 1893.

Practised for some years on the N. Circuit and Preston Sessions, then exclusively at the Parliamentary bar. A J.P. and Dept.-Lieut. for Lancashire, J.P. for the W. Riding of Yorkshire, and Chairman of the Lancashire Quarter Sessions, held at Preston. Was Recorder of Preston 1893-98. Assumed by Royal Licence the additional surname of Taylor in 1881. A Conservative. Elected for the Blackpool division of N. Lancashire in Dec. 1900 and sat until he retired in 1906. Created Bart. 1917. Died 27 June 1924. [1905]

WORTHINGTON-EVANS, Sir Laming, Bart. Continued in House after 1918: full entry in Volume III.

WORTLEY, Rt. Hon. Charles Beilby Stuart. See STUART-WORTLEY, Rt. Hon. Charles Beilby.

WRIGHT, Caleb. Westminster Palace Hotel, London. Lower Oak, Tyldesley, Lancashire. B. at Tyldesley, Lancashire 1810, his father being a Clerk. At the age of nine commenced work in a factory as a Cotton-Piecer. In 1845 he was in a position to become a Cotton Spinner on his own account, and had a very extensive business. A Magistrate for Lancashire. A Liberal and Home Ruler, strongly opposed to an hereditary legislative chamber, in favour of the abolition of the Parliamentary oath, and of the disestablishment of the Church; would support the principle of direct popular control of the sale of intoxicants. Sat for the Leigh division of Lancashire S.W. from 1885 until he retired in 1895. Died 28 Apr. 1898. [1895]

WRIGHT, Henry FitzHerbert. Yeldersley Hall, Nr. Derby. 3 Kensington Court, London. Constitutional, and Arthurs'. S. of FitzHerbert Wright, Esq., J.P., Dept.-Lieut., of The Hayes, Derbyshire, and Louise Charlotte von Beckmann of Holzendorf, Mecklenburgh-Schwerin. B. 9 Oct. 1870 at The Hayes, Derbyshire; m. 1894, Muriel Harriet, d. of Col. Henry Fletcher, Esq., C.M.G., Scots Guards. Educ. at Eton, and Trinity Coll., Cambridge. Was called to the bar at the Inner Temple 1895. Capt. 4th North Midland (Howitzer) Brigade Royal Field Artillery (T.) 1908-11; rejoined the army 1914 and posted to Territorial Reserve of Officers 5 May 1917. Gov. of Repton

School and Kingston Agricultural Coll.; J.P. and Co. Alderman for Derbyshire. A Conservative. Unsuccessfully contested the Ilkeston division of Derbyshire in 1900 and Mar. 1910. Elected for the Leominster division of Herefordshire Mar. 1912 and sat until he retired in 1918. Unsuccessfully contested Derby in 1923. Chairman of The Butterley Company Limited, 1938-44. Died 23 Feb. 1947.   [1918]

WRIGHT, Henry Smith. 4 Chelsea Embankment, London. Carlton. 3rd s. of Ichabod Charles Wright, Esq., of Mapperley, Nottinghamshire, by the Hon. Theodosia, d. of the 1st Lord Denman. B. at Quorndon, Derbyshire 1839; m. 1st, 1865, Mary, only d. of William Cartledge, Esq., of Woodthorpe, Nottinghamshire; 2ndly, 1869, Josephine Henrietta, only d. of the Rev. J. Adolphus Wright, Rector of Ickham, Kent. Educ. at Brighton Coll. and Trinity Coll., Cambridge, where he obtained a scholarship and second-class honours in the Classical Tripos. Was called to the bar at the Inner Temple 1865, and afterwards joined the Nottingham banking firm of I. and I.C. Wright and Company, retired in 1878. Author of a *Translation of the First Four Books of Homer's Iliad* and *English Hexameter Verse* (1885). A Conservative Unionist. Unsuccessfully contested Nottingham S. in 1885. First elected for Nottingham S. in 1886 and sat until he retired in 1895. Died 19 Mar. 1910. [1895]

WRIGHTSON, Sir Thomas, Bart. Neasham Hall, Darlington. Carlton, Junior Carlton, and St. Stephen's. S. of Thomas Wrightson, Esq., of Neasham Hall, Darlington. B. at Haughton-le-Skerne, Darlington 1839; m. 1870, Elizabeth, d. of Samuel Wise, Esq., Solicitor, of Ripon, Yorkshire. A Civil Engineer, a Director of Messrs. Head, Wrightson and Company, Bridge Builders, of Stockton, and of the Cramlington Colliery Company, Northumberland. A J.P. and Dept.-Lieut. for Co. Durham. A Conservative. The Unionist Small Dwellings Bill of 1899 for Housing the Working Classes was substantially the measure submitted in 1893 by him. Was an unsuccessful candidate for Stockton 1885, 1886, and 1888, but was elected there 1892 and sat until defeated 1895. First elected for E. St. Pancras in 1899 and sat until defeated in 1906. Created Bart. 1900. Died 18 June 1921. [1905]

WROUGHTON, Philip. Woolley Park, Wantage, Berkshire. Carlton. Eld. s. of Philip Wroughton, Esq., of Ibstone House, Buckinghamshire, and Woolley Park, Berkshire, by his 2nd wife Blanche, 5th d. of John Norris, Esq., of Hughenden House, Buckinghamshire. B. at Ibstone, Buckinghamshire 1846; m. 1875, Evelyn Mary, d. of Sir John Neeld, Bart., of Grittleton, Wiltshire. Was educ. at Harrow and at Christ Church, Oxford; graduated B.A. 1868. A J.P. and Dept.-Lieut. for Berkshire, and at one time Maj. Royal Berks. Yeomanry. Patron of 1 living. A Conservative. Sat for Berkshire from Feb. 1876 to 1885, and for the Abingdon division of Berkshire from 1885 until he retired in 1895. Died 7 June 1910. [1895]

WYLIE, Alexander. 1 Whitehall Gardens, London. Cordale, Renton, Dumbartonshire. Carlton. Western, Glasgow. S. of John Wylie, Esq., Colour-Maker and Calico-Printer. B. about 1838; m. 1880, d. of P. Mylrea, Esq., of Waterloo, Liverpool. Educ. at Glasgow University. A Turkey-Red Dyer and Calico-Printer, and an East Indian Merchant; a J.P., Dept.-Lieut., and County Councillor for Dunbartonshire, a Director of the Glasgow Chamber of Commerce, and was for many years Chairman of the Cardross School Board. Author of *Labour, Leisure, and Luxury*, *Physical Recreation*, and other books and papers. A Conservative and supporter of the Unionist Government, in favour of the extension of Local Government to Ireland, redistribution of seats, and peasant proprietorship. Unsuccessfully contested Dunbartonshire in 1892. Elected there in 1895 and sat until he retired in 1906. Died 13 Feb. 1921. [1905]

WYNDHAM, Rt. Hon. George. 35 Park Lane, London. Saighton Grange, Chester. Clouds, East Knoyle, Salisbury. Marlborough, Carlton, and Travellers'. S. of the Hon. Percy S. Wyndham (bro. to 2nd Lord Leconfield), by the d. of Sir Guy Campbell, Bart. B. 29 Aug. 1863 at 44 Belgrave Square, London; m. 1887, Sibell Mary, Countess Grosvenor, widow of the eld. s. of 1st Duke of Westminster. Educ. at Eton. Entered the Coldstream Guards Mar. 1883, and served at Suakim in 1885 (medal and Khedive's star); retired as Lieut. Lieut.-Col. commanding the Cheshire Yeomanry, and a J.P. for Cheshire. Was Private Secretary to the Rt.

Hon. A.J. Balfour as Chief Secretary for Ireland and First Lord of the Treasury from Apr. 1887 to 1892. Parliamentary Under-Secretary to the War Office 1898-1900, and Chief Secretary for Ireland from 1900-05, with a seat in the Cabinet in Mr. Balfour's Ministry 1902. Resigned 6 Mar. 1905. PC. Ireland 1900; PC. 1902. Lord Rector of Glasgow University 1902, and Edinburgh University 1909. Honorary D.C.L. Oxford, LL.D. Glasgow, LL.D. Edinburgh. Edited *North's Plutarch, Ronsard,* and the *Poems of Shakespeare.* A Unionist. Elected for Dover in July 1889 and sat until his death 8 June 1913. [1913]

WYNDHAM-QUIN, Windham Henry, C.B. 5 Seymour Street, London. Turf, and White's. Eld. s. of Capt. the Hon. Windham Henry Wyndham-Quin, 2nd s. of the 2nd Earl of Dunraven, by Caroline, d. of Admiral Sir George Tyler. Was heir presumptive to the Dunraven peerage. B. 1857; m.. 1885, Eva Constance Aline, d. of the 6th Earl of Mayo. Educ. at Eton, and the Royal Military Coll., Sandhurst. Entered the 16th Lancers 1878; served in the Boer War 1881; Capt. 1886; Aide-de-Camp in Madras 1886-89; Maj. 16th Lancers 1893; resigned on entering Parliament. Was Adjutant Gloucestershire Yeomanry 1890-94. Raised and commanded 4th Imperial Yeomanry in S. African War 1900-01, Lieut.-Col. Glamorgan Imperial Yeomanry. C.B. 1903. A Conservative. Represented S. Glamorganshire from 1895 until defeated in 1906. Succeeded as 5th Earl of Dunraven and Mountearl 14 June 1926. Died 23 Oct. 1952. [1905]

WYVILL, Marmaduke D'Arcy. 34 Queen's Gate Gardens, London. Denton, Ben Rhydding, Leeds. Carlton, and Travellers'. Eld. s. of Marmaduke Wyvill, Esq., J.P. and Dept.-Lieut. of Constable Burton and Denton Park, Yorkshire, by Laura, d. of Sir Charles Ibbetson, Bart. B. 1849 in London; m. 1st, 1871, Isabella, eld. d. of John Banner Price, Esq., of 32 Tregunter Road, Kensington (she died in Mar. 1895); 2ndly, 1898, Elizabeth, d. of W.H. Wilson-Todd, Esq., MP, of Halnaby Hall, Darlington. Educ. at Eton. Vice-Chairman of the Leeds and Liverpool Canal Company, a J.P. for the E. and N. Ridings of Yorkshire, and a Dept.-Lieut. for the W. Riding. A Conservative and Unionist, in favour of a United Empire, Registration

Reform, Agricultural Legislation, Old Age Pensions, and Practical Measures for the Working Classes. Contested the Bishop Auckland division of Durham Co. Dec. 1885, and the Otley division of the W. Riding of Yorkshire July 1892. First returned for the Otley division the W. Riding of Yorkshire July 1895 and sat until defeated in 1900. Died 23 Sept. 1918. [1900]

YATE, Col. Charles Edward, C.S.I. C.M.G. Continued in House after 1918: full entry in Volume III.

YEO, Sir Alfred William. Continued in House after 1918: full entry in Volume III.

YEO, Frank Ash. Sketty Hall, Swansea. Devonshire. S. of T. Yeo, Esq., of Bideford, by a d. of C. Woollacott, Esq., of Bideford. B. 1832; m. 1st, 1858, d. of R. Cory, Esq., of Cardiff (she died 1863); 2ndly, 1868, the d. of George Dowson, Esq., of Northallerton. Educ. at Bideford and also in Germany and France. A Colliery Proprietor and Patent-Fuel Manufacturer, Chairman and Director of the Swansea Bank. Chairman of the Swansea Harbour Trust from 1874 to 1886, in which year he resigned. Also a J.P. for Glamorganshire, and was Mayor of Swansea in 1874, and again in 1886. An advanced Liberal, and Home Ruler, advocating the Disestablishment and Disendowment of the Church in Wales. Sat for the Gower division of Glamorgan from 1885 until his death on 4 Mar. 1888. [1887]

YERBURGH, Robert Armstrong. 25 Kensington Gore, London. Woodfold Park, Blackburn. Carlton, and Travellers'. S. of the Rev. Richard Yerburgh, Vicar of Sleaford, Lincolnshire, by Susan, d. of John Higgin, Esq., of Greenfield, Lancaster. B. 1853; m. 1888, Elma Amy, only child of Daniel Thwaites, Esq., of Billinge, Scarr, Blackburn. Educ. at Rossall, Harrow, and University Coll., Oxford. Was called to the bar at the Middle Temple 1880, and joined the N. Circuit. Was Private Secretary to Mr. Akers-Douglas as Patronage Secretary in Lord Salisbury's Administration 1885-86, and Assistant Private Secretary to Mr. W.H. Smith, First Lord of the Treasury. A J.P. and Dept.-Lieut. for Co. Lancaster, and J.P. for Kirkcudbrightshire. President of Navy League from 1900, of the Agricultural Organization Society, and of the Urban Co-operative Banks Association. Was Maj.

2nd Volunteer Battalion Cheshire Regiment. A Unionist. Unsuccessfully contested Chester in 1885; sat for Chester from 1886 to 1906, when he was defeated; re-elected there in Jan. 1910 and sat until he accepted Chiltern Hundreds in Feb. 1916. Died 18 Dec. 1916.   [1915]

YORKE, John Reginald. Retired in 1886: full entry in Volume I.

YOUNG, Charles Edward Baring. 2 Harcourt Buildings, Temple, London. Oak Hill, East Barnet, Hertfordshire. Daylesford House, Worcestershire. Oxford & Cambridge. Eld. s. of Charles Baring Young, Esq., Merchant, by Elizabeth, d. of Stephen John Winthrop, Esq., M.D., of Little Bounds, Kent. B. 1850. Educ. at Eton, and Trinity Coll., Cambridge and called to the bar at the Inner Temple in 1876. A Conservative. Sat for Christchurch from the general election of 1885 until he retired in 1892. Died 22 Sept. 1928. [1892]

YOUNG, Edward Hilton. Continued in House after 1918: full entry in Volume III.

YOUNG, Oliver. Hare Hatch House, Twyford. Berkshire. Junior Army & Navy. S. of A.W. Young, Esq., of Hare Hatch, MP for Yarmouth and Helston. B. 1855: m. 1888, Mabel, d. of W.L. Beale, Esq., J.P. and Dept.-Lieut., of Waltham St. Lawrence. Entered the Royal Navy 1869; served in the W. Indies, S.E. America, W. Africa, and in the Mediterranean; at the bombardment of Alexandria 1882, at Suakin, etc. Retired as Commander 1887. J.P. for Berkshire, and a member of the Berkshire County Council. A Conservative. Sat for the Wokingham division of Berkshire from Mar. 1898 until he accepted Chiltern Hundreds in 1901. Died 9 Oct. 1908.   [1901]

YOUNG, Samuel. Avonmore, Derrivolgie, Belfast. National Liberal. S. of Samuel Young, Esq., of Dunavelly, Portaferry, Co. Down, by Sarah, eld. d. of Arthur Black, Esq., of Ballyhaft, near Newtownards, Co. Down. B. 14 Feb. 1822 at Dunavelly; m. 1846, d. of Edward Allen, Esq., Shipowner, of Fenchurch Street, London. Educ. at the Old Presbyterian Coll., Belfast. Head of the firm of Young, King and Company, Whisky Distillers, Belfast and Limavady, and Chairman of B. Hughes Limited, Millers and Bankers. A

J.P., and a member of the Royal Commission on the Liquor Licensing Laws. A Nationalist. First elected for E. Cavan in 1892 and sat until his death 18 Apr. 1918. [1918]

YOUNG, William. Continued in House after 1918: full entry in Volume III.

YOUNGER, Sir George, Bart. Continued in House after 1918: full entry in Volume III.

YOUNGER, William. Auchen Castle, Moffat, N.B. Naval & Military, Boodle's, and Orleans. Eld. s. of William Younger, Esq., of Auchen Castle, Moffat, N.B., by Margaret, d. of J.W. Brown, Esq., of Sydney and London. B. at Edinburgh 1862: m. 1888, Helen, d. of Sir Robert Gunter, of Wetherby Grange, Yorkshire, MP for the Barkston Ash division of the W. Riding of Yorkshire. Educ. at Worcester Coll., Oxford. Was a Lieut. 16th Lancers 1884-88; Maj. of Sherwood Rangers Yeomanry; a J.P. for Dumfriesshire and Leicestershire. A Liberal. Was an unsuccessful Unionist candidate for Orkney and Shetland in 1892. Sat for the Stamford division of Lincolnshire as a Unionist from 1895-1906, when he retired. Elected for Peebles and Selkirk as a Liberal in Jan. 1910 and sat until he retired in Dec. 1910. Created Bart. in 1911. A member of Royal Commission on Housing in Scotland from 1913-17. Died 28 July 1937.   [1910]

YOXALL, Sir James Henry. Hamilton House, Mabledon Place, Euston Road, London. 20 Kew Gardens Road, Kew, Surrey. Reform, and National Liberal. Eld. s. of Henry Houghton Yoxall, Esq., and his wife, Elizabeth, née Smallwood. B. 15 July 1857 at Redditch; m. 1886, Elizabeth, d. of Lieut.-Col. Coles, of the Royal Engineers. Educ. at the Wesleyan School, Redditch, and Westminster Training Coll. Headmaster of Sharrow Lane Board School, Sheffield. Gen. Secretary of the National Union of Teachers, 1892-1924, and at one time President. Editor of *The Schoolmaster*. Honorary M.A. Cambridge 1889 in recognition of his services to public education; Honorary M.A. Oxford 1907; Officer d'Académie (France) 1910. A J.P. Knighted 1909. Royal Commissioner on Secondary Education 1894-95; member of Government Committee on Study of Modern Languages 1916. Author of *Secondary*

Education, The Rommany Stone, Beyond the Wall, Alain Tanger's Wife, Chateau Royal, The Wander Years, The Courtier Stoops, The Villa for Coelebs, and other works. A Liberal, in favour of Home Rule for Ireland, etc. Unsuccessfully contested the Bassetlaw division of Nottinghamshire in 1892. First elected for Nottingham W. in 1895 and sat until he retired in 1918. Died 2 Feb. 1925.

[1918]

INDEX OF NAMES

This index lists all Members of Parliament who sat in the House of Commons between 1886 and 1918. Cross references are given where necessary. All names appear in the same order as in the text. Members who continued to sit after 1918, and whose full entries appear in Volume III, are marked with an asterisk. Members who sat until 1886, and whose full entries appear in Volume I, are marked with a dagger. In a few cases further information about members who sat between 1832 and 1885 has come to light. This information has been included in the main text and in the index the members concerned have been marked with a double dagger.

Abercromby, R.W. see Duff, R.W.
Abraham, W.
Abraham, Rt. Hon. W. ('M.')
Acland, Rt. Hon. A.H.D.
Acland, Sir C.T.D. see Acland, C.T.D.
Acland, C.T.D.
*Acland, Rt. Hon. F.D.
†Acland, Rt. Hon. Sir T.D., Bart.
Acland-Hood, Rt. Hon. Sir A.F., Bart.
Adam, Maj. W.A.
Adams, Maj. W.A. see Adam, Maj. W.A.
*Adamson, W.
*Addison, Rt. Hon. C.
Addison, J.E.W.
*Adkins, Sir W.R.D.
Agar-Robartes, Hon. T.C.R.
*Agg-Gardner, Sir J.T.
Agnew, Sir A.N., Bart.
Agnew, Sir G.W., Bart
‡Agnew, W.
Ainslie, W.G.
Ainsworth, D.
Ainsworth, Sir J.S., Bart.
Aird, Sir J., Bart.
Aitken, Sir W.M., Bart.
Akers-Douglas, Rt. Hon. A.
*Alden, P.
Allan, Sir W.
Allen, A.A.
Allen, C.F.E.
Allen, Maj. Rt. Hon. C.P.
†Allen, H.G.
*Allen, W.
*Allen, Maj. W.J.
†Allen, W.S.
Allhusen, A.H.E.
Allison, Sir R.A.
Allsopp, Hon. A.P.
Allsopp, Hon. G.H.
Allsopp, Hon. S.C.
Ambrose, D.
Ambrose, Dr. R.
Ambrose, W.
*Amery, L.C.M.S.
Amherst, W.A.T.
Amhurst-Tyssen, W.A. see Amherst, W.A.T.

Anderson, A.M.
Anderson, C.H.
Anderson, G.K.
Anderson, W.C.
Andrews, J.O.
Annand, J.
Anson, Rt. Hon. Sir W.R., Bart.
Anstruther, H.T.
‡Anstruther, Sir R., Bart.
Anstruther, R.H.L-.
Anstruther-Gray, Lieut.-Col. W.
Anstruther-Thomson, Lieut.-Col. W. see Anstruther-Gray, Lieut.-Col. W.
Arbuthnot, G.A.
Arch, J.
*Archdale, E.M.
*Archer-Shee, Col. M.
Arkwright, J.S.
‡Armitage, B.
*Armitage, R.
Arnold, Alfred
‡Arnold, Arthur
*Arnold, S.
Arnold-Foster, Rt. Hon. H.O.
Arrol, Sir W.
Ascroft, R.
Asher, A.
*Ashley, Lieut.-Col. W.W.
Ashmead-Bartlett, Sir E.
Ashton, T.G.
Asquith, Rt. Hon. H.H.
Astbury, J.M.
*Astor, Hon. W.
Atherley-Jones, L.A.
Atkinson, H.J. see Farmer-Atkinson, H.J.
Atkinson, Rt. Hon. J.
Attenborough, W.A.
Aubrey-Fletcher, Rt. Hon. Sir H., Bart.
Austin, Sir J., Bart.
Austin, M.

B

Baden-Powell, Sir G.S.
Baggallay, E.
Bagot, Col. J.F.
Bailey, Sir J.

Bailey, Sir J.R., Bart.
Baillie, J.E.B.
Baily, L.R.
Bain, Sir J.
Bain, J.R.
Bainbridge, E.M.
Baird, J.
Baird, J.G.A.
*Baird, J.L.
Baker, Rt. Hon. H.T.
Baker, Sir J.
Baker, J.A.
Baker, L.J.
Baker, Sir R.L., Bart.
Balcarres, D.A.E.L., Lord
Baldwin, A.
Baldwin, Rt. Hon. S.
Balfour, Rt. Hon. A.J.
Balfour, C.B.
Balfour, Sir G.
Balfour, Rt. Hon. G.W.
Balfour, J.S.
Balfour, Rt. Hon. J.B.
Balfour, K.R.
*Balfour, Sir R., Bart.
Ballantine, W.H.W.
*Banbury, Rt. Hon. Sir F.G., Bart.
Banes, G.E.
*Banner, J.S.H. see Harmood-Banner, Sir J.S.
Bannerman, Rt. Hon. H.C. see Campbell-Bannerman, Rt. Hon. Sir H.
Barbour, W.B.
Barclay, J.W.
Barclay, Sir T.
Baring, F.G.B., Visct.
Baring, Sir G., Bart.
Baring, Hon. G.V.
Baring, T.C.
Barker, Sir J., Bart.
*Barlow, Rt. Hon. Sir C.A.M-., Bart. see Montague-Barlow, Rt. Hon. Sir C.A., Bart.
Barlow, Sir J.E., Bart.
Barlow, P.
Barnard, E.B.
Barnes, A.
Barnes, F.G.
*Barnes, Rt. Hon. G.N.
*Barnett, Capt. R.W.

*Barnston, H.
Barran, Sir J., Bart.
Barran, Sir J.N., Bart.
Barran, Sir R.H.
Barratt, Sir F.L., Bart. see
   Layland-Barratt, Sir F., Bart.
*Barrie, C.C.
*Barrie, H.T.
Barrow, R.V.
‡Barry, Rt. Hon. A.H.S-.
Barry, E.
Barry, Sir F.T., Bart.
Barry, J.
Barry, Rt. Hon. R.J.
Bartlett, Sir E.A-. see Ashmead-
   Bartlett, Sir E.
Bartley, Sir G.C.T.
*Bartley-Dennis, E.R.B.
*Barton, Sir A.W.
Barton, D.P.
Barttelot, Rt. Hon. Sir W.B.,
   Bart.
Bass, H.A.
†Bass, Sir M.A., Bart.
Bateman-Hope, W.H. see
   Hope, W.H.B.
Bates, Sir E., Bart.
Bathurst, Hon. A.B.
Bathurst, Capt. Sir C.
Baumann, A.A.
Bayley, E.H.
Bayley, T.
Beach, Rt. Hon. Sir M.E.H-.,
   Bart. see Hicks-Beach, Rt.
   Hon. Sir M.E., Bart.
Beach, Hon. M.H.H-. see
   Quenington, M.H.H-B.,
   Visct.
Beach, Rt. Hon. W.W.B.
Beadel, W.J.
Beale, Sir W.P., Bart.
*Beauchamp, Sir E., Bart.
Beaufoy, M.H.
Beaumont, H.F.
Beaumont, Hon. H.G.
Beaumont, W.B.
Beaumont, Hon. W.C.B.
*Beck, A.C.T.
Beckett, E.W.
Beckett, W.
*Beckett, Hon. W.G.
Bective, T.T., Earl of
Begg, F.F.
Beith, G.
*Bell, A.C.M. see Morrison-
   Bell, A.C.
Bell, Lieut.-Col. E.F.M. see
   Morrison-Bell, Lieut.-Col.
   E.F.
Bell, R.
*Bellairs, C.W.
Belloc, J.H.P.R.
Bemrose, Sir H.H.
*Benn, A.S.
*Benn, I.H.
Benn, Sir J.W.

*Benn, Capt. W.W.
*Bennett, E.N.
Bennett, J.
Bennett-Goldney, F.
Benson, G.R.
Bentham, G.J.
Bentinck, Rt. Hon. G.A.F.C. see
   Cavendish-Bentinck, Rt.
   Hon. G.A.F.
*Bentinck, Lord H.C. see
   Cavendish-Bentinck, Lord H.
Bentinck, W.G.C. see
   Cavendish-Bentinck, W.G.
Beresford, Lord C.W. de-la-P.
‡Beresford-Hope, Rt. Hon.
   A.J.B.
Berridge, T.H.D.
Bertram, J.
Bethell, G.R.
*Bethell, Sir J.H., Bart.
Bethell, T.R.
Bhownaggree, Sir M.M.
Bickersteth, R.
Bickford-Smith, W.
Biddulph, M.
Biggar, J.G.
Bigham, J.C.
*Bigland, A.
Bignold, Sir A.
Bigwood, J.
Bill, C.
*Billing, N.P-.
Billson, A.
Bingham, G.C.B., Lord
*Bird, A.F.
Birkbeck, Sir E., Bart.
Birkmyre, W.
Birrell, Rt. Hon. A.
Black, A.W.
Black, Sir A.W.
Blades, J.H.
Blaine, R.S.
*Blair, R.
Blake, Hon. E.
*Blake, Sir F.D., Bart.
‡Blake, J.A.
‡Blake, T.
Blakiston-Houston, J.
Blane, A.
Bliss, J.
Blundell, H.B-H.
Bodkin, M.M.
Boland, J.P.
*Boles, Lieut.-Col. D.F.
Bolitho, T.B.
Bolton, J.C.
Bolton, T.D.
Bolton, T.H.
Bond, E.
Bond, G.H.
Bonsor, H.C.O.
Bontine-Cunninghame-
   Cunninghame-Graham,
   R.G. see Graham, R.G.B.C.
Boord, T.W.
Booth, F.H.

Booth, Rt. Hon. G.S. see
   Sclater-Booth, Rt. Hon. G.
Borlase, W.C.
Borthwick, Sir A., Bart.
*Boscawen, Rt. Hon. Sir
   A.S.T.G-. see Griffith-
   Boscawen, Rt. Hon. Sir
   A.S.T.
*Bottomley, H.W.
Boulnois, E.
Boulton, A.C.F.
‡Bourke, Rt. Hon. R.
Bousfield, W.R.
Bowden, Lieut.-Col. G.R.H.
*Bowerman, Rt. Hon. C.W.
Bowles, G.F.S.
*Bowles, H.F.
Bowles, T.G.
Boyd-Kinnear, J. see Kinnear,
   J.B.
Boyle, D.
Boyle, Sir E., Bart.
Boyle, J.
Boyle, W.L.
Boyton, Sir J.
*Brace, Rt. Hon. W.
*Brackenbury, H.L.
Bradlaugh, C.
Brady, P.J.
*Bramsdon, Sir T.A.
Branch, J.
Brand, Hon. A.G.
‡Brand, Hon. H.R.
Brassey, A.
*Brassey, H.L.C.
Brassey, Capt. R.B.
†Brassey, Sir T.
Bridgeman, Col. Hon. F.C.
*Bridgeman, W.C.
Brigg, Sir J.
Bright, A.H.
Bright, Rt. Hon. Jacob.
‡Bright, Rt. Hon. John.
Bright, J.A.
Bright, W.L.
†Brinton, J.
Bristowe, T.L.
Broad, H.E.
Broadhurst, H.
Brocklehurst, Col. W.B.
‡Brocklehurst, W.C.
Broderick, Hon. St. J.W. see
   Brodrick, Rt. Hon. W.St.J.F.
Brodie, H.C.
Brodrick, Rt. Hon. W.St.J.F.
Bromley-Davenport, W.
Brooke, F.R.C.G.G., Lord
Brooke, S.W.W.
Brookes, W.
Brookfield, A.M.
Brooks, J.
Brooks, Sir W.C., Bart.
*Brotherton, E.A.
Broughton, U.H.
Brown, Sir A.H., Bart.
Brown, A.L.

Brown, G.M.
Bruce, G.
Bruce, Lord H.A. *see* Brudenell-Bruce, Lord H.A.
Bruce, J.
Bruce, Hon. R.P.
Brudenell-Bruce, Lord H.A.
*Brunner, J.F.L.
Brunner, Rt. Hon. Sir J.T., Bart.
Brunskill, G.F.
Bryce, Rt. Hon. J.
Bryce, J.A.
Brymer, W.E.
Buchanan, Rt. Hon. T.R.
Buckley, A.
Buckmaster, Sir S.O.
Bucknill, Sir T.T.
*Bull, Sir W.J.
Bullard, Sir H.
*Burdett-Coutts, W.L.A.B-.
Burghley, B.H.G.C., Rt. Hon. Lord
*Burgoyne, A.H.
Burke, E.H. *see* Haviland-Burke, E.
*Burn, Col. C.R.
Burnie, R.J.D.
Burns, Rt. Hon. J.
Burnyeat, W.J.D.
‡Burrell, Sir P., Bart.
Burt, Rt. Hon. T.
Bury, A.A.C.K., Visct.
*Butcher, J.G.
Butcher, S.H.
*Buxton, C.R.
Buxton, E.N.
*Buxton, N.E.
Buxton, Rt. Hon. S.C.
Byles, Sir W.P.
Byrne, A.
Byrne, E.W.
Byrne, G.M.

C

Caine, W.S.
Cairns, T.
Caldwell, J.
Calley, T.C.P.
Cameron, Sir C., Bart.
Cameron, J.M.
Cameron, R.
Campbell, Sir A.C., Bart.
Campbell, Lieut.-Col. D.F.
Campbell, Sir G.
Campbell, H.
Campbell, H. *see* Campbell-Bannerman, Rt. Hon. Sir H.
Campbell, Rt. Hon. J.A.
Campbell, Rt. Hon. J.H.M.
Campbell, J.
‡Campbell, R.F.F.
Campbell-Bannerman, Rt. Hon. Sir H.
*Campion, W.R.
†Carbutt, E.H.

*Carew, C.R.S.
Carew, J.L.
Carew, Lieut.-Gen. Sir R.P. *see* Pole-Carew, Lieut.-Gen. Sir R.
*Carlile, Sir E.H., Bart.
Carlile, W.W.
Carmarthen, G.G.O., Marq. of
Carmichael, Sir J.M., Bart.
Carmichael, Sir T.D.G., Bart. *see* Gibson-Carmichael, Sir T.D., Bart.
Carnegie, Lieut.-Col. the Hon. D.G.
Carr-Gomm, H.W.C.
*Carson, Rt. Hon. Sir E.H.
Carvill, P.G.H.
Cassel, F.
Castlereagh, C.S.H.V-T-S., Visct.
Cator, J.
Causton, Rt. Hon. R.K.
*Cautley, H.S.
Cavan, F.E.G.L., Earl of
Cave, Rt. Hon. Sir G.
Cavendish, Lord E.
Cavendish, R.F.
Cavendish, S.C.C., Lord *see* Hartington, Rt. Hon. S.C.C., Marq. of
Cavendish, Rt. Hon. V.C.W.
Cavendish-Bentinck, Rt. Hon. G.A.F.
*Cavendish-Bentinck, Lord H.
Cavendish-Bentinck, W.G.
Cawley, Rt. Hon. Sir F., Bart.
Cawley, H.T.
Cawley, Hon. O.
Cayzer, Sir C.W., Bart.
*Cecil, Rt. Hon. E.
*Cecil, Rt. Hon. Lord H.R.H.
Cecil, Lord J.P. *see* Joicey-Cecil, Lord J.P.
*Cecil, Rt. Hon. Lord R.
Chaloner, Col. R.G.W.
Chamberlain, Rt. Hon. J.
*Chamberlain, Rt. Hon. J.A.
Chamberlain, R.
Chamberlayne, T.
Chambers, J.
Chance, F.W.
Chance, P.A.
Chancellor, H.G.
Channing, Sir F.A., Bart.
Chaplin, Rt. Hon. H.
Chapman, E.
*Chapple, W.A.
Charlesworth, A.H.
Charrington, S.
Cheetham, J.F.
Cheetham, J.M.
Chelsea, H.A.C., Visct.
Cherry, Rt. Hon. R.R.
Chesney, Gen. Sir G.T.
Chester-Master, T.W. *see* Master, T.W.C-.

*Cheyne, Sir W.W., Bart.
Childers, Rt. Hon. H.C.E.
Chiozza-Money, Sir L.G. *see* Money, Sir L.G.C.
Churchill, Rt. Hon. Lord R.H.S-.
*Churchill, Rt. Hon. W.L.S.
Clancy, J.J.
Clare, O.L. *see* Leigh-Clare, O.L.
Clark, Dr. G.B.
Clark, G.S.
Clarke, C.G.
Clarke, Sir E.G.
*Clay, Capt. H.H.S. *see* Spender-Clay, Capt. H.H.
Clayton, N.G.
Cleland, J.W.
Clive, Lieut.-Col. P.A.
Clough, W.O.
Clough, W.
*Clyde, Rt. Hon. J.A.
*Clynes, J.R.
*Coates, Sir E.F., Bart.
*Coats, Sir S.A., Bart.
Cobb, H.P.
Cobbold, F.T.
Cochrane, C.A.
Cochrane, Hon. T.H.A.E.
Cochrane-Baillie, Hon. C.W.A.N.
Coddington, Sir W., Bart.
Cogan, D.J.
Coghill, D.H.
Cohen, A.
Cohen, Sir B.L., Bart.
Cohen, L.L.
Coldwells, F.M.
Colefax, H.A.
Coleridge, Hon. B.J.S.
Collery, B.
Collings, Rt. Hon. J.
*Collins, Lieut.-Col. G.P.
Collins, Sir S.
Collins, Sir W.J.
Colman, J.J.
Colomb, Rt. Hon. Sir J.C.R.
Colston. C.E.H.A.
Colville, J.
*Colvin, Brigadier-Gen. R.B.
Combe, C.H.
Commerell, Admiral Sir J.E.
Commins, A.
Compton, Lord A.F.
Compton, F.
Compton, H.F.
Compton, W.G.S.S.C., Earl
*Compton-Rickett, Rt. Hon. Sir J.
Condon, T.J.
Connolly, L.
Connor, C.C.
Conway, M.
Conybeare, C.A.V.
Cook, E.R.
Cook, Sir F.L., Bart.

INDEX

Cook, W.T.G.
Cooke, C.W.R.
†Coope, O.E.
Cooper, Capt. B.R.
Cooper, G.J.
*Cooper, Sir R.A., Bart.
*Coote, Capt. C.R.
Coote, T.
*Coote, W.
Corbet, W.J.
Corbett, A.C.
Corbett, C.J.H.
Corbett, J.
Corbett, T.L.
*Cornwall, Sir E.A.
Cornwallis, F.S.W.
Corry, Sir J.P., Bart.
*Cory, Sir C.J., Bart.
*Cory, J.H.
*Cosgrave, W.T.
Cosgrove, J.
Cossham, H.
Cotton, Col. E.T.D. see Cotton-
Jodrell, Col. E.T.D.
Cotton, H.E.A.
Cotton, Sir H.J.S.
Cotton. W.F.
Cotton-Jodrell, Col. E.T.D.
*Courthope, Maj. G.L.
Courtney, Rt. Hon. L.H.
*Cowan, Sir W.H.
Cowell-Stepney, Sir E.A.A.K.,
Bart.
†Cowen, J.
Cox, H.
Cox, I.E.B.
Cox, J.R.
Cox, R.
Cozens-Hardy, H.H.
*Craig, C.C.
*Craig, E.
Craig, H.J.
Craig, J.
Craig, Lieut.-Col. Sir J., Bart.
Craig, N.C.
Craig, R.H.
Craig-Sellar, A. see Sellar, A.C.
*Craik, Rt. Hon. Sir H.
Cranborne, J.E.H.G.C., Visct.
Craven, J.
Crawford, D.
*Crawford, R.G.S. see
Sharman-Crawford, R.G.
Crawford, W.
Crawshay-Williams, E.
Crean, E.
Cremer, Sir W.R.
Crichton-Stuart, Lord N.E.
Crilly, D.
Cripps, Sir C.A.
*Croft, H.P.
Crombie, J.W.
Crompton, C.
*Crooks, Rt. Hon. W.
Crosfield, A.H.
Crosfield, W.

Crosland, Sir J.
Cross, A.
†Cross, Rt. Hon. Sir R.A.
Cross, Hon. W.H.
Crossley, E.
Crossley, Rt. Hon. Sir S.B.,
Bart.
Crossley, Sir W.J., Bart.
Crossman, Maj.-Gen. Sir W.
Cruddas, W.D.
Crumley, P.
Cubitt, Rt. Hon. G.
Cubitt, Hon. H.
Cullinan, J.
Cunninghame-Graham,
R.G.B. see Graham, R.G.B.C.
Curran, P.F.
Curran, T.
Curran, T.B.
Currie, Sir D.
Currie, G.W.
Curzon, Hon. G.N.
Curzon, R.G.P.C-H., Visct.
Cust, H.J.C.

D

Dalbiac, Col. P.H.
Dalkeith, J.C.M-D-S., Earl of
Dalmeny, A.E.H.M.A.P., Lord
Dalrymple, Rt. Hon. Sir C.,
Bart.
Dalrymple, Hon. H.H.
Dalrymple, J.J.H.D., Visct.
*Dalrymple-White, G.D.
Dalton, J.J.
Daly, James
Daly, John
*Dalziel, D.A.
*Dalziel, Rt. Hon. Sir J.H.
Dane, R.M.
Darling, C.J.
Darling, M.T.S.
Darwin, Maj. L.
Davenport, H.T. see Hinckes,
H.T.
Davey, Sir H.
*Davidson, J.H.
Davies, A.
†Davies, D.
*Davies, D.
*Davies, E.W.
Davies, Sir H.D.
*Davies, M.L.V. see Vaughan-
Davies, M.L.
†Davies, R.
Davies, T.H. see Hart-Davies, T.
Davies, T.
Davies, W.
Davies, Sir W. see Davies, W.
*Davies, Sir W.H.
Davies, W.R.M.
Davis, R.G. see Gent-Davis, R.
Davitt, M.
*Dawes, J.A.
Dawnay, Hon. L.P.

Dawson, R.
Deasy, J.
de Cobain, E.S.W.
de Eresby, Lord W. see
Willoughby de Eresby, G.H-
D-W., Lord
de Forest, Baron M.A.
Delany, W.
de Lisle, E.J.L.M.P.
Denison, E.W. see Beckett, E.W.
‡Denison, W.B. see Beckett, W.
*Denison, Hon. W.G. see
Beckett, Hon. W.G.
*Denison-Pender, J.C.D.
*Denman, Hon. R.D.
*Denniss, E.R.B., see Bartley-
Denniss, E.R.B.
Denny, J.M.
de Rothschild, Baron F.J. see
Rothschild, Baron F.J. de
*de Rothschild, L.N. see
Rothschild, L.N. de
*de Valera, E.
Devlin, C.R.
*Devlin, J.
Dewar, A.
Dewar, Sir J.A., Bart.
Dewar, Sir T.R.
de Worms, Rt. Hon. Baron H.
Diamond, C.
Dickinson, R.E.
Dickinson, Rt. Hon. Sir W.H.
‡Dickson, A.G.
Dickson, Rt. Hon. C.S.
‡Dickson, S.
Dickson, T.A.
Dickson-Poynder, Sir J.P., Bart.
Digby, J.K.D.W. see Wingfield-
Digby, J.K.D.
Dilke, Rt. Hon. Sir C.W., Bart.
‡Dilke, Sir C.W., Bart.
Dillon, J.
‡Dillwyn, L.L.
Dillwyn-Llewelyn, Sir J.T.,
Bart.
Dillwyn-Venables-Llewelyn,
C.L. see Venables-Llewelyn,
C.L.D.
Dimsdale, Rt. Hon. Sir J.C.,
Bart.
Dimsdale, Baron R.
Disraeli, C.R.
*Dixon, C.H.
Dixon. Rt. Hon. Sir D., Bart.
Dixon, G.
Dixon-Hartland, Sir F.D., Bart.
Dobbie, J.
Dobson, T.W.
Dodd, C.J.S.
Dodd, W.H.
‡Dodds, J.
Dolan, C.J.
Donelan, Capt. A.J.C.
Donkin, R.S.
*Donnelly, P.
Donovan, J.T.

Doogan, P.C.
Dorington, Rt. Hon. Sir J.E., Bart.
Doris, W.
Dougherty, Rt. Hon. Sir J.B.
Doughty, Sir G.
Douglas, Rt. Hon. A.A. see Akers-Douglas, Rt. Hon. A.
Douglas, C.M.
Douglas-Pennant, Hon. E.S.
Douglas-Scott-Montagu, Hon. J.W.E. see Scott-Montagu, Hon, J.W.E.D.
Doxford, Sir W.T.
Drage, G.
Drucker, C.G.A.
Duckham, T.
Duckworth, Sir J.
Du Cros, A.
*Du Cros, Sir A.P., Bart.
Du Cros, W.H.
Duff, R.W.
Duffy, W.J.
Dugdale, J.S.
Duke, Rt. Hon. H.E.
Dumphreys, J.M.T.
*Duncan, C.
Duncan, D.
Duncan, Col. F.
Duncan, J.A.
Duncan, Sir J.H.
Duncan, R.
*Duncannon, V.B.P., Visct.
Duncombe, A.
Duncombe, Hon. H.E.V.
Dunn, A.E.
Dunn, Sir W., Bart.
Dunn, Sir W.H.
Dunne, E.M.
Dunsany, J.W.P., Baron
*Du Pre, W.B.
Durant, J.C.
Durning-Lawrence, Sir E., Bart.
Dyke, Rt. Hon. Sir W.H., Bart.

E

‡Eaton, H.W.
Ebrington, H.F., Visct.
*Edge, Capt. W.
*Edwards, A.C.
Edwards, E.
Edwards, Sir F., Bart.
Edwards, Sir J.B.
*Edwards, J.H.
Edwards, O.M.
Edwards-Heathcote, J.H.
Edwards-Moss, T.C.
Egerton, Hon. A. de T.
Egerton, Hon. A.J.F.
†Egerton, Hon. F.
Elcho, H.R.C., Lord
Elibank, Master of see Murray, Rt. Hon. A.W.C.O.
Ellice, Capt. E.C.

Elliot, Hon. A.R.D.
Elliot, Sir G., Bart.
Elliot, Sir G.W., Bart.
Elliot, Hon. H.F.H.
Ellis, J.
Ellis, Rt. Hon. J.E.
Ellis, Sir J.W., Bart.
Ellis, T.E.
*Ellis-Griffith, Rt. Hon. Sir E.J., Bart.
Elton, C.I.
*Elveden, R.E.C.L.G., Visct.
Elverston, Sir H.
Emmott, Rt. Hon. A.
Engledow, C.J.
Erskine, D.C.
Esmonde, J.
Esmonde, J.L.
Esmonde, Sir T.H.G., Bart.
Essex, Sir R.W.
Esslemont, G.B.
Esslemont, P.
Evans, Sir F.H., Bart.
*Evans, Sir L.W., Bart. see Worthington-Evans, Sir L., Bart.
Evans, Sir S.T.
Evans-Gordon, Sir W.E.
Eve, H.T.
Evelyn, W.J.
Everett, R.L.
Evershed, S.
‡Ewart, Sir W., Bart.
Ewing, Sir A.O., Bart.
Eyre, Col. H.
*Eyres-Monsell, B.M.

F

Faber, E.B.
Faber, G.D.
Faber, G.H.
Faber, Lieut.-Col. W.V.
†Fairbairn, Sir A.
*Falconer, J.
*Falle, Sir B.G., Bart.
Fardell, Sir T.G.
Farmer-Atkinson, H.J.
Farquhar, Sir H.B.T., Bart.
Farquharson, H.R.
Farquharson, R.
Farrell, J.P.
Farrell, T.J.
Feilden, Lieut.-Gen. R.J.
*Fell, Sir A.
Fellowes, Rt. Hon. A.E.
Fellowes, Hon. W.H.
Fenwick, Rt. Hon. C.
Fenwick, H.T.
Ferens, Rt. Hon. T.R.
†Ferguson, R.
Ferguson, Rt. Hon. R.C.M. see Munro-Ferguson, Rt. Hon. R.C.
Fergusson, Rt. Hon. Sir J., Bart.

Fetherstonhaugh, G.
Ffrench, P.
Field, Admiral E.
Field, W.
*Fielden, E.B.
Fielden, T.
Fiennes, Hon. Sir E.E.T-W-., Bart.
Finch, Rt. Hon. G.H.
Finch-Hatton, Hon. H.H.
Finch-Hatton, Hon. M.E.G.
Findlay, A.
Finlay, Rt. Hon. Sir R.B.
Finlayson, J.
*Finney, S.
Finucane, J.
Firbank, Sir J.T.
‡Firth, J.F.B.
*Fisher, Rt. Hon. Dr. H.A.L.
Fisher, Rt. Hon. W.H.
Fison. Sir F.W., Bart.
Fitz-Gerald, J.G.
Fitzgerald, Sir R.U.P., Bart see Penrose-Fitzgerald, Sir R.U-., Bart.
Fitzgibbon, J.
Fitzmaurice, Lord E.G.P-.
Fitzpatrick, J.L.
*Fitzroy, Hon. E.A.
Fitzwilliam, Hon. W.H.W-.
Fitzwilliam, Hon. W.J.W-.
Fitzwygram, Lieut.-Gen. Sir F.W.J., Bart.
*Flannery, Sir J.F., Bart.
Flavin, M.
Flavin, M.J.
Fleming, C.J.
Fleming, Sir J.
Fleming, V.
Fletcher, B.
Fletcher, Rt. Hon. Sir H., Bart. see Aubrey-Fletcher, Rt. Hon. Sir H., Bart.
Fletcher, J.R.K. see Kebty-Fletcher, J.R.
Fletcher, J.S.
Flower, C.
Flower, Sir E.F.S.
Flynn, J.C.
Foley, P.J.
Foljambe, C.G.S.
Folkestone, J.P-B., Visct.
Folkestone, Rt. Hon. W.P-B., Visct.
Forest, M.A., Baron de see de Forest, Baron M.A.
Forster, Sir C., Bart.
Forster, Rt. Hon. H.W.
‡Forster, Rt. Hon. W.E.
Forwood, Rt. Hon. Sir A.B., Bart.
Foster, Rt. Hon. Sir B.W.
*Foster, H.S.
Foster, J.K.
Foster, Sir M.
Foster, P.S.

INDEX

Foster, Col. W.H.
Fowler, Rt. Hon. Sir H.H.
Fowler, M.
Fowler, Sir R.N., Bart.
*Fox, H.W. see Wilson-Fox, H.
Fox, J.F.
*Foxcroft, C.T.
*France, G.A.
Fraser, Lieut.-Gen. Sir C.C.
Fraser-Mackintosh, C.
Freeman-Mitford, A.B.
Freeman-Thomas, F.
Frewen, M.
Fry, L.
Fry, Sir T., Bart.
Frye, F.C.
Fulford, H.C.
Fullam, P.
Fuller, G.P.
Fuller, Sir J.M.F., Bart.
Fuller-Acland-Hood, Rt. Hon.
    Sir A., Bart. see Acland-
    Hood, Rt. Hon. Sir A.F.,
    Bart.
Fuller-Maitland, W. see
    Maitland, W.F-.
Fullerton, H.
Fulton, J.F.
Furness, Sir C.
Furness, Sir S.W., Bart.
Fyler, J.A.

G

*Galbraith, S.
Galloway, W.J.
Gane, J.L.
*Ganzoni, Capt. F.J.C.
Gardner, A.C.
*Gardner, E.
Gardner, Rt. Hon. H.C.
*Gardner, Sir J.T.A. see Agg-
    Gardner, Sir J.T.
Gardner, R.R. see Richardson-
    Gardner, R.
Garfit, W.
Gaskell, C.G.M.
Gastrell, Col. Sir W.H.H.
Gathorne-Hardy, Hon. A.E.
Gathorne-Hardy, Hon. J.S.
*Geddes, Rt. Hon. Sir A.C.
*Geddes, Rt. Hon. Sir E.C.
Gedge, S.
Gelder, Sir W.A.
Gent-Davis, R.
Gibb, J.
Gibb, T.E.
Gibbins, F.W.
Gibbons, J.L.
Gibbs, Hon. A.G.H.
*Gibbs, Col. G.A.
Gibbs, H.H.
Gibbs, Hon. V.
Gibney, J.
Gibson, Sir J.P., Bart.
Gibson, Rt. Hon. J.G.

Gibson-Carmichael, Sir T.D.,
    Bart.
*Gilbert, J.D.
Giles, A.
Giles, C.T.
Gilhooly, J.P.
Gill, A.H.
Gill, H.J.
Gill, T.P.
Gilliat, J.S.
*Gilmour, Lieut.-Col. J.
*Ginnell, L.
Gladstone, Rt. Hon. H.J.
Gladstone, Rt. Hon. W.E.
Gladstone, W.G.C.
*Glanville, H.J.
Glazebrook, P.K.
Glen-Coats, Sir T.G., Bart.
Glendinning, R.G.
Glover, T.
Glyn, Hon. P.C.
Glyn-Jones, W.S.
Goddard, Rt. Hon. Sir D.F.
Godson, Sir A.F.
Gold, C.
Goldman, C.S.
Goldsmid, Rt. Hon. Sir J., Bart.
Goldsmith, Maj. F.B.H.
Goldstone, F.W.
Goldsworthy, Maj.-Gen. W.T.
Gooch, G.P.
Gooch, H.C.
Gordon, Rt. Hon. J.
Gordon, Hon. J.E.
Gordon, Sir W.E.E. see Evans-
    Gordon, Sir W.E.
Gordon-Lennox, Rt. Hon.
    Lord W.C. see Lennox, Rt.
    Hon. Lord W.C.G-.
Gorst, Rt. Hon. Sir J.E.
Goschen, Rt. Hon. G.J.
Goschen, Hon. G.J.
*Goulding, Sir E.A., Bart.
Gourley, Sir E.T.
†Grafton, F.W.
Graham, E.J.
Graham, H.R.
Graham, R.G.B.C.
Granby, H.J.B.M., Marq. of
Grant, C.B. see Grant, J.C.
‡Grant, D.
Grant, Sir G.M., Bart.
*Grant, J.A.
Grant, J.C.
Grantham, W.
Gray, C.W.
Gray, E.D.
*Gray, E.
Grayson, A.V.
Green, Sir E., Bart.
Green, H.
Green, W.D.
Greenall, Sir G., Bart.
Greene, E.
Greene, Sir E.W., Bart.
Greene, H.D.

*Greene, W.R.
Greenwood, Sir G.G.
*Greenwood, Sir H., Bart.
*Greenwood, T.H. see
    Greenwood, Sir H., Bart.
*Greer, H.
†Gregory, G.B.
*Greig, Col. J.W.
Grenfell, C.A.
Grenfell, W.H.
*Gretton, Col. J.
Greville, Hon. R.H.F.
†Grey, A.H.G.
Grey, A. see Duncombe, A.
Grey, Rt. Hon. Sir E., Bart.
Grice-Hutchinson, G.W.
*Griffith, A.
*Griffith, Rt. Hon. Sir E.J.E-.,
    Bart. see Ellis-Griffith, Rt.
    Hon. Sir E.J., Bart.
*Griffith-Boscawen, Rt. Hon.
    Sir A.S.T.
*Griffiths, Sir J.N-.
Grimston, J.W.G., Visct.
†Grosvenor, Rt. Hon. Lord R.
    de A.
Grotrian, F.B.
Grove, Sir T.F., Bart.
Grove, T.N.A.
Groves, J.G.
*Guest, Hon. C.H.C.
*Guest, Hon. F.E.
Guest, Hon. I.C.
Guiney, J.
Guiney, P.
*Guinness, Hon. R.E.C.L. see
    Elveden, R.E.C.L.G., Visct.
*Guinness, Hon. W.E.
Gull, Sir W.C., Bart.
Gulland, Rt. Hon. J.W.
Gully, Rt. Hon. W.C.
Gunter, Sir R., Bart.
Gurdon, R.T.
Gurdon, Rt. Hon. Sir W.B.
Guthrie, D.C.
Guthrie, W.M.
Gwynn, S.L.
*Gwynne, R.S.

H

Hackett, J.
Haddock, G.B.
Hain, E.
Haldane, Rt. Hon. R.B.
Hall, A.W.
Hall, Rt. Hon. Sir C.
*Hall, D.B.
Hall, E.M.
*Hall, F.
*Hall, Sir F.
Hallett, Col. F.C.H. see
    Hughes-Hallett, Col. F.C.
Halpin, J.
Halsey, Rt. Hon. T.F.
*Hambro, A.V.

Hambro, C.E.
Hambro, C.J.T.
Hamersley, A.St.G.
Hamilton, C.E.
Hamilton, Rt. Hon. Lord C.J.
*Hamilton, C.G.C. see
    Hamilton, G.C.
Hamilton, Lord E.W.
Hamilton, Lord F.S.
*Hamilton, G.C.
Hamilton, Rt. Hon. Lord G.F.
Hamilton, J.A.E.H., Marq. of
†Hamilton, J.G.C.
Hamley, Lieut.-Gen. Sir E.B.
Hammond, J.
Hamond, Sir C.F.
Hanbury, Rt. Hon. R.W.
Hanbury-Tracy, Hon. F.S.A.
*Hancock, J.G.
Hankey, F.A.
*Hanson, Sir C.A., Bart.
Hanson, Sir R., Bart.
*Harbison, T.J.S.
Harcourt, E.W.
Harcourt, Rt. Hon. L.V.V.
Harcourt, R.V.V.
Harcourt, Rt. Hon. Sir
    W.G.G.V.V-.
Harcourt, Rt. Hon. Sir W.V. see
    Harcourt, Rt. Hon. Sir
    W.G.G.V.V-.
Hardcastle, E.
Hardcastle, F.
Hardie, J.K.
Hardy, Hon. A.E.G. see
    Gathorne-Hardy, Hon. A.E.
Hardy, G.A.
Hardy, Hon. J.S.G. see
    Gathorne-Hardy, Hon. J.S.
Hardy, Rt. Hon. L.
Hare, Sir T.L., Bart.
Harker, W.
Harland, Sir E.J., Bart.
Harman, Rt. Hon. E.R.K-. see
    King-Harman, Rt. Hon.
    E.R.
*Harmood-Banner, Sir J.S.
*Harmsworth, C.B.
*Harmsworth, R.L.
Harrington, E.
Harrington, T.C.
Harris, Rt. Hon. F.L.
Harris, F.R.
*Harris, Sir H.P.
Harris, M.
*Harris, P.A.
Harrison, C.
Harrison, Sir G.
Harrison, H.
Harrison-Broadley, Col. H.B.
Hart-Davies, T.
Hartington, Rt. Hon. S.C.C.,
    Marq. of
Hartland, Sir F.D.D., Bart. see
    Dixon-Hartland, Sir F.D.,
    Bart.

Harvey, A.G.C.
*Harvey, T.E.
Harvey, W.E.
Harwood, G.
Haslam, Sir A.S.
Haslam, J.
*Haslam, L.
Haslett, Sir J.H.
Hastings, G.W.
Hatch, E.F.G.
Hatton, Hon. M.E.G.F. see
    Finch-Hatton, Hon. M.E.G.
Havelock, Sir H.M., Bart. see
    Havelock-Allan, Sir H.M.,
    Bart.
Havelock-Allan, Sir H.M.,
    Bart.
Havelock-Allan, Sir H.M.,
    Bart.
Haviland-Burke, E.
Haworth, Sir A.A., Bart.
Hay, Hon. C.G.D.
Hayden, J.P.
Hayden, L.P.
Hayne, Rt. Hon. C.H.S-. see
    Seale-Hayne, Rt. Hon. C.H.
Hayter, Rt. Hon. Sir A.D.,
    Bart.
*Hayward, E.
Hazel, A.E.W.
Hazell, W.
Hazleton, R.
Healy, M.
Healy, T.J.
Healy, T.M.
Hearn, M.L.
Heath, A.H.
Heath, A.R.
Heath, Sir J., Bart.
Heathcote, J.H.E. see Edwards-
    Heathcote, J.H.
Heaton, J.H.
Heaton-Armstrong, W.C.
Hedderwick, T.C.H.
Hedges, A.P.
Helder, A.
Helme, Sir N.W.
Helmsley, C.W.R.D., Visct.
*Hemmerde, E.G.
Hemphill, Rt. Hon. C.H.
Henderson, Sir A., Bart.
*Henderson, Rt. Hon. A.
Henderson, Lieut.-Col. Hon.
    H.G.
Henderson, J.M.
Heneage, Rt. Hon. E.
‡Hennessy, Sir J.P.
*Henry, Sir C.S., Bart.
*Henry, D.S.
Henry, M.
*Herbert, Hon. A.N.H.M.
Herbert, Maj.-Gen. Sir I.J.C.,
    Bart.
Herbert, Hon. S.
Herbert, T.A.
Hermon-Hodge, Col. Sir R.T.

Hervey, Lord F.
Hervey, Capt. F.W.F.
*Hewart, Rt. Hon. Sir G.
Hewins, W.A.S.
Hibbert, Sir H.F.
Hibbert, Rt. Hon. Sir J.T.
Hickman, Sir A., Bart.
*Hickman, Brigadier-Gen.
    T.E.
Hicks-Beach, Rt. Hon. Sir
    M.E., Bart.
Hicks-Beach, Hon. M.H. see
    Quenington, M.H.H-B.,
    Visct.
Hicks-Beach, W.F.
Higginbottom, S.W.
Higgins, C.
Higgins, T.
Higham, J.S.
Hill, Rt. Hon. A.S.
Hill, Capt. A.
Hill, Rt. Hon. Lord A.W.
Hill, Sir C.L.
Hill, Sir E.S.
Hill, Lieut.-Gen. H.S. see
    Staveley-Hill, Lieut.-Col.
    H.S.
Hill, Sir J., Bart.
Hillier, A.P.
*Hills, J.W.
*Hill-Wood, Sir S.H., Bart.
Hinckes, H.T.
Hindle, F.G.
*Hinds, J.
Hingley, Sir B., Bart.
Hoare, E.B.
Hoare, H.E.
Hoare, Sir S., Bart.
*Hoare, Sir S.J.G., Bart.
Hobart, Sir R.H.
Hobhouse, Rt. Hon. Sir
    C.E.H., Bart.
Hobhouse, Rt. Hon. H.
*Hodge, Rt. Hon. J.
Hodge, Col. Sir R.T.H-. see
    Hermon-Hodge, Col. Sir
    R.T.
Hogan, J.F.
Hogan, M.H.
Hogg, D.C.
‡Hogg, Sir J.M.M-., Bart. see
    McGarel-Hogg, Sir J.M.,
    Bart.
Hogg, Sir L., Bart.
*Hogge, J.M.
*Hohler, G.F.
Holburn, J.G.
Holden, Sir A., Bart.
Holden, Sir E.H., Bart.
Holden, E.T.
Holden, Sir I., Bart.
Holland, Rt. Hon. Sir H.T.,
    Bart.
Holland, Hon. L.R.
Holland, Sir W.H., Bart.
Holloway, G.

Holmes, D.T.
Holmes, Rt. Hon. H.
Holt, R.D.
Hooper, A.G.
Hooper, J.
*Hope, H.
*Hope, J.F.
*Hope, Maj. Sir J.A., Bart.
*Hope, J.D.
Hope, T.
Hope, W.H.B.
*Hopkinson, Sir A.
*Hopkinson, A.
Hopwood, C.H.
Hornby, Sir W.H., Bart.
Horne, Rev. C.S.
*Horne, W.E.
Horner, A.L.
Horner, F.W.
Horniman, E.J.
Horniman, F.J.
Horridge, T.G.
Houghton-Gastrell, Col. Sir
    W.H. see Gastrell, Col. Sir
    W.H.H.
Houldsworth, Sir W.H., Bart.
Hoult, J.
*Houston, R.P.
Howard, E.S.
*Howard, Hon. G.W.A.
Howard, H.C.
Howard, John.
Howard, J.M.
Howard, Joseph.
Howell, G.
Howell, W.T.
Howorth, Sir H.H.
Hoyle, I.
Hozier, Hon. J.H.C.
Hubbard, Hon. Egerton.
Hubbard, Hon. Evelyn.
‡Hubbard, Rt. Hon. J.G.
Hudson, G.B.
Hudson, W.
Hughes, Col. Sir E.
*Hughes, S.L.
Hughes-Hallett, Col. F.C.
Hulse, E.H.
*Hume-Williams, W.E.
Humphreys-Owen, A.C.
Hunt, Sir F.S., Bart.
Hunt, R.
Hunter, Sir C.R., Bart.
Hunter, W.
Hunter, W.A.
Hunter, Sir W.G.
*Hunter-Weston, Sir A.G.
Huntington, C.P.
Huntington-Whiteley, Sir H.J.,
    Bart. see Whiteley, Sir H.J.,
    Bart.
Husband, J.
Hutchinson, C.F.
Hutton, A.E.
Hutton, J.F.
Hutton, J.

Hyde, C.G.
Hylton-Jolliffe, Hon. H.G. see
    Jolliffe, Hon. H.G.H.

I

Ibbetson, Rt. Hon. Sir H.J.S.,
    Bart. see Selwin-Ibbetson, Rt.
    Hon. Sir H.J., Bart.
Idris, T.H.W.
*Illingworth, Rt. Hon. A.H.
Illingworth, A.
Illingworth, P.H.
†Ince, H.B.
Ingleby, H.
Ingram, Sir W.J., Bart.
Isaacs, L.H.
Isaacs, Rt. Hon. Sir R.D.
Isaacson, F.W.

J

Jacks, W.
*Jackson, Hon. F.S.
Jackson, Sir J.
Jackson, J.A.
Jackson, R.S.
Jackson, Rt. Hon. W.L.
Jacobsen, T.O.
Jacoby, Sir J.A.
James, C.H.
James, F.
James, Rt. Hon. Sir H.
James, Hon. W.H.
Jameson, J.E.
Jardine, E.
Jardine, Sir J., Bart.
Jardine, Sir R., Bart.
Jarvis, A.W.
Jebb, Sir R.C.
Jeffreys, Rt. Hon. A.F.
†Jenkins, D.J.
Jenkins, J.H.
Jenkins, Sir J.J.
Jennings, L.J.
Jessel, Col. Sir H.M., Bart.
*Jodrell, N.P.
John, E.T.
Johns, J.W.
Johnson, J.
Johnson, W.
Johnson-Ferguson, J.E.
Johnston, C.N.
Johnston, W.
Johnstone, J.H.
Joicey, Sir J., Bart.
Joicey-Cecil, Lord J.P.
Jolliffe, Hon. H.G.H.
Jones, Rt. Hon. Sir D.B.
*Jones, Sir E.R.
Jones, Maj. E.R.
*Jones, H.H.
*Jones, Rev. J.T.
*Jones, Rt. Hon. L.S.
Jones, Sir P. see Pryce-Jones, Sir
    P.

Jones, W.
*Jones, W.K.
†Jones-Parry, T.D.L.
Jordan, J.
Josse, H.
*Jowett, F.W.
Joyce, M.
*Joynson-Hicks, W.

K

Kavanagh, W.M.
Kay-Shuttleworth, Rt. Hon. Sir
    U.J., Bart.
Kearley, Rt. Hon. Sir H.E.,
    Bart.
Keating, M.
Keay, J.S.
Kebty-Fletcher, J.R.
Kekewich, Sir G.W.
*Kellaway, F.G.
Kelley, G.D.
Kelly, B.
*Kelly, E.J.
Kelly, J.R.
Kemp, Sir G.
Kennaway, Rt. Hon. Sir J.H.,
    Bart.
Kennedy, E.J.
Kennedy, P.J.
Kennedy, V.P.
Kenny, C.S.
Kenny, J.E.
Kenny, M.J.
Kenny, W.
Kenrick, W.
*Kenyon, B.
Kenyon, Hon. G.T.
Kenyon, J.
Kenyon-Slaney, Col. the Rt.
    Hon. W.S.
Ker, R.W.B.
Kerans, F.H.
Kerr, J.
*Kerr-Smiley, P.
Kerry, H.W.E.P-F., Earl of
Keswick, H.
Keswick, W.
Kettle, T.M.
Kilbride, D.
Kilcoursie, F.E.G.L., Visct. see
    Cavan, F.E.G.L., Earl of
*Kiley, J.D.
Kimber, Sir H., Bart.
Kincaid-Smith, T.M.H.
King, A.J.
King, Sir H.S.
King, J.
King-Harman, Rt. Hon. E.R.
Kinloch, Sir J.G.S., Bart.
*Kinloch-Cooke, Sir C.
Kinnear, J.B.
Kirkwood, J.H.M.
Kitching, A.G.
Kitson, Rt. Hon. Sir J., Bart.
Knatchbull-Hugessen, Hon. E.

Knatchbull-Hugessen, H.T.
*Knight, Maj. E.A.
Knightley, Sir R., Bart.
Knott, J.
Knowles, Sir L., Bart.
Knox, E.F.V.
Kyffin-Taylor, Col. G.
Kynoch, G.

L

Labouchere, H.D.
Lacaita, C.C.
Lafone, A.
Laidlaw, Sir R.
Lalor, R.G.
Lamb, E.G.
Lamb, Sir E.H.
*Lambert, Rt. Hon. G.
Lambert, I.C.
Lambert, R.C.
Lambton, Hon. F.W.
Lambton, Hon. H. see Meux,
    Admiral of the Fleet Hon.
    Sir H.
Lamont, N.
Lane, W.J.
*Lane-Fox, G.R.
Langley, J.B.
*Lansbury, G.
Lardner, J.C.R.
*Larmor, Sir J.
Latham, G.W.
Laurie, Lieut.-Gen. J.W.
Laurie, R.P.
Law, Rt. Hon. A.B.
Law, H.A.
‡Lawrance, J.C.
Lawrence, Sir E., Bart. see
    Durning-Lawrence, Sir E.,
    Bart.
‡Lawrence, Sir J.C., Bart.
Lawrence, Sir J.J.T., Bart.
Lawrence, Sir J.
Lawrence, W.F.
Lawson, Hon. H.L.W.
Lawson, Sir J.G., Bart.
Lawson, Sir W., Bart. (I)
Lawson, Sir W., Bart. (II)
Layland-Barratt, Sir F., Bart.
Lea, H.C.
Lea, Sir T., Bart.
Leach, C.
Leahy, J.
Leake, R.
Leamy, E.
†Leatham, E.A.
Lechmere, Sir E.A.H., Bart.
Lecky, Rt. Hon. W.E.H.
Lee, Col. Sir A.H.
Lees, Sir E., Bart.
Leese, Sir J.F., Bart.
*Lees-Smith, H.B.
Lefevre, Rt. Hon. G.J.S. see
    Shaw-Lefevre, Rt. Hon. G.J.
Legge, Hon. H.

Legh, Hon. T.W.
‡Legh, W.J.
Lehmann, R.C.
Leicester, J.L.
Leigh, Sir J.
Leigh-Bennett, H.C.
Leigh-Clare, O.L.
‡Leighton, Sir B.
Leighton, S.
‡Le-Marchant, Sir D., Bart.
Leng, Sir J.
Lennox, Rt. Hon. Lord
    W.C.G-.
Leon, H.S.
Lethbridge, Sir R.
Leuty, T.R.
*Lever, A.L.
Lever, W.H.
Leveson-Gower, F.N.S.
Leveson-Gower, G.G.
Levy, Sir M., Bart.
Levy-Lawson, Hon. H.L.W. see
    Lawson, Hon. H.L.W.
*Levy-Lever, A. see Lever, A.L.
Lewis, Sir C.E., Bart.
‡Lewis, J.H.
*Lewis, Rt. Hon. J.H.
Lewis, T.P.
Lewisham, Rt. Hon. W.H.L.,
    Visct.
Lewisham, W.L., Visct.
Liddell, H.
Lincoln, I.T.T.
*Lindsay, W.A.
Lindsay-Hogg, Sir L., Bart. see
    Hogg, Sir L., Bart.
Little, T.S.
Llewellyn, E.H.
Llewelyn, C.L.D.V. see
    Venables-Llewelyn, C.L.D.
Llewelyn, Sir J.T.D., Bart. see
    Dillwyn-Llewelyn, Sir J.T.,
    Bart.
*Lloyd, G.A.
*Lloyd, G.B.
Lloyd, W.
Lloyd-Anstruther, R.H. see
    Anstruther, R.H.L-.
Lloyd George, Rt. Hon. D.
*Locker-Lampson, G.L.T.
*Locker-Lampson, O.S.
Lockie, J.
Lockwood, Rt. Hon. A.R.M.
Lockwood, Sir F.
Loder, G.W.E.
Logan, J.W.
Long, C.W.
*Long, Rt. Hon. W.H.
*Lonsdale, J.R.
Lonsdale, Sir J.B., Bart.
Lopes, H.Y.B.
Lorne, the Rt. Hon. J.D.S.C.,
    Marq. of
Lough, Rt. Hon. T.
Low, Sir F.
Low, W.M.

*Lowe, Sir F.W., Bart.
Lowles, J.
*Lowther, C.W.H.
*Lowther, Brigadier-Gen. Sir
    H.C.
Lowther, Rt. Hon. J.
*Lowther, Rt. Hon. J.W.
Lowther, Hon. W.
Loyd, A.K.
Loyd, Col. L.V.
Lubbock, Rt. Hon. Sir J., Bart.
Lucas, F.A.
Lucas, R.J.
Lucas-Shadwell, W.
Lundon, T.
Lundon, W.
Lupton. A.
Luttrell, H.C.F.
Lyell, Hon. C.H.
Lyell, Sir L., Bart.
Lymington, N.W., Visct.
Lynch, A.A.
Lynch, H.F.B.
Lyttelton, Rt. Hon. A.
Lyttelton, Hon. J.C.

M

MacAleese, D.
McArthur, A.
McArthur, C.
McArthur, W.A.
Macartney, Rt. Hon. W.G.E.
*McCallum, Sir J.M.
McCalmont, H.L.B.
McCalmont, Maj.-Gen. H.
McCalmont, Col. J.M.
*McCalmont, Lieut.-Gen.
    R.C.A.
McCann, J.
M'Cartan, M.
*McCartan, Dr. P.
McCarthy, J.W.
McCarthy, J.
McCarthy, J.H.
MacCaw, W.J.M.
*McCrae, G.
McCulloch, J.
*McCurdy, C.A.
McDermott, P.
Macdona, J.C.
Macdonald, Rt. Hon. J.R.
*Macdonald, Rt. Hon. J.A.M.
Macdonald, Rt. Hon. J.H.A.
McDonald, P.
Macdonald, Dr. R.
Macdonald, W.A.
Macdonnell, M.A.
M'Ewan, W.
McFadden, E.
Macfarlane, Sir D.H.
‡McGarel-Hogg, Sir J.M., Bart.
McGhee, R.
McGilligan, P.
McGovern, T.
Macgregor, Dr. D.

*McGuinness, J.
M'Hugh, E.
M'Hugh, P.A.
Macinnes, M.
MacIver, D.
McIver, Sir L., Bart.
McKane, Professor J.
Mackarness, F.M.C.
McKean, J.
McKenna, Sir J.N.
McKenna, Rt. Hon. R.
McKillop, J.
McKillop, W.
*Mackinder, H.J.
Mackintosh, C.F. see Fraser-
  Mackintosh, C.
McLagan, P.
McLaren, Rt. Hon. Sir C.B.B.,
  Bart.
McLaren, Hon. F.W.S.
*Mclaren, Hon. H.D.
McLaren, W.S.B.
*Maclean, Rt. Hon. Sir D.
Maclean, F.W.
Maclean, J.M.
Macleod, J.
*MacLeod, J.M.
Maclure, Sir J.W., Bart.
*Macmaster, D.
*McMicking, Maj. G.
McMordie, R.J.
‡Macnaghten, E.
*Macnamara, Rt. Hon. T.J.
MacNeill, J.G.S.
*Macneill, R.J.
Maconochie, A.W.
*Macpherson, Rt. Hon. J.I.
Macpherson, J.T.
Mactaggart-Stewart, Sir M.J.,
  Bart.
*McVeagh, J.
McVeigh, C.
Madden, Rt. Hon. D.H.
Maddison, F.
Maden, Sir J.H.
†Magniac, C.
*Magnus, Sir P., Bart.
Maguire, J.R.
Mahon, C.J.P.O'G.
Mahony, P.C. de L.
Mains, J.
Mainwaring, Hon. W.F.B.M.
  see Massey-Mainwaring,
  Hon. W.F.B.
Maitland, W.F-.
Majendie, J.H.A.
Makins, W.T.
*Malcolm, I.Z.
Malcolm, J.W.
*Mallaby-Deeley, H.M.
*Mallalieu, F.W.
Mallet, C.E.
Mallock, R.
Mandeville, F.
Manfield, H.
Manfield, Sir M.P.

Manners, Lord C.R.J.
Manners, Lord E.W.J.
‡Manners, Rt. Hon. Lord J.J.R.
Mansfield, H.R.
Maple, Sir J.B., Bart.
Mappin, Sir F.T., Bart.
‡March, C.H.G-L., Earl of
Marjoribanks, Rt. Hon. E.
Markham, Sir A.B., Bart.
*Marks, Sir G.C.
Marks, H.H.
Marnham, F.J.
*Marriott, J.A.R.
Marriott, Rt. Hon. Sir W.T.
*Marshall, Sir A.H.
Marshall-Hall, E. see Hall, E.M.
Martin, J.
Martin, Sir R.B., Bart.
Marton, G.B.H.
Marum, E.P.M.
Maskelyne, M.H.N.S. see Story-
  Maskelyne, M.H.N.
Mason, A.E.W.
*Mason, D.M.
Mason, J.F.
*Mason, R.
Mason, S.
Massey-Mainwaring, Hon.
  W.F.B.
Massie, J.
‡Master, T.W.C-., jun.
*Masterman, Rt. Hon. C.F.G.
Mather, Sir W.
Mathias, R.
‡Matthews, Rt. Hon. H.
Mattinson, M.W.
Maxwell, Rt. Hon. Sir H.E.,
  Bart.
Maxwell, Sir J.M.S-., Bart. see
  Stirling-Maxwell, Sir J.M.,
  Bart.
Maxwell, W.J.H.
Mayne, Rear-Admiral R.C.
Mayne, T.
Meagher, M.
Medway, J.S.G-H., Lord see
  Gathorne-Hardy, Hon. J.S.
Meehan, F.E.
Meehan, P.A.
Meehan, P.J.
Mellor, J.J.
Mellor, Rt. Hon. J.W.
Melville, B.V.
Mendl, S.F.
Menzies, R.S.
Menzies, Sir W.
Meux, Admiral of the Fleet
  Hon. Sir H.
*Meysey-Thompson, E.C.
Meysey-Thompson, Sir H.M.,
  Bart.
Micklem, N.
*Middlebrook, Sir W.
Middlemore, J.T.
†Milbank, Sir F.A.
Milbank, Sir P.C.J., Bart.

*Mildmay, Rt. Hon. F.B.
*Millar, J.D.
Mills, Hon. A.R.
Mills, Hon. C.T.
Mills, C.W.
Milner, Rt. Hon. Sir F.G., Bart.
Milnes-Gaskell, C.G. see
  Gaskell, C.G.M.
Milton, W.C.de M.W-F., Visct.
Milvain, T.
Milward, Col. V.
Minch, M.J.
Mitchell, E.
Mitchell, W.
*Mitchell, W.F.
*Mitchell-Thomson, Sir W.,
  Bart.
Molesworth, Sir L.W., Bart.
Molloy, B.C.
Molloy, M.
Molteno, P.A.
Monckton, E.P.
*Mond, Rt. Hon. Sir A.M.,
  Bart.
Money, Sir L.G.C.
Monk, C.J.
*Montagu, Rt. Hon. E.S.
Montagu, G.C.
Montagu, Hon. J.W.E.D.S-. see
  Scott-Montagu, Hon.
  J.W.E.D.
Montagu, Sir S., Bart.
*Montague-Barlow, Rt. Hon.
  Sir C.A., Bart.
Montgomery, H.G.
Moon, E.R.P.
Mooney, J.J.
Moore, Count A.J.
*Moore, Sir N.J.
Moore, W.
Moorsom, J.M.
More, R.J.
Morgan, D.J.
Morgan, Hon. F.C.
Morgan, G.H.
Morgan, Rt. Hon. Sir G.O.,
  Bart.
Morgan, J.L.
Morgan, O.V.
Morgan, W.P.
Morison, H.
*Morison, T.B.
Morley, Rt. Hon. A.
Morley, C.
Morley, Rt. Hon. J.
Morpeth, C.J.S.H., Visct.
Morrell, G.H.
Morrell, P.E.
Morris, Hon. M.H.F.
Morris, S.
*Morrison, H.
Morrison, Capt. J.A.
Morrison, W.
*Morrison-Bell, A.C.
Morrison-Bell, Lieut.-Col. E.F.
Morrogh, J.

Morse, L.L.
Morton, Sir A.C.
Morton, A.H.A.
Morton, E.J.C.
Moss, R.
Moss, S.
Moulton, Sir J.F.
*Mount, W.A.
Mount, W.G.
Mowbray, Rt. Hon. Sir J.R., Bart.
Mowbray, Sir R.G.C., Bart.
Muldoon, J.
Mulholland, Hon. H.L.
Muncaster, Lord
Mundella, Rt. Hon. A.J.
*Munro, Rt. Hon. R.
Munro-Ferguson, Rt. Hon. R.C.
Muntz, Sir P.A., Bart.
‡Muntz, P.H.
Murdoch, C.T.
Murnaghan, G.
Murphy, J.
Murphy, M.J.
Murphy, N.J.
Murphy, W.M.
Murray, Rt. Hon. A.W.C.O. (Master of Elibank)
Murray, Rt. Hon. A.G.
*Murray, Hon. A.C.
Murray, C.J.
Murray, C.W.
Murray, J.
Muspratt, M.
Myer, H.
Myers, W.H.

N

Nannetti, J.P.
Naoroji, D.
Napier, Hon. M.F.
Napier, T.B.
Naylor-Leyland, Sir H.S., Bart.
Needham, C.T.
Neilson, F.
Neville, R.
*Neville, R.J.N.
Newark, C.W.S.P., Visct.
Newdigate, F.A. see Newdigate-Newdegate, F.A.
Newdigate-Newdegate, F.A.
*Newman, J.R.P.
*Newman, Sir R.H.S.D.L., Bart.
Newnes, F.H.
Newnes, Sir G., Bart.
*Newton, H.K.
Nicholls, G.
Nicholson, Sir C.N., Bart.
*Nicholson, W.G.
Nicol, D.N.
*Nield, Sir H.
Noble, W.
†Noel, E.

Nolan, J.P.
Nolan, J.
*Norman, Rt. Hon. Sir H., Bart.
Norris, E.S.
Northcote, Hon. Sir H.S., Bart.
Norton, Capt. C.W.
Norton, R.
*Norton-Griffiths, Sir J.
Nugent, J.D.
Nugent, Sir W.R., Bart.
Nussey, Sir T.W., Bart.
Nuttall, H.

O

O'Brien, J.F.X.
O'Brien, K.E.
O'Brien, P.
O'Brien, P.J.
O'Brien, W.
O'Connor, A.
O'Connor, James
O'Connor, John (I).
O'Connor, John (II).
*O'Connor, T.P.
Oddy, J.J.
O'Doherty, J.E.
O'Doherty, K.I.
O'Doherty, P.
O'Doherty, W.
O'Donnell, C.J. O'C.
O'Donnell, J.
O'Donnell, T.
O'Dowd, J.
O'Driscoll, F.
O'Flynn, J.C. see Flynn, J.C.
Ogden, F.
O'Gorman Mahon, C.J.P.M., The see Mahon, C.J.P.O'G.
*O'Grady, J.
O'Hanlon, T.
O'Hare, P.
O'Hea, P.
O'Keefe, F.A.
O'Kelly, C.
O'Kelly, E.P.
O'Kelly, J.J.
Oldroyd, M.
O'Leary, D.
O'Mahony, P.C.de L. see Mahony, P.C.de L.
O'Mally, W.
*O'Mara, J.
O'Mara, S.
O'Neill, Hon. A.E.B.
O'Neill, C.
O'Neill, Hon. R.T.
*O'Neill, Hon. R.W.H.
Orde-Powlett, Hon. W.G.A.
Ormsby-Gore, Hon. G.R.C.
Ormsby-Gore, Hon. S.F.
*Ormsby-Gore, Hon. W.G.A.
Orr-Ewing, Sir A., Bart. see Ewing, Sir A.O., Bart.
Orr-Ewing, C.L.
O'Shaughnessy, P.J.

†O'Shea, W.H.
O'Shee, J.J.
Osmond-Williams, Sir A.
O'Sullivan, E.
O'Sullivan, T.
Oswald, J.F.
Otter, F.
Outhwaite, R.L.
Owen, A.C.H-. see Humphreys-Owen, A.C.
Owen, T.

P

*Page Croft, H. see Croft, H.P.
Paget, A.H.
Paget, Sir R.H., Bart.
†Paget, T.T.
Palmer, Sir C.M., Bart.
Palmer, G.W.
*Palmer, G.M.
Palmer, J.D.
Palmer, Sir W., Bart.
Parker, C.S.
Parker, Hon. F.
Parker, Rt. Hon. Sir H.G.G., Bart.
*Parker, J.
Parkes, Sir E.E.
Parnell, C.S.
Parnell, J.H.
Parrott, Sir J.E.
Parrott, W.
†Parry, T.D.L.J. see Jones-Parry, T.D.L.
*Parry, T.H.
Partington, Hon. O.
Paul, H.W.
Paulton, J.M.
Peacock, R.
Pearce, Sir R.
Pearce, Sir W., Bart.
*Pearce, Sir W.
Pearce, Sir W.G., Bart.
Pearson, Rt. Hon. Sir C.J.
Pearson, Sir W.D., Bart.
Pearson, Hon. W.H.M.
Pease, A.E.
Pease, A.
Pease, H.F.
*Pease, Rt. Hon. H.P.
Pease, Rt. Hon. J.A.
‡Pease, J.W.
Pease, Sir J.W., Bart.
‡Peddie, J.D.
Peel, Hon. A.G.V.
Peel, Rt. Hon. A.W.
Peel, Rt. Hon. Sir R., Bart.
*Peel, Lieut.-Col. R.F.
Peel, Hon. W.R.W.
Pelly, Sir L.
Pemberton, J.S.G.
*Pemberton-Billing, N. see Billing, N.P-.
Pender, Sir J., Bart.
Pender, Sir J.
Penn, J.

*Pennefather, J.de F.
Penrose-Fitzgerald, Sir R.U-.,
 Bart.
Penton, F.T.
‡Percy, Lord A.M.A.
Percy, H.A.G.P., Earl
*Perkins, W.F.
Perks, Sir R.W., Bart.
*Peto, B.E.
*Phillips, Maj-Gen. Sir I.
Philipps, J.W.
*Philipps, Sir O.C.
Phillips, J.
Phillpotts, A.S.
Pickard, B.
Pickersgill, E.H.
Picton, J.A.
Pierpoint, R.
Pilkington, Sir G.A.
Pilkington, R.
Pinkerton, J.
Pirie, D.V.
Pitt-Lewis, G.
Platt-Higgins, F.
Playfair, Rt. Hon. Sir L.
Plowden, Sir W.C.
Plummer, Sir W.R.
Plunket, Rt. Hon. D.R.
*Plunkett, G.N.P., Count
Plunkett, Rt. Hon. H.C.
Plunkett, Hon. J.W. see
 Dunsany, J.W.P., Baron
Pointer, J.
Pole-Carew, Lieut.-Gen. Sir R.
Pollard, Sir G.H.
*Pollock, Sir E.M.
Pollock, H.F.
Pomfret, W.P.
*Ponsonby, A.A.W.H.
Pope-Hennessy, Sir J. see
 Hennessy, Sir J.P.
Portman, Hon. E.B.
Potter, T.B.
Powell, Sir F.S., Bart.
Powell, W.R.H.
Power, P.J.
Power, R.
Poynder, Sir J.P.D., Bart. see
 Dickson-Poynder, Sir J.P.,
 Bart.
*Pratt, J.W.
*Pretyman, Rt. Hon. E.G.
Price, C.E.
Price, Capt. G.E.
Price, Sir R.J.
Price, T.P.
Priestley, Sir A.
Priestley, B.
Priestley, Sir W.E.B.
Priestley, Sir W.O.
Primrose, Rt. Hon. N.J.A.
*Pringle, W.M.R.
Pritchard-Morgan, W. see
 Morgan, W.P.
Proby, Col. D.J.
*Prothero, Rt. Hon. R.E.

Provand, A.D.
Pryce-Jones, Col. E.
Pryce-Jones, Sir P.
Pugh, D.
‡Pugh, D.
Puleston, Sir J.H.
Pullar, Sir R.
*Pulley, C.T.
†Pulley, J.
Purvis, Sir R.
Pym, C.G.
Pyne, J.D.

Q

Quenington, M.H.H-B., Visct.
Quilter, Sir W.C., Bart.
Quilter, Sir W.E.C., Bart.
Quinn, T.

R

Radford, Sir G.H.
*Raffan, P.W.
Raikes, Rt. Hon. H.C.
Rainy, A.R.
Ramsay, Hon. C.M.
†Ramsay, J.
†Ramsden, Sir J.W., Bart.
Randell, D.
*Randles, Sir J.S.
Rankin, Sir J., Bart.
*Rankin, Capt. J.S.
Raphael, Sir H.H., Bart.
Rasch, Sir F.C., Bart.
Ratcliff, Maj. R.F.
Rathbone, W.
Rattigan, Sir W.H.
*Rawlinson, J.F.P.
Rawson, Col. R.H.
Rawson-Shaw, W. see Shaw,
 W.R.
Rea, Rt. Hon. R.
*Rea, W.R.
Reckitt, H.J.
Reddy, M.
Redmond, J.E.
*Redmond, W.A.
Redmond, W.H.K.
Reed, Sir E.J.
Reed, H.B.
Rees, G.C.
*Rees, Sir J.D.
Reid, Rt. Hon. Sir G.H.
Reid, H.G.
Reid, J.
Reid, Sir R.T.
*Remnant, Sir J.F., Bart.
*Rendall, A.
Rendel, S.
Renshaw, Sir C.B., Bart.
Renton, A.L.
Rentoul, J.A.
*Renwick, G.
Reynolds, W.J.
*Rhys-Williams, Sir R., Bart.
Rice, Hon. W.F.
‡Richard, H.

Richards, H.C.
*Richards, Rt. Hon. T.
Richards, T.F.
*Richardson, A.H.H.
*Richardson, Alexander
Richardson, Arthur
Richardson, J.M.
Richardson, J.
Richardson, T. (I).
Richardson, Sir T.
Richardson, T. (II).
Richardson-Gardner, R.
*Rickett, Rt. Hon. Sir J.C. see
 Compton-Rickett, Rt. Hon.
 Sir J.
Ridley, Rt. Hon. Sir M.W.,
 Bart.
Ridley, Hon. M.W.
Ridley, S.F.
Ridsdale, E.A.
Rigby, Sir J.
Rigg, R.
Ritchie, Rt. Hon. C.T.
*Roberts, C.H.
‡Roberts, C.H.C.
*Roberts, Rt. Hon. G.H.
Roberts, J.
Roberts, J.B.
Roberts, Sir J.H., Bart.
*Roberts, Sir S.
Robertson, Rt. Hon. E.
Robertson, Sir G.S.
†Robertson, H.
Robertson, Rt. Hon. J.P.B.
Robertson, Rt. Hon. J.M.
Robertson, T.H.
Robertson, Sir W.T.
Robinson, B.
*Robinson, S.
Robinson, Sir T.
Robson, Sir W.S.
Roby, H.J.
Roch, W.F.
Roche, Hon. J.B.B.
Roche, J.
Roche, M.A.
Roe, Sir T.
Rogers, F.E.N.
Rogers, J.E.T.
Rolleston, Sir J.F.L.
Rollit, Sir A.K.
Ronaldshay, L.J.L.D., Earl of
Ropner, Sir E.H.O.R., Bart.
Roscoe, Sir H.E.
Rose, Sir C.D., Bart.
Ross, A.H.
Ross, J.
Rothschild, Baron F.J.de
*Rothschild, L.N.de
Rothschild, Hon. L.W.
Round, Rt. Hon. J.
Roundell, C.S.
Rowlands, J.
Rowlands, W.B.
Rowntree, A.S.
Rowntree, J.

Royden, T.B.
Royds, Col. C.M.
*Royds, E.
*Runciman, Rt. Hon. W. (Visct. Runciman of Doxford)
Runciman, Sir W., Bart.
Russell, Sir C.A.
Russell, Lord E.
Russell, E.R.
Russell, F.S.
Russell, Sir G., Bart.
Russell, G.W.E.
Russell, Rt. Hon. Sir T.W., Bart.
†Ruston, J.
*Rutherford, Sir J., Bart.
Rutherford, V.H.
*Rutherford, Sir W.W.
Ryder, J.H.D.
‡Rylands, P.

S

Sackville, Col. S.G.S. see Stopford-Sackville, Col. S.G.
Sadler, Sir S.A.
‡St. Aubyn, Sir J., Bart.
St. Maur, R.H.
Salis-Schwabe, Col. G.
Salt, T.
Salter, A.C.
*Samuel, Rt. Hon. Sir H.S.
*Samuel, Rt. Hon. H.L.
Samuel, J.
Samuel, M. see Montagu, Sir S., Bart.
*Samuel, S.
Samuel, Sir S.M., Bart.
Samuel-Montagu, Sir M., Bart. see Montagu, Sir S., Bart.
*Samuels, Rt. Hon. A.W.
Samuelson, Rt. Hon. Sir B., Bart.
Samuelson, G.B.
‡Samuelson, H.B.
*Sanders, R.A.
Sanderson, L.
Sandon, J.H.D.R., Visct. see Ryder, J.H.D.
Sandys, Capt. G.J.
Sandys, Col. T.M.
Sassoon, Sir E.A., Bart.
*Sassoon, Sir P.A.G.D., Bart.
Saunders, W.
Saunderson, Rt. Hon. E.J.
Savory, Sir J., Bart.
Scanlan, T.
Scarisbrick, Sir T.T.L., Bart.
‡Scholefield, J.
Schwann, C.D.
Schwann, Rt. Hon. Sir C.E., Bart. see Swann, Rt. Hon. Sir C.E., Bart.
Sclater-Booth, Rt. Hon. G.
Scoble, Sir A.R.

*Scott, A.M.
Scott, A.H.
Scott, C.P.
*Scott, L.F.
*Scott, Sir S.E., Bart.
Scott-Montagu, Hon. J.W.E.D.
Seale-Hayne, Rt. Hon. C.H.
Sears, J.E.
Seaverns, J.H.
*Seddon, J.A.
‡Seely, C.
Seely, Col. C.
Seely, Sir C. see Seely, Col. C.
Seely, Sir C.H., Bart.
*Seely, Rt. Hon. J.E.B.
Sellar, A.C.
Selwin-Ibbetson, Rt. Hon. Sir H.J., Bart.
Selwyn, Capt. C.W.
Seton-Karr, Sir H.
Sexton, T.
Shackleton, D.J.
*Sharman-Crawford, R.G.
Sharpe, W.E.T.
*Shaw, Hon. A.
Shaw, Sir T.F.C.E., Bart.
Shaw, T.
Shaw, Rt. Hon. T.
Shaw, W.R.
Shaw-Lefevre, Rt. Hon. G.J.
Shaw-Stewart, Sir M.H., Bart.
Shee, J.J. see O'Shee, J.J.
Sheehan, D.D.
Sheehan, J.D.
Sheehy, D.
*Sheffield, Sir B.D.G., Bart.
Sheil, E.
Shepherd-Cross, H.
Sheridan, H.B.
Sherwell, A.J.
Shipman, J.G.
Shirley, W.S.
*Shortt, Rt. Hon. E.
‡Shuttleworth, Rt. Hon. Sir U.J.K., Bart. see Kay-Shuttleworth, Rt. Hon. Sir U.J., Bart.
Sidebotham, J.W.
Sidebottom, T.H.
Sidebottom, W.
Silcock, T.B.
Simeon, Sir J.S.B., Bart.
Simon, Sir J.
*Simon, Rt. Hon. Sir J.A.
Sinclair, Rev. J.
Sinclair, Rt. Hon. J.
Sinclair, L.
Sinclair, W.P.
Sitwell, Sir G.R., Bart.
Skewes-Cox, Sir T.
Slack, J.B.
Slagg, J.
Sloan, T.H.
Small, J.F.
Smallwood, E.
Smeaton, D.M.

*Smiley, P.K-. see Kerr-Smiley, P.
Smith, Abel
Smith, A.H.
*Smith, Albert
Smith, Sir C.
Smith, D.
*Smith, Rt. Hon. Sir F.E., Bart.
*Smith, Harold
Smith, Harry
*Smith, H.B.L. see Lees-Smith, H.B.
Smith, H.C.
Smith, Rt. Hon. J.P.
Smith, S.
Smith, Sir S.
Smith, T.M.H.K-. see Kincaid-Smith, T.M.H.
Smith, W.
Smith, Hon. W.F.D.
Smith, Rt. Hon. W.H.
Smith-Barry, Rt. Hon. A.H. see Barry, Rt. Hon. A.H.S-.
†Smithwick, J.F.
Smyth, T.F.
Snape, T.
*Snowden, P.
Soames, A.W.
Soares, E.J.
Somervell, J.
Somervell, W.H.
Souttar, R.
Spear, Sir J.W.
Spencer, Rt. Hon. C.R.
Spencer, Sir J.E.
*Spender-Clay, Capt. H.H.
Spensley, H.
Spicer, Rt. Hon. Sir A., Bart.
Spicer, H.
Stack, J.
†Stafford, C.S-L-G., Marq. of
Stanger, H.Y.
Stanhope, Rt. Hon. E.
Stanhope, Hon. P.J.
*Stanier, Sir B., Bart.
Stanley, A.
*Stanley, Rt. Hon. Sir A.H.
Stanley, Hon. Sir A.
Stanley, Hon. A.L.
Stanley, Hon. E.G.V. see Stanley, Rt. Hon. E.G.V.S., Lord
Stanley, Rt. Hon. E.G.V.S., Lord
Stanley, E.J.
*Stanley, E.M.C.S., Lord
†Stanley, Rt. Hon. Sir F.A.
*Stanley, Hon. G.F.
Stanley, Sir H.M.
Stansfeld, Rt. Hon. Sir J.
*Stanton, C.B.
*Starkey, J.R.
Staveley-Hill, Lieut.-Col. H.S.
Steadman, W.C.
*Steel-Maitland, Sir A.H.D.R., Bart.

Stephens, H.C.
‡Stepney, Sir E.A.A.K.C., Bart.
    see Cowell-Stepney, Sir
    E.A.A.K., Bart.
Stern, S.J.
Stevenson, F.S.
Stevenson, J.C.
*Stewart, G.
Stewart, H.
Stewart, Sir M.J., Bart. see
    Mactaggart-Stewart, Sir
    M.J., Bart.
Stewart-Smith, D.
Stirling, Lieut.-Col. A.
Stirling-Maxwell, Sir J.M.,
    Bart.
Stock, J.H.
*Stoker, R.B.
Stokes, Sir G.G., Bart.
Stone, Sir J.B.
Stopford-Sackville, Col. S.G.
Storey, S.
Stormonth-Darling, M.T. see
    Darling, M.T.S.
Story-Maskelyne, M.H.N.
Strachey, Sir E., Bart.
Straus, B.S.
Strauss, A.
*Strauss, E.A.
Strong, R.
Stroyan, J.
Strutt, Hon. C.H.
Stuart, J.
Stuart-Wortley, Rt. Hon. C.B.
Sturgis, H.P.
Sturrock, P.
Sturt, Hon. H.N.
Sullivan, D.
Sullivan. M. see Sullivan, D.
Sullivan, T.D.
Summerbell, T.
Summers, J.W.
Summers, W.
Sutherland, A.
Sutherland, J.E.
Sutherland, Sir T.
Sutherland-Leveson-Gower,
    F.N. see Leveson-Gower,
    F.N.S.
*Sutton, J.E.
Swann, C.D. see Schwann, C.D.
Swann, Rt. Hon. Sir C.E., Bart.
Sweetman, J.
Swetenham, E.
Swift, R.P.W.
Swinburne, Sir J., Bart.
*Sykes, Col. Sir A.J., Bart.
Sykes, C.
*Sykes, Sir M., Bart.

T

‡Talbot, C.R.M.
*Talbot, Rt. Hon. Lord E.B.
Talbot, Rt. Hon. J.G.
Tanner, Dr. C.K.D.
Tapling, T.K.

Taylor, A.
Taylor, F.
Taylor, Col. G.K. see Kyffin-
    Taylor, Col. G.
Taylor, J.W.
Taylor, T.C.
Taylor, T.
Temple, Sir R., Bart.
†Tennant, Sir C., Bart.
Tennant, Sir E.P., Bart.
Tennant, Rt. Hon. H.J.
*Terrell, G.
Terrell, H.
Theobald, J.
Thomas, A.
Thomas, Sir A.G.
Thomas, Sir A.
Thomas, D.A.
*Thomas, Rt. Hon. J.H.
Thomas, J.A.
Thomasson, F.
*Thomas-Stanford, C.
‡Thompson, Maj. A.G.
Thompson, E.C.
*Thompson, E.C.M. see
    Meysey-Thompson, E.C.
‡Thompson, Sir H.M., Bart. see
    Meysey-Thompson, Sir
    H.M., Bart.
Thompson, J.W.H.
Thompson, Rt. Hon. R.
Thomson, F.W.
*Thomson, W.M-. see Mitchell-
    Thomson, Sir W., Bart.
Thorburn, Sir W.
*Thorne, G.R.
*Thorne, W.J.
Thornton, P.M.
Thynne, Lord A.G.
*Tickler, T.G.
*Tillett, B.
Tillett, L.J.
Tindal-Robertson, Sir W. see
    Robertson, Sir W.T.
†Tipping, W.
Tobin, A.A.
Tollemache, H.J.
Tomkinson, Rt. Hon. J.
Tomlinson, Sir W.E.M., Bart.
*Tootill, R.
Torrance, Sir A.M.
‡Tottenham, A.L.
Touche, Sir G.A.
Toulmin, Sir G.
Townsend, C.
Townsend, F.
Townsend-Farquhar, Sir H.B.,
    Bart. see Farquhar, Sir
    H.B.T., Bart.
Tracy, Hon. F.S.A.H-. see
    Hanbury-Tracy, Hon. F.S.A.
*Trevelyan, C.P.
Trevelyan, Rt. Hon. Sir G.O.,
    Bart.
Tribich-Lincoln, I.T. see
    Lincoln, I.T.T.

Tritton, Sir C.E., Bart.
Trotter, H.J.
*Tryon, Maj. G.C.
Tuff, C.
Tufnell, E.
Tuite, J.
Tuke, Sir J.B.
Tullibardine, J.G.S-M., Marq. of
Tully, J.
*Turnour, E.T., Visct. see
    Winterton, E.T., Earl
*Turton, E.R.
Twisleton-Wykeham-Fiennes,
    Hon. Sir E.E., Bart. see
    Fiennes, Hon. Sir
    E.E.T-W-., Bart.
*Twist, H.
Tyler, Sir H.W.
Tyssen-Amherst, W.A. see
    Amherst, W.A.T.
Tyssen-Amhurst, W.A. see
    Amherst, W.A.T.

U

Uniacke-Penrose-Fitzgerald,
    Sir R., Bart. see Penrose-
    Fitzgerald, Sir R.U-., Bart.
Ure, Rt. Hon. A.
Usborne, T.

V

Valentia, A.A., Visct.
Valentine, C.J.
†Vanderbyl, P.
*Vaughan-Davies, M.L.
Venables-Llewelyn, C.L.D.
Verdin, R.
Verney, Capt. E.H.
Verney, F.W.
Verney, Sir H.C.W., Bart.
Verney, Hon. R.G.
Vernon, Hon. G.R.
Vernon-Harcourt, Rt. Hon. Sir
    W.G.G.V. see Harcourt, Rt.
    Hon. Sir W.G.G.V.V-.
Vernon-Wentworth, B.C. see
    Wentworth, B.C.V-.
Verrall, G.H.
‡Villiers, Rt. Hon. C.P.
Villiers, E.A.
Vincent, Col. Sir C.E.H.
Vincent, Sir E.
*Vivian, H.H.
Vivian, Sir H.H., Bart.

W

Waddy, S.D.
Wadsworth, J.
Waldron, L.A.
Walker, H. de R.
*Walker, Col. W.H.
Wallace, J.S.
Wallace, Professor R.
Wallace, R.
Walrond, Rt. Hon. Sir W.H.,
    Bart.

Walrond, Hon. W.L.C.
Walsh, Hon. A.H.J.
Walsh, J.
*Walsh, S.
*Walters, Sir J.T.
Walton, Sir J.L.
*Walton, Sir J., Bart.
Wanklyn, J.L.
Ward, A.S.
*Ward, J.
Ward, Hon. R.A.
*Ward, W.D.
Warde, Col. C.E.
*Wardle, G.J.
Wardle, H.
Waring, Col. T.
*Waring, Maj. W.
Warkworth, H.A.G.P., Lord see
    Percy, H.A.G.P., Earl
Warmington, C.M.
*Warner, Sir T.C.T., Bart.
'Warr, A.F.
Wason, Rt. Hon. E.
*Wason, J.C.
Waterlow, D.S.
Watkin, Sir E.W., Bart.
Watson, J.
*Watson, Capt. J.B.
Watson, T.
*Watson, Hon. W.
Watt, H.A.
Watt, H.
Wayman, T.
Webb, A.J.
*Webb, Lieut.-Col. Sir H.,
    Bart.
Webb, W.G.
Webster, Sir R.E., Bart.
Webster, R.G.
Wedderburn, Sir W., Bart.
*Wedgwood, J.C.
*Weigall, Lieut.-Col. W.E.G.A.
Weir, J.G.
Welby, A.C.E.
Welby, Sir C.G.E., Bart.
Wentworth, B.C.V-.
Wentworth-Fitzwilliam, Hon.
    W.H. see Fitzwilliam, Hon.
    W.H.W-.
Wentworth-Fitzwilliam, Hon.
    W.J. see Fitzwilliam, Hon.
    W.J.W-.
†West, H.W.
West, Col. W.C.
Westlake, J.
*Weston, Col. J.W.
Weston, Sir J.D.
Weymouth, T.H.T., Visct.
Wharton, Rt. Hon. J.L.
*Wheler, G.C.H.
‡Whitbread, S.
Whitbread, S.H.
White, Sir G.
*White, Lieut.-Col. G.D. see
    Dalrymple-White, G.D.
White, J.D.

White, J.M.
White, J.B.
White, Sir L.
White, P.
Whitehead, Sir J., Bart.
Whitehead, R.E.
Whitehouse, J.H.
Whitelaw, G.A.L.
Whitelaw, W.
Whiteley, Rt. Hon. G.
Whiteley, Sir H.J., Bart.
Whitley, E.
*Whitley, Rt. Hon. J.H.
Whitmore, C.A.
*Whittaker, Rt. Hon. Sir T.P.
Whitty, P.J.
Whyte, A.F.
Wickham, W.
Wiggin, H.
Wigram, A.M.
Wiles, Rt. Hon. T.
*Wilkie, A.
Will, J.S.
*Williams, A.
Williams, A.J.
Williams, Sir A.O. see Osmond-
    Williams, Sir A.
Williams, E.C. see Crawshay-
    Williams, E.
*Williams, J.
Williams, John Carvell
Williams, John Charles
Williams, Rt. Hon. J.P.
*Williams, P.
*Williams, Sir R.R-., Bart. see
    Rhys-Williams, Sir R., Bart.
*Williams, Sir R., Bart.
Williams, T.H. see Idris,
    T.H.W.
*Williams, T.J.
Williams, W.
Williams, W.L.
Williamson, Sir A., Bart
Williamson, G.H.
Williamson, J.
Williamson, S.
*Willoughby, Hon. C.H-D-.
Willoughby, Hon. G.H-D-. see
    Willoughby de Eresby, G.H-
    D-W., Lord
Willoughby de Eresby, G.H-D-
    W., Lord
Willox, Sir J.A.
Wills, A.W.
Wills, Sir F., Bart.
*Wills, Sir G.A.H., Bart.
Wills, Sir W.H., Bart.
*Wilson, A.S.
Wilson, C.H.
Wilson, Hon. C.H.W.
Wilson, F.W.
Wilson, Lieut.-Col. Hon. G.G.
Wilson, H.J.
Wilson, I.
Wilson, J. (I)
Wilson, J. (II)

Wilson, J. (III)
Wilson, J. (IV)
Wilson, J. (V)
*Wilson, Rt. Hon. J.W.
*Wilson, J.H.
*Wilson, Lieut.-Col. L.O.
†Wilson, Sir M., Bart.
*Wilson, Maj. Sir M.R.H., Bart.
Wilson, P.W.
Wilson, Sir S.
Wilson, T.F.
*Wilson, W.T.
*Wilson-Fox, H.
Wilson-Todd, Sir W.H., Bart.
*Winfrey, Sir R.
Wing, T.E.
Wingfield-Digby, J.K.D.
Winn, Hon. R.
Winterbotham, A.B.
*Winterton, E.T., Earl
Wodehouse, Hon. A.
Wodehouse, Rt. Hon. E.R.
Wodehouse, J.W., Lord
Wolff, G.W.
*Wolmer, R.C.P., Visct.
Wolmer, W.W.P., Visct.
*Wood, Hon. E.F.L.
Wood, J.
*Wood, Lieut.-Col. Sir J., Bart.
Wood, N.
*Wood, S.H-. see Hill-Wood,
    Sir S.H., Bart.
Wood, Rt. Hon. T.M.
Woodall, W.
Woodhead, J.
Woodhouse, Sir J.T.
Woods, S.
Worsley-Taylor, H.W.
*Worthington-Evans, Sir L.,
    Bart.
Wortley, Rt. Hon. C.B.S. see
    Stuart-Wortley, Rt. Hon. C.B.
Wright, C.
Wright, H.F.
Wright, H.S.
Wrightson, Sir T., Bart.
Wroughton, P.
Wylie, A.
Wyndham, Rt. Hon. G.
Wyndham-Quin, W.H.
Wyvill, M.D'A.

Y

*Yate, Col. C.E.
*Yeo, Sir A.W.
Yeo, F.A.
Yerburgh, R.A.
†Yorke, J.R.
Young, C.E.B.
*Young, E.H.
Young, O.
Young, S.
*Young, W.
*Younger, Sir G., Bart.
Younger, W.
Yoxall, Sir J.H.